CompTIA A+®

Certification Study Guide, Ninth Edition (Exams 220-901 & 220-902)

D1604816

CompTIA A+

Certification Study Guide, Ninth Edition
(Exams 220-901 & 220-902)

Faithe Wempen
Jane Holcombe

Mc Graw Hill Education

New York   Chicago   San Francisco
Athens   London   Madrid   Mexico City
Milan   New Delhi   Singapore   Sydney   Toronto

Cataloging-in-Publication Data is on file with the Library of Congress

McGraw-Hill Education books are available at special quantity discounts to use as premiums and sales promotions, or for use in corporate training programs. To contact a representative, please visit the Contact Us pages at www .mhprofessional.com.

CompTIA A+® Certification Study Guide, Ninth Edition (Exams 220-901 & 220-902)

1 2 3 4 5 6 7 8 9   LCR   21 20 19 18 17 16

ISBN: Book p/n 978-1-25-985938-0 and CD p/n 978-1-25-985940-3
of set 978-1-25-985941-0

MHID: Book p/n 1-25-985938-X and CD p/n 1-25-985940-1
of set 1-25-985941-X

Sponsoring Editor *Hilary Flood*	**Technical Editor** *Peter Hanwith-Horden*	**Production Supervisor** *James Kussow*
Editorial Supervisor *Janet Walden*	**Copy Editor** *William McManus*	**Composition** *Cenveo Publisher Services*
Project Manager *Vasundhara Sawhney,* *Cenveo® Publisher Services*	**Proofreader** *Richard Camp*	**Illustration** *Cenveo Publisher Services*
Acquisitions Coordinator *Claire Yee*	**Indexer** *Ted Laux*	**Art Director, Cover** *Jeff Weeks*

Becoming a CompTIA Certified IT Professional Is Easy

It's also the best way to reach greater professional opportunities and rewards.

Why Get CompTIA Certified?

Growing Demand

Labor estimates predict some technology fields will experience growth of more than 20 percent by the year 2020. (Source: CompTIA 9th Annual Information Security Trends study: 500 U.S. IT and Business Executives Responsible for Security.) CompTIA certification qualifies the skills required to join this workforce.

Higher Salaries

IT professionals with certifications on their resume command better jobs, earn higher salaries, and have more doors open to new multi-industry opportunities.

Verified Strengths

Ninety-one percent of hiring managers indicate CompTIA certifications are valuable in validating IT expertise, making certification the best way to demonstrate your competency and knowledge to employers. (Source: CompTIA Employer Perceptions of IT Training and Certification.)

Universal Skills

CompTIA certifications are vendor neutral—which means that certified professionals can proficiently work with an extensive variety of hardware and software found in most organizations.

Learn

Learn more about what the exam covers by reviewing the following:

- Exam objectives for key study points.
- Sample questions for a general overview of what to expect on the exam and examples of question format.
- Visit online forums, like LinkedIn, to see what other IT professionals say about CompTIA exams.

Certify

Purchase a voucher at a Pearson VUE testing center or at CompTIAstore.com.

- Register for your exam at a Pearson VUE testing center.
- Visit pearsonvue.com/CompTIA to find the closest testing center to you.
- Schedule the exam online. You will be required to enter your voucher number or provide payment information at registration.
- Take your certification exam.

Work

Congratulations on your CompTIA certification!

- Make sure to add your certification to your resume.
- Check out the CompTIA Certification Roadmap to plan your next career move.

Learn More: Certification.CompTIA.org/aplus

CompTIA Disclaimer

CAQC Disclaimer

ABOUT THE AUTHORS

Faithe Wempen, M.A., CompTIA A+, MOS Master Instructor, has been writing and teaching about computers since 1993, with the release of her first book, *Abort, Retry, Fail: 101 MS-DOS Error Messages*. Faithe is the author/co-author of more than 150 books about computer hardware and software, including *Mike Meyers' CompTIA A+ Guide to Managing and Troubleshooting PCs Lab Manual, Fifth Edition*, as well as textbooks, magazine articles, and website content. For 15+ years she has taught A+ certification prep classes at Indiana University/Purdue University at Indianapolis (IUPUI), and her free online classes for corporate clients including Sony and HP have educated more than a quarter of a million students.

Jane Holcombe, CompTIA A+, CompTIA Network +, CompTIA CTT+, Microsoft MCSE, MCT, and CNA, pioneered in the field of PC support training. She spent 20 years as an independent trainer, consultant, and course content author, creating and presenting courses on PC operating systems taught nationwide. She co-authored a set of networking courses for the consulting staff of a large network vendor. In the early 1990s, she worked with both Novell and Microsoft server operating systems, finally focusing on the Microsoft operating systems and achieving early MCSE certification, recertifying for new versions of Windows. Since 2001 she has been the lead author, in collaboration with her husband, of 10 books and numerous book chapters.

Charles Holcombe was a programmer of early computers in both the nuclear and aerospace fields. In his 15 years at Control Data Corporation, he was successively a programmer, technical sales analyst, salesman, and sales manager in the field marketing organization. At corporate headquarters, he ran the Executive Seminar program, served as corporate liaison to the worldwide university community, and was market development manager for Plato, Control Data's computer-based education system. For the past 30 years, he has been an independent trainer and consultant, authoring and delivering training courses in many disciplines. He is a skilled writer and editor of books and online publications, and he collaborates with his wife, Jane, on many writing projects.

About the Technical Editor

Peter James Hanwith-Horden, CompTIA A+, CompTIA Network+, Security+ MCSE, MTA, MCT, technical editor, consultant, and trainer, spent 14 years in the office automation industry doing training and resolving connectivity issues in the field. Peter has traveled around South Africa lecturing at CompTIA and Microsoft courses, corporate training centers, and colleges. In 2003, he was appointed subject matter expert for CompTIA A+ to create questions for the exams. Peter currently serves on the CompTIA Network+ Certification Advisory Committee.

CONTENTS AT A GLANCE

CONTENTS

The objective of this Study Guide is to help you prepare for and pass the required exams so you can begin to reap the career benefits of CompTIA A+ certification. Because the primary focus of this book is to help you pass the exams, we don't always cover every aspect of the related technology. Some aspects of the technology are only covered to the extent necessary to help you understand what you need to know to pass the exams, but we hope this book will serve you as a valuable professional resource after your exams.

In This Book

This book is organized in such a way as to serve as an in-depth review for the latest version of the CompTIA A+ exams, released in 2015: Exam 220-901 and Exam 220-902. Each chapter covers a major aspect of the exams, with an emphasis on the "why" as well as the "how to" of IT support in the areas of installation, configuration, and maintenance of devices, PCs, and software; networking and security/forensics; diagnosis, resolution, and documentation of common hardware and software issues; troubleshooting; Internet and cloud usage; virtualization; desktop imaging; and deployment.

About the Digital Resources

The accompanying content provided electronically with this book includes additional tools to help you prepare for the exams. For more information, please see the appendix.

Exam Readiness Checklist

At the end of the Introduction, you will find two Exam Readiness Checklists. These tables have been constructed to allow you to cross-reference the official exam objectives with the objectives as they are presented and covered in this book. These checklists also allow you to gauge your level of expertise on each objective at the outset of your studies. This should allow you to check your progress and make sure you spend the time you need on more difficult or unfamiliar sections. References have been provided for each objective exactly as the vendor presents it, the section of the Study Guide that covers that objective, and a chapter and page reference.

In Every Chapter

We've created a set of chapter components that call your attention to important items, reinforce important points, and provide helpful exam-taking hints. Take a look at what you'll find in every chapter:

- Every chapter begins with the **Certification Objectives**—what you need to know in order to pass the section on the exams dealing with the chapter topic. The Certification Objective headings identify the objectives within the chapter, so you'll always know an objective when you see it!

- **Exam Watch** notes call attention to information about, and potential pitfalls in, the exams. These helpful hints reinforce your learning and exam preparation.

- **Step-by-Step Exercises** are interspersed throughout the chapters. These hands-on exercises allow you to get a feel for the real-world experience you need in order to pass the exams. They help you master skills that are likely to be an area of focus on the exams. Don't just read through the exercises; they are hands-on practice that you should be comfortable completing. Learning by doing is an effective way to increase your competency with a product.

- **On the Job** notes describe the issues that come up most often in real-world settings. They provide a valuable perspective on certification- and product-related topics. They point out common mistakes and address questions that have arisen from on-the-job discussions and experience.

- **Scenario & Solution** sections lay out problems and solutions in a quick-read format.

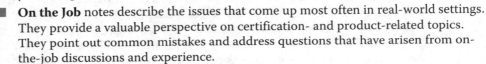

SCENARIO & SOLUTION	
My computer is part of a large corporate network. What role is my desktop computer most likely playing in this network?	A large corporate network is a client/server network. A desktop PC in this network has the role of a client.
What is the protocol suite of the Internet?	The protocol suite of the Internet is TCP/IP.
I understand that NetBEUI is very easy to install and use. Why does our corporate internetwork not use it?	A corporate internetwork consists, by definition, of interconnected networks requiring a protocol suite routable between networks. NetBEUI, as a nonroutable protocol, is therefore not used.

- The **Certification Summary** is a succinct review of the chapter and a restatement of salient points regarding the exams.

- ✓ The **Two-Minute Drill** at the end of every chapter is a checklist of the main points of the chapter. It can be used for last-minute review.

Q&A

■ The **Self Test** offers multiple-choice questions similar to those found on the certification exams. The answers to these questions, as well as explanations of the answers, can be found at the end of each chapter. By taking the Self Test after completing each chapter, you'll reinforce what you've learned from that chapter while becoming familiar with the structure of the multiple-choice exam questions. The book does not include other types of questions that you may encounter on the exams.

Some Pointers

Once you've finished reading this book, set aside some time to do a thorough review. You might want to return to the book several times and make use of all the methods it offers for reviewing the material:

■ *Re-read all of the Two-Minute Drills*, or have someone quiz you. You also can use the drills as a way to do a quick cram before the exams.

■ *Review all the Scenario & Solutions* for quick problem solving.

■ *Complete the Exercises.* Did you do the exercises when you read through each chapter? If not, do them! These exercises are designed to cover exam topics, and there's no better way to get to know this material than by practicing. Be sure you understand why you are performing each step in each exercise. If there is something you are not clear on, re-read that section in the chapter.

■ *Retake the Self Tests.* Taking the tests right after you've read the chapter is a good idea, because the questions help reinforce what you've just learned. However, it's an even better idea to go back later and do all the questions in the book in one sitting. Pretend that you're taking a live exam. When you go through the questions the first time, you should mark your answers on a separate piece of paper. That way, you can run through the questions as many times as you need to until you feel comfortable with the material.

ACKNOWLEDGMENTS

Although just two names are on the cover, this book is actually the product of many talented contributors. Our sincere thanks go to the following writing, editing, and publishing professionals.

Hilary Flood, acquisitions editor, helped get the new edition off to a good start by managing the acquisitions process. Claire Yee, editorial coordinator, expertly managed the technical editing and development phase of the project and motivated us to meet our deadlines. Peter Hanwith-Horden provided expert technical feedback and suggestions that ensured the accuracy of our manuscript. Vasundhara Sawhney, project manager, oversaw the copy editing and layout processes and kept all the balls in the air juggling multiple documents and details. Speaking of the copy editing, Bill McManus did an expert job ensuring that our language was as clear and consistent as possible. Janet Walden supervised the editorial process and cross-checked exam objectives and study questions. The professional staff of the production department at Cenveo Publisher Services turned a plain manuscript into the beautiful book you hold in your hands (or read on your screen). Proofreader Rick Camp made sure no minor mistakes slipped through the cracks, and Ted Laux indexed the book—which is no small feat for a book of this size, with hundreds of technical terms.

How to Take a CompTIA A+ Certification Exam

This section prepares you for taking the actual examination. It gives you a few pointers on methods for preparing for the exam, including how to study and register, what to expect, and what to do on exam day.

Importance of CompTIA A+ Certification

Earning CompTIA A+ certification means that you have the knowledge and the technical skills necessary to be a successful entry-level IT professional in today's environment. The exam objectives test your knowledge and skills in all the areas that today's computing environment requires. Although the exams cover a broad range of computer software and hardware, they are not vendor specific.

Both the CompTIA A+ 220-901 Exam and the CompTIA A+ 220-902 Exam are required to achieve your CompTIA A+ certification. As stated by CompTIA, together, the 220-901 and 220-902 exams "measure necessary competencies for an entry-level IT professional.... Successful candidates will have the knowledge required to assemble components based on customer requirements; install, configure, and maintain devices, PCs, and software for end users; understand the basics of networking and security/forensics; properly and safely diagnose, resolve, and document common hardware and software issues; apply troubleshooting skills; provide appropriate customer support; and understand the basics of virtualization, desktop imaging, and deployment."

Computerized Testing

The most practical way to administer tests on a global level is through a testing center, such as Pearson VUE, which provides proctored testing services for many companies, including CompTIA. In addition to administering the tests, Pearson VUE scores the exam and provides statistical feedback on each section of the exam to the companies and organizations that use their services.

On Exams 220-901 and 220-902, unanswered questions count against you. Assuming you have time left when you finish the other questions, you can return to the marked questions for further evaluation.

The standard test also marks the questions that are incomplete with a letter "I" once you've finished all the questions. You'll see the whole list of questions after you complete the last question. This screen allows you to go back and finish incomplete items, finish unmarked items, and return to questions you flagged for review.

An interesting and useful characteristic of the standard test is that questions may be marked and returned to	**later. This helps you manage your time while taking the test so you don't spend too much time on any one question.**

Question Types

The CompTIA A+ exams consist of several types of question formats, as described in a YouTube video on the test experience at http://certification.comptia.org/testing/about-testing. We strongly recommend that you take the time to watch this short video. Here is a brief overview of the question formats you may see on your exam.

Multiple-Choice Questions

Many CompTIA A+ exam questions are of the multiple-choice variety. Below each question is a list of four or five possible answers. Use the available radio buttons to select the correct answer from the given choices.

Multiple-Response Questions

A multiple-response question is a multiple-choice question with more than one correct answer, in which case, the number of correct answers required is clearly stated.

Fill-in-the-Blank Questions

A fill-in-the-blank question prompts you to type a word or phrase. Be aware that answers may be case-sensitive.

Graphical Questions

Some questions incorporate a graphical element or a video available via an Exhibit button to provide a visual representation of the problem or present the question itself. These questions are easy to identify because they refer to the exhibit in the question and there is an exhibit. An example of a graphical question might be to identify a component on a drawing of a motherboard. This is done in the multiple-choice format by having callouts labeled A, B, C, or D point to the selections.

Drag-and-Drop Questions

A drag-and-drop question is a form of graphical question in which you select a token, such as a graphic of a computer component, and drag and drop it to a designated area, in response to the question.

w a t c h   **Due to the limitations of the practice test engine software, the four online practice exams do not contain simulations of the drag-and-drop or performance-based question types.**

Performance-Based Questions

Performance-based questions include simulations and require the candidate to perform certain tasks based on multifaceted scenarios. When you encounter one of these questions, you will click a Simulation button and enter a simulated environment in which you must perform one or more tasks. You can experience a sample performance-based question here: https://certification.comptia.org/modules/performancetesting.

Study Strategies

There are appropriate ways to study for the different types of questions you may see on CompTIA A+ certification exams. The amount of study time needed to pass the exam will vary with the candidate's level of experience. Someone with several years of experience might only need a quick review of materials and terms when preparing for the exam. Others may need several hours to identify weaknesses in their knowledge and skill level and work on those areas to bring them up to par. If you know that you are weak in an area, work on it until you feel comfortable talking about it. You don't want to be surprised by a question knowing it was in your weak area.

Knowledge-Based Questions

Knowledge-based questions require that you memorize facts. These questions may not cover material that you use on a daily basis, but they do cover material that CompTIA thinks an IT professional should be able to answer. Here are some keys to memorizing facts:

- **Repetition** The more times you expose your brain to a fact, the more it sinks in, and your ability to remember it increases.
- **Association** Connecting facts within a logical framework makes them easier to remember.
- **Motor association** Remembering something is easier if you write it down or perform another physical act, like clicking the practice exam answers.

Performance-Based Questions

The first step in preparing for performance-based questions is to absorb as many facts relating to the exam content areas as you can. Of course, actual hands-on experience will greatly help you in this area. For example, it really helps in knowing how to install a video adapter if you have actually done the procedure at least once. Some of the questions will place you in a scenario and ask for the best solution to the problem at hand. It is in these scenarios that having a good knowledge level and some experience will help you.

CompTIA A+ Certification Exam 220-901

The CompTIA A+ Certification Exam 220-901 consists of four domains (categories). CompTIA represents the relative importance of each domain within the body of knowledge required for an entry-level IT professional taking this exam.

Domain	Percentage
1.0 Hardware	34%
2.0 Networking	21%
3.0 Mobile Devices	17%
4.0 Hardware & Network Troubleshooting	28%

CompTIA A+ Certification Exam 220-902

The CompTIA A+ Certification Exam 220-902 consists of five domains (categories). CompTIA represents the relative importance of each domain within the body of knowledge required for an entry-level IT professional taking this exam.

1.0 Windows Operating Systems	29%
2.0 Other Operating Systems & Technologies	12%
3.0 Security	22%
4.0 Software Troubleshooting	24%
5.0 Operational Procedures	13%

The Operational Procedures domain has switched exams in the latest exam objectives. It was in 220-801 on the **previous A+ exam, but it is in 220-902 in the new version. The content remains similar.**

Taking the Exam

The best method of preparing for the exam is to create a study schedule and stick to it. Although teachers have probably told you time and time again not to cram for tests, some information just doesn't quite stick in your memory. It's this type of information you want to look at right before you take the exam so it remains fresh in your mind. You can brush up on good study techniques from any quality study book, but here are some things to remember when preparing and taking the test:

- Get a good night's sleep. Don't stay up all night cramming for this one. If you don't know the material by the time you go to sleep, your head won't be clear enough to remember it in the morning.

- The test center needs two forms of identification, one of which must have your picture on it (for example, your driver's license). Credit cards are also acceptable forms of identification.

- Arrive at the test center a few minutes early. You don't want to feel rushed right before taking an exam.

- ■ Don't spend too much time on one question. If you think you're spending too much time on it, just flag it and return to it later if you have time.

- ■ If you don't know the answer to a multiple-choice question, think about it logically. Look at the answers and eliminate the ones that you know can't possibly be correct. This may leave you with only two possible answers. Give it your best guess if you have to, but you can resolve most of the answers to the questions by the process of elimination. Remember, unanswered questions count as incorrect whether you know the answer to them or not.

- ■ No books, calculators, laptop computers, or any other reference materials are allowed inside the testing center. The tests are computer based and do not require pens, pencils, or paper, although, as mentioned previously, some test centers provide scratch paper to aid you while taking the exam.

After the Exam

As soon as you complete the exam, your results will show up in the form of a bar graph on the screen. As long as your score is greater than the required score, you pass! The testing center will print and emboss a hard copy of the report to indicate that it's an official report. Don't lose this copy; it's the only hard copy of the report made. The testing center sends the results electronically to CompTIA.

The printed report will also indicate how well you did in each section. You will be able to see the percentage of questions you got right in each section, but you will not be able to tell which questions you got wrong.

After you pass both exams, you will receive a CompTIA A+ certificate by mail within a few weeks. You are then authorized to use the CompTIA A+ logo on your business cards, as long as you stay within the guidelines specified by CompTIA. Please check the CompTIA website for a more comprehensive and up-to-date listing and explanation of CompTIA A+ benefits.

If you don't pass the exam, don't fret. Examine the areas where you didn't do so well, and work on those areas for the next time you register to take the exams.

Exam Readiness Checklists

The following two tables, one for each of the CompTIA A+ exams (Exam 901 and Exam 902), describe each of the A+ objectives with a mapping to the coverage in the Study Guide. There are also three check boxes labeled Beginner, Intermediate, and Expert. Use these to rate your beginning knowledge of each objective. This assessment will help guide you to the areas in which you need to spend more time studying for the exams.

Exam 220-901

Exam Readiness Checklist					Beginner	Intermediate	Expert
Official Objective	**Ch #**	**Section**		**Pg #**			
901—1.0 Hardware							
1.1: Given a scenario, configure settings and use BIOS/UEFI tools on a PC.	3	Configuring a Motherboard		135			
1.2: Explain the importance of motherboard components, their purpose, and properties.	3	Motherboard Form Factors and Components		115			
	3	Configuring a Motherboard		135			
	6	Installing and Upgrading Motherboards and Onboard Components		259			
1.3: Compare and contrast various RAM types and their features.	4	Memory		156			
	6	Installing and Upgrading Motherboards and Onboard Components		259			
1.4: Install and configure PC expansion cards.	4	Expansion Cards and Built-in Adapters		164			
	6	Installing Adapter Cards		271			
1.5: Install and configure storage devices and use appropriate media.	4	Storage Devices and Interfaces		178			
	6	Installing Storage Devices		274			
1.6: Install various types of CPUs and apply the appropriate cooling methods.	3	CPUs and Their Sockets		125			
	6	Installing and Upgrading Motherboards and Onboard Components		259			
1.7: Compare and contrast various PC connection interfaces, their characteristics, and purpose.	4	Expansion Cards and Built-in Adapters		164			
	4	Storage Devices and Interfaces		178			

Exam Readiness Checklist

Official Objective	Ch #	Section	Pg #	Beginner	Intermediate	Expert
	13	Network Classifications	596			
	14	Configuring Other Common Connections	674			
1.8: Install a power supply based on given specifications.	5	Power Supplies	204			
1.9: Given a scenario, select the appropriate components for a custom PC configuration to meet customer specifications or needs.	6	Selecting Components for Custom PCs	254			
1.10: Compare and contrast types of display devices and their features.	5	Video Adapters and Displays	213			
1.11: Identify common PC connector types and associated cables.	4	Expansion Cards and Built-in Adapters	164			
	5	Video Adapters and Displays	213			
1.12: Install and configure common peripheral devices.	5	Installing and Configuring Peripheral Devices	231			
1.13: Install SOHO multifunction device/printers and configure appropriate settings.	21	Installing and Configuring Printers	940			
1.14: Compare and contrast differences between the various print technologies and the associated imaging process.	21	Printer Basics	932			
	21	Installing and Configuring Printers	940			
	21	Printer Maintenance	958			
1.15: Given a scenario, perform appropriate printer maintenance.	21	Printer Maintenance	958			
901—2.0 Networking						
2.1: Identify the various types of network cables and connectors.	13	Network Hardware	624			
2.2: Compare and contrast the characteristics of connectors and cabling.	13	Network Hardware	624			

Exam Readiness Checklist

Official Objective	Ch #	Section	Pg #	Beginner	Intermediate	Expert
2.3: Explain the properties and characteristics of TCP/IP.	13	Network Software	608			
2.4: Explain common TCP and UDP ports, protocols, and their purpose.	13	Common Ports	621			
	15	Internet Concepts	690			
2.5: Compare and contrast various Wi-Fi networking standards and encryption types.	13	Network Classifications	596			
	14	Installing and Configuring SOHO Networks	648			
2.6: Given a scenario, install and configure a SOHO wireless/wired router and apply appropriate settings.	14	Installing and Configuring SOHO Networks	648			
2.7: Compare and contrast Internet connection types, network types, and their features.	13	Network Classifications	596			
	20	Configuring and Using Mobile Device Connections	894			
2.8: Compare and contrast network architecture devices, their functions, and features.	13	Network Hardware	624			
2.9: Given a scenario, use appropriate networking tools.	3	The Hardware Toolkit	110			
901—3.0 Mobile Devices						
3.1: Install and configure laptop hardware and components.	7	Installing and Upgrading Laptops	290			
3.2: Explain the function of components within the display of a laptop.	5	Video Adapters and Displays	213			
	7	Installing and Upgrading Laptops	290			
3.3: Given a scenario, use appropriate laptop features.	7	Using Laptop Features	323			

Exam Readiness Checklist

Official Objective	Ch #	Section	Pg #	Beginner	Intermediate	Expert
3.4: Explain the characteristics of various types of other mobile devices.	20	Overview of Mobile Devices	881			
3.5: Compare and contrast accessories and ports of other mobile devices.	20	Overview of Mobile Devices	881			
	20	Configuring and Using Mobile Device Connections	894			
901—4.0 Hardware and Network Troubleshooting						
4.1: Given a scenario, troubleshoot common problems related to motherboards, RAM, CPU, and power with appropriate tools.	11	Troubleshooting Motherboards, RAM, CPUs, and Power	480			
4.2: Given a scenario, troubleshoot hard drives and RAID arrays with appropriate tools.	11	Troubleshooting Storage Devices	494			
	12	Windows Troubleshooting Tools	531			
4.3: Given a scenario, troubleshoot common video, projector, and display issues.	11	Troubleshooting Displays	503			
4.4: Given a scenario, troubleshoot wired and wireless networks with appropriate tools.	14	Using Networking Tools	644			
	16	Troubleshooting Common Network Problems	724			
	19	Configuring Windows Clients for File and Printer Sharing	842			
4.5: Given a scenario, troubleshoot and repair common mobile device issues while adhering to the appropriate procedures.	20	Mobile Device Troubleshooting	912			
4.6: Given a scenario, troubleshoot printers with appropriate tools.	21	Troubleshooting Printers	968			

Exam 220-902

Exam Readiness Checklist				Beginner	Intermediate	Expert
Official Objective	**Ch #**	**Section**	**Pg #**			
902—1.0 Windows Operating Systems						
1.1: Compare and contrast various features and requirements of Microsoft operating systems (Windows Vista, Windows 7, Windows 8, Windows 8.1).	2	Introduction to Windows Operating Systems	51			
	10	File Management	444			
	12	Windows Troubleshooting Tools	531			
1.2: Given a scenario, install Windows PC operating systems using appropriate methods.	9	Upgrading Windows	372			
	9	Installing Windows	379			
	10	Disk Management	422			
	12	Windows Troubleshooting Tools	531			
1.3: Given a scenario, apply appropriate Microsoft command-line tools.	10	Disk Management	422			
	10	File Management	444			
	12	Windows Troubleshooting Tools	531			
	19	Configuring Windows Clients for File and Printer Sharing	842			
1.4: Given a scenario, use appropriate Microsoft operating system features and tools.	9	Installing Windows	379			
	9	Configuring Windows	398			
	10	Disk Management	422			
	11	Preparing for Troubleshooting	472			
	12	Windows Troubleshooting Tools	531			

Exam Readiness Checklist

Official Objective	Ch #	Section	Pg #	Beginner	Intermediate	Expert
	14	Configuring Other Common Connections	674			
	18	Implementing a Defense Against Malware	813			
	21	Installing and Configuring Printers	940			
1.5: Given a scenario, use Windows Control Panel utilities.	5	Video Adapters and Displays	213			
	7	Power Options	313			
	9	Configuring Windows	398			
	10	File Management	444			
	12	Windows Troubleshooting Tools	531			
	14	Configuring Other Common Connections	674			
	15	Configuring Internet Settings in Windows	700			
	18	Implementing Authentication for Digital Security	794			
	18	Implementing a Defense Against Malware	813			
	19	Configuring Windows Clients for File and Printer Sharing	842			
	19	Implementing Data Security	855			
	21	Installing and Configuring Printers	940			
1.6: Given a scenario, install and configure Windows networking on a client/desktop.	14	Installing and Configuring SOHO Networks	648			

Exam Readiness Checklist

Exam Readiness Checklist

Official Objective	Ch #	Section	Pg #	Beginner	Intermediate	Expert
2.4: Summarize the properties and purpose of services provided by networked hosts.	15	Internet Concepts	690			
2.5: Identify basic features of mobile operating systems.	20	Overview of Mobile Devices	881			
2.6: Install and configure basic mobile device network connectivity and e-mail.	20	Overview of Mobile Devices	881			
	20	Configuring and Using Mobile Device Connections	894			
2.7: Summarize methods and data related to mobile device synchronization.	20	Configuring and Using Mobile Device Connections	894			
902—3.0 Security						
3.1: Identify common security threats and vulnerabilities	17	Security Threats	760			
3.2: Compare and contrast common prevention methods.	14	Configuring Other Common Connections	674			
	17	Defense Against Threats: Physical Security	777			
	18	Implementing Authentication for Digital Security	794			
	18	Implementing a Defense Against Malware	813			
	19	Implementing Data Security	855			
3.3: Compare and contrast differences of basic Windows OS security settings.	10	File Management	444			
	18	Implementing Authentication for Digital Security	794			
	19	Implementing Data Security	855			

Exam Readiness Checklist

Official Objective	Ch #	Section	Pg #	Beginner	Intermediate	Expert
3.4: Given a scenario, deploy and enforce security best practices to secure a workstation.	18	Implementing Authentication for Digital Security	794			
3.5: Compare and contrast various methods for securing mobile devices.	20	Configuring and Using Mobile Device Connections	894			
	20	Securing Mobile Devices	906			
3.6: Given a scenario, use appropriate data destruction and disposal methods.	17	Defense Against Threats: Physical Security	777			
	18	Securely Recycling or Repurposing Storage	829			
3.7: Given a scenario, secure SOHO wireless and wired networks.	14	Installing and Configuring SOHO Networks	648			
902—4.0 Software Troubleshooting						
4.1: Given a scenario, troubleshoot PC operating system problems with appropriate tools.	12	Quick Fixes	530			
	12	Windows Troubleshooting Tools	531			
	12	Windows Symptoms and Solutions	564			
	12	Troubleshooting macOS and Linux Systems	573			
4.2: Given a scenario, troubleshoot common PC security issues with appropriate tools and best practices.	12	Windows Troubleshooting Tools	531			
	18	Implementing a Defense Against Malware	813			
4.3: Given a scenario, troubleshoot common mobile OS and application issues with appropriate tools.	20	Mobile Device Troubleshooting	912			

Exam Readiness Checklist

Official Objective	Ch #	Section	Pg #	Beginner	Intermediate	Expert
4.4: Given a scenario, troubleshoot common mobile OS and application security issues with appropriate tools.	20	Securing Mobile Devices	906			
	20	Mobile Device Troubleshooting	912			
902—5.0 Operational Procedures						
5.1: Given a scenario, use appropriate safety procedures.	1	Workplace Safety and Safe Equipment Handling	2			
5.2: Given a scenario with potential environmental impacts, apply the appropriate controls.	1	Environmental Concerns for IT Professionals	19			
5.3: Summarize the process of addressing prohibited content/activity, and explain privacy, licensing, and policy concepts.	1	Dealing with Prohibited Content and Prohibited Activities	27			
5.4: Demonstrate proper communication techniques and professionalism.	1	Professionalism and Proper Communication	32			
5.5: Given a scenario, explain the troubleshooting theory.	11	Preparing for Troubleshooting	472			

Chapter 1

Operational Procedures

- ■ **902: 5.1** Given a scenario, use appropriate safety procedures

- ■ **902: 5.2** Given a scenario with potential environmental impacts, apply the appropriate controls

- ■ **902: 5.3** Summarize the process of addressing prohibited content/activity, and explain privacy, licensing, and policy concepts

- ■ **902: 5.4** Demonstrate proper communication techniques and professionalism

- ✓ Two-Minute Drill

- **Q&A** Self Test

O perational procedures for IT professionals cover many activities. They include on-the-job safety, procedures for minimizing environmental impact, policies and procedures for dealing with prohibited content and/or prohibited activity, communication skills, and workplace professionalism. Your technical skills with computers, networks, and operating systems may be excellent, but if you do not follow proper operational procedures, you may put your job and career at risk.

CERTIFICATION OBJECTIVE

■ *902: 5.1 Given a scenario, use appropriate safety procedures*

The A+ candidate must prove knowledge of appropriate safety procedures and how to participate in a safe work environment in which each person handles equipment safely to protect the equipment and prevent injury to people.

Workplace Safety and Safe Equipment Handling

Safety is everyone's job, even in an organization in which designated employees are assigned direct responsibility for safety compliance and implementation. Everyone in an organization must play an active role in maintaining a safe work environment, which includes having an awareness of, and acting to remove, common safety hazards, such as spilled liquids, floor clutter, electrical dangers, and atmospheric hazards. You must be proactive to avoid accidents that can harm people and equipment. Safe equipment handling begins with using the appropriate tools; taking care when moving equipment; protecting yourself and equipment from electrostatic discharge; avoiding damage to transmission links and data from electromagnetic interference; and taking appropriate precautions when working with power supplies, displays, and printers.

Cable Management

One often-overlooked hazard is the jumble of cables connecting the various pieces of equipment in an office. If someone trips on the cables, they may injure themselves and/or damage equipment. Therefore, control the chaos, even if you need to use cable management products to eliminate such clutter and hazards. You'll find a wide selection of cable management products on the Internet. The simplest are cable ties—either Velcro straps or plastic zip ties—that allow you to tie cables together to keep them out of the way, or cable sleeves that you use to enclose a group of cables. More sophisticated products include cable raceways (see Figure 1-1) that you can attach to furniture or walls to conceal a bundle of cables, cable trays for containing cabling within ceilings, and patch panels that network engineers use to manage the power and network cables in utility closets or server rooms.

FIGURE 1-1

A cable raceway mounted on a desk with the cover of the near section removed

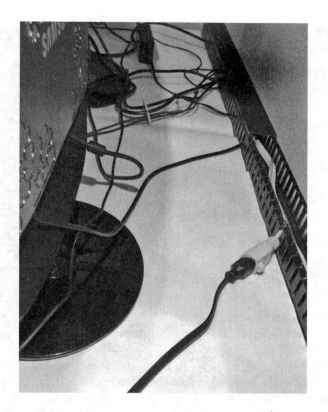

Using Appropriate Tools

The typical computer technician's toolkit is not extensive; we will discuss what it should include in Chapter 3. For now, just know that such a hardware toolkit will include various types and sizes of screwdrivers, a parts grabber, a flashlight, extra screws, and some other handy items.

Use appropriate tools to avoid damage to computer components and possible personal injury—and be meticulous about using each tool only for its intended purposes. For instance, attempting to use a flat-bladed screwdriver on a Phillips head screw can damage both the screw and the screwdriver, and it does not work very well. Worse yet, using a tool that does not fit properly may cause it to slip and damage a component such as the motherboard, or perhaps even injure yourself. Figure 1-2 shows several screwdrivers designed for specific types of screw heads.

on the **Job** **Do not carry loose objects like screwdrivers in shirt pockets or hip pockets because they can fall into computers and other equipment when you lean over or stab you if you sit down.**

FIGURE 1-2   Notice the differences in the blades of the four screwdrivers on the left—each only works with a specific screw head. The nut driver on the right works on one size of hex nut.

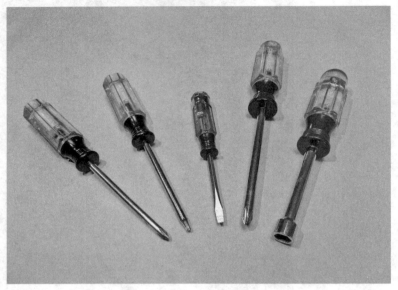

In Chapter 11, we describe methods for maintaining and cleaning computer components, and one of the tools described there is a vacuum. If you use a vacuum around open computer equipment, be sure to power down, disconnect the component, and avoid touching any power supplies with your hands or the vacuum. Further, if the vacuum does not have a filter, be sure to wear a filter mask, such as the inexpensive ones you can buy at a hardware store or pharmacy, especially when cleaning up toner. Using a vacuum can generate static, so, if available, use an antistatic vacuum—one that has a conductive path to ground to protect against causing electrostatic discharge damage to a computer during use.

If you choose to use canned compressed air to clean dust out of components, follow the instructions in Chapter 11, and wear a mask and be sure to aim the nozzle away from you to avoid blowing particles in your face.

Fire Safety

Any workplace can experience a fire, and if a fire should start, your first concern is safety for yourself and others. If you are untrained and/or are uncertain about the fuels involved in a fire, it is better to escape a fire, trigger a fire alarm, and close doors behind you than to fight a fire. The following discussion will not fully prepare you to fight a fire, but it will educate you and make you aware of the dangers and the need for proper training.

The typical workplace has a variety of potential fire sources and fuels. Look around areas such as the break room, offices, work cubicles, the wiring closet, server room, and computer workbench and imagine how a fire could start and what would fuel the fire. When working around computers, one potential fire source is a faulty computer or peripheral power supply that can result in an electrical fire. The wiring in the wall, as well as in any equipment or appliance, could develop a short, resulting in heat that could ignite the material within the equipment and spread to nearby fuels, such as paper, solvents, furniture, and more. You need to extinguish these various types by using the appropriate fire extinguisher; they come in several classes based on the fuel feeding the fire. Clearly, it is best to extinguish a fire at the source before multiple fuels are involved. Following is a description of the most common fire extinguisher classes:

Class A	Use for fires involving ordinary combustible materials, such as wood, paper, cardboard, and most plastics.
Class B	Use on fires involving flammable or combustible liquids, including gasoline, kerosene, grease, and oil.
Class C	Use on fires involving electrical equipment, such as wiring, circuit breakers, outlets, computers, and appliances. The material in a Class C extinguisher is nonconductive to reduce the risk of shock that could result from using a conductive material.
Class D	Use on chemical fires involving magnesium, titanium, potassium, and sodium.
Class K	Use on fires involving cooking oils, trans-fats, or other fats in cooking appliances. This type of extinguisher should be in commercial kitchens and restaurants.

Be sure you know what class of fire extinguisher to use for each type of fire.

Keep at least one fire extinguisher of the appropriate class or classes handy by your desk or workbench, in the wiring closet, the server room, and other locations. In some locations, you may have air-pressurized water (APW) fire extinguishers. Only use these on fires involving ordinary combustibles (see Class A in the previous list).

Some fire extinguishers contain dry chemicals, which leave a residue that reduces the chance of the fire reigniting, and some dry chemical extinguishers are rated for more than one class, which is very handy for a multiple-fuel fire. For instance, a BC extinguisher can be used on Class B or Class C fires, but be aware that it will leave a residue that must be cleaned immediately because it is corrosive. An ABC fire extinguisher is rated for all three fire types, but it leaves a sticky residue that can damage computers and electrical appliances.

Some Class B and C extinguishers contain carbon dioxide (CO_2), a nonflammable gas. One advantage of a CO_2 extinguisher is that it does not leave a residue, but because a CO_2 extinguisher relies on high pressure, it may shoot out bits of dry ice. Never use a CO_2 extinguisher on a Class A fire, because it may not smother the fire enough to fully extinguish it.

Another nonflammable gas sometimes used in Class B and C fire extinguishers is halon, with nitrogen as a propellant. Halon fire extinguishers area ideal for electronic equipment because they leave no residue; in addition, halon extinguishers are also effective on Class A fires. However, halon was classified as an ozone-depleting chlorofluorocarbon (CFC) under the Clean Air Act, and production of halon ceased in 1994. There are no federal or state regulations prohibiting the buying, selling, or use of halon extinguishers, but once the existing supply of halon has been depleted, no more will be created.

Lifting and Moving Equipment

In the United States, lifting is the number one cause of back injuries. Therefore, when lifting and moving computer equipment or any objects, take the time to do it safely, protecting yourself and the equipment, as described here.

Protecting Yourself

It is easy to injure your back when moving equipment. Therefore, the weight of what you lift and how you lift it are important factors, which means that every instance of lifting and moving is different.

Lifting Weight Limits   Ironically, as far as laws and regulations go, there are no clear limits on what an employee can lift, and the Occupational Safety and Health Administration (OSHA) has no standards written for many specific workplace lifting situations. This is because the actual circumstances differ widely, and the weight is just one consideration. Lifting hazards are very broadly addressed under the General Duty Clause of the OSH Act, specifically Section 5(a)(1). It states:

Each employer—shall furnish to each of his employees employment and a place of employment which are free from recognized hazards that are causing or are likely to cause death or serious physical harm to his employees.

The National Institute for Occupational Safety and Health (NIOSH) publishes a lifting equation so that employers can evaluate the lifting tasks for employees and establish a recommended weight limit. This is a rather complicated equation requiring considerable effort to gather information about each situation. Then, when you factor in all the human variables of every lifting situation, you understand the difficulty of attempting to calculate a maximum lifting weight.

Government agencies and other organizations have created calculators to help employees establish guidelines for lifting. One such calculator by the Ohio Bureau of Workers'

| FIGURE 1-3 | A lifting guideline tool published by the Ohio Bureau of Workers' Compensation |

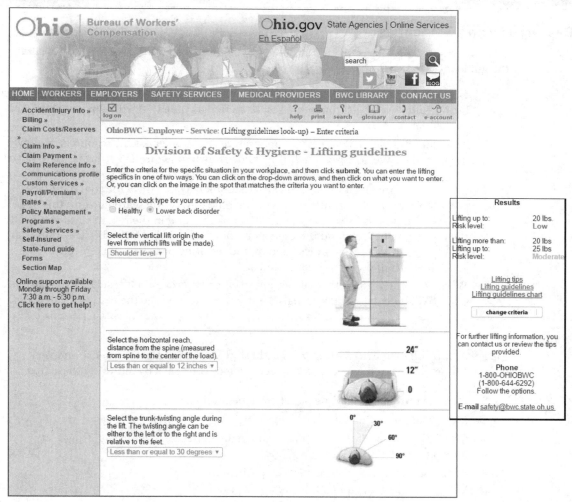

Compensation (BWC) is available online at https://www.bwc.ohio.gov. Figure 1-3 shows this calculator. This one is rather simple, requiring just a few pieces of information. When we selected lower back disorder, with a shoulder level lift, a horizontal reach of 12 inches, and a 30-degree trunk-twisting angle during the lift, the results box showed that lifting up to 20 pounds with the presented criteria resulted in a low risk level. It also showed that lifting between 20 and 25 pounds resulted in a moderate risk level. Exercise 1-1 will help you research lifting guidelines.

EXERCISE 1-1

Research Lifting Guidelines

It is important to protect yourself from injury while lifting, so take some time to research the guidelines:

1. Use your favorite Internet search engine to search on the keywords "workplace safety lifting guide." Search through the results to find a guide that will help you with your own situation.

   The Ohio Bureau of Workers' Compensation site is one possible resource, as shown in Figure 1-3. We accessed the lifting guide shown in Figure 1-3 at https://www.bwc .ohio.gov/employer/programs/safety/liftguide/liftguide.asp, but because sites tend to change their organization periodically, that link may not work for you. If it doesn't, go to their home page at https://www.bwc.ohio.gov. In the search box on this page enter **lifting guidelines**. You will need to poke around in the results until you locate the lifting guide. We found it by selecting the result labeled "OhioBWC—Employer (Safety Services)—Ergonomics," and on the resulting page we selected "Lifting guidelines" from the list of related links.

2. When you find a guide that allows you to enter criteria for a lift, such as that at the Ohio BWC site, make up a scenario, enter the data, and see the results it calculates.

Tips for Safe Lifting and Moving The best protection is common sense and very careful lifting. So, when lifting a heavy object, protect your back by following these tips:

- Plan the move and clear the path before beginning.
- Move as close to the item as possible.
- Check the weight of the equipment to see if you need assistance in lifting and moving it.
- Keep your back straight and vertical to the floor.
- Keep your head up and look straight ahead.
- Do not stoop, but bend your knees.
- Carry the item close to your body.
- Tighten abdominal muscles to help your back.
- Use slow, smooth movements, and do not twist your back while lifting.
- Don't try to carry heavy items farther than a few feet without the aid of a utility cart, such as the one shown in Figure 1-4.

A utility cart
is handy
for moving
computer
equipment.

Watch Out for Sharp Edges   Whenever handling computer components, be very careful of the sharp edges on sheet metal computer cases and in some peripherals. It is very easy to cut yourself on these. Similarly, the backs of many circuit boards contain very sharp wire ends that can cause puncture wounds. Work gloves offer protection, even if they are a bit awkward to use while handling delicate computer equipment. If you cannot wear gloves, be very cautious, checking each surface before positioning your hands.

Protecting the Equipment

While personal safety is paramount, you are also responsible for protecting the equipment you handle. Therefore, power down each piece of equipment and disconnect it from power outlets before moving it—even when moving it from one side of a desk to another. This includes laptops! Yes, they are portable devices, but if a computer has a conventional hard disk drive (HDD), moving it around while it is actively running can harm the hard drive.

Do not just flip the power switch, but select Power | Shut Down from the Windows Start menu or Start screen in Windows 8 or later (or Start | Shut Down in Windows Vista or

Windows 7). After the computer turns off, unplug the power cord. You may question always unplugging a device before moving it—even from one side of a desk to another, but we have seen too many instances in which a connected power cord caused personal injury or damage to other things. You simply are not in complete control of a device when it is still tethered to the wall.

Be very careful when moving displays. They can be fragile, and you must take care not to drop a display or put any pressure on the front of it.

Other devices require special handling when moving them. If you are unsure of the proper way to move a computer or peripheral, check out the documentation. For instance, in order to protect fragile components, a scanner may have a transportation lock that you must engage before moving it.

Hot Components

When you open up a computer or printer, be very careful to not touch hot components or let anything else touch them because some components, such as a CPU heat sink and a laser printer's fuser, remain hot enough to burn you for several minutes after powering them down. Cautiously check for hot components by holding your hand near, but not on, computer components before you touch them.

Electrical Safety

Both high voltage and low voltage can be dangerous, so be sure to follow precautions when working around high- and low-voltage devices, and avoid contact with them.

e x a m
watch   **Desktop PC power supplies and CRT monitors are high-voltage equipment. Never open them, and never wear an antistatic strap while working with either of these components.**

High Voltage

Leave servicing high-voltage peripherals such as CRT monitors, laser printers, and power supplies to technicians trained in that area. Even when unplugged for an extended period, such devices can store enough voltage to cause severe injury or death from electrical shock. Never use an electrostatic discharge (ESD) wristband or other antistatic equipment (discussed later in this chapter) when working with high-voltage devices.

Low Voltage

Although high voltage is obviously dangerous, low voltage, under certain circumstances, can also cause serious injury or death. People have died from electrical injuries involving as

exam
Watch   **Remember that both high voltage and low voltage can cause serious injuries and even death. Lack of external burns on a person who has had an electric shock does not necessarily mean that the injury is minor.**

little as 50 volts! Many variables determine the amount of damage electric shock can cause to a victim. These include (but are not limited to) the body's resistance or lack of resistance to the current, the path of the current through the body, and how long the body is in contact with the electrical current.

If the skin offers little electrical resistance (if it is wet, for instance), it may appear undamaged, although internal organs might be damaged. If the skin, due to dryness, thickness, or a combination of characteristics, offers greater resistance, it may burn badly but internal organs may not be damaged.

Electrostatic Discharge (ESD)

One of the most prevalent threats to a computer component is *electrostatic discharge (ESD)*, also known as static electricity, or simply, static. Static is all around us, especially when both the humidity and the temperature are low. When putting on a jacket makes the hair on your arm stand up, you are encountering static electricity. When you slide your feet across a carpet and then touch a person, a doorknob, or a light switch and feel a jolt, you are experiencing a static discharge.

The Dangers of ESD

ESD happens when two objects of uneven electrical charge encounter one another. Electricity always travels from an area of higher charge to an area of lower charge, and the static shock that you feel is the result of electrons jumping from your skin to the other object. The same process can occur within a computer. If your body has a high electric potential, electrons will transfer to the first computer component that you touch.

Electrostatic discharge can cause irreparable damage to your computer's components and peripherals. Typical ESD discharges range from 600 to 25,000 volts, although at tiny amperages. Most computer components can safely withstand voltages of ±12 volts, so damage to computer components can occur at as little as 30 volts—a charge you will not even detect because, under the right conditions, your body can withstand 25,000 volts.

on the
Job   **Do not count on the body's ability to withstand 25,000 volts. This ability depends on the right circumstances. Learn more about this in the next section.**

These very low-voltage static charges, or "hidden ESD," can come from many sources, including dust buildup inside a computer. Dust and other foreign particles can hold an electric charge that slowly bleeds into nearby components. This hidden ESD can cause serious problems because you will have no hint of trouble until damage has occurred and the component malfunctions. This damage is very difficult to pinpoint.

ESD can cause the immediate, catastrophic malfunction of a device, or it can cause a gradually worsening problem in a device—a process called degradation. As unlikely as it might seem, degradation damage can be more costly in lost work time and in troubleshooting and repair time than catastrophic damage. When a device suffers catastrophic damage, typically the result is immediate and obvious, so you will know to replace it right away. Degradation, on the other hand, can cause a component to malfunction sporadically, sometimes working and sometimes not. This makes pinpointing the cause harder, and the problem will persist for a longer period and be more disruptive to the user and to the support professional.

Additionally, a total failure of one component will typically not affect the usability of other components. However, degradation can cause a component to fail in ways that also result in the failure of other components.

Protection from ESD Damage and Injury

There are many ways to prevent ESD from damaging computer equipment. First, low humidity contributes to ESD; therefore, when possible, keep computer equipment in a room in which the humidity is between 50 and 80 percent. Avoid cold and dry (below 50 percent humidity) conditions, as that creates the ideal environment for ESD to occur. But do not allow the humidity to rise above 80 percent, or condensation could form on the equipment and cause it to short out.

To prevent damage to the system, you must equalize the electrical charge between your body and the components inside your computer. Touching a grounded portion of your computer's chassis will work to some extent (which CompTIA A+ 902 exam objective 5.1 calls *self-grounding*), but for complete safety, use an *ESD wrist strap* with a ground wire attached to the computer frame. See Figure 1-5 showing an ESD wrist strap with an alligator clip for attaching the ground wire to a grounded object. This will drain static charges from your body to ground. If a static charge has built up in the computer equipment, it will also bleed from the computer through your body to ground. This is true of any electrical flow; therefore, you must never use an antistatic strap attached to your body when working around high-voltage devices.

FIGURE 1-5

An ESD wrist
strap with
grounding wire
and alligator clip

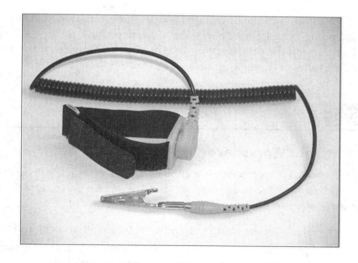

on the
job

Avoid severe electric shock caused by misuse of an ESD device. Never use one of these devices in a manner that puts your body between a power source and ground, such as when working around high-voltage devices.

Many computer assembly and repair shops use an *ESD mat* that discharges static when you stand on it. Similarly, an ESD mat on the bench table is a safe place to put expansion cards or other internal components that you have removed from the computer. An ESD mat looks like a vinyl placemat, but it has a wire lead and (usually) an alligator clip to connect it to ground.

Before you pick up a loose computer component, if you are not wearing or touching an antistatic device, discharge any static electricity on your body by touching something metal, such as a table leg or chair. Equipment placed on the mat will discharge static through it. All of these ESD devices usually have cables that you must attach to a grounded metal object. Some have a single prong that you insert into the ground socket in a regular self-grounding wall outlet. In the United States and Canada, the ground socket is the single round socket offset from the two slender blade sockets. Other cables on ESD wrist or ankle straps or on ESD mats may use alligator clips for making this attachment. Components like memory sticks and adapter cards may come in antistatic packaging, often an antistatic bag, and you should store used components in antistatic bags if their original packaging is not available. Do not remove the item from the packaging or bag until you are prepared to install it, and never place it on top of its antistatic packaging, since the outside does not offer any protection.

on the
job

An antistatic bag provides no protection when used like a potholder to handle components. (Yes, we've seen people doing this.) There's no protection provided on the outside of the bag. ESD protection occurs only when the component is inside the bag. That's because the bag functions as a Faraday cage. (Google that if needed.)

In addition to the ESD/antistatic products mentioned in this section, there are others, including gloves, finger cots, labels, cleaners, bins, meters, and spray. Exercise 1-2 will lead you through the process of protecting your workspace and computer from ESD damage using some of these products.

EXERCISE 1-2

ESD-Proofing Your Workspace

Whether your workspace is a cubicle or desk at which you do minor repairs, or a computer workbench where you do more extensive service on computers and peripherals, follow these simple steps to ESD-proof your workspace:

1. Maintain the room's humidity between 50 percent and 80 percent.
2. Spray your clothing and the work area with antistatic spray. Never spray directly on the computer, its components, printers, or scanners.
3. Place an ESD mat on the workspace and attach its alligator clip to something stationary and metal, such as the leg of a table.
4. Remove all jewelry, including rings.
5. Put an ESD strap around your wrist, and attach the other end to a stationary metal object (if it has an alligator clip) or plug it into a wall outlet's ground socket (only if the grounding strap has an outlet prong).

Electromagnetic Interference (EMI)

Another problem related to electricity is *electromagnetic interference (EMI)*, which is the disruption of signal transmission caused by the radiation of electrical and magnetic fields. Equipment such as electric motors, high-voltage transformers, electrical panels, and fluorescent lights are sources of EMI. The EMI from these devices can temporarily interfere with the functioning of some types of computer equipment, such as older CRT monitors. EMI interference can cause a CRT to have a jittery or distorted picture, but removing the source of the interference, or moving the monitor, will cause the picture to return to normal. The biggest problem with EMI is that it can disturb the transmission of data over copper wires, such as network cables.

Putting magnetic business cards and refrigerator magnets on a computer is highly risky. Remember, a traditional hard drive's read/write head is actually a tiny electromagnet that writes magnetic information on a magnetic surface, so erasing data by putting a magnet near it is easy. Keep magnets away from computers!

Working Safely with Power Supplies

The power stored in the capacitors in a computer's high-voltage power supply is enough to cause injury or death. Simply turning off the power switch is not enough. Even when turned off, the power supply in a computer or printer can provide electricity, and most motherboards continue to have power applied—a technology called soft power that we describe in Chapter 5. To be safe, unplug the power supply and never wear an ESD wrist strap when replacing or handling a power supply. Also, never open a power supply.

Display Devices

Although flat-panel displays have replaced CRT monitors, there are still a few CRTs still out in the field. Remember—like power supplies, CRT monitors are high-voltage equipment and can store a harmful electrical charge, even when unplugged. Never open a CRT case, and never wear a wrist strap when handling a CRT. You do not want to provide a path to ground through your body for this charge.

Printers

Printers have many moving parts, so you need to follow several basic safety procedures whenever you work with or around a printer. Do not allow long hair, clothing, jewelry, or other objects near the moving parts of a printer, because of the danger of their being entangled in the moving parts, including feed or exit rollers. In particular, a necktie or scarf itself may build up a static charge that it can pass to the component if it touches it. When wearing a tie or scarf, make sure you either tuck it into your shirt or use some kind of clip or tie tack. Figure 1-6 shows an open printer and the cartridge assembly, which rapidly moves back and forth when operating.

Furthermore, do not try to operate a printer with the cover off. The cartridge in an inkjet printer, and the print head in a dot matrix printer, move rapidly back and forth across the page, and getting your hands or other objects caught is possible, damaging both you and the printer. The laser beam in a laser printer can cause eye damage. Most printers do not work when their covers are open anyway.

FIGURE 1-6 Keep loose clothing and jewelry away from open printers.

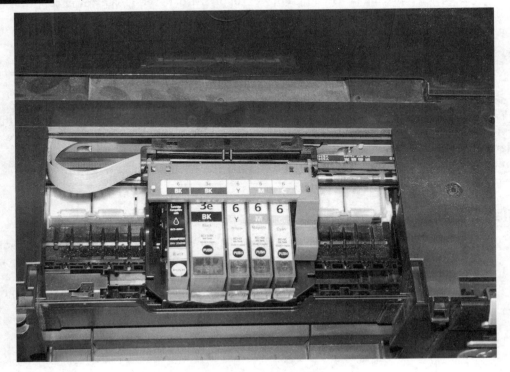

FIGURE 1-7   A laser printer with the toner cartridge removed, showing the potentially very hot fusing area deep in the back

The fusing assembly and the power supply pose the two biggest dangers associated with working with a laser printer. Avoid touching the fusing roller in a laser printer because it can be hot enough to burn. Power down a laser printer and allow it to cool off before opening it. Laser printers also use both high-voltage and low-voltage/high-current power supplies. Make sure you power off and unplug the laser printer before opening it. See Figure 1-7.

Compressed Air

You can use compressed air to clean dirt and dust out of computers, as described in Chapter 11. When using canned compressed air to blow dust out of computers and peripherals, take care to keep the can upright while spraying and avoid tilting or turning the can upside down because the liquid gas that forces the air out may spill and cause freeze burns on your skin and/or damage components. Never use compressed air from an air compressor because the pressure is too high and it can damage delicate components.

Additionally, when you use compressed air to clean anything, you should wear eye protection, such as safety goggles, and even an air filter mask to keep from inhaling dust and getting airborne particles in your eyes. Figure 1-8 shows these items, ready to use.

FIGURE 1-8

A can of
compressed air,
eye protection,
and a filter mask

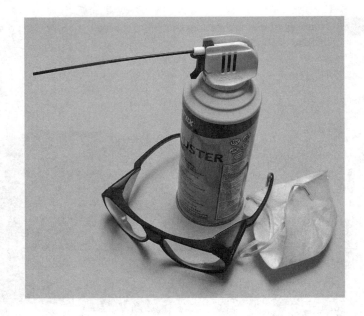

SCENARIO & SOLUTION

I need to remove a Phillips head screw from a computer case, but I don't have a Phillips head screwdriver that will fit. I would like to try a flat-bladed screwdriver. Should I do it?	Don't use a flat-bladed screwdriver in a Phillips head screw unless it is an emergency. To avoid damaging the screw or the computer, wait until you can obtain the correct tool.
Since a laptop is portable, is there any reason why I should not move it from desk to desk while it is operating?	A laptop's portability does not apply when it is up and running with the hard drive spinning. Before moving any PC, even a laptop, shut it down. After the computer turns off, unplug the power cord.
We have excellent climate control in our computer server room and equipment closet, but the manager prefers to keep the setting very cool and with a humidity level below 50 percent. Is this OK?	Such very low humidity levels create a perfect environment for ESD. At the very least, the manager should adjust the climate controls so that the humidity is above 50 percent, and raise the temperature to a comfortable level for employees.

CERTIFICATION OBJECTIVE

■ *902: 5.2   Given a scenario with potential environmental impacts, apply the appropriate controls*

The A+ candidate must prove knowledge of the dangers posed by inappropriate disposal of computer equipment and chemical solvents that contain materials hazardous to the environment. Similarly, the A+ exams will test your knowledge of how to discover proper disposal methods in your community.

Environmental Concerns for IT Professionals

As an IT professional, you will be concerned with the environment of the workplace and its effect on the health of people and equipment. Earlier, we detailed the issues of safety in the workplace, which is just one part of addressing your workplace environment. Next, we will look at protecting people and equipment from the airborne particles generated by manufacturing or computer equipment, and then we will examine proper disposal of computer waste without causing a negative impact on the environment.

Working in a Harsh Environment

Computers and peripherals, as well as the people who use and support them, often operate in harsh work environments that can negatively affect both the equipment and the people. These workplaces can be too hot, too cold, dusty, dirty, and noisy. Further, some worksites do not have the reliable, consistent power computers require. Now we'll look at measures you can take to protect people and equipment from problematic work environments.

Protection from Dust, Debris, and Other Airborne Particles

When cleaning computer equipment with compressed air or a vacuum, you might stir up a cloud of dust, debris, or other particles that you don't want in your lungs. For example, toner (which is a blend of iron and plastic powder) can be hazardous to breathe in. The dust and debris that build up inside a PC case can also cause coughing and breathing difficulties if inhaled.

When cleaning dusty items with compressed air or a vacuum, wear an air filter mask and safety goggles to keep all that dust and debris out of your eyes, nose, and mouth. In addition, when using a vacuum to clean up spilled toner, make sure it is a model designed for electronics use, not a regular household vacuum. That's because the electronics vacuum has a finer filter on it; on a standard vacuum, the particles can pass right through the air filter and circulate out into the air you breathe.

Providing the Proper Environment for Equipment

Extremes of heat, humidity, and airborne particles are damaging to computers and peripherals. To find the actual temperature and humidity extremes listed in the user or technical manual for a PC or component, look under "Operating Environment." A recommended operating environment is in the range of 50 to 90 degrees Fahrenheit (10 to 32 degrees Centigrade) with relative humidity between 50 and 80 percent. A rough guideline: if you are not comfortable, the PC is not either.

Therefore, the best operating environment for computers is a climate-controlled room with a filtration system to control these three enemies of electronics. However, since this is not always possible, consider an appropriate enclosure or case that will provide better ventilation and filtration.

Providing Good Power

Matching power requirements for equipment with power distribution is important. Therefore, ensure a power supply in a computer can handle the requirements of the components it supplies. Learn more in the discussion of power supplies, electrical terminology, and power requirements for PC components in Chapter 5, and learn about power requirements for laptops in Chapter 7.

When you consider a proper environment for computer equipment, you must also think of the power it receives. Therefore, you should never plug critical equipment into a wall outlet without some provision to protect it from the vagaries of the power grid. While sags in power below the 115V U.S. standards can cause your computer to reboot or power off, a power surge can do significant damage. A *power surge* is a brief, potentially damaging increase in the amount of electrical power. A simple power strip offers no protection because it is nothing more than an extension cord with several power outlets. At a minimum, use a surge suppressor to protect all computer equipment, including modems and phone and cable lines.

Surge Suppressor   At first glance, a *surge suppressor* (also called a *surge protector*) may look like an ordinary power strip, but it protects equipment from power surges. Your PC's power supply will also do this for small power fluctuations above the 115V U.S. standard, but it will eventually fail if it is the first line of defense. Therefore, plug your PC into a surge suppressor that has a protection rating of more than 800 joules. (A joule is a unit of energy.) Look for a surge suppressor that carries the Underwriters Laboratories label showing that it complies with UL standard 1449; this is the least expensive power protection device.

To distinguish a surge suppressor from a simple power strip, look for the UL label showing a protection rating of more than 800 joules.

Beyond Surge Suppressors   Do not just buy the minimum; buy the best power protection you can afford, which should include protection from power fluctuations, brownouts, and blackouts. *Power fluctuations* involve all sorts of inconsistencies in the delivery of electrical power—both too much (surges) and too little. A *brownout* is a period during which heavy demand or other problems cause a reduced flow of power, which can cause computers to behave erratically and suddenly power off. A *blackout* is a complete loss of power. The duration of a brownout or blackout depends on the cause and the ability of responsible parties, such as electrical utilities, to correct the problem. Blackouts can last hours or days, and your first concern related to a brownout or blackout is to have enough time to safely save your data and shut down your computer. The most common device that protects from power brownouts and blackouts while giving you time for these tasks is an *uninterruptible power supply (UPS)*. A UPS will also normally protect from power surges. A UPS is more expensive than a simple surge suppressor, but UPS prices have come down as more manufacturers have introduced consumer-level versions of these devices, such as the one shown in Figure 1-9. Notice the ports labeled Battery Backup and Surge Protection at the top and the ports labeled Surge Protection on the bottom. Plug your computer and display into the Battery Backup ports and they will be doubly protected. Plug less critical equipment into the second type of port to protect it from surges only, not from power outages.

FIGURE 1-9   This type of UPS contains a battery backup that provides battery power for a limited period in the event of a power outage.

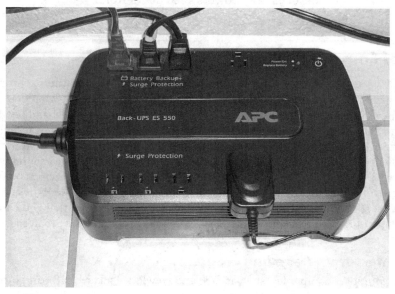

In order to select a UPS, first determine the power requirements in watts for each device you will connect to the UPS and add them up. Then decide how much time you would require to save your data when main power fails.

A computer or other device plugged into a UPS battery backup port is truly isolated from line power because during normal operation, the device runs directly off the battery through an inverter, which takes the direct current (DC) power stored in the battery and converts it to 110V, 60-cycle alternating current (AC) power. The battery is continually charging from line power, and when it loses line power, the battery continues to power the computer for a short period. The time the battery can power the computer is limited and varies by the capacity of the battery in the UPS and by how much power the computer draws. Unless line power comes back on quickly, you probably have a window of just minutes to save your data and to power down the computer. For this reason, a UPS device usually includes a data cable and software. Once the software is installed and the UPS senses a power outage, the software warns you to shut down. If no one is at the keyboard to respond, it will automatically save open data files, shut down the operating system, and power down the computer before the UPS itself runs out of battery power. A UPS is more expensive than a surge suppressor, but it gives excellent power protection.

In a real disaster, power can be off for days or weeks. If you work with mission-critical systems in certain industries, like banking and hospitals, the organization should have backup power generators that can kick in and provide power. Propane or diesel usually powers such generators.

Disposing of Computing Waste

Lead, mercury (including the mercury in laptop backlights), cadmium, chromium, brominated flame retardants, polychlorinated biphenyls (PCBs)—what do they all have in common? They are toxic to the environment and to humans if mishandled. They are widely used in electronics, including computers, printers, and monitors, so you must dispose of or recycle these items in the proper manner. You should never discard them directly into the trash where they will end up in landfills and potentially pollute the ground water.

In addition, electronics contain plastic, steel, aluminum, and precious metals—all of which are recoverable and recyclable. Provide containers in which to collect these components for proper sorting and disposal. Check with local agencies to ensure that you comply with local government regulations concerning disposal of all computer waste materials.

Manufacturers' Recycling Programs

Some computer companies, such as Dell and Hewlett-Packard (HP), and other electronics companies such as Nokia, are using more environmentally friendly components and working to recycle components from discarded computers. In fact, there is a relationship between these two activities. The more a manufacturer is involved in recycling the wastes from its products, the more changes that company makes to use more eco-friendly material. If companies don't use environmentally hazardous materials in electronic components in the first place, then the environment is in less danger. Manufacturers are a long way from eliminating hazardous materials from electronics, however, so we need to continue recycling for both hazardous and nonrenewable materials, such as gold, copper, and aluminum. In spite of efforts by several manufacturers to help users recycle computer components, estimates are that only 10 to 15 percent of electronics are recycled.

Batteries

Many batteries contain environmentally hazardous materials, such as lithium, mercury, or nickel and cadmium, so you cannot just put them in the trash where they will end up in a landfill. Many communities have special recycling depots that accept batteries so they do not introduce harmful elements into the environment; they may also periodically conduct hazardous material pickups in which you can hand over toxic materials, such as batteries and paint, for proper disposal.

Never store computer batteries for extended periods, and never leave batteries in equipment being stored for extended periods because battery casings are notorious for corroding, allowing the chemicals inside to leak or explode out. Leaking or exploding chemicals can cause a large mess within the equipment, destroy nearby components, and cause skin burns if you touch them.

Laser Printer Toner Cartridges

Laser printer toner cartridges contain the toner, which is the print medium for laser printers, and they often contain other components important to the printing process, such as the photosensitive drum. *Toner* is the medium for laser printers and is normally available packaged within a *toner cartridge*. The toner consists of very fine particles of clay combined with pigment and resin. Although the chemical makeup of laser toner may not be harmful, the super-fine powder of laser toner poses a hazard to your lungs. For this reason, be careful when cleaning up toner residue, using a damp cloth for any residue outside the printer, and a filtered vacuum (antistatic, if possible) when cleaning up spilled toner inside a printer that has been powered down and unplugged from a power source.

on the **job**

When working with laser printers and handling toner cartridges, avoid breathing in the toner powder.

The cartridges for many laser printers also contain the cylindrical photosensitive drum, the cleaning blade, and other components that are also considered consumables, because

FIGURE 1-10   A laser printer toner cartridge

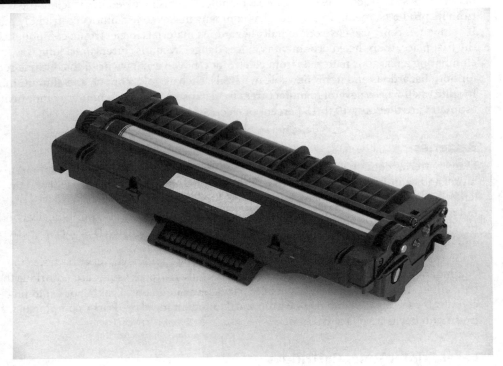

you normally replace the entire cartridge together with its contents once the toner is gone. Therefore, you will need to dispose of many toner cartridges over the life of a laser printer.

Laser printer toner cartridges also provide a potential environmental hazard due in part to their large numbers and the space they can take up in a landfill. For this reason, you should not simply throw them away. Fortunately, most toner cartridges have reusable components. That is, many companies will buy back used toner cartridges, refill and recondition them (if necessary), and then resell them. Figure 1-10 shows a laser toner cartridge removed from a printer. Learn more about the laser printing process in Chapter 21.

Ink Cartridges

The most common color printers found in homes and offices are inkjet printers that use wet ink that comes in cartridges. These cartridges are reusable, or you can recycle them for the plastic and other materials they contain. A large number of organizations accept used inkjet cartridges for recycling. Some, such as retailers, have collection containers

FIGURE 1-11   Used inkjet cartridges ready for recycling

for printer cartridges and other computer waste, and will give you credit toward new or recharged cartridges. Some organizations apply the profit from recycling the cartridges to some worthy cause. We use special preaddressed envelopers we received from a charity. Once we have enough to fill the envelope, we mail it in. It is easy to do this and it helps the environment as well as a charity of your choice. Do this with used cartridges, as well as those unused cartridges we often are left with after a printer fails and we discard it. Figure 1-11 shows print cartridges and a mailer for sending them in to a recycling center.

Display Devices

Because CRTs are obsolete, you will probably encounter some that you'll need to dispose of. CRT displays contain lead, which is toxic to the environment, but it is also a useful recyclable metal. Therefore, never throw CRTs in trash destined for a landfill. Always search for ways to recycle a CRT.

Flat-panel displays, including those in laptop computers, use fluorescent lamps that contain toxic material, so these displays, too, must be recycled. Call your local waste disposal organization and arrange to drop monitors off at its site. Many communities advertise locations and hours for these recycling services.

Chemical Solvents and Cans

All chemical solvents are potentially hazardous to the environment, so you must dispose of them properly. If you are unsure of the proper handling or disposal procedures for a chemical, look for its *material safety data sheet (MSDS)*. An MSDS is a standardized document that contains general information, ingredients, and fire and explosion warnings, as well as health, disposal, and safe transportation information about a particular product. Any manufacturer that sells a potentially hazardous product must issue an MSDS for it.

If an MSDS did not come with a particular chemical, contact the manufacturer or search for it on the Internet. A number of websites contain large lists of MSDSs. There have been some major changes in these websites. Therefore, if you wish to find an MSDS on a particular product or type of product, use a search engine with appropriate keywords, including MSDS and terms associated with the product.

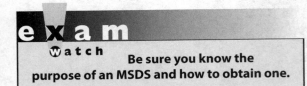

Many communities collect solvents and paints and make them available for recycling. Residents can go to the recycling center and obtain the solvents or paints for free or at a reduced cost. Those solvents and paints deemed unsafe for recycling are disposed of properly. Look for a hazardous material pickup or depot in your area.

Similarly, empty cans, including aerosol cans, should be disposed of in an appropriate manner. Contact your local waste disposal company for the proper handling and disposal of empty cans that once held solvents or other toxic materials. They may be as dangerous as their previous contents. Exercise 1-3 can help you get started researching the recycling options in your area.

EXERCISE 1-3

Researching Recycling Centers

Research the recycling options in your community.

1. First, use the local phone book and look under the local government listings for recycling. List the center nearest your home here:_____.
2. Call the center and determine if it accepts the following items: computer monitors, chemicals, empty paint and solvent cans, circuit boards, old computers, or batteries.
3. Find out the days and times when the center accepts these items for recycling and list them here:_____.
4. Ask if the center has private home pick-up service for recycling, and ask how to arrange it.
5. Ask if the center has a business pick-up service for recycling, and ask how to arrange it.

SCENARIO & SOLUTION

You work for a new small business that is planning to create an equipment room to house their network servers, network connection devices, and cabling. Describe the temperature and humidity ranges that are generally safe for this equipment.	The recommended operating environment for computer equipment is in the range of 50 to 90 degrees Fahrenheit (10 to 32 degrees Centigrade) with relative humidity between 50 and 80 percent.
What may happen to a computer when power to it sags below the 115V U.S. standard?	The computer may reboot or power off.
What documentation should a manufacturer provide that describes the proper disposal information for a chemical?	A material safety data sheet (MSDS) is a standardized document that contains general information, ingredients, and fire and explosion warnings, as well as health, disposal, and safe transportation information about a particular product.

CERTIFICATION OBJECTIVE

■ ***902: 5.3*** *Summarize the process of addressing prohibited content/activity, and explain privacy, licensing, and policy concepts*

The A+ exam will test your knowledge of the general concepts surrounding prohibited content in the workplace and how you, as an IT professional, should handle the discovery of prohibited activity.

Dealing with Prohibited Content and Prohibited Activities

Access to the Internet gives you access to the world with all its imperfections. Similarly, access to a corporate network gives you access to all types of content owned and managed by the corporation. As an IT professional, you need to be aware of issues related to the types of content available on the Internet, and, on a smaller scale, on a corporate network and local computers. In the following sections, we will discuss prohibited content and activities, and the government agencies and institutions that define and combat them. Then we will look at what you need to know about how you should respond on the job to discovery of prohibited content or activities.

Defining Prohibited Content and Behavior

Prohibited content is any content that an organization or government deems is harmful to the institution in general and to all persons or a class of persons for which it is responsible. An example of a class of persons is children, who can be harmed by content deemed pornographic or violent. In the case of an organization, the persons for whom this content is defined may be their employees, customers, or members. For a government, it covers their citizens and anyone who enters the country or, in the case of the Internet, communicates over the Internet. Content may also be prohibited in certain situations because it exposes the company to potential legal liability or gives away trade secrets or demographic information that a competitor could exploit.

As an IT professional, it is not usually your job to define what content should be prohibited in a particular environment; your job is to help enforce the guidelines or regulations that your employer provides by identifying, documenting, and reporting violations.

Policies Concerning Prohibited Content and Behavior

While governments have laws concerning prohibited content and behavior, most organizations have, or should have, documents defining how laws and the corporations' rules apply to employees and what they must do to comply. These may fall under a set of organizational policies and procedures, security policies, or both. Such policies vary by organization, but should cover certain areas and define prohibited behavior.

Acceptable-Use Policy

An *acceptable-use policy* is a security policy that defines what actions can be taken on data and computing resources, including—but not limited to—storing, accessing, deleting, disseminating, and sharing of that data through computers and networks. Such policy must comply with all applicable laws as well as the policies and rules of the organization. An acceptable-use policy normally defines how acceptable use is managed, ownership of data, what acceptable use is for various types of data and computing resources, and what incidental use of computing resources (e-mail, Internet access, fax machines, printers, copiers, etc.) is allowed for employees for personal use. We'll discuss some of the topics you should expect to find in an acceptable-use policy.

In defining how acceptable use is managed, the policy will define who is responsible for defining and maintaining this policy, who is responsible for training and educating employees about the acceptable-use policy, who is responsible for establishing a formal review cycle for the acceptable-use policy, and the initiatives that result from it.

Further, the acceptable-use policy will define an incident-report policy describing to whom employees should report any prohibited activity, what proof is needed to substantiate the claim, and what methods should be used to make a report.

An acceptable-use policy should define classes of data, depending on the type of organization. Confidential data is often organized into categories, such as patient medical data, patient/customer financial data, product data, research data, and many others.

An acceptable-use policy usually defines ownership of all data created and stored on the organization's computer systems as belonging to the organization. It also will state that, as part of managing acceptable use, designated employees have the right to monitor and/or log all employee use of such data and may access all such data stored at any time without employee knowledge.

An acceptable-use policy will also define the behavior of employees expected as part of acceptable use. This is usually a long list of requirements as well as prohibited behaviors. For instance, it will require that employees report any indication of a problem with computer security to the appropriate support staff. This includes unusual system behavior that could indicate a security threat. Employees are also required to report incidents of possible misuse or violation of the policy through the processes defined in the acceptable-use policy and to the appropriate staff. Other stipulations of an acceptable-use policy will prohibit users from sharing their user accounts (network, e-mail, and others) and related passwords, personal identification numbers (PINs), smart cards and similar security tokens, and other means of accessing accounts. Some organizations define a separate e-mail policy for employees, while others may combine these policies to include all user accounts.

Remember that your first response to prohibited behavior should be to identify the behavior, report through proper channels, and preserve the data (logs, etc.) or devices containing evidence of the prohibited behavior.

If incidental use of the organization's computer resources is allowed, the policy will define that use and most certainly will stipulate that the use must not result in any direct cost, legal action against, or embarrassment to the organization. Further, the acceptable use must not interfere with normal performance of the employee's job.

Educating Employees on Policies and Procedures

Organizations use a range of methods to educate employees on policies and procedures. These include documents, such as an employee handbook, which may serve as an introduction to policies and procedures, as well as a reference. A new employee may have to sign a receipt and acknowledgement document stating that they received the handbook and have read and understand the content.

Ongoing training is also important for educating employees about policies and procedures, especially in an organization, such as a hospital or clinic, which comes under strict laws concerning patients' confidentiality. Further, an organization may require that employees sign confidentiality and nondisclosure documents.

Additionally, some organizations will post signs reminding employees of required behavior, as well as informing customers/patients of their part in preserving their confidential data. For instance, we are all familiar with the signs in pharmacies requesting that clients line up an adequate distance from the pharmacy window to give others privacy while discussing and purchasing prescriptions.

Responding to the Discovery of Prohibited Content and/or Behavior

So, what should you do when you become aware of prohibited behavior? Perhaps you discover confidential patient information displayed on the screen of an unattended PC against company policy, or you find evidence of a coworker's access to a known pornographic website on their work PC. The answer is, "It all depends." Let's look at the three components of a first response to the two scenarios presented here.

Once you have clearly identified prohibited behavior, your first response will depend on the actual behavior as well as the company's policies and procedures. The following sections explain the procedures to follow when identifying and reporting prohibited behavior.

Identify the Problem

Identify the problem by asking yourself if it is truly a case of inappropriate behavior. In the case of the unattended PC with confidential patient information, this is inappropriate behavior, but you may need to determine if any harm has been done, and how you react also depends on the urgency of the situation and if harm has actually been done. Are unauthorized persons within viewing range of the computer screen? If so, then do whatever you can to change the screen content to hide such information. Is the responsible employee nearby? If so, then call it to that person's attention and have it corrected. Once you have identified that inappropriate behavior has occurred, you need to comply with company policies and procedures to determine if you are required to report the problem.

Report Through Proper Channels

In the case of finding clear evidence of or upon witnessing a coworker's access to prohibited content, you are required as an IT professional to report the incident through proper channels as defined in the organization's policies and procedures documents.

Document Your Findings

Accusing someone of breaking a law or violating company policies can have serious consequences and you should not take it lightly. Therefore, you will need to document your observations that resulted in the accusation. This may require that you write a few simple statements or it may require that you fill out forms. Whatever the case, when documenting any prohibited behavior, be sure to avoid expressing personal opinion and conjecture. Simply state what you observed.

Maintain Chain of Custody

Because such reporting can result in consequences to the employee, as an IT professional you will need to preserve and track evidence of the improper or even illegal behavior and present it to the proper person. It must be clear who has had access to the evidence, even digital evidence. This record of who has access or possession of evidence is called the chain of custody, and you will need to follow the procedures described in the policies and procedures documents. Someone—maybe you—must be responsible for tracking the evidence and documenting the entire process.

Data/Device Preservation

Take steps to carefully preserve any data or device involved in the use of prohibited content; that includes capturing data that proves prohibited behavior. The steps you take will depend on the location of this data and/or device. If the data was stored on a local PC, you may need to remove the PC and store it in a secure location. If the incriminating data is stored on a network server, you may need to find a way to protect the data and leave it unaltered on the server, at the same time ensuring that no unauthorized person has access to it.

SCENARIO & SOLUTION

You suspect that another employee is involved in prohibited activities. What should you do?	If all you have is a suspicion, you really cannot take action. Wait until you have proof.
You are unsure what is defined as prohibited content and prohibited behavior regarding the use of computer equipment in your organization. How can you learn more?	Go to a supervisor and tell her of your concern. Most organizations have manuals defining acceptable-use policy and also offer training to all employees.
Your company has a searchable policy document defining acceptable use. What term should you search to discover what actions you must take in order to file a claim against an employee for prohibited behavior?	Search on "incident report" or similar language in order to find to whom you report, what proof is needed, and the procedures required to file a claim.

CERTIFICATION OBJECTIVE

■ **902: 5.4** *Demonstrate proper communication techniques and professionalism*

CompTIA requires an A+ candidate to demonstrate knowledge of appropriate interpersonal communication skills and professionalism in the workplace. Real communication between people consists of both the verbal and nonverbal behavior that results in exchanging thoughts, messages, or information. Not only must you say the right words, but your body language must convey the same message as your words. Professionalism includes your behavior in all interactions, as well as how you treat property belonging to your employer and customers.

Professionalism and Proper Communication

You show professionalism on the job in the way you dress and behave, as well as in how you communicate with customers and colleagues. In this section, we'll explore the intertwined topics of professionalism and proper communication. In short, it isn't just what you say—it's how you say it and what you do while you are saying it.

Professionalism

Professionalism is a set of behaviors that each of us should use whether we are being observed or not. Many professions have a formal code of ethics that defines professionalism framed in the context of that profession. In this section, we will explore a general definition of professionalism for an IT worker, as it applies to behavior in dealing with others and in the treatment of property.

Professional Dress and Good Hygiene

Although not explicitly listed in the objectives for the A+ exams, good grooming, cleanliness, and proper dress are part of professional behavior. Wear freshly laundered clothes appropriate for the tasks required and that fit into your work environment. If you support computers for a group of attorneys, you may need to wear pressed slacks, shirt, and even a jacket. Tank tops are not appropriate in any office; skimpy clothes and flip flops are for picnics and the beach, not for work. Wear closed-toe shoes with nonskid soles. Even if your employer allows blue jeans, consider upgrading yourself to neatly pressed khakis to look a bit more professional.

exam

ⓦatch Unfortunately, any job in which you provide a service involves encounters with difficult customers, so expect some scenario-based questions on the exam involving your response to such situations.

Respect Toward Others—Even the Difficult Customer

Professional behavior is respectful and ethical. This includes being pleasant, reasonable, and positive in the face of the variety of events that can occur in the work environment, such as dealing with difficult customers or situations. Ethics includes how you react to a wide variety of situations.

Proper Language

Jargon is not necessarily bad—it is simply using words or acronyms, often technical and uncommon, that only people who share a common profession or interest understand. It is okay to use jargon when both parties understand it. It is not okay, or professional, to use jargon with people unfamiliar with it, such as the ordinary computer user you may encounter on the job, or nontechnical customers and coworkers. Similarly, be very careful to avoid common or vulgar slang expressions.

on the job Every profession has its own jargon. Because professions tend to be separate cultures, the use of jargon, abbreviations, acronyms, and slang among peers is generally acceptable, but do not let this spill over to your communications with people who are not part of your specific culture.

Listen and Do Not Interrupt

When a coworker or customer is explaining something to you—for example, when describing the symptoms of a problem—do not interrupt. Allow them to complete their statements. Do not jump to conclusions. If necessary, without interrupting, clarify customer statements by asking pertinent questions or restating your understanding in your own words. This shows that you are listening, and helps you to avoid making incorrect assumptions.

exam

ⓦatch Listening without interruption may be the most important communication skill you can develop, and you should expect scenario-based questions that test how well you embrace this idea.

Get Acknowledgment

Frequently confirm that the customer understands what you are saying by asking questions like, "Does that make sense?" "Does that sound okay to you?" "Would you like to go through those steps while I am here?" Think of the conversation as a train, with you as the engineer. The customer is a passenger waiting on the platform; if you do not stop or slow down, the customer cannot get on the train, and you will find yourself at the destination, but the customer will still be back at the station. Slow down and confirm that he is on board before you race ahead with a technical explanation that would please your coworkers but bewilder the customer.

Deal Appropriately with Customers' Confidential Materials

Deal appropriately with customers' confidential materials using tact and discretion, two very important components of effective communication. Tact involves showing consideration for others. Tactful communication is more about what you do not say than what you do say. Take care to not offend, no matter what you may think of the other person or what your own situation is. Being discreet includes not revealing information about someone that would be harmful to or embarrass her.

People often see *discretion* and tact as synonyms, but there is a subtle difference between them. For instance, a tactful person avoids embarrassing or distressing another. But discretion assumes a measure of good judgment based on the situation. It doesn't matter whether your encounters with customers are face-to-face, by phone, or purely via electronic messages (e-mail, newsgroups, or messaging)—you must still use tact and discretion.

Be culturally sensitive. In today's world, you may be dealing with people from around the globe. A smart-aleck comment that may be amusing in your own culture may be very offensive to a person from another culture. Be cautious and tactful when dealing with people from other cultures.

Be Tactful   Many times we have seen a customer who does not seem to understand the connection between the power switch and the computer, but still manages to figure out how to customize the Windows desktop with family photos on the background, customized pointers, and a desktop cluttered with dozens of files, folders, and shortcuts. Unless you are there specifically to help him clean up the desktop, stick to the purpose for the visit, and don't offer your opinion. This is using tact. After you have solved the technical problem, you might inquire if he has had end-user training on using the Windows desktop. If the answer is "Yes," then just drop the subject. If he lets you know that his own desktop actually bewilders him and he would like help cleaning it up and organizing his files, then you can go ahead and help him.

Be Discreet   Being discreet requires that you deal appropriately with confidential materials located on a customer's computer, desktop, printer, etc. Whatever you see on her desk or in her computer is her property, and to be discreet, you don't reveal it to anyone. Further, don't reveal unnecessary information to customers or coworkers. Gossiping about other people, company policies, or other proprietary information about the company is indiscreet. If the information would hurt or offend a third party or harm your company—keep it to yourself.

If you do not follow this advice and you divulge information you have no authority to share, you will find it difficult to build trust with other people. Even when someone seems to enjoy hearing the information, your behavior tells her that you are not trustworthy.

Be Cautious   Be careful with what you share with the customer. Sometimes technicians go too far in empathizing with the customer's plight and speak negatively about the equipment or software that the company pays you to support. The customer does not need to know that you think the printer the company bought for her is a poor one, or even that you dislike driving out to her office because of the terrible traffic conditions.

Avoid Arguing or Being Defensive   Avoid arguing with customers or coworkers, even if you feel the other person is being especially difficult. If you discover something that makes you angry, work to calm yourself before engaging about the problem. When others approach you angrily, stay calm and avoid becoming defensive. Resist falling into the payback trap of acting toward them the way they are acting toward you. These measured responses can defuse a potentially volatile situation.

Maintain a Positive Attitude   Work to maintain a positive attitude and tone of voice. A positive attitude takes practice and discipline; everyone has personal problems and challenges in their lives, along with all the job issues such as politics, personalities, work goals, and more. You need to literally compartmentalize your life. Hold an image in your mind such that when you are at work the other parts of your life are behind doors. Try to keep the doors to these other parts of your life closed when you are at work, and only open them at an appropriate time. When you become successful at this, you will find that you are more effective in all the areas of your life, because you can give each area the full attention it deserves at the appropriate time.

Do Not Minimize Others' Concerns   Never minimize another person's problems and concerns. You are minimizing when you interrupt an explanation or show through body language, such as a dismissive wave of the hand, that his concern is not important to you. Do not tell the customer about someone else who has a worse predicament—that is irrelevant to him. Imagine how you would feel if you could not get some work completed on time due to a computer problem, and while trying to explain your plight to a technician, she minimized or dismissed your concern as being unimportant.

You must also strike a balance between not minimizing and assuring the customer that you have an easy fix for the problem. An easy fix just means that you can solve the problem soon; it does not mean the customer has no reason to mourn the lost time, lost deadline, or loss of productivity.

Avoid Judgmental Behavior   Avoid being judgmental and/or insulting to anyone. Never resort to name-calling, which is damaging to any relationship and is completely unprofessional. For instance, if computer hardware and software fascinate you, you may find it difficult to be patient with those people who cannot seem to understand or even care how a computer works, and who frequently need help with hardware or software. It is just a small baby step to behaving judgmentally toward the customer.

Maintain Confidentiality and Respect for Privacy   When interacting with people, we learn things about one another; some of what we learn is personal, and we should not share it with others. Being professional includes knowing when to keep your mouth shut; this includes both company matters and someone's personal life. Being discreet shows respect for the privacy of others. Keeping such information to yourself helps you gain the trust of your coworkers and customers. Of course, being respectful of someone's privacy, you do not try to gain personal information, but sometimes you learn it inadvertently. However you learn such information, keep it to yourself.

Even if your organization does not formally provide a privacy policy, you should have your own personal policy that should be part of your personal standards of behavior.

Avoid Distractions

Distractions reduce your productivity and value as an employee. Some jobs are filled with distractions—ringing phones, conversations, music, construction noise, traffic noise, and more. Many distractions are unavoidable, but you can control some distractions, and how you control them is a measure of your professionalism. Personal calls, personal interruptions, and talking to coworkers while helping customers are distractions you must avoid because they show disrespect.

Taking Personal Calls   Because you can only make personal calls, such as calls to your doctor or child's school during normal business hours when doctors have hours and schools are open, if your workplace permits these, don't abuse the privilege. Keep them very short.

Talking to Coworkers   A productive work environment normally involves a community of people who treat each other professionally and work as a team. Therefore, in most jobs, you will have frequent conversations with coworkers—on both personal and professional topics. Personal discussion with coworkers should not occur within earshot of customers.

When you are talking to a customer, he should have your full attention. The only excuse for a side conversation is if it concerns solving the customer's problem, and you should even do that outside the customer's hearing if possible. The best rule is not to talk to coworkers while interacting with customers.

Minimizing Personal Interruptions   Personal interruptions come in many forms, such as personal calls, leaving the office during working hours for personal business, a family member or friend visiting the workplace, and attending to personal business in any way during work hours. Try especially hard to avoid these while helping a customer. Avoid personal interruptions as much as possible, and when such an interruption is necessary, be sure to minimize its impact on the customer by keeping it very brief and don't extend its effect by sharing details of the interruption with the customer.

Set and Meet Expectations

Many things, both actual and perceived, influence a customer's expectations. Your company may set expectations by describing your department and/or job function and the services it will provide to customers. This expectation exists even before you answer the customer's call or walk into their office.

Beyond that, you control the expectations—either consciously or unconsciously. Be aware of ways in which you do this. If a customer makes an unreasonable demand, do not simply smile without comment. This sets the expectation that you will deliver according to his demand. If you must disappoint, do it as soon as possible, so a simple disappointment doesn't turn into the perception that you broke a commitment—perceived or otherwise.

Control expectations, beginning with the expectation that you will be on time. If delayed, be sure to contact the customer, apologize, and provide a reliable estimate of when you will arrive. Then, once you have determined what the problem is, be sure to give the customer your best and most honest estimate of the timeline for solving the problem. When possible, offer different repair or replacement options because they give the customer a sense of control of a situation.

At the conclusion of a service call or visit, provide the customer with proper documentation on the services you provided. Sit down with the customer and review all that you did. If appropriate, have her sign a receipt confirming the work you performed.

Follow up with each customer later to verify satisfaction. This is important because people don't always tell you when they are not happy, and a quick phone call or e-mail might alert you to their dissatisfaction and give you a chance to rectify the situation.

SCENARIO & SOLUTION

How can I avoid a confrontation when someone else shows anger toward me?	Try to stay calm, avoid becoming defensive, and do not reciprocate the anger.
I try to put customers' concerns into perspective for them by telling them about others who are worse off. Is this a good practice?	No, this is not a good practice, because the customers will believe (rightly so) that you are minimizing their concerns.
If the company gives me a laptop to take home, do I have the right to use it for personal purposes?	No. Unless you have an unusual arrangement, you are to use the laptop given to you by the company for business purposes only. Using it for personal purposes is unprofessional.
I get very bored with talking to customers at the front counter, and I find that I can pick up my e-mail while listening to a customer's description of a problem. My boss has told me not to do this. Why is that?	This behavior is inappropriate for many reasons. Just one is that you are not showing the customer respect by letting him know that you are listening. And you may miss important information if you do not use active listening techniques.
I enjoy sharing information about office politics and unannounced changes in company policy. My boss has reprimanded me for this, but people seem to enjoy listening. Why is doing this a problem?	This behavior is inappropriate for many reasons. At the very least, revealing this information shows a lack of discretion and does not engender trust in you, even though people may seem to enjoy hearing the information.

CERTIFICATION SUMMARY

This chapter explored operational procedures, first by examining appropriate safety and environmental procedures, and then by detailing the handling of prohibited content and activities and the use of communication skills and professionalism in the workplace. Safety in an organization is everyone's responsibility. Always be aware of potential safety hazards and practice safe equipment handling to protect both yourself and equipment. Always dispose of computer components properly. Handle components carefully when you store them. Keep them out of hot or damp places, and keep magnetic storage devices away from EMI-emitting devices.

Candidates for an A+ certificate must understand the communication skills required for success on the job. This includes listening and communicating clearly while employing tact and discretion with all interpersonal contacts. Be conscious of your body language to ensure that your words and actions are not sending conflicting messages.

You should understand what your organization and all applicable laws define as prohibited content and prohibited activity. Know how to respond to an instance of use of prohibited content or prohibited activity, including how to report it through proper channels, how to preserve the data or devices involved, how to document it, and the proper chain of custody for the evidence.

TWO-MINUTE DRILL

Here are some of the key points covered in Chapter 1.

Workplace Safety and Safe Equipment Handling

❑ Organize cables to avoid tripping hazards, and use each appropriate repair tool only for its intended purpose.

❑ Common tools for working on computers include Phillips screwdrivers, a parts grabber, a flashlight, extra screws, and cleaning equipment such as a vacuum designed for electronics.

❑ Learn about fire safety, including the types of possible fire fuels and the appropriate fire extinguisher to use for each.

❑ Protect your back when lifting and moving equipment by following published guidelines for what and how to safely lift.

❑ Turn off all equipment and disconnect the power cord before moving it, even laptops. Moving any computer while powered up could damage the hard drive(s).

❑ Avoid touching hot components, even after powering the equipment off.

❑ Do not try to service high-voltage peripherals, such as CRTs, laser printers, and power supplies.

❑ Do not use an ESD wristband when working with high-voltage devices.

❑ Both high-voltage and low-voltage devices can cause serious injury or death under certain circumstances.

❑ Electrostatic discharge (ESD) can cause damage to equipment, and low humidity contributes to ESD.

❑ Use ESD devices (ESD wrist straps, ESD mats, and antistatic bags) when working with and storing computer equipment, especially internal components.

❑ Electromagnetic interference (EMI) usually causes temporary problems and is more of a danger to data than to equipment.

❑ Once removed from a computer, a component is susceptible to damage unless it is properly stored to protect it from ESD and extremes of heat, cold, and humidity.

❑ Take extra precautions when working with a printer because long hair, loose clothing, and jewelry can catch in the moving parts or pass ESD to the printer.

❑ Do not try to operate a printer with the cover off.

❑ You can use compressed air to clean dirt and dust out of computers. Take care to blow the debris away from you, and to clean up any mess.

Environmental Concerns for IT Professionals

- ❑ You need to be aware of the workplace environment and its effect on the health of people and equipment.
- ❑ When cleaning dusty items with compressed air or a vacuum, wear an air filter mask and safety goggles to keep all that dust and debris out of your eyes, nose, and mouth.
- ❑ Use a climate-controlled environment whenever possible for both people and equipment.
- ❑ If you cannot maintain a good working environment for equipment, consider using an appropriate enclosure or case that will provide better ventilation and filtration.
- ❑ The power a computer receives is also part of its working environment. Use equipment to protect crucial equipment from power fluctuations. A surge suppressor with a rating of 800 joules or better is the least expensive protection from power surges.
- ❑ An uninterruptible power supply (UPS) protects from power fluctuations, brownouts, and blackouts.
- ❑ Toxic metals and chemicals used in computers and peripherals include mercury, cadmium, chromium, brominated flame-retardants, and polychlorinated biphenyls (PCBs).
- ❑ When a computer or component reaches the end of its useful life, dispose of it appropriately for proper handling of the toxic and reusable components.

Dealing with Prohibited Content and Prohibited Activities

- ❑ Prohibited content is any content that an organization or government deems is harmful to the institution in general and to all persons, or a certain class of persons, for which it is responsible.
- ❑ When prohibited content or behavior is discovered, be sure to document your findings, report the finding to the proper authorities, and maintain the chain of custody for any evidence.
- ❑ Governments have laws about prohibited content and behavior, and many organizations have documents defining how laws and the corporations' rules apply to the employees and what employees must do to comply, published as policies and procedures and/or security policies.

Professionalism and Proper Communication

- ❑ Professionalism is a set of behaviors that you should do whether you are being observed or not.
- ❑ Always practice tact and discretion in interactions with other people.
- ❑ Professional behavior is respectful and includes having a positive attitude, avoiding confrontation or having a judgmental attitude, and never minimizing others' concerns.
- ❑ When you are respectful, you are attentive and you respect confidentiality and privacy.

SELF TEST

The following questions will help you measure your understanding of the material presented in this chapter. Read all of the choices carefully because there might be more than one correct answer. Choose all correct answers for each question.

Workplace Safety and Safe Equipment Handling

1. Which of the following is the correct fire extinguisher class for an electrical fire?
   A.   A
   B.   B
   C.   C
   D.   D

2. Which statement is a true general comparison of the effects of EMI versus ESD?
   A.   ESD can damage hardware; EMI harms data.
   B.   EMI can harm hardware; ESD harms data.
   C.   ESD and EMI are identical.
   D.   EMI can cause injury or death; ESD is less harmful to people.

3. You plan to replace the power supply in a computer. What is the most important safety measure you should take to protect yourself?
   A.   Wear an antistatic wristband.
   B.   Do *not* ground yourself.
   C.   Bend your knees when you lift it.
   D.   Buy a name-brand power supply.

4. A client has a large CRT. It is now malfunctioning, and none of the external buttons on the monitor help, nor can you fix it using the Properties settings in Windows. Although the monitor is quite old, the client likes it, and wants it to be repaired if possible. What should you do?
   A.   Open the CRT case and look for a loose connection.
   B.   Take it to a qualified repair center.
   C.   Immediately discard it.
   D.   Recycle it.

5. What can you use to protect a PC from power sags?
   A.   Surge suppressor
   B.   Power supply
   C.   UPS
   D.   APS

6. What should you do before moving any computer equipment?
   A. Power down and disconnect the power cord.
   B. Wear work gloves.
   C. Put on a facemask.
   D. Remove the power supply.

7. What is the ideal environment for ESD to occur?
   A. Hot and humid
   B. Cold and humid
   C. Hot and dry
   D. Cold and dry

8. You are getting ready to install a new component, a memory stick that came in its own antistatic bag. What is the correct way to handle this component and the bag?
   A. Remove the component from the bag and place it on top of the bag until ready to install.
   B. Remove the component from the bag and immediately discard the bag.
   C. Leave the component in the bag until you are ready to install it.
   D. Remove the component from the bag and turn the bag inside out before placing the component on the bag.

9. When should you wear an air filter mask and goggles?
   A. When changing a toner cartridge
   B. When using compressed air to clean dust out of a PC case
   C. When installing RAM
   D. When disassembling a monitor

Environmental Concerns for IT Professionals

10. When a computer system is no longer functioning and is not repairable, how should you dispose of it?
    A. Put it in the trash.
    B. Donate it to a charity.
    C. Send it to a recycling center.
    D. Send it to a landfill.

11. You do not know the proper handling of an old solvent previously used in your company, and now you need to discard it. How can you find out more about it?
    A. Contact the manufacturer and ask for an MSDS.
    B. Send it to a recycling center.
    C. Transfer it to a glass jar for safe storage.
    D. Call 911.

12. What should you do with a large number of used batteries accumulated in your office?
    A. Dispose of them in the trash.
    B. Find a recycling center that will accept them.
    C. Send them back to the manufacturers.
    D. Let them accumulate and dispose of them about once a year.

13. Which of the following protects against blackouts?
    A. Power strip
    B. Surge suppressor
    C. Inverter
    D. UPS

Dealing with Prohibited Content and Prohibited Activities

14. Which of the following is a document that defines what actions can be taken on data and computing resources in a company?
    A. Acceptable-use policy
    B. Chain of custody
    C. Statement of libel
    D. User manual

15. You believe you have witnessed prohibited behavior, and you have clearly identified it by referring to company policies. What should you do next?
    A. Evaluate whether the policy is a good one and should be enforced.
    B. Report the incident through proper channels.
    C. Minimize the importance of the violation by finding a rationale.
    D. Wait until you observe a second violation of the same policy.

Professionalism and Proper Communication

16. When you are explaining something technical to a customer, which of the following is the best technique to use to confirm the customer understands your explanation?
    A. As you explain, intersperse questions such as, "Does that make sense?"
    B. After the explanation, give the customer a quiz.
    C. Give the customer a printed explanation to read as you speak.
    D. Maintain eye contact.

17. When someone has explained something to you, how can you make sure you heard and understood what she said?
A. Focus.
B. Repeat it back in your own words.
C. Imagine how you sound and appear to the other person.
D. Nod your head frequently.

18. Which of the following is a technique you would use to show respect to a customer? Select all that apply.
A. Be as clear as possible and correct any misunderstandings.
B. Show the customer your company's security policy.
C. Do not minimize the importance of what someone else tells you.
D. Treat others the way you like to be treated.

19. When a customer is explaining a problem, what is the single most important thing you must do?
A. Nod your head to show understanding.
B. Empathize.
C. Allow the customer to explain the problem without interruption.
D. Show respect.

20. What behavior shows a positive and professional attitude? Select all that apply.
A. Avoiding confrontation
B. Avoiding judgmental behavior
C. Showing respect
D. Minimizing another's concerns

SELF TEST ANSWERS

Workplace Safety and Safe Equipment Handling

1. ☑ **C.** Class C is the correct fire extinguisher class for an electrical fire.
☒ **A, B,** and **D** are all incorrect because they are the classes for, respectively, ordinary combustible materials, flammable or combustible liquids, and chemical fires.

2. ☑ **A.** ESD can damage hardware; EMI harms data. This general comparison is true concerning the effects of EMI versus ESD.

☒ **B** is incorrect because the opposite is true. **C** is incorrect because there is a difference. **D** is incorrect because ESD is potentially more harmful.

3. ☑ **B.** The most important safety measure you should take to protect yourself is to not ground yourself, because you do not want to make your body a path for electricity to take to ground. Wearing an antistatic wristband, standing on a grounding mat, or touching something already grounded would do this and put you in danger.
☒ **A** is incorrect because this would expose you to possible electrical shock. **C** is incorrect because replacing a power supply should not require heavy lifting. **D** is incorrect because this is not a safety measure.

4. ☑ **B.** Take it to a qualified repair center.
☒ **A** is incorrect because it is dangerous to open a CRT, and only highly trained technicians should open a CRT case. **C** is incorrect because this is an extreme reaction until you know more about the nature of the problem and whether the CRT can be repaired. If it cannot, then recycle it, rather than "discard" it. **D** is also incorrect until you have more information about the problem and whether the CRT can be repaired. If you cannot get it repaired, then you will need to recycle it.

5. ☑ **C.** A UPS will protect a PC from power sags because it provides conditioned power, free from the surges, spikes, and sags coming from the power company.
☒ **A** is incorrect because a surge suppressor only protects from power surges, not from power sags. **B** is incorrect because a power supply does not protect a PC from power sags. **D** is incorrect because APS is not a standard acronym for a power protection device.

6. ☑ **A.** Power down and disconnect the power cord before moving any computer equipment.
☒ **B** is incorrect because you only need to wear gloves when you are moving something with sharp edges, and not all computer equipment has sharp edges. **C** is incorrect because a facemask is only needed if you expect to be exposed to airborne particles. **D** is incorrect because this is a very extreme and unnecessary action to take before moving computer equipment.

7. ☑ **D.** Cold and dry is the ideal environment for ESD to occur. This should be avoided because ESD can damage equipment.
☒ **A, B,** and **C** are all incorrect because none of these is as ideal an environment for ESD as is a cold and dry environment.

8. ☑ **C.** Leave the component in the bag until you are ready to install it.
☒ **A** is incorrect because the outside of the bag may hold a static charge. **B** is incorrect because you may want to reuse the bag if you need to store this or another component at some time. **D** is incorrect because this procedure is not recommended and could expose the component to ESD.

9. ☑ **B.** Compressed air is likely to stir up dust and other debris that could get in your eyes and lungs. Protect yourself with a mask and goggles.
☒ **A** is incorrect because changing a toner cartridge is not likely to release much toner into the air. **C** is incorrect because installing RAM is not likely to stir up any airborne contaminants. **D** is incorrect because disassembling a monitor would not likely stir up airborne contaminants (and you should not be disassembling a monitor anyway).

Environmental Concerns for IT Professionals

10. ☑ **C.** Send it to a recycling center. Even a nonfunctioning computer has material in it that can and should be recycled.
☒ **A** is incorrect because something put into the trash will usually end up in a landfill (see response to **D**). **B** is incorrect because donating something that is beyond repair is not ethical, and is passing on the responsibility for disposing of the computer. **D** is incorrect because computers contain components that can contaminate the environment and components that should be recycled.

11. ☑ **A.** Contact the manufacturer and ask for an MSDS because this document will contain instructions on safe handling and safe disposal of the chemical.
☒ **B** is incorrect, although this is what you may ultimately do. You first need to know how to safely handle the chemical. **C** is incorrect because no information is available to lead you to believe the original container is not adequate. **D** is incorrect because there is no emergency.

12. ☑ **B.** Find a recycling center that will accept batteries is correct.
☒ **A** is incorrect because you should never throw batteries in the trash. They contain environmentally dangerous components and chemicals. **C** is incorrect in general. Some manufacturers may have a program for used batteries, but first locate a recycling center. **D** is incorrect because batteries stored for long periods can leak toxic chemicals.

13. ☑ **D.** UPS is correct. This is an online power protection device.
☒ **A** is incorrect because this provides no power protection whatsoever. **B** is incorrect because a surge suppressor only protects against power surges, and is not an online power protection device in the way that a UPS is, providing full-time power from the battery, and **C** is incorrect because an inverter takes low-voltage DC power and transforms it to 110V 60-cycle AC output.

Dealing with Prohibited Content and Prohibited Activities

14. ☑ **A.** An acceptable-use policy defines what can be done with data and computing resources in a company in order to preserve the company's interests.
☒ **B** is incorrect because chain of custody refers to the disciplined documentation of who has ownership of an item at any given time. **C** is incorrect because a libelous statement is one that is false, malicious, and defamatory and appears in print. **D** is incorrect because a user manual would explain how to operate a certain piece of hardware or software, but would not provide an overall policy for a company.

15. ☑ **B.** Report the incident through proper channels.
☒ **A, C,** and **D** are all incorrect. It is not your job to evaluate the policy, minimize the importance of the violation, or wait for a second violation.

Professionalism and Proper Communication

16. ☑ **A.** As you explain, intersperse questions such as "Does that make sense?" to confirm the customer's understanding.

☒ **B** is incorrect because giving a quiz is not the best technique and would probably make the customer angry. **C** is incorrect because this is not the best way to treat a customer. **D** is incorrect because although this should always be part of face-to-face interactions, eye contact is not the best technique to use to confirm understanding.

17. ☑ **B.** Repeat it back in your own words. This confirms that you heard and understand.

☒ **A** is incorrect, although focusing on the customer and the problem is an important thing to do. **C** is incorrect, although this is a good habit when you are the one doing the speaking. **D** is incorrect because, although this tells the speaker that you are listening, nodding does not confirm that you heard and understood what she said.

18. ☑ **A, C,** and **D.** These are all correct techniques for showing respect.

☒ **B** is incorrect because although this is an important policy for an organization, this behavior does not directly show respect at the personal level.

19. ☑ **C.** Allow the customer to explain the problem without interruption is the most important thing you must do when a customer is explaining a problem.

☒ **A, B,** and **D** are all incorrect because although you should use all of these in your interactions with the customer, the most important thing to do in this case is to allow the customer to explain without interruption.

20. ☑ **A, B,** and **C.** These are all correct behaviors that show a positive and professional attitude.

☒ **D** is incorrect because this is negative and unprofessional behavior.

Chapter 2

Operating System Fundamentals

I f you lump together all the Windows versions currently in use and count them as a single operating system (OS), Windows is the most widely used PC operating system for home and business. Therefore, technicians should prepare themselves to work with recent versions of the Microsoft Windows client operating systems. Like many people, you may have used Windows for much of your life, and you can competently do ordinary tasks, such as navigating folders, saving files, downloading files, and running programs. With such proficiency, you may wonder why you need to study the operating system any further. It's because you need a far different set of skills and knowledge to support Windows than you need to simply use it. Those skills include understanding it enough to competently install, configure, troubleshoot, and maintain it.

On the other hand, you do not need to be a systems programmer who understands the OS's source code. You only need a base of knowledge, a sharp mind, good powers of observation, and patience.

The coverage of Windows begins in this chapter with an overview of the versions included on the A+ exam, moves to a brief survey of important considerations you should know before installing or upgrading Windows, and finishes with a tour of the user interface. It also looks at the macOS user interface, and points out some of the features of that operating system.

Discussion of Windows continues in Chapters 8, 9, 10, 12, and 19. Each chapter will take you through a different aspect of supporting Windows, from working with Windows client virtualization (Chapter 8), then installing and upgrading Windows—either into a virtual machine or more conventionally on a physical PC (Chapter 9), managing disks and files (Chapter 10), troubleshooting and maintaining Windows (Chapter 12), and finally, supporting Windows as a network client (Chapter 19).

CERTIFICATION OBJECTIVE

■ **902: 1.1** *Compare and contrast various features and requirements of Microsoft operating systems (Windows Vista, Windows 7, Windows 8, Windows 8.1)*

CompTIA A+ 902 exam objective 1.1 requires that you understand the differences among various editions of four versions of Windows: Windows Vista, Windows 7, Windows 8, and Windows 8.1, including the implications of using the 32-bit or 64-bit versions of each. Be sure that you know the minimum system requirements for each of these versions, their system limits, and upgrade paths. You should be able to recognize the user interface and identify features in Windows Vista and Windows 7 such as Sidebar, Aero, gadgets, Compatibility Mode, virtual XP Mode, Windows Easy Transfer, Administrative Tools, Windows Defender, Windows Firewall, Security Center, and Event Viewer. Understanding file structure and paths will also help you support Windows, and you should know how to work with Windows User Account Control (UAC). In Windows 8 and 8.1, you should be familiar with side-by-side apps, the Metro (Modern) UI, pinning, OneDrive, the Windows Store, multi-monitor taskbars, charms, the Start screen, PowerShell, Live sign-in, and the Action Center.

Even though you have to study Windows 8 and 8.1 for the 220-902 exam, you won't deal with these versions much on the job. Because upgrading from Windows 8 to Windows 8.1 was rolled out through Windows Update automatically, you'll be hard-pressed to find an actual Windows 8 machine in the field. For that matter, you won't find a lot of Windows 8.1 machines either, because Microsoft made upgrading free from Windows 7/8/8.1 to Windows 10 for the first year (ending that offer in July 2016). We suggest installing Windows 8.1 in a virtual machine such as Hyper-V to do your exam prep.

Introduction to Windows Operating Systems

In this section, you will learn the purpose of operating systems, the differences among versions of the Windows operating system, the characteristics of 32-bit versus 64-bit Windows OSs, and the importance of updates and service packs. This section also contains an overview of selected features, and an explanation of Microsoft Support Lifecycle.

The Purpose of Operating Systems

The purpose of an *operating system (OS)* is to control all of the interactions among the various system components, the human interactions with the computer, and the network operations for the computer system. An OS is actually a group of programs that accomplishes its tasks by building an increasingly complex set of software layers between the lowest level of a computer system (the hardware) and the highest levels (user interactions). An important type of software that works closely with the OS is a *device driver*—program code that allows the OS to interact with and control a particular device. Many device drivers come with Windows and you can easily add others to the OS. That is why new hardware comes packaged with a disc containing a device driver for one or more versions of Windows and other OSs.

The OS is responsible for managing the computer's files in an organized manner and allowing the user to manage data files. The OS keeps track of the functions of particular files and brings them into memory as program code or data when needed. Furthermore, the OS is responsible for maintaining file associations so data files launch in the proper applications. The OS is also responsible for managing the computer's disks, keeping track of each disk's identification, and managing disk space use.

A *user interface (UI)* is both the visual portion of the operating system and the software components that allow the user to interact with the OS for starting programs, creating data, saving files, and other user tasks. A *graphical user interface (GUI)* is a user interface that takes advantage of a computer's graphics capabilities to make it easier for the user to interact with the OS by manipulating graphic objects on the desktop to accomplish a multitude of tasks.

An operating system also works with one or more computer architectures. A *computer architecture* (sometimes called the platform) is the basic design of a computer describing the data pathways and the methods the computer's CPU uses to access other components with the computer. In physical terms, the main components are the CPU, BIOS, and chipset—all of which you will study in Chapter 3.

The Many Flavors of Windows

Windows comes in many "flavors" involving versions and editions, and updates and service packs from Microsoft occasionally modify each of these. We will clarify the differences among these terms.

Windows Versions

Each Microsoft Windows *version* is a new level of the venerable operating system, with major changes to the core components of the operating system as well as a distinctive and unifying look to the GUI. The Windows versions included on the CompTIA A+ 220-902 exam include Windows Vista, Windows 7, Windows 8, and Windows 8.1. The exam objectives do not include Windows 10 yet.

ⓦatch Server versions of Windows, like client versions, come in several editions for each version. However, no server versions are covered on the current CompTIA A+ exams, so you don't have to study them.

Pre-Vista Versions This section provides a brief history of the early 32-bit Windows OSs to help you understand how Microsoft arrived at the design of Windows Vista, the earliest version of the OS you are expected to be familiar with for the CompTIA A+ 220-902 exam.

In 1995 and 1998, respectively, Microsoft released two 32-bit desktop versions, Windows 95 and Windows 98—both more or less based on the MS-DOS kernel and targeted to the consumer market, although Windows 98 was widely accepted in the corporate world. At the same time, Microsoft had an entirely different line of server operating systems, called Windows NT, based on a much more robust kernel and with better built-in security features.

Microsoft built both their Windows 2000 Workstation product for business desktops and Windows 2000 Server products on the same kernel with the same GUI. With the same GUI on the desktop as on servers, IT professionals thought that going forward life would be a bit easier for those who supported both desktop Windows and Windows Server. However, that was not going to last, because in 2000 Microsoft also introduced Windows Me (Millennium edition) for home users with new features and a significantly changed look. This product was not successful, and Windows XP, yet another version targeted at the desktop and with a different GUI than the server products, followed it a year later.

FIGURE 2-1

The Windows
Vista desktop

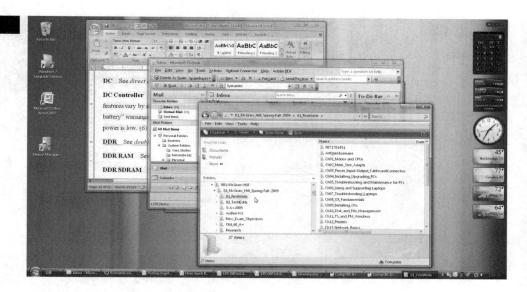

Microsoft released Windows XP in 2001 as a desktop operating system. The Windows XP default desktop was different from that of Windows 2000 in the overall look, if not in functionality. Windows XP was designed to be useful for both the home and business markets—no more separation, as there had been with Windows 2000 and Windows Me. It also had a cleaner look because the only icon on the desktop by default was the *Recycle Bin*, which pointed to the location where Windows sends deleted files. In addition, Microsoft redesigned and reorganized the Start menu to have two columns rather than just one.

Windows Vista   Microsoft released Windows Vista in 2007. Seen more as an upgrade to the extremely popular Windows XP, it included improvements in how Windows handles graphics, files, and communications. With enhancements to the GUI, Vista is attractive (see Figure 2-1), but it was not widely adopted due to problems with slow speed and high hardware requirements. As a result, Microsoft extended the support lifecycle of Windows XP, allowing sales of new PCs with Windows XP preinstalled until October 22, 2010.

Windows 7   Released in 2009, Windows 7 (see Figure 2-2) includes an enhanced GUI, improved speeds in just about any way you want to measure an OS, and nearly identical hardware requirements as Windows Vista. Given that computers became faster and cheaper (as they do) in the two years between the release of Windows Vista and the introduction of Windows 7, the hardware requirements for Windows 7 are not the burden on the customer that they were for Windows Vista.

Windows 8   Windows 8, released in October 2012, was a faster and leaner Windows OS with some surprising (and controversial) new features. The most obvious was the new Modern GUI (previously called Metro, and still called that in the A+ exam), an updated

FIGURE 2-2

The Windows 7
desktop

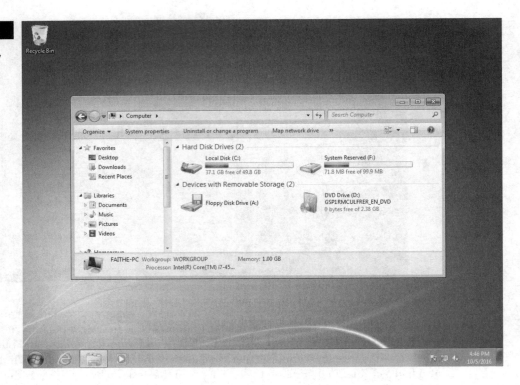

tile-based user interface. The Start screen shown in Figure 2-3 contained one tile for every installed application, and these tiles showed active content, such as news feeds, stock quotes, slideshows, and more, depending on the application. A Charms bar on the right side of the screen provided icons for common tasks. Touch screen support was emphasized, to the point where users with regular non-touch desktop PCs were at a disadvantage. The Windows desktop still existed, but you had to click a tile on the Start screen to access it. Clearly, Microsoft meant for users to begin phasing out of the desktop environment and into the Modern/Metro environment.

Users hated all these changes, and hated Microsoft's "trust us, we know what's good for you" attitude about it. Windows 8 was a flop.

Windows 8.1   Only 12 months after Windows 8's release, a chastened and apologetic Microsoft released Windows 8.1 as an "update" to Windows 8. Although it's technically a new operating system version, it was released as a free, automatically downloaded update for all Windows 8 PCs. That's why you will seldom see a PC running the original Windows 8 anymore. Windows 8.1 restored the desktop as the default interface (see Figure 2-4), brought back the Start button on the desktop (although it just opened the Start screen, not a Start menu as in Windows 7 and earlier), and deemphasized the much-hated Charms bar.

FIGURE 2-3

The Windows 8
Start screen

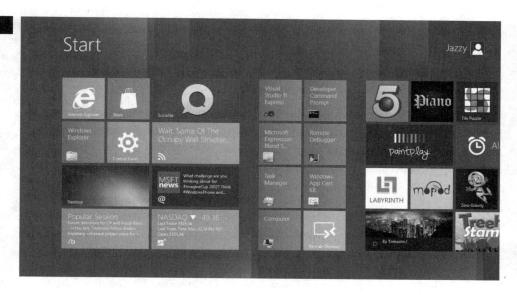

FIGURE 2-4 The Windows 8.1 desktop

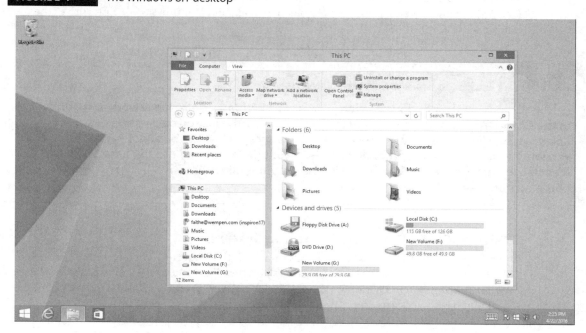

Windows 10 Windows 10, released in 2015, wiped the slate clean of that unpleasant business of Windows 8/8.1, and returned to what people wanted from Windows: a solid, easy-to-use desktop-centric operating system. Furthermore, Microsoft offered a free upgrade to Windows 10 for all existing Windows 7, 8, and 8.1 PCs that would support it, so Windows 10 is the predominant OS today, at least on newer PCs. Microsoft announced that Windows 10 would be the last Windows version sold, with future updates rolled out for free through Windows Update.

The CompTIA A+ 220-902 exam doesn't cover Windows 10, so we won't cover it heavily in this study guide. However, you will want to familiarize yourself with it on your own, because it's increasingly going to be the OS used on the client PCs you support as an IT professional.

Editions

Microsoft brings out an entirely new group of products for each version of Windows. What distinguishes each of these *editions* from one another is the mix of features in each that is designed for a specific target market. For example, Windows 7 could be purchased for home use (Home Basic, Home Premium), for business use (Professional), for large-scale business deployment via volume licenses (Enterprise), or as a top-of-the-line product containing all the available features (Ultimate). Windows 8 and 8.1 were released in three versions, Windows 8/8.1 (the basic version, designed for home and casual use), Windows 8/8.1 Pro (the professional version, designed for business use), and Windows 8/8.1 Enterprise (the big-business edition).

exam

ⓦatch In the previous version of the CompTIA A+ exam, you needed to know the specifics of each edition of each version. You don't have to go that deep with it anymore. Just remember that the basic and home versions don't allow you to connect to a Windows-domain network and don't offer sophisticated encryption or security services, while the business versions don't contain features of use to home users, like multimedia utilities.

32-Bit vs. 64-Bit Windows Operating Systems

Operating systems tie closely to the CPUs on which they can run. Therefore, we often use CPU terms to describe an operating system's abilities. For instance, Windows 2000 was a *32-bit operating system*. Windows Vista, Windows 7, and Windows 8/8.1 all come in both 32-bit and 64-bit versions.

TABLE 2-1	Edition	RAM Limit in 32-bit Windows	RAM Limit in 64-bit Windows
	Windows Vista Ultimate/Enterprise/Business	4 GB	128 GB
Windows Memory Usage Limits	Windows Vista Home Premium	4 GB	16 GB
	Windows Vista Home Basic	4 GB	8 GB
	Windows Vista Starter	1 GB	N/A
	Windows 7 Ultimate/Enterprise/Professional	4 GB	192 GB
	Windows 7 Home Premium	4 GB	16 GB
	Windows 7 Home Basic	4 GB	8 GB
	Windows 7 Starter	2 GB	N/A
	Windows 8/8.1	4 GB	128 GB
	Windows 8/8.1 Pro	4 GB	512 GB
	Windows 8/8.1 Enterprise	4 GB	512 GB

The biggest difference between the 32-bit and 64-bit versions of Windows is in the maximum address space used by both system random access memory (RAM) and other RAM and read-only memory (ROM) in your computer (see Table 2-1).

You may have noticed that calculating 2 to the 32nd power comes out to approximately 4 GB, which is where the RAM limit comes from for 32-bit Windows. So you might be thinking that a 64-bit system could handle 2 to the 64th power bits, right? That's about 2 billion gigabytes of RAM. In theory, yes, there are enough addresses to work with that much RAM in a 64-bit environment. However, in practice, 64-bit Windows is limited to between 8 GB and 512 GB, depending on the version and edition. Part of that is marketing (with the cheaper editions supporting less RAM), but part of that is also the physical logistics of the motherboard and the amount of RAM that today's motherboards can support. Chapter 3 explains those components in more detail.

A *64-bit operating system* requires 64-bit applications, although Microsoft has offered ways to support older applications in each upgrade of Windows, described later in this chapter in "Running Old Applications in Windows." To determine if a computer is running 32-bit or 64-bit Windows, follow the steps in Exercise 2-1.

Updates

Computer hardware technology does not stand still; therefore, operating systems must change to keep up. Each of the major operating systems is modular, so incremental updates can make some changes to the existing OS version. In Microsoft terminology, an *update* contains one or more software fixes or changes to the operating system. Some updates add abilities to the OS to support new hardware, and some resolve problems discovered with the operating system. This second type of update is often required to fix security problems. A *hotfix* or *patch* is a software fix for a single problem. However, Microsoft tends to call them all "updates" generically in newer Windows versions.

on the **job**

At one time, these updates, whether for functional or security problems, were issued without a predictable timetable. In recent years, Microsoft has assigned the second Tuesday of each month as the release day for updates. This day is widely called "patch Tuesday." Plan accordingly if your IT department lets users download and install their own updates.

Service Packs

A *service pack* is a bundle of patches or updates released periodically by a software publisher. Windows service packs are major milestones in the life of a Windows version. For that reason, some devices and applications will require not simply a certain version of Windows, but also a certain service pack. Microsoft is lately moving away from releasing big clusters of updates in named service packs, in favor of silently and gradually shipping them out via Windows Update.

EXERCISE 2-1

Viewing the Windows Version, Edition, and Service Pack Information

Here is an easy way to determine the version, edition, and service pack level for Windows Vista and Windows 7:

1. Open the Start menu and right-click Computer in the column on the right.
2. Select Properties.
3. Look for the version, edition, and service pack information near the top of the window, as shown in Figure 2-5.

Here are the steps for Windows 8.1:

1. Right-click the Start button and click System.
2. Look for the version, edition, and service pack information near the top of the window.

FIGURE 2-5

This System dialog box shows that the version is Windows 7, the edition is Ultimate, and it includes Service Pack 1.

Microsoft Support Lifecycle

Each version of Windows has a *support lifecycle*, as defined in Microsoft's Support Lifecycle Policy, first announced in 2002 and updated since then. A support lifecycle defines the length of time Microsoft will support a product, as well as the support options. It applies to most of their products that fall into two broad categories: Business and Developer products and Consumer, Hardware, and Multimedia products. All versions of Windows are included in the support lifecycle.

The lifecycle for each product moves through two phases: first is the Mainstream Support phase, followed by the Extended Support phase. Table 2-2, derived from information on Microsoft's Support Lifecycle page, illustrates the support options available during these two phases.

The lifecycle of each version also ties to the installed service pack level. Presently, Microsoft's policy is to end the support of a service pack 24 months after the next service pack releases or at the end of the product lifecycle, whichever comes first.

The current lifecycle for consumer versions of Windows is ten years, as announced in February 2012. Therefore, support for Windows Vista ends April 11, 2017, and for Windows 7 the end date is January 14, 2020. So we can count on updates and security patches for these products until those dates.

To learn more about the lifecycle for a specific product, enter the keywords "Microsoft support lifecycle" into your favorite search engine and select the result that points to the Microsoft Support Lifecycle page. From there, you can do a search on a product, such as Windows 7.

TABLE 2-2 Microsoft Support Phases — Available Support	Mainstream Support Phase	Extended Support Phase
Paid support	X	X
Security update support	X	X
Nonsecurity hotfix support (to fix a specific problem)	X	*
No-charge incident support	X	
Warranty claims	X	
Design changes and feature requests	X	
Product-specific information available in the online Microsoft Knowledge Base	X	X
Product-specific information available by using the Support site at Microsoft Help and Support	X	X

* Extended Support only available with an extended hotfix agreement purchased within 90 days of the end of mainstream support.

Considerations for Installing or Upgrading Windows

Unless you buy or build a custom computer, when you purchase a PC from a major manufacturer, it will come with the latest version of Windows installed. But what if you wish to install the latest version on your existing PC? It turns out you need to do a bit of homework before you make that step. First, you need to see if your computer meets the recommended system requirements. Then you will want to determine if the new version will be compatible with your existing hardware and applications. And finally, you need to know the upgrade paths to the new version because, in some cases, you cannot upgrade from the installed version and need to be prepared to take the correct steps to successfully install the new version. This section will prepare you for the actual installation or upgrade of Windows as presented in Chapter 9.

System Requirements

Each revision or version of an OS has specific minimum requirements for the level of CPU, amount of memory, and amount of free hard disk space. To determine if it will run on your existing computer, check the *system requirements* listed on the package and published on Microsoft's website. This will describe the minimum CPU, RAM, free hard disk space, and video adapter required. In early versions you could count on the system requirements being greater as you moved from one version to another, as from Windows Vista to Windows 7. However, the system requirements are the same for Windows 7, Windows 8/8.1, and Windows 10.

Another system requirement is the computer platform on which a given OS will run. Windows runs on the Microsoft/Intel platform, with a range of CPUs (from Intel and makers of compatible products, such as AMD), BIOSs, and chipsets compatible with Microsoft OSs. Some call this the *Wintel* architecture. We make another distinction between x86 systems, which are Wintel computers that support 32-bit Windows, and x64 systems, which support the 64-bit Windows. To make things a bit more complicated, Windows 8 supports both 32-bit and 64-bit Wintel systems, plus (in a special version) the ARM architecture, named for the manufacturer of these ultra-small CPUs and chipsets designed for mobile devices, such as tablets and smartphones.

e x a m

ⓦ a t c h **Given information about a computer's CPU, RAM, and free hard disk space, make sure you can identify which versions of Windows would run well on that computer.**

Table 2-3 describes the system minimums for the versions of Windows covered on the CompTIA A+ 220-902 exam. Additionally, an optical drive is required if you want to install from the Windows optical disc (CD or DVD). But these requirements are modest and far less than you will find in the most minimally configured new desktop PC.

TABLE 2-3		Windows Vista	Windows 7 Windows 8/8.1 Windows 10
Windows System Minimums			
	CPU	800 MHz	1 GHz (32-bit or 64-bit)
	RAM	512 MB	1 GB (32-bit) or 2 GB (64-bit)
	Free Hard Disk Space	15 GB	16 GB (32-bit) or 20 GB (64-bit)
	Video Adapter	Support for Super VGA graphics	DirectX 9 adapter with WDDM 1.0 or higher device driver
	Optical	CD if installing from disc	DVD if installing from disc

You would be very unhappy trying to work on a PC with a minimal configuration, because the programs most people choose to run on desktop computers have grown in their hardware requirements; you will want many hundreds of GBs of hard drive space for the programs you add and the data you will create with those programs. Therefore, the recommended configuration for 64-bit Windows 7 through Windows 10 is 2 GHz 64-bit multicore processor, 2+ GB of system memory, a 120 GB hard drive, and a DirectX 11 adapter with 256 MB graphics memory. Many of the features available with Windows require additional hardware support. For instance, Windows Media Center features (Windows 7, 8, or 8.1) need more video RAM and specialized hardware like a TV tuner. Windows Vista's Windows XP Mode requires an additional 1 GB of RAM and an additional 15 GB of available hard disk space, as well as a processor that supports hardware virtualization.

Application and Hardware Compatibility

After Microsoft releases a new Windows version, there is a transition time during which many individuals and organizations choose to stay with the old version; some move to the new version right away, and others make the change gradually. Not everyone immediately embraces the new OS and replaces their old OS with the new one. There are many reasons for this.

System Requirements

Old hardware may be below the system requirements. Therefore, if the old operating system is functioning adequately, individual users, as well as businesses, will not simply reflexively upgrade to the new OS until they have a compelling reason to do so.

Hardware Compatibility

The BIOS in an older PC may not support critical features of the new OS, and if the manufacturer does not offer a BIOS upgrade, the computer will not support the new OS. Hardware compatibility problems extend to peripherals when manufacturers do not create new device drivers for a new OS.

Software Compatibility

Some applications are written to take advantage of certain features (or weaknesses) in older versions of Windows. Large organizations have often delayed upgrading to a new OS until they could either find a way to make the critical old applications run in the new OS or find satisfactory replacements that would work in the new OS.

Upgrade Advisor/Upgrade Assistant/Get Windows 10

Although the recent versions of Windows test the compatibility of the hardware and (in the case of an upgrade) software early in the installation process, you would be smart to run this test yourself before you start the installation process—even before purchasing the new OS. Microsoft provides a utility for each of its recent upgrades that lets you test your computer and hardware for compatibility. This program is Upgrade Advisor for Windows Vista and 7, and was renamed Upgrade Assistant for Windows 8/8.1. The Windows 10 version is called Get Windows 10.

If you already have the installation media for the OS to install, you can check the compatibility as part of the Setup process. If you want to assess the system *before* purchasing a version of Windows, you can download the appropriate assessment utility from the Internet. Check out the Microsoft website to locate the Upgrade Advisor, Upgrade Assistant, or Get Windows 10 app for the specific version of Windows to which you want to upgrade.

After testing the hardware and the software, the utility produces a report providing valuable information and recommendations or tasks that you need to perform before installing the next version of Windows, and it may show tasks to perform after the installation. You may find the tasks needed to make a computer meet the compatibility and minimum system requirements are too expensive to perform on an older computer and decide to postpone your move to the new version until you are ready to replace the old system.

Exercise 2-2 provides the steps for acquiring and running the Windows 7 Upgrade Advisor for upgrading Windows XP and Vista systems to Windows 7. Exercise 2-3 does the same for checking upgradability from Windows 7, 8, or 8.1 to Windows 10. Chapter 9 includes details on the practice of upgrading an installed Windows OS with a new Windows OS.

The Acronyms lists for both the CompTIA A+ 901 and 902 Exam Objectives include the now-obsolete hardware compatibility list (HCL), a list of **compatible hardware that was included on the Windows distribution discs and maintained by Microsoft at their website. The Upgrade Advisor/Assistant replaced it.**

EXERCISE 2-2

Running Upgrade Advisor for Windows 7

Upgrade Advisor is somewhat dated in real-life usage, but it's still listed in CompTIA A+ 902 exam objective 1.4. You can use it to see if your Windows computer hardware and application software will be compatible with Windows 7. You will need a broadband Internet connection to successfully complete this exercise. Do this exercise on a PC running Windows XP or Windows Vista.

1. Open your Internet browser and enter the keywords **windows upgrade advisor** into your favorite search engine.
2. From the results, select a link (within the Microsoft.com domain) for the Windows 7 version of Upgrade Advisor.
3. Download and save the Upgrade Advisor file to the desktop.
4. When the download completes, locate the file on the desktop and double-click it to run the Advisor.
5. When the Upgrade Advisor completes, it will display a task list similar to the one in Figure 2-6. Print this out or save it.

EXERCISE 2-3

Checking for Windows 10 Compatibility with the Get Windows 10 App

The Windows 10 system requirements are the same as those of Windows 7 and 8.1, as you saw in Table 2-3, so compatibility is much less of a concern than it was with earlier version upgrades. The Get Windows 10 app runs a compatibility check as a precursor to the actual

FIGURE 2-6

A portion of
the Windows 7
Upgrade Advisor
task list

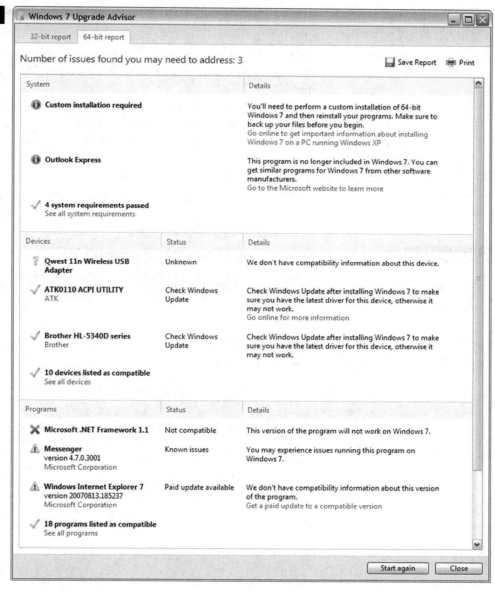

upgrade, and you can view a compatibility report from its initial step without performing the upgrade.

1. Open your favorite web browser and navigate to **www.microsoft.com/windows10**.
2. From the results, select a link (within the Microsoft.com domain) for the Get Windows 10 app.
3. Click the Download Now link, and when prompted to run or save, click Run. The Get Windows 10 app runs and performs a quick check of the system.
4. A screen appears with a View Report hyperlink. Click that hyperlink to see a report, as in Figure 2-7.
5. Close the app without performing the upgrade now.

FIGURE 2-7   The Get Windows 10 app reports any compatibility problems it finds.

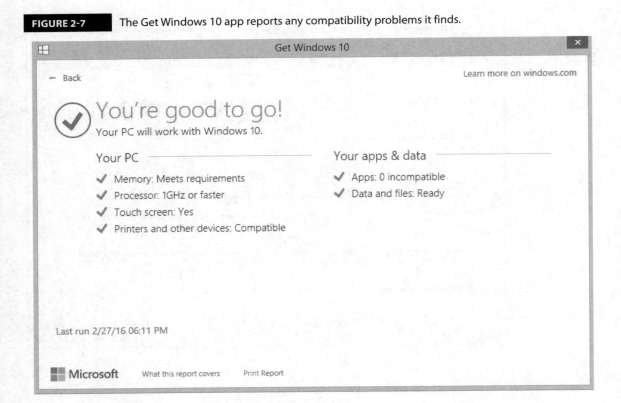

Running Old Applications in Windows

Some older programs don't run well under newer Windows versions. It's usually because they were written to assume certain things about the host OS that are no longer true. For example, some applications require a certain display resolution that Windows no longer supports (like 640 × 480), or a certain way of handling sound, memory, or CPU usage. An older program may fail to install under the newer Windows version, or may install but fail to run. You might or might not see an error message.

Fortunately, you can often trick an older program into installing and running in a newer version of Windows that it otherwise wouldn't accept by using Compatibility Mode. With some versions of Windows 7, you can also run Windows XP Mode, which may enable an application written for Windows XP to run on a Windows 7 machine that otherwise wouldn't support it. We'll examine each of these options next.

Compatibility Mode

Many older applications will work just fine in newer Windows versions, but there are always a few stubborn ones that won't. For such programs, you can set up *Compatibility Mode*, which sets up a custom sandbox in which the application can run with the settings it needs. You can set up Compatibility Mode manually in the Properties box for the application's executable or shortcut, or you can run the Program Compatibility Troubleshooter (which is called the Program Compatibility Wizard in Windows Vista) via the Help and Support Center. The compatibility settings are saved for the executable or shortcut, so they apply whenever you run it. In Exercise 2-4, you will practice using Compatibility Mode by configuring it both automatically and manually.

on the job

If you always want the program to run with certain compatibility settings, set up Compatibility Mode for the executable. If you want the option of running different compatibility settings at different times, create shortcuts to the executable (for example, on the desktop) and configure Compatibility Mode separately for each shortcut.

Compatibility Mode does not set up MS-DOS applications to run in a DOS environment; it only works for older Windows versions. In addition, not all older Windows versions are compatibility-supported in all versions. Windows Vista and Windows 7 both support all the Windows client versions all the way back to Windows NT 4.0 (Service Pack 5), plus Windows Server 2003. Windows 7 also includes Vista and Windows Server 2008 (Service Pack 1) as well. Windows 8/8.1 goes back as far as Windows 95 in client support, but supports no server versions. Windows 10 goes back only as far as Vista, and also supports no server versions.

on the **job**

Only use Compatibility Mode for old productivity applications (word processing, spreadsheet, and so on). Never use Compatibility Mode for antivirus programs, backup programs, or system programs (such as disk utilities and drivers) because these types of programs require more access to the disk and other resources than they will be allowed within Compatibility Mode.

EXERCISE 2-4

Exploring Compatibility Mode Settings

You can do this exercise in any version of Windows (Vista through 10), although the modes available will vary, and the automated method (Part I) isn't available in Vista.

Part I: Troubleshooting Compatibility Automatically   One way to troubleshoot compatibility is to use the automated wizard. In Windows 7 or later, you can do the following:

1. Right-click the shortcut or executable file you want to set up for Compatibility Mode. This shortcut can be on the desktop, on the Start menu or Start screen, or in a Windows Explorer or File Explorer window.
2. Click Troubleshoot Compatibility.
3. In the Program Compatibility Troubleshooter window, click Try Recommended Settings.
4. Click Test the Program. Windows will attempt to run the program. Try out the program to make sure it works. Then return to the Program Compatibility Troubleshooter window, and click Next.
5. If the program worked okay, click Yes, Save These Settings for This Program. If it didn't, click No, Try Again Using Different Settings.
6. If you chose to try again, click to check the check boxes for the problems you found, and then click Next.
7. The screens that appear after this point depend on what you chose in Step 6, so follow along with the prompts to complete the process until the application is working.

Part II: Troubleshooting Compatibility Manually   If the automatic compatibility settings don't solve your problems, you can try adjusting the settings manually. (Actually, you might want to adjust the settings manually anyway if you think you know what's wrong.)

1. Right-click the shortcut or executable file you want to set up for Compatibility Mode.
2. Click Properties, and then click the Compatibility tab.

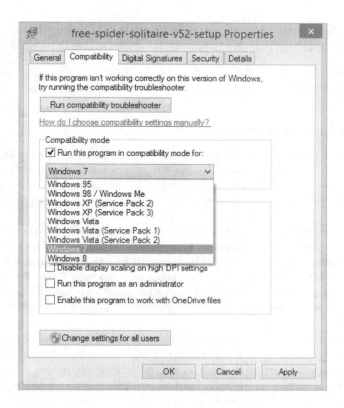

FIGURE 2-8

Setting the
Compatibility
Mode manually

3. Click to place a check mark in the Run This Program in Compatibility Mode For check box, and then choose the desired Windows version from the drop-down list. See Figure 2-8.
4. In the Settings area, click to place a check mark in any of the check boxes corresponding to options that you think might help correct the compatibility issues. You might need to experiment.
5. Click OK to apply the new settings, and then try running the application to see if your new settings helped. Repeat as needed.

Windows XP Mode and Windows Virtual PC

If Compatibility Mode does not enable an old program to run properly, and if you are running Windows 7 Professional, Enterprise, or Ultimate edition, then you can use Windows XP Mode, which is Microsoft Virtual PC with a fully licensed version of

XP installed. Windows XP Mode is not designed for 3-D games and other programs with high-end graphics needs, and it may not work with certain hardware, such as TV tuners. Once again, use this for the business productivity program that you need but cannot upgrade to a compatible version. We'll hold off on further discussion of Windows XP Mode until Chapter 8, where we explore the topic of operating system virtualization.

Clean Install vs. an Upgrade

A clean install, as the name implies, wipes out the system drive's entire content and starts fresh. The PC loses all data files, settings, and installed applications. You'll do a clean install on a new PC or when changing operating systems where there is no upgrade path from the old OS to the new OS. (See the next section for details about upgrade paths.)

Prior to Windows 8, sometimes a clean install was necessary to solve the thorniest OS problems. However, Windows 8, 8.1, and 10 all include a Reset feature as an alternative to doing a clean install for repair purposes. Reset has an advantage over a clean install, in that you can keep your files. (You'll still have to reinstall applications, though.) You can access it by booting from the installation media or, if Windows will boot, from the Settings app (Update & Security | Recovery).

An upgrade of an operating system, also called an *in-place upgrade*, is an installation of a newer operating system directly over an existing installation. An upgrade has the benefit of saving you the trouble of reinstalling all your programs and creating all your preference settings. Upgrades may not correct all previous system problems, however, and there is not always an upgrade path from the old to the new operating system.

Upgrade Paths

In order to do an upgrade installation, there must be a valid *upgrade path* from the old version to the new one. One global limitation is that you can't cross platforms (32-bit vs. 64-bit). Changing between those requires a clean install. Another limitation is that you can't upgrade when it would cause you to go backward edition-wise. For example, you can't upgrade Windows Vista Ultimate to Windows 7 Home Premium, because you would be losing some features that might be in use (like NTFS encryption or connection to a network domain). Tables 2-4 and 2-5 outline the upgrade paths from Vista to 7 and from 7 to 8, respectively.

Why would you want to upgrade from Windows 7 to the much reviled Windows 8 instead of upgrading directly 8.1? Because when you upgrade from Windows 7 directly to Windows 8.1, you can only keep personal files, not applications. If you do an interim upgrade, first to Windows 8 and then to Windows 8.1, you get to keep the applications. Table 2-6 provides the upgrade paths to Windows 8.1.

TABLE 2-4	From Windows Vista	Upgrade to Windows 7
Upgrade Paths from Windows Vista to Windows 7	Home Basic	Home Basic, Home Premium, Ultimate
	Home Premium	Home Premium, Ultimate
	Business	Professional, Enterprise, Ultimate
	Enterprise	Enterprise
	Ultimate	Ultimate

TABLE 2-5	From Windows 7	Upgrade to Windows 8
Upgrade Paths from Windows 7 to Windows 8	Starter	Windows 8, Windows 8 Pro
	Home Basic	Windows 8, Windows 8 Pro
	Home Premium	Windows 8, Windows 8 Pro
	Professional	Windows 8 Pro, Windows 8 Enterprise
	Enterprise	Windows 8 Enterprise
	Ultimate	Windows 8 Pro

TABLE 2-6	From Windows 7 or 8	Upgrade to Windows 8.1
Upgrade Paths from Windows 7 or 8 to Windows 8.1	Windows 7	Windows 8.1 (keep only files, not applications)
	Windows 8	Windows 8.1, Windows 8.1 Pro
	Windows 8 Pro	Windows 8.1 Pro, Windows 8.1 Enterprise
	Windows 8 Pro with Media Center	Windows 8.1 Pro, Windows 8.1 Enterprise
	Windows 8 Enterprise	Windows 8.1 Pro, Windows 8.1 Enterprise

Migrating Data and Settings

When preparing to move to a new version of Windows from an older version, whether you plan to do a clean install or an in-place upgrade, you will want to migrate your data and settings from the old to the new. Microsoft has provided tools for doing this, including *Windows Easy Transfer (WET) Wizard*, a utility introduced in Windows Vista. Learn more about this and other data migration tools in Chapter 9.

SCENARIO & SOLUTION	
What's the functional difference between 32-bit and 64-bit Windows versions?	A 64-bit Windows OS can access more RAM than a 32-bit version. The 32-bit version is limited to 4 GB of RAM, whereas 64-bit versions have a maximum that varies between versions and editions, ranging from 8 GB to 192 GB. If your PC has more than 4 GB of RAM, use the 64-bit version of Windows. Otherwise, it doesn't really matter.
Can I do an upgrade install from a 32-bit version of Windows to a 64-bit version or vice versa?	No, changing between 32-bit and 64-bit versions requires a clean install.
What is "patch Tuesday?"	Patch Tuesday is the second Tuesday of the month—the day when Microsoft releases regular updates to their products.
Why isn't support available for Windows XP anymore?	The product has reached the end of its lifecycle. A product's lifecycle ends ten years after its last service pack.
If my PC can run Windows 7, can it run Windows 8.1?	Probably. Their system requirements are the same.

Windows Features That Vary by Version

CompTIA A+ 902 exam objective 1.1 asks you to compare and contrast features and requirements among the various versions of Windows. So far in this chapter we have looked at the system requirements and interface differences between the versions; next we look at an assortment of individual features that the exam objective mentions specifically.

File Structure and Paths

Different versions of Windows store files and handle file paths slightly differently. The following sections review some of the differences.

File Management Application

In Windows Vista and Windows 7, the file management application is called Windows Explorer. When you open a certain location from the Start menu like Computer, Documents, or Pictures, you are really opening Windows Explorer to different locations. In Windows 8 and later, this utility is called File Explorer.

Another difference between versions is the name of the file management location where icons for all the local drives can be viewed. In Windows Vista and Windows 7, it's called Computer, and it includes only the local drive letters. In Windows 8/8.1 and Windows 10, it's called This PC and it includes shortcuts to some other locations too, such as the user's personal folders.

In Windows 7, 8/8.1, and 10, there's a shortcut to the file management utility on the taskbar. In Windows 7, this shortcut opens the Computer location. In Windows 8/8.1, it opens the This PC location if libraries are not enabled (see the next section), or the Libraries location if they are. In Windows 10, the shortcut opens a location called Quick Access, which shows shortcuts for frequently used folders and recently accessed files.

Libraries

Windows 7 introduced a file management feature called Libraries that was supposed to make file management easier, but that many people failed to understand. This feature still exists in Windows 8/8.1 and Windows 10, but it is no longer enabled by default.

Whereas in Windows Vista each user account has a Documents, Pictures, and Music folder of its own, Windows 7 has libraries with those names. A library is a virtual location that aggregates the content from multiple locations, making it seem like the files are all in a single location even if they are actually in many different folders. There are four default libraries (Documents, Pictures, Music, and Videos), and you can also create your own libraries.

In the navigation pane in Windows Explorer in Windows Vista, under the Favorite Links heading, you see shortcuts to personal folders. In Windows 7, in contrast, you see a Libraries heading in the navigation pane, under which are shortcuts to the libraries. When you open a library, such as Documents, you see the contents of two folders: My Documents and Public Documents. (You can also add other folders.) In Windows 8/8.1, shortcuts appear under This PC for those basic locations, but these aren't libraries; they're individual folders, like they were in Windows Vista. Figure 2-9 compares the navigation panes in the three versions. You can optionally enable the Libraries feature in Windows 8/8.1 by right-clicking an empty area of the navigation pane and clicking Show Libraries.

File Paths

Windows, like most operating systems, stores files on drives, within folders. The complete address of a particular file is its *path*. A path includes a drive letter, the folders (in order of closest to the root to furthest down), and the filename itself, like this:

C:\Users\Faithe\Documents\cports\readme.txt

The file's path can be represented with text, as in this example, or graphically in a *folder tree*, like the one in File Explorer shown in Figure 2-10. In a folder tree, the drive (volume) is

FIGURE 2-9

Navigation pane in Windows Vista (left), Windows 7 (center), and Windows 8.1 (right)

FIGURE 2-10

A folder tree like this one appears in the left pane in File Explorer in Windows 8.1.

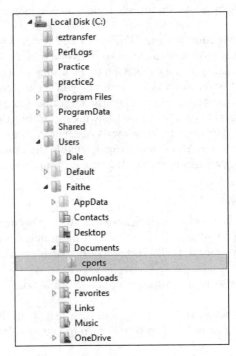

at the top level, and indented beneath it are the names of each folder. Under each folder are its subfolders, and so on. The individual files don't appear in the folder tree. In File Explorer, the folder tree levels can be expanded or collapsed. A white triangle means the level is collapsed; a black triangle means it is expanded. Click a triangle to change its state.

The folder trees and navigation panes are very similar across the Windows versions. However, in Windows Vista, the Folders portion of the navigation pane is hidden by default; you have to click the Folders button in the lower-left corner of the Windows Explorer window to display it.

File Locations

Each version of Windows has a few default folders that it uses for specific purposes. Some of these vary depending on the Windows version.

- **Program Files**   When you install a 64-bit desktop application on a 64-bit version of Windows, or a 32-bit desktop application on a 32-bit version of Windows, the Setup program usually creates a folder for it in the Program Files folder.
- **Program Files (x86)**   On a 64-bit Windows system, if you install a 32-bit desktop application, the Setup program usually creates a folder for it in the Program Files (x86) folder. This keeps the 32-bit programs separate from the 64-bit ones.
- **Windows**   The files that Windows itself needs to run are stored here. This doesn't vary; it's the same for all Windows versions and editions.
- **Users**   The files specific to each user are stored here, in folders with the user names. In Figure 2-10, for example, the Users folder contains a user folder for Faithe, and also one for Dale, and also one for Default (which is dimmed, indicating it is a hidden folder).

on the **job**

C:\Users\username\AppData is another important folder to know about for troubleshooting purposes. (It's hidden by default. To find it, display hidden files, as explained in Chapter 10.) The AppData folder holds settings for various applications that are specific to that user. For example, if you have Microsoft Word installed, its Normal.dotm template is stored in C:\Users*username*\AppData\Roaming\Microsoft\Templates.

Aero

Aero is a visual enhancement to the desktop that Microsoft introduced in Windows Vista and continues in most editions of Windows 7. (Aero features are deemphasized in Windows 8, and removed altogether in Windows 10.) Aero is disabled in Windows Vista and Windows 7 if the display adapter isn't adequate to handle it, or if the Windows edition is Home Basic or Starter.

FIGURE 2-11

Using Flip 3D in
Windows 7

Aero enables some interesting and handy effects like:

- **Aero Glass**   Aero is responsible for the semitransparent look (called Glass) of the taskbar and window borders. This is available only in Windows 7; in Windows 8, the taskbar is semitransparent, but windows aren't.
- **Flip 3D**   Press WINDOWS KEY-TAB to see your open windows in a three-dimensional stack that you can quickly flip through, as shown in Figure 2-11. (This doesn't work in Windows 8. Instead, in Windows 8, WINDOWS KEY-TAB activates a new task switcher that switches between Metro/Modern apps.)
- **Taskbar thumbnails**   Hover the mouse over a taskbar button for an open window to display a preview of the window.
- **ALT-TAB switching**   When Aero is enabled and you press ALT-TAB to switch between items, you see live previews of the windows for each open program.
- **Aero Peek**   Hover the mouse pointer over a taskbar thumbnail. The window you're hovering over will be displayed and all other windows will be temporarily transparent. This feature is called Peek (without the Aero moniker) in Windows 8.
- **Aero Snap**   Drag a window border to the left or right side of the screen and quickly release it to resize the window to take up half the screen. This only works if you drop quickly after dragging.
- **Aero Shake**   Click and hold a window's title bar and "shake" the window back and forth by rapidly moving your mouse. All other windows become minimized. Shake it again to bring them back.

FIGURE 2-12

The Sidebar in
Windows Vista
with several
gadgets

To enable Aero in Windows 7, switch to a desktop theme that is
in the Aero section of the Themes list. To switch themes, right-click
the desktop and click Personalize and then make your theme
selection. You don't have to enable it in Windows 8; what features
remain from Aero are automatically enabled, although they are no
longer called Aero.

Sidebar and Gadgets

The *Sidebar* was introduced in Windows Vista and removed from
subsequent versions. It is a vertical bar located by default on the right
side of the Vista desktop with the purpose of containing gadgets. A
gadget is a mini-program that shows information, such as time and
temperature in various locations, stock quotes, and handy tools such
as a small yellow notepad or calculator. The Windows Vista Sidebar,
shown in Figure 2-12, fits nicely on wide displays where you have
enough real estate to keep it visible while working at your normal
tasks. You can choose the various gadgets you wish to display, move
gadgets off the Sidebar where some of them will automatically grow
larger, or choose to eliminate the Sidebar altogether. Microsoft
removed the Sidebar from Windows 7 as unnecessary, since gadgets
can reside anywhere on the desktop.

To enable a gadget in Windows 7, simply right-click an empty
spot on the desktop and click Gadgets to open the Gadget Gallery,
shown along with some active gadgets in Figure 2-13. Double-click a
gadget to have it appear on the desktop.

Because of security vulnerabilities associated with gadgets,
Microsoft has discontinued them, and no longer provides them
for download from their website. Windows Vista and Windows 7
can continue to use their existing gadgets, however. Windows 8/8.1 doesn't include the
capability of using them.

Control Panel

The Control Panel provides access to utilities and settings that enable users to customize
Windows in various ways. Upcoming chapters explore many of these utilities and settings.
For now, though, let's look at one particular aspect of the Control Panel: Category View
versus Classic View.

Each utility or settings panel in the Control Panel is known as an *applet*, and is
represented by an icon. Before Windows Vista, all of the applet icons were displayed
together in the Control Panel folder. In Windows Vista and all subsequent Windows

FIGURE 2-13

On the left is the Windows 7 Gadget Gallery where you can select a gadget. On the right are several active gadgets.

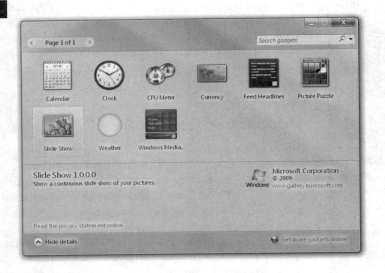

versions, Microsoft offers an alternative structure in which icons are organized into hierarchical groups. This look and organization is called *Category View*, because the many applets are organized into a handful of categories. In Vista, click Category View or Classic View in the navigation pane on the left to switch among the two views.

In Windows 7 and 8/8.1, you have three choices: Small Icons, Large Icons, and Category. Small Icons and Large Icons are different variations of Classic View, in which each applet has its own icon. To switch between Control Panel views in Windows 7 and 8/8.1, click the down arrow next to Category in the top right of the Control Panel folder. Then select Large Icons or Small Icons, either of which will change Control Panel to Classic View. Figure 2-14 shows the Windows 8.1 Control Panel in Category View.

Administrative Tools

Administrative Tools is a collection of utilities for system administration and troubleshooting. To access the Administrative Tools folder, open the Control Panel, click System and Security, and click Administrative Tools. In some versions of Windows you can also access Administrative Tools from the Start menu.

The actual utilities shown vary among Windows versions, and even among editions of a version. Figure 2-15 shows the Administrative Tools folder in Windows 8.1.

FIGURE 2-14   Windows 8.1 Control Panel in Category View

Event Viewer is one of the tools in Administrative Tools specifically called out in CompTIA A+ 902 exam objective 1.1. It's an administrative tool for logging errors, warnings, and other events that occur in Windows. If someone is having a problem with their computer and reports seeing an error in Windows but cannot recall what it said, open Event Viewer and search for the error. Beyond retrieving fleeting error messages, Microsoft has improved Event Viewer over the years to become a great tool for troubleshooting problems, allowing you to pinpoint the source of a problem. You will learn how to use Event Viewer in Chapter 12, and we will explore other tools available in Administrative Tools in later chapters.

FIGURE 2-15   Administrative Tools in Windows 8.1

Security Tools

We have two entire chapters devoted to security, but A+ 902 exam objective 1.1 explicitly lists several Windows features, so we will introduce them here, explain security fundamentals in Chapter 17, and show you how to use security tools in Chapter 18.

- *User Account Control (UAC)* is a security feature introduced in Windows Vista to prevent unauthorized changes to Windows. It has been modified and improved in newer versions of Windows.

- *BitLocker drive encryption* is a drive encryption technology introduced in Windows Vista Enterprise and Ultimate editions and continues to be improved in newer versions of Windows, although only available in certain editions.

- *Windows Defender* is an antispyware program, built into Windows since Windows 7, and a free download for Windows Vista. In Windows 8, 8.1, and 10, Windows Defender also includes antivirus protection. Prior to Windows 8, users could download Microsoft Security Essentials for free antivirus protection alongside Windows Defender.

- *Windows Firewall* is Microsoft's free personal firewall, which is software that guards against unauthorized network access to a single computer. First available in Service Pack 2 for Windows XP, it has been built into Windows since then.

- *Windows Security Center* is the Windows Vista page of the Control Panel that presents security status and gives access to Windows security tools.

- *Action Center* is the Windows 7 and later replacement for Windows Security Center. It provides not only security recommendations but also system maintenance recommendations.

System Restore and Shadow Copy

System Restore enables you to roll back the system configuration to an earlier time (a *restore point*) to correct recently introduced system problems. For example, if you install a bad driver or a buggy application that causes Windows to crash, you can correct the problem by using System Restore to roll back to a time before the bad change.

System Restore automatically creates a restore point once a day. You can also create your own restore points any time.

When System Restore creates its restore points, it makes a backup called a *shadow copy* of certain important system files. A shadow copy is a hidden backup that's only accessible through certain utilities. Some versions and editions of Windows can also make shadow copies of your data files, so you can restore previous versions of them if you accidentally save bad changes to them. Through the Previous Versions feature in Windows Vista Business, Enterprise, and Ultimate editions, and in all Windows 7 editions, you can browse and restore earlier versions of data files. Windows 8 and 8.1 don't support restoring previous data file versions, although System Restore still works just fine. Windows 10 brought back the ability to restore previous versions of data files, but the feature for making such copies is disabled by default. You'll learn more about the System Restore feature and shadow copies in Chapter 12.

ReadyBoost

ReadyBoost is included in Windows Vista and newer versions of Windows. It enables certain types of flash drives and solid-state storage cards (such as SD and CompactFlash cards) to be used as a write cache between the hard drive and RAM, to improve the computer's performance. When you plug in a flash drive, the AutoPlay dialog box offers an option to use the drive to speed up the system, and a ReadyBoost tab appears in the drive's Properties dialog box. From that tab you can allocate some of the drive's space to be used as a cache and keep the rest of it for storage. The minimum cache size is 250 MB, and the maximum is 4 GB in Vista or 32 GB (if NTFS is used on the drive being cached) for Windows 7 and newer versions. In Windows Vista you are limited to one device used this way at a time; in Windows 7 and newer you can use up to seven devices this way, at 32 GB each for up to 256 GB in cache altogether.

Why is a write cache a good thing? Because RAM is faster than a hard drive, and a flash drive is basically the same stuff as the main memory in your computer. By employing the faster medium as a cache, you reduce the amount of read operations the hard drive has to do, and speed up performance overall.

Easy Transfer

Windows Easy Transfer is a utility in Windows Vista, 7, 8, and 8.1 that helps transfer personal files and settings from one computer to another. It eases the pain and reduces the hassle of moving to a new computer. Windows 10 discontinued Windows Easy Transfer, and instead provides a free version of Laplink's PCmover Express utility.

Features Specific to Windows 8/8.1

As you learned earlier in this chapter, Windows 8 and 8.1 made some significant changes to the user interface. Windows 8 was a critically panned flop, largely because it was too focused on touch screen users and not convenient enough for desktop users. Windows 8.1 was released as quickly as Microsoft could possibly get it out there, correcting some of the shortcomings users complained most bitterly about (like not having a Start button, for example). Microsoft was aggressive about rolling out Windows 8.1 as a free upgrade, so as a result, you will rarely see a Windows 8 PC in the field today. The CompTIA A+ 220-902 exam officially does cover Windows 8, but most questions about it will also pertain to Windows 8.1. In the following sections we outline the features listed under 902 exam objective 1.1 that originated in Windows 8/8.1. (Some of them are still present in Windows 10 and some have been abandoned, but you don't need to know those details for the exam.) The upcoming Exercise 2-5 walks you through exploring several of the version-specific Windows 8/8.1 features you'll need to know.

Live Sign-in

In Windows 8/8.1, there are two available types of Windows user accounts. A *local account* is the traditional type of account; it exists only on the local PC. A *Microsoft account* (the default) is tied to a specific e-mail address which is then registered with a Microsoft server. Windows 8/8.1 encourage users to have Microsoft accounts by providing special features available only to Microsoft accounts, such as the ability to automatically transfer settings and appearance preferences between different PCs where the signed-in user is the same, and to access your OneDrive storage (described later in the chapter) without having to sign in separately. Windows 10 is the same; it also strongly pushes Microsoft accounts.

902 exam objective 1.1 refers to Microsoft account sign-in as "Live sign in" because Microsoft previously branded its sign-in process as Microsoft Live, and this naming has carried over. However, you won't see that naming in Windows itself.

The Start Screen

The Start screen serves the same purpose as the Start menu did in earlier Windows versions (and does again in Windows 10). It provides shortcuts for installed applications. In Windows 8 and 8.1, you can open the Start screen from the desktop by pressing the WINDOWS key. Windows 8.1 also has a Start button on the desktop that opens the Start screen.

The Start screen, at least as it initially opens when you summon it, does not provide shortcuts to every installed application. It starts out with a generic assortment of pinned items, but you can customize that as needed. It is like a bulletin board, in that you can *pin* items to it that you use frequently, and unpin the items you don't use much. To unpin an item, right-click its tile and click Unpin from Start, as shown in Figure 2-16.

To pin an application to the Start screen, you must pull up a list of all installed applications. To do so in Windows 8.1, click the down arrow at the bottom of the Start screen. Then locate the application, right-click it, and choose Pin to Start.

Windows 8 has no Start button. The Start button in Windows 8.1 appears in the lower-left corner of the screen, as you would expect from earlier Windows versions, but clicking it only opens the Start screen; it doesn't have its own menu.

However, the Start button in Windows 8.1 does have one great feature: if you right-click it, you get a menu of shortcuts to commonly used utilities like Control Panel, Device Manager, and Task Manager. (The Windows 10 Start button has that feature too.)

FIGURE 2-16 The Start screen in Windows 8.1

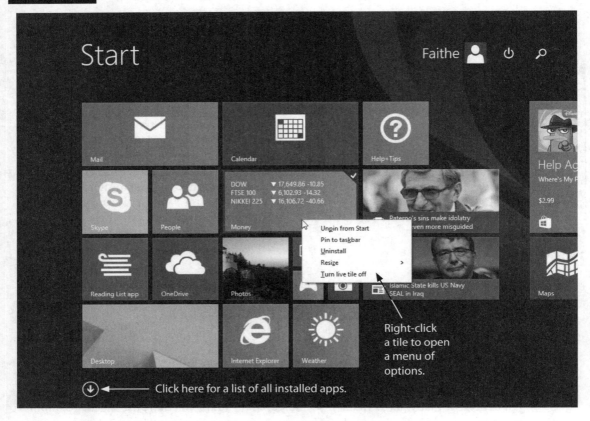

Start Faithe

Mail

Calendar

Help+Tips

Skype

People

DOW ▼ 17,649.86 -10.85
FTSE 100 ▼ 6,102.93 -14.32
NIKKEI 225 ▼ 16,106.72 -40.66

Money

Paterno's sins make idolatry even more misguided

Help Ac
Where's My P

$2.99

Unpin from Start
Pin to taskbar
Uninstall
Resize
Turn live tile off

Reading List app

OneDrive

Photos

Islamic State kills US Navy SEAL in Iraq

Maps

Desktop

Internet Explorer

Weather

Right-click
a tile to open
a menu of
options.

Click here for a list of all installed apps.

The Charms Bar

The Charms bar, a completely new feature in Windows 8/8.1, is a bar containing five special-purpose icons. You can bring it into view by swiping in from the right (on a touch screen) or moving the mouse pointer to the lower-right corner of the screen. Figure 2-17 shows the Charms bar in Windows 8.1. The icons, from top to bottom, are New image for this edition.

- **Search** Opens a Search box, in which you can search for anything (files, applications, stuff on the Web).
- **Share** Depending on the context, provides links to different ways of sharing the screen's current content. You might have the option to take a screenshot, for example, or send an e-mail.
- **Start** Returns you to the Start screen.

■ **Devices**   Depending on the devices available, may connect you to a projector, a printer, or some other device.

■ **Settings**   Opens a Settings task pane (see Figure 2-18), from which you can access the Control Panel, get information or help, adjust the volume, turn off the computer, and more. You can also click Change PC Settings to open the Settings app, which is an alternative to the Control Panel and provides some of the same settings and some different ones.

FIGURE 2-17

The Charms bar in Windows 8.1

FIGURE 2-18

The Settings task pane in Windows 8.1

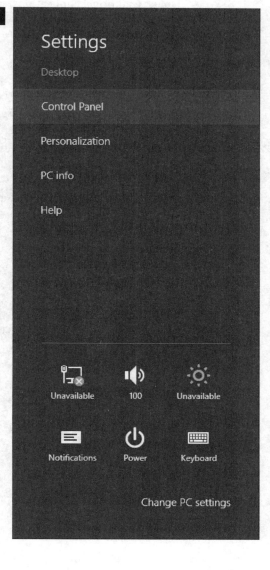

Metro/Modern Apps

As part of the new interface for Windows 8/8.1, Microsoft also released a radically new type of application, optimized for touch screen use. At first this was called the Metro user interface (UI), but due to some trademark complications, Microsoft rebranded it as the Modern UI. This new app type does not have menus or toolbars. Instead, users are expected to right-click or swipe to bring up command bars containing commands. Figure 2-19 shows an example of a Modern app.

Unlike traditional applications, which were purchased on discs and via downloads from websites, Modern apps are acquired online through the *Windows Store app*, which comes with Windows 8/8.1. Because there is a single source for all Modern apps, and Microsoft

FIGURE 2-19   Windows 8 introduced Modern apps such as this one.

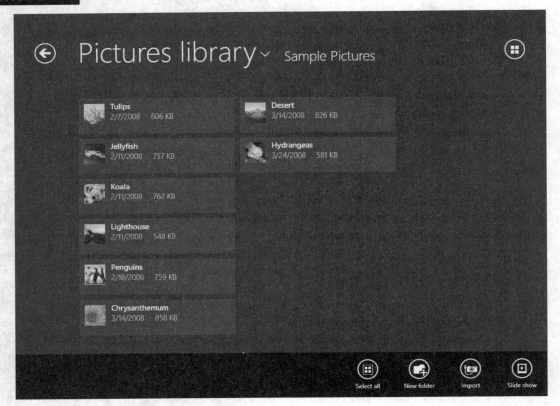

controls it, strict compatibility and quality controls can be enforced, cutting down on apps that crash, perform poorly, or introduce malware.

Most people already familiar with Windows hated Modern apps initially, because they seemed so foreign, aside from an arrow button to go back one screen. These apps originally lacked a title bar with window controls, as you can see in Figure 2-19, and the commands on the command bars weren't logically organized in many cases. So, when Microsoft revamped Windows for Windows 8.1, they also made some changes to how Modern apps are handled. For example, when you move the mouse pointer up to the top of the screen, a title bar appears for the Modern app, including that all-important Close button (X). In Windows 10, Modern apps still exist, but they stand out less because most of them can be windowed, so they look very much like desktop applications (except for a few cosmetic details).

Side-by-Side Apps

Modern apps are designed to run full-screen. However, there are times when you really need to see multiple apps at once, so Windows 8 included a side-by-side feature (aka *Snap*) that allowed you to "snap" a Modern app to either the left side or right side of the screen. You could then open a second Modern app in the other side, or view the desktop on the other side (including whatever desktop application was running on it at the time). The original Windows 8 implementation of this idea was wonky, however, and worked only if your screen was at least a certain width. In Windows 8.1, Snap works better, and with all screen resolutions. However, you still can't adjust the relative sizes of the two panes. In Windows 10, the split bar between them is adjustable.

To arrange two apps side by side, open one app, and then position the mouse pointer at the top of the screen and drag downward until the app image becomes smaller, like a window. Then drag it to the left or right and drop it on one side of the screen. Then return to the Start screen (press the WINDOWS key) and open another app to fill in the other side. See Figure 2-20. A dividing line appears between the two panes; to maximize one pane and minimize the other, drag the divider all the way in one direction or the other.

Application Switching

In all versions of Windows you can use ALT-TAB to switch between applications. Hold down the ALT key as you tap the TAB key to cycle through thumbnails of the open applications, and then release ALT to select one.

In Windows 8/8.1, there is an additional way of switching between Modern apps. Move the mouse pointer up to the top-left corner and pause for a thumbnail image to appear. If the thumbnail is of the app you want to switch to, click it. If not, move the mouse downward slightly to make a black bar appear with thumbnails of all the open Modern apps.

FIGURE 2-20   Side-by-side Modern apps in Windows 8.1

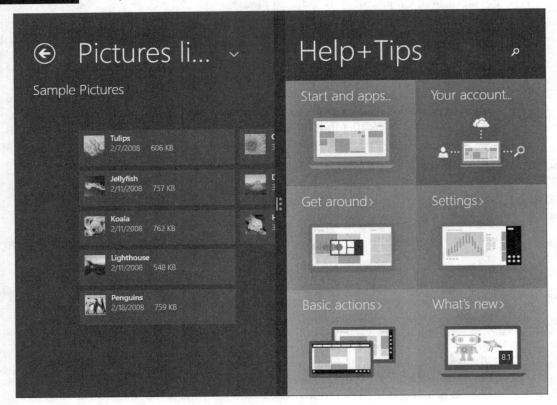

(The desktop and all its apps appear as a single thumbnail in that bar.) Click the desired thumbnail to switch to a different Modern app, or to the desktop. You might be thinking "That's really awkward; why in the world would Microsoft do that?" It is awkward with a mouse, but with a touch screen it makes a bit more sense.

Multi-monitor Taskbars

In previous Windows versions, when you have multiple monitors and you extend the desktop across them, the taskbar appears in only one monitor. In Windows 8, 8.1, and 10, on a multi-monitor setup, you can choose to enable the taskbar across displays. Right-click the taskbar and choose Properties. On the Taskbar tab, in the Multiple Displays section, check or clear the Show Taskbar on All Displays check box. You can then optionally adjust other settings as well for the multi-monitor taskbars.

Windows PowerShell

Windows PowerShell offers a more powerful version of the command-line interface than the standard command prompt. It comes with Windows 8, 8.1, and 10. To run it, click the Start button and then type **Power**, and then click Windows PowerShell in the search results. (In contrast, to run the standard command prompt, right-click the Start button and click Command Prompt.)

PowerShell offers more than just a command prompt, however. It is also an automation platform and .NET scripting language. It has a built-in editor for writing, testing, and debugging scripts, many keyboard shortcuts, and extensible add-ons.

Microsoft OneDrive

Microsoft OneDrive is a cloud storage location. Anyone can sign up for a certain amount of free storage space there, and you can buy more as needed. You can access OneDrive from any web browser, regardless of operating system version. However, Windows 8, 8.1, and 10 users who sign in with Microsoft accounts get access to their OneDrive storage in Windows without having to separately sign in to OneDrive.

There are several ways to access OneDrive. The easiest is via the OneDrive shortcut in File Explorer's navigation pane. It's important to note that this shortcut points to the OneDrive staging area in the active user's local files, not directly to the online storage. For better performance, OneDrive content is cached locally in the signed-in user's personal folder (C:\Users) and then uploaded and synchronized with online storage in the background.

Another way to access OneDrive is to use a web browser to go to https://onedrive.live .com. You can also go to https://www.office.com and sign in to your Microsoft account to use Office apps online and store the files in your OneDrive storage.

There is also a Modern-style OneDrive app that you can access from the Start screen in Windows 8/8.1.

EXERCISE 2-5

Exploring Windows 8.1 Features

This exercise reviews several of the version-specific Windows 8/8.1 features that you need to know about for 902 exam objective 1.1. Follow these steps in Windows 8.1:

1. Sign in to Windows 8.1 using a Microsoft account.
2. Open Notepad, and create a new file there. (Put whatever text you want in it.) Save it to OneDrive using the OneDrive navigation shortcut in the Save As dialog box in Notepad.

3. Open the Windows Store app. Download a free app (such as a game) and install it.
4. Open your newly downloaded app, and then open the Weather app in side-by-side split screen with it.
5. Switch between the Modern apps using the upper-left-corner mouse method.
6. Pin your new app to the Start screen. Then resize its tile (right-click to access that command) and then unpin it. Then uninstall it.
7. Open a web browser, navigate to **https://onedrive.live.com**, find the file you just created, and delete it. (If it doesn't appear there yet, wait for your PC to synchronize with OneDrive.)
8. Use the Settings charm to display the Settings task pane, and then click Change PC Settings. Review the available settings in the Settings app by clicking the entries in the navigation bar on the left. Then close the Settings app without making changes.

SCENARIO & SOLUTION

How do I remove pinned shortcuts from the Start menu in Windows 7, or the Start screen in Windows 8/8.1?	Right-click the item and choose Unpin from Start Menu (Windows 7) or Unpin from Start (Windows 8/8.1).
What's the difference between a personal folder like Documents and a library?	Libraries are not real folders; they are virtual locations that show the content of multiple locations. Where it gets confusing is that the Documents library's default folder is the signed-in user's Documents personal folder.
What if I don't know which category a particular utility is located under in the Control Panel?	Switch to Large Icons or Small Icons view (Windows 7 and later) or switch to Classic view (Windows Vista) to see all the icons at once
How do I remove a Metro/Modern app in Windows 8/8.1?	Right-click it on the Start screen and choose Uninstall.
How do I get to the Settings app in Windows 8/8.1?	Display the Charms bar, click the Settings charm, and then click Change PC Settings.

CERTIFICATION OBJECTIVE

■ *902: 2.1*   *Identify common features and functionality of the Mac OS and Linux operating systems*

CompTIA A+ 902 exam objective 2.1 is new to the latest version of the CompTIA A+ exam objectives. It asks that you be able to navigate Linux and Mac systems proficiently, including using common features and utilities to maintain the system and troubleshoot any problems that may occur. In the rest of this chapter you will learn how to install, upgrade, and configure Mac systems and how to use a few basic macOS features that the exam objectives specifically mention. Chapter 10 covers many of the basic Linux commands and Chapter 12 touches on a variety of macOS tools and best practices.

Configuring and Using macOS

As a CompTIA A+ certified technician, you probably won't spend a lot of time working on Macs, but when you do, you ought to be able to sit down at a Mac workstation and navigate with confidence. This section points out the specific macOS features listed under CompTIA A+ 902 exam objective 2.1. It's not a comprehensive list of important-to-know OS features, but it's a good start. We'll continue this topic in Chapter 12, when we look at OS utilities for maintaining a system. At that point we'll look at topics like backups, updates, and antimalware in a macOS context.

watch   **In September 2016, Apple changed the name of its desktop operating system from OS X to macOS, concurrently with the release of a new version called Sierra. (The previous version was OS X El Capitan.) We use this new naming convention throughout the book.**

The macOS Interface

macOS is a GUI, as is Windows, so the principles of navigation are the same. It has a colorful background, icons, toolbars, menus, and windows. The key landmarks of the interface are the Dock, Finder, and Apple menu. Many of the features to be covered are shown in Figure 2-21.

Dock

The *Dock* is the ribbon-like toolbar across the bottom of the screen in Figure 2-21. It's roughly the equivalent of the Start screen in Windows 8/8.1. It's like a bulletin board where you can pin shortcuts to the things you use the most. It comes with some shortcuts already pinned to it, but you can customize it completely, adding and removing items as needed.

FIGURE 2-21   The macOS desktop

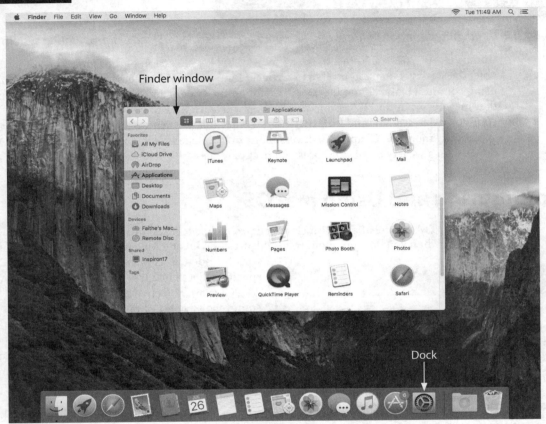

A black dot under an item on the Dock means it is running. In Figure 2-21, there is a black dot under the Finder icon (the leftmost icon).

To add an item to the Dock, drag and drop it onto the Dock, in the desired position. To remove an item from the Dock, right-click its icon on the Dock, point to Options, and click Remove from Dock.

Finder

Finder (the open window in Figure 2-21) is the equivalent of File Explorer in Windows. It's your file management interface. If Finder isn't open, you can open it from the Dock by clicking the Finder icon (shown with the black dot under it in Figure 2-21).

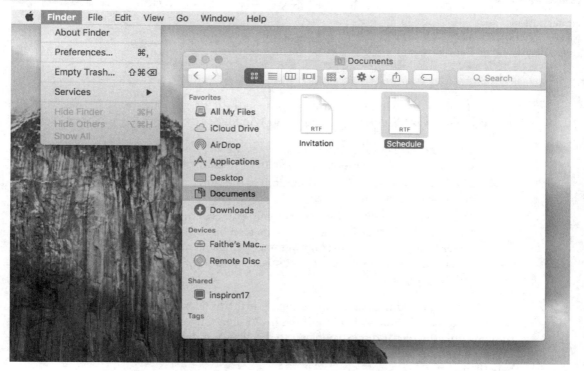

FIGURE 2-22 Menus appear for the active application.

Along the left side of the Finder window is a navigation pane, containing shortcuts to commonly accessed locations. In Figure 2-21, the Applications shortcut has been selected, so that the icons that appear are those of installed applications. You can start an application from here, by choosing its icon.

In macOS, a menu system for the active application appears in the upper-left corner of the screen. In Figure 2-22, you can see that because Finder is open, a Finder menu appears. The menu with the name that matches the program name (in this case, the Finder menu) contains commands for controlling the application. Most applications (Finder is an exception) have a Quit command on this menu, for exiting the application. There is also always a Help menu. The other menus vary depending on the application.

The buttons across the top of the Finder window help you navigate between locations and display content, similar to the ones in File Explorer/Windows Explorer in Windows. Figure 2-23 points out the buttons and their purposes.

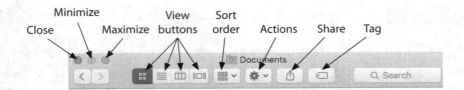

FIGURE 2-23

Finder buttons
for controlling
the display listing

A word about the window control buttons, on the left side of Figure 2-23. They work
mostly the same as the equivalent buttons in Windows, except for a few minor quirks:

- The Maximize button (green) maximizes the window such that you can't see the
  window controls anymore. Press ESC to un-maximize a window.
- The Minimize button (yellow) minimizes the running program or window to an icon
  on the right end of the Dock.
- The Close button (red) does not actually exit a running application; it just hides it.
  You can tell it's still running because its icon on the Dock appears with a black dot
  under it. If you want to exit a program, open its menu in the upper-left corner of
  the screen and choose Quit. (That doesn't work for Finder because Finder is not an
  ordinary application.)

One important thing to know about Finder is that it doesn't show you *all* the files the
way File Explorer/Windows Explorer does in Windows. It keeps nontechnical users safe by
showing only the files it thinks you want to see, like your data files and your applications.
Everything else is hidden. (Stuff like this is why newbies love Macs and most techies
hate them.)

e x a m

ⓦatch   One of the commands
on the Apple menu is Force Quit. You can
use this to quit an unresponsive program.
It's similar to using the Task Manager in
Windows to end a program.

Apple Menu

Click the apple symbol in the upper-left corner
of the screen to open the Apple menu. From
here you can shut down, log out, view system
preferences, visit the App Store, and more.
See Figure 2-24.

Running Applications

Clicking the rocket icon on the Dock opens Launchpad, a screen of icons for the installed
programs. Click an icon to run that program. Yes, many of these are the same as the ones on
the Dock, but this is a more complete collection.

FIGURE 2-24

The Apple menu

Another way to run an application is to open Finder and then click the Applications shortcut in the navigation bar. The resulting set of application icons is sorted somewhat differently than the ones in Launchpad, but you should be able to find them all here. If you don't see the application you want, begin typing its name in the Search box.

Using Multiple Desktops

macOS enables you to have multiple desktops running at once, each with different open applications. That way you can start with a clean slate without having to close running applications and windows. Microsoft Windows 10 has a similar feature.

To access this feature, called Mission Control, run the Mission Control application from Launchpad or the Applications list in Finder. A bar appears across the top of the screen; this is your management interface. There are two items on it by default: Dashboard and Desktop. Dashboard is a shortcut collection of commonly needed utilities, like a calculator, calendar, and clock. Desktop is your current desktop. Click the plus sign on the right end of this bar to create a new copy of the desktop, as shown in Figure 2-25. You can then switch back and forth between them by pressing CTRL-LEFT ARROW or CTRL-RIGHT ARROW.

Storing Passwords

The Keychain feature safely stores your Safari website user names and passwords, so you don't have to remember them or continually type them. It can also keep the accounts you use in Mail, Contacts, Calendar, and Messages up to date across all your Mac devices. When you set up a Mac initially, you are asked if you want to enable the Keychain feature. If you choose not to, you can do so later.

FIGURE 2-25   Mission Control enables you to have multiple desktops.

To enable Keychain, on the Apple menu, choose System Preferences | iCloud. Scroll down to Keychain, and if there is not a check mark next to it, click to place one. Then work through the prompts.

Searching

Click the magnifying glass icon in the upper-right corner of the screen to open Spotlight search. It searches the local system for files and applications, but it can also search the Internet for you as well.

Using Gestures

Gestures are shortcuts that you can perform to navigate using a touchpad or touch screen. Here's a good way to learn about them: From Finder, choose Help | Get to Know Your Mac. Click Next until you see information about Gestures. Then read that page to learn how to use Scroll, Navigate, Zoom, and Secondary Click a touchpad.

Accessing iCloud

iCloud is an online storage area, free to Mac users, equivalent to OneDrive in Windows. To access iCloud, open Finder and, in the navigation pane, click iCloud Drive. You can drag and drop files to and from your iCloud drive (for example, from the desktop).

Dual-Booting with Windows

Boot Camp is a utility that helps you install Microsoft Windows on a Mac and then switch between the two operating systems. To use Boot Camp, make sure you have a Windows disk image (an ISO file). Then using Finder, click Applications | Utilities | Boot Camp Assistant. Work through the on-screen instructions to repartition the startup disk, download the needed drivers, and install Windows.

Using Another Computer's Optical Drive

Remote Disc provides a way for a Mac that doesn't have an optical drive, such as a Mac Mini, to borrow another Mac's optical drive via a network.

To allow sharing, from the Mac that *does* have the optical drive, do the following: From the Apple menu click System Preferences, and then click Sharing. Click DVD or CD Sharing to place a check mark next to that feature.

Then to use the remote disc on the computer that does *not* have the optical drive, do the following: In Finder, under Devices in the navigation bar, click Remote Disc. If a computer on your LAN is sharing an optical drive with you, that computer will appear as an icon. Double-click the icon to access the drive. To make the connection, you might need to click Ask to Use and then click Accept on the Mac that has the optical drive.

You can also share an optical disk from a Windows PC with your Mac, but you have to download a utility to help with that. Go to https://support.apple.com/kb/DL112?locale=en_US to download the needed file on the Windows PC, and run the Setup program. Then open the Control Panel, open Hardware and Sound (in Category View), and click DVD or CD Sharing Options. Click the check box to enable the feature.

CERTIFICATION SUMMARY

Before you can install and support computers, you must develop an understanding of the concepts beyond those required to simply use an OS. This begins with understanding the purpose of operating systems; knowing the differences among the major operating systems; and understanding updates, service packs, and revision levels. The versions of Windows presently included in the CompTIA A+ 902 exam objectives are Windows Vista, Windows 7, and Windows 8/8.1. These versions have many GUI elements in common, but with each new version, Microsoft has made changes, such as modifications to the Start menu (Start screen in Windows 8/8.1), additions of GUI elements, and the visual enhancements of Aero that were introduced in Windows Vista, and improved upon in Windows 7.

macOS is the operating system for Apple Mac computers (desktops and laptops). It is a GUI, like Windows. The key features are the Dock, the desktop, Launcher, the Apple menu, and Finder.

TWO-MINUTE DRILL

Here are some of the key points covered in Chapter 2.

Introduction to Windows Operating Systems

❑   An OS controls all the interactions among the various system components, human interactions with the computer, and network operations for the computer system.

❑   Microsoft Windows comes in versions, such as Windows Vista, Windows 7, Windows 8, Windows 8.1, and Windows 10.

❑   Each Windows version also comes in editions, such as Windows 7 Starter, Windows 7 Home Premium, Windows 7 Professional, Windows 7 Ultimate, and Windows 7 Enterprise.

❑   Operating systems tie closely to the CPUs on which they run. Therefore, CPU terms such as 32-bit and 64-bit may also describe an OS. Windows XP, Windows Vista, Windows 7, and Windows 8, and Windows 8.1 all have both 32-bit and 64-bit versions.

❑   Windows updates are software fixes to the operating system code to fix problems or enhance security. A patch is a fix for a single problem. A service pack is a bundle of patches or updates released periodically by a software publisher.

❑   The Microsoft Support Lifecycle specifies the services available for different Microsoft products, such as Windows. Microsoft ends support for a Windows version 10 years after the last update to it.

Considerations for Installing or Upgrading Windows

❑ Each version of an OS has a certain set of system requirements, which includes the computer platform and the amount of RAM and disk space.

❑ Each new OS also introduces hardware and software compatibility issues. Windows has features for managing incompatible applications, including Compatibility Mode. In addition, Windows 7 has Windows XP Mode, which uses Windows Virtual PC with an instance of a fully licensed Windows XP Professional edition.

❑ Each edition of Windows at each version level has unique upgrade paths that allow you to upgrade directly, performing an in-place installation, from certain earlier editions of Windows. In some cases, such as when changing between 32-bit and 64-bit, you cannot upgrade from a previous version or specific edition and must do a clean installation.

Windows Features That Vary by Version

❑ In Windows Vista and 7, the file management tool is Windows Explorer; in Windows 8 and later it is File Explorer.

❑ Libraries were introduced in Windows 7, as virtual storage locations that combine the contents of multiple folders. The feature is available but not enabled by default in later Windows versions.

❑ 64-bit Windows versions have a Program Files (x86) folder for 32-bit application files, and a Program files folder for 64-bit ones. 32-bit Windows versions have only a Program Files folder.

❑ Aero is a set of visual enhancements for the display in Windows Vista and 7. It is deemphasized and no longer named Aero in Windows 8/8.1.

❑ The Sidebar is a Vista-only feature that allows automatically updating gadgets to sit on the desktop. Gadgets sit directly on the desktop in Windows 7, and Windows 8/8.1 do not allow gadgets because of security concerns.

❑ Security tools that vary by Windows version and edition include User Account Control (UAC), BitLocker, Windows Defender, Windows Firewall, and the Action Center.

❑ System Restore takes system snapshots that you can roll back to when system configuration issues occur. When System Restore creates its snapshots, or restore points, it makes a backup called a *shadow copy* of certain important system files.

❑ ReadyBoost enables certain types of flash drives and solid-state drives to be used as a write cache.

❑ Easy Transfer helps transfer personal files and settings between PCs. It is not present in Windows 10, replaced by a free version of Laplink PCmover Express.

Features Specific to Windows 8/8.1

❑ Windows 8/8.1 encourage you to sign in with a Microsoft account tied to an e-mail address, and provide extra features such as OneDrive integration if you do. This is also known as Live sign-in.

❑ Windows 8/8.1 have a Start screen, rather than a Start menu. Windows 8 has no Start button on the desktop, but Windows 8.1 does.

❑ The Charms bar in Windows 8/8.1 provides five icons called charms: Search, Share, Start, Devices, and Settings. The Charms bar is not present in Windows Vista or Windows 7, nor in Windows 10.

❑ Windows 8/8.1 have access to Modern/Metro apps acquired through the Windows Store; they are more like apps on a tablet or phone, and their installation and removal is simplified compared to desktop applications.

❑ Metro/Modern apps usually run full-screen but you can run two side by side in Windows 8/8.1 by snapping the open app to one side of the screen or the other.

❑ In Windows 8/8.1 you can move the mouse to the upper-left corner of the screen to browse thumbnails for the running Metro/Modern apps.

❑ In versions of Windows prior to Windows 8, when using multiple monitors, the taskbar appears on just one monitor. In Windows 8/8.1, you can optionally have the taskbar on multiple monitors.

❑ Windows PowerShell is a command-line interface, automation platform, and scripting language in Windows 8/8.1 that advanced users may prefer to use instead of the regular command-line interface.

Configuring and Using macOS

❑ The current CompTIA A+ 902 exam objectives expect you to know how to navigate a macOS system.

❑ The important features to understand involving everyday operation of macOS include the Dock, Finder, Mission Control, Apple menu, Keychain, Spotlight, iCloud, Gestures, Remote Disc, and Boot Camp.

❑ Chapter 12 will cover important macOS utilities you should know about.

SELF TEST

The following questions will help you measure your understanding of the material presented in this chapter. Read all of the choices carefully because there might be more than one correct answer. Choose all correct answers for each question.

Introduction to Windows Operating Systems

1. Which of these is *not* a responsibility of the operating system?
   A. Connecting to a network
   B. Interacting with hardware
   C. Providing a user interface
   D. Performing the power-on self-test

2. Which of these is a 16-bit version of Windows?
   A. Windows 95
   B. Windows XP
   C. Windows 8
   D. None of the above

3. Which of these is the correct chronological order for Windows versions from oldest to newest?
   A. Windows XP, Windows Vista, Windows 7
   B. Windows Vista, Windows XP, Windows 7
   C. Windows 7, Windows XP, Windows Vista
   D. Windows XP, Windows 7, Windows Vista

4. Windows 7 is a version; what is Windows 7 Ultimate?
   A. An OEM release
   B. An edition
   C. A patch
   D. An update

5. What is the benefit of using a 64-bit version of Windows?
   A. Faster
   B. Supports more applications
   C. Supports more memory
   D. Supports larger hard drives

6. What Microsoft policy defines the length of time Microsoft will support a product, as well as the support options for that product?
   A. Software Assurance
   B. Support Lifecycle
   C. Upgrade Advisor
   D. Compatibility Wizard

Considerations for Installing or Upgrading Windows

7. What is the minimum CPU speed required for Windows 8.1?
   A. 800 MHz for 32-bit and 1 GHz for 64-bit
   B. 1 GHz for 32-bit and 2 GHz for 64-bit
   C. 1 GHz for both 32-bit and 64-bit
   D. 2 GHz for both 32-bit and 64-bit

8. Which of the following is one of the system requirements Microsoft specifies for a particular version of Windows?
   A. Hard disk type (magnetic vs. solid state)
   B. Amount of RAM
   C. Form factor of case
   D. Brand of sound card

9. Which of the following does *not* have a direct upgrade path from Windows Vista Business?
   A. Windows 7 Professional
   B. Windows 7 Home Premium
   C. Windows 7 Enterprise
   D. Windows 7 Ultimate

10. Before you install Windows 7 or Windows 8.1, download the latest version of this free program to determine if your computer's hardware and software are compatible with the new OS.
    A. Windows Setup
    B. Get Windows
    C. Upgrade Advisor/Upgrade Assistant
    D. Help | About

11. If an old app will not run in Windows 7 Professional, Enterprise, or Ultimate editions, even after trying other methods to help it run, use this free Microsoft tool, which includes a fully licensed version of Windows XP installed in a virtual machine.
    A. Administrative Tools
    B. Windows Virtual PC
    C. Windows XP Mode
    D. Compatibility Mode

Windows Features That Vary by Version

12. Which version of Windows uses libraries by default for personal file management?
   A. Windows Vista
   B. Windows 7
   C. Windows 8.1
   D. All of the above

13. Which of these is an Aero feature in Windows 7?
   A. BitLocker
   B. Themes
   C. Flip 3D
   D. Metro

14. Why are there no gadgets in Windows 8.1?
   A. No longer useful
   B. No more Sidebar
   C. Copyright issues
   D. Security issues

15. If you wanted to browse the Control Panel without using categories in Windows Vista, which view could you switch to?
   A. Classic
   B. Small Icons
   C. Large Icons
   D. Details

Features Specific to Windows 8/8.1

16. Live sign-in occurs when you log in to Windows 8 with what type of account?
   A. Standard
   B. Microsoft
   C. Local
   D. Administrator

17. What does the Start button do when clicked in Windows 8.1?
   A. Opens the Start screen
   B. Opens the taskbar
   C. Minimizes all open windows
   D. Nothing; Windows 8.1 has no Start button

18. How do you install new Metro/Modern apps in Windows 8/8.1?
    A. Control Panel
    B. Settings app
    C. Windows Store
    D. Start screen

Configuring and Using macOS

19. Which feature provides file system browsing on a Mac?
    A. Launchpad
    B. Notepad
    C. Finder
    D. Keychain

20. How do you shut down a Mac?
    A. Start | Shut Down
    B. Apple menu | Force Quit
    C. Finder menu
    D. Apple menu | Shut Down

SELF TEST ANSWERS

Introduction to Windows Operating Systems

1. ☑ **D.** The power-on self-test (POST) occurs before the operating system loads.
    ☒ **A, B,** and **C** are all incorrect because connecting to a network, interacting with hardware, and providing a user interface are all OS responsibilities.

2. ☑ **D.** None of these are 16-bit versions. The last 16-bit version was Windows 3.1.
    ☒ **A** is incorrect because Windows 95 was a 32-bit version. **B** and **C** are incorrect because Windows XP and Windows 8 both come in both 32-bit and 64-bit versions.

3. ☑ **A.** Windows XP is the oldest, followed by Vista, and then Windows 7.
    ☒ **B, C,** and **D** are all incorrect because they list the chronology in incorrect orders.

4. ☑ **B.** Windows 7 Ultimate is an edition of the Windows 7 version.
   ☒ **A** is incorrect because that describes any edition of Windows that is bundled with a computer. **C** is incorrect because a patch is a software fix for a single problem. **D** is incorrect because an update is software that contains fixes to problems in Windows, often security issues.

5. ☑ **C.** 64-bit versions can support more memory. A 32-bit version is limited to 4 GB of RAM.
   ☒ **A** is incorrect because the 64-bit version is not necessarily faster. **B** is incorrect because there are not more applications for 64-bit; if anything, there are more 32-bit applications. **D** is incorrect because 32-bit vs. 64-bit has no effect on the hard drive size limitations.

6. ☑ **B.** Support Lifecycle is the Microsoft policy that defines the length of time Microsoft will support a product.
   ☒ **A** is incorrect because this is Microsoft's software purchasing, volume licensing, and support plan for large organizations. **C** is incorrect because this is a utility for determining if an existing installation of Windows can be successfully upgraded to a newer version. **D** is incorrect because this is a Microsoft wizard for applying compatibility settings for the application program.

Considerations for Installing or Upgrading Windows

7. ☑ **C.** The minimum CPU speed for Windows 8.1 is 1 GHz regardless of 32-bit or 64-bit.
   ☒ **A** is incorrect; that is the minimum for Windows Vista. **B** is incorrect because Windows 8.1's requirements do not change for 32-bit vs. 64-bit. **D** is incorrect because the minimum is 1 GHz, not 2 GHz.

8. ☑ **B.** Amount of RAM is important in the system requirements for a Windows version.
   ☒ **A** is incorrect because the OS doesn't care what technology the hard disk uses. **C** is incorrect because this describes the dimensions of a hardware device, not the system requirements for an OS. **D** is incorrect because Windows can accept almost any sound card, provided the manufacturer supplies a driver.

9. ☑ **B.** Windows Vista Business cannot be directly upgraded to Windows 7 Home Premium because a business edition cannot be upgraded to a home edition.
   ☒ **A, C,** and **D** are all incorrect because you can upgrade to any of them from Windows Vista Business.

10. ☑ **C.** Upgrade Advisor (Windows 7) or Upgrade Assistant (Windows 8/8.1) is the program that will determine if your computer has hardware and software compatible with Windows 7 or Windows 8/8.1.
   ☒ **A** is incorrect because Windows Setup is the setup program for the new version of Windows itself, located on the installation media. It is not a free download. **B** is incorrect because it is not a real program. There is a Get Windows 10 app that checks upgradability for Windows 10, however. **D** is incorrect because this is a menu choice in many programs that will provide version information, not hardware and software compatibility information.

11.   ☑   **C.** Windows XP Mode is a virtual machine with a fully licensed version of XP installed that is a free feature for Windows 7, used to run incompatible older apps.
      ☒   **A** is incorrect because this is simply a Start menu item that gives access to several helpful utilities. **B** is incorrect because, by itself, it is only one part of Windows XP Mode. **D** is incorrect because this is simply a tool for tweaking the Windows environment in which an incompatible app runs; it is not Windows XP Mode, which is Microsoft Virtual PC with a fully licensed version of XP installed.

Windows Features That Vary by Version

12.   ☑   **B.** Windows 7 uses libraries by default.
      ☒   **A** is incorrect because libraries were not yet introduced in Vista. **C** is incorrect because, although libraries are available in Windows 8.1, they are not enabled by default. **D** is incorrect because A and C are incorrect.

13.   ☑   **C.** Flip 3D is an Aero feature that enables you to flip through a 3D stack of open windows to switch applications.
      ☒   **A** is incorrect because this describes a drive security program in some versions of Windows. **B** is incorrect because themes are available even when Aero is not available. Some themes are Aero-enabled, but not all. **D** is incorrect because it is a new type of application introduced in Window 8, also called Modern.

14.   ☑   **D.** Microsoft discontinued gadgets because of security concerns in Windows 8 and higher.
      ☒   **A** is incorrect because gadgets did not lose their usefulness. **B** is incorrect because Windows 7 does not have a Sidebar (as Vista does), but still has gadgets. **C** is incorrect because there is no copyright problem with gadgets.

15.   ☑   **A.** In the Windows Vista Control Panel, there are two viewing options: Classic and Category.
      ☒   **B** and **C** are both incorrect because these views are available only in Windows 7 and newer Windows versions. **D** is incorrect because it is a view in File Explorer/Windows Explorer, not in the Control Panel.

16.   ☑   **B.** Live sign-in refers to signing in with a Microsoft account, connecting the user to online resources.
      ☒   **A** and **D** are both incorrect because Standard and Administrator are levels of permission for the account. **C** is incorrect because a local account is one that exists only on the local PC, the opposite of a Microsoft account.

17.   ☑   **A.** Clicking the Start button in Windows 8.1 opens the Start screen.
      ☒   **B** is incorrect because Windows 8.1 has no Start menu. **C** is incorrect because the taskbar does not require opening. **D** is incorrect because Windows 8.1 does have a Start button; Windows 8 did not, however.

18. ☑ **C.** Windows Store is the source of Metro/Modern apps.
☒ **A** is incorrect because it's where you uninstall desktop applications. **B** is incorrect because this app has no connection to installed apps of any kind. **D** is incorrect because there is nothing on the Start screen for installing new apps.

Configuring and Using macOS

19. ☑ **C.** Finder is the file management utility in macOS.
☒ **A** is incorrect because it is an interface for running applications. **B** is incorrect because it is a text editor in Windows. **D** is incorrect because it is the password management feature in macOS.

20. ☑ **D.** To shut down a Mac, open the Apple menu and click Shut Down.
☒ **A** is incorrect because it is the Windows method of shutting down. **B** is incorrect because it is a means of shutting down an unresponsive application. **C** is incorrect because it does not contain a Shut Down command.

Chapter 3

Personal Computer Components: Motherboards and Processors

CERTIFICATION OBJECTIVES

■ **901: 1.1** Given a scenario, configure settings and use BIOS/UEFI tools on a PC

■ **901: 1.2** Explain the importance of motherboard components, their purpose, and properties

■ **901: 1.6** Install various types of CPUs and apply the appropriate cooling methods

■ **901: 2.9** Given a scenario, use appropriate networking tools

✓ Two-Minute Drill

Q&A Self Test

Together, this chapter and Chapters 4 and 5 introduce you to basic computer technology concepts, including categorizing, explaining, and identifying common components. Consider the contents of these three chapters to be the basic technical knowledge computer professionals need when working with PCs and laptops. Familiarity with the components, as well as a good working knowledge of their function, will enable you to work comfortably with most types of computers, in spite of different layouts or new component designs.

Once you have a good sense of how the parts of a computer system work together, you will be on the road to becoming a PC technical professional. This knowledge will aid in all the technical tasks ahead of you and in passing your CompTIA A+ Certification exams. Later chapters will give you an opportunity to learn skills for installing and troubleshooting these components.

CERTIFICATION OBJECTIVE

■ **901: 2.9** *Given a scenario, use appropriate networking tools*

CompTIA A+ 901 exam objective 2.9 requires that you know when and how to use appropriate networking tools—that is, hand tools used specifically for network connection and maintenance. The following hardware toolkit is composed of tools listed under exam objective 2.9, the list of tools in the A+ Proposed Hardware and Software List, and some additional tools we felt should also be mentioned. We are presenting the entire list here, but we will revisit many of these tools in scenarios in coming chapters.

The Hardware Toolkit

As a new PC technician, you might begin with a repair toolkit that is not very extensive: perhaps a small assortment of screwdrivers and nut drivers, a small flashlight, and an assortment of screws and nuts. You'll add tools as you need them for special jobs. For this, you may decide to purchase a basic computer technician's toolkit, or assemble the components yourself. Figure 3-1 shows some of the most basic tools a computer technician uses on the job, and following that is a more complete list of components you should have in your kit, depending on your responsibilities. For instance, if you are not required to

FIGURE 3-1

An assortment of basic tools

test network equipment, you will not need a toner probe, and if you never need to crimp connectors onto lengths of cables, you will not need a crimper.

- You should have an assortment of Phillips head, flathead, and Torx screwdrivers, as well as varying sizes of nut drivers.

- It is helpful to carry some of the most common small parts used on desktop and laptop PCs, including various sizes of screws, nuts, nonconductive washers, and *stand-offs* (spacers used to hold the motherboard off the case floor).

- *Slot covers* are the metal brackets that cover the openings (slots) in the back of a PC for accommodating expansion cards. A slot cover serves to keep dust out when an expansion slot is empty and helps cooling airflow.

- A *parts grabber*, also called an *extending extractor*, is a pen-sized tool has a plunger at one end, which, when pressed, causes small, hooked prongs to extend from the other end of the tool. These are useful for retrieving dropped objects, such as jumpers or screws, from inside a computer. Be very careful not to touch any circuitry when using one.

- An *extension magnet* is a long-handled tool with a magnet on the end. Use it like a parts grabber, only it has a magnet that attracts small objects that contain iron. This is handy for picking up objects that fall on the floor, but the potential dangers may not be worth the convenience. Never use an extension magnet near a circuit board or any peripherals that contain magnetic storage because the magnet can damage data.

- A flashlight helps illuminate dark places.

- A small container is useful for holding extra screws and other small parts (a pill bottle works well).

- An *ESD wrist strap* helps prevent damage from static electricity when working on any component except the power supply, monitor, and laser printers. We discussed ESD wrist straps in Chapter 1.

- An *ESD mat* provides a static charge with a path to ground and is designed for the desktop or floor of a workspace. While this mat may not fit in your toolkit, it is something that should be available at any PC technician's workbench.

- *Field replaceable units (FRUs)* should be included in your hardware toolkit. An FRU is any component that you can install into a system onsite. This includes such items as memory modules, heat sinks, motherboard batteries, various adapter cards, hard drives, optical drives, keyboards, mice, fans, AC adapters, spare cables and connectors, power supplies, and even spare motherboards. Of course, all of this depends on the scope of your job and how cost-effective it is to have these items on hand.

- A *multimeter* is indispensable in determining power problems from a power outlet or from the power supply. You'll use this handheld device to measure the resistance, voltage, and/or current in computer components (see Figure 3-2) using two probes (one negative, one positive) that you touch to power wires in the equipment you are testing.

A simple
multimeter

■ A *power supply tester* is a specialized device for testing a power supply unit, and is a bit safer to use than a multimeter for this purpose. A power supply tester comes with connectors compatible with the output connectors on a standard power supply, rather than with just the simple probes of a multimeter. An LCD display or LEDs show the test results.

■ A *cable tester*, also called a *continuity tester*, is a machine that detects if a cable can correctly carry a signal. See Figure 3-3. You can test some kinds of cable with a multimeter by checking each wire individually, but a cable tester is much quicker because it tests all the pins/wires at once. Several types of cable testers are available, such as those for copper Ethernet and phone cables, fiber-optic cable testers, and coaxial cable testers.

A network cable
tester (Photo:
Rainer Knäpper;
Free Art License,
http://artlibre.org/
licence/lal/en/)

- A *toner probe* is a cable tester that generates a tone on one end of a cable and evaluates the signal received on the other end. The part that generates the tone is called a *tone generator*. We will revisit cable testers in Chapter 16.
- A *loopback plug* is a plug wired to send signals back to a specific port type (such as USB) or device, such as an Ethernet adapter, as a test of the device. It reroutes the sending pins from the port or device to the receiving pins, thus allowing you to test the ability to send and receive without connecting to an external device or network.
- A digital camera will enable you to document the condition of a computer before you begin troubleshooting. One important way we use a digital camera is to document the cabling and connections—both external and internal—before making any changes, so that we can reconnect all components correctly. A camera is also handy for capturing low-level error messages that cannot be captured with a software screen capture utility.
- Wire cutters are used for cutting various types of wires, but especially for Ethernet cables.
- A *punch down tool* is a hand tool with a screwdriver-type handle and one or more specialized blades used for inserting various types of wire into appropriate wiring panels. The wiring may be for electrical power or network cabling. See Figure 3-4.
- A *crimper*, also called a *crimp tool*, resembles a pair of pliers, but is used to terminate a multistranded cable into a connector, clamping each wire in place in the connector so that the wires line up with the wires in the connector.

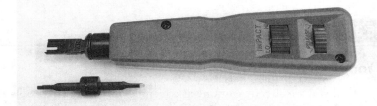

■ A *cable stripper* is a cross between a pair of pliers and scissors and is designed to strip the insulation from around the wires in a cable.

■ A *POST card* is an adapter card used to run a special diagnostic test on a computer as it powers up. These tests go beyond those performed by the computer's own BIOS-based testing that occurs as it starts up. We'll revisit POST cards in Chapter 11.

■ *Thermal paste* is an electrically insulating, heat-conductive paste that helps increase the transfer of heat between a hot chip and a heat-dissipating fan or heat sink. It is also called *thermal grease* or *heat sink compound*. You apply it in a thin layer between the components. Depending on the type, it may or not have adhesive properties; usually when it aids in adhesion, it is called *thermal adhesive*.

■ A *Wi-Fi analyzer* detects nearby Wi-Fi signals. There are two kinds: software and hardware. The hardware type can also monitor bandwidth utilization and record data sent over the network. Fluke is one popular brand of Wi-Fi analyzer for professional use.

■ A *SATA to USB connector* enables you to use an internal hard drive (using a serial ATA connector) as an external hard drive (using a Universal Serial Bus connector). It may be called a *drive enclosure* if it contains a plastic shell into which you can mount the drive to make it easier to handle and transport.

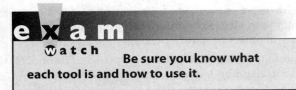

Be sure you know what each tool is and how to use it.

EXERCISE 3-1

What's in Your Toolkit?

1. If you are already working as a technician, gather your tools and compare them to the previously mentioned list. What would you add to the printed list? What is in the list that you would like to add to your toolkit?

2. If you are not a technician, find one who will talk to you about the tools of the trade. You may find this person at work, school, or even at a local PC repair business. Ask the technician to tell you which tools he uses the most and what he recommends you have in a basic toolkit.

CERTIFICATION OBJECTIVE

■ **901: 1.2**   *Explain the importance of motherboard components, their purpose, and properties*

The motherboard is the real estate on which a PC is built; all PC components are directly or indirectly connected to this large printed circuit board. This section introduces all of the topics of CompTIA A+ 901 exam objective 1.2, including motherboard sizes (ATX, Micro-ATX, ITX, and Mini-ITX), expansion slots, RAM slots, CPU sockets, chipsets, power connections and types, fan connectors, front panel connectors, and bus speeds.

Motherboard Form Factors and Components

The average desktop PC that resides in most offices may look like a simple device—a box connected to a display, keyboard, and mouse—but it is an extremely complicated piece of equipment that includes a vast array of technologies in its components. As a computer technician, you do not really need to be overly concerned about the actual inner workings of these components, but you must understand their general functions.

We will begin with the motherboard, the foundation of every PC. Each internal and external PC component connects, directly or indirectly, to a single circuit, the motherboard. The *motherboard*, also referred to as the *mainboard*, the *system board*, or the *planar board*, is made of fiberglass, typically brown or green, and with a meshwork of copper lines, called *traces*. Power, data, and control signals travel to all connected components through these pathways. A group of these wires assigned to a set of functions is collectively called a *bus*.

Safety first! Hands-on experience is important for preparing for your CompTIA A+ exams, and as you study you will want to install and remove components on a PC system. Therefore, you must thoroughly understand safety procedures, as detailed in Chapter 1.

In this section, we focus on types of motherboards, their typical integrated components, and the differences between the motherboard's communication busses and what components can connect to a motherboard through these various busses.

Sizes/Form Factors

A motherboard *form factor* defines the type and location of components on the motherboard, the power supply that will work with it, the size of the motherboard, and the corresponding PC case that will accommodate both. There are several motherboard form factors, each with different layouts, components, and specifications. A motherboard will use only certain CPUs and types of memory, based on the type of CPU and memory sockets installed. Therefore, if you decide to build a computer from components, you must ensure that the motherboard, power supply, CPU, memory, and case will all work together.

Personal computer motherboards have evolved over the past several decades, and continue to do so. Although motherboards can vary from manufacturer to manufacturer, Intel Corporation, a major manufacturer, has developed several form factors over the years, including the early AT and NLX, ATX, and ITX form factors. Form factor standards also have smaller variations. We will discuss their sizes, typical components, and prevalence next.

CompTIA A+ 901 exam objective 1.2 does not mention the term "form factor," but it does mention "sizes," under which it lists the ATX, Micro-ATX, Mini-ITX, and ITX form factors. Be sure to pay attention to the differences among these form factors. Size is just one feature of a motherboard form factor. We discuss these form factors, as well as others that have some relevance to the exams, even if they are not listed in the objectives.

NLX

New Low-profile eXtended (NLX) was an Intel standard for motherboards targeted to the low-end consumer market. It used a riser card to install expansion boards parallel to the motherboard. NLX no longer is listed in the CompTIA A+ exam objectives but it is an acronym on the CompTIA A+ Acronyms list.

on the job
If you work with experienced PC technicians, read trade publications, or visit technical websites, you'll probably see the slang term *mobo* used in place of motherboard.

ATX

The *Advanced Technology eXtended (ATX)* motherboard standard was released by Intel Corporation in 1996 and has been updated many times over the years—both officially and through proprietary variations by manufacturers. Counting all the variations, it is the most commonly used form in PCs. The original ATX motherboard measures approximately 12" wide by 9.6" from front to back (305 mm × 244 mm), keeping it from interfering with the drive bays, which was a problem with the now-ancient AT motherboards. The processor socket is located near the power supply, so it will not interfere with full-length expansion boards. Finally, the hard drive and disk drive connectors are located near the drive bays. Figure 3-5 shows a motherboard with the CPU next to the power supply along with various cables connected between the power supply and motherboard.

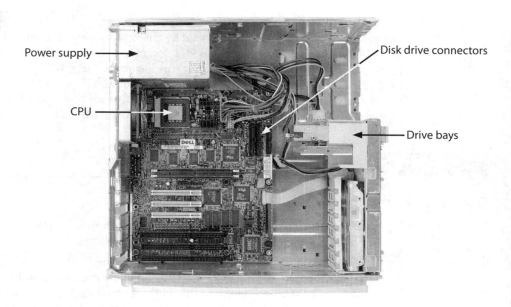

FIGURE 3-5

An ATX
motherboard
installed in a case
with the CPU
and some cables
visible

Power supply

CPU

Disk drive connectors

Drive bays

When first introduced, the ATX motherboard included integrated parallel and serial ports (I/O ports) and a mini-DIN-6 (PS/2) keyboard connector. Depending on the manufacturer and the intended market, todays ATX motherboard will contain memory slots for the latest RAM types, support for BIOS-controlled power management, multimedia, Intel or AMD CPU sockets, both PATA and SATA disk drive connectors, and support for USB and IEEE 1394 (also known as FireWire).

There are at least three additional size variations in the ATX form factor, as shown in Table 3-1. The only variation specifically mentioned in the 901 exam objectives, however, is Micro-ATX.

TABLE 3-1

Motherboard
Approximate Size
Comparison

Form Factor	Approximate Size
ATX	12" × 9.6" (305 mm × 244 mm)
Micro-ATX	9.6" × 9.6" (244 mm × 244 mm)
Flex-ATX	9" × 7.5" (228.6 mm × 190.5 mm)
Mini-ATX	5.9" × 5.9" (150 mm × 150 mm)
ITX	8.5" × 7.5" (215 mm × 191 mm)
Mini-ITX	6.7" × 6.7" (170 mm × 170 mm)
Nano-ITX	4.7" × 4.7" (120 mm × 120 mm)
Pico-ITX	3.9" × 2.8" (100 mm × 72 mm)
Mobile-ITX	2.9" × 1.77" (75 mm × 45 mm)

ITX

ITX, originally named EPIA, was developed by chipset-company VIA in 2001 for use in low-power CPUs (such as very small desktop PCs designed to be part of home entertainment systems) and chipsets in low-cost PCs, but was never used in production. Subsequent designs—the Mini-ITX, Nano-ITX, Pico-ITX, and Mobile-ITX—have been progressively smaller and targeted to embedded systems. See Table 3-1 for their specifications. The only ones listed in the current 901 exam objectives are ITX and Mini-ITX.

EXERCISE 3-2

Compare Motherboards

1. From a computer with an Internet connection, use your browser to search on the ATX and ITX form factors and their smaller variations.
2. Notice the locations of the CPU, expansion bus, and memory slots.
3. If possible, open a desktop PC, following the safety guidelines outlined in Chapter 1, and determine the form factor of the motherboard by measuring its dimensions and comparing them to those in Table 3-1. Do not disconnect or remove any components within the case.
4. Keep the computer open while you complete this chapter, locating as many of the components described as you can.
5. When you are finished, close the computer case, reconnect the computer, and make sure that it works as well as it did before you opened it.

Motherboard Components

The components built into a motherboard include sockets for various PC components, including the CPU and memory, expansion slots (such as PCIe), built-in components such as network, display, and sound adapters, hard drive controllers, support for various port types (such as USB and FireWire), and the chipset. Following is an explanation of all of these, with the exception of hard drive controllers, which we will describe in Chapter 4 during the discussion of storage type.

RAM Slots

A motherboard has slots, or sockets, for system memory. Depending on the vintage and the manufacturer of a motherboard, special sockets accept one of the various types of RAM chips attached to small circuit boards called *memory modules* or, less formally, *memory sticks*. There have been many different types over the years, but the ones you need to know today are all some type of *Dual Inline Memory Module (DIMM)*. Different DIMMs include Double Data Rate (DDR), DDR2, DDR3, and Small Outline DIMM (SODIMM). You'll learn about these in Chapter 4.

Some motherboards have paired RAM slots, in a configuration called *dual-channel architecture*, in order to improve RAM performance. In such motherboards, DIMMs must be installed in matched pairs in the slots with matching colors. For example, there might be two blue slots and two black ones. Dual-channel is a function of the motherboard, not the RAM itself; ordinary RAM is used in dual-channel slots.

on the ①ob

How do you find out what memory modules will work on a specific motherboard? You read the motherboard user guide. If you cannot find one for your computer, find the manufacturer's name and the model of the motherboard (or computer system) and query your favorite Internet search engine. You will often find the right manual in PDF format.

Bus Architecture

The term *bus* refers to pathways that power, data, or control signals use to travel from one component to another in the computer. Standards determine how the various bus designs use the wires. There are many types of busses on the motherboard, including the *memory bus* used by the processor to access memory. In addition, each PC has an *expansion bus* of one or more types. The most common types of expansion bus architectures are PCI, PCI-X, PCIe, and Mini PCIe, and we discuss these next. The following bus types are those that you can expect to see in PCs today.

on the ①ob

The terms *bus*, *system bus*, and *expansion bus* are interchangeable. A bus refers to either a system bus or an expansion bus attached to the CPU.

PCI   *Peripheral Component Interconnect (PCI)* is an expansion bus architecture released in 1993 but still around on many motherboards today for backward compatibility. In some documentation it is called *conventional PCI* to distinguish it from the more modern PCIe.

The PCI bus transfers data in parallel over a 32-bit or 64-bit data bus. (The 32-bit type is much more common.) Over the years several variants of the PCI standard were developed, and data transfer speeds vary depending on the variant and the bus width. The original 32-bit PCI bus ran at 33.33 MHz (megahertz) with a transfer rate of up to 133 megabytes per second (MBps).

PCI slots are 3" long and are typically white. PCI cards and slots are not compatible with those of other architectures. PCI was the assumed slot type for almost all expansion boards for various functions for many years, and motherboards typically had a lot of them. Figure 3-6 shows a motherboard with several PCI slots.

A set of
conventional
PCI slots (Photo:
Jonathan Zander)

PCI was originally developed for video (back in the days when PCI was the fastest bus around), but few video cards are PCI anymore because there are faster alternatives. Nowadays a typical motherboard will have only one or two PCI slots, with the rest of them being PCIe.

PCI-X   PCI-X is a 64-bit parallel interface that is backward compatible with conventional 32-bit PCI cards. It was introduced in 1998, and has never been very popular, but A+ 901 exam objective 1.2 does mention it. A PCI-X slot looks like a conventional PCI slot except it's longer. See Figure 3-7. When 32-bit PCI cards fit into it, they fit into only the first two segments, and the third segment remains vacant.

Some PCI-X slots.
(Photo: https://
commons
.wikimedia.org/
wiki/File:64bitpci
.jpg [Creative
Commons
license])

PCIe   *Peripheral Component Interconnect Express (PCIe)* differs from PCI in that it uses serial communications rather than parallel communications as well as different bus connectors. Also called PCI Express and PCI-E, it has, for the most part, replaced PCI and is incompatible with conventional PCI adapter cards. Although PCIe programming is similar to PCI, the newer standard is not a true bus that transfers data in parallel, but rather a group of serial channels. The PCIe connector's naming scheme describes the number of serial channels each handles, with the designations x1, x4, and x16 indicating 1, 4, and 16 channels, respectively.

On the motherboard, a PCIe x1 connector is approximately 1½" long, whereas PCIe x4 is about 2" long, and PCIe x16 is close to 4" long. Figure 3-8 shows several PCIe slots, and one conventional PCI slot.

The PCIe transfer rate depends on which version of the standard the bus installation supports. For instance, PCIe 1.0 supports data transfers at 250 MBps per channel, with a maximum of 16 channels. Therefore, the maximum transfer rate for 16-channel PCIe 1.0 is 4 GBps. PCIe 2.0, released in late 2007, added a signaling mode that doubled the rate to

FIGURE 3-8   From top to bottom: PCIe x4, x16, x1, x16, and conventional PCI (Photo: https://commons .wikimedia.org/wiki/File:PCIExpress.jpg [Creative Commons license])

500 MBps per channel. This rate was redoubled to 1 GBps per channel with the PCIe 3.0 standard, expected to support a signaling mode of 1 GBps per channel but be downward compatible with existing PCIe products.

Mini PCI and Mini PCI Express   Mini PCI has a 32-bit data bus, like conventional PCI. The biggest difference is that Mini PCI is much smaller than PCI—both the card and the slot. If a laptop has an installed Mini PCI slot, it is usually accessible via a small removable panel on the bottom of the case. Mini PCI cards also come in three form factors: Type I, Type II, and Type III. Types I and II each have 100 pins in a stacking connector, whereas Type III cards have 124 pins on an edge connector.

Mini PCIe cards have replaced Mini PCI slots in newer laptops. (Depending on the manufacturer, this is also called *PCI Express Mini Card*, *Mini PCI Express*, *Mini PCIe*, or simply *MiniCard*.) This specification provides much faster throughput with a 64-bit data bus. At 30 mm × 26.8 mm, it is much smaller than a Mini PCI card and has a 52-pin edge connector. Figure 3-9 compares a Mini PCI card to a Mini PCI Express card.

FIGURE 3-9

Comparison of Mini PCI and Mini PCI Express

Motherboard Power Connectors

If you carefully examine a motherboard, you will see many connectors that range from tiny 3-pin connectors to long 24-pin connectors. These range from power connectors to connectors for onboard components, such as audio, I/O interfaces, and more. These will normally be labeled and well documented in the motherboard user's manual.

The main power connector for the motherboard is a 24-pin connector with many different wire colors. In addition, look for one or more 4-pin or 6-pin connectors to the motherboard. The 4-pin variety is also called P4 or ATX12V, and delivers extra 12-volt power. This is necessary on many newer systems because they require more 12-volt power than the few 12-volt (yellow) wires in the 24-pin power supply connector can deliver. The 6-pin type is an auxiliary connector (AUX), which supplies extra 3.3V and 5V current to the motherboard. (You can distinguish it because it uses red, white, and black wires, but no yellow ones. Yellow is for 12V.)

on the
j o b

Older motherboards may have a 20-pin power connector. Some power supplies have a 24-pin connector where the last 4 pins snap off the end, so the connector can be used on a 20-pin motherboard. This is called a 20+4 connector.

There may also be an additional 6-pin or 8-pin power connector on the power supply, called a PCIe power connector, designed to give PCIe cards a power boost. These are 12V connectors, and will have yellow and black wires only. On some high-end (that is, power-hungry) systems you may see an 8-pin connector labeled EPS12V. (It is sometimes called EATX12V or ATX12V 2×4.) As the "12" in the name implies, it provides even more 12V power to the motherboard.

The CPU fan, a system fan, and auxiliary fans will have 3-pin connectors, which the manufacturer will usually clearly label so that you can identify them.

Front/Top Panel Connectors

In addition to the main power connectors on the motherboard, there are also a series of tiny pins onto which very small connectors attach, with only two or three wires each. Each of these small connectors provides power to a component on the front or top panel of the case, for items such as a power button, power LED, disk activity LED, and reset button. There might also be connectors to attach for USB ports on the front of the case. (USB ports on the back of the case are generally built directly into the side of the motherboard.) In addition, if the case has audio controls on the front, small wires might connect them to the motherboard or sound card as well.

Firmware and Chipsets

Firmware refers to software instructions, usually stored on *read-only memory (ROM)* chips—special memory chips that retain their contents when the computer is powered off. Most PC components, such as video adapters, hard drives, network adapters, and printers, contain firmware. Firmware built into the motherboard controls the basic functions, capabilities, and configurability of a computer system. Firmware on the motherboard includes the chipset and system BIOS.

A critical component of the motherboard firmware is the *chipset*. When technicians talk about the chipset, they are usually referring to one or more chips designed to control and manage the data movement within the motherboard. It is the chipset that determines which CPUs and memory the motherboard will accept and how fast the various buses move data. Choosing a motherboard appropriate to the system you are building involves understanding the motherboard chipset's capabilities.

In older motherboards, there were two main chips that formed the chipset: a *Northbridge* that handled the fast components (like the memory, CPU, and video card) and a *Southbridge* that handled the slower components (like the expansion slots, the BIOS, the drives, and the external ports). Those terms are still present in the 220-901 exam objectives, but on modern systems the chipset design doesn't break down that way anymore. Instead, the functions formerly managed by the Northbridge are now directly on the CPU, and the Southbridge has been renamed the Input/Output Controller Hub (ICH) for Intel systems and the Fusion Controller Hub (FCH) in AMD systems. Some of the newest systems further move the Southbridge features to a Platform Controller Hub (PCH), which connects directly to the CPU. Another important firmware component is the system BIOS, which we will discuss later in this chapter in "Configuring a Motherboard." But first we explore the topic of CPUs.

SCENARIO & SOLUTION

What are the most common bus architectures in use today?	PCI and PCIe are most common today.
You have opened a PC, looking for the PCIe slots, and you see two sets of long slots in the expansion area; some are light in color, and others are dark in color and slightly longer than the others. Which is more likely to be a PCIe x16 slot?	The longer dark-colored slots are more likely to be PCIe x16. A PCIe x16 slot is the longest kind of slot found on a modern motherboard.

CERTIFICATION OBJECTIVE

■ *901: 1.6   Install various types of CPUs and apply the appropriate cooling methods*

CompTIA A+ 901 exam objective 1.6 includes the following subtopics: socket types, characteristics, and cooling. It does not require that you memorize the hundreds, or perhaps thousands, of CPU models you will encounter on the job.

CPUs and Their Sockets

A personal computer is more than the sum of its parts. However, the most important part, without which it is not a computer, or even a useful tool, is the *central processing unit (CPU)*, also called the *processor*. But a CPU may not be the only processor in a PC. Other components may include a processor for performing the intense work of the component. The most common example of this is the *graphics processing unit (GPU)* found on modern video adapters, used to render the graphics images for the display. GPUs were integrated onto system boards along with the video adapter, and now there is a trend of integrating the GPU into some CPUs. Wherever it is located, the GPU saves the CPU for other system-wide functions and improves system performance. The following is an overview of CPUs, their purposes and characteristics, manufacturers and models, technologies, and the motherboard sockets into which they fit.

CPU Purposes

In a PC, the CPU is the primary control device for the entire computer system. The CPU is simply a chip containing a set of components that manages all the activities and does much of the "heavy lifting" in a computer system. The CPU interfaces with, or connects to, all of the components such as memory, storage, and input/output (I/O) through busses. The CPU performs a number of individual or discrete functions that must work in harmony in order for the system to function. Additionally, the CPU is responsible for managing the activities of the entire system.

What Goes On Inside a CPU

A CPU is printed in a single operation onto a silicon wafer, not assembled from discrete parts. Nevertheless, inside each CPU is a variety of component parts, each with a specific function. These include the control unit, the arithmetic logic unit (ALU), registers, buses, and memory caches. Each of these is explained in an upcoming section.

The Machine Cycle

The CPU's internal components perform four basic operations that are collectively known as a *machine cycle*. The machine cycle includes fetching an instruction, decoding the instruction, executing the instruction, and storing the result. Figure 3-10 provides an overview of this process. Understanding this process upfront will make the discussions of the individual components more relevant.

Control Unit

The *control unit* is the "traffic cop" inside the CPU. It uses electrical signals to direct the CPU's overall operation. It signals to other parts of the computer system what they should do. The control unit interprets instructions and initiates the action needed to carry them out. First it *fetches*, which means it retrieves an instruction or data from memory. Then it *decodes*, which means it interprets or translates the instruction into strings of binary digits that the computer understands.

ALU

The *arithmetic logic unit (ALU)* is the part of the CPU that executes the instructions (Step 3 in Figure 3-10). It performs arithmetic operations on the data (add, subtract, multiply, and divide), and also performs logical operations such as comparing two data strings and determining whether they are the same.

FIGURE 3-10   The four-step machine cycle employs the control unit, ALU, and registers.

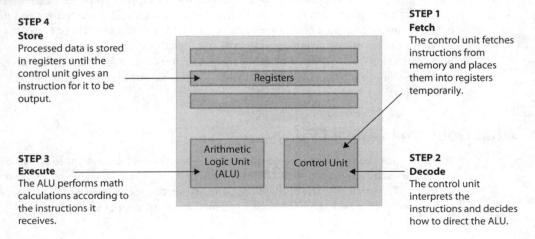

STEP 4
Store
Processed data is stored in registers until the control unit gives an instruction for it to be output.

STEP 1
Fetch
The control unit fetches instructions from memory and places them into registers temporarily.

Registers

Arithmetic Logic Unit (ALU)

Control Unit

STEP 3
Execute
The ALU performs math calculations according to the instructions it receives.

STEP 2
Decode
The control unit interprets the instructions and decides how to direct the ALU.

Registers

A *register* is a memory location inside the CPU, temporary storage used as a scratch pad for calculations. There are two types of registers used in modern systems: dedicated registers and general-purpose registers. Dedicated registers are usually for specific functions such as maintaining status or system-controlled counting operations. General-purpose registers are for multiple purposes, typically when mathematical and comparison operations occur. Placing data into a register is the *storing* step of the machine cycle (Step 4 in Figure 3-10).

Buses

Buses, generically speaking, are pathways over which data travels. External buses, such as the *front-side bus*, carry data to and from the CPU, and internal buses in the CPU itself move data between its internal components.

Cache Memory

Because the CPU is so much faster than the computer's other components, it can potentially spend a lot of time idle, waiting for data to be delivered or picked up. The farther the data has to travel to get to the CPU, the longer the delay. To help minimize these delays, modern CPUs have multiple caches. A *cache* (pronounced "cash") is a pool of extremely fast memory that's stored close to the CPU and connected to it by a very fast pathway. Only when the needed data isn't found in any of the caches does the system have to fetch data from storage (for example, the main memory of the PC, or a hard drive).

When the CPU needs some data, it looks first in the L1 (level 1) cache, which is the one closest to the CPU. The L1 cache is an *on die cache*; that means when the CPU is stamped into the silicon wafer, the L1 cache is stamped into the same piece of silicon at the same time.

It is important to remember the locations and general purpose of cache memory, especially L1, L2, and L3, for the exam. In general, you won't be asked the sizes, though the concepts of large and small amounts of memory are important.

The L1 cache is quite small, so it can't hold everything the CPU has recently used or may need to use soon. If the data needed isn't found in the L1 cache, the system looks in the L2 cache. On older systems, the L2 cache was on the motherboard, but on modern systems, it's in the CPU package, next to the silicon chip. If the data isn't in the L2 cache, the system checks the L3 cache, which is larger and slightly farther away from the CPU, although still within the ceramic chip that we call the CPU. On a multicore CPU (discussed later in this chapter), all of the cores share a common L3 cache.

CPU Technologies and Characteristics

There are a number of technologies employed in a CPU, based on both standards and proprietary designs, which are constantly changing. This section describes common CPU technologies and characteristics you should know for the exam.

Architecture

A CPU supports a certain *word size,* which is the size of the chunk of data that can enter and exit the CPU in one operation. This is also called the chip's *architecture,* and on modern PC CPUs it is either 32-bit or 64-bit. The architecture is significant because it determines what version of the operating system the PC can use. On a 32-bit CPU, you are limited to the 32-bit version of Windows, which supports a maximum of 4 GB of RAM. A 64-bit CPU can handle either 64-bit or 32-bit Windows.

Speed

The *clock speed* of a CPU is the speed at which it can potentially execute instructions. CPU clock speed is measured in billions of cycles per second, or gigahertz (GHz). A CPU of a certain type and model may be available in a range of clock speeds.

All other features being equal, the CPU with the faster clock speed will be more expensive. However, when comparing different models of CPUs, the faster clock speed alone will not determine the fastest CPU. Manufacturers use many technologies to speed up CPUs. For example, the number of clock cycles required for completing the same operation can vary among CPU models. To the end user, the perceived speed of a PC, or lack of it, may involve other aspects of the computer's total design, such as the cache size, the amount and speed of the RAM, the speed of the busses, and the speed of the hard drive. Some experts give the "actual" speed of a CPU as the speed determined by the manufacturer through testing each CPU. This speed then becomes part of the rating for that CPU. There are software tools for measuring the speed of the CPU while performing certain operations, the results of which you could consider the "real" speed.

Overclocking is the practice of forcing a CPU or other computer component to run at a higher clock rate than the manufacturer intended. This is done by increasing the clock speed of the motherboard. It works because a CPU doesn't really have a speed of its own; it only has a maximum speed for which it is rated. The actual cadence of the operations on the PC depend on the motherboard's system clock. PC hobbyists and gamers often overclock their systems to get more performance out of CPUs, video cards, chipsets, and RAM. The downside to this practice is that overclocking produces more heat and can cause damage to the motherboard, CPU, and other chips, which may explode and/or burst into flames.

Hyperthreading

A *thread,* or thread of execution, is a portion of a program that can run separately from other portions of the program. A thread can also run concurrently with other threads.

Hyperthreading, also known as *simultaneous multithreading (SMT)*, is a CPU technology that allows two or more threads to execute at the same time within a single execution core. This is considered partially parallel execution. Intel introduced hyperthreading in the Pentium 4 Xeon CPU, referring to it as Hyper-Threading Technology (HT Technology).

Multicore

The most visible change in CPUs in recent years has been the introduction of *multicore CPUs* with more than one core on the same integrated circuit. Each *core* is essentially a CPU with its own set of control unit, ALU, and registers. The first of these were *dual-core* CPUs containing two CPU cores. Quad-core CPUs are commonly available, and manufacturers offer 6-core, and more—even 128-core Superchip CPUs.

Server computers have long been available with multiple CPUs, so why not simply install two or more single-core CPUs on the same motherboard? Two cores on the same chip can communicate and cooperate much faster than two single-core processors. A dual-core CPU can simultaneously process two threads in true parallel execution, and each core has its own L1 cache; triple-core CPUs can simultaneously process three threads, and so on. On top of the advantage of using multiple cores, the manufacturers have made other changes to the CPU architecture to make them faster and more energy efficient.

Virtualization Support

Virtualization is a big topic that we will discuss more in Chapter 8. For now, understand that most modern CPUs include virtualization support—the ability to manage multiple operating systems running at once through virtual machines—enabled through BIOS settings. In Intel CPUs, the name of the group of technologies involved is *Virtualization Technology (VT)*, which may have an additional symbol or letter associated with a particular CPU model. AMD's virtualization technology is *AMD-V*.

Integrated GPU

Some systems have a separate video card (display adapter) installed in a motherboard slot; others have a graphics chip on the motherboard, known as an *integrated graphics processing unit (GPU)*. In the past, integrated GPUs were found mostly on low-end systems, and their performance lagged behind that of dedicated display adapter cards. On newer motherboards, however, some integrated GPUs have performance levels equivalent to dedicated cards.

Execute Disable Bit

Execute Disable Bit (EDB or XDB) is a security feature built into Intel CPUs. It allows the CPU to classify memory areas where application code can execute or not. This helps prevent worms from attempting to insert code in a buffer. When that happens, the CPU disables code execution, preventing the damage. For this feature to work, the PC must have a CPU that supports it, the feature must be enabled in BIOS, and the operating system must support the feature. You can identify an EDB-enabled CPU by Intel because there's a J after the model number.

CPU Manufacturers and Models

There are many CPU manufacturers, but the prevailing ones in the PC market today are *Intel Corporation* and *Advanced Micro Devices, Inc. (AMD)*. Intel received a huge boost when IBM selected their 8088 processor for the original IBM-PC in 1981. For over a decade, AMD produced "clones" of Intel CPUs under a licensing agreement granted to them at a time when Intel's manufacturing capacity could not keep up with the demand for CPUs. Since 1995, AMD has designed and produced their own CPUs. Both companies manufacture more than CPUs, but their competition in the CPU market gets more attention in the trade and business press since AMD emerged as Intel's major competitor.

The world has gotten a bit more complicated for those supporting PCs, laptops, and tablet PCs, because beginning with Windows 8, Microsoft has included an additional supported architecture built around the ARM CPU by ARM Holdings. This architecture is designed for very small devices like tablet PCs and smartphones that need tiny but powerful chips with low power needs. Windows 8 comes in separate editions for the Intel/AMD 32- or 64-bit architectures, as well as ARM. Because only Intel and AMD are listed in the objectives, the following discussion includes a sampling of CPU models from these two manufacturers.

Intel

Over time, Intel Corporation has released a number of CPU models ranging from the Intel 8086 in 1978 to the latest generation of processors, which come with a variety of model names. In earlier days, Intel released CPUs such as Pentium, Pentium II, Pentium 3, and Pentium 4 for standard usage, Celeron for economy models, and Itanium or Xeon for high-end server models. Today, however, Intel classifies a generation of CPUs by its *microarchitecture*, which is expressed as a code name such as Haswell (2013), Broadwell (2014), and Skylake. Within a microarchitecture family, the low-end CPUs are classified as Celeron or Pentium, the midrange models as i3 and i5, and the high-end models as i7 and i7 Extreme.

What is important for a tech to understand is that each of the CPU brands includes many—even dozens—of individual models and the various models are categorized by the purposes for which they were designed, such as desktop, server, workstation, notebooks, and Internet devices. Additionally, Intel designed an entire category of CPUs for the embedded and communication devices markets.

AMD

Advanced Micro Devices, Inc. (AMD) is Intel's greatest competitor in the CPU arena. They manufacture a large variety of products based on integrated circuits. Like Intel, they categorize their CPUs by their design purposes, such as desktop, server, workstation, notebooks, and embedded devices. They also stay competitive with Intel by offering each brand in a variety of multicore configurations. They target the AMD Opteron CPU brand for use in servers, whereas the AMD FX brand is used in high-end desktops and graphics workstations. Several AMD brands target different levels of laptop uses. For instance, you'll find the A-Series CPUs with integrated GPU on laptops targeted for the home market. AMD targets some Athlon and Sempron CPU models to desktop computers. As with Intel, this is all subject to change, but look for more simplification in the product lines from both manufacturers, even as they continue to bring out dozens of CPU models each year.

CPU Sockets

The *CPU socket* connects a CPU to the motherboard. Every motherboard contains at least one CPU socket, and the location varies from one motherboard standard to another. Early CPUs were pressed into a socket and held in place by friction, but modern CPU sockets have an arm or bracket that raises to allow the CPU to drop in easily, and then lowers to hold the CPU in place. This is called a *zero insertion force (ZIF)* socket.

For many years both manufacturers used some variation of *pin grid array (PGA)* CPU packaging, meaning that the underside of the CPU chip has a grid of pins (numbered in the many hundreds) that insert into matching holes in the socket on the motherboard. One variation is *pin grid array 2 (PGA2)*, which was used with Intel Pentium processors, and later the *staggered pin grid array (SPGA)* came along, in which the pin rows are staggered to allow for a higher pin density than PGA.

More recently, Intel has moved to the *land grid array (LGA)* socket. An LGA CPU has pads rather than pins. These pads on the processor contact pins in the socket on the motherboard and permit a higher density than possible with PGA. In many cases, with both PGA and LGA processors, a number that indicates the number of pins or pads in the array follows the word "socket." For instance, an Intel LGA CPU with 775 pads is referred to as using Socket 775, but Intel also has alternative names for the sockets, as shown in Table 3-2, which lists the Intel socket types named in CompTIA A+ 901 exam objective 1.6, along with the year Intel introduced each of them.

While AMD has used LGA, a survey of their recent models shows that they are still using some form of PGA. Table 3-3 lists the AMD sockets named in exam objective 1.6, along with the number of pins and the year AMD introduced each of them.

TABLE 3-2	Socket Name/Pins	Year Introduced
	Socket T/775	2004
Intel LGA CPU Sockets	Socket B/1366	2008
	Socket H/1156	2009
	Socket H2/1155	2011
	Socket R/2011	2011
	Socket H3/1150	2012

TABLE 3-3	Socket Name/Pins	Socket Type	Introduced
	AM3/940 or 941	PGA	2009
AMD CPU Sockets	AM3+/942	PGA	2011
	FM1/905	PGA	2011
	FM2/904	PGA	2012
	FM2+/906	PGA	2014

Read the motherboard and CPU documentation very carefully to be sure the CPU and socket match, because there are many versions of PGA and LGA sockets. Learn how to install a processor on a motherboard in Chapter 6.

Cooling Systems

The more powerful PCs become, the more heat they generate within the case. Heat is your PC's enemy, and it should be yours, too. An overheated CPU will fail. Rather than allow heat to cause damage, several techniques—both passive and active—are used to maintain an optimum operating temperature. Some components will even slow down so they produce less heat before any damage occurs. Manufacturers have struggled to keep ahead of the heat curve and provide sufficient cooling for the entire system. These methods involve fans, heat sinks, thermal compounds, and even liquid cooling systems.

CPU and Case Fans

Early PCs relied on the design of the PC case and the power supply fan to provide all the cooling for the computer's interior. During this era, the typical PC had vents in the front through which the power supply fan pulled cool air and in the back through which the heated air was exhausted. Today, we usually employ additional methods, but the power supply fan still plays an important part in cooling the PC. It is very common to see a fan mounted directly over the CPU, as shown in Figure 3-11, in which the *CPU fan* is clearly visible in the center of the photo.

FIGURE 3-11

An open PC with the CPU fan visible in the center and the power supply at the top left

One or more case fans may also supplement a power supply fan. A *case fan* is a fan mounted directly on the case, as opposed to a power supply fan, which is inside the power supply. Figure 3-11 also shows a black case fan on the far left, just below the power supply. Systems that do not come with a case fan may have mounting brackets for adding one or more case fans.

Heat Sinks and Fanless/Passive Cooling

Another device that works to cool hot components is a *heat sink*. This is usually a passive metal object with a flat surface attached to a component, a chip, for instance. The exposed side of a heat sink has an array of fins used to dissipate the heat. Look for the light-gray heat sink that is partially visible at the bottom of Figure 3-11, just below the CPU fan. A combined heat sink and fan may even attach directly to a chip with thermal adhesive.

Early CPUs used standard heat sinks for cooling, and they worked well enough for those CPUs because those CPUs didn't run very hot. On systems made in the last two decades, though, standard fanless (passive) heat sinks haven't cut it; powerful fans have been required to pull the heat away effectively. Motherboards still employ passive heat sinks for other chips besides the CPU, like the Northbridge chip or the GPU, but not the CPU itself.

However, new generations of fanless cooling devices released lately have been challenging the assumption that a fan is always required for the CPU. These vary in their construction, but generally include copper heat pipes and a large stack of nickel-plated aluminum fins.

Thermal Compounds

As you learned earlier in the chapter, *thermal paste* is an electrically insulating, heat-conductive paste that helps increase the transfer of heat between a hot chip and a heat-dissipating fan or heat sink. It is also called *thermal grease* or *heat sink compound*.

You apply it in a thin layer between the components. Depending on the type, it may or not have adhesive properties; usually when it aids in adhesion, it is called *thermal adhesive*.

Liquid Cooling Systems

Many of today's motherboards for sale on the Internet or at large electronics stores feature one or more *liquid cooling systems*, which range from sealed liquid cooling systems that transfer heat by conduction from several components, to active systems that use tiny refrigeration units. Liquid cooling is generally more effective than standard cooling, so it is sometimes employed in overclocked systems to help keep the CPU cool enough to function at the higher speed. But it is also more expensive, more difficult to install, and can cause serious system damage with short-circuiting in the event of a leak.

Case Design

The design of each case allows for maximum airflow over the components. Part of this design is the placement of vents, positioned to either bring in fresh air or to exhaust air. If this airflow is disturbed, even by additional openings, the system may overheat. Therefore, be sure that all the expansion slot openings on the back of the PC are covered. The expansion card's bracket covers each opening that lines up with an occupied expansion slot. A metal slot cover covers an empty slot in order to preserve the correct airflow.

EXERCISE 3-3

Check Out Your Cooling System

If you have access to a PC with the conventional case fan cooling system, check it out now.

1. Without opening the computer case, look for vents in the case.
2. If the computer is running, and if it is of a conventional design, you should hear a fan running in the power supply and see the vent from the power supply. You may hear another fan running and see a set of vents for that fan.
3. Are there vents that do not appear to have a case fan behind them?
4. Hold your hand by the vents you located and determine if air flow is going into or out of the computer case. Is the power supply fan blowing in or out? If you located a case fan, is it blowing in or out?
5. Make note of your findings and discuss with your classmates or coworkers.

SCENARIO & SOLUTION

Briefly describe hyperthreading.	Hyperthreading is a CPU technology that allows two or more threads to execute at the same time within a single execution core.
You are planning to build a custom PC and want to use the most standard CPUs, so you plan to use one of the two major manufacturers of CPUs. Who are they?	The two major manufacturers of CPUs are Intel Corporation and Advanced Micro Devices, Inc., better known as AMD.
What is the relationship of the CPU socket number to the PGA or LGA layout?	The number corresponds to the number of connection points in the grid array. For example, LGA 775 has 75 connection points.

CERTIFICATION OBJECTIVE

■ **901: 1.1** *Given a scenario, configure settings and use BIOS/UEFI tools on a PC*

■ **901: 1.2** *Explain the importance of motherboard components, their purpose, and properties*

CompTIA A+ 901 exam objective 1.1 requires that you understand how a BIOS is upgraded through flash BIOS, what information you can glean from the BIOS-setting program, how to make important configuration settings to the BIOS using the built-in BIOS, and what BIOS settings will monitor the health of a computer. You should also be able to differentiate between a traditional BIOS and UEFI. From exam objective 1.2, this section covers one topic: the CMOS battery on the motherboard.

Configuring a Motherboard

After you physically install a motherboard and attach components to it, the next step is to configure the motherboard to perform optimally with the installed hardware. On very old motherboards, a few key settings are configured using jumpers. On the majority of modern motherboards, however, all setup is done through a firmware (BIOS or UEFI) setup utility.

Setting Jumpers

Older motherboards and other circuit boards sometimes have jumpers used to configure, enable, or disable a feature. A *jumper* is a small connector that slides down on a pair of pins jutting up from a circuit board. There are often a number of pins side by side on the board.

Each possible jumper configuration is interpreted by the system firmware as a setting. Check the user manual that came with the motherboard or other circuit board to discover how to configure the settings you desire.

Two decades ago, nearly all circuit boards had one or more jumpers. Jumpers were used on motherboards to change settings such as the system clock rate and memory type, and on expansion boards to assign system resources. Today, however, most of the motherboard settings are configured in BIOS setup and expansion cards are assigned resources via plug and play. You may still see one or two jumpers on a motherboard for special purposes, like resetting BIOS setup. Jumpers are not covered on the 220-901 exam.

Understanding BIOS and UEFI

Each computing device has a chip on its main circuit board with some basic firmware that helps the device start up and communicate with the operating system and the other hardware. This firmware is traditionally known as the *basic input/output system (BIOS)*. A PC's BIOS resides on the motherboard, and is called the *system BIOS*. Each expansion card also has its own BIOS chip that, among other things, reports the device's plug and play settings to the motherboard's BIOS and to the OS.

The system BIOS is responsible for performing the *power-on self-test (POST)*, a hardware test during startup, and informing the processor of the devices present and how to communicate with them. Whenever the processor makes a request of a component, the BIOS steps in and translates the request into instructions that the component can understand. That was true for many years and is true today, up to the point when an operating system loads, whereupon drivers loaded by the OS take over most of the BIOS functions.

The traditional PC system BIOS is a 16-bit program that requires x86-compliant hardware. However, newer systems that have large hard drives (3+ terabytes) bump up against a limitation there. Enter *Unified Extensible Firmware Interface (UEFI)*, which has lately taken the place of a traditional BIOS on newer and higher-end motherboards.

In simplistic terms, UEFI is a 32-bit or 64-bit BIOS alternative that adds some features and benefits. From an end-user and PC technician point of view, it's roughly equivalent to a BIOS. (Its setup program is very similar to a BIOS setup program, for example.) The main advantages of UEFI are that it supports file systems that enable booting to large drives (2.2 terabytes and up), it supports 32-bit or 64-bit booting, and it's not dependent on x86 firmware. Many technicians use the term BIOS (or CMOS; see the next section) to refer to both BIOS and UEFI firmware.

A Brief History of the PC System BIOS

BIOS was originally stored on a *read-only memory (ROM)* chip that was completely inaccessible for user changes. To get a BIOS update, you had to replace the BIOS chip on the motherboard. As you can imagine, that was a hardship, especially because back in those days, there was no plug and play. If your BIOS didn't recognize a certain type of drive or other hardware, you couldn't use it.

As a workaround, systems began offering BIOS written on *erasable programmable ROM (EPROM)* chips. These BIOS chips had a little clear window in the top. You could put the chip in a special machine that would flash a strong light into that window that erased the BIOS chip. Then the machine would reprogram the chip. That's how the name *flash BIOS* or *flash ROM* originated.

But even that was a pain. End users didn't have the needed machine, and many small repair shops didn't either. So the next evolutionary step was to make a BIOS chip that could be erased with a strong pulse of electricity, rather than light. This was known as *electrically erasable programmable ROM (EEPROM)*. An EEPROM update could be done in-place on the motherboard using a software utility. Big improvement!

The problem with EPROM and EEPROM chips was that, except when using their special update procedures, you couldn't write changes to them. That meant that each time the PC turned on, it was a blank slate. The PC couldn't remember what drives or memory were installed, what user settings were desired, or even the current date and time. To get around this, motherboards had another chip, a *complementary metal-oxide semiconductor (CMOS)*. This was a special kind of dynamic RAM (DRAM) chip that stored the exceptions to the BIOS settings. First the BIOS would load its basic settings, and then the CMOS chip would load the changes to the defaults. The CMOS chip required electricity to hold its data, but it was a very small amount of electricity. Motherboard manufacturers supplied that electricity with a small battery on the motherboard.

As technology advanced, electrically rewriteable ROM chips became faster and less expensive, to the point where device makers were using them as a substitute for magnetic disk storage in systems. (USB flash drives and solid-state hard drives are two examples.) Motherboard makers began using this type of memory to hold the user customizations to the BIOS settings, rather than CMOS chips. Such chips don't require the motherboard's battery to retain their settings. So technically in modern motherboards there is no longer a CMOS chip, nor a need for a battery.

The utility used to write the user changes to the CMOS chip was known as *CMOS setup* or *BIOS setup*, depending on the BIOS brand and model. Even though you won't find a CMOS chip on a motherboard anymore today, the term CMOS setup is still very common, referring to the firmware setup program.

Updating the Firmware

Motherboard manufacturers and PC makers periodically release firmware updates for their motherboards. These updates may correct bugs in the code, and may add extra features, like support for a new type of device. Most PCs function just fine with the original firmware version they came with, but occasionally a problem can crop up that can be solved by updating the firmware to the latest version.

Updating the firmware involves running a program to "flash" the BIOS or UEFI. In modern terms, what that really means is to update the programming on the memory chip on the motherboard that holds the firmware. There's not really any flashing going on anymore, although the name persists. You can download a firmware update and accompanying utility for installing it (perhaps in a single executable) from the website of the motherboard or PC manufacturer.

It is very important to follow the directions given by the manufacturer when updating the firmware. A botched update can render the system inoperable and require a replacement chip from the manufacturer.

Modern motherboards include a great many more devices and capabilities than older motherboards—often more than can be adequately supported by the motherboard firmware. Therefore, when you purchase a motherboard, it will come with a driver disc, containing utilities to install in specific operating systems to work with motherboard features like built-in display, sound, and networking adapters. You will learn about installing and configuring motherboards and using the driver disc in Chapter 6. Companies such as Phoenix Technologies and AMI specialize in manufacturing BIOSs for PC manufacturers, and many PC and/or motherboard manufacturers make their own BIOSs.

Configuring the Firmware

The most common way to optimize a motherboard is to modify the BIOS or UEFI setup configuration program, also called the *BIOS setup* or *CMOS setup*. Literally hundreds of settings are available in different computers; we discuss the most common basic and advanced settings here. The choices available, and the methods for selecting them, may vary from one manufacturer to another. The best reference for using the firmware setup menus is the motherboard manual.

Accessing Firmware Settings

To access the computer's firmware settings, closely watch the computer screen at startup. Following the system hardware test, a message appears indicating the proper key sequence you should use to enter the firmware setup program. It may simply say "Setup" followed by a key or key sequence name. This key or key combination varies among computers but is typically F2, DELETE, or CTRL-ALT-ESC. In most systems, the message will appear for only three to five seconds, and you must use the indicated key combination within that allotted time.

On PCs with Windows 8 and higher and UEFI, if the Secure Boot feature is enabled in the firmware settings, you might not see a prompt as the PC starts telling you to press a key to enter setup. On such systems, there is an alternate method of getting into the setup program through the Settings app. See Exercise 3-4 for details.

EXERCISE 3-4

Booting into Firmware Setup

This exercise provides two methods of entering firmware setup. Use Method 1 if possible because it is easier.

Method 1   Use this method if you see a message about a key to press at startup.

1. Reboot your PC, and as it reboots, watch the screen for a message telling you what key to press to enter Setup.
2. When you see that message, press the key as quickly as you can. If you see the Windows splash screen, you missed the window of opportunity; allow Windows to finish loading, and then restart and try again.

Method 2   Use this method if you are running Windows 8/8.1 or Windows 10 and don't see any message about a key to press at startup.

1. In Windows 8 or 8.1, display the Charms bar, click the Settings charm, and click Change PC Settings. Or, in Windows 10, choose Start | Settings.
2. In the Settings app, click Update and Recovery (Windows 8 or 8.1) or Update and Security (Windows 10). Then in the navigation bar, click Recovery.
3. Under the Advanced Startup heading, click Restart Now. Then at the Choose an Option screen, click Troubleshoot, and then click Advanced (Windows 8 or 8.1) or Advanced Options (Windows 10).
4. At the Advanced Options screen, click UEFI Firmware Settings. If using Windows 10, click Restart. The PC reboots and opens the setup application.

Navigating in the Firmware Setup Program

Firmware setup programs differ widely. Some allow you to use the mouse, and some only the keyboard. The names of the settings might also vary slightly. Use the program's Help feature or on-screen prompts for information about how to navigate through the program and save or discard your changes. Usually, though, pressing the ESC key quits without saving, and pressing the F10 key quits and saves. The RIGHT and LEFT ARROW keys usually move between screens, the UP and DOWN ARROW keys move the highlight to select a different option, and pressing ENTER usually selects whatever option is highlighted.

EXERCISE 3-5

Viewing the Firmware Settings

1. Enter the firmware setup program by completing Exercise 3-4.
2. Look at the bottom of the screen for navigation instructions, as well as how to access the Help utility (normally the F1 key).
3. Page through the screens carefully, and if you have a digital camera handy, take a picture of each screen.
4. Locate the settings described in the following sections.
5. When you have finished, use the indicated key combination to exit *without* saving any changes.

Backing Up Firmware Settings

Make notes about the current firmware settings before you change them, in case you need to change them back. We prefer to do this using a digital camera, taking a picture of each screen without making any changes. Also, look for a firmware-settings backup utility in the firmware setup menus, sometimes located on a Tools menu, or check out the firmware manufacturer's website for backup instructions. Alternatively, look for a third-party firmware backup program.

Main Settings

A main settings screen will be mostly informational. Only such settings as System Time and System Date will be configurable from this screen. You don't have to go into the firmware settings to change the date and time on your computer, though. In Windows, you simply click the real-time clock display on the right end of the taskbar, click Date and Time Settings (or Adjust Date/Time in Windows 7), and make the changes.

Aside from date and time, this screen has a great deal of information about your computer. For instance, on the Dell Inspiron laptop used to write this chapter, this screen displays the component information shown in Table 3-4.

Notice the information in this screen, such as the amount of RAM installed (System Memory and Extended Memory taken together makes 16 GB in this case), the size and model of the hard drive (Fixed HDD), and the model and type of optical drive installed (SATA ODD), as well as the model of the CPU and its speed and the size and types of CPU cache.

watch Although there are easier methods for seeing at least most of this system information from within Windows, CompTIA A+ 901 exam objective 1.1 requires that you understand where and how to find this information in the BIOS setup program.

TABLE 3-4	Setting Name	Actual Configuration
	BIOS Version	A13
Example of	Product Name	Inspiron 17 7000 Series 7737
Details Shown in	CPU Type	Intel Core i7-4500U CPU @ 1.80 GHz
Main Screen of	CPU Speed	1.80 GHz
Firmware Setup	CPU Cache	
	L1 Cache	32 KB
	L2 Cache	256 KB
	L3 Cache	4096 KB
	Fixed HDD	ST1000LM014-1EJ164 –(S0) 1000 GB
	SATA ODD	PLDS DVD+/–RW DU-8A –(S1) ATAPI
	AC Adapter Type	90 W
	System Memory	628 KB
	Extended Memory	16384 KB
	Memory Speed	1600 MHz
	Keyboard Type	Backlight Keyboard

Advanced Settings

Continuing to use the Dell laptop system BIOS as our model, we find an advanced menu with plenty of items we can configure. Table 3-5 lists some of these items, along with a brief explanation. Notice the virtualization setting that enables hardware-level support for running virtualization software on your computer. This is important to know for the exam, and you will learn more about virtualization in Chapter 8.

Security Settings

Depending on the BIOS make and version, you might have the option to configure up to three passwords in the Security section of firmware setup: Supervisor/Admin, User/System, and Hard Disk Drive (HDD). All are disabled by default.

on the **Job**

Except in special high-security situations, we don't recommend using the firmware-level passwords. It's too easy to forget that they're set when you pass along a PC to a new owner, or to forget a password in times of distress, like when you need to get into the firmware setup to correct a problem in the middle of a tight deadline project.

The User or System password restricts booting the PC. A Supervisor or Admin password restricts access to the firmware-settings program itself or to change user passwords. Most firmware setup programs require that you first set a Supervisor/Admin password before it allows you to set a User/System password. Some systems also have an HDD password, which must be entered before a user can access the hard drive.

TABLE 3-5   Advanced Screen of a BIOS Setting Menu

Setting Name	Setting State	Description
Intel SpeedStep	Enabled	Turns on a feature of the CPU that "steps" the CPU up when more power is needed, and steps it down when it is not needed so as to conserve power usage.
Virtualization	Enabled	Enables Intel Virtualization Technology (VT-x).
Integrated NIC	Enabled	Enables or disables the onboard network interface card (NIC).
USB Emulation	Enabled	Determines whether the system BIOS controls Universal Serial Bus (USB) keyboards and mice. When enabled, the system BIOS controls USB keyboards and mice until a USB driver is loaded by the operating system.
USB Powershare	Enabled	Allows USB devices plugged into certain USB ports to charge from the PC's battery.
USB Wake Support	Disabled	When enabled, allows a USB mouse or keyboard to wake a computer from sleep.
SATA Operation	AHCI	Advance Host Controller Interface (AHCI) enables full capabilities of SATA. Choose AHCI when using a recent version of Windows that works with SATA. Choose ATA, which will emulate the old PATA interface, for an older OS.
Adapter Warnings	Enabled	When enabled, the system will warn you if you attempt to use a power adapter with too little capacity.
Function Key Behavior	Function Key	When "Function Key" is selected, the FN key must be pressed before pressing one of the alternate functions on the laptop's function keys. If "Multimedia Key" is selected, only the function key (F1, F2, etc.) with the alternate function needs to be pressed. Disabled during startup so that you can call up the System menu with the F2 key.
Intel Smart Connect Technology	Enabled	Wakes the PC from sleep mode periodically to update applications that get their data from the Internet, so that fresh data is waiting for you when you restore the PC from sleep.
Intel Rapid Start Technology	Enabled	Enables a "deep sleep" state that is quicker to wake up from than normal hibernation, but drains no power, unlike regular sleep mode.

Some systems also have an option that allows you to enable the BIOS interface to connect to a for-pay antitheft service. Enabling this option involves signing up for the service over the Internet and downloading additional software. Once you have enabled and subscribed to the service and connected the computer to the Internet, the software installed in your OS will contact the service's servers and check for a theft report, as well as transmitting the

exam

Watch CompTIA A+ 901 exam objective 1.1 uses the spelling "lo-jack," which is incorrect. If you see that spelling on the exam, assume it to mean "LoJack."

system and GPS tracking information concerning the location of the computer. This service may have a product name attached to it, such as Computrace or LoJack.

Even formatting or replacing the existing hard drive will not bypass this security because it takes advantage of the built-in *Trusted Platform Module (TPM)*, an embedded security chip that stores encrypted passwords, keys, and digital certificates. Various services can use the TPM chip. Even without a for-pay location service, when you combine the use of TPM with a BIOS-level Administrator password and a User password required at power-on, the computer is virtually useless to a thief. Learn more about other security measures in Chapters 17 and 18.

on the Job Considering how often users forget passwords, using the combination of TPM, Administrator password, and a required User password at power-on may make a computer useless to the user! Use these security measures only where and when required, such as protecting mobile computers that contain sensitive information.

A less common firmware security feature found on some models is a chassis *intrusion detection system (IDS)*. When turned on, if this feature detects that someone has opened the case, then on the next reboot, it will display a message such as "Alert! Cover was previously removed." This is useful in a situation in which someone steals computer components out of computers, but, with the trend toward integrating more and more components on the motherboard, it may be more sensible to secure the building against the theft of the entire computer system.

The *Secure Boot* feature is enabled/disabled in firmware setup, but also relies on the PC having Windows 8 or later and UEFI. Provided all three of those pieces are present, Secure Boot helps prevent malware (such as a rootkit replacing the Windows boot loader) and unauthorized OSs from loading during the system boot process. Secure Boot is enabled by default on systems where it is available. One drawback of it is that you can no longer press a key at startup to enter firmware; you have to go in through Windows, as in Exercise 3-4. The Secure Boot feature may be controlled from the Security section or the Boot section in firmware setup, depending on the firmware brand and version.

Boot Sequence

Your system firmware will no doubt have a setting for selecting the order in which the system will search devices for an OS. You can normally select from among a variety of possible boot devices, including C: or Hard Disk, CD/DVD drive, removable drive, USB devices, and even the network. In the last case, the firmware will boot via your network interface card (NIC). All modern network cards support the ability to start a computer over the network, without relying on a disk-based OS, using an Intel standard called Preboot eXecution Environment (PXE).

If you plan to install a new OS on a system using a bootable optical disc, you will need to go into the firmware setup program and change the boot order so that the optical drive precedes the hard drive. With this turned on, every time the system restarts with a bootable disc in the optical drive, you briefly see a message to press any key to boot from the optical disc. After installing a new OS, you might change the boot order back to start from the hard drive first. Then it only searches other drives at startup if it does not find an OS on the hard drive.

Firmware-Based Diagnostics and Monitoring

In addition to the configuration settings program, some firmware setup programs include built-in diagnostics and monitoring features, depending on the manufacturer and the type of system to which it is targeted, such as desktop, laptop, or tablet.

Power-on Self-Test

The *power-on self-test (POST)* is actually a group of tests stored in the BIOS and performed every time a PC boots up. These tests check for the presence and status of recognized components. A visual (text) error message on the screen, or a series of beeps, typically indicates errors found during the POST. Your firmware setup program may allow you to customize the POST, such as disabling a thorough check of memory at startup (often called Quick Boot) and suppressing on-screen text at startup (often called Quiet Boot).

Optional Tests

Further, a firmware setup program may also include additional tests that you can initiate through the menus to perform more advanced tests on components. If you poke around in a setup program you may discover diagnostic tests for the motherboard components and memory. Some manufacturers install special diagnostic software for their hardware when they preinstall Windows on a system. Browse through the Start menu for clues to such a program.

BIOS-Based Monitoring and Alerts

Some firmware setup programs include the ability to monitor the health of a computer, including such indicators of possible problems as CPU and system temperatures, CPU and case fan speeds, CPU core voltage, and voltages supplied to the motherboard. A couple of older systems we support have this feature, and in those instances, the monitoring is always happening, but you can optionally choose a setting to turn on alarms and even shut down the computer for some of the more critical indicators, such as fan failure and CPU temperature.

SCENARIO & SOLUTION

You need to access a PC's firmware setup program; in general terms, how will you do that?	Restart the computer and watch carefully for a brief message that may say "Setup" followed by a key or key combination name. Press that key or combination to enter setup. If that doesn't work, follow the steps in Exercise 3-4, Method 2.
You need to boot a computer from an optical disc, but every time you try, it immediately boots from the hard drive and loads Windows. What can you do?	Go into the firmware setup and add the optical disc to the boot order, making sure it precedes the hard drive.
You want to change the system time and date on your PC. What is the easiest way to do this?	Although this is a firmware setting, the easiest way to do this is from the OS.

CERTIFICATION SUMMARY

Common computer components include the processor, memory, storage devices, and input and output devices. All of these devices have specific functions, and your familiarity with them will help you to determine when to upgrade or replace a component.

This chapter described general characteristics of motherboards, installed motherboard components and form factors, and CPU technologies. You must use a motherboard that supports the selected CPU and RAM. Motherboards have many integrated functions. This chapter introduced several of the technologies that the CompTIA A+ exams may test you on. A good knowledge of these concepts is also important when you are repairing or upgrading a computer system. Chapters 4 and 5 will continue with explanations of other important PC components, and Chapter 6 will describe how to install and upgrade PC components.

 # TWO-MINUTE DRILL

Here are some of the key points covered in Chapter 3.

The Hardware Toolkit

❑ Start out with a basic toolkit of an assortment of screwdrivers and nut drivers, a small flashlight, and an assortment of screws and nuts.

❑ In addition to a variety of tools and replacement parts, consider keeping a digital camera handy to document the physical condition of a computer before you begin troubleshooting, and to capture low-level error messages that you cannot capture otherwise.

Motherboard Form Factors and Components

❑ All components, including external peripherals, connect directly or indirectly to the motherboard.

❑ A motherboard form factor defines the type and location of the components on the motherboard, the power supply that will work with that motherboard, and the PC case the components will fit into.

❑ ATX remains the standard for motherboards; several smaller-size versions include Micro-ATX, Flex-ATX, and Mini-ATX.

❑ ITX is a small-form-factor alternative to ATX, and comes in several sizes as well.

❑ Motherboard components include sockets for various PC components, including the CPU and memory, built-in components such as video and sound adapters, hard drive controllers (PATA and SATA), support for various port types, and the chipset.

❑ Memory slots can include DIMM on motherboards for desktop systems, and SODIMM on laptop motherboards.

❑ Every motherboard contains at least one CPU socket, and the location varies, based on the form factor.

❑ The most common types of bus architectures are PCI (obsolete but still supported on some motherboards) and the current standard: PCIe. PCIe comes in several slot lengths, including x1, x4, and x16. PCI-X was originally proposed as a 64-bit version of PCI, but has lost popularity. Mini PCI and Mini PCI Express are versions of PCI and PCIe, respectively, in notebook PCs.

❑ A variety of connectors attach to the motherboard, including a large 24-pin connector from the power supply.

❑ The chipset is one to three separate chips on the motherboard that handle very low-level functions relating to the interactions between the CPU and other components.

CPUs and Their Sockets

❑ The CPU chip is the primary control device for a PC. A GPU is a processor on a video adapter, dedicated to the rendering of display images.

❑ The CPU connects to all of the components, such as memory, storage, and input/output, through communication channels called buses.

❑ The machine cycle consists of fetching, decoding, executing, and storing.

❑ CPU components include the control unit, the arithmetic logic unit (ALU), registers, and cache memory (L1, L2, L3).

❑ Hyperthreading is a technology that allows a CPU to execute two threads at the same time.

❑ A multicore processor contains two or more processing cores and can process multiple threads simultaneously, performing true parallel execution.

❑ Intel Corporation and AMD (Advanced Micro Devices, Inc.) are the two top manufacturers of PC CPUs.

❏ The socket types to know for the 220-901 exam are Intel 775, 1155, 1156, 1366, 1150, and 2011. The AMD socket types to know are AM3, AM3+, FM1, FM2, and FM2+.

❏ CPUs require cooling, as do some other hardworking chips, such as the graphic processor. Cooling is usually active (involving a fan), but can also be passive (with no moving parts).

Configuring a Motherboard

❏ Older motherboards may have jumpers to set for configuration, but most modern motherboards are configured via a firmware setup utility.

❏ The basic input/output system, or BIOS, is firmware that informs the processor of the hardware that is present and contains low-level software routines for communicating with and controlling the hardware. Configured through a BIOS setup program, you may also need to upgrade, or flash, an older BIOS.

❏ UEFI is the more modern replacement for BIOS. On a system with Window 8, 8.1, or 10 with UEFI, additional BIOS features are available such as Secure Boot.

❏ To access BIOS setup, press the key indicated onscreen at startup. To access UEFI firmware setup you must go through the operating system.

❏ Follow the onscreen instructions to navigate in a firmware setup program.

❏ The power-on self-test (POST) is a group of tests stored in BIOS and performed every time a PC boots up. It issues error messages on the screen or a series of beeps when it discovers errors.

❏ Additional monitoring options and diagnostics tests are available with some BIOSs.

SELF TEST

The following questions will help you measure your understanding of the material presented in this chapter. Read all of the choices carefully because there might be more than one correct answer. Choose all correct answers for each question.

The Hardware Toolkit

1. Use this tool to detect if a cable has a broken wire in it.
    A. Stand-off
    B. FRU
    C. Cable tester
    D. POST card

2. What would you use to measure the resistance, voltage, and/or current in computer components using two probes?
   A. Multimeter
   B. FRU
   C. Cable tester
   D. Punch down tool

Motherboard Form Factors and Components

3. Which is the most common type of RAM slot on modern desktop motherboards?
   A. RIMM
   B. SIMM
   C. SODIMM
   D. DIMM

4. Which of the following statements is true?
   A. The motherboard must always be in a horizontal position.
   B. Each internal and external PC component connects to the motherboard, directly or indirectly.
   C. The "lines" on the motherboard provide cooling.
   D. A system board is an unusual motherboard variant.

5. Which of the following describes a motherboard form factor?
   A. The size and color of a motherboard
   B. The processor the motherboard supports
   C. The type and location of components and the power supply that will work with the motherboard, plus the dimensions of the motherboard
   D. Mid-tower

6. This variant of the most enduring and popular motherboard form factor measures 9.6" on each side.
   A. Mini-ATX
   B. ATX
   C. Mobile-ITX
   D. Micro-ATX

7. On modern systems, where are the functions that used to be part of the Northbridge?
   A. Directly on the CPU
   B. On the Input/Output Controller Hub
   C. On the Fusion Controller Hub
   D. On the Platform Controller Hub

8. Which of the following describes a difference between PCI and PCIe?
   A. PCIe is only used for graphics adapters; PCI is used by a variety of adapters.
   B. PCI uses parallel data communications; PCIe uses serial communications.
   C. PCIe uses parallel data communications; PCI uses serial communications.
   D. PCIe is used by a variety of adapters; PCI is only used by video adapters.

9. What type of local bus connector is used for video cards on modern systems?
   A. PCIe x16
   B. PCIe x1
   C. AGP
   D. USB

CPUs and Their Sockets

10. What is the purpose of the control unit?
    A. Performs math calculations
    B. Evaluates logical statements
    C. Fetches instructions or data from memory
    D. Temporarily stores data to be processed

11. What is the purpose of the L1 cache?
    A. Holds data that the CPU is likely to need soon, so it doesn't have to be retrieved from memory.
    B. Holds applications loaded from the hard disk drive
    C. Swaps out data between main memory and the hard disk drive
    D. Performs the POST.

12. What component in a CPU is responsible for all logical and mathematical operations?
    A. ALU
    B. Registers
    C. Control unit
    D. Processor bus

13. What CPU component temporarily stores data inside the CPU as it is being processed?
    A. Registers
    B. Processor
    C. Control unit
    D. Bus

14. What Intel CPU technology allows two threads to execute at the same time within a single execution core?
    A. Hyperthreading
    B. Core
    C. Cache memory
    D. Microcode

15. Where is the L1 cache located on modern CPUs?
  A.   In the registers
  B.   In the ALU
  C.   In the motherboard chipset
  D.   On the CPU chip

16. In a system with an integrated GPU, into what component is the GPU integrated?
  A.   Motherboard
  B.   CPU
  C.   Memory
  D.   L2 cache

17. What CPU feature helps prevent worm infection?
  A.   ROM-BIOS
  B.   Multicore design
  C.   Integrated GPU
  D.   Execute Disable Bit

18. Which socket is an AMD PGA with 904 pins?
  A.   Socket T
  B.   Socket H2
  C.   AM3
  D.   FM2

Configuring a Motherboard

19. What does an Admin or Supervisor password in BIOS setup prevent unauthorized people from doing?
  A.   Booting the PC
  B.   Accessing BIOS setup
  C.   Accessing the hard disk drive
  D.   Removing the hard disk drive

20. What is UEFI?
  A.   A type of RAM that the BIOS can automatically detect
  B.   An alternative to the traditional system BIOS
  C.   A motherboard driver on an optical disc
  D.   A POST routine

SELF TEST ANSWERS

The Hardware Toolkit

1. ☑ **C.** A cable tester is the tool to use to detect if a cable can connect properly end to end and determine if there is a short.

    ☒ **A** is incorrect, because stand-offs are small, washer-type parts used to ensure that a motherboard does not come in contact with a computer case. **B** is incorrect because FRU stands for field-replaceable unit—any computer component that you can install into a system onsite. **D** is incorrect because a POST card is an adapter card used to run a special diagnostic test on a computer as it is powering up.

2. ☑ **A.** A multimeter is the device you would use to measure the resistance, voltage, and/or current in computer components using two probes.

    ☒ **B** is incorrect because an FRU is a field-replaceable unit, or any component that you can install into a system onsite. **C** is incorrect because a cable tester is usually used for network cables to test if a cable can connect properly end to end. **D** is incorrect because it is a hand tool used for inserting various types of wire into appropriate wiring panels.

Motherboard Form Factors and Components

3. ☑ **D.** DIMM RAM slots are the most common type of RAM slots on desktop motherboards.

    ☒ **A** and **B** are both incorrect because they are old technologies not likely to be found on new desktop motherboards. **C** is incorrect because this type of RAM slot is usually found on laptops.

4. ☑ **B.** Each internal and external PC component connects to the motherboard, directly or indirectly.

    ☒ **A** is not true because the motherboard can be oriented in whatever position the case requires. **C** is not true because the lines on the motherboard do not provide cooling but carry signals and are part of various busses installed on the motherboard. **D** is not true; system board is simply another name for motherboard.

5. ☑ **C.** A motherboard form factor is the type and location of components and the power supply that will work with the motherboard, plus the dimensions of the motherboard.

    ☒ **A** is incorrect because, while size may be part of a form factor, color has nothing to do with the form factor. **B** is incorrect because the processor the motherboard supports is not, by itself, a description of a form factor. **D** is incorrect because mid-tower is a case size, not a motherboard form factor.

6.   ☑ **D.** The Micro-ATX variant of the ATX form factor measures 9.6" × 9.6".
     ☒ **A** is incorrect because mini-ATX measures 5.9" × 5.9". **B** is incorrect because ATX measures 12" × 9.6". **C** is incorrect because Mobile-ITX measures just 2.9" × 1.77".

7.   ☑ **A.** Northbridge functions are now directly on the CPU.
     ☒ **B** is incorrect because the ICH is the Intel replacement for the Southbridge. **C** is incorrect because the FCH is the AMD replacement for the Southbridge. **D** is incorrect because the PCH is a newer alternative to the Southbridge that connects directly to the CPU.

8.   ☑ **B.** PCI uses parallel data communications; PCIe uses serial communications.
     ☒ **A** and **D** are incorrect because both PCIe and PCI are used by a variety of expansion cards. **C** is incorrect because the very opposite is true. PCIe uses serial data communications, and PCI uses parallel data communications.

9.   ☑ **A.** PCIe x16 is the fastest bus available on modern systems, and is used by most video cards.
     ☒ **B** is incorrect because PCIe x1 is too small a bus to effectively handle video card traffic. **C** is incorrect because AGP is an old, obsolete expansion slot type for video cards. **D** is incorrect because USB is a peripheral bus, not a bus connector on the motherboard in which an expansion card is installed.

CPUs and Their Sockets

10.   ☑ **C.** The control unit fetches instructions or data from memory.
      ☒ **A** is incorrect because it is a function of the ALU. **B** is incorrect because it is also a function of the ALU. **D** is incorrect because it is a function of the registers.

11.   ☑ **A.** The function of the L1 cache is to hold data that the CPU is likely to need soon.
      ☒ **B** is incorrect because it is a function of the system's main memory, not the L1 cache. **C** is incorrect because it is a function of the paging file. **D** is incorrect because it is a function of the BIOS.

12.   ☑ **A.** The ALU is the CPU component that is responsible for all logical and mathematical operations.
      ☒ **B** is incorrect because the registers are just holding areas. **C** is incorrect because the control unit is the component responsible for directing activities in the computer and managing interactions between the other components and the CPU. **D** is incorrect because the processor bus is just a pathway among components in the CPU.

13.   ☑ **A.** Registers temporarily hold data in the CPU.
      ☒ **B** is incorrect because processor is just another name for CPU. **C** is incorrect because the control unit does not store temporary data. **D** is incorrect because the bus is just a group of wires used to carry signals.

14. ☑   **A.** Hyperthreading is the CPU technology that allows two threads to execute at the same time within a single execution core.
    ☒   **B** is incorrect because a core is a CPU with its own cache, controller, and other CPU components. **C** is incorrect because cache memory is usually a relatively small amount of expensive, very fast memory used to compensate for speed differences between components. **D** is incorrect because microcode is the name for the low-level instructions built into a CPU.

15. ☑   **D.** The L1 cache is built into the CPU chip.
    ☒   **A** and **B** are incorrect because they are each a different part inside the CPU. **C** is incorrect because the L1 cache is located on the CPU, not on the motherboard.

16. ☑   **A.** An integrated GPU is built into the motherboard.
    ☒   **B** is incorrect because the GPU is not a part of the CPU. **C** is incorrect because a GPU is a processing chip, which could not be resident in memory. **D** is incorrect because the L2 cache is also a type of memory.

17. ☑   **D.** Execute Disable Bit is a CPU feature that prevents certain malware infections, including some worm attacks.
    ☒   **A** is incorrect because it is the system BIOS chip, not a CPU feature. **B** is incorrect because although having multiple processor cores makes a system faster, it does nothing to prevent malware. **C** is incorrect because it integrates the display adapter into the motherboard, but does nothing for security.

18. ☑   **D.** The FM2 is a PGA CPU produced by AMD with 904 pins.
    ☒   **A** is incorrect because Socket T is an Intel CPU with 775 pins. **B** is incorrect because Socket H2 is an Intel CPU with 1155 pins. **C** is incorrect because AM3 is an AMD CPU with 940 or 941 pins.

Configuring a Motherboard

19. ☑   **B.** An Admin or Supervisor password will prevent unauthorized people from accessing BIOS setup.
    ☒   **A** is incorrect because it is what a User or System password will prevent. **C** is incorrect because it is what an HDD password will prevent. **D** is incorrect because there is no password that can prevent the HDD from being physically removed.

20. ☑   **B.** UEFI is a modern alternative to the traditional system BIOS.
    ☒   **A** is incorrect because UEFI is not RAM, and because the motherboard can automatically detect all types of RAM anyway. **B** is incorrect because UEFI is built into the motherboard on a chip, and is not a driver that would come on a disc. **D** is incorrect because it is a startup hardware check performed by the BIOS or UEFI at startup.

Chapter 4

Personal Computer Components: Memory, Adapters, and Storage

This chapter is a continuation of the survey of PC concepts and components begun in Chapter 3, which provided the purposes and technologies of PC motherboards, CPUs, and cases. In this chapter, you will continue along the same vein and explore RAM memory, adapter cards, and storage devices. Further, we'll define the connection interfaces, connectors, and ports associated with the expansion cards and storage devices. Chapter 5 will continue this survey of PC concepts and components, and then in Chapter 6 we'll put it all together by installing components in a PC.

CERTIFICATION OBJECTIVE

■ **901: 1.3** *Compare and contrast various RAM types and their features*

This section introduces all of the topics listed in CompTIA A+ 901 exam objective 1.3, including types of RAM, parity versus nonparity, ECC versus non-ECC, single-sided versus double-sided, buffered versus unbuffered, and single channel versus dual channel versus triple channel. RAM types for laptops will be discussed in Chapter 7.

Memory

In Chapter 3, you learned about a type of memory chip called read-only memory (ROM) and about the programs, called firmware, stored on those chips. However, when people discuss computer *memory*, they are usually referring to *random access memory (RAM)*, so called because data and programs stored in RAM are accessible in any (random) order. Most of the memory in a PC is volatile RAM (also called *dynamic RAM*, or *DRAM*), meaning that when the computer is off and the RAM no longer receives power, the contents of this memory are lost. Computers use several types of RAM, each with a different function and different physical form. Chapter 3 described the various types of RAM memory slots used to connect RAM modules to motherboards, and we will complete that discussion in this chapter by describing how RAM and ROM are used, and features and configurations of RAM chips and modules. But first we will define how we measure data quantities and the speeds of electronic components.

From Bits to Exabytes

When we talk about storing data—whether it is in RAM or ROM or on storage devices like disk drives—we casually throw out terms describing the amount of data, or the amount of memory or storage capacity. These terms begin with the lowly *binary digit (bit)*. Think of a single bit as being like a light switch: it can represent two states—either on or off. In computer storage, when a switch is on, it represents a one (1); when it is off, it represents a zero (0). This is the basis for binary numeric notation, and binary works well with computers because RAM, ROM, and storage devices all use binary, two-state methods of storing data. We won't go into just how they do this, just understand that they do.

In computing, we combine bits into groups to create a code or define memory or storage capacity. We call each group of bits a *byte*. Although a byte can be other sizes, it is usually a number divisible by eight. A single 8-bit byte may represent a character, like the letter A in a word processing document, or a very simple command, like the command to move down one line in a document. When we talk about memory and storage capacity, it is most commonly in terms of 8-bit bytes, and when you have 1024 bytes, you have 1 kilobyte (2 to the 10th power—"kilo" means one thousand). Other terms we use represent larger quantities, which Table 4-1 shows. We tend to think about these values in round numbers, so a kilobyte is about a thousand, a megabyte is about a million, a gigabyte is about a billion, a terabyte is about a trillion, and so forth. However, this type of rounding can be deceptive, as you can see that a gigabyte is actually almost 74 million bytes larger than you may expect it to be.

Hertz to Gigahertz

When we talk about the speed of electronics, such as RAM memory modules, we use the word *hertz (Hz)*, a unit of measurement representing the number of electrical cycles or vibrations per second. One hertz is one cycle per second. Then, a *kilohertz (KHz)* is one thousand cycles per second, a *megahertz (MHz)* is one million cycles per second, and a *gigahertz (GHz)* is one billion cycles per second. Watch for these terms a little later when we discuss memory speeds.

Overview of RAM and ROM

When a user makes a request, the CPU intercepts it and organizes the request into component-specific tasks. Many of these tasks must occur in a specific order, with each component reporting its results back to the processor before it can go on to complete the next task. The processor uses RAM to store these results until they can be compiled into the final results.

TABLE 4-1

Common Values Used to Measure Data

	Calculation	Result in Bytes
One kilobyte (KB)	2^{10}	1024
One megabyte (MB)	2^{20}	1,048,576
One gigabyte (GB)	2^{30}	1,073,741,824
One terabyte (TB)	2^{40}	1,099,511,627,776
One petabyte (PB)	2^{50}	1,125,899,906,842,624
One exabyte (EB)	2^{60}	1,152,921,504,606,846,976

RAM also stores instructions about currently running applications. For example, when you start a computer game, a large set of the game's instructions (including how it works, how the screen should look, and which sounds must be generated) is loaded into memory. The processor can retrieve these instructions much faster from RAM than it can from the hard drive, where the game normally resides until you start to use it. Within certain limits, the more information stored in memory, the faster the computer will run. In fact, one of the most common computer upgrades is to increase the amount of RAM. The computer continually reads, changes, and removes the information in RAM, which is *volatile*, meaning that it cannot work without a steady supply of power, so when you turn your computer off, the information in RAM disappears.

Unlike RAM, ROM is read-only, meaning the processor can read the instructions it contains, but cannot store new information in ROM. As described in Chapter 3, firmware is typically stored on ROM chips on circuit boards such as the motherboard and adapter cards. ROM has an important function; it is rarely changed or upgraded, and even then, instead of being physically replaced, it is more often "flashed," as described in Chapter 3, to change the information. So ROM typically warrants less attention by most computer users.

Features and Configurations of RAM Chips and Modules

When shopping for RAM, you need to understand the features and configurations of RAM chips and modules, such as the error-checking methods, single-sided versus double-sided, and single-channel versus multichannel. You should also understand the types of RAM and how to select among the various generations of double data rate (DDR) synchronous dynamic RAM (SDRAM), depending on the requirements and capabilities of a motherboard, which are described in a motherboard manual.

Memory Error Checking

Earlier you learned that RAM memory is volatile, so you should realize that memory can be error-prone. The fact is that modern memory modules are very reliable, but there are methods and technologies that you can build into RAM modules to check for errors. We'll look at two of these methods: parity and error-correcting code (ECC).

Parity   In one type of memory error checking, called *parity*, every 8-bit byte of data is accompanied by a ninth bit (the parity bit), which is used to determine the presence of errors in the data. Of course, *nonparity* RAM does not use parity. There are two types of parity: odd and even.

In *odd parity*, the parity bit is used to ensure that the total number of ones in the data stream is odd. For example, suppose a byte consists of the following data: 11010010. The number of ones in this data is four, an even number. The ninth bit will then be a one to ensure that the total number of ones is odd: 110100101.

Even parity is the opposite of odd parity; it ensures that the total number of ones is even. For example, suppose a byte consists of the following data: 11001011. The ninth bit would then be a one to ensure that the total number of ones is six, an even number.

Parity is not failure-proof. Suppose the preceding data stream contained two errors: 101100101. If the computer was using odd parity, the error would slip through (try it; count the ones). However, creating parity is quick and does not inhibit memory access time the way a more sophisticated error-checking routine would.

A DIMM is 64-bits wide, but a parity-checking DIMM has 8 extra bits (1 parity bit for every 8-bit byte). Therefore, a DIMM with parity is $64 + 8 = 72$ bits wide. Although parity is not often used in memory modules, there is an easy way to determine if a memory module is using parity—it will have an odd number of chips. A nonparity memory module will have an even number of chips. This is true even if the module only has two or three chips total.

If your system supports parity, you must use parity memory modules. You cannot use memory with parity if your system does not support it. The motherboard manual will define the memory requirements.

on the **Job**

Be aware that the majority of today's motherboards do not support memory that uses parity. Other computing devices use parity, however. One example of parity use is in some special drive arrays, called RAID 5, mostly found in servers. Therefore, understanding the basics of parity is useful.

ECC   *Error-correcting code (ECC)* is a more sophisticated method of error checking than parity, although it also adds an extra bit per byte to a stick of RAM. Software in the system memory controller chip uses the extra bits to both detect and correct errors. Several algorithms are used in ECC. We call RAM that does not use this error checking and correcting method *non-ECC RAM*.

Buffered vs. Unbuffered Memory

The terms *buffered* and *unbuffered* are somewhat dated, although the CompTIA A+ 901 exam objective 1.3 still uses them; the more modern usage is *registered* and *unregistered*. We use the older terminology here to correlate more closely with the exam.

One factor limiting how much memory a motherboard can support is the electrical load on the memory controller. *Buffered memory* uses a buffer (also called a *register*) between the DRAM and the memory controller. This helps the system to reliably support more RAM than it otherwise could. Buffered memory is more expensive than unbuffered, so it's used mostly in systems where a lot of RAM is required, like in servers. Most (but not all) buffered memory is also ECC memory.

You can't swap freely between buffered and unbuffered memory; if the motherboard requires it, you must use it. If the motherboard doesn't accept it, you must not. Some motherboards accept but do not require it, but even if that's the case you must not mix buffered and unbuffered modules in the same system.

Single-Sided vs. Double-Sided Modules

The DIMMs discussed in this chapter come in both single-sided and double-sided versions. *Single-sided modules* have chips mounted on just one side of the memory circuit card, while *double-sided modules* have chips mounted on both sides. Most memory sticks are single-sided because there are incompatibility problems—mainly involving space—with the double-sided modules and motherboards.

Do not confuse being single-sided or double-sided in terms of chip mount with the *single* and *double* in Single Inline Memory Module (SIMM) and Dual Inline Memory Module (DIMM). The latter refers to the way the pins are read in the memory slot. On a SIMM (a now-obsolete type of RAM), each metal pin on the bottom edge of the module wrapped around the bottom, so it was the same pin on both sides. On a DIMM (which is what all modern system RAM is), the metal pin on one side of the module is a different pin from the corresponding one on the other side.

SRAM

Static RAM (SRAM) (pronounced "ess-ram") can hold its data without constant electrical stimulation. Although SRAM is very fast to access compared to DRAM, it is also very expensive. For this reason, PC manufacturers typically use SRAM only for caches. As you learned in Chapter 3, cache memory stores frequently accessed instructions or data for the CPU's use. On modern systems, the L1, L2, and L3 caches are all built into the CPU package.

DRAM

Dynamic RAM (DRAM) (pronounced "dee-ram") was developed to combat the high cost of SRAM. Although DRAM chips provide much slower access than SRAM chips, they are still much faster than accessing data from a hard drive. They can store several hundreds of megabytes of data on a single chip (or even gigabytes, when packaged together on a "stick").

You can think of a DRAM chip as a tiny spreadsheet with billions of individual cells, arranged in rows and columns. The number of columns corresponds to the bus width of the RAM; a 64-bit chip has 64 columns. Every "cell" in a DRAM chip contains one transistor and one capacitor to store a single bit of information. This design makes it necessary for the DRAM chip to receive a constant power refresh from the computer to prevent the capacitors from losing their charge. This constant refresh makes DRAM slower than SRAM and causes a DRAM chip to draw more power from the computer than SRAM does.

Because of its low cost and high capacity, manufacturers use DRAM as "main" memory (system memory) in the computer. Modern DRAM operates at a speed dictated by the motherboard's system clock (a.k.a. system timer). Since it is synchronized with the system clock, it is known as synchronous DRAM, or SDRAM. Originally SDRAM operated at the same speed as the system clock, but more modern types operate at a multiple of that speed, and are known as double data rate (DDR) SDRAM. The following sections explain the various types of DDR SDRAM.

Dual-Channel and Triple-Channel Architecture   One way of increasing the speed of the system RAM is to access it using two or more channels. With *dual-channel architecture*, the system alternates between reading two physically separate memory modules, to read and write data twice as fast. With triple-channel, it alternates between three modules. Quad-channel architecture also exists but is not explicitly mentioned in the 220-901 exam objectives.

Multichannel is a function of the motherboard, not of the RAM itself. Motherboards that support the DDR SDRAM types you'll learn about in the next several sections also employ multichannel architecture to achieve speed improvements.

w a t c h   For the CompTIA A+ 901 exam, be sure to understand the difference between single-, dual-, and triple-channel architecture, as well as single-sided versus double-sided modules.

The important thing to remember about a multichannel-enabled motherboard is that the RAM must be installed in identical modules across a set of slots. For example, if you see two blue RAM slots and two black ones, the memory in the two blue slots must be identical in capacity, features, and all the other particulars, and the memory in the two black ones must be identical. The same goes for triple-channel, except there are three slots to identically match. That's because the motherboard treats these sets of slots as if they were a single slot logically.

DDR1 SDRAM   People often call any version of double-data rate SDRAM (DDR SDRAM) simply "DDR RAM," but there are several versions. The first version, now called *DDR1 SDRAM*, doubled the speed at which standard SDRAM processed data by accessing the module twice per clock cycle. In addition, when you combine DDR memory with dual-channel or triple-channel architecture, you get even faster memory access.

The JEDEC Solid State Technology Association (once known as the Joint Electron Device Engineering Council, or JEDEC) defines the standards for DDR SDRAM. There are two sets of standards involved here—one for the module (the "stick") and another for the chips that populate the module. The module specifications include PC1600, PC2100, PC2700, and PC3200. This labeling refers to the total bandwidth of the memory, as opposed to the old standard, which listed the speed rating (in MHz) of the SDRAM memory—in that case, PC66, PC100, and PC133. The numeric value in the PC66, PC100, and PC133 refers to the MHz speed at which the memory operates, which should match the motherboard's clock speed. Each module specification pairs the stick with chips of a certain chip specification.

A stick of DDR SDRAM memory is an 184-pin DIMM with a notch on one end so it can only fit into the appropriate DIMM socket on a motherboard. It requires only a 2.5V power supply, compared to the previous 3.3V requirement for SDRAM.

TABLE 4-2	DDR2 Chip Specification	Chip Operating Speed	I/O Clock Speed	DDR2 Module Specification
	DDR2-400	100 MHz	200 MHz	PC2-3200
JEDEC Speed Standards for DDR2 SDRAM Chip and Module Combinations	DDR2-533	133 MHz	266 MHz	PC2-4200
	DDR2-667	166 MHz	333 MHz	PC2-5300
	DDR2-800	200 MHz	400 MHz	PC2-6400
	DDR2-1066	266 MHz	533 MHz	PC2-8500

DDR2 SDRAM   *Double-data-rate two SDRAM (DDR2 SDRAM)* replaced the original DDR standard, now referred to as DDR1. Due to some improvements in electrical characteristics, DDR2 can handle faster clock rates than DDR1 can, beginning at 400 MHz, while using less power. DDR2 achieves much of its speed increase by clock doubling the I/O circuits on the chips and adding buffers.

As with DDR1, there are specifications for the chips, as well as for the modules. Table 4-2 shows the JEDEC speed standards for DDR2 SDRAM chip and module combinations.

DDR2 sticks are compatible only with motherboards that use a special 240-pin DIMM socket. The DDR2 DIMM stick notches are different from those in a DDR1 DIMM. A DDR2 DIMM only requires 1.8V compared to 2.5V for DDR1. Manufacturers of motherboards and processors were slow to switch to support for DDR2, mainly due to problems with excessive heat. Once manufacturers solved the problems, they brought out compatible motherboards, chipsets, and CPUs for DDR2.

DDR3 SDRAM   First appearing on new motherboards in 2007, *double-data-rate three SDRAM (DDR3 SDRAM)* chips use far less power than the previous SDRAM chips—1.5V versus DDR2's 1.8V—while providing almost twice the bandwidth, thanks to several technology improvements on the chips and modules. As with DDR2, the DDR3 DIMMs have 240 pins and they are the same size. However, they are electrically incompatible and come with a different key notch to prevent you from inserting the wrong modules into DDR3 sockets. DDR3 modules can take advantage of dual-channel architecture, and you will often see a pair of modules sold as a dual-channel kit. And it gets better—memory controller chips (MCCs) that support a triple-channel architecture (switching between three modules) are available, and DDR3 memory modules are sold in a set of three as a triple-channel set. DDR3 SDRAM is quickly replacing DDR2 SDRAM.

As with DDR1 and DDR2, there are specifications for the chips, as well as for the modules. Table 4-3 shows the JEDEC speed standards for the DDR3 SDRAM chip and module combinations.

TABLE 4-3	DDR3 Chip Specification	Chip Operating Speed	I/O Clock Speed	DDR3 Module Specification
Some JEDEC Speed Standards for DDR3 SDRAM Chip and Module Combinations	DDR3-800	100 MHz	400 MHz	PC3-6400
	DDR3-1066	133 MHz	533 MHz	PC3-8500
	DDR3-1333	166 MHz	667 MHz	PC3-10600
	DDR3-1600	200 MHz	800 MHz	PC3-12800
	DDR3-1866	233.33 MHz	933.33 MHz	PC3-14900
	DDR3-2133	266.66 MHz	1066.66 MHz	PC3-17000

The low-voltage version of DDR3 is called *DDR3L*. It runs at 1.35V, in contrast to the 1.5V or 1.65V of standard DDR3. Low-voltage RAM is important in situations where there's a lot of RAM in the works, like in a data center or server farm. It runs cooler and decreases electricity usage. It doesn't make much difference in an individual desktop PC. The motherboard must support DDR3L for it to work, although it is slot-compatible with regular DDR3.

DDR4 SDRAM   DDR4 came out in 2014. As you might expect, it's faster, higher density, and lower voltage than DDR3. One big difference is that DDR4 changes how the channels are accessed, using a point-to-point architecture whereby each channel connects to a single module. This is a departure from the multichannel architectures of DDR1, DDR2, and DDR3. DDR4 comes on 288-pin DIMMs, so it's not compatible with slots that take earlier types. It is not listed on the current 220-901 exam objectives.

e x a m
ⓦatch
The CompTIA A+ Acronyms list at the end of both sets of exam objectives includes many useful acronyms that you should be sure to understand. However, several of the listed acronyms are for outdated technologies. For instance, *FPM* is an acronym for *fast page mode*, a memory technology that is faster than the original DRAM, but far behind the curve when compared to newer RAM technologies.

RAM Compatibility

Before purchasing RAM modules for a computer, you should read the motherboard manual or other documentation from the manufacturer to determine what RAM is compatible with the motherboard. Normally, all RAM modules must match the features supported by the motherboard and chipset, including the features described in the following sections, as well as speed. The manual will describe any acceptable exceptions to this "perfect match" rule.

Keep in mind that even if the motherboard and chipset support differences in RAM modules, such as different speeds, this will not be the optimum configuration and it is fraught with potential for problems. It is best to have identical modules.

SCENARIO & SOLUTION

What kind of RAM is this?	Solution
184-pin DIMM with a notch on one end	DDR1
240-pin DIMM labeled PC2-6400	DDR2
240-pin DIMM labeled 1.35V	DDR3L

CERTIFICATION OBJECTIVES

■ **901: 1.4**   *Install and configure PC expansion cards*

■ **901: 1.7**   *Compare and contrast various PC connection interfaces, their characteristics, and purpose*

■ **901: 1.11**   *Identify common PC connector types and associated cables*

This section introduces the various types of adapter cards listed under CompTIA A+ 901 exam objective 1.4, including sound, video, and network cards, various I/O cards, modem cards, TV tuner cards, video capture cards, and riser cards, but the discussion of storage cards is later in the chapter under "Storage Devices and Interfaces." In this section, we also examine various connection interfaces, including all the interfaces listed in 901 exam objective 1.7, except the video-related ones (VGA, DVI, and HDMI), which we include in Chapter 5. We will also delay the discussion of various wireless cellular cards and devices until Chapter 7.

This section also explores those connectors listed in 901 exam objective 1.11 that you should expect to see on the adapter cards described here, and at the end of this section is a very brief overview of cable types. We'll describe connectors on storage interfaces in the following section and other connectors in the appropriate chapter for the connector type. We will save the actual installation of, and configuration of, the components described in this section for Chapter 6.

Expansion Cards and Built-in Adapters

Traditionally, an *expansion card* or *adapter card* is a printed circuit board installed into an expansion slot in the motherboard to add functionality. However, in modern systems, many add-on devices do not fit that traditional description because they are external, connecting to a computer via a USB, FireWire, or eSATA port or built into the motherboard itself.

Examples of common adapter cards include display adapters, network interface cards (NICs), sound cards, and cards that add various types of ports, such as FireWire. As you read about these types of devices, keep in mind that PC motherboards contain increasing numbers of these functions so they no longer need an adapter card added to the system. For example, a decade ago, most desktop PCs had adapter cards for display, sound, and network, but today most motherboards have these built in. Therefore, although the CompTIA A+ 901 exam objective 1.4 lists each of these as cards, we will refer to them as *adapters*, which is what they are whether the device is on a separate circuit card or built into the motherboard. The functions, however, remain as described in the following sections that describe each of the most common adapters. The difference, of course, is in the necessity of physically installing expansion cards.

on the **Job**

The term "adapter" has two meanings. One is as described in this section— display adapter, network adapter, and so on. The other meaning, as used in 220-901 exam objective 1.11, refers to a connector that converts one interface to another, such as a PS/2-to-USB converter for a keyboard or mouse.

Display Adapter

A *display adapter* (also called a *video adapter*) controls the output to the display device. This function may either be built into the motherboard of a PC or provided through an expansion card installed into the PCIe expansion bus (preferably the x16 slot, but not always; x4 and x1 adapters are also available). You'll learn more about display adapters in Chapter 5 when we look at the various display technologies along with monitors that connect to the displays adapters and the various connectors for attaching monitors to display adapters.

Sound Cards

A *sound card* (or *audio adapter*) converts digital information from computer programs into analog sounds that come out of your speakers. This is called a digital-to-analog converter (DAC). Sound cards convert in the other direction too, taking analog input from microphones and turning it into digital samples that can be stored on a PC. That's called an analog-to-digital converter (ADC). Sound cards can also process digital-to-digital input and output. Sound cards come in a full range of prices, based on the quality of the components and the number of features.

A typical configuration of sound card connectors consists of three or more audio ports, or "jacks." All of these are 3.5 mm mini jacks (small round holes). Sometimes they are color coded; other times they have symbols that tell their functions. Table 4-4 lists the commonly used colors and symbols.

On a full-featured sound card you might also see an Optical Out port, which looks like a rounded square with a plastic flap inside. This port is used to send digital (optical) data out to an AV receiver, such as in a home theater system. It's not as good as High-Definition

TABLE 4-4	Sound Card Port Colors and Symbols		
Color	**Function**	**Connector**	**Symbol or Label**
Pink	Analog microphone input.	3.5 mm round	A microphone or MIC
Light blue	Analog line input.	3.5 mm round	Arrow going into a circle or LINE IN
Light green	Analog speakers or headphones; if there are multiple speaker jacks, this one is for the front speakers.	3.5 mm round	Headphones, or an arrow going out one side of a circle into a wave, or FRONT
Orange	Analog line output for center channel speaker and subwoofer.	3.5 mm round	SUB/C/SL
Black	Analog line output for rear or surround speakers.	3.5 mm round	REAR/SR

FIGURE 4-1

The ports on the Sound Blaster Audigy RX sound card (Image courtesy of Creative Technology Ltd)

Multimedia Interface (HDMI) in terms of quality, but it's better than the red/white/yellow composite AV cables that older home-theater systems used.

Figure 4-1 shows a typical midrange SoundBlaster Audigy sound card made by Creative Labs. It includes most of the ports from Table 4-4 (although they aren't color-coded) as well as an Optical Out port.

Musical Instrument Digital Interface (MIDI) is both a sound clip format and a physical interface. It is no longer a part of the main exam objectives, but it still shows up on the CompTIA A+ Acronyms list. Sound clips with a .mid extension have been created by a digital music-making device, such as an electronic keyboard, rather than recorded from an analog source with a microphone. The MIDI interface is a 15-pin D-Sub connector where the pins/holes are arranged in two rows (unlike the 15-pin D-Sub connector used for VGA, where the pins are in three rows). The MIDI cable is coaxial. The MIDI port is sometimes called a *gameport*, because early joysticks used it. The MIDI interface has been obsolete for quite a while now, having been replaced by the ubiquitous USB port on nearly all music-related devices. Consequently, newer sound cards do not usually have a MIDI port.

e x a m
ⓦ a t c h
S/P DIF, sometimes written as SPDIF, stands for Sony-Philips Digital Interface Format. It is a digital sound interface no longer covered on the current CompTIA A+ exam, but it still appears in the A+ Acronyms list.

Video Capture and TV Tuner Cards

A *video capture card* is a category of adapter card that accepts and records video signals to a PC's hard drive in digital form, storing both the digital image and sound. One type of capture card, called a *TV tuner card*, brings a TV signal into a computer in order to record TV programs onto a hard drive, thus turning your computer into a digital video recorder (DVR). Some capture cards simply capture video from a VHS tape or other video format, while others are for editing video files, regardless of how they were obtained.

Port Adapter Cards

PCs have evolved, and, with the invention of more and more I/O devices, manufacturers have continued to integrate these new capabilities into the motherboard. While your PC has various I/O technologies built in, you may still wish to add an expansion card to give you additional ports. For example, you might want to add FireWire (IEEE 1394).

Typically, the term *connector* refers to the plug at the end of a cable, and *port* refers to the socket where the cable attaches to the device or computer. Even though we refer to connectors and ports, remember the port is also a connector. The following sections contain descriptions of some common I/O interfaces and the connector types related to each.

USB

The *Universal Serial Bus (USB)* interface has become the interface of choice for PCs, making both parallel and serial ports obsolete and even replacing SCSI and FireWire/IEEE 1394 (discussed later in this chapter). All PCs manufactured in the last decade have at least one USB port, and many PCs literally bristle with USB connectors located conveniently on the front, as well as the back, of a desktop PC case, and on the sides and back of a laptop. So, you are not likely to need to add a USB expansion card to a system. If you do need more USB ports, you can add a USB hub, a multiport connecting device for USB devices.

USB is an external bus that connects into the PC's PCI bus. With USB, you can theoretically connect up to 127 devices to your computer. There have been several versions of the USB standard; most notable are 1.0, 1.1, 2.0, and 3.0.

on the **Job**

On some systems, there are different USB ports with different versions. They may be color-coded: black for USB 1.0/1.1, royal blue for USB 2.0, and gray for USB 3.0. If you look at the tab in the end of the cable's connector, it may be similarly color-coded; a cable designed for a USB 2.0 device will have a blue tab, for example. USB 2.0 and 3.0 ports might also have lettering on or near them indicating their speed.

USB 1.0 and 1.1   The low-speed 1.0 and 1.1 versions transmit data up to 1.5 Mbps (megabits per second), whereas the full-speed 1.1 standard is rated at 12 Mbps. Communications are controlled by the host system and can flow in both directions, but not simultaneously. This one-way-at-a-time transmission is called *half-duplex communication*.

Hi-Speed USB 2.0 *Hi-Speed USB 2.0* transmits data at speeds up to 480 Mbps, which equals 60 MBps (megabytes per second), in half duplex. You can attach a low-speed device like a mouse to a Hi-Speed port, but devices designed for Hi-Speed require, or run best, when attached to a USB port that is up to the 2.0 standard. USB hubs and peripherals are downward compatible with hardware using the older standard, but when you plug an older device into a Hi-Speed USB port, or connect a Hi-Speed USB device to a full-speed USB 1.1 port, the resulting speed will be at the lower rate, a maximum of 12 Mbps.

SuperSpeed USB 3.0 The *SuperSpeed USB 3.0* standard was introduced in the third quarter of 2008, and is now common on new PCs and laptops. USB 3.0 operates at up to 5 Gbps (625 MBps), which is ten times the speed of USB 2.0 and faster than the present 300 MBps eSATA speed (more about eSATA later in this chapter). USB 3.0 also supports *full-duplex communication*, the ability to communicate in both directions at once. Figure 4-2 shows a SuperSpeed USB 3.0 port on a laptop with the familiar forked USB symbol and the letters "SS" indicating SuperSpeed. Look for this symbol identifying a SuperSpeed USB 3.0 port. Manufacturers now integrate USB 3.0 into chipsets, so look for these fast ports on recently manufactured computers. Aside from physical marking on a USB 3.0 port, if you open the Universal Serial Bus Controllers node in Device Manager (as described in Exercise 4-2 a bit later), it may identify the USB level for the USB Host Controller and Root Hub as 2.0 or 3.0.

Power for USB Devices Until USB 3.0, only low-power devices, such as flash drives, keyboards, and mice, could receive power through the USB bus, and some rechargeable devices could recharge via a USB 2.0 port. However, USB 2.0 could only output 500 milliamps. USB 3.0 outputs 900 milliamps, which permits faster charging and supports more power-hungry devices. Additionally, USB 3.0 is actually more efficient in its use of power compared to USB 2.0.

USB Ports, Connectors, and Cables A standard USB port on a computer is rectangular and acts as a receiver for a USB type-A connector measuring 1/2" by 1/8" (look back at Figure 4-2). Most computers and devices clearly identify USB ports with a trident (fork-shaped) symbol. A plastic device in the port holds the four wires for USB 1.x or 2.0, and USB 3.0 has an additional five wires positioned behind the first four so that the connectors and ports from 3.0 are downward compatible with older ports and connectors.

FIGURE 4-2

A SuperSpeed
USB 3.0 port

FIGURE 4-3

A USB cable showing the USB 2.0 type-B connector on the left with a USB 2.0 type-A connector on the right

This, together with a similar plastic device in the connector, polarizes the connectors, which keeps the two from connecting incorrectly.

The connector on the device end of a USB cable is a type-B connector, but there are several sizes of type-B connectors. Figure 4-3 shows a USB cable with a 2.0 type-A connector on the right and a full-size, nearly square 2.0 type-B connector on the left. Notice that the two corners of the type-B connector are beveled so that it cannot be inserted incorrectly. A USB 3.0 type-B connector has a smaller connector containing the additional five wires, mounted on top of what looks like a 2.0 type-B connector.

There are also variations of small USB type-A and type-B connectors found on portable devices. The micro-B connector measures about 1/4" × 1/16". The mini-B D connector is the same width as the micro-B connector, but it is twice as thick, measuring about 1/4" × 1/8". Figure 4-4 shows an example of a micro-B and mini-B connector.

USB cables have a maximum length based on the version. For instance, USB 2.0 has a cable length limit of five meters, while USB 1.0 had a limit of three meters. The USB 3.0 specification does not give a maximum cable length, so it depends on the quality of the cable needed to maintain the speed of USB 3.0, which could limit the cable to as little as three meters. Further, a USB type-A connector has an additional pair of wires, but this type-A connector can still connect to a USB type-A port.

FIGURE 4-4

Connectors on two separate cables: the one on the left has a USB mini type B, and next to it is a USB micro type B.

USB 3.0 is downward compatible with USB 2.0, meaning that you can plug a USB 2.0 device and cable into a USB 3.0 port. You can also plug a USB 3.0 type-A connector to a USB 2.0 type-A computer port, even though the USB 3.0 type-A connector has an additional pair of wires. The USB 3.0 device at the other end of this cable will only run at USB 2.0 speed. Further, you cannot use a USB 3.0 cable with an older USB device, and a USB 3.0 device cannot use a USB 2.0 cable. This is because the USB 3.0 type-B connector that plugs into a device does not fit into the USB 2.0 type-B port on a device.

USB hubs take you beyond these limits, but the connecting cables still must be within the prescribed limits. You can also find a USB cable that has a hub built in to extend the length, but this only works to connect one device to a computer.

Another type of USB cable is a simple extension cable that has a type-A connector on one end and a receiving USB port connector on the other end. These come in varying lengths, and we keep several on hand. You never know when you might want to connect to a USB port on the back of a computer or on the front of a computer that is out of reach, such as under a table or in a cabinet. Plug in the extension cable and run it to your desk, where it is handy for plugging in your flash drives or other devices. Short extension cables also have their use. Many USB devices described in this book are very small and come without a cable. You simply connect the device to a USB port and it juts out from the computer, barely visible, but vulnerable. One wrong move and you can ruin the device or the port into which it is plugged. Our solution is to purchase and keep handy a couple of short (about 9") USB extension cables. Then the device sits on the desk, tethered to the port, and bumping it won't damage the device or the port.

on the **j** o b

Keep USB extension cables on hand for connecting devices to hard-to-reach ports or to protect a device.

EXERCISE 4-1

Research USB Connectors

There are many variations of USB connectors. If you have a computer with an Internet connection, research USB connectors.

1. Open your favorite Internet search engine, such as Google or Bing.
2. Search on the keywords **usb connectors**.
3. Search the results for a site that gives you a range of connectors, as well as photos of each type.
4. Keep track of the number of variations you find, looking for the differences in the USB 2.0 and USB 3.0 connectors.

EXERCISE 4-2

Explore Your System's USB Ports

Follow these steps in Windows (version 7 or newer) to check out your USB ports:

1. Open Device Manager. There are lots of ways to do this; you can go through the Control Panel, or in Windows 8.1 or 10 you can right-click the Start button and choose Device Manager.

2. Double-click Universal Serial Bus Controllers to expand that category, and then double-click Generic USB Hub to open its Properties dialog box.

3. Click the Advanced tab and look in the Hub Information. You might see something like "Hub is operating at high-speed." That's USB 2.0.

4. Click the Power tab. Make a note of any devices listed under Attached Devices. These are devices plugged into that hub. They may not be actually plugged in; some built-in devices appear there, such as built-in Bluetooth.

5. Examine the information on the other tabs, and then close the Properties dialog box.

6. Repeat Steps 2–4 for the USB Root Hub entry.

7. Check out the properties for any other items that appear under Universal Serial Bus Controllers. Then close Device Manager.

USB Plug and Play   USB supports *plug and play*, meaning the computer firmware and operating system recognize a USB device when you connect it, and the operating system automatically installs and configures a device driver (if available). Always check the documentation for a USB device, because many require that you install a device driver before you connect the device. USB ports also support *hot swapping*, which is the act of safely disconnecting and connecting devices while the computer is running, giving you instantly recognized and usable devices.

Adding More USB Hubs   If a PC has too few USB ports for the number of USB devices a user wishes to connect, the easiest fix is to purchase an external USB hub and connect it to one of the PC's USB connectors. In fact, you can add other hubs and devices in this way. Although the USB standard allows for daisy-chaining of devices, manufacturers do not support this capability because they prefer to use hubs connected directly to the USB controller, which includes the root hub. There is a limit of five levels of hubs, counting the root hub. Each hub can accommodate several USB devices, possibly creating a lopsided tree. USB supports different speeds on each branch, so you can use devices of varying speeds. Figure 4-5 shows a PC with an internal root hub. Connected to this hub are a USB keyboard and another USB hub. Several devices connect to the first USB hub, including yet another hub, which in turn has several devices connected to it.

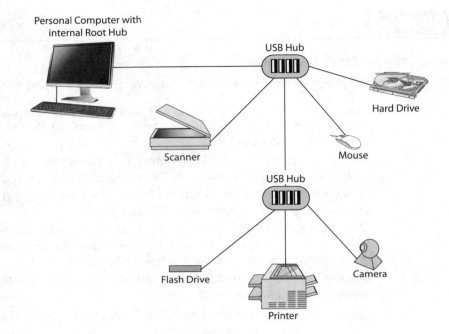

FIGURE 4-5

USB hubs can add more USB ports to a PC.

Personal Computer with internal Root Hub

USB Hub

Hard Drive

Scanner

Mouse

USB Hub

Flash Drive

Printer

Camera

IEEE 1394/FireWire

The *Institute of Electrical and Electronics Engineers (IEEE)* is an international nonprofit organization that sets standards as part of its charter. You will encounter many IEEE standards, represented by "IEEE" followed by a number assigned to that standard. Like USB, the *IEEE 1394* standard describes an external serial bus that connects to the internal PCI bus. The CompTIA A+ 901 exam objectives use the term *FireWire*, which is Apple's trademarked name, but it is also the commonly used name (including in this book). Sony calls their implementation of IEEE 1394 i.LINK, and Texas Instruments uses the name Lynx.

Some PC motherboards have FireWire support built in with an external FireWire port. Each FireWire device can be part of a daisy chain to more devices. A single FireWire port can support up to 63 daisy-chained devices. Therefore, adding ports to the computer itself is not usually necessary, although you may add them by installing an expansion card.

The original standard, now called *IEEE 1394a*, supports speeds up to 400 Mbps with maximum individual cable length of 4.5 meters. Many in IT call this *FireWire 400*. A standard 1394a six-pin FireWire port is about half an inch long, with one squared end and one three-sided end to guarantee the cable connector is connected correctly. As with USB, the wires connect to a plastic device. Alternatively, you will find smaller four-wire ports, especially on laptops. Most computers and devices clearly identify FireWire ports and cable connectors with a Y-shaped symbol. Figure 4-6 shows a FireWire port on a computer, while Figure 4-7 shows two connectors on a FireWire cable.

At top, FireWire port with an identifying label. Below it are two USB ports.

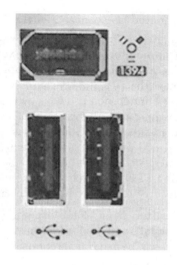

Be sure you understand the differences between USB and FireWire and are able to describe the ports and connectors, as well as how multiple devices are normally connected.

In 2003, the IEEE released the *IEEE 1394b* specification, with cable distances of up to 100 meters and top speeds of 800 Mbps (a.k.a. *FireWire 800*), 1600 Mbps, and 3.2 Gbps. A significant limit is that one 1394a device in a chain will cause any 1394b devices to operate at the lower speed. In addition, although 1394b is generally downward compatible with 1394a, 3.2 Gbps is only available with special hardware that is not downward compatible with 1394a devices, and the IEEE 1394b cable terminates with a connector that resembles an Ethernet RJ-45 connector, but uses nine wires.

A subsequent standard, *IEEE 1394c-2006*, came out in 2007 and is a major departure from the old standards in that it uses Category 5e twisted-pair cable with RJ-45 connectors, combining Ethernet and FireWire, meaning that it can connect to either an Ethernet network interface card or a FireWire device. In 2008 these updates combined into *IEEE 1394-2008*.

A FireWire cable with two 6-pin connectors

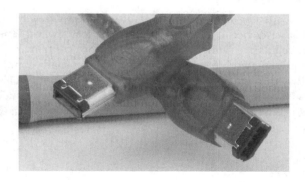

Thunderbolt

Thunderbolt is a high-speed interface used primarily in Apple computers. It carries DisplayPort data (for monitors) and also PCI Express data. Carrying data outside the PC case using the PCI Express bus is unique to Apple; the Intel/IBM-compatible platform doesn't currently have that. It's good because PCI Express is faster than both USB and FireWire. How fast? Thunderbolt provides two separate channels on the same connector with 10 Gbps throughput in both directions. Thunderbolt 2, the next generation of Thunderbolt, increases that to 20 Gbps. This is 40 times faster than USB 2.0, 25 times faster than FireWire 800, and 4 times faster than USB 3.0. It can also be used to daisy-chain multiple high-speed devices without using a hub or switch.

One cool additional feature is that you can purchase a Thunderbolt chassis, which is essentially an enclosure designed to hold PCIe cards, and connect that chassis to the main PC to access all the expansion slots within it.

PS/2

PS/2 is a round, 6-pin port and connector that was used in systems to connect keyboard and mouse before USB became popular. CompTIA A+ 901 exam objective 1.11 mentions it as a device cable and connector to know, but it has been obsolete for quite a while. You should be able to recognize it and identify devices that use it (keyboard and mouse), and you should be able to select and use a converter that allows a PS/2 keyboard to connect to a USB port and vice versa.

Communication Adapters

We have used the term "communication" many times in this and the preceding chapter, mostly in talking about communication between components within the PC. Now we will talk about the communication devices that connect a PC to a network, whether it is a local area network (LAN) or the Internet. Once again, the motherboards of most PCs now have these functions built in, and it is not usually necessary to add an adapter card to a computer for communications.

Network Adapters

A network adapter (or network card), often called a *network interface card (NIC)*, connects a PC or other device to a type of network, such as a wired Ethernet network or a wireless Wi-Fi or cellular network. Most PCs and laptops contain an Ethernet NIC because most PC users require network communications and can usually connect to the Internet—directly or indirectly—through an Ethernet network. Many computers also include a wireless NIC— either Wi-Fi (the most common) or another wireless type, such as cellular, Bluetooth, or near field communication (NFC), all of which are covered in Chapter 13.

On the job, a typical desktop PC is connected to a LAN, which in turn may be connected to a larger private network and, ultimately, to the Internet. At home, you may connect two or more PCs via a LAN connection to share a digital subscriber line (DSL) or cable modem Internet connection. The network adapter in the PC may be an Ethernet wired network adapter or a wireless adapter, depending on whether you wish to connect to a wired Ethernet LAN or a wireless LAN. We will save the larger discussion of networking for Chapters 14, 15, and 16, and in Chapter 7 we will describe the various types of wireless adapters found in laptops.

The most common connector for Ethernet NICs is RJ-45. A *registered jack (RJ)* connector is rectangular in shape and has a locking clip on one side. The number designation of an RJ connector refers to its size rather than to the number of wire connections within it. RJ-45 contains eight wires and most commonly attaches twisted-pair cables to Ethernet network cards. Figure 4-8 shows an RJ-45 port with the small notch to accommodate the locking clip on a cable connector labeled with a symbol representing a network.

Modem Adapters

A *modem*, so named for its combined functions of *mod*ulator/*dem*odulator, allows computers to communicate with one another over existing phone lines, a type of communication called dial-up that will be described in Chapter 14 when we look at how to connect to networks. A modem may be internal in the motherboard, or it may be an adapter card in the expansion bus. An external modem connects to a port on the computer, either serial or USB. Whether internal or external, a modem connects to a regular telephone wall jack using the same connector as a phone.

This type of modem is an *analog modem* as opposed to the data communication devices used to connect to a cable network or to phone lines for DSL service. "Modem" is actually a misnomer for the devices used on cable or DSL networks because the signals involved are all digital signals, and, therefore, there is no modulating or demodulating of the signal. However, because they are physically between the computer and the network, much like a modem is, manufacturers use the term "modem."

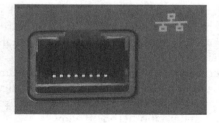

FIGURE 4-8

The RJ-45 Ethernet port on this laptop is labeled with a symbol resembling three computers connected to a network.

An analog modem adapter card with two RJ-11 connectors on the left side and a cable with an RJ-11 plug attached resting on top of the card

Be prepared to demonstrate that you understand the differences between RJ-11 and RJ-45 connectors. Remember their uses and the number of wires in each.

An RJ-11 port is where you attach a phone cable to a modem (analog or other) and to a wall-mounted phone jack. It is similar to an RJ-45 port—only slightly smaller, and it contains either two or four wires. Figure 4-9 shows two RJ-11 connectors on a modem adapter: one that connects to the wall jack, and the other that attaches to a phone set. A cable with an RJ-11 connector attached is resting on top of the card. (That's a joystick port on the right side, by the way, which is the same pin configuration as the MIDI port you learned about earlier. Its presence signals that this is an older modem card.)

Riser Cards

Riser cards are used in slim or low-profile cases. The riser card contains expansion slots, like the motherboard normally would. The riser card is mounted in a dedicated slot on a specially designed motherboard, and then the actual expansion cards are mounted in the riser card. This results in the expansion cards being able to sit parallel to the motherboard, rather than perpendicular to it, so the case can be smaller. Ironically, you will find riser cards both in the largest network servers and in the smallest of low-profile desktop computer cases. In the case of network servers, the use of a riser card allows the addition of more cards than the standard motherboard allows.

Adapters and Converters

For CompTIA A+ 901 exam objective 1.11, make sure you are aware of the various types of adapters (aka converters) that can be used in situations where you need to connect a device to a PC that doesn't have the right type of port. There are converters available for every combination of all the major types of display adapters, including DVI, HDMI, VGA (all covered in Chapter 5), and Thunderbolt. You can also convert between PS/2 and USB, between USB type-A and USB type-B (or any of the mini and micro variants), and between USB and Ethernet.

Characteristics of External Connection Interfaces

CompTIA A+ 901 exam objective 1.7 asks that you know the characteristics of various interfaces, many of which we've already looked at in this chapter. Use Table 4-5 to review these characteristics in one place. The objective asks you to identify whether each interface is analog or digital; in this table they are all digital, so we haven't included that column. Quality of transmission may vary with the distance traveled (that is, the length of the cable).

Note that Table 4-5 doesn't include network interfaces like Ethernet, Wi-Fi, Bluetooth, or NFC, as those are covered in Chapter 13. It also doesn't include display adapter connectors like VGA, DVI, and HDMI, which are covered in Chapter 5.

TABLE 4-5   Characteristics of Common External Connection Interfaces

Interface	Used For	Max. Distance	Max. Speed	Connector
USB 1.1	General	3 meters	12 Mbps (half duplex)	USB A, USB B
USB 2.0	General	5 meters	480 Mbps (half duplex)	USB 2.0 A USB 2.0 B Mini USB 2.0 B Micro USB 2.0 B
USB 3.0	General	No official limit, depends on cable quality	5 Gbps (full duplex)	USB 3.0 A USB 3.0 B Mini USB 3.0 B Micro USB 3.0 B
FireWire 400 (IEEE 1394A)	General	4.5 meters	400 Mbps	1394A
FireWire 800 (IEEE 1394B)	General	100 meters	800 Mbps, 1600 Mbps, or 3.2 Gbps	1394B
Thunderbolt 2.0	Display and general (Apple)	3 meters	10 Gbps per channel	Thunderbolt
Thunderbolt 1.0	Display and general (Apple)	3 meters	20 Gbps per channel	Thunderbolt

EXERCISE 4-3

View Adapter Cards in Device Manager

Look at the list of adapter cards in Device Manager in Windows 7.

1. Select Control Panel | Device Manager.
2. In the list of devices in the Device Manager window, note those for adapters named in the previous section. This list will include, but not be limited to, display adapters, network adapters, and various controllers.
3. Close the Device Manager window.

SCENARIO & SOLUTION

What type of expansion card would you install in order to make a dial-up connection to the Internet?	Modem
What type of device would you install in a PC if you wanted to record TV programs onto a hard drive?	TV tuner card
What digital port on a sound card might you use to connect to a home theater system?	Optical Out

CERTIFICATION OBJECTIVES

- **901: 1.5** *Install and configure storage devices and use appropriate media*
- **901: 1.7** *Compare and contrast various PC connection interfaces, their characteristics, and purpose*

This section introduces the storage types listed in CompTIA A+ 901 exam objective 1.5, hard disk drives (HDDs), tape drives, optical drives, and solid-state drives (SSDs). We'll also define special configurations of drives, called RAID, and the various media types and capacities of storage devices. However, Chapter 6 presents the actual installation and configuration of storage devices. This section also covers the interfaces related to storage devices, from CompTIA A+ 901 exam objective 1.7.

Storage Devices and Interfaces

In computing, the function of a *mass storage device* is to hold, or store, a large amount of information, even when the computer's power is off. Unlike information in system RAM, files kept on a mass storage device remain there unless the user or the computer removes or alters them. In this section, we will first explore the types of interfaces for connecting storage devices to computers, and then we'll explore various types of storage devices in use today.

Drive Interfaces

Drive interfaces have changed quite a bit in the last decade. The older parallel ATA (PATA) drives are now obsolete, and nobody will miss them, with their awkward jumper-based master/slave configuration and their bulky ribbon cables. Nobody is likely to miss SCSI ("skuzzy") either, which had even more complicated configuration requirements. Today, the dominant interface for internal drives is serial ATA (SATA). For external drives, external SATA (eSATA) is popular, along with USB and FireWire, which you learned about earlier in the chapter.

There are several obsolete terms related to storage on the CompTIA A+ Acronyms list in the published exam objectives. Two important ones are parallel advanced technology attachment (PATA)**, which was the ancestor of the current SATA, and** small computer system interface (SCSI)**, a very old but powerful alternative to PATA that was popular on high-end systems and servers.**

SATA

Serial ATA (SATA) is the dominant standard for connecting internal drives such as hard disk drives, solid-state drives, and optical drives. You might occasionally see an old-style ribbon cable for a parallel ATA drive, but it's becoming less and less common every day. (You might benefit from knowing how to configure PATA drives on the job, but it's no longer on the A+ exam, so we won't cover it here.)

A motherboard typically has at least four SATA connectors, like the ones shown in Figure 4-10. SATA cables (such as the one connected to the lower-left connector in Figure 4-10) are thin and compact (compared to the bulky old ribbon cables of the past), and can be up to 39.4 inches long. Because each SATA device has a direct connection to the SATA controller, it does not have to share a bus with other devices, and therefore it provides greater throughput. Unlike PATA, SATA also supports hot swapping.

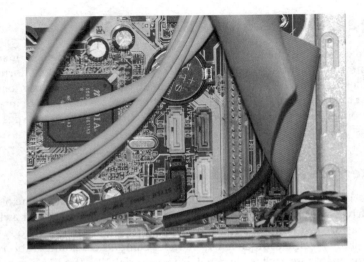

FIGURE 4-10

A cluster of four SATA connectors on a motherboard. The long vertically oriented connector to their right is a PATA connector.

Even the first two SATA standards, SATA 1.5 Gbps (150 MBps) and SATA 3 Gbps (300 MBps), far exceeded the PATA speeds. The SATA 3.0 standard, or SATA 6 Gbps, released in May 2009, is fast enough for solid-state drives (SSDs). SATA 3.1 includes support for SSDs in mobile devices, or *mSATA* (also called *Mini-SATA*), defining a scaled-down form factor. Figure 4-11 shows the SATA ports on the back of an internal hard drive. The power port on the right has 15 contacts, while the SATA data port to the left of it has 7 contacts. Figure 4-12 shows the corresponding connectors on a power cable and a SATA data cable.

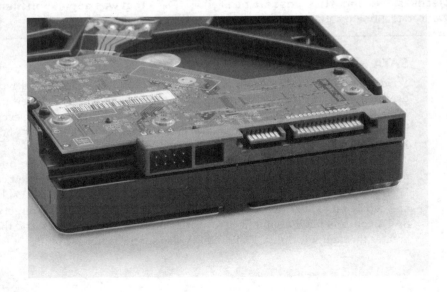

FIGURE 4-11

The SATA power and data ports on a hard drive. The power port is the long one on the right, and the data port is immediately to its left.

FIGURE 4-12

The power cable on the left connects to the power connector on a SATA drive, while the SATA data cable with its smaller connector is next to it.

eSATA

External SATA (eSATA) is an extension of the SATA standard for external SATA devices, with the same speeds as the SATA standard it supports, which at present is 300 MBps. Internal eSATA connectors are included in newer motherboards, in which case, cabling is required to connect them to an eSATA port on the PC case. Use eSATA adapter cards to add eSATA to older motherboards without built-in support. eSATA is replacing FireWire and at least competing with USB. Figure 4-13 shows an eSATA port on an external hard drive enclosure, and Figure 4-14 shows the connectors on either end of an eSATA cable.

FIGURE 4-13

An eSATA port on an external hard drive enclosure

FIGURE 4-14

The eSATA connectors on either end of an eSATA cable

	Interface	Used For	Max. Distance	Max. Speed	Connector
TABLE 4-6	SATA1	Internal storage	1 meter	1.5 Gbps	SATA
	SATA2	Internal storage	1 meter	3 Gbps	SATA
Characteristics of SATA and eSATA	SATA3	Internal storage	1 meter	6 Gbps	SATA
	eSATA	External storage	2 meters	2.4 Gbps	eSATA

Table 4-6 lists the characteristics of the various SATA types, which you will need to know as part of 901 exam objective 1.11.

Mass Storage Devices

Many types of mass storage devices are available, including those that store data on magnetic media, devices that use optical technologies, and devices based on solid-state technology. Note that this list includes both removable and fixed (nonremovable) devices. Further, certain of these, depending on their interfaces, are hot-swappable devices, and many are considered backup media. Let's explore all these dimensions.

Magnetic Mass Storage

Magnetic mass storage devices used with computers store digital data on magnetized media, such as the metal platters in hard disk drives and magnetic tape used in tape drives. Unlike dynamic RAM, which loses its data when power to the device is off, this type of storage is *nonvolatile*. Read/write heads create magnetic patterns on the media that stay there until altered. Following are descriptions of two types of devices covered on the 220-901 exam that can save data onto magnetic media: hard disk drives and tape drives.

Hard Disk Drives   A *hard disk drive (HDD)* stores data using patterns of positive or negative magnetic polarity on metal platters. Hard drives are available in a wide range of capacities, and new hard drives now have a capacity between several hundred gigabytes and several terabytes.

Inside a hard disk casing is a stack of metal platters, spaced on a spindle so they do not touch. Each side of each platter has its own *read/write head* on an *actuator arm* that moves it in (toward the center of the platter) and out (toward the edge). The heads all move together as a single unit. The space between each platter and its read/write head is so small that even a tiny speck of dust could interfere with it; therefore the components are encased in a sealed metal box assembled in a clean room. Each hard disk drive has a controller on a circuit board mounted on the outside of its casing; this controller communicates with the motherboard to read and write data. The original term for a drive having a built-in controller was *Integrated Drive Electronics (IDE)*, and you may sometimes still see hard drives described as IDE or Enhanced IDE (EIDE).

FIGURE 4-15

An internal hard
drive

Figure 4-15 shows a 2 TB hard disk drive designed for internal installation. It has connectors for a SATA cable and for a connection to the PC's power supply.

Hard drives designed for external use have a protective case around both the hard drive and its circuit board, and usually require an external power cord and a USB, FireWire, or eSATA connector to an external port on the PC. You can buy a drive enclosure that converts an internal hard disk drive to an external one by adding a protective case and converting the data and power interfaces.

When buying a new computer or additional hard drive, look for the preferred interface (SATA or eSATA), the capacity, and the speed of the drive, and try to buy the largest, fastest drive you can afford. The most common way to measure drive speed is the rate at which the platters spin—called *spindle speed*—measured in *revolutions per minute (rpm)*. Commonly available speeds in existing and new hard drives include 5400 rpm, 7200 rpm, 10,000 rpm, and 15,000 rpm. Data transfer rates tend to favor the higher rpms; prices vary accordingly.

Tape Drives   A *tape drive* is a mass storage device primarily used for backing up data from computers. It uses special removable magnetic data tape cartridges. People often choose tape drives for archiving data and backups because the media is relatively inexpensive and long lasting. Because data must be stored sequentially on tape, the access time for restoring individual files is slow. However, some high-end tape drives can write data to tape at transfer rates that compare well to hard drive speeds. Small tape drives designed for individual systems are no longer popular because there are so many faster and easier backup media available. However, for large-scale business use, you may still see them, and they are still covered on the CompTIA A+ 220-901 exam.

Normally, tape drives read and write just one tape size and format, such as the venerable *Digital Linear Tape (DLT)* technology. Developed in the 1980s, this technology was improved upon over the years as the *Super DLT (SDLT)* technology, and variations of this standard are still in use today. Both DLT and SDLT are one-half inch (12.7 mm) wide and contained within a cartridge that you insert into a tape drive without touching the tape itself. These data tapes are guaranteed to store data reliably for up to 80 years, under controlled conditions.

Optical Disc Drives

An optical disc drive is a drive that can accept, read, and sometimes write to compact discs (CDs), digital versatile discs (DVDs), and/or Blu-ray discs. Note that the terminology differs slightly between optical and magnetic media; in magnetic media it's disk (with a *k*) and in optical media it's disc (with a *c*). Generally speaking, drives are backward compatible with earlier formats. For example, DVD drives can also read CDs, and Blu-ray drives can read all three types. Most drives sold today are *burners*, in that they can also write to blanks of the formats they support.

The standard CD, DVD, or Blu-ray disc is approximately 4.75 inches (12 cm) in diameter, but there are minidiscs that measure about 3.125 inches (8 cm). The surface is smooth and shiny with one labeled side and one plain side (unless it's a double-sided disc, in which case both sides are equally shiny). The data, music, or video is stored on the disc using microscopic depressed and raised areas called *pits* and *lands*, respectively, which are covered by a protective transparent layer. A laser beam and a light sensor are used read the data from the disc. You can access data much faster from a hard drive than from an optical disc, but optical storage is more portable. Optical disc capacity is generally much smaller than commonly available hard drives.

Now that you know what they have in common, we will drop the phrase "optical drive" and "optical disc" and talk about the various types, mainly CD, DVD, and Blu-ray, and the variations of each.

CD Drives and Media   CD drives were the first generation of optical drives. Initially they were just for music, but they later became used to store digital computer data as well. CDs can hold up to 700 MB of data, or 80 minutes of audio.

Discs that you purchase containing music or software are *compact disc–read-only memory (CD-ROM)* discs, meaning they are only readable; you cannot change the contents. Writeable CD drives can write to two different kinds of blank discs: CD-R (recordable), which can be written only once and then they become read-only, and CD-RW (rewriteable), which can be written to multiple times.

A CD drive has a speed rating, expressed as an "x factor." The first CD drives transferred (read) data at 150 KBps, a speed now called 1x. CD drives are now rated at speeds that are multiples of this and have progressed up through 72x, which is 10,800 KBps. In the case of a writeable CD drive, there will be three numbers, such as 52x24x16x. In this case, the drive is rated at 52x for reads, 24x for writes, and 16x for rewrites.

DVD Drives and Media   Originally created for video storage in 1995, *digital video discs* have evolved into *digital versatile discs (DVDs)* and are used extensively on PCs for all types of data storage.

DVD drive speeds are expressed in terms similar to those of CD drives, although the rotational speed of a 1x DVD drive is three times that of a 1x CD drive, and a 1x DVD drive transfers data faster than a 9x CD drive. When looking at advertisements for DVD drives or PCs that include DVD drives, you will see the combined drive types followed by a combination of drive speeds, depending on the drive's operating modes. For instance, "DVD+R/RW 40x24x40x" indicates the three speeds of this drive for reading, writing, and rewriting because each drive has a different potential speed for each type of operation.

However, you need to read the manufacturer's documentation to know the order. As a general rule on DVD drives, reads are fastest, writes may be as fast as or a bit slower than reads, and rewrites are the slowest. DVD discs are the same physical size as CD discs but have a higher storage capacity and several other differences, as we'll discuss in this section.

The DVD discs sold at retail stores containing video or software are *DVD-ROM* discs, meaning they are only readable; you cannot change the contents. DVD-ROM has a maximum capacity of 15.9 GB of data. Read-only DVD discs are used to distribute standard-definition movies, computer applications, and collections of data files like clip art.

on the **job**

Because CDs and DVDs have no protective covering, handling them with care is important. Scratches, dust, or other material on the surface can prevent data from reading correctly. Because data is located on the bottom side of the disc, always lay the disc label-side down.

Whereas CDs only store data on a single side, DVDs come in both a conventional *single-sided DVD (SS DVD)* and a *dual-sided DVD (DS DVD)* variant that stores data on both sides, requiring that you turn the DVD over to read the second side. In addition, the format on each side may be *single-layer (SL)* or *dual-layer (DL)*, indicated as DVD SL or DVD DL. Although the SL format is similar to the CD format in that there is only a single layer of pits, the DL format uses two pitted layers on each data side, with each layer having a different reflectivity index. This is true for both DVD-ROM discs and the writeable versions as well. Table 4-7 shows DVD capacities based on the number of data sides and the number of layers per side.

There are several standards for recordable DVD media. The use of the "minus" (−) or "plus" (+) has special significance. The minus, used in the first DVD recordable format and written hyphenated as DVD-R and DVD-RW, indicates an older standard than those with the plus. *DVD-R* and *DVD-RW* are generally compatible with older players. *DVD-R*

TABLE 4-7	Type	Sides	Layers	Capacity
DVD Capacities	SS DVD SL	Single	Single	4.7 GB of data, or over two hours of video
	SS DVD DL	Single	Dual	8.54 GB of data, or over four hours of video
	DS DVD SL	Dual	Single	9.4 GB of data, or over four and a half hours of video
	DS DVD DL	Dual	Dual	17.08 GB of data, or over eight hours of video

and *DVD+R* media are writable much like CD-Rs. DVD-RAM, DVD-RW, and *DVD+RW* are writable and rewritable much like CD-RW. When shopping for a DVD drive, or a PC that includes a DVD drive, you will see the previously described types combined as DVD+R/RW, DVD-R/RW, and simply DVD-RAM. Drives may also be labeled with the combined + and −, showing that all types of DVD discs can be used.

DVD-RAM is a format used primarily in camcorders and personal video recorders. This format doesn't appear on the current CompTIA A+ exam. It does, however, appear in the Acronyms list.

Blu-ray   Blu-ray is a high-capacity optical disc format that was originally developed for high-definition movie distribution, but has also come to be widely used for computer data. There were originally two competing standards: High-Definition DVD (HD-DVD) and Blu-ray Disc (BD), but Blu-ray emerged victorious as the industry standard in 2008. Blu-ray drives use a blue-violet laser to read the discs, compared to the standard DVD, which uses a red laser. The blue laser, combined with a special lens, allows for a more focused laser, which results in higher density data storage.

Following the CD and DVD precedence, different types of Blu-ray discs are *BD-ROM* (read-only) and *BD-R* (write once), with a third designation, *BD-RE*, that describes the rewritable Blu-ray disc. Blu-ray discs are the same physical size as CD and DVD discs but have a much higher storage capacity. And, like the CD and DVD technologies, Blu-ray disc drives can read from and write to the older CD and DVD discs.

Recall the discussion of layers when describing DVDs, because Blu-ray discs come in single-, double-, triple-, and quadruple-layer versions. Single-layer Blu-ray discs hold 25 GB, double-layer discs hold 50 GB, triple-layer discs hold 100 GB, and quadruple-layer discs hold 128 GB. Movie titles available in Blu-ray format were on 25 GB discs until November 2007, when the first title appeared on 50 GB discs. Blu-ray disc isn't just for video. Like DVD, you can use Blu-ray to store any type of data.

Solid-State Storage

Up to now, the storage devices we have looked at use magnetic or optical technologies. However, a growing category of storage devices uses integrated circuits, which are much faster than these other technologies. Generically called *solid-state storage, solid-state drives (SSDs),* or *flash memory,* this technology has no moving parts and uses *nonvolatile memory,* meaning it does not require power to keep the stored data intact. These devices are more expensive on a per-gigabyte basis than conventional hard drives, but there are many uses for these very lightweight, quiet, and fast devices.

Many people assume that because this memory is able to be written and rewritten to, and is nonvolatile, that it is a type of static RAM (SRAM). However, the memory in most solid-state storage is actually a variant of electrically erasable programmable read-only memory (EEPROM). Yes, it can be written to, but it is written in blocks, not written in bytes the way RAM is written. All that is invisible and irrelevant to the end user, of course.

SSDs come in a range of form factors. There are external and internal models. SSDs designed to replace HDDs in desktop or notebook PCs come in packages the same size and shape as the equivalent HDDs they replace (3.5" for desktop and 2.5" for notebook).

Because SSDs are so much more expensive than HDDs, drive manufacturers came up with a way to create a *hybrid drive* that has many of the benefits of SSDs but at a lower cost. A hybrid drive looks and acts like a regular HDD, but it contains some nonvolatile memory like an SSD, and it uses it to store the most frequently used data, such as operating system files. As a result, users with hybrid drives can expect faster disk access than with a standard HDD.

There are also smaller SSDs for mobile devices. One popular variant for embedded applications such as digital cameras, smartphones, navigational systems, and tablets is the *embedded Multi-Media Controller (eMMC)*. This is a unit containing the flash memory and an integrated controller for it on the same silicon die, in a ball grid array (BGA) package.

A *flash drive* is an inexpensive, highly portable type of external SSD, and is also called a *thumb drive*, *jump drive*, or *USB drive*. Flash drives can hold up to hundreds of gigabytes of data, with different capacities available to suit any budget, in a device about the size and shape of a human thumb. When plugged into your computer, it appears as an ordinary drive with a drive letter assigned to it.

Solid-state memory can also exist on tiny plastic wafers, called *memory cards*, that can be removed from their reading device (a *card reader*). Flash memory cards are commonly used in a variety of devices, such as in digital cameras, smartphones, and navigation devices. A prolific photographer will carry several memory cards, swapping out full cards for empty ones. Although many cameras come with software and cables for transferring the photos from the camera's memory card to a computer and/or printer, another method does not require either cable or software. In this method, you remove the card from the camera and insert it into a special slot on the PC or printer. Whether the card is in a camera or inserted directly into the computer's card reader, it is treated like a drive. There are many types of flash memory cards using various solid-state technologies, some with trademarked names. Figure 4-16 shows some of the most common sizes.

FIGURE 4-16 Common flash memory cards (Photo: https://commons.wikimedia.org/wiki/File:Flash_memory_cards_size_comparison_(composite).svg)

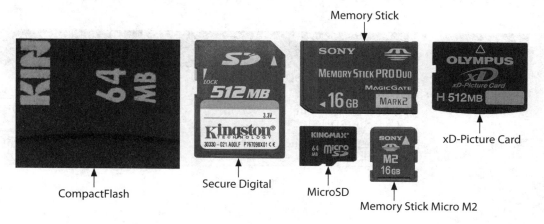

CompactFlash (CF), by SanDisk, first appeared on the scene in 1994, making it a very early SSD, but it is still popular in its updated variations, now standardized through the CompactFlash Association. Dozens of manufacturers have produced CF cards.

The xD-Picture Card, by Olympus and Fujifilm, was used in digital cameras in the early and mid-2000s and had a capacity up to 2 GB, but is no longer used in new cameras. The xD-Picture Card is smaller than the standard SD card (discussed next), but larger than miniSD and microSD form factors.

Secure Digital (SD) cards are high capacity yet tiny and support high-speed data transfer. SD cards are used in portable devices, such as digital video recorders, digital cameras, handheld computers, audio players, and cell phones.

SD cards come in several capacities and three major form factors. The standard form factor measures 32 mm × 24 mm × 2.1 mm, while the mini form factor measures 21.5 mm × 20 mm × 1.4 mm, and the micro form factor measures 15 mm × 11 mm × 1.0 mm. Table 4-8 shows the major capacities and form factors for SD cards.

The *Memory Stick (MS)* is a Sony flash memory card format measuring roughly 5/8" × 1 3/4" in its original form factor. It was available in capacities between 4 MB and 128 MB, and was followed by the *Memory Stick Pro (MSP)*, which held up to 1 GB. Then came the physically smaller *Memory Stick Duo (MSD)*, with a capacity of a mere 128 MB. The improved *Memory Stick PRO DUO (MSPD)* followed with at first a 16 GB maximum, followed soon after with a version with a 32 GB maximum. Inevitably, Sony, together with Sandisk, improved on this standard with the verbosely named *Memory Stick PRO Format for Extended High Capacity* with a maximum capacity of 2 TB. As shown in Figure 4-16, there is also a micro version. The Memory Stick format is not on the 220-901 exam.

A slot that can read an SD card may also be able to read a *MultiMediaCard (MMC)*, which has a form factor similar to the standard SD card. At 24 mm × 32 mm × 1.4 mm, MMC is just slightly thinner, but pin-compatible. This format is not on the 220-901 exam either.

Because some of the sizes are so similar, card readers with multiple slots use labels to help you figure out which slot to use. Figure 4-17 shows the front panel of a PC with a variety of flash memory slots, including one labeled MMC/SD. If a card reader is not built into your PC, and you require one, you can buy a bus card or an external USB card reader to add one to your PC.

TABLE 4-8		Maximum Capacity	Form Factors
Capacities and Form Factors for SD Cards	Standard-capacity SD (SDSC or SD)	2 GB	Standard, miniSD, microSD
	Secure Digital High Capacity (SDHC)	32 GB	Standard, miniSDHC, microSDHC
	Secure Digital eXtended Capacity (SDXC)	2 TB	Standard, miniSDXC, microSDXC

FIGURE 4-17

FIGURE 4-17

This computer is ready to read a variety of memory cards.

EXERCISE 4-4

Identify Your Storage Devices

Use Windows to view your connected storage devices.

1. Open Computer (Windows Vista or Windows 7) or open File Explorer and view This PC. This will show you all the attached disk drives.
2. Identify the drives displayed. What kinds of drives do you have? For example, is there an optical drive? Does it have a disc in it? Is there more than one internal HDD or SSD? Are there any removable drives connected, such as a USB flash drive?

Hot-Swappable Drives

A *hot-swappable drive* (sometimes called *hot-pluggable*) can be connected or disconnected without shutting down the system. SATA and all external drive interfaces used today are hot-swappable, so it's no longer the big deal it once was to be hot-swappable. (PATA drives were not hot-swappable.)

This doesn't mean you can just "pull the plug," so to speak, any old time. In order to avoid losing data, you need to ensure the disk is not in use before disconnecting it. Close any applications or windows that may be using the drive, and then take the steps necessary, depending on your operating system. In Windows, use the Safely Remove Hardware applet found in the notification area on the right end of the taskbar.

EXERCISE 4-5

Safely Disconnect External Storage

Follow these steps to practice disconnecting a USB flash drive safely before removing it. You will need a flash drive and Windows.

1. Connect the USB flash drive to the PC.
2. Look in the notification area (system tray) for a Safely Remove Hardware icon. It appears there after the OS recognizes the flash drive.

3. Click the icon. A menu appears.
4. Click the Eject option. (It will contain the name of the flash drive, such as Eject Data Traveler.)
5. Wait for a message to appear that it is now safe to remove the flash drive, and then disconnect it.

RAID Arrays

Redundant array of independent disks (RAID) is a group of schemes designed to provide either better performance or fault-tolerant protection for data through the use of multiple hard drives. Often (but not always) RAID uses specialized hardware called a *RAID controller*. RAID can also be achieved using specialized software, but it always requires multiple drives configured to work together to use one of the RAID schemes. We call this set of disks collectively a *RAID array*. The drives should be of equal size, or you will waste space. We identify each RAID scheme by the word "RAID" followed by a number. Figure 4-18 shows a small RAID array for a home or small office.

Fault tolerance is the ability to survive a failure of a part of a system. When speaking of RAID arrays, fault tolerance is the ability to protect data from a failure. This is done through data redundancy or through a special algorithm. Only RAID 1 and RAID 10 provide fault tolerance through data redundancy, and RAID 5 provides fault tolerance through the use of an algorithm. Learn how these different RAID levels work.

FIGURE 4-18

A small RAID array

RAID 0   *RAID 0* defines a simple striped set without parity. It gives improved drive read and write speeds. The operating system sees the separate physical drives in the array as a single hard drive, and each time data must be written to the drive array, the controller writes a portion of the data to each drive in the drive array, which is called a *stripe*. RAID 0 uses the total disk space in the array for data storage, without any fault-tolerant protection of the data from drive failure. If one of the drives in a RAID 0 array fails, all the data is lost.

RAID 1   *RAID 1*, also called *mirroring*, provides fault tolerance by writing all data simultaneously to the two drives in the *mirrored set*. If one of the drives should fail, the data still exists on the surviving drive. You may experience some improved performance on reads with RAID 1, depending on the operating system.

RAID 5   *RAID 5*, also called *striping with distributed parity* or *striping with interleaved parity*, requires at least three physical drives. As data is written to the striped set, it is written in blocks on each drive. In each stripe, the block written on just one of the drives (different with each write) is not the actual data, but the result of an algorithm performed on the data contained in the other blocks in the stripe. A single drive in a RAID 5 striped set can fail without a loss of data, because until the drive is replaced, the blocks in each stripe on the surviving drives are either the data itself (if the parity block was on the failed drive) or a parity block. Therefore, the controller uses the surviving data block and parity block in each set to reconstruct the data. Once the missing drive is replaced, the RAID controller will automatically rebuild the data as it existed on the failed drive, using the existing data and parity blocks. Also, until you replace the missing member of the set, the reads from the striped set are slower, due to the need to run the algorithm in order to produce the data.

RAID 10   A *RAID 10* array is a stripe of mirrors, requiring a minimum of four identical disks paired into two mirrored sets. Data is written in a stripe across the two mirrored sets as if they were simply two disks in a RAID 0 array. This gives you the fault tolerance of a mirror and the performance of RAID 0.

on the **job**

In most organizations, RAID is valued for the protection of data through redundancy, available with RAID levels 1 and 5. Therefore, expect to encounter these types of RAID on the job, especially on servers. Outside IT departments, gamers are very savvy about RAID, but they lean toward RAID level 0, which gives performance gains without redundancy protection.

RAID for Everybody   RAID isn't just for expensive server systems anymore. Built-in drive controllers on modern desktop motherboards are often RAID controllers because they include the ability to support one or more levels of RAID. Similarly, when you shop for a separate drive controller to install in a PC, you will find many that include RAID support.

RAID created using specialized RAID controllers is invisible to the operating system. This is a good thing, because managing a RAID array is a job that your operating system shouldn't see, and a RAID controller will do that for you. Many operating systems support software RAID, only requiring the correct number of drives, not a special RAID controller.

What is possible, however, is not always advisable. That is true of software RAID. RAID controllers are now much less expensive and widely available. One may exist in your own desktop computer. Therefore, if you want to install a RAID array in a computer, use a hardware RAID controller and configure it per the controller's documentation. Normally, configuring a RAID controller is much like configuring system BIOS/UEFI settings, with the addition of a utility for configuring the desired RAID level. Doing software RAID is interesting, and something many of us did more as a lab exercise years ago when it was cheaper to simply install multiple hard drives and use software RAID just for the experience of working with RAID than to purchase an expensive RAID controller. That was then, and things are much different now.

SCENARIO & SOLUTION

What type of drive is required to play high-definition video movies on optical discs?	Blu-ray Disc drive
You are asked to recommend a computer to be a file and print server for a small business. What RAID configuration should you recommend to the small business owner to add data redundancy to the system?	RAID level 1; consider mirroring to give the server redundancy. RAID 5 could also be an option, as it also provides redundancy. You would not, however, recommend RAID 0.
When shopping for internal storage for a desktop PC, you should look for an HDD or SSD with what interface?	SATA
What kind of internal storage device combines some of the benefits of SSD with the lower price of HDD?	Hybrid drive
If you see an optical drive described as 52x24x16, what does the smallest number mean?	Rewrite speed

CERTIFICATION SUMMARY

Identifying personal computer components and their functions is the first step in becoming a computer professional. While PC component technologies are ever-changing, understanding the basics of the components and their functions today will help you to understand newer technologies as they are introduced. This chapter described the important features of memory, expansion cards, and storage. It isn't enough to understand the technologies of these important components; you also need to understand the various connection interfaces related to them and the connectors and related cables, which were included in this chapter.

TWO-MINUTE DRILL

Here are some of the key points covered in Chapter 4.

Memory

❑ Data storage capacity is described in terms of bits, bytes, kilobytes, megabytes, and terabytes.

❑ The speed of electronics, such as RAM, is often described in terms of hertz (Hz), kilohertz (KHz), megahertz (MHz), and gigahertz (GHz).

❑ RAM is volatile, and used to store active programs and data. ROM is nonvolatile, and used to store firmware on motherboards and adapters.

❑ Most memory modules do not perform error checking. Some older memory modules use an error-checking method called parity, and others may use a more complex method called ECC.

❑ Buffered memory, also called registered memory, uses a buffer between the DRAM and the memory controller to take some of the strain off the controller so the system will reliably support more RAM.

❑ DIMMs come in both single-sided and double-sided versions.

❑ SRAM is very fast and very expensive, and is used for system cache in most systems.

❑ DRAM is slower than SRAM. It is less expensive, has a higher capacity, and is the main memory in the computer.

❑ DRAM technologies include SDRAM, DDR1 SDRAM, DDR2 SDRAM, DDR3, and DDR4 SDRAM.

❑ To avoid compatibility problems, read the motherboard manual before buying and installing additional RAM modules in a computer.

Expansion Cards and Built-in Adapters

❑ Common expansion cards (adapters) include display adapters, network interface cards (NICs), sound cards, and cards that add various types of ports, such as FireWire or Thunderbolt. Most expansion cards are PCIe.

❑ The need for expansion cards has diminished as PC motherboards contain more functions.

❑ Riser cards are used in low-profile cases to allow expansion cards to sit parallel to the motherboard to fit more cards in a small space.

Storage Devices and Interfaces

❑ SATA is the standard interface for internal mass storage, and eSATA, USB, and FireWire are all common interfaces for external storage devices.

❑ A mass storage device holds large amounts of information, even when the power is off.

❑ Mass storage devices come in three general categories: magnetic, optical, and solid-state storage.

❑ Hard disk drives and tape drives are examples of magnetic mass storage devices that store digital data on magnetized media.

❑ Optical drives include CD, DVD, and Blu-ray drives, each of which has a variety of capacities and speeds.

❑ Solid-state storage, a.k.a. solid-state drives (SSDs), have no moving parts and use large-capacity, nonvolatile memory, commonly called flash memory.

❑ Hot-swappable drives can be connected or disconnected without shutting down the system. Some hard drive systems are hot-swappable, depending, in large part, on the interface.

❑ Hard drives with USB, FireWire, SATA, or eSATA interfaces are usually hot-swappable, as is nearly any USB or FireWire device.

❑ RAID, which stands for redundant array of independent (or inexpensive) disks, is a group of schemes designed to provide either better performance or improved data reliability through redundancy.

❑ RAID 0 defines a striped set without parity. It gives improved drive read and write speeds.

❑ RAID 1, also called mirroring, provides fault tolerance because all the data is written identically to the two drives in the mirrored set.

❑ RAID 5, also called striping with distributed parity or striping with interleaved parity, requires at least three physical drives.

❑ RAID 10 is a stripe of mirrors, requiring a minimum of four identical disks, paired into two mirrored sets, with data written in a stripe across the two mirrored sets.

SELF TEST

The following questions will help you measure your understanding of the material presented in this chapter. Read all of the choices carefully because there might be more than one correct answer. Choose all correct answers for each question.

Memory

1. This type of memory is volatile, used as temporary workspace by the CPU, and loses its contents every time a computer is powered down.
   A. ROM
   B. DRAM
   C. CMOS
   D. Solid state

2. Cache memory uses which type of RAM chip because of its speed?
   A. DRAM
   B. VRAM
   C. DIMM
   D. SRAM

3. This type of SDRAM doubled the speed at which standard SDRAM processed data by accessing the module twice per clock cycle.
   A. Dual-channel
   B. Multichannel
   C. Double-sided
   D. DDR1

4. This type of RAM module uses a special 240-pin DIMM socket and requires far less power than the previous modules, while providing almost twice the bandwidth.
   A. DDR1 SDRAM
   B. DDR2 SDRAM
   C. DDR3 SDRAM
   D. EEPROM

5. This specialized type of DDR3 runs at 1.35V, which decreases electricity used.
   A. DDR4
   B. Dual-channel
   C. DDR3L
   D. Double-sided

6. This type of SDRAM module has memory chips mounted on both sides.
   A. Single-sided
   B. Double-sided
   C. ECC
   D. Dual channel

7. This chip manages the main memory on a motherboard.
   A. CMOS
   B. DRAM
   C. MCC
   D. DDR3

Expansion Cards and Built-in Adapters

8. Which of the following is *not* a technology for connecting external devices?
   A. Thunderbolt
   B. USB
   C. IEEE 1394
   D. Serial

9. Name a common communications adapter card used to connect PCs to a LAN or to take advantage of a DSL or cable modem Internet connection.
   A. NIC
   B. Modem
   C. USB
   D. Serial

10. This category of adapter card accepts and records video signals to a PC's hard drive.
    A. Network adapter
    B. Modem
    C. Capture card
    D. Video adapter

Storage Devices and Interfaces

11. This is a component in a hard drive system that reads and writes data.
    A. Spindle
    B. Head
    C. Platter
    D. Cable

12. Name the rotating shaft to which a hard drive's platters attach.
- A.   Head
- B.   Cable
- C.   Pin
- D.   Spindle

13. Which of the following is an example of a magnetic mass storage device?
- A.   SSD
- B.   DVD drive
- C.   HDD
- D.   Flash drive

14. Name two common interfaces for external hard drives.
- A.   PATA and SATA
- B.   Serial and parallel
- C.   USB and eSATA
- D.   Modems and hubs

15. This DVD type stores 17.08 GB of data, or over eight hours of video.
- A.   Dual sided, dual layer
- B.   Single sided, dual layer
- C.   Dual sided, single layer
- D.   Single sided, single layer

16. This type of optical mass storage device was developed to read and write high-definition video.
- A.   DVD-18
- B.   CD-RW
- C.   Blu-ray Disc
- D.   DVD-RW

17. Which version of SATA allows a cable length of two meters and transfers data at up to 2.4 Gbps?
- A.   SATA1
- B.   SATA2
- C.   SATA3
- D.   eSATA

18. This feature indicates that a drive can be connected or disconnected without shutting down the system.
- A.   External
- B.   RAID
- C.   USB
- D.   Hot-swappable

19. This magnetic mass storage device type stores data sequentially and has been primarily used as backup storage for servers.
   A. USB flash drive
   B. Tape drive
   C. Optical drive
   D. HDD

20. This is a group of standards defining several schemes for using multiple identical hard drives, working together in an array with the goal of achieving either better performance or redundancy.
   A. RAID
   B. eSATA
   C. USB
   D. Serial

SELF TEST ANSWERS

Memory

1. ☑ **B.** Dynamic RAM (DRAM) is the type of volatile memory used by the CPU as workspace.
   ☒ **A** is incorrect because this type of memory is not volatile; its contents are not lost every time the PC is powered off. **C** is incorrect because it is special battery-powered support memory that holds basic system configuration information used by the computer as it powers up. **D** is incorrect because this is a type of storage device that is nonvolatile and is not used by the processor in the manner described.

2. ☑ **D.** SRAM is the type of RAM used for cache memory because of its speed.
   ☒ **A** is incorrect because this is slower than SRAM. **B** is incorrect because although it is fast, this type of RAM is used on video adapters. **C** is incorrect, as it is a RAM connector/slot type, not a type of RAM chip.

3. ☑ **D.** DDR1 SDRAM doubled the speed at which standard SDRAM processed data by accessing the module twice per clock cycle.
   ☒ **A** and **B** are incorrect because both are used to describe an architecture that speeds up memory access by having the MCC access each module on a different channel. **C** is incorrect because it describes a RAM module with chips populating both sides.

4. ☑ **C.** DDR3 SDRAM is the type of RAM module that uses a special 240-pin DIMM socket and requires far less power than the previous modules, while providing almost twice the bandwidth.
☒ **A** is incorrect because it uses a 184-pin DIMM socket, not a 240-pin DIMM socket. **B** is incorrect because although it also uses a (different) 240-pin DIMM socket, it requires more power than the previous RAM module type (DDR1 SDRAM). **D** is incorrect because it is ROM, not RAM.

5. ☑ **C.** DDR3L is correct, as this type of DDR3 is low-voltage.
☒ **A** is incorrect because DDR4 is not a type of DDR3 RAM. **B** is incorrect because dual-channel is a function of the motherboard, not of the RAM. **D** is incorrect because being single-sided or double-sided has no effect on voltage.

6. ☑ **B.** Double-sided is correct because this type of RAM module has memory chips mounted on both sides.
☒ **A** is incorrect because a single-sided memory module only has chips mounted on one side. **C** is incorrect because this stands for error-correcting code, which is an error detecting and correcting mechanism used by some memory modules. **D** is incorrect because this refers to a technique for speeding up memory access in which the MCC switches between two memory modules, effectively doubling the memory speed.

7. ☑ **C.** MCC, or memory controller chip, is correct because this chip controls the main memory on a motherboard.
☒ **A** is incorrect because the CMOS chip is a special battery-supported chip that retains the system settings. **B** is incorrect because this is a type of RAM used for the main memory itself; it is not a memory controller. **D** is incorrect because this is a type of SDRAM, not a controller chip.

Expansion Cards and Built-in Adapters

8. ☑ **D.** Serial is not a technology, but a way that data travels through a cable (one bit at a time).
☒ **A, B,** and **C** are all incorrect because they are external connection technologies.

9. ☑ **A.** A network interface card (NIC) is a common communications adapter card used to connect PCs to a LAN or to take advantage of a DSL or cable modem Internet connection.
☒ **B** is incorrect because, although it is a communications adapter card, it is used for a dial-up connection, not for a LAN connection. **C** is incorrect because it is an I/O interface, not a communications adapter. **D** is incorrect because it is an I/O interface, not a communications adapter, although some external modems can connect to a serial port.

10. ☑ **C.** A capture card is a type of adapter used to record video signals to a PC's hard drive.
☒ **A** is incorrect because this type of adapter is used for network communications. **B** is incorrect because it is used for a dial-up connection, not for recording video signals. **D** is incorrect because it is used to drive a display device, not to capture video signals.

Storage Devices and Interfaces

11. ☑ **B.** The head is the component in a hard drive system that reads and writes data. There is one head for each platter side.
    ☒ **A** is incorrect because this rotating pole holds the platters in a hard drive. **C** is incorrect because this component holds the data. **D** is incorrect because a cable connects a device to a computer but does not read data from a hard drive.

12. ☑ **D.** The spindle is the rotating shaft to which a hard drive's platters are attached.
    ☒ **A** is incorrect because this component reads and writes data. **B** is incorrect because a cable connects a device to a computer and is not a rotating shaft. **C** is incorrect because a pin is a component of a cable plug, not the rotating shaft in a hard drive.

13. ☑ **C.** A hard disk drive (HDD) is a magnetic storage device.
    ☒ **A** and **D** are incorrect because both are types of solid-state storage, not magnetic. **B** is incorrect because it provides optical storage.

14. ☑ **C.** USB and eSATA are two common interfaces for external hard drives.
    ☒ **A** is incorrect because these are interfaces for internal hard drives, not for external hard drives. **B** is incorrect because these are not interfaces for external hard drives. **D** is incorrect because these are not common interfaces for external hard drives.

15. ☑ **A.** A dual-sided, dual-layer disc stores 17.08 GB of data, or over eight hours of video.
    ☒ **B** is incorrect because it only holds 8.54 GB of data, or over four hours of video. **C** is incorrect because it only holds 9.4 GB of data, or over four and a half hours of video. **D** is incorrect because it only holds 4.7 GB of data, or over two hours of video.

16. ☑ **C.** Blu-ray disc was developed to read and write high-definition video.
    ☒ **A, B,** and **D** are all incorrect because, although they are all optical mass storage devices, none of them can handle high-definition video formats.

17. ☑ **D.** External SATA (eSATA) allows for a two meter cable length and 2.4 Gbps throughput.
    ☒ **A, B,** and **C** are all incorrect because they all have a maximum cable length of one meter.

18. ☑ **D.** Hot-swappable is a feature that indicates that a drive can be connected or disconnected without shutting down the system.
    ☒ **A** is incorrect because while some external drives are also hot-swappable, the term "external" itself does not indicate that a drive has this feature. **B** is incorrect because although drives that are part of a RAID array may be hot-swappable, the term "RAID" itself does not indicate that a drive has this feature. **C** is incorrect because, although some hot-swappable drives use the USB interface, the term "USB" itself does not indicate that a drive has this feature.

19. ☑ **B.** A tape drive is a magnetic mass storage device type that stores data sequentially, and it has been primarily used as backup storage for servers.
    ☒ **A** and **C** are incorrect because neither is a magnetic mass storage device type, and neither has ever been primarily used as backup storage for servers. **D** is incorrect because, although it is a magnetic mass storage device type, it has not been primarily used as backup storage for servers.

20. ☑ **A.** RAID is the acronym for redundant array of independent (or inexpensive) disks, a group of schemes designed to provide either better performance or improved data reliability through redundancy.

☒ **B** is incorrect because this is a standard for an external version of the serial ATA interface. **C** is incorrect because this is the Universal Serial Bus standard. **D** is incorrect because this is another interface, not a standard for disk arrays.

Chapter 5

Power Supplies, Display Devices, and Peripherals

T his chapter explores power supplies, display devices (both video adapters and displays), and peripheral devices, identifying the connector types and cables associated with these computer components. Also included are instructions for installing and configuring each type of device, with the exception of the physical installation of video adapter cards, which will be described in Chapter 6 as part of the how-to instructions for installing any expansion card.

CERTIFICATION OBJECTIVE

■ *901: 1.8* *Install a power supply based on given specifications*

This section describes power supply types and characteristics. You will learn about voltage, wattage, capacity, power supply fans, and form factors. Also included are descriptions of power cables and connectors. This section prepares you to select an appropriate power supply, remove an older power supply, and install a new one.

Power Supplies

A *power supply*, or *power supply unit (PSU)*, is the device that provides power for all other components on the motherboard and is internal to the PC case. Every PC has an easily identified power supply; it is typically located inside the computer case at the back, and parts of it are visible from the outside when looking at the back of the PC. On a desktop computer (PC or iMac), you will see the three-prong power socket. Most PCs also have a label, and sometimes a tiny switch. Figure 5-1 shows the interior of a PC with a power supply on the upper left. Notice the bundle of cables coming out of the power supply. These cables supply power to the motherboard and all other internal components. Each component must receive the appropriate type and amount of power it requires, and the power supply itself has its own requirements. Therefore, you should understand some basic electrical terminology and apply it to the power supply's functions.

Electrical Terminology

Electricity is the flow of electrons (*current*) through a conductor, such as copper wire, and we use it in two forms: *direct current (DC)* and *alternating current (AC)*. In DC, the type of electrical current generated by a battery, the flow of negative electrons is in one direction around the closed loop of an electrical circuit. In AC, the flow of electrons around the electrical circuit reverses periodically and has alternating positive and negative values. AC is the kind of electricity that comes from a wall outlet.

FIGURE 5-1

FIGURE 5-1

The power supply, shown in the upper left, is usually located in the back of the computer case, with a three-prong power socket visible on the exterior of the PC.

A *volt (V)* is the unit of measurement of the pressure of electrons on a wire, or the electromotive force. A *watt (W)* is a unit of measurement of actual delivered power. An *ampere (A* or *amp)* is a unit of measurement for electrical current, or rate of flow of electrons, through a wire. When you know the wattage and amps needed or used, you calculate volts using the formula volts = watts / amps. When you know the voltage and amps, you can calculate wattage used or required with the formula watts = volts × amps. And if you need to know the amps but only know the wattage and voltage, use the formula amps = watts / volts. All these calculations are versions of Ohm's Law, which represents the fundamental relationship among current, voltage, and resistance.

Voltage

The power supply is responsible for converting the AC voltage from wall outlets into the DC voltage that the computer requires: ±12 VDC, ±5 VDC, or ±3.3 VDC (volts DC). The PC power supply accomplishes this task through a series of switching transistors, which gives rise to the term *switching-mode power supply.*

A device, such as a laser printer or a cathode-ray tube (CRT), that requires high voltage has its own *high-voltage power supply (HVPS).*

Typical North American wall outlets provide about 110 to 120 volts AC (VAC) at a frequency of 60 Hertz (Hz—cycles per second), which is also expressed as ~115 VAC at 60 Hz. The *frequency* is the number of times per second that alternating current reverses direction. Elsewhere in the world, standard power is 220 to 240 VAC at 50 Hz.

Power supplies manufactured for sale throughout the world *are dual voltage*, providing either the U.S. standard or the international standard. Dual-voltage options in power supplies come in two categories: power supplies that automatically switch and those that must be manually switched. An *auto-switching power supply* can detect the incoming voltage and switch to accept either 120 or 240 VAC, but a *fixed-input* power supply will have a switch on the back for selecting the correct input voltage setting. Figure 5-2 shows the back of a power supply with the *voltage selector switch* for selecting 115 VAC or 240 VAC. It is the tiny slide switch positioned below the power connector.

Wattage and Size

How big a power supply do you need? First, we are not talking about physical size, but the capacity or wattage a power supply can handle. Figure 5-3 shows the label on a power supply. Notice that this is a 300-watt power supply. Notice also that the label specifies this power supply will run on either 120 VAC or 240 VAC and at either 50/60 Hz, which means it will run in almost any country. Just a few years ago power supplies ranging from 300 to 500 watts were considered more than adequate for PCs; today you will find many modestly priced PCs with 700-watt or greater power supplies. Higher-end computers use 800- to 1500-watt power supplies. Therefore, to answer the question, you need a power supply with a capacity that exceeds the total watts required by all the internal components, such as the motherboard, memory, drives, and various adapters.

The total power is not the only factor to consider, however. How that power is allocated among multiple rails also matters. A *rail*, in power supply terms, is a pathway that delivers a specific voltage of power to a specific connection. Modern power supplies are designed for systems that need a lot of 12V power, far more than just the modest amount provided

FIGURE 5-2

The back of a power supply, with power connector socket and the voltage selection switch below it

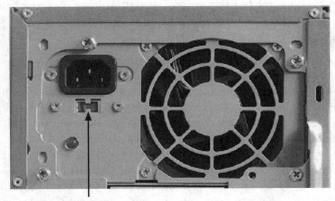

Voltage selection switch

The maximum wattage supported by a power supply appears on the Total Power line.

Model No	XS700							
AC Input	110-240 Vac ~ 10-5A 50 - 60Hz							
DC Output	+3.3V	+5V	+12V1	+12V2	+12V3	+12V4	-12V	+5Vsb
Max Output Current	36A	30A	18A	18A	18A	18A	0.5A	3.0A
Max. Combined Power	155W		680W				20W	
Total Power			700W	Total output current for this subject power supply is 70A Maximum combined current for the 12V outputs shall be 50A				

12V Output Distribution List	
Output Voltage	Device
12V1	CPU1
12V2	PCI-E2/CPU2
12V3	M/B accessory
12V4	PCI-E1

WARNING! HAZARDOUS AREA
SAFETY INSTRUCTIONS:
DO NOT REMOVE THE COVER
NO SERVICEABLE COMPONENTS INSIDE.
REFER SERVICING TO QUALIFIED SERVICE PERSONNEL.

CAUTION! HAZARDOUS AREA
SAFETY INSTRUCTIONS:
DO NOT REMOVE THE COVER
NO SERVICEABLE COMPONENTS INSIDE.
REFER SERVICING TO QUALIFIED SERVICE PERSONNEL.

Tested To Comply
With FCC Standards
FOR HOME OR OFFICE USE

CB   CE   224636   E243823   N

on the P1 connector (the big 24-pin connector to the motherboard). They provide one or more extra 12V connectors, as you learned in Chapter 4. Notice in Figure 5-3 that in the DC Output row there are four +12V rails listed, each one with 18 amps allocated to it. The 12V Output Distribution List in the lower left corner of the label explains how each of those rails is allocated.

EXERCISE 5-1

Check Out the Wattage on PCs and Other Devices

1. Look at the back of a PC and find the power supply label. Record the wattage information. If wattage is not shown but the volts and amps are, multiply those two numbers to calculate the wattage.

2. Make a note of the voltages and watts for different rails, if that information is provided on the label.

3. Do the same on computer peripherals that are available to you, such as displays, printers, and scanners.

4. Similarly, check out the wattage on noncomputer devices in the classroom or at home.

Fans

Another function of a power supply is to dissipate the heat that it and other PC components generate. Heat buildup can cause computer components (including the power supply) to fail. Therefore, power supplies have a built-in exhaust fan that draws air through the computer case and cools the components inside. For more information on cooling, flip back and review the section on cooling systems in Chapter 3.

AC Adapters

Another form of power supply is an AC adapter used with portable computers and external peripherals. An *AC adapter* converts AC power to the voltage needed for a device. Like the power supply in a desktop PC, it converts AC power to DC power. The connector between the AC adapter and the laptop or device may be one of several types. The traditional connectors are various sizes of coaxial connectors, but AC adapters also come with one of several types of Universal Serial Bus (USB) connectors. Figure 5-4 shows an AC adapter for a laptop with a coaxial connector on the right. On the far left is the cable that connects the adapter to a wall socket via a grounded plug. Notice the smaller three-prong plug that connects to the matching socket on the AC adapter. Not all of them are three-prong; some are two.

If you must replace an external adapter, simply unplug it and attach a new one that matches the specifications and plug configuration of the adapter it is replacing. Since AC adapters have different output voltages, only use an AC adapter with output voltage that exactly matches the input voltage for the laptop. Previously, laptop power supplies were *fixed-input power supplies* set to accept only one input power voltage. Now, many laptop AC adapters act as *auto-switching power supplies*, detecting the incoming voltage and switching to accept either 120 or 240 VAC. The part of the cord that plugs into the wall can be switched out depending on the country you are in.

FIGURE 5-4

An AC adapter
for a laptop

Power Supply Form Factors and Connectors

When building a new computer, a power supply may come with the computer case, or you can purchase one separately, but you need to consider both wattage and form factor. Like motherboards and cases, computer power supplies come in a variety of form factors to match both the motherboard and case. The most common power supply form factor for desktop PCs is referred to as the *ATX power supply*, used in most case desktop sizes, except the smallest low-profile cases and the largest, jumbo-sized full-tower cases. A smaller version of the ATX power supply is the *micro-ATX power supply*, which works in many of the smaller cases with the micro-ATX and similar motherboard form factors. There are many other form factors that are variations on the ATX PSU form factor. Whenever you need to match a power supply with a computer, start with the motherboard manual, and pay close attention to all the features required by the motherboard. Then consider the case and what will fit in it. In fact, when putting together a custom computer, a PSU will often come with the case.

In response to the demands of PC-based servers and gamers, power supply manufacturers have added proprietary features beyond those in any standards. You can find power supplies that offer special support for the newest Intel and AMD CPU requirements and greater efficiency, which saves on power usage and reduces heat output.

The form factor of the power supply determines the motherboard it works with and the type of connector used to supply power to the motherboard. Most motherboards use 24-pin connectors, called *P1 power connectors*. (Some are 20-pin in older systems.)

The power supply will likely also offer some additional connectors to the motherboard. On most modern systems, a separate cable will connect to the motherboard with a 4-, 6-, or 8-pin connector. Under the *ATX 12V* standard, a 4-pin, *P4 connector*, also called a *P4 12V connector*, supplies 12 volts in addition to that provided by the P1 connector, or, based on the *ATX 12V 2.0* standard, a 24-pin main connector and a 4-pin secondary connector. Some motherboards require EPS12V connectors, which include a 24-pin main connector, an 8-pin secondary connector, and an optional 4-pin tertiary connector.

There are several types of 6-pin and 8-pin connectors. A now-obsolete 6-pin connector, called the *AUX power connector*, added 3.3 volts or 5.0 volts to AMD dual-processor motherboards. A newer type of connector is the *PCI Express (PCI-e) power connector*, which comes in 6-pin or 8-pin configurations. A PCIe power connector attaches to a connector on a motherboard (if available) or to a connector on a specialized expansion card.

Some high-end non-ATX motherboards used in network servers and high-end workstations include a 4-pin or 8-pin connector to provide additional power to the CPU, which also derives power through its own motherboard socket.

ATX and other power supplies and motherboards work together to provide a feature called *soft power*. Soft power allows software to turn off a computer rather than only using a physical switch. Most PCs have soft power. A computer with soft power enabled has a pair of small wires leading from the physical switch on the case to the motherboard. Usually, there is a system setting that controls just how this feature is used. For safety's sake, you should always consider soft power as being on, because when you have enabled soft power, turning the power switch off means that although the computer appears to be off, the power supply is still supplying ±5 volts to the motherboard. This means you can never trust the power button to turn the computer completely off. Some PCs come equipped with two power switches. One is in the front, and you can consider it the "soft" off switch. The other is on the back of the case, in the power supply itself, and this is the "real" off switch. Even so, the safest thing to do is to unplug the power cable from the wall outlet to ensure no power is coming to the motherboard.

Connecting Power to Peripherals

In addition to providing power to the motherboard, power supplies have ports and connectors for providing power to internally installed peripherals—mainly various drives, but sometimes to expansion cards. Power supplies often have cables that are permanently connected to the PSU, and they may have additional ports to which you connect additional cables, allowing for expansion. (A power supply that lets you connect cables to it is called a *modular power supply*.) The cable connections on the peripheral end vary based on the type of device and power requirements.

Two traditional peripheral connectors are the 4-pin *Molex connector*, measuring about 7/8" wide, and the much smaller 4-pin *miniconnector*. The Molex and miniconnector each provide 5 and 12 volts to peripherals. Molex connectors traditionally connected to most parallel ATA internal devices, while the miniconnector mainly connected to floppy drives. Figure 5-5 shows a power splitter cable with a single Molex connector on one end and two miniconnectors on the other. Both are usually white.

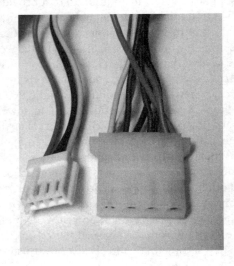

FIGURE 5-5

A mini connector (left) and Molex connector (right) (Photo: https://commons.wikimedia.org/wiki/File:Molex1.jpg [Creative Commons license])

FIGURE 5-6

A SATA power connector to a drive (Photo: https://commons .wikimedia.org/ wiki/File:SATA_ Power_Cable_ with_3.3_V .jpg [Creative Commons license])

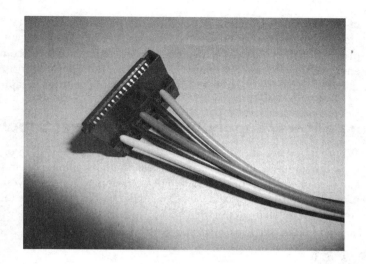

On modern systems, most of the drives you will want to connect require a serial ATA (SATA) connector from the power supply, as shown in Figure 5-6. Look for a SATA power cable coming off the power supply with a 15-pin connector, usually black, for connecting to most optical or hard drives. If an older power supply does not have this cable, use a Molex-to-SATA power connector adapter to connect the SATA power cable to a Molex connector from the power supply. Small SATA storage devices have a tiny 15-pin micro SATA power connector. The pins in a SATA power connector supply different voltages for SATA devices, including 3.3V (orange), 5V (red), and 12V (yellow), and they support hot-swapping SATA devices. There is also a slimline version (found on portable computers) that has only 6 pins and delivers only 5V power, and a micro version used with 1.8-inch drives that uses 9 pins to deliver 3.3V and 5V power.

Some SATA connectors do not have the orange wire (they have only four wires) and do not supply 3.3V power. In addition, if you use an adapter to convert a Molex connector to a SATA one, you won't get the 3.3V rail. That's not a problem for most magnetic and optical drives, as they don't use the 3.3V power anyway. However, some solid-state drives and other specialty storage devices do require it, so check the power supply requirements for the drive if in doubt.

Energy Efficiency

Although not directly a power supply issue, energy efficiency in all PC components has become a very important feature and affects the selection of a power supply. We seem to need bigger and bigger power supplies to accommodate the increasing number and types of components we include in our PCs: more memory, larger hard drives, more powerful video adapters, and so on. The good news is that the power requirements have not grown proportionally with the performance improvements of these components, which are more energy efficient and have features that reduce their power consumption during idle times. Learn more about managing these energy-saving features in laptops in Chapter 7.

Removing a Power Supply/Installing a Power Supply

Whether you are purchasing a power supply for a new system or replacing an old one, you have the same set of concerns when selecting, installing, or removing a power supply. Power supplies in existing computers do fail from time to time, and you can replace them using the procedure outlined in Exercise 5-2, which provides basic steps for removing an old power supply and replacing a new one.

EXERCISE 5-2

Replacing a Power Supply

Do this exercise on a desktop PC.

1. Turn off the power and remove the power connector from the wall socket. Use appropriate ESD protective measures.
2. Remove the power connector(s) from the motherboard, grasping the plastic connector, not the wires.
3. Remove the power connectors from all other components, including hard, floppy, and optical drives.
4. Using an appropriately sized screwdriver, remove the screws that hold the power supply to the PC case. Do not remove the screws holding the power supply case together!
5. Slide or lift the power supply away from the computer.
6. Reverse these steps to install a new power supply.

Recall that power supplies can still hold a charge when turned off, especially if you use only the soft power switch. Before removing any power supply, even a failed one, be sure to unplug it from the wall outlet. To avoid the danger of electric shock, do not wear an antistatic wristband while working with power supplies.

CERTIFICATION OBJECTIVES

■ ***901: 1.10***   *Compare and contrast types of display devices and their features*

■ ***901: 1.11***   *Identify common PC connector types and associated cables*

■ ***902: 1.5***   *Given a scenario, use Windows Control Panel utilities*

■ ***901: 3.2***   *Explain the function of components within the display of a laptop*

This section introduces all of the topics covered by CompTIA A+ 901 exam objective 1.10, including the various types of display devices (projectors, OLEDs, plasma, and LCDs), display technologies, and display settings, as listed in CompTIA A+ 901 exam objective 3.2. Control Panel Display resolution settings are described here, per 902 exam objective 1.5. Also included here are two areas of 901 exam objective 1.11: display connector types and display cable types. Other cable and connector types were covered in Chapter 4.

Video Adapters and Displays

The quality of the image you see on a PC display depends on both the capabilities and configuration of the two most important video components: the video adapter and the display device (also called a monitor, when it is a separate unit). The technologies used in video adapters and displays have become a more complex topic as we transitioned from the old analog technologies to the digital technologies in use today. We will explore that transition in this section, as well as important display settings and how they affect output to a display.

Analog vs. Digital

Video adapters, as part of inherently digital computing systems, have long been digital devices, meaning that a video adapter uses a *digital signal* composed of discrete on-off signals or pulses representing digits to compose the video image before sending it to a display. However, historically these adapters were connected to *analog displays* that accepted only an *analog signal*, meaning that it was a continuously variable signal. Therefore, the adapter had to translate the digital data to an analog signal. The upside to analog displays was that they could display continuously varied colors. A digital display, on the other hand, accepts digital signals, and although it does not display continuously variable colors, the typical digital display shows more complex colors and intensities not possible on an analog display. In the days when analog displays prevailed, the video adapter translated that image to an analog signal before sending it to the display. In the following discussion of video interface modes, we begin with the analog video technologies based on the old VGA standard and end with the several digital standards in use today.

Video Adapters

The video adapter controls the output from the PC to the display device. Although the video adapter contains all the logic and does most of the work, the quality of the resulting image depends on the modes supported by both the adapter and the display. If the adapter is capable of higher-quality output than the display, the display limits the result—and vice versa. In this section, we will explore video interface modes, screen resolution and color depth, the computer interfaces used by video adapters, and the connectors used to connect a display to the video adapter.

Computer Interfaces

When purchasing a video adapter card, pay attention to the interface between the video adapter and the computer so that you select one you can install into your PC. If the motherboard contains a video adapter, it still accesses one of the standard busses in the computer. If the video adapter is a separate expansion card, it installs into a PCIe slot (usually an x16 slot). We discussed PCIe in Chapter 3. You will find the current version of the video standards mentioned here available with any of these interfaces.

Video Modes and Technologies

In order to be compatible with older displays and software, even the latest video adapter supports many of the less-capable modes that preceded it. Therefore, the following is a survey of these modes.

The most basic of video modes are text and graphics. As a PC boots, and before the operating system takes control, the video is in text mode and can only display the limited ASCII character set. Once the operating system is in control, it loads drivers for the video adapter and display, and it uses a graphics mode that can display bitmapped graphics. Today these graphics modes—commonly called video modes—support millions of colors. Many video modes have been introduced since the first IBM PC in 1981. However, we will only discuss the video modes you can expect to encounter on the CompTIA A+ exams, as well as in businesses and homes today. Along with each new mode comes the supporting technology, along with a specific type of connection between the video adapter and the display. These connectors will be identified in the following discussion of video modes and technologies.

Be able to identify on sight the various types of connectors and the video mode or technology associated with them.

VGA *Video Graphics Array (VGA)* is a video adapter standard introduced with the IBM PS/2 computers in the late 1980s. VGA sends analog signals to the display, producing a wide range of colors. VGA is an old technology today because we have gone far beyond it in capabilities, but some software packages still list it as a minimum requirement for installing the software, and the connector used on VGA adapters is in use today on many video adapters that also support more advanced video modes—although newer connectors are also available, often on the same adapter. VGA mode most often consists of a combination of 640 × 480 *pixels* (a contraction of *picture elements*), the tiny dots used to create an image, and 16 colors. In text mode, VGA has a maximum resolution of 720 × 400 and can produce around 16 million different colors, but can only display up to 256 different colors at a time, a VGA color setting known as 8-bit high color ($2^8 = 256$).

For nearly two decades, technicians only needed to work with one video display connector—the DE-15 (also called HD15 or VGA). Now other options are available that go with newer technologies. As you study the various video technologies, you will learn about common display connectors. Figure 5-7 shows the back of a video adapter with three connectors: (from left to right) DVI Dual Link, S-Video, and DE-15. The last is often labeled "VGA." S-Video is no longer covered on the CompTIA A+ exams, so we don't cover it in this book.

exam

Watch While many sources incorrectly call a VGA connector DB-15, technically a DB-15 connector has 15 pins in two rows of 7 and 8, and is not used for video. The correct terminology for the three-row 15-pin VGA connector is DE-15, HD-15, or VGA.

The DE-15 connector, also called a 15-pin D-Sub connector or a VGA connector, is used on video adapters for connecting to both traditional CRT monitors and many flat-panel displays. It has three rows of five pins each, slightly staggered. This connector is also commonly called a VGA connector, or *Video Electronics Standards Association (VESA)*, for the standards organization that developed this standard, as well as many others. This name does not reflect the ability of the video adapter, but only the fact that the earliest VGA video adapters used it. The connector on the monitor cable is male, whereas the connector on the video adapter (the computer end) is female. A male port or connector has pins, and a female port or connector is a receiver with sockets for the pins of the male connector.

Liquid crystal display (LCD) displays use a digital signal. Although video adapters actually store information digitally in video RAM, they have long been able to convert the digital signal to analog for CRT displays. Therefore, LCD displays that connect to these traditional video adapters (as distinguished by the DE-15 connector on the LCD's interface cable) must include the ability to reconvert the analog signal back to digital! We call such a display an *analog LCD display* (in spite of its digital nature).

FIGURE 5-7

DVI-I Dual Link, S-Video, and DE-15 connectors on a video adapter card

on the **job**

If you have a choice between VGA and DVI to connect a monitor to a computer, go with DVI. However, be aware that not all DVI is all-digital, as you'll learn in the upcoming "DVI" section.

SVGA   In the past two decades, video standards have advanced nearly as fast as CPU standards. *Super video graphics array (SVGA)* is a term that was first used for any video adapter or monitor that exceeded the VGA standard in resolution and color depth. But improvements to SVGA's early 800 × 600–pixel resolution led to resolutions of 1024 × 768, 1280 × 1024, 1600 × 1200, and 1680 × 1250. Although SVGA also supports a palette of 16 million colors, the amount of video memory present limits the number of colors SVGA can simultaneously display. This is also true of the newer digital video standards, which are designed to work with flat-panel LCD and other digital display devices, including Digital Visual Interface (DVI), High-Definition Multimedia Interface (HDMI), and DisplayPort.

DVI   Digital Video Interface (DVI) may be one term, but there are actually five different variations of it, each with its own pin arrangement on the connectors and each transmitting a different kind of signal. All standard DVI type connectors measure 1" by 3/8" with a variety of pin configurations, including one or two grids of pins and a flat blade off to the side of the pin grid area.

You should be able to distinguish the five variations by looking at a connector. Figure 5-8 provides the layouts.

FIGURE 5-8

DVI connector
pin layouts for
DVI-I, DVI-D,
and DVI-A

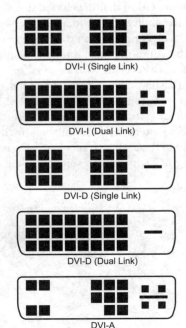

DVI-I (Single Link)

DVI-I (Dual Link)

DVI-D (Single Link)

DVI-D (Dual Link)

DVI-A

The digital mode of DVI, *DVI-D*, is partially compatible with HDMI (described later). A DVI-D connector is digital only and comes in two varieties called Single Link and Dual Link. The DVI-D Single Link connector has two 3 × 3 grids of 9 pins each, whereas the DVI-D Dual Link has a single 24-pin 3 × 8 grid. Dual Link doubles the bandwidth in the cable to support higher resolution video modes.

A *DVI-A* connector supports only analog signals, with four pins positioned around the blade to the side of the main pin grid area. It has two other groupings of pins: the first contains eight pins in a 3 × 3 grid (the ninth position is empty); the second group contains two sets of two pins with space between them.

DVI-I, or DVI-Integrated, supports both DVI-D and DVI-A signals and can control both digital and analog displays.

Depending on the exact implementation of DVI, it supports several screen resolutions and color densities. Common resolutions include 1920 × 1200 *Wide UXGA (WUXGA)* running at 60 Hz, 1280 × 1024 *Super XGA (SXGA)* running at 85 Hz, and 2560 × 1600 *Wide Quad XGA (WQXGA)* running at 60 Hz. There are several connector types to support these modes.

Be sure you recognize the pin compatibility issues with the various types of DVI connectors.

When connecting using any interface, you have to match this type of display with an adapter card with the appropriate connector. However, in the case of DVI, you also need to match the pins, because several different configurations of DVI connectors look alike until you compare them closely.

DVI-I is interchangeable, supporting either analog or digital signals. It also comes in Single Link and Dual Link versions. Both versions resemble their DVI-D counterparts, with the addition of the four pins around the blade to support analog mode.

Apple briefly used a smaller version of the DVI connector called a Mini-DVI, which they have since phased out. The Mini-DVI connector is about the same width as a standard USB connector, but is twice as thick, containing four rows of eight pins. Yet another miniaturized version, the Micro-DVI connector, was briefly used by ASUS and Apple. This DVI-D-compatible connector was almost the exact size of a USB connector.

HDMI   *High-Definition Multimedia Interface (HDMI)* is a relatively recent interface standard for use with devices that output high-definition digital video signals, such as DVD/Blu-ray players, *digital television (DTV)* players, set-top cable or satellite service boxes, camcorders, digital cameras, and other devices. It combines audio and video signals into an uncompressed signal and has a bandwidth of up to 10.2 Gbps. HDMI is integrated into many PCs, replacing DVI, and many home theater PCs (HTPCs) use this interface. Further, it supports a *digital rights management (DRM)* feature called *High-Bandwidth Digital Content Protection (HDCP)* to prevent illegal copying of Blu-ray discs. HDMI has added support for 3D video, as well as high-speed Ethernet communications.

HDMI is backward compatible with the DVI standard as implemented in PC video adapters and displays. Therefore, a DVI video adapter can control an HDMI monitor, provided an appropriate cable and converter are used. The audio and remote control features of HDMI, however, will not be available via a DVI video adapter, nor will 3D and Ethernet. One specially designed cable with an HDMI connector is all you need now between a compatible video device and the TV. Previously, several cables were required.

Five types of HDMI connectors are available: A, B, C, D, and E. Type A and Type B were part of the original specification, whereas Type C is defined in the 1.3 version of the specification, and Type D was defined in the 1.4 version. Type A is electrically compatible with DVI-D Single Link. Type B includes the same support as Type A, plus it supports very-high-resolution displays, such as WQUXGA (3840 × 2400). It is electrically compatible with DVI-D Dual Link.

Two types of HDMI connectors are designed for use in laptops and other small devices. The first is the Type C *Mini-HDMI* connector, defined by the version 1.3 standard. It has

FIGURE 5-9

An HDMI socket on a computer

the same 19 pins as a Type A connector but some changes in assignments. Figure 5-9 shows an HDMI socket for a Type C Mini-HDMI connector, and Figure 5-10 shows Type C Mini-HDMI connectors on a cable. The second connector for small devices is the Type D Micro-HDMI connector, introduced in the HDMI 1.4 specification. HDMI also introduced the Type E Automotive Connection System for use in video systems installed in cars. The Type E Automotive Connection system is both a cable and connector designed for the stresses placed on equipment installed in cars. The connector has a special locking mechanism to

FIGURE 5-10

Two Type C Mini-HDMI connectors on a cable

prevent it from working loose, but you will not see this connector on PCs, laptops, and other portable devices. Table 5-1 describes the HDMI Type A through D pins and plug dimensions.

Before any HDMI device or cable can display the HDMI logo, it must be licensed by HDMI Licensing, LLC, the licensing agent for the HDMI Founders. Look for this logo on any HDMI products. There are five HDMI cable types to match the various HDMI standards. Those standards include HDMI Standard, HDMI Standard with Ethernet, HDMI Standard Automotive, HDMI High Speed, and HDMI High Speed with Ethernet. Cables terminated with all but the B connector type have 19 wires, while those with B connectors have 29 wires. Most HDMI cables that you will encounter for computers and HDTV, the standard for digital high-definition TV, are rounded and about 1/4" thick.

TABLE 5-1	Connector Type	Number of Pins	Plug Dimensions
HDMI Connectors	A	19	13.9 mm × 4.45 mm approximately .5" × .18"
	B	29	21.2 mm × 4.45 mm approximately .8" × .18
	C (Mini-HDMI)	19	10.2 mm × 2.42 mm approximately .4" × .1"
	D (Micro-HDMI)	19	6.4 mm × 2.8 mm approximately .1" × .25"

DisplayPort   *DisplayPort*, a digital display interface standard developed by VESA, is the newest of the standards discussed here. Like HDMI, it supports both video and audio signals and contains HDCP copy protection. It is unique in that it is royalty-free to manufacturers and has some important proponents, such as Apple, Hewlett-Packard, AMD, Intel, and Dell. At first, industry experts observed that we did not need this standard after the wide acceptance of HDMI, but that changed after DisplayPort received a huge boost in the fall of 2008 when Apple introduced new MacBooks with DisplayPort replacing DVI. DisplayPort neither supports all the color options supported by HDMI, nor is it electrically compatible with DVI, whereas HDMI is backward compatible with DVI. DisplayPort also includes copy protection for DVDs in the form of DisplayPort Content Protection (DPCP).

At less than 1/4" thick, a DisplayPort cable is slimmer than those of its predecessor,

FIGURE 5-11

A Mini DisplayPort socket

and the connectors are much smaller and do not require thumbscrews like those on DVI plugs. Some manufacturers include both DisplayPort and HDMI in the same devices, evidenced by the presence of both connectors. DisplayPort comes in two sizes: standard and Mini DisplayPort. Figure 5-11 shows a Mini DisplayPort socket on a computer. Figure 5-12 shows a Mini DisplayPort connector on a cable end.

FIGURE 5-12

A Mini DisplayPort connector on a cable

Composite Video   The next time you watch television, take a close look at the image. You will notice variations in both brightness and color. The traditional transmission system for television video signals, called *composite video*, combines the color and brightness information with the synchronization data into one signal. While television sets have long used separate signals, called *luminance*—brightness, measured in units called *lumens*—and *chrominance* (color), they receive composite signals and have to separate out the luminance and chrominance information. Errors in separating the two signals from the composite signal result in on-screen problems, especially with complex images. Composite video uses a single RCA connector, usually yellow. It carries only video, not audio, so it is typically paired with white and red stereo audio plugs. It's typically found on low-end TV systems, and seldom seen on computer equipment.

Component Video   Component video splits the video display into three separate signals: red, green, and blue. Component video requires three separate, color-coded RCA cables. Component video was used on some CRT monitors a decade or more ago, because providing the red, green, and blue data separately for each of the CRT's electron guns increased the rate at which data could be sent. However, component video is seldom seen anymore on modern computer equipment. You'll still find it on some standard-definition television equipment.

Screen Resolution and Color Depth

As fast as new standards are developed and adopted by manufacturers, they are modified and improved upon. Table 5-2 gives a summary of screen resolution and color depth typical of the listed video standards. There are additional standards available, particularly those starting with "W," which apply to widescreen monitors. Keep in mind the best resolution and color depth you will see on your display depends on the capabilities of both the video adapter and display and, increasingly, the aspect ratio of the screen. Widescreen monitors have different resolutions, which are expressed in columns and rows, as in 1920 columns by 1200 rows. We will discuss aspect ratio, refresh rates, and other display features later in this chapter in the sections "Display Types" and "Display Settings."

Miscellaneous Connectors and Cables

In this section, we'll describe several connector types listed under 901 exam objective 1.11 that are not associated with the technologies detailed so far. Then we'll look at some basic cable types that you will encounter when working with computers.

RCA   *RCA connectors* have been around for a long time. They consist of a coaxial plug with an outer shield. The center plug goes into the socket, while the shield slides around the outside of the socket completing the connection. Figure 5-13 shows an RCA Y-adapter. Used to connect audio components for decades, they have connected video components for many years as well. They are inexpensive, and you can buy them anywhere. Better quality ones are gold plated.

TABLE 5-2   A Selection of Video Standards and Their Resolution, Color Palette, and Color Depth

Name	Maximum Graphics Resolution	Number of Colors in Palette	Number of Colors Displayed Simultaneously in Standard Color Depth
Video Graphics Array (VGA)	640 × 480	Over 16 million	16
eXtended Graphics Array (XGA), an IBM standard	1024 × 768	Over 16 million	256 or 65,536
Extended Video Graphics Array (EVGA), a VESA standard	1024 × 768	Over 16 million	256 or 65,536
Super Video Graphics Array (SVGA)	1600 × 1200	Over 16 million	Over 16 million*
Super XGA (SXGA)	1280 × 1024	Over 16 million	Over 16 million*
Super XGA Plus (SXGA+)	1400 × 1050	Over 16 million	Over 16 million*
Ultra XGA (UXGA)	1600 × 1200	Over 16 million	Over 16 million*
Wide UXGA (WUXGA)	1920 × 1200 (widescreen)	Over 16 million	Over 16 million*
Wide Quad XGA (WQXGA)	2560 × 1600 (widescreen)	Over 16 million	Over 16 million
Wide Quad UXGA (WQUXGA)	3840 × 2400 (widescreen)	Over 16 million	Over 16 million

*The actual number of simultaneous colors depends on the video adapter and the amount of video memory installed.

BNC   The acronym BNC used for this connector is the subject of some debate. It may stand for "Bayonet-Neill-Concelman" or "British Naval Connector." *BNC connectors* attach coaxial cables to BNC ports. The cable connector is round and has a twist-lock mechanism to keep the cable in place. BNC connectors have a protruding pin that corresponds to a receiver socket in the port.

Mini-DIN-6 Connectors   *DIN connectors* get their name from Deutsche Industrie Norm, Germany's standards organization. Most (but not all) DIN connectors are round with a circle or semicircle of pins. The mini-DIN connector, or more accurately, the *mini-DIN-6* connector, gets its name from the fact that it is smaller than the original *DIN-6* keyboard connector found on early PCs. Mini-DIN connectors commonly connected mice and keyboards prior to USB becoming the default interface for those components. Because these connectors first appeared on IBM's Personal System/2 (PS/2) computers in the 1980s, mini-DIN connectors are also known as PS/2 connectors. Figure 5-14 shows two mini-DIN-6 connectors at the top of the back panel of a PC, one for a keyboard and another for a mouse. You won't find these on new PCs today.

FIGURE 5-14

The back panel
of a PC showing
two mini-DIN-6
connectors at
the top

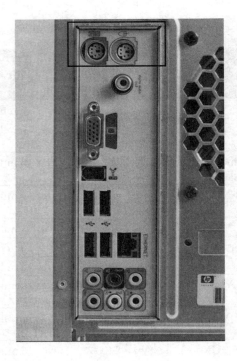

Cable Basics: What's Inside a Cable?   A wide variety of cables physically connect computer components and networks. These cables carry electronic signals for power, control of devices, and data. But what's inside these cables? The basic cable types you will encounter are straight pair, twisted pair, multicore twisted pair, fiber optic, and coaxial. A *straight-pair cable* consists of one or more metal wires surrounded by a plastic insulating sheath. A *twisted-pair cable* consists of two sheathed metal wires twisted around each other along the entire length of the cable to avoid electrical interference, with a plastic covering sheath surrounding it. A *multicore twisted-pair cable* has multiple pairs of twisted wires, but in practice even the multicore twisted pair is simply called "twisted pair." A *fiber-optic cable* has a core made of one or more optical fiber strands surrounded by a protective cladding, which is in turn reinforced by strength fibers; all of this is enclosed in an outer jacket. Fiber-optic cable carries light pulses rather than electrical signals, so it is not susceptible to electromagnetic interference (EMI). A *coaxial cable* contains a single copper wire, surrounded by at least one insulating layer, a woven wire shield that provides both physical and electrical protection, and an outer jacket. Figure 5-15 displays these five basic cable types. We will revisit the use of various cables in future chapters.

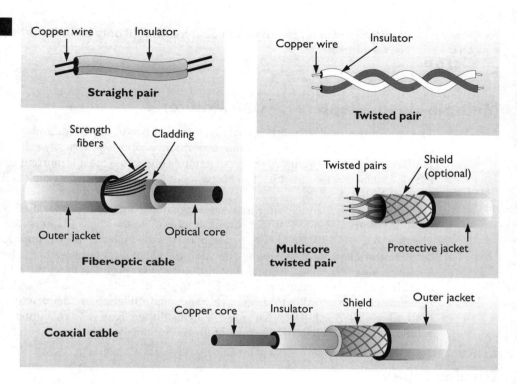

FIGURE 5-15

Common cable types used to connect computer components and networks

Straight pair — Copper wire, Insulator

Twisted pair — Copper wire, Insulator

Fiber-optic cable — Strength fibers, Cladding, Outer jacket, Optical core

Multicore twisted pair — Twisted pairs, Shield (optional), Protective jacket

Coaxial cable — Copper core, Insulator, Shield, Outer jacket

Multiple Displays

For some years, people who work with simultaneously open multiple documents or who have large spreadsheet or image requirements have used *multi-monitor* configurations that extend the desktop to two or more displays. People in certain jobs, such as engineering, stock day trading, and software development, use multiple monitors on one computer. Multi-monitors previously required expensive hardware and special software, but today it is easy to have two or more monitors. These days a "dual-headed" video adapter won't break most budgets, and with the correct drivers, a modern operating system manages the image placement. Today's video adapters, which have large amounts of dedicated RAM available, manage these tasks without taking a big performance hit. Monitors can be analog, digital, or both, depending on the video adapter. Laptops have long supported two monitors, but for many years the second monitor was a replacement for the laptop display—something a user attached to a laptop while in the office. Once operating systems supported multiple displays, people caught on to using the desktop monitor, not as a replacement, but as an extension of the built-in monitor.

Multi-monitor is also known as dual-monitor (if only two), multi-display, and even multi-head.

Multiple Video Adapters for One Monitor

The opposing model to multi-monitor is the use of two or more video adapters to drive one display to improve video graphics performance. This is generically called a *multi-GPU solution*, because the graphics processing unit is one of the most important components of the video adapter. Two manufacturers stand out for their proprietary multi-GPU systems: ATI and NVIDIA.

Although each manufacturer has several possible configurations for their multi-GPU solutions, both now offer a direct connection between the video adapters that are working together in a PC. This direct connection bypasses the PCIe bus for communications between the adapters, thus avoiding an additional load on the shared bus. The ATI solution is commonly called *CrossFire*, and the third-generation products carry the ATI CrossFireX or AMD CrossFireX brand name. The NVIDIA multi-GPU solution is branded *Scalable Link Interface (SLI)*. In addition to specific video adapter models, both manufacturers require motherboards with chipsets that support their solution. Expect to encounter multi-GPU solutions in systems that must render high-performance graphics.

Display Types

The function of a PC video *display* device is to produce visual responses to user requests. Often called simply a display or *monitor*, it receives computer output from the video adapter, which controls its functioning. The display technology—which you have already learned about—must match the technology of the video card to which it attaches, so in this section we will explore types of displays and display settings. Until a few years ago, most desktop computers used CRT monitors, but today flat-panel displays (FPDs) are inexpensive and universally available. This is true both for computer displays and for televisions.

CRTs

A *CRT monitor* is bulky because of the large cathode ray tube it contains. A CRT uses an electron gun to activate phosphors behind the screen. Each pixel on the monitor has the ability to generate red, green, or blue, depending on the signals it receives. This combination of colors results in the display you see on the monitor. CRT monitors are obsolete, but there are a few still in use. CRTs have extremely high-voltage capacitors inside, so do not open a CRT for any reason. If a CRT is malfunctioning, dispose of it.

Flat-Panel Displays

A *flat-panel display (FPD)* is a computer display that has a form that is very thin—many are thinner than 1/2" and take up far less desk space (at least front to back) than the traditional CRT displays. Some of the newer FPDs go beyond the standard two-dimensional images, offering *three-dimensional (3D)* images with realistic depth that require HDMI video adapters that can output the 3D video signals. Let's look at FPD technologies, which are common to both computer displays and TVs.

LCD Displays An *LCD* and a *light-emitting diode (LED) display* are both actually types of LCDs because each has a layer of liquid crystal molecules, called subpixels, sandwiched between polarizing filters, that are backlit when the display is powered on. The biggest difference between LCD and LED displays is the backlight source. In an LCD display, the source is one or more *cold cathode fluorescent lamps (CCFLs)*, a type of lamp that provides a bright light but is energy efficient and long-lasting. On the other hand, the light source in an LED panel is a grid of many tiny light bulbs called *light-emitting diodes*, positioned behind the glass enclosing the liquid crystals. When power is applied to the diodes, the bulbs glow. In the following discussion, references to LCD will apply to both backlighting methods, unless we specify one or the other. When necessary to make the distinction, an LED backlit display will be referred to as an *LED-lit LCD*.

In a color LCD display, the individual molecules of liquid crystal are called *subpixels*. A see-through film in front of the crystal liquid consists of areas colored red, green, and blue. Each cluster of this trio of colors makes up a *physical pixel*. Images and colors are created by charging subpixels within the physical pixels.

An LCD display requires less than half the wattage of a comparably sized CRT. Add to this the power-saving features built into displays, such as the features defined by VESA's *Display Power-Management Signaling (DPMS)* standard. Rather than needing to turn off a display manually when you leave your desk or are not using the computer, DPMS-compliant displays automatically go into a lower power mode after a preconfigured amount of time without any activity.

LCD Technologies The most common technology for an LCD monitor is twisted nematic (TN). This was the first type of LCD panel widely produced. LCD monitors are thin, clear, and inexpensive to produce, and support higher refresh rates than IPS (discussed next), but they can suffer from uneven backlighting, motion blur, limited viewing angles, poor viewing in sunlight, and input lag.

In-Plane Switching (IPS) is a newer technology that improves viewing angles and color reproduction. The contrast ratio (explained in the next section) is also better, and the color accuracy is good. However, the response rate and maximum refresh rate is not as good as TN. Therefore, IPS monitors are more suitable for graphic design than for game playing.

A Vertical Alignment (VA) panel is a compromise between TN and IPS, offering advantages of both. VA panels support higher refresh rates, like TN panels, but support the higher color reproduction and better brightness and viewing angles of IPS.

LCD Contrast Ratio *Contrast ratio*, the difference in value between a display's brightest white and darkest black, is an area in which the early LCD displays could not compete with CRTs. Today, however, even inexpensive LCD and LED displays offer a dynamic contrast ratio of 3000:1 or a static contrast ratio of 800:1 or greater, which is excellent.

Display Aspect Ratio The *aspect ratio* is the proportion of the width to the height. For instance, a traditional CRT monitor has a width-to-height aspect ratio of 4:3. LCD panels come in the traditional 4:3 aspect ratio as well as in wider formats, of which the most common is 16:9, which allows you to view wide-format movies. Less common but sometimes seen is 16:10.

When viewing a widescreen movie video on a 4:3 display, it shows in a *letterbox*, meaning the image size reduces until the entire width of the image fits on the screen. The remaining portions of the screen are black, creating a box effect. Figure 5-16 shows an LCD display with a 16:9 aspect ratio.

OLED Yet another type of thin display technology uses *organic light-emitting diode (OLED)*, which does not require backlighting. OLED diodes use organic compounds for the electroluminescence. There are *passive-matrix OLED (PMOLED)* displays and *active-matrix OLED (AMOLED)* displays. A PMOLED display panel relies strictly on the electroluminescent layer to light the screen and does not use a *thin-film transistor (TFT)*

FIGURE 5-16

An LCD display with a 16:9 aspect ratio

backplane, as does an AMOLED. OLED screens are found in a wide range of devices from smartphones and tablets to computer displays and TVs. Samsung calls their version of AMOLED technology *Super AMOLED Plus*, and uses this in the display on many products, including the Galaxy Tab, which has a high-resolution 1280 × 800, 7.7" screen. Presently, the organic materials in OLED displays degrade over time, making this technology more appropriate for devices that are not powered on for several hours a day, but intermittently turned on, as with a smartphone or tablet.

Plasma Displays   *Plasma display* technology is offered mostly for HDTVs, although today a TV usually can double as a computer display by simply cabling the computer and TV. Plasma HDTV sizes begin at about 32" due to the large pixel size.

Much like the difference between LCD and LED displays, plasma displays have yet another method for lighting the screen: they use phosphorous cells in place of liquid crystals, and the phosphors do not require backlighting. Plasma displays are also less expensive than LED displays. The downside to plasma displays is that they are generally thicker and require more power to run. Previously, plasma displays had better image quality when subjected to careful testing, but tests on recent LED-lit LCDs, especially in HDTVs, have shown better image quality compared to plasma displays. Plasma displays have a wide viewing angle.

Projectors

A *projector* takes video output and projects it onto a screen for viewing by a larger audience. Most digital projectors pass the light from a high-intensity bulb through an LCD panel to project an image on a screen. There are also projectors that use *digital light processing (DLP)* chips that yield a larger, brighter image, and small projectors that use LEDs or lasers. DLP projectors are also used in rear-projection televisions. Projector brightness is measured in *lumens*. Projectors that offer higher lumen levels tend to cost more and project better at large sizes.

Digital projectors have been available for years, but they were bulky and expensive. Today the prices of projectors have dropped to the point where they are usable as TVs because they can use video as well as digital sources. Their physical size has dropped as well, and now some tiny digital projectors fit in the palm of your hand and can be used with a laptop computer for presentations to small groups. They are available in many video modes, including XGA, SVGA, WXGA, and SXGA, among others. Add to this built-in support in Windows operating systems and the ability to network these devices by name or IP address, and you have a very popular device.

Touch Screens

A *touch screen* is a video display that allows you to select and maneuver screen objects by touching, tapping, and sliding your finger or a stylus on the screen, making a touch screen an input device, as well as an output device. Touch-screen technology was developed in the late 1960s, appeared on special-use systems as early as the 1970s, and continued to be popular for use in kiosk-based computer systems. Touch screens for personal computers have been around almost as long as personal computers, but have never enjoyed a great deal of popularity for general use. Today's touch screens are so improved over those of 20 years ago that there is very little resemblance. They are now found on many handheld devices, such as smartphones like the Android and the Apple iPhone, global positioning system (GPS) navigation systems, electronic reading devices, and the increasingly popular tablets, such as the Apple iPad and Samsung Galaxy models. New touch-screen devices accept many more subtle gestures than previously.

Screen Filters (Privacy and Antiglare)

There are several types of screen filters, all of which are translucent and often made of a plastic film placed over a display screen. An *antiglare filter* reduces the glare created by light coming from the display backlight, while an *antireflective filter* blocks ambient light that would bounce off the screen. A *privacy screen filter* provides privacy from onlookers attempting to see your confidential information by viewing it over your shoulder by reducing the viewable angle for the display. On a TV a wide viewing angle is a desirable feature, but you may not want people to be able to see your screen while you are entering a password or working on a confidential document while sitting in a coffee shop or airport. Some screen filters fulfill more than one purpose, and manufacturers such as 3M have screen filters to fit almost any screen—desktop, laptop, or handheld.

Display Settings

Some settings are only available from a special menu built into your display. This menu is independent of your operating system, and you access it through buttons mounted on the monitor, as long as the monitor is powered up, regardless of the presence or absence of a PC. Other settings are accessible from within the Display settings in Windows. You will want to locate this in your version of Windows and search for these settings as you read through the following sections. In Windows 7 and newer, simply open the Start menu, type **display** in the Search box, and then press the ENTER key. You will then have to search for

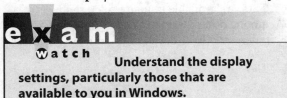

Understand the display settings, particularly those that are available to you in Windows.

the individual settings. You can also right-click the desktop and choose Personalize to access display settings in Windows Vista, and then click Display Settings. You can access the screen resolution settings directly by right-clicking and choosing Screen Resolution (Windows 7 and 8) or Display Settings (Windows 10).

Vertical Position/Horizontal Position

The built-in menu on an LCD display will have the *vertical position* setting, which adjusts the viewable area of the display vertically, and the *horizontal position* setting, which adjusts the viewable area of the display horizontally.

Display Resolution

Display resolution is the displayable number of pixels. A CRT display may easily support several different display resolutions, so if you have a CRT, you can play with this setting, along with others, until you have the most comfortable combination of resolution, color depth, and refresh rate. On an LCD display, however, you should keep this setting at the *native resolution* of the display, which is the number of physical pixels, horizontally and vertically, such as 1920 × 1080, beyond which it cannot operate. In addition, if you set a display at a lower resolution, the image degrades. For this reason, always set an LCD display at its native resolution, as stated on the box and in the display documentation. It is usually the highest available resolution in the Windows Display applet and is labeled "recommended," as shown in Figure 5-17. Also, notice that this is a dual-display system, and the resolution shown is for the display on the left.

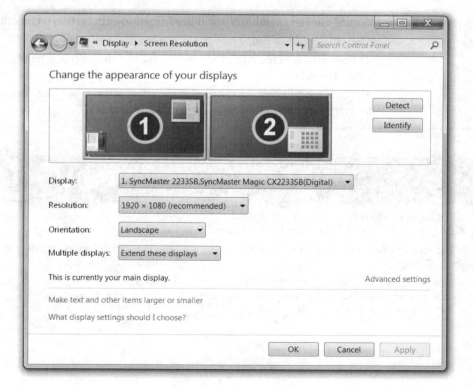

FIGURE 5-17

The Screen Resolution page of the Windows 7 Display applet

The 1920 × 1080 pixel screen resolution is the screen resolution of an HDTV. It is also shown as *1080p*.

Color Quality

The Colors setting refers to the number of bits used to describe the color of each pixel. Also called *color depth*, this setting may be expressed in terms of 16 bits or 32 bits. In modern Windows versions, 32-bit is the standard color depth. Exercise 5-3 will walk you through the steps for locating the color quality setting in Windows 7.

EXERCISE 5-3

Check Out the Color Quality Setting in Windows 7

1. Open the Start menu, type **display** in the Search box, select the Display result, and press the ENTER key.
2. Click Adjust Resolution to open the Screen Resolution page.
3. Locate the Advanced Settings link near the lower right, and click this link.
4. Click the Monitor tab.
5. At the bottom of the Monitor tab page, notice the spin box labeled Colors and click to see the selections.
6. You can experiment with changing the color setting, but be sure to set it back to your preferred setting.

SCENARIO & SOLUTION	
What aspect ratio is desirable on a flat-panel display intended for viewing wide-format videos?	16:9
What resolution should you always use on an LCD display?	The native resolution, which is the highest resolution available
When shopping for a digital projector, what factor should you consider if you plan on projecting onto a very large screen in a big auditorium?	Lumens

CERTIFICATION OBJECTIVE

■ *901: 1.12 Install and configure common peripheral devices*

This section defines the types of peripheral devices listed in 901 exam objective 1.12.

Installing and Configuring Peripheral Devices

Although the processor is the central component of a PC, it would not have anything to process without input, and that processing doesn't do any good unless you can get it out of the computer some way—output. Therefore, it is fair to say that computers are all about input and output—both within the system box and between the system box and a variety of external devices. The term *input/output (I/O)* covers both types of these interactions and the various devices that must connect to a computer for the users' interaction.

Examples of common input devices include the keyboard and any pointing device (mouse, trackball, pen, etc.). Data can also be input from devices that also take output, such as storage devices and network cards. The most common output devices are the display, sound card, and printer. Less common I/O devices include bar code readers, biometric devices, touch screens, and KVM switches. Today's computers come with a variety of connectors to internal interfaces to accommodate a huge selection of peripheral devices.

You have already learned about display interfaces and connectors, so we will begin with installing displays. Then we'll describe how to install the most common input devices as well as the various classic multimedia devices and the interfaces used for I/O peripherals. You will learn about installing printers in Chapter 21.

Installing Displays

An easy and satisfying PC upgrade is a new, larger, and better-quality display. In most cases, this will not require replacing the video adapter, since even inexpensive video adapters in recently manufactured PCs provide excellent output at high resolutions. In addition, many PC tasks are so much easier with two displays. Therefore, you might not be replacing a display, but augmenting it with a second display so that you can spread your on-screen work across the real estate of two displays.

Removing a Display

In order to remove a display, power down the computer and the display, unplug the display from the power outlet, and disconnect the display data cable from the computer.

Installing a Single Display

In order to install a display, simply attach the display's cable to the proper connector on the computer and plug in the power cord. Then power up both the display and the computer. Windows will normally recognize a display and install an appropriate driver if one is needed. Some digital displays come with a disc containing utilities or drivers to access advanced features. Once the display is connected and the driver installed, take a look at the display settings discussed earlier in this chapter, and check out the resolution and color quality.

A CRT, being analog, doesn't require or use a driver. However, some CRTs came with "driver" discs containing information files (.inf extension). These information files let the operating system know the monitor's maximum resolution and refresh rate settings so it could set the limits appropriately in the OS.

Installing Multiple Displays on a Single PC

As for a multi-monitor configuration, most laptops come with the ability to support both the built-in screen and an external display, but a desktop PC normally has a video adapter with just one connector, supporting a single display. Therefore, to add a second display (or more) to a PC, you will need to install additional video adapters. Most motherboards have only one PCIe x16 slot, though, so the additional video adapters will need to fit into slots with lesser throughput, like PCIe x4 or x1. For this reason, it is often better to replace the PC's single-output video adapter with a video adapter that has multiple monitor connectors, so two monitors can run off the faster PCIe x16 bus. If the PC's primary video adapter is built into the motherboard, you won't be able to replace it; just add another video adapter in the fastest slot available.

Once the adapter is installed, connect to each of the two displays exactly as you would connect to one, and power up after everything has been connected. Then, using the disc that came with the new video adapter, run the setup program. After that you will need to go into the Control Panel in Windows and configure one of the monitors to be the main monitor and the other one (or more) to have the desktop extend onto it. If you don't extend the desktop onto the second monitor, the two monitors will simply display the exact same thing.

Once you extend the desktop, the main monitor will contain the taskbar and desktop icons, while the other will contain any windows or objects you wish to place there. Figure 5-17 in the previous section shows a dual display configuration in the Screen Resolution page of the Windows 7 Screen Resolution section of the Control Panel.

In Windows 8, there is also another way to control multiple monitors. You can display the Charms bar and click Devices | Project | Second Screen | Extend.

Installing Touch Screen Displays

A touch screen will take just a few more steps to connect and install on a PC. First, we are assuming you have a free-standing PC and wish to install a retail touch screen display, rather than convert a conventional display to a touch screen display. Most touch screen monitors will have two interfaces—a standard video connector for the video output to the screen, and a USB connector for the input from the touch screen component of the monitor. Before you purchase a touch screen, be sure the interfaces will work with the computers to which you will connect them. Connect the cables, power up the display and computer, and then install the device drivers.

Some models of touch screen displays require a reboot after installing the drivers. With a conventional display, your job would be done at this point, but with a touch screen display, you still need to calibrate it. Run the calibration program that comes with the display. It will require that you perform several tasks, touching the screen at specific spots, to enable the touch screen interface to line itself up with the images on the screen. After calibration, test the programs you wish to use on this computer. If you are not happy with the results, run the calibration program again. If it still is not satisfactory, you may need to contact the manufacturer to see if a driver upgrade is available.

Selecting Input Devices

An input device sends signals into a computer. The two most common input devices are the keyboard and a pointing device, such as a mouse. In retail settings, and any other venue in which it is important to control inventory, specialized scanners called bar code readers are a very common input device. Devices used where a retail sale occurs, such as at a checkout stand, are often categorized as *point of sale (PoS)* devices. And multimedia devices, which were once optional for desktop and laptop computers, are now ubiquitous on consumer-grade computers. An output device, such as a display, printer, or even a sound card, receives outgoing data from a computer. Most of the devices detailed here are input devices, with the exception of audio devices.

Keyboards

For the vast majority of PC users, the *keyboard* is their primary input device for entering numbers, letters, and symbols. There are several types of keyboards, including 84- and 101-key designs. Newer keyboards might include a variety of additional keys for accessing the Internet, using Microsoft Windows, and performing other common functions. Some keyboards even include a pointing device, such as a mouse or touch pad.

There are also several keyboard layouts. The keyset on an ergonomic keyboard's physical form factor (see Figure 5-18) is split in half and each half slants outward to provide a more relaxed, natural hand position. The layout of the keys themselves can also vary, regardless of the form factor. Typical English-language keyboards (even ergonomic keyboards) have a QWERTY layout (see Figure 5-19), named after the first six letters on the second row of the keyboard. The Dvorak keyboard has an entirely different key layout (also shown in Figure 5-19), and allows for faster typing speeds. Unfortunately, the Dvorak keyboard has not been widely adopted. Accurately learning and using both layouts is exceptionally difficult, so most people stick to the old QWERTY standby that they learned in school.

FIGURE 5-18

An ergonomic keyboard has a different structure from a conventional keyboard.

FIGURE 5-19

QWERTY and Dvorak keyboard layouts

QWERTY

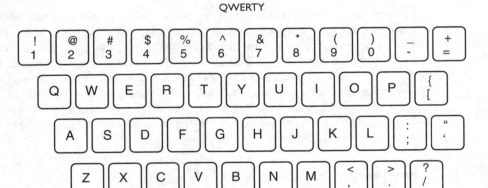

Dvorak

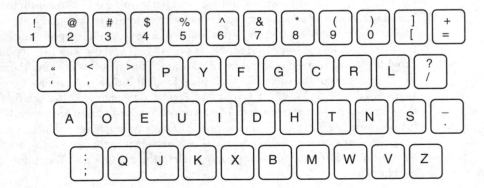

Pointing Devices

A *pointing device* is used to manipulate a pointer and other items on the computer display for input. The *mouse* is by far the most popular pointing device. Users learn mouse operations quickly; the movement of a mouse over a surface translates into the movement of the pointer across the screen. Two or more buttons on the mouse allow the user to perform various operations such as selecting items and running programs. Another popular pointing device is the *trackball*, a device that is generally larger than a mouse but remains stationary, so it requires less desk space. The user moves the pointer by rolling a ball mounted in the trackball device. A trackball will also have buttons that you use like the buttons on a mouse.

The *touchpad* on a notebook PC is a touch-sensitive panel that you can move your finger across to move the mouse onscreen. External touchpads are also available, so you can add touchpad capability to a desktop or tablet (provided it has the right input port and the OS will accept the driver for it).

Installing Keyboards and Pointing Devices

Very old keyboards and mice have mini-DIN-6 (PS/2) connectors, while newer ones have USB connectors. Most keyboards and mice will work without the need for add-on device drivers. The standard mouse and keyboard drivers installed with the operating system will be sufficient. To access nonstandard keyboard and mouse features, or to use one of many other types of pointing devices, you will need to install and configure a device driver in Windows and sometimes in a special application. See the section "Installing USB Devices," later in the chapter, for instructions on installing a USB keyboard or mouse.

Some keyboards and mice come with one of the short-range wireless radio frequency (RF) interfaces that we will describe in Chapter 14. The most common is Bluetooth, and a less common one today is infrared (IR). Bluetooth and infrared require a transceiver device attached to the computer—usually via USB—unless the transceiver is built in, which is often the case with laptops and tablets. An important difference between using a Bluetooth device and an infrared device is that with Bluetooth, you are primarily concerned about keeping the device and receiver within the appropriate distance for the signal. With infrared, line-of-sight is as important as proximity because the infrared signal must not be blocked by anything in its way.

Joysticks

A *joystick* is an input device that has a slender gimbaled stick that can move around a single axis in two dimensions, allowing the user to move a computer's cursor or other graphical objects around the screen. As input devices for computer games go, the joystick is the oldest, showing up on the old commercial game consoles, such as *Pac-Man* and others seen in bars and game rooms, before the PC appeared in our homes and offices. The joystick also owes both its functional movements and name to aviation, since that was the name given to an airplane's control stick decades before it showed up on game consoles. A joystick is the basic accessory for using Microsoft's venerable *Flight Simulator*. A modern computer joystick will have several controls on it, including a trigger, switches, and various configurable buttons.

A joystick will connect to a PC either via USB or wirelessly. Read the manufacturer's instruction before installing either type. The later section "Installing USB Devices" gives general directions. For a wireless device—either Bluetooth or infrared—you will need to install a receiver that will usually connect to the computer via USB. Again, follow the manufacturer's instructions for installing the receiver. Then you will need to install the software for controlling the device and configure any programmable buttons—either through the joystick's software or through the gaming software.

Game Pads

A *game pad* is a much more elaborate computer game control device than a joystick, although one or more joysticks will usually be included in the gamepad, along with programmable buttons and directional pads. Many gamepads also provide feedback in the form of vibration. Connecting a gamepad is much like connecting and configuring a joystick.

Motion Sensors

A *motion sensor* allows a user to control the computer with hand gestures. The Leap controller, made by Leap Motion, is the best known of these. It plugs into a USB port, and has its own software that enables you to use a hand or finger in the air as a pointing device. In 2014, the company introduced an update that can work with a virtual reality headset such as the Oculus Rift. Installation is simple; just plug it into a USB port and run the included setup software.

Digitizers

A *digitizer* (a.k.a. a *drawing tablet* or *digitizing tablet*) is a touch-sensitive input device with a surface that responds to input from a finger, stylus, light pen, or other pointing device. The tiny touchpad on a laptop is a form of digitizer, and recent laptop touchpads accept the many gestures of the latest touch screens. But when we speak of a digitizer we usually are referring to the type of digitizer used by engineers, artists, and designers to create elaborate drawings and schematics. It is usually an external device that connects to a computer via USB or Bluetooth, and it converts analog data to digital data, the analog data being the lines traced across the surface of the tablet with a pointing device. A digitizer tablet may be pressure sensitive to thousands of levels and sense the tilt angle of a pen or stylus, produce high-resolution drawings, and may come with several interchangeable nibs for the stylus. Digitizers come in formats measuring from several inches square to very large formats such as 2' × 3' and 3' × 4'. Figure 5-20 shows a Wacom digitizer, called a pen tablet, with an overall size of approximately 12" × 8" and with a tablet surface measuring 7" × 5". This one also has ten spare nibs that allow you to produce different drawing effects.

FIGURE 5-20

A small digitizer
with stylus and
spare nibs

After installing the drivers for a digitizer and connecting it, you will need to calibrate it, much as you calibrate a touch screen. The installation program will take you through the calibration process.

Bar Code and Smart Card Readers

On nearly every item you buy, every package you ship, and membership card you carry, there is a small rectangular image with a unique pattern of black bars and white space. This is a *bar code*, which contains information appropriate to the type of use and can be optically scanned and interpreted by computer software. On product packaging, a bar code will contain vendor, inventory, and pricing information. On your library card, it will identify you as a registered user. A *bar code reader* is a device used to optically scan the bar code. The design of the reader must match the type of code on the item it scans in order to interpret it. The bar code reader uses a laser beam to measure the thicknesses of the lines and spaces. This information is converted to digital data and transferred to a computer. At the grocery store, the computer is in the cash register, which tallies up your total and sends inventory information to a central computer.

There are various types of bar code readers, so select the reader that best meets your needs. The most common readers that you will encounter for PCs are handheld scanners and stationary scanners, such as those you see in retail stores.

To install a USB bar code scanner, follow the instructions for installing a USB device provided in the "Installing USB Devices" section, later in the chapter.

A *smart card* is a plastic card (like a credit card or an ID badge) with a built-in microprocessor or memory, used for storing personal identification, financial transactions, or other data. Many credit cards also have chips on them that make them "smart cards."

To access the data on a smart card, you need a smart card reader. These readers can be contact readers, such as machines you swipe or insert cards in, or contactless readers that sense the proximity of nearby smart cards and read their data. Card readers are available that interface with PCs to process the data from smart cards. These card readers come with their own setup applications and most models plug into USB ports.

Scanners

A *scanner* is a device that can optically examine a piece of paper and create a bitmap image of what it sees in full color or in black and white. In some small scanners you pass the scanner over the paper slowly to get an image, but most scanners are able to scan an entire page of text. The form factor of flatbed scanners lets you lay the paper to scan on the glass plate, close the cover (usually called a platen) on the paper, and press the scan button. Some flatbed scanners open up so you can scan a thick object such as a book. Multifunction devices generally include a scanner with a document feeder, a printer, and a fax machine in one box. Many multifunction devices are able to scan one side of the paper and then automatically turn the paper over to scan the other side. The latest scanners are able to simultaneously scan both sides of a page very rapidly, up to 20 pages a minute, or three seconds per page, and their document feeders let you insert many pages at a time, even ones of different sizes, for automatic scanning.

Install a scanner per the manufacturer's instructions, paying close attention to whether the driver must be installed before or after connecting and powering up the scanner.

Modern scanners support the Microsoft Scan Service (WS-Scan) protocol, and that's how they communicate with Windows and its applications. However, older scanners may instead conform to the *TWAIN* set of standards (this is not an acronym) for scanners and cameras, and is often called a "TWAIN driver."

Optional *optical character recognition (OCR)* software allows scanned text to be converted into editable text in a word processor. Your computer sees a scanned image as a graphic bitmap image, which is fine for a photo or other image, but when the scanned image is of a printed page and you want to be able to edit the document, you will need OCR software to interpret the pattern of dots in the image as alphanumeric characters. There are several very good OCR software programs to convert a scanned bitmap image to editable text. Your scanner may or may not come with one.

Multimedia

A variety of multimedia input devices are available for PCs. The short list includes Web video cameras, digital still cameras, MIDI devices, microphones.

Cameras

The most common type of camera attached to a PC is a *Web camera*, or *Webcam*. This type of digital video camera broadcasts video images (usually live) over the Internet. A Webcam is an inexpensive and easy-to-use addition to a PC that provides a visual component for meetings and other business communications, as well as entertainment and security functions.

A handheld *digital video camera*, as opposed to a Webcam, does not spend its useful life tethered to a computer, but only connects to a computer to transfer its digital video files to the PC for review, editing, and distribution by the user.

A *digital camera* is a camera type that has taken the world by storm, replacing film-based cameras for amateur photographers, as well as for many professional photographers. Today, most digital cameras have some limited video capability. Like the digital video camera, a digital still camera spends much of its time detached from a PC, connecting only to upload digital photographs or movies to the computer to be reviewed, modified, and printed.

The most common interface for a digital camera or Webcam is USB, but some higher-end models may use IEEE 1394 (FireWire). The images or videos stored on the camera may be stored on a flash card. You can connect the camera directly to a computer to read data from it like you would any external drive, or you can remove the flash card and read the data using a card reader.

MIDI

The Musical Instrument Digital Interface (MIDI) is a standard for connecting electronic musical instruments, such as a synthesizer keyboard, to computers or among themselves. This allows musicians to input their music for mixing and to convert it to musical notation. Modern MIDI devices have USB connectors, and therefore, you will normally need to install the driver before connecting the MIDI device to a USB port on the computer.

Sound Output

Sound is generated by a *sound card* and output to a sound device, such as a set of speakers or a pair of headphones. Sound cards normally have connectors for both types of devices. The classic connector for these devices is the 1/8" single-pin mini-audio connector, but some handheld devices use the 3/32" single-pin submini audio connector. They come in both mono and stereo versions. The mono version will have a single black ring around the front end of the pin, and the stereo version will have two black rings. If you are connecting a CD or DVD player to an amplifier or speaker, you will need the consumer version of the Sony/Philips Digital Interface Format (S/P DIF). Simply insert the correct connector firmly into the socket.

Microphones

As a PC input peripheral, a microphone gives a remote meeting attendee a voice at the meeting, and the latest voice recognition programs allow a user to dictate entire documents with a very low error rate. A microphone typically connects to a PC's sound card using a mini-audio connector.

Installing Multimedia Devices

Most multimedia devices are fairly simple to connect and use. Many multimedia devices, such as Webcams, digital cameras, and MIDI, often use a USB interface, which usually requires that you install the device driver before attaching the device to a USB port, as described later in the section "Installing USB Devices." Microphones or headsets only need to be connected to the correct port(s) and do not usually require a special device driver.

Video capture cards can take a bit more work to install. These cards are available as bus cards (PCI or PCIe) and as USB devices. However, the bus cards are generally less expensive and have more features than the USB devices. If you decide on a bus card, you will install it like most other adapter cards. Either interface will require a special driver and software. Follow the instructions that come with the card. For a bus card, you will normally install the drivers and software after the physical installation. The software that comes with the device may install as part of the driver installation, or you may need to initiate that install. Once the software is installed, shut down the computer and connect the device to the appropriate TV input, whether cable TV, satellite TV, or broadcast TV. The types of cables you will need depend on the input. For instance, coaxial cable is used for cable TV, while composite or component cables are used for other inputs.

Smart TVs and Set-Top Boxes

Now that TVs and home theater equipment are increasingly "smart" (meaning they have built-in computing capabilities such as CPU, RAM, and storage), the natural next step is to connect them to PCs and networks. Most modern high-definition digital TVs can connect to a PC via HDMI cable, so you can use the TV as a large-screen monitor for the PC.

If the TV has an Ethernet port or Wi-Fi support, you can also connect it to your local network, and from there to the Internet, to download online content from streaming services like Hulu and Netflix. A smart TV may automatically detect a network connection, and it may also have a Network Setup utility you can run from its system software to adjust network settings. Set-top boxes such as cable boxes, digital video recorders (DVRs), and DVD players can also be "smart," containing their own CPU, memory, and system software, and can also connect to your PC and your local network.

Biometric Devices

A *biometric* device uses a measurement of a body part, such as a fingerprint or retina scan, to provide greater authentication security than simply supplying a user name and password.

You must install a biometric device as an I/O device, as well as a security device. We will save the detailed discussion of security devices for Chapter 17, and only concern ourselves at this point with the local installation of a fingerprint scanner as a representative biometric device. Some laptops come with a fingerprint scanner physically installed. When adding one to a computer, read the instructions and install the scanner as you would any device, installing the drivers at the appropriate time. The software that comes with a fingerprint scanner requires a fingerprint to compare with the scanned print. It may store the fingerprint locally, or it may store it in a central database. We will discuss the latter scenario in Chapter 17. In the case of a locally stored fingerprint, typically done when using a portable device, you will run a special program after installing the device. This program will take a baseline scan of your fingerprint and store it locally. After that, you simply follow the instructions for the placement of your finger in order to gain access to the computer.

KVM Switches

A *KVM switch* is a device traditionally found in server rooms to control multiple computers with one keyboard, mouse, and monitor. The acronym KVM stands for keyboard, video, and mouse. A KVM switch is a box to which you connect one local monitor, keyboard, and mouse. Ports on the switch provide a number of keyboard, mouse, and video connectors for cables to each of the computers being controlled. KVM switches are now divided into two broad categories: local KVM and remote KVM.

Local KVM Switches

The *local KVM switch* category is still the norm in server rooms, where it creates a one-to-many connection that allows you to control any one of the servers connected through the switch. Some local KVM switches have USB ports for the shared devices and may share additional types of devices, such as speakers. Other KVM switches reverse this model, connecting two or more sets of keyboards, displays, and mice to one computer. This model is commonly used in a kiosk scenario where the public has access through one set of peripherals, and an administrator has access via another set. In either situation, control is switched through the KVM switch using software and special keyboard commands, and such a KVM switch is called an *active KVM switch* or *electronic KVM switch*. You control an *inactive KVM switch*, the least expensive type of KVM switch, through a mechanical switch on the box itself. Inactive switches have many limitations and problems; you are unlikely to encounter them, so we will describe how to install a local active switch.

Before installing a local active KVM switch, read the installation instructions and assemble the cabling, devices, and computers you wish to connect. Memorize the keystrokes required to switch control from one computer to another. Check for the needed drivers. In our experience, these are not necessary because the KVM switch itself captures the keystrokes and changes the focus from computer to computer based on your keyboard commands.

Installing a local active KVM switch is just a bit more complicated than connecting a keyboard, display, and mouse to a computer. In fact, the first thing you do is connect your keyboard, display, and mouse to the appropriate connectors on the KVM switch. You will find them grouped together, and there may even be more than one type of connector for the mouse or keyboard and it may have speaker ports. Once the devices are connected to the switch, you can connect the KVM switch to the computers you wish to control. This requires special cables that are usually bundled together with the connectors split out on each end. This bundling ensures that you won't mistakenly connect a cable from one set to two different computers. If you do not have bundled cables, bundle them yourself.

Once all the computers are connected to the KVM switch, power up the switch and then power up each PC. During bootup, the PC should recognize the KVM switch as the keyboard, video, and mouse devices.

Remote KVM Switches

The *remote KVM switch* category is further divided into two types: local remote KVM and KVM over IP. A *local remote KVM switch* uses either Ethernet cable or USB cabling. A local remote KVM switch using Ethernet cabling can be used to control computers over a distance of up to 300 meters, using a proprietary protocol (not IP) and special hardware. A remote KVM switch using USB cabling has a distance limit of up to five meters.

A *KVM over IP switch* uses specialized hardware to capture the keyboard, video, and mouse signals, encodes them into IP packets, and sends them over an IP network. They can connect a keyboard, video display, and mouse to a special remote console application that allows the user to control multiple computers across a LAN or WAN. They are also used in one-to-one situations; for example, in hospitals or clinics with a centralized records system and consoles in the locations where they do not want system units (for a variety of reasons, including sanitation). The console consists of a keyboard, video display, and pointing device—all connected to a KVM device, such as a KVM port extender. There are many possible configurations, but in medical installations, the console may connect to the central system (directly or indirectly) to access and update patient records.

The physical connection of a KVM over IP switch is much like connecting a computer to a network, which you will learn about in Chapter 14. Once the device connects to the network, follow the manufacturer's instructions for installing the software. You will need guidance from your network administrator in order to log in and access the remote data.

Installing USB Devices

Today, most input devices come with a USB interface and are plug and play. Even some devices that traditionally had a dedicated interface, such as keyboards and mice, now usually come with a USB interface. In spite of the variety of devices using USB, installation and removal are simple because of the plug-and-play interface. As always, read the manual before installing any device, but the general rule for a USB device is to run the setup software that comes with the device before connecting the device. At some point in the setup process, you will be prompted to connect the USB device.

One caution: With the newer and faster USB interfaces, be sure that any high-speed device is matched to a high-speed USB port, especially when connecting a newer device to an older PC. The speed of the connection will be limited by the slower component. Refer to the Chapter 4 discussion of the various USB speeds and connectors.

CERTIFICATION SUMMARY

This chapter wraps up the discussion of PC components begun in Chapter 3 and continued in Chapter 4, describing power supplies, display devices, and peripheral devices, and how to install them.

Because power supplies provide the DC voltages required by various other components, they produce heat. Therefore, a typical power supply has a fan that dissipates the heat the power supply creates, as well as contributes to cooling the entire system. In most PCs, this is not sufficient, so additional methods are used to keep PCs cool enough for the components to function safely.

Display technologies have changed a great deal since the days of the analog CRT. The most recent developments include support for both video and audio through a single interface, connection, and cable. The physical form of the cable, and the connectors and ports used with a cable, depend on the purpose and design of the interface used and the device or devices that use the cable.

There are many types of interfaces for connecting peripherals, but, excluding display devices, most peripherals today connect to a PC using a USB connection, although some use wireless Bluetooth or infrared connections. Always read the documentation that comes with a device and follow the instructions for connecting and installing the drivers and other software.

 # TWO-MINUTE DRILL

Here are some of the key points covered in Chapter 5.

Power Supplies

❑ A power supply provides power for all components on the motherboard and those internal to the PC case.

❑ A volt is the unit of measurement of the pressure of electrons. A watt is a unit of measurement of actual delivered power. An ampere (amp) is a unit of measurement for electrical current or rate of flow of electrons through a wire.

❑ A power supply converts alternating current (AC) voltage into the direct current (DC) voltage required by the computer.

❑ Power supply capacity is measured in watts, with power supplies for desktop computers ranging up to about 1500 watts.

❑ An AC adapter is a form of power supply used with portable computers and external peripherals.

❑ Select a power supply that is of the correct form factor for both the motherboard and the case, and select one that has sufficient wattage for the internal components you expect to have.

❑ Older ATX motherboards used a 20-pin ATX (P1) connector to provide power. Some recent motherboards require two ATX12V 2.0 connectors—one is a 24-pin main connector, and the other is a 4-pin secondary connector. Other newer motherboards require EPS12V connectors, which include a 24-pin main connector, an 8-pin secondary connector, and an optional 4-pin tertiary connector.

Video Adapters and Displays

❑ The video adapter controls the output from the PC to the display device. Display adapters support a variety of display modes and technologies, including VGA, SVGA, DVI, HDMI, and DisplayPort.

❑ A video adapter may be built into the motherboard or may be a separate circuit board that plugs into a PCIe connector. For maximum performance, use an x16 slot.

❑ Display connectors include DE-15 (VGA), DVI, HDMI, DisplayPort, Composite Video, and Component Video.

❑ Classic multimedia interfaces include MIDI and a variety of audio ports using the 1/8" single-pin mini-audio connector.

❑ Mini-DIN-6 (PS/2) was used to connect keyboards and mice prior to USB becoming the dominant interface for input devices.

❑ Common electronic cables used with PCs include straight pair, twisted pair, and coaxial.

❑ Fiber-optic cable carries data in pulses of light, rather than via electricity.

❑ Multi-monitor systems have two or more displays on a single computer.

❑ Flat-panel displays (FPDs) have replaced CRT displays. Most FPDs use a form of LCD, LED, or plasma technology, with tablet PCs using OLED or AMOLED.

❑ Projectors take video output and project it onto a screen for viewing by a larger audience. A touch screen is a video display element that allows you to select and maneuver screen objects by touching, tapping, and sliding your finger or stylus on the screen.

❑ To install a display, connect it to the PC and then to a power outlet. A touch screen display requires an extra step to calibrate the touch screen with the images on the computer desktop.

❑ Some display settings, such as vertical position/horizontal position, are available only through a menu on the display itself.

❑ Display resolution is a setting that you can control through Windows.

Installing and Configuring Peripheral Devices

❑ Displays, printers, and sound cards are the most common output devices. Keyboards, pointing devices, bar code readers, and many multimedia devices are input devices. A special category of device, a KVM switch, is used in a variety of scenarios, but most commonly to allow a single person using one keyboard, video display, and pointing device to control many computers.

❑ A biometric device must be installed as an I/O device and also configured as a security device.

❑ To install a KVM switch for the purpose of controlling two or more computers using one keyboard, video display, and mouse, first connect the keyboard, display, and mouse to the device in the properly marked connectors. Then connect each computer to the appropriate connectors on the switch.

❑ The installation and configuration of an I/O device depends on the interface. Always read the documentation for the device before installing.

SELF TEST

The following questions will help you measure your understanding of the material presented in this chapter. Read all of the choices carefully because there might be more than one correct answer. Choose all correct answers for each question.

Power Supplies

1. Which statement is true?
   A. A PC power supply converts wattage to voltage.
   B. A PC power supply converts voltage to wattage.
   C. A PC power supply converts AC to DC.
   D. A PC power supply converts DC to AC.

2. What is the name of the main power connector that goes between an ATX power supply and an ATX motherboard?

   A. P3

   B. P1

   C. P2

   D. P4

3. The capacity of a power supply is normally stated in these units.

   A. Volts

   B. Watts

   C. Amperes

   D. Ohms

4. What type of current is required by internal PC components?

   A. Alternating current (AC)

   B. Direct current (DC)

   C. Lumens

   D. PSU

5. Which of the following calculations would you use to determine the capacity you require in a power supply?

   A. Add the voltage for all internal components.

   B. Add the wattage for all internal components.

   C. Add the voltage for all external components.

   D. Add the wattage for all external components.

6. This component of a typical power supply dissipates heat.

   A. Heat sink

   B. P1 connector

   C. Fan

   D. AC adapter

7. What is a common term for a laptop power supply?

   A. PSU

   B. Heat sink

   C. AC adapter

   D. Thermal compound

8. Select all the items that should be considered when selecting a new power supply.

   A. Wattage

   B. CPU

   C. Form factor

   D. Power connectors

9. What equipment should you never use when working with a power supply?
   A. Screwdriver
   B. Connectors
   C. Motherboard
   D. Antistatic wrist strap

Video Adapters and Displays

10. This venerable video interface standard was introduced with the IBM PS/2 computer in the 1980s.
   A. DisplayPort
   B. HDMI
   C. DVI
   D. VGA

11. Which of the following video interface standards supports both analog and digital signals?
   A. DisplayPort
   B. HDMI
   C. DVI
   D. VGA

12. This video standard supports both digital video and audio and has the thinnest cable and the smallest connectors.
   A. DisplayPort
   B. HDMI
   C. DVI
   D. VGA

13. Cold cathode fluorescent lamps (CCFLs) are a feature of what kind of display?
   A. CRT
   B. LED
   C. LCD
   D. Plasma

14. This type of display device takes up less desk space and replaces an older technology that uses more power.
   A. CRT
   B. FPD
   C. ATX
   D. USB

15. Which of the following connectors is *not* used to connect a display to a digital video interface?

    A. DVI

    B. DE-15

    C. HDMI

    D. DisplayPort

16. Which of the following is *not* a DVI connector type?

    A. DVI-A

    B. DVI-B

    C. DVI-I

    D. DVI-D

17. After physically connecting a touch screen and installing necessary device drivers, what important configuration task must you perform?

    A. Record a fingerprint scan.

    B. Calibrate.

    C. Upgrade Windows.

    D. Wash the screen.

Installing and Configuring Peripheral Devices

18. This type of input device is ideal for the more elaborate computer games.

    A. Joystick

    B. Digitizer

    C. Bar code reader

    D. Game pad

19. When adding this type of device to a PC, you will normally have two cables for two separate connections between the device and the PC.

    A. Printer

    B. Touch screen

    C. Touch pad

    D. Joystick

20. The local version of this type of device is found in server rooms, connecting multiple servers to a single set of I/O devices (mouse, display, and keyboard).

    A. Scanner

    B. Biometric

    C. KVM switch

    D. Multimedia

SELF TEST ANSWERS

Power Supplies

1. ☑   **C.** A PC power supply converts AC to DC.
    ☒   **A** and **B** are not true, because wattage equals volts times amps; wattage is a calculated value, not something that can be converted. **D** is not true because it does just the opposite.

2. ☑   **B.** P1 is the main power connector used between an ATX power supply and an ATX motherboard.
    ☒   **A** is incorrect because the chapter mentioned no such connector. **C** is incorrect because the chapter mentioned no such connector. **D** is incorrect because this is a four-wire 12V connector used in addition to the P1 connector.

3. ☑   **B.** The capacity of a power supply is stated in watts.
    ☒   **A** is incorrect because volts is a measurement of electrical potential. **C** is incorrect because amperes is a measurement of electrical current, or rate of flow of electrons through a wire. **D** is incorrect because ohms is a measurement of resistance.

4. ☑   **B.** Direct current (DC) is the type of current required by internal PC components.
    ☒   **A** is incorrect because this is the type of current that is provided through the typical wall outlet. **C** is incorrect because lumens is a measurement of the brightness of a projector; it is not related to electricity. **D** is incorrect because it is an acronym for "power supply unit."

5. ☑   **B.** Add the wattage for all internal components to determine what capacity you require in a power supply.
    ☒   **A** is incorrect because this is not the correct measurement required. **C** and **D** are both incorrect because external components normally have their own power supplies and do not need to draw power from the computer's power supply.

6. ☑   **C.** The fan is the component in a typical power supply that dissipates heat.
    ☒   **A** is incorrect because a heat sink is something that draws heat off something and dissipates it in some passive manner, such as via metal fins. **B** is incorrect because this is a power supply connector, not a part of a power supply that dissipates heat. **D** is incorrect because an AC adapter converts electrical power; it does not dissipate heat.

7. ☑   **C.** AC adapter is the common term for a laptop power supply.
    ☒   **A** is incorrect because this is an acronym for "power supply unit." **B** is incorrect because heat sinks dissipate heat. **D** is incorrect because thermal compound is used to increase the heat conductivity among components.

8. ☑ **A, C,** and **D.** These are all correct because you should consider wattage, form factor, and power connectors when selecting a new power supply.
    ☒ **B** is incorrect because although its wattage requirements are important, the CPU itself is not an issue when selecting a power supply.

9. ☑ **D.** You should never use an antistatic wrist strap when working with a power supply.
    ☒ **A** is incorrect because it may be necessary to remove the screws holding a power supply to the case. **B** is incorrect because you must work with the connectors from the power supply to the motherboard and other components. **C** is incorrect because you may need to work with the power supply connectors on the motherboard.

Video Adapters and Displays

10. ☑ **D.** VGA is the video interface standard introduced with the IBM PS/2 computer in the 1980s.
    ☒ **A, B,** and **C** are all incorrect because they are recent standards.

11. ☑ **C.** DVI is the video interface standard that supports both analog and digital signals.
    ☒ **A** and **B** are incorrect because DisplayPort and HDMI only support digital signals. **D** is incorrect because VGA is an analog video interface standard.

12. ☑ **A.** DisplayPort supports both digital video and audio and has the thinnest cable and the smallest connectors.
    ☒ **B** is incorrect because, although HDMI supports both video and audio, it does not have the thinnest cable and smallest connectors. **C** is incorrect because DVI does not support both digital video and audio. **D** is incorrect because VGA only supports analog video.

13. ☑ **B.** LCD is the type of display that includes CCFLs.
    ☒ **A** is incorrect because a CRT monitor uses an electron gun. **B** is incorrect because an LED uses a light-emitting diode. **D** is incorrect because a plasma screen does not use CCFLs.

14. ☑ **B.** A flat-panel display (FPD) takes up less desk space and replaces an older (CRT) technology that uses more power.
    ☒ **A** is incorrect because it takes up more desk space than a flat-panel display and uses more power. **C** is incorrect because ATX is a motherboard and power supply form factor, not a type of display. **D** is incorrect because USB is an I/O interface.

15. ☑ **B.** A DE-15 connector is not used to connect a display to a digital video interface.
    ☒ **A, C,** and **D** are all incorrect because these connectors are all used to connect a display to a digital video interface (of the same name).

16. ☑ **B.** DVI-B is not a DVI connector type.
    ☒ **A, C,** and **D** are all incorrect because DVI-A, DVI-I, and DVI-D are all DVI connector types.

17. ☑ **B.** Calibrate is correct because this will allow the touch screen interface to line itself up with the images on the screen.
    ☒ **A** is incorrect because a touch screen is not intended to scan fingerprints. **C** is incorrect because screen calibration is the task required by a touch screen display. **D** is incorrect because, although you will want to do this from time to time for any screen (using the correct method), this is not a configuration task.

Installing and Configuring Peripheral Devices

18. ☑ **D.** A game pad is a type of input device that is ideal for the more elaborate computer games because it typically comes with programmable buttons and directional pads and one or more joysticks.

    ☒ **A** is incorrect because a joystick is a rather primitive input device when compared to a game pad. **B** is incorrect because a digitizer is not an appropriate input device for a game, but more appropriate for working with drawings and schematics, converting the analog data (lines) to digital data. **C** is incorrect because a bar code reader is a device that optically scans a unique pattern of bars and white space that is interpreted by computer software.

19. ☑ **B.** A touch screen that you add to a PC will normally have two cables between the device and the PC: one for video signals and the other for input from the touch screen component of the monitor.

    ☒ **A** and **D** are incorrect because they normally have one cable between the device and the PC. **C** is incorrect because a touch pad normally is part of a laptop or keyboard, and, as such, doesn't have a cable to connect to the PC. An external touch pad will have a single cable.

20. ☑ **C.** A local KVM switch connects multiple computers to a single keyboard, video display, and mouse.

    ☒ **A** is incorrect because a scanner optically scans an image; it is not used as described in the question. **B** is incorrect because a biometric device uses a measurement of a body part, such as a fingerprint or retina, to use in authentication. **D** is incorrect because a multimedia device cannot be used to connect multiple computers to a single set of I/O devices.

Chapter 6

Installing and Upgrading PC Components

T his chapter begins with examples of custom computer configurations for various needs and then it moves on to describe and demonstrate how to install and replace common PC components. With a little practice, you will be capable of performing these tasks on most personal computers, in spite of different layouts or new component designs.

CERTIFICATION OBJECTIVE

■ **901: 1.9** *Given a scenario, select the appropriate components for a custom PC configuration, to meet customer specifications or needs*

This certification objective requires that you understand how to select the right components for building or ordering a custom computer for a specific job. The custom computers listed under this objective are a graphic/computer-aided design (CAD)/computer-aided manufacturing (CAM) design workstation, an audio/video editing workstation, a virtualization workstation, a gaming PC, a home theater PC, a standard thick client, a thin client, and a home server PC. The past three chapters have prepared you to understand the decisions you need to make for each configuration.

Selecting Components for Custom PCs

In Chapter 3, you learned about motherboards, CPUs, and cases; in Chapter 4, you learned about storage devices, memory, and adapter cards; and Chapter 5 detailed the features of power supplies, cooling systems, and peripherals. This section draws on the knowledge you gained in those three chapters by giving examples of the components you would select when building a custom PC to meet specific needs.

First, notice that some of the configurations described next are called "workstations" while others are called "PCs." What is the difference? While these terms are often used interchangeably, when a distinction is made, a *personal computer (PC)* is a computer intended for home or standard office productivity work and intended for the use of a single user, while a *workstation* is a computer that is more powerful than the average office or home desktop PC, with more expensive, higher-performance components, although it also may be dedicated to a single user. Despite the distinction, the latter is most often still called a PC, though a powerful PC targeted for a specific use.

When selecting a motherboard, you cannot tell which components it supports solely by knowing the form factor of the motherboard. Therefore, you must always check the manufacturer's documentation before you select a motherboard and the components you wish to install on it. To do this, check the manufacturer's website for the specifications for each model with a list of installed and supported components, such as chipset, CPUs (models, speeds, and number of CPUs), and memory (type, speed, data width, and maximum amount of memory the motherboard will support), as well as the speed of the motherboard's front-side bus (FSB).

Most desktop PCs take standard, interchangeable parts. A benefit of a standardized platform is that it is easy to customize. You can design modifications to a basic PC computer that will allow it to fulfill specific requirements.

What kind of requirements are we talking about? They range from a thin client machine that really only requires enough CPU power, random access memory (RAM), and communication ability to handle basic applications and function as a terminal, up through a gaming PC that needs a powerful multicore processor, a high-end video or specialized graphics processing unit (GPU), a better sound card, and high-end cooling capability, to a graphics/CAD/CAM design workstation with even higher requirements.

Today's computers are so powerful that an appropriately configured laptop, such as one with a multicore central processing unit (CPU), 8+ GB of RAM, and a 1+ TB hard drive can serve in several of these configurations. Let's look at seven custom configurations.

Graphics/CAD/CAM Design Workstation

Designers, engineers, and architects need computer systems capable of creating very complex graphics. The software they use must do complex graphics rendering for design and manufacturing.

One category of software used by engineers and architects is *computer-aided design (CAD)*, which allows them to design a wide variety of objects from machine parts to extremely complex products such as aircraft, cars, or boats. CAD software allows you to view the design in 2-D or 3-D from all angles and from different distances. Another type of software sometimes combined with CAD is *computer-aided manufacturing (CAM)*. A CAM system can control the machines used to manufacture an object. A combined *computer-aided design/computer-aided manufacturing (CAD/CAM)* system allows the engineer to go from design directly to manufacturing. The software's graphics product is usually a vector graphic, which defines images using algorithms for defining lines and shapes, rather than explicitly describing an image as a map of dots (a bitmap).

A design workstation requires a powerful processor to handle all the required computation, a high-end video card driving a high-quality industry-certified graphics display, a lot of disk space, and a lot of RAM. How much RAM? Sixteen GB is good; 32 GB is better. On the extreme high end 128 GB is great. The CPU could be a 64-bit four-, six-, or eight-core processor or two four-core processors. You'll need fault-tolerant RAID 1, 5, or 10 capability so as to not risk losing valuable design data.

Furthermore, a designer, engineer, or architect working at a graphics workstation will usually want a pointing device such as a light pen or digitizing tablet that has finer control than you have with an ordinary mouse. You will also need to select an appropriate printer

for rendering images and specifications, such as a large format printer or plotter—both of which are more expensive than your average office printer. A plotter is a specialized high-precision device used by engineers and architects that creates images in black and white or color using special pens rather than ink cartridges. They can print on paper up to 44" wide and of any reasonable length.

Audio/Video Editing Workstation

An audio/video editing workstation requires a specialized audio and video card for the highest fidelity possible while editing. A large monitor, preferably two, is required, and you need large and very fast Serial Advanced Technology Advancement (SATA) hard drive(s). An effective configuration is three hard drives: one for system and application programs, one for video streaming while rendering, and one for storing the edited video. A bottleneck for an editing workstation is the vast amount of data it moves on and off disks, so these drives should be very fast; standard 7200 rpm drives are good; 10,000 rpm drives work better. You need a high-wattage power supply to feed all this equipment too. You can add specialized equipment such as stereo 3-D capture and editing capability and real-time effects.

Virtualization Workstation

A *virtualization workstation* is a computer used to support the on-screen simulation of a computing environment. It can be a simulation of a complete computer including hardware, desktop or server operating system, and running applications. Or it may be virtualization of an application and all the supporting software, but not an entire operating system and desktop, allowing you to run an incompatible application on a computer isolated from the OS and hardware of the computer. A single instance of such a simulation is a *virtual machine*, and there can be multiple virtual machines running on the same workstation, as long as there is sufficient computing power, memory, and disk space to support them.

A virtualization workstation needs a very fast multicore CPU, and both the CPU and BIOS/UEFI must physically support virtualization. In Intel CPUs and chipsets, look for the term Virtualization Technology (VT), and in AMD CPUs and chipsets, look for the term

According to CompTIA A+ 901 exam objective 1.9, the most important components of a virtualization workstation are maximum RAM and CPU cores. In addition, there is yet another crucial requirement: both the CPU and BIOS must support virtualization.

AMD-V. The technologies were introduced in Chapter 3, but virtualization will be further detailed in Chapter 8.

A virtualization workstation must also have lots of RAM, not only to handle the virtualization process, but also to allow for the real work the virtual programs are doing. Of course, the scale of virtualization you intend to do is also important and affects how much RAM and hard drive space you need, and even how many cores or even additional CPUs you will use. If you only wish to run a single virtual machine in order to test a new version of Windows, a quad-core CPU, 8 GB of RAM, and about 20 GB of additional space for the virtual machine may be all you need. If this workstation is going to run many virtual machines, you will want more CPU power, more RAM, and more disk space. High-speed data busses help too. If you intend to do server virtualization, then you need fast network interface cards (NICs) connected to a high-speed network.

Gaming PC

Gamers require a very powerful processor to handle all the graphics calculations. You'll want at least 16 GB of RAM installed, a motherboard that enables SATA3, a 1 TB or 2 TB 7200 rpm or faster hard drive (or a solid-state hard drive if you can afford it), and a high-end video GPU card with at least 1 GB of RAM in it. You'll want a high-end sound card as well. Gamers often overclock the CPU, which increases the heat output considerably,

Remember that the most important components of a gaming PC are a powerful CPU, high-end video with a specialized GPU, a high-quality sound card, and high-end cooling.

so you'll want to install high-end cooling capability, perhaps even going to liquid cooling if overheating problems recur. In addition to a keyboard and mouse, a gamer will want the appropriate peripherals, such as gamepads, joysticks, and wheels. Multichannel sound, up to 7.1 channel high-definition (HD) surround sound, which provides a subwoofer and six surround speakers, helps with the realism.

Home Theater PC

A *home theater PC (HTPC)* is a computer that houses components for a home theater system. It often comes in a smaller format that can fit inside your entertainment console. The HTPC should contain a medium-speed CPU and 8 GB or 16 GB of RAM with multiple large hard drives in a RAID 1, 5, or 10 configuration because it stores movies and music that you don't want to lose. You'll need a TV tuner card that lets you access cable TV, broadcast, Internet, or other signal sources. A popular option is to install digital video recorder (DVR) software that takes video input from the TV tuner and records it.

A single HTPC box can replace several boxes, but, of course, you need to connect it to a high-definition TV (HDTV), using High Definition Multimedia Interface (HDMI) or Digital Visual Interface (DVI) cables. And don't forget to install a high-end sound adapter card that outputs 7.1 channel (or higher) HD surround sound to great speakers. Further, install the latest Blu-ray combo drive for playing and burning DVDs and Blu-ray discs, and connect your HTPC to a high-speed local area network (LAN), preferably one supporting Gigabit Ethernet or Wi-Fi to stream video to other computers or TVs in the house.

Standard Thick Client

A *client* is software that connects over a network to related server software, such as a file and print client that accesses a file and print server for saving, retrieving, and printing files. Or an e-mail client that connects to an e-mail server. The operating system running under these clients may also be referred to as the client, as is true of Windows versions that are not explicitly server versions. In fact, the file and print client is part of Windows. In a broader sense, we may speak of the computer underneath all that as a client. A *thick client* is just another name for a typical network-connected desktop PC with various applications installed—one that you would see on most desktops at work, school, and the home office. The word "client" implies that the computer connects to a network as a client to various services for e-mail, network browsing, file sharing, and more that you will learn about in Chapter 19. A thick client meets the recommended requirements for CPU, memory, and disk storage for Windows and all installed desktop applications. A reasonably fast Internet connection is desired, and the desktop applications are usually Microsoft Office, or an equivalent productivity suite, along with one or more Internet browsers and other applications required or desired by the user.

Thin Client

A *thin client* is a low-cost, scaled-down PC used primarily for Internet access and not requiring a full suite of local applications. Therefore, a PC configured as a thin client only needs to meet the minimum requirements of the Windows version installed, because it is assumed that all work is done and saved out on the network (private or Internet) somewhere. However, a fast Internet connection would be very important for the user. Basic applications would include an Internet browser, an e-mail client (unless the user accesses e-mail solely via the Internet browser), and something for some basic word processing, although this may not be required. You won't see many thin clients in the field because they've been overshadowed and replaced by tablet PCs and netbooks, with similar cost and better portability.

e x a m

ⓦatch **Remember that the most important components of a thin client are just basic applications and a system that meets the minimum requirements for running Windows.**

Home Server PC

Depending on your needs, we see a home server PC as a combination of the HTPC described earlier and a home office file-sharing PC. The HTPC aspects should include media streaming capabilities and any of the other HTPC components desired. All of this would require a high-speed LAN, preferably Gigabit Ethernet using a Gigabit Ethernet NIC, and the system must have a high-speed Internet connection.

As a home office file-sharing computer, it should include a Windows OS that supports media streaming as well as file and print sharing. And because you will store your personal and maybe business data on this system, consider configuring multiple drives as a fault-tolerant RAID 1, 5, or 10 array.

e x a m

ⓦatch **Remember that the most important components of a home server PC are support for media streaming, file sharing, and print sharing. The computer should also have a Gigabit Ethernet NIC and a RAID array.**

CERTIFICATION OBJECTIVES

- **901: 1.2** *Explain the importance of motherboard components, their purpose, and properties*
- **901: 1.3** *Compare and contrast various RAM types and their features*
- **901: 1.6** *Install various types of CPUs and apply the appropriate cooling methods*

Strictly speaking, the requirements for exam objectives 1.2, 1.3, and 1.6 of the CompTIA A+ 901 exam have been satisfied in Chapters 3 and 4 where you explored these computer components. However, what is the sense of understanding motherboards and their components, RAM, and CPUs if you don't know how to physically work with them? Therefore, in this section, you will look at how to install and configure these components.

Installing and Upgrading Motherboards and Onboard Components

Installing and upgrading a motherboard requires that you understand the CPU models that will work with the motherboard, as well as the appropriate type of memory compatible with both the CPU and motherboard and the amount of memory they can handle. Your best source for this information is the motherboard manual.

Whenever you install or replace a computer component that involves opening the case, you must turn the computer's power off and ensure that you follow the electrostatic discharge (ESD) procedures discussed in Chapter 1. All the exercises described in this book assume that you have taken steps to protect yourself, and the computer, from harm.

Replacing a Motherboard

Replacing a motherboard is not a common occurrence. If a motherboard fails while a computer is under warranty, it will be replaced as part of that coverage. Therefore, only if you work for a company that does such warranty work will motherboard replacement be a big part of your job. If a motherboard fails after the warranty period, you need to decide whether a suitable replacement is available and whether you will be able to use all your old components with a newer motherboard. In many cases it may make more sense to simply replace the entire computer.

Because most components attach physically to the motherboard, replacing it can be a very time-consuming task. If you are replacing one motherboard with another of exactly the same brand and version, you should make notes about any BIOS settings and jumper positions (if there are any jumpers) for the old motherboard in case you need to change them on the new board. You will use the BIOS settings the first time you start up the computer after the installation, but make the physical jumper changes, if any, before securing the new motherboard in the case. The jumpers may not be as easy to reach after the motherboard is installed, especially if you don't do it until after you install other components. Once you have done this, you are ready for the real work.

When it comes to replacing a motherboard versus building an entirely new system from scratch, doing the latter may be easier, because you can buy all the pieces at once from one source and request their help and guarantee that all the components will play nicely together.

Installing a Motherboard

When installing or replacing a motherboard, you should follow the instructions in the motherboard manual, your most important tool. In addition to listing the components supported, the typical motherboard manual includes instructions on installing the motherboard in a case and installing components, such as the CPU, memory, and power supply. The manual will explain how to set appropriate jumpers on the motherboard and how to attach all the various power and data cables. These include all the drive interface cables and connections to both front and back panel connectors for the various interfaces, such as Universal Serial Bus (USB), FireWire, external SATA (eSATA), and even video, sound, and networking, if any of those components are built in.

Exercise 6-1 will guide you through the task of removing an old motherboard.

Before you open a computer case, be sure to unplug any power cords and turn off the power supply. Then, to prevent damage to the system, equalize the electrical charge between your body and the components inside your computer. If nothing else, touch a grounded portion of your computer's chassis. A better option is to place the computer on a grounded mat, which you touch before working on the PC. You could also wear an antistatic wrist strap. Warning: Do not use an antistatic wrist strap when working with high-voltage devices, such as power supplies, cathode ray tube (CRT) monitors, and laser printers.

EXERCISE 6-1

Removing an Old Motherboard

If possible, use a digital camera to record the steps, beginning with pictures of the unopened PC from all sides, then at each point before and after you make a change, such as opening the case and removing components. This can serve as your documentation for reassembling the computer.

1. If you haven't done this already, power down and unplug the PC's power cord.
2. Remove all expansion cards and cables from the motherboard.
3. If the drives and/or the drive bays interfere with access to the motherboard, remove them.
4. Remove any screws or fasteners attaching the motherboard to the case, lift the board out of the case, and put it aside. Be sure to carefully save any screws you remove.

The first three steps of Exercise 6-2 describe a recommended procedure for handling a motherboard, which applies to any circuit board. The remainder of Exercise 6-2 includes general steps for installing a motherboard. It assumes that the BIOS, complementary metal oxide semiconductor (CMOS), CMOS battery, and chipset have come preinstalled on the motherboard (as is customary). Always check the instructions included with the motherboard or other component.

EXERCISE 6-2

Properly Handling and Installing a Motherboard

1. Before unpacking a new motherboard, ensure that you have grounded your body properly. One method is to wear a static safety wrist strap, as described in Chapter 1. Your work area should include a grounded antistatic mat.

2. Hold the board by its edges and avoid touching any contacts, integrated circuit (IC) chips, or other components on the surface.

3. Place the board on a grounded antistatic mat (described in Chapter 1).

4. Install the CPU and memory on the motherboard, per manufacturer's instructions.

5. Follow the motherboard manual's instructions for setting any jumpers on the motherboard, and pay attention to instructions for how to attach screws and stand-offs, which keep the motherboard from touching the metal floor or wall of the case. Now you are ready to install the board.

6. To place the new motherboard in the computer, line it up properly on the chassis screw holes, and fix it into place.

7. Attach the power and drive connectors, as well as connectors to the correct ports on the case (both front panels and back panels).

Upgrading a CPU

Upgrading a CPU is uncommon anymore, but not unheard of. If your motherboard accepts multiple speeds of CPUs and your current one isn't at the top of that range, you might be able to switch out the CPU for a faster one. This might not provide the performance boost that you hope for, though. Motherboards typically accept CPUs in a rather narrow range of speeds. The performance difference between two CPUs in the same basic class (that is, two CPUs that would run on the same motherboard) is not likely to be a game-changer. You'll likely see much more dramatic performance increases when you add more RAM, or install a better video adapter.

Be sure to consult the manufacturer's documentation for your motherboard to determine which processors and speeds it supports. In some cases, you will need to configure the board for the new speed or model using a set of jumpers, but many newer motherboards allow you to make such changes through BIOS system setup. You can run a software test to see what CPU is installed. For instance, the free program CPU-Z will scan your computer and report on many onboard components, including the CPU, caches, the motherboard, memory, memory speed, and graphics.

on the **Job**

When we mention free software in this book, we are only using it as an example; it's not an endorsement of that product. If you download and install such software, note that most of the websites offering free software also show links to download other software, and sometimes those links are positioned so that you might inadvertently download a program other than the one you intend. The installation program of the software you desire may also include installing add-ons to your browser. Watch for these, and do not install anything you do not explicitly want.

Removing a CPU

How you remove an installed CPU depends on the type of socket. Once again, read any manuals available for your motherboard or computer. You may need to consult the manufacturer for more information.

on the **Job**

The existing CPU will have a heat sink and/or fan attached to it. If possible, remove the CPU without removing these attachments. However, if they interfere with the mechanism for releasing the processor, you may need to remove them.

There are two basic socket types, as you learned in Chapter 3: pin grid array (PGA) and land grid array (LGA). The main difference you will see between PGA and LGA sockets is that LGA sockets have a cover in addition to the lever. The cover holds the CPU firmly in place, while only the lever and the fit of the pins in the holes hold a CPU in a PGA socket. The steps for removing CPUs from both types of sockets are similar, with one important difference, as shown in Exercises 6-3 and 6-4. Both are *zero insertion force (ZIF)* sockets, meaning you do not have to apply any downward pressure to seat the CPU in the socket.

on the **Job**

The processor will be very hot when you first turn off a PC. You can burn your fingers if you touch a hot CPU chip. Always allow at least five minutes for the chip to cool before you remove it.

EXERCISE 6-3

Removing a PGA Processor from Its Socket

1. First, ensure that you have an antistatic bag at hand.
2. Lift the socket lever. You might have to move it slightly to the side to clear it from a retaining tab.
3. Lift out the processor. Because this is a ZIF socket, you should encounter no resistance when you remove the CPU.
4. Place the CPU in an antistatic bag. (Remember, putting it on top of the bag provides no protection.)

EXERCISE 6-4

Removing an LGA Processor from Its Socket

1. First, ensure that you have an antistatic bag at hand.
2. Lift the socket lever and cover.
3. Lift out the processor.
4. Place the CPU in an antistatic bag.

Installing a CPU

The CPU socket on the motherboard will usually have a mechanism to make it easier to install the CPU without damaging any pins. As described earlier, CPUs designed for PGA and LGA sockets have levers, but the LGA sockets also have a cover.

When installing a CPU into a socket, raise the lever and position the CPU with all pins inserted in the matching socket holes. Then close the lever, which lets the socket contact each of the CPU's pins. Exercise 6-5 describes how to install a CPU in an LGA socket. In all cases, do not count on these simple instructions alone, but follow those provided in the manuals that come with the motherboard and CPU.

EXERCISE 6-5

Installing a Processor in an Empty LGA Socket

1. First, open the antistatic packaging containing the CPU, including any packing securing the CPU, but keep it within the packaging until you are ready to install it in the socket. Do not place the CPU on top of the packaging, because that will expose it to static.
2. Lift the socket lever and cover.
3. Align the CPU over the socket.
4. Position the cover over the CPU.
5. Press the lever down.

on the
ᴊob

When handling a CPU, grasp it by the sides—never touch the underside of a CPU, where the pins or contacts are.

Removing and Installing Cooling Systems

As a rule, the typical PC comes with a cooling system that is adequate for the standard components delivered with the PC. Once you start adding hard drives, memory, and additional expansion cards, you should give some thought to supplementing the existing cooling system. How far you go with this depends on just how much you add to the PC.

An overheated computer may slow down, thanks to built-in technology in some motherboards that senses the temperature of the motherboard and slows down the processor when the temperature exceeds a certain limit. This reduces the heat the processor puts out. In the extreme, overheating can damage PC components. The other side of this is that modern cooling systems also use heat sensors, and as temperatures rise they will adjust their performance to keep the system cool. Newer power supply and case fans will change speed to match the temperature.

Common Sense First

Before you consider spending money on a new cooling system, check that the currently installed cooling systems is not being impaired in any way. Maybe if you just corrected its problems, it would be adequate. Begin by ensuring that the PC case is closed during operation, that all slot covers are in place, that airflow around the case is not obstructed, and that the computer system is not installed in an unventilated space, such as an enclosed cabinet. Also, check to see if ribbon cables are blocking air flow inside the case. Use plastic ties to secure cables out of the way. Correct these problems before spending money supplementing the cooling system.

In addition, open the case and give the interior of the PC a good vacuuming before you spend money on upgrading the cooling system. Excessive dust and dirt on components will act as an insulator, keeping the heat from dissipating and causing a computer to overheat, which in turn can cause it to slow down, stop operating, or be permanently damaged. Learn more about vacuuming a PC and other maintenance tasks in Chapter 11.

on the **Job**

Notebook PCs are prone to overheating too, because they have components crammed into such a tight space. Make sure that you do not block any fans on the bottom or sides of the notebook PC, and operate the notebook on a hard flat surface, not on your lap. A hot notebook PC sitting directly on your lap not only can overheat, but can also burn your legs. If a notebook PC frequently overheats, consider disassembling it to clean out any dust or hair inside that may be interfering with air flow and fan operation.

Case Fan

New PCs often come with both a power supply fan and a separate case fan. Perhaps you can simply upgrade the present case fan. Also, check to see if the PC has an empty bay or bracket for a case fan. A case fan is a very inexpensive upgrade, cheaper than a latte and muffin at your favorite coffee shop. The only requirement is a bracket or bay in the case that will accommodate a case fan, and the appropriate power connector.

When shopping for a case fan, you will need the dimensions of the fan bay (usually stated in millimeters), rated voltage, and power input. Features to compare are fan speed in revolutions per minute (rpm), airflow in cubic feet per minute (CFM), and noise level in decibels. A *decibel (dbA)* is a commonly used measurement of sound. The fan speed and airflow reflect the fan's effectiveness for cooling. The noise level is an important consideration because fans and drives are the only moving parts in a PC and generate the most noise. Look for fans with a noise decibel rating in the 20s or below. In addition, check out the power connector on new case fans. Many come with a Molex connector that can connect directly to the power supply, and some have a special connector that must connect directly to the motherboard. Figure 6-1 shows a 100-mm-wide case fan with a Molex connector.

CPU Fans and Heat Sink

If you are installing a CPU, then you will also need to install a cooling system for it. Today's processors typically require a fan/heat sink combination, which may also include some other cooling technology as well. Often, the cooling system and the CPU are packaged together, making the choice for you. Pay attention to the power connector for the fan, and locate the socket for this connector on the motherboard ahead of time. It is unlikely that you will replace an existing CPU fan and/or heat sink unless the CPU fan has failed.

FIGURE 6-1

A case fan

Even then, considering the complexity of it and the danger of damaging the CPU, it may be easier to replace the entire CPU if the same or similar model is available.

Liquid Cooling Systems

Liquid cooling systems are not just for gamers anymore. Like most technologies, as manufacturers improve liquid cooling systems, more people adopt them, and the prices for the improved systems drop. If you decide to look into this option, do your homework because these systems have several issues. For one, they require special skills to install, and they take up considerable space inside a computer because they require specific tubing, reservoirs, fans, and power supplies to work effectively.

Removing a Cooling System

If a cooling system fails or is inadequate, you will need to remove it from the PC. In that case, turn the computer's power off and ensure that you follow the ESD procedures. Then reverse the steps for installing the component, unplugging power and motherboard connectors, unscrewing mounting screws, and lifting it out of the case.

Installing and Configuring a Cooling System

When installing a new cooling system, be sure to read the documentation for the new components as well as for the motherboard, if appropriate. Assemble the components required, and follow good practices to avoid damaging the computer or injuring yourself. Turn the computer's power off, disconnect the power cord, and ensure that you follow the ESD procedures discussed in Chapter 1.

When installing a new case fan, affix the fan to the case in the appropriate bracket or bay, using the screws that came with either the case or the fan. Connect the power connector and any required motherboard connectors.

When installing a heat sink and/or fan on a CPU, be sure to apply thermal compound according to the instructions, and carefully connect the heat sink or fan using the clip provided. Plug the fan into the appropriate power socket on the motherboard.

SCENARIO & SOLUTION

I would like to build a PC. Is it best to shop for the best price on each component (motherboard, CPU, memory, etc.) from several sources?	No. The best strategy, especially if you are new to this, is to buy all the components from one source and get a guarantee that they will work together.
I read that I might have to upgrade my BIOS before installing the next Windows operating system. Does this mean I have to replace the physical BIOS chip?	You probably will not have to do something that drastic. Most BIOSs today are actually flash BIOS chips that can be electronically upgraded using software from the BIOS manufacturer.
The PC I want to build will be used mostly for running standard office productivity software. Should I consider a water-cooled system?	Generally, a water-cooled system would be overkill in a PC running standard office productivity software, but some new motherboards have built-in sealed (passive) liquid cooling systems.

Optimizing a System with RAM

One function of RAM is to provide the processor with faster access to the information it needs. Within limits, the more memory a computer has, the faster it will run. One of the most common and effective computer upgrades is the installation of more system RAM.

The optimal amount of memory to install is best determined by considering the requirements of the operating system you are installing and how you will use the computer. On an existing system, you can run a software test that will scan your memory, report on what it finds (including the type and quantity of installed memory), the number of memory slots, and the number of available (empty) memory slots. It will then recommend upgrade requirements right down to the specifications you will need to select and purchase the correct RAM modules. One such software test is available at www.crucial.com. Exercise 6-6 will walk you through running the Crucial System Scanner.

on the **Job**

Recall the earlier warning about downloading and installing free software. If you choose to use the Crucial System Scanner, be sure that you only download the scanner, and that you do not agree to make any changes, such as an add-in to your web browser.

EXERCISE 6-6

Running a Memory Scanner

For this exercise, you will need a computer with Internet access. Depending the browser and your security settings in the OS, the process for downloading the utility may vary slightly from what's described here.

1. Enter the URL **www.crucial.com/usa/en/systemscanner** into the address box of your web browser. (If you are running a Mac OS, you will be automatically redirected to a page from which you can download the Crucial Mac System Scanner.)

2. Click the Agree to the terms & conditions check box (after reading the terms and conditions).

3. Click the Download the scanner button.

4. If you are asked whether you want to save or run the file, choose Save. Save it in your Downloads folder, or wherever you prefer.

5. In the Downloads folder, locate and click CrucialScan.exe.

6. In the User Account Control dialog box, click the Yes button (if you are logged on as an administrator) or enter the administrator password if you are not logged on as an administrator.

7. If you are prompted to choose which application to use to run the utility, select your current or favorite web browser. A Scan In Progress message will appear followed by a page of results.

8. Review the results.

A scan of a laptop computer shows two slots, each of them containing one 8 GB SO-DIMM, and no empty slots. To upgrade this computer, you would need to replace at least one of the SO-DIMMs with a higher-capacity SO-DIMM. Before doing this, though, you would check the documentation for the computer to make sure the motherboard will accept 16 GB SO-DIMMs. You would also check the maximum amount of RAM the OS can support; if you flip back to Table 2-1 in Chapter 2, you'll see that 64-bit Windows 7 Home Premium can use only 16 GB of RAM, for example. If that were your OS, a RAM upgrade would be of no value until you moved to a different OS that supported more.

Installing and Removing DIMMs

Dual Inline Memory Module (DIMM) sockets are often dark in color with plastic clips at each end. DIMM sockets for PCs are 184-pin for DDR1 synchronous dynamic RAM (SDRAM) or 240-pin for both DDR2 SDRAM and DDR3 SDRAM sticks. They are all keyed differently to fit into slots that support just one type of DDR RAM, and they are not interchangeable. You do not have to install DIMMs in pairs unless the motherboard is dual-channel architecture. If a motherboard has two types of memory slots, such as four DIMM slots supporting DDR2 and two DIMM slots supporting DDR3, it is an either/or situation: you can install one or the other type of memory. If you install both, the system will not boot up.

The technique for installing DIMMs is described in Exercise 6-7. A notch in each type of module is positioned to only fit in the appropriate type of memory socket, where a matching socket key will prevent you from installing the wrong type of module. So even if the number of pins is the same, you will not be able to install one type of module in the socket for another. When installing a memory module, pay attention to the location of the key on both the module and in the socket, and orient the module notch to line up with the socket key. Then open the retention clips on the socket and align the module vertically with the socket holding the module upright. Chapter 7 will detail how to install small outline DIMMs (SODIMMs) in laptops.

EXERCISE 6-7

Installing and Removing a DIMM

1. Open the retention clips on the socket and align the module with the slot, keeping it upright so the notches in the module line up with the tabs in the slot.

2. Gently press down on the module. The retention clips on the side should rotate into the locked position. You might need to guide them into place with your fingers.

3. To remove a DIMM, press the retention clips outward, as shown in Figure 6-2, which lifts the DIMM slightly, and then grasp the DIMM and lift it straight up.

CERTIFICATION OBJECTIVE

■ *901: 1.4 Install and configure PC expansion cards*

Chapter 4 described features and characteristics of the expansion cards listed in CompTIA A+ 901 exam objective 1.4. In this section, we will expand that discussion to describe the installation and configuration of expansion cards.

FIGURE 6-2

Removing a DIMM

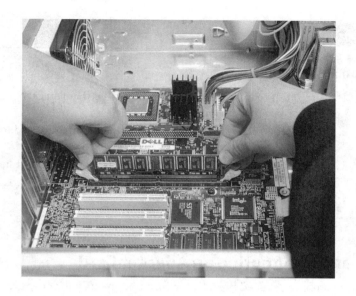

Installing Adapter Cards

Even with the large number of features built into PCs, technicians need to know how to add new adapter cards to PCs in order to add new functionality. Installing an adapter card requires that you open up the case and install the card in an available expansion slot.

Before you buy an adapter card, consider the alternatives. Would you be able to achieve the same result (at the same performance level) from an external device using a USB, FireWire, or eSATA port? Both USB and FireWire allow you to have multiple devices hanging off a single port. (USB achieves this with a USB hub, and FireWire does so by daisy-chaining devices.)

In some cases, however, you can't avoid working with adapter cards. For example, if you don't have a certain kind of port, an adapter card will add it, like FireWire or USB 3.0. And if you want to add or replace a video adapter, that's always an adapter card (because of the bus speed required for good display performance).

Removing an Adapter Card

Before removing an adapter card, be sure you have an antistatic bag in which to store the removed adapter card. Exercise 6-8 describes the general steps for removing an adapter card.

EXERCISE 6-8

Removing an Adapter Card

1. Turn off the computer, unplug it, and ensure that you carry out proper ESD procedures, as described in Chapter 1.
2. Use a screwdriver to remove the screw fastening the card to the slot in the back of the computer case.
3. Grasp the adapter card with both hands and pull straight up to remove it from the socket.
4. Place the card in an antistatic bag.

Installing and Configuring an Adapter Card

Once you have selected the adapter card that meets your needs, you will need to install it in the PC. Exercise 6-9 provides general steps for installing an adapter card. Although installing and configuring most adapter cards is straightforward, you must understand the card's purpose. Before you begin, check the documentation for both the adapter card and the motherboard, and note any variations from this general procedure. Check if the adapter card has any physical jumpers that you need to position. (Modern cards usually don't, as they are configured via their BIOS or the operating system, but it doesn't hurt to check.) Be sure to have any device driver disc handy so that you can install the device driver and any related software after you install the adapter card; also, test the card after installing the driver and before securing the case cover, as described in the exercise.

EXERCISE 6-9

Installing an Adapter Card

1. Set any jumpers identified in the documentation for the card. Jumpers are uncommon on modern cards.
2. Turn off the computer, unplug it, and ensure that you carry out proper ESD procedures, as described in Chapter 1.
3. Remove the slot cover for the appropriate expansion slot, removing whatever hardware is holding the slot cover in place.
4. Position the adapter card upright over the empty slot, aligning the card's slot cover with the opening behind that expansion slot. (See Figure 6-3.)

FIGURE 6-3

Installing an
adapter card

5. Place your thumbs along the top edge of the card and push straight down.
6. Secure the card to the case using the existing screw holes.
7. After the board is installed but the case is still open, connect all necessary cables and start up the computer.
8. After the operating system starts up, install the device driver and test the device. (Learn more about installing drivers in Windows in Chapter 9.) Once the device is working, turn the computer off and secure the case cover.
9. Restart the computer to ensure that replacing the case cover did not disturb any cables and connectors.

CERTIFICATION OBJECTIVE

■ *901: 1.5* *Install and configure storage devices and use appropriate media*

Chapter 4 introduced the various PC storage devices and media that are listed in CompTIA A+ 901 exam objective 1.5, but we delayed coverage of the installation and configuration of these devices for this chapter.

Installing Storage Devices

Replacing storage devices is a common task because those storage devices with moving parts tend to fail more than other components. Adding more storage space is also a common upgrade. Fortunately, because most drives are standardized, they can be recognized by any PC and don't need special configuration.

New hard disk drives (and their SSD equivalents) must be partitioned and formatted before use. Some of them come prepartitioned and preformatted, especially external ones, but you can make changes. If you do want to change the drive's partitioning and formatting, the best time to do so is when the drive is new and contains no data. Chapter 10 explains partitioning and formatting procedures.

Removing an Internal Storage Device

To remove an internal storage device of any type, check the documentation for the device. Exercise 6-10 provides general steps that will work for all types of internal storage devices.

EXERCISE 6-10

Removing a Drive

1. Remove the power supply and data cables from the back of the drive. Ensure that you grasp the plastic connector, not the wires themselves. If the connector doesn't come out easily, try gently rocking it lengthwise parallel to the socket from end to end (never side to side) while you pull it out.

2. Remove the screws that attach the drive to the drive bay, or push to release the retaining clips that hold the drive's rails into the bay. These are usually located on the sides of the drive. Be sure to carefully save any screws you remove. On some cases, before you can remove the screws on one side of a drive, you have to remove the whole metal frame into which the drive is mounted.

3. Slide the drive out of the computer.

4. If the drive used rails to slide into the bay, remove the screws holding the rails to the drive.

Installing Optical Drives

Physically installing and removing an internal CD or DVD drive is the same as installing and removing hard drives, except that the CD or DVD drive must be installed into a bay with a front panel that allows access to the drive for inserting and removing discs.

 On really old systems you might see a small colored-wire cable running between the optical drive and the sound card. This analog cable was used on early multimedia PCs to play audio CDs through the sound card. However, modern systems (Windows XP and later) send all audio through the same data cable as used for the drive itself, so the separate audio cable is no longer required.

Normally, the BIOS will automatically recognize the CD or DVD drive, but it may be necessary to enable the ATA channel to which it is connected in the BIOS settings. If the computer doesn't recognize, or can't communicate with, the new drive, you need to load a driver for it. Learn about installing device drivers in Chapter 9.

Blu-ray drives are becoming the optical drive of choice on modern systems, not only for their high-capacity data storage, but also for their ability to play HD movie discs on a PC. When selecting a drive, carefully consider the reason for the upgrade. Will it only be used for storing nonvideo data, or will it be used to run Blu-ray movies? You can add a Blu-ray drive for storing nonvideo data to a system without upgrading the video system, but in order to run Blu-ray movies, the video system must support HD resolutions, usually stated as 720 pixels, 1080i, or 1080p over a digital connection. Further, the PC must also support High-Definition Content Protection (HDCP) at the graphics chipset level and display level. Part of this is the requirement that the digital connection between the video adapter and display support be either DisplayPort or HDMI to support the HDCP signal. This extends to an HDCP-compliant graphics driver and disc-playback software.

Finally, before installing an optical drive to support the running of high-definition video content, be sure you have a multicore CPU and at least 2 GB of RAM under Windows Vista or newer. Otherwise playback may be choppy or poor quality.

 You can usually install hard drives and other devices on their sides with no impact on operation or performance. Never install a conventional hard drive upside down, however. Solid-state storage can be installed at any orientation.

Installing Solid-State Storage

Solid-state storage is available for nearly every storage need. At the low end of the price scale, thumb drives provide a solution for someone needing ease of use and portability when transferring data among computers. Similarly, we use a variety of storage devices such as flash memory cards in smartphones and cameras, often connecting these devices, or their solid-state cards, to our PCs to transfer data. And SSDs are offered as a lighter-weight option compared to conventional hard drives in laptops because they add very little weight. At the high end, SSDs are available for large server systems at a higher price than comparably sized hard drive systems, but they offer better reliability and power savings over conventional hard drives. Low-end solid-state storage will plug into a PC's bus through a media reader, whereas high-end solid-state storage is more likely to come with the SATA interface.

Because high-capacity solid-state storage that replaces a system's main hard disk drive is expensive, some drive manufacturers have created *hybrid drives*. A hybrid drive is a traditional magnetic hard disk drive with an integrated SSD with a fairly low capacity compared to the mechanical portion (usually around 8 GB). The SSD storage is used for frequently or recently accessed data, improving the drive's performance somewhat.

Installing Drives on SATA Channels

Each SATA device has its own dedicated channel and does not require setting jumpers. Simply connect one end of the SATA data cable to a SATA channel and connect the other end to the drive's data connector.

Generally speaking, SATA devices require a SATA power connector. You can use an adapter to convert a Molex connector to a SATA power connector if needed. Some older SATA devices may have two power connectors on the drive, one 4-pin Molex connector and one 15-pin SATA power connector. This is an "either-or" situation; use only one of these power connectors. If both are used, the drive will be damaged. Exercise 6-11 provides general instructions for installing an internal SATA drive. Be sure to follow the instructions in the manual for your motherboard and drive when installing a SATA drive. Figure 6-4 shows a SATA data cable alongside a SATA power cable.

FIGURE 6-4

A SATA data cable connector (left) next to a SATA power connector (right)

EXERCISE 6-11

Installing a SATA Drive

1. Secure the drive to an available drive bay.
2. Locate an available SATA connector on the motherboard or on a SATA expansion card. Plug one end of the SATA cable into the motherboard and the other end to the drive. (The plugs on the ends of the cable are different so you will have no trouble plugging the cable in correctly.)
3. Locate a power connector coming from the power supply that matches the power connector on the SATA drive and connect it to the drive. Figure 6-5 shows an installed SATA drive connected to a SATA channel on the motherboard. Notice the three open SATA channel connectors at the bottom left, just above and to the right of the one into which the cable is connected.

FIGURE 6-5

Installed SATA drive (top) connected to SATA channel on motherboard (bottom left)

Installing RAID Arrays

Not too many years ago, if you wanted RAID, you had to add a special RAID controller adapter card to your computer. Today, many desktop and server motherboards come with a RAID controller built in. Therefore, if you need to create a RAID array on a recently manufactured computer, you will probably only need to add the appropriate number of hard drives. If this is not true of the computer you wish to add RAID to, then you will need to purchase an adapter and install it.

The physical installation of a RAID adapter is identical to installation of any other bus adapter. After installing it, you will need to install and connect each drive in the array to the controller, and then start the computer and run the RAID controller setup program.

The setup program will be similar whether the controller was integrated on the motherboard or on a separate controller card. You access it while starting up the machine. In the case of an integrated controller, the RAID setup program may be on the system BIOS Setup menu, normally on an advanced menu. In the case of a separate RAID controller, watch during bootup for a prompt to press a key to enter the RAID setup. From there, you simply follow the menus and select the RAID level you desire.

Removing and Installing an External Storage Device

Today, the market is practically flooded with inexpensive external storage devices of all types and sizes, including USB flash drives, external optical drives, external HDDs, and external SSDs, as well as flash cards and their corresponding readers.

Most flash memory drives come with a USB interface, and external HDDs and SSDs have USB, IEEE 1394 (FireWire), or eSATA interfaces. Newer computers come with eSATA ports for attaching external eSATA devices. An eSATA port connects to the motherboard's SATA bus. If you wish to connect an eSATA device to a computer without SATA support, you will need to add an adapter card.

Traditional external HDDs also come in a full range of sizes from the low gigabytes to hundreds of gigabytes and even terabytes. The tiny two-inch format drives, like the thumb drives, do not need power supplies because they draw their power from the USB interface. The more conventionally sized drives require their own power supplies that plug into the wall outlet. All of these drives are so simple to use that they hardly need instructions. Plug one in, and your OS will recognize the drive, assign it a drive letter, and include it in the drive list. You can then browse the contents of the drive and manage data on the drive using the Windows interface.

Take care when removing a USB-connected storage device. Many people simply unplug their thumb drive when they finish with it, but they risk losing their data or damaging the thumb drive. Windows requires an important step before the drive is disconnected: Click the Safely Remove Hardware icon in the system tray area of the taskbar, and select the external storage device from the list that pops up. This will notify the operating system that the device is about to be removed so the operating system "stops" the device. If files are open, Windows may issue a message that the device cannot be stopped. Wait until the status message declares that it is safe to remove the device before unplugging it from the USB port. The same is also true for IEEE 1394 (FireWire) devices.

CERTIFICATION SUMMARY

This chapter led you through the processes required to install, upgrade, and configure PC components. You also learned the important issues for selecting each type of component, because whether you are building a system from scratch or just upgrading one or more components, you need to go through a selection process to ensure that the components will function well together. For this, use the knowledge gained in Chapters 3, 4, and 5 about the basic technologies and features of the components. Then, follow the appropriate step-by-step instructions from the manufacturer for the component you are installing. Never fail to read all the appropriate documentation for both a component and the PC or, specifically, the motherboard.

TWO-MINUTE DRILL

Here are some of the key points covered in Chapter 6.

Selecting Components for Custom PCs

❏ The most important components of a graphics/CAD/CAM design workstation are a powerful CPU, high-end video, and maximum memory.

❏ The most important components of an audio/video editing workstation are specialized audio and video cards, a large, fast hard drive, and dual displays.

❏ According to CompTIA A+ 901 exam objective 1.9, the most important components of a virtualization workstation are maximum RAM and a powerful CPU. In addition, there is yet another crucial requirement: both the CPU and BIOS must support virtualization.

❏ The most important components of a gaming PC are a powerful CPU, high-end video with a specialized GPU, a high-quality sound card, and high-end cooling.

❏ The most important components of a home theater PC are a surround-sound audio system, HDMI output (required by high-quality HDTVs), the HTPC compact form factor so that the box fits in the entertainment cabinet, and a TV tuner.

❑ The most important components of standard thick clients are desktop applications and a system that meets the recommended minimums for running Windows.

❑ The most important components of a thin client are just basic applications and a system that meets the minimum requirements for running Windows.

❑ The most important components of a home server PC are support for media streaming, file sharing, and print sharing. The computer should also have a Gigabit Ethernet NIC (at least 1 Gbps) and, ideally, a RAID array.

Installing and Upgrading Motherboards and Onboard Components

❑ Select motherboard, CPU, and memory modules that are compatible with each other by researching the specifications of each.

❑ When installing a motherboard, follow the instructions in the motherboard manual.

❑ The ability to upgrade an existing CPU depends on the limits of the motherboard.

❑ One of the most common and most effective PC upgrades is the installation of more RAM.

❑ An overheated PC will slow down, stop functioning altogether, or become damaged.

❑ The typical PC comes with a cooling system adequate for the standard components delivered with it.

❑ Supplement the cooling system when adding hard drives, memory, and additional expansion cards or if the PC must function in a hot environment.

Installing Adapter Cards

❑ Select an adapter card that will add the functionality you need and that also fits an available expansion port on the motherboard.

❑ Read the documentation for the adapter card and the motherboard before installing the card.

❑ Physically install an adapter card; then restart the computer and install any necessary device driver and related software, and then test the adapter.

Installing Storage Devices

❑ Only one SATA device connects to each SATA channel, so there are no configuration issues.

❑ Newer PC BIOSs often support at least one or two types of RAID arrays. Install the correct number of drives for the type of array, and configure the array through BIOS setup.

❑ Various external storage devices, such as those with eSATA, USB, or IEEE 1394 connectors, are available today. These devices are truly plug and play, and once one is plugged in, the system recognizes it and assigns it a drive letter.

❑ To disconnect an external storage device, use the Safely Remove Hardware icon in the system tray area of the Windows taskbar to stop the device, and only after it is stopped, unplug it.

SELF TEST

The following questions will help you measure your understanding of the material presented in this chapter. Read all of the choices carefully because there might be more than one correct answer. Choose all correct answers for each question.

Selecting Components for Custom PCs

1. What category of software is used by engineers to design complex products, allowing you to view a design in 2-D or 3-D?
   A. CAM
   B. CAD
   C. Device driver
   D. Graphics

2. This type of custom computer configuration often uses a special small-format case in order to fit into an entertainment console.
   A. Audio/video editing workstation
   B. Graphics workstation
   C. Home theater PC
   D. Standard thin client

3. Which of the following is an appropriate set of components for a custom audio/video editing workstation?
   A. Basic applications and minimum requirements for running Windows
   B. Powerful processor, high-end video/specialized GPU, better sound card, and high-end cooling
   C. Maximum RAM and CPU cores and hardware support for virtualization
   D. Specialized audio and video card; large, fast hard drive; and dual monitors

4. What is the generic term for a single instance of an on-screen simulation of a complete computer?
   A. CAD
   B. CAM
   C. Virtual PC
   D. Virtual machine

Installing and Upgrading Motherboards and Onboard Components

5. How can you determine which CPU and memory modules to use with a certain motherboard?
   A. All ATX motherboards accept all Intel and AMD CPUs and DIMMs.
   B. Each motherboard is unique; check the manual.
   C. Check the CPU documentation.
   D. Check the RAM module documentation.

6. What's a common name for a CPU socket that uses a lever for aligning the contacts and a cover for firmly securing a CPU?
   A. PGA
   B. LGA
   C. HTPC
   D. DIMM

7. How should you handle a motherboard?
   A. Grasp the largest component on the board.
   B. Grasp the handle.
   C. Hold it by the edges.
   D. Use a parts grabber.

8. Which of the following must you do when installing a DIMM?
   A. Open the retention clips on the socket and tilt the DIMM at a 45-degree angle to the socket.
   B. Open the retention clips on the socket and align the DIMM vertically with the socket.
   C. Close the retention clips on the socket and tilt the DIMM at a 45-degree angle to the socket.
   D. Close the retention clips on the socket and align the DIMM without tilting.

9. What prevents you from installing a DDR2 module into a DDR3 socket?
   A. DDR3 installs at a 45-degree angle; DDR2 installs vertically.
   B. Socket key
   C. Socket notch
   D. DDR2 and DDR3 have a different number of pins.

10. What do modern PC cooling systems use to detect when to adjust the performance of the cooling system to keep the system cool?
    A. CAM
    B. Heat sensors
    C. Case fan
    D. Liquid cooling

11. Which of the following could impair the functioning of the installed cooling system? (Select all that apply.)
    A. Keeping the case open during PC operation
    B. Removing slot covers behind empty expansion slots
    C. Vacuuming the interior
    D. Dirt and dust

12. Adding this cooling component is an easy and cheap cooling system upgrade.
    A. Liquid cooling system
    B. Case fan
    C. CPU heat sink
    D. CPU fan

Installing Adapter Cards

13. You have just purchased a new device that requires the latest version of USB, but your USB ports are only at USB 1.1. What is a good solution?
    A. Buy a new computer.
    B. Buy a converter for the device so it can use a parallel port.
    C. Install a USB adapter card with the latest version of the USB standard.
    D. Exchange the device for one with a parallel interface.

14. Before installing an adapter card in a computer, check the documentation and do one of the following, if necessary.
    A. Set jumpers.
    B. Install the driver.
    C. Upgrade the card's BIOS.
    D. Partition the card.

Installing Storage Devices

15. To remove a modern internal storage device, which of these do you *not* need to do?
    A. Run a utility to position the read/write heads in a safe location.
    B. Release the drive from its bay, usually by removing screws.
    C. Disconnect the power connector from the drive.
    D. Disconnect the data connector from the drive.

16. How should you choose a bay for an optical drive in the PC case?
    A. It should be in the rear of the case.
    B. It should be adjacent to the bays containing other drives.
    C. It should be an externally accessible bay.
    D. It should be one of the smallest bays.

17. Which of these is *not* solid-state storage?
    A. Optical drive
    B. Micro-SD
    C. USB flash drive
    D. CompactFlash

18. A hybrid drive is a combination of what two types of drives? (Choose two.)
    A. Optical drive
    B. Magnetic HDD
    C. Solid-state drive
    D. Tape drive

19. How many SATA drives can be connected to a single data cable?
    A. 1
    B. 2
    C. 3
    D. 4

20. Which of these interfaces would not be used to connect external storage?
    A. eSATA
    B. USB
    C. IEEE 1394
    D. PCIe

SELF TEST ANSWERS

Selecting Components for Custom PCs

1. ☑ **B.** CAD (computer-aided design) software is used by engineers to design complex products, allowing you to view a design in 2-D or 3-D.
   ☒ **A** is incorrect because computer-aided manufacturing (CAM) integrates with manufacturing equipment; it does not, by itself, include design. **C** is incorrect because a device driver is simply the software that allows the OS to control a device. **D** is incorrect because although CAD software allows you to work with graphics, it is a specialized type of software, allowing for designing and viewing in both 2-D and 3-D.

2. ☑ **C.** A home theater PC often uses a special small-format case in order to fit into an entertainment console.

☒ **A, B,** and **D** are all incorrect because none of these systems is likely to be installed in an entertainment console.

3. ☑ **D.** Specialized audio and video card; large, fast hard drive; and dual monitors is an appropriate set of components for a custom audio/video editing workstation.

☒ **A** is incorrect because basic applications and minimum requirements for running Windows is appropriate for a thin client. **B** is incorrect because powerful processor, high-end video/specialized GPU, better sound card, and high-end cooling are appropriate for a gaming PC. **C** is incorrect because maximum RAM and CPU cores and hardware support for virtualization are appropriate for a virtualization workstation.

4. ☑ **D.** Virtual machine is the term for an on-screen simulation of a complete computer.

☒ **A** is incorrect because CAD is an acronym for computer-aided design, a type of software. **B** is incorrect because CAM is an acronym for computer-aided manufacturing, a type of software. **C** is incorrect because virtual PC is not the generic term used for on-screen simulation of a complete computer.

Installing and Upgrading Motherboards and Onboard Components

5. ☑ **B.** Each motherboard is unique; check the manual.

☒ **A** is incorrect because it states that all ATX motherboards accept all Intel and AMD CPUs and DIMMs. Each motherboard is unique in the components it will support. **C** is incorrect because checking the CPU documentation will not tell you if the motherboard itself will support this CPU. **D** is incorrect because this will not tell you if the motherboard itself will support this RAM module.

6. ☑ **B.** LGA (land grid array) is correct because this type of socket uses both a lever for aligning the contacts and a cover for firmly securing a CPU.

☒ **A** is incorrect, because while PGA uses a lever, it does not use a cover. **C** is incorrect because this is the acronym for home theater PC. **D** is incorrect because this is the acronym for Dual Inline Memory Module, a type of RAM.

7. ☑ **C.** Hold a motherboard by the edges.

☒ **A** is incorrect because you should never touch any components on the board. **B** is incorrect because circuit boards do not have handles. **D** is incorrect because you will not be able to remove or install a circuit board with a parts grabber.

8. ☑ **B.** Open the retention clips on the socket and align the DIMM vertically with the socket.

☒ **A** is incorrect because you must install DIMMs in an upright position. **C** is incorrect because you cannot insert a module if the clips are closed, and you do not insert a DIMM at an angle to the socket. **D** is incorrect, only because you must open the clips first.

9. ☑ **B.** The socket key in the DDR3 socket will only allow for the notch in a DDR3 RAM module. ☒ **A** is incorrect because they both install vertically, aligned with the socket. **C** is incorrect because a socket has a key that fits the notch in the correct type of module. **D** is incorrect because they both have 240 pins.

10. ☑ **B.** Heat sensors are used by modern cooling systems to detect when to adjust the performance of the cooling system to keep the system cool. ☒ **A** is incorrect because CAM is an acronym for computer-aided manufacturing. **C** is incorrect because this is a part of a cooling system, not something that would be used to detect a temperature problem. **D** is incorrect because this is a type of cooling system, not something that would be used to detect a temperature problem.

11. ☑ **A, B,** and **D.** They are all actions that would impair the functioning of the cooling system. **A** and **B** disturb the airflow design for the case. **D** acts as insulation and reduces the cooling ability. ☒ **C** is incorrect because this will remove dirt and dust from components, improving the efficiency of cooling and not impairing it.

12. ☑ **B.** Adding a case fan is an easy and cheap cooling system upgrade, as long as there is a place to mount the fan in the case and power is available. ☒ **A** is incorrect because this is the most difficult and most expensive cooling system upgrade. **C** is incorrect because adding a heat sink would not be easy, although it may be cheap, unless the CPU is damaged in the process. **D** is incorrect because adding a CPU fan would not be easy, although it may be cheap, unless the CPU is damaged in the process.

Installing Adapter Cards

13. ☑ **C.** Installing a USB adapter card with the latest version of the USB standard is a good solution. ☒ **A** is incorrect because buying a new computer is not necessarily the solution to a single outdated component on a PC. **B** is incorrect because you do not know that this is even possible with the device or that the PC has a parallel port. **D** is incorrect because most devices have a USB interface, not parallel, and many PCs do not have parallel ports.

14. ☑ **A.** Set jumpers, if necessary, before installing an adapter card in a computer. ☒ **B** is incorrect because you will install the driver the first time you start the computer after installing the card. **C** is incorrect because you cannot update the card's BIOS until after it is installed. **D** is incorrect because partitioning is not something you do to an adapter card.

Installing Storage Devices

15. ☑ **A.** You do not have to run any utility or set the read/write heads in any certain way before removing a drive. ☒ **B, C,** and **D** are all incorrect because they represent the three things that you *do* need to do in order to remove a modern internal storage device. You must remove the drive from its bay and disconnect the power and data connectors.

16. ☑   **C.** An optical drive should be in an externally accessible bay so that its tray can eject optical discs without opening the PC's case.

☒   **A** is incorrect because externally accessible bays are all located in the front of the case, not the rear. **B** is incorrect because a drive's position in relation to other installed drives is irrelevant. **D** is incorrect because optical drives are large drives and will not fit in the small bays designed for hard disk drives.

17. ☑   **A.** An optical drive is not solid-state; it is a mechanical drive that relies on moving parts.

☒   **B** and **D** are incorrect because Micro-SD and CompactFlash are two types of memory cards, which are solid-state. **C** is incorrect because these drives are also solid-state.

18. ☑   **B** and **C.** A hybrid drive combines a traditional magnetic HDD with a small amount of SSD storage.

☒   **A** is incorrect because an optical drive is a completely different kind of drive, reading CDs and DVDs. **D** is incorrect because a tape drive is also a completely different kind of drive, reading data from magnetic tape.

19. ☑   **A.** Each SATA cable supports only one drive.

☒   **B, C,** and **D** are all incorrect because SATA supports only one drive per cable, not two, three, or four. PATA drives (now obsolete) supported up to two drives per cable.

20. ☑   **D.** PCIe is an internal interface, and would not support an external drive.

☒   **A, B,** and **C** are all incorrect because eSATA, USB, and IEEE 1394 are all common types of external storage connections.

Chapter 7

Configuring and Using Laptops

CERTIFICATION OBJECTIVES

- **901: 3.1** Install and configure laptop hardware and components

- **901: 3.2** Explain the function of components within the display of a laptop

- **901: 3.3** Given a scenario, use appropriate laptop features

- **902: 1.5** Given a scenario, use Windows Control Panel utilities

✓ Two-Minute Drill

Q&A Self Test

L aptop sales surpassed the sales of desktop PCs in 2005, well over a decade ago, as the public demanded greater portability and convenience for their computing. Today's laptops are not much more expensive than desktop PCs, and offer screen sizes, processor power, RAM configuration, and hard disk size and performance equivalent to desktops. Consequently, as a technician you may spend quite a bit of time configuring and servicing laptop PCs. You may also be frequently called upon to configure and troubleshoot smaller computing devices too, such as tablets and smartphones.

This book covers laptops and other mobile devices in three chapters. Chapter 7 covers configuration and installation of laptops and their components. Chapter 12 looks at troubleshooting and maintenance for laptops. Then in Chapter 20, you'll learn about supporting other mobile devices.

CERTIFICATION OBJECTIVES

- **901: 3.1** *Install and configure laptop hardware and components*
- **901: 3.2** *Explain the function of components within the display of a laptop*

In this section, we cover CompTIA A+ 901 exam objective 3.1, describing how to install and configure laptop components. This includes information about laptop-specific expansion slots, laptop devices, and how to replace those devices, including the keyboard, hard drive, memory, optical drive, wireless card, screen, direct current (DC) jack, battery, touchpad, plastics, speaker, system board, and central processing unit (CPU). To prepare for CompTIA A+ 901 exam objective 3.2, be sure that you understand the components of a laptop display.

Installing and Upgrading Laptops

This section defines laptop computers, as distinguished from other portable computers, and then provides an overview of opening up a laptop and the proper procedure for disassembly and reassembly of a laptop. Finally, it introduces you to some laptop-specific components and peripherals, describing installation and upgrading procedures where applicable. In all cases, when you consider installing a new component or replacing an old one, you should first check with the manufacturer for any firmware upgrades. If one is available, install it before you proceed.

What Is a Laptop?

A *portable computer* is any type of computer that you can easily transport and that has an all-in-one component layout. In addition to the size difference, portable computers differ from desktop computers in their physical layout and their use of battery power when not plugged into an alternating current (AC) outlet. Portable computers fall into two broad categories: laptops (by several different names) and handhelds, but they all are integral to mobile computing.

A *laptop* (also called a *notebook*) generally weighs less than seven pounds, fits easily into a tote bag or briefcase, and has roughly the same dimensions as a one- to two-inch-thick stack of magazines. The top contains the display, and the bottom contains the keyboard and the rest of the computer's internal components. A typical laptop uses a liquid crystal display (LCD) and requires small circuit cards that comply with modified versions of the bus standards found in full-size PCs. A laptop, as seen in Figure 7-1, opens in the same manner as a briefcase.

Initially, people called most portable computers "laptops" because they could fit on the user's lap, although early laptops were a little heavy to do this comfortably. As technology improved, laptops became smaller and lighter, and the term "notebook" came into use to reflect this smaller size.

As circuitry shrinks, we discover smaller and smaller portable computers and newer terms, such as *ultra-portable* or *mini-notebook* for a laptop that weighs less than three pounds and gives up features to keep the weight down and maintain the highest battery life. *Netbook* is a term for scaled-down laptops in the ultra-portable category, designed mainly for Internet access. People purchase netbooks as a second (or even third) computer for traveling, as a teaching aid for schoolchildren, and as a first computer for people in developing countries. At the other extreme, many purchase laptops as full-featured desktop replacements in which performance is more important than battery life. These have large screens and weigh in at the top of the range. Regardless of the size and type of portable computer, throughout this book we will use the term "laptop" to encompass all of these types.

One key feature of laptops is the ability to run the same basic OS as their desktop counterparts. For example, a Windows laptop uses the same Windows product as a Windows desktop, and the same goes for Linux and Macintosh laptops. Some ultra-portable devices like tablets and smartphones use other operating systems, or special scaled-down OS editions; these devices are covered in Chapter 20.

FIGURE 7-1

A typical laptop

Opening a Laptop Case

Many laptop configuration and installation tasks are software or BIOS based, but occasionally you'll need to do something that involves partially or fully disassembling a laptop, like upgrading the memory or replacing a screen or keyboard. If you do need to open the case, make sure you follow the safety precautions outlined in Chapter 1.

The tricky part about opening a laptop case is that there's not much standardization among brands and models. Components aren't located in standard places, and the disassembly procedures can vary widely. For example, on one model you might be able to access the hard disk drive from an access panel on the bottom of the laptop, whereas on another model you might have to remove the keyboard and touchpad to find it. Consequently, you should arm yourself with a service manual for the particular model before getting started. (Service manuals are typically available online for most laptops.) A service manual will show you where all the screws are, and will tell you which ones you need to remove to replace specific components.

A laptop has two sources of power: the AC adapter and the battery. Therefore, for your own safety, ensure that there is no power to components. Always unplug the AC adapter and remove the battery before opening the case in any way.

Use Appropriate Hand Tools

After reading the manufacturer's documentation, and before beginning, assemble all the hand tools you expect to use. Refer to Chapter 3 for a list of tools. Most laptops use standard Phillips screws, although a few may use Torx or flathead.

Don't use magnetic screwdrivers when working on PCs, including laptops. If you have no choice, take care to keep the screwdriver tip well away from anything other than the screws.

Organize Parts

Have containers ready to temporarily hold the screws and other parts that you will remove (small pill bottles work well), and have antistatic bags handy for any circuit boards you remove. After you reassemble the laptop, you should not have any extra parts except for those that you replaced.

If there are multiple types of screws used in various spots, find a way to keep each type separate, and make notes about which type goes where. For example, there might be long screws holding parts of the case together, and short screws that mount a disk drive.

Document and Label Cable and Screw Locations

This important step is also one that many people would rather skip. For internal component replacements, you will begin by removing screws from the body of the laptop. Before you open the laptop compartment, take photos with a digital camera or make a rough sketch of the exterior portion involved, and label cable and screw locations. You don't have to be an artist to do this—simple lines and shapes, carefully labeled, will suffice. Once you have removed any panels, photograph or sketch the inside, labeling any components and their cables so you will be able to reassemble the laptop after replacing or adding a part.

Laptop Components

Laptop components that distinguish one manufacturer's models from others are at least partially proprietary, but most manufacturers use at least some generic components, such as the CPU, memory, and hard drives. Therefore, if a laptop component fails, a carefully worded query in an Internet search engine should reveal sources for an appropriate replacement part or the name of a company that will replace the part for you. Both interior and exterior replacement parts are available, even plastic exterior components, such as the case, LCD lid, LCD bezels, palm rest, button panels, doors, and compartment covers for some popular laptop models. Always research whether replacing the part is more cost effective than replacing the entire laptop.

Plastics

The portable nature of a laptop and the tendency of a laptop owner to take for granted that a laptop can survive the rigors of travel mean a laptop will typically experience rough treatment during its short lifetime. Although designed for portability, manufacturers do not design most laptops to survive harsh treatment. Those models purposely designed for rough treatment sell for a premium price that most users cannot justify.

Unless you work for an organization that requires the use of laptops under extreme conditions, you will work on the more vulnerable commonplace laptops, so you need to know what to do in case the plastic that makes up the laptop case falls victim to a mishap that doesn't damage the internals. Cracked or broken laptop case corners can happen. If the laptop is out of warranty but new enough to be valuable to the owner, you need to research replacing the laptop case or some part of it. You could attempt a repair, using epoxy glue for cracks and epoxy putty to fill voids, but if you do this, be very careful not to drip the glue or putty into the interior.

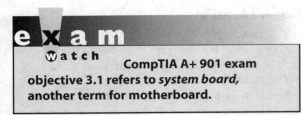

Motherboard

Although laptops run standard PC operating systems and applications, laptop motherboards have different form factors than those in desktop PCs because of the miniaturization required. A laptop motherboard contains specialized versions of the components you would expect to find in a desktop PC, such as the CPU, chipset, random access memory (RAM), video adapter (built in), and expansion bus ports.

If you find that a motherboard has failed, and your research and evaluation shows that a replacement is available and cost effective, be sure the replacement exactly matches the form factor and all electrical connections. This type of repair is fraught with failure potential, so you risk going to the expense and trouble of replacing a motherboard but botching the repair. Then you face the expense of the repair plus the cost of replacing the failed laptop.

CPU

Both Intel and AMD have a number of CPUs designed especially for laptops that include mobile computer technologies such as power-saving and heat-reducing features and throttling that lowers the clock speed and input voltage when the CPU is idle. Different models of mobile processors are available, including high-performance models requiring more power that are appropriate for desktop replacement laptops, and CPUs that run at lower voltage and reduced clock speeds to give the best battery life. Many mobile CPUs support Wi-Fi networking. Learn about wireless networking in Chapters 14 and 15.

If a laptop CPU fails, or if you wish to replace it in the hopes of obtaining better performance, contact the manufacturer for specifications for a replacement CPU. You may discover the CPU is not replaceable because they soldered it to the motherboard. Manufacturers will not usually sell you a replacement CPU, so if you find the CPU is replaceable, use the specifications to find a compatible CPU. Or, if the CPU is still functioning, you can download a utility program from either the Intel or AMD website that will give you the specs of the currently installed CPU. Note the information from the utility program, especially the voltage and power draw, and then look for a chip that matches the specs. Power-wise, you want a chip with a voltage and a power draw that is equal to or less than the one you are replacing.

To replace the CPU, you will need to open up the area inside the case that houses it. Refer to the earlier section "Opening a Laptop Case." No doubt you will need to remove a heat sink from the installed CPU; set this aside. Once the CPU is exposed, you will need to release it by loosening a screw or other locking mechanism and lifting it out. Remove the old thermal compound from the heat sink with isopropyl alcohol and a lint-free rag. When the heat sink is dry, apply a very thin layer of thermal paste to the top of the new CPU. Attach the heat sink to the new CPU and install it into the laptop socket, being sure to lock it in place again. Reassemble the system and start it up, taking care to go into the BIOS setup program to check that it recognizes the CPU.

External Expansion Slots

A laptop typically has a variety of external expansion slots for connecting different devices. Many of these are the same as on a desktop PC, such as USB, IEEE 1394, display ports like DVI, HDMI, and VGA, and 3.5-mm sound input and output jacks. However, there are a couple of external expansion ports and slots that are found solely or mostly on laptops.

Older External Expansion Slots   On old laptops you might find PCMCIA, PC Card, or CardBus external expansion slots, depending on the age of the machine. These were all standards for expansion cards inserted in slots in the side of the laptop; most cards were approximately the size and shape of a very thick credit card. None of these expansion cards are covered in the current CompTIA A+ exams, although you will find PCMCIA (Personal Computer Memory Card International Association) in the A+ Acronyms list in the exam objectives. They're mentioned here only for historical context.

ExpressCard   The modern type of external expansion slot is called ExpressCard. The current version is ExpressCard 2.0, supporting PCIe and USB 3.0 with transfer rates of up to 5 Gbps. ExpressCard devices are not compatible with any of the earlier external slot standards, like PC Card.

on the **job**

An adapter is available that allows a PC Card device to be used in an ExpressCard slot, but it may be a smarter strategy to replace the PC Card device than to buy the adapter.

The ExpressCard interface has 26 contacts in a form referred to as a *beam-on-blade connector*. Although all ExpressCard modules have the same number of contacts (also called "pins"), there are currently two sizes of modules: both are 75 mm long and 5 mm high, but they vary in width. See Figure 7-2. The form factor known as *ExpressCard/34* is 34 mm wide, whereas *ExpressCard/54* is 54 mm wide. ExpressCard/34 modules will fit into ExpressCard/54 slots, but the opposite is not true.

ExpressCard supports a variety of device types, including local area network (LAN) and wide area network (WAN) adapters, cards that add IEEE 1394 ports to the system, cards that provide interfaces for Serial Advanced Technology Attachment (SATA) and solid-state drives (SSDs), USB hubs, micro hard drives, and much more.

ExpressCard technology is not only for laptops. The ExpressCard interface is also available as standard bus cards for desktops. However, that's a very uncommon usage, and requires an add-on ExpressCard reader; desktop PCs don't come with them.

A comparison of ExpressCard/ 34 and ExpressCard/54. Both have the same 26-contact connector. (Photo: https:// commons .wikimedia.org/ wiki/File:PCCard-ExpressCard .svg [Creative Commons license])

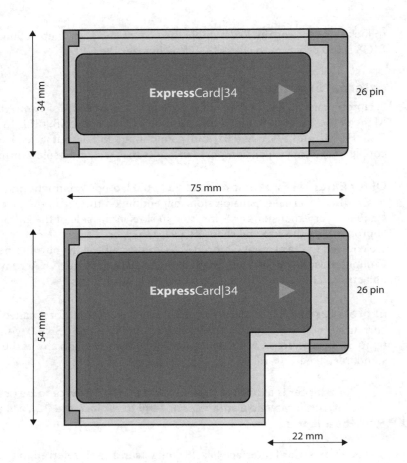

ExpressCard devices are all plug and play (as were earlier external card types like PC Card). You simply slide the card into the appropriate slot, pushing it in until it feels firmly seated. When removing a card, look for a small button next to the slot that releases the card.

Internal Expansion Slots

Some laptops also have one or more special mini-expansion slots inside the case. Two, based on the full-size PCI and PCIe expansion bus found in a desktop PC, are Mini PCI and Mini PCIe. Another is mSATA, a physically smaller form of the SATA interface. We described PCI, PCIe, and SATA in Chapters 3 and 4.

TABLE 7-1	Card Type	Dimensions in mm (depth × length × width)
Dimensions of the Various Types of Mini PCI Cards	IA	7.5 × 70 × 45
	IB	5.5 × 70 × 45
	IIA	17.44 × 70 × 45
	IIB	5.5 × 78 × 45
	IIIA	2.4 × 59.6 × 50.95
	IIIB	2.4 × 59.6 × 44.6

Mini PCI   Mini PCI is a standard based on PCI (see Chapter 3). The biggest difference (although there are others) is that Mini PCI is much smaller than PCI—both the card and the slot. Mini PCI has a 32-bit data bus. If a laptop has an installed Mini PCI slot, it is usually accessible via a small removable panel on the bottom of the case. Mini PCI cards also come in three form factors: Type I, Type II, and Type III. Types I and II each have 100 pins in a stacking connector, whereas Type III cards have 124 pins on an edge connector. Each type is further broken down into A and B subtypes, as Table 7-1 shows.

Mini PCIe   A newer standard for Mini Cards has replaced the Mini PCI standard on laptop motherboards. That is the *Mini PCIe Card* (depending on the manufacturer, this is also called *PCI Express Mini Card, Mini PCI Express, Mini PCI-E*, or simply *MiniCard*). This specification provides much faster throughput with a 64-bit data bus. At 30 mm × 26.8 mm, it is much smaller than a Mini PCI card and has a 52-pin edge connector. Figure 7-3 shows a Mini PCIe slot and card.

mSATA   Today's laptops and other mobile devices may use a mass-storage interface designed for mobile devices called mSATA (or Mini-SATA), as described in Chapter 4. Introduced in 2009, the SATA 3.1 standard is a scaled-down form factor of the SATA mass storage interface with added support for SSDs in mobile devices.

Memory

Laptop memory modules come in small form factors. The most commonly used is *Small Outline DIMM (SODIMM)*, which measure about 2 5/8", or about half the size of a Dual Inline Memory Module (DIMM). First-generation SODIMMs had 30 pins, and the next generation had 72 pins. These had a data bus width per module of 8 bits and 32 bits, respectively. Next came the 100-pin, 32-bit SODIMMs. Look for 64-bit 144-pin and 200-pin SODIMMs in older laptops. Recent laptops will have 64-bit 204-pin SODIMMs.

As with DIMMs, SODIMMs have notches in them so that they only fit into the properly keyed SODIMM slots. The 144-pin SODIMMs have a single notch just off center. However,

200-pin SODIMMs have at least three different locations for the notch, depending on the DDR level, as described in Chapter 4. At this time, you can find 200-pin DDR1, DDR2, and DDR3 SODIMMs, although the latter are more common in new laptops. All have a single notch that is off center and in a different location for each type (DDR1, DDR2, and DDR3). Figure 7-4 shows a 200-pin DDR3 SODIMM. There are also 204-pin SODIMMs available with DDR3 RAM that have a notch that is just off center.

Figure 7-5 shows a laptop with the battery removed and the access panel open to expose two 204-pin DDR3 SODIMMs, each populated with 4 GB of RAM. The top one (at bottom)

FIGURE 7-5

A laptop with
access panel
removed to
expose the two
DDR3 SODIMMs

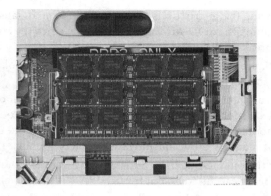

has eight chips on it, and it covers up half of the module under it, showing only its top four chips. Visible near them are 102 of the top module's 204 pins, as well as the module notch. Also visible on the sides of each module are the clips used to secure them in place.

MicroDIMM, a RAM module designed for smaller laptops, is half the size of a SODIMM and allows for higher-density storage.

You can add RAM to most laptops if there is a RAM slot available. If none is available, you must swap out the existing RAM module or modules for denser modules. Some systems include extra RAM slots within the chassis, which requires either opening the computer's case or removing the compartment cover and inserting the RAM module in an available slot. Exercise 7-1 describes the steps for installing memory in a laptop and for verifying that the system recognizes it.

EXERCISE 7-1

Installing SODIMM Memory

For this exercise, you will need a way to ground yourself and/or your work area. You will also need a new module of SODIMM memory appropriate for your laptop in an antistatic bag, the user's manual, a spare antistatic bag, and a small nonmagnetic screwdriver for opening the case. If you do not have a new module, simply remove an already installed module and reinstall it. In this case, you will just need an antistatic bag in which to place the module should you need to set it down.

1. Ground yourself using one of the methods described in Chapter 1.
2. Turn off the computer and all external devices.
3. Unplug the computer and disconnect all exterior cables and devices. Remove the laptop battery.

4. Following the instructions in the laptop user manual, open the compartment containing the SODIMM slots. Be careful, since the cover may have retaining tabs that break off easily.

5. Your laptop may have one or two memory slots. Look for numbers near any open slots and fill the lowest numbered slot first.

6. If you are replacing memory, remove the module or modules you are replacing. To remove a module, press down on the retaining clips located on the sides, lift the edge of the module to a 45-degree angle, and gently pull it out of the slot, being careful to hold it by its edges without touching the contacts or chips.

7. Place the old module in an antistatic bag. Remove the new module from its antistatic bag, being careful to hold it by its edges without touching the contacts or chips.

8. Align the notch of the new memory module with that of the memory slot, as shown here, and gently insert the module into the slot at a 45-degree angle. Carefully rotate the module down flat until the clamps lock it in place.

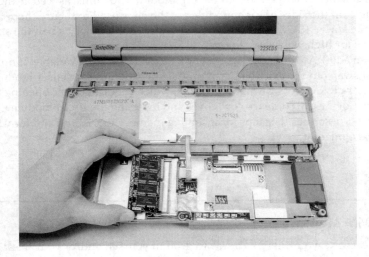

9. Close the memory compartment, reinstall the battery, and reconnect the power cable.

10. Power up the computer, and, if necessary (according to the user manual), configure memory in BIOS setup, although this is not normally required.

11. Perform a normal startup in Windows, and check the System Properties applet in the Control Panel to see if it recognized the new memory.

You may notice the memory count during bootup does not quite add up to the total memory installed, which means your laptop may be using some of your system RAM for the video adapter, which often is the case with integrated video adapters if they do not have their own volatile RAM (VRAM). Main RAM memory used in this way is *shared video memory* and is not available to the operating system.

Memory Card Reader

A laptop today will often come with a built-in, solid-state card reader. While we often lump all of these devices together as flash memory, they have several formats (see Chapter 4). Therefore, be sure your laptop supports the format you use, such as CompactFlash (CF), miniSD, MultiMediaCard (MMC), Secure Digital (SD), and Memory Stick (MS).

Fans

Before considering replacing a seemingly failed laptop fan, open the laptop and clean the fan blades. If the fan still does not work, attempt to replace the fan. This process will require the usual search for a suitable fan. Once you locate one and determine that the cost is worth the effort, follow the manufacturer's instructions to replace the failed fan, being careful to remove and replace the *heat pipe*, a tubular device that works with the fan to draw heat away from the interior of the laptop. If the installation is successful, you should hear the fan when you power up the laptop.

Storage Devices

For years, laptops came with two mass storage devices: a hard drive and an optical drive. Today you will still find an optical drive in most full-size laptops, but in high-end and/or very lightweight laptops an SSD may replace the hard drive. As the price of SSDs comes down, this will become more and more common. Recall the discussion of SSDs in Chapter 4.

Although the optical drives in laptops are low profile, they still must accommodate 4.75" optical discs. Most laptops typically use 2.5" hard drives versus the 3.5" hard drives used in desktop PCs. Very small laptops have 1.8" hard disk drives.

The biggest change in laptop mass storage in the last several years has been large-capacity SSDs replacing hard drives at all price points of the newer ultra-portable models. SSDs in laptops are desirable because they are faster than hard drives, lighter, and less vulnerable to damage from impacts or excess motion. As you learned in Chapter 4, hybrid drives offer some of the speed benefits of SSD by combining a standard mechanical hard drive with a smaller SSD drive in the same unit.

After you power down the computer, use the same precautions you would use with a PC case before proceeding. Accessing an internal storage device may be as simple as removing a plastic access cover on the bottom or side of the laptop. In that case, simply slide the drive out, and then replace it with a new drive and replace the cover. On the other hand, replacing a storage

Chapter 5 covered the difference between fluorescent (CCFL) and LED backlighting, so make sure you review that material in the context of laptops as well as desktops. This topic is newly added to CompTIA A+ 901 exam objective 3.2 for the latest exam.

device may involve removing the keyboard or the entire bottom of the case. This is where the service manual comes in handy, to find out where the hard drive is located and how to access it.

Displays and Video Adapters

A laptop has a flat-panel display integrated into the "lid" of the case and connected to the integrated video adapter. A laptop display is usually some form of LCD display as described in Chapter 5—most often lit with *light-emitting diodes (LEDs)*. Many small-screen laptops or touch screen tablets have organic LED (OLED), active matrix OLED (AMOLED), or Super AMOLED screens, also described in Chapter 5. Some high-end laptop displays support 3-D, which also requires a built-in High Definition Multimedia Interface (HDMI) video adapter. An LCD screen requires an internal *inverter* to convert the DC current from the power adapter or battery to the AC current the display requires.

Most laptop video adapters can drive two displays—the integrated flat-panel display and an external display. There may be a VGA, HDMI, DVI, Thunderbolt (Mac), or Mini DisplayPort (Mac) port, or perhaps more than one of those. You can use the external display as a replacement for the integrated display, display the same desktop on both simultaneously, or use the external display in addition to the built-in display in a multi-monitor configuration, as described in Chapter 5. Converters are available between nearly every combination of display port type and every other type, including Thunderbolt to/from DVI and HDMI to/from VGA.

To activate multiple monitor support, press the FN key in conjunction with whatever key is defined as the Display Mode key. (It varies depending on the keyboard, but is usually one of the function keys. There will be a graphic on the key indicating its purpose.) You'll learn more about the FN key later in this chapter, in the "Special Function Keys" section. If you don't have a Display Mode key, or can't find it, you might be able to choose a display mode via the OS. See Exercise 7-2 to learn how to do this in Windows 8.1 or 10.

Thunderbolt and Mini DisplayPort are new additions to 901 exam objective 3.1, due to the addition of Macintosh technologies to the exams. These two ports look identical and both can be used for displays. However, a Thunderbolt port has a lightning-bolt symbol next to it, and it can accommodate other types of devices besides displays (for example, a Gigabit Ethernet adapter). A Mini DisplayPort is more limited in the range of devices it can accommodate.

EXERCISE 7-2

Extending Windows to an Additional Monitor

You'll need a PC with Windows 7, 8.1, or 10 installed on it, and an external monitor. You'll also need for the laptop to have at least one kind of video port (VGA, DVI, or HDMI), and an appropriate cable to run from the external monitor to that port.

If you have Windows 8.1 or 10, follow these steps:

1. Connect the external monitor to the PC's display port.
2. Connect the power cord to the external monitor and power it on.
3. Press WINDOWS KEY-P to open the Second Screen pane (Windows 8.1) or Project pane (Windows 10).
4. Click Extend. The desktop extends to the second monitor.

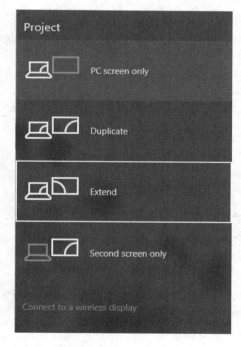

5. Repeat Steps 3–4 and click PC Screen Only to return to normal viewing.
6. Power off the external monitor and disconnect it from the laptop.

If you have Windows 7, follow these steps. (These steps also work as an alternative method in Windows 8.1 and 10.)

1. Connect the external monitor to the PC's display port.
2. Connect the power cord to the external monitor and power it on.
3. Right-click the desktop and click Screen Resolution. Two monitors appear in the graphic in the center of the dialog box, labeled 1 and 2.
4. Click the 2 monitor on the graphic.
5. Open the Multiple Displays drop-down list and click Extend These Displays.

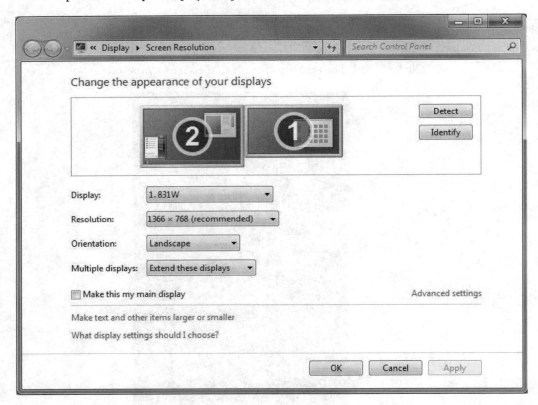

6. Click OK.
7. Repeat Steps 3–6, but in Step 5, select Duplicate These Displays. Now both monitors show the same thing.
8. Power off the external monitor and disconnect it from the laptop.

The display is one of the most expensive laptop components, and one of the most difficult to replace. If you have a failed laptop display and manage to find a suitable replacement, follow the manufacturer's instructions for removing the old display and installing the replacement.

There typically isn't much you can do to upgrade or repair a video adapter in a laptop because it is usually built into the motherboard. You would have to replace the entire motherboard. However, you can affect a video adapter's performance by updating its driver. You can download driver updates from the PC manufacturer or from the video adapter manufacturer; sometimes these updates add new features as well as fix problems.

I/O Devices

As with a PC, the primary input devices for a laptop are the keyboard and a pointing device. The primary output device is the display. We will now look closer at the display, keyboards, and other I/O devices designed for portability.

Keyboards   Due to size constraints, the built-in keyboard in a laptop has thinner keys that do not have the vertical travel that those on traditional keyboards do, so they do not give the same tactile feedback. If you often work in low-light environments, you may want a laptop with a *keyboard backlight*, a feature that gently lights the keyboard for ease of use. Just a few years ago, this feature was in only a few premium laptops, but in the last few years manufacturers have created more models with this feature, or offer it as an upgrade option. If you choose a laptop with a backlit keyboard, accept the fact that using it will be yet another draw on the battery. (There may be an FN key combination you can press to toggle the backlighting on/off. See "Special Function Keys," later in this chapter.) You can also purchase an external keyboard with this feature.

A laptop keyboard has the alphanumeric keys, ENTER key, function keys (F1, F2, ... F12), and some of the modifier keys (SHIFT, CTRL, ALT, and CAPS LOCK) in the same orientation to one another as on a full-size keyboard. But many of the special keys—the directional arrow keys and the INSERT, DELETE, PAGE UP, and PAGE DOWN keys—are in different locations.

The separate numeric keypad disappeared a long time ago from most laptops. Rather, the keypad is completely absent or the function integrates into the alphanumeric keys, and small numbers on the sides of keys or in a different color on the top of each key indicate what number they are. Each alphanumeric key normally produces two characters—one when pressing the key alone and another when NUM LOCK is toggled on to enable the keypad. On many mobile keyboards an indicator light illuminates when NUM LOCK is on. On some laptops the keypad characters may be controlled by pressing the function-modifying FN key while pressing certain marked keys. See "Special Function Keys," later in this chapter, for more information about the FN key and its functions.

Like other laptop components, you can replace the built-in laptop keyboard if you can find a suitable replacement. If a laptop keyboard became damaged and you decide that you must replace it and you have determined that it is cost effective to do so, follow

FIGURE 7-6

A laptop
touchpad

the manufacturer's instructions. Alternatively, you might just decide to use an external keyboard—a very inexpensive alternative since you simply plug it into a USB port.

Pointing Devices When shopping for a new laptop, you can expect to find a built-in pointing device on all the popular models. After experimenting with a variety of such devices, most manufacturers have settled on the *touchpad* (or *touch pad*), a smooth, rectangular, touch-sensitive panel sitting in front of the keyboard, as shown in Figure 7-6. Moving your finger across the surface of the touchpad moves the pointer on the display, and you use the buttons next to the touchpad as you would use those on a mouse or trackball. Alternatively, you can tap the touchpad in place of clicking a button.

Although mostly obsolete now (except on some IBM/Lenovo laptops), you may encounter a *pointing stick* (or *point stick*)—a very tiny, joystick-type device that usually sits in the center of the keyboard, sometimes between the G, H, and B keys. Barely protruding above the level of the keys, this device usually has a replaceable plastic cap for traction and two buttons located in the front of the keyboard. You operate a pointing stick by pushing it in the direction you want to drive the on-screen pointer. If the installed pointing device fails, replacing it is much like replacing the keyboard because you need to locate a suitable replacement and then open the computer and install it. If your touchpad fails and the laptop is not still under warranty, consider using an external pointing device.

Digitizers A *digitizer* is a touch-sensitive input device that allows you to input data and commands using your finger or a stylus pen. If the laptop has a touch screen, the screen has a built-in digitizer. A touchpad is technically also a digitizer, although it isn't commonly lumped into that category.

A touch screen's digitizer hardware is a separate feature from the output component of the screen (that is, the display image). It's a transparent, built-in overlay on top of the screen. The digitizer could be broken while the screen is just fine, and vice versa. However, it's difficult to find them separated as replacement parts, so when one goes bad, you usually end up replacing the entire touch screen unit.

I/O Ports and Adapters

Don't have the correct port for the device you need to use? There's probably an adapter available for it. For example, you can get adapters that plug into a USB port and provide Ethernet (RJ-45) connectors, Wi-Fi, Bluetooth, FireWire, Thunderbolt, and just about any other external connector for I/O devices. Make sure you know about the range of adapters available; 901 exam objective 3.1 specifically mentions the following:

- **Thunderbolt** and **DisplayPort**   Know the difference between them (explained in the "Displays and Adapters" section, earlier in this chapter).
- **USB to RJ-45** or **USB to Wi-Fi dongle**   Know what a dongle is (it's a short cord or cable with a port or device hanging off it, and connecting to an external port).
- **USB to Bluetooth**   Be aware that you can install Bluetooth capability through a USB port device.
- **USB to optical drive**   External optical drives connect to the USB port, making it possible for lightweight laptops to function without a full-time optical drive to weigh them down.

Media/Accessory Bay

To save space, a laptop may contain a *media bay*, a compartment that holds a single media device that you can switch with another. For instance, you may switch an optical drive or a secondary hard drive into and out of a single bay, but you can use only one device in the bay at a time. Figure 7-7 shows a media bay and two drives that you can alternate in the bay. This type of bay, also called an *accessory bay*, is now less common, since so many external accessories and drives are available with USB, FireWire, or external SATA (eSATA) interfaces, including external media bays that hold optical drives or hard drives. However, it is still mentioned in 901 exam objective 3.1.

Wireless Communications

Laptop computers are designed for portability, so it is only natural that they should have built-in wireless communication. Wi-Fi is a given, of course, but most laptops also support Bluetooth, and some also support less common wireless standards as well, such as WiMAX and/or cellular wireless (4G).

FIGURE 7-7

A media bay in a laptop, with two drives that you can swap into this bay

Wi-Fi   Most new laptops today come with a Wi-Fi adapter built in. For those laptops without built-in Wi-Fi, you can purchase Mini PCIe or USB add-ons. We will describe Wi-Fi in more detail in Chapter 14 and talk about configuring a Wi-Fi adapter in Chapter 15.

Figure 7-8 shows a Wi-Fi wireless LAN adapter installed in a Mini PCIe slot. This particular adapter is actually two in one, as it is both a Wi-Fi adapter and a Bluetooth adapter. The antennas for this card run through the small black cable visible on the upper right of the card and running to the upper left. It leads up through the lid hinge into the lid behind the screen. If the antenna fails, it requires dismantling the screen of the laptop.

on the job

The switch to enable or disable a wireless adapter is often very easy to accidently trigger, causing the wireless to turn off. If you support laptop users, educate yourself on the method used on each laptop so that you can help a client who accidently disables the wireless adapter.

Bluetooth   *Bluetooth* is another wireless standard. Bluetooth devices use radio waves to communicate with each other. Some laptops come with a Bluetooth adapter built in. If not, you can purchase one—often along with one or more wireless devices that use the Bluetooth

FIGURE 7-8

A Mini PCIe
WLAN card
installed in a
laptop

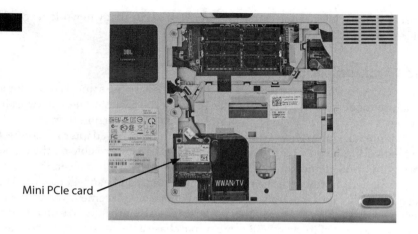

Mini PCIe card

standard. A popular peripheral package is a Bluetooth keyboard and mouse bundled with
a Bluetooth transmitter adapter using a USB interface. Many cell phones have Bluetooth
built in for use with wireless headsets and for communicating with a Bluetooth-enabled
computer to share the phonebook and other data stored in the phone.

Although one thinks of Bluetooth as mainly a very-short-distance communications
standard, there are actually three classes of Bluetooth, each with its own power
requirements, and each with a power-dependent distance. Class 1 Bluetooth devices have
a distance limit of about 100 meters, whereas Class 2 devices are limited to about 10 meters,
and Class 3 are limited to 1 meter. The class we describe in this chapter is Class 3. Microsoft
Windows operating systems have included support for the Bluetooth standard since
Windows XP. On laptops with an integrated Bluetooth adapter, you use a switch on the case
or a key combination to enable or disable the adapter. This may be the same mechanism
used to enable or disable a Wi-Fi adapter, if both are integrated.

Cellular WAN   A cellular network is a wireless wide area network (WWAN), or *cellular
WAN*. Participation in a cellular network requires some type of subscription plan with the
cellular provider. The major cellular telecommunications providers now offer a variety
of options for data communications over the cellular networks, but unlike Wi-Fi, laptop
manufacturers do not usually build cellular adapters into their systems, although several
providers bundle their adapter and a contract plan with certain e-book readers and tablets.
Some laptops have a slot available for an optional WWAN adapter. Although this is not
usually considered something a user should add, it makes it easy for the manufacturer or
supplier to add a WWAN card as an option when you custom-order your laptop. Notice in
Figure 7-8 the Mini PCIe slot is reserved for either a WWAN adapter or a TV tuner card.

If there is no cellular adapter installed, or an appropriate internal slot is not available, you
need to contact a cell provider, sign up for the service, and buy a cellular adapter from that

provider. You must be sure the card they offer is of a type that will work in your laptop. Then install it as you would any device in that format.

Wired Communications

When it comes to wired communications, the choices are the same as those for a desktop PC—dial-up modem or Ethernet. Chapter 14 offers the basics of these networking technologies and Chapter 15 tells you how to install and configure them.

Most, if not all, laptops now come with a built-in Ethernet adapter for connecting to a wired network. The only part of a built-in Ethernet adapter visible on the outside of the case is an RJ-45 connector (described in Chapter 4). If your built-in Ethernet adapter fails, you will need to research the replacement options, and you will face the same choice between the higher cost but convenience of an internal replacement versus the lower cost and inconvenience of an external Ethernet adapter—also now the size of a flash drive. Either buy one that comes on its own USB cable or purchase an extension cable so that the device isn't vulnerable to damage from jostling. Recall our On the Job tip in Chapter 4, in which we recommended using USB extension cables.

Power and Electrical Input Devices

Laptops come with two sources of electrical input: an AC adapter for when AC power is available and a built-in battery for when external power is not available.

Laptop Batteries When not plugged into a wall outlet, a laptop computer gets its power from a rechargeable battery. The typical laptop today has a *lithium ion (Li-Ion) battery*. You may also run into *nickel metal hydride (NiMH)* batteries in older laptops, or a very old laptop may have a heavy, inefficient, and obsolete *nickel-cadmium (NiCD)* battery. A Li-Ion battery is smaller and lighter than its predecessors and produces more power. These rechargeable batteries have a battery life between recharges in the range of five to eight hours at best.

Laptop batteries have only a few years of life, so expect to replace a laptop battery as it approaches two years of age. Purchase replacement batteries from the laptop manufacturer or other sources that specialize in laptop parts or batteries. Laptops allow easy access to the battery to change it. In many cases, the battery fits into a compartment on the bottom or on the side of the computer. Look for a release mechanism, such as a slide, to remove the battery. Figure 7-9 shows a Li-Ion laptop battery removed from a laptop, turned upside down, and resting on the case.

The AC adapter recharges the battery, but if you are not near a wall outlet when the battery's power fades, you will not be able to work until you replace the battery with a fully charged one or until AC power is available again. People who do important, time-sensitive work on a laptop often travel with an extra battery for this reason.

FIGURE 7-9

A Li-Ion laptop
battery removed
from the case

DC Controller   Most laptops include a *DC controller* that monitors and regulates power usage, providing just the correct amount of DC voltage to each internal component. The other features of DC controllers vary by manufacturer, but typically, they provide short-circuit protection, give "low battery" warnings, and can be configured to shut down the computer automatically when the power is low.

AC Adapter   As described in Chapter 5, the AC adapter is your laptop's external power supply that you plug into an AC power source. Like the power supply in a desktop PC, it converts AC power to DC power. If you must replace an external adapter, simply unplug it and attach a new one that matches the specifications and plug configuration of the adapter it is replacing. Furthermore, AC adapters have different output wattages. An AC adapter will show its wattage on its label; if you are using an AC adapter other than the one that came with the laptop, read the label first and make sure it matches the wattage of the original AC adapter for that unit. An AC adapter with a lower wattage than the original may not work at all, or it may partially work but be lacking in some way (such as powering the laptop but not charging its battery).

DC Jack   A *DC jack* is the connector on a laptop to which an AC adapter connects. The actual socket in the jack will vary, as described in Chapter 5. If a DC jack becomes damaged and must be replaced, you may be able to find one from the manufacturer or another source. The entire DC jack assembly is usually no bigger than a single die from a pair of gaming dice. To install it, you must disconnect the power cord, remove the battery, and open the case. Then remove the old DC jack assembly and install the replacement. The tricky part about this replacement is not so much the jack itself, but the fact that you may have to disassemble the laptop to get to it.

CMOS Battery   Like a PC, an older laptop has a battery on the motherboard that supports the CMOS chip that holds the system's BIOS settings. (Newer models use flash memory instead.) If a laptop shows signs of a failing CMOS battery—namely, losing the date and time when the computer is off and also out of main battery power—you will need to investigate the type and location of the battery in the laptop and purchase a replacement only if the laptop's documentation describes how to open it to replace the CMOS battery. While some laptop components are accessible under easy-to-remove panels, the CMOS battery usually requires that you dissemble the case. For instance, some models hide the battery under the palmrest—the area in front of the keyboard that contains the touchpad. A laptop CMOS battery may resemble the typical lithium battery, also called a coin-cell battery, or it may be an entire battery pack of coin-size batteries shrink-wrapped in plastic with a special connector on one end.

Multimedia Components

Laptops have much the same multimedia components as desktop PCs, although smaller of course, and more difficult to get to if they must be replaced.

Webcam   A built-in video camera, or *Webcam*, typically appears at the top of the screen on a laptop, embedded in the bezel. Webcams have a variety of uses, including facial recognition, motion detection, and video chatting, depending on the software used with them.

The Webcam may not be separable from the screen, or from the lid of the laptop; you may need to replace the entire screen if the Webcam isn't working, or resort to using an external USB Webcam replacement. Check the service manual for the laptop to determine how to access and replace the Webcam if needed.

Microphone   A laptop will have a built-in microphone, which the user can employ for voice pattern recognition security, speech recognition for data input, and audio recordings, among other things. The quality of the built-in microphone generally isn't very good, so power users of those features (especially those who convert speech to written text) may prefer to add an external microphone. An external microphone may plug into the Mic port on the laptop (if there is one) or to a USB port.

To access and replace the built-in microphone, consult the service manual for the laptop. It is probably located somewhere toward the front of the keyboard (that is, close to the person using the laptop), but designs vary greatly.

Speakers   Laptops often come with very small speakers that provide marginally adequate sound. If these speakers fail, you may be able to find suitable replacements, but a better alternative is to plug external speakers into the laptop using either the earphone jack, if that is all that is available, or other audio-out jacks. Replacing internal laptop speakers is nearly as involved as replacing a video adapter, along with all the inherent dangers of opening the laptop, but plugging in external speakers is risk-free, takes only a few seconds, and will improve the sound output. Be sure to test the speakers after replacing or adding them.

When a PC has more than one set of speakers available (such as with a laptop that has both a built-in speaker and external speakers), you must tell the operating system which speaker(s) to prefer for playback. To do that in Windows, open the Control Panel and choose Hardware and Sound. Under the Sound heading, click Manage Audio Devices, and then on the Playback tab, select the desired speaker(s) and click Set Default.

SCENARIO & SOLUTION

What important step in the disassembly of a laptop will help the most when you attempt to reassemble it?	Document and label cable and screw locations.
When I plug in an external monitor, how do I get the display to extend to that monitor?	On many laptops there is an FN key combination that enables the external display. You can also configure the display in the Display Properties in the Control Panel. In Windows 8.1 and later, you can also extend the display onto an external monitor through the Action Center.

CERTIFICATION OBJECTIVE

■ *902: 1.5* *Given a scenario, use Windows Control Panel utilities*

CompTIA A+ 902 exam objective 1.5 contains a long list of Windows Control Panel utilities with a wide range of functionality. We will discuss most of these in later chapters, as appropriate, but here we will address an important subset for use on laptops, the power options. In this section you'll learn about Windows power management features that power down the screen and hard drive when it detects no activity, and power-saving modes called Hibernate, Sleep, Standby, and Suspend. You'll also learn about various power options as well as when and under what circumstances these various power plans are used.

Power Options

Nearly every component in a modern laptop has some sort of *power management* feature, a group of options in the hardware and the operating system that allows you to minimize the use of power—especially, but not exclusively—to conserve a laptop's battery life. In fact, even desktop computers come with power-saving features. Many devices, like the hard drive, will power down when not in use, and CPUs and other circuitry will draw less power when they have less demand for their services. Displays will power down after a configurable period of time during which there was no activity from the mouse or keyboard. If a component is not drawing power, it is not creating heat, so power management and cooling go hand-in-hand.

Power Management Standards

Supporting the power management features in laptop hardware requires that the system BIOS, the chipset, the operating system, and device drivers be aware of these features and be able to control and manage them. Several standards and practices have come together for power management to work at both the hardware and operating system level. They include SMM, APM, ACPI, and ASPM.

System Management Mode

For over two decades, Intel CPUs have included a group of features called *System Management Mode (SMM)*, and other CPU manufacturers have followed suit. SMM allows a CPU to reduce its speed without losing its place, so to speak, so it does not stop working altogether. In addition, a CPU using SMM mode triggers power savings in other components. System BIOSs and operating systems take advantage of SMM. Intel took the first two steps for involving the BIOS and operating system in power management when they developed two standards, APM and ACPI.

Advanced Power Management

Advanced Power Management (APM) defines four power-usage operating levels: Full On, APM Enabled, APM Standby, and APM Suspend. Details of these operating levels are not important, as they are now a subset of the next standard, ACPI.

Advanced Configuration and Power Interface

Advanced Configuration and Power Interface (ACPI) includes all the power-usage levels of APM, plus two more. It also supports the soft-power feature described in Chapter 5. ACPI defines how to configure the power management feature in the BIOS settings and has seven power-usage levels, called *power states*. These range from a power state in which the computer is fully on and all devices are functional, through several sleeping states to two power-off states. The details of ACPI are not important, as long as you know how to configure power management in Windows.

Active State Power Management

Active State Power Management (ASPM) is a standard for PCI Express that allows power to be incrementally reduced to individual PCIe serial links (paths). Windows enables or disables a link based on several parameters, including the system power plan, PCIe capabilities, and more. In the Windows graphical user interface (GUI), this is called *Link State Power Management.*

Configuring Power Management in Windows

Getting the most out of your laptop battery depends on how you manage the use of the battery's power. Using the Power Options Control Panel utility in Windows, you can configure the power management settings to minimize the power usage of laptop components. While this utility is available in Windows on all computers, you will find some differences in it when you compare Windows installations on desktops versus laptops and in different Windows versions.

Figure 7-10 shows the Windows 7 Power Options utility on a Dell laptop on which Windows 7 was preinstalled. Notice the references to the Dell Battery Meter and the Dell plan. Also notice the screen brightness control at the bottom. Dimming the screen helps conserve power use, and many find dimming the screen in low-light environments is a bit easier on their eyes. There is also a setting in the left pane for choosing what closing the lid does—a very laptop-centric setting. This option is not shown in the retail version of Windows 7 installed on a desktop PC (see Figure 7-11). Missing also is any branded information, such as the Dell Battery Meter and Dell power plan. Power Options on a PC does not include a battery meter, because the desktop computer would never need to run on battery. Windows 8 and 8.1 have similar power management options to those in Windows 7. The Windows 10 power management options can be configured via the Control Panel, the same as earlier versions, or they can be configured via the Settings app if you prefer. (You don't have to study Windows 10, though, because it's not on the exams.)

Using Power-Saving Modes

Power-saving modes let you set the computer to use little or no power without shutting it down completely. The computer's current state (including all OS settings and open applications) is preserved, so that when you resume work, the computer comes back up to full operation within seconds. You can configure these power modes via the Power Options applet in the Control Panel in all modern Windows versions. You can place the computer in one of the low-power modes manually from the menu on or adjacent to the Power or Shut Down command on the Start menu/Start screen. (The exact placement depends on the Windows version.)

FIGURE 7-10

Windows 7
Power Options
on a Dell laptop
computer

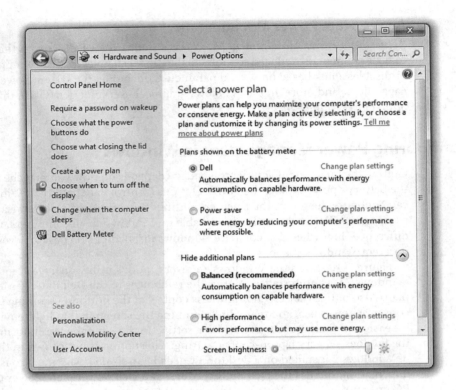

On very old computers, some power-saving modes may be built into BIOS setup, but don't use those settings, as they can conflict with the OS power management configuration. Leave any BIOS-based power management turned off.

Sleep Mode   *Sleep mode* uses just enough power to keep the RAM powered on the computer, and shuts down everything else (CPU, disk drives, display, and so on). The computer appears to be off, but it springs back to life, already booted up, when you press the power button. Sleep mode extends the length of the battery charge considerably, while keeping the machine state preserved so you don't have to close applications and shut down (and then restart everything later). You might use Sleep mode when packing up your work PC to go home if you plan on working when you get home, for example. In earlier Windows versions, Sleep mode was called Standby (Windows XP) or Suspend (Windows 95).

FIGURE 7-11   Windows 7 Power Options on a generic desktop PC

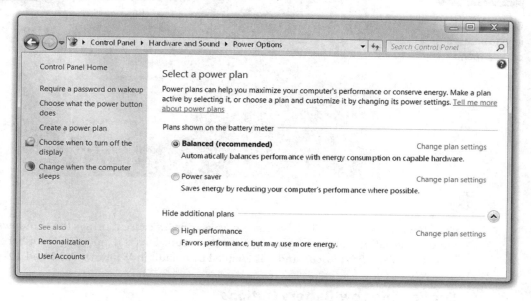

Sleep mode is good for short-term pausing (less than a day or so), but for longer stretches of time, if the PC is on battery power, the battery eventually runs out of power. What happens at that point depends on the power management settings configured in Windows. It could shut down (not optimal, because you lose any unsaved work), or it could switch over into Hibernate mode (described next). When power management is set up to switch over to Hibernate when the battery charge falls below a certain amount, that's known as *Hybrid sleep*, and it's available in Windows Vista and newer versions.

Hibernate Mode   The *Hibernate* power-saving mode uses hard drive space to save all the programs and data that are in memory at the time you choose this mode. The computer then completely shuts down, using no power while it is hibernating. Like Sleep, Hibernate lets you stop work on your computer but quickly pick up where you left off. It takes slightly longer to go into and out of Hibernate than it does to go into and out of Sleep. Hibernate is a safer option if you aren't sure how long you'll be away from your computer, as it does not require any power since everything is saved to disk.

Windows 8/8.1 and 10 add another twist to the Hibernate feature. When you shut down a Windows 8, 8.1, or 10 computer using the Shut Down command, Windows actually uses a form of hibernation—not the entire saving-all-your-programs-and-data-to-disk hibernation, but a saving to disk of the Windows OS kernel as it appears in memory at the moment you

Click the battery
icon to access a
pop-up menu.

shut down. As a result, Windows startup is very fast because it brings the Windows kernel out of hibernation, fully configured and ready to run. This startup using the hibernated kernel is called *Hybrid Boot*, and it is enabled by default in Windows 8/8.1 and 10.

Configuring Low-Battery Options

On a laptop, the Windows notification area of the taskbar displays a tiny battery icon that serves as an indicator of battery charge level. Hover the mouse pointer over this icon to see battery charge status. Click the icon to display a pop-up menu (Figure 7-12 shows the Windows 8.1 version, but others are similar) that will allow you to switch power plans, adjust the screen brightness, or open Power Options for even more choices. To quickly change power plans from here, click the radio button next to the plan you wish to select. To view and change plan settings, click the battery icon, and then click More Power Options.

Exploring Power Plans/Power Schemes

Windows has preconfigured power settings, called Power Plans. Of the preconfigured plans, the Balanced Power Plan is a good bet for most laptop users because it balances power savings with performance. However, if better performance is more important to you than battery life, select the High Performance power plan. If you need every minute of battery power you can squeeze out of your laptop while away from the office, select the Power Saver power plan.

Exercise 7-3 will guide you as you create a new plan in Windows 7 or 8.1.

EXERCISE 7-3

Exploring Power Options on a Laptop

For this exercise, you will need a computer with Windows 7 or 8.1 installed. It is not necessary to have a laptop for this, although there will be some differences. For instance, the screen brightness and lid-closing settings will not be available.

1. Open the Control Panel and (in Category View) click Hardware and Sound | Power Options.
2. Notice which plan is selected.
3. In the left pane, click Create a Power Plan.

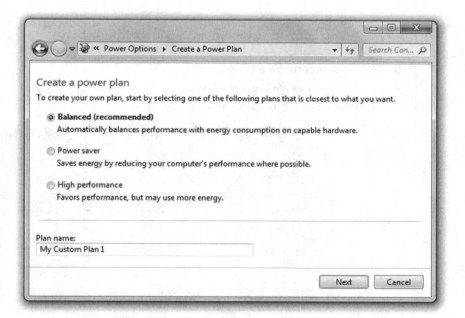

4. In the Create Power Plan window, select one of the plans and click Next.
5. If you are using a laptop, notice the two groups of settings—one for when you're on battery and one for when the laptop is plugged in. If using a desktop, you'll see only one set of settings.

6. Make changes to the settings.
7. Click Create to save the new plan.
8. The new plan is now listed in Power Options.

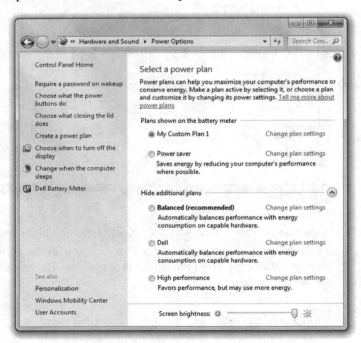

Changing Power Settings

To dig even deeper into power settings, open Power Options, and click Change Plan Settings for the current power plan. Then, in the Edit Plan Setting window, click Change Advanced Power Settings. This will display the Advanced Settings tab of the Power Options dialog box, shown in Figure 7-13, where you can scroll through a long list of settings, each of which varies based on whether the computer is on battery or plugged in and, with the exception of the Require a Password on Wakeup setting, controls the power management for an individual component. The actual items in this list may vary, based on what hardware is present (note the Intel Graphics Settings). Following is a sample list of settings found in

FIGURE 7-13

In the Edit Plan Settings window, click Change Advanced Power Settings; then use the scrollbar to view and/or change various power settings.

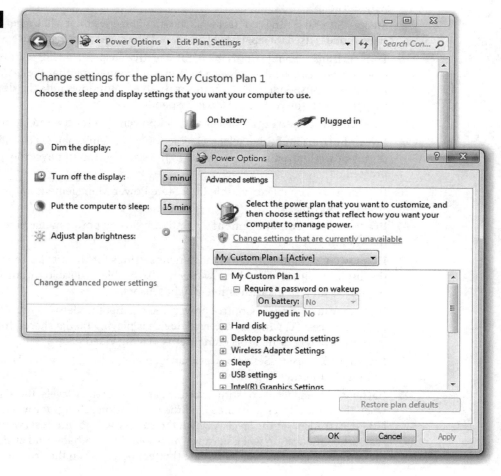

both Windows 7 and Windows 8/8.1. You might have to click Change Settings That Are Currently Unavailable to access some of these options, depending on your Windows version and edition and hardware.

- **Require a password on wakeup**   Select Yes if you want to lock the screen and require a password to unlock the computer when it wakes from Sleep.
- **Hard disk**   Control how long the system waits after no activity before turning off the hard disk.
- **Desktop background settings**   If the desktop background is a slideshow, this setting will control whether it is available or paused.
- **Wireless Adapter Settings**   Save power by enabling the power-saving mode for the wireless adapter.
- **Sleep**   Several settings control what length of inactive time will trigger sleep and which sleep mode is used (Sleep, Hybrid Sleep, or Hibernate). Also configure wake timers.
- **USB settings**   Enable or disable USB selective suspend, a USB feature whereby a device driver can send a message to Windows requesting that the OS put the device into an idle (suspended) state. If this is disabled, Windows puts the device into suspend when the rest of the OS is suspended.
- **Intel Graphics Settings**   Select an Intel power plan for the Intel graphics adapter.
- **Power buttons and lid**   Select what action will occur when (1) the lid is closed, (2) the power button is pressed, and (3) the sleep button (if physically present) is pressed.
- **PCI Express**   Enable or disable Link State Power Management implementation of ASPM power plans.
- **Processor power management**   Configure several power management settings for the system CPU.
- **Display**   Configure power management settings for the display to control when the display is dimmed and by how much. Also enable or disable automatic (adaptive) brightness on systems with ambient light sensors.
- **Multimedia settings**   Control power management under two sets of circumstances: (1) when an external device is playing media shared from this computer, and (2) when this computer is playing video.
- **Internet Explorer**   Select power management settings for when JavaScript is running in Internet Explorer.
- **Battery**   Define what constitutes critical and low battery levels, the actions taken when the critical level is reached, and the notification settings for when low-battery level exists. Also, set the level at which the battery will go into reserve power mode. A smart configuration will issue a warning sound for both low and critical, and place the computer into Sleep or Hibernate (better choice) when the critical level is reached.

on the **!** ob

Power management isn't just for laptops, although some features, such as battery management, only apply to laptops. However, minimizing power usage of desktop computers is important to both individuals and big organizations. Therefore, you will want to apply what you learn here to the desktop computers that you support.

SCENARIO & SOLUTION

I use my laptop at work, carrying it with me from meeting to meeting in order to take notes. How can I avoid the hassle of waiting for it to power up at the beginning of each meeting?	Select Sleep from the shutdown options.
When traveling, I would like to save all my work and the desktop when I shut down, and have the laptop start up with my work state exactly as it was when I stopped. How do I achieve this, plus conserve as much battery life as possible?	Enable Hibernate in the Power Options applet in Control Panel, and then, when you are ready, select Hibernate from the shutdown options.
How do I configure a different set of behaviors for when my laptop is on battery as opposed to when it is plugged in?	Open the Power Options applet and click Change Plan Settings for the current plan. In the Edit Plan Settings dialog box, you can configure one group of settings for when the laptop is on battery and another set for when it is plugged in.

CERTIFICATION OBJECTIVE

■ *901: 3.3   Given a scenario, use appropriate laptop features*

In this section, we cover the many special function keys on a laptop, including the all-important FN key and all the commands it enables. We also take a look at some physical characteristics of laptops, such as docking stations, laptop security, and rotating or removable screens.

Using Laptop Features

This section covers four important topics: special function keys, docking stations, laptop security, and rotating/removable screens. Each of these features is unique to laptops, and each one solves a particular problem or difficulty unique to laptops.

Special Function Keys

Laptops have less room for a keyboard than desktops, which means their keyboards tend to have fewer keys. They don't typically have separate numeric keypads, for example. Laptops also have several additional hardware options to enable/disable that desktops don't have, like changing the brightness and contrast on the built-in screen and turning Wi-Fi capability on/off. Because a laptop actually needs *more* keys, while it has room for *fewer* keys, laptop makers needed a way of providing more different keys in a smaller space.

They achieved this goal by creating an additional modifier key, called the FN key. Like the CTRL and ALT keys, holding down FN while pressing a function key executes the special function indicated by the symbol on the key. As shown in Figure 7-14, a laptop keyboard has an FN key near the lower-left corner, next to the CTRL key. On the function keys (F1, F2, etc.) are pictures indicating the special functions that happen when you press them in conjunction with the FN key. For example, in Figure 7-14, the ESC key's special function is Lock, the F1 key's special function is to mute the sound, and so on. Notice that the F8 key's special function is Display Mode, which switches between internal and external display sources (901 exam objective 3.3 calls Display Mode *dual displays*).

The special functions listed in CompTIA A+ 901 exam objective 3.3 are given in Table 7-2 that you should be able to identify and use on a laptop. See how many of these you can find on your own laptop. Not every laptop has all of them; for example, if you don't have a backlit keyboard, you won't have an FN function for it. And, not every laptop handles every function with an FN key; some of them have a separate hardware button for enabling and disabling Wi-Fi or Bluetooth, for example. When troubleshooting a non-functioning built-in component, such as GPS or Bluetooth, check to see whether the component may have been toggled off by inadvertent pressing of its FN key combination.

FIGURE 7-14

A laptop's FN key provides access to special command assignments for certain keys.

FN key

TABLE 7-2	Special Function Keys for Laptop Use	
Function	**Description**	**Symbol (May Vary)**
Display Mode (Dual Displays)	Toggles between built-in display, external display, and both	One or more monitors
Wireless (Wi-Fi) On/Off	Toggles built-in Wi-Fi on/off	Triangular tower with waves radiating from the top
Cellular On/Off	Toggles built-in cellular on/off	Varies
Volume Settings	Mutes volume, increases or decreases volume	Usually three separate buttons, each with some form of speaker on it
Screen Brightness	Increases or decreases screen brightness	Usually two separate buttons, with some variation of a shining sun on them plus an up or down arrow
Bluetooth On/Off	Toggles built-in Bluetooth on/off	May show a Bluetooth logo
Keyboard Backlight On/Off	Toggles keyboard backlight on/off	A key with rays radiating from it
Touch Pad On/Off	Toggles touchpad on/off	Varies
Screen Orientation	Toggles the screen between horizontal and vertical orientation	Varies
Media Options	Controls the playback of audio and video clips in some applications	Usually several buttons, including Play/Pause, Fast Forward, and Rewind
GPS On/Off	Toggles a built-in GPS on/off	Varies
Airplane Mode	Toggles settings needed for safe use of the device on an airplane, including turning off all wireless communication	Airplane image

Port Replicators and Docking Stations

The laptop owner who uses a laptop while traveling, but also as a desktop replacement, usually has a "base of operations" office. This office is where the owner will use external devices such as a keyboard, printer, display, mouse, and external hard drive storage. The user must connect and disconnect the laptop from these components every time he or she returns to or leaves the office with the laptop. The solution to that inconvenience is a port replicator or docking station.

A *port replicator*, a device that remains on the desktop with external devices connected to its ports, can make this task less time-consuming by providing a single connection to the laptop and permanent connection to these external devices.

A more advanced (and more expensive) alternative to the port replicator is a *docking station*. In addition to the ports normally found on a port replicator, a docking station may include full-size expansion slots and various drives. In the past, port replicators and docking stations were always proprietary—often only fitting one model of laptop. If the manufacturer did not make one of these devices to fit your laptop, you had no options. Now you can easily find an inexpensive "universal" port replicator or docking station that interfaces with a laptop via a USB port. Whether you have a proprietary device that fits your laptop or one that uses a USB connector, be sure to read the documentation that comes with the docking station or port replicator and follow the instructions for connecting and disconnecting the device.

Physical Security Devices

Most laptops have a security slot, usually on the rear-left corner of the case, which is easy to overlook at approximately 1/4" × 1/8". This slot accepts a lock head from a laptop security device—usually a cable lock resembling a bicycle cable lock. The cable is usually made of high-quality woven wire—sometimes combined with other materials for added strength, and usually covered with a plastic sleeve. To secure a computer with a cable lock, first wrap the cable around a strong stationary object and then pass the lock head through the loop on the opposite end of the cable before inserting it into the security slot. Engage the lock to secure it within the slot. These locks are available from several manufacturers and come with a variety of locking mechanisms, such as a key or combination lock. Kensington is one popular manufacturer—so popular that the slot on a laptop that accepts the cable is sometimes called a *K-slot*.

Rotating and Removable Screens

Some specialty laptops are convertible between being a clamshell-style laptop and a slate-style tablet. To convert to a tablet, you either rotate the screen and fold it back or remove the screen entirely. The key with this type of unit is not to force it. The screen should rotate or come apart easily; if it doesn't, you are doing something wrong. Look for a release button, for example, or make sure you are turning it the correct direction.

SCENARIO & SOLUTION

I plug my laptop into an external display, printer, and keyboard every time I return to the office. Is there an easier way to do this?	Yes. Plug each of these devices into a port replicator and leave them there. To access the devices, simply attach your laptop to the port replicator.
I can't figure out what the symbols represent on the function keys that go with the FN key.	Consult the laptop's documentation online, or deduce their uses by a process of trial-and-error and then make notes for future use.

CERTIFICATION SUMMARY

Most PC technicians will need to understand laptop technologies and how to replace components in them since use of these portable computers remains widespread in both the workplace and the home—even as the sales of newer tablet computers cut into the number of laptops sold each year. Laptops come in many sizes, from the very lightweight ultra-portables or netbooks to desktop replacements.

Although laptops are basically compatible with standard PC operating systems like Windows, macOS, and Linux, they use smaller integrated components that, for the most part, do not conform in either form or size with the standard PC components.

A technician should know how to conserve battery usage, and the best Windows tool for doing that is Power Options. A technician should also know how to use the FN functions, and how to connect and disconnect from docking stations and manipulate removable or rotating screens.

TWO-MINUTE DRILL

Here are some of the key points covered in Chapter 7.

Installing and Upgrading Laptops

❑ A portable computer is any type of computer you can easily transport and that has an all-in-one component layout.

❑ A laptop is a portable computer that can run the same operating systems as a desktop PC, with a keyboard in the base and a display in a hinged top.

❑ Internal and integrated laptop hardware, such as the display, keyboard, pointing device, motherboard, memory, hard drives, and expansion bus, has special scaled-down form factors, but a laptop can use most standard external PC peripherals.

❑ Your laptop disassembly and reassembly processes should include consulting the manufacturer's documentation, using appropriate hand tools, organizing parts, and documenting and labeling cable and screw locations.

❑ Although laptop components are at least partially proprietary, you can find replacement parts from the original manufacturer or from other sources. Always research the cost-effectiveness of replacing parts rather than replacing the entire laptop.

❑ ExpressCard is the lone remaining standard still in use for external expansion slots in laptops, and it has lost favor with manufacturers and is rarely seen on new laptops.

❑ Internal expansion slots include Mini PCI, Mini PCIe, and mSATA.

❑ You add memory to a laptop in the form of SODIMMs installed into slots inside the case.

❑ Most laptops use 2.5" hard drives, but some smaller models use 1.8" hard drives. Drives can be either magnetic or solid state. Hybrid drives are also available.

❑ The flat-panel display built into a laptop is likely some form of LCD, backlit with LEDs or CCFL, or organic LED (OLED). To extend the display to an external monitor, use the appropriate FN key combination or a command in the OS.

❑ Laptops have many of the same I/O ports and adapters that desktops have, including one or more display ports (such as HDMI or DVI), multiple USB ports, and audio ports.

❑ Some laptops have a media/accessory bay holding a single device that you can switch with another device that fits in the bay.

❑ Laptops often come with built-in communications adapters—including Wi-Fi and Ethernet for LAN connections, Bluetooth for short-distance wireless communications, and cellular adapters for connecting to cellular networks.

❑ A laptop comes with two sources of electrical power: a rechargeable battery and an AC adapter.

❑ A laptop will usually have a built-in microphone and one or more built-in speakers. There will be ports for external sound input and output as well.

Power Options

❑ You can use the Windows Power Options utility to configure power management settings in laptops that comply with power management standards through the operating system to shut down the display, the hard drive, and even the entire system after a period of inactivity and/or when the battery is low.

❑ Hibernate is a Windows state that uses hard drive space to save all the programs and data that are in memory at the time you choose this mode. The computer then completely shuts down and requires no power while it is hibernating.

❑ Sleep is a state that conserves power while saving your desktop in RAM memory in a work state; it requires a minimum amount of power.

❑ Hybrid Sleep starts out in Sleep mode but converts to Hibernate mode when the battery runs low.

Using Laptop Features

❑ The FN key is an additional modifier key that, when pressed along with certain other keys, performs special functions like changing the display brightness or enabling/disabling Wi-Fi. Refer to Table 7-2 to review.

❑ Port replicators and docking stations provide permanent connections for external devices used in the laptop user's office. Universal docking stations and port replicators have USB interfaces and, therefore, connect in the same manner as other USB devices.

❑ Physical security measures such as cables and locks make laptops more difficult to steal. Many laptops have a hole or slot in the side designed for a cable or locking device.

❑ Convertible laptops have rotating or removable display screens. Take care to rotate or remove these according to the manufacturer's instructions to prevent damage.

SELF TEST

The following questions will help you measure your understanding of the material presented in this chapter. Read all of the choices carefully because there might be more than one correct answer. Choose all correct answers for each question.

Installing and Upgrading Laptops

1. How many pins does a DDR3 SODIMM have?
    A. 102
    B. 200 or 204
    C. 204 or 256
    D. 144

2. What is the name for system memory used by the video adapter and, therefore, unavailable to the operating system?
    A. VRAM
    B. SODIMM memory
    C. Shared video memory
    D. SRAM

3. What built-in component allows laptop use for short periods (hours) without an outside power source?
    A. Keyboard
    B. Touchpad
    C. Pointing stick
    D. Battery

4. A replacement motherboard must match the form factor of the one being replaced and which of the following?
    A. Weight
    B. Manufacturer
    C. Serial number
    D. Electrical connections

5. Which type of external expansion slot is most likely to be found in a modern laptop?
   A. PC Card
   B. CardBus
   C. PCMCIA
   D. ExpressCard

6. Which of the following is a laptop component used to convert the DC power from the power adapter or battery to the AC power required by the LCD display?
   A. Inverter
   B. Converter
   C. Power switch
   D. Generator

7. What is the most common laptop memory module?
   A. SORIMM
   B. MicroDIMM
   C. SODIMM
   D. DIMM

8. Which is a common size for a laptop hard drive?
   A. 2.5"
   B. 5"
   C. 3.5"
   D. 1"

9. Which of the following allows you to attach nearly any type of desktop component to a laptop?
   A. Port replicator
   B. Enhanced port replicator
   C. Extended port replicator
   D. Docking station

10. Select the two names for a compartment in some laptops that can hold a media device (secondary hard drive, optical drive, floppy drive, etc.) that you can swap with another device.
    A. Slot
    B. Media bay
    C. USB port
    D. Accessory bay

11. How is Mini PCIe different from Mini PCI?
    A. Larger card
    B. 64-bit data bus
    C. Fits in an ExpressCard slot
    D. All of the above

12. Where is the hard disk located on a laptop?
   A. Under the keyboard
   B. On the side, in a removable slot
   C. On the underside, next to the battery
   D. Varies depending on the model

13. Which wireless communications standard is used between a laptop and nearby devices, and is limited to devices within a few meters of the computer?
   A. Cellular
   B. Wi-Fi
   C. Bluetooth
   D. Wired Ethernet

14. What is a battery type commonly used in recently built laptops?
   A. Lithium ion
   B. AC adapter
   C. DC controller
   D. Nickel metal hydride

15. What type of external display connector are you likely to find on a Mac laptop?
   A. Thunderbolt
   B. PCIe
   C. VGA
   D. DVI

16. On a touch screen, what component allows the screen to function as an input device?
   A. Video adapter
   B. Shared memory
   C. Digitizer
   D. Touchpad

Power Options

17. What Windows utility can you use to configure low-battery options for a laptop?
   A. Power Options
   B. System Properties
   C. Battery Options
   D. BIOS setup

18. What is the name for the power-saving mode supported by Windows Vista and newer versions of Windows whereby the contents of memory are saved into RAM as well as to disk?
    A. Hybrid Boot
    B. Suspend
    C. Hybrid Sleep
    D. Fast Start

Using Laptop Features

19. What key, which is not found on desktop keyboards, acts as a modifier to assign special roles to function keys and other keys?
    A. ALT
    B. SHIFT
    C. F1
    D. FN

20. What kind of device can be used to quickly connect and disconnect a laptop from a variety of external devices all at once?
    A. Docking station
    B. External monitor
    C. K-slot
    D. KVM switch

SELF TEST ANSWERS

Installing and Upgrading Laptops

1. ☑ **B.** A DDR3 SODIMM has either 200 or 204 pins, depending on the type, with 204 being the more recent.
    ☒ **A** is incorrect because it is not, at this writing, a valid number for pins on any SODIMM, although it is the number of pins on one side of a 204-pin SODIMM. **C** is incorrect because those are not valid numbers of pins on any SODIMM. **D** is incorrect because that is the number of pins found in some older SODIMMs.

2. ☑   **C.** Shared video memory is the name for system memory used by the video adapter and, therefore, is unavailable to the operating system.

☒   **A** is incorrect because volatile RAM (VRAM) is the type of memory used on a video adapter. A video adapter with VRAM installed does not need to use system memory. **B** is incorrect because, although a SODIMM is the physical memory module used in most laptops, the name for the portion of this memory used by the video adapter is what the question asks for. **D** is incorrect because SRAM (static RAM) is simply a type of very high-speed RAM.

3. ☑   **D.** It provides power to the laptop when not plugged into AC power.

☒   **A, B,** and **C** are all incorrect because although they may be built into a laptop, they do not make it possible for a laptop to be used for short periods without an outside power source.

4. ☑   **D.** Electrical connections must match when replacing a laptop motherboard.

☒   **A** is incorrect because weight is irrelevant in selecting a replacement motherboard. **B** is incorrect because replacement motherboards are available from many manufacturers. **C** is incorrect because even the exact model motherboard from the same manufacturer will have a unique serial number.

5. ☑   **D.** ExpressCard slots are the most recent of the types listed and the most likely to be found in a modern laptop.

☒   **A, B,** and **C** are all incorrect because they are older standards for external expansion slot devices.

6. ☑   **A.** This component converts DC power to the AC power required by an LCD panel.

☒   **B** is incorrect because a converter does just the opposite, converting AC power to DC power. **C** is incorrect because the power switch simply turns the main power to the laptop on and off. **D** is incorrect because this is not a component of a laptop. A generator generates power using an engine powered by fuel such as gasoline or diesel.

7. ☑   **C.** SODIMM is the most common memory module. It is a scaled-down version of the DIMM memory module.

☒   **A** is incorrect because this is a now-obsolete memory module form not discussed in the book. **B** is incorrect because this module is half the size of SODIMM and is used in handheld computers and less often in laptops. **D** is incorrect because this is a full-size memory module for desktop PCs.

8. ☑   **A.** 2.5" is the most common size of a laptop hard drive.

☒   **B** is incorrect because this very large size is not used in laptops. **C** is incorrect because this is also a large size that is not used in laptops but is common in desktop PCs. **D** is incorrect (at this writing) because it is not a size commonly used in laptops.

9. ☑   **D.** A docking station allows you to attach nearly any type of desktop component to a laptop. The docking station can remain on the desk with all the desired devices installed or connected to it. To access these devices, simply plug the laptop into the docking station.

☒   **A** and **B** are incorrect because they do not allow access to the number and variety of devices that a docking station does. **C** is incorrect because this is not a real type of portable system component.

10. ☑ **B** and **D**. Media bay and accessory bay are the correct names for the compartment some laptops have for swapping between one device and another.
    ☒ **A** is incorrect because a slot is the socket a circuit card plugs into. **C** is incorrect because a USB port is what a USB cable plugs into.

11. ☑ **B**. Mini PCIe is a 64-bit card, whereas Mini PCI was 32-bit.
    ☒ **B** is incorrect because Mini PCIe is smaller than Mini PCI. **C** is incorrect because no PCI or PCIe cards fit in that slot. **D** is incorrect because A and C are incorrect.

12. ☑ **D**. Hard disk placement varies depending on the model. It can be in any of the locations listed, or in a different place.
    ☒ **A, B,** and **C** are incorrect because although they are all possible locations, there is no guarantee. You must consult the service manual to find the correct location or, if the manual is not available, disassemble the laptop and locate the hard drive visually.

13. ☑ **C**. Bluetooth is for short-range communications only. The others listed have longer ranges.
    ☒ **A** is incorrect because cellular technology can be used to connect a laptop to the Internet from cell towers several miles away. **B** is incorrect because Wi-Fi connects a laptop to a wireless local area network (WLAN) at distances of several hundred feet. **D** is incorrect because this is a wired technology requiring cable.

14. ☑ **A**. Lithium ion (Li-Ion) is the battery type commonly used in recently built laptops.
    ☒ **B** is incorrect because this is the laptop's power supply that plugs into an AC power source. **C** is incorrect because this is not a battery type, but a laptop component that monitors and regulates power usage. **D** is incorrect because this type of battery is more common in older laptops.

15. ☑ **A**. Thunderbolt is the port used for external displays on a Mac.
    ☒ **B** is incorrect because PCIe is a standard for internal expansion slots, not displays. **C** and **D** are incorrect because these display connectors are not present on Macs.

16. ☑ **C**. The digitizer is the part of the display that is touch-sensitive and enables touch input.
    ☒ **A** is incorrect because a video adapter allows the screen to function as an *output* device. **B** is incorrect because shared memory is system RAM, not an input device. **D** is incorrect because although this is an input device, it has no connection with the touchscreen.

Power Options

17. ☑ **A**. Power Options is the utility where you can configure a low-battery alarm for a laptop.
    ☒ **B** is incorrect because you cannot configure a low-battery alarm in System Properties. **C** is incorrect because there is no such utility in standard Windows. **D** is incorrect because BIOS setup is not in Windows, but at the system level of the computer.

18. ☑ **C.** Hybrid Sleep is the name for the power-saving mode supported by Windows Vista and newer whereby the contents of memory are saved into RAM, as well as to disk.
☒ **A** is incorrect because Hybrid Boot is the method used by Windows 8 at startup in which the hibernated kernel from the last shutdown is quickly brought into memory to speed up startup. **B** is incorrect because Suspend is simply an old term for power management features, such as Standby, Sleep, and Hibernate. **D** is incorrect because it is not even a term discussed in this book.

Using Laptop Features

19. ☑ **D.** The FN key modifies other keys to allow a laptop computer to have extra keyboard shortcuts. It is not found on a desktop keyboard.
☒ **A** and **B** are incorrect because both are found on desktop keyboards too. **C** is incorrect because not only is F1 found on desktop keyboards too, but it is also not a modifier key.

20. ☑ **A.** A docking station provides a quick and easy way to connect to multiple external peripherals at once.
☒ **B** is incorrect because an external monitor provides only one external device (itself), not a variety. **C** is incorrect because a K-slot is a slot for inserting a security cable. **D** is incorrect because a KVM switch enables multiple computers to share a common set of keyboard, video, and mouse, but does not allow a laptop to quickly connect from the devices all at once.

Chapter 8

Client-Side Virtualization

- **902: 2.2** Given a scenario, set up and use client-side virtualization
- ✓ Two-Minute Drill
- **Q&A** Self Test

IT professionals who support desktop or server systems need to keep up to date on the newest operating systems and applications. This can become expensive if they use dedicated computers for testing new software. But many do not. Instead they use virtualization software to run the desktop or server OSs in a test environment, isolated from their organization's network. You can too, once you learn how to work with the latest technologies in virtualization.

In Chapter 6, when we described components for a virtualization workstation, we defined a few terms associated with virtualization, saving the bulk of the information for this chapter. Those terms defined in Chapter 6 include virtualization workstation and virtual machine. In this chapter we give the big picture of virtualization with examples of the different types. Then we will compare server-side virtualization with client-side virtualization, and provide more details on client-side virtualization to guide you through the hands-on experience of installing and configuring the software that supports desktop virtualization as an example of client-side virtualization.

CERTIFICATION OBJECTIVE

■ *902: 2.2   Given a scenario, set up and use client-side virtualization*

As you prepare for the CompTIA A+ certification exams, be ready to answer questions about the basics of client-side virtualization, including being able to define a hypervisor and install and use one. You should understand the purpose of virtual machines and be able to describe resource requirements for client-side virtualization, emulators, and networks, as well as the security requirements. In this chapter we go somewhat beyond the actual CompTIA A+ exam objectives to give you a broader understanding of client-side virtualization because, for over a decade, we have found it to be a very useful tool, and feel almost evangelical about bringing this knowledge to new IT workers. To that end, this chapter begins with an overview of virtualization, introducing the many purposes of virtualization and the part that hypervisors play in virtualization of operating systems. Then we will look at the specifics of Windows client virtualization, beginning with your choices for doing it, the hardware requirements, and the types of virtual machines, and ultimately we home in on client-side virtualization and give you an opportunity for hands-on experience. When you complete this chapter, you will have installed a hypervisor and created a virtual machine for a Windows operating system. Then, in Chapter 9 you can choose to install Windows into the virtual machine you create in this chapter.

Introduction to Virtualization

In this section, we expand on the limited definition of virtualization provided in Chapter 6 to detail the many purposes of virtualization and to compare server-side virtualization versus client-side virtualization. Finally, we will explore the types of client-side virtualization in preparation for the section that follows in which you will implement client-side virtualization.

Purposes of Virtualization

Virtualization is the creation of an environment that seems real but isn't, and today it seems like virtualization is everywhere, and there are many types. As an IT professional, your professional life will be touched by some form of virtualization.

For example, you can explore a *virtual world*, such as Second Life or one of many massively multiplayer online games. Each of these virtual worlds contains a simulated environment within which participants create an online community. Within a virtual world a user often selects an *avatar*, an animated computer-generated human or animal image, to represent him or her. Virtual worlds are used in online training, in marketing of products, and in games because virtual worlds usually allow your avatar to interact with those of other people.

A *virtual classroom* is an eLearning tool for distance learning, usually provided as a service from an Internet-based source, such as eLecta Live (www.e-lecta.com) or iLinc (www.ilinc.com). If you have taken online classes you have probably experienced virtual classrooms, used by instructors for presenting interactive lectures, and even completion of coursework. Figure 8-1 shows a virtual classroom in which the presenter is sharing a web page with a student.

Many organizations use *storage virtualization* in which client computers can utilize many networked hard drives as though they are one drive or location. Network engineers work with *network virtualization* in which they create a network address space that exists within one or more physical networks. It is logically independent of the physical network structure, and users on computers accessing this virtual network are not aware of the underlying network. A *virtual network* can exist over a physical network, or one can be fully virtualized within a host computer.

FIGURE 8-1

The eLecta Live virtual classroom

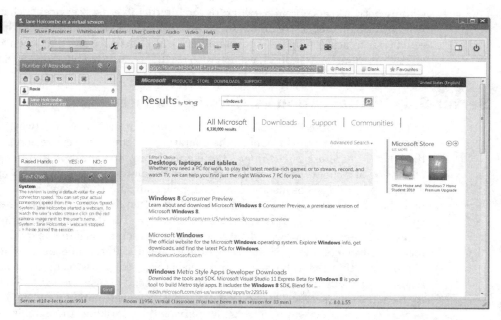

Then there is *server virtualization*, in which a single computer hosts one or more server operating systems, each in a virtual machine and each performing tasks independently from the other virtual machines and from the host. Companies that provide low-cost web hosting services can create a separate virtual web server for each customer. Many organizations use server virtualization for a large number of reasons, including but not limited to, the ease of centrally managing servers, efficient use of server hardware, improved server availability, as a disaster recovery tool, for testing and development, and, of course, to reduce costs.

With only a small leap from server virtualization, we come to *desktop virtualization*. This is virtualization of a desktop computer, into which you can install a desktop operating system, its unique configuration, and all the applications and data used by (normally) a single person. Each simulation of a machine is a virtual machine—whether you install a desktop or server OS. We have used desktop virtualization for over a decade for testing beta versions of software and various configurations. Desktop virtualization has also been a great tool for acquiring screenshots of things you cannot normally capture, such as the early stages of an OS installation or the startup of a computer.

Today, desktop operating systems and their installed apps are clients to numerous services on private and public networks. The typical computer user seamlessly connects to a home network, corporate network, or the Internet to access services such as file and print sharing, e-mail, media streaming, social networking, and much more. For that reason, we often refer to desktop operating systems as clients, and it follows that when you create a virtual machine for Windows, we may also use the term *Windows client virtualization*.

Server-Side Virtualization vs. Client-Side Virtualization

In Chapter 6 we described a client as software that connects over a network to related server software. The client can also mean the operating system, or the entire computer beneath that client. Therefore, *client-side virtualization* is any virtualization that happens on the client side of a client–server relationship. And usually, but not always, it means the physical client side of things. For instance, in desktop virtualization, you can host the virtual desktops on either the client side or the server side. Quite often they are hosted on the server side in specialized servers. This is *server-side virtualization*. The desktop environment—in most cases, a version of Windows—displays on the user's screen as if the operating system was local. The value of this approach is that the local computer can be an older, less powerful computer (a thin client) because it only needs to run software to connect to the server, transfer video downstream to the thin client, and send mouse and keystrokes upstream to the app on the server. This hosting of the desktop environments and applications on servers centralizes all support tasks, simplifying the upgrading and patching of the operating

FIGURE 8-2

Windows 8 running in a virtual machine in macOS on an iMac

system and applications in the virtual machines within the server or servers. This same centralization gives IT more control over the security of the desktop.

The term used today for hosting and managing multiple virtual desktops (often thousands) over a network is *virtual desktop infrastructure (VDI)*. The term is attributed to VMware in distinguishing its virtual desktop server products from the products offered by competitors, specifically Citrix and Microsoft. Today VDI applies to any server product that provides full virtual desktop support.

You can host one or more virtual machines on your PC if it meets the requirements for both the hypervisor and for each guest OS. Common examples of client-side virtualization of desktop environments include hypervisors that allows you to run Windows, Linux, Unix, and even DOS guest OSs in virtual machines on Windows, Linux, Unix, or macOS host OSs. Figure 8-2 shows a macOS desktop with a window open to a virtual machine that is running Windows 8. The hypervisor in this case is Oracle VM VirtualBox, a free and very capable hypervisor.

Types of Client-Side Virtualization

While we will use desktop virtualization in our working examples, client-side virtualization is not just about desktops. In recent webcasts from Microsoft, they featured three types of client-side virtualization: desktop virtualization, application virtualization, and presentation virtualization. We have already defined desktop virtualization, and will soon move into more details about that type. Here we will describe presentation virtualization and application virtualization.

In *presentation virtualization,* a user connects to a server from their desktop or laptop and accesses an application rather than an entire desktop environment. The application user interface (window) is "presented" on the user's desktop as if it were running locally, but it is actually running on the server. This allows the user to use an application that is incompatible with their local operating system or that cannot run on the local computer because the computer hardware is old or underpowered. Microsoft currently uses Windows Server running Windows Terminal Services for presentation virtualization. Notice that this is client-side virtualization, but it physically occurs on the server side and is presented on the client side, as shown in Figure 8-3. Specialized software sends the screens to the client computer and returns all input to the application on the server.

Another type of client-side virtualization is *application virtualization,* in which the application runs in a virtualized application environment on the local computer. The application is isolated from the surrounding system, interacting with the hardware

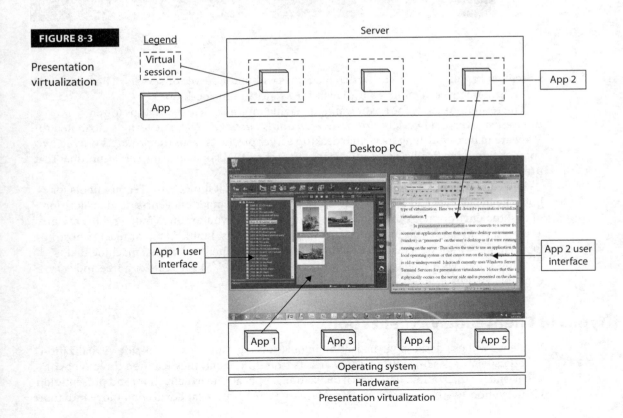

FIGURE 8-3

Presentation virtualization

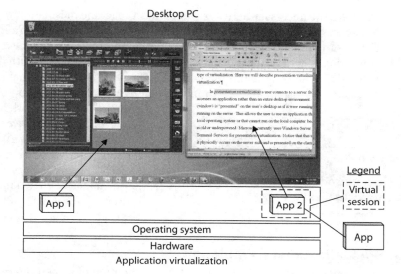

FIGURE 8-4

Application virtualization

Desktop PC

Legend

Virtual session

App

Application virtualization

(and user) through application virtualization software, a virtual machine with only the support required by the app. See Figure 8-4. This isolation of the application on the desktop computer requires a sufficiently powerful computer, but it has the advantage of being a compatibility solution when older, critical apps will not run on newer hardware or software. Another benefit is that a virtualized app is under IT control because they can install or update it over a network as a complete application without concern for the underlying system beyond the application virtualization software. Microsoft's current implementation of application virtualization is *Microsoft Application Virtualization (App-V)*.

Implementing Client-Side Desktop Virtualization

In this section we begin by describing hypervisors, the software that supports desktop virtualization. Then we will look at specific hypervisors and their resource and network requirements. Finally, we guide you through the process of selecting and installing a hypervisor on a desktop computer and creating one or more virtual machines in preparation for installing an OS into that virtual machine.

Hypervisors

To do desktop or server virtualization, you first need a hypervisor. A *hypervisor*, also called a *virtual machine monitor (VMM)*, is the software that creates a virtual machine, providing access to the necessary hardware on the host machine in isolation from other virtual machines and the host operating system, if present. This allows multiple operating systems to run simultaneously on a single physical computer, such as a network server or desktop computer. A hypervisor must create a virtual CPU compatible with that of the underlying machine—mainly either an Intel or an AMD CPU. This means that the installed OS must be capable of installing directly on the underlying computer. Also, today's hypervisors require, or at least work best on, computers with *Hardware-Assisted Virtualization (HAV)* features, either Intel Virtualization Technology for x86 (Intel VT-x) or AMD Virtualization (AMD-V). HAV supports and improves the performance of virtual machines on the host. Both Intel and AMD CPUs have supported HAV since 2006.

Be sure you understand what a hypervisor is and the role it plays in client-side virtualization.

Virtualization vs. Emulation

You may have heard the term *emulation* or mention of something called an *emulator*. At first glance, emulation and virtualization seem synonymous, but in computing these terms are very different. Emulation differs very much from the virtualization of servers or desktops we discuss here. The key is compatibility. When we use a virtual machine, the hypervisor that creates and manages it must create a virtual machine compatible with the underlying virtual machine, even while isolating the virtual machine from the underlying hardware.

An *emulator*, on the other hand, is software that allows you to run an OS or device on hardware with which it is completely incompatible. This is done in order to run a critical application designed for an old type of computer system that is no longer available. In fact, in the early days of PCs many organizations used special adapter cards and software on PCs to emulate the old dumb terminals that connected to their large mini- or mainframe computer systems. Now we do this with terminal emulation software, such as the VT Series terminal emulators from Ericom (www.ericom.com) used to emulate physical terminal hardware systems by DEC, Compaq, and Hewlett-Packard. Vendors such as Ericom offer versions of their terminal emulation software that will run on Windows, macOS, or Linux operating systems. Today developers wanting to write apps for phones running the Android OS can use software that will emulate the underlying CPU and other hardware of an Android phone and run an Android OS—all on their desktop computer.

All things being equal, an emulator requires more computing resources (processing power and RAM) than a hypervisor needs for a virtual machine, and the OS or applications generally run much slower in the emulator than they would on the original hardware due to the translation and redirection of commands from within the emulator to the underlying computer. On the other hand, apps running in a virtual machine with no need for emulation will often run nearly as fast as they would on the physical machine.

Having made the distinction between virtualization and emulation, we acknowledge that people still use the term "emulate" for what a hypervisor does in creating a virtual machine, saying that the virtual machine is an emulation of the underlying hardware. Sometimes they are correct. In some instances, the hypervisor must do emulation. While virtualization requires that the virtual machine must have a virtual CPU that is compatible with that of the underlying computer, if the chipset in the computer is incompatible with the OS to be installed in the virtual machine, the hypervisor can emulate the compatible chipset within the virtual machine and translate or redirect instructions from the OS installed in the virtual machine to the underlying chipset. Think of this as partial emulation, but as with any emulation, there is a performance cost for this. If the chipset were compatible, these instructions would only need the hypervisor to pass them on to the chipset, with little effect on performance, but when the hypervisor must redirect and translate these instructions, things slow down. So, when necessary, modern hypervisors do some emulation as well as virtualization. One example of this is when we use a hypervisor on an Apple computer running macOS to create a virtual machine for running Windows. A modern Apple computer running macOS has an Intel CPU, but a different chipset than a Wintel computer for which Windows is written.

Types of Hypervisors

There are two types of hypervisors, Type I and Type II, as Figure 8-5 shows. A *Type I hypervisor*—sometimes called a *bare-metal hypervisor*—can run directly on a computer without an underlying host operating system and then manage one or more virtual machines. A *Type II hypervisor* requires a host operating system, such as Windows, macOS, or Linux. The Type II hypervisor actually runs as an app in that host operating system, putting more software layers between each virtual machine and the hardware.

Type I Hypervisors   Type I hypervisors first appeared on high-powered servers running server OSs in virtual machines. Examples of current Type I server hypervisors include VMware ESXI, Citrix XenServer, and Microsoft Hyper-V. Type I hypervisors are very appealing because, when compared to an equivalent Type II hypervisor, a Type I hypervisor has a smaller layer of software between each *guest OS* running in a virtual machine and the underlying hardware.

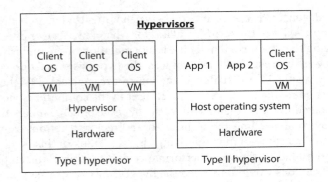

FIGURE 8-5

Comparison of
Type I and Type II
hypervisors

Type I client hypervisors are a solution to the problem of centrally distributing images of Type I hypervisors with client operating systems, fully configured with installed apps, to large numbers of desktops and laptops. You may say that you can already do that by centrally distributing more conventional images to the desktop without having a hypervisor and virtual machine as part of the image. However, consider an image that includes a Type I client hypervisor with two virtual machines—one with security locked down for the user to use at work or when traveling, and another that grants the user a much higher level of privilege for their personal use—and the user can easily switch between the two virtual machines as needed.

If a user loses a laptop and needs the same image installed on a new one, the image can be sent to the new computer over the network, taking only minutes before the user is up and working again. In fact, some Type I client hypervisor products are targeted specifically at laptops, and the distribution service for the hypervisor may have a feature that allows a central administrator to issue a kill command to remotely wipe out a stolen laptop when the thief connects it to the Internet.

This targeting of specific hardware can be one of the drawbacks, since each Type I hypervisor may support only certain computer (usually laptop) models because of their close relationship to the hardware. Although some Type I hypervisors run on a large number of PC and laptop models, some will run on any computer with a CPU that supports Intel's VT-x technology, which includes the majority of new PCs and laptops.

Type II Hypervisors   The hypervisors we use in our examples and exercises in this chapter are all Type II hypervisors requiring an underlying operating system, the host OS, which is the operating system installed directly on the computer, and one or more guest OSs, which are the operating systems running within virtual machines.

You have several choices for Type II hypervisors for desktops. The major sources of hypervisors are VMware, Citrix, Parallels, Microsoft, and Oracle. There are many other players in the field, with virtualization topics appearing in the technical press every week. You can install a Type II hypervisor on your Linux, Windows, or macOS desktop and test another operating system without the expense of a separate computer.

Implementing Desktop Virtualization

To implement desktop virtualization, you must first determine what desktop OS you will use as a guest OS. When it comes to selecting and installing a hypervisor, the general considerations and steps remain the same, whether you are planning server virtualization or desktop virtualization. For our purposes, we will focus on selecting and installing a Type II client hypervisor on a desktop computer for testing Windows and Linux operating systems. In this case, the available computer may drive your choice of hypervisor, so we will first select a computer and then a hypervisor. We'll then prepare the computer for installation of the hypervisor, install the hypervisor, and create one or more virtual machines based on the operating system or systems we plan to install.

Security for Virtual Machines

We cannot emphasize enough that you must keep your guest OS as secure as the host OS. At minimum, you should create a strong password for the account used to log in to the guest OS and install security software in your guest OS. Chapters 17 and 18 give the bigger story of computer security, and you can flip forward to those chapters for details. However, there are many excellent free security suites from third parties and Microsoft has free solutions. For Windows Vista and Windows 7, consider the free Windows Security Essentials available for download from Microsoft. Windows 8 and later has security software preinstalled.

Networking Requirements

While it is possible to do desktop virtualization on a computer without an Internet connection, it would be very awkward for several reasons. First, the easiest way to obtain a hypervisor is over the Internet, and updates to the hypervisor, host OS, and guest OS are easily available with an Internet connection. Furthermore, if you create a virtual machine to test an operating system or other software for use in a normal environment, then you certainly should include testing how it works on a network. Therefore, the hypervisors we use simulate a network card within each virtual machine, as well as a network on the host, so that multiple virtual machines can communicate with each other and the underlying host. Then, through a virtual connection to the host computer's physical network adapter, each VM has access to an external network, and through that to the Internet, if available. Of course, you can turn off these and other features for a VM, if you desire.

Selecting a Guest OS for Desktop Virtualization

The selection of a guest OS for virtualization may be less selection and more necessity. Perhaps you need to learn Linux for a class you are taking, but you do not have a spare computer. Or maybe you would like to look at the next version of Windows without installing it over your present OS. Or maybe you just need to select an OS so that you can experiment with desktop virtualization. Whatever the reason, you will need a legal license to install it, just as you do on any computer. If you plan to install Linux, you will find many free versions online, and if you are testing a pre-release version of Windows, simply download it and save it as an ISO file, something we will talk about in Chapter 9 when we install Windows on our real or virtual machines.

Recall that while a network may not be required for a virtual machine, it is essential to have network access in order to easily update all the software and to create a real-world environment in which a computer is connected to a network.

If you are looking for an OS to install just for learning to work with virtualization, consider using an older version of Windows, if you happen to have an old disc around along with the product key. A *product key* is a string of alphanumeric characters, usually five groups of five each, printed on the packaging for retail editions of Microsoft software. You must provide this product key during the installation, or within 30 days, or the software will be disabled. This is Microsoft's protection against piracy.

While we will talk about installing a hypervisor and creating a virtual machine in preparation for installing an OS, we will save the details of installing the Windows OS for the next chapter.

Selecting a Host OS for Desktop Virtualization

Deciding on the host OS and a host computer for desktop virtualization seems like the chicken and egg situation—which comes first? First, it depends on what is available to you. However, since the CompTIA A+ exams focus mainly on the Windows OS, we will use the Windows OS as our host OS in the following exercises. But if you have a Linux system, there are hypervisors for Linux hosts. Over the years, we have mainly used various versions of Windows as the host OS, but we have had equally good experiences in the last year using an Apple iMac with macOS as the host OS.

Selecting a Host Computer for Desktop Virtualization

If possible, select as the host computer a PC that supports HAV. Not all hypervisors require it, but most will take advantage of the feature if it's available. Without HAV, some hypervisors will limit you to 32-bit installations of some operating systems.

How can you discover if your computer supports HAV? You may already know if you completed Exercise 3-4 in Chapter 3. One of the BIOS settings on a computer with HAV support will be virtualization and the ability to enable or disable it. If you are uncertain, rerun that exercise and make sure virtualization is present.

Alternatively, you can run a software test. If your computer is running one of the following operating systems, you can use Microsoft's Hardware-Assisted Virtualization Detection Tool:

■ Windows Vista Home Basic, Home Premium, Business, Enterprise, or Ultimate (Service Pack 1 or 2)

■ Windows XP Professional Service Pack 2 or 3

■ Windows 7 Home Basic, Home Premium, Professional, Enterprise, or Ultimate

Exercise 8-1 describes the test for locating, downloading, and running this test on your Windows computer. Exercise 8-2 shows how to test an Intel CPU for HAV support.

on the **job**

If you have Hyper-V installed, diagnostics may incorrectly report that your system does not support HAV. Remove Hyper-V (it's one of the optional Windows components) and reboot, and your system will once again know that it has HAV support (for example, to run Oracle VM VirtualBox).

EXERCISE 8-1

Testing a Windows XP, Vista, or 7 Computer for HAV Support

1. Using your web browser, navigate to https://www.microsoft.com/en-us/download/details.aspx?id=592.

2. Download and run the Hardware-Assisted Virtualization Detection Tool. You may need to respond to a User Account Control dialog box, and you will need to accept the license terms before the utility will run.

3. If the tool finds that your computer has HAV and it is enabled, you will see the message shown here and you can click OK.

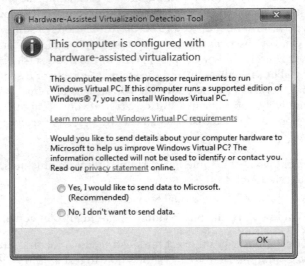

4. If you run the tool and see the message shown here, change your BIOS settings to enable HAV. The web page referenced in the hyperlink gives example instructions for specific PC models.

5. If your computer does not support HAV, you will need to use a hypervisor that does not require HAV—we will discuss this later.

EXERCISE 8-2

Testing an Intel CPU for HAV Support

If you couldn't do Exercise 8-1 because you didn't have a supported OS, but you do have an Intel CPU, try this exercise instead to collect the same type of information via an Intel utility.

1. Using your web browser, navigate to http://tinyurl.com/zoyvqc3. (Or, if that link doesn't work, go to https://downloadcenter.intel.com/download/7838/Intel-Processor-Identification-Utility-Windows-Version.)
2. Click the pidenu44.msi button to download the utility.
3. Run the downloaded file to install the utility. Then run the utility.
4. On the CPU Technologies tab in the utility, check the Intel Virtualization Technology setting.

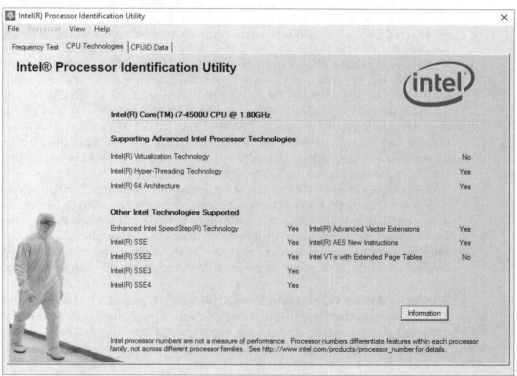

5. If the setting is No, look in BIOS setup to see if there is a setting you can change to enable virtualization. Otherwise you will need to use a hypervisor that does not require HAV for the OS version you want to install. More on that later in the chapter.

Selecting a Type II Client Hypervisor

You have several options—both commercial and free—for running Linux, DOS, or Windows on a Windows desktop computer. At this writing, you cannot run any version of macOS in a virtual machine on a PC, due more to licensing issues than technical issues.

If you want to use a Microsoft hypervisor, your choice will be dictated by the Windows version on your host machine.

- For Windows XP or Vista, use Microsoft Virtual PC 2007. (We don't cover Microsoft Virtual PC 2007 in this book, as not many people use Windows XP or Windows Vista as their host OS.)
- For Windows 7, use Windows Virtual PC.
- For Windows 8 and newer (64-bit Pro and Enterprise editions) or Windows Server 2008 or 2012, use Hyper-V Manager.

If you don't have one of the supported Windows versions for Hyper-V or Windows Virtual PC, consider a non-Microsoft hypervisor instead. Of the non-Microsoft hypervisors, we selected Oracle VirtualBox to cover in this chapter because it works on both platforms (macOS and Windows) that we have in our office, and it simply works well for us.

There are other free hypervisors, most notably VMware Player, which doesn't have a version for macOS. The free VMware Player also has fewer features than the industry-leading hypervisor, VMware Workstation (the retail product), which also does not come in a version for macOS hosting. The entire suite of VMware products is very popular in large organizations, so you may want to download and install VMware Player on your own to become familiar with the VMware virtualization look and feel. All of these hypervisors are downloadable from the Internet and they all work in a similar way, so working with one will teach you the basics of working with desktop virtualization.

This chapter would not be complete without some mention of Parallels, a very popular hypervisor for macOS hosts. It does not come in a free version, only a 14-day trial, which you may want to download from their website (www.parallels.com). While Parallels has versions for Windows and Linux hosts, their main efforts go to their product for macOS hosts, and the other versions are not kept as up to date. Therefore, since we work on both Windows and macOS hosts, at this time we prefer to use Oracle VirtualBox on both platforms.

Windows Virtual PC and Windows XP Mode   Windows XP Mode is a virtual PC preconfigured to run a single virtual machine, with a legally licensed instance of Windows XP preinstalled. If you have some stubborn Windows XP applications that simply won't run on Windows 7, Windows XP Mode could solve the problem. (Before going to that extreme, though, try Compatibility Mode.) When you install Windows XP Mode, you are actually installing two components: Windows Virtual PC and the VM image for XP Mode. After Windows Virtual PC is installed, you can also create VMs to run other guest systems.

Once installed, Windows Virtual PC is so well integrated into Windows 7 that you can start programs installed in the Windows Virtual PC VM from Start menu shortcuts of the host OS. Beyond that, if you have a certain data file type that you prefer to run in a program that is in the VM, you can assign that file type to the program in the host. Then, double-clicking such a data file will launch the VM and the program within it. These capabilities are part of the Windows Virtual PC Virtual Applications feature.

All editions of Windows 7 support Windows Virtual PC, but you cannot install Windows XP Mode in the Home editions. If your host OS is the Basic or Home Premium edition, you need to install Windows Virtual PC, create your own virtual machine for Windows XP, and then install Windows XP using a valid, licensed setup disc or downloaded Windows XP installation files.

The system requirements for Windows Virtual PC are as follows:

- 1 GHz 32-bit/64-bit CPU
- 2 GB RAM or higher
- 15 GB hard disk space per virtual machine
- **Host OS**   Windows 7 Home Basic, Home Premium, Enterprise, Professional, and Ultimate
- **Guest OS** (clients)
  - **Windows XP**   The Virtual Applications feature is only supported in Windows XP Professional with Service Pack 3 (SP3).
  - **Windows Vista**   The Virtual Applications feature is only supported in Windows Vista Enterprise and Ultimate editions.
  - **Windows 7**   The Virtual Applications feature is only supported in Windows 7 Enterprise and Ultimate editions.

Windows XP Mode and Windows Virtual PC originally required HAV technology, but a 2010 update removed this requirement.

You can download Windows XP Mode for Windows 7 at the Windows Virtual PC home page. Because URLs change, we recommend that you enter the search string **windows virtual pc** into your favorite search engine and then select the result that points to the Virtual PC home page at Microsoft.com.

FIGURE 8-6

FIGURE 8-6

Create a virtual machine in Windows Virtual PC

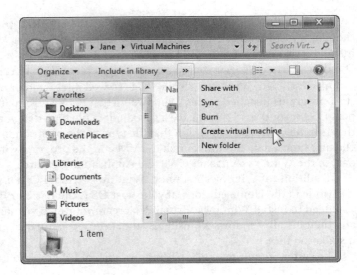

Once Windows Virtual PC is installed, you can create additional virtual machines by opening Windows Virtual PC from the Start menu. Then, in the Virtual Machines console, if the Create Virtual Machine button is on the button bar, click it; if it is not visible, click the chevrons (>>) to open the drop-down menu shown in Figure 8-6 and select Create Virtual Machine. Follow the instructions on each screen, keeping the default settings until you are more comfortable working with virtual machines. You will need to provide a name for the virtual hard disk, which will be the name for the virtual machine. When you are finished, you should have a new virtual machine listed, ready for you to install a new guest OS.

Hyper-V Hyper-V comes with the 64-bit Pro and Enterprise editions of Windows 8 and newer. It has more features than Windows Virtual PC, and more configuration options.

The system requirements for Hyper-V are as follows:

- 1.4 GHz 64-bit CPU with Hardware-Assisted Virtualization
- Hardware-enforced Data Execution Prevention must be available and enabled. This setting is configured in BIOS setup, and may be called Intel XD (execute disable) or AMD NX (no execute).
- 512 MB or more RAM
- At least one network adapter
- **Host OS** 64-bit Windows 8 Pro or Enterprise, Windows 8.1 Pro or Enterprise, Windows 10 Pro or Enterprise

Hyper-V client software is available on 32-bit versions of Windows 8 and higher, but it doesn't allow you to create new guest virtual machines, only to run existing ones. Don't be confused by this. If you run Hyper-V and a lot of the commands seem to be missing, including those for creating new VMs, check your host OS. You probably have a 32-bit version.

- **Guest OS** (clients)
    - Windows 10 (all editions)
    - Windows 8 and 8.1 (all editions)
    - Windows 7, with or without Service Pack 1, in 32-bit or 64-bit Ultimate, Enterprise, and Professional editions
    - Windows Vista with Service Pack 2, Business, Enterprise, and Ultimate editions, including N and KN editions
    - Windows XP Professional 32-bit with Service Pack 3
    - Windows XP x64 Professional Edition with Service Pack 2
    - Linux versions (CentOS and Red Hat Enterprise Linux, Debian, SUSE, Oracle Linux, Ubuntu, FreeBSD)

You may be able to run other OSs in Hyper-V besides the ones on the preceding list. That preceding list contains *supported* guest OSs, which means support may be available through Microsoft for helping you get them set up. It's not a comprehensive list of what will or won't work.

Hyper-V has some quirks, like not allowing USB drive access from within the guest OS and not automatically setting up network support, which may ultimately make you prefer Oracle VirtualBox (covered in the next section). However, as a technician, you need to know the basics of its setup and configuration.

EXERCISE 8-3

Enabling Hyper-V Manager

Some editions enable Hyper-V Manager by default; others don't. In this exercise you will check for Hyper-V, and enable it if necessary. You'll need 64-bit Windows 8.1 or 10 Pro or Enterprise.

1. Click Start, and type **Hyper-V** in the Search box. If Hyper-V Manager appears in the search results, click it to start the application, and you're done. Go on to Exercise 8-4. Otherwise proceed to Step 2.

2. Right-click the Start button and click Control Panel. Then choose Programs | Turn Windows Features On or Off.

3. Check the Hyper-V check box and click OK.

4. Follow the prompts to set up Hyper-V and then click Close.

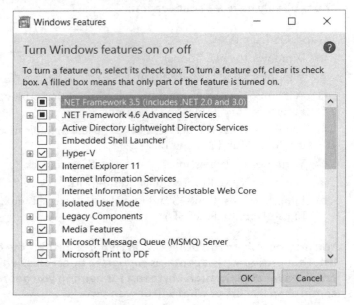

Setting Up a Virtual Switch in Hyper-V

Hyper-V doesn't detect the host system's network or Internet connection automatically; you have to set up a virtual switch, and then assign that virtual switch to the guest OS. This exercise creates a virtual switch, which you can then assign to a guest VM in Exercise 8-5.

1. Start the Hyper-V Manager application.

2. In the Actions list on the right, click Virtual Switch Manager.

3. Click New Virtual Network Switch.

4. Click External, and then click Create Virtual Switch.
5. Assign a name to the virtual switch.
6. Under Connection type, choose External Network.
7. Choose the network adapter on the host PC that provides the Internet connection.
8. Click OK. If you see a warning, click Yes.

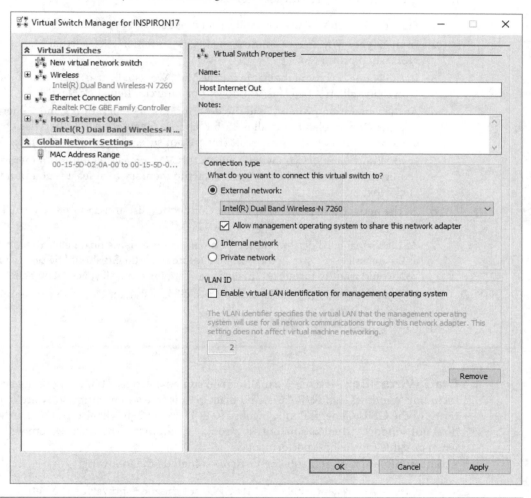

EXERCISE 8-5

Creating a VM in Hyper-V

Now you're ready to create a VM in Hyper-V. We won't actually install an OS on it right now, but we'll get the VM ready for later use.

1. Start the Hyper-V Manager application if needed.
2. In the Hyper-V Manager window, click New, and then click Virtual Machine. Click Next when prompted.
3. In the Name box, type the name for the VM. We usually use the name of the OS we plan to install on it (such as Windows 7 or Linux). Then click Next.
4. At the generation prompt, read the descriptions of Generation 1 and Generation 2. If the OS you plan to install is 32-bit, choose Generation 1. Otherwise choose Generation 2. (For this exercise, if you are not sure, choose Generation 1.)
5. If you know what OS you will install on this VM, check its minimum memory requirements, and set the amount of startup memory to at least that amount. Then click Next.
6. At the networking prompt, open the Connection list and choose the virtual switch you created in Exercise 8-4. Then click Next.
7. At the virtual hard disk prompt, type a name in the Name box. Leave the location set at the default. Set a size in the Size box. (Note that 100 GB should be plenty for any OS you would want to install; go smaller if you are low on disk space.) Then click Next.
8. When prompted for installation options, click Install an Operating System Later. Then click Next.
9. Click Finish.

Oracle VirtualBox Oracle VirtualBox will run on a variety of host operating systems, including Windows, Linux, Solaris, and macOS. It is free, open source software under the terms of the GNU General Public License (GPL) version 2. It will also run on hardware that does not support virtualization, but we strongly recommend you use a system with HAV when possible for the best performance.

The minimum requirements for VirtualBox include the following:

- **CPU** Any recent Intel or AMD CPU, but the more powerful, the better.
- **Disk space** It all depends on the VirtualBox features you select, but we recommend about 1 GB of disk space just for the VirtualBox software, plus several GB per virtual machine. The exact VM requirements depend on the guest OS and the programs and data you will add to the VM.

- **Memory**   Memory depends on the guest OS, but at least 512 MB and at least 1 GB for Windows XP and 2 GB for Windows 7 or Windows 8.
- **Host OS**   Windows, Linux, Solaris, or macOS.
- **Guest OS**   Versions of Windows, Linux, Solaris, Open Solaris, OS/2, Open BSD, or DOS.

Learn more about VirtualBox at the VirtualBox website (www.virtualbox.org), where you will find the online user manual and a link to download the software. To complete Exercise 8-6, you will need to download VirtualBox. To do that, click the Downloads link on the home page. On the Download VirtualBox page, shown in Figure 8-7, locate the version for the host

FIGURE 8-7   Select the correct download for your host OS

OS you plan to use and select it for download. In our case, we clicked the link for VirtualBox for Windows hosts. Once it completes downloading, you are ready to install it on your system. The screens and steps will vary depending on the version of VirtualBox and the host OS you use. For instance, the file downloaded to a macOS host (described on the VirtualBox download page as simply "OS X") will have a .dmg extension.

EXERCISE 8-6

Installing Oracle VirtualBox

Using the file you downloaded, run the VirtualBox installation wizard to install it on your Windows computer. To complete this exercise, you will need a system that meets the hardware and host OS requirements listed earlier, and we recommend at least 2 GB of memory if you hope to install Windows as a guest OS when you install Windows 7 in Chapter 9. In addition, you will need the following:

- The user name and password of an administrator account for this computer
- A broadband Internet connection

The installation steps are as follows:

1. Locate and double-click the installation program. Your version will be newer than the one we used, called "VirtualBox-5.0.22--108108-Win.exe."
2. Run the downloaded file, following the prompts to install the application. If prompted with a warning about network interfaces, click Yes.
3. At the end of the setup process, click Finish.
4. If you see a prompt about having an old version of an extension pack, click Download and wait for the new one to be downloaded, and then click Install and wait for it to be installed.

Congratulations! Oracle VM VirtualBox Manager is now installed. Move on to Exercise 8-7.

EXERCISE 8-7

Create a Virtual Machine in VirtualBox

This exercise picks up where Exercise 8-6 left off. You've installed VirtualBox, and now you'll create a new virtual machine.

1. On the application's toolbar, click New.

2. Type the name for the VM in the Name box. We usually use the name of the OS to be installed on it, for example. For this exercise, call it **Windows 7 Test**.

3. Open the Type drop-down list and select the OS you plan to install, and then open the Version drop-down list and select the version. For this exercise, choose Microsoft Windows as the type and Windows 7 as the version. Then click Next.

4. On the Memory Size page, drag the slider to 1 GB (1024 MB) and then click Next.

5. On the Hard Disk page, click Create a Virtual Hard Disk Now and click Create.

6. On the Hard Disk File Type page, click VDI (unless you have a reason to select something else) and click Next.

7. On the Storage on Physical Hard Disk page, leave Dynamically Allocated selected and click Next.

8. On the File Location and Size page, leave the default of 25 GB selected and click Create.

Congratulations! You now have a VM in VirtualBox Manager, ready to go for exploration of Windows 7 installation in Chapter 9.

Capturing and Releasing the Mouse and Keyboard in a Guest OS

Once you have a guest OS installed into a virtual machine, the guest OS and host OS are sharing the same physical hardware, but each physical device can serve only one master at a time.

Most hypervisors have extensions for most modern operating systems that allow control of the keyboard and mouse to pass seamlessly back and forth between the VM and the host system. (These are called *guest additions* in VirtualBox. You learn how to enable them in the next section.) When the VM window is active, the keyboard and mouse work within it. When the mouse moves outside the VM window and clicks, control returns to the host OS.

However, with some OSs, that smooth transfer doesn't happen automatically. In some cases you may be able to install extensions that enable the feature, but in other cases you may need to press a certain key sequence to release the mouse from the guest OS window each time you want to return to the host OS. This is called the *host key*.

The hypervisor assigns a host key. For instance, VirtualBox on a Windows computer uses the right CTRL key as the host key. VirtualBox on a macOS system uses the left COMMAND key, while Windows Virtual PC and Hyper-V both use the right ALT key.

Improving Guest OS Performance

After you install a guest OS into a guest VM, no matter which hypervisor you use, you may find that the screen and performance are not quite up to par, with only a low resolution available to you. Hypervisors usually have special software that you can install into the guest OS. For instance, VirtualBox has special drivers and other software called collectively Guest

Additions, and you install them after you install a guest OS. To do this, you start up your guest OS, and then access the VirtualBox menu on the window containing your guest OS, and click the Devices menu, as shown in Figure 8-8. Click Install Guest Additions and follow the instructions to run the program, which is presently named VBoxWindowsAdditions.exe (for a Windows guest OS). You will need to respond to a User Account Control prompt and at another point click Install in a Windows Security prompt. Notice that it installs dozens of files over several minutes. The result should be better performance overall, and you may find that Windows will have more resolution options for configuring your display.

When the Guest Additions are installed, you will be prompted to reboot the virtual machine. This is necessary before the changes take effect. Oracle VirtualBox configures your guest client to check for updates to the Guest Additions, so after you reboot the VM, if you are connected to the Internet through the host OS, you may see a message stating that there are updates—even if, as we did, you downloaded and installed VirtualBox on the same day.

FIGURE 8-8

Oracle VM
VirtualBox
Manager with
Windows Vista as
the guest OS

on the
Job

> **Each hypervisor has its own set of drivers and other programs to improve the virtual machine performance, but they are all guest-OS-specific, and each vendor gives their group of guest OS drivers and programs a different name.**

CERTIFICATION SUMMARY

A technician should understand the basics of client-side virtualization, the purpose of virtual machines, and the various requirements, including resources on the host computer, emulator needs, security, and network. Also important is understanding what a hypervisor is and the types of hypervisors available.

TWO-MINUTE DRILL

Here are some of the key points covered in Chapter 8.

Introduction to Virtualization

- ❑ Virtualization is the creation of an environment that seems real, but isn't.
- ❑ Virtualization is used for many purposes, such as a virtual world, a virtual classroom, storage virtualization, network virtualization, server virtualization, and desktop virtualization.
- ❑ Client-side virtualization occurs on the client side of a client-server arrangement.
- ❑ Server-side virtualization occurs on the server side of a client-server relationship.
- ❑ Virtual desktop infrastructure (VDI) is the hosting and managing of multiple virtual desktops on network servers.
- ❑ Examples of desktop virtualization include Windows, Unix, or Linux virtual machines running on Windows, macOS, or Linux systems.
- ❑ Examples of client-side virtualization include presentation virtualization, application virtualization, and desktop virtualization.

Implementing Client-Side Desktop Virtualization

- ❑ A hypervisor, also called a virtual machine monitor (VMM), is the software that creates a virtual machine, providing access to the necessary hardware on the host machine in isolation from other virtual machines, and from a host operating system, if present.
- ❑ Most hypervisors require or, at least work better, with Hardware-Assisted Virtualization (HAV), features of Intel Virtualization Technology for X86 (Intel VT-x) or AMD Virtualization (AMD-V).

❑ In virtualization, the hypervisor must create a virtual machine compatible with that of the underlying machine, whereas emulation allows you to run an OS or device on hardware with which it is completely incompatible. Sometimes a virtual machine may emulate some piece of hardware in the virtual machine that is either not present or not compatible in the underlying hardware.

❑ Emulators usually require more computing resources than hypervisors require for virtual machines.

❑ Internet access is important for working with virtual machines and keeping the hypervisor and its guest OSs up to date. A hypervisor will provide virtual network adapters, as well as a virtual network, on the host computer.

❑ The security requirements for a guest OS are the same as those for the host system. Therefore, immediately after installing a guest OS, install a security suite.

❑ In Windows 7, Windows Virtual PC is available as a hypervisor. In Windows 8 and newer, it's Hyper-V. (Not all editions are supported; refer to the specs in the chapter.)

❑ Oracle VM VirtualBox Manager is a free hypervisor that runs on a variety of platforms, and is easy to set up and use.

SELF TEST

The following questions will help you measure your understanding of the material presented in this chapter. Read all of the choices carefully because there might be more than one correct answer. Choose all correct answers for each question.

Introduction to Virtualization

1. You may use one of these animated graphic objects to represent you in a virtual world.
   A. Gadget
   B. Guest
   C. Avatar
   D. Snap-in

2. What type of virtualization is used in distance learning for interactive presentations by instructors?
   A. Server-side virtualization
   B. Virtual classroom
   C. Client-side virtualization
   D. Application virtualization

3. This type of virtualization only provides support for an app's user interface, and the user interface itself exists on a client computer, while the app runs on a server.
   A. Application virtualization
   B. Storage virtualization
   C. Presentation virtualization
   D. Server virtualization

4. In network virtualization, what portion of a network exists within one or more physical networks, creating a virtual network?
   A. Network adapters
   B. Network address space
   C. Switch
   D. Router

5. What acronym represents the term for hosting and managing of multiple virtual desktops on a network?
   A. VMM
   B. HAV
   C. VDI
   D. App-V

6. In this type of client-side virtualization, a user runs an application in a virtualized application environment on the local computer, isolating the application.
   A. Storage virtualization
   B. Application virtualization
   C. Virtual world
   D. Thin client

Implementing Client-Side Desktop Virtualization

7. Which acronym is a generic term for virtualization support found in modern CPUs?
   A. VMM
   B. VDI
   C. HAV
   D. App-V

8. Which of the following terms is used in computers to describe the use of software that allows you to run an OS or device on hardware with which it is completely incompatible?
   A. Virtualization
   B. Hardware-Assisted Virtualization
   C. Emulation
   D. Linux

9. Which of the following is a free hypervisor by Oracle with versions for Linux, Windows, and macOS hosts?
   A. VirtualBox
   B. Parallels
   C. Player
   D. Virtual PC

10. Which of the following does not require a host OS?
    A. Type II hypervisor
    B. Type I hypervisor
    C. Virtual PC 2007
    D. Windows Virtual PC

11. Which of the following terms is synonymous with hypervisor?
    A. Type I
    B. Virtual machine manager (VMM)
    C. Type II
    D. Remote Desktop

12. Which hypervisor is available in 64-bit versions of Windows 8, 8.1, and 10 Pro and Enterprise?
    A. Hyper-V
    B. Virtual PC 2007
    C. Windows Virtual PC
    D. VirtualBox

13. What legal issue must you consider when installing a guest OS in a virtual machine?
    A. Security
    B. Licensing
    C. Copyright
    D. Credentials

14. Which of the following will release the mouse and keyboard from control of a virtual machine?
    A. Host key
    B. Guest key
    C. WINDOWS key
    D. Product key

15. Two critical apps written for Windows XP will not run on your new Windows 7 computer, and Compatibility Mode only solved the problem for one app. Which of the following is the least expensive choice for running the old app on Windows 7?

    A. Windows XP Mode

    B. Microsoft Virtual PC 2007

    C. VMware Workstation

    D. Oracle VirtualBox

16. You must enter this within 30 days of installing a retail edition of Microsoft software.

    A. Host key

    B. Guest key

    C. WINDOWS key

    D. Product key

17. Put the following steps in order: (1) Install guest OS; (2) Install hypervisor; (3) Create virtual machine; (4) Install security software.

    A. 1, 2, 3, 4

    B. 1, 4, 3, 2

    C. 2, 3, 1, 4

    D. 4, 1, 3, 2

18. Which of the following is true?

    A. No emulation is possible by the hypervisors studied in this chapter.

    B. No emulation is possible by the hypervisors studied in this chapter unless the client OS is macOS.

    C. Some emulation of incompatible hardware is possible by the hypervisors studied in this chapter, as long as the CPU is compatible.

    D. Some emulation of incompatible hardware is possible by the hypervisors studied in this chapter, as long as the CPU is incompatible.

19. Which of the following identifies Intel's CPUs with Hardware-Assisted Virtualization technology?

    A. HAV

    B. App-V

    C. VMM

    D. VT-x

20. Which of the following describes a Type I hypervisor?

    A. App-V

    B. Guest OS

    C. VDI

    D. Bare-metal hypervisor

SELF TEST ANSWERS

Introduction to Virtualization

1. ☑ **C.** Avatar is an animated, computer-generated human or animal image that represents a computer user in a virtual world.

   ☒ **A** is incorrect, as a gadget is a small program. **B** is incorrect because the only use of the term "guest" in this chapter is in the context of "guest OS," the OS running within a VM. **D** is incorrect because a snap-in is a utility module added to a Microsoft Management Console.

2. ☑ **B.** Virtual classroom is a type of virtualization used in distance learning for interactive presentations by instructors.

   ☒ **A** and **C** are both incorrect because these are simply terms for the hosting location of virtualization. **D** is incorrect because this is a type of client-side virtualization.

3. ☑ **C.** Presentation virtualization is a type of virtualization in which only support for an app's user interface, and the user interface itself, exist on a client computer, while the app itself runs on a server.

   ☒ **A** is incorrect because in this type of virtualization the entire app is virtualized and the user interface is not separated from the app, but is isolated in a VM. **B** is incorrect because this type of virtualization allows client computers to utilize many networked hard drives as though they are one drive or location. **D** is incorrect because in server virtualization a single machine hosts one or more server operating systems, each in a virtual machine and each performing tasks independently from the other virtual machines and from the host.

4. ☑ **B.** Network address space exists within one or more physical networks, creating a virtual network.

   ☒ **A** is incorrect, as it is the address space that is virtualized in network virtualization. **C** and **D** are incorrect, as these are both types of network hardware not described in this chapter, and are not used to create a virtual network.

5. ☑ **C.** VDI, virtual desktop infrastructure, describes the hosting and managing of multiple virtual desktops over a network.

   ☒ **A** is incorrect because virtual machine monitor (VMM) is another term for hypervisor. **B** is incorrect because Hardware-Assisted Virtualization (HAV) is hardware-level support for virtualization found in Intel and AMD CPUs. **D** is incorrect because Application Virtualization (App-V) is the term for Microsoft's application virtualization software.

6. ☑ **B.** Application virtualization is the type of client-side virtualization in which a user runs an application in a virtualized application environment on the local computer, isolating the application.

☒   **A** is incorrect because storage virtualization allows client computers to utilize many networked hard drives as though they are one. **C** is incorrect because a virtual world is an artificial environment that users can explore, often using an avatar. **D** is incorrect because a thin client is a low-cost PC that runs software to connect to a server, transfer video downstream to the thin client, and send mouse and keystrokes upstream to the application on the server.

Implementing Client-Side Desktop Virtualization

7.   ☑   **C.** HAV (Hardware-Assisted Virtualization) is the generic term for virtualization support found in modern CPUs.
☒   **A** is incorrect because virtual machine manager (VMM) is simply another term for a hypervisor. **B** is incorrect because virtual desktop infrastructure (VDI) is a term for the creation and management of multiple virtual desktops. **D** is incorrect because App-V is a Microsoft term for their application virtualization software.

8.   ☑   **C.** Emulation is the use of software that allows you to run an OS or device on hardware with which it is completely incompatible.
☒   **A** is incorrect, as virtualization is the creation of an environment that seems real, but is not. While that is close to emulation, in the context of virtualization on computers, these terms are often kept separate. **B** is incorrect because Hardware-Assisted Virtualization (HAV) is simply hardware support for virtualization built into modern CPUs. **D** is incorrect because Linux is simply an operating system.

9.   ☑   **A.** VirtualBox is the free hypervisor by Oracle with versions for Linux, Windows, and macOS hosts.
☒   **B** is incorrect because Parallels is not by Oracle and is not free. **C** is incorrect because Player is by VMware not Oracle, and it does not come in a version for macOS hosts. **D** is incorrect because Virtual PC is by Microsoft, not Oracle, and it does not come in a version for macOS hosts.

10.   ☑   **B.** Type I hypervisor is correct because it does not require a host OS.
☒   **A** is incorrect because a Type II hypervisor does require a host OS. **C** and **D** are both incorrect because they are both Type II hypervisors that require a host OS.

11.   ☑   **B.** Virtual machine manager (VMM) is synonymous with hypervisor.
☒   **A** and **C** are incorrect because while they are types of hypervisors, Type I and Type II are not synonymous with hypervisor. **D** is incorrect because it is a Windows feature that enables you to remotely access other systems; these are real systems, not virtual machines, and no hypervisor is involved.

12.   ☑   **A.** Hyper-V is available in 64-bit versions of Windows 8 and higher in Pro and Enterprise editions.
☒   **B** and **C** are incorrect because while both are hypervisors, they are not available in Windows 8 and higher. **D** is incorrect because VirtualBox is an Oracle product, not included in any version of Windows.

13.   ☑   **B.** Licensing of the guest OS is very important.
☒   **A** is incorrect because although security is very important for both the guest and host OSs, it is not strictly speaking a legal issue. **C** and **D** are incorrect because neither is a legal issue with a guest OS.

14. ☑ **A.** A host key is a special key or key combination that will release the mouse and keyboard from control of a virtual machine.

☒ **B** is incorrect because a guest key is not the key or key combination that will release the mouse and keyboard from control of a virtual machine. **C** is incorrect because this special key works within Microsoft software on its own and in combination with other keys, and is many things other than a host key. **D** is incorrect, as the product key is not an actual key on the keyboard, but a string of characters used by Microsoft for piracy protection.

15. ☑ **A.** Windows XP Mode is the least expensive option because it provides for free both a hypervisor and a fully licensed version of Windows XP.

☒ **B** is incorrect because although Microsoft Virtual PC 2007 is free and would work, it does not include Windows XP, so you would have to provide that client OS at your expense. Also, Virtual PC 2007 does not support HAV, so it would run slower on the computer with HAV support. **C** is incorrect because VMware Workstation is not free, and it does not include a free license for Windows XP. **D** is incorrect because although Oracle VirtualBox is free, you would still need to provide a licensed version of Windows XP as the client.

16. ☑ **D.** A product key, a string of alphanumeric characters that comes on the packaging for Microsoft software, must be entered within 30 days of installing the software or the software will be disabled.

☒ **A** is incorrect because a host key is a key used to release the keyboard and mouse from a virtual machine. **B** is incorrect; this is not what you must enter within 30 days, and guest key is not a term found in this chapter. **C** is incorrect because the WINDOWS key is a key on a PC keyboard, not something you would enter at the keyboard.

17. ☑ **C.** (2) Install hypervisor; (3) Create virtual machine; (1) Install guest OS; (4) Install security software.

☒ **A, B,** and **D** are all incorrect because they are not in the proper order as described in this chapter.

18. ☑ **C.** Some emulation of incompatible hardware is possible by the hypervisors studied in this chapter, as long as the CPU is compatible.

☒ **A, B,** and **D** are all incorrect because they are all incorrect statements.

19. ☑ **D.** VT-x identifies Intel's CPUs with Hardware-Assisted Virtualization technology.

☒ **A** is incorrect because HAV is simply the acronym for the generic term. **B** is incorrect because App-V is the abbreviation for Microsoft Application Virtualization. **C** is incorrect because VMM is the acronym for virtual machine manager, another term for hypervisor.

20. ☑ **D.** Bare-metal hypervisor describes a Type I hypervisor because it does not require a host OS between it and the hardware.

☒ **A** is incorrect because App-V is Microsoft's application virtualization technology. **B** is incorrect because the guest OS is the OS running within a virtual machine. **C** is incorrect because virtual desktop infrastructure (VDI) describes hosting and managing multiple virtual desktops (often thousands) over a network.

Chapter 9

Upgrading, Installing, and Configuring Operating Systems

In this chapter, you will learn how to install and configure Microsoft Windows. Whether you are upgrading from an older version of Windows or installing from scratch (a clean install), you must follow certain guidelines and procedures, including basic preparation and installation steps and post-installation tasks. Post-installation configuration involves many components, including network connections, registration and activation, updating, applications and Windows components, devices, power management, and, occasionally, virtual memory. They are all included in this chapter. We'll also take a look at some of the common features and functionality of the macOS and Linux operating systems.

CERTIFICATION OBJECTIVE

■ *902: 1.2* *Given a scenario, install Windows PC operating systems using appropriate methods*

CompTIA A+ 902 exam objective 1.2 asks you to determine the best way to install or upgrade Microsoft Windows on a PC, given a particular scenario. This section looks at boot methods and types of installations, as well as file system choices and post-installation configuration processes like adjusting region and language settings and installing additional drivers and updates. First we'll look at upgrading, because that's a more common activity; then we'll turn our attention to clean installations.

Upgrading Windows

In this section, we will look at why you would upgrade Windows rather than do a clean install, what tasks you should perform before an upgrade, and how to do an upgrade. The next section will detail how to do a clean install.

Why Upgrade?

An in-place upgrade installation of Windows involves installing the new version of Windows directly on top of an existing installation. During an in-place upgrade, Windows reads all the previous settings from the old *registry* (a database of all configuration settings in Windows), adapts them for the new registry, and transfers all hardware and software configuration information, thus saving you the trouble of reinstalling applications and reconfiguring your desktop the way you like it.

An upgrade can also cost less than a full installation. Some Windows versions/editions are available in Upgrade versions, which are less expensive than the full product, but which require a previous licensed copy of Windows already installed.

on the job

Depending on the version/edition, you *might* be able to do a clean install with an upgrade version disc, provided you have a licensed copy of an eligible previous version available to insert in your optical drive when prompted during the setup process.

Pre-upgrade Tasks

Before attempting an OS upgrade, check the requirements of the new version and verify compatibility with the existing system's hardware and software. Then do whatever you can to clean up the existing system and safeguard its data, including backing up files, deleting unwanted files, and defragmenting the hard drive. The following sections explain these tasks in more detail.

Checking Requirements and Compatibility

When upgrading Windows, pay close attention to compatibility issues, run the Upgrade Advisor/Assistant, as described in Chapter 2 in "Upgrade Advisor/Upgrade Assistant/Get Windows 10," and be ready to resolve any problems you find. For example, if it shows that the new operating system does not have a driver for your network adapter and you proceed with the upgrade, you will not be able to access the network through the existing adapter. If the Upgrade Advisor/Assistant found incompatible hardware or software, take steps to resolve these problems before you upgrade.

Resolving Software Incompatibility

If an upgrade is available for an incompatible application program, obtain it and check with the manufacturer. Upgrade the application before upgrading the OS, unless advised otherwise by the manufacturer.

Remove any programs that will not run in the new OS from the computer before upgrading. There are also programs that interfere with the Windows Setup program but are compatible with the new Windows version after installation. This is often true of antivirus software. The Upgrade Advisor/Assistant report will list these, in which case follow the instructions under Details report. You may need to uninstall the program before the upgrade and reinstall it after the new version of Windows runs successfully.

If you have a critical app that is incompatible but you must use it in the new version of Windows, then use whatever compatibility options are available in the Windows upgrade after it is installed. Recall the Program Compatibility Troubleshooter described in Chapter 2, or Windows XP Mode for Windows 7 described in Chapter 8.

Resolving Hardware Incompatibility

When it comes to hardware incompatibility, usually the device driver, not the hardware, is the source of incompatibility with an operating system. The Upgrade Advisor/Assistant will identify incompatibilities with your hardware. If any are found, contact the manufacturer to see if they have an updated driver that will work. If so, obtain the driver beforehand, and follow the manufacturer's instructions. You may need to wait to upgrade the device driver until after the Windows installation is completed.

If your research shows that a hardware incompatibility cannot be resolved, remove the hardware in question, and replace it with a component that has a driver that works with the new OS.

Cleaning Up the Hard Drive

Before upgrading your computer to a new version of Windows, clean up the hard drive, especially the C: volume. This cleanup should include removing both unwanted programs and unnecessary files.

Removing Unwanted Programs The programs you should consider removing are those nifty programs you installed on a whim and now find you either dislike or never use. They are all taking up space on the hard drive.

Open Control Panel and use the Programs and Features applet to find and remove the unwanted application.

Removing Unnecessary Files It's amazing how fast hard drive space fills up. One way it fills up is with large data files, especially music, video, and picture files. Another, less obvious way hard drive space fills up is with temporary files, especially temporary Internet files that accumulate on the local hard drive while you are browsing the Internet. Windows has a nifty utility for cleaning up these files—Disk Cleanup. Exercise 9-1 walks you through the process of using the utility.

EXERCISE 9-1

Using Disk Cleanup

In this exercise, you will use the Disk Cleanup utility to remove unnecessary files in preparation for a Windows upgrade. You will need a PC with Windows Vista, 7, or 8.1 installed. If at any point UAC prompts you, click Continue to move past the warning. (That's more likely to occur in Windows Vista than in the other versions.)

1. Do one of the following to open Windows Explorer or File Explorer and display a list of local drives:
   - **Windows Vista or Windows 7** Click Start | Computer.
   - **Windows 8.1** Click the File Explorer icon on the taskbar, and then, if needed, click This PC in the navigation bar.
2. Right-click the C: drive and click Properties.
3. On the General tab, click Disk Cleanup.
4. Do one of the following to specify that all files should be cleaned up:
   - **Windows Vista** Click Files from All Users on This Computer.
   - **Windows 7 or Windows 8.1** Click Clean Up System Files.

5. Check or clear check boxes as needed to fine-tune the cleanup. Then click OK to begin the cleanup.

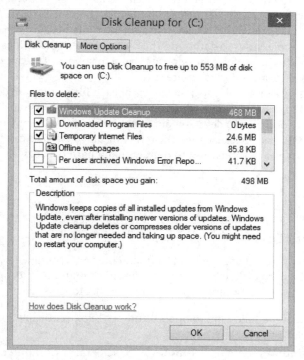

6. At the warning message, click Delete Files.
7. Wait for the cleanup to complete and its dialog box to close. Then click OK to close the Properties box.

If you select the Recycle Bin, Disk Cleanup will only delete the contents, not the Recycle Bin folder itself.

Backing Up Data

Back up any data from the local hard drive. Installing a new OS should not put your data in danger, but you just never know. Upgrading makes many changes to your computer, replacing critical system files with those of the new OS. If your computer loses power at an inopportune time, it could become unusable. This is a rare but real danger, especially if the computer is very old. Besides, surely you need to back up your hard drive. Backing up can be as simple as copying the contents of your Documents folder onto an external hard drive or flash drive. In Windows 7 and earlier, you can also use the built-in Windows Backup program (covered in Chapter 10).

Defragmenting the Hard Drive

Because of the way files are stored on a magnetic hard disk, the changes you make to a file may be written in a different spot on the disk than the original file. Such a file is fragmented. It takes longer to retrieve a fragmented file because the disk's read/write head must move multiple times to gather up the pieces. When lots of files are fragmented, disk read performance can suffer. (This doesn't apply to solid-state drives [SSDs], because the technology used to store files is different.)

Defragmenting a drive relocates the pieces of each file so they are contiguous, and relocates files as needed to create as much contiguous blank space as possible. Before upgrading Windows, it's a good idea to defragment the main hard drive to maximize the amount of contiguous blank space because then the newly installed OS files can be installed contiguously.

Follow the steps in Exercise 9-2 to defragment a hard disk drive.

EXERCISE 9-2

Defragmenting a Disk Drive

In this exercise, you will use the Disk Defragmenter or Optimize Drives utility in Windows to defragment a hard disk drive, as a preparation for upgrading its operating system. You can use Windows Vista, Windows 7, or Windows 8.1 for this exercise (any edition).

1. Do one of the following to open Windows Explorer or File Explorer and display a list of local drives:
   - **Windows Vista or Windows 7**   Click Start | Computer.
   - **Windows 8.1**   Click the File Explorer icon on the taskbar, and then, if needed, click This PC in the navigation bar.
2. Right-click the C: drive and click Properties.
3. On the Tools tab, click Defragment Now (Windows Vista or 7) or click Optimize (Window 8/8.1).
4. If a UAC box appears, click Continue.
5. Click Defragment Now.
6. Make sure the check box is marked for the C: drive (Windows Vista), or make sure the C: drive is selected from the Current Status list (Windows 7) or Status list (Windows 8.1). Defragmenting other drives is optional.
7. Click OK (Windows Vista) or click Defragment Disk (Windows 7) or click Optimize (Windows 8/8.1).
8. Wait for the defragmentation to complete. It may take up to several hours. You can continue to use the computer while the defragmentation is happening.
9. Click Close and then click Cancel to close the open dialog boxes.

Upgrading from Older Versions to Newer Versions

The title of this section might be a bit confusing, but there is a difference between running an upgrade from earlier versions to new versions of Windows and running an upgrade from a less capable edition of a particular version to a more capable edition of the same version. Therefore, in this section, we will describe an older-version-to-newer-version upgrade, and in the next section, we will discuss upgrading from one edition to another.

For any installation, you have to decide if the installation will be unattended (run from a script) or attended. Unattended installations are usually done in large organizations to distribute software to many computers. We will discuss unattended installation later in this chapter. An *attended installation*, also called a *manual installation*, is an installation of Windows that is not automated, but requires someone present to initiate it and respond to the prompts from the Setup program. And then we have attended clean installations (described later) and attended upgrades, described here.

To start an attended upgrade from earlier versions of Windows to Windows Vista, Windows 7, or Windows 8/8.1, start the existing version of Windows and place the distribution disc into the drive. Wait several seconds to see if the Setup program starts on its own. If it does not start, use Windows Explorer (or File Explorer) to browse to the CD or DVD and launch the Setup program. The Setup program will then detect the existing version of Windows. If it is a version that you can directly upgrade, Upgrade will be an active option in the Setup program. For example, Figure 9-1 shows an Upgrade option from Windows Vista to Windows 7. If the OS cannot be upgraded, this option will be grayed out.

FIGURE 9-1

Choose Upgrade in the Setup utility.

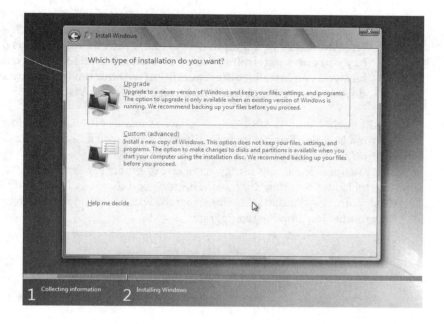

Click Next to continue with an upgrade, and Setup will continue in a manner similar to a clean installation (covered later in this chapter), but with fewer interruptions for information, and you will not be prompted to create a new partition for the OS (something we'll look at later in this chapter) since that would wipe out the installed OS and programs. You will need to provide a product key for any retail version, full or upgrade.

Upgrading to a Different Edition of the Same Windows Version

Windows Vista and Windows 7 both come in several editions: Starter, Home Basic, Home Premium, Business (Vista) or Professional (7), Enterprise, and Ultimate. If you have a computer with a less capable edition, such as Home Premium, and you discover it is lacking a feature you require, such as the ability to join your employer's corporate Microsoft domain, you can very easily upgrade.

To upgrade to a different edition in Windows Vista, you must have the installation media and a product key for the desired edition. Run the Setup utility on the installation media from within the current edition's desktop environment and follow the prompts.

In Windows 7, upgrades are even easier than that. From the Start menu in Windows 7, type **anytime upgrade** in the Search box and click Windows Anytime Upgrade in the search results.

on the
ⓙob

The Windows 7 installation disc actually includes all editions on it; the product key you enter determines which version is installed. By purchasing a new product key, you can install a different edition without having to buy an additional disc or download anything. That's not true of Windows Vista.

Although Windows 8/8.1 does not have as many editions as Windows 7, it does have the Anytime Upgrade feature, under a different name. You'll find it in the Control Panel as Add Features to Windows 8.

If you upgrade editions using a retail disc of a more capable edition, Windows 7 Setup will still launch Anytime Upgrade. This is a good thing because it will save you time. Using either path, the Windows Anytime Upgrade wizard will open (shown in Figure 9-2). Follow the prompts to complete the upgrade.

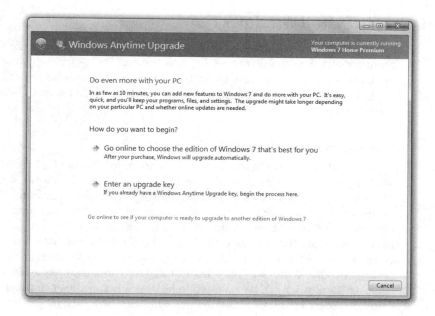

FIGURE 9-2

The Windows
Anytime
Upgrade screen

CERTIFICATION OBJECTIVES

■ *902: 1.2*   *Given a scenario, install Windows PC operating systems using appropriate methods*

■ *902: 1.4*   *Given a scenario, use appropriate Microsoft operating system features and tools*

In this section we continue the coverage of CompTIA A+ 902 exam objective 1.2 with coverage of clean installations to individual computers and other installation options and types, such as installing from an image, from a recovery disc, and from a factory recovery partition.

CompTIA A+ 902 exam objective 1.4 covers a broad range of operating system features and tools, but just two items in that extensive list are part of this chapter: Windows Easy Transfer and the User State Migration Tool (USMT).

Installing Windows

Performing a clean install of a new operating system is not a one-step process—in fact, it occurs in three stages. In the first stage, you perform necessary tasks to prepare for the installation; in the second stage, you actually install the operating system; and in the third stage, you implement follow-up tasks. In this section, you will learn the necessary tasks for the first two stages when performing a clean installation of Windows.

Preparing to Install Windows

Prepare to install Windows by first ensuring the computer meets the minimum requirements. You should then verify hardware and software compatibility, understand the basics of disk preparation for installation as well as the choice of file systems (where appropriate), and finally, take steps to migrate data from a previous Windows installation to a new installation.

Hardware Requirements

Table 9-1 summarizes the minimum hardware requirements for installing the various Windows versions covered on the CompTIA A+ exams. (This is the same data as in Table 2-3, repeated here for your convenience.) Remember that minimums are just that: the lowest level of CPU, the minimum amount of RAM, and the minimum free hard disk space needed. You will need a more powerful computer, in terms of hard drive space and RAM, to run a suite of office productivity tools. The good news is that a basic consumer-grade computer today far surpasses the system minimums for all current versions of Windows. Notice also that Windows 7, 8, 8.1, and 10 all have identical requirements, so a system running Windows 7 can be assumed to be basically capable of running any of the others (provided there are no incompatibilities with specific hardware or software installed).

Verifying Hardware and Software Compatibility

Besides minimum system requirements, you must also consider the compatibility of the specific components installed in the PC.

The Windows Setup program (Windows 7 and newer) should check for incompatibilities automatically when it runs. As you learned in Chapter 2, you can also run the Upgrade Assistant (or Upgrade Advisor) to check compatibility.

Don't forget about the issues of 32-bit versus 64-bit Windows and hardware and software compatibility. Most 32-bit Windows applications will run on the 64-bit version of Windows, but the reverse is not true; you cannot run 64-bit applications on a 32-bit version of Windows.

TABLE 9-1 Windows System Minimums		Windows Vista	Windows 7 Windows 8/8.1 Windows 10
	CPU	800 MtHz	1 GHz (32-bit or 64-bit)
	RAM	512 MB	1 GB (32-bit) or 2 GB (64-bit)
	Free Hard Disk Space	15 GB	16 GB (32-bit) or 20 GB (64-bit)
	Video Adapter	Support for Super VGA graphics	DirectX 9 adapter with WDDM 1.0 or higher device driver
	Optical	CD if installing from disc	DVD if installing from disc

Locating Third-Party Drivers for Storage

Some storage devices, particularly those using RAID or SCSI controllers, aren't automatically recognized by Windows Setup. If you plan on installing Windows on a system where some sort of unconventional storage device must be accessed to complete the installation, make sure you have a Windows driver for that device ready to supply if needed. At some point during the beginning of the Setup process (the exact point varies depending on the Windows version) you might be prompted to press a key to load a third-party driver; after you do so, you'll be prompted for the location of that driver. It can be on a USB flash drive, an optical disc, or a hard disk drive that the Setup program recognizes.

Preparing a Storage Device

CompTIA A+ 902 exam objective 1.2 lists *dynamic, basic, primary, extended, logical,* and *GPT* under the Partitioning topic. These are all covered in Chapter 10 also, but we bring them up now too because you might need to make some decisions involving them when doing a clean install of an OS.

If you install Windows on an unpartitioned hard disk, the Setup program will automatically prompt you to create a partition, assign a drive letter, and format the partition. If you accept the defaults, it will create a partition of the maximum size available on the primary hard drive, assign the drive letter C: to the partition, and format it with the New Technology File System (NTFS) file system. After that, the actual installation of Windows will proceed.

We will take a few pages here to define partition tables (GPT versus MBR), storage types (basic versus dynamic), partition types (primary versus extended), and file systems, and in Chapter 10 you will work with Disk Management, the utility you use after Windows is installed to manage and maintain your storage devices.

Disk Storage Types   Microsoft introduced the concept of storage type—dynamic and basic—in Windows 2000, and they continue to use these types in the newer versions of Windows. The storage type applies to the entire disk, but it is not a physical characteristic of a disk. It is a logical characteristic that has to do with how it allocates and manages space.

The *basic storage* type was the only storage type for hard disks from the days of Microsoft DOS (MS DOS) until Windows 2000. In fact, it has only been since Windows 2000 that the term basic storage has been used, and a disk using basic storage, a *basic disk*, is somewhat limited. What defines a basic disk is the use of the partition table, saved on disk in the first physical sector and called the *master boot record (MBR)*. Dynamic storage uses another location and method for storing disk configuration information. Basic storage is the default storage type when you install Windows. Techs may call a basic disk an MBR disk.

Basic disks that use MBR cannot support drives larger than 2.2 TB, so in the past one reason to go with dynamic disks has been large drive support. However, on systems with UEFI firmware (discussed in Chapter 3), you may be able to use GPT rather than MBR to circumvent that limitation, as discussed in the next section, while still keeping the disk a basic one.

Dynamic storage is an alternative way to allocate disk space and manage hard disks. The feature was introduced in Windows 2000 and continues in today's Windows versions. When a disk storage type is changed from basic to dynamic, it is then a *dynamic disk*, and does not have the limits imposed on basic disks (which we will describe when we talk about partitioning). The following statements are true of dynamic disks:

- When you work with dynamic disks, the term "partitions" goes away, and what formerly was a partition is now a *volume.*

- The number of volumes on a dynamic disk is not limited.

- A volume can extend to include available space on any hard disk in the computer, and therefore a dynamic disk can support redundant array of independent disks (RAID) fault-tolerance levels described in Chapter 4. That means you can create a software-based RAID using Windows.

- Configuration information for a dynamic disk, the *dynamic disk database*, can be rather complex, as compared to basic disks, and this information is stored on the disk space beyond the first physical sector outside of any volume on the hard disk. This is set aside and not visible when you use File Explorer (or Windows Explorer) to view your disks, folders, and files. If a disk was previously configured, the conversion to dynamic disk may need to make room for this database and remove an older partition.

Once the operating system is up and running, you may choose to convert a basic disk to a dynamic disk, but the benefits of dynamic disks really aim at the needs of network servers or high-end workstations, not the needs of most desktop computers. In fact, only one RAID type, disk mirroring, is available in client versions of Windows. Other, more advanced features are available only in the Windows Server products.

GPT vs. MBR Partition Tables *GPT (GUID Partition Table)* is a partition table alternative to MBR on a basic disk. GPT has two main advantages: it works with disks larger than 2 TB in capacity, and it allows up to 128 partitions per drive (as opposed to the usual limit of 4).

Macs with Intel hardware can boot macOS from a disk that uses GPT, as can a variety of Linux and Unix operating systems, both 32-bit and 64-bit. Most Windows versions (Vista and newer) can read/write a GPT volume, but require UEFI firmware to boot from it. Table 9-2 outlines the requirements for client OS versions. (Server versions of Windows have their own requirements, which are not covered on the CompTIA A+ exam and thus are not covered here.)

If the disk isn't larger than 2 TB and you don't need more than four partitions, go with MBR on a Windows system.

TABLE 9-2	Operating System	Read/Write Support for GPT	Boot Support for GPT
OS Support for GUI Partition Tables	Linux (most versions)	Yes	Yes
	macOS (10.4.0 and later) with Intel hardware	Yes	Yes
	Windows Vista 32-bit	Yes	No
	Windows Vista 64-bit	Yes	Yes, with UEFI
	Windows 7 32-bit	Yes	No
	Windows 7 64-bit	Yes	Yes, with UEFI
	Windows 8/8.1 32-bit and 64-bit	Yes	Yes, with UEFI
	Windows 10 32-bit and 64-bit	Yes	Yes, with UEFI

Basic Disk Partition Types   Before a basic disk can store data, it must be partitioned and formatted. *Partitioning* means dividing the disk into one or more areas that you can treat as separate logical drives, each of which can be assigned a different drive letter. You must format each logical drive with a *file system*, and each can have a different file system (although you will probably want NTFS for most logical drives on Windows systems).

Most people think of a partition and a logical drive as roughly the same thing, and it's easy to make that assumption because a partition usually contains only one logical drive. However, a partition can be either primary or extended (explained in the next section), and an extended partition can have multiple logical drives. It's therefore not always a one-to-one relationship.

Normally, you wouldn't want to divide a hard disk into multiple logical drives, so you create a single partition that uses the entire drive. On basic disks, a partition table within the MBR or GPT holds a record of the partition boundaries on a disk. A basic disk using MBR can have up to 4 partitions, and a basic disk using GPT can have up to 128 partitions.

Primary Partitions   Each *primary partition* can have only one logical drive assigned to it encompassing the entire partition. Because a computer can only boot from a primary partition that is also marked as active, a Windows PC with basic disks must have at least one primary partition.

Extended Partitions   An *extended partition* is not bootable, but it can have more than one logical drive (each with a drive letter). The main advantage of an extended partition is that it can be divided up into any number of logical drives, whereas a primary partition can have only one logical drive. If you're using a basic disk with MBR, the disk is limited to four partitions in total; if you need it to have more than four logical drives, you have to make one of the partitions extended.

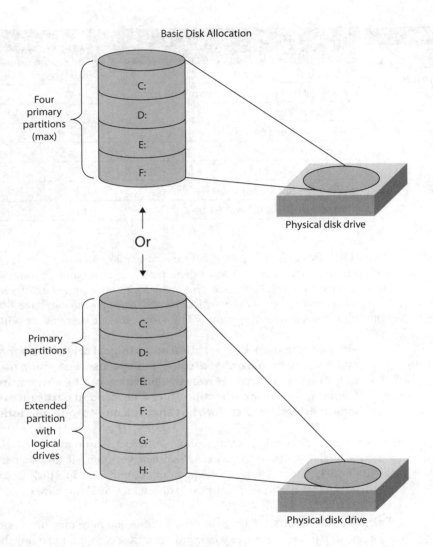

FIGURE 9-3

Basic disk with MBR allocation allows for a maximum of four partitions.

Figure 9-3 shows two scenarios for a basic disk with MBR. The first one has four primary partitions, each of which has a single logical drive letter. The second one has three primary partitions and one extended partition, and the extended partition is divided up into three logical drives.

Designating the Active Partition   In order for Windows to boot from a partition, that partition must be a primary partition marked as active. This is because the startup procedure common to all PCs looks for an *active partition* on the first physical drive from which to start an OS. Installing Windows on a new unpartitioned hard drive creates a primary partition and makes it active.

Partition Size Limits   When you partition a drive, the maximum partition size is the lesser of two values: the maximum partition size supported by the hardware or the maximum partition size supported by the file system. The older file systems that predated NTFS will be the limiting factors if you plan to format a partition with one of them. For instance, the FAT32 file system has a partition size limit of 2 terabytes (2 trillion bytes).

If you use NTFS, which is the default file system when you install Windows, the hardware will be the limiting factor. In the versions of Windows included on the CompTIA A+ exams (that is, the client versions of Windows Vista, 7, and 8/8.1), the NTFS file system has a partition size limit of 16 exabytes (an exabyte is 1 billion billion bytes). Now, this is obviously theoretical, because the hardware limit on a computer with a BIOS (versus UEFI firmware) is much smaller. Most modern BIOSs have a 2.2 TB limit. UEFI firmware breaks that limitation, but only if you use GPT rather than MBR as the partition table manager for the drive.

Selecting a File System for Windows   A *file system* is the means an operating system uses to organize information on disks. When you format a disk, you place the file system on the disk. That is, the format program creates the supporting logical structure on the disk, which is the most important component of a file system. Windows Setup can format a hard disk with your choice of several file systems, including FAT32 and NTFS. Unless you have a special reason for selecting one of the older file systems, you should choose the NTFS file system during Windows installation.

FAT32 is the 32-bit file system used in Windows 95 through Windows Millennium Edition (ME). It supports long file names but it has many limitations that make it undesirable for use on modern systems, such as a 32 GB partition size limit on Windows systems.

on the job **FAT32 can actually support up to 16 TB partitions, but Microsoft limits FAT32 file systems to 32 GB per partition in Windows.**

NTFS is the default file system in Windows. It not only supports large partitions but also has many useful encryption and compression features, and in some Windows versions it allows you to set up disk quotas and other administrative features.

If you are installing Windows on a drive that has been previously formatted, you may be offered a Quick Format option. Quick Format does not perform a sector-by-sector physical inspection and erasure of the disk; it simply refreshes the file system components on the disk, zeroing out all directory entries so that the disk appears empty. In reality, the old data is still written to disk after a quick format, but is difficult (but not impossible) to retrieve. In contrast, a full format does all that a quick format does, plus it overwrites the data space. A full format takes much longer (as much as an hour or more), but may be desirable under two special conditions: 1) you want to ensure the drive is wiped for security reasons, or 2) you suspect physical errors on the disk and want each physical sector to be inspected.

Learn more about file systems and how to manage them in Chapter 10.

Selecting a File System for Other Operating Systems   New to the CompTIA A+ 902 exam objectives are the file systems that are used primarily on Linux systems: ext3 and ext4. When you are installing a Linux distro on an unpartitioned drive, you'll be asked to make a choice of file systems.

Ext4, which was released in 2008, has these benefits over ext3:

- Larger maximum file size (16 TB versus 2 TB)
- Larger maximum partition size (1 EB versus 32 TB)
- Up to 64,000 subdirectories in a directory (up from 32,000 in ext3)
- Backward compatibility with ext3 file systems without upgrading them
- A multitude of features that improve performance

However, ext3 has one important benefit: You can share an ext3 partition with Windows. So if you multiboot your system (see the next section) and one of the drives must be accessed under both Windows and Linux, make sure that drive uses ext3.

Preparing for a Multiboot Installation

It is possible to configure a computer to boot into multiple operating systems, meaning that at startup you select the OS you wish to boot. This is called *multiboot* or, in the case of multibooting between just two OSs, *dual boot*. This is one way to try out a new version of Windows without replacing your old Windows installation. (Another way is virtualization, which you learned about in Chapter 8.)

When you start up a multiboot-configured system, a menu displays for several seconds. During that time, you can select the OS; if you do not make a selection, the default OS will be started.

On a multiboot system, you should dedicate a partition to each OS. While in the distant past we have dual-booted between two different OSs installed on the same partition, that is not the most desirable configuration, nor is it always possible. If the PC has two physical hard drives, each OS should have its own hard drive. If not, each should at least have its own logical drive, if not its own partition.

We have a computer, for example, that dual-boots between Windows 7 and Windows 8.1. This PC came with Windows 7 preinstalled on a 600 GB hard drive, and the entire drive set up as a single primary partition. To prepare the computer to dual-boot, we opened the Disk Management utility and used the Shrink Volume option to shrink the volume (really a partition, since this is a basic disk) by 60 GB. Then, in the space we freed up, we created a new partition, formatted it, and were ready to boot into the Windows 8.1 setup. We installed Windows 8.1 into the newly created partition, and when it detected the other installation of Windows, it automatically installed the appropriate files and configuration so that now when we boot up we see an OS Selection menu.

CompTIA A+ 902 exam objective 1.2 uses the term multiboot, but in practice we more often use the term dual-boot. Look for multiboot on the exam.

on the job

A good rule of thumb when setting up a multiboot system is to install "oldest to newest." In other words, if you have to install more than one OS, install the oldest one first, and work up toward the newest one. There are two reasons for this. One is that newer versions tend to be able to recognize the presence of older OSs better than older versions can recognize newer ones. The other is that as technology advances, the multiboot management interface improves, so by installing the newest one last, you get the latest and greatest updated multiboot manager.

Using Data Migration Tools

The most valuable files on a PC are not the OS and applications, but the user's data. Therefore, when upgrading the OS or moving the user to a new computer, you must plan for a successful *data migration*—the moving of data from one storage device to another. When you do an in-place upgrade, you retain all the user settings and data, so data migration is a nonissue. However, when you do a clean installation on a computer that has an older version of Windows, you often need to ensure that the settings and/or data from the old installation migrate to the new installation. Or, when you purchase a new computer with a new version of Windows, you face migrating settings and/or data files from an older computer.

Microsoft provides the Windows Easy Transfer utility in Windows Vista, Windows 7, and Windows 8/8.1. This utility brings over your data and places it in the correct locations on the hard drive to fulfill the basic task of data migration. It also goes further by migrating the settings for Windows and certain Windows applications, including desktop preferences and preferences for Internet Explorer and all Microsoft applications installed on both the old and the new computers. The utility does not install any applications on the new PC, however, so you must install your applications on the new PC before migrating the data and settings from the old PC.

exam

watch   In addition to Windows Easy Transfer's appearance under CompTIA A+ 902 exam objective 1.4, 902 exam objective 1.1 lists "easy transfer" under operating system features, in a more generic sense.

Windows Easy Transfer for Windows Vista, Windows 7, and Windows 8   The Windows Easy Transfer utility was described briefly in Chapter 2. It comes with Windows Vista, Windows 7, and Windows 8. (There is also a Windows 8.1 version, but it's different, and discussed separately in the next section.) Use it when doing a single transfer of data and settings to a new Windows computer from an older Windows computer. It is not practical to use this utility for multiple computers because it only works on a one-to-one basis with each old and new pair. The three transfer methods are via an Easy Transfer cable (a special USB cable available from many sources), via network, or via an external hard disk or USB flash drive. Two of these methods, the cable and network, require two separate computers, while the third method can also be used when you are planning to replace (not upgrade) the current Windows installation with a new, clean installation.

Depending on the transfer method you use, the wizard will guide you through the process of installing the utility into the older version of Windows and gathering the files.

Windows Easy Transfer for Windows 8.1   Microsoft has stripped much of the functionality out of Windows Easy Transfer in Windows 8.1. Here are its limitations compared to earlier versions:

- It accepts incoming transfer data only from Windows 7, Windows 8, and Windows RT.
- It doesn't save the current computer's data for transfer elsewhere; it only accepts incoming data.
- You can't use the Easy Transfer cable or network options to transfer data; it only accepts data saved on an external drive.

Data Migration for Windows 10   Microsoft has removed Windows Easy Transfer entirely in Windows 10. One alternative is the PCmover utility (either Express or Professional edition), by Laplink. For information about it, see http://pcmover-10.laplink.com.

User State Migration Tool   The *User State Migration Tool (USMT)* is an advanced tool that only works in a Windows server–based domain network. This is the tool for network administrators in such a network who either need to migrate data from many computers or need to perform what Microsoft calls a "wipe-and-load migration" from and to the same computer. Compared to simpler utilities like PCmover Express and Windows Easy Transfer, USMT takes longer to prepare, involving creating custom scripts, but it results in an automated process that occurs in two stages. The first stage collects files and settings, and the second stage installs the files and settings on the target computer.

USMT has been available since Windows XP, although it has gone through several updates. The current version can be downloaded in the Windows Assessment and Deployment Kit (Windows ADK) for the version of Windows you plan on migrating to. You'll find the Windows 10 version at https://developer.microsoft.com/en-us/windows/hardware/windows-assessment-deployment-kit#adkwin10. Download and run the Setup utility for the Windows ADK, and then during the setup process, you can check the check boxes for the utilities you want. One of these is User Sate Migration Tool (USMT), as shown in Figure 9-4.

Selecting Boot Media and Methods

When installing Windows on a new computer that does not have an OS on the hard drive, you will need to boot into the Setup program. How you do this depends on the computer, but your choices today include optical drive, USB device, External Serial Advanced Technology Attachment (eSATA) device, or Preboot eXecution Environment (PXE) boot (for an over-the-network installation). The most common method for starting Windows Setup for the standard retail version is to boot up from the optical disc media, and most computers will do that by default.

FIGURE 9-4 Install Windows ADK and make sure the USMT tool is included in the features to be installed.

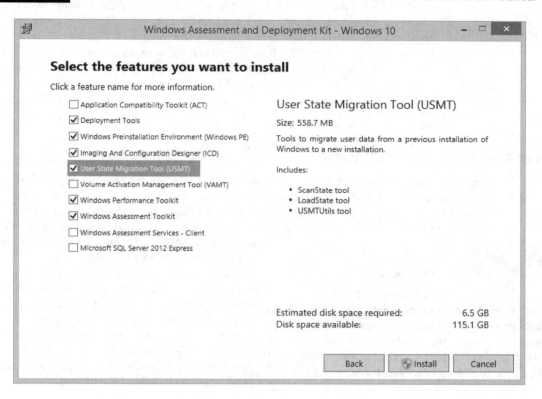

Modifying the Boot Order

If you want to boot from a device other than the one that the PC currently prefers (probably the hard disk or the optical drive), you must use firmware setup to change the boot order for the system.

Recall from the firmware configuration discussion in Chapter 3 that one important configuration setting is the boot sequence or boot priority order.

Before you begin a clean installation requiring that you boot into the Windows Setup program, go into your firmware settings, as described in Chapter 3, and ensure that the device you need to boot from is either first in the list or not preceded by a bootable device. Then, for most of these options, you simply reboot and Windows Setup begins.

Booting from the Network (PXE Boot or NetBoot)

All modern network cards support the ability to start a computer over the network, without relying on a disk-based OS, using an Intel standard called *Preboot eXecution Environment (PXE)*, or more simply *PXE Boot*. If network boot is selected in firmware setup, the network card will initiate the startup of the computer, downloading the initial bootup files from a network server. Then it is ready to perform a task, such as installing the new OS over the network or running centralized maintenance tests on the computer. However, someone has to do the prep work of preparing a server running the Microsoft *Windows Deployment Services*. This service responds to PXE Boot requests from network clients and supplies the boot environment needed to boot up. Then, usually through a script, the client computer is directed to connect to the network share containing the Windows installation files and run the Setup program over the network. On Macs, the equivalent technology is NetBoot, which enables Macs to boot from a network.

Over-the-Network Installation

A network installation can involve an image installation, an attended installation, or an unattended installation. Any of these network installation methods requires quite a bit of prep work, but what they have in common is the basic steps for preparing for the installation. Here, we will describe the steps required for either an attended or unattended network installation. Later, we will address an over-the-network image installation.

To prepare for an attended or unattended network installation, first, copy the Windows source files into a shared folder on the server; second, configure the client computer to boot up and connect to the server; and third, start the Setup program itself. The actual steps for doing this are extensive, often requiring trained personnel and testing of the procedure.

e x a m
watch CompTIA A+ 902 exam objective 1.2 only requires that you understand the differences among the various installation methods. You do not need in-depth, hands-on experience with the unattended or drive-imaging methods.

Installing from a Recovery Disc

Many manufacturers ship computers with original equipment manufacturer (OEM) Windows installed (whatever version), but most of them do not ship an OEM Windows disc with the computer. They may ship what they call a recovery disc, or they give you the option of creating a set of recovery discs yourself from a utility installed with Windows. In this case, *don't skip creating these discs*.

However you acquire the recovery media, be sure to keep it in a safe place. Without the OEM Windows disc, the recovery disc is your only source of your legally licensed Windows. If you need to reinstall Windows from a recovery disc, all you need to do is boot up the disc and the recovery program will run. The sad part is that it returns your computer to the state it was in the day you unpacked it and first turned it on. It wipes out all your installed programs and data, and you will have to reinstall the programs and then restore your data from backups. Sometimes installing from a recovery disc is your only option, but not always. In Chapter 13, we will look at how to diagnose operating system failures and how to recover from certain types of failures without reinstalling Windows.

Installing from a Factory Recovery Partition

If a manufacturer does not ship a recovery disc with a Windows computer or include a utility for creating this disc, they may offer another option, which is a factory recovery partition containing an image of the drive partition on which Windows is installed. The recovery partition itself is hidden and only accessible by a method the manufacturer provides for restoring the system to its fresh-from-the-factory state. Check the manufacturer's documentation long before you need to resort to installing from a factory recovery partition. In many cases, you enter the factory recovery partition utility by pressing a function key as the system starts up. If you install a new version of Windows on a computer with a recovery partition, the new OS may overwrite a critical part of the Windows partition containing information for calling up the recovery program, so check with the manufacturer before upgrading.

Attended Clean Windows Installation

Installing Windows requires inputting certain unique information for each computer. During an *attended installation* of Windows, also called a *manual installation*, you must pay attention throughout the entire process to provide information and to respond to messages. A Setup Wizard guides you through the process. The installation process takes about an hour, and you spend most of that time watching the screen. Most of the process is automated, with user interaction required only at the beginning and end. Feel free to walk away as the installation is taking place, because, if it needs input, the installation program will stop and wait until you click the correct buttons.

The following description is of a clean install, meaning the partitioning and formatting of the hard disk will occur during the installation. You would perform this type of installation on a new computer, or on an old computer when you want a complete new start. A clean install avoids the potential problems of upgrading, which we will describe later in "Updating Windows."

Gathering Information

Before you begin an attended installation from a retail version of Windows, gather the specific information you need, which depends on whether you are installing a PC at home or in a business network. Either way, gather the appropriate information, including the following:

- The product ID code from the envelope or jewel case of the Windows optical disc, or a digitally acquired product key, such as one purchased online or provided by an employer.
- A 15-character (or less) name for the computer, which must be unique on the local network; you can make up a name yourself on a workgroup or home network.

■ The name of the workgroup or domain the computer will join. You may need to get this information from a network administrator. Anyone can create and join a workgroup, but to join a domain, an administrator must create accounts in the domain for both you and your computer.

■ If the computer will be joining a domain, the user name and password assigned to the user account to be set up first on this PC.

■ The necessary network configuration information. Ask your network administrator for this information, but the Windows default will configure the computer to receive an address automatically, which should work for you in a corporate setting, at home, and at school. Learn more about how a computer receives network addresses in Chapter 13.

In addition, gather the discs and/or setup files for any device drivers for the computer and its installed peripherals, especially the network adapters. (Everything else can be downloaded later, but the network card must be working in order to download anything.) You may need to download device drivers from manufacturers' websites. Windows may have appropriate drivers for all your devices, but if it does not, Windows Setup may prompt you to provide them. You can do that during Setup, or you can let Windows install minimal generic drivers during Setup, and then install or update the drivers after Setup is complete.

Installing Interactively

Begin the attended Windows installation by booting into the Window Setup program from one of the sources described earlier. In most cases, when installing to a single computer you will begin by inserting the Windows distribution disc and booting the computer. Beyond that, there are some differences in how Setup runs for the various versions of Windows. All the versions examine your hardware configuration early on.

on the job

All versions of Windows that we are studying here include an option to repair an existing installation early in the Setup process. You can use that instead of doing a clean install when a system is so badly damaged or corrupted that Windows won't start normally. If the PC is running Windows 8 or newer, another possibility in such a situation is to refresh or restore the Windows installation, as explained in Chapter 12.

When you start up Windows Vista or newer from a disc or other media with Setup files, the *Windows Preinstallation Environment (Windows PE)* starts. This is a scaled-down Windows operating system with limited drivers for basic hardware. Windows Vista, Windows 7, and Windows 8/8.1 Setup screens are nearly identical. The steps of the process include copying Windows files, expanding Windows files, installing features, installing updates, and completing installation.

Near the beginning of the installation process, you are prompted to select the language and other *regional settings*, such as date, time, and currency formats, and keyboard or input method. See Figure 9-5. A feature called the *Multilingual User Interface (MUI)* allows you to install a language other than English as the only language or as an additional language.

FIGURE 9-5

Select a language on this Windows 7 Setup page.

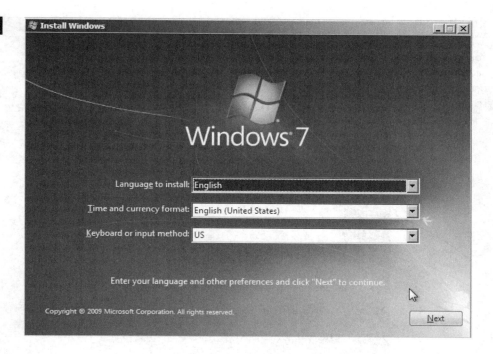

In all versions, when prompted, enter your *product key*. Windows will use the product key when activating after Setup completes. When the End User License Agreement (EULA) appears, read it and follow the instructions to acknowledge acceptance of the agreement and to continue. This is mandatory, as it is your agreement to comply with your license to use Windows that allows you to install Windows on one computer for each license that you own. The product key tells the Setup program which edition of Windows you have purchased; different editions use different keys. The product key is usually located on the DVD sleeve in a retail box version of Windows.

Windows Setup will display a list of existing partitions and unpartitioned space. On most systems, this page will show a single disk, and you will simply click Next. Figure 9-6 shows this page. Although it is not obvious, in this case the disk is a virtual hard drive in a virtual machine, and the virtual hard drive is smaller than we would normally choose for a typical desktop, but otherwise, this is what you would expect to see. If you click Next, the disk will be partitioned using all available space, and it will be formatted with NTFS. If you need to load a third-party driver for the hard disk, click Load Driver. If you want to do anything different than the default, click Drive Options (Advanced). For instance, if the disk has enough space, you might want to create more than one partition, or install Windows into a folder other than the default. We don't recommend straying from the defaults for the majority of situations.

Setup copies files to the location you indicated or to the newly formatted partition. Unless you specify another location, Setup creates a folder named Windows in C:\, into which it installs the OS, creating appropriate subfolders below it. After it finishes copying

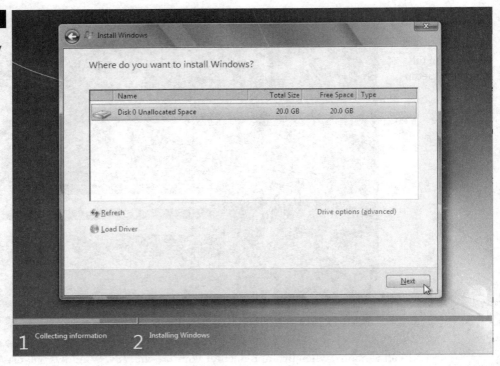

FIGURE 9-6

You will normally accept the defaults on this screen.

the base set of files to this location, your computer reboots. At this point the PC reboots and returns to the graphical mode, usually at a higher screen resolution than before the restart because it is now using the newly installed drivers rather than the drivers used by PE. All versions of Windows Setup will restart multiple times during the Setup process.

Near the end of the Setup process, you will be asked some questions about the PC's configuration; follow the instructions on the screen, accepting the defaults when you are unsure.

If Setup detects a network card, the network components will install and configure with default settings. All versions will give you a chance to personalize Windows by user name and password, computer name, and information for joining a Windows workgroup or for connecting to a Windows Domain (if applicable).

As a summary of this previous explanation of an attended installation, Exercise 9-3 will walk you through the steps for performing a clean installation of Windows 7.

EXERCISE 9-3

Installing Windows 7

In this exercise, you will do a clean installation of Windows 7. To complete this exercise, you will need the Windows 7 installation disc and the information listed earlier under

"Gathering Information." You can install on a separate PC, or you can use one of the virtual machines that you created in Chapter 8.

1. Insert the Windows disc and boot the computer. Watch the screen for instructions to boot from the optical drive. A plain black screen will briefly flash, followed by a black screen with the message "Windows is loading files…" while Windows PE is loaded and started. The Starting Windows screen signals that Windows PE is starting and will soon load the GUI for Windows 7 Setup.

2. On the first Install Windows page, select a language, time, currency format, and keyboard input methods and select Next.

3. The most prominent feature of the next screen is the Install Now button, but you should notice two important links. One is labeled What to Know Before Installing Windows; click it to see if you have overlooked a preparation step. The second link, labeled Repair Your Computer, is an important one to remember. If at any time after you install Windows 7 your system will not start, and if it also will not start in Safe Mode, pull out your Windows 7 disc, boot from it, and select Repair Your Computer.

4. On the license page, read the Microsoft Software License Terms, click to place a check in the box labeled I Accept the License Terms, and click the Next button.

5. On the next page, you are asked which type of installation you want. Select Custom to perform a clean installation.

6. On the next page, you need to select the target drive for the installation (see Figure 9-6).

7. Windows 7 Setup goes through the phases of the installation, restarting several times, and returning to a page that displays the progress with a green check mark by each completed phase.

8. At the completing installation phase, the message "Setup will continue after restarting your computer" displays. After this, as Windows 7 restarts, the message "Setup is checking video performance" displays. Then you will need to enter a user name for the first user and a name for the computer.

9. Next create the password for the first user account, entering it twice, and type a password hint that will help you to recall the password but not reveal it to others. The password hint will display any time you enter an incorrect password when logging on.

10. On the next page, you will need to enter the product key and check the box labeled Automatically Activate Windows When I'm Online." Already checked by default, this means it will activate automatically if your computer connects to the Internet. You must activate Windows within 30 days of installation. After that it will stop functioning. Click Next to continue the final configuration steps.

11. On the next page, configure the Automatic Update Settings. You would normally click the first option: Use Recommended Settings. Windows Setup will then continue.

12. On the next page, select your time and date settings, and click Next. Now select your computer's current location. If you are at home, select Home Network; if you are at

school or work, select Work Network; if your computer has mobile broadband or you are using a public Wi-Fi network, select Public Network. There will be a short delay while Windows connects to the network and applies settings.

13. The Welcome page displays, followed by a message "Preparing your desktop..." Soon after the desktop will display and, depending on the setting you selected for updating and if you have an Internet connection, you will see a message that Windows is downloading and installing updates. Some updates require restarting Windows to complete installing the update.

After Setup is complete, your job is not finished. You will now need to configure Windows to personalize it for the user. We'll talk more about that topic after we look at unattended installations.

Unattended Installation

An *unattended installation* is one in which the installation process is automated. There are two general types of unattended installations:

- A scripted installation using *answer files* and *Uniqueness Database Files (UDFs)*, which provide the data normally provided by a user during an attended installation
- An image installation, using either Microsoft software tools or a third-party tool

Scripting for Unattended Installations

A scripted installation uses scripts that someone has prepared ahead of time. Organizations with large numbers of desktop computers needing identical applications and desktop configurations use this. This type of installation normally requires trained people who plan and implement the installation using a variety of automation methods, including scripts and access to the Windows source files on a *distribution server*.

A typical scripted installation scenario involves placing the Windows source files from the distribution disc onto a file share on a server, which is then called a *distribution share*. This assumes sufficient licenses for the number of installations from these source files. Then, each desktop computer boots up, either from the local hard drive or from another source, and runs a script that connects to the distribution server to begin the installation.

Although we place scripted installations under unattended installations here, the amount of interaction required ranges from none to as much as is required for an attended installation. In fact, certain software on the server side, such as Microsoft's System Center Configuration Manager (SCCM) can, with proper configuration of each client computer, push an installation down from the server with no one sitting at each desktop. This can include an automated installation of user applications on top of the newly installed Windows OS.

Drive Imaging

In organizations that want to install the same OS and all the same application software on many desktop PCs, drive imaging is often used. A *drive image*, or *disk image*, is an exact duplicate of an entire hard drive's contents, including the OS and all installed software, applied to one or more identically configured computers. CompTIA A+ 901 exam objective 1.2 calls this type of installation *image deployment*.

Microsoft has developed an entire suite of tools for deploying Windows to large numbers of desktop computers. These tools and sets of recommended procedures cover the planning, building (of the images), and deployment phases. Even an overview of these tools would take a great deal of time and space, and CompTIA A+ 902 exam objective 1.2 only requires that you understand the basics of image installations. Therefore, we will simply list and briefly describe the tools for the build and deployment phases.

- **Microsoft Deployment Toolkit** A technician uses this tool to create and manage both the distribution share and the various images. Plus, this tool will configure several deployment sources, including a single server, a deployment share, a DVD ISO image, or a directory that contains all the files needed for a customized deployment from a server running Microsoft's System Center Configuration Manager (SCCM) software.
- **Windows System Image Manager** This tool allows a technician to create the components for automating custom installs using custom scripts.
- **ImageX** Use this tool to create the disk images.
- **Windows Preinstallation Environment (Windows PE)** PE is a bootable environment that gives operating system support during three types of operations: installing Windows, troubleshooting, and recovery.
- **User State Migration Tool (USMT)** Technicians use this tool for migrating files and settings to many desktop computers. It does not migrate programs, however, just data files, operating system settings, and settings from Microsoft applications.

Microsoft is not the only source for such tools: many third-party vendors offer an array of imaging and deployment tools. Learn more about these tools by searching on the Internet.

CERTIFICATION OBJECTIVES

- **902: 1.4** *Given a scenario, use appropriate Microsoft operating system features and tools*
- **902: 1.5** *Given a scenario, use Windows Control Panel utilities*

CompTIA A+ 902 exam objectives 1.4 and 1.5 include a large list of features and utilities. This section covers only two of them: Windows Update (from 1.4) and Virtual Memory (from 1.5).

Configuring Windows

After installing Windows, you have a few post-installation and configuration tasks. They include verifying network access (assuming connection to a network exists), registering and activating Windows, and installing any available Windows updates. After those essentials are taken care of, you may choose to customize the desktop interface, install new devices and applications, and adjust virtual memory settings.

Network Configuration

Once you have completed the installation, if the computer is on a network, verify that it can communicate with other computers on the network. If it cannot, you may need to add a device driver for the network adapter and/or configure the network components. Network connectivity is important because this is the best way to download updates to your newly installed operating system—a task you must do as soon as you have Internet access.

Checking Network Connectivity

Browse the network to determine if you can see any computers on the network besides your own. In Windows Vista and Windows 7, look for a shortcut named Network on the Start menu. In Windows 8/8.1, open File Explorer and click the Network shortcut in the navigation bar on the left. Only computers with the file and print sharing enabled will appear.

Adding a Network Adapter Device Driver

If you are installing network drivers or other drivers after the installation, wait until after the final reboot, and then follow the manufacturer's instructions for installing the device driver(s). Download the latest driver from the manufacturer (using a different computer, obviously, since the one you are working on doesn't have network connectivity yet). Learn more about installing and configuring network components in Chapter 15.

Registration and Activation

Many people confuse registration and activation. These are two separate operations. *Registration* informs the software manufacturer who the owner or user of the product is, and provides contact information such as name, address, company, phone number, e-mail address, and so on, about them. Registration of a Microsoft product is still entirely optional.

Activation, more formally called *Microsoft Product Activation (MPA)*, is a method designed to combat software piracy, meaning that Microsoft wishes to ensure that only a single computer uses each license for Windows.

Mandatory Activation Within 30 Days of Installation

Activation is mandatory, but you may skip this step during installation. You will have 30 days in which to activate Windows, during which time it will work normally. If you don't activate it within that time frame, Windows will automatically disable itself at the end of the 30 days. Don't worry about forgetting, because once installed, Windows frequently reminds you to activate it with a balloon message over the tray area of the taskbar. The messages even tell you how many days you have left.

on the job

Understanding activation is important because most Microsoft products require it, and Microsoft is not the only software vendor using an activation process. Software purchased with a volume license agreement does not require product activation.

Activation Mechanics

When you choose to activate, the product ID, generated from the product key code that you entered during installation, combines with a 50-digit value that identifies your key hardware components to create an installation ID code. This code must go to Microsoft, either automatically if you have an Internet connection, or verbally via a phone call to Microsoft, which then gives you a 42-digit product activation code.

MPA does not scan the contents of the hard disk, search for personal information, or gather information on the make, model, or manufacturer of the computer or its components. Nor does it gather personal information about you as part of the activation process.

Reactivation

Sometimes reactivation is required after major changes to a computer. To understand why, you need to understand how MPA creates the 50-digit value that identifies your hardware. MPA generates this hardware identifier value used during activation, called the "hardware hash," by applying a special mathematical algorithm to values assigned to the following hardware:

- Display adapter
- Small Computer System Interface (SCSI) adapter
- Integrated Development Environment (IDE) adapter
- Network adapter Media Access Control (MAC) address
- RAM amount range
- Processor type
- Processor serial number
- Hard disk device
- Hard disk volume serial number
- Optical drive

MPA will occasionally recalculate the hardware hash and compare it to the one created during activation. When it detects a significant difference in the hardware hash, you will be required to *reactivate*, and you may need to contact Microsoft and explain the reason for the reactivation. This is Microsoft's way of ensuring that you did not install the product on another computer.

Adding new hardware will not necessarily require reactivation, but replacing any components in the preceding list, or repartitioning and reformatting a drive, will affect the hardware hash. We have had to reactivate after making a number of changes to a computer and again when we decommissioned a computer and installed the licensed retail version of Windows on a different computer. In both instances, we had to do this over the phone because we had to explain the circumstances to the representative.

Updating Windows

Windows will automatically begin updating as part of Setup. The program that manages that, Windows Update, connects to Microsoft servers online and then downloads and installs any updates, patches, and other fixes that it finds.

Configuring Automatic Update Settings

Although Windows Update is configured to automatically download and install updates, you can change these settings by opening Windows Update from the Control Panel and selecting Change Settings from the Task pane on the left. Then you can configure updates to occur at a regular interval. Figure 9-7 shows the Change Settings page in Windows 7, which is nearly identical to that in Windows Vista and Windows 8/8.1.

Corporate Policies that Prohibit Automatic Updating

In spite of ease of updating Windows over the Internet, how you actually obtain updates will depend on the organization (school or business) that manages the computer, if it's not your own.

Updates can bring their own problems. Therefore, many organizations with IT support staff disable automatic updates, waiting until they have conducted their own internal tests before distributing them to users' desktops and laptops. This is especially true of service packs. In some organizations, the IT department may distribute updates intended for new installations on optical disc in order to install them before a computer ever connects to a network. Other organizations may make them available on a shared folder on the network, but many large organizations use a central management system for distributing and installing all desktop software—from the operating systems to applications and updates.

Uninstalling an Update

Sometimes an update will create new problems on specific PCs. If you experience problems with an update, you can remove the update via the Control Panel. Navigate in the Control Panel to Programs and Features, and then click View Installed Updates. Select the update you think is causing the problem and click Uninstall to remove it, just as you would remove any other software.

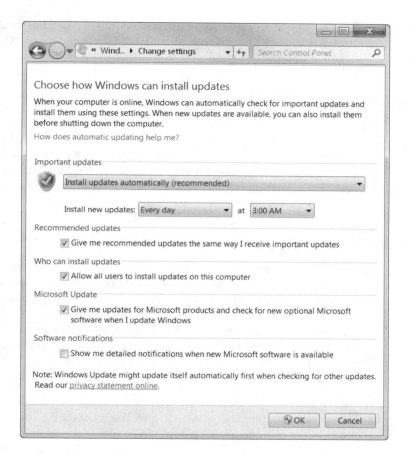

FIGURE 9-7

The Windows Update Change Settings page in Windows 7

Installing Applications and Additional Windows Components

After installing Windows and updating it, install and configure any security software, and then install the applications the user requires, including a third-party backup utility, if so desired. For the majority of applications—those that are proven compatible with the new version of Windows—you will simply follow the manufacturer's instructions for installing and configuring the program. Applications will install into a folder named Program Files, located in the root of the disk volume where you installed Windows. After installing each program, be sure to update it and to configure automatic updates for the application, if available. This is particularly important for Microsoft Office, which has frequent and important updates.

On a 64-bit Windows system, there will also be a Program Files (x86) folder, which holds the program files for any 32-bit applications that are installed. On a 32-bit Windows system, there is only one folder for program files, and it's called Program Files.

It is possible that an application that worked fine in an earlier version of Windows may not work in the new version you've installed. In that case, use Compatibility Mode (described in Chapter 2) to find a settings workaround.

Migrating Data

At this point, restore any data and/or settings you migrated from an old Windows installation. If you used a migration tool on the settings and data on the old system, run the migration tool on the new system and provide the location of the migrated data—either a network location or media, such as discs, solid-state drive (SSD), or external hard drive. Similarly, if you used a backup utility to back up your data on the old system, run the restore option of the Windows or third-party backup utility.

Installing New Devices

Installing a new device involves attaching the device and waiting while Windows recognizes it and installs the appropriate device driver. (That process is called plug and play, and all modern devices support it.) If Windows does not have a driver, it will prompt you to supply a location (disc drive, hard drive, or network) or connect to the Internet and search for it. A few devices may require that you run the device installation program before connecting the device. When that's the case, it's usually because it's important that the device use the driver that comes on the installation disc rather than the default Windows driver that Windows assigns.

Adequate Permissions

In order to install or uninstall device drivers, you must log on as the administrator or a member of the Administrators group. We discuss user accounts in Chapter 18 and permissions in Chapter 19. If you attempt to install a device driver while logged on with a non-administrator account, you will see a message stating that you have insufficient security privileges to install or uninstall a device. However, once installed, an ordinary user may disconnect and reconnect the device without restriction.

Driver Signing

A device driver becomes a part of the operating system with access to the core operating system code. Therefore, a poorly written device driver can cause problems—even system crashes. Drivers have long been a major cause of operating system instability. To prevent this problem, Microsoft works with manufacturers to ensure that driver code is safe to use.

Approved driver files have a *digital signature*, which is encrypted data placed in a file. The all-encompassing term for this is *code signing*, and when applied to device drivers, it is called *driver signing*. Microsoft began signing all of the operating system code starting with Windows 2000.

When you attempt to install a file, Windows looks for a digital signature. If it finds one, it uses a process called *file signature verification* to unencrypt the signature data and use the information to verify that the program code in the file was not modified since the signature was added. If it sees tampering, you will receive a warning and can stop the installation.

The 32-bit versions of Windows Vista and Windows 7 allowed you to install an unsigned driver by clicking Continue Anyway at a dire warning that appeared, but 64-bit Windows Vista and Windows 7 and all editions of Windows 8 and newer do not allow unsigned drivers at all. You can find workarounds online for installing unsigned drivers in Windows versions that don't permit it, but we don't recommend those.

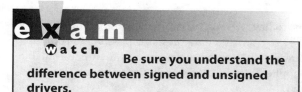

Be sure you understand the difference between signed and unsigned drivers.

If you absolutely must install an unsigned driver, you should first back up all your data. When you install an unsigned driver, Windows will automatically create a restore point before making any changes. Use System Restore to undo the driver installation if it proves to cause problems.

Automated vs. Manual Driver Installation

When Windows detects a newly installed device, the operating system does an automated search for an appropriate device driver. If it finds one, it installs it and configures the device. You may have to answer a few questions during the configuration process.

The driver it finds during this automated search may be one that came with Windows or one that you preinstalled before installing the device. If Windows cannot find a driver during this automated search, it will prompt you to insert media or browse to the folder containing the driver.

Verifying Driver Installation

After installing a device and its driver and associated utility program, verify the success of the installation. Do this by checking Device Manager and by testing the functionality of the new device. If a device does not work, check the documentation. You may have skipped a configuration step or need to supply more information before it is fully configured.

Device Manager   Immediately after installing a new device, open Device Manager and look for the device you just installed by browsing for it. If the device is in the list and does not have a yellow circle with an exclamation mark over its icon, the system considers it to be functioning properly.

Functionality   You should also test the functionality of the new device, because sometimes Device Manager does not detect a problem, but when you try to use the device, it does not function properly. This is usually due to a configuration option that does not show up as a problem in Device Manager. An example of this is a network adapter that is functioning okay from Device Manager's point of view but will not allow you to access the network. There are higher-level configuration options for a network adapter that must be correct before it will work. Learn more about configuring network adapters in Chapter 14.

Optimizing Windows

Windows performs self-optimizing tasks automatically at pre-configured intervals, such as defragmenting the hard drive and managing virtual memory. Normally, you should allow Windows to manage such tasks. In this section, we'll look at the virtual memory settings for a Windows computer and an optional extension feature for virtual memory called ReadyBoost.

Virtual Memory

Windows allows you to *multitask*—that is, to have several programs open in memory at the same time. When you multitask with large program and data files, it is possible to run out of space in physical RAM. When a Windows computer is running low on memory available for the operating system and any loaded applications, rather than limit your activities, it employs a technique called virtual memory.

Virtual memory is the use of a portion of hard disk as a temporary storage space for data that would ordinarily be in the PC's RAM. This temporary storage space exists inside a special file called *PAGEFILE.SYS*, which is stored by default in the root directory of the C: drive. Virtual memory works by determining what data in RAM is the least likely to be needed soon (that is, has been least recently called for by the OS), and sending that data to the paging file for storage. It then creates a placeholder marker so the data can be found again later, and then makes that freed-up block of RAM available for other use. When a program calls for the paged data, it "swaps" the paged data back into actual RAM, moving whatever was in its place to the paging file. Because of this swapping of data into and out of RAM, a paging file is also called a *swap file*.

As a rule, Windows manages virtual memory just fine without intervention. We recommend that you don't change it unless you have a specific reason to. For 32-bit versions of Windows, the default paging file size is 1.5 times the amount of physical RAM. For 64-bit versions, Windows will dynamically adjust the paging file size as system usage dictates, within minimum and maximum values. Table 9-3 explains the minimum and maximum values for the paging file for 64-bit versions of Windows (for more information, see https://support.microsoft.com/en-us/kb/2860880). Windows 8 and newer are tricky and don't have precise values for the minimum, as you can see in the table; the more errors the system has that require a crash dump (that is, blue-screen stop errors), the larger the paging file becomes. This is called Automatic Memory Dump.

The general idea to take from Table 9-3 is that the optimal paging file size is not simple to calculate, and in most cases you're better off allowing Windows to perform that calculation for you by leaving the paging file set to a system-managed size.

In Exercise 9-4, you will view the virtual memory settings on your computer. The default location of the paging file is on drive C:. If you are running out of free disk space on drive C:—and if you have other internal hard drive volumes—consider moving the paging file to another drive that has more free space. In particular, if you have a solid-state drive that is not your primary hard drive, and nowhere near being full, consider relocating the paging file to that drive, because it is likely to be your fastest drive and you'll get the best performance.

TABLE 9-3	Windows Version	Minimum Paging File	Maximum Paging File
Size Ranges for System-Managed Paging Files in 64-bit Windows Versions	Windows Vista Windows 7 Windows Server 2008 Windows Server 2008 R2	1× the amount of physical RAM	3× the amount of physical RAM or 4 GB, whichever is larger
	Windows 8 Windows Server 2012	Varies depending on the crash dump setting, but generally, 1× the amount of physical RAM plus 257 MB	3× the amount of physical RAM or 4 GB, whichever is larger
	Windows 8.1 Windows Server 2012 R2	Varies depending on the crash dump setting, but generally, 1 GB	3× the amount of physical RAM or 4 GB, whichever is larger

You can also have more than one paging file, but this is not normally necessary on a desktop or laptop computer. Never place the paging file on an external hard drive, because it may not be available during startup and this could prevent Windows from launching.

EXERCISE 9-4

Viewing the Virtual Memory Settings

You can easily view the present virtual memory settings for your computer.

1. Open the System page of the Control Panel. To do so, open the Control Panel, click System and Security (in Category View), and then click System.
2. Click Advanced System Settings in the navigation bar at the left. The System Properties dialog box opens.
3. In the System Properties dialog box, select the Advanced tab.
4. Under Performance, click Settings.
5. In the Performance Options dialog box, select the Advanced tab.
6. Under Virtual Memory, click Change to view the virtual memory settings for all the hard drives on your computer (see Figure 9-8).
7. If you wanted to make changes, you would clear the Automatically Manage Paging File Size for All Drives check box. However, for this exercise, just look and don't touch.
8. If you made no changes, click Cancel three times to close the three dialog boxes: Virtual Memory, Performance Options, and System Properties.

FIGURE 9-8

The Virtual
Memory dialog
box

ReadyBoost

ReadyBoost was mentioned in Chapter 2. This performance feature, introduced in Windows
Vista and improved in Windows 7 and newer, further blurs the line between RAM and
storage, allowing you to use the memory on USB flash cards and other SSD devices as cache
memory to replace or supplement the use of the hard drive for virtual memory.

**If the system disk on a computer is an SSD, ReadyBoost may be automatically
disabled as unnecessary, since the speed of the SSD would make it a good
location for the swap file and it would not be improved by using a separate
device as additional cache memory.**

So how do you take advantage of ReadyBoost? You need to connect a compatible device
and make changes on the ReadyBoost folder in the device's Properties dialog box. See
Figure 9-9. Exercise 9-5 describes the steps to do this.

EXERCISE 9-5

Enabling ReadyBoost for a Flash Drive

If your computer is running low on memory, you can easily speed things up by allowing Windows to use a flash drive. You can try this exercise in Windows Vista or any newer version.

1. Connect a USB flash drive with at least 1 GB of available space.
2. Open File Explorer/Windows Explorer and display the local drives. (Depending on the Windows version, this may be called Computer or This PC.)
3. Right-click the USB flash drive and click Properties. Then click the ReadyBoost tab.
4. Click Dedicate This Device to ReadyBoost (this will automatically use the maximum space), or select Use This Device (this allows you to select a lesser amount). See Figure 9-9.
5. Click OK. ReadyBoost will configure the device, and whenever it is connected to your computer, it will be used for system memory.

FIGURE 9-9

The ReadyBoost page for a compatible flash drive

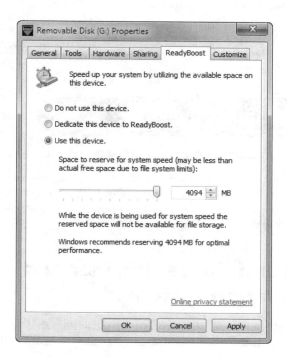

Power Management

Another configuration task to consider is power management. In Chapter 7, you learned about the power management features in Windows, how to configure the features that are especially important to a laptop (Hibernate and Sleep), and how to set the sleep timers for your settings. Power management is available on all Windows computers and is very important for saving power under all circumstances, not just for laptops. Therefore, after you install a new version of Windows, open the Power Options applet from Control Panel and explore the options.

SCENARIO & SOLUTION	
How do I boot into the Windows Setup program on a computer with an unpartitioned hard disk?	If the computer can boot from the optical drive (as most can), place the Windows distribution disc into the drive, and start the computer.
Windows is prompting me to activate my upgrade of Windows, but I do not want to send personal information to Microsoft. Should I activate Windows?	Although the activation process is mandatory, it does not send personal information to Microsoft. Registration, which is optional, sends personal information.
Will Windows 8.1 or Windows 10 run on my Windows 7 PC?	Very likely. The basic system requirements are identical. However, you should check for compatibility with specific hardware and software that is already installed.

CERTIFICATION OBJECTIVE

■ *902: 2.1* *Identify common features and functionality of the Mac OS and Linux operating systems*

Mac and Linux systems are less common in the field, so you may not have much experience with them yet. Review the section "Configuring and Using macOS" in Chapter 2 for the basics of macOS functionality, and study the following section to learn about installing and upgrading those operating systems.

Installing and Upgrading Mac and Linux Operating Systems

The current CompTIA A+ exams do not require that you know how to install and upgrade Mac and Linux systems, so this is a section you can skip if you're just here for the exam prep. However, CompTIA A+ 902 exam objective 2.1, which is addressed in the next two chapters, requires you to know how to work with various features of both Mac and Linux systems, and in order to practice those skills you are going to need a working macOS system and a working Linux environment. Therefore, a few words about installing and upgrading these systems are in order.

Installing macOS

Macs come with macOS preinstalled as the operating system. You can't buy the macOS operating system separately, so you will probably never do a clean install of macOS. Instead you'll download and install an OS upgrade via the App Store. The process is mostly invisible and free of choices, so there's not much you need to learn about it.

on the **job**

It's technically possible to install macOS on a virtual machine under VirtualBox, but it's neither easy (i.e., there are lots of steps, and some of them involve manually editing command strings) nor legal.

However, suppose for some reason you *do* want to do a clean install of macOS, replacing the current OS. You might do this to fix a pernicious problem you've been having that defies troubleshooting, or for security reasons (such as to wipe out all evidence of a previous user and his activities). Exercise 9-6 explains how to do it.

EXERCISE 9-6

Clean-Installing macOS

For this exercise you will need a working macOS system and a blank USB flash drive that is at least 8 GB in capacity.

1. Back up any files you need to save. Use the Time Machine utility or the Migration Assistant tool for the Mac.
2. Find a blank USB flash drive that is at least 8 GB in capacity. Then use the Disk Utility (located in the Utilities folder in the Applications folder) to format the USB drive. For the format type, choose Mac OS Extended (Journaled). Keep the default volume name (untitled). Then click Erase.
3. Download the OS upgrade. It will appear as a file in your Applications folder.
4. Create a bootable USB disk for the downloaded OS. The easiest way is to use a utility called DiskMaker X (found at http://diskmakerx.com). As an alternative, you can use a Terminal window:
   a. Open the Terminal app, type the following, and press ENTER (this example assumes the version is El Capitan):

      sudo /Applications/Install\ OS\ EL\ Capitan.app/Contents/Resources
   b. Enter your user password when prompted. Then let the utility do its thing. It will erase the USB drive and copy the installer files to the disk.

5. Restart the Mac and hold down the OPTION key. Choose the USB drive containing the macOS version you are installing.

6. Select Disk Utility and then your main hard drive. Click Erase.

7. Return to the main menu and click Install macOS. Select your hard drive, and then follow the prompts to finish the installation.

Installing Linux

Compared to macOS, Linux is refreshingly easy to get and install. You'll need to study Linux in upcoming chapters as part of your exam prep, so take a few minutes now to acquire and install a copy of Linux on a virtual machine in VirtualBox or Hyper-V on a Windows PC, or directly onto the hard drive of any spare PC you happen to have around.

There are many distributions ("distros") of Linux, and some are easier to use than others. We recommend Ubuntu Desktop for the activities in this book. Exercise 9-7 walks you through the process of downloading Ubuntu and creating a bootable DVD for it, and then installing Ubuntu in VirtualBox (one of the hypervisors you learned about in Chapter 8).

EXERCISE 9-7

Installing Ubuntu Linux

For this exercise you'll need a writeable DVD drive and a blank DV-R disc, or a USB drive of at least 8 GB capacity with nothing on it that you want to keep. If you want to install on a virtual machine, you'll also need a hypervisor such as VirtualBox.

1. Download Ubuntu Desktop from www.ubuntu.com/download. The 64-bit version is better if your hardware will support it. (The host system's firmware should support virtualization if you're going with the 64-bit version. You learned in Chapter 8 how to determine this.)

2. Use an ISO burning program to burn the downloaded .iso file to an optical disc. You must use a burning program that creates bootable discs; don't just copy the file over, or it won't be bootable. There are many good burning programs that will do this. Tuxboot is just one example (https://sourceforge.net/projects/tuxboot). Or, you can use a utility that creates bootable USB flash drives, and go that route instead. (You can't use the USB method with Hyper-V, though, because Hyper-V doesn't recognize the host system's USB flash drives.)

3. Boot the PC from the DVD. Or, if you are installing on a virtual machine, boot up the VM you created in Chapter 8, or create a new one for Ubuntu. Boot to the DVD or flash drive you created in Step 2, and follow the steps to install Ubuntu Linux. (You'll have the options of Try Ubuntu and Install Ubuntu; go with Install, so you'll have it for upcoming chapters.)

CERTIFICATION SUMMARY

You have many decisions to make before installing a new version of Windows. Will this be a clean installation or an upgrade? Will it be an attended installation or a fully automated unattended installation? What tasks should you perform before installing or upgrading Windows? What tasks should you perform after installing Windows? Finally, what will improve the startup and running performance of Windows?

The answers to all of these questions are important to understand for passing the CompTIA A+ exams, and for doing your job.

TWO-MINUTE DRILL

Here are some of the key points covered in Chapter 9.

Upgrading Windows

- ❑ An upgrade installs the new version of Windows directly on top of an existing installation, transferring all the settings from the old installation into the new one.
- ❑ An upgrade version of Windows is less expensive than a full retail version, but will only install into a previous legal installation of Windows.
- ❑ Before upgrading, test for incompatible software and hardware, and then resolve any incompatibilities.
- ❑ Before upgrading, back up all data, clean up the hard drive, and then defragment it.

Installing Windows

- ❑ Installing Windows involves three stages: preparation, installation, and follow-up tasks.
- ❑ Preparation tasks include verifying the target computer meets the physical hardware requirements, as well as the hardware and software compatibility requirements.
- ❑ Windows 7 and Windows 8/8.1 both have the same basic system requirements.
- ❑ It is important to plan how to start setup and the location of the source files.
- ❑ Choose a storage type for the system disk: basic or dynamic. For a basic disk, choose MBR or GPT. Choose a file system (probably NTFS for Windows or ext3 or ext4 for Linux). Plan the partitions on the disk if you are going to have more than one.
- ❑ When setting up a multiboot system, put each OS on its own partition, and install them in oldest to newest order.
- ❑ Setup can be started from an optical disc, a flash drive, an external hard drive, a network share, a recovery disk, or a factory recovery partition.
- ❑ An attended installation requires the presence of a person who can respond to occasional prompts for information.

❏ Scripts that answer the Setup program's questions automate an unattended installation.

❏ A drive or disk image is an exact duplicate of an entire hard drive's contents, including the OS and all installed software.

Configuring Windows

❏ After installation, test network connectivity and, if necessary, add and configure a network adapter driver.

❏ Activating Windows is mandatory, but registration is optional.

❏ As long as you have an Internet connection, you should consider having Windows update automatically. Windows Vista and Windows 7 have Automatic Updates turned on by default.

❏ After completing a Windows installation and performing the most urgent configuration tasks, you should install and configure security programs and then install and configure other applications.

❏ If you must install an old application that is not compatible with the newly installed version of Windows, first attempt to get the program to run by configuring Compatibility Mode. If that does not work, and if you are trying to get a Windows XP application to run in Windows 7, use Windows XP Mode.

❏ Install any device drivers not installed during setup.

❏ Sometimes the virtual memory settings need to change to improve performance. The use of ReadyBoost can also improve performance.

❏ Check the Power Options applet in Control Panel to see if you should make any changes to improve power management.

Installing and Upgrading macOS and Linux Operating Systems

❏ Macs come with the macOS preinstalled, and OS updates and new versions are provided via the App Store, so you will seldom need to install macOS.

❏ You can download a Linux distro for free, burn it to a DVD or flash drive, and then install it on an empty hard disk or a virtual machine.

SELF TEST

The following questions will help you measure your understanding of the material presented in this chapter. Read all of the choices carefully, because there might be more than one correct answer. Choose all correct answers for each question.

Upgrading Windows

1. Which of these is *not* a benefit of upgrading instead of doing a clean install?
   A. An upgrade edition may be less expensive.
   B. An upgrade may solve persistent system problems that a clean install cannot.
   C. You can keep your old files and settings.
   D. You don't have to reinstall all the applications.

2. What should you do before an upgrade if you discover incompatible software or hardware?
   A. Nothing. The incompatibility will be resolved during the upgrade.
   B. Buy a special version of Windows for incompatibility problems.
   C. Resolve the incompatibility before beginning the upgrade.
   D. Repartition and format the hard drive.

Installing Windows

3. Which of the following refers to the lowest level of CPU, the minimum amount of RAM, and the free hard disk space needed to install an OS?
   A. Hardware compatibility
   B. Software compatibility
   C. Hardware requirements
   D. Hardware optimizing

4. What is the task order when preparing a new hard drive for a new OS installation?
   A. Format, then partition, then install the OS
   B. Partition, then install OS, then format
   C. Format, then install OS, then partition
   D. Partition, then format, then install OS

5. What is the preferred file system for Windows?
   A. NTFS
   B. FAT16
   C. FAT32
   D. ext3

6. Which of the following boot sources for Windows Setup is designed to initiate an over-the-network installation?
   A. eSATA
   B. PXE Boot
   C. Optical drive
   D. USB device

7. What type of installation requires a person's real-time response to prompts?
   A. Unattended
   B. Image
   C. Scripted
   D. Attended

8. What installation method places an exact copy of a hard drive containing a previously installed operating system and applications (from a reference computer) onto the hard drive of another computer?
   A. Attended
   B. Scripted
   C. Image
   D. Unattended

9. What are the two general types of unattended installations? Select all that apply.
   A. Drive image
   B. Scripted
   C. Upgrade
   D. USMT

10. No discs came with a computer purchased with Windows 7 preinstalled. What sources could potentially be used to reinstall the OS without spending more money? Select the two best answers.
    A. Windows 7 full retail DVD
    B. Recovery disc made using a DVD-R disc
    C. Factory recovery partition
    D. Windows 7 Upgrade

11. Windows Setup requires a product key for the retail box version of Windows 8.1 you are installing. Where are you most likely to find it?
    A. Inner flap of the box
    B. On the protective sleeve that the DVD came in
    C. Outside of box, above the UPC code
    D. On a website that you access after Setup

12. Which of the following statements is true of the Windows 7 Setup?
    A. The computer will restart one or more times during Setup.
    B. If the computer restarts during Setup, something has gone wrong.
    C. The installation steps are identical to those for Linux.
    D. You must install English as the primary/first language.

13. What bootable environment gives operating system support during three types of operations: installing Windows, troubleshooting, and recovery?
    A. USMT
    B. MUI
    C. Aero
    D. Windows PE

Configuring Windows

14. What purpose does Microsoft Product Activation (MPA) serve?
    A. Product compatibility
    B. Prevention of software piracy
    C. Product registration
    D. Prevention of malware infection

15. What is the consequence of not completing the activation process for Windows within the required time period?
    A. There is no consequence.
    B. Windows will continue to work but you do not receive updates.
    C. Windows is disabled.
    D. You will not receive e-mails about new products.

16. What task should you do as soon as possible after installation for the sake of stability and improved security?
    A. Upgrade Windows.
    B. Activate Windows.
    C. Run Windows Update.
    D. Partition the hard disk.

17. What may MPA require if you make too many hardware changes to a Windows computer?
    A. Reinstallation
    B. Removal of Windows
    C. Reactivation
    D. Update

18. What is the term that describes disk space used by the operating system when it runs out of physical memory?
    A. Virtual memory
    B. RAM memory
    C. ROM memory
    D. Flash memory

Installing and Upgrading macOS and Linux Operating Systems

19. How do Macs receive OS updates?
    A. Users purchase retail DVD upgrades.
    B. Apple mails update DVDs to your registered address.
    C. They are downloaded from the App Store.
    D. Macs never need OS updates.

20. What is the least expensive way to acquire a desktop version of Linux?
    A. Purchase a download from an authorized website.
    B. Buy a used DVD on an auction site.
    C. Buy a retail box version.
    D. Download a distro and burn a bootable DVD.

SELF TEST ANSWERS

Upgrading Windows

1. ☑ **B.** An upgrade may solve persistent system problems that a clean install cannot is not true and is, therefore, the correct answer. The opposite of that statement is actually correct; a clean install can solve problems that an upgrade may not fix.
   ☒ **A, C,** and **D** are incorrect because they are all true.

2. ☑ **C.** Resolve the incompatibility before beginning the upgrade is the correct action to take before an upgrade if you discover incompatible software or hardware.
   ☒ **A** is incorrect because the incompatibility will not be resolved during the upgrade. **B** is incorrect because there is no such version. **D** is incorrect because this will not solve the problem; it is extreme and will void the ability to install an upgrade.

Installing Windows

3. ☑   **C.** Hardware requirements are the CPU, minimum amount of RAM, and free hard disk space needed to install an OS.

☒   **A** is incorrect because hardware compatibility refers to the actual make and model of the hardware, not the level of CPU and quantity of RAM and free hard disk space. **B** is incorrect because software compatibility does not refer to the CPU, RAM, and free hard disk space. **D** is incorrect because hardware optimizing does not refer to the level of CPU and quantity of RAM and free hard disk space.

4. ☑   **D.** Partition, then format, then install OS, is the correct order for preparing a new hard drive.

☒   **A, B,** and **C** are all incorrect because the steps are out of order and actually impossible to complete.

5. ☑   **A.** NTFS is the preferred file system for Windows.

☒   **B, C,** and **D** are all incorrect because none of them is the preferred file system for Windows. FAT16 and FAT32 are obsolete versions of DOS and Windows file systems, and ext3 is for Linux systems.

6. ☑   **B.** PXE Boot uses a feature of a network card that will initiate the startup of the computer, downloading the initial bootup files from a network server, after which it is ready to perform a task, such as installing the new OS over the network or running centralized maintenance tests on the computer.

☒   **A, C,** and **D** are all incorrect because while they are valid sources for starting an OS and going into Windows Setup, none of them was specifically designed for an over-the-network installation.

7. ☑   **D.** Attended installation is the type that requires a person's real-time response to prompts.

☒   **A** is incorrect because this type of installation does not require a person's real-time response to prompts. **B** is incorrect because this method replaces Setup altogether. **C** is incorrect because you could use this term to describe an unattended installation.

8. ☑   **C.** Image installation places an exact copy of the operating system and applications (from a reference computer) onto the hard drive of another computer.

☒   **A** is incorrect because attended installation does not place an exact copy of a hard drive onto another computer. **B** is incorrect because scripting is just part of an installation, not a method of installation. **D** is incorrect because this method may or may not include an image.

9. ☑   **A** and **B.** These are the two general types of unattended installations.

☒   **C** is incorrect because you can upgrade as either an attended or unattended installation. **D** is incorrect because USMT is a tool for migrating user settings and data.

10. ☑   **B** and **C.** The manufacturer will normally give you one of these options. When the system was new, the user may have been prompted to insert a DVD-R to make a recovery disc. If not, the system may be bootable into a factory recovery partition.

☒   **A** is incorrect because, although this would work, it requires spending more money. **D** is incorrect because this would cost money. It will also only work if your original Windows 7 OS is still working.

11. ☑ **B.** On the protective sleeve that the DVD came in is the standard location for the product key for a retail-purchased copy of Windows.

☒ **A** is incorrect because, unlike some software vendors, Microsoft doesn't place the product key in the inner flap of the box. **C** is incorrect because if the code were on the outside of the box, it could be stolen and used by someone other than the purchaser. **D** is incorrect because you would not be able to access the Web until after Setup had completed. You can buy Windows product keys online for downloadable Setup files, but this question specifically stated a Windows retail box version.

12. ☑ **A.** The computer will restart one or more times during Setup. It is normal for this to occur, and nothing to worry about.

☒ **B, C,** and **D** are all incorrect because these statements are false.

13. ☑ **D.** Windows PE (Windows Preinstallation Environment) is a bootable environment that gives operating system support during three types of operations: installing Windows, troubleshooting, and recovery.

☒ **A** is incorrect because USMT is an advanced tool that only works in a Windows server–based domain network. **B** is incorrect because MUI is a feature that allows you to install a language other than English as the only language or as an additional language in Windows. **C** is incorrect because Aero is a feature of the Windows GUI.

Configuring Windows

14. ☑ **B.** Prevention of software piracy is the purpose of Microsoft Product Activation.

☒ **A, C,** and **D** are all incorrect because none of these is the purpose of MPA.

15. ☑ **C.** Windows is disabled is the immediate consequence of not completing the activation process for Windows within the required time.

☒ **A** is incorrect because there is a consequence. **B** is incorrect because Windows will not continue to work. **D** is incorrect because this may be a consequence of not registering.

16. ☑ **C.** Run Windows Update is the task you should do as soon as possible for the sake of stability and security.

☒ **A** is incorrect because upgrading Windows is not a task you should do for the sake of stability and improved security. **B** is incorrect because activating Windows is not a task you should do for the sake of stability and improved security. **D** is incorrect because partitioning the hard disk is a task for preparing a hard drive for use.

17. ☑ **C.** MPA may require that you reactivate if you make too many hardware changes to a Windows computer.

☒ **A** is incorrect because MPA will not require reinstallation if you make too many hardware changes. **B** is incorrect because MPA won't require you to remove Windows. **D** is incorrect because MPA will only require reactivation, not upgrading, if you make too many hardware changes.

18. ☑ **A.** Virtual memory is the term that describes disk space used by the operating system when it runs out of physical memory.
☒ **B, C,** and **D** are all incorrect because none of these describes disk space used by the OS when it runs out of physical memory.

Installing and Upgrading Mac and Linux Operating Systems

19. ☑ **C.** Mac computers prompt the user to download an update from the App Store whenever one becomes available.
☒ **A** is incorrect because macOS is not available on retail DVDs. **B** is incorrect because you do not need to share your mailing address with Apple in order to receive an update. **D** is incorrect because Macs, like all operating systems, need upgrades periodically.

20. ☑ **D.** Downloading a distro and burning a bootable DVD costs nothing.
☒ **A, B,** and **C** are all incorrect because most desktop distros of Linux are free. You should not have to pay anything to acquire one.

Chapter 10

Disk and File Management

T his chapter starts by covering disk management tools, both at the command line and in a GUI. We focus mostly on Windows, but will also review some essential Mac disk management tools as well. We'll discuss file systems and attributes, contrasting Windows with Mac and Linux systems, and look at the tools and utilities each OS provides for file management.

CERTIFICATION OBJECTIVES

- **902: 1.2** *Given a scenario, install Windows PC operating systems using appropriate methods*
- **902: 1.3** *Given a scenario, apply appropriate Microsoft command-line tools*
- **902: 1.4** *Given a scenario, use appropriate Microsoft operating system features and tools*
- **902: 2.1** *Identify common features and functionality of the Mac OS and Linux operating systems*

In Chapter 9 you learned about disk partitioning and file systems conceptually; now in this section you will learn how to manage disk partitions and file systems as a practical matter, using the actual GUI and command-line tools that you would use in the field. You'll use the Disk Management tool in Windows (902 exam objectives 1.2 and 1.4), learn about key disk management command-line utilities (902 exam objective 1.3), and survey the available disk management tools in the macOS and Linux operating systems (902 exam objective 2.1).

Disk Management

PC technicians need to understand how to prepare a disk for use, a topic introduced in Chapter 9, which focused on OS installation. You learned in that chapter about basic and dynamic disks, MBR versus GPT partition management, and commonly chosen file systems like NTFS for a Windows system and ext3 and ext4 for Linux systems.

The following sections expand on that knowledge via the Disk Management utility and some other tools in Windows and some equivalent tools in other operating systems. Since basic disks are the most common type used on Windows computers, the coverage of dynamic disks will include only those topics that are part of the objectives for the CompTIA A+ exams and only what applies to dynamic disks. The coverage of basic disks includes some characteristics that are common for both storage types, such as drive letter assignments, mount points, and drive paths.

Managing Disks in Windows

The main tool for managing disks in Windows is the Disk Management console, which lets you see disk drives as more than the drive letters, folders, and files you see in File Explorer or Windows Explorer. As with many Windows programs and features, there are several ways to launch Disk Management. For instance, it is a part of the Computer Management console, which you will find in Administrative Tools. However, we like to open the separate Disk Management console separately. To do that in any Windows version, press WINDOWS KEY-R to open the Run dialog box, type **diskmgmt.msc**, and press ENTER. Or use one of these methods instead, depending on the Windows version:

- **Windows Vista**   Click Start, and then in the Start Search box, type **diskmgmt.msc** and press ENTER.
- **Windows 7**   Click Start, and then in the Search Programs and Files box, type **diskmgmt.msc** and press ENTER.
- **Windows 8**   From the Start screen, type **disk management**, and then click Create and Format Hard Disk Partitions.
- **Windows 8.1** and **Windows 10**   Right-click the Start button and click Disk Management.

In this section we will use two scenarios. In the first we will use Disk Management to view the only disk in a computer and use this example to talk about the basic disk storage type. Then we will move on to a system in which we already have two physical disk drives and wish to add a third disk, exploring options including both basic disks and dynamic disks and what can be done with each storage type.

Viewing a Basic Disk

A basic disk, as described in Chapter 9, uses the traditional method for creating partitions, including use of a single partition table per disk that resides in the first physical sector of a hard disk. The partition table occupies a mere 64 bytes of the 512 bytes in the sector. This sector, called the master boot record (MBR), also contains the initial boot program loaded by BIOS during startup. This program and the partition table are created or modified in this sector when someone partitions the disk. (Recall also that GPT is a more advanced alternative to MBR, available on some systems with UEFI firmware. Here, we are referring to both MBR and GFT generically as MBR for simplicity.)

Figure 10-1 shows Disk Management on a Windows 7 computer with a single physical hard disk drive that came with Windows preinstalled with three volumes (we later created the fourth volume). Notice the volume information in the top pane displayed in labeled columns. The Status column shows the status for each volume. This same information is displayed in the rectangle representing each volume in the graphical pane below the volume information. Information on the status of the physical disk (Disk 0) and the DVD drive (labeled CD-ROM 0) is on the left. The status for the hard disk is Online, and the status for the DVD drive is No Media. If you have a Windows computer handy, open Disk Management and keep it open as you read through this section. You will have different disks and volumes, of course.

Disk
Management
showing
information for
the volumes on
Disk 0

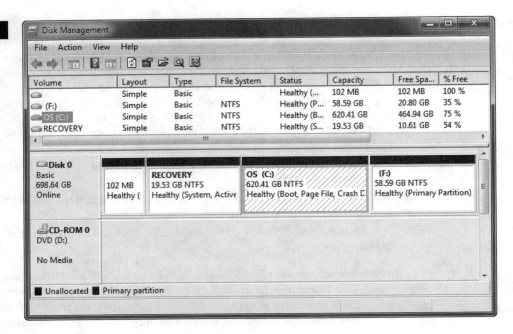

Each volume of the basic disk in Figure 10-1 is shown with the layout designation, *simple volume*. A basic disk has a four-volume-per-disk limit (because, as you learned in Chapter 9, an MBR disk can be divided into no more than four partitions).

The CompTIA A+ 220-902 exam objectives use the term "partition," as we did in Chapter 9. However, in Windows GUI tools such as Disk Management, you will see the terms volume and partition used loosely and interchangeably. Microsoft has in some reference sources tried to differentiate by saying that "partitions" exist on basic disks and "volumes" exist on dynamic disks. However, even Microsoft is not consistent with that differentiation.

A simple volume can reside on either a basic disk or dynamic disk. In our example, the original volumes were probably created as an image by the manufacturer. The first volume is unallocated, and it allows space to hold the dynamic disk database should we convert

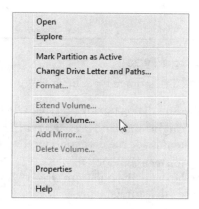

FIGURE 10-2

Shrinking a
volume in Disk
Management

the disk to dynamic. The second is a recovery volume created by Dell to allow us to revert
the disk to the factory-installed state. The third is the system volume, drive C:, where
Windows 7 was installed at the factory.

The fourth volume takes a little explaining. Soon after we acquired the computer, we
opened Disk Management, right-clicked the graphical representation of drive C:, and
selected Shrink Volume from the menu, shown in Figure 10-2. This option is referred to as
"splitting partitions" in the Disk Management topic of CompTIA A+ 902 exam objective 1.4.
We shrunk the volume holding logical drive C: so that we could create another volume into
which we installed Windows 8. This created a dual-boot system with Windows 7 on drive C:
and Windows 8 on Drive F:.

One consequence of shrinking the volume and creating an additional volume is that the
physical disk now has four volumes (partitions)—the maximum number allowed on a basic
disk. If we wanted to shrink the volume again and create yet another smaller volume, that
would require a fifth volume, which is not allowed on a basic disk type. At that point, we
would be prompted to change the storage type to dynamic to accommodate more than four
volumes—just one of the capabilities of dynamic disks.

on the
job

**If you wanted more than four volumes on a disk but you didn't want to convert
to a dynamic disk, you could make that fourth partition an extended one,
and then create multiple logical drives within it. Recall from Chapter 9 that
extended partitions can have any number of logical drives on them. However,
you can't create extended partitions with Disk Management. You would have to
use some other disk tool to create the partition. The DISKPART utility will do it,
for example.**

Exercise 10-1 walks you through opening Disk Management and checking out the storage
type.

EXERCISE 10-1

Viewing the Disk Storage Type

You can view the disk storage type on your Windows computer by following these steps.

1. Open the Run dialog box by pressing WINDOWS KEY-R.
2. Type **diskmgmt.msc** and press ENTER. There will be a short delay while Disk Management reads the disk configuration information.
3. In Disk Management, look for Disk 0. Disk 0 is normally your first internal hard disk drive, and usually the one from which Windows boots. Just below the words "Disk 0," you will see the storage type.
4. Determine the answers to these questions:
   - Is it a basic disk or a dynamic disk?
   - How many volumes are on Disk 0?
   - How many physical disks are in your computer?
5. Leave Disk Management open as you continue through the following section on adding a physical drive.

Configuring a New Physical Drive in Windows

Let's say you have added a hard disk drive to your Windows desktop computer. What storage type should it be? For most everyday desktop PCs, the basic storage type is fine. You should convert to dynamic storage only if you have a specific reason to do so, such as if you need more than four volumes on a disk or want to create a spanned, striped, or mirrored volume. Dynamic disks have their drawbacks. For starters, a dynamic disk can be used only under Windows; you can't use part of it for a Linux install, for example. Another issue is that managing one of these multiple-disk configurations adds to the operating system's workload. Redundant array of independent disks (RAID) configurations are best done at the hardware level, with the RAID controller managing the disks and presenting multiple disks to the operating system as a single volume.

To manage dynamic disks, Windows stores a special configuration database on each dynamic disk outside the area occupied by volumes. (It's like the MBR or GPT but more full-featured.) This provides the flexibility of allowing you to move the drive or array from one Windows computer to another, as long as the version of Windows understands dynamic disks. That means the Windows version must be Windows 2000 or later, and it is best to do this between computers with the same version of Windows. Older versions of Windows, such as Windows XP and Windows 95/98/Me, cannot read dynamic disk volumes.

 **Dynamic disks store a special configuration database on the disk outside the area used by volumes.**

After installing an internal disk drive or connecting an external drive, open Disk Management and locate the new physical drive. Figure 10-3 shows the Windows 8.1 version of Disk Management displaying three physical disks: Disk 0, Disk 1, and Disk 2. The last one was recently added and the space is unallocated, so it does not have a volume listed in the top pane.

on the **job**

A new disk drive, especially an external drive, may come preformatted with a file system, usually FAT32. You can delete any existing volumes and start over.

All three physical disks in Figure 10-3 are basic disks, and by right-clicking Disk 2, the pop-up menu shows the actions we can take. Keep in mind that a spanned volume, striped volume, mirrored volume, and RAID 5 volume are all forms of *disk arrays* in that each volume type uses multiple physical disks in a single volume. These were covered in detail in Chapter 4. If you wish to add an array to your computer, simply add the drives required; then in Windows open Disk Management and select the drives and the type of array you wish to create. These options are unavailable in Figure 10-3 because there is only one physical disk with unallocated space on it that could be used for a RAID. If you connected a second disk, these options would be available, with one exception: RAID 5 is not supported in desktop versions of Windows—only in Windows Server editions.

FIGURE 10-3

The pop-up menu on Disk 2 shows the available options.

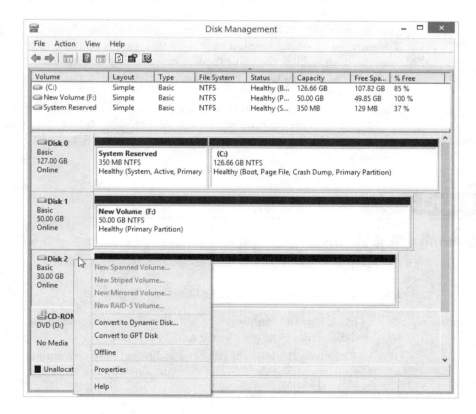

on the **job**

If you wish to create a disk array of any type, we strongly recommend that you explore doing it at the hardware level, rather than with Windows. Many computers today have firmware and disk controllers that control this at the hardware level. In that case, the multiple disks would be hidden from Windows and from Disk Management. You would see a single volume for each array. Then, the hard work of managing the array is left to the hardware and its firmware, not to the operating system, which already has plenty to do.

Notice that on the shortcut menu in Figure 10-3 you can also convert to a dynamic disk. If you set up one of the RAID options on the upper portion of the shortcut menu, that happens automatically, but you can also do it as a separate activity.

Also on the shortcut menu is a command for conversion to a GPT disk. This conversion causes you to lose all the data on all volumes of the disk, but since this is a brand-new disk in Figure 10-3, that wouldn't matter.

Volume Layout and Formatting

Take another look at Figure 10-3, and notice that the new Disk 2 does not appear anywhere in the Volume list at the top of the Disk Management window. That's because there are currently no volumes on it. Whether you leave the disk as basic or convert it to dynamic, it will not appear in the Volume list until you create a volume.

The most common volume layout you would create is a simple volume. In Disk Management, right-click the empty square representing the unallocated space to bring up a menu that now includes Create Simple Volume (or New Simple Volume, depending on the Windows version).

Now suppose this is a typical scenario, and your selected disk is a basic disk, and you want to create a simple volume. Select New Simple Volume from the menu, and the New Simple Volume Wizard will guide you through the process. Exercise 10-2 walks you through this activity.

EXERCISE 10-2

Creating a New Volume

In this exercise, you first remove any existing volumes from a disk if needed, and then you create a new simple volume.

For this exercise you will need one of the following:

- A virtual machine running Windows 7 or 8.1, configured for an additional virtual hard disk other than the one containing the OS.

- A PC running Windows that has an additional hard disk connected to it other than the one containing the OS, and that contains nothing you want to keep, or already contains nothing.

1. From the Disk Management window, locate the disk you will be working with. Make sure it contains nothing you want to keep.

2. If there is already a volume shown in the lower portion of the Disk Management window, right-click the volume and click Delete Volume. Click Yes to confirm.

3. Right-click the unallocated space and click New Simple Volume. The New Simple Volume Wizard runs. Click Next.

4. When prompted for the volume size, stay with the default setting, which is the maximum size (the entire physical disk capacity). Then click Next.

5. When prompted to assign a drive letter, stay with the default setting, which is the next available drive letter. Then click Next.

6. When prompted about formatting the volume, choose NTFS with the default allocation unit size. For the volume label, use anything you like, or stay with the default.

7. Leave the Perform a Quick Format check box checked. Click Next.

8. Click Finish. After a brief pause, the new volume appears. Its status shows as Healthy (Primary Partition).

Logical Drives, Drive Paths, and Mounted Volumes

When it comes to assigning drive letters to volumes, you can select from the 26 letters of the alphabet, with the first two letters, *A* and *B*, normally reserved by Windows for floppy disk drives, but with floppy drives not present, you can also use these letters. Windows assigns drive letters automatically in a specific order. During an upgrade installation, it will preserve the drive letter assignments that existed under the previous version of Windows. The drive letter assignments are saved in the Windows registry in a location called MountMgr.

During a fresh install of Windows, the Setup program will assign letter *C* to the first volume it detects, marking it as active. It will then assign drive letters (*D*, *E*, etc.) to any other formatted volumes it detects. Once assigned, these drive letters are persistent until changed from the Disk Management console.

Windows also has a pair of features called drive paths and mounted drives that allow you to avoid using drive letters in some special cases. These features are available on both basic and dynamic disks. A *mounted drive* is a volume that is mapped to an empty folder on an NTFS volume. It does not need to have a drive letter assigned at all, but instead can be "connected" to an empty folder on another logical drive. This connection point to a folder is a *mount point*, and the path to the volume is a *drive path*, which requires the NTFS file system on the volume hosting the drive path. A volume can have both a drive letter and one or more drive paths. In Computer/This PC, the mount point is listed along with local folders, but with a drive icon, as shown in Figure 10-4 where a mount point is labeled "Utility"; the contents of the mounted volume appear in the right pane (not shown). Exercise 10-3 shows how to create a mount point.

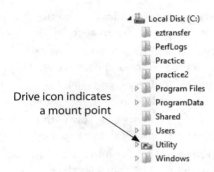

Notice the drive icon by the mount point Utility.

Drive icon indicates a mount point

EXERCISE 10-3

Mounting a Volume to a Folder

In this exercise, you will mount a volume to an empty folder on your primary hard drive. This exercise starts where Exercise 10-2 ends; you should have Disk Management open, and access to more than one formatted volume.

1. Using File Explorer/Windows Explorer, create a new empty folder in the root directory of your C: drive. Name it **Utility**.

2. In File Explorer/Windows Explorer, browse to Computer/This PC and confirm that the volume appears as a drive letter.

3. From the Disk Management window, in the Volumes list (upper pane), locate the new volume you created in Exercise 10-2, and right-click it. Choose Change Drive Letter and Paths. Note that there is a drive letter assigned to it.

4. Select the drive letter and click Remove. Click Yes to confirm.

5. Right-click the volume and choose Change Drive Letter and Paths again to reopen the dialog box.

6. Click Add.

7. Click Mount in the following empty NTFS folder.

8. Click Browse. Locate the folder you created in Step 1, select it, and click OK.

9. Click OK.

10. In File Explorer/Windows Explorer, browse to Computer/This PC and confirm that the volume no longer appears as a drive letter.

11. In the navigation pane, expand the contents of the C: drive, and confirm that the Utility folder appears with a drive icon, as in Figure 10-4.

12. Right-click the volume and choose Change Drive Letter and Paths again to reopen the dialog box.

13. Click Add.

14. Click Assign the Following Drive Letter. Make sure the letter is set to the same letter as before.
15. Click OK.
16. Close the Disk Management window and File Explorer/Windows Explorer.

Using Storage Spaces

Windows 8 and newer include a new feature called Storage Spaces. It allows you to combine the storage space from multiple drives of various types and interfaces into a single large pool of storage that you can access as a single large volume. Storage Spaces is essentially a RAID tool, enabling you to create RAID 1 and RAID 5 volumes. Its main advantage is that you can combine disks of any sizes and types. USB flash drives and memory cards won't work, but every kind of HDD and SSD will. (Be aware, however, that if you combine disks with radically different data transfer speeds, the overall speed is going to be only a bit higher than the speed of the slowest disk.)

You can't use your system volume in Storage Spaces, and you can't boot from a Storage Spaces volume. Storage Spaces is primarily a tool for mass data storage. For example, you could use a Storage Spaces volume to hold backups, File History settings, or system recovery images, or to store your entire music and video collection on a single volume.

To get started with Storage Spaces, search for the feature from the Start screen/Start menu, or navigate in the Control Panel to System and Security | Storage Spaces. Select the drives you want to include. Make sure they don't contain anything you want to keep, because they will be reformatted.

During the setup, you'll be prompted to choose a Resiliency setting. Resiliency in this context means the ability to protect the data in the event that one of the disks fails. You have four choices:

- **Simple (no resiliency)**   Requires at least one drive and does not protect data. It allows you to combine multiple drives as one large drive, but if one disk fails, all data is lost on the entire volume. It is similar to RAID 0. It is suitable for storing large temporary files, but not for anything important that you don't have backed up elsewhere.
- **Two-way mirror**   Requires at least two drives, and is similar to RAID 1 (mirroring). Protects against one drive failure.
- **Parity**   Requires at least three drives and protects against one drive failure. This is similar to RAID 5. Read performance is slower than on a two-way mirror; use this for large files that do not change often.
- **Three-way mirror**   Requires at least five drives, and protects against two simultaneous drive failures. It is similar to RAID 10.

Choose thoughtfully, because you can't switch the resiliency type later without disassembling the entire space and reformatting. You can, however, add more drives to an existing storage space later.

Managing Disks at the Windows Command Prompt

All modern versions of Windows include Disk Management, and that is where you will go to manage disks unless your system has a major problem that prevents you from accessing Disk Management. In such cases you may need to use a non-GUI disk management tool in the Windows Recovery Environment or Windows Safe Mode with Command Prompt. You will learn about those in Chapter 13. However, since we're working with disks in this chapter, we want to at least mention the utility available in those environments for managing disks: DISKPART.

DISKPART is an advanced utility for disk management that understands basic and dynamic storage types. You can run it at a command prompt or use it in automated scripts. If you enter the command **diskpart** at the command prompt, it actually loads its own command interpreter with a prompt that looks like this: diskpart>. At this prompt, you enter commands that DISKPART accepts with the correct syntax, and then you type **exit** to exit from DISKPART.

e x a m

ⓦatch   The command for opening a command prompt is COMMAND. It's mentioned in 902 exam objective 1.4. You wouldn't type it at an already-open prompt, of course, but you might use it in a batch file or startup instructions, or type it in the Run dialog box (WINDOWS KEY-R) in Windows.

Once you get into DISKPART, you can type HELP for a list of commands that it accepts. However, DISKPART is not intuitive to use, and mistakes can be costly in terms of lost data, so we recommend you study an online reference for the command before attempting to use it for anything more than simply viewing current disk settings. Exercise 10-4 provides the most cursory of looks at the utility; don't go far beyond that without some study.

EXERCISE 10-4

Using DISKPART

In this exercise, you will use DISKPART to check out your system's volumes.

1. Open a Command Prompt window with administrative privileges. In Windows 8.1, you can do this by right-clicking the Start button and choosing Command Prompt (Admin).
2. Type **help** and press ENTER. You see a list of commands. Notice that the LIST command displays a list of objects.
3. Type **list** and press ENTER. A list of valid parameters for that command appears.

4. Type **list disk** and press ENTER. A list of the physical disks on your system appears. This list is similar to the lower pane in Disk Management.

5. Type **list volume** and press ENTER. A list of volumes appears. This list is similar to the upper pane in Disk Management. Note the volume number for the volume you created in Exercise 10-2. (Ours is Volume 3.)

6. Type **select volume 3** (or whatever number you noted in Step 5) and press ENTER. Be careful; make sure you have selected the empty volume from Exercise 10-2, not your system volume, or you could be in real trouble.

7. Type **help format** and press ENTER. You see the syntax for formatting a volume.

8. Type **format fs=ntfs label="Ready" quick** and press ENTER.

9. Type **exit** and press ENTER.

10. Close the Command Prompt window.

11. Open Computer/This PC and note the volume label on the empty drive (Ready).

Managing Disks in macOS

In macOS, the Disk Utility program is the equivalent of Disk Management in Windows. To access it, click the Launchpad icon on the Dock, then click the Other folder, and then click Disk Utility. The main screen is shown in Figure 10-5. The navigation pane on the left enables you to select physical disks (top level of the hierarchy) and logical volumes on them. In Figure 10-5 there is only one physical disk and only one volume on it.

As you can see, across the top of the window are five buttons:

- **First Aid** Diagnoses and fixes disk problems. Click First Aid, and then click Run.
- **Partition** Allows you to view and adjust partitions, including creating new partitions and resizing existing ones. If this command isn't available, make sure you have selected a physical disk in the navigation pane.
- **Erase** Wipes out existing data on a volume. This isn't available for the system volume, for safety reasons.
- **Unmount** Disconnects the volume logically from the OS. This one also isn't available for the system volume.
- **Info** Provides information about the selected disk or volume.

Managing Disks in Linux

In Linux, the disk management tool is called Disks. You can access it from the Ubuntu GUI by searching for Disks or by browsing applications.

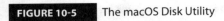

FIGURE 10-5 The macOS Disk Utility

Notice on the left in Figure 10-6 that, as with the macOS Disk Utility shown in Figure 10-5, the disks appear in a navigation pane. To change which volume is represented, click the desired volume. To access the commands for managing the selected volume, click the More Actions button (gears symbol) under the colored bar representing the volume, opening a menu like the one shown in Figure 10-6. To work with the disk itself (the physical disk), click the More Actions button (single gear) in the upper-right corner of the window.

SCENARIO & SOLUTION

How do I open Disk Management without going through Computer Management?	You can run the diskmgmt.msc command, or in Windows 8.1 or 10 you can right-click the Start button and choose Disk Management.
Can I set up a software-based RAID 5 array through Disk Management?	Yes, but only in server versions of Windows. The command is unavailable on client versions of Windows.
I added a new hard disk, so why doesn't it show up in the Volumes list in Disk Management?	You have to partition and format it first.
How do I manage disks on a Mac?	Use the Disk Utility application.
How do I manage disks in Ubuntu Linux?	Use the Disks application.

FIGURE 10-6   The Ubuntu Linux Disks utility

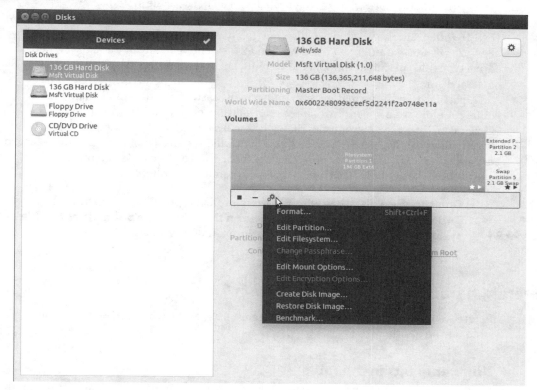

CERTIFICATION OBJECTIVE

■ *902: 1.2   Given a scenario, install Windows PC operating systems using appropriate methods*

This section explores portions of CompTIA A+ 902 exam objective 1.2 relating to file systems. You'll learn about the features, limitations, and compatibility issues among all the file systems covered in the exam objectives, including FAT32, exFAT, NTFS, CDFS, NFS, ext3, and etx4.

File Systems

File management begins with understanding the underlying file system that supports the saving, retrieving, deleting, and other management tasks for files. Windows has several file systems that it supports, so we will compare those file systems. Although most file management tasks remain the same across all the file systems supported by Windows, you will learn about features that are not available in all of these file systems.

All modern versions of Windows fully support several file systems, including NTFS, FAT16 (often simply called File Allocation Table, or FAT, or the FAT file system), and FAT32. The Format utility in Windows can format a drive in any of these file systems. Some drive types also permit additional file systems, such as exFAT for flash drives and CDFS for optical discs.

A partition can be formatted with only one file system at a time, and changing to a different file system generally requires reformatting, erasing all current content. The General tab of a drive's Properties dialog box will show which file system is on a drive.

Windows can use the FAT, FAT32, and NTFS file systems on either disk type—basic or dynamic—and on any volume type. Once you partition a basic disk, you may format it with any of these file systems. This is also true of dynamic disk volumes.

on the **Job**

Don't confuse disk type with file system. Disk type affects the entire disk underlying the partitions or volumes on the drives. The boundaries of a file system lie within the partition or volume in which it resides.

General Characteristics of a File System

Before we take a look at individual file systems, let's review what differentiates one file system from another.

Number of Bits in the Table

Each file system maintains a table that tells what is stored in each physical location on the disk. Depending on the file system, this may be called the *File Allocation Table (FAT)* or the *Master File Table (MFT)*. (Because the file system itself is also called FAT, sometimes this table is referred to redundantly as the *FAT table*.) The table uses a certain number of binary digits to describe each addressable location on the disk. FAT16 is a 16-bit system, whereas FAT32 and NTFS are both 32-bit file systems. The more bits, the more addressable locations, and therefore the larger the maximum volume capacity.

Cluster Size

Each disk's storage is divided into sectors of 512 bytes each. However, if a file system were to address each sector individually, the file allocation table would run out of space quickly. For example, a 16-bit FAT would only be able to store information for about 33.5 MB (2^{16} bytes times 512 bytes). Therefore, sectors are grouped into *clusters*, also called *allocation units*. A cluster is the smallest individually addressable storage unit on the disk. Each entry in the FAT or MFT refers to the starting location of a different cluster.

	File System	Volume Size	Default Cluster Size
TABLE 10-1 Default Cluster Sizes	NTFS	7 MB to 16 TB	4 KB (8 sectors)
	NTFS	16 TB to 32 TB	8 KB (16 sectors)
	NTFS	32 TB to 64 TB	16 KB (32 sectors)
	NTFS	64 TB to 128 TB	32 KB (64 sectors)
	NTFS	128 TB to 256 TB	64 KB (128 sectors)
	FAT32	32 MB to 64 MB	512 bytes (1 sector)
	FAT32	64 MB to 128 MB	1 KB (2 sectors)
	FAT32	128 MB to 256 MB	2 KB (4 sectors)
	FAT32	256 MB to 8 GB	4 KB (8 sectors)
	FAT32	8 GB to 16 GB	8 KB (16 sectors)
	FAT32	16 GB to 32 GB	16 KB (32 sectors)
	FAT16	8 MB to 32 MB	512 bytes (1 sector)
	FAT16	32 MB to 64 MB	1 KB (2 sectors)
	FAT16	64 MB to 128 MB	2 KB (4 sectors)
	FAT16	128 MB to 256 MB	4 KB (8 sectors)
	FAT16	256 MB to 512 MB	8 KB (16 sectors)
	FAT16	512 MB to 1 GB	16 KB (32 sectors)
	FAT16	1 GB to 2 GB	32 KB (64 sectors)
	FAT16	2 GB to 4 GB	64 KB (128 sectors)

When you format a disk, you can choose a cluster size, or you can accept the default cluster size, which is based on the volume size. Table 10-1 lists the default cluster sizes for NTFS, FAT32, and FAT16.

Notice how when the disk size is small, default cluster size is small, because that's preferable, but as the volume size grows, the clusters get larger to circumvent addressing limitations. You want to keep cluster sizes small to avoid wasting storage space. For example, suppose a file with a size of 8 KB is stored on a disk. On a disk with 4 KB clusters (that is, 8 sectors per cluster), it occupies 8 KB. But on a disk with 64 KB clusters (that is, 128 sectors per cluster), it occupies 64 KB. If you store a lot of small files, this difference can really add up.

Special Features

Besides the raw storage capacity, a file system can also have special features, such as compression, error correction, and security encryption. NTFS is a much more feature-rich file system than either FAT or FAT32. We'll explain its features later in the chapter.

FAT

The *FAT file system* has been around for several decades and was the file system implemented by Microsoft in the MS-DOS operating system. We have long been tempted to declare this file system dead or irrelevant, but it is still around, supported by almost any operating system you may encounter. It is also used on small storage devices because it is a file system that takes up very little space on disk for its own use, as compared to NTFS, which takes up a great deal of space (overhead), even while providing many benefits in exchange. We also include this discussion because FAT32 are listed in CompTIA A+ 902 exam objective 1.2 and both FAT and FAT32 are in the Acronyms list for both exams.

FAT File System Components

When Windows formats a disk with the FAT file system, it places the FAT file system's three primary components on the disk. These components are the boot record, the FAT table, and the root directory. They reside at the very beginning of the disk, in an area called the system area. The space beyond the system area is the data area, which can hold files and subdirectories.

- **Boot record**   The *boot record* or *boot sector* is the first physical sector on a FAT-formatted hard drive partition. The boot record contains information about the OS used to format the disk and other file system information. It also contains the boot code involved in the boot process, as described earlier.

- **FAT table**   The *File Allocation Table (FAT)* is the file system component in which the OS creates a table that serves as a map of where files reside on disk.

- **Root directory**   A *directory* (also commonly called a *folder*) is an organizing unit for file storage. The *root directory* is the top-level directory on the volume, and the only one created during formatting. The entries in a directory point to files and to the next level of directories. The root directory, therefore, contains information about any files stored at the top level of the volume and also about any folders stored at the top level.

FAT12

FAT12 is for floppy disks and very small hard drives—too small to worry about today. If you format a floppy disk in Windows, it automatically formats it with the FAT12 file system. Because it's a 12-bit file system, it is limited in the size of drive it can access, but floppy disks are so low-capacity (1.44 MB) that it's not a problem. Using a 12-bit file system rather than 16-bit saves a few bytes of storage on the disk. Not much by today's standards, of course, but when the entire disk is only 1.44 MB in capacity, a few bytes seems more significant.

FAT16

The *FAT16* file system, as implemented in the versions of Windows included in this book, is limited to 65,525 clusters (because of the 16-bit size of its file allocation table, as we discussed earlier). That means its maximum capacity per volume is 4 GB, which is inadequate for today's hard disks. You won't see FAT16 in use much anymore.

FAT32

The *FAT32* file system was introduced by Microsoft in a special release of Windows 95, over 20 years ago. This improved version of the FAT file system can format larger hard disk partitions (up to 2 TB) and allocates disk space more efficiently. A FAT32-formatted partition will have a FAT table and root directory, but the FAT table holds 32-bit entries, and there are changes in how it positions the root directory. The root directory on both FAT12 and FAT16 was a single point of failure, since it could only reside in the system area. The FAT32 file system allows the OS to back up the root directory to the data portion of the disk and to use this backup in case the first copy fails.

e x a m

ⓦ a t c h   **The important file systems to focus on when preparing for the CompTIA A+ exams are FAT, FAT32, NTFS, Compact Disc File System (CDFS), HFS+ (macOS), and ext3 and ext4 (Linux).**

NTFS

All modern Windows versions support an improved version of a file system introduced in Windows NT: the New Technology File System (NTFS). From its beginnings, NTFS has been a much more advanced file system than any form of the FAT file system.

Master File Table

In contrast to the FAT file system, NTFS has a far more sophisticated structure, using an expandable *Master File Table (MFT)*. This makes the file system adaptable to future changes. NTFS uses the MFT to store a transaction-based database, with all file accesses treated as transactions, and if a transaction is not complete, NTFS will roll back to the last successful transaction, making the file system more stable.

Fault Tolerance

In another improved feature, NTFS also avoids saving files to physically damaged portions of a disk, called bad sectors. This is a form of fault tolerance.

NTFS on Small-Capacity Media

Windows will not allow you to format a floppy disk with NTFS, because it requires much more space on a disk for its structure than FAT does. This extra space is the file system's overhead. You may format a small hard disk partition with NTFS, but because of the overhead space requirements, the smallest recommended size is 10 MB. That's megabytes, not terabytes, so it is pretty much a nonissue today.

While a USB flash drive normally comes formatted with FAT32 (and is readable by your Windows OS), you can format one with NTFS. However, once you do this, it becomes more important to use the Safely Remove Hardware applet before removing the drive to prevent damaging data on the drive. Although we recommend doing that for any USB drive, you are more likely to damage data on an NTFS-formatted flash drive if you remove it without using this applet to stop all processes that are accessing the drive.

As much as we favor NTFS for all its advanced features, it is very much a Microsoft-only file system. FAT32, however, is supported by many operating systems, including macOS and variations of Unix and Linux. When we want to use an external hard drive or USB flash drive on our PC as well as on our Apple iMac, we make sure to format it with FAT32.

NTFS Indexing

The indexing service is part of Windows and speeds up file searches on NTFS volumes. If this service is on, indexing of any folder that has the index attribute turned on will occur so that future searches of that folder will be faster.

NTFS Compression

NTFS supports *file and folder compression* to save disk space, using an algorithm to reduce the size of a file as it writes it to disk. You can turn it on for an individual file or for the entire contents of a folder, and this is a very nice feature if you are running low on disk space. However, the tradeoff is that it takes Windows more time to write a file to disk when it has to compress it, and also more time to expand a compressed file as it brings it into memory when you open the file.

NTFS Security Features

NTFS offers encryption at the file and folder level in a feature called *Encrypting File System (EFS). Encryption* is the conversion of data into a special format that cannot be read by anyone unless they have a software key to convert it back into its usable form. The encryption key for EFS is the user's authentication. Therefore, once a user encrypts a file or folder, only someone logged on with the same user account can access it.

While all modern Windows versions support EFS, not all editions do; look for it only in the Business, Enterprise, and Ultimate editions (Windows Vista and 7), Windows 8/8.1 Pro and Enterprise editions, and Windows 10 Pro, Enterprise, and Education editions.

In addition, on NTFS volumes you can apply permissions to folders and files for added security. A *permission* is the authorization of a person or group to access a resource—in this case, a file or folder—and take certain actions, such as reading, changing, or deleting. This is one of the most important differences between NTFS and FAT file systems.

The Properties dialog box of each folder and file on a drive formatted with NTFS will have a Security tab showing the permissions assigned to that folder or file. Learn more about file and folder permissions in Chapter 18.

on the Job While Windows uses the term "folder" and shows a folder icon in the GUI, many of the dialog boxes and messages continue to use the old term "directory" for what we now know as a disk folder. People frequently use these two terms interchangeably. In this book, we generally use "folder" when working in the GUI and "directory" when working from the command line.

exFAT

Extended File Allocation Table (exFAT) is a file system Microsoft introduced in Service Pack 1 for Windows Vista. Since then, all versions of Windows support this file system, which was not intended for use on hard drives, but as a replacement for FAT32 on small solid-state storage devices such as USB flash drives and SSD cards. The Format utility in Windows makes it available as an option when you are formatting SSDs, as shown in Figure 10-7, but not when formatting regular hard drives.

The exFAT file system includes the following advantages over FAT32:

■ 256 TB maximum volume size.

■ A single folder/directory can hold up to 100 high-definition movies, 60 hours of high-definition audio, or 4000 RAW images. A *RAW image* file contains unprocessed image data from a digital camera, image scanner, or digital movie scanner.

■ Faster file saves, so that solid-state devices can save at their full speed.

■ Cross-platform interoperation with many operating systems; Apple added exFAT support to macOS beginning with Snow Leopard (10.6.5).

■ The file system is extensible, meaning that manufacturers can customize it for new device characteristics.

Resilient File System

Resilient File System (ReFS) is a new file system expected to replace the NTFS file system on Windows Server. It retains many of the features of the NTFS file system, but discards some features and adds many others for servers to support really large hard drives and RAID-style systems with very advanced performance and fault tolerance support.

FIGURE 10-7

When a solid-state device is selected, exFAT is available in the Format dialog box.

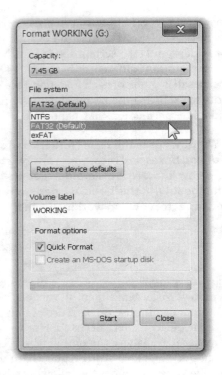

 You will not see questions concerning the Resilient File System on the CompTIA A+ 220-901 or 220-902 exams. In fact, you will not see this file system on desktop computers for a long while, since it is currently available only in Windows Server products. However, what appears on Windows Server products eventually trickles down to the desktop products, so you will eventually see it on the job.

Mac File Systems

macOS's native file system is Hierarchical File System Plus (HFS+). That's the file system that the system drive comes with, with the OS preinstalled on it. Don't try to change that.

macOS also supports FAT32 and exFAT (for flash drives). It reads NTFS file systems but can't write to them. macOS doesn't read any of the Linux file systems (ext2, ext3, or ext4).

Linux File Systems

Linux's native file system is ext3 or ext4. We reviewed the differences between ext3 and ext4 in Chapter 9 in the section "Selecting a File System for Other Operating Systems." Turn back there now if you need a reminder.

In addition, Linux can also support ext2 (for older Linux system compatibility), FAT (for broad compatibility with nearly every kind of system), NTFS (for compatibility with modern Windows systems), and an encrypted version of ext4. It can read and write HFS+ (but doesn't format disks using it).

Other File Systems

Although NTFS is the most important file system for anyone supporting Windows PCs, several other file systems exist, and we will briefly examine them. These include CDFS, UDF, and DFS.

CDFS

Compact Disc File System (CDFS) is an ISO 9660–compliant file system used by Windows to read CDs, DVDs, and CD-ROMs. While UDF has replaced CDFS, Windows still supports CDFS to use with optical discs that do not support UDF.

UDF

UDF is an acronym with multiple identities. In Chapter 9, UDFs made an appearance as "Uniqueness Database Files," files used in a scripted installation of Windows, and now we have another use for this acronym: *Universal Data Format (UDF)*, a file format used for optical discs. This format is for movie DVDs. Windows Vista was the first Windows version to support writing the UDF format, so prior to Windows Vista, if you wanted to write to disc using UDF, you needed a third-party program like Roxio. In addition, some versions of Windows could read UDF-formatted discs, but could not write to them.

DFS

Distributed File System (DFS) is a service implemented on Windows Servers that hides the complexity of the network from end users, in that it makes files that are distributed across multiple servers appear as if they are in one place. Unless you are managing Microsoft Servers, you will not come in close contact with DFS, but it is included in the CompTIA A+ Acronyms list for the 220-901 and 220-902 exams.

NFS

Network File System (NFS) is included in CompTIA A+ 902 exam objective 1.2, but you are not likely to encounter it on the job. It's not equivalent to the other file systems you have learned about in this chapter; instead, it's a distributed file system protocol developed by Sun Microsystems that allows a client computer to access network storage locations.

SCENARIO & SOLUTION

What is the preferred file system for Windows?	NTFS is the preferred Windows file system.
Which file system is best for an external drive that will be shared among Windows, macOS, and Linux computers?	FAT32 is the safest choice, because they all accept that. macOS has only read-only support for NTFS and doesn't read ext3 or ext4, while Windows doesn't support HFS+.
Which file system is best for a USB flash drive that will be used on both macOS and Windows systems?	exFAT is a good choice because both platforms read and write it natively for flash drives. FAT32 would also work, but exFAT has more features.
Why wouldn't you always use the smallest cluster size when formatting a disk?	A smaller cluster size may not allow for large enough volumes. For example, a FAT32 volume with 4 KB clusters can be a maximum of 8 GB. This is less of an issue on NTFS volumes; the limits are much higher.

CERTIFICATION OBJECTIVES

- **902: 1.1**   *Compare and contrast various features and requirements of Microsoft Operating Systems (Windows Vista, Windows 7, Windows 8, Windows 8.1)*
- **902: 1.3**   *Given a scenario, apply appropriate Microsoft command-line tools*
- **902: 1.5**   *Given a scenario, use Windows Control Panel utilities*
- **902: 3.3**   *Compare and contrast differences of basic Windows OS security settings*

This section explores the few details of CompTIA A+ 902 exam objective 1.1 not addressed in Chapter 2. These include an examination of file structure and paths by defining the default locations where each of the listed Windows versions stores certain files and folders, including critical Windows OS system, program, and user files.

We also address a small portion of CompTIA A+ 902 exam objective 3.3 by describing how to show or hide protected system files and hidden files in file listings, leaving the discussion of more robust types of file and folder-level security for Chapter 19.

Finally, this section addresses the use of several of the command-line tools for file management listed in CompTIA A+ 902 exam objective 1.3, and the Folder Options settings mentioned in 902 exam objective 1.5.

File Management

File management is an end-user skill, so it's assumed background knowledge for technicians. Make sure you can move, copy, rename, delete, and restore files and folders, and create, delete, and rename folders. We aren't going to go into those skills in detail here. Instead, the following sections look at some technical specs about files that may not be obvious from working with files in the Windows GUI.

Naming Rules

MS-DOS and early versions of Windows into the 1990s used the 8.3 naming rules, in which the filename could be a maximum of eight characters long and the file extension was a maximum of three characters long. A *long filename (LFN)* is any file or folder name that breaks the 8.3 file-naming convention. Modern versions of Windows support LFNs on all file systems on all media, including hard drives, flash drives, optical discs, and even floppy disks.

The support for long filenames in Microsoft's FAT file systems (FAT12, FAT16, and FAT32) is provided by a technology Microsoft calls the *virtual file allocation table (VFAT)*. Using VFAT, all versions of Microsoft Windows since Windows 95 can create filenames beyond the 8.3 limit by simply using multiple directory entries. For each file or directory with a long filename, VFAT stores a long file up to 255 characters, including spaces, which were not allowed in 8.3 filenames. In addition, it creates a legacy 8.3 filename for each long filename entry.

File Attributes

A *file attribute* is a component of a file or directory entry that determines how an operating system handles the file or directory. In all the variations of the FAT, FAT32, and NTFS file systems, the standard file attributes are read-only, archive, system, and hidden. Two special attributes, also in all Windows file systems, are volume label, which allows you to give a name to the volume (recall the Volume Label option in the New Simple Volume Wizard), and directory, which identifies an entry as a directory. The operating system modifies these attributes, as do certain programs such as file backup utilities. NTFS supports many more types of file attributes beyond these six.

The following are explanations of each of the four standard file attributes.

Read-Only Attribute

The read-only attribute was designed to ensure that a file or folder will not be modified, renamed, or deleted accidentally—with emphasis on accidentally. In Windows, if you try to modify, rename, or delete a read-only file, you will receive a warning message requiring confirmation, but you can still proceed with the action.

Archive Attribute

By default, Windows turns on the archive attribute for all files when they are created or modified. This attribute, when turned "on," marks a file as one that needs backing up. Most backup utilities provide the option to back up only files that have been created or modified since the last backup. One way this is tracked is by looking for the archive attribute. A backup program can turn off the archive attribute as it backs up a file, allowing the backup program to do subsequent backups that only back up files with the archive attribute turned on, thus backing up only those files created or modified since the last backup.

System Attribute

The OS or an application gives certain folders and files the system attribute automatically to identify it as a system file. Most system files also get the hidden attribute to keep users from viewing them. From Windows Explorer (File Explorer in Windows 8), you can neither see the system attribute nor turn it on or off.

Hidden Attribute

A file or folder with the hidden attribute turned on will not show in Computer/This PC or Windows Explorer unless the View settings allow it to be shown.

Additional Windows File Attributes

The NTFS file system has these original file attributes, as well as additional file attributes. In fact, NTFS saves a file's actual contents as one or more file attributes. NTFS allows for future expansion of attributes—making this file system more expandable.

The General tab of the Properties dialog box for a file or folder will show two of the traditional attributes: read-only and hidden. On an NTFS file or folder, clicking the Advanced button will display the status of four attributes: archive, index, compress, and encrypt (see Figure 10-8). Index, compress, and encrypt are special NTFS file attributes. Turning on the index attribute will make file searches much faster, as the file contents and properties will be indexed by the *Windows Indexing Service*. Use the compress attribute on a folder to compress the contents, and use the encrypt attribute to encrypt the contents of a folder using the Encrypting File System (EFS). These two attributes are mutually exclusive. You cannot both compress and encrypt, but you can apply one or the other of these attributes to a file or folder.

File Types

Windows computers use several file types, including, in broad terms, data files and program files. Data files contain the data you create with application programs. Program files (also called "binary files") contain programming code (instructions read by the OS or special interpreters). Program files include those that you can directly run, such as files with the .com or .exe extension (called "executables"), and those that are called up by other programs, such as files with the .dll extension.

FIGURE 10-8   The Advanced Attributes dialog box shown in Windows 7

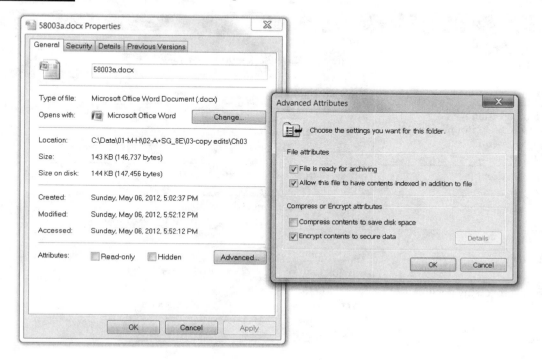

Data Files

When it comes to file management, you should only manage data files. Leave management of program files to the operating system. There are a large number of data file types. A short list of some common Windows file types and associated extensions is shown in Table 10-2.

System Files and Folders

The essential files needed to boot and run Windows are considered *system files*. Some of them have the System and/or Hidden attribute assigned to them, but not all. They are mainly located in the C:\Windows folder (that's the default system folder location, although on some systems it may have been changed at installation). There are dozens of subfolders within the C:\Windows folder, and you don't need to be able to identify them for the exam. However, there are also some system files in the root directory of the C: drive.

By default, Windows hides certain system files to protect them. You can choose whether or not you want this by following the steps in Exercise 10-5.

TABLE 10-2	Common File Extensions

File Type	Associated Extension(s)
Compressed files	.zip: WinZip
Database files	.accdb: Microsoft Access 2007 or later .mdb: versions of Microsoft Access prior to Access 2007
Graphic files	.bmp, .dib, .gif, .jpg, .tif, .png, and others
Microsoft Management Console files (Computer Management, Disk Management, etc.)	.mmc
Presentation files	.pptx: Microsoft PowerPoint 2007 or later .ppt: Versions of Microsoft PowerPoint prior to PowerPoint 2007
Spreadsheet files	.xlsx: Microsoft Excel 2007 or later .xls: versions of Microsoft Excel prior to Excel 2007
Text files	.txt
Video files	.mpg, .mp3, .mp4, corresponding to several file formats defined by the Moving Picture Experts Group (MPEG)
Word-processing document files	.docx: Microsoft Word 2007 or later .docm: Microsoft Word 2007 or later; document file with macros enabled .doc: versions of Microsoft Word prior to Word 2007 and some other word processors

exam **watch**

Make sure you know how to hide and show file extensions in File Explorer/Windows Explorer. It's mentioned in CompTIA A+ 902 exam objective 1.5. In Windows 7 and earlier, you have to open the Folder Options dialog box, as in Exercise 10-5. In Windows 8 and newer, there is a check box on the View tab in File Explorer. Familiarize yourself also with the General and View tabs in the Folder Options dialog box, which provide configuration options for how files appear in File Explorer.

EXERCISE 10-5

Showing or Hiding Protected System Files

In this exercise, you will learn how to include or exclude system files in file listings. You will need Windows Vista, 7, 8/8.1, or 10.

1. Open File Explorer/Windows Explorer.
2. Open the Folder Options dialog box. To do this:
   - ■ Windows Vista or Windows 7: Click Organize | Folder and Search Options.
   - ■ Windows 8/8.1 or Windows 10: Click View | Options.
3. In the dialog box, click the View tab.
4. Clear the Hide Protected Operating System Files (Recommended) check box. At the warning that appears, click Yes.
5. Click OK.

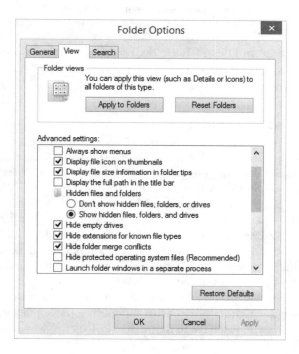

Some of the system files are hidden using several layers of security; you just turned off one layer. Another layer is that the individual files have the Hidden attribute turned on. When Windows is set to show hidden files, they appear in file listings with dimmed icons; when it's set to hide hidden files, they don't appear at all.

6. Browse to the root directory of the C: drive. Do you see any of the hidden files in the listing? They may include bootmgr and pagefile.sys, for example.
7. Repeat Steps 2–3 to reopen the Folder Options dialog box and redisplay the View tab.
8. Under Hidden Files and Folders, note the current setting. (It is either *Don't show hidden files, folders, or drives* or *Show hidden files, folders, and drives*.)

9. Change the setting, and then click OK. Check out how the file listing for the root directory has changed.

10. Repeat Steps 7–9 to change the setting back. While you're there, re-hide the protected operating system files as well.

Program Files and Folders

Whereas system files keep Windows itself running, program files serve individual programs. When you install an application, it copies the files it needs to your hard drive, usually in one of two places:

- **Program Files**   This folder holds subfolders for each installed application.
- **Program Files (x86)**   If you are running a 64-bit version of Windows, any 32-bit program files are stored here. This folder doesn't exist on a 32-bit Windows system.

User Files and Folders

The C:\Users folder holds a separate folder for each local user account. This folder includes a variety of subfolders that work together to store all the system preferences, application settings, and data files for that user. For example, this is where the individual user's Documents, Music, Downloads, OneDrive, Pictures, and Videos folders reside.

Some programs store data based on the signed-in Windows account, so that different users of the same PC can retain separate settings for that program. Those files are generally stored in C:\Users*username*\AppData. (That's a hidden folder.) Sometimes when you are troubleshooting a problem with an application, you will need to browse this folder to locate a certain file to modify or delete, so make sure you remember that it's hidden and you have to display hidden files in order to access it.

Within the AppData folder are Local, LocalLow, and Roaming folders. If you're not on a domain network, they are not that different; some applications save settings to one versus another and you just have to figure out (or look up) where each one operates if you need to find the files.

If you are on a domain network, though, there's a difference. The Local and LocalLow folders store data that does not roam with the user (if the user logs in to the network from a different PC in the network). The Roaming folder holds user-specific data that should roam with the user. When the user signs out, the roaming data is updated on the network, and when the user signs in, the roaming data is transferred to the other PC for the application(s) to use.

So then what's the difference between Local and LocalLow? LocalLow is used for "low integrity" applications to write their user-specific data to, such as Internet Explorer add-ons. A low-integrity app is one that can't be trusted to not harm the computer, so it's assigned fewer privileges.

There is also a hidden ProgramData folder, in the root directory of the C: drive. This folder is used to hold general user settings that don't pertain to a specific user account, for applications that normally store settings in C:\Users*username*\AppData. That might be useful if someone who logged in with the Guest account wanted to run the app, for example.

File Management at the Windows Command Prompt

As we noted earlier, this chapter doesn't cover file management skills in the Windows GUI, because we're assuming that by the time you get to the point where you are studying for a CompTIA A+ exam, you are already a competent Windows user with the requisite user skills. Being able to move, copy, rename, and delete files and folders in File Explorer is assumed.

However, the same cannot be said for file management at a command prompt. In our experience, many people who are otherwise Windows power users today lack this skill, simply because they have grown up in a computing environment where it wasn't needed. So let's spend some time reviewing command-line file management.

Back in the days of MS-DOS, the command line was the only interface available for running programs and managing files. It persists today in the form of a Command Prompt application included in Windows. Using this application, you can issue commands in a text prompt environment that is similar to that original MS-DOS environment.

We strongly suggest that, under normal circumstances, you do not attempt file management from the command line, because you can only use text-mode commands that give you very little feedback, and a minor typo can result in disaster.

However, as a support person, you might find yourself working at a special command-line interface such as in the Windows Recovery Environment (RE) in cases where the system will not start normally. Therefore, prepare for the time when you may need to work with these command-line interfaces by practicing now with the Windows Command Prompt. In Chapter 13 you will learn about working with the Command Prompt in the recovery environment.

Opening the Command Prompt

In Windows Vista or Windows 7, you can launch the Command Prompt window with Start | All Programs | Accessories | Command Prompt. In Windows 8.1 or 10, you can right-click the Start button and choose Command Prompt.

Most of the time the regular Command Prompt environment will work fine. However, if you see a message that *the requested operation requires elevation*, close the Command Prompt window and reopen it using administrator privileges. (That's most likely to occur when you are using network-related commands.) To open an elevated command prompt in Windows Vista or Windows 7, right-click the Command Prompt command on the Start menu and click Run as Administrator. In Windows 8.1 or 10, right-click the Start button and click Command Prompt (Admin).

Windows 8 is a special case; none of the methods explained previously work in it because it has neither a Start menu nor a Start button. Instead, when you right-click the bottom left of the screen, a context menu appears. From this menu, you can select either Command Prompt or Command Prompt (Admin). The second choice will run Command Prompt as an administrator.

Managing Files at the Command Prompt

There are two commands for creating and deleting directories (folders) at the Command Prompt: md (Make Directory) and rd (Remove Directory). Use the dir (directory) command to view listings of files and directories. Move around the directory hierarchy at the Command Prompt using the cd (Change Directory) command. Use two dots together (..) to indicate the directory immediately above the current directory. You can use these in many command-line commands. For instance, if you only want to move up one level, type **cd ..** and press ENTER. (Commands are not case sensitive; most people use lowercase when typing them because it is easier.)

You can use wildcards from the Command Prompt. The most useful one is the asterisk (*). Use the asterisk to represent one or more characters in a filename or extension. For instance, enter the command **dir *.exe** to see a listing of all files in the current directory ending with "exe." Using *.* will select all files and directories. Use a question mark to indicate a single character.

When you are working at the Command Prompt, the previous commands and messages remain on the screen until they scroll off. To clear this information from the screen, use the cls (clear screen) command.

When you want to copy files, you have a choice of commands. The simplest is copy, which is a very, very old command that does not understand directories. To use this command on files in different directories, you must enter the path to the directory or directories in the command. It helps to first make either the source directory or the target directory current before using this command. We rarely use copy because of its limits. We prefer the xcopy command, because it is a more advanced command that understands directories. In fact, you can tell xcopy to copy the contents of a directory simply by giving the directory name. The simple syntax for both of these commands is *<command> <from_source> <to_destination>*. Both copy and xcopy will accept either filenames or folder names in the source and destination arguments. For instance, the command xcopy monday tuesday can be entered to copy the contents of the folder Monday into the folder Tuesday.

A far more advanced command is *Robust File Copy*, which has the command name *robocopy*. It is a folder copier, meaning that you must enter folder names as the source and destination arguments. It will not accept filenames or wildcard characters in the source or destination arguments, although it copies all the files within the specified folder. In addition, robocopy has a list of advanced features, such as the ability to stop a copy operation that is interrupted by a disconnected network. It then resumes upon reconnection with the network. It also allows you to mirror two entire folder structures. This is a handy but tricky feature, because those files on the destination that are no longer present on the source will be deleted from the destination. There are many more robocopy features—all of which are accessed with the appropriate arguments. A simple example of a command that would mirror the DATA folder on two different drives is robocopy c:\data d:\data /mir.

Exercise 10-6 walks you through using various command-line commands for managing files and folders.

Managing Directories and Files at the Command Prompt

Practice working with directories and files from the Command Prompt.

1. Open the Command Prompt window, and note the location shown on the prompt. This is the active location. It is the user folder for the currently signed-in user, like this: C:\Users\Faithe, if you opened a standard command prompt, and C:\Windows\System32, if you opened an elevated command prompt.

2. Type **help** and press ENTER. A list of all valid commands appears, but it scrolls by very quickly. Scroll the window upward so you can see the whole list, and then scroll down again to the prompt.

3. Type **dir /?** and press ENTER. An explanation of all the switches for the dir command appears. Note that one of them is /w for the wide list format.

4. Type **dir /w** and press ENTER. A listing of files and directories within the directory will display. The /w switch uses a compact, multicolumn listing.

5. Type the command again with the pause switch: **dir /p**. If prompted, press the SPACEBAR to advance the display one screenful at a time to the end of the listing.

6. Type the clear screen command, **cls**, and press ENTER to clear the screen.

7. Type **cd ** and press ENTER to go to the root directory.

8. Type **cd %homepath%** and press ENTER to go to the home directory for the signed-in user.

9. Type **cd documents** and press ENTER to change to the Documents directory. Because it is a subdirectory of the current location, you can just use its name, and not its full path.

10. Type **md testdata** and press ENTER. This creates a new directory in the Documents directory.

11. Type **copy nul > file.txt** and press ENTER. That creates a blank text file, just to have a file to work with.

12. Type **copy file.txt testdata** and press ENTER. That copies the new file into the testdata directory.

13. Type **del file.txt** and press ENTER.

14. Type **rd testdata** and press ENTER. You get an error because only empty directories can be removed.

15. Type **del testdata*.*** and press ENTER.

16. Type **Y** and press ENTER to confirm.

17. Type **rd testdata** and press ENTER. This time it is removed.

The following illustration shows Steps 7 through 17.

18. Type **exit** and press ENTER to close the Command Prompt window.

Checking a Disk for Errors from the Command Prompt

The chkdsk (Check Disk) command is the text-mode version of the GUI Error-Checking program you can access from the Tools page of the Properties dialog box for a disk. It checks disks for physical and logical errors. You must use an elevated command prompt to run this utility. Figure 10-9 shows a chkdsk operation in progress.

Running chkdsk without the /f parameter only analyzes the disk. It makes no corrections. If errors are found, rerun the command with the /f parameter and it will fix disk errors. Use the /r parameter together with the /f parameter, and chkdsk will both fix the disk errors and attempt to recover the data in the bad space by moving it.

If the volume is in use (as is always the case with drive C:), you might see a message asking if you would like to schedule the volume to be checked during the next system restart. Press Y and ENTER to schedule this. Be aware that chkdsk can take as much as an hour or more to check and repair a large hard drive.

Formatting a Disk from the Command Prompt

The format command will allow you to format a hard drive or other media, such as the rare floppy disk or the more common SSD from a Command Prompt. Once again, the preferred

| FIGURE 10-9 | A chkdsk check underway via an elevated command prompt window |

way is to format from the GUI, where you are less likely to make an error when doing this. The choice of GUI tool is either the Disk Management console or File Explorer/Windows Explorer.

Figure 10-10 shows the command for formatting the D: drive. Notice that it does not proceed until you press Y. Press N to cancel. This command will wipe out the contents of the drive. Using the proper syntax, you can format a hard drive with any of the file systems supported by Windows for the target disk.

Checking System Files with sfc

System files have very privileged access to your computer. Therefore, malicious software (malware) targets system files so that it can have the same access (more on malware when we describe security threats in Chapter 18). At one time, system files were easy targets for such malware, but recent versions of Windows come with protections, both at the file system level (through assigned permissions) and through the use of a service that protects system files.

FIGURE 10-10
Press Y to continue with the formatting of the D: drive.

Windows Resource Protection (WRP) is a Windows component that maintains a cache of protected files. If a file is somehow damaged, WRP will replace the damaged file with an undamaged copy from the cache. It also provides similar protection for registry keys. Learn more about the Windows registry in Chapter 13.

The *System File Checker (SFC)* is a handy utility that uses the WRP service to scan and verify the versions of all protected system files. The syntax for this program is as follows:

```
sfc [scannow] [scanonce] [scanboot] [revert] [purgecache] [cachesize=x]
```

When you run the sfc command with the /scannow parameter, you will see a message box showing a progress bar while it checks that all protected Windows files are intact and in their original versions. If SFC finds any files that do not comply, it will replace them with the correct signed file from the cache.

Managing Files at the Linux or macOS Command Prompt

Linux is a command-line environment at its basic level; the friendly GUI shell you see on top of it in distros like Ubuntu is just a façade. It's no wonder, then, that Linux has a broad selection of commands to work with at a command prompt—a larger and more robust set than Windows provides.

New to the 220-902 exam is the requirement that you know some basic Linux command-line commands. We'll look here at the ones that pertain to file and folder management, and others we'll save for upcoming chapters on PC troubleshooting, maintenance, security, and networking. Because both macOS and Linux are based on Unix, macOS and Linux have the same Terminal window capabilities and accepts the same Linux commands, so you can use either macOS or Linux to practice the commands covered in this section.

Commands in the macOS and Linux command environments are case-sensitive; commands in the Windows command environment are not.

Opening a Command Prompt in Ubuntu Linux or macOS

The command-line interface in Linux is called Terminal. Press CTRL-ALT-T to open it, or click the Ubuntu icon in the upper-left corner, type **terminal**, and click the Terminal application. In macOS, click Launchpad | Other | Terminal to open a Terminal window.

Creating and Editing Files with the vi Editor

CompTIA A+ 902 exam objective 2.1 includes mention of the *vi editor*, which is a text editor designed to be used in the command-line environment in Linux or macOS. There is no modern equivalent for the Windows command prompt.

To enter the vi editor from a Terminal window, type **vi** and press ENTER. Depending on your Linux distro, instead of the traditional vi editor, you may see a program called VIM (Vi IMproved). It is very similar.

Vi has two modes: command mode and insertion mode. It starts out in command mode. In command mode, you can move the insertion point and do text selection and deletion. You can return to command mode at any time by pressing ESC.

To issue a command, you first type a colon (:). Here are some common commands:

- **:x** Exit and save your changes.
- **:q** Quit, as long as there are no unsaved changes.
- **:q!** Quit and ignore any changes.

In insertion mode, you can use one of these commands.

There isn't room in this book for a full discussion of vi, so check out a command reference online for it, such as this one: www.lagmonster.org/docs/vi.html. Use Exercise 10-7 for some quick practice creating a text file with vi. You'll need to do this exercise, or create a file in some other way, in order to complete Exercise 10-8.

EXERCISE 10-7

Creating a Text File in vi

For this exercise you will need some version of Linux (such as Ubuntu) or macOS.

1. At the Linux desktop GUI, press CTRL-ALT-T. Or, at the macOS desktop, click Launchpad | Other | Terminal.
2. Type **vi** and press ENTER.
3. Type **I am typing this document.** and press ENTER twice.
4. Use the following directional keys to move the insertion point around onscreen:
   - H to move left
   - J to move down
   - K to move up
   - L to move right
5. Using the directional keys, position the insertion point on the "d" in the word "document."
6. Type **i** (to insert). Now you are in insertion mode.
7. Type **excellent**.
8. Press ESC to return to command mode.
9. Type **:w excellent.txt**. This saves the file with that name.
10. Type **:q** to quit.

TABLE 10-3   Comparison of Linux/macOS and Windows File Management Commands

Activity	Linux and macOS	Windows
List the content of the active location	ls	dir
Change to a different location on the same drive	cd	cd
Rename a file or folder	mv	rn
Delete a file	rm	del
Copy a file	cp	copy
Print current directory name	pwd	No equivalent command
Create a directory	mkdir	md or mkdir
Remove a directory	rmdir	rd or rmdir
Search for a file	find	dir –r
Search for a file that contains certain text	grep	findstr
Duplicate data across devices, files, partitions, and volumes	dd	No equivalent command
Change security permission on a file or folder	chmod	No equivalent command
Change the owner of a file or folder	chown	No equivalent command

Using Basic File Management Commands in Linux or macOS

Linux does all the same file management tasks as Windows, but the commands and syntax are different. Table 10-3 compares the Windows and Linux commands. As you prepare for the 220-902 exam, make sure you study each of the commands in the Linux column of this table, as well as its syntax. macOS is based on Unix (as is Linux), so its commands and syntax are the same as in Linux.

EXERCISE 10-8

Managing Files at the Linux Terminal Window

This exercise begins where Exercise 10-7 ends and helps you explore many of the commands in Table 10-3. Complete Exercise 10-7 first so you have the file to work with for this exercise.

1. At the Linux desktop GUI, press CTRL-ALT-T to reopen a Terminal window. Or, on the macOS desktop, click Launchpad | Other | Terminal.
2. Type **ls** and press ENTER. Notice that excellent.txt is among the files listed, from Exercise 10-7. The default location shown is the user folder for the currently logged-in user. If you're working in Ubuntu Linux, the folder names are blue and the filenames are white.

3. Type **cp excellent.txt Documents** and press ENTER. This command copies the file into the Documents folder in your user folders.

4. Type **ls Documents**. A listing of the contents of the Documents folder appears. The copied file is there.

5. Type **cd Documents**. The active directory changes to that folder. Notice how the prompt changes to include /Documents.

6. Type **mv excellent.txt great.txt** and press ENTER. This renames the file.

7. Type **rm great.txt** and press ENTER. This deletes the file. Type **ls** and press ENTER to confirm that it is gone.

8. Type **mkdir Stuff** and press ENTER. This creates a new folder. Type **ls** and press ENTER to confirm that it exists.

9. Type **rmdir Stuff** and press ENTER. The new folder is deleted. Type **ls** and press ENTER to confirm it is gone.

10. Type **pwd** and press ENTER. The current folder's name appears. Its full path appears, not just the portion that was in the prompt.

   The following illustration shows Steps 2–10.

11. Type **clear** and press ENTER. Notice that unlike in Windows, when the cls command actually cleared the screen, the clear command only scrolls the window down so you don't see your previous commands; you can scroll up to see them again if you like.

12. Type **cd** and press ENTER. You return to the top level of your user folders.

13. Type **find *.txt** and press ENTER. A list of files with that extension appears. (There is only one.)

14. Type **grep "excellent" *.txt** and press ENTER. The content of the excellent.txt file appears, showing the word *excellent* highlighted in red.

15. Close the Terminal window.

You might have noticed that we didn't let you practice the dd command in the preceding exercise. That was on purpose. You should know what dd is because it's included in the objectives, but it's not in the same league as the other basic file-handling commands you've just learned. It's a serious administrator-type tool for Linux power users, and can be a dangerous command in the hands of the inexperienced. You can use it to create an ISO disk image from a CD-ROM, to restore a hard drive backup image, and to clone partitions or drives. Consult reputable online references to learn more about dd.

Using the Shutdown Command

Strictly speaking, the shutdown command is not a disk or file management tool, but rather a system management tool. It allows you to shut down the local computer or a remote computer using the command prompt, either immediately or after a certain delay you specify. Both Windows and Linux support this command (and so does macOS, since it's Linux based), although the syntax is different between the Linux/Mac and the Windows versions.

Shutdown Command in Windows

The syntax and arguments for the shutdown command differ among Windows versions. Here's a good reference that explains the full syntax for each version: www.computerhope .com/shutdown.htm. In this section we'll provide a few basic switches that work in all versions.

To specify the kind of shutdown you want, use one of these switches:

- **/s** for a shutdown.
- **/r** for a restart.
- **/h** to hibernate.
- **/hybrid** to shut down and prepare the PC for fast startup. This option isn't available prior to Windows 8.

To specify a time delay, use /t and then provide a number of seconds. The default is 30. So, for example, to restart after 60 seconds, you would use this:

```
shutdown /r /t 60
```

You can also use shutdown to shut down a remote computer. To do this, use the \m switch, like this:

```
shutdown -s /m \\Server01
```

Since Windows has a perfectly good GUI shutdown method, why would you want
to use a command-line shutdown? One reason is to create your own custom
shutdown shortcuts on the desktop that have different settings. Right-click
an empty area of the desktop and select New, and then select Shortcut. In the
Create a Shortcut wizard, enter the string for the shutdown command with the
parameters you desire, then click Next and enter a name for the shortcut.

Shutdown Command in Linux

In Linux, the command syntax uses dashes rather than slashes for the switches. Use this
reference for a complete list of switches: www.computerhope.com/unix/ushutdow.htm.
Here are a few of the most common ones.

To specify what happens during the shutdown, use one of these (case-sensitive) commands:

- **−P** for a shutdown and power down
- **−r** for a restart

To specify a time delay, use **−t** and then provide a number of seconds between sending
processes the warning and the kill signal.

To specify a particular time of day, use the time argument. (It doesn't have a switch
associated with it.) The time can be in hours and minutes, like 20:00, or in +m, where m is
the number of minutes to wait. The word "now" is the same as +0. Here are some examples:

- To restart after 5 minutes: **shutdown −r +5**
- To shut down and power off immediately: **shutdown −P now**

CERTIFICATION SUMMARY

As a computer support professional, you need to arm yourself with knowledge of operating
system disk and file management. Disk management in Windows begins with understanding
both basic and dynamic storage types. Technicians working with Windows PCs should
understand the differences between basic and dynamic storage types while focusing on
creating primary partitions on basic disks.

Most file management tasks remain the same across all the file systems supported by
Windows. NTFS is the preferred file system for Windows, providing more advanced file
storage features and file and folder security. You should perform file management from

the GUI tools, but a technician should be familiar with command-line file management methods for certain troubleshooting scenarios. You should understand file-naming conventions, file attributes, file types, and text file editors, and be able to organize files into folders. You should know the techniques and rules for moving and copying files in the GUI.

Windows comes with a number of utilities, specialized programs used to configure, optimize, and troubleshoot Windows and networks. A technician should be familiar with both GUI tools and command-line tools.

TWO-MINUTE DRILL

Here are some of the key points covered in Chapter 10.

Disk Management

❑ In Windows, the Disk Management tool is used to view and work with disks. Access it from the diskmgmt.msc command or through Computer Management.

❑ Disks can be basic or dynamic. Dynamic disks offer some additional flexibility and features, such as RAID arrays, but most desktop and notebook systems do not need those features.

❑ A basic disk can have up to four partitions. Either all four partitions can be primary, or the disk can have a combination of up to three primary partitions and one extended partition. Primary partitions are preferred.

❑ A PC with one or more basic disks must have at least one primary partition in order to boot Windows.

❑ Windows Setup creates a basic disk with a primary, active (bootable) partition and formats the partition with a file system.

❑ A dynamic disk allows more than four partitions per disk, and can be used to create spanned, striped, and RAID 5 volumes that combine multiple physical disks into a single logical volume.

❑ A mounted drive is a volume that is mapped to an empty folder on an NTFS volume.

❑ A quick format does not actually overwrite or test the entire volume, but simply puts the file system components on the disk, refreshing the directory and allocation information so that the disk appears empty, whether it is or not. A full format overwrites all the data space, as well as the directory information.

❑ Storage Spaces is a feature in Windows 8 and newer that allows you to combine the storage space from multiple drives of various types and interfaces into a single large pool of storage.

❑ DISKPART is a command-line utility that performs many of the same operations as Disk Management.

❑ On a macOS system, the Disk Utility program is the equivalent of Disk Management in Windows. Its utilities include First Aid, Partition, Erase, Unmount, and Info.

❑ In Ubuntu Linux, the disk utility is called Disks. To access the commands for managing the selected volume in Disks, click the More Actions button (gears symbol) under the colored bar representing the volume.

File Systems

❑ Most file management tasks remain the same across all the file systems available in Windows: FAT12, FAT16, FAT32, and NTFS.

❑ The key characteristics of a file system include number of bits in the table (either FAT or MFT), cluster size, and special features like encryption and compression.

❑ Sectors are grouped into clusters to make addressable allocation units. Disks store files more efficiently with smaller cluster sizes, but to support large volumes, larger cluster sizes may be required. Refer to Table 10-1.

❑ FAT systems include FAT16 and FAT32, the numbers referring to the number of bits in the file allocation table. FAT12 was used for floppy disks, now obsolete.

❑ NTFS is the preferred file system for modern Windows systems because it works with larger hard drives, is more stable, and offers file and folder security and compression that is not available in the FAT file systems.

❑ exFAT is a file system designed for use on small solid-state storage devices such as USB flash drives and SSD cards.

❑ Resilient File System (ReFS) is a new file system expected to replace the NTFS file system on Window Server.

❑ The native file system on a Mac is HFS+; the native file system on Linux is ext3 or ext4.

❑ CDFS is an older file system used on optical disks; it has been largely replaced by UDF.

❑ NFS is a distributed file system protocol developed by Sun Microsystems that allows a client computer to access network storage locations.

File Management

❑ Windows supports the standard file attributes of read-only, archive, system, and hidden. It also supports additional file attributes in NTFS, including index, compress, and encrypt.

❑ Filenames can be up to 255 characters, including spaces.

❑ The four basic on/off flags (attributes) a file has are read-only, system, hidden, and archive. In addition, a file may have other attributes specific to the OS, such as NTFS attributes in Windows.

❑ Windows determines a file's type by looking at its extension. Refer to Table 10-2 for some common extensions.

❑ System files and folders are hidden by default. They mostly reside in the C:\Windows folder and in the root directory of the system volume.

❑ Program files are used by individual applications. They are mostly stored in C:\ Program Files and C:\Program Files (x86).

❑ The Users folder has subfolders for each user. Within a user's folder are subfolders for Documents, Music, Downloads, and other categories of personal files.

❑ A user's personal folder contains a hidden folder called AppData that holds user-specific settings for applications.

❑ You can manage files from a command-line interface within Windows using basic commands like dir, copy, del, rename, xcopy, cd, rd, and md.

❑ Use chkdsk to check a disk for errors at the command prompt. Use format to format a disk from the command prompt. Use sfc to check system files.

❑ macOS and Linux have the same underlying structure so they have the same command-line commands and syntax. To open a Terminal window in Linux, press CTRL-ALT-T. In macOS, choose Launchpad | Other | Terminal.

❑ You should know how to use the vi editor to create and save text files from the Linux command prompt.

❑ The important Linux commands you need to know for the 220-902 exam are ls, cd, mv, rm, cp, pwd, mkdir, rmdir, find, grep, and dd.

❑ Windows and Linux both have a shutdown command that enables you to shut down the PC from a command prompt, but they have different syntax.

SELF TEST

The following questions will help you measure your understanding of the material presented in this chapter. Read all of the choices carefully, because there might be more than one correct answer. Choose all correct answers for each question.

Disk Management

1. Which disk storage type should you use on a typical Windows desktop PC?
   A. Dynamic
   B. Basic
   C. Primary
   D. Extended

2. Which of the following describes a partition from which Windows can boot?
   A. Primary extended
   B. Active extended
   C. Primary active
   D. Simple extended

3. Which GUI tool should you use to create a partition on a new drive after installing Windows?
   A. My Computer
   B. Device Manager
   C. Disk Defragmenter
   D. Disk Management

4. How many logical drives are on a primary partition?
   A. 1
   B. 2
   C. 3
   D. Up to 24

5. What is the maximum number of volumes allowed on a dynamic disk?
   A. One.
   B. Two.
   C. Three.
   D. There is no limit.

6. If you want to create a striped or spanned volume, what type of disk must you have?
   A. Basic
   B. Dynamic
   C. Mirrored
   D. RAID 5

File Systems

7. Which file system supports file and folder security?
   A. FAT12
   B. NTFS
   C. FAT16
   D. FAT32

8. Which file system supports file compression and encryption?
   A. FAT32
   B. FAT12
   C. FAT16
   D. NTFS

9. Which feature of NTFS makes file searches faster?
   A. Compression
   B. Encryption
   C. Indexing
   D. MFT

10. What file system feature determines the number of addressable locations on a volume, and therefore the maximum volume capacity?
    A. Sector size
    B. Encryption support
    C. Compression support
    D. Number of bits in the FAT or MFT

11. What is the maximum capacity for a FAT16 volume?
    A. 4 GB
    B. 64 KB
    C. 128 sectors
    D. 32 GB

File Management

12. Which of the following file attributes cannot be changed in a file's Properties dialog box?
    A. Read-only
    B. Archive
    C. System
    D. Hidden

13. Instead of a file allocation table, what does an NTFS volume have?
    A. MFT
    B. Allocation units
    C. Boot sector
    D. Cluster

14. Which of the following can you use for managing files and folders?
   A. Control Panel
   B. Notepad
   C. File Explorer
   D. Disk Management

15. What disk error-checking program can you run from the Command Prompt to analyze the disk for physical and logical errors?
   A. chkdsk
   B. vi
   C. format
   D. grep

16. What is stored in the Program Files (x86) folder on a 32-bit Windows system?
   A. 32-bit programs.
   B. 64-bit programs.
   C. All programs.
   D. No such folder exists.

17. What should you do if the AppData folder is missing from a user's personal folder?
   A. Copy it from the Public profile.
   B. Copy it from the Windows Setup DVD.
   C. Restore the AppData file from a full system backup.
   D. Enable the display of hidden items.

18. What is the purpose of opening an elevated command prompt?
   A. More full-featured interface
   B. Larger window
   C. Greater security permission
   D. Better help system

19. What is the purpose of the pwd command in Linux?
   A. Set password
   B. Show the active directory path
   C. Find a text string in a file
   D. List the contents of the active directory

20. What Windows command-line command scans and verifies the versions of protected system files?
   A. chkdsk
   B. defrag
   C. scanboot
   D. sfc

SELF TEST ANSWERS

Disk Management

1. ☑ **B.** Basic is the disk storage type you should use on a typical Windows desktop PC.
    ☒ **A** is incorrect because this disk type is more suited for a network server. **C** and **D** are incorrect because both are partition types, not a disk storage type.

2. ☑ **C.** Primary active describes a partition from which Windows can boot.
    ☒ **A** is incorrect because it describes two different partition types. **B** is incorrect because you cannot mark an extended partition as active; only a primary partition can be marked as active. **D** is incorrect because Windows cannot boot from an extended partition (and "simple extended" is not a term that is normally used).

3. ☑ **D.** Disk Management is the GUI tool you should use for creating a partition on a new hard drive after installing Windows.
    ☒ **A** is incorrect because this is not a tool for creating a partition. **B** is incorrect because this utility is for managing devices. **C** is incorrect because Disk Defragmenter is a tool for defragmenting files on a drive.

4. ☑ **A.** One, because it is the only number of logical drives that you can create on a primary partition.
    ☒ **B, C,** and **D** are all incorrect because a primary partition can contain only one logical drive.

5. ☑ **D.** There is no limit (theoretically) to the number of volumes allowed on a dynamic disk.
    ☒ **A, B,** and **C** are all incorrect because each places a limit on the number of volumes allowed.

6. ☑ **B.** A dynamic disk is required for a spanned or striped volume.
    ☒ **A** is incorrect because a basic disk does not allow spanned or striped volumes. **C** and **D** are incorrect because both are types of RAID that can be set up only on dynamic disks.

File Systems

7. ☑ **B.** NTFS is the file system that supports file and folder security.
    ☒ **A, C,** and **D** are all incorrect because none of these file systems support file and folder security.

8. ☑ **D.** NTFS supports file compression and encryption.
    ☒ **A, B,** and **C** are all incorrect because none of these file systems support compression or encryption.

9.   ☑   **C.** Indexing, an NTFS feature, makes file searches faster.
☒   **A** and **B** are incorrect because although both are NTFS features, they do not make file searches faster. **D** is incorrect because although MFT is a core component of NTFS, it does not make file searches faster.

10.   ☑   **D.** The number of bits in the FAT or MFT determines the number of addressable locations.
☒   **A** is incorrect because sector sizes never vary; they are always exactly 512 bytes. **B** and **C** are incorrect because they make no difference in capacity.

11.   ☑   **A.** With a 64-bit cluster size, a FAT16 volume can support a 4 GB volume.
☒   **B** is incorrect because 64 KB is the cluster size, not the capacity. **C** is incorrect because number of sectors is not a capacity. **D** is incorrect because 32 GB is the maximum size for a FAT32 volume.

File Management

12.   ☑   **C.** System is the file attribute you cannot change in the file's Properties dialog box.
☒   **A, B,** and **D** are all incorrect because they can all be changed in the file's Properties dialog box.

13.   ☑   **A.** MFT, the Master File Table of NTFS, is the equivalent of the file allocation table, keeping track of volume contents.
☒   **B** and **D** are incorrect because they are synonyms that refer to a group of sectors. **C** is incorrect because the boot sector is the first sector on a disk, not strictly a part of a file system.

14.   ☑   **C.** You can use File Explorer for managing files and folders in Windows 8/8.1 and Windows 10. It is called Windows Explorer in earlier Windows versions, but it's the same utility.
☒   **A** is incorrect because the Control Panel is a special folder containing applets for configuring many aspects of the Windows system. Although you can adjust hidden file and folder settings from the Folder Options applet, this is not the correct answer. **B** is incorrect because Notepad is simply a text file editor. **D** is incorrect because the Disk Management tool is used for managing disk partitions.

15.   ☑   **A.** chkdsk is the disk error-checking program that you can run from the Command Prompt to do an analysis of the disk for physical and logical errors.
☒   **B** is incorrect because this command opens a text editor at a Linux command prompt. **C** is incorrect because the format command overwrites the contents of a drive with file-system components. **D** is incorrect because the grep command in Linux searches for files based on text strings in their contents.

16.   ☑   **D.** No such folder exists on a 32-bit Windows system. That folder is present only on a 64-bit Windows system, to store 32-bit programs.
☒   **A** is incorrect because although 32-bit programs are stored in that folder on a 64-bit system, the question specifies a 32-bit system. **B** is incorrect because 64-bit programs are not present on a 32-bit system. **C** is incorrect because not all programs appear in this folder when it is present.

17.   ☑   **D.** Enabling the display of hidden items is the most likely solution. This folder is hidden by default, so it might seem to be missing.
☒   **A** is incorrect because the Public profile would not contain the right settings. **B** is incorrect because the whole point of AppData is that it contains customized settings. **C** is incorrect because AppData is hidden by default; it's probably not actually gone.

18.   ☑   **C.** Greater security permission is the purpose of opening an elevated command prompt.
☒   **A, B,** and **D** are all incorrect because there is no difference in any of those factors between a standard command prompt and an elevated command prompt.

19.   ☑   **B.** Showing the active directory path is the purpose of pwd, which stands for print working directory.
☒   **A** is incorrect because the command for setting the password is passwd, not pwd. **C** is incorrect because it describes what the grep command does. **D** is incorrect because it describes what the ls command does.

20.   ☑   **D.** The sfc command stands for System File Checker and is used to scan and verify the versions of protected system files.
☒   **A** is incorrect because chkdsk checks the entire disk for errors, not specifically the system files. **B** is incorrect because defrag defragments the volume. **C** is incorrect because scanboot is an argument you can use with sfc, not a separate command on its own.

Chapter 11

PC Hardware Troubleshooting and Maintenance

T he most common procedures you will perform as a computer technician are troubleshooting and resolving computer problems. The more familiar you are with a computer's components, the easier it will be for you to find the source of a problem and implement a solution. Build your comfort level by studying the previous chapters in this book and by gaining experience. In this chapter, you will first learn troubleshooting theory, and then you will progress to basic diagnostic procedures and troubleshooting techniques, practice isolating PC component issues, discover the appropriate troubleshooting tools, and become proactive using common preventive maintenance techniques.

CERTIFICATION OBJECTIVES

- **902: 1.4**   *Given a scenario, use appropriate Microsoft operating system features and tools*
- **902: 5.5**   *Given a scenario, explain the troubleshooting theory*

For A+ 902 exam objective 5.5, CompTIA requires that you understand the troubleshooting theory, procedures, and techniques that this section details. It also covers a single topic, Device Manager, from A+ 902 exam objective 1.4.

Preparing for Troubleshooting

Troubleshooting is the act of discovering the cause of a problem and correcting it. It sounds simple, and if you watch an experienced technician, it may appear to be. However, troubleshooting a PC requires patience, instinct, experience, and a methodical approach. In this section, we will explore a methodical approach to troubleshooting theory and techniques. You will need to acquire the experience on your own, and you will find that your experiences will hone your instincts.

Protecting Systems and Gathering Tools

When faced with a computer-related problem, resist the urge to jump right in and apply your favorite all-purpose solution. Rather, take time to do the following:

1. Make sure you understand the corporate policies and procedures relating to computer usage, and consider the larger impact of any changes you might make to a computer system. For example, if you need to take an important server offline to fix it, you ought to know what times of day the server is used the least, so you can schedule the downtime accordingly.

2. Before you make any changes to a user's computer, verify that you have a recent set of backups of the user's data. If you find there isn't one, perform backups of data (at minimum) and the entire system—providing the system is functional enough for these tasks. If backups are not available and there is no way to do a backup, inform the customer that they may lose all their data. Bad news is best served up immediately, but gently.

3. Always have a pad and pencil, tablet PC, smartphone, or other means to record your actions, findings, and outcomes. A digital camera or device with a camera built in is also handy for documenting the hardware before and after and at various stages of disassembly. Recording your actions will be critical to the documentation you create at the end of the entire process.

4. Assemble troubleshooting tools—both hardware and software tools. Check out the hardware toolkit described in Chapter 3. Many software troubleshooting tools are built into Windows, and we will describe some in this chapter, and more in Chapter 12 where we list important software tools.

5. Apply the troubleshooting theory, described next.

Troubleshooting Theory

Experienced IT professionals find that six procedures, taken in order, are important for solving most problems and for documenting the problems and solutions for future reference and training. CompTIA A+ 902 exam objective 5.5 lists the following procedures, and we describe each in more detail in the following paragraphs.

1. Identify the problem.
2. Establish a theory of probable cause (question the obvious).
3. Test the theory to determine the cause.
4. Establish a plan of action to resolve the problem, and then implement the solution.
5. Verify full system functionality and, if applicable, implement preventative measures.
6. Document findings, actions, and outcomes.

Identify the Problem

Clearly identify the problem. Always gather as much information as you can about the computer and its peripherals, applications, operating system, and history. Do this even when the solution seems obvious.

Examine the Environment   Ideally, you will be able to go onsite and see the computer "patient" in its working environment so you can gather information from your own observations. Once onsite, you may notice a situation that contributed to the problem or could cause other problems. If you cannot go onsite, you may be able to diagnose and correct software problems remotely, using Remote Assistance or Remote Desktop, methods you will explore in Chapter 12. Otherwise, you must depend solely on the user's observations. Whether onsite or remote, you are looking for the cause of the problem, which is often a result of some change, either in the environment or to the computer directly.

When troubleshooting a system that is not functioning properly, make it a practice to always perform a visual inspection of all cables and connectors, making sure all connections are proper before you invest any time in troubleshooting.

Question the User: What Has Happened?   The best source for learning what happened leading up to a problem is the person who was using the computer when the problem occurred. Your first question to the user should be, "What happened?" This question will prompt the user to tell you about the problem—for example, "The printer will not work." Ask for a specific description of the events leading up to the failure and the symptoms the user experienced.

"Do other devices work?" This question will help you isolate the problem. If one or more other devices also do not work, you know you are dealing with a more serious, device-independent problem.

Ask about a problem device's history. "Did this device ever work?" If the user tells you that it is a newly installed device, you have a very different task ahead of you than if you learn that it has worked fine until just now. The former indicates a flawed installation, whereas the latter points to a possible failure of the device itself.

If the user mentions an error message, ask for as much detail about the error message as possible. If the user cannot remember, try to re-create the problem. Ask if this error message is new or old and if the computer's behavior changed after the error. For example, the computer might issue a warning that simply informs the user of some condition. If the error code points to a device, such as an optical drive, ask device-related questions.

The Event logs in Windows save many error messages, so if the user cannot remember the error messages, check the Event logs. Learn more about the Windows Event logs in Chapter 12.

Sometimes customers are reluctant to give you all the details of the problem because they fear being embarrassed or held responsible. Treat the customer in a respectful manner that encourages trust and openness about what may have occurred. In Chapter 1, you learned how important good communication skills are and how to apply them every day.

Question the User: What Has Changed?   You should also find out about any recent changes to the computer or the surroundings. Ask if a new component or application was recently installed. If so, ask if the computer has worked at all since then. The answer to this question could lead you to important information about application or device conflicts. For example, if the user tells you the audio has not worked since a particular game was loaded, you can surmise that the two events—the loading of the new game and the audio failure— are related. When troubleshooting, remove the software or any other upgrades installed shortly before the problem occurred.

Establish a Theory of Probable Cause

When you have determined the symptoms of a problem, try to replicate the problem and begin an analysis from which you will develop your theory of probable cause. Question the obvious. That is, if the user says the printer does not work, have him send another print job to the printer. Watch closely as he performs the task. Take note of any error messages or unusual computer activity that he may not have noticed. Observation will also give you a chance to see the process from beginning to end. Looking over the user's shoulder (so to speak) gives you a different perspective, and you may see a mistake, such as an incorrect printer selection or the absence of an entry in the Number of Copies to Print field, that caused the problem.

exam

ⓦ **a t c h**   CompTIA A+ 902 exam objective 5.5 explicitly states "question the obvious." Be prepared for scenario-based questions in which the answer may not be exactly "question the obvious," but a choice that could be an example of doing that, as described here.

Vendor Documentation   As you work to pinpoint the source of the problem, check out any vendor documentation for the software or hardware associated with the problem. This may be in the form of hard copy or information posted on the vendor's website. For example, you might discover from the user forums on the website that there is a known incompatibility between a certain application and a certain brand of display adapter that can be resolved with a driver update. (That example is actually pretty common. Out-of-date display drivers can cause many problems that are not obviously display related.)

Hardware or Software   From your observations and the information you gather from the user, try to pinpoint the cause of the problem. It may be obvious that a device failed if the device itself will not power up. If the source of the problem is not yet apparent, however, you need to narrow down the search even further by determining whether the problem is hardware or software related. We consider a hardware problem to include the device as well as its device drivers and configuration. Software problems include applications, operating systems, and utilities.

One of the quickest ways to determine if hardware or software is at fault is to use Windows *Device Manager*, a Windows GUI utility for viewing the status of devices and installing, removing, and updating devices. The list available to Device Manager, called the *hardware profile*, is a list in the registry of all devices that have been installed on Windows and not uninstalled (drivers have not been removed), even if the physical devices are removed or disabled. This gives Device Manager access to the listed hardware and their status. Device Manager will indicate any conflicting or "unknown" devices. But even if Device Manager offers no information about the problem, it does not mean it is not hardware related; it only means Windows has not recognized it. Exercise 11-1 shows you how to open Device Manager and look for problem devices, an important task when troubleshooting hardware.

EXERCISE 11-1

Troubleshooting with Device Manager

1. Open the Run dialog box (WINDOWS KEY-R), enter **devmgmt.msc**, and click OK. That works in any Windows version; if you are running Windows 8.1 or newer, you can alternatively right-click the Start button and click Device Manager.

2. In the Device Manager window, you will see the devices on your computer organized under types of hardware, such as Computer, Disk Drives, Display Adapters, DVD/CD-ROM Drives, and Human Interface Devices, as Figure 11-1 shows.

3. If Windows detects a problem with a device, it expands the device type to show the devices. In the case of a device with a configuration problem, you will see an exclamation mark on the device icon. Figure 11-1 has two such exclamation marks, on entries under the Network Adapters heading. When Windows recognizes a device but does not understand its type, it places the device under a type named Other Devices, and you will see a question mark.

4. If you see an exclamation mark or question mark on an icon, double-click the item to open its Properties dialog box. If not, double-click the Network Adapters category and then double-click any network adapter.

5. Look on the General tab in the Device status box. It will either say *This device is working properly* or display an error message or code. You can look up error messages or codes online for further troubleshooting ideas.

FIGURE 11-1

Device Manager,
showing the
types of devices
installed

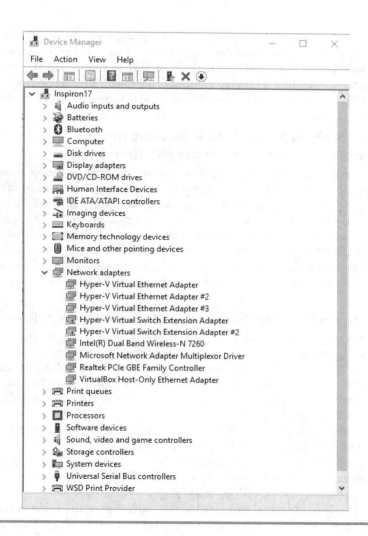

Probable Causes   From your observations and research, compile a list of probable causes, and if any of them has a simple solution, apply it first. If that does not solve the problem, then investigate the other items on your list.

Test the Theory to Determine Actual Cause

After establishing a theory of probable cause, test the theory. You may need to do this on a test system, isolated from the rest of the network, or, if that is not an option, simply test the theory on the problem system. Whatever you do, you need to find a way to test your theory in a manner that does not endanger the user's data and productivity. Does this solution extend beyond a single user's desktop or beyond your scope of responsibility? If so, you must escalate the problem to another department, such as network administration. Once you have tested the theory and found it to be successful, you can move to the next step.

Establish an Action Plan to Resolve the Problem and Implement the Solution

After successfully testing your theory of probable cause, you now move on to the planning stage. Now you need to think through both the actions you must take and the possible consequences of those actions, involving people from all areas affected by the problem and by the effects of the solution. Possible business areas to consider include accounting, billing, manufacturing, sales, and customer service, among others. You also need to check with all IT support areas that must take part in the solution. The plan should then include the steps to take, the order in which to take them, and all testing and follow-up needed. This will include steps required to minimize any possible bad effects.

Verify Full System Functionality and Implement Preventative Measures

Whether the problem and solution involve a single computer or an entire enterprise, you must always verify full system functionality. If you are dealing with a single desktop system, once you have applied the solution, restart the system and the device (if appropriate), and test to be sure everything works. If your solution seems to have negatively affected anything, take additional steps to correct the problem—you may find yourself back in the troubleshooting loop.

Once you have successfully tested a solution, have the user verify and confirm that your solution solved the problem. This verification should begin just like the user's workday begins: with the user restarting the computer and/or logging on and opening each application used in a typical day and then using all peripherals such as printers. Have the user confirm that everything is working.

This is a very important step to take, regardless of the scope of the problem and solution. Our experience has been that once you touch a problem system, even though you might solve the problem, the person in charge or individual user will associate you with the next thing that goes wrong. Then you will receive a call stating that "such and such" has not worked since you were there, even though "such and such" does not relate to any changes you made.

Therefore, once everything is working normally and both you and the client have tested for full system functionality, have them sign off on it to document the satisfactory results. If this last step is not an accepted procedure in your organization, you should suggest adopting it because it adds commitment to both sides of this transaction. You are committed to testing and confirming a successful solution, and the user is committed to acknowledging the solution worked.

Document Findings, Actions, and Outcomes

Document all findings, actions, and outcomes! Take notes as you work, and once you have resolved the problem, review the notes and add any omissions. Sit down with the client and review what you did. This is your statement to the client that you made certain changes. You should be clear that you made no other changes to the system.

These notes, whether informal or formal, such as comments entered into a help desk database, will be useful when you encounter identical or similar problems. It's a good idea to incorporate some of the lessons learned during troubleshooting into training for both end users and support personnel.

Training

Well-trained personnel are the best defense against problems. Therefore, an important troubleshooting technique is ongoing training for both end users and support personnel. The delivery methods and training materials should suit the environment, as many options are available for high-quality online training, starting with the help programs available in most operating systems and applications, user manuals, installation manuals, and Internet or intranet resources. All personnel involved should know how to access any training resources available. End users can often solve their own problems by checking out the help program or accessing an online training module, cutting down on the number of service calls and associated loss of productivity.

SCENARIO & SOLUTION

What should I do before making any changes to a computer?	Verify there is a recent set of backups; if a set does not exist, perform a backup of data and the operating system.
If I believe I know the solution, then why should I question the user before trying the solutions I know?	You should learn what happened and what has changed and gather all the information before jumping to any conclusions about the solution.
You have found a solution, applied it, and successfully tested it. What is the final step you need to take?	Document the troubleshooting activities and outcomes.

CERTIFICATION OBJECTIVE

■ *901: 4.1 Given a scenario, troubleshoot common problems related to motherboards, RAM, CPU, and power with appropriate tools*

CompTIA A+ 901 exam objective 4.1 requires that you be able to explain and interpret common symptoms and, when faced with a scenario, know how to detect problems, troubleshoot, and repair or replace computer components. This section describes both common symptoms and tools.

Troubleshooting Motherboards, RAM, CPUs, and Power

This section discusses procedures for troubleshooting common component problems, physical symptoms that can occur with various devices, power-on self-test (POST) audio and text error codes, and, for certain components, specific symptoms and solutions. For each component problem, we describe scenarios, probable causes, and solutions.

Procedures

When troubleshooting PC components, first do all that you can without opening the PC. If you do not find the source of the problem and a potential solution through nonintrusive methods, then you will have to open the PC. Follow these steps, which will take you from the least intrusive to the most intrusive:

1. Check for proper connections (external device).
2. Check for appropriate external components.
3. Check installation: drivers, driver settings, and physical settings.
4. Check proper seating of components (internal adapter card, memory, and so on).
5. Simplify the system by removing unneeded peripherals. If the problem goes away, then you must isolate the problem peripheral.

While the traditional PC cases—towers and desktop system units—are convenient to open for adding or replacing components, the same is not true of the newer all-in-ones. These systems resemble the Apple iMacs in that all the components normally found inside a computer case are inside the display case, and opening the case in most cases voids the warranty, and is very difficult to do without causing damage. This makes it even more imperative that you make every effort to troubleshoot using the least intrusive tactics.

Even the most knowledgeable technician cannot repair some problems with computers or components. That is why it is important to pay attention to warranties on equipment.

In large organizations, warranties are managed through contracts with companies that provide the hardware and support it. In those cases, the contractor removes the failed equipment and replaces it. But if you, or your company or school, do not have such an arrangement, someone needs to be tracking the computer equipment as managed assets, and they must pay close attention to warranties—whether they are the basic warranty that comes with the item or a purchased extended warranty.

Manufacturers allow for returns of in-warranty equipment, but you need to contact the manufacturer and make arrangements, which will usually involve reporting the failure, and receiving what amounts to permission to return the equipment. This permission is a *returned materials authorization (RMA)*, which now often comes by e-mail, and you must wait to receive this before packing up and returning the item. The RMA usually has a number that must be displayed somewhere on the packaging.

General Symptoms

Inspect a computer and its peripherals for physical symptoms. Several symptoms can apply to any of several components, such as excessive heat, loud noise, odors, status light indicators, and visible damage to the device itself or cabling. When one of these symptoms occurs, take appropriate action based on the symptom and the device.

Lockups, Shutdowns, and Crash Screens

There are many possible causes of system instability problems with symptoms like system lockups, spontaneous shutdowns, and OS-specific crash screens, like the Blue Screen of Death (BSOD) in Windows. We tend to suspect software, especially device drivers, but these symptoms can and do occur after a failure of a motherboard component. We will discuss troubleshooting software-caused problems in Chapter 12. However, if you see any of these symptoms, first do basic troubleshooting of your hardware, especially the motherboard and associated components. Here are descriptions of these system instability symptoms so that you recognize them:

- **System lockups** These appear as a screen that will not change or show any response to mouse movement. In some cases, the mouse pointer still moves but shows an hourglass, or whatever symbol it normally shows when the system or an app is busy and cannot respond to input.
- **System shutdowns/unexpected shutdowns** These are just what the terms imply: the system simply shuts down—usually without any warning. You may see an error message beforehand, but not necessarily.
- **OS-specific crashes** The BSOD, more conventionally called the *stop screen*, appears when the Windows operating system detects a critical error and literally stops the system so that the error doesn't cause loss of data (or further loss of data).

All operating systems have some form of the stop screen, and the Windows stop screen displays an error message indicating what software component failed. You can use this information to troubleshoot the cause of the problem. Learn more about working with the BSOD error information in Chapter 12. On a Mac, instead of BSOD, you get the Pinwheel of Death, an endlessly spinning mouse pointer and failure to respond to keyboard or mouse input.

Excess Heat/Overheating

If a device is giving off excessive heat, smoke, a burning smell, or other odors, or if wires or cables are hot, turn it off until you can replace it or otherwise solve the problem. Later in this chapter, we will discuss power supplies and cooling systems—components related to these symptoms. Unusual noises may occur if a device has moving parts, such as a fan or printer. In these cases, a new or different noise usually means a component, such as a fan bearing, is failing. This will reduce the fan's effectiveness and cause an unusual noise.

Indicator Lights

Many devices, such as printers and network adapters, have one or more *status light indicators*—usually a *light-emitting diode (LED)*, a semiconductor resembling a tiny light bulb. These usually indicate a problem with the device by changing the color of the light, by blinking or remaining steady, or by a combination of both. Look for labels on the device itself defining the function of each light. For example, a network interface card (NIC) may have a light with a label of "ACT" for "activity," indicating the card is indeed transmitting data. A multispeed NIC might have a different colored light for each of its speeds. These same indicators are often duplicated as icons in the status area (also called the notification area) of the taskbar on the Windows desktop. The applet associated with the icon will issue alerts when a device malfunctions.

Other physical symptoms include damage to a device, such as an area of melted plastic on a case or cable, a broken cable or connector pin, or a socket device not getting the appropriate signals (often due to a loose connection). Of course, when inspection of a device or cabling shows physical damage, such as a break or the appearance of melted plastic, you need to determine the extent of the damage and the right solution for the problem, such as replacing the device or cable.

Only the Fan Works

If you can hear the power supply fan and/or a case fan, but nothing else seems to work, including the display, then power the system off, open the case, and check out all power connectors between the power supply and the motherboard, reseating all of them. Also, look for some sort of debris that could be shorting out the motherboard and remove it.

Something else that can cause the motherboard to short out is an incorrectly installed standoff—a washer-like part made of nonconductive material designed to keep the motherboard from coming in contact with the case. Yet another possible cause of this symptom is a failed CPU (although usually if the CPU doesn't work, the fan doesn't spin).

Intermittent Device Failure

If one device fails periodically, there are several causes to investigate. First, there could be an incorrect BIOS system setting or wrong device driver. Heat can cause such symptoms, in which case the device works fine until the system heats up. Because people use computers in all types of environments, we often forget that they work best in a low-to-moderate ambient temperature, around 75 degrees Fahrenheit. Of course, the internal temperature is higher than that, so the computer's own cooling system has to work harder as the environment gets hotter. If you witness intermittent device failure that coincides with a rise in ambient temperature, take steps to cool the environment and/or to augment the internal cooling system, or replace the entire system with a more rugged system designed to survive the higher temperatures.

Another possible cause of intermittent device failure could be the power supply unit providing too little or too much power or not maintaining a constant supply to the system. Test the power supply, as described later in this chapter.

Troubleshooting Motherboard Problems

A properly configured motherboard will typically perform flawlessly for several years. Things that can change that happy state include power problems, actual component failure, and incorrect changes to the system. A major motherboard failure will prevent the computer from booting properly. However, if the firmware can run a POST, it might report a problem with the motherboard. In either case, consult the motherboard manual and the manufacturer's website for solutions to the problem.

POST Audio and Visual Errors

A faulty motherboard can cause many different symptoms and can even make it appear that a different component is at fault. This is because a motherboard problem might manifest in one particular area, such as a single circuit or port, causing the failure of a single device only. For example, if the video card's expansion slot on the motherboard stops working, it will appear that the display system has a problem. In this case, you are likely to discover the motherboard as the point of failure only after checking all other components in the video system.

In Chapter 3 we briefly described the power-on self test (POST) that occurs when a PC starts up. The POST checks for the presence and status of existing components. A visual (text) error message on the screen or POST code beeps typically indicate errors found during the POST. A single beep or two quick beeps at the end of the POST normally means that it detected no errors and the system should continue booting into the operating system. If you hear any other combination of beeps, or if the system does not continue the normal startup, consult the motherboard manufacturer's documentation.

On some systems, POST text error messages appear in the upper-left corner as white characters on a black screen, and can point you in the right direction for troubleshooting an error at startup. For instance, if a firmware manufacturer uses the traditional codes 1*xx*, 2*xx*, and 3*xx* (where *xx* = a range of numbers from 00 to 99), they can indicate system board, memory, or keyboard failures, respectively. Similarly, the 17*xx* error codes may indicate a hard disk controller or hard drive problem. These are the original POST error codes. If you see numeric digits during a failed startup, check out the website of the firmware manufacturer to find a list of codes so that you can interpret them.

If you believe a motherboard component is failing but no type of error code displays, a POST card (one of the tools listed in the hardware toolkit in Chapter 3) will give you more information. Consider buying one if you support many computers with the same or similar motherboard. Install a POST card into a motherboard expansion slot, then power up the computer. A small two-character LED display will show hexadecimal codes for errors detected on startup, and the documentation that comes with the POST card will help you decipher the error codes. Then you will know what component is failing and you can make a decision about how to fix it. If it is an embedded component that is not easily replaced, such as a problem with the chipset, you may need to replace the entire motherboard. You can usually remedy a problem with an embedded video adapter or drive controller by installing a replacement into an expansion slot.

 Sometimes called PC analysis cards, POST cards come in a wide range of prices and with connectors for one or two types of expansion slots. Check out the specifications before purchasing, but an inexpensive card will usually suffice.

Physical Changes

Physical sources of motherboard problems can include jumper or switch settings, front panel connectors, back panel connectors, sockets, expansion slots, and memory slots. Because jumpers and switches are mechanical elements, they won't change unless someone has opened the system and fiddled with them. If you think someone has opened the system, double-check the jumper and switch settings and compare them with the manufacturer's documentation. If you are 100 percent sure that someone made a change that caused the present problems, determine the correct settings and then return the jumpers or switches to those settings. Jumpers are present mainly on old motherboards; newer ones use firmware settings instead to control board settings.

Another possible physical motherboard problem source is loose or improperly made connections. These could include improper insertion of adapter cards into expansion slots,

FIGURE 11-2

Distended capacitors on a motherboard, with residue on the tops indicating physical failure (Photo: https://en.wikipedia.org/wiki/Capacitor_plague#/media/File:Al-Elko-bad-caps-Wiki-07-02-17.jpg [Creative Commons license])

or of memory sticks into memory slots, or of the cables connecting onboard I/O ports to front or back panel connectors.

Distended Capacitors/Swollen Batteries

A physical inspection of the motherboard may show one or more capacitors that are distended (swollen) or have some sort of brownish residue on them. These capacitors are typically mounted on their ends, sitting perpendicular to the motherboard, as shown in Figure 11-2. Such a motherboard should be replaced, even if it is currently exhibiting no problems. Electronics experts may attempt to change out the capacitors themselves (since the motherboard is going to have to be discarded otherwise), but must nonprofessionals will choose to replace the whole motherboard.

A mobile device battery (such as the removable battery on a smartphone or tablet) can also become distended or swollen, indicating that it is failing. Do not use a mobile device if its battery appears physically abnormal; have the device serviced right away.

Firmware Problems

Older motherboards come with a small coin-size battery, such as a 3-volt lithium battery, to support the nonvolatile RAM, called CMOS RAM, where the BIOS settings are stored.

We discussed this briefly in Chapter 3. Since this battery supports the date and time tracking, the classic symptoms of a failed battery is a system that does not keep the correct time after turning it off. If that occurs, open the case and remove the battery, much as you would remove a watch battery. Then find a replacement for it that matches the voltage and designation number of the old battery. On newer motherboards, settings are stored in nonvolatile memory, so a battery is not required. Exercise 11-2 walks you through the battery replacement process.

If the system repeatedly loses track of time when turned off, you probably need to replace the battery. This is usually a simple process, requiring opening the case and exchanging the old battery for a new one.

EXERCISE 11-2

Replacing the Motherboard Battery

For this exercise you will need a desktop system with a motherboard that has a battery. Such systems are typically older, so they will have BIOS rather than UEFI firmware.

1. Enter the computer's BIOS setup program and make a backup copy of the current BIOS settings, using whatever method is available to you. You may want to take a digital picture with your camera, smartphone, or other device. Or simply write down the settings.
2. Turn off the computer and remove the cover, ensuring you carry out the proper electrostatic discharge (ESD) procedures.
3. Locate the battery on the motherboard.
4. Slide the battery out from under the retaining clip. The clip uses slight tension to hold the battery in place, so you do not need to remove the clip or bend it outward.
5. Note the battery's orientation when installed, and install the new battery the same way.
6. Restart the computer. Enter the system's setup program again and restore the BIOS settings you recorded in Step 1.

If your system will not support a new device, you may need a firmware update. Before doing this, be sure to back up the firmware settings or make note of them in some way— such as photographing each screen with a digital camera. Then, using the manufacturer's utility, install the firmware update, either from a local drive or from a source over the Internet.

How is it possible to update something that is "read-only"? The answer is that you actually can change many modern ROMs, but only by special means. Today, that is normally a special program from the manufacturer. This is why reading the documentation before updating the firmware is important. We often call upgrading firmware *flashing the BIOS*. This applies to system-level firmware, as well as to the firmware on an individual adapter.

Become familiar with the firmware setup menu screens and practice navigating through these menus, as described in Exercises 3-4 and 3-5 in Chapter 3. This means booting the system and selecting the keyboard option after the POST that lets you access system setup. The first thing you should then do is look for the help hints, usually at the bottom or in a sidebar on every screen. Then find out how you can exit from the BIOS without saving changes. Knowing this is important, because almost everyone who explores these menus gets confused about whether they have inadvertently made a change, and the best way to back out of that situation is to select Exit Without Saving, if it is available. If not, look for two exit methods. For instance, you might use the F10 function key for Save and Exit and the ESC key for Exit. Now you know how to exit without saving.

Although the exact BIOS menu organization varies by manufacturer, the main menu will have the most basic settings, such as system date and time, detected drives, and drive interfaces. An advanced menu will often have the settings for the CPU, the chipset, onboard devices, the expansion bus configuration, and overclocking, an option that boosts CPU performance. You do not need to use overclocking on computers designated for simple office tasks, but people often use it for computers requiring higher CPU performance, such as for gaming and other tasks requiring maximum performance. (Overclocking may cause the CPU to overheat, and may void the system warranty, so beware.) Other advanced BIOS settings may involve configuring the PCIe bus and Universal Serial Bus (USB) settings.

Incorrect BIOS settings can have many permutations because there are BIOS settings for a great variety of system elements, including the hard drives, the boot sequence, keyboard status, and parallel port settings. An incorrect setting will manifest as an error relating to that particular device or function, so pinpointing a specific source of a problem can be difficult. However, when you need to change or update firmware settings, enter the firmware setup program, as described in Exercise 3-4 in Chapter 3. Make the appropriate change(s), save the new setting(s), and restart the computer.

Troubleshooting RAM Problems

If you turn on the computer and it does not even complete the POST, or it does nothing at all, and you have eliminated power problems, the main memory might have a problem.

Sometimes the motherboard will emit multiple beeps at startup when memory is at fault. Check out a beep code reference online for the firmware brand you're working with, like the one at www.computerhope.com/beep.htm.

The solution to a memory problem is to remove the offending component and replace it with a new one. If the error persists, the memory might be in a damaged slot or socket on the motherboard. In this case, replace the motherboard, or the entire PC.

One important thing to keep in mind is that the computer may not report some RAM errors at all. That is, if an entire memory module does not work, the computer might just ignore it and continue to function normally without it. At startup, watch the RAM count on the screen (if firmware configuration allows this), or check the reported memory amount in the OS, to ensure the total amount available matches the capacity installed in the machine. If this amount comes up significantly short, you will probably have to replace a memory module.

Troubleshooting CPUs

In most cases, CPU problems are fatal, meaning the computer will not boot at all. These problems also closely relate to motherboard problems, such as CPU socket failure, so it can be difficult to pinpoint which component is actually at fault without having spare parts you can swap out.

If you turn on the computer and it does not complete the POST, or it does nothing at all, and you have eliminated power problems, you might discover the processor has a problem. A persistent error indicates a possible problem with the slot or socket that the processor connects to the motherboard with. In this case, you need to replace the motherboard. Check the system warranty before taking any action, because the warranty could cover motherboard failure. If you determine the problem is isolated to the CPU, then you will have to replace it, in which case you must replace it with an exact match for the motherboard, including the socket type, speed, number of cores, internal cache, power consumption, and other features. Use the motherboard documentation or information for the motherboard at the manufacturer's website to determine the exact requirements before purchasing a new CPU.

Considering today's low PC prices, if you encounter a CPU or motherboard problem on a computer not covered by a warranty, consider replacing the entire system. First, however, check to see if it is a leased computer and what the lease agreement says about component failures, service, and replacement.

A computer that has become slower can be a symptom of overheating. The CPU may have reduced its clock speed in response to overheating, a practice called *throttling*. A processor that has activated thermal throttling will run slower. Why is the computer overheating? Perhaps because of dust, blocked vents, or a failed cooling fan. Check out these possibilities and remedy any that you find.

Troubleshooting Power Supplies

Power supplies can experience either total or partial failures, resulting in inconsistent or displaced symptoms. However, to pinpoint the problem, you can check a few common symptoms of power supply failure; we discuss those symptoms here.

When the power supply fails, replace it. Never try to open or repair a power supply, because it can hold enough charge to injure you seriously, and the time spent on such a repair is more valuable than the replacement cost of a power supply.

When installing a new power supply in a PC, check the wattage and capacity, the availability and types of connectors, and the output voltage required by the computer components to ensure it will have sufficient power and the correct connections.

As suggested in Chapter 3, you can use either a multimeter or a power supply tester to make sure that a power supply is putting out the correct voltages. A multimeter requires more knowledge of electricity to use and is a more sophisticated instrument, measuring resistance, voltage, and/or current in computer components. Figure 11-3 shows a digital multimeter, with a digital display. Analog multimeters exist (with a needle that swings to show values), but they are mostly obsolete.

FIGURE 11-3

A digital multimeter (Photo: https:// commons. wikimedia.org/ wiki/File:Digital_ Multimeter_Aka .jpg [Creative Commons license])

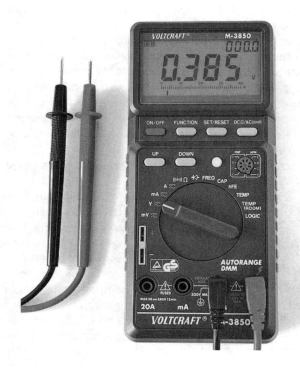

To use a multimeter, you connect two probes (red and black) to the meter, and set the meter to what you want to measure. For instance, set it to AC Volts to measure wall line voltage, DC Volts to measure the voltage coming from the power supply, or Ohms to measure resistance. Take a measurement by touching the ends of the probes to power wires in the equipment you are testing. For example, to check a yellow wire in a Molex connector coming from the power supply, you would insert the red (live) probe into one of the holes for the yellow wire, and insert the black (ground) probe into the hole for a black wire in the same connector. If the multimeter is set for DC Volts and it reports a measurement of around +12V, you know that the yellow wire is doing its job.

New technicians are sometimes intimidated by the prospect of probing live electrical connections, thinking they could be electrocuted. When checking voltages on a motherboard, though, the voltage is so low that there's no danger.

Some connectors can't be checked unless they are plugged in. For example, the P1 connector from the power supply to the motherboard must be connected to the motherboard for the power supply to operate, so you can't disconnect it and stick a probe down into one of the holes. In cases like that, you stick the probe down into the place where the wire enters the connector, from the back. This is called *back-probing* and is detailed in Exercise 11-3.

To measure resistance, you touch the probes to the circuit you want to measure. For example, to check a cable to make sure there are no broken wires, touch the red probe to a pin at one end, and touch the black probe to the corresponding pin at the other end. Consult a pin-out diagram for that cable as needed to determine which pins correspond.

To measure current, you must break the circuit so the electricity goes through the meter. Disconnect a connector, and then touch the red probe to a pin on the cable and the black probe to the corresponding pin or hole on the connector that the cable normally is plugged into.

Most meters today are auto-ranging, meaning you don't have to choose a specific range; they change ranges on their own.

For the exam, as well as for your own safety, remember that, like displays, power supplies can cause serious personal injury. Never open the case of a power supply!

A power supply tester tests voltage output from a power supply unit and is much easier to use than a multimeter. Even an inexpensive power supply tester has several types of sockets to accommodate the variety of plugs available on power supplies. Simply connect the output connectors from a power supply to the matching socket, turn on the power supply, and a set of LEDs or a liquid crystal display (LCD) display indicates whether the power supply is functioning correctly.

EXERCISE 11-3

Checking a P1 Connector

For this exercise you will need a desktop system and a multimeter. This exercise gives you plenty of experience with back-probing; by the time you've checked all the wires, you'll be confident about doing it.

1. Place the computer on its side, so the motherboard is lying flat. Remove the computer's case cover, so you can see the motherboard. Turn the computer on if it is not already on.
2. Set the multimeter to DC Volts.
3. Locate the P1 connector, the 20-pin or 24-pin connector that connects the power supply to the motherboard.
4. Carefully stick the tip of the red probe down as far as possible into the connector where a yellow wire enters the connector. If the probe tip is too wide to make contact with the bare wire, stick a steel pin (like you would use in sewing) or an open safety pin down to make contact, and then touch the probe to the pin.
5. Carefully stick the tip of the black probe down as far as possible into the connector where a black wire enters the connector.
6. Read the value shown on the multimeter. It should be +12V, plus or minus about 10 percent.
7. On another PC, do a Google Images search for "pin out P1" to locate a chart that tells the expected voltages for the various wires on the P1 connector.
8. Check each of the remaining wires on the P1 connector, and confirm that they are delivering the correct voltages. You don't have to move the black probe; just move the red probe from wire to wire.
9. Remove all probes from the connector, shut off the multimeter, and replace the computer's cover.

Symptoms Associated with Power Supply Problems

Failed or failing power supplies have many symptoms. A failed power supply is dormant, and so is the entire computer, so the cause is not hard to determine once you have eliminated the simpler causes, such as the power button being in the off position or an unplugged power cord. A failing power supply will cause symptoms in other components, leading you down the wrong troubleshooting path.

Nothing Happens When the Computer Is Turned On   A few things can cause a total lack of activity at system startup. These include a bad processor or memory, but the most likely suspect is the power supply.

First, check that the power supply connects properly to an electrical outlet. In addition, check the power selector (on the back of the computer near the power cord connection and the on/off switch) to ensure it has the right setting for your geographic region. Because you can switch many power supplies to use either 120 or 230 volts, verify that someone did not change the supply to the wrong voltage setting. North America is 110–120 VAC at 60 Hz and Europe is 220–240 VAC at 50 Hz.

If the power supply's fan stops working, you must replace the entire power supply, not just the fan.

When the power supply stops working, so does the computer's fan, which is typically the first thing you hear (along with the hard drive) when you turn on the computer. Therefore, if you do not hear the power supply fan at startup (or any fan or hard drive noise), you should suspect a power supply problem and turn off the computer immediately. Some power supplies will shut down if the fan is not working.

Be aware that the power supply fan may not work if the motherboard or CPU is dead, because the power supply requires a load (that is, power to be drawn from it) in order to operate. Therefore, don't assume that a lifeless-seeming power supply automatically means a dead power supply.

If only the power supply fan failed, then once the computer is off, try cleaning the fan from the outside of the case using an antistatic vacuum. Dust, lint, or hair can cause the fan to stop rotating. If cleaning does not resolve the problem, you must replace the entire power supply.

If the problem is not so easily isolated to the power supply fan because the system simply will not turn on, try removing all the power supply connections to internal components and turning the PC back on.

Also, check that the power cables attach properly to the motherboard and other necessary devices, including the computer's power button.

Memory Errors   A memory error can be an indication of a failing power supply because it can provide inadequate power to the RAM sticks. If on each reboot, the memory error identifies a different location in memory, then it is more likely to be a power problem than a memory error. A real memory error would identify the same memory location on each reboot.

The Computer Reboots Itself, or Some Components Sporadically Stop Working   A computer with a bad power supply may continuously reboot itself without warning. If the power supply provides power only to some devices, the computer will behave irregularly; some devices will seem to work, whereas others will work only part of the time or not at all. Check that all power plugs connect properly.

Cooling Systems

Excessive heat can be a symptom of cooling system failure. Inadequate cooling will cause components to overheat, in which case they might work sometimes but not at other times, and very commonly, an overheated computer will simply shut down or spontaneously reboot. Try cleaning the power supply fan without opening the power supply itself by vacuuming the fan vents. If this does not solve the problem, replace the power supply or consider adding another case fan, if one will fit in your computer. Many cases come with brackets to add one or more case fans.

Missing Slot Covers

Believe it or not, the removable slot covers at the back of the computer are not there solely to tidy up the appearance of the computer. They keep dust and other foreign objects out of the computer, and if you leave the slot covers off, you run the risk of allowing dust to settle on the PC's internal components, especially the empty expansion slots (which are notoriously difficult to clean). Missing slot covers can also cause the computer to overheat. The design of the computer places the devices that generate the most heat in the fan's cooling air flow. Missing slot covers mean the cooling air's path through the computer could be changed or impeded, resulting in improper cooling of the components inside.

Noisy Fan

There are more cooling fans inside a computer than the one on the power supply. Today's computers have one (slot) or two cooling fans on the CPU. There can also be one or more strategically placed cooling fans inside the case.

When a fan begins to wear out, it usually makes a whining or grinding noise. When this happens, replace the fan, unless it is inside the power supply. In that instance, replace the entire power supply.

CPU Cooling Issues

Considering the reliability of computer circuitry, you do not expect a CPU to fail, but modern CPUs generate a great deal of heat and they must be properly installed. Proper installation requires high standards for applying thermal compound and correctly inserting the CPU into the CPU socket on the motherboard and attaching a heat sink and/or a CPU fan. Systems assembled in tightly controlled facilities by experienced technicians who practice excellent quality control methods should not fail due to overheating during normal operation. Normal computer operation usually means the CPU and/or busses are not modified to operate beyond their default system settings, or in an environment with temperature and humidity beyond the manufacturer's specified operating range for the system.

e✗am
ⓌＡＴＣＨ   **Memory failures may not cause a system to appear to malfunction at all. Most modern systems will simply ignore a malfunctioning memory module** **and normal operations will continue. The user may note performance loss, however, which is a key symptom of a memory module failure.**

Adapter Cards

If you must replace or upgrade an adapter card in a motherboard, follow the steps to remove the old one in Exercise 6-8 in Chapter 6, followed by the instructions for installing a new adapter card in Exercise 6-9. If the adapter card is a video card, ensure the replacement card has the correct interface.

SCENARIO & SOLUTION

The computer does not maintain the date and time when powered on. What should I do?	Replace the motherboard's battery.
What should I do with a computer that keeps rebooting itself?	Test the power supply. You may need to replace it. Also suspect overheating issues, if the rebooting occurs after the PC has been running for 20 minutes or more.

CERTIFICATION OBJECTIVE

■ **901: 4.2**   *Given a scenario, troubleshoot hard drives and RAID arrays with appropriate tools*

This section looks at common symptoms of storage device problems, as described in 901 exam objective 4.2. It also covers tools such as screwdrivers and external enclosures, as listed in that same objective.

Other 901 exam objective 4.2 tools not covered here are discussed in other chapters: partitioning and defragmentation tools in Chapter 9, formatting in Chapter 10, and file recovery software in Chapter 12.

Troubleshooting Storage Devices

The steps you take when troubleshooting problems with storage devices vary based on the type of storage device. We will look at hard disk drives (HDDs), solid-state drives (SSDs), removable storage such as optical discs, and external storage such as USB flash drives.

Tools Required

To work on internal storage devices, your single most important tool will be a Phillips-head screwdriver. You'll need this to open the computer's case (unless it has some kind of latch or lever that opens it), and you'll need it to remove the drive from the case (unless the drive is on sliding rails that don't require screws to be removed).

When troubleshooting a drive, you might want to take it to another computer to see if it can be read there. If the other computer has an internal drive bay for it—great. But you might prefer to have a *drive enclosure* handy. A drive enclosure is basically a plastic box with drive connectors inside it. You can put an internal disk drive in there, and then connect the plastic box to a USB port on any computer, turning an internal drive into an external one. Drive enclosures are designed for hard disks, but you can make one work in a pinch for an optical drive too, if you don't close up the enclosure but just leave the drive dangling off its wires. (Not preferred, but it works for temporary use.)

Hard Disk Drives

Many things can go wrong with a hard drive, each of which can result in a number of different symptoms, so it can be difficult to determine the cause of the problem. You should replace a hard drive that begins corrupting data before all the information stored on it is lost. In Chapter 12, you will learn about using specialized utilities to correct data problems on hard drives, including corrupted and fragmented files. We discuss the most common hard drive symptoms and problems in the sections that follow.

Computer Attempts to Boot to Incorrect Device

If a computer attempts to boot from the incorrect device and will not boot from the system drive (usually drive C:), the cause could be as simple as you inadvertently pressed a key as the system was starting up and it attempted to boot from the optical drive, or it could be a more serious cause. Therefore, once this occurs, restart the system, taking care not to touch the keyboard until the system has completed the startup. We have even found that a messy desk can be the root cause, because a book, papers, or other detritus on a desk touches the keyboard as the system boots up.

If the system still fails to boot up from the correct drive, then go into the BIOS setup program and check out the boot order settings. Put the usual boot device first in the order and restart your computer.

If this still does not work, you may have a failed disk controller or hard drive, or the operating system might be corrupt. When the main hard disk doesn't appear to contain a usable operating system, the firmware skips it and tries the next-priority device, and that's probably what is happening. It might not appear to have a usable operating system because it doesn't work at all, or because the interface to which it is connected has failed, or because its content has become corrupted. Troubleshoot for the hardware problems first, reseating any existing connections and try to boot once again. Chapter 12 describes how to recover from damage to the operating system. Try one of those methods before replacing the hard drive, which will require reinstalling or restoring the OS, your applications, and your data.

Failure to Boot

If your computer fails to boot due to a hard drive or controller failure, you might receive a POST error message with an error code in the 1700 to 1799 range if your BIOS POST uses the traditional error codes. You could also get a message stating that there is no hard drive present. Typically, these errors are not fatal, and you can still boot the computer using some other bootable disk, such as a USB flash drive or optical disc.

This type of error means the computer does not recognize, or cannot communicate with, the hard drive. First, restart the computer and go into the firmware settings. In the firmware drive configuration, check that it has correctly detected the hard drive's model and capacity.

If the firmware settings are correct and the drive still will not work, or if the firmware cannot detect the hard drive, the system could have a cabling problem. Power the system off and check any connections to the disk in question; then replace any problem cables and reseat connectors. If there is another SATA connector available on the motherboard, try switching the drive's cable to that connector.

If the disk is recognized by the firmware but the OS does not start normally, check out the information in Chapter 12 on various Windows OS recovery options.

Exercise 11-4 walks through the steps in troubleshooting a nonworking hard disk drive.

EXERCISE 11-4

Troubleshooting a Drive Failure

1. Reboot the computer, start the firmware system setup program (see Exercise 3-4 if needed), and check the settings for the drive and the interface (PATA, SATA, etc.), as appropriate. If you make any changes, restart and check to see if the problem is resolved. If it is not resolved, continue to the next step.

2. Turn off power to the computer and open the case.

3. Ensure the connections are all secure. A serial ATA (SATA) drive does not require any jumper configuration, so settings should not be an issue.

4. Reboot the computer and see if the drive is now working.

If the drive is still not working, if possible, remove it from the PC and install it in a different, known-working PC to see if it will be recognized there. You can also use a drive enclosure to convert an internal hard drive to an external one that then can be connected to any PC via USB or FireWire port.

S.M.A.R.T. Error

S.M.A.R.T. (yes, it's always written like that, with the periods) stands for Self-Monitoring And Repair Tool. It's a feature built into all modern magnetic hard drives that allows them to signal the user when a failure is imminent, so the user can pull off any critical data before that happens. The operating system *should* pass along any errors from S.M.A.R.T. to you, so no news is good news. However, you can also check S.M.A.R.T. anytime for your own peace of mind.

Windows doesn't have a graphical interface for checking S.M.A.R.T. status, but you can download third-party utilities that will do it. You can also check a drive's status by entering the following commands at a command prompt:

```
wmic
diskdrive get status
exit
```

Read/Write Failure

If you see a message containing the words "read/write failure," it means that the BIOS cannot find the information it needs in the first sector of the disk, where it expects to find information for either booting up from the disk or reading data from the disk. The possible causes can include a "head crash"—a collision that can occur in a classic hard drive system between the disk drive's read/write heads and the platters containing the data. This is often unrecoverable if it occurs in a critical portion of the disk, such as in the first few sectors, but recoverable if it occurs elsewhere, depending on how extensive the damage is. If the read/write error message appears as you boot up, the error is most likely in a critical area, but if it occurs after the operating system is running and does not cause any other problem with the OS, it is in a less critical area, and may present itself as a read/write error message within the OS. If you see that, you may be able to use a disk repair tool such as CHKDSK to find and fix the error, as explained in Chapter 12.

Slow Performance

Slow performance can be a symptom that is difficult to quantify in a casual way, because what may seem like a slow hard drive may be a slow system caused by overheating or other problems. However, if you or a client perceive that the hard drive is slow and you have eliminated system performance as a symptom, then the problem is most likely with the file system. Try running a disk repair tool to find and fix storage errors that may be slowing down the system, or try using the Disk Defragmenter/Optimizer tool in Windows (the name varies depending on the OS version) to optimize file read/write performance.

Loud Clicking Noise

A loud clicking noise is a very ominous symptom for a hard drive. If you can isolate this noise to your drive and the drive is not functioning, it is probably physically damaged beyond repair. The smartest thing to do if you cannot access any data on the drive is to replace it and restore your data from the latest backup.

OS Not Found

Once firmware finishes the POST, it looks for the presence of an OS on the hard drive. If the BIOS does not find a special OS pointer in the drive's master boot record, it assumes that no OS exists and it will display a message that the OS was not found. If you have not yet installed an OS, you must do so at this point. Chapter 9 describes how to install Windows. If an OS exists but is not accessible, refer to Chapter 12 for steps to take to recover from this situation.

SATA and eSATA Interfaces

The SATA and eSATA interfaces are pretty simple. They connect a single drive to the motherboard or controller board using a single cable per drive. There's no drive configuration required, so any problems can immediately be narrowed down to one of three things: the motherboard or controller, the cable, or the drive itself. Check all connections to make sure they are snug, and swap out components as possible to isolate the source of the problem.

If you are connecting an external device, the eSATA cables must connect to an eSATA adapter card. Although it's possible to do so, you should not use SATA cables designed for internal use to connect a removable eSATA device. That's because the cables are not sturdy enough, and won't hold up well with you constantly connecting and disconnecting them. eSATA cables and their connectors are designed for thousands of connection and removal cycles, but the SATA cables and connectors are designed for only about 50 such cycles.

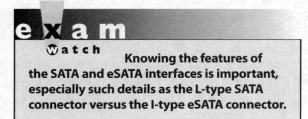

Fortunately, the cables are keyed differently, with the I-type eSATA cable plug having a simple narrow oblong connector and the L-type SATA connector having a notch in the female connector and a corresponding key on the cable plug.

RAID Arrays and Controllers

If a single drive in a RAID array fails, you will need to replace the drive with a comparable drive that will work in the array. After that, restart the computer and enter the RAID setup program, which may be part of the firmware system setup program or, as in the case of a RAID bus adapter, may be a program in the adapter's firmware that you can also enter during startup. Once in the RAID setup program, the steps you need to take depend on the level of RAID used.

If a drive in a RAID 0 array fails, you have lost the entire volume, because this type of RAID involves data written across the drives in the array, without any special algorithm for rebuilding the stripes in the array and recovering lost data should a drive fail. Therefore, once you replace a failed drive, run the RAID setup program, and re-create the array combining the drives into what appears to your operating system as a single logical drive. Then you must format the drive and restore your data from your latest backups. Chapter 10 discusses formatting disks and data backup.

If a drive in a RAID 1 array fails, the system will continue working, writing to the surviving member of the array mirror, but it will no longer mirror the data. This may result in an error message at the time of the failure and at each startup, or you might find a record of a RAID error event in one of the computer's log files. Once you determine that one of the drives in the mirror failed, do a full backup, replace the failed hard drive, and re-create the mirror using the RAID setup program.

However, if you see a message such as "RAID not found" or if the entire RAID array stops working without a clear message and you cannot access the drives at all, then you need to do some serious hardware troubleshooting, beginning with checking the connections. Then, if it is software-level Windows RAID, open Disk Manager and attempt to use it to determine if just one member of the array is failing, and if you can replace it and re-create the array.

ⓦａｔｃｈ **When a RAID array fails with a RAID-specific error, troubleshoot the RAID controller or, if it is a Windows-based RAID, open Disk Management to see the status. Also remember to troubleshoot as you would any hard drive system.**

If it is hardware-level RAID, check the manufacturer's documentation to see if there is a diagnostics procedure you can follow, along with diagnostic utilities—sometimes this is built into the controller. Or test the array in another computer, which can be problematic if the RAID is hardware-level RAID built into the first computer. Then you will need to find an identical system to test the drives in. If the hardware-level RAID is based on a separate RAID card, test the card and the drives in another computer.

When a single drive in a RAID 5 array fails, an error message will appear, but the system will continue to write to the array in a stripe across the drives. The system will not be able to create a recovery block on one drive in each stripe, however, so you will have lost your fault tolerance, and reads will be slower, as it re-creates the lost data on each read. Do a backup before replacing the failed drive, and then restart the computer and run the RAID setup utility. The system will then rebuild the array without losing the data on the drive, re-creating the data on the replaced drive by using the data on the remaining drives and the algorithm block, when necessary.

Solid-State Storage Devices

When supporting SSDs, there are specific concerns for troubleshooting and caring for these devices. One is loss of data from incorrectly removing an external SSD from a computer. We describe this later in this chapter in "External Storage." Other issues are exposure to dirt and grime, and recovering lost data from SSDs.

Dirt and Grime

Solid-state storage seems indestructible, or at least considerably more stable than conventional hard drives, which are sensitive to movement or being dropped while operating. But with external SSDs, the very portability of these devices makes them vulnerable to dirt, dust, and magnetic interference. People often carry thumb drives on lanyards around their necks, or on keychains, exposing them to a great deal of abuse—including food and beverage spills. Instruct your customers to always keep their solid-state storage devices protected. Thumb drives should always have a protected cap on when not connected to a computer. Each internal SSD has exposed connectors, and you should either install the SSD into a computer or portable device, or keep it in the plastic case it came in. Cleaning up one of these devices involves carefully removing dirt and debris from the contacts on the device's connectors.

Recovering Lost Data from SSDs

If you are helping someone who lost data on a solid-state storage device, either from deleting the data or from mishandling the device, all may not be lost. Programs are available for recovering files from solid-state devices, such as CompactFlash, Memory Stick, Secure Digital Card, and MultiMediaCard. You must be able to access the device from your computer, and many of these utilities run in Windows.

Removable Storage

Removable media, as described in Chapter 4, includes all the storage types in which you can remove the media from the drive. These include optical discs, tape, and solid-state drives. We will discuss optical and tape media here.

Optical Drives and Media

CD, DVD, and Blu-ray Disc drives and media are functionally similar, so you can use similar methods to troubleshoot them. A common problem with any of these devices is that the computer may report that it cannot read the disc. In that case, first check that you inserted the disc the correct way. If the drive is oriented horizontally, the label must be inserted face up so the drive can access the data on the underside of the disc. Next, visually inspect the disc. Scratches or smudges may prevent the computer from reading the disc. Learn how to clean optical discs later in this chapter when we explore maintenance issues in "Maintenance and Cleaning of Computer Components."

To rule out the media as the cause, try inserting a different disc in the optical drive. When you experience problems reading more than one disc in an optical drive, cleaning the lens may solve the problem. Sometimes a damaged optical disc will read in one drive but not in another, although the problem drive reads other discs just fine. If this is true, try making a copy of the disc, and then test the new disc in the original drive.

If the drive is the problem, check Device Manager to ensure the computer recognizes it. Reload the device's driver if necessary, and check its system resources. If the problem persists, check the cable connection and any jumper settings. Try the drive in another computer to confirm or rule it out as the cause of the problem.

Tape Drives

If a newly installed drive does not work, review the installation procedure and make sure you did not skip a step. Make sure that the adapter card is properly seated and that any cable connectors are fully engaged. Check for damage to cables. If the drive is a SCSI tape drive, check to see that it has the correct SCSI configuration and that it is not in conflict with other devices on the chain. If no other devices on the chain work, check for proper termination per the manufacturer's instructions. If other devices work properly, the device itself may be the problem. Most manufacturers recommend cleaning the heads at regular intervals following instructions you will find in the documentation. Even a new tape drive may need to have the heads cleaned.

Check the tape media to be sure the drive manufacturer certified it. Any other tape could damage the tape drive heads. Only use tapes with the capacity recommended by the manufacturer. Test the drive with a new tape from a different box than the tape used when the problem occurred.

External Storage

External storage devices come in every storage type. A hard drive or optical drive that has its own case and power supply and connects to a computer via an external cable is external storage. These devices can connect using USB, FireWire, eSATA, and even Ethernet (not discussed here) and still qualify as external storage. There are even external *media readers*

FIGURE 11-4

Safely Remove Hardware
12:23 PM

The Safely
Remove
Hardware icon
in the taskbar

(also called *card readers*) for reading a variety of solid-state cards. Of course, all forms of thumb drives are external storage.

Whatever the storage media, when experiencing problems with an external device, first check the data cable and connectors between the device and computer as well as the power cable, unless the device is a very low-power USB device that is powered through the USB cable. Most drives, other than SSDs, require more power than is available through USB, so check the power cable. If the cable and its connections are okay, restart the computer and see whether the situation changes. Connect the device to another computer—if it works, the problem is with the interface on the first computer.

Although newer external devices using USB or FireWire are plug and play, you should never disconnect an external storage device from a Windows computer while it is powered up unless you first close all applications that may be using the device. Then use the Safely Remove Hardware applet available as an icon in the notification area on the right of the taskbar (see Figure 11-4). A single click on this icon opens a list of removable devices. From this list, select the external drive you wish to remove, wait for the Safe to Remove Hardware message to appear, and then disconnect the device.

SCENARIO & SOLUTION

After moving a desktop PC to a new office, it fails to recognize the hard drive. What should you check first?	Look inside the case to make sure no cables have come loose from the jostling around involved in moving the PC.
When you try running your favorite game, you see an error message about a disk read error in Windows. What should you do?	Check the disk for errors with CHKDSK or some other disk utility. If the error persists, uninstall and reinstall the game.

CERTIFICATION OBJECTIVE

■ *901: 4.3*   *Given a scenario, troubleshoot common video, projector, and display issues*

CompTIA A+ 901 exam objective 4.3 lists several common symptoms of video and display problems, which we describe in this section. Problems with video adapters and displays can be frustrating because many of the symptoms leave you with no visual means to troubleshoot in the operating system, so we provide common solutions for these problems that will help you on the job as well as in preparing for the exam.

Troubleshooting Displays

A computer's video system includes, at minimum, the video adapter, one or more displays, and necessary cable and connectors. It may also include a video capture card or TV tuner, so diagnosing and resolving problems can be a bit tricky. Another difficulty in resolving video problems is that, without a working display, you cannot see the OS or BIOS settings in order to remedy the problem. Flat-panel displays (FPDs) are now the norm for desktop PCs, and all laptops have this type of display.

PC technicians typically do not repair monitors without special training beyond that required for A+ certification. Monitors are so inexpensive today that just replacing them is the best course of action if you aren't trained in how to repair one. Of course, the display is only a part of a computer's video system, and therefore not the only source of problems. Therefore, we will talk about problems tied to all video components, including the device drivers, video adapters, displays, and cables and connectors. Following are some common video system symptoms and their most likely causes and solutions.

No Image on Screen

If, during the POST, the computer sounds the audio error code for a video problem and the display remains blank, the video adapter may not connect to a display or the adapter may be damaged. First, check the connection between the display and the video adapter. Next, check the video card function. If the video adapter is not a motherboard-integrated adapter, and if you have a spare computer, install the adapter in another computer to determine whether it is functioning. If it does not work in another computer, install a new adapter into the problem computer.

If the video adapter is integrated into the motherboard—a common configuration today—check the motherboard documentation for how to disable it. You might be able to disable it in firmware setup, for example. Then, install a replacement video adapter card. If you cannot get the new adapter to work, you may need to replace the motherboard or the computer system itself, if it isn't cost effective to replace the motherboard.

The Computer Goes into Low-Resolution VGA Mode

If a display goes into a low-resolution Video Graphics Array (VGA) mode (640 × 480 or 600 × 800), you'll know right away because images and icons will be extra-large, and colors may appear dithered or washed out (because there are fewer colors to choose from than usual). First determine if the PC is in Safe Mode, which is pretty hard to miss, since the words

"Safe Mode" are displayed right on the screen in the corners. If it is in Safe Mode, and if you did not purposely put it into Safe Mode, then flip forward to Chapter 12 to learn how to solve problems in Safe Mode.

If the display is in low resolution but not in Safe Mode, determine what has changed. Go back to questioning all that happened. Perhaps the user actually made display setting changes that put the video into low resolution. If that is the case, use the Control Panel to change the screen resolution. Perhaps Windows updated and is now not compatible with the display driver.

In Windows Vista or Windows 7, right-click the desktop and select Personalize to open the Personalization applet in the Control Panel. Then select Display from the left pane, and in the Display applet select Adjust Resolution at the top of the left pane. This opens the Screen Resolution page of the Control Panel, where you can make changes. We showed the Screen Resolution page in Chapter 5 in Figure 5-17. In Windows 8/8.1 or 10, right-click the desktop and click Display Settings. Then click Advanced Display Settings, and use the Resolution drop-down list to make a change.

Another cause for the symptom of low resolution is a corrupted or incorrect video driver. If the driver was recently updated, there may be a problem with the update. First make sure you have tried to change to a higher resolution. If that doesn't work, then troubleshoot for a bad driver update. Whenever Windows updates a device driver, it saves a copy of the previous version of the device driver. To check if this is a possible cause, open the Properties dialog box of the display adapter, as shown in Figure 11-5. You can access this dialog box by

FIGURE 11-5

If the Roll Back Driver button is active, the driver was updated.

opening Device Manager (as in Exercise 11-1), expanding the Display Adapters section, and double-clicking the display adapter. Click the Driver tab to see driver details. In Figure 11-5, the Roll Back Driver button is grayed out, indicating that the driver has not been updated. If this button is active and you are troubleshooting a video problem, click it to remove the updated video driver, restart the computer, and see if the video returns to normal. You may need to go in and adjust the resolution settings.

Blank Screen at Startup

If the display shows no image at all at startup and the computer does not issue a beep code, check the video system components. Start with the display's connection to the power supply and ensure the display is on. Check the data cable and verify that none of the pins on the connector are bent; straighten them if necessary. Also, ensure the brightness is set at an adequate level.

You can determine if the display itself is at fault by swapping it with a known-good one. If the new display works in the system, you can assume the original display is the problem. Again, because display costs have decreased so much in the last few years, it is less expensive to simply replace the display with a new one than to have a technician professionally repair it. It seems counterintuitive, and you still have to dispose of the old display appropriately, but that's today's reality. Chapter 1 describes proper disposal of PCs and their components.

If a problem continues after you have eliminated the display as a cause, and if the video adapter is a bus card, check for proper seating of the video card in the expansion slot. Some video cards do not seat easily, so press the card firmly (but not too hard), and listen for an audible click to tell you the card seats properly.

Screen Suddenly Shuts Down

If the screen seems to be functioning normally and then suddenly shuts down, the first thing you should do is move the mouse or press a key on the keyboard. This will reactivate the system if the screen is blank because of a screen saver or a power mode setting that causes it to go blank after a specified period. For any other component, we would have you check the connections first, but it takes so little effort to move the mouse or press a key, that it is the best first step in this case.

If moving the mouse or pressing a key does not solve the problem, the PC may have suddenly shut itself off due to power management settings. Windows may be set to put itself into Sleep or Hibernate mode automatically after a certain triggering event occurs, such as being idle for a certain amount of time or, in the case of a notebook PC, reaching a critical threshold in remaining battery charge. If the PC has a battery, make sure the PC is running on AC power at the moment.

A sudden black screen can also mean that the monitor has overheated—perhaps due to a very hot environment. This is more common with older CRT monitors than with flat-panel displays, which use less power. Do whatever you can to lower the temperature in the room where the computer resides.

If the ambient temperature is reasonable (around 75 degrees Fahrenheit), then troubleshoot for a problem with either the display or the video adapter. Switch out the display and see if the same problem occurs on a different display. If it does, then the video adapter is the source of the problem. If switching the display solves the problem, then the original display is damaged or defective and you should replace it, since displays are not user serviceable.

Screen Artifacts

Screen artifacts are tiny, pixel-size spots that randomly appear and disappear on the display screen. You can tell they are not physical, permanent spots because they come and go. Determine the software in use at the time, because the video adapter overheating can cause this symptom—in particular, the graphics processing unit (GPU) overheats when using software that is very video graphics intensive, such as photo-editing software. Test it by closing any photo-editing or other graphics-intensive software. If the artifacts disappear, then find a way to supplement the system's cooling system and/or replace the GPU or the entire video adapter with one designed for better cooling.

Burn-In

Burn-in is permanent discoloration of certain areas on a screen, as a result of the screen displaying the same image for a very long time. You sometimes see this on old video arcade games, where the opening screen of the game can still be faintly seen as a ghost image even after the unit is turned off. Burn-in happens on phosphor-based displays (such as CRTs and plasma displays).

There isn't anything you can do to fix burn-in; it's permanent damage. However, you can prevent burn-in by not allowing the same image to display on the monitor for very long at a time. Screen savers—moving pictures that appear on a monitor when the computer is idle— were invented for this purpose. Set a display to either show a screen saver or turn off entirely after a certain period of idle time.

Fuzzy Display on FPD

A FPD looks good only at its maximum, native resolution. If the display doesn't appear crisp and clear, the first thing to check is whether the display resolution has been set for a lower setting than the maximum. Exercise 11-5 explains how to check and change this setting and, while you're at it, how to optimize the color depth and refresh rate settings too. (Refresh rate is covered in the next section.)

EXERCISE 11-5

Optimizing Screen Resolution, Color Depth, and Refresh Rate

For this exercise you will need Windows 7 or 8.1. In this exercise you will set the screen resolution, color depth, and refresh rate.

1. Ensure that the display is using the highest recommended resolution.
   a. Right-click the desktop and click Screen Resolution.
   b. Check the Resolution setting and choose a higher setting if one is available.
2. Ensure that the display is using the highest color mode.
   a. Click Advanced Settings.
   b. Click the Monitor tab.
   c. Check the Colors setting and choose a higher setting if one is available.
3. Ensure that the screen is using a high enough refresh rate.
   - On an FPD you might not have a choice; it may be set to 60 Hertz and that's that.
   - On a CRT:
     - If Windows correctly identifies your monitor model, set the refresh rate to the highest setting. (Windows will know what that setting is.)
     - If Windows does not correctly identify your monitor, set the fresh rate to a moderate setting such as 90 Hertz. (You shouldn't set it for the highest setting if the monitor isn't correctly identified, because the monitor might not be able to support that setting.)
4. Click OK, and then OK again to close all open dialog boxes. If you are asked to confirm the new setting(s), click Yes or OK to respond to the prompts as needed.

Flickering Image

A flickering image on a display has causes that depend on whether the display is a CRT or an FPD.

Flickering on a CRT

A flickering CRT display may be a symptom of a faulty one. But before you jump to that conclusion, check to see if there is a motor or a fluorescent light very close to the display causing electromagnetic interference (EMI). Workers often have fluorescent lights in their office cubicles, and many add small fans to cool their workspace. Either of these can cause flickering, which goes away as soon as you remove or turn off the motor or fluorescent light.

If possible, look on the other side of the wall partition, where you might find a source of EMI, such as an electrical panel. If you cannot remove the source from the display, move the display away from the source.

A too-low refresh rate setting can also cause the display to flicker. See Exercise 11-5 to learn how to adjust the refresh rate in Windows.

The standard refresh rate for CRT displays is 75 Hz. CRTs have much less noticeable flickering at higher refresh rates, such as 90 Hz or higher. However, setting the OS to force a higher refresh rate than the CRT is capable of can result in a darkish, distorted display image, and if run that way for long, it can cause damage to the CRT.

Flickering on an FPD

A flickering FPD display is a sign of a failing component within the display—either the backlight or the inverter. Both are reasons to replace the display, but before you go to that expense, perform a small experiment. Test a known-good display on the computer. If the test display has the same problem, the video adapter is the cause—if the test display works just fine, then replace the flickering display. Only open an FPD display if you were trained on how to do it, because there is a serious risk of electrical shock if you do. The inverter supplies alternating current (AC) power at a high voltage, and to make it worse, an inverter may still retain a charge after you remove power—whether unplugging the power cord or, in the case of a laptop, both unplugging the power cord and removing the battery.

Screen Image Is Dim

Something as simple as a maladjusted brightness control on the display itself can cause a dim screen image. Most displays have buttons on the case in addition to the power button. Pressing one of these opens a hardware-level menu for adjusting the display. One of the many options on the menu is brightness. Related to this are the special keys on a laptop that control brightness on the display. Therefore, if your FPD on your desktop or laptop seems too dim, check these controls. And while you are at it, also use the display's controls to adjust contrast, which can also contribute to a perception that the display is dim.

On a notebook computer, the most common cause of a dim screen is that the computer is running on battery power and the OS's power management settings have been configured to dim the screen to save battery life.

A more serious case of a dim display is a bad inverter that simply isn't providing enough power to the display's light source. Once again, this may be justification for replacing the display. Recall the cautions in the previous section concerning attempting to open and repair an FPD.

Dead and Stuck Pixels

Flat-panel display LCD screens, described in Chapter 5, have special pixilation problems related to the LCD or related technology. These screens have three transistors per pixel, one transistor each for red, green, and blue, called subpixels. The transistors turn on and off to create a combination of colors. When a transistor turns off permanently (not by design, but through failure), it shows as a dark spot on the screen called a *dead pixel*. Another, nearly opposite problem is a *lit pixel* (also called a *stuck pixel*). This occurs when a transistor is permanently turned on, causing the pixel to constantly show as red, green, or blue. When pixels contiguous to each other are all in this lit-pixel state, they show as the color derived from their combination.

 Before you decide you have a defective FPD, be sure to wipe it clean with a soft, antistatic cloth, very slightly dampened with mild nonammonia glass cleaner.

You may have bad or lit pixels on your FPD without noticing it because the dead pixels are not visible when displaying an image with dark colors in the defective area, and lit pixels may not show when displaying an image showing the colors that result from the dark pixels. A few defective pixels are normal; it is nearly impossible to find an FPD without some. It only becomes a problem if many bad pixels are located together and cause the image to be distorted or unreadable. To test for dead or lit pixels, you need to configure the desktop with a plain white background, close all windows, and configure the taskbar so it hides. This will give you a completely empty, white screen. Now examine the screen, looking for nonwhite areas. These may appear as the tiniest dot, about the size of a mark made by a fine-point pen on paper. Black dots indicate dead pixels, whereas any other color indicates a lit pixel. You will need to determine if the number you find is acceptable and what, if any, actions you will take.

Image Distortion or Discoloration

Improper display resolution or a driver issue can cause a distorted image. However, first check the display cable for damage or a bad connection. Check the manual settings on the display itself and reset it to the original settings (a common option). If this still doesn't resolve the problem, check the display resolution and refresh rate. If both appear to be at the recommended settings, check the manufacturer's website for a driver update. If an update is available, install and test the display with the update.

With CRT monitors, a few other possibilities exist. A magnet close to the edge of the monitor glass can cause distortion (for example, putting a refrigerator magnet on the side of the monitor), and a too-high refresh rate setting can darken and distort an image. See Exercise 11-5 to learn how to change the refresh rate on a CRT.

If the on-screen image doesn't appear to be a rectangle (for example, if one or both of the sides are bowed in or out, or the whole screen image is trapezoidal), the *screen geometry* may need adjusted. The monitor's built-in controls may be able to make a correction. Use the buttons on the front of the monitor to access a menu system, and then look for options that contain the word *shape* or *geometry*.

Projector Issues

In some ways, a digital projector is a lot like any other monitor. It connects to one of the computer's monitor ports, like VGA or DVI. It has a maximum resolution at which it can display. It is subject to various types of image problems, such as fuzziness and dimness. The solutions for its problems are often different from the solutions for the same problems on an FPD or CRT, however. Table 11-1 lists some of the most common problems with digital projectors and some possible solutions.

TABLE 11-1 Common Projector Problems and Possible Solutions

Problem	Possible Solution
Nothing appears on the projection screen.	Make sure the projector is powered on and connected to the PC. Make sure you have removed the lens cap. Make sure the projector's lamp is installed properly and not burnt out.
The projector's startup screen displays briefly but not the computer image.	Make sure the connection is snug between the PC and the projector, and that the cable is good. On a notebook PC, make sure the externally accessible monitor port is enabled. There may be an FN keyboard shortcut for this.
Image is too dim.	Adjust the projector's brightness level. If the brightness level is already at maximum, replace the lamp (it may be failing) or move the projector closer to the screen so the image is smaller and more compact (which will also make it brighter).
Screen is truncated.	Make sure the display resolution in Windows is not set for a higher resolution than the projector can handle.
Image isn't centered on the display screen.	Reposition the projector. If the projector has horizontal or vertical position controls, adjust these.
Image is fuzzy.	Adjust the focus on the projector (usually a ring around the lens that you can turn). Move the projector toward or away from the projection screen.
Image is backward.	Check to make sure the projector is not operating in Rear Projection mode.
Image is upside down.	Check to make sure the projector is not operating in Ceiling mode.

Troubleshooting Keyboards and Pointing Devices

A keyboard and a pointing device such as a mouse or trackball are necessities when it comes to navigating a graphical operating system like Windows. The following sections discuss some common issues with them.

Common Keyboard Issues

Compared to the rest of a computer, a keyboard is pretty simple and low-tech. Most of its problems are mechanical in nature: a key is stuck down, for example, or a key doesn't respond when you press it. Table 11-2 lists come common keyboard problems and solutions. Most apply both to desktop and mobile computers that have hardware keyboards.

TABLE 11-2   Common Keyboard Issues and Possible Solutions

Problem	Possible Solution
The keyboard is not responding at all to keypresses.	Check that the keyboard is snugly plugged into the PC (if corded), or that the USB receiver is connected to the PC and the keyboard's batteries are fresh (if cordless).
There is a Keyboard Stuck error message at startup.	Make sure nothing is sitting on top of the keyboard that might be holding one of the keys down.
Certain keys don't respond.	There is probably something lodged under the key that isn't working. Try turning the keyboard upside down and shaking it to dislodge any debris that's stuck in there. Try blowing compressed air under the keys. Removing a key to troubleshoot underneath it is a last resort, because both removing it and putting it back carry a risk of damaging the contacts.
	If it's a laptop, and multiple keys aren't responding, try this: power down, unplug AC power, and remove the battery. Then press and hold the Power button for at least 30 seconds. Strangely enough, this sometimes corrects software-related keyboard issues.
Character on screen does not match key pressed.	Restart Windows. If that doesn't solve the problem, turn the keyboard upside down and shake it to dislodge any debris. If that doesn't work, there may be a problem with the keyboard driver in Windows (unlikely) or you may need to replace the keyboard (likely).
Spilled liquid on the keyboard.	Unplug the keyboard immediately from the computer to avoid short-circuiting the keyboard. Turn the keyboard upside down immediately to allow liquid to drain out.
	If the liquid did not contain sugar (plain water, diet drinks), let the keyboard air dry for 72 hours and then try it again; it will probably work.
	If the liquid contained sugar, wash the keyboard in a dishwasher, in the top rack, on the shortest, gentlest cycle possible, without heated drying. Let it air-dry for 72 hours more, and then try it again.

| TABLE 11-3 | Common Mouse Issues and Possible Solutions |

Problem	Possible Solution
The pointer moves in only one direction, or only sporadically; pointer hesitates or stutters when moved.	Clean the device. If it's an old ball-style mechanical mouse, take the ball out and clean the chamber where it was. If it's an optical mouse, wipe any debris from the sensor(s).
The pointer bounces around the screen erratically, so badly that so you can barely use the mouse.	Reboot. If that doesn't help, update the display driver. This is usually a problem with the display driver, not with the mouse or its driver.
The pointer doesn't respond to the device at all.	Check that the device is snugly connected to the PC (either cord or USB receiver). Confirm that the device's On/Off switch is set to On (if it has one). If the device has a battery, check that it is fresh. Make sure a driver is installed for the device. In Windows, look in Device Manager (see Exercise 11-1) to make sure Windows sees the device.
The pointer moves too slowly or to quickly for your preference.	Adjust mouse settings via the operating system.
Mouse pointer "drifts" or moves on its own on a laptop. This is sometimes called a "ghost cursor."	If your laptop has a pointing stick, disable it in firmware setup, or open up the laptop and disconnect the cable for the pointing stick.

Pointing Device Issues

Pointing devices such as mice, trackballs, and touchpads should respond accurately and immediately by moving the pointer on screen. When that doesn't happen, user frustration goes through the roof. Table 11-3 provides some troubleshooting help for pointing devices.

Troubleshooting USB and FireWire Ports and Peripherals

Have you noticed that many formerly popular connector types have virtually disappeared from new computers? USB has replaced them. USB has been least troublesome interface of any we have worked, but occasionally you may encounter problems even with these devices.

Table 11-4 provides some ideas for troubleshooting devices that connect to USB and FireWire ports. IEEE 1394/FireWire ports and connections are included here because they have the same kinds of problems and solutions as USB.

TABLE 11-4	Common USB and FireWire Issues and Possible Solutions
Problem	**Possible Solution**
The OS doesn't detect the device.	Disconnect and reconnect the device.
	Try the device in a different port.
	Make sure the port is of adequate speed (USB 2.0, USB 3.0) for the device's requirements.
	Try the device on a different PC.
The OS detects the device but reports a problem with it, and the device doesn't work.	Check the documentation to see whether a special device driver may be required to be installed.
	Check that the device is certified to work with your OS version.
	Try all the solutions for "OS doesn't detect the device."
	The device may be defective.
An error message reports that the device requires a higher standard than the port supports.	Plug the device into a higher-level port if one is available (USB 2.0 or 3.0). Some PCs have ports of different standards; others do not.
An error message reports that the power to the device is inadequate.	Plug the device into a different port if one is available.
	Plug the device directly into the PC, not into an unpowered hub or extender.
	Check the power draw on the hub being used (see Exercise 11-6) if the device is not directly connected to the PC.
A USB printer or multifunction device is missing some of its features or isn't working properly.	Disconnect the printer, and uninstall its driver in Device Manager. In the Control Panel, remove any applications related to the printer. Then reboot the computer and rerun the setup program for the printer, and connect the printer to the PC only when prompted by the setup program to do so.

EXERCISE 11-6

Checking USB Hub Power Usage

For this exercise, use a Windows 7, 8/8.1, or 10 system with at least one USB device connected. If you have an external USB hub, connect that to the PC for this exercise, but it's okay if you don't.

1. Open Device Manager (see Exercise 11-1) and double-click the Universal Serial Bus Controllers category.
2. Double-click one of the USB Root Hub or Generic USB Hub entries. A Properties dialog box opens.

3. Click the Power tab and read the total power available in the Hub Information section.

4. Look in the Attached Devices section to see which devices are connected to that hub and what power they require. As long as the required amount of power is less than the amount supplied by the hub, power to the devices should not be an issue.

5. Close the Properties dialog box and Device Manager.

Using a Loopback Plug

A *loopback plug* is a plug that connects to an external port (such as an Ethernet or USB port) for testing purposes. It allows the port to send out a signal, and then the plug "loops back" the signal to be incoming data for that port. Without any other device, you can thusly check a port's ability to both send and receive data. Loopback plugs are generally used in conjunction with port testing software; by themselves they aren't much good. PassMark Software is one popular brand of both the testing software and the plug hardware.

Preventive Maintenance Techniques

The old adage "an ounce of prevention is worth a pound of cure" applies to computers as much as it does to anything else. Begin by providing each computer and all peripherals with a well-ventilated location. Then take time to schedule and perform preventive maintenance on the PCs for which you are responsible. This includes regular visual and aural inspections, being aware of temperature fluctuations, and component cleaning.

Visual and Aural Inspection

Frequent visual inspections will alert you to problems with cables and connections. This is true of your own personal computer as well as other people's computers. Make yourself consciously look at a computer for connection problems and environmental problems. Things change. You may discover that you have inadvertently piled papers on top of a powered USB hub in a corner of your desk, and it is getting hot. You may find that a computer or peripheral moved, which stretched the data cable or power cables to the point of nearly coming out of the sockets.

An aural inspection involves listening for a noisy fan or hard drive. A squealing fan or hard drive may be a sign of a pending problem. Correct it before you lose the fan or hard drive. Clean and/or replace the fan. Immediately back up a hard drive that makes an unusual noise, and take steps to replace it.

Managing Environmental Temperature

Some components within a PC are thermally sensitive. These components should only operate within the recommended operating environment, as stated previously in this chapter.

Thermally sensitive devices include motherboards, CPUs, adapter cards, memory, and printers. They operate best in cool environments; in hot environments, they may overheat.

Transporting a PC or other thermally sensitive device requires being aware of the environment. For instance, if you live in a cold climate and bring a new PC home when it is 20 degrees Fahrenheit below zero, be sure to let it acclimate before plugging it in and turning it on. If the PC feels cold to the touch when you unpack it, this acclimation time should be extended to several hours, because, as it warms up, some condensation will occur on internal components, and the PC needs time to dry out!

Cleaning Computer Components

Computer components will last longer and function better with some basic and regular maintenance and cleaning. For example, by regularly cleaning the fans in the power supply and case, you can ensure they properly cool the computer's internal components, preventing system slowdown and potential damage to components.

Cleaning Products

A variety of cleaning products are available for PCs. The following list includes some of the most common:

- Disposable moistened cleaning wipes
- Canned compressed air
- Antistatic vacuum cleaner
- Nonabrasive liquid cleaning compound, such as isopropyl alcohol

When using any cleaning products, first ensure that you are protected from any dangers involved in their use, as described in Chapter 1, and wear eye protection when doing any work that could stir up dust. Use compressed air to blow dust out of components, ensuring that you are not blowing it into other components.

Internal Components

One of the most common reasons to clean the insides of a computer is to remove dust build-up to protect the system from overheating. Recall that the power supply's fan draws air out of the computer. Outside air comes in through ports and is distributed over the internal components, bringing with it dust. Because dust can cause ESD and lead to overheated components, cleaning the inside of the computer regularly is important. Pay particular attention to the system board, the bottom of the computer chassis, and all fan inlets and outlets on both the power supply fan and case fans. Of course, make sure you turn off and unplug the computer before you start cleaning it.

One of the easiest ways to remove dust from the system is to use compressed air to blow the dust out. Compressed air comes in cans roughly the size of spray-paint cans.

Typically, liquid Freon in the can compresses the air and forces it out when you depress the can's nozzle. Do not tilt the can, because this can cause Freon to spill onto your skin or components. Liquid Freon can cause freeze burns on your skin and can damage the computer's components.

You can also use compressed air to blow dust out of the keyboard, expansion slots, and ports. Use only canned compressed air, not high-pressure air from a compressor. Whatever you use to blow out dust from a computer, be aware of where you are blowing the dust so that you are not blowing the dust off one component only to have it settle on or in another.

Another common method for removing dust from inside a computer is to use an antistatic vacuum cleaner—one that has a conductive path to ground to protect against causing electrostatic discharge damage to a computer during use. This has the advantage of removing dust without allowing the dust to settle elsewhere. It is best to use a handheld vacuum that allows you to get into smaller places and clean the computer without accidentally hitting and damaging other internal components. Take the nozzle out of the computer, and move the vacuum cleaner away before turning it off.

External Components

Finally, you can use a lint-free cloth to wipe off dusty surfaces, such as displays, keyboards, printers, and the outside of the PC case. Use a clean antistatic cloth to remove dust and dirt from display screens. Avoid using the newer dust cloths that work by "statically attracting" dust. Remember, static is harmful to the computer.

For dirt you cannot dust off, use disposable moistened cleaning wipes on optical discs and most plastic, metal, and glass exterior surfaces, such as display screens. Do not use glass cleaner containing ammonia (such as Windex) on a monitor screen, as the ammonia can damage the protective coating on the screen. If working with a spray bottle of liquid, spray it on the cloth and wipe; do not spray directly on the screen.

A liquid cleaning compound, such as isopropyl alcohol, can come in handy for cleaning gummy residue from the surface of the PC case or a peripheral. Manufacturer's instructions may also suggest using this for cleaning components inside the PC or other device, but only do this per the manufacturer's instructions.

Storage Devices

Common storage devices also require regular maintenance for better performance. The following sections describe simple tasks for maintaining hard drives and optical drives.

Hard Drives   Hard drive maintenance includes running a utility called a disk defragmenter (Defrag) or disk optimizer to reorganize fragmented files on disk, and Check Disk (CHKDSK) or Scandisk to discover problems with the disk. Run these utilities on a regular basis, perhaps once a week on a drive in which you save many new files and delete old files. Chapter 12 will explain the details of the problems both types of utilities resolve.

Optical Media and Drives   You can prevent damage to your optical drives by keeping the discs clean. Commercial optical disc cleaning and repair kits are readily available to restore optical discs. But you can simply wipe any type of optical disc (CD, DVD, or Blu-ray) clean with an antistatic cloth. For more stubborn dirt, use plain water or isopropyl alcohol on the cloth. Ensure the disc is completely dry before inserting it into a drive. The Blu-ray Discs (also called "BD") have a hard coating—beyond what you will find on older types of optical discs—that resists scratches.

If a disc is too badly scratched, you may need to replace it, or if it is irreplaceable or too expensive to replace and you have nothing to lose, consider polishing the disc.

Never clean an optical drive that is working properly, but if you find you must clean a drive, use compressed air to blow dirt out of the drive. If your optical drive has the lens in the disc tray, you will see it when the tray extends. You can carefully clean this type of drive with an antistatic cloth dampened with isopropyl alcohol. Be careful that you do not use too much alcohol and damage the drive. "Dampened" does not mean "dripping."

Be wary of kits for cleaning optical drives, because some of these use a small brush or felt pad to clean the lens of the drive, which can have unintended consequences, such as scratching the lens. If you decide to use one of these kits, make sure you follow the directions carefully, as improper use may cause more problems than it solves.

Cleaning Input Devices   For input devices, such as keyboards, mice, and trackball devices, schedule frequent cleaning. For the keyboard, this involves vacuuming the crevices between the keys. Simply turning a keyboard upside down over a wastebasket and shaking it will remove a surprising amount of dust and debris, depending on the environment and the habits of the user. You may need to protect a keyboard in a dirty environment, such as an auto repair shop, with a special membrane cover that allows use of the keyboard, but keeps dirt, grease, solvents, and other harmful debris out of it. You can find such covers on the Internet or in computer supply catalogs under the keyboard protector category. For devices that are rarely used, consider using dust covers that remain on the device until needed.

To clean an optical mouse, simply turn the mouse over, locate the tiny lens, and wipe it with a soft, static-free cloth. To clean a trackball, simply remove the ball, and wipe the socket with a soft, static-free cloth. To clean rollers on a traditional mouse, carefully dismantle it, remove the ball, and clean the inside, including the rollers.

SCENARIO & SOLUTION

You are visiting a customer whose computer is running slowly. The computer is in a fabric store that generates a great deal of dust and fibers. In addition to your basic tools, what should you take along?	Be sure to take a vacuum—an antistatic vacuum, if possible. Overheating due to dust and fibers covering the internal components may cause the slow running.

CERTIFICATION SUMMARY

Understanding troubleshooting theory and taking a structured and disciplined approach will not only help you arrive at a solution, but also help you quickly resolve similar problems in the future. If you determine that you have a software problem, check the application's configuration, or try uninstalling and then reinstalling the program. If the problem is hardware related, identify the components that make up the failing subsystem. Starting with the most accessible component, check for power and that the component properly attaches to the computer. Check the device's configuration and the presence of a device driver. Finally, swap suspected bad components with known-good ones.

Assemble the right tools for troubleshooting and maintenance before you need them. Take time to perform regular maintenance tasks on computers and peripherals to prevent future problems.

As a computer technician, you will be required to locate and resolve the source of computer problems. If you have a good knowledge of the functions of the computer's components, you will be able to quickly troubleshoot problems that occur.

However, there are other telltale signs of failed components. For example, you can use POST error codes to determine a problem's cause. Although the troubleshooting procedures differ from component to component, and even for different problems within the same component, many of the procedures involve cleaning the component, ensuring it is properly attached to the computer, or finally, replacing the component.

TWO-MINUTE DRILL

Here are some of the key points covered in Chapter 11.

Preparing for Troubleshooting

❑ Arm yourself with appropriate troubleshooting tools, including software and hardware tools.

❑ The six steps of the troubleshooting theory are: (1) identify the problem; (2) establish a theory of probable cause (question the obvious); (3) test the theory to determine the cause; (4) establish a plan of action to resolve the problem and then implement the solution; (5) verify full system functionality and, if applicable, implement preventative measures; and finally, (6) document findings, actions, and outcomes.

❑ Protect computers and data by performing backups of data and the operating system before making any changes to try to resolve problems.

❑ Ongoing user training can prevent many problems and ensure that users know how to respond to common problems.

Troubleshooting Motherboards, RAM, CPUs, and Power

❑ Procedures should move from least intrusive to most intrusive, checking proper connections, appropriate components, drivers, settings, and component seating for internal devices.

❑ General symptoms, such as excessive heat, noise, odors, and visible damage, can apply to any of several components.

❑ Various system instability problems are most likely to be software related, but they also may have a hardware-based cause. These include system lockups, system shutdowns, unexpected shutdowns, and OS-specific crash screens like BSOD.

❑ Never open a power supply because there is a danger of severe shock.

❑ POST error codes, such as 1*xx*, 2*xx*, and 3*xx*, can indicate system board, memory, or keyboard failures, respectively.

❑ Most CPU problems are fatal, which requires replacing the CPU or system. Check your warranty if you suspect a problem with the CPU because it may require replacing the motherboard.

❑ Incorrect firmware settings can affect a variety of system components. Check and correct these problems by running the system setup and changing the settings.

❑ Motherboard batteries last from two to ten years. A computer that does not maintain the date and time when powered off is a symptom of a failed battery.

❑ Most system board, processor, and memory errors are fatal, meaning the computer cannot properly boot up.

❑ Motherboard errors can be the most difficult to pinpoint and, due to the cost and effort involved in replacement, should be the last device you suspect when a subsystem or the entire computer fails.

Troubleshooting Storage Devices

❑ Replace a hard drive that begins to develop corrupted data before all the information stored on it is lost. S.M.A.R.T. technology may report an impending failure. A loud clicking noise also signals that the drive will fail soon.

❑ Failure to boot can be due to a bad drive, a loose connection, or corrupted or missing OS startup files.

❑ An L-type SATA connector is used for internal drives; it's bent like an L. An I-type eSATA connector is for external SATA, and is straight.

❑ When a drive in a RAID fails, you can usually replace it without taking the RAID offline. The RAID controller can rebuild the data that was formerly on the missing disk on a new disk.

❑ When disconnecting external storage, make sure you use the Safely Remove Hardware feature in Windows to stop the drive before unplugging it.

Troubleshooting Displays

❑ If no image appears on the screen, first check all connections and then check the video card functionality.

❑ When a system goes into low-resolution VGA Mode, first determine if it is in Safe Mode. If it is in Safe Mode, follow the instructions in Chapter 12. If the display is in low-resolution VGA Mode but not in Safe Mode, determine what has changed, looking for a recently updated device driver or other newly installed software.

❑ Some displays automatically shut down when overheated. Check ambient temperature and cool it down, if possible. Switch displays to see if the problem is in the display or video adapter.

❑ Dead pixels are pixels that are off, creating dark spots on the screen. This is only a problem if bad pixels cause the image to be distorted or unusable.

❑ An overheating video adapter can cause screen artifacts that randomly appear and disappear—in particular, the GPU overheats when using software that is very video graphics intensive, such as photo-editing software. Find a way to supplement the system's cooling system and/or replace the GPU or the entire video adapter with one designed for better cooling.

❑ A fuzzy FPD display may indicate that the OS is running in a lower resolution than the device's maximum that is supported.

❑ Something as simple as a maladjusted brightness control on the display can cause a dim display image. Troubleshoot by adjusting the brightness control on a PC or laptop display. A more serious cause is a bad inverter, in which case, it may be wise to replace the display rather than try to repair it.

❑ A flickering image on a CRT may be due to EMI from a nearby motor. Remove the source. Or, it can be that the refresh rate setting for the CRT is incorrect.

❑ A flickering FPD display is a sign of a failing component within the display—either the backlight or the inverter. Replace the display.

❑ Improper display resolution or a driver issue can cause a distorted image. You should first check the display cable for damage or a bad connection.

❑ Projector problems most commonly arise from lack of connectivity to the PC, projector positioning, burned-out lamp, and adjustment of projector controls such as focus.

Troubleshooting Keyboards and Pointing Devices

❑ If a keyboard key isn't working, turn the keyboard upside down and shake it.

❑ If a keyboard or mouse isn't working, check its cable (if wired) for connectivity to the PC. If it's wireless, make sure its battery is fresh and that it's turned on (if it has an on/off switch).

❑ The most common mouse problem is irregular movement, which can be resolved by cleaning the internal rollers of a mechanical mouse or the bottom surface of an optical mouse.

Troubleshooting USB and FireWire Ports and Peripherals

❑ USB and FireWire are similar, both being external general-purpose ports. If the OS doesn't detect a device, disconnect and reconnect it, and try a different port or a different PC to narrow down the problem.

❑ Both USB and FireWire have had different standards as they evolved. If you plug a slower device into a faster port, there's no issue, but the opposite may cause problems.

Preventive Maintenance Techniques

❑ Schedule regular preventive computer maintenance, such as visual and aural inspections, driver and firmware updates, cleaning, and verifying a proper environment.

❑ Schedule regular preventive component maintenance for displays, power devices, and drives. Protect thermally sensitive devices by cleaning regularly and ensuring proper airflow.

❑ Acquire and learn how to use appropriate cleaning products, such as cleaning wipes, canned compressed air, an antistatic vacuum cleaner, and nonabrasive cleaning compounds, such as isopropyl alcohol.

SELF TEST

The following questions will help you measure your understanding of the material presented in this chapter. Read all of the choices carefully because there might be more than one correct answer. Choose all correct answers for each question.

Preparing for Troubleshooting

1. Which of the following is a hardware diagnostics tool that you insert into an expansion slot in a motherboard?
   A. POST card
   B. Loopback plug
   C. Video adapter
   D. Nut driver

2. What should you do before making any changes to a computer?
   A. Turn off the computer.
   B. Use a grounding strap.
   C. Restore the most recent backup.
   D. If no recent backup of data and/or the operating system exists, perform a backup.

3. According to troubleshooting theory, what should you do immediately after establishing a theory of probable cause?
   A. Identify the problem.
   B. Test the theory to determine the cause.
   C. Document findings, actions, and outcomes.
   D. Establish a plan of action to resolve the problem.

Troubleshooting Motherboards, RAM, CPUs, and Power

4. Reorder the following troubleshooting steps from the least intrusive to the most intrusive.
   A. Check proper seating of internal components.
   B. Check for proper connections to external devices.
   C. Check installation: drivers, driver settings, and physical settings.
   D. Check for appropriate external components.

5. You want to narrow down the source of a problem to one of what two broad categories?
   A. Power or data
   B. Operating system or application
   C. Motherboard or component
   D. Hardware or software

6. How do you narrow down the problem to one hardware component?
   A. Remove the data cables.
   B. Run specialized diagnostics.
   C. Swap each suspect component with a known-good one.
   D. Restart the computer.

7. After you apply and test a solution, what should you have the user do as part of evaluating the solution?
   A. Ground themselves using an antistatic wrist strap.
   B. Disconnect the problem component.
   C. Test the solution and all commonly used applications.
   D. Print out the user manual.

8. What should you do if you are unsure if a problem is limited to the single application that was in use at the time the problem occurred?
   A. Remove and reinstall the application.
   B. Upgrade the application.

    C.   Use more than one application to perform the actions that resulted in the problem.

    D.   Upgrade the driver.

9.   A customer reports that the computer spontaneously reboots after being used for about 20 minutes, and will not restart until it has sat idle for a few minutes. Furthermore, even when the computer does start, the fan does not make as much noise as before. What is the likely cause of these problems?

    A.   The power supply

    B.   The system board

    C.   The processor

    D.   The RAM

10. Which of the following is the safest and easiest device for measuring the voltage output from a power supply?

    A.   Multimeter

    B.   Power supply tester

    C.   UPS

    D.   Power Options

11. Your computer consistently loses its date and time settings. Which procedure will you use to solve the problem?

    A.   Replace the motherboard battery.

    B.   Flash the battery using a manufacturer-provided disk.

    C.   Use the computer's AC adapter to recharge the battery.

    D.   Access the firmware setting programs at startup and select the low-power option.

Troubleshooting Storage Devices

12. Which of the following symptoms could *not* be caused by a RAM error?

    A.   The POST cannot be completed.

    B.   When you turn on the computer, nothing happens.

    C.   The system reports a No Operating System error.

    D.   The RAM count at startup does not match the capacity of the installed RAM.

Troubleshooting Displays

13. Your video display is blank. Which of the following should you do first?

    A.   Swap the display with a known-good one.

    B.   Replace the video adapter with a known-good one.

    C.   Check the power and data cables.

    D.   Check the seating of the video adapter.

14. Which of the following is a possible cause of a display going into low-resolution VGA Mode?
    A. Incorrect brightness setting
    B. Lit pixel
    C. Corrupt video driver
    D. Disconnected cable

15. Which of the following is a possible cause of a display suddenly shutting down?
    A. Overheating
    B. Incorrect resolution
    C. EMI
    D. Incorrect brightness setting

Troubleshooting Keyboards and Pointing Devices

16. A user reports that the mouse pointer does not move smoothly across the screen. Which of the following is most likely to remedy the problem?
    A. Reinstall the mouse driver.
    B. Ensure that the mouse cable connects securely to the computer.
    C. Replace the mouse with a trackball. Ensure there are no IRQ conflicts between the mouse and another device.
    D. Clean the mouse.

17. What is the best way to clean debris out from under an unresponsive key on a keyboard?
    A. Pry off the key and wipe underneath it.
    B. Wash the keyboard in a dishwasher.
    C. Turn the keyboard over and shake it.
    D. Poke a sharp object under the key.

Troubleshooting USB and FireWire Ports and Peripherals

18. A USB hard drive with its own separate AC power cord works, but transfers data very slowly. What is likely its problem?
    A. It is plugged into a USB 1.1 port.
    B. It is not receiving enough power from the hub.
    C. It is plugged into a FireWire port instead of USB.
    D. The disk is unpartitioned.

Preventive Maintenance Techniques

19. Which cleaning product blows dirt and dust out of PC components?
   A. Antistatic display cleaner
   B. Canned compressed air
   C. Liquid cleaning compound
   D. Antistatic vacuum cleaner

20. What should you use to clean a CD or DVD disc with sticky residue on it?
   A. A small toothbrush
   B. Canned compressed air
   C. Isopropyl alcohol
   D. An abrasive pad

SELF TEST ANSWERS

Preparing for Troubleshooting

1. ☑ **A.** A POST card is a hardware diagnostics tool that you install into an expansion slot. Then, when the computer boots up, the POST card performs diagnostics and reports an error code that you can look up to determine where the boot process is halting.
☒ **B** and **D** are incorrect because, although these are examples of hardware tools, neither is insertable into an expansion slot. **C** is incorrect because this is not a hardware diagnostics tool, but a common PC component.

2. ☑ **D.** If no recent backup of data and/or the operating system exists, perform a backup. This is correct because you do not want to risk losing the user's data.
☒ **A** is incorrect because it is rather irrelevant, although after taking care of the backup, you may want to restart the computer. **B** is incorrect because until you have narrowed down the cause, you do not know if using a ground strap will be necessary. You must do a backup before you reach this point. **C** is incorrect because you have no idea if restoring the most recent backup is even necessary at this point.

3. ☑ **B.** Test the theory to determine the cause.
☒ **A** is incorrect because you should identify the problem before you establish a theory of probable cause. **C** is incorrect because documenting findings, actions, and outcomes is the very last procedure (sixth) of troubleshooting theory, while the procedure in question is the third procedure. **D** is incorrect because establishing a plan of action to resolve the problem comes after testing the theory to determine the cause.

Troubleshooting Motherboards, RAM, CPUs, and Power

4. ☑ **B, D, C, A** is the correct order.
   ☒ Any other order is incorrect.

5. ☑ **D.** Hardware and software are the two broad categories of problem sources.
   ☒ **A** is incorrect because, although you may have problems in these areas, they are not the two broad categories of problem sources. **B** is incorrect because these are both types of software, and software is just one of the two broad categories of problem sources. **C** is incorrect because these are both types of hardware, and hardware is just one of the two categories of problem sources.

6. ☑ **C.** Swapping each suspect component with a known-good one will narrow down a hardware problem to one component.
   ☒ **A** is incorrect because, although cable removal may be part of removing a component, this alone will not help you narrow down the problem to one component. **B** is incorrect because specialized diagnostics lead to general areas, not specific components. **D** is incorrect because restarting will not indicate one component, although it might cause the problem to disappear.

7. ☑ **C.** The user should test the solution and all commonly used applications to confirm the fix works and to assure herself that the changes you made were not harmful.
   ☒ **A** is incorrect because grounding is something a technician would do when working inside a PC. **B** is incorrect because without the problem component connected you cannot evaluate the solution. **D** is incorrect because printing the manual has little to do with evaluating the solution.

8. ☑ **C.** Use more than one application to perform the actions that resulted in the problem. If the problem only occurs in the one application, then focus on that application.
   ☒ **A** is incorrect because, although this may be a fix for the problem, you must first determine that the problem only occurs with that application before doing something so drastic. **B** is incorrect because, although upgrading the application may be a fix for the problem, you must first narrow it down to the one application. **D** is incorrect because, although this may be a solution, you must first narrow down the cause to specific hardware before upgrading the driver.

9. ☑ **A.** The power supply is the most likely cause of these symptoms. When a power supply begins to fail, it often manifests in a number of different, sporadic symptoms. If the power supply's fan stops working, the computer will overheat and spontaneously reboot itself. If the components are still excessively hot when the system restarts, the computer may not start at all.
   ☒ **B, C,** and **D** are all incorrect because failure of any of these components does not cause the specific set of symptoms mentioned in the question. The system board does not include a fan, so would not affect fan noise, and if the system board were faulty, the PC would not boot at all. Although an overheated processor could cause the system to reboot, it would not be associated with the lack of noise from the power supply fan. A RAM failure will not cause the computer to reboot (unless all RAM fails).

10. ☑ **B.** A power supply tester is the safest and easiest device for measuring the voltage output from a power supply.
    ☒ **A** is incorrect because a multimeter requires much more knowledge of electricity to use and is a more complex device. **C** is incorrect because a UPS is not a device for measuring voltage output from

a power supply, but an uninterruptible power supply device. **D** is incorrect because Power Options is a Windows Control Panel applet for managing the power-saving features of your computer.

11. ☑ **A.** You should replace the battery. When the computer "forgets" the time and date, it is most likely because the motherboard battery, which normally maintains these settings, is getting low on power and you must replace it.

☒ **B** is incorrect because it suggests flashing the battery. This procedure (flashing) applies to the upgrade of a firmware chip, not a battery. **C** is incorrect because it suggests recharging the battery with the computer's AC adapter. Although this procedure will work with a portable system battery, you cannot recharge motherboard batteries with an AC adapter. **D** is incorrect because it suggests selecting a "low-power" option in the firmware settings program. Any low-power setting in the firmware settings refers to the function of the computer itself, not to the battery. You cannot adjust the amount of power the firmware chip draws from its battery.

Troubleshooting Storage Devices

12. ☑ **C.** The No Operating System error message is not associated with a memory error, but with a disk error on the system disk.

☒ **A, B,** and **D** are all incorrect because these are all typical symptoms of bad memory. If the memory has totally failed, the firmware cannot conduct or complete the POST—it is also possible that the firmware might not even be able to initiate the processor. This problem might make it appear that the computer does absolutely nothing when turned on. A bad memory stick may not cause an error, but will not work, and if you watch the memory count during startup, you may notice the count does not match the installed RAM.

Troubleshooting Displays

13. ☑ **C.** Check the power and data cables is correct because it is the least intrusive action. If this does not resolve the problem, check the brightness setting, and then continue to **A, D,** and **B,** in that order.

☒ **A** is incorrect because swapping the display is more trouble than simply checking the cables. **B** and **D** are incorrect because these are very intrusive actions and should not be attempted until you have performed less intrusive actions.

14. ☑ **C.** A corrupt video driver can cause a display to go into low-resolution VGA Mode.

☒ **A** is incorrect because this would only cause the display to be too bright or too dim. **B** is incorrect because this would only cause a pixel to constantly display just one of its three colors; it would not result in VGA Mode. **D** is incorrect because a disconnected cable would simply result in a blank display.

15. ☑ **A.** Overheating can cause a display to suddenly shut down.

☒ **B** is incorrect because incorrect resolution would not cause the display to shut down. **C** is incorrect because, although EMI can cause flickering problems with a CRT, it does not cause a display to shut down. **D** is incorrect because an incorrect brightness setting would only cause the display to appear too dim or too bright.

Troubleshooting Keyboards and Pointing Devices

16.   ☑   **D.** Cleaning the mouse is most likely to remedy the problem of a mouse pointer that does not move smoothly on the screen.
        ☒   **A** is incorrect because if the mouse does not have a proper driver, it will not work at all. Driver problems for any device will cause that device to stop functioning altogether or to work sporadically. **B** is incorrect because if the mouse does not connect to the computer, it will not respond at all. If the mouse connector is loose, the operation of the mouse could be sporadic, working at some times, and not working at all on other occasions. **C** is incorrect because although this solution may resolve the problem caused by a dirty mouse, it is more extreme than cleaning the mouse.

17.   ☑   **C.** Shaking a keyboard is likely to dislodge debris from under a key, and is not intrusive or likely to break the keyboard.
        ☒   **A** is incorrect because prying off the key may damage the keyboard and it may be difficult to get the key back on. **B** is incorrect because you would do something drastic like that only in the event that the keyboard is otherwise ruined; for example, if you spilled a sugary beverage on it. **D** is incorrect because although this solution may resolve the problem, it is likely to damage the keyboard.

Troubleshooting USB and FireWire Ports and Peripherals

18.   ☑   **A.** A USB hard drive plugged into a USB 1.1 port will transfer data at the speed of USB 1.1, which is much slower than the hard drive is capable of performing.
        ☒   **B** is incorrect because the drive has its own AC power and does not draw power from the hub. **C** is incorrect because a USB cable would not fit into a FireWire port. **D** is incorrect because an unpartitioned disk would not transfer any data at all, nor be recognized by the OS.

Preventive Maintenance Techniques

19.   ☑   **B.** Canned compressed air is the cleaning product used to blow dirt and dust out of PC components. The drawback to this is that it can also blow dirt and dust into components, and if used improperly, the liquid Freon within the can could spill onto the skin or computer components, causing injury or damage.
        ☒   **A** and **C** are both incorrect because you use these wet cleaning products to wipe off the screen and other surfaces. **D** is incorrect because an antistatic vacuum cleaner draws the dust in, rather than blowing it out. This more expensive product is preferred for cleaning out a PC.

20.   ☑   **C.** Isopropyl alcohol will dissolve the sticky residue without scratching the disc surface.
        ☒   **A** and **D** are both incorrect because they will damage the surface. **B** is incorrect because it is inadequate to remove sticky residue.

Chapter 12

Operating System Troubleshooting and Maintenance

■   **902: 4.1**   Given a scenario, troubleshoot PC operating system problems with appropriate tools

■   **902: 4.2**   Given a scenario, troubleshoot common PC security issues with appropriate tools and best practices

✓   Two-Minute Drill

Q&A   Self Test

I n the last chapter, you learned some important hardware troubleshooting skills. In this chapter, we turn our attention to troubleshooting operating systems, looking at problems large and small that might prevent an OS from functioning well. We focus mainly on Windows because it is the most popular OS, but we also provide some basic assistance for macOS and Linux, to the extent dictated by the 220-902 exam's objectives. We also look at some common preventive maintenance tasks that can help avoid problems down the road.

CERTIFICATION OBJECTIVE

■ *902: 4.1*   *Given a scenario, troubleshoot PC operating system problems with appropriate tools*

We kick off this chapter by covering a single topic from CompTIA A+ 902 exam objective 4.1: Uninstall/reinstall/repair (listed under Tools). Later sections in this chapter dig into 902 exam objective 4.1 much more deeply and cover more topics.

Quick Fixes

Perhaps you've heard of Occam's razor, a.k.a. the law of parsimony? Roughly paraphrased, it states that "among competing hypotheses, the one with the fewest assumptions should be selected." In other words, "try the simplest solution first." That applies very well to computer OS troubleshooting.

This chapter contains a lot of very detailed troubleshooting information and technique that you should know as a CompTIA A+ certified PC technician, for very specific situations. However, in everyday tech work, the majority of the problems you face can be fixed by one of these general-purpose methods:

- ■ **Reboot**   Often a system restart is all that's required to clear up a problem.
- ■ **Verify**   Make sure the software or device you are attempting to install or troubleshoot is compatible with the hardware and software of the PC.
- ■ **Repair**   If the problem is with a specific application, go into the Control Panel's Programs and Features applet, select the application, and click Repair (or Change), if that command is available. If the problem is with Windows itself, use a repair technique (dependent on Windows version) such as one of the techniques discussed later in this chapter when looking at the Windows Recovery Environment (Windows RE).
- ■ **Uninstall/reinstall**   If the problem is with a specific device, remove it physically from the PC, and then remove its driver and all its software from the OS. Check for any updates for its driver or software online, and then reinstall.

CERTIFICATION OBJECTIVES

- ■ *901: 4.2*   *Given a scenario, troubleshoot hard drives and RAID arrays with appropriate tools*
- ■ *902: 1.1*   *Compare and contrast various features and requirements of Microsoft Operating Systems (Windows Vista, Windows 7, Windows 8, Windows 8.1)*
- ■ *902: 1.2*   *Given a scenario, install Windows PC operating systems using appropriate methods*
- ■ *902: 1.3*   *Given a scenario, apply appropriate Microsoft command-line tools*
- ■ *902: 1.4*   *Given a scenario, use appropriate Microsoft operating system features and tools*
- ■ *902: 1.5*   *Given a scenario, use Windows Control Panel utilities*
- ■ *902: 1.7*   *Perform common preventive maintenance procedures using the appropriate Windows OS tools*
- ■ *902: 4.1*   *Given a scenario, troubleshoot PC operating system problems with appropriate tools*
- ■ *902: 4.2*   *Given a scenario, troubleshoot common PC security issues with appropriate tools and best practices*

Don't let this long list of objectives intimidate you! This section does cover a lot of ground, but part of the reason for the large number of objectives listed is that several of this section's topics appear under multiple objective numbers. For example, Event Viewer is listed under the 902 exam objectives 1.1, 4.1, and 4.2, and System Restore/System Protection is included in four separate places, in the 902 exam objectives 1.1, 1.4, 1.5, and 4.2.

There is also some overlap of topics across the exams. 901 exam objective 4.2 is included in this section because it duplicates several tools that are also listed in 902 exam objectives 1.3 (CHKDSK, BOOTREC, DISKPART) and 1.4 (DEFRAG).

e x a m

ⓦ a t c h CompTIA A+ 902 exam objective 4.2 refers to two topics that are specific to Windows XP: Recovery Console and Automated System Recovery (ASR). Since Windows XP is no longer covered on the current CompTIA A+ exams, it is unclear whether retaining those topics in the objectives was an oversight on the part of the exam developers or whether they intended to continue to require knowledge of them. We don't cover these features in this book, but you may wish to explore them on your own.

Windows Troubleshooting Tools

In this section, you'll learn about the many Windows tools for troubleshooting operating system problems. We'll look at Action Center, System Information, the Registry, the Microsoft Management Console (MMC), Register Server (REGSVR32), ODBC Data Source Administrator, Task Manager, System Configuration (MSCONFIG), and Windows Memory Diagnostic. We'll also look at alternative start modes from the Boot Options menu, System Restore, Shadow Copy, DirectX Diagnostics, and the Windows Recovery Environment (RE). That's a pretty ambitious tour, so let's get started!

BIOS/UEFI for OS Troubleshooting

When you think about entering BIOS/UEFI setup for troubleshooting purposes, perhaps the first thing that comes to mind is hardware troubleshooting, such as investigating why a disk drive isn't being recognized. However, some firmware settings also can affect the OS. For example, when Safe Boot is enabled in a UEFI BIOS, you aren't able to use F8 to enter Advanced Boot Options at startup, and when Virtualization support is disabled, virtual machines might not run well. Review Chapter 3 for help entering BIOS/UEFI setup and making settings changes there.

Command Prompt/Terminal

Keep in mind that the Command Prompt window is always available from within the Windows GUI, as you learned in Chapter 10. Many of the utilities we explain in upcoming sections run either from a command line or from the Run dialog box (WINDOWS KEY-R).

Remember also from Chapter 10 that on Mac and Linux systems, the command prompt is known as Terminal.

The Windows Recovery Environment (Windows RE), explained later in this chapter, also has an option that enables you to work from a command prompt, for system troubleshooting when the GUI doesn't start properly.

Action Center/Problem Reports and Solutions

The *Problem Reports and Solutions* applet in the Control Panel exists only in Windows Vista. It gives you feedback and possible solutions for security issues and problems your computer reports to Microsoft using the Windows Error Reporting service. Click a solution to have it applied to Windows. Then, manually remove the resolved items.

Windows 7 and newer have an improved reporting tool, called *Action Center*, which reports security and maintenance status and includes links to troubleshooting and recovery tools. Open Action Center via the Control Panel when you want to take a quick look at the beginning of the troubleshooting process to see if it shows any problems in the Security or Maintenance areas (which pretty much cover everything). Once you identify a problem area, click a link to open a helpful tool, such as Performance and Information, Backup and Restore, Windows Update, System Restore, and the Troubleshooting tool. Figure 12-1 shows Action Center in Windows 8.1, for example.

Select the Troubleshooting link in Action Center and it opens a menu of categories with troubleshooters that walk you through a solution. For instance, the Programs category contains a link that opens the Program Compatibility troubleshooter in which you identify the older program that will not run properly, and then the troubleshooter walks you through a variety of settings for that application.

In addition to the Programs category, Troubleshooting has troubleshooters for Hardware and Sound, Network and Internet, System and Security, and (in Windows 7 only) Appearance and Personalization. The last category is not included in this tool in Windows 8 and newer, because the Appearance and Personalization troubleshooter in Windows 7 addresses problems with Windows Aero, which is not included in Windows 8 and newer.

System Information (MSINFO32.EXE)

You sit down at a Windows computer you have never touched before. You know little about it, but you need to gather information to troubleshoot a problem. Where do you start? One of the first things you should do is learn as much as you can as quickly as you can. What version, edition, and service pack of Windows are installed? How much memory is installed? What CPU? This information and more is displayed as a summary of the hardware, operating system, and other installed software in *System Information*. You can access it through the graphical user interface (GUI), or you can type its command (**msinfo32.exe**) from the Start menu or in the Run dialog box (WINDOWS KEY-R). Figure 12-2 shows this utility in Windows 8.1.

FIGURE 12-1 Action Center, available in Windows 7 and newer, provides feedback and possible solutions for security and system problems.

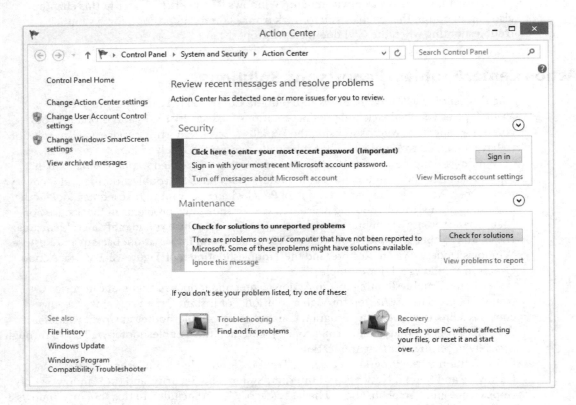

Registry

A basic knowledge of the registry is required of anyone supporting Windows. As defined in Chapter 9, the Windows registry is a database of all Windows configuration settings for both hardware and software. As Windows starts up, it reads information in the registry that tells it what components to load into memory and how to configure them. After startup, the OS writes any changes into the registry and frequently reads additional settings as different programs load into memory. The registry includes settings for device drivers, services, installed applications, OS components, and user preferences.

FIGURE 12-2 System Information, a.k.a. MSINFO32

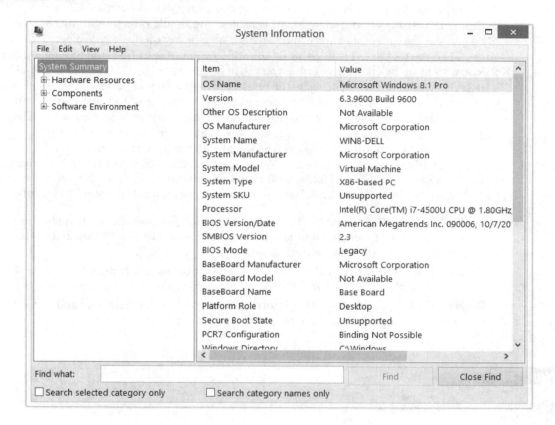

Changing the Registry

The registry is created when Windows installs; however, configuring Windows and adding applications and devices continually modifies it. Here are the actions that cause registry changes:

- Windows starts up or shuts down
- Windows Setup runs
- Changes are made through a Control Panel applet
- Installing a new device
- Any changes made to the Windows configuration
- Any changes made to a user's desktop preferences
- Installing or modifying an app
- Any changes made to an app's user preferences

Using Registry Editor

The best way to change the registry is indirectly, using various tools in the GUI, such as the Control Panel applets and some MMC consoles. You should directly edit the registry only when you have no other choice and you have specific instructions from a very reliable source. Then the tool to use is Registry Editor, which you can start from the Run dialog box (WINDOWS KEY-R) by entering **regedit**. You might be prompted by UAC to allow access.

In Registry Editor, you can navigate the registry folders with your mouse in the same way you navigate disk folders. Each folder represents a *registry key*, an object that may contain one or more settings as well as other keys, each of which is a *subkey* of its parent key. The top five folders, as seen in Figure 12-3, are *root keys*, often called *subtrees* in Microsoft documentation. Each of these subtrees is the top of a hierarchical structure.

A setting within a key is a *value entry*. When you click the folder for a key, it becomes the active key in Registry Editor. Its folder icon opens, and the contents of the key appear in the right pane, as shown in Figure 12-3. Here is an overview of each subtree and its contents:

- **HKEY_CLASSES_ROOT**   The relationships (associations) between applications and file types. Shown as a root key, it is actually all the information located in HKEY_LOCAL_MACHINE\Software\Classes.
- **HKEY_CURRENT_USER**   The user profile for the currently logged-on user, which consists of the NTUSER.DAT file for the user, along with any changes since logon.
- **HKEY_LOCAL_MACHINE**   Information about detected hardware and software, security settings, and the local security accounts database.

FIGURE 12-3

Use Registry Editor (REGEDIT) to view the registry components.

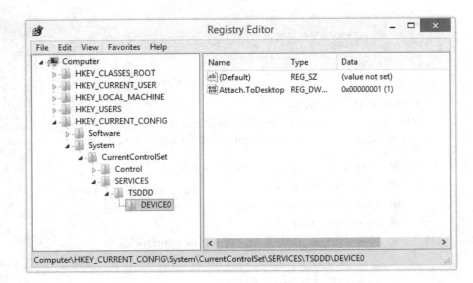

- **HKEY_USERS** All user profiles that are loaded in memory, including the profile of the currently logged-on user, the default profile, and profiles for special user accounts for running various services.
- **HKEY_CURRENT_CONFIG** Configuration information for the current hardware profile, which are settings defining the devices, the list of files associated with each device, and configuration settings for each. It also contains a set of changes to the standard configuration in the Software and Systems subkeys under HKEY_LOCAL_MACHINE.

Editing the registry is not difficult, but it can be dangerous if done improperly, causing system problems that can prevent Windows from starting or running properly. When you research a system problem online, you may find some recommended registry edits proposed as solutions. Be wary. Make registry edits with care, and only after making a backup of the registry or a particular section. Exercise 12-1 helps you make a backup of a registry key and then practice restoring a backup.

Video

EXERCISE 12-1

Backing Up and Restoring the Registry

In this step-by-step exercise, you will back up a section of the Windows registry. You would do this before making a change to the registry, as a safeguard. You could then restore the backup if the change you made caused system instability. You can back up the entire registry (although that creates a large file), or the individual key that you plan on editing. You can use Windows 7 or newer for this exercise.

1. Run REGEDIT to open Registry Editor. You can use the Run dialog box (WINDOWS KEY-R) or open the Start menu/screen and type **regedit**.
2. Click HKEY_CURRENT_USER to select that key.
3. Click File | Export. In the Export Registry File dialog box, change to a location where you can save temporary files (we use a folder called C:\Temp).
4. In the File Name box, type **HKEY_CURRENT_USER Backup** and today's date.
5. Click Save.
6. Click File | Import. In the Import Registry File dialog box, navigate to the folder you chose in Step 3.
7. Select the file you backed up.
8. If this were an actual import, you would click Open at this point, but instead click Cancel.

Microsoft Management Console (MMC)

The Microsoft Management Console (MMC) is a user interface for Windows administration tools that is flexible and configurable. Most Control Panel applets and administrative applets that run within the Windows GUI open in an MMC window. *Computer Management* is a preconfigured version of the MMC with several common modules already loaded. You can access Computer Management in one of the following ways:

- **Windows Vista and 7** Click Start and then right-click Computer and select Manage.
- **Windows 8** Open the Control Panel and choose System and Security, then Administrative Tools, and then Computer Management. (This method works in all other Windows versions too.)
- **Windows 8.1 and 10** Right-click the Start button and click Computer Management.

Figure 12-4 shows the Computer Management window. Notice the grouping of tools on the left. The tools (such as Task Scheduler and Device Manager) are all *snap-ins* to the Computer Management console, meaning they are MMC nodes that can be added to an MMC console.

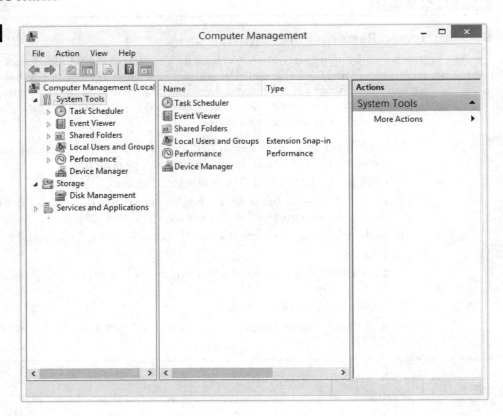

FIGURE 12-4

Computer Management console

An administrator can build his own custom consoles, consisting of individual snap-ins. To do this, you enter the command **mmc.exe** in the Run dialog box, which opens a blank console window on the desktop. By choosing File | Add/Remove Snap-ins, you can select one or more administrative snap-ins to create your custom console. Consoles have an .msc file extension, and you can call up your favorite tool directly by entering the correct filename and extension. For instance, to start Computer Management, shown in Figure 12-4, click the Start button or open the Start screen and then type **compmgmt.msc**.

Following are overviews of three MMC-based tools that are useful in both troubleshooting and preventing problems. They are Device Manager, Task Scheduler, and Performance Monitor.

Device Manager

Chapter 11 featured Device Manager as a troubleshooting tool for several types of hardware problems, so we will only briefly revisit it here to emphasize that it is an MMC snap-in. Device Manager allows an administrator to view and change device properties, update device drivers (you normally will use the manufacturer's program to update a driver), configure device settings, roll back an updated driver that is causing problems, and uninstall devices. You can access Device Manager from the Control Panel. Alternatively, you can open the Run dialog box (WINDOWS KEY-R) and enter **devmgmt.msc**. This will open it into a separate MMC console window.

Task Scheduler

Task Scheduler allows you to view and manage tasks that run automatically at preconfigured times. Use Task Scheduler to automate daily backups and updates. You can open Task Scheduler from the Run dialog box by entering **taskschd.msc**; then expand the Task Scheduler Library to see folders for the many categories of tasks. You will be surprised at the number of scheduled tasks. Most, if not all, of the tasks you will find there were not created by you directly, but were added to Task Scheduler when you installed a new app and configured it to automatically check for updates. We cover Task Scheduler in more detail later in the chapter, in the context of scheduling maintenance utilities to run automatically.

Performance Monitor

Network administrators use performance monitoring to watch for potential problems and to ensure quality of service. Desktop versions of Windows don't usually require monitoring, but they nevertheless come with several tools for monitoring performance and the overall health of the system.

The performance tool specifically mentioned in CompTIA A+ 902 exam objective 1.3 is Performance Monitor. You can run it via the Run dialog box (WINDOWS KEY-R) by typing **perfmon**, or by searching for Performance Monitor. Performance Monitor tracks and gathers performance data for memory, disks, processors, networks, and more so that you can see if one of these items is showing performance problems.

FIGURE 12-5 Performance Monitor in Windows 7

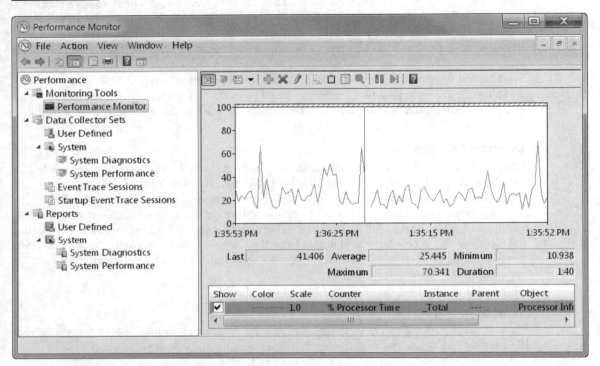

Each item you can monitor, such as physical disks, memory, processor, and network interface, is an *object* and it has one or more characteristics, called *counters*, that you may select for monitoring. Performance Monitor displays the data in real time in a report, line graph, or histogram (bar chart) format. Figure 12-5 shows Performance Monitor displaying processor performance information.

Event Viewer

Windows automatically saves most error messages in Event logs for later viewing in Event Viewer. You can open Event Viewer from Administrative Tools or by typing its filename, **eventvwr.msc**, in the Run dialog box. Become familiar with Event Viewer before a problem occurs, so you will be comfortable using it to research a problem. Use Event Viewer to view logs of system, security, and application events, paying attention to the warning and error logs for messages you can use to solve problems.

Event Viewer has three standard categories of events: system, application, and security. Other Event logs may exist, depending on the Windows configuration. For instance, Internet Explorer creates its own Event log.

Event Viewer displays a list of Administrative events, which is a selection of events from all the log files that show a status of Warning or Error. This saves scrolling through all the Information events to find an event indicating a problem. To see the individual logs, select the Windows Logs folder in the left pane and select each Event log in turn:

■ The System log records events involving the Windows system components (drivers, services, and so on). The types of events range from normal events, such as startup and shutdown (called Information events), through warnings of situations that could lead to errors, to actual error events. Even the dreaded "Blue Screen of Death" error messages show up in the System log as STOP errors. The System log, shown in Figure 12-6, is the place to look for messages about components, such as a driver or service. Details for the selected event, including the actual message, display in the pane below the events list. The message itself may lead you to the solution. Each event also has an ID number. Search the Microsoft website for a solution, using either a portion of the error message or the event ID.

FIGURE 12-6   Windows 7 Event Viewer showing the System log

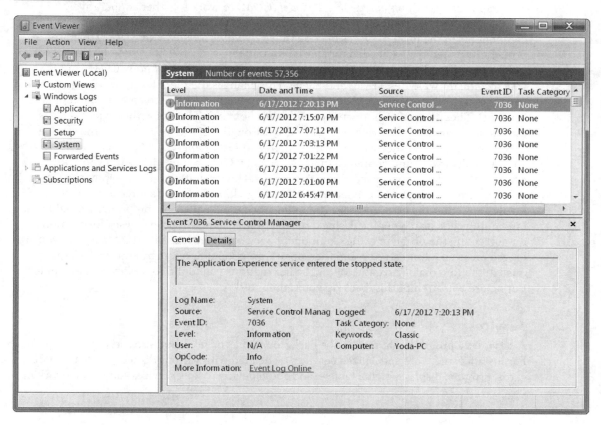

- The Application log shows events involving applications. These applications may be your office suite of applications or Windows components that run in the GUI, such as Windows Explorer or Document Explorer. If you see an error on your screen that mentions an application, you will find the error listed in the Application log.

- The Security log will log events such as a successful or failed logon attempt. It will also log events relating to access to resources, such as files and folders. Several types of security events are logged by default, and an administrator can enable and disable logging of security events. See the section "Local Security Policy" in Chapter 19 to learn how to control what security messages are logged.

To learn more about Event Viewer, use the help command from within Event Viewer.

Component Services

Windows allows applications to work together in a number of ways. Applications called COM apps use the *Component Object Model (COM)* to work together cooperatively. A COM app will have an executable program that opens the app for the user and various components in the form of pieces of code called *dynamic link libraries (DLLs)* that are brought into memory as needed for special functions.

The next complexity level includes the *Component Object Model Plus (COM+)* apps, which come in two types: server and client. This changes the model from working cooperatively to one of a component (a server) providing a service to another component (a client). These server components provide the client components with services such as transactions, queuing, and role-based security through DLLs associated with the service.

When apps install, such as the various Microsoft Office apps, they normally automatically install and configure their COM and COM+ applications, and you are neither aware of nor concerned about these tasks. However, if you see an error message that includes the words "COM Server" or "missing dll," contact the source of the software involved or enter the error message (including the actual names of components or DLLs) into an Internet search engine. Using a reliable source, you will probably see instructions for correcting the problem using Component Services, an MMC snap-in. Make sure you are logged on as an administrator, and then open Component Services by entering **compexp .msc** in the Run dialog box and follow the instructions you found for resolving the problem. But before you attempt this, back up your computer!

Services

A *service* is a program that runs in the background, has no GUI, and supports other programs. For instance, there are specialized services associated with various devices, such as smart cards, printers, displays, digital tablets, and audio devices. Many services support networking

FIGURE 12-7 The Windows 7 Services console

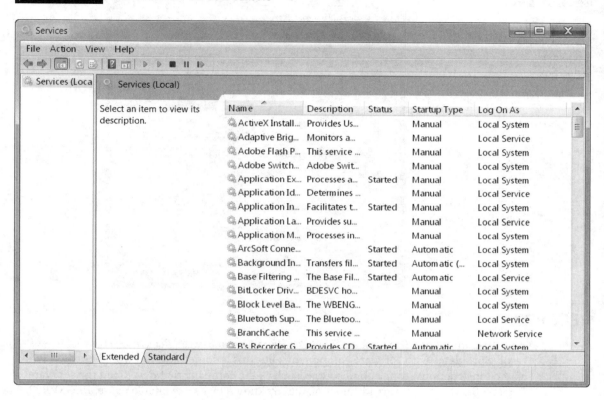

and security, and the list goes on. Open the Services console by entering **services.msc** in the Run dialog box. The Services console, shown in Figure 12-7, lets you manage services.

You normally should not need to make any changes to services, but if you must make changes, use this tool rather than others. In the Services console, you can start, stop, pause, resume, and disable services. You can also

CompTIA A+ 902 exam objective 1.4 lists Services twice: once under Services, and once under its filename, SERVICES.MSC.

configure the recovery options for what should occur when an individual service fails. To access that feature, you need to right-click a service in the Services console and select Properties. In the Properties dialog box for the service, click the Recovery tab, as shown in Figure 12-8. The recovery options include Take No Action, Restart the Service, Run a Program, and Restart the Computer.

FIGURE 12-8

The Recovery
tab on a service's
Properties
dialog box

REGSVR32

As with Component Services, described earlier, you can use the *Register Server tool* to
resolve problems with software components, but this is something you would only use with
explicit instructions from a good source, such as the company that developed the software.
Register Server is a command-line tool, mainly known by its executable name, *REGSVR32*,
and is used to register or unregister software components, such as dynamic link libraries
(DLLs) and ActiveX controls. If a software publisher recommends that you use this tool,
you will need the exact command-line options
and instructions from them. First do a complete
backup of your system; then open the Command
Prompt as administrator and carefully enter the
command with options. Follow the software
publisher's instructions for interpreting any
resulting error messages and do testing to see if
the problem is resolved.

e x a m
ⓦ a t c h CompTIA A+ 902 exam
objective 4.1 lists REGSRV32 under the
Tools topic. This is a typo, because the
name of this tool is REGSVR32 (notice the
"VR" in the correct spelling).

System File Checker (SFC)

System File Checker (SFC) is a command-line utility that scans the important Windows system
files to make sure none of them are missing or corrupted, and makes any repairs needed.

This utility can be used for, among other things, repairing the DLL cache. Run SFC from an elevated (Administrator) command prompt.

To scan all protected system files and replace corrupted files with a cached copy, use **sfc /scannow**. The cache is a compressed folder located in C:\Windows\System32\dllcache. If you see a message *Windows Resource Protection could not perform the requested action*, reboot into Safe Mode and retry the operation.

Data Sources

Yet another tool you would only use with explicit instructions is *ODBC Data Source Administrator*. You can launch it from Administrative Tools in Control Panel or from the Run dialog box by entering **odbcad32.exe**. This opens a tabbed dialog box where you can manage database drivers and data sources. To understand why you would use this tool, we need to define a few terms. *Open Database Connectivity (ODBC)* is program code for connecting to *database management systems (DBMSs)*. A DBMS is a program that manages the creation, storage, retrieval, and modification of data on a computer. Theoretically, ODBC can be used with any operating system and any DBMS through the use of a special driver that, like a driver for a hardware component, acts as a translator. In the case of a hardware driver, it translates between the hardware component and the operating system, whereas an ODBC driver translates between the application and the DBMS.

As long as the correct ODBC driver is installed, a DBMS-compliant app can access any DBMS. Common data sources on Windows computers are Microsoft Excel spreadsheet files, Microsoft Access database files, and dBase files. When an ODBC-compliant program installs, it will normally install the correct ODBC driver. If you see an error message that an ODBC connection cannot be made, first back up data on that computer, and then reinstall the problem application. If that does not correct the problem, contact the software publisher and obtain a new ODBC driver or instructions for changes you can make in ODBC Data Source Administrator.

Task Manager

Task Manager is a utility for examining running processes and services and shutting them down if needed. It changes and improves with each Windows version, and in all modern versions it includes multiple tabbed pages. In Windows 8 and later, the default Task Manager window is a simple, single window with no tabs, and you will need to click More Details to see the tabs.

To open Task Manager, press CTRL-SHIFT-ESC, or right-click an empty area of the taskbar and choose Task Manager or Start Task Manager.

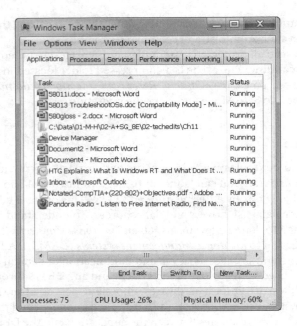

FIGURE 12-9

Windows 7
Task Manager,
Applications tab

Applications Tab

The Applications tab (see Figure 12-9) is the one from which you view and manage GUI applications. If an application is not responding, and you cannot close the application any other way, open Task Manager, select the nonresponding application, and click End Task.

w a t c h

CompTIA A+ 902 exam objective 1.3 includes the TASKKILL command, which will stop a running program. This command-line command has many options that you can explore with the /? switch. Here is an example that will stop the Microsoft Paint program, assuming it will not stop normally: taskkill /f /t /im mspaint.exe. In practical use, however, you would be more likely to stop a nonresponsive program via Task Manager than from a command line.

Processes Tab

Select the Task Manager Processes tab to see the Process list, showing each active process currently running in memory. A program runs in memory as one or more processes. A single *process* consists of memory space, program code, data, and the system resources required by the process. Each process has at least one thread, which is the program code executed by the process. An operating system has many active processes at any given time. Add to that the processes for such programs or applications as File Explorer and Microsoft Word, and you have dozens of active processes running in memory at one time performing various functions. A *background process* is one that runs "behind the scenes" and has a low priority, does not require input, and rarely creates output. Many of the processes in the Process list are background processes. In Task Manager, the image name (filename) and *process ID (PID)* identifies a process, which is a number dynamically assigned by the operating system as it starts each process. The Processes tab also shows the amount of memory and the CPU usage of the process.

When a programmer creates a program, she gives it a *process priority level*, also called a *base priority level*, which determines the order in which the program code's process or processes execute in relation to other active processes. There are six levels, listed from the lowest to the highest: Low, Below Normal, Normal, Above Normal, High, and Real Time. A program that has a High priority level has the potential to tie up the processor, and one with a Real Time priority level can cause system crashes. The operating system can adjust these levels to some degree, and you can temporarily adjust the level of an active process by right-clicking a process and selecting Set Priority. We do not recommend that you do this.

To view all running process, select Show Processes from All Users at the bottom left of the window.

To view the priority level of active processes, first select the Processes tab, and then open View | Select Columns. In the Select Process Page Columns dialog box, click to place a check mark in the Base Priority box. This adds the Base Priority column. Most of the processes will have a Base Priority level of Normal, with a few High priorities and perhaps one or two Below Normal. The High Priority processes should be part of the operating system, such as csrss.exe, dwm.exe, or some (but not all) programs associated with a specialized device, such as a digital tablet.

CompTIA A+ 902 exam objective 1.3 includes the TASKLIST command. Run TASKLIST without parameters to see a list of process IDs for all running tasks. Use the /? switch to learn more.

So how do you use this knowledge of processes in troubleshooting? If a system is slow, noting which processes are running with a high priority at the times of slow performance may tell you which ones are taking processing time away from others. Perhaps the answer is to evaluate the need for that app. If it is critical that you continue to use it, and the software publisher does not have a solution, you may need to run it on a more powerful computer.

Services Tab

Click the Services tab to see the list of services loaded into Windows. If you look at the status in Task Manager, you will see that not all of the listed processes are actually running.

Many are stopped because they are only started when needed. Some processes and services are associated, and when you right-click a service that is running and select Go To Process, it will open the Processes tab and highlight the associated process. However, if you do that on a running service and no process is highlighted, the process may be hidden and you will need to select Show Processes from All Users, as described earlier. You can learn more about the current services by clicking the Services button on the bottom right of this page. This will open the Services MMC.

Performance Tab

The Performance tab is a "lite" version of Performance Monitor. Open this for a quick look at the current performance of CPU and memory. The most important object to check here is CPU, which you'll see in a real-time line graph. The graph measures the percentage of CPU usage in a separate window for each CPU or core. CPU usage usually bounces up and down as various processes execute. However, sustained usage above about 80 percent indicates that the CPU is inadequate for the task. This may indicate a problem with the CPU from overheating or another cause, or it may simply mean it is time to upgrade the CPU or entire computer.

Networking Tab

The Networking tab in Task Manager gives performance and state information about your network connections. If a network seems slow, open Task Manager, click Networking, and you will find a real-time line chart showing the bandwidth usage for each network connection. With this open, do whatever type of networking function seems to slow things down, such as a large download from a file-sharing site. Even that should not tax the network connection much. Network bottlenecks are usually beyond your local connection at an Internet router. Chapter 16 will show you how to find such a bottleneck.

Users Tab

The Users tab in Task Manager shows the currently logged-on users, including you, in a Session type of console, along with any users who are connected to a share on your computer over a network. When a network user is connected, their computer name will show up under the Client Name column. What will *not* show up are the various special user's accounts that run services on your computer.

From this tab you can disconnect or log off a user. If it is a network user, you should click the Send Message button to send them a warning so that they can close any files they have open on your computer.

Exploring Windows 8.1 Task Manager

In this exercise you will start an application and then pretend that it has become unresponsive and shut it down manually using Task Manager. It's good practice for when an application actually does become unresponsive in Windows. For this exercise, use Windows 8.1 if you have it available. Its tabs are somewhat different from those in Windows 7, so it will be good for you to compare and contrast them.

1. In Windows 8.1, start the Notepad app.
2. Right-click the taskbar and click Task Manager.
3. Click More Details or Fewer Details, whichever one appears, to toggle between the two display modes. When you're finished trying that out, end up with the tabs hidden (fewer details). Notice that only the running applications appear. Then click More Details. Notice that the applications appear on the Processes tab in an Apps section, and there is also a rather large Background Processes section with other processes.
4. Click the Memory column. The processes become sorted by the amount of memory they are using. If the largest amount doesn't appear at the top, click Memory again to reverse the sort. Then click the Name column to return the sort order to the default.
5. Click each of the other tabs to see what it contains. Mentally compare these to the tabs from the Windows 7 version of Task Manager.
6. Go back to the Processes tab and click Fewer Details.
7. Click Notepad, and click End Task.
8. Close the Task Manager window.

System Configuration (MSCONFIG.EXE)

Beginning with Windows XP, and continuing through later versions of Windows, Microsoft includes the *System Configuration* utility, also known as *MSCONFIG*. In Windows Vista and Windows 7, among this utility's many functions is the ability to exclude certain items from automatically loading at startup, so you can isolate the source of a startup problem. Once you determine what program or service is causing a problem, you can uninstall the program or permanently disable the service so it will not run when the computer boots. However, in Windows 8 and newer, this functionality has been moved to Task Manager. There is still a Startup tab in later versions of System Configuration, but it's just an empty stub with a hyperlink to the new location in Task Manager.

As they do with Task Manager, the current CompTIA A+ exam objectives cover the Windows 7 version of System Configuration, so we will cover that version here too. Keep in mind that in Windows 8 and newer, the startup configuration we explain here will actually be performed in Task Manager.

While you can call this program up from the GUI, the quick way to launch it from any version is by entering **msconfig** in the Run dialog box (WINDOWS KEY-R).

CompTIA A+ 902 exam objective 1.4 lists this utility twice: under the Administrative topic it is listed by its GUI name, System Configuration, and then the next topic is titled MSCONFIG. Be prepared to see either name in CompTIA's A+ 220-902 exam. This same utility is also referenced again in 902 exam objective 4.2, in the context of accessing Safe Mode from the Boot tab, and also in 902 exam objective 4.1.

General Tab

The General tab contains quick startup options to help you isolate a cause of a startup problem. Normal Startup will simply start up Windows normally, and is what you should choose after you have used other options. Diagnostic Startup will temporarily disable all but basic services and drivers before starting up. If the problem persists after using Diagnostic Startup, then the source is within Windows base components, not in an installed driver or service. Selective Startup lets you choose three categories of items to disable or enable at startup. Use this to isolate the problem to system services or other programs that normally start up with Windows.

Take time to practice using the System Configuration utility before you need to use it for troubleshooting.

Boot Tab

From the Boot tab, you can restart Windows in Safe Mode by selecting the Safe Boot option and clicking OK. Then a message box displays, giving you the opportunity to either restart or exit without restarting. If you restart, you will be in Safe Mode, where you can continue your troubleshooting. When finished working in Safe Mode, open System Configuration again, clear the Safe Mode option from the Boot page, return to the General page, and select Normal Startup. You will see the same prompt, where you will need to click the Restart button, and Windows will restart normally. Figure 12-10 shows System Configuration open to the Boot tab.

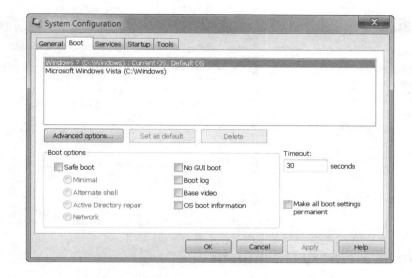

FIGURE 12-10

The System
Configuration
Boot tab

Services Tab

The System Configuration Services tab lets you select services to disable for a restart. This is one way to test if a certain service is causing a problem. Like the other tabs, when you click OK, you will be prompted to restart or cancel. Do not consider this the place to manage services, because there is a full-featured Services MMC (services.msc).

Startup Tab

The Startup tab (in Windows 7 and Vista) lists every program that loads when Windows starts up. System Configuration is great to use when you want to prevent a program from launching at startup to see if it is the cause of a problem. Using System Configuration saves you from needing to search all the possible startup locations. The value of System Configuration today is that it will let you test "what-if" scenarios for startup. For instance, you can temporarily disable the startup of one or more programs, restart, and see if that eliminated the program; if it did, make the change permanent so that the problem will not reoccur. In Windows 8 and newer, you can click the hyperlink on this tab to accomplish these same changes via Task Manager.

Tools Tab

The Tools tab in System Configuration contains a long list of troubleshooting and administrative tools, giving you yet another way to launch them. Select a tool in the list, and then click the Launch button.

FIGURE 12-11

Schedule a
memory scan
using Windows
Memory
Diagnostic.

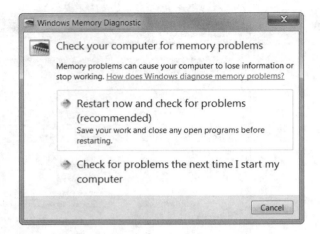

Windows Memory Diagnostic

The *Windows Memory Diagnostic* tool (see Figure 12-11) is actually a memory diagnostics scheduler. You can open it by entering **mdsched.exe** in the Run dialog box (WINDOWS KEY-R). Then, choose either to have the computer restart immediately to run the diagnostics or to have it run them on the next restart. When the system shuts down and restarts the diagnostics, it runs in character mode. It can take several minutes to run the tests, and then the computer will automatically restart. The next time you log on, the results will display. By default, Windows Memory Diagnostic runs a standard set of tests, but if you press F1 while the diagnostics are running, you can select to either run a basic set that won't take as long, or run a more rigorous extended set that runs several more tests. While it is running, the screen will occasionally look as if it has stalled, but be patient, let it complete, and restart your computer.

Advanced Boot Options Menu

Advanced Boot Options, shown in Figure 12-12, is a menu that you can trigger at Windows startup. In some Windows versions this menu appears automatically upon reboot if Windows failed to start normally last time. In some Windows versions it is named Boot Options.

To access the Advanced Boot Options menu in Windows Vista and Windows 7, restart the computer and press F8 before the graphical Windows start screen appears. On systems with Safe Boot enabled by UEFI setup, which is common on systems with later Windows versions on them, you won't be able to use the F8 method. On such systems, we recommend using MSCONFIG instead to restart in Safe Mode for troubleshooting.

Following is a brief description of the startup options available from the Advanced Boot Options menus.

FIGURE 12-12   The Windows 7 Advanced Boot Options menu

```
                        Advanced Boot Options

Choose Advanced Options for: Windows 7
(Use the arrow keys to highlight your choice.)


   Repair Your Computer


   Safe Mode
   Safe Mode with Networking
   Safe Mode with Command Prompt

   Enable Boot Logging
   Enable low-resolution video (640x480)
   Last Known Good Configuration (advanced)
   Directory Services Restore Mode
   Debugging Mode
   Disable automatic restart on system failure
   Disable Driver Signature Enforcement


   Start Windows Normally

Description: View a list of system recovery tools you can use to repair
             startup problems, run diagnostics, or restore your system.


 ENTER=Choose                                          ESC=Cancel
```

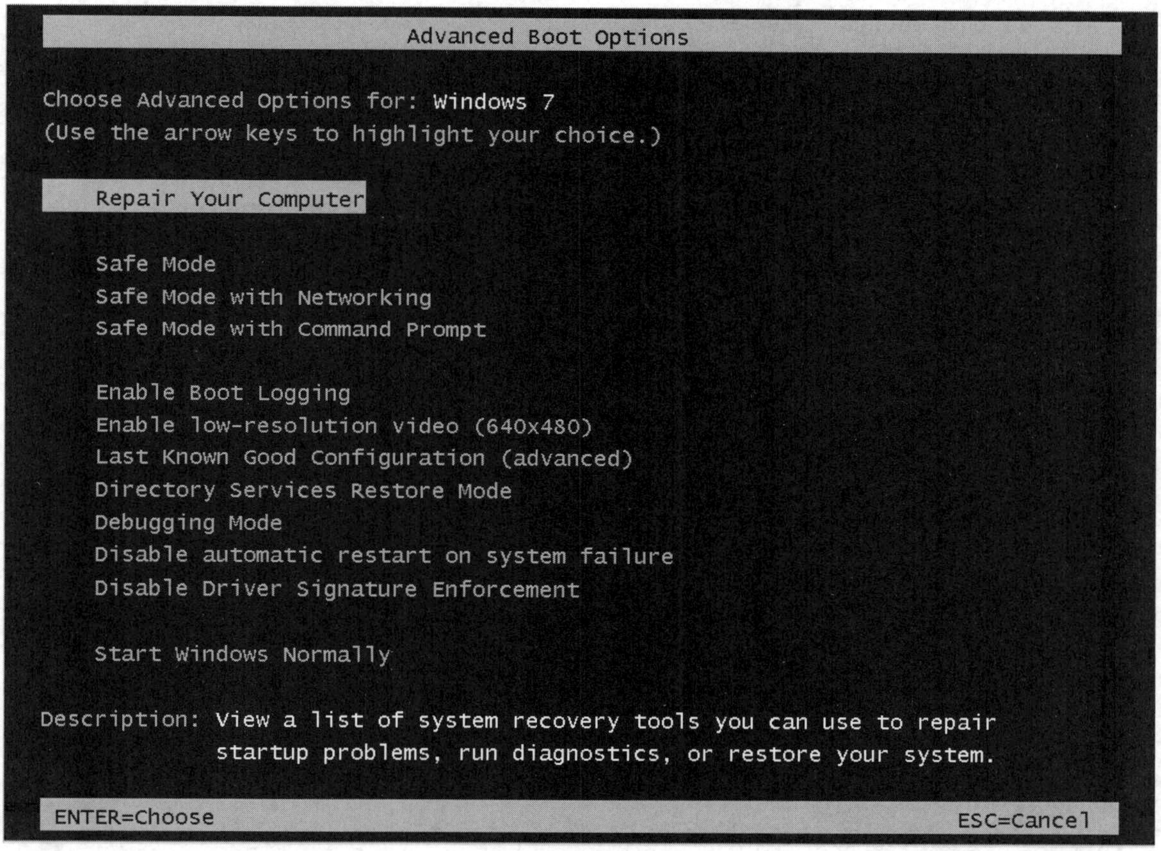

Repair Your Computer (Windows 7 and Windows 8 Only)

Repair Your Computer is available on the Advanced Boot Options menu in both Windows 7 and Windows 8, but this description is specific to Windows 7, and varies a bit from Windows 8. When you select this option, Windows PE (the Windows Preinstallation Environment defined in Chapter 9) loads and first requires that you supply a keyboard input method, and then requires that you log on, and finally displays the System Recovery Options screen, described later in this chapter under "Recovery Options."

Safe Mode

Safe Mode is a startup mode for starting Windows with certain drivers and components disabled, but many troubleshooting and recovery tools do work in Safe Mode. Figure 12-13 shows Safe Mode in Windows 7. Notice that the background is all black and the words "Safe Mode" appear in the corners. If Windows will not start normally but starts just fine in Safe Mode, use Device Manager within Safe Mode to determine if the source of the problem is a faulty device. You can run System Restore while in Safe Mode and roll back the entire system to before the problem occurred. Safe Mode does not disable Windows security. You are required to log on in all three variants of Safe Mode, and you can only access those resources to which you have permissions.

FIGURE 12-13   The Windows 7 Safe Mode screen

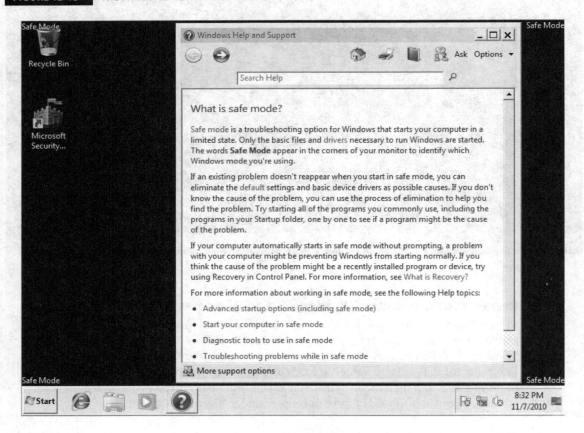

There are actually three Safe Mode variants available: Safe Mode, Safe Mode with Networking, and Safe Mode with Command Prompt.

- *Safe Mode* starts up without using several drivers and components that it would normally start, including the network components. It loads only very basic, non-vendor-specific drivers for mouse, video (loading Windows' very basic VGA.sys driver), keyboard, mass storage, and system services.

- *Safe Mode with Networking* is identical to plain Safe Mode, except that it also starts the networking components. Use the following debug sequence with Safe Mode with Networking:

  - If Windows will not start up normally but it starts fine in plain Safe Mode, re-start and select Safe Mode with Networking.

  - If it fails to start in Safe Mode with Networking, the problem area is network drivers or components. Use Device Manager to disable the network adapter driver (the likely culprit), and then boot up normally. If Windows now works, replace your network driver.

  - If this problem appears immediately after upgrading a network driver, use Device Manager while in Safe Mode to roll back the updated driver. When an updated driver is available, install it.

- *Safe Mode with Command Prompt* is Safe Mode with only a command prompt as a user interface. Windows would normally load your GUI desktop, but this depends on the program EXPLORER.EXE, the GUI shell to Windows. In place of this GUI shell, Safe Mode with Command Prompt loads a very limited GUI with a Command Prompt (CMD.EXE) window. This is a handy option to remember if the desktop does not display at all. Once you have eliminated video drivers as the cause, corruption of the EXPLORER.EXE program itself may be the problem. From within the Command Prompt, you can delete the corrupted version of EXPLORER.EXE and copy an undamaged version. This requires knowledge of the command-line commands for navigating the directory structure, as well as knowledge of the location of the file that you are replacing. You can launch programs, such as the Event Viewer (eventvwr.msc), the Computer Management console (compmgmt.msc), or Device Manager (devmgmt.msc), from the Command Prompt.

Enable Boot Logging

While boot logging occurs automatically with each of the three Safe Modes, selecting *Enable Boot Logging* turns on boot logging and starts Windows normally. Boot logging causes Windows to write a log of the activity (programs loaded into memory and programs started) during Windows startup in a file named NTBTLOG.TXT, and it saves it in the *systemroot* folder (usually C:\Windows). This log file contains an entry for each component in the order in which it loaded into memory. It also lists drivers that were not loaded, which alerts an administrator to a possible source of a problem.

Enable VGA Mode/Enable Low-resolution Video (640 × 480)

This option starts Windows normally, except that the video mode is changed to the lowest resolution (640 × 480), using the currently installed video driver. It does not switch to the basic Windows video driver. Select this option after making a video configuration change that the video adapter does not support and that prevents Windows from displaying properly.

Last Known Good Configuration (Not Available in Windows 8/8.1)

Last Known Good Configuration is a startup option that starts Windows normally and selects the configuration that existed at the last successful user logon (the "last known good configuration"), ignoring changes made after the last logon. This works if you made changes that caused obvious problems. On the very next restart, selecting this option will discard the changes. The problem is that if you have logged on since the changes occurred, those changes will be part of the last known good configuration, so it won't work. This rather crude system-restore method only works if you did not restart and log on since making the change.

Directory Services Restore Mode (Not Available in Windows 8/8.1)

The *Directory Services Restore Mode* option only works on Windows Servers acting as domain controllers, and Microsoft finally removed it in Windows 8.

Debugging Mode

The *Debugging Mode* is a very advanced option in which Windows starts normally, and information about the activity (programs loaded and programs started) during Windows startup is sent over a cable to another computer that is running a special program called a debugger. We consider this option to be obsolete.

Disable Automatic Restart on System Failure

The default setting for Windows is for it to restart after a system crash. However, depending on the problem, restarting may simply lead to another restart—in fact, you could find yourself faced with a continuous loop of restarts. If so, access the Advanced Boot Options menu and select the *Disable Automatic Restart on System Failure* option. Then Windows will attempt to start normally (just once for each time you select this option) and may stay open long enough for you to troubleshoot. Do not attempt to work with any data file after restarting with this option, because the system may be too unstable. If you are not able to solve the problem, then you will need to restart in Safe Mode to troubleshoot.

Disable Driver Signature Enforcement

If you are unable to install a driver because it has not been digitally signed and is being disabled by driver signing and you trust the manufacturer, select *Disable Driver Signature Enforcement*, which will start Windows normally, disabling driver signature enforcement just for one startup.

Disable Early Launch Anti-Malware Driver (Windows 8/8.1 Only)

While it is a good thing to have your antimalware driver launch early so that it is ready to protect your computer, this very behavior may be tied to a startup problem. To eliminate this as the possible cause, select the *Disable Early Launch Anti-Malware Driver* option in Windows 8 or 8.1, which will only apply to one startup.

Start Windows Normally

Use the *Start Windows Normally* option to start Windows normally with no change in behavior. You would use this after accessing the Advanced Boot Options menu and deciding to continue with a normal startup. It does not restart the computer, but continues the startup.

Return to OS Choices Menu (Multiboot Only)

Selecting the *Return to OS Choices Menu* option on a multiboot computer will return to the OS Choices Menu (OS Loader menu) where you can select the OS you want to load.

EXERCISE 12-3

Working in Safe Mode

In this step-by-step exercise, you will start Windows in Safe Mode. Although we will use Windows 7 in the steps, the steps are similar in Windows Vista. If you wish to use Windows 8/8.1 or 10 for this exercise, we recommend that you use the System Configuration utility (MSCONFIG) and select Safe Boot from the Boot tab. The screens will not be identical, but you can experience Safe Mode in any of these OSs. Be prepared to provide credentials to access Safe Mode because security is still in place in Safe Mode. Once in Safe Mode, you can run most Windows troubleshooting tools just as you would after a normal start.

1. Restart the computer, pressing F8 as soon as the power-down completes and before the splash screen appears.
2. On the Advanced Boot Options menu, use the UP and DOWN ARROW keys to move the cursor around. Position the cursor on Safe Mode and press ENTER.

3. When prompted, provide credentials. Safe Mode loads with a black desktop background and the words "Safe Mode" in the corners of the screen. It also opens Windows Help and Support to the page on Safe Mode. Browse through the help information and click the link labeled Diagnostic Tools to Use in Safe Mode.

4. On the resulting page, locate links to start several very handy tools in Safe Mode. In the following steps, practice opening some of these utilities.

5. Click the link labeled Click to Open Recovery. On the Recovery page, notice the links to other tools. Click the button labeled Open System Restore. On the page labeled Restore Files and Settings, click Next to see a list of the restore points on your computer. Click Cancel to leave System Restore, and close the Recovery windows to return to Help and Support.

6. Next use the link that will open Control Panel. You can open most tools you would need from this page.

7. When you finish exploring Safe Mode, close all open windows, and either shut down or restart Windows, allowing it to start normally.

System Restore

If you have ever added the latest software or new device to your Windows computer, only to find that nothing seems to work right after this change, System Restore will come to your aid. If you can't access the GUI, you can access System Restore via the System Recovery Options menu, described later in this chapter under "Recovery Options."

System Restore creates *restore points*, which are snapshots of Windows, its configuration, and all installed components. Windows creates restore points automatically when you add or remove software or install Windows updates and during the normal shutdown of your computer. You can also choose to force creation of a restore point before making changes. If your computer has nonfatal problems after you have made a change, or if you believe it has a malware infection, you can use System Restore to roll it back to a restore point.

During the restore process, only settings and programs are changed—no data is lost. Your computer will include all programs and settings as of the restore date and time. This feature is invaluable for overworked administrators and consultants. A simple restore will fix many user-generated problems.

To open System Restore, open the Control Panel and navigate to System and Security | System | System Protection. That opens the System Properties dialog box to the System Protection tab. See Figure 12-14.

Click the System Restore button to start the System Restore wizard, and then work through its steps. You will be prompted to select a restore point, as in Figure 12-15. Usually the most recent one is a good choice, unless you know specifically when the problem started and can choose a point right before that.

FIGURE 12-14

The System
Protection tab
of the System
Properties
dialog box

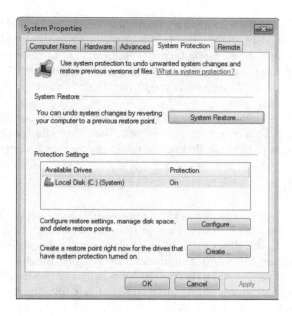

FIGURE 12-15

Select a
restore point.

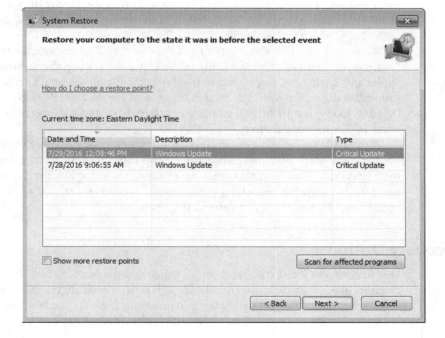

You don't have to just rely on the automatic creation of restore points. You can create a restore point at any time. In Windows 7 do this from the System Protection tab in the System Properties dialog box (see Figure 12-14) by clicking the Create button. Type a description for your restore point and then click Create. This is something to consider doing before making changes that might not trigger an automatic restore point, such as directly editing the registry.

System Restore is on by default, and uses some of your disk space to save restore points each day. To turn System Restore off (disable) or change the disk space, click the Configure button on the System Protection tab of the System Properties dialog box (Figure 12-14).

Shadow Copy

While System Restore tracks and maintains snapshots of the Windows files, it is not concerned with user data files, or it wasn't until Microsoft added Shadow Copy to System Restore in Windows Vista. Shadow Copy was briefly defined in Chapter 2. Previously only available on Microsoft Windows Server systems, Shadow Copy tracks and maintains backup copies of versions of data files. As long as System Restore is on, Shadow Copy is also on for the volume containing the Windows OS, providing that it is a New Technology File System (NTFS) volume. While Microsoft calls this feature Shadow Copy, in the GUI the two features, System Restore and Shadow Copy, are called *System Protection*. In Windows Vista and Windows 7, Shadow Copy, like System Restore, is only turned on for the system drive—the drive containing the operating system files, and only if that drive is formatted with NTFS, which is the default.

Windows 8 includes the ability to add drives other than the system drive to Shadow Copy. To create or configure Shadow Copy in Windows 8/8.1, open the System Control Panel applet and select System Protection from the task list on the left. This will open the System Properties dialog box with the System Protection tab current. By default, System Protection (Shadow Copy) is only turned on for the system drive, but you may also turn it on for any other NTFS-formatted drive.

With Shadow Copy/System Protection turned on in any of these versions of Windows, you can right-click a file on the protected drive in Windows Explorer and select Restore from Previous Versions. This brings up a Properties dialog box for the file opened to the Previous Versions tab page. It may take several seconds for the list of previous versions to be populated. Once it is, select a version and restore it.

Recovery Options

When Windows won't start, and you've exhausted the features described so far in this chapter (like System Restore and MSCONFIG), your next step is the recovery tools. These involve booting into a preinstallation environment (PE). As you learned in Chapter 9, a PE is a special graphical environment designed to run diagnostic and troubleshooting tools on

Windows itself, and repair any problems found. The preinstallation environment options vary somewhat depending on the Windows version; for example, Windows 8/8.1 provide Refresh and Reinstall options that earlier versions do not.

Entering the Windows Recovery Environment (Windows RE)

In Chapter 9, you learned about the Windows Preinstallation Environment (Windows PE), a scaled-down Windows operating system with limited drivers for basic hardware and support for the NTFS file system, TCP/IP, certain chipsets, mass storage devices, and 32-bit and 64-bit programs. That description belies the power of this environment, because when needed, it supports a powerful group of diagnostics and repair tools called the *Windows Recovery Environment (Windows RE)*. Computer manufacturers have the option of adding their own repair tools to Windows RE.

Windows RE Startup at Failure   When a Windows Vista, Windows 7, or Windows 8/8.1 computer fails to start, if the damage is not too extensive, Windows RE will start and load the Windows Error Recovery page with two options: Launch Startup and Repair (Windows RE's built-in diagnostics and recovery tool), and Start Windows Normally. It is always worth trying the second option to see if the cause of the problem was something transient. Then, if it still doesn't start up normally, select Launch Startup and Repair and follow the instructions on the screen.

Starting Windows RE from the Advanced Options Menu   You can also call up Windows RE from the Advanced Boot Options menu, which you learned about earlier in this chapter. Windows 7 and newer include the Repair Your Computer options, which loads the Windows RE System Recovery Options menu. This option requires a local administrator password.

Starting Windows RE from Windows Media   Another option is to start Windows RE by inserting the Windows DVD in the drive and restarting the computer. When prompted, press a key to start from disc. Select language, time and currency format, keyboard or input method, and click Next. On the following page, click Repair Your Computer (on the bottom left). This brings up the Windows RE System Recovery Options dialog box. Select the operating system you want to repair and click Next, and the System Recovery Options menu appears.

   If Windows came preinstalled on your computer, the manufacturer may have installed this menu as is or customized it, or they may have replaced it with their own recovery options.

Starting Windows RE from Within Windows (Windows 8/8.1/10)   If the Windows RE files are available on the local hard disk, and you can boot into Windows (even if it's having problems), you can boot into Windows RE in one of these ways:

- **Windows 8 or 8.1** Press WINDOWS KEY-I and click the Power icon. Then hold down SHIFT and click Restart. Click Troubleshooting | Advanced Options.
- **Windows 8.1 or 10** Press WINDOWS KEY-X or right-click the Start button, and then click Shut Down or Sign Out. Hold down SHIFT and click Restart. Click Troubleshooting | Advanced Options.

Using the Windows Vista or 7 Recovery Environment

In Windows Vista or Windows 7, the Windows RE tools are as follows:

- **Startup Repair** This tool replaces missing or damaged system files, scanning for such problems and attempting to fix them.
- **System Restore** This tool restores Windows using a restore point from when Windows was working normally.
- **System Image Recovery (Windows Vista)/Windows Complete PC Restore (Windows 7)** If you previously created a complete PC image backup, this tool will let you restore it.
- **Windows Memory Diagnostic** This tool, described earlier, tests the system's RAM (a possible cause for failure to start). If it detects a problem with the RAM, replace the RAM before trying to restart Windows.
- **Command Prompt** This tool provides a character-mode interface where you can use Command Prompt tools to resolve a problem, as explained in the following section.

Windows RE Command Prompt

In the Windows RE Command Prompt, you can run some (but not all) commands you normally run within the Windows Command Prompt. The value of this command prompt is the ability to run such tools to repair the disk or BCD file when Windows will not start.

To see a list of Windows RE utilities, simply enter **help** at the prompt. To learn more about an individual command, enter the command name followed by /**?**. Here is a brief description of a few handy commands:

- **DISKPART** Performs disk partitioning
- **EXIT** Exits the recovery environment and restarts your computer
- **FIXBOOT** Writes a new partition table from the backup master file table on disk
- **FIXMBR** Repairs the master boot record (MBR)
- **HELP** Displays a Help screen

- **LOGON** Logs on to a selected Windows installation (if more than one is installed)
- **SYSTEMROOT** Sets the current directory to the location of the Windows system files—usually C:\Windows

You can also run a tool, BOOTREC, that is not available to you from within a normal Windows Command Prompt. Following are the BOOTREC commands you can run at the Windows RE Command Prompt for repairing a system partition:

- **bootrec /fixmbr** Repairs the MBR without overwriting the partitionable portion of the disk.
- **bootrec /fixboot** Overwrites the boot sector with one compatible with the Windows version installed.
- **bootrec /scanos** Scans all disks, looking for compatible Windows installations, and then displays the results.
- **bootrec /rebuildbcd** In addition to the scanning performed by /scanos, this option lets you select an installation to add to the BCD store. Do this if an installation on a multiboot system does not show as an option in the Boot Management menu.

Refreshing or Restoring Your PC (Windows 8/8.1 Only)

In Windows 8/8.1, if you can get into Windows at all (even in Safe Mode), you can run the Refresh utility, which is similar to Startup Repair. It refreshes system files without losing any data. To access it, select the Settings charm, and then choose PC Settings | Update and Recovery | Recovery, and then under the Refresh Your PC Without Affecting Your Files heading, click Get Started (see Figure 12-16). Then just follow the prompts. You can also choose to restore (reinstall) Windows from this same screen, losing all your applications and files.

If some of the needed files are missing, you'll see a message that your Windows installation or recovery media will provide these files. If you get that message, boot the Windows Setup DVD to access the recovery environment, and use the Refresh option from there.

DirectX Diagnostic Tool

The *DirectX Diagnostic Tool (DXDIAG)* is a GUI utility, but it's launched from a command line. Launch this program when experiencing video problems, such as poor performance or the inability to display video motion in two dimensions or three dimensions. Use this tool when you suspect that the display or its adapter is causing a problem, especially with a specific application.

FIGURE 12-16 Refresh or restore your PC in Windows 8.1.

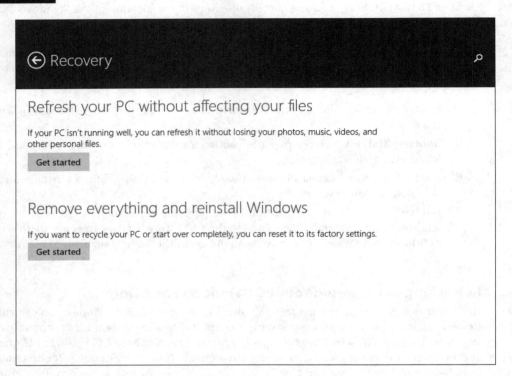

CERTIFICATION OBJECTIVE

■ *902: 4.1 Given a scenario, troubleshoot PC operating system problems with appropriate tools*

This section details the possible solutions for the symptoms listed in CompTIA A+ 902 exam objective 4.1, along with appropriate tools for diagnosing and solving problems. Many of these solutions involve the tools you learned about earlier in this chapter.

Windows Symptoms and Solutions

Operating system failures occur for a variety of reasons, but just a few types—startup, device driver, and application failures—account for the majority. These often occur at startup. Operational problems are those that occur while Windows is running, as opposed to those that occur during startup. These may be instability problems, and they may involve

OS components, including drivers, or application components. Regardless of the source of the problem, watching for error messages and familiarizing yourself with common error messages is important.

OS Instability Problems

What does OS instability look like? Instability includes a variety of symptoms, such as STOP errors, missing graphical interface, lockups of applications or the OS itself, and failure to open programs or files. The next several sections provide some guidance for various types of system instability situations.

Bluescreen (STOP) Error

A fatal error is one that could cause too much instability to guarantee the integrity of the system. Therefore, when the operating system detects a fatal error, it will stop and display a text-mode screen with white letters on a blue background. This screen is officially a STOP screen, but unofficially people call it the Blue Screen of Death (BSOD). We mentioned it in Chapter 11 as well, because it is more often than not caused by hardware (or a hardware driver). It displays a message and multiple numbers that are the contents of the registers and other key memory locations. This information is usually not overly useful to a computer technician, but it can provide a great deal of information to developers and technical support professionals as to the nature of the failure. It is a good idea to capture that information before you contact customer support.

If you are present when a STOP error occurs, read the first few lines on the screen for a clue. If the system reboots before you can read this information, you can view it in the System log after the reboot. Open Event Viewer and look in the System log for a STOP error.

For example, suppose the error message looks something like this: "STOP [several sets of numbers in the form 0x00000000] UNMOUNTABLE_BOOT_VOLUME." If you search www.microsoft.com using just the last part of this message (UNMOUNTABLE_BOOT_VOLUME), you may find sufficient information to determine the cause and the action to take by examining the values that preceded it.

Freezes and Spontaneous Restarts

Sometimes the OS may stop responding to commands; this is called locking up, or freezing. The mouse pointer may or may not still work depending on the nature of the underlying problem. If this happens once in a great while, don't worry about it; reboot and try again. But if it happens repeatedly (say, more than once a week), dig a little deeper.

First, assess whether this may be a problem with overheating or power. Overheating is the most common cause of system lockups, and it usually happens 15 to 30 minutes after the PC is started up. Check the CPU's heat sink and cooling fans for proper operation; you might need to install additional cooling methods. Spontaneous restarts are almost always due to inadequate cooling or a failing power supply.

If cooling doesn't seem to be the problem, there are probably some corrupted system files. On a Windows system, try using the Windows Recovery Environment to repair the Windows installation, or System File Checker. Both were covered earlier in this chapter.

Improper shutdown can cause instability problems. All operating systems require a proper shutdown in order to close and save all open files. An improper shutdown can cause damage to open system and data files. Windows has controls built in that make this less likely to occur, such as the ability to configure the power button on your computer to not actually power down the computer but to send a shutdown command to the OS. Use the Power Options utility, described in Chapter 7, to configure your power button to shut down, hibernate, or put the computer to sleep.

Windows Boots to Safe Mode

If Windows spontaneously boots to Safe Mode, there is a failure with an operating system component and you can troubleshoot from Safe Mode. All of the recovery tools described earlier in this chapter that normally run in Windows also run within Safe Mode. First try using System Restore to restore the system to a previous point in time. If that doesn't help, then follow the instructions in the "Advanced Boot Options Menu," section earlier in this chapter.

Missing Graphical Interface/Fails to Load

The graphical interface is such an integral part of the OS that when it doesn't load, you know you've got some serious OS problems. Use the Windows Recovery Environment to repair your Windows installation, as described earlier in the chapter.

Slow System Performance

Perhaps your system was zipping along nicely, and then after a restart, it suddenly slowed to a crawl. The root cause is probably the last thing you changed or installed. Use System Restore to go back to a previous restore point; this usually clears up the problem.

If your system gets slower gradually over time, you might have too much extraneous stuff running in the background. Check the Startup tab in Task Manager (Windows 8/10) or System Configuration/MSCONFIG (Windows Vista and 7) to see if there is anything loading that doesn't need to be loaded. You can also look in the Programs list in the Control Panel to see if there are any programs you can uninstall. This may help if one or more of the programs you are getting rid of is adware, or if your hard disk is nearly full.

Hard disk fullness can cause system slowdown because of the paging file. When the hard disk gets close to being full, Windows allocates less space to the paging file, so you have less virtual memory to work with.

Slow performance can also be a symptom of virus infection. Make sure your antivirus program and definitions are up to date. Boot into Safe Mode with Networking and use your browser to do a system scan using a free service like Trend Micro or AVG Online.

Failure to Open Applications

When an application that has opened before doesn't open, it's sometimes a system problem rather than an application problem. Restarting the OS is usually effective in clearing it up. If an application still doesn't open normally after a reboot, try repairing the application in the Programs and Features applet in the Control Panel; then try uninstalling and reinstalling the application.

Multiple Monitor Misalignment

When you have multiple monitors arranged on a desk, Windows has no way of knowing their actual physical positioning. Therefore, you might need to rearrange the monitors logically in the OS.

Right-click the desktop and click Screen Resolution. Thumbnail images of your monitors appear. Drag them so that they represent the actual positions of the monitors. Click Identify to see the numbers on the screens so you can tell them apart.

Startup Error Messages

An IT professional must recognize and interpret common error messages and codes. These range from messages that appear during the early stages of a failed startup, through a variety of operational error messages. Once-fleeting messages that were not available after the fact are now logged in many cases, and a knowledgeable computer technician learns where to find them, as you will see in the sections that follow. Some of these refer to devices, services, or applications, but they appear at startup, rather than when those items are actually accessed.

When an OS fails in the early stages of startup, the problem often stems from corruption or loss of essential OS files. If this is the case, you may need to reinstall the OS, but before you take such a drastic step, consider other actions, such as the recovery options detailed earlier in this chapter.

Inaccessible Boot Drive

This error may show as a bluescreen STOP error, in which case the exact wording is Inaccessible Boot Device. This fatal error has several possible causes and solutions. Here are just a few:

- A boot-sector virus has infected the computer. Learn more about boot-sector viruses at https://support.microsoft.com.

■ A resource conflict exists between the two disk controllers. This conflict is most likely to occur after the installation of an additional controller. In that case, remove the new controller and reboot. If Windows starts up normally, then troubleshoot the new controller for a configuration that conflicts with the boot controller.

■ The boot volume is corrupt. If you have eliminated other causes, then remove the boot hard drive system and install it in another computer that has a working installation of the same version of Windows. Configure it as an additional drive, boot into the existing operating system, and then run CHKDSK (Check Disk, discussed later in this chapter) on the hard drive to diagnose and fix errors.

Missing Operating System

"Missing operating system" or "Operating system not found" may appear on a black screen when you start Windows. Then, because you cannot start up from the hard drive at all, you can try to boot from the Windows Setup disc and start the Recovery Environment. At that point, if you see the message "Setup did not find any hard drives installed on your computer," the cause is most likely one of the following:

■ BIOS/UEFI did not detect the hard drive.
■ The hard drive is damaged. Run CHKDSK.
■ The MBR (located in the first physical sector) or GPT is damaged.
■ An incompatible partition is marked as Active.

To troubleshoot for this, restart the computer and access the BIOS/UEFI setup menu, as explained in Chapter 3. Check to see that the BIOS/UEFI recognizes the hard drive. If it is not recognized, check the computer or motherboard manufacturer's documentation to enable the BIOS/UEFI to recognize the hard drive and learn how to run diagnostics once the drive is recognized.

If the BIOS/UEFI still does not recognize the hard drive, power down, open the computer case, and check the data cable and power cable connections to the hard drive. If you find and correct a problem with the connectors, close the system up, restart and run the BIOS/UEFI setup again, and see if the drive is recognized. If it still fails, then the drive may be irreparable. But before you give up on the drive, restart again with the Windows Setup disc in the drive.

In Windows Vista or Windows 7, boot from the Setup disc and select Repair Your Computer; this loads the System Recovery Options dialog box. Select your operating system (unless your computer multiboots, there will only be one option). Then the System Recovery Options list will open. Select Command Prompt.

Regardless of the version of Windows you are attempting to repair, there are two utilities that are most useful for this problem: CHKDSK and FIXMBR.

CHKDSK will check for damage to the file system within the logical drive. We recommend using this before trying FIXMBR. Run the CHKDSK command by entering **chkdsk c: /f /r**.

The CHKDSK command can take hours to run, but we have been able to recover hard drives that seemed hopeless. After the command completes, restart the computer. If it boots into the operating system, you are good to go, but if not, repeat the steps to get back to the Command Prompt through the Recovery Options menu and then run FIXMBR. To run FIXMBR, it is best to specify the exact hard drive with the problem unless there is only one. If there is only one, you simply enter **fixmbr** at the Command Prompt, and the program will locate the backup copy of the master boot record and overwrite the damaged one. Hard disks are numbered beginning with zero (0). So, if the disk is the second hard disk in the computer, run FIXMBR by entering **fixmbr \device\harddisk0**. If this fails to correct the problem, the disk may simply be too damaged to repair.

Missing NTLDR and Missing Boot.ini

A couple of Windows XP errors still appear in the exam objectives, although Windows XP is no longer covered.

CompTIA A+ 902 exam objective 4.1 lists Missing NTLDR as one of the conditions to troubleshoot, but this error is found only in Windows XP and earlier, so you won't see it in modern systems. On a Windows XP system, you would copy the missing file from the Windows installation media to the root directory of the boot drive to fix this error.

It also lists Missing Boot.ini as a condition to troubleshoot; Boot.ini was a configuration file in Windows XP. Among other things, it pointed the system to the NTOSKRNL file needed to start Windows. When Boot.ini was missing, Windows would try to load NTOSKRNL from a default location, and that activity would fail if it wasn't found in C:\Windows\System32. Therefore, a message about a missing NTOSKRNL was more likely an indication that Boot.ini was missing or corrupted.

Device Has Failed to Start

If you see the message "Device has failed to start" or a similar message, open Device Manager and double-click the device name to open the device's Properties dialog box. On the General tab, look in the Device Status box for an error code. Troubleshoot in accordance with the error code. You may search the Microsoft website for this error code and find a recommended solution.

If the driver is corrupted, you will need to uninstall the driver, click the Action menu in Device Manager, and select Scan for Hardware Changes to reinstall the driver. Another common solution is to select Update Driver in Device Manager. This will start the Hardware Update Wizard, which will walk you through the update process.

Sometimes, you do not see an associated error message when a device fails to start. This usually happens just as you attempt to use a device, such as a camera, scanner, or printer, and Windows does not recognize it and cannot install a driver (assuming this is the first time it was connected). First check that the device is properly connected and powered on, and then try again. Recall the quick fixes at the beginning of this chapter and power down the device and Windows. Turn power on to the device and power up the computer and try again. If the problem persists, contact the manufacturer and/or do a search on the problem.

Device Referenced in Registry Not Found

If you see an error message stating that a device referenced in the registry was not found, use the instructions given in the preceding section, "Device Has Failed to Start," to either update the driver or uninstall and reinstall the driver.

Service Has Failed to Start

If you see the error message "Service has failed to start" or a similar message, open the Services console (services.msc). In the contents pane, scroll down until you see the service that failed to start and right-click it. From the context menu, click Start. It may take several minutes for the service to start. If it starts normally, without any error messages, then do not take any further steps unless the problem recurs, in which case you will need to research the problem. Do this by searching the Microsoft site on the service name, adding the word "failed" to the search string.

Program Referenced in Registry Not Found

If you see an error message stating that a program referenced in the registry was not found, uninstall and reinstall the program.

Missing DLL File

This error message may occur during startup or after you call up an application. Record the name of the DLL file, such as DIRECTX.DLL or MSVCR100D.DLL, and then use a search engine to research the error, or go to https://support.microsoft.com and enter a search string including "missing" and the filename. This error occurs when a program install or uninstall did not complete properly. You may need to reinstall a program or manually uninstall a program, based on instructions from either Microsoft or the publisher of the program, if it is a third-party program.

In a related but less common problem, the files in the DLL cache become corrupt, in spite of being in a protected location. The files in the DLL cache folder (%systemroot%\system32\dllcache) are used as a backup set in case the DLLs in the default location (%systemroot%\system32) become corrupt. In spite of many protections put in place to preserve both the installed DLL files and this cache of "spares," the cache location can be damaged. To repair it, use the System File Checker command-line tool, as described earlier in this chapter.

CompTIA A+ 902 exam objective 1.3 lists the EXTRACT command, but there is no EXTRACT command in any of the covered Windows versions. This was a command-line utility in Windows 95 and 98 for extracting specific missing files from Windows and Office compressed setup files (called cabinet files). Read this article for details: https://support.microsoft.com/en-us/kb/132913.

Troubleshooting Applications

Common problems with applications include the failure of an application to start and problems when running legacy applications in Windows.

Inability to Open Applications

If programs or files won't run or open at all, that's a serious system problem. Repair your Windows installation. If programs appear at first not to run at all but are just painfully slow to open, see the earlier section, "Slow System Performance."

Application Locks Up or Terminates Unexpectedly

If a particular application stops responding, you might be able to wait it out. Just let the PC sit for a few minutes, especially if the hard disk activity light is flashing vigorously on the PC. Things might come back to life again. If waiting it out (5 minutes or so should be enough) doesn't do anything, terminate the unresponsive program with Task Manager. If the same application locks up again, investigate. Run the Repair function for that program in Programs in the Control Panel, and try uninstalling and reinstalling the application. Make sure the display adapter's driver is up to date also.

Application Fails to Start

When an application won't start, a reboot will often solve the problem, because the problem is often a lack of available memory. Sometimes a program or process will claim memory and then fail to release it, leaving inadequate memory for other applications to run.

If a particular application still won't start after a reboot, repair/reinstall it. If multiple applications won't start, that's a system problem; repair Windows.

Application Compatibility Errors

Let's say you start an old application in a new version of Windows and it does not run correctly. Maybe the screen doesn't look quite right, or perhaps the program frequently hangs up. To solve this problem, first check for program updates from the manufacturer and install those. If this does not help, try reinstalling the program. If that also does not work, then use the Program Compatibility Troubleshooter (or Program Compatibility Wizard in Vista) for the version of Windows you are running. We described the Program Compatibility Troubleshooter in Chapter 2. After running the Program Compatibility Troubleshooter, test the program to see if there is an improvement. If Compatibility Mode does not solve the problem for a program that ran well under Windows XP, and if you are running Windows 7, you have another option, which is Windows XP Mode, described in Chapter 8. Use this option before doing something that would be less desirable, such as creating a dual-boot configuration. That would require booting the computer into Windows XP just to run the old app and back into Windows 7 for other tasks. If Windows XP Mode does not work, consider dual-booting or finding an alternate app that will run in your Windows version.

File Fails to Open

To troubleshoot why a file fails to open, first look at the method used for opening the file. There are two frequently used methods for opening files. One is to locate the file using Windows Explorer and double-click the file to launch it in the associated program. Another is to first open the app, such as Microsoft Word, and open a file from within the app. For instance, in Microsoft Word click the File tab in the upper-left corner of the window and either select the file from the Recent Documents list or select Open and browse to the file's location.

When a file fails to open when you use the first method, it is most likely that the file type is not associated with any installed program. This happens frequently on a brand-new computer when someone attempts to open a PDF file. The reason it cannot open is most likely because the computer does not have a PDF reader, such as Adobe Acrobat Reader. Locate a free PDF reader on the Web, download it, and install it. Caution: Only download from a website you trust, and be careful because a web page containing free download will often have a bigger and more obvious button for downloading something you may not even want, and it is easy to click the wrong button.

If a file fails to open from a recent list—whether it is the Recent list within the application or the Recent Items list on the Start menu—suspect that the file got moved or renamed since the last time it was opened in an app. Open File Explorer and do a search for the filename you recall. If that fails to locate your file, do another search for a string of characters you know is contained in the document.

CERTIFICATION OBJECTIVES

- ■ *902: 2.1* *Identify common features and functionality of the Mac OS and Linux operating systems*
- ■ *902: 4.1* *Given a scenario, troubleshoot PC operating system problems with appropriate tools*

This section covers the few Linux and Mac troubleshooting techniques covered on the A+ exams. You won't be expected to be an Apple Genius or Linux guru, but you should at least know the basics. For CompTIA A+ 902 exam objective 2.1, we'll explain the ps, su, sudo, and apt-get commands. For 902 exam objective 4.1, we'll look at three specific problems: missing GRUB/LILO, failure to load the graphical interface, and kernel panic.

Troubleshooting macOS and Linux Systems

Entire books are written on Linux and macOS troubleshooting; in this chapter we look only at specific items from the CompTIA A+ exam objectives.

Managing Tasks with ps

Linux has a command-line equivalent to Windows Task Manager, called ps. From a Linux or Mac Terminal window, type **ps** and press ENTER to see a list of running processes.

When troubleshooting, you might want to know which processes are consuming the most CPU or memory, because those may be malfunctioning processes. To do this from a Terminal window, use switches that ask for the list to be sorted. For example, to display the top five processes consuming most of the CPU time, use the following command:

```
ps -aux –sort -pcpu
```

Check the man page for the ps command for complete details.

Taking Administrative Control with su/sudo

When you run Linux commands that attempt to fix system problems, you need to do so as the root user. The root user is roughly equivalent to the Administrator account on a Windows system. Normal Linux users run with reduced permissions, like a Standard account in Windows.

The su command (short for superuser) switches to the root user when you run it with no switches. (Just type **su** and press ENTER.) You can also use it to switch to other user accounts; for example, **su mary** switches to the mary account.

The sudo command is a prefix you add to individual commands to execute them with root privileges without actually switching to the root user. There's an example in the "Getting Missing Files with apt-get" section coming up.

Starting the Linux Graphical Shell Manually

On a Linux system that boots to Terminal, an easy way to start the graphical shell is to type **startx** at the prompt.

If no graphical shell loads at that point, perhaps one is not installed. See the next section.

Getting Missing Files with apt-get

The apt command is short for Advanced Packaging tool, a popular Linux package manager. One possible parameter you can specify for the command is get, used to get missing files.

Let's look at an example. Suppose the Linux graphical shell doesn't load. Maybe you don't have it on the machine you're working on. Some administrators leave it off to save overhead. Here's how you would get it with the apt command:

```
sudo apt-get install -re-install ubuntu-desktop
```

As previously described, sudo instructs Linux to run the command as a superuser. The get parameter tells the apt command what you want to do (in this case, get something). The ubuntu-desktop parameter describes the package that contains the graphical desktop environment for Ubuntu.

Missing GRUB/LILO

GRUB (Grand Unified Bootloader) and LILO (Linux Loader) are boot loading utilities; GRUB is the more popular of the two. If you have a multiboot system with Windows and Linux, you might have one of these utilities that manages the boot loading process. Occasionally they become corrupted. This can happen, for example, when you install Windows on a system that already has Linux on it and Windows tries to replace GRUB with its own boot loader.

To re-enable GRUB, start up the PC from the Linux installation media, and run a boot loader repair tool such a Boot-Repair (included with Ubuntu Linux). Different Linux distros may have different tools.

Kernel Panic

Kernel panic is a cute term for a serious system error that the system cannot recover from without a reboot. The term is used mostly to describe this condition in Linux and macOS, and it is the equivalent to the Windows Blue Screen of Death. In Linux, the keyboard LEDs blink during a kernel panic condition. A less serious variant in Linux is known as a kernel oops, where the kernel keeps running after killing the process causing the error.

On newer versions of macOS (10.8 and newer), the computer reboots automatically and displays a message that lets the user know that the computer restarted because of a problem.

When kernel panic occurs, restarting usually corrects the problem. If kernel panic reoccurs, start investigating hardware and hardware drivers, applications, and the OS itself.

CERTIFICATION OBJECTIVES

- **902: 1.7** *Perform common preventive maintenance procedures using the appropriate Windows OS tools*
- **902: 2.1** *Identify common features and functionality of the Mac OS and Linux operating systems*

CompTIA A+ 902 exam objective 1.7 describes a list of best practices for preventive maintenance of Windows, macOS, and Linux computers. You should know how to schedule important maintenance tasks, such as backups, checking disks for errors, defragmentation, OS updates, patch management, driver or firmware updates, and antivirus /antimalware updates. Also listed are the tools you should use for many of these tasks, including Backup, System Restore, recovery image, and disk maintenance utilities. The following section will describe how you use these tools to perform important maintenance tasks. This section also includes some macOS and Linux maintenance tools as well, such as Time Machine on macOS.

OS Preventive Maintenance

Preventive maintenance for operating systems includes tasks that either prevent certain problems from occurring or guarantee that you can quickly recover from a problem or disaster with a minimum loss of time or data.

Preventive maintenance best practices include the following:

- Scheduled backups
- Scheduled disk checking for errors
- Scheduled defragmentation
- Operating system updates
- Patch management
- Driver/firmware updates
- Antivirus/antimalware updates

New in the CompTIA A+ 220-902 exam is the expectation that you will know how to do these things not only in Windows but also in macOS. In the following sections we address the Windows utilities first, and then explain the equivalent macOS utilities.

Scheduled Backups

The data created and stored on computers is far more valuable for individuals and organizations than is the computer hardware and software used to create and store the data. So your backup strategies, the hardware and software used for backup, and the actual habit of backing up are critical to maintaining both data and computers. In case of the accidental destruction of data, and/or the disks containing the data, having a recent backup on removable media can be the difference between personal or professional disaster and the relatively minor inconvenience of taking the time to restore the data.

A Backup utility creates a backup disk set that compresses and stores multiple files in a single large backup file that requires decrypting with the same Backup program in the event that the backups must be restored. The advantage of this is the compression; the backup data can fit in less storage space than it could if the files were uncompressed. The disadvantage, obviously, is convenience. You can't just browse the backup disc and pick out the file you want to restore.

Backup utilities like the ones that come with Windows and Mac operating systems are very basic, small-potatoes programs. Large companies don't use them; instead they have dedicated backup servers or network appliances that back up data using the company's network during off-hours.

Windows 8.1 and Windows 10 do not include a Backup utility. Backup utilities have fallen out of favor, as other backup solutions have become more desirable. However, Windows Vista, Windows 7, and Windows 8 each include a Backup utility, and you'll need to know about these for your exam prep.

Using Windows Backup

Windows Backup and Restore can back up to network locations as well as to internal and external local drives. Open it by entering **backup** in the Start Search box and selecting Backup and Restore from the results (or Backup and Restore Center in Windows Vista).

The interface for the Backup utility and the exact steps for using it vary somewhat among Windows versions. Figure 12-17 shows Backup and Restore in Windows 7 with settings for the location and information about the next scheduled backup, the last scheduled backup, the contents of the backups, and the schedule. All of this information is missing when you first open Backup and Restore. In its place is a simple statement, "Windows Backup has not been set up," and a shortcut labeled Set Up Backup. Click this to select what you want to back up and to choose a location for the backups. You can have Backup and Restore back up files in certain folders (and you choose the types of files you want backed up from those

FIGURE 12-17   Click Change Settings to make changes to the backup settings.

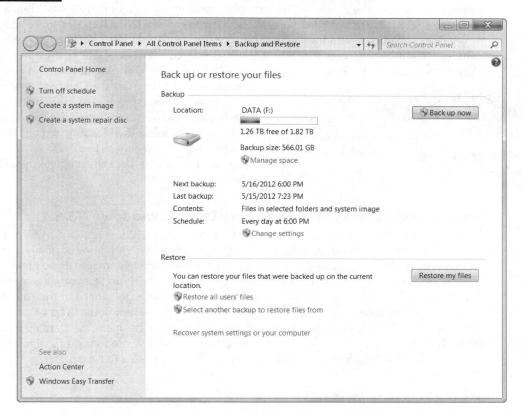

folders), and you can have it create a system image (Windows 7 only). We do both (files and system), and we recommend that you do this also. The computer in the example backs up to an external hard drive, and has been backing up to the drive for the last several months. We allow Windows Backup and Restore to manage the space, automatically deleting old backups as necessary to preserve space, and we still have 1.26 TB of space free on the backup disk. We also configured backup to run every evening at 6 P.M.

If possible, occasionally test your backups by restoring them. Now, you need to be careful when doing this, because if the backup is even minutes old and you have made changes to files since the backup, you will end up restoring on top of the changed files and lose your new work. Therefore, if possible, test your backups by restoring to another identically configured computer—perhaps one you use for testing or training purposes.

Creating a System Image in Windows 7

A *system image* (or *recovery image*) is a complete backup of the hard drive containing an operating system. There are third-party tools that you can use to create a system image for previous versions of Windows without this option, but Windows 7 Backup and Restore includes the option to Create a System Image. (This feature isn't available in any other Windows version.) You can create an image backup on a hard disk, one or more DVDs, or a network location. Start the Create a System Image wizard from the task list in the left pane of the Backup and Restore utility (see Figure 12-17). In the wizard, select the location, and follow the instructions. If you choose to use DVDs, you may need a stack of them to complete the image backup.

System image is referred to as Recovery image in CompTIA A+ 902 exam objective 1.7.

Create a System Repair Disc/Recovery Drive in Windows 7/8/8.1

Windows 7 and Windows 8/8.1 have a utility that will create a *system repair disc*, an optical disk that you can use to boot your computer when Windows will not boot normally, and it contains system recovery tools that you can use to restore a system image (if you created a system image beforehand) or do other repairs to Windows without restoring the image. (Windows 8/8.1 calls it a *recovery drive*.) Create a system repair disc ahead of time and keep it on hand for an emergency. To do this in Windows 7, type **system** in the Start | Search box and select Create a System Repair Disc from the results list. This opens the Create a System Repair Disc dialog box where you can choose an optical drive to use to create a repair disc. In Windows 8/8.1, search instead for **recovery** and select Create a Recovery Drive.

Use Backup Tools in macOS

macOS doesn't use the same kind of backup program that Windows does. Rather than making you run a utility (or having one run automatically) to back things up at certain times, macOS uses a real-time backup utility called *Time Machine*. You can connect an external drive to your Mac, and as you work, your files will be backed up hourly. Time Machine keeps hourly backups for the past 24 hours, daily backups for the past month, and weekly backups for all previous months. When the backup disk becomes full, the oldest backups are deleted.

To enable Time Machine, connect an external drive to your Mac. Then open System Preferences (cog icon in the Dock) and click Time Machine. Click Select Disk to choose the disk to use, and then drag the Time Machine slider to On if it doesn't set itself that way automatically. See Figure 12-18. You might be prompted to erase the disk if its current file system is incompatible with macOS.

To access your backups, on the Dock click Launchpad. Click the Other folder, and click Time Machine. Scroll through the available backups with the up and down arrow buttons, and then select the file(s) to restore and click Restore.

FIGURE 12-18

Time Machine
backs up
every hour
automatically.

Use Backup Tools in Linux

Different Linux distros have different backup tools. In Ubuntu, there's a utility called Deja-Dup that you can access in the GUI. Click System Settings and then click Backups. This simple utility enables you to choose which folders to save and which to ignore, where to store the backups, and on what schedule to do the backing up. You can choose to back up once a day or once a week (not hourly as on the Mac).

Scheduling Disk Maintenance

Disk maintenance can include defragmenting a disk, checking it for errors, and deleting unwanted files. These utilities were covered in Chapters 9 and 10. They work somewhat differently in different Windows versions, and have different names. (In Windows 8.1, for example, Disk Defragmenter has been renamed Optimize Drives.) These activities can also be scheduled in macOS and Linux.

These utilities are fairly straightforward to use; you can run them from the Properties dialog box for any hard disk drive, on the Tools tab. However, what may not be obvious is that you can schedule them to run automatically at certain intervals using the Task Scheduler utility. Depending on the Windows version, some disk maintenance utilities also include a means for scheduling them within the applications themselves. To schedule disk maintenance, run the Task Scheduler utility. Exercise 12-4 demonstrates how to use it.

EXERCISE 12-4

Scheduling Disk Maintenance

In this exercise you will use Windows 7 or 8.1 to practice scheduling a task using Task Scheduler.

1. Click Start, type **task**, then click Task Scheduler (Windows 7) or Schedule Tasks (Windows 8.1).

2. In the navigation pane on the left, expand folders to open Task Scheduler Library | Microsoft | Windows. Within that folder you'll find folders for many utilities you can set up to run automatically at specific times.

3. Click Defrag. Look in the upper section of the center pane. The scheduled defrag already exists.

4. Click each of the tabs in the lower section of the center pane to examine the settings for this scheduled task.

5. If you are using Windows 8.1, click Chkdsk in the navigation pane on the left. A task has been scheduled for Check Disk. If you are using Windows 7, you won't have a Check Disk task prescheduled.

6. Click Windows in the navigation pane and then click Action | Create Basic Task. The Create Basic Task Wizard appears. This is the way you would create additional tasks.

7. If you would like to try creating a task, do so, using Chkdsk or any utility. Or, if you think you've got this without the practice, click Cancel.

Updates and Patch Management

An important part of OS maintenance is making sure that available updates are installed in a timely manner. Updates are sometimes called *patches* because they tend to fix problems. CompTIA A+ 902 exam objectives 1.7 and 2.1 refer to "Patch management," and what they mean by this is the cumulative collection of all available updates, including OS, applications, drivers, and firmware.

Getting Updates and Patches in Windows

Windows has the Windows Update feature, previously introduced in the "Updating Windows" section in Chapter 9. Windows Update downloads updates for Windows itself, as well as for certain Microsoft applications. It can also download updates for some hardware drivers. However, it does not update most non-Microsoft applications or firmware; you must update them within the individual applications or by downloading and installing new versions manually.

You can check for driver updates for most devices through Device Manager. Open the Properties dialog box for the device and click the Driver tab, and then click Update Driver and follow the prompts.

Getting Updates and Patches in macOS

In macOS, you can set your update preferences by opening the System Preferences and clicking App Store. Then make sure that all the check boxes are checked in the dialog box, as shown in Figure 12-19, to allow all updates to download and install automatically. The operating system handles all driver updates along with the OS updates, so you do not have to search manually for updated drivers.

Notice in Figure 12-19 that software updates are available. You can click Show Updates to open the App Store window with the updates listed for all your installed applications. You can also get to that same place by opening the App Store separately and then clicking Updates.

FIGURE 12-19

Configure
updates to occur
automatically
in macOS.

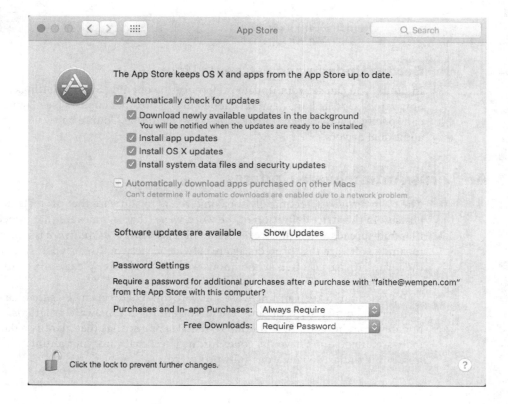

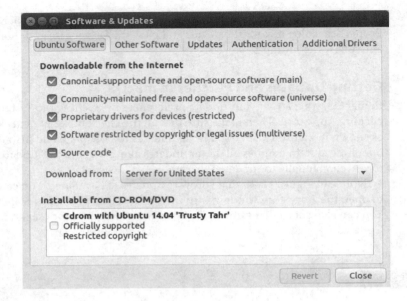

Getting Updates and Patches in Linux

In Linux, you can set your update preferences by opening System Settings and clicking
Software & Updates. In the multi-tabbed dialog box that appears (see Figure 12-20), you
can specify exactly which updates you want, including Ubuntu software, other software, and
additional drivers.

Antivirus/Antimalware Updates

The term *antivirus*, technically speaking, refers to software that protects only against
viruses, in the strict definition of the word *virus* (that is, malware that infects executable
files and spreads when those executable files are run). *Antimalware* is a broader term
meaning software that protects against a wide variety of threat types. In practice, however,
the term antivirus is often synonymous with antimalware. We use the term antimalware to
refer to both.

It's essential to keep antimalware software up to date on any PCs that have network
or Internet connectivity. Updates are important for antimalware programs because these
updates contain malware definitions—telltale code strings that identify a particular piece of
malware. If you don't have the codes for the latest malware, your antimalware software can
miss some things, so you aren't fully protected.

Besides keeping it updated, you don't have to do anything with antimalware software; it runs in the background and alerts you if it finds any problems. Most antimalware software has a command that enables you to do a full system scan immediately, but you don't have to manually do this unless you suspect a problem.

Windows Antivirus and Antimalware

Windows Vista and newer come with Windows Defender, an antimalware utility. However, up until Windows 8, it did not include antivirus capabilities; it only protected against certain other types of malware, like adware and cookie trackers, that were more likely to invade your privacy than to cause system problems. Therefore, if you are running Windows Vista or Windows 7, you need an add-on antivirus program in addition to Windows Defender.

Microsoft supplied a free program called Microsoft Security Essentials for Windows Vista and Windows 7, available for download. It replaced Windows Defender, providing both antivirus and antimalware protection. In Windows 8 and newer, Microsoft has rebranded Microsoft Security Essentials as Windows Defender, so they are no longer two separate programs, and has included it in all editions of Windows.

That doesn't mean, however, that you can't use a third-party antivirus or antimalware product, or even a multifunction third-party security suite that includes not only those capabilities but also a more robust firewall, e-mail filtering, and other security tweaks.

Windows Defender updates are downloaded automatically along with Windows OS updates. If you use a third-party program, you can set it to automatically update itself at regular intervals.

macOS and Linux Antivirus and Antimalware

macOS and Linux do not come with any antivirus or antimalware software, although both receive security patches and updates along with OS updates. Most people will tell you that a full-featured antimalware program is not necessary, because nobody writes malware for Mac and Linux systems. While that seems rather overoptimistic, it is by and large true. You can buy third-party antimalware software for the macOS, however, from all the same major third-party players that make Windows antimalware software, such as Symantec and McAfee.

Malware exists for the Mac that poses as antimalware software. Watch out for free antivirus software with the names MacDefender, MacProtector, and MacSecurity. These are all names of known Mac malware.

CERTIFICATION SUMMARY

As an IT professional, you must have a foundation of knowledge about operating systems in order to troubleshoot common problems, beginning with a few quick fixes to try before going any further in researching symptoms. Then, if the quick fixes don't work, attempt to pinpoint the problem's source to a single application or to the operating system in general. Ensure that a computer meets the minimum requirements for the installed OS and apps and has no known compatibility issues.

Familiarize yourself with the utilities and tools for troubleshooting. Begin with documentation resources available to you for troubleshooting and training yourself in using and supporting Windows and applications. Practice using Registry Editor, Device Manager, Task Manager, Task Scheduler, Performance Monitor, System Configuration (MSCONFIG), and Windows Memory Diagnostic. Also practice modified startups using the various Safe Mode options. Ensure that you know the recovery options for Windows Vista, Windows 7, and Windows 8.1. Make sure you know the macOS and Linux equivalents of the Windows troubleshooting tools as well; although they're not included in the A+ objectives, you may need them in your work.

You should recognize common symptoms and understand the possible causes and solutions to these problems. Recognize common error messages and codes, and understand how to work with Event Viewer.

Practice preventive maintenance on Windows computers, including defragmenting hard drive volumes, turning on automatic updates for both Windows and applications, scheduling backups, testing restores, and configuring System Restore. Make sure you also know the equivalent utilities and practices on Mac and Linux systems.

TWO-MINUTE DRILL

Here are some of the key points covered in Chapter 12.

Quick Fixes

❑ Try quick fixes such as rebooting before assuming that more in-depth troubleshooting is required.

❑ Verify that the software or device you are attempting to install or troubleshoot is compatible with the hardware and software of the PC.

❑ For application problems, use the Control Panel's Programs and Features applet to repair an application.If that doesn't work, uninstall and reinstall the application.

Windows Troubleshooting Tools

❑ Some BIOS/UEFI settings can affect OS functionality; check firmware setup for any settings that may be interfering with specific OS features.

❑ You can access a command-line interface in Windows, macOS, or Linux. In the latter two it is called Terminal. You can run command-line commands there, or call the executable filenames for GUI programs. In Windows, you can also run individual command lines from the Run dialog box (WINDOWS KEY-R) or, in some Windows versions, from the Search box on the Start menu.

❑ Action Center provides feedback and possible solutions for security and system problems.

❑ Use the System Information utility (MSINFO32.EXE) to quickly learn about a system you must troubleshoot or support.

❑ The registry is a database of all Windows configuration settings that is best modified indirectly through many configuration tools, although administrators can use Registry Editor (REGEDIT) to view and directly edit it.

❑ The GUI for many Windows utilities is an MMC window. Some tools available in the MMC are Device Manager, Task Scheduler, Performance Monitor, Event Viewer, Component Services, and Services.

❑ Event Viewer enables you to examine error logs to determine when and how often problems are occurring.

❑ REGSVR32 is a command-line tool for resolving problems with software components.

❑ System File Checker (SFC) scans Windows to make sure no important system files are missing or corrupted and makes any repairs needed.

❑ Use Task Manager to stop a program that has stopped responding and that cannot be stopped any other way.

❑ Use the System Configuration utility (MSCONFIG.EXE) to modify startup configuration settings without having to alter the settings directly. You can test startup settings without making them permanent until you are satisfied with the results.

❑ Windows Memory Diagnostic is a tool that will schedule a group of diagnostic tests of your memory after a reboot.

❑ You can access the Windows Advanced Boot Options menu by pressing F8 as the computer is restarting. It contains many alternative ways to start Windows when you are troubleshooting startup problems.

❑ Select from three Safe Mode options to troubleshoot and solve Windows problems. They are Safe Mode, Safe Mode with Networking, and Safe Mode with Command Prompt.

❑ System Restore creates restore points, or snapshots that Windows created automatically, including its configuration and all installed programs. If your computer has nonfatal problems after you make a change, you can use System Restore to roll it back to a restore point.

❑ Windows Shadow Copy is turned on when System Restore is, adding the ability to track and maintain backup copies of data file versions for files on an NTFS volume. Windows Vista and Windows 7 can only use Shadow Copy on the system volume, while Windows 8/8.1 allows you to add other NTFS volumes.

❑ To enter the Windows Recovery Environment (Windows RE), boot from Windows installation media or choose it from the Advanced Options menu. It might also load automatically after a startup failure.

❑ The Windows RE command prompt supports a subset of the normal command-line tools. One of these tools, BOOTREC, is not available except in Windows RE. It repairs the master boot record or boot sector and can rebuild the BCD store.

❑ In Windows 8/8.1, you can use Refresh to repair your Windows installation without losing data or programs.

❑ If your computer cannot take advantage of DirectX video, sound, and input required by some applications, use the DirectX Diagnostic Tool (DXDIAG) from the Run dialog box to diagnose the problem.

Windows Symptoms and Solutions

❑ OS instability problems include STOP errors, freezes and spontaneous restarts, booting into Safe Mode, missing graphical interface, and slow system performance.

❑ Slow system performance can mean insufficient memory, corrupt system files, a bad driver, or a virus. There are many possible causes. Try System Restore to go back to a time before performance degraded.

❑ Be familiar with command error messages and their possible solutions. Use Event Viewer to see error messages you missed.

❑ Sometimes if an application locks up, it will start working again if you wait a few minutes. If it does not, shut it down with Task Manager. Troubleshoot by repairing or reinstalling it, and check its compatibility with the installed Windows version.

❑ When an application fails to start but there are no other obvious symptoms, suspect that insufficient memory is the problem.

Troubleshooting Mac and Linux Systems

❑ In Linux, the ps command-line utility shows information about running processes.

❑ The su command changes to the superuser account; sudo runs a single command as the superuser.

❑ If the Linux graphical shell doesn't start automatically, type startx at the Terminal prompt.

❑ The apt command is a Linux package manager. Use apt-get to get software that you don't have.

❑ GRUB and LILO are boot loading utilities. They sometimes get disabled by Windows on a multiboot system. Use a boot loader repair tool to fix this.

❑ Kernel panic is the Mac and Linux equivalent to the Blue Screen of Death in Windows. Reboot if the system does not automatically reboot.

OS Preventive Maintenance

❑ Schedule regular backups of both the OS and data files using either the Backup utility in Windows or a third-party backup program. Test a restore of your data to ensure that it will work when you really need it.

❑ In macOS, the Time Machine utility handles automatic backups if you connect an external drive or specify another backup destination. In Linux, one popular backup tool is Deja-Dup.

❑ Schedule disk maintenance via the Task Scheduler. You may want to automate Defrag and Check Disk, for example.

❑ Make sure the OS is configured to receive automatic system updates. Depending on the OS, there may be separate procedures for receiving driver, firmware, and application updates.

❑ It is important to keep antimalware software up to date. Malware is less of a problem on Linux and Mac systems, and those OSs do not come with antimalware utilities.

SELF TEST

The following questions will help you measure your understanding of the material presented in this chapter. Read all of the choices carefully because there might be more than one correct answer. Choose all correct answers for each question.

Quick Fixes

1. Which of the following is *not* a quick fix that you should at least consider before further investigation of a problem?
   A. Reboot the computer.
   B. Restore a system image.
   C. Uninstall a recently installed app.
   D. Uninstall a recently installed device.

Windows Troubleshooting Tools

2. How can you access Safe Mode at startup?
   A. Start menu
   B. Advanced Boot Options menu
   C. Control Panel
   D. System Properties

3. What is the name of the executable file for System Information?
   A. MSINFO32
   B. MSCONFIG
   C. SYSINFO
   D. REGEDIT

4. Which of the following is a tool for making changes to the registry?
   A. MSINFO32
   B. MSCONFIG
   C. REGSVR32
   D. REGEDIT

5. Computer Management is a preconfigured version of what utility?
   A. Compatibility Mode
   B. MSINFO32
   C. MSCONFIG
   D. MMC

6. What mode can you try to allow a legacy application to run well in Windows 7?
   A. GUI Mode
   B. Legacy Mode
   C. Compatibility Mode
   D. Virtual Mode

7. What GUI tool do you use to stop an application that is not responding to mouse and keyboard commands?
   A. Startup disk
   B. Task Manager
   C. System Configuration Utility
   D. Device Manager

8. What tool enables you to control which applications and services load at startup in Windows 7?
   A. Device Manager
   B. Safe Mode
   C. Notepad
   D. MSCONFIG

9. Where does System Restore store its restore points?
   A. In RAM
   B. On the local hard disk
   C. On a network share
   D. On removable drives

10. What command-line tool can you use to repair damaged system files?
    A. TASKKILL
    B. REGSVR32
    C. SFC
    D. TASKLIST

11. Which of these is a way of starting the Windows Recovery Environment?
    A. Boot from a Windows Setup disc.
    B. Restart the computer in Safe Mode.
    C. Run Device Manager.
    D. Press CTRL-ALT-DELETE.

Windows Symptoms and Solutions

12. How do you recover after a STOP error?
    A. Restart the computer.
    B. Press ESC.
    C. Open Event Viewer.
    D. Use System Restore.

13. What should you suspect if Windows spontaneously reboots frequently?
    A. Hard disk error
    B. Corrupted registry
    C. Failing power supply
    D. Missing DLLs

Troubleshooting Mac and Linux Systems

14. What Linux command enables you to see a list of running processes at a Terminal window?
    A. sudo
    B. ps
    C. startx
    D. apt-get

15. What are GRUB and LILO?
    A.   Boot loading utilities
    B.   Linux GUI environments
    C.   Boot loader repair tools
    D.   Security utilities

16. Which version of Windows comes with a Backup and Restore utility that allows you to make a recovery image?
    A.   Windows 10
    B.   Windows Vista
    C.   Windows 8.1
    D.   Windows 7

17. What is the backup utility in macOS?
    A.   Task Manager
    B.   Time Machine
    C.   Backup and Restore
    D.   Launchpad

OS Preventive Maintenance

18. What application allows you to schedule system maintenance actions?
    A.   Task Scheduler
    B.   Task Manager
    C.   System Configuration
    D.   System File Checker

19. In which OS do you get system updates through the App Store?
    A.   Windows
    B.   macOS
    C.   Linux
    D.   All of the above

20. What free Microsoft-supplied program supplements Windows Defender in Windows 7 and Windows Vista to provide antivirus services?
    A.   apt-get
    B.   Norton Antivirus
    C.   Microsoft Security Essentials
    D.   Time Machine

SELF TEST ANSWERS

Quick Fixes

1. ☑ **B.** Restore a system image is not a quick fix, when compared to the other three options, which are quick fixes that would not have further impact. You would need much more investigation before you would restore a system image.
☒ **A, C,** and **D** are all incorrect answers because they are quick fixes, as opposed to restoring a system image.

Windows Troubleshooting Tools

2. ☑ **B.** The Advanced Boot Options menu is the place where you can access Safe Mode. Get to this menu by pressing the F8 key immediately after restarting your computer.
☒ **A, C,** and **D** are all incorrect because these are all part of the Windows GUI, and the Advanced Options menu is something you use before you start Windows.

3. ☑ **A.** MSINFO32 is the executable for System Information.
☒ **B** is incorrect because it is the executable for System Configuration. **D** is incorrect because it is the executable for Registry Editor. **C** is incorrect because it is not a valid command.

4. ☑ **D.** REGEDIT is a registry-editing tool.
☒ **A** is incorrect because MSINFO32 is a tool for viewing information about the hardware and software on a computer. **B** is incorrect because MSCONFIG is a utility for testing alternate startup settings. **C** is incorrect because REGSVR32 is a command-line tool for resolving a certain type of software problem.

5. ☑ **D.** Computer Management is a Microsoft Management Console (MMC) preloaded with several snap-ins.
☒ **A** is incorrect because Compatibility Mode is a method of running older programs on newer Windows versions. **B** is incorrect because MSINFO32 is the executable for the System Information utility. **C** is incorrect because MSCONFIG is the executable for the System Configuration utility.

6. ☑ **C.** Compatibility Mode may allow a legacy application to run well in Windows 7.
☒ **A, B,** and **D** are all incorrect because none of these modes exist.

7. ☑ **B.** Task Manager is the GUI tool used to stop an application that is not responding to mouse and keyboard commands.
☒ **A** is incorrect because this is neither a GUI tool nor the tool to use to stop a nonresponsive application. **C** and **D** are incorrect because neither is the correct GUI tool to use to stop a nonresponsive application.

8. ☑ **D.** MSCONFIG is the tool that will allow you to control which applications and services load at startup in Windows 7. In Windows 8/8.1, this is done in Task Manager.
☒ **A** is incorrect because Device Manager works solely with device drivers, not with the Windows startup settings. **B** is incorrect because Safe Mode is simply a startup mode that allows you to troubleshoot and make changes using a variety of tools. **C** is incorrect because Notepad is simply a Windows text editor.

9. ☑ **B.** System Restore stores its restore points on the local hard disk.
☒ **A** is incorrect because you would not want restore points to be stored in volatile RAM. **C** and **D** are incorrect because a network share and removable drives may not always be available.

10. ☑ **C.** SFC (System File Checker) is a command-line tool that you can use to repair system files.
☒ **A** is incorrect because TASKKILL is a command-line tool for stopping a running program. **B** is incorrect because REGSVR32 is a command-line tool that is used to register or unregister software components, such as DLLs, and ActiveX Controls. **D** is incorrect because TASKLIST is a command-line tool for viewing running tasks.

11. ☑ **A.** Boot from a Windows Setup disc and choose Repair to enter the Windows Recovery Environment.
☒ **B** is incorrect because Safe Mode is not connected to Windows RE. **C** is incorrect because Device Manager is a utility for analyzing installed hardware. **D** is incorrect because that key sequence opens a menu from which you can open Task Manager.

Windows Symptoms and Solutions

12. ☑ **A.** Restart the computer. The computer must be restarted after a STOP error because it won't do anything until that happens.
☒ **B** is incorrect because the computer is locked up and ESC will do nothing. **C** is incorrect because you cannot run any programs until you restart. **D** is incorrect because you cannot run System Restore until you restart.

13. ☑ **C.** A failing power supply frequently causes spontaneous reboots.
☒ **A, B,** and **D** are all incorrect because none of these things would cause spontaneous reboots.

Troubleshooting Mac and Linux Systems

14. ☑ **B.** The ps command shows a list of running processes.
☒ **A** is incorrect because sudo runs the associated command as the superuser. **C** is incorrect because startx starts the Linux GUI. **D** is incorrect because apt-get gets a specified application.

15. ☑ **A.** GRUB and LILO are boot loading utilities that enable multiboot systems.
☒ **B** is incorrect because these are not GUI environments. **C** is incorrect because these do not repair the boot loader; they *are* the boot loader. **D** is incorrect because these are not security utilities.

16.   ☑   **D.** Windows 7 is the only version in which Backup and Restore includes a recovery image utility.

☒   **A** is incorrect because it does not come with a Backup utility. **B** is incorrect because the Windows Vista Backup and Restore utility does not have a recovery image utility. **C** is incorrect because Windows 8.1 does not come with a Backup utility.

17.   ☑   **B.** Time Machine is the backup program in macOS.

☒   **A** is incorrect because Task Manager is a Windows utility that shows running tasks. **C** is incorrect because Backup and Restore is the Windows 7 utility for backups. **D** is incorrect because Launchpad is the macOS utility for displaying installed applications you can run.

OS Preventive Maintenance

18.   ☑   **A.** Task Scheduler allows you to schedule system maintenance tasks.

☒   **B** is incorrect because Task Manager is a Windows utility that shows running tasks. **C** is incorrect because System Configuration manages system services and startup options. **D** is incorrect because SFC is the utility that checks and repairs system files.

19.   ☑   **B.** macOS updates are accessed via the App Store.

☒   **A** is incorrect because Windows gets its updates via Windows Update. **C** is incorrect because Linux gets its updates from Update Manager. **D** is incorrect because **A** and **C** are incorrect.

20.   ☑   **C.** Microsoft Security Essentials supplements the Windows 7 and Vista versions of Windows Defender, which do not include antivirus protection.

☒   **A** is incorrect because apt-get is the command-line utility in Linux for acquiring software. **B** is incorrect because, although Norton Antivirus can supplement Windows Defender, it is neither a Microsoft product nor free. **D** is incorrect because Time Machine is a macOS backup utility.

Chapter 13

Network Basics

Computer networks provide users with the ability to share files, printers, resources, and e-mail globally. Networks have become so important that they provide the basis for nearly all business transactions.

Obviously, a discussion of the full spectrum of network details and specifications is too broad in scope to be contained in this book. However, as a computer technician, you should be aware of basic networking concepts so you can troubleshoot minor problems on established networks. This chapter focuses on basic concepts of physical networks; Chapter 14 guides you through simple small office/home office (SOHO) network installation, and Chapter 16 provides the basis for troubleshooting common network problems.

CERTIFICATION OBJECTIVES

- **901: 1.7** *Compare and contrast various PC connection interfaces, their characteristics, and purpose*
- **901: 2.5** *Compare and contrast Wi-Fi networking standards and encryption types*
- **901: 2.7** *Compare and contrast Internet connection types, network types, and their features*

This section begins by describing the types of networks based on how they are connected (topology) and based on the area they service (LAN, WAN, PAN, and MAN), along with wide area network (WAN) technologies and connection types, as required by CompTIA A+ 901 exam objective 2.7. The discussion of the wireless networking standards contains the information as required by CompTIA A+ 901 exam objective 2.5, but a portion of that objective, Encryption types, is covered in Chapter 15. CompTIA A+ 901 exam objective 1.7 is included here only for the brief explanation of interfaces used in a PAN, such as infrared and Bluetooth.

Network Classifications

For a computer professional working with PCs, the networked computer is the norm, not the exception. A computer not connected to a network is a *standalone computer*, and this has become a nearly extinct species, as more and more PCs network together—even within homes.

To understand networks, you must first be familiar with basic network performance and classifications, which describe networks by speed, geography, and scale, beginning with the smallest networks up to globe-spanning ones.

We classify networks by geographic area types, and there are specific technologies designed for each of them. Network builders select these technologies for the capabilities that match the distance needs of the network.

Personal Area Network

You may have your own *personal area network (PAN)*, if you have devices such as smartphones, tablets, or printers that communicate with each other and/or your desktop computer. A PAN may use a wired connection, such as Universal Serial Bus (USB) or FireWire, or it may communicate wirelessly using one of the standards developed for short-range communications, such as Infrared (IR), also known as Infrared Data Association (IrDA), or Bluetooth.

Infrared (IR) is not a popular technology anymore, but you may still encounter it on old laptops or peripherals, such as old wireless keyboards and mice. IR-enabled devices can communicate with each other over a very short distance (1 meter), and because IR uses an infrared light, the communicating devices must maintain line-of-sight between the IR ports on the two devices.

watch **The term PAN is included** in CompTIA A+ 901 exam objective 2.7; the wireless technologies used in a PAN are also included, in 901 exam objective 1.7, so be	**familiar with them and their distance limit, which is 1 meter for infrared and 10 meters for Bluetooth (see Chapter 7).**

As you learned in Chapter 7, Bluetooth uses radio waves, which do not require line-of-sight, but the signal can be disrupted by physical barriers as well as interference from other signals. The Bluetooth standard describes three classes, with power requirements and distance limits. The Bluetooth standard commonly used with computer peripherals and mobile devices is Class 3, limited to a distance of 1 meter, or Class 2, limited to about 10 meters.

Local Area Network

A *local area network (LAN)* is a network that covers a much larger area than a PAN, such as a building, home, office, or campus. Typically, distances measure in hundreds of meters. A LAN may share resources such as printers, files, or other items. LANs operate very rapidly, with speeds measured in megabits or gigabits per second, and have become extremely cost effective. While there are many LAN technologies, the two most widely used in SOHO network installations are Ethernet and several Wi-Fi standards.

Ethernet

Most wired LANs use hardware based on standards developed by the 902.3 subcommittee of the Institute of Electrical and Electronics Engineers (IEEE). *Ethernet* is the word created to describe the earliest of these networks, and we continue to use this term, although there really are many Ethernet standards—all under the 902.3 umbrella. These standards define, among other things, how computer data is broken down into small chunks, prepared, and packaged before the Ethernet network adapter (also known as a network interface card, or NIC) places it on the Ethernet network as a chunk of data called an Ethernet *frame*. Ethernet standards also define the hardware and media that control and carry the data signals.

Early implementations of Ethernet were *half-duplex*, meaning that while data could travel in either direction, it could only travel in one direction at a time. Later implementations are capable of *full-duplex* communication, in which the signals travel in both directions simultaneously, but they usually auto-negotiate and automatically use either half- or full-duplex, depending on what is in use on the network. Networks today are usually full-duplex, unless a network has very old hardware.

Depending on the exact implementation, Ethernet supports a variety of transmission speeds, media, and distances. All Ethernet standards using copper cabling, either unshielded twisted-pair (UTP) or shielded twisted-pair (STP), support a maximum cable length of 100 meters between a NIC and a hub or switch. Learn more about hubs and switches later in this chapter, in the section "Devices for Connecting to LANs and the Internet." The maximum distances for fiber-optic cable (a.k.a. fiber) installations vary, depending on the exact cable type in use. Here is a summary of several Ethernet levels and their speeds:

- **10BaseT/Ethernet** For many years the most widely used implementation, 10BaseT transfers data at 10 Mbps over UTP copper cabling in half-duplex mode with a maximum cable length of 100 meters.

- **100BaseT/Fast Ethernet** Using the same cabling as 10BaseT, 100BaseT or *Fast Ethernet* operates at 100 Mbps and uses different NICs, many of which are also capable of the lower Ethernet speeds, auto-detecting the speed of the network and working at whichever speed is in use. Early 100BaseT NICs were half-duplex, but later ones support full-duplex.

- **1000BaseT/Gigabit Ethernet** Supporting data transfer rates of 1 Gbps over UTP, there are several *Gigabit Ethernet* standards, but the most common one is 1000BaseT. It is capable of full-duplex operation using four-pair UTP cable with standard RJ-45 connectors (see the description of cable later in "Transmission Medium").

- **10 GbE/10-Gigabit Ethernet** WANS and some high-end LANs use one of the many standards of *10-Gigabit Ethernet*, which operates at speeds of up to 10 Gbps in full-duplex mode over either copper (10GBaseT) or fiber. There are many 10-Gigabit Ethernet fiber standards for both WANs and LANS, and we will only briefly mention two of them here. The *10GBaseSR* standard is one of the standards used for fiber-optic LANs, whereas *10GBaseSW* is one of the standards used for fiber-optic WANs.

Wireless LAN (WLAN)

Wireless LAN (WLAN) communication (local area networking using *radio frequency*, or *RF*) is very popular. The most common wireless LAN implementations are based on the IEEE 802.11 group of standards, also called *Wireless Fidelity (Wi-Fi)*. There are several 802.11 standards, and more were proposed. These wireless standards use either 2.4 GHz or 5 GHz frequencies to communicate between systems. The range on these systems is relatively short, but they offer the advantage of not requiring cable for network connections.

In many homes and businesses, Wi-Fi networks give users access to the Internet. In these instances, the wireless communications network uses a wireless router connected to a broadband connection, such as a cable modem or digital subscriber line (DSL) modem.

Wi-Fi, long a standard feature on laptops, is also available on most smartphones and tablets. In large corporations, users with wireless-enabled laptops and other devices can move around the campus and continue to connect to the corporate network through a Wi-Fi network that connects to the corporate wired network. And many public places, such as libraries, restaurants, and other business, offer free or pay access to Wi-Fi networks that connect to broadband Internet services. Such a point of connection to the Internet through a Wi-Fi network is called a *hotspot*. On an interesting twist on this concept, cellular providers and manufacturers of cellular-enabled mobile devices have cooperated to provide a newer type of service called a *mobile hotspot*. You can create a mobile hotspot by connecting to the Internet with your smartphone's cellular service, and then using the smartphone's Wi-Fi connectivity to allow other nearby Wi-Fi-enabled devices to share that Internet connection.

Here is a brief description of several 802.11 standards and their features:

- **802.11a**   The *802.11a* standard was developed by the IEEE at the same time as the slower 802.11b standard, but the "a" standard was more expensive to implement. Manufacturers, therefore, tended to make 802.11b devices. 802.11a uses the 5 GHz band, which makes 802.11a devices incompatible with 802.11b and the subsequent 802.11g devices. Because 802.11a devices do not provide downward compatibility with existing equipment using the 802.11b or newer 802.11g standards, they are seldom used. An 802.11a network has speeds up to 54 Mbps with a range of up to 150 feet.

- **802.11b**   The *802.11b* standard was the first widely popular version of Wi-Fi, with a speed of 11 Mbps and a range of up to 300 feet. Operating in the 2.4 GHz band that is also used by other noncomputer devices such as cordless phones and household appliances, these devices are vulnerable to interference if positioned near another device using the same portion of the radio spectrum.

- **802.11g**   *802.11g* replaced 802.11b. With a speed of up to 54 Mbps and a range of up to 300 feet, it also uses the 2.4 GHz radio band. 802.11g devices are normally downward compatible with 802.11b devices, although the reverse is not true.

- **802.11n**   The *802.11n* standard has speeds of up to 100+ Mbps and a maximum range of up to 600 feet. The standard defines speeds of up to 600 Mbps, which actual implementations do not achieve. *MIMO (multiple input/multiple output)* makes 802.11n speeds possible using multiple antennas to send and receive digital data in simultaneous radio streams that increase performance.

- **802.11ac**   The *802.11ac* standard has multistation throughput of 1 Gbps, and a single-link throughput of 500 Mbps. It accomplishes these higher speeds by using a wider RF bandwidth than 802.11n, more MIMO streams (up to eight), and high-density modulation.

When considering a wireless network, determining its speed and range can be nebulous at best. In spite of the maximums defined by the standards, many factors affect both speed and range. First, there is the limit of the standard, and then there is the distance between the wireless-enabled computer and the *wireless access point (WAP)*, a network connection device at the core of a wireless network. Finally, there is the issue of interference, which can result from other wireless device signals operating in the same band or from physical barriers to the signals. In Chapter 14, you will learn about installing a WLAN to avoid interference and devices that will extend the range of the signals. You will also learn about the configuration options for wireless networks, including the use of identifiers for the wireless devices, secure encryption settings, and settings for keeping intruders out.

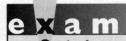

Be sure you understand that Wi-Fi alone does not give you a connection to the Internet, because it is a LAN technology. The reason people are able to connect to the Internet through a Wi-Fi connection is that the Wi-Fi network connects to a broadband connection through a device called a *wireless router*, a combination WAP and router.

Metropolitan Area Network

A *metropolitan area network (MAN)* is a network that covers a metropolitan area, connecting various networks together using a shared community network, and often providing WAN connections to the Internet. A MAN usually runs over high-speed fiber-optic cable operating in the gigabits-per-second range. *Synchronous Optical Networking (SONET)* is one long-established fiber-optic WAN technology. Although people tend to be less aware of MANs, they nonetheless exist. In fact, a MAN may well be somewhere between you and the Internet.

For the CompTIA A+ 220-901 exam, be sure that you understand the distinctions between the various network types, including PAN, LAN, MAN, and WAN.

Wide Area Network

A *wide area network (WAN)* can cover the largest geographic area. A *WAN connection* is the connection between two networks over a long distance (miles). The term WAN is used to describe a wired WAN connection versus a *wireless wide area network (WWAN)*, a wireless connection between two networks over a long distance. The generic term for these connected networks is an *internetwork*, if it is a public network. The most famous, and largest, internetwork is the *Internet* itself. An *intranet* is a private internetwork, generally owned by a single organization. Your Internet connection from home is a WAN connection, even when the network at home consists of but a single computer. WANs, which traditionally used phone lines or satellite communications, now also use cellular telecommunications and cable networks.

WAN speeds range from thousands of bits per second up into the billions of bits per second. At the low end today are 56 Kbps analog modems (56,000 bits per second). At the high end of WAN speeds are parts of the Internet backbone, the connecting infrastructure of the Internet, running at many gigabits per second.

on the Job

The speed of your communications on any network is a function of the speed of the slowest part of the pathway between you and the servers you are accessing. The weakest link affects your speed.

Dial-Up WAN Connections

A *dial-up* network connection uses an analog modem (described in Chapter 2) rather than a network card, and uses regular phone cables instead of network cables. In a dial-up connection, you configure the client computer to dial the remote host computer and configure the host computer to permit dial-up access. Once a dial-up connection is established, the client communicates with the host computer as though it were on the same LAN as that computer. If the host computer is already part of a LAN, and if the host configuration allows it, the client computer can access the network to which the host is connected. Some home PCs still use a modem connection for dial-up Internet access. In this case, the host computer is just a gateway to the Internet. This is the slowest, but cheapest, form of Internet access, and in some areas, it may be all that is available.

Broadband WAN

WAN connections that exceed the speed of a typical dial-up connection come under the heading of *broadband WAN*. Broadband speeds are available over cellular, Integrated Services Digital Network (ISDN), DSL, cable, and satellite technologies. WAN connections can connect private networks to the Internet and to each other. Generally, these connections are "always on," meaning that you do not have to initiate the connection every time you wish to access resources on the connected network, as you do with dial-up. If you wish to browse the Web, you simply open your web browser. Unless you are using dial-up, your connection to the Internet is a broadband WAN connection, and we will explore your Internet connection options here.

Line-of-Sight Wireless   As implied by the name, *line-of-sight wireless* technology cannot tolerate obstructions such as forests, mountains, or buildings between the service provider tower and the Internet-connecting site. On-site equipment includes a dish to receive and transmit microwave signals to and from the tower, as well as a modem device connected to a computer.

One technology that uses both line-of-sight and non-line-of-site is *Worldwide Interoperability for Microwave Access (WiMAX)*. Line-of-sight is much faster than non-line-of-site, and both types of WiMAX are used in cellular networks (described next) as well as by various Internet service providers (ISPs) and carriers as a wireless "last mile" connection option for homes and businesses, in which case it is line-of-sight wireless service.

Cellular   Long used mainly for voice, the cell networks provide cellular WAN Internet data connections, also referred to as wireless WAN (WWAN). These data services vary in speed from less than dial-up speeds (28.8 Kbps) to a range of broadband speeds, depending on the cellular provider and the level of service you have purchased. Because the trend in cellular is to provide broadband speeds, we include it under broadband WAN.

In the United States, the move away from the original analog cellular networks (the first and second generations) to all-digital cellular networks supports this trend to higher speeds. The first two common digital cellular networks in the United States were based on two standards: *Code Division Multiple Access (CDMA)*, used by Verizon and Sprint, and *Global System for Mobile Communications (GSM)*, used by T-Mobile and AT&T. Cell providers add other technologies that speed things up. For instance, both Verizon and Sprint have used *Evolution Data Optimized (EVDO)* on their networks in the past. Both CDMA and GMS are *Third Generation (3G)* digital mobile broadband technologies.

A later and faster 3G technology is High Speed Packet Access (HSPA), with various implementations. The earlier 3G ran at a minimum of 144 Kbps, but eventually 3G service ranged from 400 Kbps to over 4 Mbps.

The next big technology leap was *Fourth Generation (4G)*, which is less of a standard and more of a marketing term associated with several different standards with a range of speeds. The expectation is that a 4G network provides many megabits per second, but the actual speeds vary by cellular provider (carrier). At this writing, a number of large cities in the United States enjoy 4G access offered by several cell providers. The 4G technologies include HSPA+, WiMAX, and LTE. T-Mobile and AT&T both use HSPA+ 21/42. The 21 and 42 indicate maximum speeds of 21 Mbps and 42 Mbps, but actual tests are usually much lower—around 10 Mbps. Sprint's 4G service for mobile devices is called Worldwide Interoperability for Microwave Access (WiMAX), with speeds around 10 Mbps over a maximum distance of 30 miles. T-Mobile and Verizon use *Long Term Evolution (LTE)*; both call their offering *4G LTE*, although it lacks some of the technical criteria for true 4G. More carriers are moving to LTE.

ISDN   *Integrated Service Digital Network (ISDN)* was an early international standard for sending voice and data simultaneously over digital telephone wires. These days, newer technologies such as DSL and cable have largely replaced it. ISDN uses existing telephone circuits or higher-speed conditioned lines to get speeds of 64 Kbps or 128 Kbps. In fact, the most common ISDN service, Basic Rate Interface (BRI), includes three channels: two 64 Kbps channels, called B-channels, that carry the voice or data communications, and

FIGURE 13-1

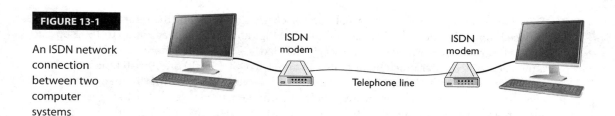

FIGURE 13-1

An ISDN network connection between two computer systems

one 16 Kbps D-channel that carries control and signaling information. ISDN connections use an ISDN modem on both ends of the circuit. Figure 13-1 shows an ISDN connection between two computers. This connection uses a conditioned phone line provided by the phone company.

DSL   *Digital subscriber line (DSL)* uses existing copper telephone wire for the communications circuit. A DSL modem splits the existing phone line into two bands to accomplish this; voice transmission uses the frequency below 4000 Hz, and data transmission uses everything else.

Figure 13-2 shows the simplest configuration with a single computer connected directly to the DSL modem. If you have multiple computers, you would connect a router between the computer and the modem and then have each computer connect to the router, either via wireless signal or Ethernet cable. If your DSL modem also contains a built-in router, so much the better—all the computers would then connect to the combo device. Not shown in the figure is that you can also connect your phones, adding a special filter to each phone jack in your house or office and connecting the phones via phone cable and RJ-11 connectors. DSL separates the total bandwidth into two channels: one for voice, the other for data. Voice communications operate normally, and the data connection is always on and available.

DSL service is available through phone companies, which offer a large variety of DSL services, usually identified by a letter preceding DSL, as in ADSL, CDSL, SDSL, VDSL, and many more. Therefore, when talking about DSL in general, the term *x*DSL is often used. Some services, such as *asymmetrical digital subscriber line (ADSL)*, offer asymmetric service in that the download speed is higher than the upload speed. The top speeds, including the newer variations of ADSL (ADSL2 and ADSL2+), can range from 1.5 Mbps to 25 Mbps for download and between 0.5 Mbps and 3.3 Mbps for upload. An inexpensive version of DSL, Consumer

FIGURE 13-2

A DSL connection

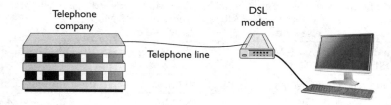

DSL (CDSL) service, targets the casual home user with lower speeds than this range. CDSL service is limited to download speeds of up to 1 Mbps and upload speeds of up to 160 Kbps. It is now rare to see a provider offer a service labeled "CDSL." Other, more expensive services aimed at business offer much higher rates. Symmetric DSL (SDSL) offers matching upload and download speeds. Table 13-1 shows some DSL services and their maximum data transfer speeds. Most of these services are available as second-generation services with higher speeds, indicated with a "2" at the end of the name, as in ADSL2, ADSL2+, VDSL2, and HDSL2.

Cable Cable television service has been around for several decades, but in the last decade, providers have also been offering broadband Internet service as well. Cable is currently the fastest available Internet service for home use, with speeds of between 30 and 100 Mbps depending on the plan you buy. However, whereas DSL service is point-to-point from the client to the ISP, a cable client shares the network with their neighboring cable clients. It is like sharing a LAN that, in turn, has an Internet connection, so speed degrades as more people share the local cable network. Cable networks use coaxial cable to connect a cable modem to the network. Many cable modems also function as wireless routers, to share the Internet connection with multiple computers in the home or office.

TABLE 13-1   DSL Download and Upload Services with Maximum Speeds

Service	Maximum Speed Download	Maximum Speed Upload	Comments
ADSL	1.5–12 Mbps	0.5–1.8 Mbps	Speeds vary among versions approved between 1998 and 2007.
ADSL2	1.5–12 Mbps	0.5–3.5 Mbps	Speeds vary among versions approved between 2002 and 2007.
ADSL2+	24 Mbps	1.3–3.3 Mbps	Speeds vary among versions approved between 2003 and 2008.
Consumer DSL (CDSL)	1 Mbps	16–160 Kbps	Different upload and download speeds. Also called DSL-Lite (G.Lite).
High-data-rate DSL (HDSL)	1.544 Mbps in North America; 2.048 Mbps elsewhere	1.544 Mbps in North America; 2.048 Mbps elsewhere	Same upload and download speeds.
Symmetric DSL (SDSL)	1.544 Mbps in North America; 2.048 Mbps elsewhere	1.544 Mbps in North America; 2.048 Mbps elsewhere	Same upload and download speeds.
Very high data-rate DSL (VDSL)	13–55 Mbps	1.5–15 Mbps	Different upload and download speeds.
VDSL2 long reach	55 Mbps	30 Mbps	Different upload and download speeds.
VDSL2 short reach	100 Mbps	100 Mbps	Same upload and download speeds.

T-Carrier Developed by Bell Labs in the 1960s, the *T-carrier system* multiplexes voice and data signals onto digital transmission lines. Where previously one cable pair carried each telephone conversation, the *multiplexing* of the T-carrier system allows a single pair to carry multiple conversations. Over the years, the T-carrier system has evolved, and telephone companies have offered various levels of service over the T-carrier system. For instance, a *T1* circuit provides full-duplex transmissions at 1.544 Mbps, carrying digital voice, data, or video signals. A complete T1 circuit provides point-to-point connections, with a *channel service unit (CSU)* at both ends. On the customer side, a T1 multiplexer or a special LAN bridge, referred to as the *customer premises equipment (CPE)*, connects to the CSU. The CSU receives data from the CPE and encodes it for transmission on the T1 circuit. T1 is just one of several levels of T-carrier services offered by telephone companies over the telephone network.

Satellite *Satellite communications* systems have come a long way over the last several years. Satellite communications systems initially allowed extensive communications with remote locations, often for military purposes. These systems usually use microwave radio frequencies and require a dish antenna, a receiver, and a transmitter. Early satellite communications systems were very expensive to maintain and operate. Today, a number of companies offer relatively high bandwidth at affordable prices for Internet connections and other applications. Satellite connections are available for both fixed and mobile applications, with speeds ranging from 5 to 25 Mbps. Different satellite speed plans are available to fit different budgets. An average speed is around 10 Mbps at this writing. As with TV satellite service, you must have a place to mount the dish antenna with a clear view of the southern sky.

on the
job

The problem with satellite service is not so much the raw speed, but the latency (that is, the delay) between a request and a response. Because the signal must travel into space and back, there is an unavoidable delay each time your computer requests data, which makes satellite service seem slower than raw speed tests would have you believe.

Fiber In order to compete with cable companies, AT&T, Verizon, and a few other telecommunications companies offer fiber-optic cabling to the home in most areas. Where available, subscribers can have the combined services of phone, Internet, and television. The Internet access speeds vary by provider and service level, but look for speeds greater than 100 Mbps.

Permanent Virtual Circuit (PVC) A *virtual circuit (VC)* is a communication service provided over a telecommunications network or computer network. A VC logically resembles a circuit passing over a complex routed or switched network, such as the phone company's *frame relay or asynchronous transfer mode (ATM)* network. A *permanent virtual* *circuit (PVC)* is a virtual circuit, created and remaining available, between two endpoints that are normally some form of data terminal equipment (DTE). Telecommunications companies provide PVC service to companies requiring a dedicated circuit between two sites that require always-on communications.

Virtual Private Network (VPN)   A *virtual private network (VPN)* is not in itself a WAN connection option, but rather a way to create a simulated WAN-type point-to-point connection across a complex unsecured network. For instance, at one time, if you wanted to connect the computers in a small district office to your employer's private internetwork, you either used a very slow dial-up connection or a fast but expensive physical point-to-point connection. Today, you would connect a single computer or network to the private internetwork over the Internet in a way that keeps your data secure and appears to be a point-to-point connection. You would still need a physical connection to the Internet, preferably a WAN connection, and on top of that you would run special software on both ends of the connection that create a VPN. This is one of several *tunneling* techniques used to secure network traffic by encapsulating the original packets within other packets. A VPN uses special tunneling protocols for this purpose, and each endpoint of the tunnel must be assigned an IP address.

EXERCISE 13-1

Testing Broadband Speeds

Regardless of the broadband service you use, they all vary in the actual speeds they provide from moment to moment. Connect to one of the many broadband speed-testing sites on the Internet and test yours now.

1. Open your favorite search engine and enter a search string that will locate an Internet speed testing website. We used **network speed test**.

2. From the results listed in the search engine, select a site (we chose www.internetfrog .com). Often sites suggest downloading and running other software to test your computer, so be careful to only select the speed test and not to download or run programs you do not want.

3. Follow the instructions for testing your connection. Some sites test as soon as you connect, and some test sites ask you to select a city near you. The test may take several minutes.

4. View the results (see Figure 13-3). Are the results congruent with the service you expect from your broadband connection?

5. Time permitting, try this at another time, or even on another day, and compare your results.

FIGURE 13-3	The speed of a broadband Internet connection can vary.

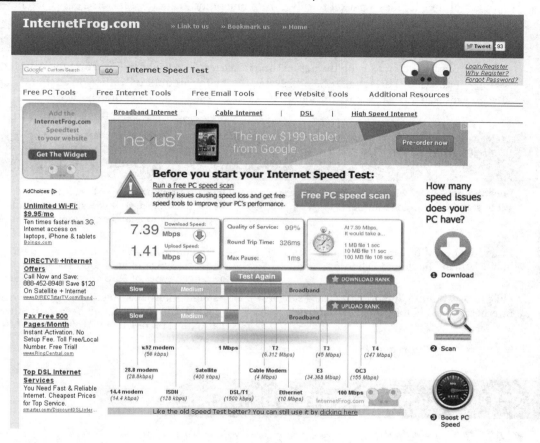

Bandwidth and Latency

While the range of a network, the distance over which signals are viable, is one important defining characteristic of a network, bandwidth is another. *Bandwidth* is the amount of data that can travel over a network within a given time. It may be expressed in kilobits per second (Kbps), kilobytes per second (KBps), megabits per second (Mbps), and even gigabits per second (Gbps)—that is, thousands of bits per second, thousands of bytes per second, millions of bits per second, and billions of bits per second, respectively.

Another network characteristic related to bandwidth is latency. *Latency* is the amount of time it takes a packet to travel from one point to another. In some cases, latency is determined by measuring the time it takes for a packet to make a round trip between two points. This can be a more important measurement, as it is does not measure the speed at which the packets travel, but the length of time it takes a packet to get from point A to point B. It is like measuring the actual time it takes you to travel by car from Los Angeles to San Francisco. The actual time of travel varies by the amount of traffic you encounter and the interchanges you pass through. The same is true for a packet on a network.

SCENARIO & SOLUTION

I need to buy a new wireless router for home. What standard should it support?	Get a router that supports 802.11ac, the newest standard, so it will support all the latest network adapters and equipment you may buy in the future.
I want the fastest possible Internet service at home. Which one should I choose?	At the moment, cable is the fastest in most areas, topping out at around 100 Mbps. Certain advanced types of DSL are in second place.
I like to play online games. I have heard satellite Internet is no good for games. Is that true?	Satellite Internet isn't good for games where quick reaction time is important because it inherently has quite a bit of latency. However, for turn-based games, satellite is fine.

CERTIFICATION OBJECTIVES

■ *901: 2.3   Explain the properties and characteristics of TCP/IP*

■ *901: 2.4   Explain common TCP and UDP ports, protocols, and their purpose*

This section details the topics required for CompTIA A+ 901 exam objective 2.3, including a comparison of IPv4 and IPv6, the types of IP addresses based on usage (public, private, and APIPA), the two methods for assigning IP addresses (static and dynamic), and such important TCP/IP terms as client-side DNS, DHCP, subnet mask, and gateway. Coverage of CompTIA A+ 901 exam objective 2.4 is also included in this section because it is part of the TCP/IP story. It includes an explanation of both TCP and UDP protocols, as well as other TCP and UDP protocols and related services, and the ports used by TCP and UDP.

Network Software

The software on a network is what gives us the network that we know and use. This is the logical network that rides on top of the physical network. In this section, we'll explore several aspects of networking that are controlled by software, including the network roles, protocol suites, and network addressing of the logical network.

Network Roles

You can describe a network by the types of roles played by the computers on it. The two general computer roles in a network are *clients*, the computers that request services, and *servers*, the computers that provide services.

Peer-to-Peer Networks

In a *peer-to-peer network*, each computer system in the network may play both roles: client and server. They have equal capabilities and responsibilities; each computer user is responsible for controlling access, sharing resources, and storing data on their computer. In Figure 13-4, each of the computers can share its files, and the computer connected to the printer can share the printer. Peer-to-peer networks work best in a very small LAN environment, such as a small business office, with fewer than a dozen computers and users. Microsoft calls a peer-to-peer network a *workgroup*, and each workgroup must have a unique name, as must each computer.

Client/Server-Based Networks

A *client/server-based network* uses dedicated computers called *servers* to store data and provide print services or other capabilities. Servers are generally more powerful computer systems with more capacity than a typical workstation. Client/server-based models also allow for centralized administration and security. These types of networks are scalable in that they can grow very large without adding administrative complexity to the network.

FIGURE 13-4

A peer-to-peer network

Laser printer

A client/server environment where dedicated servers perform assigned functions

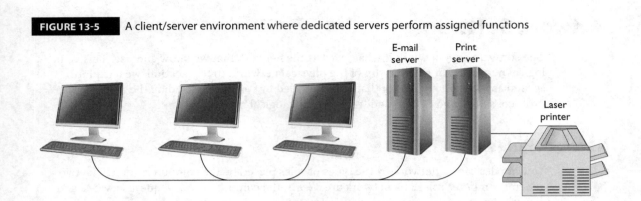

A large private internetwork for a globe-spanning corporation is an example of a client/server-based network. When configuring the network, the network administrator can establish a single model for security, access, and file sharing. Although this configuration may remain unchanged as the network grows, the administrator can make changes, if needed, from a central point. Microsoft calls a client/server network with Microsoft servers a *domain*. The domain must have a unique name, and each client or server computer must have a unique name.

Organizations use client/server environments extensively in situations that need a centralized administration system. Servers can be multipurpose, performing a number of functions, or dedicated, as in the case of a web or e-mail server. Figure 13-5 shows a network with servers used for e-mail and printing. Notice in this example that each of the servers is dedicated to the task assigned to it.

Network Operating System

A *network operating system (NOS)* is an operating system that runs on a network server and provides file sharing and access to other resources, account management, authentication, and authorization services. Microsoft Windows Server operating systems, UNIX and Linux are examples of network operating systems. The distinction is clouded somewhat by the ability of desktop operating systems to allow file sharing, but desktop operating systems do not provide the robust services that, coupled with high-performance servers and fast network connections, add up to reliable server operating systems.

Network Client

A *network client* is software that runs on the computers in a network and that receives services from servers. Windows, macOS, and Linux, when installed on desktop computers that have a network connection, automatically install a basic network client that can connect to servers and request file and print services. In each case, the automatically installed clients can only connect to a certain type of server. In the case of Windows, it is a Windows server. Novell has client software that comes in versions the Linux and Windows operating systems can use for accessing Novell servers.

Beyond a basic file and print client, Windows and other OSs usually come with an e-mail client, a browser (web client), and other clients, depending on the options you select during installation. You can add other clients. For instance, if you install an office suite such as Microsoft Office, you will have a more advanced e-mail client (Outlook in the case of Office) than the one that comes with the OS.

TCP/IP

Every computer network consists of physical and logical components controlled by software. Standards, also often called *protocols*, describe the rules for how hardware and software work and interact together. Ethernet, detailed earlier in this chapter, is a standard for the physical components, such as cabling and network adapters, as well as for the software that controls the hardware, such as the firmware in the network adapters and device drivers that allows the network adapters to be controlled from the operating system.

However, in most discussions about networks and related documentation, the term "protocol" describes certain software components that work on top of such underlying protocols as Ethernet. These protocols control communication at a higher level, including the addressing and naming of computers on the network, among other tasks. They combine into suites that include a group of protocols built around the same set of rules, with each protocol describing a small portion of the tasks required to prepare, send, and receive network data.

The CompTIA 220-901 and 220-902 exams require that A+ candidates understand the basics of the *TCP/IP* protocol suite because it is the most common protocol suite used on LANs and WANs, as well as on the Internet. It actually involves several protocols and other software components, and together, we call these a "protocol stack."

TCP/IP replaced two older protocol suites that were used on many early computer networks—namely, Microsoft's NetBEUI and Novell's IPX/SPX. You may encounter these in some organizations or hear about them from long-time network techs.

Transmission Control Protocol/Internet Protocol (TCP/IP) is by far the most common protocol suite on both internal LANs and public networks. It is the Internet's protocol suite. TCP/IP requires some configuration, but it is robust, usable on very large networks, and routable (a term that refers to the ability to send data to other networks). At each junction of two networks is a router that uses special router protocols to send each packet on its way toward its destination.

Although the TCP/IP suite has several protocols, the two main ones are the Transmission Control Protocol (TCP) and the Internet Protocol (IP). There are many subprotocols, such as UDP, ARP, ICMP, and more. We'll describe UDP later in the discussion about common ports, *Address Resolution Protocol (ARP)* is used to resolve an IP address to a MAC address, and Internet Control Message Protocol (ICMP) is described in Chapter 16.

Although TCP/IP is actually a protocol suite, techs commonly refer to this suite as "the TCP/IP protocol." On the job, take your cue from the experienced techs, and use the terms they use for easy communication.

TCP/IP allows for cross-platform communication, meaning that computers using different OSs (such as Windows and Linux) can send data back and forth, as long as they are both using TCP/IP. We now briefly describe the two cornerstone protocols of the TCP/IP suite as well as NetBIOS, a leftover from the NetBEUI suite.

The CompTIA A+ 220-901 and 220-902 exams only expect you to understand the basics of TCP/IP, how to configure IP, and the purpose of the various protocols and their associated ports.

Internet Protocol

Messages sent over a network are broken up into smaller chunks of data, and each chunk is placed into a logical container called a *packet*. Each packet has information attached to the beginning of the packet, called a *header*. This packet header contains the IP address of the sending computer and that of the destination computer. The *Internet Protocol (IP)* manages this logical addressing of the packet so that routing protocols can route it over the network to its destination. We will describe addressing later in "Network Addressing."

Transmission Control Protocol

When preparing to send data over a network, the *Transmission Control Protocol (TCP)* breaks the data into chunks, called datagrams. Each *datagram* contains information to use on the receiving end to reassemble the chunks of data into the original message. TCP places this information, both a byte-count value and a datagram sequence, into the datagram header before giving it to the IP protocol, which encapsulates the datagrams into packets with addressing information.

When receiving data from a network, TCP uses the information in this header to reassemble the data. If TCP is able to reassemble the message, it sends an *acknowledgment (ACK)* message to the sending address. The sender can then discard datagrams that it saved while waiting for an acknowledgment. If pieces are missing, TCP sends a non-*acknowledgment (NAK)* message back to the sending address, whereupon TCP resends the missing pieces.

An excellent 13-minute movie describing how TCP/IP works in an amusing and interesting fashion is available for viewing at www.warriorsofthe.net and is well worth watching.

NetBIOS vs. NetBEUI

Networked Basic Input/Output System (NetBIOS) and *Networked Basic Input/Output System Extended User Interface (NetBEUI)* are very old technologies that you may never encounter. However, the CompTIA A+ 220-901 and 220-902 exam objectives include both of these in their Acronyms list, so here is the short lecture. People often confuse NetBEUI with NetBIOS, perhaps because NetBEUI was the original protocol suite within which NetBIOS was a single protocol. NetBEUI was the default protocol suite on Microsoft networks in the 1980s and 1990s. It was appropriate only for small networks because it was limited to a single network segment and could not route network traffic beyond that segment. TCP/IP has replaced NetBEUI as well as other outdated network protocol suites.

NetBIOS is a single protocol for managing names on a network. In a Windows network, you can use NetBIOS names and the NetBIOS protocol with the TCP/IP suite. NetBIOS only requires a computer name and a workgroup name for each computer on the network. NetBIOS naming has limited value in modern networks, and the Internet-style names of the DNS protocol (which requires TCP/IP) have replaced it. Learn more about DNS later in the topic "DNS Server."

NetBT

NetBIOS over TCP/IP (NetBT) is a software component that supports the NetBIOS naming system and name resolution on a TCP/IP network. While even Microsoft has pretty much abandoned the use of the NetBIOS naming system, some organizations are still using old apps that depend on finding network resources based on the old NetBIOS system. Since virtually all networks today use the TCP/IP protocol suite, these systems must have NetBT enabled, as must the servers or networked printers that the old software is accessing.

NetBT on the client computer uses several methods to resolve a NetBIOS name to an IP address. First, it looks in the local computer's local NetBIOS cache of recently resolved NetBIOS names. If it does not find the name in the cache, it then sends a query to the WINS server (described a bit later in the section "Primary WINS Server"). If the WINS server does not have the name in its list of NetBIOS names and IP addresses, the client sends out a NetBIOS broadcast on the local network querying for the name. If the server/computer in question has NetBT enabled and it is functioning, it will respond and the client is done searching. That may be more than you will ever need to know about NetBT, but in Chapter 16 we revisit this topic and how to troubleshoot for NetBT problems.

Network Addressing

Identifying each computer or device directly connected to a network is important. We do this at two levels: the hardware level, in which the network adapter in each computer or network device has an address, and the logical level, in which a logical address is assigned to each network adapter.

FIGURE 13-6

The physical
address of a NIC,
labeled "MAC
Address," and
shown on the NIC

Hardware Addressing

Every NIC, and every device connected to a network, has a unique address, placed in ROM
by the manufacturer. This address, usually permanent, is called by many names, including
Media Access Control (MAC) address, physical address, Ethernet address (on Ethernet
devices), and NIC address. For the sake of simplicity, we will use the term "physical address"
in this book.

A MAC address is 48 bits long and usually expressed in hexadecimal. You can view
the physical address of a NIC several ways. It is usually, but not always, written on a label
attached to the NIC. Figure 13-6 shows the label on a wireless USB NIC. The words "MAC
Address" appear above the physical address. The actual address on this NIC is six two-digit
hexadecimal numbers, but on this label, the numbers are not separated. It is easier to read
these numbers if separated by a dash, period, or space, like this: 00-11-50-A4-C7-20.

Locating this address is not always so easy. You can also discover the address of a NIC
through Windows. Use the *IPCONFIG* command-line utility that is installed on a Windows
computer with the TCP/IP protocol suite. This command lets you view the IP configuration
of a network connection and perform certain administrative functions. To see the physical
address as well as the rest of the IP configuration for a connection, simply open a Command
Prompt window (as described in Chapter 10) and type the **ipconfig /all** command.
The physical address is in the middle of the listing. Notice that it shows six two-digit
hexadecimal numbers, each separated by a dash.

This physical address identifies a computer located in a segment of a network. However,
you use logical addresses to locate a computer that is beyond the local network segment.

Logical Addressing/IP Addressing

In addition to the hardware address, a computer in a TCP/IP network must have a logical
address that identifies both the computer and the network. This address comes under the
purview of the IP protocol. Internet Protocol version 4 (IPv4) and its addressing scheme
have been in use for over the past three decades. It offers almost 4.3 billion possible IP
addresses, but the way they have been allocated throughout the world reduces that number.
The Internet is currently transitioning to Internet Protocol version 6 (IPv6) with a new
addressing scheme that provides many more addresses.

An IP address identifies both a computer, a *host* in Internet terms, and the logical network on which the computer resides. This address allows messages to move from one network to another on the Internet. At the connecting point between networks, a special network device called a *router* uses its routing protocols to determine the route to the destination address before sending each packet along to the next router closer to the destination network. Each computer and network device that directly attaches to the Internet must have a globally unique IP address. Both versions of IP have this much and more in common. Following are explanations of these addressing schemes to help you distinguish between them.

IPv4 Addresses   An IPv4 address is 32 bits long, usually shown as four decimal numbers, 0–255, each separated by a period—for example, 192.168.1.41. Called *dotted-decimal notation*, this format is what you see in the user interface. However, the IPv4 protocol works with addresses in binary form, in which the preceding address looks like this: 11000000.101 01000.00000001.00101001.

IPv4 addresses are routable because an IP address contains within it both the address of the host, called the *host ID*, and the address of the network on which that host resides, called the *network ID (netID)*. A mask of 1s and 0s separates the two parts. When you put the mask over an address, the 1s cover up the first part, or network ID, and the 0s cover up the remaining part, or host ID. The address portion that falls under the 1s is the network address, and the address portion that falls under the 0s is the host address. In the preceding example, with a mask of 11111111.11111111.11111111.00000000, or 255.255.255.0, the network ID is 11000000.10101000.00000001.00000000, and the host ID is 00101001 (see Figure 13-7). In dotted-decimal form, the network ID is 192.168.1.0, and the host ID is 41. Often called a *subnet mask*, this mask is an important component in a proper IP configuration. After all, the IP address of a host does not make any sense until masked into its two IDs. When you enter the subnet mask into the Windows user interface in the Properties dialog box of the NIC, you will enter it in dotted-decimal notation, but we commonly use a shorthand notation when talking about the subnet mask, and you will see this notation in some user interfaces. For instance, a subnet mask of 255.255.255.0 is easily represented as /24. Therefore, using our example address from earlier, rather than saying the IP address is 192.168.1.41, with a subnet mask of 255.255.255.0, you can put it together as 192.168.1.41/24.

FIGURE 13-7

The subnet mask defines the network ID and host ID portions of an IP address.

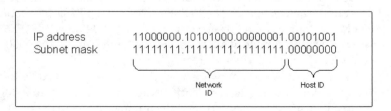

IP address   11000000.10101000.00000001.00101001
Subnet mask   11111111.11111111.11111111.00000000

Network ID   Host ID

TABLE 13-2	Class	First Octet (Network ID)	Address Range	Hosts per Network
IPv4 Class IDs	A	1–126	1.0.0.0–126.255.255.255	16,277,214
	B	128–191	128.0.0.0–191.255.255.255	65,534
	C	192–223	192.0.0.0–223.255.255.255	254
	D	224–239	224.0.0.0–239.255.255.255	N/A because this is a multicast class
	E	240–255	240.0.0.0–255.255.255.255	Reserved

The *Internet Assigned Numbers Authority (IANA)* oversees the allocation of IP addresses for use on the Internet. They did this directly in the early years, and now do it through a group of *Regional Internet Registries (RIRs)* that allocate IP addresses to the largest Internet service providers. In the early years of IPv4, IANA divided the IP address pool into groupings of addresses, called *Class IDs*, with five classes, each defined by the value of the first octet of the IP address, as Table 13-2 shows.

So, the organization that received a Class A network ID of 12 actually has more than 16,277,214 host IDs. Obviously, this scheme is a very inefficient way to allocate IP addresses. In fact, the organization can subnet this Class A network into smaller networks, wasting individual host IDs in the process. Today some organizations have returned all or part of their original allotment, and the large ISPs give out portions of these classful networks using subnetting rules called Classless Inter-Domain Routing (CIDR).

w a t c h   **You do not have to identify the various classes and their IP address ranges, but make sure you understand CIDR, and can explain how it improves upon classful network IP assignments.**

IPv6 Addresses In preparation for the day when ISPs and the Internet routers are fully IPv6 ready, all modern Windows versions support both IPv6 and IPv4, as do most new network devices. In fact, some high-speed internetworks already use IPv6. IPv6 has 128-bit addressing, which theoretically supports a huge number of unique addresses—340,282,366,920,938,463,463,374,607,431,768,211,456 to be exact. We show an IPv6 address in eight groups of hexadecimal numbers separated by colons, such as this: 2002:470:B8F9:1:20C:29FF:FE53:45CA. Sometimes the address will contain a double colon (::)—for example, 2002:470:B8F9::29FF:FE53:45CA. This means there are consecutive groups of all 0s, so :: might be shorthand for :0000:0000:0000. *Global unicast* addresses, the public IPv6 addresses, have a prefix of 001.

IPv6 addresses use a network mask the same way IPv4 addresses do—to distinguish which portion of the address identifies the network. As is often done with IPv4, the mask is expressed with a front slash (/) and the number of bits in the mask; for example, 2002:470:B8 F9:1:20C:29FF:FE53:45CA/64 implies a 64-bit network mask.

June 6, 2012, was international World IPv6 Launch Day. Major websites such as Google, Facebook, Yahoo!, and others enabled IPv6 on their websites to assess real-world connectivity for a 24-hour period, but until ISPs around the globe enable IPv6 routing, true end-to-end IPv6 connectivity on the Internet will not be realized.

You can see both IPv4 and IPv6 data by using IPCONFIG at a command prompt, or from a GUI interface. In Windows Vista or Windows 7, access IP address information by clicking Start and entering **network connections** in the Search box. From the results list, select View Network Connections. Then in the Network Connections section of the Control Panel, double-click the connection you wish to view. This opens the Connection Status dialog box for the connection. Click the Details button to display the Network Connection Details dialog box. Figure 13-8 shows the details for a single network connection as seen in the Windows 7 Network Connection Details dialog box. Notice that this connection has both IPv4 (dotted-decimal) and IPv6 (hexadecimal) addresses. Only the IPv4 protocol has addresses for the default gateway, DHCP server, and DNS server, indicating that this computer is configured for a IPv4 network. These three addresses are described in the next section.

FIGURE 13-8

The Network Connection Details dialog box in Windows 7

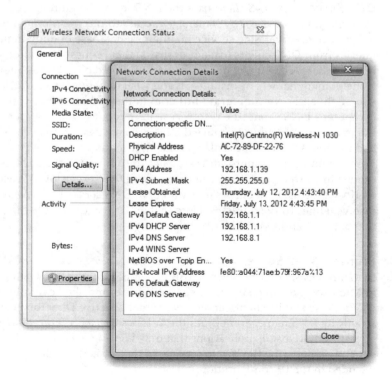

Addresses for IP Configuration

When you view the IP configuration for the NIC on your PC, you may be surprised to see other IP addresses besides that of the NIC. These include addresses labeled Default Gateway, DHCP Server, DNS Servers, and (sometimes) Primary WINS Server.

Default Gateway   When your IP protocol has a packet ready to send, it examines the destination IP address and determines if it is on the same IP network (in the earlier example, this is 192.168.1.0) as your computer. If it is, then it can send the packet directly to that computer (host ID 41 in the example). If the destination IP address is on another IP network, then your computer sends it to the IP address identified as the *default gateway*. This address is on your network (same IP network ID), and it belongs to a router that will send the packet on to the next router in its journey to its destination. Without a default gateway, your computer does not know what to do with packets that have a destination address beyond your IP network. IPv6 also requires a default gateway setting to route packets to remote networks. This can be configured manually or delivered via a Dynamic Host Configuration Protocol (DHCP) device that supports IPv6.

DNS Server   A *DNS client* uses the DNS server IP address for name resolution. The *Domain Name Service (DNS)* manages access to Internet domain names, like mcgraw-hill.com. The server-side service maintains a database of domain names and responds to queries from DNS clients (called resolvers) that request resolution of Internet names to IP addresses. A client will do this before sending data over the Internet, when all it knows is the domain name. For instance, if you wish to connect to a McGraw-Hill web server, you might enter **www.mcgraw-hill.com** in the address bar of your browser. Then, your computer's DNS client (the resolver) sends a request to a DNS server, asking it to resolve the name to an IP address. Once the DNS server has the answer (which it most likely had to request from another DNS server), it sends a response to your computer. The IP protocol on your computer now attaches the address to the packets your computer sends requesting a web page. IPv4 clients query a DNS server for "A" records, which map to an IPv4 address. IPv6 clients query an IPv6 DNS server for "AAAA" (quad A) records to resolve names to IP addresses. Note that an IPv6 address (128 bits) is four times longer than an IPv4 address (32 bits)!

Primary WINS Server   *Windows Internet Name Service (WINS)* has a function similar to that of DNS, but it resolves NetBIOS names rather than DNS host names. WINS works in Microsoft networks, but the need for it has diminished over the years. Newer versions of Windows and its client/server environment, Active Directory, can locate computers strictly by DNS name. Sometimes the WINS service is required on a network because of old operating systems or applications that only know how to work with NetBIOS names and depend on querying the WINS service. In that case, the address of the WINS server must be included in the IP configuration.

Assigning IP Addresses to NICs   There are two ways to assign an IP address to a network host: manually (or statically) and automatically (or dynamically). We will discuss assigning an address manually here and automatically in the next section when we discuss DHCP. When you assign an address manually in Windows, you must open the Properties dialog box for the NIC and enter the exact IP address (obtained from your network administrator), subnet mask, and other configuration information, which includes the addresses for the default gateway, DNS server, and (if necessary) WINS server. An IP address configured in this manner is a *static address*. This address is not permanent, because an administrator can easily change it, but some documentation uses the term permanent rather than static.

e x a m
ⓦ a t c h

Be sure you understand how the subnet mask divides the host ID and network ID of an IP address. Also make sure that you understand the purpose of the	following addresses as used in an IP configuration: default gateway, DNS server, WINS server, and DHCP server.

DHCP Server   When you install any nonserver version of Windows, the Setup program installs the TCP/IP protocol suite and configures the computer (or its network card, to be more specific) as a *DHCP client*, meaning it configures it to obtain an IP address automatically from a DHCP server. A NIC configured as a DHCP client will send a request out on the network when Windows starts.

Now, you would think that a client computer without an IP address would not be able to communicate on the network, but it can in a very limited way. Using a special protocol called *BOOTP*, the computer sends a very small message that a *Dynamic Host Configuration Protocol (DHCP)* server can read. It cannot communicate with other types of servers until it has an IP address. A properly configured *DHCP server* will respond by sending the DHCP client an IP address and subnet mask (also using BOOTP). This configuration is the minimum it will assign to the client computer. In most cases, the server will provide the other IP configuration addresses, including default gateway, DNS server, and primary WINS server. Only Windows networks that require this last address get that one.

A DHCP server does not permanently assign an IP address to a client. It leases it. *Lease* is the term used, even though no money changes hands in this transaction between a DHCP client and a DHCP server. When one-half of the leased time for an IP address (and its associated configuration) has expired, the client tries to contact the DHCP server in order to renew the lease. As long as the DHCP server has an adequate number of unassigned IP addresses, it will continue to reassign the same address to the same client each session. In fact, this happens every day for a computer that is turned off at the end of the workday, at which point the DHCP client will release the IP address, giving up the lease.

Exercise 13-2 walks you through using a command that displays the physical address and IP address for your network card.

EXERCISE 13-2

Viewing the Physical and IP Addresses of a NIC

To view the physical and IP addresses of a NIC, follow these steps:

1. Open a command prompt.
2. In the Command Prompt window, enter the command **ipconfig /all** and press ENTER.
3. The result should look something like Figure 13-9 (Windows 7), only with different addresses.
4. The address of the NIC is in the middle, labeled Physical Address. Notice that the physical address is six pairs of hexadecimal numbers separated by hyphens.
5. Three lines below that is the NIC's IPv6 address, and one line below that is the IPv4 address.
6. Locate the other addresses discussed in the preceding text, including those of the default gateway, DNS server, DHCP server (if present), and WINS server (if present).
7. When you run this command on a Windows Vista, Windows 7, or Windows 8/8.1 computer, you will also see IPv6 information.

FIGURE 13-9

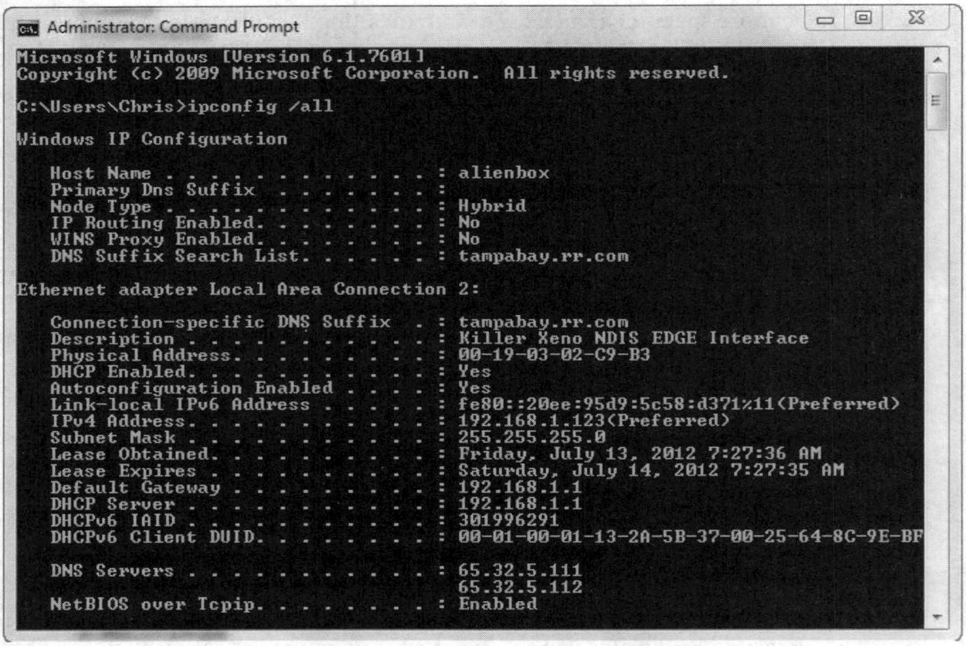

Use the ipconfig /all command to view the physical address and the IP address of a NIC and the other addresses that are part of the IP configuration.

```
Administrator: Command Prompt                                    □  ▣  ✕

Microsoft Windows [Version 6.1.7601]
Copyright (c) 2009 Microsoft Corporation.  All rights reserved.

C:\Users\Chris>ipconfig /all

Windows IP Configuration

   Host Name . . . . . . . . . . . . : alienbox
   Primary Dns Suffix  . . . . . . . :
   Node Type . . . . . . . . . . . . : Hybrid
   IP Routing Enabled. . . . . . . . : No
   WINS Proxy Enabled. . . . . . . . : No
   DNS Suffix Search List. . . . . . : tampabay.rr.com

Ethernet adapter Local Area Connection 2:

   Connection-specific DNS Suffix  . : tampabay.rr.com
   Description . . . . . . . . . . . : Killer Xeno NDIS EDGE Interface
   Physical Address. . . . . . . . . : 00-19-03-02-C9-B3
   DHCP Enabled. . . . . . . . . . . : Yes
   Autoconfiguration Enabled . . . . : Yes
   Link-local IPv6 Address . . . . . : fe80::20ee:95d9:5c58:d371%11(Preferred)
   IPv4 Address. . . . . . . . . . . : 192.168.1.123(Preferred)
   Subnet Mask . . . . . . . . . . . : 255.255.255.0
   Lease Obtained. . . . . . . . . . : Friday, July 13, 2012 7:27:36 AM
   Lease Expires . . . . . . . . . . : Saturday, July 14, 2012 7:27:35 AM
   Default Gateway . . . . . . . . . : 192.168.1.1
   DHCP Server . . . . . . . . . . . : 192.168.1.1
   DHCPv6 IAID . . . . . . . . . . . : 301996291
   DHCPv6 Client DUID. . . . . . . . : 00-01-00-01-13-2A-5B-37-00-25-64-8C-9E-BF

   DNS Servers . . . . . . . . . . . : 65.32.5.111
                                       65.32.5.112
   NetBIOS over Tcpip. . . . . . . . : Enabled
```

Special IP Addresses   You use public IP addresses on the Internet, and each address is globally unique. But there are some special IP addresses that are never allowed for computers and devices connected directly to the Internet. They are as follows:

- **Loopback addresses**   Although it is generally believed that the address 127.0.0.1 is the IPv4 loopback address, any Class A address with a network ID of 127 is a loopback address, used to test network configurations. If you send a packet to a loopback address, it will not leave your NIC. Sounds like a useless address, but you will use it for testing and troubleshooting in Chapters 14 and 16. Also, note that the IPv6 loopback address is ::1 (0:0:0:0:0:0:0:1).

- **Private IPv4 addresses**   If a network is not directly connected to the Internet, or if you wish to conceal the computers on a private network from the Internet, you use private IP addresses. Millions of locations all over the world use these addresses and they are, therefore, not globally unique because they are never used on the Internet. In Chapter 14, we will describe how you can use these addresses on your private network, yet still access resources on the Internet, thanks to methods that hide your address when you are on the Internet. The private address ranges include the following:
  - 10.0.0.0 through 10.255.255.255 (1 Class A network)
  - 172.16.0.0 through 172.31.255.255 (16 Class B networks)
  - 192.168.0.0 through 192.168.255.255 (256 Class C networks)

- **Private IPv6 addresses**   The FC00::/7 range has been set aside for private IPv6 network addressing. These addresses will not be routable by IPv6 Internet routers, but internal routers within an organization can route them much like they do IPv4 private addresses. The proper term for this type of address is a Unique Local Address (ULA).

- **Automatic Private IP Addressing (APIPA) address**   If a DHCP client computer fails to receive an address from a DHCP server, the client will give itself an address with the 169.254 /16 network ID. If a computer uses this range of addresses, it will not be able to communicate with other devices on the network unless they also have addresses using the same network ID, which means the other computers must also be using an APIPA address. These clients will not have a default gateway address and, therefore, will not be able to communicate beyond the local network. IPv6 behaves similarly, except that the self-assigned IPv6 address will have a prefix of FE80 and is always present, even if a routable IPv6 address was configured either statically or via DHCP. This is referred to as a "link local address."

Common Ports

It isn't enough for a packet to simply reach the correct IP address; each packet has additional destination information, called a *port*, which identifies the exact service it is targeting. For instance, when you want to open a web page in your browser, the packet requesting access to the web page includes both the IP address (resolved through DNS) and the port number of the service. In this case, it would be HTTP for many web pages and HTTPS for a secure web page where you must enter confidential information. All the services you access on the Internet have port numbers. These include the two services just mentioned, plus FTP, POP3, SMTP, Telnet, SSH, and many more. Each port is also associated with a protocol. The most common protocols for communicating with Internet applications are TCP and UDP. TCP is used for communications that are connection-oriented, which is true of most services you are aware of using, whereas *Universal Datagram Protocol (UDP)* is used for connectionless communications, in which each packet is sent without establishing a connection. Therefore, in Table 13-3, we identify the protocol along with the port number for common TCP/IP services.

SCENARIO & SOLUTION

Is it better to assign IP addresses to individual workstations through static addressing or dynamic addressing?	Dynamic addressing is better because it prevents most IP address conflicts.
When would I use an IPv6 address?	The Internet still runs on IPv4 at this writing, but is expected to switch over to IPv6 at some point. Some Internet providers have started using IPv6, so you should follow the lead of your provider.
My PC has an automatically assigned IP address of 169.254.2.1. Why?	That's an APIPA address, and you have it because your router's DHCP server failed to assign the PC an address. Investigate the router settings.

TABLE 13-3 Protocol and Port Numbers for Common Internet Services

Service	Port	Descriptions
Apple Filing Protocol (AFP)	TCP 548 or 427	Formerly called AppleTalk Filing Protocol; file services for macOS
Common Internet File System (CIFS)	TCP 445	A version of Server Message Block (SMB)
Domain Name System (DNS)	UDP 53	Used by DNS clients to perform DNS queries against DNS servers
File Transfer Protocol (FTP)	TCP 20/21	Transfers files between an FTP client and FTP server
Hypertext Transfer Protocol (HTTP)	TCP 80	Web page transmission to web browser

| | TABLE 13-3 | Protocol and Port Numbers for Common Internet Services (*continued*) |

Service	Port	Descriptions
HTTP over Secure Sockets Layer/Transport Layer Security (HTTPS)	TCP 443	Secure transmission of web pages
Internet Message Access Protocol Version 4 (IMAP4)	TCP 143	Retrieves e-mail; advanced features beyond POP3, such as folder synchronization
Lightweight Directory Access Protocol (LDAP)	TCP 389	A standard method of accessing a network database; often used for authenticating user accounts during user logon
Post Office Protocol Version 3 (POP3)	TCP 110	Retrieves e-mail from a POP3 mail server
Remote Desktop Protocol (RDP)	TCP 3389	Used to remotely access a Windows desktop
Secure File Transfer Protocol (SFTP)	TCP 22	Uses an SSH-encrypted connection to transfer files
Secure Shell (SSH)	TCP 22	Secure (encrypted) terminal emulation that replaces Telnet
Server Message Block (SMB)	TCP 445 or TCP 137–139	Windows file and print sharing service
Simple Mail Transfer Protocol (SMTP)	TCP 25	Sending e-mail
Simple Network Management Protocol (SNMP)	UDP 161	Queries network devices for status and statistics
Telnet	TCP 23	Terminal emulation; all data sent in clear text
Trivial File Transfer Protocol (TFTP)	UDP 69	Differs from FTP in that there is no option for authentication

CERTIFICATION OBJECTIVES

■ ***901: 2.1*** *Identify the various types of network cables and connectors*

■ ***901: 2.2*** *Compare and contrast the characteristics of connectors and cabling*

■ ***901: 2.8*** *Compare and contrast network architecture devices, their functions, and features*

In this section we will detail the features and characteristics of network cabling, including fiber-optic, twisted-pair, and coaxial cabling, as well as their connectors, as required by CompTIA A+ 901 exam objectives 2.1 and 2.2. We will also survey the various hardware devices used on networks—some of them for connecting networks to each other, and some for allowing client computers and devices to access networks. Knowledge of these is required for CompTIA A+ 901 exam objective 2.8.

Network Hardware

Network hardware includes many network connection devices that are part of the infrastructure of small networks, as well as large internetworks, and of the largest internetwork, the Internet itself. We limit the hardware we describe in this section to the network adapters used in PCs, the medium that connects these adapters to the network, the devices that connect networks to one another, and a few miscellaneous devices included in the CompTIA A+ 220-901 exam objectives.

Network Adapters

While we previously mentioned network interface cards in this chapter, we now focus on this particular type of network hardware device. Each computer on a network must have a connection to the network provided by a NIC, also called a *network adapter*, and some form of network medium that makes the connection between the NIC and the network. NICs are identified by the network technology used (Ethernet or Wi-Fi) and the type of interface used between the NIC and the PC, such as the PCI and PCIe interfaces introduced in Chapter 3, or the USB or FireWire interfaces defined in Chapter 4, or for a laptop, the PC Card or ExpressCard interfaces explored in Chapter 7.

Most NICs come with status indicators, as lights on the card itself, and/or software that displays the status on the notification area of the taskbar. You can use these when troubleshooting, as described in Chapter 16.

Transmission Medium

The transmission medium for a network carries the signals. These signals may be electrical signals carried over copper-wire cabling, light pulses carried over fiber-optic cabling, or infrared or radio waves transmitted through the atmosphere. In these examples, the copper wire, fiber-optic cable, and atmosphere are the media. When it comes to wired media, one important issue is plenum versus PVC, which we will explore next, and then we'll look at the basics of twisted-pair, coaxial, and fiber-optic cabling.

Plenum vs. PVC

Many commonly used network cables use a *polyvinyl chloride (PVC)* outer sheath to protect the cable. PVC is not fire resistant, and, by code, you cannot use it in overhead or *plenum* areas in offices, those spaces in a building through which air conditioning and heating ducts run. *Plenum cable* uses a special fire-resistant outer sheath that will not burn as quickly as PVC. Plenum cable frequently costs more, but most areas require it. Most of the standard cables discussed in this chapter are available in plenum-grade ratings.

Twisted Pair

Twisted-pair cable is the most popular cable type for internal networks. The term "twisted pair" indicates that it contains pairs of wires twisted around each other. These twists help "boost" each wire's signals and make them less susceptible to *electromagnetic interference (EMI)*. The most common type of twisted-pair wiring is *unshielded twisted-pair (UTP)*, which, although it has a plastic sheathing, does not have actual metal shielding.

There are several standards for twisted-pair cables, each with a different number of wires, certified speed, and implementation. We often refer to these standards as CAT (short for "category") followed by a number—for example, CAT3 or CAT4. Currently, CAT5, CAT5e, and CAT6 are the most common twisted-pair cable types. Table 13-4 summarizes twisted-pair cable standards. CAT5e is an enhanced and more stringently tested version of CAT5 that offers better transmission characteristics than CAT5. CAT6 and CAT7 cable offer even higher bandwidth and improved signal-handling characteristics.

The telecommunications standards organization, *Telecommunication Industry Association/Electronics Industry Alliance (TIA/EIA)*, developed the *TIA/EIA 568* standards for telecommunications cabling. TIA/EIA standards are now labeled per the standards group, the American National Standards Institute (ANSI), with an ANSI prefix. A portion of these standards, now called *ANSI/TIA/EIA-568-B* standard, includes pin assignments for connecting eight-wire cabling to Ethernet connectors. One pin assignment is called *T568A*, and the other is *T568B*. Technically, as long as you standardize on one pin assignment, either is fine. However, T568B is recommended, and the use of T568A is only recommended if you want to create a cross-over cable, which you can accomplish by using the T568A standard on one end and the T568B standard on the other, as the main difference is in the assignment of the two wires that these two standards reverse.

According to the ANSI/TIA/EIA standard for CAT5e copper cable (TIA/EIA 568-5-A), the maximum length for a structured wiring cable segment, is 100 meters (328 feet) without need for a switch or a hub (repeater). With a repeater, you can run up to five segments for 10BaseT.

TABLE 13-4	Type	Speed	Common Use
Cable Categories	CAT1	1 Mbps	Phone lines
	CAT2	4 Mbps	Token Ring networks
	CAT3	16 Mbps	Ethernet networks
	CAT4	20 Mbps	Token Ring networks
	CAT5	100 Mbps	Ethernet networks
	CAT5e	1 Gbps	Ethernet networks
	CAT6	10 Gbps	Ethernet networks
	CAT7	10 Gbps	Ethernet networks

For 100BaseT, you can use two hubs for a cable run of up to 200 meters (656 feet). Using modern switches with 100M and Gigabit LANs raises these limits. Consult the switch vendor's specifications for details.

Twisted-pair cable is also available as *shielded twisted-pair (STP)*, with an extra insulating layer that helps prevent data loss and blocks EMI. However, due to the expense of STP, UTP is more commonly used.

You can identify a twisted-pair cable by its use of RJ-45 connectors, which look like regular RJ-11 phone connectors but are slightly larger, as they contain eight wires, whereas RJ-11 connectors contain four wires.

The oldest cabling you should normally encounter in a business is CAT5, although it is certainly possible to find very old installations of CAT3 cabling, which is not adequate for modern networks.

Coaxial Cable

The type of cabling used to connect a cable modem to a cable network is coaxial cable, which consists of a central copper wire surrounded by an insulating layer, which is itself surrounded by a braided metal shield that protects the signals traveling on the central wire from outside interference. We also described coaxial cabling in Chapter 5, with a drawing of a cable and its components shown in Figure 5-15. A plastic jacket encases all of this. Coaxial cable used for standard cable television and high-definition TV (HDTV), as well as cable-modem Internet access, is usually RG-6 cable with a 75 Ohm rating. Theoretically, signals can travel up to 300 meters at 500 Mbps over RG-6 coax cables, but the practical limit is 50 Mbps, which still makes this medium very popular for broadband Internet connections. The specific distance and speed vary, depending on the type of signal and the devices generating the signal. Sometimes people use RG-59 cable to carry closed-circuit TV (CCTV) signals, although modern CCTV implementations use standard network cabling such as CAT5e UTP. Compared to RG-59, RG-6 cabling has a thicker conductive core and as a result can transmit data over longer distances. Expect an RG-6 cable to connect to the cable wall jack and cable modem with either F-connectors that you must securely screw on or Bayonet Neill-Concelman (BNC) connectors that lock with a simple quarter-turn twist.

A *splitter* is a box that allows two cables to join to a single cable. Splitters are most common on coaxial cable, such as when splitting the incoming signal from a cable TV/Internet provider into two branches: one for the TV and one for the cable modem. Splitters do affect signal strength, so don't use them unnecessarily. If you think that splitting may be degrading the signal to the point where errors are occurring, ask a service technician from the cable company to check the lines.

Splitters are also available for UTP cable, but you probably don't want one. If you want to share a single incoming network signal with multiple devices, use a switch or router.

Fiber-Optic Cable and Connectors

Fiber-optic cable (*fiber* for short) has commonly been used to join separate networks over long distances, but until recently, LANs seldom used fiber-optic cable. Increasingly, however, many new homes, apartments, and businesses have both fiber and copper wiring installed when being built. Also, some phone companies are using fiber to connect directly to homes and businesses.

Fiber transmits light rather than electrical signals, so it is not susceptible to EMI. It is capable of faster transmission than other types of cable, but it is also the most expensive cable.

A single light wave passing down fiber cabling is a *mode*. Two variants of fiber used in fiber-optic cables are *single-mode fiber (SMF)* and *multimode fiber (MMF)*. Single-mode fiber allows only a single light wave to pass down the cable, but supports faster transmission rates over longer distances. Multimode fiber allows multiple light waves to pass simultaneously and is usually larger in diameter than single-mode fiber; each wave uses a certain portion of the fiber cable for transmission. There are many Ethernet standards for fiber-optic cabling, with a wide range of maximum speeds and distances. Multimode fiber is used most often in LANs with speeds up to 1 Gbps and a maximum range of 1000 meters, whereas single-mode fiber has a range of dozens of miles with speeds in the terabits per second.

Fiber-optic data transmission requires two cables: one to send and another to receive. Connectors enable fiber-optic cable to connect to transmitters, receivers, or other devices. Over the years, the various standards for connectors have continued to evolve, moving toward smaller connectors. Here are brief descriptions of four types of connectors used with fiber-optic cable:

- **Straight-tip (ST)**   A straight, round connector used to connect fiber to a network device. It has a twist-type coupling.
- **Subscriber connector (SC)**   A square snap coupling, about 2.5 mm wide, used for cable-to-cable connections or to connect cables to network devices. It latches with a push-pull action similar to audio and video jacks.
- **Lucent connector (LC)**   Also called *local connector*, has a snap coupling and, at 1.25 mm, is half the size of the SC connector.
- **Mechanical Transfer Registered Jack (MT-RJ)**   Resembles an RJ-45 network connector and is less expensive and easier to work with than ST or SC.

Figure 13-10 shows ST and SC connectors.

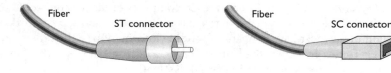

FIGURE 13-10

The ST and SC connectors used with fiber-optic cable

Devices for Connecting to LANs and the Internet

Most LANs now connect to other LANs or through WAN connections to internetworks, such as the Internet. A variety of network connection devices connects networks. Each serves a special purpose, and a single device may contain two or more of these functions.

Repeater

A *repeater* is a device used to extend the range of a network by taking the signals it receives from one port and regenerating (repeating) those signals to another port. Repeaters are available for various networks. For instance, on an Ethernet network, you would use an Ethernet repeater, and on a Wi-Fi network you would use a wireless repeater (often called a signal booster) to boost the signal between wireless networks. In both cases, the repeater must be at the appropriate level and speed for the network (Ethernet, Fast Ethernet, Gigabit Ethernet, 802.11b, 802.11g, 802.11n, etc.).

Bridge

A *bridge* is a device used to connect two networks, and it passes traffic between them using the physical address of the destination device. Bridges segment large networks into smaller networks and only forward network traffic to the segment where the recipient station resides. A bridge is specific to the hardware technology in use. For instance, an Ethernet bridge looks at physical Ethernet addresses (MAC addresses) and forwards Ethernet frames with destination addresses that are not on the local network. Bridges are now seldom used since a switch functions as both a bridge and a hub.

Hub

A *hub* is a device that is the central connecting point of a classic 10BaseT Ethernet LAN. It is little more than a multiport repeater, because it takes a signal received on one port and repeats it on all other ports. An *active hub* will regenerate the signal and send it on to all devices connected to the network. A *passive hub* is simply a wiring panel or punch-down block for connecting or disconnecting devices.

Router

Connections between networks usually require some form of routing capability. In the case of a connection to the Internet, each computer or device connected to the network requires a TCP/IP address. In order to reach a computer on another network, the originating computer must have a means of sending information to the other computer. To accomplish this, routes are established, and a *router*, a device that sits at the connection between networks, stores information about destinations.

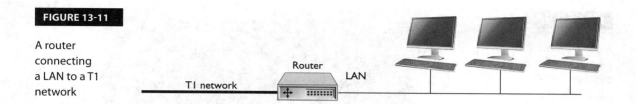

FIGURE 13-11

A router
connecting
a LAN to a T1
network

A router is specific to one protocol suite. The type of router used to connect TCP/IP networks is an *IP router*, using routing protocols that work with the IP protocol. Routers use several specialized router protocols to update their list of routes dynamically, such as *routing information protocol (RIP)*, a protocol that dates to the 1980s and is now essentially obsolete even though it has been updated a few times and most routers still support it. An IP router knows the IP addresses of the networks to which it connects and the addresses of other routers on those networks. At the least, a router knows the next destination to which it can transfer information.

Many routers include bridging circuitry, a hub, and the necessary hardware to connect multiple network technologies together, such as a LAN and a T1 network, or a LAN to any of the other broadband networks. The Internet has thousands of routers managing the connections between the millions of computers and networks connected to it. Figure 13-11 shows a router between a LAN and a WAN.

Switch

After the introduction of 100BaseT, the *switch* replaced the classic hub. This is a more intelligent device that takes an incoming signal and sends it only to the destination port. This type of switch is both a bridge and a hub. At one time switches were very expensive, but now small eight-port switches are inexpensive and commonly used, even in very small LANs. As always, each computer or other device in a network attaches to a switch of the type appropriate for the type of LAN. For example, computers using Ethernet cards must connect to an Ethernet switch; wireless devices attach wirelessly to a wireless hub, more often called a *wireless access point (WAP)* or wireless router. Devices may combine these functions, as in the case of a WAP or wireless router that includes an Ethernet switch (look for one or more RJ-45 connectors). This last scenario is very common.

Patch Panels

In corporate networks with many clients, the sheer number of individual Ethernet cables running from individual PCs to routers is staggering. A *patch panel* can help keep the cable connections orderly by providing a central point into which the cables for many workstations can connect. See Figure 13-12. Some high-capacity switches also serve as patch panels, physically organizing a large number of cables as well as distributing local network data.

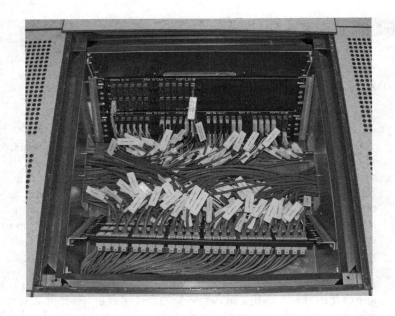

Power over Ethernet (PoE) Injector

Power over Ethernet (PoE) passes electrical power through twisted-pair Ethernet cabling. It allows one cable to serve as both data and electrical conduit to a device. It allows you to set up network devices in locations where there is no AC outlet, and power them via the same Ethernet cable that connects them to the network. PoE is popular for use with security cameras, paging systems, wall clocks that get the time from the network, and routers placed in out-of-the-way locations.

A switch that supports PoE has power injection built in. In other words, it is able to inject power into the cables that run to the PoE devices. A device called a *midspan injector* (or *PoE injector*) can be used to add PoE capability to regular non-PoE network switches and routers.

Wireless Access Point

A *wireless access point (WAP)* allows wireless clients to connect to a wired network. Most access points also have built-in routing capability and, as such, are called *wireless routers*. Modern access points are configurable in "isolation mode," which isolates wireless clients from one another, usually for security or privacy purposes.

Modem

Note that this discussion does not apply to DSL or cable modems. Computers are digital devices. Most local telephone lines are still analog. A *modem* allows computer-to-computer communication over analog telephone lines. Modems can be external devices that connect to a piece of computing equipment via a serial cable, or they can be internal expansion cards.

Either way, they have at least one RJ-11 telephone jack so that they can plug into an analog phone line. Many network administrators still use modems today to remotely connect to network equipment (such as a router) in case the Internet connection fails or the router is misconfigured.

Firewall

A *firewall* restricts or allows the flow of network traffic based on a set of rules. A firewall can be a hardware device or it can be software. Hardware firewalls run on network devices such as dedicated firewall appliances or routers or on a dedicated computer. Software firewalls run within an operating system and apply *IP packet filtering*, a service that inspects (or filters) each packet that enters or leaves the network; apply a set of security rules defined by a network administrator; and do not allow packets that fail inspection to pass between networks. When you change the rules to allow a certain type of traffic through a firewall, you are making an *exception*. To allow or deny traffic, you can base a firewall rule on many attributes, including:

- **Type of packet** Defined by port; TCP 80 (HTTP website) traffic might be allowed where TCP 25 (SMTP outbound e-mail) traffic might be denied.
- **Source/destination** SMTP traffic to a specific host might be allowed, but all other destination SMTP hosts could be denied.

Ethernet over Power (EoP)

Ethernet over Power (EoP) is a type of broadband Power Line Communication (PLC), an alternative to traditional networking. (Don't confuse it with Power over Ethernet, PoE, described earlier in this overview of connection devices.) EoP uses the existing power lines in a home or office as conduits for network data, using adapters to translate and send the data. The HomePlug AV standard (IEEE 1901) is the specification that defines this type of equipment. At one point, EoP was poised to become an important technology, because it allowed people to create Ethernet networks without running cable through the walls of existing buildings. However, because of the popularity of Wi-Fi, it has never realized its potential.

EXERCISE 13-3

Identifying Network Hardware

See what network hardware you can identify in your home, office, or school.

1. If you have a PC in your home and it has a connection to the Internet, locate and identify the network components.

2. If you use a dial-up connection, look for the modem, the telephone cable between the modem and the phone jack on the wall, and the RJ-11 connectors at either end of the telephone cable.

3. If you have a DSL connection, look for the Ethernet cable that runs between your computer and the hub/switch or modem. Examine the RJ-45 connectors on either end of the cable. The cable may connect to a single box that performs all of these functions.

4. If you have cable Internet service, look for an Ethernet cable between your computer and the cable modem, and then look for a coaxial cable between the modem and the wall connector.

5. At school or work, all you may find is an Ethernet cable connecting your computer to a wall jack that connects to the cable in the walls that connects to the network. Ask the network administrator to describe how you connect to the Internet through the network.

SCENARIO & SOLUTION

I need to set up some security cameras in locations where there is no power outlet. How can I power them?	Power them with Power over Ethernet (PoE). Use PoE injectors if needed to inject power into the connections provided by your existing switches, or use switches with PoE capability.
What good does it do me to memorize TCP port numbers?	You can allow or block access to certain ports in your firewall program, and you can understand security reports that show certain ports being used. It will also help you pass the CompTIA A+ 220-901 exam.
What's the difference between a switch and a router?	A switch handles only local network traffic; a router provides a path out of the local network, to another network such as the Internet.

CERTIFICATION SUMMARY

IT professionals preparing for the CompTIA A+ 220-901 and 220-902 exams must understand the basic concepts of computer networks. More in-depth knowledge is required for other exams, such as the CompTIA Network+, Security+, and Server+ exams. Basic concepts include network topologies—the geographic classifications of networks into LANs, MANs, and WANs. You must understand LAN technologies, such as Ethernet and Wi-Fi, and the various WAN connection methods, including dial-up and broadband WAN connections like ISDN, cable, DSL, satellite, and cellular. Be able to identify the most common cabling types, connectors, and common network adapters used in PCs.

Understand that TCP/IP is a protocol suite designed for the Internet and now used on most LANs and interconnected networks. Understand network-addressing concepts, including physical addresses assigned to network adapters and logical addresses assigned and used through the network protocols.

Understand the various addresses that are part of an IP configuration and their roles. These include the IP address and subnet mask of the network adapter, default gateway, and the DNS server, DHCP server, and WINS server addresses.

Be prepared to distinguish between various network hardware, including adapters, the transmission medium, network-to-network connection devices (repeater, bridge, and router), and devices for connecting computers to a network (hub and switch).

TWO-MINUTE DRILL

Here are some of the key points covered in Chapter 13.

Network Classifications

❏ Networks fall into several classifications, including PAN, LAN, MAN, and WAN.

❏ PAN technologies include the use of standards for wireless transmissions over very short distances. These include infrared (IR/IrDA), limited to about 1 meter, and Bluetooth, which has a range of up to 10 meters.

❏ Common LAN technologies include Ethernet in wired LANs and Wi-Fi in wireless LANs.

❏ Ethernet has several implementations, each with increasing speeds, including 10BaseT at 10 Mbps, 100BaseT at 100 Mbps, 1000BaseT at 1 Gbps over UTP, and 10GBaseT with speeds up to 10 Gbps. In addition, fiber-optic cable supports very high speeds.

❏ The Wi-Fi standard 802.11a supports speeds up to 54 Mbps using the 5 GHz frequency. Other Wi-Fi standards are more popular. These include 802.11g, which also supports speeds of up to 54 Mbps but uses the same frequency (2.4 GHz) as its predecessor, 802.11b. 802.11g equipment is usually downward compatible with the slower and older 802.11b equipment.

❏ The 802.11n Wi-Fi standard provides speeds of up to 100 Mbps and beyond. The standard actually defines speeds of up to 600 Mbps. The 802.11ac standard hits 1 Gbps.

❏ Dial-up WAN connections are the slowest and require initiation of the connection every time a user wishes to connect to a remote resource.

❏ Broadband WAN connections, all offering speeds faster than dial-up, include cellular, ISDN, DSL, cable, T-carrier, satellite, line-of-sight wireless, PVC, VPN, and fiber.

Network Software

❏ The roles played by the computer on the network describe the network. The two most general roles are those of clients and servers.

❏ A network in which any computer can be both a client and a server is a peer-to-peer network.

❏ A client/server network is one in which most desktop computers are clients and dedicated computers act as servers.

❏ An NOS is an operating system that runs on a network server and provides file sharing and access to other resources, account management, authentication, and authorization services. Examples of NOSs are Microsoft Windows Server operating systems, Novell Server operating systems, and Linux.

❏ A network client is software that requests services from compatible servers. Windows, macOS, and Linux, when installed on desktop computers that have a network connection, automatically install a basic network client.

❏ A protocol suite is a group of related protocols that work together to support the functioning of a network. TCP/IP is the dominant protocol suite as well as the protocol suite of the Internet.

❏ TCP/IP supports small-to-large networks and interconnected networks called internetworks. The Internet is the largest internetwork.

❏ Network addressing occurs at both the physical level and the logical level. Every Ethernet network adapter from every Ethernet NIC manufacturer in the world has a unique physical address, also called a MAC address, which is 48 bits long and is usually shown in hexadecimal notation.

❏ Internet Protocol is concerned with logical addresses. An IPv4 address is 32 bits long and is usually shown in dotted-decimal notation, as in 192.168.1.41. IPv6 has 128-bit addressing, which theoretically supports a huge number of unique addresses.

❏ An IPv4 and IPv6 address configuration includes a subnet mask, which determines the host ID and network ID portions of the address. In addition, the IP configuration may include addresses for a default gateway, DNS server, primary WINS server, and DHCP server.

❏ In addition to an IP address, a packet will contain a port number identifying the service on the target computer that should receive the packet's contents.

Network Hardware

❏ A network adapter provides the connection to the network medium. Network adapters (network interface cards) are available for the various networking technologies, such as Ethernet and Wi-Fi.

❏ Physical transmission media include twisted-pair, fiber-optic, and coaxial cable.

❑ Networking requires various network connection devices. A repeater is a device used to extend the range of a network by taking the signals it receives from one port and regenerating (repeating) those signals to another port.

❑ A bridge is a device used to connect two networks and pass traffic between them based on the physical address of the destination device.

❑ A hub is a device that is the central connecting point of a 10BaseT Ethernet LAN, with all network devices on a LAN connecting to one or more hubs.

❑ More intelligent devices called switches or switching hubs now replace hubs on Ethernet networks. These take an incoming signal and send it only to the destination port.

❑ An IP router sits between networks and routes packets according to their IP addresses.

❑ Many routers combine routing and bridging, and connect multiple network technologies, such as a LAN and a T1 network.

❑ A patch panel is like a switchboard for networking connections, helping to organize cables.

❑ Power over Ethernet (PoE) enables you to deliver power to devices through the same network cable that carries its data. A midspan injector can add PoE capability to non-PoE equipment.

❑ A wireless access point (WAP) is a wireless switch.

❑ A dial-up modem uses a telephone line to connect to a remote network.

❑ A firewall is hardware or software that restricts the flow of network traffic based on a set of rules.

❑ Ethernet over Power (EoP), also called HomePlug AV, allows you to use the existing power wires in a building as LAN data cables.

SELF TEST

The following questions will help you measure your understanding of the material presented in this chapter. Read all of the choices carefully because there might be more than one correct answer. Choose all correct answers for each question.

Network Classifications

1. What is the standard for fiber-optic Ethernet WANs?
   A. 10GBaseSR
   B. 1000BaseT
   C. Fast Ethernet
   D. 10GBaseSW

2. Which of the following statements is true about a LAN versus a WAN?
   A. A LAN spans a greater distance than a WAN.
   B. A WAN spans a greater distance than a LAN.
   C. A LAN is generally slower than a WAN.
   D. A WAN is used within a home or within a small business.

3. Which of the following is a PAN technology?
   A. Ethernet
   B. Satellite
   C. Bluetooth
   D. 802.11a

4. What is the type of network that connects many private networks in one metropolitan community?
   A. PAN
   B. MAN
   C. WAN
   D. LAN

5. Of the following technologies, which is downward compatible with 802.11b?
   A. 802.11a
   B. 802.11g
   C. Bluetooth
   D. IrDA

6. Which of the following is usually the slowest WAN connection?
   A. Dial-up
   B. DSL
   C. Cable
   D. Satellite

7. Which of the following WAN technologies uses a network originally created for television transmissions?
   A. DSL
   B. Cellular
   C. Cable
   D. Dial-up

8. Which of the following is a term that describes the amount of time it takes a packet to travel from one point to another?
   A. Bandwidth
   B. KBps
   C. Latency
   D. MBps

Network Software

9. Which statement describing IPv4 versus IPv6 differences is correct?
   A. IPv6 uses a subnet mask, while IPv4 uses 128-bit addressing.
   B. IPv4 uses 128-bit addressing, while IPv6 uses 32-bit addressing.
   C. IPv4 uses 32-bit addressing, while IPv6 uses 128-bit addressing.
   D. IPv4 uses double colons to indicate consecutive groups of 0s.

10. Which port is the correct one for Hypertext Transfer Protocol (HTTP) and web page transmission to a browser?
    A. TCP 80
    B. UDP 53
    C. TCP 443
    D. TCP 110

11. What protocol used on the Internet is concerned with the logical addressing of hosts?
    A. TCP
    B. IP
    C. UDP
    D. ARP

12. What protocol adds the old Microsoft naming system to TCP/IP?
    A. NetBEUI
    B. NetBIOS
    C. DHCP
    D. DNS

13. What divides an IP address into its host ID and network ID components?
    A. Default gateway
    B. DNS server
    C. DHCP server
    D. Subnet mask

14. A NIC has this type of a permanent address assigned to it by the manufacturer.
    A. IP address
    B. Physical address
    C. Host ID
    D. Automatic address

15. A packet with a destination address not on the local network will be sent to the address identified by which label in the IP configuration?
    A. Default gateway
    B. DNS server
    C. DHCP server
    D. Subnet mask

Network Hardware

16. Which of the following statements is correct?
    A. CAT5 cable can transmit 1 Gbps.
    B. CAT6 cable can transmit 10 Gbps.
    C. CAT5, CAT5e, and CAT6 segments can all be a maximum of 200 meters long.
    D. CAT5e cable can transmit 10 Gbps.

17. Which of the following is not a network medium?
    A. Plenum
    B. Twisted-pair cable
    C. Fiber-optic cable
    D. Atmosphere

18. Which type of cable uses ST, SC, LC, or MT-RJ connectors?
    A. STP
    B. UTP
    C. Fiber-optic
    D. Coaxial

19. Thousands of this type of device exist on the Internet between networks, direct the traffic of the Internet using the destination IP address of each packet, and pass the packets to their destinations along the interconnected networks of the Internet.
    A. Router
    B. Modem
    C. NIC
    D. Hub

20. Which of these uses the electrical wires in a home or business network to transmit Ethernet data?
   A. EoP
   B. WAP
   C. PoE
   D. Repeater

SELF TEST ANSWERS

Network Classifications

1. ☑ **D.** 10GBaseSW is the standard for fiber-optic Ethernet WANs.
   ☒ **A** is incorrect because 10GBaseSR is the standard for 10-Gigabit Ethernet over twisted-pair cable. **B** is incorrect because 1000BaseT is the standard for 1 Gbps Ethernet on twisted-pair cable. **C** is incorrect because Fast Ethernet is the common name for 100BaseT, which carries data at 100 Mbps on twisted-pair cable.

2. ☑ **B.** A WAN spans a greater distance than a LAN.
   ☒ **A, C,** and **D** are all incorrect because they are not true.

3. ☑ **C.** Bluetooth is a personal area network (PAN) technology used to connect devices and computers over very short distances.
   ☒ **A, B,** and **D** are all incorrect because none of these is a PAN technology. Ethernet is a wired LAN technology, satellite is a WAN technology, and 802.11a is a set of WLAN standards.

4. ☑ **B.** MAN, a metropolitan area network, is the type of network that connects many private networks in one community.
   ☒ **A** is incorrect because a PAN is a personal area network that only connects devices in a very small (usually a few meters) area. **C** is incorrect because this type a wide area network connects over long distances. **D** is incorrect because a local area network is limited to a distance of hundreds of meters and would not span an entire metropolitan community.

5. ☑ **B.** 802.11g is downward compatible with the slower 802.11b standard because they both use the 2.4 GHz bandwidth.
   ☒ **A** is incorrect because the 802.11a Wi-Fi standard operates in the 5 MHz band, which makes it totally incompatible with 802.11b. **C** is incorrect because Bluetooth is a standard for very short distances and is not downward compatible with 802.11b. **D** is incorrect because IrDA is a standard for very short-range infrared communications, which is totally incompatible with 802.11b.

6. ☑ **A.** Dial-up is usually the slowest WAN connection, at an advertised rate of 56 Kbps but with a top actual rate of about 48 Kbps.
   ☒ **B, C,** and **D** are all incorrect because each of these is a broadband service with maximum speeds that go up to many times that of dial-up.

7. ☑ **C.** Cable is the WAN technology that uses a network originally created for television transmissions.
   ☒ **A** is incorrect because DSL uses the telephone network, not a network created for television transmissions. **B** is incorrect because cellular uses the cellular network, originally created for voice transmissions but which was upgraded to digital and can be used for broadband data transmissions. **D** is incorrect because dial-up uses the telephone network, not a network created for television transmissions.

8. ☑ **C.** Latency is the term for the time it takes a packet to travel from one point to another.
   ☒ **A** is incorrect because bandwidth is the amount of data that can travel over a network within a given time. **B** and **D** are both incorrect because these terms mean kilobytes per second and megabytes per second, respectively, which describe the amount of data that can travel over a network.

Network Software

9. ☑ **C.** IPv4 uses 32-bit addressing, while IPv6 uses 128-bit addressing.
   ☒ **A** is incorrect because IPv4 uses 32-bit addressing. IPv6 can use a subnet mask also. **B** is incorrect because it is just the opposite. **D** is incorrect because it is IPv6 that uses the double colons to indicate consecutive groups of 0s.

10. ☑ **A.** TCP 80 is the correct port number for HTTP and web page transmission to a web browser.
    ☒ **B** is incorrect because UDP 53 is the port for Domain Name Service used by clients to perform DNS queries against DNS servers. **C** is incorrect because TCP 443 is the port for secure web page transmission. **D** is incorrect because TCP 110 is the port for Post Office Protocol that retrieves e-mail from a POP3 mail server.

11. ☑ **B.** IP is the protocol used on the Internet that is concerned with the logical addressing of hosts.
    ☒ **A** is incorrect because TCP is not concerned with the logical addressing of hosts. **C** is incorrect because UDP is not concerned with the logical addressing of hosts. **D** is incorrect because ARP is not concerned with the logical addressing of hosts.

12. ☑ **B.** NetBIOS is the protocol that adds the old Microsoft naming system to TCP/IP.
    ☒ **A** is incorrect because this old Microsoft network protocol suite had NetBIOS as just a part. **C** is incorrect because DHCP is the protocol used for automatically allocating IP addresses. **D** is incorrect because DNS is the protocol that supports Internet-style names.

13. ☑ **D.** A subnet mask divides an IP address into its host ID and network ID components.
☒ **A** is incorrect because the default gateway is the name of the router address to which a computer directs packets with destinations beyond the local network. **B** is incorrect because the DNS server is where a network client sends queries to resolve DNS names into IP addresses. **C** is incorrect because the DHCP server is what automatically assigns IP addresses to DHCP client computers.

14. ☑ **B.** The physical address is the type of permanent address assigned to a NIC by the manufacturer.
☒ **A** is incorrect because an IP address is not a permanent address but a logical address not permanently assigned to a NIC. **C** is incorrect because the host ID is the portion of an IP address that identifies the host. **D** is incorrect because an automatic address usually refers to an IP address assigned to a PC by a DHCP server.

15. ☑ **A.** The default gateway is the address to which the router sends packets that have addresses not on the local network.
☒ **B** is incorrect because this server resolves DNS names. **C** is incorrect because the DHCP server assigns IP addresses automatically. **D** is incorrect because a subnet mask is not an address but a mask used to divide an IP address into its host ID and network ID components.

Network Hardware

16. ☑ **B.** CAT6 can indeed transmit 10 Gbps.
☒ **A** is incorrect because CAT5 can only transmit 100 Mbps. **C** is incorrect because each of these cable categories requires a repeater or a switch at 100 meters. **D** is incorrect because CAT5e can only transmit 1 Gbps.

17. ☑ **A.** Plenum is not a network medium, but rather a characteristic of certain network media (cables), indicating the cable sheath is fire resistant and appropriate to run in plenum space.
☒ **B, C,** and **D** are all incorrect because all are networking media.

18. ☑ **C.** Fiber-optic cable uses ST, SC, LC, or MT-RJ connectors.
☒ **A, B,** and **D** are all incorrect because they do not use ST, SC, LC, or MT-RJ connectors.

19. ☑ **A.** A router is the device that exists on the Internet and passes IP packets from many sources to destinations along the Internet.
☒ **B** is incorrect because a modem does not pass packets along the Internet, although it is a beginning point for a single computer to send packets. **C** is incorrect because a network interface card (NIC) is simply a device for connecting a single computer to a network. **D** is incorrect because a hub is an older device used at the heart of a LAN but not an Internet device.

20. ☑ **A.** Ethernet over Power (EOP) uses power lines for Ethernet networking.
☒ **B** is incorrect because a wireless access point (WAP) does not user power lines. **C** is incorrect because Power over Ethernet (PoE) delivers electrical power over UTP Ethernet cable. **D** is incorrect because a repeater amplifies an Ethernet signal via standard Ethernet cable, not power lines.

Chapter 14

Installing a Small Office/Home Office (SOHO) Network

■   **902: 3.2**   Compare and contrast common prevention methods

■   **902: 3.7**   Given a scenario, secure SOHO wired and wireless networks

✓   Two-Minute Drill

Q&A   Self Test

I n this chapter, you will learn the tasks required to install and configure client computer access to a local area network (LAN) or wireless local area network (WLAN), focusing on a small network, such as you would find in a small office or home office (SOHO).

CERTIFICATION OBJECTIVE

■ *901: 4.4*   *Given a scenario, troubleshoot wired and wireless networks with appropriate tools*

We start out this chapter by reviewing the hardware tools for creating and maintaining networks covered in CompTIA A+ 901 exam objective 4.4. Some of these were also mentioned in Chapters 1 and 3, but in the following section they get full coverage.

Using Networking Tools

Networking tools—at least the hardware ones—are mainly required to make wired connections and test those connections. We described those tools in Chapter 3, and we explain their role in installing networks here. As you read through the descriptions for using these tools, and the discussion in the next section on connecting a wired NIC to a network, recall the information in Chapter 5 in the section titled "Cable Basics: What's Inside a Cable?"

Crimper and Wire Stripper

To create your own UTP network cables, you will need bulk unshielded twisted-pair (UTP) cabling, RJ-45 connectors, and a crimper. Use a *wire stripper* (often built into the crimper) on each end of the cable to expose the four wire pairs. Ensure the wires are in the correct

FIGURE 14-1

Using a wire-
crimping tool to
attach an RJ-45
connector to a
UTP cable

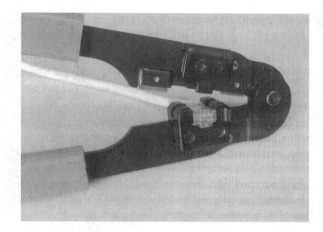

order and place them into an RJ-45 connector. Insert the RJ-45 connector into the crimper
and squeeze the crimper handles. The RJ-45 connector has eight small metal probes or
needles, each of which will pierce one of the eight wires. Figure 14-1 shows a crimper with a
crimped network cable.

Punch Down Tool

Network installers have the responsibility of running network cables through walls and
creating RJ-45 wall outlets in offices. This is done by hard-wiring the cable to the wall outlet
at one end, and to a patch panel in the wiring closet at the other end.

First, a network installer runs cable through the walls of the building, with one end
terminating in the wiring closet, and the other end poking out of a small hole in the office
receiving the wall outlet. Then at the office end, the installer uses a *punch down tool*
(see Figure 14-2, and also Figure 3-3 in Chapter 3) to insert each of the bare wires into the
back of a port mounted in a wall plate, and then attaches that plate to the wall.

Next, the installer goes to the wiring closet and uses the wire stripper and punch down
tool again to connect the wires inside the cable to the back of an RJ-45 port on a patch
panel. Now the cable has been hard-wired from the wall outlet to the wiring panel. Next,
the installer uses a short cable to connect the newly wired RJ-45 port on the wiring panel to
a switch or router, being careful to label the short cable to describe the location of the office
being connected.

on the
job

**Why not just directly hard-wire the cable into the switch or router? You can
probably guess the answer. If you need to replace the switch or router, you
don't want to have to rewire dozens of ports.**

FIGURE 14-2

A punch down tool helps insert bare wires into connectors. (Photo: https:// commons .wikimedia.org/ wiki/File:Ideal_ punchdown_ tool,_side .jpg [Creative Commons license])

Multimeter

You can test the electrical properties of a cable or circuit with a multimeter. You could test, for example, the continuity of a power cable, or you could test that a power supply Serial Advanced Technology Attachment (SATA) hard disk connector is supplying the proper voltage. Set the multimeter to ohms (resistance), and touch the probes to corresponding wires at each end of a cable. If you get anything other than 0 (or very nearly 0), you have a break in the cable. Figure 3-2 in Chapter 3 shows a multimeter.

Tone Generator and Probe

Wiring rooms can sometimes look like a packrat's nest—complete and utter chaos. To determine exactly which cable in the wiring room maps to a network jack in another room, use a tone generator and probe (defined in Chapter 3). A tone generator and probe work together as a pair. The tone generator connects to a cable or network jack and sends a tone along the cable. As you pass the probe near the cable carrying the tone, the probe gets louder. This helps you isolate a specific cable in a cable bunch.

Cable Tester

Sometimes network cables look fine, but some wires inside may be bent and broken. Testing STP and UTP network cable continuity is easy with a *cable tester*; it has two RJ-45 ports where you plug in each end of the cable. Indicator lights tell you whether wires inside the cable are intact. Figure 3-4 in Chapter 3 shows a cable tester.

Loopback Plug

A *loopback plug* connects to a port, such as a serial or RJ-45 port. Inside the device, it reverses the receive and transmit wires so you can determine whether a port is functional. It's employed along with software that sends and receives the signal through the port and interprets the results.

Wireless Locator

A wireless locator is an electronic device that lets you know what wireless networks are within range and some basic information about them, such as the Service Set Identifier (SSID), channel, signal strength, encryption type, geographical coordinates (working in conjunction with GPS), and many other details. Used often during wireless site surveys to detect nearby WLANs and their channels, the tool can also be used during a security audit to test WLAN visibility, distance, and security. A wireless locator can be a specialized handheld device or software installed on a smartphone, tablet, laptop, or PC.

A tablet or smartphone can be used as a basic wireless locator without any special software. Just pull up the settings screen where you choose a wireless network, and watch the list of available networks as you move around.

CERTIFICATION OBJECTIVES

- **901: 2.5** *Compare and contrast various Wi-Fi networking standards and encryption types*
- **901: 2.6** *Given a scenario, install and configure a SOHO wireless/wired router and apply appropriate settings*
- **902: 1.6** *Given a scenario, install and configure Windows networking on a client/desktop*
- **902: 3.7** *Given a scenario, secure SOHO wireless and wired networks*

A CompTIA A+ certification candidate must know how to connect desktop and laptop computers to a LAN. This requires understanding how to install and configure common network hardware, and how to configure the OS to recognize and work with the hardware.

In this section we cover the wireless encryption types listed in CompTIA A+ 901 exam objective 2.5, and the router configuration settings from 901 exam objective 2.6.

On the A+ 220-902 exam side, this section covers setup and configuration of Windows networking on a client (902 exam objective 1.6), and most of the router security settings from 902 exam objective 3.7.

Installing and Configuring SOHO Networks

A *small office/home office (SOHO)* is an office consisting of a single computer or just a few computers. The location may be in a home or in a commercial office. Computers in a SOHO environment need to connect to the Internet, requiring the same steps you would take in a larger environment. A connection to a LAN requires a network adapter for each computer— whether it is a wired NIC (Ethernet), a Wi-Fi NIC, or an analog modem for making a dial-up connection. Therefore, the first step in connecting a computer to a network is to install a NIC appropriate for the type of network—wired or wireless. Once you've installed the NIC and driver, you need to configure the NIC with an appropriate IP configuration, along with any other settings appropriate to the type of network. In this section, we describe the software tools and settings required for installing and configuring a network and then describe the steps for configuring a typical SOHO network.

Installing a Network Adapter

Most computers have a built-in wired Ethernet adapter, but add-on adapters are also available. A network adapter can be internal (using a PCIe card) or external (using a USB port or ExpressCard slot). You learned in Chapter 4 how to install an internal expansion card. If your network adapter is built into the motherboard, you can enable or disable it via the motherboard BIOS/UEFI, and perhaps adjust some of its settings there too as well. You learned how to access that in Chapter 3.

To connect a computer to a LAN, plug one end of an Ethernet cable into the network adapter on the computer, and plug the other end into a switch or router. Use UTP cable of no more than 100 meters that conforms to the CAT5e or CAT6 standard. Connect the other computers in the network to the same switch or router, and voila, you have a LAN. Most switches and routers have at least four wired Ethernet ports on them (in addition to any wireless device connection capabilities they might have), as shown in Figure 14-3.

Connecting a Network Adapter to a Switch or Router

The next step is to make a physical connection between the network adapter and the switch or router. Most SOHO switches are also *broadband routers*, meaning they are designed to allow several computers to share an Internet (broadband) connection. You connect an Ethernet cable from the broadband modem (usually cable or DSL) to the router via a specially labeled port on the router (usually something like WAN or Internet). In Figure 14-3, for example, the cable is being plugged into the WAN port.

FIGURE 14-3

This SOHO router acts as a switch for the LAN and also provides a connection to a cable or DSL modem.

Older routers may have an uplink port, in addition to the WAN or Internet port. An uplink port is a reverse-wired port, designed to be used with a crossover cable to connect two routers. Don't confuse this with the WAN port, which is what you plug the Internet cable into.

Configuring a Network Adapter

A network adapter will usually work pretty well without any special configuration in a SOHO environment. However, familiarize yourself with these settings, both for those unusual situations you may encounter and for CompTIA A+ 902 exam objective 1.6.

QoS

Some data you receive via network is not time-sensitive. For example, when you receive an e-mail message, the packets may arrive out of order, and that's okay; they are assembled into a message before you open it. Other network data, however, needs a stable and reliable connection for time-sensitive data. For example, when you are video chatting, you need the packets to arrive in the correct order and with the least delay.

Quality of Service (QoS) includes many techniques and technologies that attempt to solve the problem of delivering content that cannot suffer delays and lost packets. A variety of QoS features are found in network adapters and routers, including features that prioritize types of traffic, giving higher priority to traffic like a video call. You'll find these settings in your router's Setup page (which you'll learn to access later in this chapter.)

As for the network adapter's QoS settings, you can enable or disable the QoS Packet Scheduler. Open the Network and Sharing Center (from the Control Panel). Next to Connections you'll see a hyperlink for the current network connection. Click it to open a Status dialog box, and then click Properties. Make sure that QoS Packet Scheduler appears here, and that it has a check mark next to it. If it doesn't, click Install and add it. It is enabled by default.

Wake on LAN

Wake on LAN enables a computer to wake up from a very low power state when it receives a wake-up pattern. This pattern can be what's called a "magic packet" that contains the MAC address of the network adapter, or it can be a request directed at the OS's definition of the network adapter (such as its NetBIOS name or IPv4 or IPv6 address).

There may be a Wake on LAN setting in BIOS/UEFI setup (see Chapter 3). If there is, it must be set to Enabled for Wake on LAN to work. Check this first, and then check the network adapter's settings in the OS.

To check the network adapter's Wake on LAN setting in Windows, open Device Manager and double-click the network adapter to open its Properties dialog box. On the Advanced tab, select the Wake on LAN or Wake on Magic Packet setting. If needed, change its Value setting (Enabled/Disabled). See Figure 14-4. This setting controls only waking on a magic

FIGURE 14-4

Look for a Wake settings in the Properties dialog box for your network adapter.

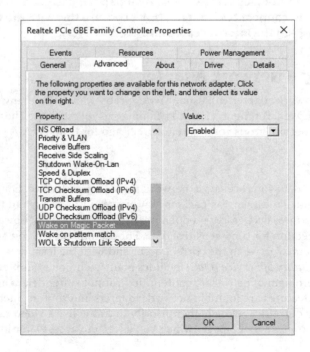

packet (the MAC address). Then check the Wake on Pattern Match setting, which controls waking based on an OS-level request such as a NetBIOS name resolution broadcast for the local computer name or an ARP packet for the IPv4 address of the network adapter.

So what about when you want to actually wake a remote computer via LAN? Here's a good resource to learn about that, and to get a utility: https://www .depicus.com.

Speed and Duplex

When data is sent on a cable in only one direction, that's called *simplex*. For example, a monitor cable sends data to the monitor, but the monitor doesn't send anything back. When the two connected devices send data back and forth but only one sends at a time, that's called *half-duplex*. Half-duplex requires special signaling in the communication to let each device know when it is its turn to send. When two connected devices can send and receive simultaneously, that's *full-duplex*. In Chapter 13, in the "Local Area Network" section, you learned how duplex applies to Ethernet. Nearly all Ethernet today is full-duplex. A device's duplex setting was important many years ago, before devices could negotiate their duplex setting automatically.

The same goes with network adapter speed. Early communications between devices required a speed to be specified, such as 10 Mbps, 100 Mbps, or 1000 Mbps, but today most devices negotiate the speed automatically.

To control both speed and duplex for a network adapter, go back to that same Properties dialog box that you worked with in the preceding section, from Device Manager. On the Advanced tab (see Figure 14-4), select Speed & Duplex and make sure Auto Negotiation is selected (unless you have a specific reason to use some other setting).

Creating a Wi-Fi Network

Before you install a wireless network, you must consider some special issues for selecting and positioning wireless hardware. These issues include obstacles between the computers and the WLAN, the distances involved, any possible interference, the standards supported by the devices on the Wi-Fi network, and the wireless mode for your WLAN. Then you should take steps to update the firmware on the wireless access point (WAP), if necessary.

Obstacles and Interference

Certain devices emit radio signals that can interfere with Wi-Fi networks. These devices include microwave ovens and cordless telephones that use the 2.4 GHz radio band, as well as other nearby WAPs. WAPs normally support channel selection. Therefore, if you have a 2.4 GHz cordless phone that supports channel selection, configure the phone to use one channel (channel 1, for instance), and the WAP and each wireless NIC to use another channel, like channel 11. In addition, metal furniture and appliances, metal-based ultraviolet

(UV) tint on windows, and metal construction materials within walls can all block or reduce Wi-Fi signals.

When a computer or other physical device connects to a network, it is called a *node*.

Certain businesses and organizations require a professional site survey, a set of procedures to determine the location of obstacles and interference that would disrupt wireless signals. WAP placement is then determined from this site survey. Although a professional site survey is too costly for a small business or home owner, you can use the site survey feature of your wireless NIC to discover which channel nearby wireless networks are using. The name of the site survey feature may simply be Available Network, which shows a list of wireless networks. Clicking a network in the list reveals the channel in use and other important information. Alternatively, use a wireless locator, described earlier in this chapter.

Distances and Speeds

A huge issue with wireless networks is the signal range of the communicating devices. All of the Wi-Fi standards used give maximum outdoor signal ranges of 75 to 125 meters, but that is for a signal uninterrupted by barriers, such as walls that may contain signal-stopping materials like metal lath. Position a WAP in a central location within easy range of all devices, NICs, and access points.

watch CompTIA A+ 902 exam objective 3.7 lists "Radio power levels" as a topic of interest. Make sure you understand that the radio power level of the WAP affects signal strength and maximum distance.

The farther a wireless NIC is from a WAP, the more the signal degrades and the greater the chance of slowing down the connection speed. Actual ranges for these devices once in place vary greatly. For instance, the documentation for our 802.11g WAP shows that the outdoor range of this device is 40 meters at 54 Mbps and 300 meters at 6 Mbps or less. Indoor range is 15 meters at 54 Mbps and 120 meters at 6 Mbps. For devices that use multiple bands to achieve their throughput, like 802.11ac, a WAP will be described in its marketing with the number of streams it supports. The theoretical maximum for 802.11ac is eight streams, but most SOHO routers support either two or three.

The ranges for the various standards are shown in Table 14-1.

In the past, we preferred to use USB NICs attached to a USB cable (see Figure 14-5) rather than bus or PC Card NICs that were internal to the computer. The cable gives you more flexibility in positioning the wireless antenna for best signal reception.

TABLE 14-1	IEEE Standard	Operating Frequency	Typical Data Rate	Maximum Data Rate	Indoor Range	Outdoor Range
	802.11b	2.4 GHz	6.5 Mbps	11 Mbps	~35 meters	~100 meters
Summary of Common Wi-Fi Standards	802.11g	2.4 GHz	25 Mbps	54 Mbps	~25 meters	~75 meters
	802.11n	2.4 GHz or 5 GHz	200 Mbps	540 Mbps	~50 meters	~125 meters
	802.11ac	5 GHz	2.5 Gbps	6.9 Gbps	~50 meters	~125 meters

However, unless you can find a Wi-Fi NIC with a USB 3.0 interface (5 Gbps), the 480 Mbps speed of USB 2.0 is slower than the maximum data rate for 802.11ac of 1.3 Gbps. Alternatively, you can find bus Wi-Fi NICs with antennas attached via a cable to the NIC, allowing you some flexibility for positioning the antenna.

When a wireless network spans buildings, you encounter special problems. For instance, the material in the building's walls may interfere with the signal. Now you need to get creative. For instance, consider a wireless NIC with a directional dish antenna that you can position in a window and point directly toward the WAP. Another option is a wireless range extender—a device that resembles a WAP but is designed to boost the signals from a WAP and extend its coverage distance.

Once you find the ideal location for each WAP, you may discover that you do not have a power connection available to each one, but you do have a nearby run of Ethernet cabling to tap into so that the WAP/router can connect to an Ethernet network. It requires the correct Ethernet cable and *PoE splitter*. (You may recall Power over Ethernet, PoE, from

Chapter 13.) The Ethernet cable from the network plugs into the splitter, which splits the signal and sends it to two connectors: an Ethernet jack and a power connector. You then connect the WAP by Ethernet cable to the jack, and by power cable to the power connector.

In addition to WAPs and wireless routers, all types of networked devices, such as security cameras, IP phones, and Ethernet switches, use PoE.

Compatibility

Another issue is the standard supported by each device. If possible, for each wireless network installation, select NICs and WAPs that comply with the exact same Wi-Fi standard. A single device that supports only a lower standard on a higher-standard WAP will slow down the entire WLAN. For example, while an 802.11b NIC can communicate with an 802.11ac WAP, all other traffic on that router will suffer in performance as long as it is connected.

In addition, use devices from the same manufacturer, when possible, because some manufacturers build in special proprietary features—support for higher speeds or greater range—that are only available in their device. However, this rule is difficult to enforce in practice, especially when you add a laptop with a built-in wireless NIC to your network.

Setting Up a WAP

SOHO WAPs also typically include routing capabilities, for Internet connection sharing, and are referred to as *wireless routers*. The one pictured in Figure 14-6 includes a dedicated

FIGURE 14-6

A wireless access point

Ethernet port for connecting to a broadband modem, plus a four-port Ethernet switch. The wireless nodes (including the WAP) communicating together in infrastructure mode make up a *Basic Service Set (BSS)*.

on the job

The WAP in Figure 14-6 has only one antenna, but many WAPs have more than one. Where there are two antennas, one is generally for transmission and one for reception. On WAPs that support multiple input/multiple output (MIMO), like 802.11ac models, there may be one or two separate antennas for each stream. Some WAPs have internal antennas, though, so you can't rely on an antenna count to know how many streams a WAP supports.

Position a WAP in the center of all the computers that will participate in the wireless network. If there are barriers to the wireless signals, you will need to determine if you can overcome them with the use of an enhanced antenna on the WAP, or a wireless signal booster to reach computers that are beyond the WAP's range.

In order to configure a new WAP, you normally connect to it using an Ethernet cable between a computer with an Ethernet NIC and the WAP. Check the documentation that comes with the WAP in case you need to use a special cable. Direct connection via the Ethernet port is required only for initial setup of the WAP. Once it is up and running, you can connect from any computer on the network, wired or wirelessly, and modify the configuration.

It only takes a few minutes to set up a WAP physically and then to configure it to create your wireless LAN. You will need a WAP and its user manual, a computer with an Ethernet NIC, two Ethernet cables (one may have come with the WAP), and the WAP's IP address, obtained from the user manual. If you will be using the router to connect PCs to the Internet, you will need the DSL or cable modem already set up and ready to go. With all the materials assembled, follow these general instructions for connecting and configuring a WAP that is a DSL/cable router, commonly called a wireless router. The actual steps required to configure a WAP may vary from these steps. These general instructions work for most WAPs we have used:

1. Before connecting the WAP, turn off the computer and the DSL or cable modem.
2. Connect one end of an Ethernet cable to the WAN port of the WAP, and connect the other end of the cable to the DSL or cable modem.
3. Take another network cable and connect one end of the cable to your computer's Ethernet NIC and the other end to one of the Ethernet ports on the WAP.
4. Turn power to the modem on, and wait for the lights on the modem to settle down.
5. Turn the WAP's power on by connecting the power cable that came with the WAP, first to the WAP and then to an electrical outlet. If the WAP has a power switch, turn it on now.

6. Turn the computer's power on.
7. Now look at the WAP and verify that the indicator lights for the WAN and WLAN ports light up. Ensure that the indicator light for the LAN port to which the computer connects is lit as well.

Once you have completed these steps, you can test the connection to the WAP, and if all works well, you can configure the WAP settings. Exercise 14-1, later in the chapter, will walk you through testing the WAP connection and then using your web browser to connect and configure the WAP settings.

Status messages will appear over your notification area when a wireless connection is first established and when a wireless connection fails. These messages only display briefly, so most NICs also change the appearance of the icon, showing perhaps a blue or green icon when the NIC is connected and a red icon, or an icon with an *x* over it, when the NIC is disconnected. A laptop with an integrated wireless adapter will usually have a hardware switch to enable or disable the wireless connection. Be sure you have this turned on.

Accessing a Configuration Utility

Several of the upcoming sections refer to changes you can make in the WAP's configuration utility, so before you go any further, you should learn how to access this utility. (This is the same for routers and wired switches as well.)

Depending on the WAP, you initially might have to access the configuration utility via a wired Ethernet connection rather than wirelessly. Let's assume that is the case, for now. Connect an Ethernet cable from a desktop or laptop PC's Ethernet port to any of the Ethernet ports on the back of the WAP (except one of the special ones like WAN or Uplink).

Consult the documentation for the WAP to find out its default IP address. It probably starts with 192.168. Then open a web browser, and in the address bar, type **http://** and then the IP address. You're in! Figure 14-7 shows the configuration utility for an AT&T U-Verse combination device that is both a DSL modem and a Wi-Fi router. The layout and look varies dramatically between makes and models.

You might see a prompt for a user name and password, either initially or when you try to change certain settings. Consult the documentation for the WAP to find out the default user name and password, and enter these. Use the configuration utility in the web browser to configure various settings on the WAP, such as the ones described in the following sections.

If the WAP is also a cable/DSL modem, you may see settings for the Internet connectivity in the configuration utility. Leave those settings alone unless directed by a qualified cable/DSL technician.

FIGURE 14-7   An example configuration utility; yours may look very different.

Updating Firmware

A WAP has its own firmware (BIOS) that holds its low-level settings. Before you spend a lot of time configuring it, you might want to check to make sure the firmware is up to date, because installing a firmware update may wipe out any custom settings, returning the WAP to factory defaults. (Whether or not this happens depends on the brand and model.) Updated firmware may correct problems, add more features or more compatibility with newer devices, and be less vulnerable to hacking and malware.

To check the firmware version, find the System Information (or similar) page in the configuration utility, and note the Firmware or Software Version setting. Then go online, to the support website for the make and model of the WAP, and see whether a firmware update is available for download. Compare its version number to the one you have, and if the downloadable one is newer, go ahead and get it. Follow the instructions on the support website for downloading and installing it.

Configuring DHCP

As you learned in Chapter 13, a Dynamic Host Configuration Protocol (DHCP) server assigns IP addresses to the connected devices. By default, a WAP or wireless router has DHCP enabled, but you might need to disable DHCP on a WAP for some reason (such as another device or server on your network fulfilling that function). You should find the DHCP on/off setting in the WAP's configuration utility, in the DHCP section. You should also be able to specify DHCPv4 Start Address and Stop Address, which defines the range of addresses to be assigned to devices in the LAN. For example, on my WAP, the range is 192.168.1.64 to 192.168.1.253.

If you turn off DHCP, and no other DHCP server is operating on the LAN, you will need to manually assign static IP addresses to each device. That skill is covered later in this chapter, in the section "Assigning Static IP Addresses at the Router."

exam

ⓦatch   For the CompTIA A+ 220-901 and 220-902 exams, be aware that most of the topics discussed here under "Securing a Wireless Network" apply to both wired and wireless networks. Those that apply only to a wireless network include Wi-Fi Protected Setup (WPS), changing the Service Set Identifier (SSID), disabling SSID broadcasts, and the wireless standards discussed under the topic "Wireless Encryption." You can apply much of what you learn here to configure a router/firewall on a wired network, although the examples given here and in Exercise 14-1 are of a wireless network.

Securing a Wireless Network

There are several techniques for protecting a wireless network—both through maintaining physical security and through the configuration utility for a WAP or wireless router. Even devices designed for the consumer market have sophisticated security technologies, and any technology or feature that applies rules to control access between networks is a firewall technology. On top of that, many of these devices automatically and securely configure themselves while walking you through the process.

We will review important tasks for securing a wireless network next, and in the upcoming Exercise 14-1, you will see the steps required to configure settings for most of these.

Physical Security

Ensure that you physically protect the heart of the wireless network, the WAP or wireless router, both from theft and from harmful conditions. Then consider the physical security of the computers and devices that connect to the network; because many of them are small mobile devices, those two characteristics make them vulnerable to theft. Therefore, consider taking steps to protect those devices and the data on them. For instance, using Apple's iCloud service, you can configure an iPad so that if it is lost or stolen, you can see its location via the Internet and the use of GPS. You can remotely lock it or erase it. Learn more about mobile devices in Chapter 20.

Wi-Fi Protected Setup (WPS)

Newer wireless routers support an automatic configuration method called *Wi-Fi Protected Setup (WPS)*. WPS makes connecting wireless clients to a wireless network easy, because you can simply press a button on the wireless router and on any compatible wireless NIC to securely connect them. However, if a wireless device is not WPS enabled, you will need to manually configure it with the settings, including the password to access the wireless network, explained in the next section.

Wireless Encryption

Wireless transmissions are vulnerable because they travel over radio waves, which are easy for anyone with the right equipment to pick up and read the data. Therefore, you should take steps to encrypt any data sent over a wireless network. There are three sets of standards for this: WEP, WPA, and WPA2. One concept to understand is that wireless encryption (as well as other encryption methods) depends on the use of a code called an *encryption key* (also simply called a *key*) that is issued automatically by the encryption software. The key is used by other devices or users for decrypting the encrypted data. The types of keys and how they are used is one of the features that distinguishes the standards.

Wired Equivalent Privacy (WEP) is the oldest of the Wi-Fi encryption standards. It uses 64- or 128-bit encryption that is easily broken. It does not encrypt the actual data in a packet, just the portion that contains the source and destination information. Another security issue with WEP is that it issues a single static key that is not changed from session to session and that all network clients share. Further, WEP has no way to perform user authentication on the packet, something added to later standards. Consider WEP obsolete and do not use it unless it is the only wireless encryption standard supported by your hardware, which would make your hardware very old and due for being replaced.

Wi-Fi Protected Access (WPA) is a data encryption standard based on the IEEE 802.11i security standard for wireless networks. It corrects many of the problems with WEP. It issues keys per-user and per-session and includes encryption key integrity checking. On top of the WPA data encryption, it uses a *Temporal Key Integrity Protocol (TKIP)* with a 128-bit encryption key for authentication. WPA was considered transitional because it supported most older NICs, and, once hackers broke the TKIP encryption key, it, too, became obsolete.

At this time, the latest wireless encryption standard is *Wi-Fi Protected Access 2 (WPA2)*, which complies with the 802.11i security standard in that it does not support older network cards and offers both secure authentication and encryption, thus providing true end-to-end data encryption with authentication. It uses *Extensible Authentication Protocol (EAP)*, which defines a type of wrapper for a variety of authentication methods. A *wrapper* is program code that acts as a logical container for other code or data. Wireless devices generally use *EAP with Personal Shared Key (EAP-PSK)*, which involves using a string of characters (a shared key) that both communicating devices know. WPA2 uses an encryption standard approved by the U.S. government—*Advanced Encryption Standard (AES)*.

When preparing for the CompTIA A+ 220-901 exam, remember that WEP is an obsolete wireless encryption standard, and that WPA was an improvement, but its 128-key TKIP encryption was soon broken, making it also obsolete. The latest and most secure of these standards is WPA2, which uses AES encryption.

Each computer that connects must have a wireless NIC that is compatible with the version of wireless encryption in use on the WAP/router, and will be required to enter a password. Normally, you can configure your wireless NIC to remember the password and use it every time it connects to that Wi-Fi network. Learn how to do this a bit later in Exercise 14-1, "Configuring a WAP or Wireless Router."

Changing SSID and Disabling SSID Broadcast

A *Service Set Identifier (SSID)* is a network name used to identify a wireless network. Consisting of up to 32 characters, the SSID travels with the messages on the wireless network, and all of the wireless devices on a WLAN must use the same SSID in order to communicate. Therefore, assigning a SSID is part of setting up a wireless network. A WAP or wireless router comes from the manufacturer with a preconfigured SSID name. You must change this name in the WAP; in fact, some configuration programs assign a random new name for you every time you run the configuration utility, but allow you the option to provide a different name if you wish. You can also disable SSID broadcast through the configuration menus on a WAP or wireless router. This means that before any clients can connect, someone must manually enter the WLAN name into the configuration for that client's NIC.

Changing Default Administrator User Name and Password

WAPs and wireless routers come with a default administrator user name and password, which you must change immediately so that no one can easily log on to the WAP and change its configuration. Here again, the configuration program in many wireless routers will prompt you to do this.

Enabling MAC Filtering

Another way to limit access is by enabling and configuring *MAC filtering* on the WAP or wireless router. As you learned in Chapter 13, a Media Access Control (MAC) address is a unique hardware address assigned to every NIC, including Wi-Fi and Bluetooth NICs. The MAC address of the sending NIC is contained within each packet that travels the network. You can enable MAC filtering to allow or deny specific MAC addresses from connecting to your wireless network. One way to see the MAC address for a NIC is to open a Command Prompt and enter **ipconfig /all**.

Disabling Ports

Recall the section in Chapter 13 titled "Common Ports" and the description of the services that use each port. A wireless broadband router limits incoming traffic from the Internet that was not initiated from inside the wireless network. It does this by disabling incoming ports in the router's settings. By default, most wireless broadband routers have all incoming ports disabled, requiring a request from the local wireless network to open a port. For instance, when you browse to web pages on the Internet, the router recognizes that the website is responding to your requests.

Firewall Settings

We mention firewall settings as a separate topic here mainly because A+ 902 exam objective 3.7 calls it out separately, but firewall settings are not one simple, well-contained feature. *Firewall* describes a whole class of features and options.

A firewall blocks unauthorized port usage. A firewall can be a separate hardware device, software utility running in the OS (like Windows Firewall), or a collection of settings on the router or WAP. The configuration utility for your WAP or router may contain a Firewall section, and in it you may find settings for packet filtering and network address translation (NAT), both of which are covered in upcoming sections.

FIGURE 14-8   This WAP allows you to specify certain games that should be allowed to circumvent the firewall settings.

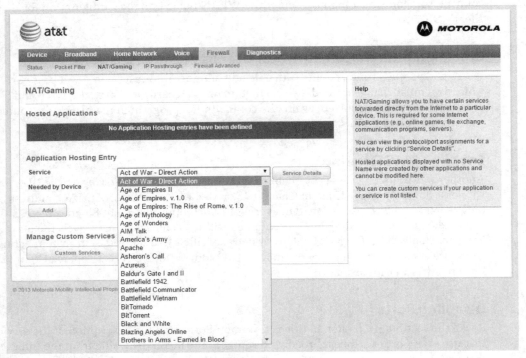

One of the most commonly configured firewall settings on a WAP or router is Hosted Applications. People who play multiuser games have the option in some games of hosting a game on their computer, to which other players connect via Internet. A firewall would normally prevent such connections, but you can configure the WAP or router to allow them. Our WAP, for example, has a list of services we can choose to allow past its firewall, as shown in Figure 14-8.

NAT Routing

In a home or small business, a broadband router (wired or wireless) is the connection point between the wired or wireless LAN. This router will contain a DHCP server that automatically assigns a private IP address on the LAN, and the device will also act as a *NAT router*, although you can turn this on or off without affecting the DHCP settings. The default is to turn on *NAT routing*, a firewall technology that uses *network address translation (NAT)*, a TCP/IP protocol that hides IP addresses on a private network from hosts beyond the router—usually on the Internet. When you access the Internet through a router using NAT routing (almost everyone does), it "remembers" your internal address, but changes the source address in each IP packet from your computer to the router's external address. When packets come back from the Internet in response to your computer's requests, the NAT router recalls that your computer made that request and sends the return packet to your computer. Therefore, malicious code outside your network does not know your internal address and cannot target you directly using your IP address.

Port Forwarding

If you have a server on your private network that you would like to receive traffic from the Internet, then you will need to enable *port forwarding*, which you do through the router's settings, mapping the port to the IP address of the server (a static IP address). Then outsiders can access that server. The technique involved in doing port forwarding is called *destination network address translation (DNAT)*. A situation in which you may need to enable port forwarding that does not involve what you normally think of as a server is when you want to allow Remote Desktop Protocol (RDP) access from a computer beyond the router to an internal host. Upcoming Exercise 14-1 includes instructions for configuring this on the router.

Port Triggering

While port forwarding requires that the host within the private network have a static address, you can use *port triggering* to allow incoming traffic to reach a host that receives its address via DHCP and is behind a NAT router (true of wireless broadband routers). See the previous section titled "NAT Routing." To enable port triggering, you specify a range of outgoing ports, and when an interior host makes an outgoing connection through a port in that range, a specified incoming port will open for a brief period of time. Exercise 14-1 shows an example of port triggering to enable Internet Relay Chat (IRC), which is an online chat system.

Universal Plug and Play (UPnP)

Universal Plug and Play (UPnP) uses Internet and web protocols to help various types of devices to connect to a network and automatically know about each other. It's an extension of the plug and play technology in individual PCs that allows a PC to identify new hardware components as they are installed. With UPnP, a new device connecting to a network can configure itself, acquire an IP address, and let other devices on the network know about its existence. For example, when you connect a new computer to an existing network, UPnP would allow that computer to discover the available printers on the network and install drivers for them automatically.

If your router or WAP supports UPnP, there will be a setting for it in the configuration utility. When it's enabled, it allows applications running on PCs to open inbound ports to receive information from other network devices. Some security experts warn that UPnP increases a network's vulnerability to worm and malware attacks, and they recommend configuring port forwarding manually instead. However, for a SOHO network, you may decide that the convenience outweighs any risks.

You can also enable or disable UPnP in Windows itself for individual PCs, although the feature has a different name in Windows. From the Network and Sharing Center, click Change Advanced Sharing Settings. In the Network Discovery section, choose to turn network discovery on or off.

DMZ

A standard firewall feature is support for something called a *demilitarized zone (DMZ)*, a network between firewalls. The way it works is one firewall is at the gateway between an internal network and the Internet, and another firewall is at the connecting point between the first internal network and another internal network. You place servers you want accessible from the Internet on the first network, the DMZ, and you open ports on the external firewall for the services on these servers. Then, on the internal firewall, you close those ports. An inexpensive broadband router (wireless or wired) will have a DMZ feature that opens ports just for certain MAC addresses on the internal network.

Assigning Static IP Addresses at the Router

Any NIC accessing a Wi-Fi network must be assigned an IP address with the same network ID as the Wi-Fi network. The DHCP server on most WAPs and wireless routers will do this by default. However, you can configure static addresses—either through the WAP's or router's DHCP settings or in the settings for the NIC in each computer's OS.

The section "Static IP Addressing," later in this chapter, specifically addresses how to assign static IP addresses in Windows. (That's the most common way of doing it.)

If you assign a static address through the DHCP settings on the WAP or router, you will need the MAC address for each NIC you wish to allow to connect to the network. Sometimes the WAP or router helps in this regard, displaying the MACs of detected NICs, and you can then associate a static IP address to the NIC. Technically, this isn't a static address, since it is assigned through DHCP, but it has the same result in that the same address is always given to the same MAC address (which DHCP tries to do anyway), but it also keeps a NIC with a different MAC address from connecting.

e x a m
ⓦ a t c h   The best way to prepare for the networking objectives in both CompTIA A+ 220-901 and 220-902 exams is to get as much hands-on experience connecting wired and wireless computers to a network as you can. Also, if you have access to any type of router, access it remotely, as shown in the upcoming Exercise 14-1, and browse through the settings. If you are concerned about the stability of the network, do not change any settings. If you are permitted, go directly to Step 13, back up the existing settings, and then experiment with modifying settings described in the exercise.

Content Filtering/Parental Controls

Some (but not all) SOHO routers include content filtering, which can block certain websites at the network level. This obviates the need for each individual client PC to have filtering software installed on it. It's only useful for blocking or allowing a few specific sites that you enter, though; it won't block all adult sites, or sites by a particular topic or category. The few routers that do provide a real filtering solution have special filtering software built in, which usually requires you to sign up (and pay for) the service.

Another option if you want to implement content filtering throughout your network is to use a DNS-based filtering solution, such as OpenDNS. It doesn't require any special hardware or software on your network. All you have to do is change the DNS server addresses on your router to addresses that point to a filtering DNS service.

Individual users can bypass DNS filtering by setting a different DNS address on their individual devices. However, you can thwart them by setting the port filtering feature on the router to block users from accessing port 53 to all IP addresses except the IP addresses of the DNS-based filtering solution you are using. Users are effectively blocked from using any other DNS servers besides the one you specify.

EXERCISE 14-1

Configuring a WAP or Wireless Router

You will need to obtain the IP address for the WAP and then use the PING command to test the connection between the computer and the WAP. Once you determine that the connection works, you can connect and configure the WAP.

1. Open a Command Prompt window in Windows.

2. Test the connection using the PING command. Type **ping *ip_address_of_WAP*** where *ip_address_of_WAP* is the IP address of the wireless access point. A successful test will show results similar to those shown in Figure 14-9.

3. Open a web browser, and in the address box, enter the address you successfully tested in Step 2.

4. If prompted for a user name and password, use the one provided in the WAP's user manual. At your first opportunity, change this user name, as well as the password, so no one else familiar with the default settings can connect and change the settings. (If you're doing this in a classroom, or with someone else's router or WAP, make sure you document the change.)

5. The next screen might be a setup utility for the WAP. If you see setup questions, follow the instructions and provide the type of Internet access, using information from your Internet service provider (ISP). Perform other steps appropriate to your

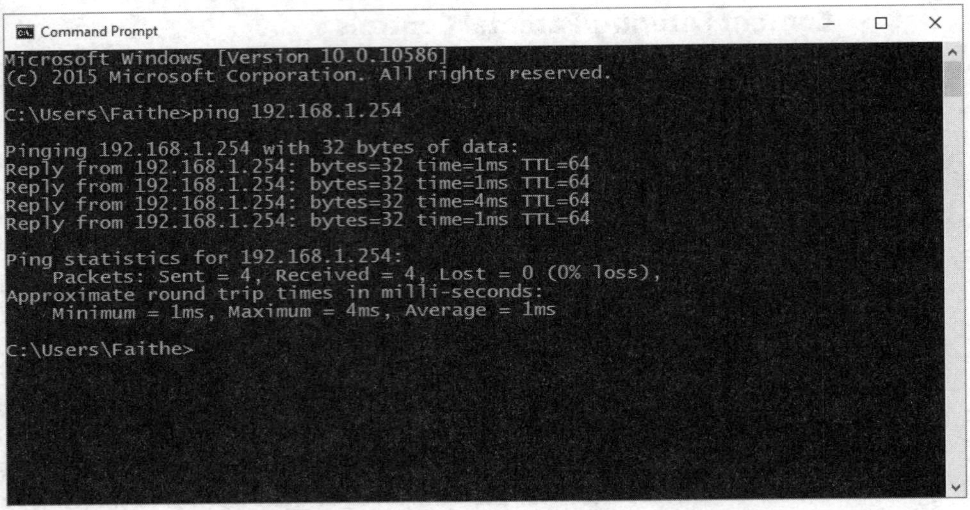

FIGURE 14-9

A successful test of the Ethernet connection to the WAP

```
Command Prompt                                                    —    □    ×
Microsoft Windows [Version 10.0.10586]
(c) 2015 Microsoft Corporation. All rights reserved.

C:\Users\Faithe>ping 192.168.1.254

Pinging 192.168.1.254 with 32 bytes of data:
Reply from 192.168.1.254: bytes=32 time=1ms TTL=64
Reply from 192.168.1.254: bytes=32 time=1ms TTL=64
Reply from 192.168.1.254: bytes=32 time=4ms TTL=64
Reply from 192.168.1.254: bytes=32 time=1ms TTL=64

Ping statistics for 192.168.1.254:
    Packets: Sent = 4, Received = 4, Lost = 0 (0% loss),
Approximate round trip times in milli-seconds:
    Minimum = 1ms, Maximum = 4ms, Average = 1ms

C:\Users\Faithe>
```

type of Internet access, and if needed, provide the user name and password required for Internet access so the router can connect to the Internet.

6. Most WAPs, by default, act as DHCP servers, running the DHCP service and giving out private IP addresses to computers on the internal WLAN and LAN (if appropriate). If there is no other DHCP server on your network, leave this as the default. If there is a DHCP server for your LAN, disable DHCP for the LAN (all Ethernet connections), but leave it enabled for the WLAN (all wireless connections).

7. A screen will appear, in which you can configure other settings for the wireless router. The look of the screen and the settings available will vary widely. There will probably be multiple tabs, and perhaps multiple levels of tabs within each major section. One setting you might see, as in Figure 14-10, is Network Mode, which determines if older Wi-Fi clients can connect. A setting of Mixed means the wireless router will allow connections from 802.11b, 802.11g, and 802.11n clients. Look for the SSID setting, and change it from the default name to a unique name; for additional security, consider disabling SSID broadcast. You can also change the standard channel if there is interference from other devices.

8. Figure 14-11 shows how you can permit specific device access using MAC address filtering. Locate the equivalent screen in your utility.

FIGURE 14-10

WPS, network mode, channel, and SSID wireless configuration settings

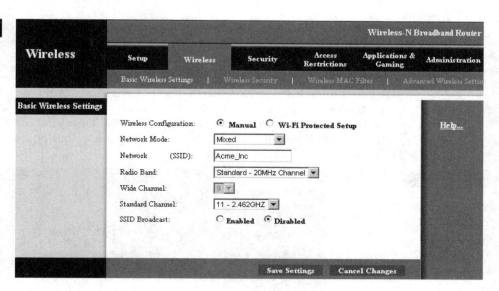

FIGURE 14-11

Wireless access point MAC address filtering

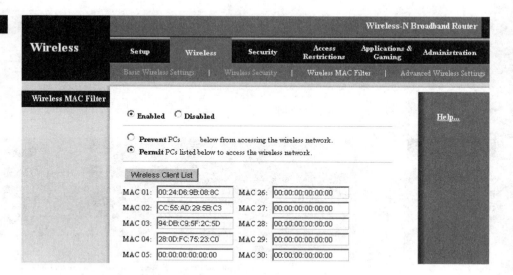

9. Figure 14-12 shows a port-forward configuration allowing RDP access to an internal host (192.168.1.166) on port 3389. By default, the wireless router does not allow inbound traffic to internal hosts. Locate the equivalent screen in your utility.

10. Figure 14-13 shows a port-triggering configuration for IRC. In this example, the wireless router will monitor internal clients that connect to IRC servers between ports 6660–7000 and open an inbound port (113) since IRC servers authenticate users by connecting back to them on port 113, which, by default, will not work through most firewalls. Locate the equivalent screen in your utility.

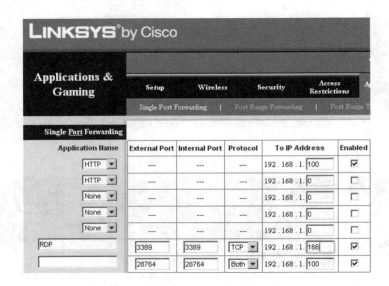

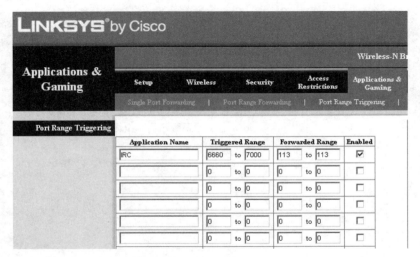

11. Configure wireless encryption. In Figure 14-14, we enabled WPA2 encryption with the passphrase of P@$$w0rd. Connecting stations (see Figure 14-15) must use this same passphrase (security key) to connect to the wireless network. Locate the equivalent screen in your utility. If your connecting devices support it, choose Advanced Encryption Standard (AES); it is considered more secure than Temporal Key Integrity Protocol (TKIP).

FIGURE 14-14

Configuring WPA2 wireless encryption

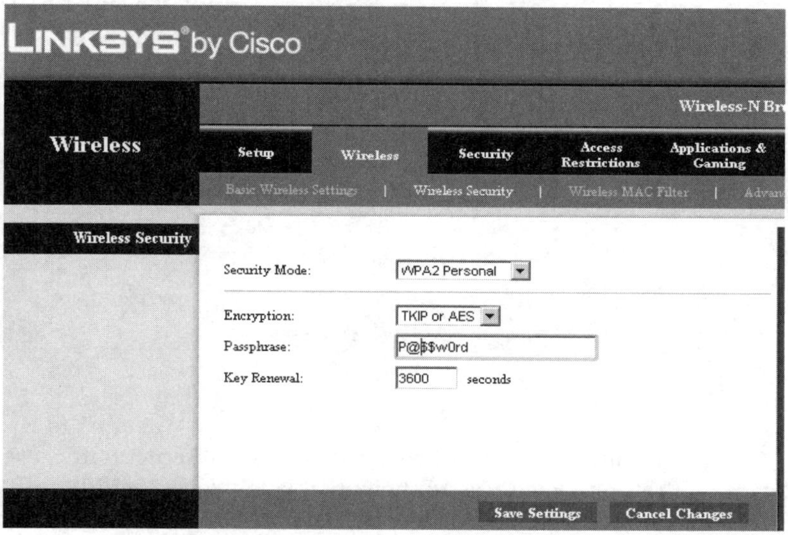

FIGURE 14-15

Connecting to a WPA2-encrypted wireless network from Windows 7

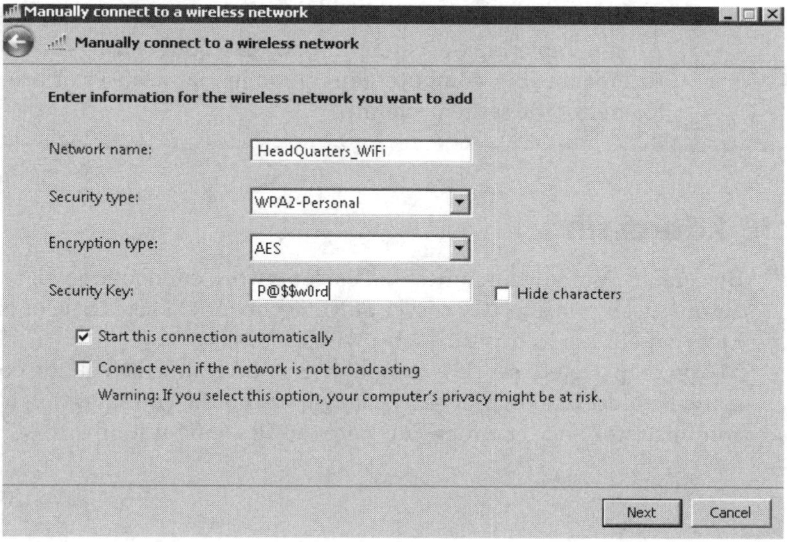

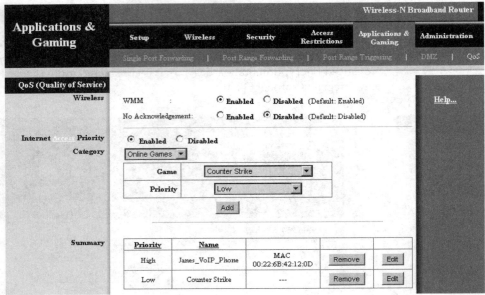

12. If you want to prioritize certain types of Internet traffic, use your wireless router QoS settings. Figure 14-16 shows that Jane's Voice over IP (VoIP) phone has priority over playing the game Counter Strike on the Internet since VoIP network traffic is time-sensitive; Counter Strike network traffic will have to wait if Jane is using her VoIP phone at the same time. Locate the equivalent screen in your utility.

13. After completing the configuration, save your settings and back up the configuration to a file on your computer (an option in many WAPs or broadband routers), and then log out of the setup program.

Static IP Addressing

By default, Windows assumes that each network connection will receive an IP address automatically via a DHCP server on your network. This is true of connections made via an Ethernet NIC as well as through a wireless NIC.

You may need to set up a computer on a LAN in which all the computers are assigned static IP addresses. In that case, you will obtain the configuration information from a LAN administrator and then manually enter an IP configuration into Windows. This information

| TABLE 14-2 |
IP Configuration Setting	Setting Value
IP address	192.168.227.138
Subnet mask	255.255.255.0
Default gateway	192.168.227.2
DNS server	192.168.227.3
WINS server (rarely used)	192.168.227.4

Sample IP
Configuration
Settings

should include the IP configuration addresses described in Chapter 13. The list will resemble Table 14-2, although the actual addresses will be unique to your network. Notice that these are private IP addresses. Add the address for a WINS server only if the computer is part of a routed network that requires Windows Internet Naming Service (WINS).

If you need to manually configure IP settings, make a list similar to that in Table 14-2, showing the required settings that you received from your network administrator. Then open the IP configuration dialog for your network adapter. Exercise 14-2 describes how to do this in Windows Vista and newer.

EXERCISE 14-2

Video

Configuring a Static IP Address

The following steps will guide you through entering IP configuration settings into Windows Vista, Windows 7, Windows 8.1, or Windows 10.

1. Open the Network and Sharing Center in Control Panel.
2. In Windows Vista, select Manage Network Connections from the list of tasks in the left pane to open the Network Connections window. Or, in Windows 7, 8.1, or 10, select Change Adapter Settings.
3. Right-click the icon for the network connection you wish to configure and select Properties from the context menu.
4. Locate the list of items used by the connection and double-click Internet Protocol Version 4 (TCP/IPv4) to open the Properties dialog box. Click the radio button labeled Use the Following IP Address.
5. Enter the IP Address, Subnet Mask, and Default Gateway settings.
6. If you have a DNS server address to use, click the radio button labeled Use the Following DNS Server Addresses and enter the Preferred DNS Server. If you have an address for the Alternate Server, enter that address, too.

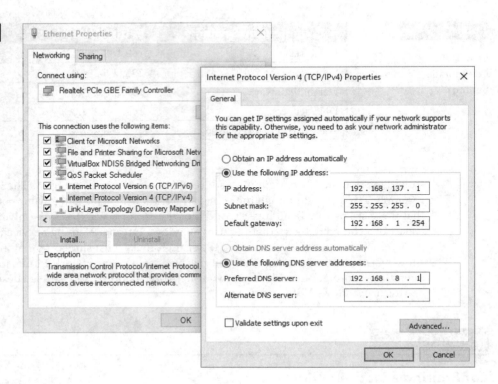

Static IP information in the Internet Protocol Version 4 (TCP/IPv4) Properties dialog box

7. If you have a WINS server address, click the Advanced button, select the WINS tab, click the Add button, and enter the address. Click Add and click OK to close the Advanced TCP/IP Settings dialog box.

8. The Internet Protocol Version 4 (TCP/IPv4) Properties dialog box should resemble Figure 14-17. Check the numbers you entered, click OK to accept these settings, and then click the Close button in the Properties dialog box for the connection.

9. To test your settings, open a Command Prompt window and ping the gateway address to ensure your computer can communicate on the LAN. If your configuration is correct, and if the gateway router is functioning, you should see four replies.

SCENARIO & SOLUTION

What kind of cable do I need to connect an Ethernet port on a PC to a broadband router?	Use CAT5e or CAT6 cable.
Which port on the router should I connect to my cable modem?	Use the WAN port (or Internet port).
Which Wi-Fi standard is going to give me the maximum range?	802.11n and 802.11ac both have an indoor range of about 50 meters.
How do I access a wireless router's configuration utility?	Through a web browser, by entering its IP address in the address bar. Look up its IP address in its manual if needed.

CERTIFICATION OBJECTIVES

- **901: 1.7** *Compare and contrast various PC connection interfaces, their characteristics, and purpose*
- **902: 1.4** *Given a scenario, use appropriate Microsoft operating system features and tools*
- **902: 1.5** *Given a scenario, use Windows Control Panel utilities*
- **902: 1.6** *Given a scenario, install and configure Windows networking on a client/desktop*
- **902: 2.1** *Identify common features and functionality of the Mac OS and Linux operating systems*
- **902: 3.2** *Compare and contrast common prevention methods*

In the following section, we review a variety of specialty connections common in the SOHO environment, including various other wireless technologies such as Bluetooth and NFC (A+ 901 exam objective 1.7).

This section hits several topics from A+ 902 exam objective 1.6, including VPN, Remote Desktop Connection, and Remote Assistance. VPN is also mentioned in 902 exam objective 3.2.

The Remote Desktop Connection feature is also included in several other objectives, including A+ 902 exam objective 1.4 (where its executable, MSTSC, is specified) and 902 exam objective 1.5 (where Remote Settings are mentioned as part of the Control Panel). The Mac equivalent of Remote Desktop, called Screen Sharing, is included from 902 exam objective 2.1.

Configuring Other Common Connections

This section looks at several other technologies for making connections. It includes alternatives to Wi-Fi such as Bluetooth, IR, and NFC, and also secure alternatives to standard unsecure Internet transmission like VPN. We also look at Remote Desktop and Remote Assistance, two features that allow screen sharing in Windows.

Bluetooth

Bluetooth is a short-range wireless connection used for wireless peripherals like headsets and wireless speakers. Bluetooth can also be used for data transfer between two Bluetooth-enabled computing devices, such as between your smartphone and your laptop. There are different classes of Bluetooth devices, based on their transmit power (measured in milliwatts, or mW). Each class has a different range. Table 14-3 summarizes them. Most wireless peripherals are Class 2.

Pairing

Establishing a connection between two Bluetooth-enabled computing devices is called *pairing*. Pairing can occur between two computing devices (like two tablets), or between a computing device and a peripheral (like a smartphone and a wireless headset). To pair devices, you must first enable Bluetooth on both devices. Many mobile devices have Bluetooth disabled by default to extend battery life.

Some Bluetooth devices are automatically discoverable by other devices whenever Bluetooth is enabled; on other devices (like laptops), you must issue a separate command to put them in Pairing (or Discovery) mode. Consult the documentation for each of the devices to find out how to do this. (Look for Bluetooth in the Settings app on Android and iOS devices.)

On some devices, a security confirmation is required when pairing. (This is usually the case when both devices have a display screen, and not the case when one of them doesn't.) One device will provide an authorization code on its screen, and that same code must be confirmed on the other device.

TABLE 14-3	**Device Class**	**Transmit Power**	**Intended Range**
Bluetooth Classes	Class 1	100 mW	100 meters (328 feet)
	Class 2	2.5 mW	10 meters (33 feet)
	Class 3	1 mW	Less than 10 meters

Transferring Data with Bluetooth

If you are accustomed to sharing files wirelessly between computers on a Wi-Fi network, you might expect to be able to do the same when the two computers are connected via Bluetooth—just open Windows Explorer/File Explorer and drag and drop the files between locations, right? Unfortunately, Bluetooth file transfer doesn't work that way. Bluetooth file transfer is not true network sharing of a location; it's only the sending and receiving of individual files between mobile devices.

Near Field Communication (NFC)

Near Field Communication (NFC) is a specialized, low-power, short-range radio frequency (RF) wireless communication method. You may have encountered NFC at a cash register at your local superstore, where you had the option to tap your credit card on the reader instead of swiping it. Bringing your card near the reader (within a few inches) enables it to read it. NFC is found more often on smartphones than on PCs. If a smartphone has NFC, it can share certain kinds of files with other nearby phones. It works great with photos, but it doesn't share most other types of files.

Infrared (IR)

Infrared (IR) is a line-of-sight wireless technology that was popular before Bluetooth for connecting wireless peripherals and quick device-to-device transfers. It's not popular anymore because the line-of-sight requirement limits its flexibility. You may find an IR port on a very old laptop or handheld device.

Virtual Private Network (VPN)

If you connect over the Internet to your work network, your data is at risk because your messages are traveling over an unsecured network. Therefore, you and your employer will want to protect that connection with a virtual private network (VPN), which was briefly introduced in Chapter 13. A VPN creates a virtual tunnel that encapsulates your traffic using special protocols.

Before you can configure a VPN, you must have the specific configuration information, which you obtain from whoever is providing the VPN connection. You need the host name or IP address of the VPN, a valid user name and password, and any custom technical configuration details that may be required.

In Windows Vista and newer, open the Network and Sharing Center, and click Set Up a New Connection or Network. Then click Connect to a Workplace, click Next, and click

FIGURE 14-18

Setting up a VPN
connection

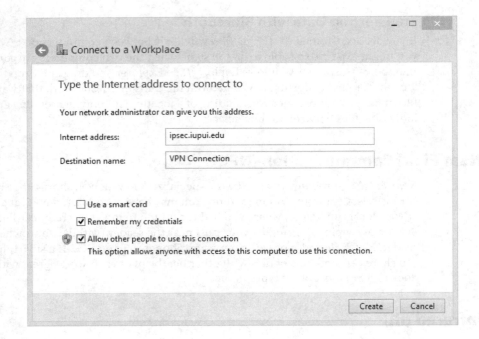

Use My Internet Connection (VPN). Fill in the details of the connection in the boxes
provided (see Figure 14-18), and then click Create.

Remote Desktop

Since Windows XP, Microsoft has included *Remote Desktop* as a feature that depends
on the *Remote Desktop Protocol (RDP)*. Remote Desktop allows you to connect remotely
to a computer running Windows XP or newer and log on to the desktop, just as if you
were physically sitting at that computer. It does not require an "invitation," but it does
require that you configure the computer to which you will connect with Remote Desktop
beforehand. While connected, the local computer screen is logged out; only the Remote
Desktop user sees the Windows desktop. Not every edition of Windows fully supports
Remote Desktop. The Home and Starter editions can use Remote Desktop to connect to
other host computers, but cannot use Remote Desktop to allow other machines to connect
to them.

Remote Desktop must be enabled on the host machine (that is, the one that others will
connect to). To enable it, from the Control Panel choose System and Security | System |

FIGURE 14-19

Enabling Remote
Desktop in
Windows 8.1

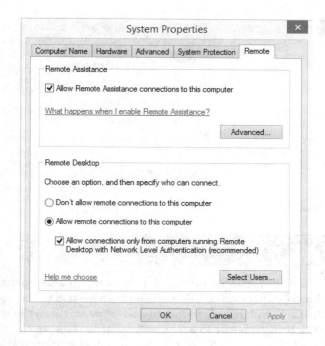

Remote Settings. On the Remote tab in the System Properties dialog box, make sure Allow
Remote Assistance Connections to This Computer is selected, as shown in Figure 14-19. If
you are signed in as an Administrator account, you see a check box where you can choose
whether or not to allow connections only from computers running Remote Desktop with
Network Level Authentication. Use that unless the connection request is coming from
a non-Microsoft OS or a version of Windows prior to Vista. In the Windows Vista and
Windows 7 version of Figure 14-19, instead of two radio button options and a check box,
you have three radio button options, but the settings are the same.

Members of the local Administrators group can always connect via Remote Desktop, but
you can click the Select Users button to add any user account. Enabling Remote Desktop
will allow inbound port 3389 traffic in Windows Firewall on that computer, and if the
incoming Remote Desktop connection is coming from within your LAN, you will not need
to do anything else. If it is coming over the Internet, or any other location on the other side
of a router, you will need to configure the router, as described back in Exercise 14-1.

Figure 14-20 shows the Remote Desktop Connection client software. Search for Remote
Desktop Connection from the Start screen/Start menu, or run its executable file from a
prompt (**mstsc**). You can connect to either the friendly host name (e.g., Toronto_Server1) or
the IP address.

FIGURE 14-20

The Remote
Desktop
Connection
client

---

exam
watch

The macOS version of Remote Desktop Connection is called Screen Sharing. Make sure you are able to locate and run it in macOS. If you have both a Mac and a Windows PC on the same LAN, try setting up Windows as the remote desktop host,	**and then using the Screen Sharing client in macOS to connect to it. Make sure you have cleared the check box in Figure 14-19 that requires the clients to have Network Level Authentication.**

Remote Assistance

Remote Assistance is another service that is available for connecting to computers running Windows XP or newer. Like Remote Desktop, it relies on the RDP protocol. The major difference between Remote Assistance and Remote Desktop is that Remote Assistance requires that the user needing assistance send an invitation. A remote assistant cannot connect without this invitation.

There are two requirements for using Remote Assistance:

■ Both computers must be running Windows XP or newer.
■ Both computers must be connected via a network (or the Internet).

Preparing for Remote Assistance

The computer seeking assistance must have Remote Assistance turned on. Do this on the requesting computer from the Control Panel by opening the System applet, clicking Remote

Settings, selecting the Remote tab (refer to Figure 14-19), and placing a check in the box labeled Allow Remote Assistance Connections to This Computer. Click OK to close the dialog box.

Before requesting remote assistance, check your firewall settings—both your computer's software firewall and any firewall between the two computers, such as a wireless broadband router—and configure it to allow this traffic through as an exception.

Requesting Remote Assistance

You request remote assistance by sending an invitation. To make a request for assistance, you need to open the Windows Remote Assistance Wizard. To do this in Windows Vista or Windows 7, simply enter **remote assistance** in the Start | Search box. In Windows 8/8.1, open the Control Panel and enter **remote** in the Search box, and then from the results select Invite Someone to Connect to Your PC and Help You, Or Offer to Help Someone Else. In addition to requesting assistance, you can offer remote assistance help to someone from this wizard. To request assistance, click the option labeled Invite Someone You Trust to Help You (in all versions). Then continue through the wizard, choosing to send an e-mail invitation or to create a file that you will manually send to the assistant.

SCENARIO & SOLUTION

What class of Bluetooth is my wireless headset?	It's probably Class 2. Most devices are Class 2, with a range of 10 meters (33 feet).
My company wants me to use VPN to work from home. How do I set that up?	From the Network and Sharing Center, click Set Up a New Connection or Network, and then choose Connect to a Workplace.
How can I access the desktop computer in my basement when I'm at my laptop in the living room?	Set up your desktop computer as a Remote Desktop host, and then use the Remote Desktop Client application from the laptop to connect to it.

CERTIFICATION SUMMARY

Be able to identify basic network tools and describe their use, including crimper, wire stripper, punch down tool, multimeter, tone generator, cable tester, loopback plug, and wireless locator.

Understand the steps in setting up and configuring a SOHO wired or wireless network, including configuring many settings in the configuration utility of a SOHO router or wireless access point. In particular, make sure you can configure Wi-Fi encryption, and differentiate among the available encryption standards. Be able to establish static IP addresses for specific Windows client PCs, including subnet mask and default gateway.

Be able to explain additional wireless technologies, such as Bluetooth, IR, and NFC, and to configure a VPN connection. Make sure you can create a Remote Desktop connection, and ask for and provide help through Remote Assistance.

TWO-MINUTE DRILL

Here are some of the key points covered in Chapter 14.

Using Networking Tools

❑ Crimpers are used to create network cables. Use a punch down tool to connect network cabling to the inside of an RJ-45 wall jack and to a punch down block. Use a wire stripper to prepare the wires to be punched down.

❑ A multimeter tests the electrical properties of a cable or circuit. Cable testers test for broken wires inside network cables. A tone generator helps identify cable ends by sending a signal through the cable that the probe can pick up.

❑ A loopback plug reverses the receive and transmit wires on a port so you can test if the port is functional.

Installing and Configuring SOHO Networks

❑ Each computer on a network requires a NIC (wired or wireless) in order to connect. The NIC may be an Ethernet NIC, a Wi-Fi NIC, or, when using a dial-up connection, the NIC is an analog modem.

❑ Decide how a NIC should interface with your computer (bus, USB, or other interface), and select a NIC for the type of network you require—LAN or WLAN.

❑ First install the NIC; then connect the cable, and finally, start the computer and install the drivers.

❑ When installing a NIC, you will connect the NIC to the port or slot, connect the NIC to the network, and then start the computer and let Windows recognize the NIC. When prompted, provide a disc or the location of driver files.

❑ If required, enable a NIC's Wake on LAN feature.

❑ QoS is a feature that supports stable and reliable transmission of time-sensitive content, such as streaming music or video.

❑ When connecting to a wired Ethernet network, use CAT5e/6 UTP cabling with an RJ-45 connector. Connect one end to the NIC and the other to the wall jack, or directly to a hub or switch.

❑   When creating a Wi-Fi network, check for possible obstacles and interference sources that can block the signal. Signals degrade over distance, causing slower data speeds, so verify that the distances between the wireless devices are well within the published signal range for the devices.

❑   A Service Set Identifier (SSID) is a network name used to identify a wireless network. All of the wireless devices on a WLAN must use the same one.

❑   To connect a wireless network directly to another network, you need to use a wireless access point (WAP) for all nodes on the network.

❑   You normally do the initial setup of a WAP with a directly wired Ethernet connection between a PC and the WAP. You can make subsequent changes over the wireless network.

❑   With a single press of a button, Wi-Fi Protected Setup (WPS) automatically sets up a secure wireless network.

❑   Most WAPs run the DHCP service to give out IP addresses on the WLAN. Most can also do the same over their Ethernet port or ports.

❑   Change the default SSID of a WAP to a unique name, change the default user name and password to ones that will not be easily guessed, enable MAC address filtering and wireless encryption, and set other security options, as appropriate for your WLAN.

❑   Port forwarding allows external stations to connect through a wireless router to internal network services such as Remote Desktop.

❑   Port triggering dynamically opens inbound ports when certain outbound port traffic is detected.

❑   Once a NIC connects to the network and the drivers are installed, configure the TCP/IP properties. If your network has a DHCP server, you can leave these settings at their default, and your computer will acquire an IP address automatically from the DHCP server.

❑   If you do not use a DHCP server and wish to communicate beyond a single network, you must configure IP settings manually (static IP), including IP address, subnet mask, default gateway, DNS server, and (rarely) WINS server.

Configuring Other Common Connections

❑   Bluetooth is a wireless connection commonly used for wireless peripherals. It comes in three classes, of which Class 2 is the most common. Connecting devices with Bluetooth is called pairing.

❑   Near Field Communication (NFC) is a specialized, low-power, short-range wireless method. One of its uses is to read data from credit cards at a cash register. Another is to transfer data between smartphones.

❑ Infrared (IR) is an older technology that uses line-of-sight to connect older wireless peripherals to computers.

❑ Configure a VPN for a secure connection over the Internet to a private network. It requires a VPN server on the private network, but Windows has a wizard that will walk you through the configuration for a VPN.

❑ Remote Desktop must be enabled on the host PC, and the host PC must be running a professional version of Windows. Another PC then uses the Remote Desktop client app to connect to it via LAN or Internet.

❑ Remote Assistance uses the same technology as Remote Desktop but it requires the permission of the person using the host PC to make the connection.

SELF TEST

The following questions will help you measure your understanding of the material presented in this chapter. Read all of the choices carefully because there might be more than one correct answer. Choose all correct answers for each question.

Using Networking Tools

1. What tool would you use to connect a CAT5 cable to a patch panel?
   A. Crimper
   B. Punch down tool
   C. Loopback plug
   D. Multimeter

Installing and Configuring SOHO Networks

2. Which of these is a SOHO network?
   A. Two hundred computer workstations in a client/server network
   B. A customer connecting to the Amazon.com website
   C. A broadband router in a coffee shop that provides free Internet access to customers
   D. All of the above

3. What kind of cable connects a NIC to a switch in a SOHO network?
   A. Fiber optic
   B. Coaxial
   C. CAT3
   D. CAT5e

4. What kind of activity is QoS most likely to improve?
   - A. Shopping
   - B. Video chatting
   - C. E-mail
   - D. Downloading files from an FTP site

5. Which of these terms is associated with Wake on LAN?
   - A. QoS
   - B. Magic packet
   - C. Full duplex
   - D. Static IP address

6. Which Wi-Fi standard has the highest maximum data rate?
   - A. 802.11ac
   - B. 802.11b
   - C. 802.11g
   - D. 802.11n

7. Which of the following is the acronym for the name that identifies a wireless network?
   - A. VPN
   - B. DHCP
   - C. SSID
   - D. WAP

8. What radio band does 802.11g use?
   - A. 2.4 GHz
   - B. 4.2 GHz
   - C. 5 GHz
   - D. 7 GHz

9. What happens as you move a wireless NIC and host computer farther away from a WAP?
   - A. Signal increases
   - B. Connection speed increases
   - C. No change
   - D. Connection speed decreases

10. How do you access the configuration utility of a WAP?
   - A. FTP
   - B. Web browser
   - C. E-mail
   - D. NetBIOS

11. What should you update on a WAP to ensure it has all available updates and fixes?
    A. OS
    B. Applications
    C. Firmware
    D. Administrator account

12. What kind of wireless encryption is the most secure, and the one you should use when available?
    A. WEP
    B. WPS
    C. WPA
    D. WPA2

13. What routing feature hides the IP addresses on a private network from hosts beyond the router?
    A. DHCP
    B. NAT
    C. DNS
    D. DMZ

14. Which of these do you specify when configuring a static IP address? Select all that apply.
    A. DMZ server
    B. DHCP server
    C. Default gateway
    D. Subnet mask

Configuring Other Common Connections

15. How do you connect a Bluetooth microphone headset to a laptop?
    A. Pairing
    B. Infrared
    C. NFC
    D. VPN

16. What is the RF technology that enables two smartphones to share data by being placed within a few inches of each other?
    A. Bluetooth
    B. NFC
    C. VPN
    D. Infrared

17. What is the advantage of a VPN connection over standard Internet communication?
     A. Bandwidth
     B. Cost
     C. Speed
     D. Security

18. What Windows features use RDP? Select all that apply.
     A. Remote Desktop
     B. Remote Assistance
     C. Virtual private networking
     D. Internet Explorer

19. What is the macOS version of Remote Desktop called?
     A. Screen Sharing
     B. Remote Assistance
     C. Launchpad
     D. Finder

20. If you cannot connect to another computer using a Remote Assistance invitation you have received, what should you check? Select all that apply.
     A. FTP server
     B. Windows edition (not all editions support it)
     C. Firewall settings on both PCs
     D. Firewall settings on the router

SELF TEST ANSWERS

Using Networking Tools

1. ☑ **B.** Use a punch down tool to connect a cable to a patch panel.
    ☒ **A** is incorrect because a crimper attaches an RJ-45 connector to a CAT5 cable. **C** is incorrect because a loopback plug is used in testing a port. **D** is incorrect because a multimeter tests cables for continuity and tests electrical circuits.

Installing and Configuring SOHO Networks

2. ☑ **C.** A SOHO network is a network in a small office or home office, and a coffee shop meets the criteria for being a small office.

   ☒ **A** is incorrect because a client/server network with 200 computers is a much larger network than a SOHO network. **B** is incorrect because it is an example of a wide area network (WAN). **D** is incorrect because A and B are incorrect.

3. ☑ **D.** CAT5e is an eight-wire UTP cable suitable for connecting a NIC to a switch.

   ☒ **A** is incorrect because fiber-optic cable is costly and difficult to install, and is used only in high-traffic network areas. **B** is incorrect because coaxial is the kind of cable used to deliver cable and satellite TV and Internet signal to a modem. **C** is incorrect because CAT3 is also a UTP cable but, unlike CAT5e, is of insufficient quality for networking. CAT3 is typically used for analog telephone lines.

4. ☑ **B.** Quality of Service (QoS) settings are most likely to help an activity where packets must arrive in the correct order, like with video chatting.

   ☒ **A, C,** and **D** are all incorrect because they are activities where packet order is not important.

5. ☑ **B.** A magic packet is the packet that contains the target PC's MAC address that wakes it up.

   ☒ **A** is incorrect because QoS is associated with packet delivery order and quality. **C** is incorrect because full duplex describes the flow of data through a cable. **D** is incorrect because the IP address assignment method has nothing to do with Wake on LAN.

6. ☑ **A.** 802.11ac has the highest maximum data rate of the standards listed.

   ☒ **B** is incorrect because 802.11b has a maximum data rate of 11 Mbps. **C** is incorrect because 802.11g has a maximum data rate of 54 Mbps. **D** is incorrect because 802.11n has a maximum data rate of 540 Mbps.

7. ☑ **C.** SSID, or Service Set Identifier, is the term that describes a name that identifies a wireless network.

   ☒ **A** is incorrect because a VPN is a virtual private network, a private tunnel across a public network such as the Internet. **B** is incorrect because DHCP is a service that assigns IP addresses to connected devices. **D** is incorrect because a wireless access point (WAP) is a hub for a wireless network.

8. ☑ **A.** 2.4 GHz is the band used by 802.11g.

   ☒ **B** and **D** are both incorrect because none of the Wi-Fi wireless standards use these radio bands. **C** is incorrect because the 5 GHz band is not used by 802.11g. It is used by 802.11n as one of two options (the other being 2.4 GHz) and by 802.11ac.

9. ☑ **D.** Connection speed decreases as you move a wireless NIC and host computer farther away from a WAP.

   ☒ **A** is incorrect because the opposite happens as you move a wireless NIC and host computer farther away from a WAP. **B** is incorrect because the opposite happens as you move a wireless NIC and host computer farther away from a WAP. **C** is incorrect because connection speed definitely decreases because the signal degrades as distance increases.

10. ☑ **B.** You use a web browser to access the configuration utility of a WAP via its IP address.
    ☒ **A** is incorrect because FTP is a protocol for sending and receiving files. **C** is incorrect because the configuration utility cannot be accessed via e-mail. **D** is incorrect because NetBIOS is an alternative network addressing method used on some older LANs.

11. ☑ **C.** Firmware, the low-level software settings stored on a chip in the device, may need to be updated on a wireless access point to make sure it is up to date.
    ☒ **A** is incorrect because WAPs do not have OSs, at least not in the traditional sense. **B** is incorrect because WAPs do not have applications. **D** is incorrect because an Administrator account would not need a downloaded update.

12. ☑ **D.** Wi-Fi Protected Access 2 (WPA2) is the most secure of the methods listed.
    ☒ **A** is incorrect because Wired Equivalent Privacy (WEP) is a very old encryption standard, and not very secure. **B** is incorrect because Wi-Fi Protected Setup (WPS) is a method of configuring security between a WAP and a device by pressing a button. **C** is incorrect because WPA is an older and less secure version of WPA2.

13. ☑ **B.** Network address translation (NAT) hides the IP addresses from external hosts to keep them secure.
    ☒ **A** is incorrect because Dynamic Host Configuration Protocol (DHCP) is a means of dynamic IP address assignment. **C** is incorrect because Domain Name Service (DNS) is a means of translating addresses between IP addresses and domain names on the Internet. **D** is incorrect because a DMZ is a network between firewalls.

14. ☑ **C and D.** When setting up a static IP address, you must specify the default gateway and subnet mask.
    ☒ **A** is incorrect because there is no such thing as a DMZ server. **B** is incorrect because a DHCP server assigns dynamic IP addresses, not static.

Configuring Other Common Connections

15. ☑ **A.** Pairing is the process of connecting a Bluetooth peripheral to a Bluetooth-enabled computing device.
    ☒ **B** and **C** are both incorrect because Bluetooth, infrared, and NFC are all different technologies. **D** is incorrect because VPN is a virtual private network, used for sending secure data over the Internet, not connecting to local devices.

16. ☑ **B.** Near Field Communication (NFC) allows devices to share data when they are very close to one another.
    ☒ **A** is incorrect because Bluetooth has a range of 10 meters, so devices do not need to be within inches of each other. **C** is incorrect because a VPN is a type of secure tunnel through the Internet, not an RF technology. **D** is incorrect because infrared is not an RF technology; it works with light rather than radio waves.

17. ☑ **D.** The advantage of a VPN connection is security.

    ☒ **A** and **C** are both incorrect because they refer to the transmission rate, and VPN does not improve transmission rate. **B** is incorrect because VPN is not a lower-cost alternative; it is the same cost or possibly higher if you consider the time people spend setting it up and connecting with it.

18. ☑ **A** and **B.** Remote Desktop Protocol (RDP) is used by both Remote Desktop and Remote Assistance.

    ☒ **C** is incorrect because virtual private networking does not use RDP. **D** is incorrect because Internet Explorer is a web browser, using protocols such as HTTP.

19. ☑ **A.** The macOS version of Remote Desktop is called Screen Sharing.

    ☒ **B** is incorrect because Remote Assistance runs in Windows, not macOS. **C** is incorrect because Launchpad is a macOS app for running programs. **D** is incorrect because Finder is a macOS app for managing files.

20. ☑ **C** and **D.** Firewall settings are likely to be the problem when Remote Assistance fails.

    ☒ **A** is incorrect because an FTP server is an Internet server with no direct connection to the local PC. **B** is incorrect because Windows edition makes a difference only when setting up a Remote Desktop host; it has no restrictions on Remote Assistance.

Chapter 15

Internet and Cloud Basics

I n this chapter, you will learn about the services, protocols, and applications that comprise the world's largest network: the Internet. You'll learn how the Internet addresses clients and servers, what protocols make activities like the Web and e-mail possible, and what kinds of servers businesses and organizations make available online to provide the services that people rely on in their daily lives. You'll also learn what cloud computing entails, and the levels of services that cloud providers offer.

CERTIFICATION OBJECTIVES

■ *901: 2.4*   *Explain common TCP and UDP ports, protocols, and their purpose*

■ *902: 2.4*   *Summarize the properties and purpose of services provided by networked hosts*

This section examines the nuts and bolts of the Internet, including some of the common protocols and services listed in CompTIA A+ 901 exam objective 2.4. It also looks at the roles of various types of servers listed in 902 exam objective 2.4, including web servers, file servers, mail servers, proxy servers, and so on. This section also covers Internet appliance concepts and legacy/embedded systems, also listed in 902 exam objective 2.4.

Internet Concepts

You probably use the Internet every day as a consumer, but there's a lot more to it than meets the eye. In this section you'll learn about the physical structure of the Internet, how service providers make a living while helping people connect, and how domain names, IP addresses, protocols, and services create a balanced online ecosystem. You'll also learn about the types of Internet-based servers, and about embedded systems and Internet appliances.

How the Internet Is Structured

The Internet is a huge, global wide area network (WAN), with the hardware provided collaboratively by businesses all over the world. No one company "owns" the Internet because it is a joint venture. Physically the Internet's layout resembles a mesh of routers, with many alternate paths available between any two points. This redundancy makes the Internet a fairly reliable and stable network, because even if many pathways are blocked at once, there is nearly always a way for a packet to reach its destination.

The group of main routes of the Internet, its super-highway system, is referred to as the backbone. This *backbone* is composed of high-speed fiber-optic networks that join together at connections called *network access points*. A small number of companies own these high-speed backbone networks; those companies are called Tier 1 providers. Tier 1 providers work cooperatively; they do not charge each other fees to connect to one another. You probably don't know the names of these Tier 1 providers, because they don't sell anything directly to the public, so they don't advertise where you would be likely to see it.

Tier 1 providers make their money from Tier 2 providers, who own smaller, regional Internet segments. The big-name companies in this arena, like Earthlink and Comcast, are Tier 2 providers. Tier 2 providers manage their own small segments of the Internet, and they rent the use of their segments to individuals on a monthly basis, functioning as *Internet service providers (ISPs)*. They also sell connectivity to smaller providers, Tier 3 providers, who are even smaller and more localized.

The lesson from that overview of the tier system is simply that you can't connect to the Internet directly, all by yourself. You have to contract with an ISP, which is either a Tier 2 or Tier 3 provider, and which grants you the right to connect into their little segment of the Internet and from there gain access to the rest of the world.

Internet Service Providers

As we mentioned in the preceding section, an Internet service provider (ISP) is a company in the business of providing Internet access to users. When you connect to the Internet from your home or office, you connect through your ISP. While you are on the Internet, your ISP relays all data transfers to and from locations on the Internet. Traditionally, ISPs were phone companies, but now ISPs include cable companies and organizations that lease phone or cable network usage.

The ISP you select will depend on the type of connection available to you. For instance, a cellular provider will be your ISP if you chose to connect to the Internet via the cellular network, and a cable company will be your ISP if you connect over the cable network. As for DSL, at first local phone companies mainly offered this service, but many other companies now offer DSL using the telephone network, and some telephone companies are now offering Internet access via their fiber-optic networks. Meanwhile, some ISPs specialize in satellite Internet access. See Chapter 13 for in-depth discussions of connectivity types.

In addition to Internet connection services, ISPs now provide a number of other services. Some of these services, such as e-mail, are free, and the cost of others, such as hosting web servers, is based on the complexity of the web services provided. For example, an e-commerce site in which you sell products and maintain customer lists is a service that would come at additional cost. You also are not limited to purchasing Internet services from your ISP. You now have a huge variety of sources for all of these services.

Domain Names, IP Addresses, and DNS Servers

Whenever you visit a website, you enter or select the *Uniform Resource Locator (URL)* of the website you want to visit—in other words, its web address. A URL consists of a domain name, such as microsoft.com, plus additional information that points to a particular folder and page on that website, like this:

https://www.microsoft.com/en-us/windows

Let's break down that URL into its component parts.

We'll start at the beginning. A URL starts with the protocol, which is https in the example. HTTPS is a secure form of Hypertext Transfer Protocol, the main protocol used for web pages.

The next part, www.microsoft.com, is known as a *fully qualified domain name (FQDN)*. It's called that because it contains both a host name (www) and a domain (microsoft.com). Let's look at these parts separately:

- The *host name* is the name of the server or service within the domain. Some small websites have only one host, and it's usually www (traditional for websites). However, larger sites may have several hosts, representing different services or services. For example, Microsoft has support.microsoft.com and www.microsoft.com, to name only two of many.

- The domain includes a *top-level domain*, or TLD (in this case, com), and a *second-level domain*, or SLD (in this case, microsoft). The top-level domain describes the general category of domain; com is short for "commercial," for example. There are several dozen top-level domains, with names like edu (for education), gov (for government), mil (for military), and org (for organization), as well as individual country codes like ca (for Canada) and uk (for United Kingdom).

- The ending part of the address is the file path of the host's server—in this case, en-us/windows. Just like in local file paths, slashes separate directories. On the host server, there is a folder called en-us, and within that is a folder called windows.

on the **Job**

If you leave off the host name when typing a URL into a browser, the browser will usually assume www as the host name.

The irony of all these text-based names is that the Internet (as a computer network) doesn't actually use any of them. They are a figment of our collective imagination. The real addresses on the Internet are IP addresses, assigned by the Internet Assigned Numbers Authority (IANA). So how do the IP addresses and domain names connect to one another? They do so through a series of servers called *Domain Name System (DNS)* servers.

A DNS server receives a domain name and looks it up in a giant table it maintains to find its IP address match. Then it provides that IP address to the requesting computer. That's all it does, millions of times a minute, 24/7. There are thousands of DNS servers all over the world performing this task, all at once.

Maintaining a complete table of every IP address and domain name would be nearly impossible for any single DNS server, no matter how capable, and looking up addresses would take too long. Therefore, the work of DNS servers is split up according to top-level domains. One DNS server only parses between top-level domains, routing a request to the appropriate server. For example, a server says "microsoft.com, that's a dot-com, so I'll send it to the dot-com DNS server." Then another server receives the request that has a table of only the dot-com IP addresses and domains. It looks up the IP address for the requested domain, and sends it back to the requesting computer.

e x a m

watch   Make sure you understand the purpose of a DNS server, and that you can explain the concepts of top-level domain and fully qualified domain name.

e x a m

watch   Not all of the protocols in this section are listed in any specific exam objective, but they appear in the CompTIA A+ Acronyms list. At a minimum, you should know what each acronym stands for and what kind of activity it describes.

Internet Services and Protocols

There are many Internet services, enabling activities like web browsing, mail delivery, and instant messaging. In this section, we will describe a few of these services. Some of them have been covered elsewhere in the book, but we provide them here for easy study reference, all being related to Internet usage.

Simple Mail Transfer Protocol (SMTP)

Simple Mail Transfer Protocol (SMTP) transfers e-mail messages between mail servers (discussed later in this chapter). Clients also use this protocol to send e-mail to mail servers. When configuring a computer to access Internet e-mail, you will need the address or name of an SMTP server to which your mail client software will send mail.

Post Office Protocol (POP)

Post Office Protocol (POP) is the protocol used to allow client computers to pick up (receive) e-mail from mail servers. The current version is POP3.

Internet Message Access Protocol (IMAP)

Internet Message Access Protocol (IMAP) is a protocol used by e-mail clients for communicating with e-mail servers. IMAP allows users to connect to e-mail servers and not only retrieve e-mail, which removes the messages from the server as they do with the POP protocol, but also manage their stored messages without removing them from the server. The current version is *IMAP4.*

Hypertext Markup Language (HTML)

Hypertext Markup Language (HTML) is the language of web pages. Web designers use the HTML language to create web page code, which your web browser converts into the pages you view on your screen.

Hypertext Transfer Protocol (HTTP)

The *World Wide Web (WWW)* is the graphical Internet consisting of a vast array of documents located on millions of specialized servers worldwide. The *Hypertext Transfer Protocol (HTTP)* is the information transfer protocol of the Web. Included in HTTP are the commands web browsers use to request web pages from web servers and then display them on the screen of the local computer.

Secure Sockets Layer (SSL)

The *Secure Sockets Layer (SSL)* is a protocol for securing data for transmission by encrypting it. Encryption is the transformation of data into a code that no one can read unless they have a software key or password to convert it back to its usable form (decrypt it). When you buy merchandise online, you go to a special page where you enter your personal and credit card information. These web merchants almost universally use some form of SSL encryption to protect the sensitive data you enter on this page. When you send your personal information over the Internet, it is encrypted and only the merchant site has the key to decrypt it. As with most computing technologies, there are improvements to SSL, and a newer encryption technology, *Transport Layer Security (TLS)*, for secure transmission over the Internet.

Hypertext Transfer Protocol Secure (HTTPS)

Hypertext Transfer Protocol over Secure Sockets Layer (HTTPS) is a protocol that encrypts and decrypts each user page request, as well as the pages downloaded to the user's computer. The next time you are shopping on a website, notice the address box in your browser. You will see the Uniform Resource Locator (URL) preceded by "HTTP" until you go to pay for your purchases. Then the prefix changes to "HTTPS," because the HTTPS protocol is in use on the page where you will enter your personal information and credit card number.

Telnet

At one time, all access to mainframes or minicomputers was through specialized network equipment called *terminals*. At first, a terminal was not much more than a display, a keyboard, and the minimal circuitry for connecting to the mainframe. People called it a "dumb terminal." With the growing popularity of PCs in the 1980s, it wasn't unusual to see both a terminal and a PC on a user's desktop, taking up a great deal of space. Eventually, by adding both software and hardware to a PC, the PC could emulate a terminal and the user would switch it between terminal mode and PC mode.

The *Telnet* utility provides remote terminal emulation for connecting to computers and network devices running responsive server software, and it works without concern for the actual operating system running on either system. The original Telnet client was character based, and it was a popular tool for network administrators who needed to access and manage certain network equipment, such as the routers used to connect networks.

Secure Shell (SSH)

Although Telnet supports the use of credentials for a terminal emulation session, it sends those credentials in clear text that many methods can pick up, such as a device that connects to the network and collects the traffic. To overcome that limit, the *Secure Shell (SSH)* service has replaced Telnet because it secures all traffic using a tunneling technique similar to a VPN (described in Chapter 14). It is used to connect to terminal servers that require sophisticated security protocols.

File Transfer Protocol (FTP)

File Transfer Protocol (FTP) is a protocol for computer-to-computer (called host-to-host) file transfer over a TCP/IP network. The two computers do not need to run the same operating system; they only need to run the FTP service on the server computer and the FTP client utility on the client computer. FTP supports the use of user names and passwords for access by the FTP client to the server. FTP is widely used on the Internet for making files available for download to clients.

Secure Copy and SFTP

Another file transfer method is *secure copy (SCP)*, which uses Secure Shell (SSH) for encrypting data. SCP lacks the file management capabilities of other methods, such as Secure FTP (SFTP). Therefore, SFTP, which also uses SSH, is often preferred.

Internet Relay Chat

The *Internet Relay Chat (IRC)* protocol supports text messaging over a TCP/IP internetwork in real time, something commonly called *chat*. The latest version is *Internet Relay Chat web extension (IRCwx)*, but it is still widely referred to as IRC. Groups of people can chat simultaneously using IRC, or it can be used between just two people.

Network News Transfer Protocol (NNTP)

The *Network News Transfer Protocol (NNTP)* is used by *news servers* that support newsgroups, to which users can subscribe. Using *news reader* software, the client to the news server, a subscriber connects and selects articles to read.

Network Time Protocol (NTP)

Windows computers (and many others worldwide) keep their date and time settings up to date thanks to a time service. *Network Time Protocol (NTP)* is an Internet protocol that has been improved upon over its 30-year lifespan as a service that synchronizes a computer's real-time clock (described in Chapter 3) with a network time server. Windows is configured to synchronize with an Internet-based time server. To view the time server settings on your computer, open the Control Panel Date and Time applet and click the Internet Time tab. The time server for the Windows computers in our office is time-a.nist.gov. You can select another time server by clicking the Change Settings button on the Internet Time tab.

Challenge-Response Protocols

Often, when you create a new account of almost any type on the Internet, after you have created your user name (often an e-mail address) and password, you may encounter a challenge test—a test that a human can easily pass but a computer cannot. You enter a response to continue. A popular type of challenge-response is *Completely Automated Public Turing test to tell Computers and Humans Apart (CAPTCHA).* A CAPTCHA usually consists of an image of one or two hard-to-read words, or at least a string of characters. To pass the test and proceed with creating your new account, you must enter the characters you see into a box. This ensures that a computer program is not attempting to automatically create accounts for nefarious reasons, such as for sending spam. To learn more about CAPTCHA, point your browser to www.captcha.net.

Server Types

Servers are essential to Internet operation. Different kinds of servers perform different important roles in your Internet experience, and you probably don't even notice what kind of server is serving you at any given moment. For example, the DNS server (discussed earlier in the "Domain Names, IP Addresses, and DNS Servers" section) makes it possible for you to visit websites by typing user-friendly, text-based domain names instead of having to remember an IP address consisting of a long string of numbers.

Make sure you understand the role of each of these server types. We cover them here in the Internet chapter because the majority of them pertain to the Internet, but several of these could be part of any network, not necessarily an Internet-enabled one.

Web Server

While the World Wide Web (the Web) is just one on the many services that exist on the Internet, it alone is responsible for most of the huge growth in Internet use that began after the Web's introduction in the 1990s. Web technologies changed the look of Internet content from all text to rich and colorful graphics. A *web server* provides the graphical content, called web pages, that we access by client software, called a *web browser*. There are many choices of web server software, but the most popular may be *Apache HTTP Server*, open source software that runs on a wide range of operating systems including Windows and several versions each of Linux and UNIX.

Microsoft's web server software, *Internet Information Services (IIS)*, only runs on Windows and supports the traditional HTML content as well as the transfer services HTTP and HTTPS web transfer services. It also supports other services, such as File Transfer Protocol (FTP), Simple Mail Transfer Protocol (SMTP), and Network News Transfer Protocol (NNTP).

File Server

A file server, as the name implies, makes files available to users. There are file servers on business networks that deliver private files to employees, and there are file servers on the Internet that provide the same service to the public, or to users who have the appropriate credentials with which to log in.

One common type of file server uses the FTP protocol (File Transfer Protocol), and is referred to as an FTP server. An FTP server can be open to the public to log into via an anonymous connection, or can require a user name and password. As you learned in Chapter 14, FTP is not particularly robust in security, so some FTP servers use SFTP (Secure FTP) instead.

Users can access an FTP server via most web browsers, although the interface may be somewhat awkward. Most people who use FTP servers frequently use special FTP software, such as the free program FileZilla.

Print Server

A print server manages multiple printers that connect to it, and makes those printers available to users. Print servers are much more common on business networks than on the Internet. Part of a print server's job is to hold the incoming print jobs in memory until they can be parsed out to the available printers. A print server can be a full-fledged computer with printers attached to it, or it can be a network appliance that's basically just a box with a network connection and some printer ports. In the latter case, you would configure the print server by talking to it via a web browser using its IP address.

DHCP Server

As you learned in Chapter 14, a DHCP server assigns IP addresses to clients that request them. Your ISP may have a DHCP server that it uses to assign IP addresses to its customers, providing dynamic IP addressing for Internet usage. That's the norm, because it is most efficient. Unused IP addresses can be dynamically assigned to other customers whenever they become available. An alternative is a static IP address assignment, which you would want if you were hosting your own web server. Most ISPs charge more if you want that.

DNS Server

We talked about DNS servers earlier in this chapter; recall that they translate between IP addresses and domain names. There are DNS servers all over the Internet, publicly available for use. The use of a DNS server is invisible to the end user.

Mail Server

A *mail server* manages e-mail accounts. A company might have its own e-mail server, for example, that stores incoming messages for each user and then forwards them to the individual client PC whenever that user's e-mail application connects to the server. (That's called a *store-and-forward system*.) Similarly, your ISP has its own mail servers that receive mail on your behalf and then deliver it to you when you open your e-mail program and connect. Some ISPs have a single mail server for both incoming and outgoing mail; others have two separate servers (more common).

When you configure an e-mail application, you might need to enter the addresses of your mail server(s). These are usually three-part names with the parts separated by periods, like this: pop.mymail.com. The incoming mail servers are usually either POP or IMAP, and the outgoing mail server is usually SMTP. You learned about these and other protocols earlier in this chapter, in "Internet Services and Protocols."

Authentication Server

An *authentication server* is in charge of logging users into and out of a secure system. Corporate networks use authentication servers to allow users to access networked computers on a domain; if you sign in to your company's network each morning at work, you can thank an authentication server. The Internet also has authentication servers. For example, if you sign into your account at an online store like Amazon.com, an authentication server checks your credentials and grants you access.

Proxy Server

In many instances, an Internet connection includes a *proxy server*, a network service that handles the requests for Internet services, such as web pages, files on an FTP server, or mail for a proxy client, without exposing that client's IP address to the Internet. There is specific proxy server and client software for each type of service. Most proxy servers combine these services and accept requests for HTTP, FTP, POP3, SMTP, and other types of services. The proxy server will often cache a copy of the requested resource in memory, making it available for subsequent requests from clients without having to go back to the Internet.

A client PC can be configured to use a specific proxy server. Some content filtering programs do that, for example—they set the PC to go through a proxy server online that only allows "clean" content through, according to the rules of the filtering. Some ISPs also recommend you use their proxy server for better performance. Satellite Internet providers sometimes provide a proxy server on which commonly accessed pages are cached. To learn how to configure a Windows client to use a proxy server, see "Using a Proxy Server," later in this chapter.

Legacy and Embedded Systems

CompTIA A+ 902 exam objective 2.4 lists legacy/embedded systems. While it's not clear what CompTIA may be referring to here, we surmise that they want you to be aware that there are embedded systems nearly everywhere you look around you, and that there are servers all over the world that talk to them.

Most people think of the typical desktop or laptop PC when they picture an Internet connection, or perhaps a smartphone or tablet connection. All those are great for single-user Internet connectivity, of course, but a wide variety of devices connect to the Internet that you might not think of, from street lights and traffic signals to wristwatches and refrigerators. These computing components are called *embedded systems*. Believe it or not, it is estimated that 98 percent of all microprocessors manufactured today are for embedded systems, not for personal computers. For example, there's probably a microprocessor in your car that can report error codes to a technician, and in some cases can even upload those error codes to a server.

The "legacy" part may refer to the fact that these systems typically stay in service for many years, long past their technology being state-of-the-art. One of the dangers of a legacy system is that it may be more subject to hacking because it lacks the latest security precautions. For example, an ATM running on Windows XP is (theoretically) more easily hacked than one running Windows 10, because support for Windows XP ended in 2014 and Microsoft has not released any new security patches for it.

Internet Appliances

There are two different meanings to the term "Internet appliance." If you enter the term into your search engine of choice, you will probably find that an Internet appliance is described as a consumer device whose main function is to provide easy access to Internet services. A modern example of this might be a Chromebook, for example—a lightweight, skimpily equipped laptop that runs Chrome OS and that does very little except connect to the Internet.

However, if you look at the subtopics under "Internet appliance" in A+ 902 exam objective 2.4, you'll realize that the preceding definition is not what CompTIA means. Instead, the exam objective is referring to a class of server applications and services designed to protect servers (and thereby protect users). While as a PC technician you will not be called upon to set up or configure such services, you should understand what they are and what they do. The objectives specifically refer to three kinds of Internet appliance: IDS, IPS, and UTM.

An *intrusion detection system (IDS)* is a security application that monitors packets, looking for evidence of security intrusions such as worms, viruses, and password-cracking attempts. Even though IDS is listed under the umbrella of Internet appliances, an IDS is useful on any network, not just on the Internet. An IDS can't take direct action to prevent an intrusion, but it can report what it detects to another application, like a firewall, and can signal to a human network administrator to look out for a problem.

An *intrusion prevention system (IPS)* is similar to an IDS in that it also actively monitors network traffic, but it has more muscle behind it—an IPS can stop an attack on its own. That makes it a more effective tool in the fight against malicious attacks, but it also can bog down the network, so it's not used on systems where latency can cause a problem.

Unified threat management (UTM) is the principle of creating a unified package of appliances that work together to reduce the threat of harm from attacks. A UTM solution might include IDS, IPS, VPN, firewalls, antimalware applications, and other tools.

CERTIFICATION OBJECTIVES

- **902: 1.5** *Given a scenario, use Windows Control Panel utilities*
- **902: 1.6** *Given a scenario, install and configure Windows networking on a client/desktop*

In this section, we cover the Internet options listed under CompTIA A+ 902 exam objective 1.5. The specific items listed in the objective are actually the names of tabs in the Internet Options dialog box, and we go through that dialog box tab by tab here. One of the settings in that dialog box deals with using a proxy server, so we use that opportunity to cover the proxy settings topic listed under 902 exam objective 1.6.

Configuring Internet Settings in Windows

When it comes to Internet-related settings, Windows is merciful to PC techs, providing most of the available settings in one place: the Internet Options (or Internet Properties) dialog box. This dialog box contains many important settings that affect the user's Internet usage experience, including security, privacy, connectivity, and convenience.

To access the Internet Options dialog box, you can use either of these methods:

- Open the Internet Explorer browser and then choose Tools | Internet Options.
- Open the Control Panel and choose Network and Internet | Internet Options.

on the Job

The dialog box has a different title depending on the method you choose for opening it. When opening through IE, it's Internet Options; when opening through the Control Panel, it's Internet Properties. The dialog box content is the same either way.

Some of the settings in this dialog box pertain only to the Internet Explorer browser; they don't affect Windows in general. For example, if you delete the browsing history, it's deleted only for IE, not for any other browsers you might have installed. Other settings affect your entire Internet connection, regardless of browser, like the proxy server setting.

FIGURE 15-1

The General tab
of the Internet
Options dialog
box

The Internet Options dialog box contains seven tabbed pages, and in the following
sections we look at each of them in depth.

General Settings

On the General Settings tab, shown in Figure 15-1, there are many settings that affect the
overall operation and appearance of Internet Explorer.

- **Home Page**   You can specify the URL of the page that you want to always open
  when you start IE. You can specify additional pages to have multiple tabs open at
  startup; place each URL on its own line in the Home Page box.

**An easy way to set a home page is to display that page and then, on the General
tab, click Use Current.**

- **Startup**   Choose whether to start with the home page (specified previously) or with
  the tabs from the last session.

You can clear
your browsing
history, both for
privacy and to
save disk space.

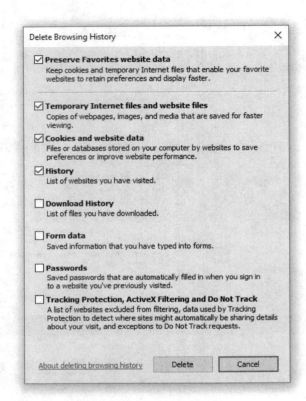

- **Tabs**   Click the Tabs button to open the Tabbed Browser Settings dialog box. From here you can fine-tune how tabs are used. For example, you can choose what to display on a new tab when opened, and you can enable tab groups.
- **Browsing History**   You can clear your browsing history by clicking Delete and specifying in the Delete Browsing History dialog box what information you want to clear. See Figure 15-2. The Settings button in this section opens the Website Data Settings dialog box, where you can control how history data is cached to your hard drive. For example, you can set a limit for the size of temporary Internet files, and you can choose how many days of browsing history should be retained.
- **Appearance**   The buttons in this section enable you to change how Internet Explorer appears. You can control the colors, languages, fonts, and accessibility.

Security Settings

Security in a browser context means the ability to prevent your computer from being harmed by malware. When you crank up the security settings to a high level, you minimize the chance that visiting a website with malicious code will infect your computer and cause problems.

Change the security settings for a particular zone.

High security settings may prevent some websites from performing as intended, though; for example, some shopping sites won't work with security settings at their highest levels.

The security zones feature of the Security tab (see Figure 15-3) allows you to differentiate between risky sites and safe ones. A *security zone* is a group of settings that is applicable to a certain trust level for websites. There are four zones: Internet, Local Intranet, Trusted Sites, and Restricted Sites. Internet is the default zone. The other three zones enable you to assign websites to them. To control which sites are in a zone, click the zone and then click the Sites button. Using zones enables you to have different security settings for sites that you trust, like your banking institution, and sites that you don't trust, like an adult content site (not that you would ever visit one of those).

To change the security level for a zone, click the zone icon at the top, and then drag the slider bar up or down. You can also click Custom Level and fine-tune the security settings for the chosen zone.

Privacy Settings

Privacy in a browser context means the ability to limit the amount of your personal information that gets shared with others. This can include your browsing history, your

On the Privacy
tab you can
control the use
of cookies and
pop-ups.

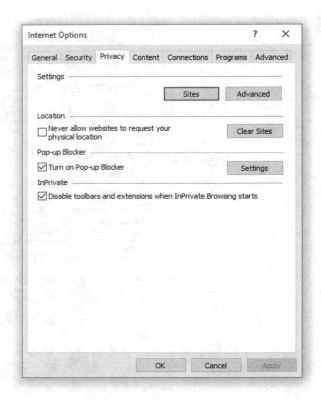

location, and any information stored in cookies. You can choose which information you
want to share through the Privacy tab (see Figure 15-4).

Controlling Cookies

A *cookie* is a small text file stored on your computer that remembers your settings for a
particular website. If you ever revisit a website where you've previously signed in and the
page greets you by name, that's a cookie at work.

Cookies come from two different sources. A *first-party cookie* comes from the website
you are actually visiting. First-party cookies can actually be helpful. A *third-party cookie*
comes from another source, such as an advertisement on the web page. Third-party cookies
have no benefit to you as a user.

On the Privacy tab, you can click the Advanced button to open the Advanced Privacy
Settings dialog box. From there you can choose how to handle first-party and third-party
cookies. Your choices are to allow them, block them, or prompt each time one tries to write
to your hard disk. You can click the Sites button on the Privacy tab to open a dialog box
where you can indicate certain websites to always allow or always block from using cookies.

Blocking Pop-Ups

Also on the Privacy tab you can allow or prevent websites from requesting your physical location, and you can enable and configure the Pop-Up Blocker feature. Click the Settings button next to Pop-up Blocker to open a dialog box where you can allow certain websites to use pop-ups, while continuing to forbid most websites in general from doing so. You can also set an overall blocking level (Medium is the default).

InPrivate Browsing

In Figure 15-4 notice that you can choose whether to disable toolbars and extensions in InPrivate mode. This is a special high-privacy browsing mode that IE provides. You might use it when visiting a website that you don't trust, for example, or one that you don't want any record to be made of your having visited. By default this mode disables all toolbars and extensions. However, if there's an app on the website that requires a certain extension to be loaded, you might need to allow toolbars and applications.

To use InPrivate browsing, press CTRL-SHIFT-P, or press ALT to see the menu bar and then choose Tools | InPrivate Browsing.

Content Settings

On the Content tab (see Figure 15-5), you can control what security certificates are allowed, and you can view the certificates and publishers you have chosen to trust. You can also clear the SSL state, so that any security that is currently in effect must be reauthenticated.

Also on the Content tab you can manage AutoComplete, which is the setting that fills in previously typed data for you after you type the first few letters of it. It's very handy, but it can also be a privacy concern if you don't want someone who sits down at your computer to see previous information that's been saved, like your address or phone number that you've typed into an online registration form.

You can also adjust settings for feeds and Web Slices here. *Feed* refers to a Really Simple Syndication (RSS) feed, which can deliver updated content from some websites. Web Slices is a different brand of content syndication.

Connections Settings

The Connections tab controls settings for all of Windows, not just for Internet Explorer. On it you can click Setup to run a Windows wizard that steps you through the process of connecting to the Internet (if you don't already have a connection). You can also add a dial-up or VPN connection here. (The main thing you may want to explore on the Connections tab, though, is setting up a proxy server, explained next.

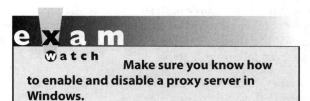

FIGURE 15-5

On the Content
tab you can
control security
certificates,
AutoComplete,
and feed settings.

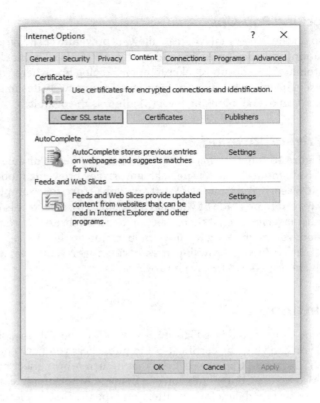

Using a Proxy Server

If your network has a proxy server, you can configure your browser to send requests to the proxy server, which will forward and handle all requests. If you set this up from within other browsers, like Chrome or Firefox, it applies only when using them. However, when you set up a proxy server using the Internet Options dialog box in IE, or the Internet Properties dialog box from the Control Panel, the proxy server applies to Windows itself (all browsers).

Windows provides options for four types of proxy servers: HTTP, Secure (HTTPS), FTP, and Socks. You should already be familiar with the first three of those. Socks is a proxy server protocol. If you have a proxy server for other services not supported by Windows, you will need to install a proxy client provided by the vendor of the server software.

To configure Windows to use a proxy server, follow these steps:

1. On the Connections tab of the Internet Options dialog box, click the LAN Settings button to open the Local Area network (LAN) Settings dialog box.
2. Under Proxy Server, click to place a check in the box labeled Use a Proxy Server for Your LAN (These Settings Will Not Apply to Dial-up or VPN Connections).

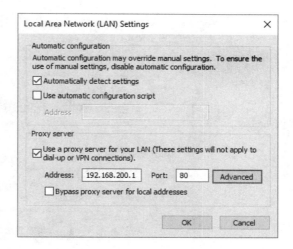

3. Enter the IP address in the Address box and the port number (obtained from your network administrator or from the documentation for the proxy server) in the Port box. Click Advanced if you need to add more addresses and ports for other services. Figure 15-6 shows this dialog box.

4. Click OK twice to close all open dialog boxes, or click only once to keep the Internet Options dialog box open for the next section.

Programs Settings

On the Programs tab (see Figure 15-7), you can control what programs operate using your Internet connection. You can control add-ons, set a default HTML editor, and access Windows' default programs and file associations controls. (You can also access those controls from the Control Panel directly; the buttons in the dialog box are just shortcuts to those.) Of these, the most important setting to know about for exam prep is the one for managing browser add-ons, covered next.

Add-Ons

You can add functionality to a browser by installing an *add-on*, a small program that is inserted into an app (such as a browser) but not fully controlled by the app. Also called a *plug-in* or *browser helper object (BHO)*, an add-on is usually free and available as a download. For instance, if you have the Adobe Acrobat add-on installed, you can view PDF files in your browser.

FIGURE 15-7

The Programs tab

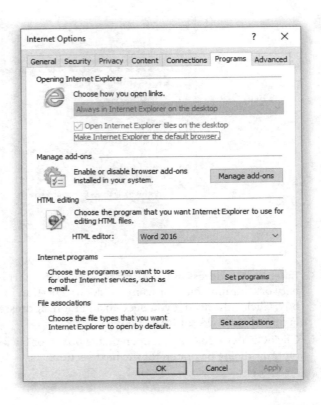

Because the browser does not fully control an add-on, add-ons are malware targets. As a result, the trend is moving away from using add-ons and using HTML5 instead to create rich, interactive web page content that does not require an add-on.

To control add-ons, click the Manage Add-ons button on the Programs tab, opening the Manage Add-ons dialog box. From here you can enable or disable toolbars and extensions, specify your default search provider, work with accelerators, and enable or disable tracking protection.

■ **Toolbars and Extensions**   These are the traditional kinds of add-ons, adding some capability to the browser. Select an item and then view its details in the lower pane. Click Enable or Disable to turn it on or off. See Figure 15-8.

- **Search Providers**   When you type keywords directly into the address bar in IE, a default search provider takes them and runs a query. You can control which search provider does this work for you. The default one for IE is Bing, Microsoft's search engine. To add others to the list, click the Find More Search Providers hyperlink at the bottom of the dialog box.

- **Accelerators**   An *accelerator* is a helper program that works with certain kinds of content. For example, you might have a translation accelerator that works when it detects a foreign language in use. You can choose which accelerator to use for various kinds of content. Click Find More Accelerators at the bottom of the dialog box to get others besides the default-provided Microsoft ones.

- **Tracking Protection**   Some advertisers attempt to track you across multiple websites that you visit. If you've ever shopped for an item and then seen an ad for that same item minutes later in Facebook, you know you've been tracked. You can get and enable tracking protection lists that deny your information to any advertisers on the tracking list provided. Click Get a Tracking Protection List Online to find lists.

FIGURE 15-8   The Manage Add-ons dialog box

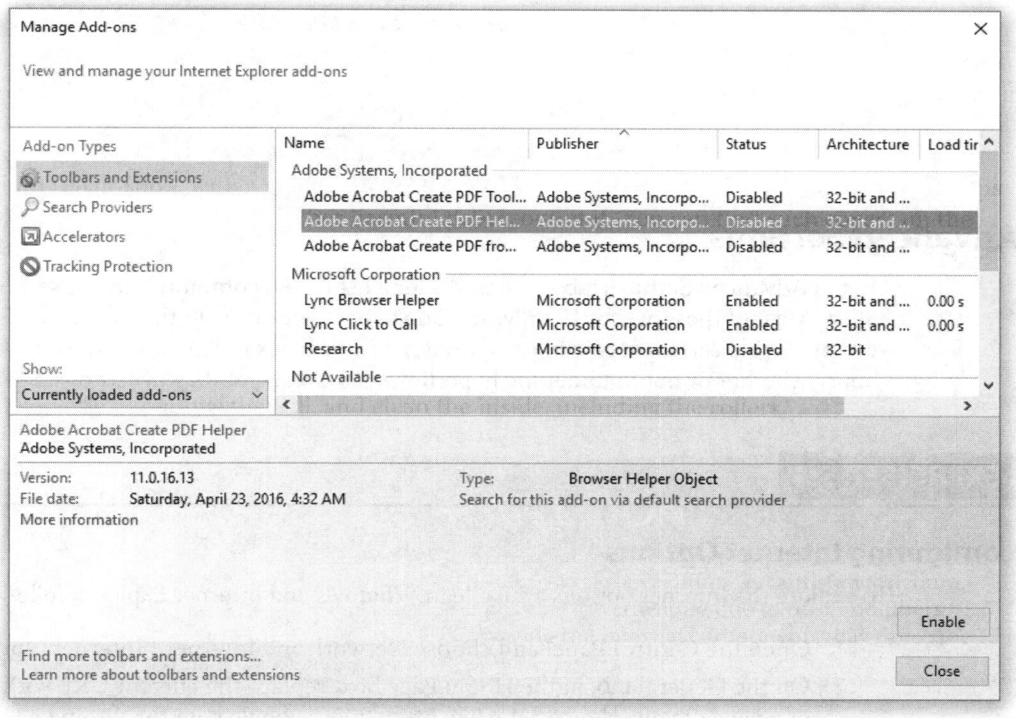

The Advanced tab

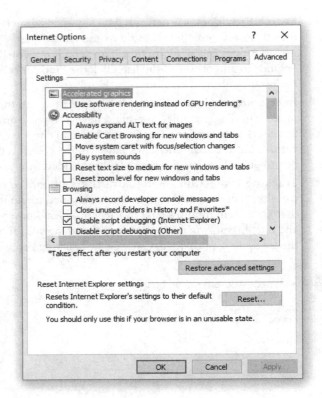

*Takes effect after you restart your computer

Advanced Settings

On the Advanced Settings tab you'll find a long list of less common browser settings you can adjust. Most of these are for IE only, and don't affect your use of other browsers. For example, you can enable certain accessibility options, allow or block certain kinds of content, and choose whether or not to underline hyperlinks. It's a real grab-bag of settings! See Figure 15-9.

EXERCISE 15-1

Configuring Internet Options

To explore the Internet options available in Windows and Internet Explorer, follow these steps:

1. Open the Control Panel and choose Network and Internet | Internet Options.
2. On the General tab, in the Home Page box, replace the current URL with the URL of a page of your choice. (We like http://news.google.com for a home page to get the latest news headlines, but choose one that you will enjoy.)

3. On the General tab, click Settings, and then click the History tab. Change the Days to Keep Pages in History value if desired. Click OK.

4. Click the Security tab. Click Trusted Sites, and click the Sites button. Add a site to your list of trusted sites, and then click Close.

5. On the Security tab, click the Custom Level button. Examine the custom security settings available. Make a change, and click OK. Notice that the slider is gone.

6. Click Default Level to return the security settings to their defaults. The slider returns.

7. On the Privacy tab, click Advanced. Set Third-party Cookies to Block, and click OK.

8. On the Content tab, click the Settings button for AutoComplete. Review the settings there. Adjust any as desired and click OK.

9. On the Programs tab, open the HTML Editor drop-down list to see your choices for HTML editing. Make a different choice if desired.

10. Click OK to make the changes and close the dialog box, or click Cancel to abandon the changes.

SCENARIO & SOLUTION

How can I change the cookie-handling policy for IE?	On the Privacy tab of the Internet Options dialog box.
Where do I configure a proxy server?	On the Connections tab of the Internet Options dialog box.
Where can I change the default search provider in IE?	On the Programs tab of the Internet Options dialog box, click Manage Add-ons.

CERTIFICATION OBJECTIVE

■ *902: 2.3* *Identify basic cloud concepts*

This section covers all the topics from CompTIA A+ 902 exam objective 2.3, which deals with cloud computing. These topics include characteristics of a cloud environment, types of cloud services, and types of cloud deployment. For the CompTIA A+ exams you don't need to know how to actually implement cloud services, but you should be able to describe how clouds work.

Cloud Concepts

A *cloud* is an online location that offers one or more types of computing services to users. For example, a cloud-based file storage system like OneDrive or Dropbox enables people to store, access, and share files from any Internet-connected computing device. A cloud-based application might allow users to perform tasks online that normally are accomplished on a local PC, like editing a business document, or to interact with an online application to place orders or collaborate with others. In the following sections we'll look at some key cloud-related terms you should understand.

w a t c h These five characteristics are listed in A+ 902 exam objective 2.3, so make sure you can explain each of them.

Characteristics of a Cloud Environment

The National Institute of Standards and Technology (NIST) defines cloud computing as having five key characteristics. The following descriptions of those characteristics come directly from NIST SP 800-145, "The NIST Definition of Cloud Computing."

- **On-demand self-service** A consumer can unilaterally provision computing capabilities, such as server time and network storage, as needed automatically without requiring human interaction with each service provider.
- **Broad network access** Capabilities are available over the network and accessed through standard mechanisms that promote use by heterogeneous thin or thick client platforms (e.g., mobile phones, tablets, laptops, and workstations).
- **Resource pooling** The provider's computing resources are pooled to serve multiple consumers using a multi-tenant model, with different physical and virtual resources dynamically assigned and reassigned according to consumer demand. There is a sense of location independence, in that the customer generally has no control over or knowledge of the exact location of the provided resources, but may be able to specify location at a higher level of abstraction (e.g. country, state, or datacenter). Examples of resources include storage, processing, memory, and network bandwidth.
- **Rapid elasticity** Capabilities can be elastically provisioned and released, in some cases automatically, to scale rapidly outward and inward commensurate with demand. To the consumer, the capabilities available for provisioning often appear unlimited and can be appropriated in any quantity at any time.
- **Measured service** Cloud systems automatically control and optimize resource use by leveraging a metering capability at some level of abstraction appropriate to the type of service (e.g., storage, processing, bandwidth, and active user accounts). Resource usage can be monitored, controlled, and reported, providing transparency for both the provider and consumer of the utilized service.

on the !ob

For more information about NIST publication SP 800-145, see http://nvlpubs.nist .gov/nistpubs/Legacy/SP/nistspecialpublication800-146.pdf.

Cloud Service Models

Three basic cloud service models are defined in NIST SP 800-145, based on what is being provided. An organization can choose among these to find the best fit for the services they wish to implement.

Software as a Service (SaaS) enables users to run software from the cloud's server, rather than downloading and installing it on their own individual computers. For example, Microsoft Office Online is SaaS.

Platform as a Service (PaaS) provides developers a cloud-based environment on which to deploy their own applications that they can in turn offer to consumers in a cloud environment. For example, if a company wanted to provide a Human Resources application to their employees that could be accessed online, they might use PaaS to develop it.

Infrastructure as a Service (IaaS) allows companies and developers to create and control their own platform. They can provision servers, storage, networks, and virtual machines as needed to create PaaS and SaaS to offer to consumers. For example, a company might create their own fully immersive suite of tools online, including a nonstandard user interface.

Deployment Models

Another way that NIST SP 800-145 classifies clouds is according to where the hardware and software running the cloud are located or hosted.

A *private cloud* is operated on a network that only one company or organization has access to. It may be managed either internally within the company or by a contractor, but the key feature here is that the server or virtual machine being used is for internal use only. It's hosted at the company's own data center, where all the data is protected behind a firewall. A private cloud scores high on control and security, but it can be expensive to maintain.

---

exam

ⓦatch

An *intranet* is an internal network that uses web software and protocols to share information internally within a company. That sounds like the definition of a private cloud, doesn't it?	Cloud computing uses some more advanced designs and services than simple web technology, but a private cloud can basically be thought of as a fancy intranet.

A *community cloud* is a cloud where several companies or organizations have agreed to cooperate to share a private cloud. It's the equivalent of a co-op of friends buying a house together. It cuts down on costs, but there is more administration involved because the parties must agree on its management.

A *public cloud* operates on a network open for public use, such as the Internet. The cloud content is hosted at the vendor's data center, and the vendor is responsible for server management and security. Even though you don't manage the server's security, your data remains separate from that of other customers, and you can still require people using your cloud services to sign in securely.

A *hybrid cloud* is a conjunction of two or more of these cloud types. They remain separate clouds, but they are connected in some way. For example, a business might have two clouds: a private one for sensitive internal data, and a public one for interacting with customers. Those two clouds could be joined together to provide employees seamless access to both kinds of data.

CERTIFICATION SUMMARY

Be able to explain how the Internet is structured, including Tier 1, 2, and 3 providers, domain names, IP addresses, and DNS servers. Make sure you can identify the protocols and services involved in Internet usage, including those for web, mail, file transfer, chatting, time lookup, and authentication.

Be able to explain the functions of the many kinds of servers in use on the Internet, including web, file, print, DHCP, DNS, mail, authentication, and proxy, and understand the presence and purpose of legacy and embedded systems and Internet appliances.

Know how to access the Internet Options dialog box in Windows and what settings you can configure on each of its tabs.

Make sure you understand the cloud concepts outlined in the publication NIST SP 800-145, including the five characteristics of cloud computing, the differences among SaaS, PaaS, and IaaS, and various deployment models, such as private, community, public, and hybrid.

TWO-MINUTE DRILL

Here are some of the key points covered in Chapter 15.

Internet Concepts

❑ The Internet is a huge, global WAN. No one company owns it. Its major pathways collectively are called the backbone.

❑ Backbone networks are owned by Tier 1 providers. Tier 2 providers are large ISPs that purchase access from Tier 1 providers. Tier 3 providers are small ISPs and individual companies.

❑ Which ISP you should select depends on the type of connection you want. Some ISPs provide only one kind of connection; others offer a choice, such as DSL versus dial-up.

❑ A website's address is its Uniform Resource Locator (URL). In a URL, the first part is the protocol, such as http. The next part is the host name, such as www. The domain name consists of a top-level domain like .com and a second-level domain like microsoft. Forward slashes (/) separate the parts of the page's path on the host.

❑ A domain name that includes a host name as well as a top-level domain and a second-level domain is a fully qualified domain name (FQDN).

❑ Domain Name System (DNS) servers translate between domain names and IP addresses.

❑ Protocols for mail delivery include SMTP, POP, and IMAP.

❑ HTML is the language of web pages. HTTP is the protocol used to display web pages.

❑ Secure web pages use SSL or TLS to encrypt the data for transmission, and use HTTPS as the protocol to display the pages.

❑ Telnet is a very old protocol used to emulate a terminal environment. SSH is a secure version of Telnet.

❑ FTP is a file transfer protocol employed by many online file servers. Secure copy (SCP) uses SSH for encrypting data. SFTP is a secure version of FTP.

❑ IRC is a protocol for online text messaging. It is used as part of the very popular Internet Relay Chat service.

❑ NNTP is a protocol that accesses news servers that support newsgroups.

❑ NTP is a protocol that is used to keep clocks synchronized online.

❑ CAPTCHA is a service used to create a test that only a human can pass, such as finding text in a graphical image, so online users can prove they are not a machine.

❑ A web server is an online server that provides web pages to requesting clients.

❑ A file server makes files available to users.

❑ A print server manages multiple printers and makes them available to users.

❑ A DHCP server assigns IP addresses dynamically to clients.

❑ A mail server stores and forwards e-mail messages on behalf of clients.

❑ An authentication server manages and checks user identities to safeguard secure resources.

❑ A proxy server points Internet requests for data to an alternative server that manages the requests, such as directing them to cached copies or declining to display certain content.

❑ A legacy system is one with old hardware or software. An embedded system is a computer that is inside an object that is not primarily a computer, like a microwave oven or a clock/radio.

❑ The term Internet appliance can refer to a consumer device that accesses the Internet or (per 902 exam objective 2.4) to a class of server applications and services designed to protect Internet servers. In that latter meaning, two key types are IDS and IPS.

❑ Unified threat management (UTM) is the principle of creating a unified package of appliances that work together to reduce the threat of harm from attacks.

Configuring Internet Settings in Windows

❑ In Windows you can access Internet settings from the Control Panel or from inside Internet Explorer. The two methods produce identical dialog boxes except for the names, Internet Properties and Internet Options, respectively.

❑ On the General tab of the dialog box you can change the home page, configure IE tabs, and manage browsing history.

❑ On the Security tab you can define the security settings for different security zones: Internet, Local intranet, Trusted sites, and Restricted sites.

❑ On the Privacy tab you can control cookie settings and block pop-ups, as well as configure InPrivate browsing.

❑ On the Content tab you can control security certificates and publishers and clear the SSL state. You can also manage AutoComplete, feed, and Web Slices settings.

❑ On the Connections tab you can set up a new Internet connection, including dial-up, VPN, or LAN. You can also configure a proxy server.

❑ On the Programs tab you can control add-ons, which include toolbars and extensions, search providers, accelerators, and tracking protection.

❑ On the Advanced tab is a long list of less common browser settings you can adjust.

Cloud Concepts

❑ The five characteristics of a cloud environment are: on-demand self-service, broad network access, resource pooling, rapid elasticity, and measured service.

❑ Software as a Service (SaaS) allows users to run software from the cloud's server.

❑ Platform as a Service (PaaS) provides developers a cloud-based environment on which to deploy their own applications.

❑ Infrastructure as a Service (IaaS) allows companies to create and control their own platform.

❑ A private cloud is hosted on a private server inside a company's firewall.

❑ A community cloud is a cloud where several companies share a private cloud.

❑ A public cloud operates on an open network, such as the Internet. Even though the network itself is public, you can still require users to sign into your cloud.

❑ A hybrid cloud is a joining of two or more other cloud types.

SELF TEST

The following questions will help you measure your understanding of the material presented in this chapter. Read all of the choices carefully because there might be more than one correct answer. Choose all correct answers for each question.

Internet Concepts

1. Which type of companies own and control the Internet backbone?
   A. Tier A
   B. Tier B
   C. Tier 1
   D. Tier 2

2. From what kind of company do individuals get Internet connectivity?
   A. ISP
   B. DNS
   C. Tier 1
   D. DHCP

3. Which of these is a FQDN?
   A. http
   B. www
   C. sycamoreknoll.com
   D. www.sycamoreknoll.com

4. Which of these is a host name?
   A. http
   B. www
   C. sycamoreknoll.com
   D. www.sycamoreknoll.com

5. What kind of server translates between IP addresses and domain names?
   A. DHCP
   B. ISP
   C. DNS
   D. FQDN

6. Which of these is a mail protocol?
   A. HTML
   B. IMAP
   C. Telnet
   D. FTP

7. Which of these is the protocol for a secure web page?
   A. SFTP
   B. HTTPS
   C. SSH
   D. POP

8. Which of these is a protocol for synchronizing clocks?
   A. NNTP
   B. IRC
   C. FTP
   D. NTP

9. What kind of server would you use for FTP?
   A. Web
   B. File
   C. Mail
   D. Authentication

10. What kind of server assigns IP addresses to clients?
    A. Web
    B. DNS
    C. File
    D. DHCP

11. What kind of server handles requests for Internet services for a client without exposing the client's IP address to the Internet?
    A. DNS
    B. Proxy
    C. Mail
    D. Authentication

12. What can an IPS do that an IDS can't?
    A. Detect security intrusions
    B. Manage printers
    C. Stop a detected attack
    D. Host an FTP site

Configuring Internet Settings in Windows

13. On which tab of the Internet Options dialog box can you change the home page used for IE?
    A. Appearance
    B. General
    C. Advanced
    D. Home

14. Internet, Local intranet, Trusted sites, and Restricted sites are the four types of what?
    A. Security zones
    B. Cookies
    C. Privacy settings
    D. Web servers

15. What kind of cookie comes from the website you are visiting?
    A. First-party
    B. Second-party
    C. Third-party
    D. Fourth-party

16. _____ is a high-privacy browsing mode in Internet Explorer.
    A. First-party
    B. InPrivate
    C. Add-on
    D. Proxy

17. HTTP, HTTPS, FTP, and Socks are four types of what?
    A. DHCP servers
    B. Websites
    C. LANs
    D. Proxy servers

Cloud Concepts

18. Which of these is *not* one of the five characteristics of cloud computing?
   A. Rapid elasticity
   B. Resource pooling
   C. Measured service
   D. Private server

19. Which of these refers to users running applications from a cloud's server, rather than downloading the application?
   A. Infrastructure as a Service
   B. Platform as a Service
   C. Software as a Service
   D. Hardware as a Service

20. A cloud that operates via the Internet is a _____ cloud.
   A. Hybrid
   B. Community
   C. Public
   D. Private

SELF TEST ANSWERS

Internet Concepts

1. ☑ **C.** Tier 1 providers own and control the backbone.
   ☒ **A** and **B** are both incorrect because tiers are numbered, not lettered. **D** is incorrect because this refers to large ISPs.

2. ☑ **A.** Individuals contract with an Internet service provider (ISP) for Internet service.
   ☒ **B** is incorrect because DNS is a type of server that translates between IP addresses and domain names. **C** is incorrect because Tier 1 refers to an owner of the Internet backbone; Tier 1 owners do not provide Internet accounts to individuals. **D** is incorrect because DHCP is a service that dynamically assigns IP addresses to clients.

3. ☑ **D.** A fully qualified domain name (FQDN) includes both a host and a domain.
☒ **A** is incorrect because it is a protocol. **B** is incorrect because it is a host name. **C** is incorrect because it is a domain name but it lacks a host name.

4. ☑ **B.** www is a host name.
☒ **A** is incorrect because it is a protocol. **C** is incorrect because it is a domain name but it lacks a host name. **D** is incorrect because it is an FQDN.

5. ☑ **C.** A Domain Name System (DNS) server translates between IP addresses and domain names.
☒ **A** is incorrect because a DHCP server dynamically assigns IP addresses to clients. **B** is incorrect because ISP refers to an Internet service provider, a company that provides Internet service. **D** is incorrect because FQDN describes a web address that includes a host name.

6. ☑ **B.** IMAP, Internet Mail Access Protocol, is a mail protocol.
☒ **A** is incorrect because HTML is the language used to create web pages. **C** is incorrect because Telnet is a terminal emulation protocol. **D** is incorrect because FTP is a file transfer protocol.

7. ☑ **B.** HTTPS is a secure form of HTTP, a web protocol.
☒ **A** is incorrect because SFTP is a protocol for secure file transfer. **C** is incorrect because SSH is for secure terminal emulation or file transfer. **D** is incorrect because POP is a mail protocol.

8. ☑ **D.** Network Time Protocol (NTP) is for synchronizing clocks.
☒ **A** is incorrect because NNTP is a protocol for news feeds. **B** is incorrect because IRC is a protocol for online text messaging. **C** is incorrect because FTP is a protocol for file transfers.

9. ☑ **B.** A file server would be used for FTP, which is a file transfer protocol.
☒ **A** is incorrect because a web server delivers web pages. **C** is incorrect because a mail server is used for e-mail. **D** is incorrect because an authentication server verifies user identities.

10. ☑ **D.** A Dynamic Host Configuration Protocol (DHCP) server assigns IP addresses.
☒ **A** is incorrect because a web server delivers web pages. **B** is incorrect because a DNS server translates between IP addresses and domain names. **C** is incorrect because a file server allows users to upload and download files.

11. ☑ **B.** A proxy server protects the client's IP address from the Internet, among its other benefits.
☒ **A** is incorrect because a DNS server translates between IP addresses and domain names. **C** is incorrect because a mail server sends and receives e-mail. **D** is incorrect because an authentication server verifies user identities.

12. ☑ **C.** An intrusion prevention system (IPS) can stop a detected security attack.
☒ **A** is incorrect because both an IPS and an IDS can detect security intrusions. **B** and **D** are both incorrect because they are not functions of either an IPS or an IDS.

Configuring Internet Settings in Windows

13. ☑ **B.** You can set the home page on the General tab.
    ☒ **A** is incorrect because Appearance is not an Internet Options tab; it is a button on the General tab. **C** is incorrect because the Advance tab contains advanced settings (not including the home page). **D** is incorrect because Home is not an Internet Options tab.

14. ☑ **A.** These are all security zones, found on the Security tab.
    ☒ **B, C,** and **D** are all incorrect because they are not classified using these types.

15. ☑ **A.** A first-party cookie comes from the website you are visiting.
    ☒ **B** and **D** are incorrect because there is no such thing as second-party or fourth-party cookies in cookie classification. **C** is incorrect because a third-party cookie is a cookie from an advertiser.

16. ☑ **B.** InPrivate is the high-privacy browsing mode in IE.
    ☒ **A** is incorrect because first-party is a kind of cookie. **C** is incorrect because an add-on is an extension that adds new features to the browser. **D** is incorrect because a proxy is a type of server.

17. ☑ **D.** HTTP, HTTPS, FTP, and Socks are four types of proxy servers.
    ☒ **A, B,** and **C** are all incorrect because HTTP, HTTPS, FTP, and Socks are not types of these items. HTTP and HTTPS are protocols for delivering web pages, and FTP is a file server protocol.

Cloud Concepts

18. ☑ **D.** Private server is not one of the five characteristics.
    ☒ **A, B,** and **C** are all incorrect because each is one of the five characteristics.

19. ☑ **C.** Software as a Service (SaaS) is the term for running an application from a cloud.
    ☒ **A** is incorrect because IaaS refers to creating an entire infrastructure environment in the cloud. **B** is incorrect because PaaS refers to having developers create their own cloud applications on a supplied platform. **D** incorrect because Hardware as a Service is not a recognized cloud service model.

20. ☑ **C.** A public cloud is one that operates via a public network such as the Internet.
    ☒ **A** is incorrect because a hybrid cloud joins two or more other types of clouds. **B** is incorrect because a community cloud is a deployment in which several organizations share a private cloud. **D** is incorrect because a private cloud is a deployment where the company running it also controls and manages the server and network.

Chapter 16

Troubleshooting Networks

Although there are many network problems only a trained network specialist can resolve, there are also many common and simple network problems that you will be able to resolve without extensive training and experience. You can also run certain tests that will give you important information to pass on to more highly trained network specialists, such as those in a large corporation or at your local Internet service provider (ISP).

In this chapter, you will explore the tools and techniques for troubleshooting common network problems. You will also learn about preventive maintenance tasks for networks.

CERTIFICATION OBJECTIVES

■ **901: 4.4** *Given a scenario, troubleshoot wired and wireless networks with appropriate tools*

■ **902: 2.1** *Identify common features and functionality of the Mac OS and Linux operating systems*

For CompTIA A+ 901 exam objective 4.4, be prepared to identify hardware and software tools for basic network troubleshooting and demonstrate that you understand how they are used. You should practice and review troubleshooting techniques for networks. In this section we also cover a single topic from A+ 902 exam objective 2.1, on the Linux/Mac side: IWCOFIG/IFCONFIG.

Troubleshooting Common Network Problems

To troubleshoot networks, a PC professional must call on all the skills required for hardware and software support, applying a structured approach to determining the problem, applying solutions, and testing. However, keep in mind that if you make all the connections properly, and all the hardware is working properly, the most common problems will involve the TCP/IP configuration of network interface cards (NICs).

Tools for Network Troubleshooting

The tools you will use for network troubleshooting include hardware tools and software tools. The hardware tools and some software tools were described in Chapter 14 as tools needed to create a network, but you also need them to troubleshoot network problems. In this chapter, as we visit troubleshooting problems, we will describe which of those tools to use and how to use them. But first, we would like to briefly talk about some command-line utilities that play a big role in troubleshooting.

Be sure you also know how each of the following hardware tools is used for troubleshooting networks: cable tester, tone generator and probe, loopback plug, punch down tool, and crimper. Refer back to Chapter 14 to review these.

When the TCP/IP protocol suite installs into Windows, it also installs a variety of command-line tools, such as IPCONFIG, PING, TRACERT, NETSTAT, NBTSTAT, and NSLOOKUP. These are the handiest and least expensive tools you can use for network troubleshooting or a variety of problems—those both local to and far removed from the computer, such as Domain Name Service (DNS) and Dynamic Host Configuration Protocol (DHCP) problems.

Each utility provides different information and is most valuable when used appropriately. For instance, you should first view the IP configuration using the *IPCONFIG* utility and verify that the configuration is correct for the network to which you are connected. If you discover any obvious problems when you view the IP configuration, correct them before proceeding. Then, select the tool that will help you diagnose and—in some instances—resolve the problem.

Most of these utilities have many optional parameters you can enter at the command line to change the command's behavior. In this book, we provide the simplest and/or most often used syntax. If you would like to learn more about each command, in Windows, simply open a Command Prompt window and enter the command name followed by a space, a slash, and a question mark, and then press ENTER. For the IPCONFIG command, enter the following: **ipconfig /?**.

A *parameter* is a string of characters entered at the command line along with the command. Some parameters are data, such as the IP address you enter with the PING command, and other parameters are switches, which alter the behavior of the command, such as the "/?" switch that requests help information about a command. Most command-prompt commands will accept either a hyphen (-) or a slash (/) character as part of a switch. When entering commands at the command line, separate the command name, such as "ipconfig," from any parameters with a space. In the case of **ipconfig /?**, the slash and question mark together comprise a parameter, which is separated from the command name with a space. Do not insert a space between the slash or hyphen and what follows, such as "?" or "all." If additional parameters must be used, separate each parameter with a space.

On the Mac and Linux side of things, the command is *IFCONFIG*, rather than IPCONFIG as it is in Windows. It stands for interface configuration. This is actually an older command; the newer version is the IP command. Either one will work, but ifconfig is specifically mentioned in the A+ 220-901 and 220-902 exam objectives. Note that IFCONFIG is only for wired connections; *IWCONFIG* is the corresponding command for wireless network interfaces.

Now that you understand some of the basics of command-line tools, we will look at some common network problems. Some require hardware tools, but most require that you use command-line tools—both to test for a problem and to resolve a problem.

Connectivity Problems

Connectivity problems are more obvious because the user simply fails to connect to a computer and usually receives an error message. For the PC technician troubleshooting connectivity problems involving the Internet, there are literally worlds of possible locations for the problems. When you suspect that a computer does not have network connectivity, check the network hardware, and use a variety of utilities to determine the cause, as described in the following sections. Learn how to pinpoint the location of a connection problem, from the local computer to Internet routers.

Checking Network Hardware

When there is a connectivity problem, first check the hardware. Check the NIC, cables (for a wired network), hub, switch, wireless access point (WAP), and router. Check the NIC by examining the status indicator lights on it, if available. On a bus NIC, the lights are on the card's bracket adjacent to the RJ-45 connector. Status indicator lights typically indicate link (a connection to a network), activity, and speed. Since most NICs receive power from the PC, any light is a good indication that the NIC's connection to the PC is working (or at least the power lines are). Look closer to check the connection. The Link light (usually green), when steady, indicates the connection to the network is live, and it will usually blink when sending or receiving. Multispeed NICs may have a separate Link light for each speed the NIC supports, and the lights may be labeled 100M for 100 Mbps and 1000M for 1000 Mbps (1 Gbps). If a Link light is off, there is either no power to the NIC or the connection is broken, which may be caused by a broken connector or cable.

Indicator Lights on NICs and Switches   Status indicators for network hardware include light-emitting diode (LED) lights on the physical device itself and/or software installed along with the device driver. With a quick glance at the lights on a device, or at the icons and messages on your computer screen, you will know that the device is powered up, that it is receiving and transmitting data, and (in the case of wireless devices) the strength of the signal. Many NICs have at least an *activity (ACT)* light that blinks to indicate network activity. These lights also indicate problems when they flash or change color. Read the device's documentation so you understand what these lights mean when troubleshooting.

Most NICs—both Ethernet and Wi-Fi—install with a configuration utility that can be opened from an icon in the taskbar's system tray. A balloon message may appear over the notification area when the status of one of these devices changes. The icon may also change to indicate the device's current status, and you can pause your mouse over one of these icons to display the status of the devices. For example, you might see a message such as "A network cable is unplugged," and the icon might have a red X over it.

If you see an amber light, especially on an older NIC, this may be a collision light, flashing as collisions are detected on the network. It will usually be on an older NIC because modern Ethernet switches make the need for this light obsolete, since a switch is designed to minimize collisions. If you do see a collision light on an old NIC on an old Ethernet network, then pay attention to it, because if it is blinking so excessively that it almost appears steady, this means there are excessive collisions on the network, and it could indicate that there is more traffic than the network can handle. The solution is to swap out the hub (which allows collisions) for a switch.

In addition, some wireless NICs have five LEDs that indicate signal strength, much like the bars on a cell phone. One lit light indicates a poor connection, and five lit lights indicate an excellent connection.

With many Ethernet and wireless NICs now built into computers, you often do not have physical status lights but must rely on status information provided in Windows. Check the notification area on the taskbar for an icon for the NIC.

If you have determined that a NIC has power, but there is no evidence of a connection (Link lights or status icon), take steps to correct this. In the case of a wired Ethernet NIC, check for a loose or damaged cable and examine the RJ-45 connectors for damage. Follow the cable to the hub or switch. We recommend the use of a cable tester since broken wires inside the cable are not revealed by visual inspection.

If the cable tests okay, check that the hub, switch, WAP, and router are functioning. Check for power to each device. These devices also have status lights similar to those of NICs. If all the lights are off, check the power supply. In the case of an Ethernet hub or switch, if it has power, look at the status light for each Ethernet connection on the device. If the light is out for the port to which the computer connects, swap the cable with a known-good cable, and recheck the status. Also check the cable standard that is in use. You may still find very old CAT3 cabling in use on a Fast Ethernet network. Upgrade the cabling to, at minimum, CAT5e. Remember that network devices such as switches and WAPs are computers. So, for example, if all users connected to the same WAP have the same network problem, consider restarting the WAP.

Check for any source of electrical interference affecting the cabling. Unshielded twisted-pair (UTP) cabling does not have shielding from interference, relying instead on the twists in the cable pairs to resist electromagnetic interference (EMI). Many things can cause EMI. Heavy power cables running parallel to network cabling emit signals that can cause interference, especially if there are intermittent loads on the power cable, such as when a large electric motor starts and stops. *Radio frequency interference (RFI)* can also affect networks if a source of RFI, such as a poorly shielded electronic device, is located near network cabling. If you find such a situation, take steps to move the cabling or the source of the interference.

If you cannot find any physical problems with the NIC, cabling, hub, switch, or WAP, and cannot find a source of interference, check the status of the NIC in Network Connections

FIGURE 16-1 Check the status of the NIC.

(in the Control Panel, choose Network and Internet | Network and Sharing Center | Change Adapter Settings and double-click the name of the NIC).

Figure 16-1 shows the Status dialog box from a Windows 7 computer with a connection problem (left) and a Windows Vista computer with no problem indicated (right). (This dialog box hasn't changed in newer Windows versions.) A lack of error in the Vista version doesn't necessarily mean there is absolutely no problem with the NIC on the Vista computer, but when you are first troubleshooting a network problem, accept this opinion at least temporarily and perform other tests before doing anything drastic, like replacing the NIC. In the case of the Windows 7 computer, we eventually found that we had a problem with the device driver. Installing the correct driver solved the problem.

Testing a Cable   To test for a broken cable, use a cable tester, such as the one shown in Figure 16-2. Notice that there are two separate components: a master unit and a smaller remote terminator. This makes it possible to connect to each end of a cable when those ends are in separate rooms or even on separate floors, in which case, you will need a troubleshooting partner on the other end. Of course, before you can test for a broken cable, you must locate both ends of the same cable. If the far end is connected to a punch down

FIGURE 16-2

A cable-testing
tool

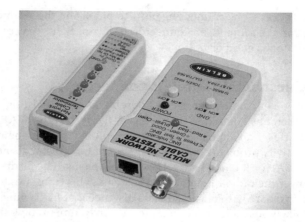

block, you will need to connect a tester to the correct RJ-45 socket, which can be a challenge if the punch down block in the wiring closet is not properly labeled. That is where a tone generator and probe comes in handy. Chapter 14 described how to use a tone generator and probe. Of course, this assumes you can access the cable bunch near the punch down block.

Once you find both ends of a cable, plug one end into the master unit and the other end into the remote unit. Turn on the master unit and watch the lights on the remote unit. (It helps to have a helper on one end.) The LEDs on the remote terminator will light up in turn as the master unit sends signals down each pair of wires. If the cable wiring is intact, the LEDs corresponding to each pair will be green. If there is damage to the cable wiring, the LEDs will not light up at all, or may first be green and then turn red. This is true for each pair of wires tested.

Some cable testers will test more than one type of cabling, but in most LANs, being able to test Ethernet cable is very useful and may be all you need.

on the
j o b

If you use your favorite search engine to query "cable tester," you will find a large selection of cable testers. You are sure to find one that fits your budget and needs. Some vendors, such as LANshack (www.lanshack.com), publish free tutorials on working with various types of cables.

If you find problems with a cable, you may need to run a new cable, which also means getting out the punch down tool for attaching cable to a punch down block and digging into your supply of spare RJ-45 connectors and crimping new ones onto the ends of cables before connecting the ends to the hubs/switches and NICs.

Testing Network Ports   Loopback plugs test whether or not a physical port, such as an RJ-45 port on a switch, or the RJ-45 port in a wall jack, are working. Some variations of this device are essentially a single plastic RJ-45 connector with two very short internal looped wires—one connecting pin 1 to pin 3, and the second wire connecting pin 2 to pin 6, all within the same RJ-45 connector. Indicator lights may be present to let you know if the connection is good or not.

Troubleshooting Wireless Connectivity

When you encounter connectivity problems on an existing wireless network that involve more than one computer, try the easier fix: restart the WAP/broadband router. In our home offices, this is an almost guaranteed solution. If this is a new wireless network, wireless connectivity problems may be the result of too great a distance between the wireless NICs and a WAP or it could be interference problems. The farther a Wi-Fi NIC is from a WAP, the lower the radio frequency (RF) signals. This translates to slower network speeds. But what if you are within a reasonable distance that had a much better signal before? The three most likely suspects are changes to the environment, new signal-impeding obstructions, or interference. Snow storms in the winter and thick foliage in the summer can affect your signal. Higher-gain antennae on the WAP and the Wi-Fi clients (if feasible) can help.

Using an *RF spectrum analyzer*, a generally expensive hardware device, you can do an RF spectrum analysis to discover interference from other nearby devices using the same frequency range, be they wireless local area networks (WLANs), cordless phones, microwave ovens, and so on. Assuming you don't have the budget for an RF spectrum analyzer, there are many inexpensive or free wireless locators (defined in Chapter 14) that only detect Wi-Fi networks. Figure 16-3 shows the result of using a wireless locator application called inSSIDer

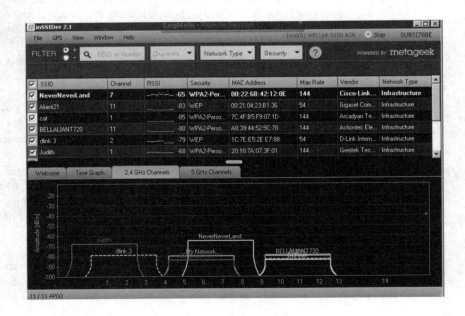

FIGURE 16-3

Scanning for wireless networks using inSSIDer

(www.metageek.net/products/inssider). It discovered six wireless networks and displays information it detected by analyzing the signals from each network. Because a software wireless locator like inSSIDer depends on your Wi-Fi adapter to detect signals, it will not detect the broad range an RF spectrum analyzer can, but it will detect nearby Wi-Fi networks.

Once you run one of these tools, the solution here is to configure the WAP to use a channel as far away from the interfering frequencies as possible. Each channel actually uses a different frequency, although adjacent channels—for example, channels 2 and 3—are so close together that changing from channel 2 to 3 will not make a difference.

Another common problem with Wi-Fi is that the expected SSID is not found. Users want to connect to your Wi-Fi network, but as far as they can tell, it doesn't exist. This happens when the WAP isn't broadcasting the SSID, which may be for any number of valid reasons. For example, perhaps you turned it off to increase security. Users can find the network by setting it up manually in their OS. For example, in Windows, open the Network and Sharing Center and click Set Up a New Connection or Network, and then choose Manually Connect to a Wireless Network. This starts a wizard that walks you through the prompts to establish a connection with an access point by manually entering its SSID. If you set up this connection to automatically reconnect, you shouldn't have to reconfigure it again after that initial setup.

Troubleshooting Limited Connectivity

Limited connectivity should mean that you only have a local LAN or WLAN connection, but a router of some sort is present and you cannot communicate beyond the LAN. However, network connection status messages vary depending on the version of the installed operating system. For Windows Vista, "limited local connectivity" sometimes means an IPv4 address could not be acquired via DHCP but there is a local IPv6 address (prefix of FE80). In this case, open the Properties dialog box for the NIC involved and deselect Internet Protocol Version 6 (TCP/IPv6). Click OK to accept that change and then open a Command Prompt window. Then, in the Command Prompt window, type **ipconfig /release** followed by **ipconfig /renew**. This command forces the DHCP client to release any IP address it may have and request a new IP address. It may take several seconds before you see a response, but it should receive a new address if it is able to reach the DHCP server. The output from the command will make it clear whether the computer receives an address. Remember this command because it is very useful, and we will recommend this command as a solution at least two more times in this chapter.

If your computer is a member of a HomeGroup, you will want to enable IPv6 after solving the limited connectivity problem because IPv6 is required for a HomeGroup. Learn more about HomeGroups in Chapter 19.

There are other possible causes for "limited or no connectivity" messages, and we will review some scenarios and possible solutions:

- For encrypted wireless networks, ensure your wireless NIC supports the encryption method. For example, perhaps your card only supports Wired Equivalent Privacy

(WEP) but the wireless network is using Wireless Protected Access 2 (WPA2). Check the configuration on both ends of the wireless connection. You may need to upgrade your NIC. If they both are using the same encryption method, ensure you have correctly entered the wireless encryption passphrase.

■ From the Command Prompt, type **ipconfig**. If the NIC's IP address begins with 169.254, this means it issued itself an Automatic Private Internet Protocol Addressing (APIPA) address because it did not reach a DHCP server to receive a valid IP configuration. If other stations are experiencing the same issue, consider restarting the DHCP server—bear in mind, however, the DHCP server might be your wireless router. If only this station is having problems, type **ipconfig /release** and then type **ipconfig /renew**.

e x a m
ⓦatch
The Linux/macOS ifconfig command doesn't have a direct equivalent to the ipconfig /release and ipconfig /renew commands. Instead, you use the dhclient command. The equivalent of ipconfig /release is dhclient –r eth0, **where eth0 is the network interface. (eth0 stands for Ethernet 0, the first Ethernet connection; wlan0 would represent the first wireless connection.) The equivalent of ipconfig /renew is** dhclient eth0.

■ Ensure you have the latest stable driver for your wireless NIC and that Device Manager is not reporting a problem. Consider uninstalling and reinstalling the driver.

■ Use **ipconfig /all** to ensure you have a valid default gateway and DNS server configured.

■ If your computer has more than one NIC (for example, a wired NIC and a wireless NIC), consider enabling one at a time and testing network connectivity individually.

■ Reset the NIC. Open Network Connections in the Control Panel, right-click the name of the NIC, select Disable in the Status dialog box (refer to Figure 16-1), and when that completes, right-click again and select Enable. Wait a few minutes before testing connectivity.

■ If disabling and enabling the network adapter does not resolve the problem, then run diagnostics. From the Network Connections screen in the Control Panel, right-click the NIC and select Diagnose. In both cases, Windows will attempt to detect and repair the problem.

■ On a wireless network, interference usually causes intermittent connectivity problems. Try configuring the wireless router to use a different channel.

- Check that the configuration of installed antimalware or firewall programs is not interfering with network operations.
- Check the router to see if Media Access Control (MAC) address filtering is preventing WLAN connections.

on the job

As the Internet and the world in general move to IPv6, you will want to learn more about working with it. Some of the traditional command-line commands work with IPv6—some requiring special parameters. For instance, to release and renew an IPv6 DHCP address, the commands to enter are ipconfig /release6 **and** ipconfig /renew6**. Use** ipconfig /? **for more IPv6 options.**

Testing IP Configuration and Connectivity

If you have eliminated obvious and easy-to-check connectivity issues, then use IPCONFIG to first check that the IP configuration is correct and then use PING to test connectivity. To test for slow communications over a routed network, use the TRACERT command, and use the NETSTAT command to troubleshoot some connection errors.

Verifying IP Configuration with IPCONFIG   When you are troubleshooting network connectivity problems on an IP network, after eliminating an obviously disconnected or failed NIC, use the IPCONFIG command to verify the IP configuration. Ensure that the IP address is within the correct range and has the appropriate subnet mask and DNS settings. If you completed Exercise 13-2 in Chapter 13, you already saw what this command can do, but you will now learn how to use the information.

Remember that IP addresses must be unique on a subnet. DHCP servers are smart enough to only assign unused IP addresses to clients, but it is possible for somebody to manually configure an IP address already in use on the network—Windows is not shy about telling you there is an IP address conflict. When you see this message, first check the IP configuration on the computer reporting that problem. If it has a static address and there is no good reason for that, change it to automatic (DHCP) and use the command **ipconfig /release** followed by **ipconfig /renew**. If that does not solve the problem, check the IP addresses in use on the DHCP server (or in your WAP or router). If you have more than a handful of computers on the network, this can be a tedious task.

When you open a Command Prompt and enter **ipconfig /all**, it will display the IP configuration of all network interfaces on the local computer, even those that receive their addresses and configuration through DHCP. In fact, if your NIC is a DHCP client, this is the

exam *watch*   **An IP address conflict (called an "IP conflict" in the list of topics under CompTIA A+ 901 exam objective 4.4) will keep a computer from communicating on a network and will result in an IP address conflict error message.**

best way to see the resulting IP configuration quickly in all versions of Windows. In Windows XP and older versions, there were no good graphical user interface (GUI) options for displaying this information in Windows, since the TCP/IP Properties dialog box for a DHCP client connection will only show that it is configured to receive an IP address automatically, and it will not show its IP configuration. Windows Vista and newer versions display the IP configuration information, regardless of how the NIC received it, in the Network Connection Details dialog box, as shown in Figure 13-8 in Chapter 13. You can only view this information for one connection at a time, so techs still like to use **ipconfig /all** to see information about all connections at once. Figure 16-4 shows an example of running the **ipconfig /all** command on a Windows 7 computer with multiple network adapters.

FIGURE 16-4

The result of running the ipconfig /all command

```
D:\Windows\system32\cmd.exe                                              _ □ X

Microsoft Windows [Version 6.1.7601]
Copyright (c) 2009 Microsoft Corporation.  All rights reserved.

D:\Users\Yoda>ipconfig /all

Windows IP Configuration

   Host Name . . . . . . . . . . . . : Yoda-PC
   Primary Dns Suffix  . . . . . . . :
   Node Type . . . . . . . . . . . . : Hybrid
   IP Routing Enabled. . . . . . . . : No
   WINS Proxy Enabled. . . . . . . . : No

Ethernet adapter Local Area Connection 3:

   Connection-specific DNS Suffix  . :
   Description . . . . . . . . . . . : Realtek PCI GBE Family Controller
   Physical Address. . . . . . . . . : 00-27-19-CD-2F-C2
   DHCP Enabled. . . . . . . . . . . : Yes
   Autoconfiguration Enabled . . . . : Yes
   Link-local IPv6 Address . . . . . : fe80::40dc:bc77:14ee:9cf3%18(Preferred)
   IPv4 Address. . . . . . . . . . . : 192.168.1.134(Preferred)
   Subnet Mask . . . . . . . . . . . : 255.255.255.0
   Lease Obtained. . . . . . . . . . : Friday, July 13, 2012 7:26:28 AM
   Lease Expires . . . . . . . . . . : Saturday, July 14, 2012 7:26:33 AM
   Default Gateway . . . . . . . . . : 192.168.1.1
   DHCP Server . . . . . . . . . . . : 192.168.1.1
   DHCPv6 IAID . . . . . . . . . . . : 452994841
   DHCPv6 Client DUID. . . . . . . . : 00-01-00-01-14-2D-C9-A0-00-27-19-CD-2F-C2

   DNS Servers . . . . . . . . . . . : 192.168.8.1
   NetBIOS over Tcpip. . . . . . . . : Enabled

Ethernet adapter VirtualBox Host-Only Network:

   Connection-specific DNS Suffix  . :
   Description . . . . . . . . . . . : VirtualBox Host-Only Ethernet Adapter
   Physical Address. . . . . . . . . : 08-00-27-00-98-C5
   DHCP Enabled. . . . . . . . . . . : No
   Autoconfiguration Enabled . . . . : Yes
   Link-local IPv6 Address . . . . . : fe80::bc35:1a2:a311:2433%14(Preferred)
   IPv4 Address. . . . . . . . . . . : 192.168.56.1(Preferred)
   Subnet Mask . . . . . . . . . . . : 255.255.255.0
   Default Gateway . . . . . . . . . :
   DHCPv6 IAID . . . . . . . . . . . : 336068647
   DHCPv6 Client DUID. . . . . . . . : 00-01-00-01-14-2D-C9-A0-00-27-19-CD-2F-C2

   DNS Servers . . . . . . . . . . . : fec0:0:0:ffff::1%1
                                       fec0:0:0:ffff::2%1
                                       fec0:0:0:ffff::3%1
```

When the output from the IPCONFIG command shows an IP address other than 0.0.0.0, you know that the IP settings have been successfully bound to your network adapter. "Bound" means that there is a linking relationship, called a "binding," between the network protocol and the adapter. A binding establishes the order in which each network component handles network communications.

In addition, when viewing the IP configuration information, verify that each item is correct for the IP network segment on which the NIC is connected. There are three rules to keep in mind when evaluating an IP configuration:

- The network ID and the subnet mask of each host on an IP segment must match.
- The default gateway address must be the IP address of a router on the same subnet.
- Each host on an IP segment must have a unique host ID.

Therefore, if there are other hosts on the same subnet, run IPCONFIG on each of them to determine if all the hosts comply with these rules. If not, correct the problem.

Finally, if the computer in question has an IP address that begins with 169.254, this is an APIPA address—an address that a DHCP client can assign to itself when it cannot reach a DHCP server. If this is a very small network of just a few computers in which all of the computers use APIPA, this may be okay, but in most cases, consider this address a sign of a failure. If possible, check to see if the DHCP server is available. For a large network, you will need to contact a network administrator.

In a small office or home office (SOHO) network, the DHCP server may be part of a broadband router. In that case, reset the router. If you wait long enough, the DHCP server should assign an address to the DHCP client computer, and if you wish to take control of the process, use the command **ipconfig /release** followed by **ipconfig /renew**.

Troubleshooting Connection Errors with the PING Command   The *PING* command is useful for testing communications between two hosts. The name of this command is an acronym for Packet Internet Groper. We prefer to think (as many do) that it was named after the action of underwater sonar. Instead of bouncing sound waves off surfaces, the PING command uses data packets, sending them to specific IP addresses and requesting a response (hence, the idea of pinging). Then, PING listens for a reply.

If you completed Exercise 14-1 or 14-2 in Chapter 14, you know the simplest syntax of the PING command, which is **ping *target-IP-address*.** However, you do not always need to know a target's IP address. You can also ping a domain name, such as mcgraw-hill.com, and on a network running Windows computers, you can ping the computer name. Use the PING command to test a new network connection and, for troubleshooting, a connection failure. The following is a suggested order for doing this.

1. Ping the local NIC using the command: **ping localhost**. The standard host name *localhost* is assigned by the IP protocol to the loopback network interface and no packets will leave the NIC, and if it is functioning, it will send the normal response back. Recall the discussion of loopback in Chapter 14. If the ping results in four responses, move on to the next step. If this fails, troubleshoot the NIC as you would any hardware component. If you have another identical NIC known to work, swap it with the current NIC. If the replacement NIC works, replace the original NIC.

2. Ping the IP address of the default gateway. If this does not work, verify that the gateway address is correct. If there are other computers on the network, compare the IP configuration settings. If the address for the default gateway matches those of other hosts on the network, ping the default gateway address from another computer.

3. Ping the IP address or DNS name of a computer beyond the default gateway.

This order tests, first, if the NIC is working. It also tests that the address works within your LAN, because the default gateway address is on the LAN and has the same network ID as the local NIC. Finally, successfully pinging an address beyond the gateway confirms at least two things: the router works, and the NIC of the target host is functioning and can respond to ping requests. If you cannot ping any computer beyond the router, the problem may be in the router itself.

PING has several switches. Use the -t switch when you want to ping an address repeatedly. The default is to ping an address four times. It will continue until you stop it. Pressing the CTRL-BREAK key combination will cause it to display statistics and then continue. To stop this command, press the CTRL-C key combination. Figure 16-5 shows the output from PING with this switch.

Another default of the PING command is the size (or length) of the data it uses. The default size is 32 bytes, which is not a very heavy load for any connection. Therefore, administrators sometimes test a connection by sending more data. Do this with the -l switch followed by a space and the size, such as 1024. For instance, type the command **ping 192.168.1.1 -l 1024**. A connection that can easily handle the 32-byte size with zero percent loss of data may show some data loss with the 1024-byte size.

Now for some technical information about PING and related commands. The PING command uses a subprotocol of IP called the *Internet Control Message Protocol (ICMP)*. This little protocol has a big job in a TCP/IP internetwork. It detects problems that can cause errors. Such problems include congestion and downed routers. When ICMP detects these problems, it notifies other protocols and services in the TCP/IP suite, resulting in routing of packets around the problem area.

When you use PING, it sends *ICMP echo packets* to the target node. An echo packet contains a request to respond. Once the target node receives the packets, it sends out one response packet for each echo packet it receives. You see information about the received packets in the lines that begin with "Reply from." Pay attention to the time information on

FIGURE 16-5

Using the PING
command with
the -t parameter

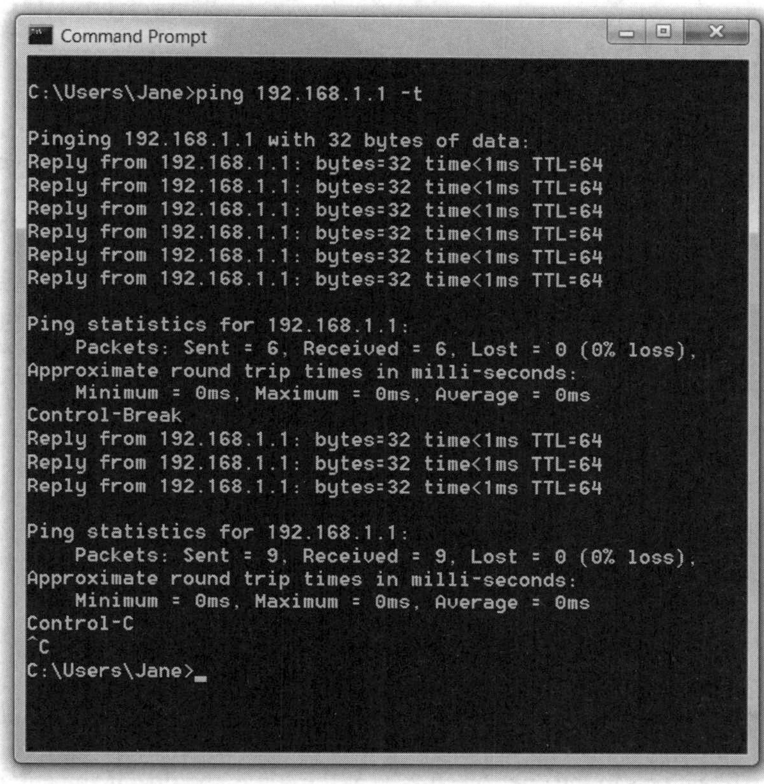

```
Command Prompt                                                    _ □ X

C:\Users\Jane>ping 192.168.1.1 -t

Pinging 192.168.1.1 with 32 bytes of data:
Reply from 192.168.1.1: bytes=32 time<1ms TTL=64
Reply from 192.168.1.1: bytes=32 time<1ms TTL=64
Reply from 192.168.1.1: bytes=32 time<1ms TTL=64
Reply from 192.168.1.1: bytes=32 time<1ms TTL=64
Reply from 192.168.1.1: bytes=32 time<1ms TTL=64
Reply from 192.168.1.1: bytes=32 time<1ms TTL=64

Ping statistics for 192.168.1.1:
    Packets: Sent = 6, Received = 6, Lost = 0 (0% loss),
Approximate round trip times in milli-seconds:
    Minimum = 0ms, Maximum = 0ms, Average = 0ms
Control-Break
Reply from 192.168.1.1: bytes=32 time<1ms TTL=64
Reply from 192.168.1.1: bytes=32 time<1ms TTL=64
Reply from 192.168.1.1: bytes=32 time<1ms TTL=64

Ping statistics for 192.168.1.1:
    Packets: Sent = 9, Received = 9, Lost = 0 (0% loss),
Approximate round trip times in milli-seconds:
    Minimum = 0ms, Maximum = 0ms, Average = 0ms
Control-C
^C
C:\Users\Jane>_
```

this line. It should be below 200 ms; if the time is greater than 500 ms, there is a connectivity issue between the two hosts. Of course, a little common sense may tell you that it will take a longer time to receive a response from the other side of the world.

on the job

Practice working with these command-line tools before your network has a problem. Then you will be more comfortable with the tools and their screen output.

Using TRACERT to Troubleshoot Slow Communications   You may have situations in which you can connect to a website or other remote resource, but the connection is very slow. If this connection is critical to business, you will want to gather information so a network administrator or ISP can troubleshoot the source of the bottleneck. You can use the TRACERT command to gather this information. *TRACERT* is a command-line utility that traces the route taken by packets to a destination.

Be sure you understand the type of results you get from each of the command-line commands.

When you use TRACERT with the name or IP address of the target host, it will ping each of the intervening routers, from the nearest to the farthest. You will see the delay at each router, and you will be able to determine the location of the bottleneck. You can then provide this information to the people who will troubleshoot it for you.

Understanding *time to live (TTL)* is also important. Each IP packet header has a TTL field that shows how many routers the packet can cross before being discarded. Like PING, TRACERT creates ICMP echo packets. The packet sent to the first host or router has a TTL of 1. The TTL of each subsequent packet is increased by one. Each router, in turn, decreases the TTL value by one. The computer that sends the TRACERT waits a predetermined amount of time before it increments the TTL value by one for each additional packet. This repeats until the destination is reached. This process has the effect of pinging each router along the way, without needing to know each router's actual IP address.

Consider a scenario in which your connection to the Google website (www.google.com) is extremely slow. You are working from a small office that has a cable modem connection to the Internet, and you are accustomed to very fast responses when you browse the Web. You have connected in the last few minutes to other websites without significant delay, so you believe there is a bottleneck between you and Google.

Use TRACERT as described in Exercise 16-1 and report the results to your ISP. TRACERT will reveal the address of the router that is the bottleneck between you and a target host. Normally, the first and last numbered lines in the output represent the source IP address and the target IP address. Every line in between is a router located between your computer and the target. You can verify that the last line is the target by matching the IP address to the one you entered at the command line. If you entered a DNS name at the command line, the IP address will display below the command line.

EXERCISE 16-1

Video

Using TRACERT

In this exercise, we use Google as the target, but you can substitute another domain name or IP address.

1. Open a Command Prompt.
2. Type **tracert www.google.com**.
3. In Figure 16-6, one of the routers shows a value that is much greater than the others, but it is not greater than 500 ms, so there is a bottleneck relative to the others, but it is not a serious one. If your test shows a router with a much greater value, report this to your ISP or to a network professional in your company, if appropriate.

FIGURE 16-6

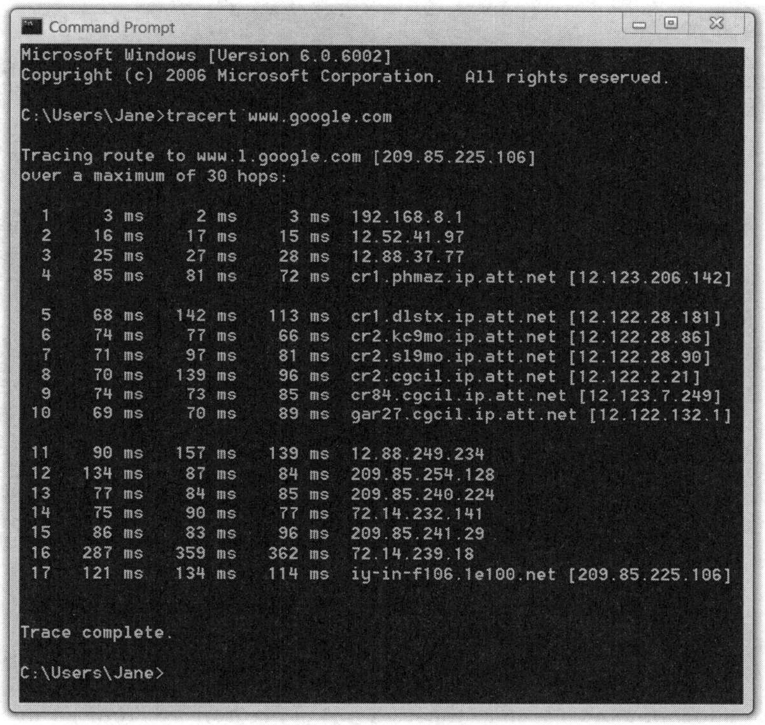

Using TRACERT
to trace the route
to www.google
.com

FIGURE 16-6

Using TRACERT to trace the route to www.google.com

```
Command Prompt                                                        _ □ ☒

Microsoft Windows [Version 6.0.6002]
Copyright (c) 2006 Microsoft Corporation.  All rights reserved.

C:\Users\Jane>tracert www.google.com

Tracing route to www.l.google.com [209.85.225.106]
over a maximum of 30 hops:

  1     3 ms     2 ms     3 ms  192.168.8.1
  2    16 ms    17 ms    15 ms  12.52.41.97
  3    25 ms    27 ms    28 ms  12.88.37.77
  4    85 ms    81 ms    72 ms  cr1.phmaz.ip.att.net [12.123.206.142]

  5    68 ms   142 ms   113 ms  cr1.dlstx.ip.att.net [12.122.28.181]
  6    74 ms    77 ms    66 ms  cr2.kc9mo.ip.att.net [12.122.28.86]
  7    71 ms    97 ms    81 ms  cr2.sl9mo.ip.att.net [12.122.28.90]
  8    70 ms   139 ms    96 ms  cr2.cgcil.ip.att.net [12.122.2.21]
  9    74 ms    73 ms    85 ms  cr84.cgcil.ip.att.net [12.123.7.249]
 10    69 ms    70 ms    89 ms  gar27.cgcil.ip.att.net [12.122.132.1]

 11    90 ms   157 ms   139 ms  12.88.249.234
 12   134 ms    87 ms    84 ms  209.85.254.128
 13    77 ms    84 ms    85 ms  209.85.240.224
 14    75 ms    90 ms    77 ms  72.14.232.141
 15    86 ms    83 ms    96 ms  209.85.241.29
 16   287 ms   359 ms   362 ms  72.14.239.18
 17   121 ms   134 ms   114 ms  iy-in-f106.1e100.net [209.85.225.106]

Trace complete.

C:\Users\Jane>
```

Using NETSTAT to Troubleshoot Connection Errors   The *NETSTAT* command will give you statistical information about the TCP/IP protocols and network connections involving your computer, depending on the parameters you use when you enter the command. Although NETSTAT has many options, there are a few you should remember. For instance, running netstat without any parameters, as shown in Figure 16-7, will show the current connections by protocol and port number. NETSTAT by itself can show you a connection that is not working—perhaps because an application has failed. Running netstat –s displays statistics on outgoing and incoming traffic on your computer. If this test shows there is no traffic in one direction, you may have a bad cable.

Troubleshooting with the NET Command

The Windows *NET* command is a command-prompt utility that can be used to perform a variety of administrative and troubleshooting tasks. We have even used this command to create scripts for automating the creation of user accounts in a Windows

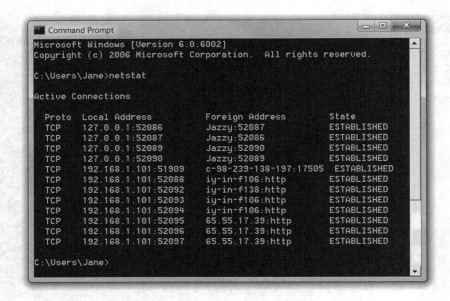

FIGURE 16-7

The NETSTAT command shows current connections.

domain—an advanced task. You can use the NET command to start and stop network services. To learn more about the NET command, enter **net help** to display a list of subcommands, such as those shown in Figure 16-8. You can then learn more about a single subcommand. For instance, the command for starting network services is **net start** *service*, where *service* is the name of the network service you wish to start. Enter **net stop** *service* to stop a service. To see a list of the services you can start, enter this command: **net help start**. To see a list of the services you can stop, enter this command: **net help stop**. You will see fewer services listed for the STOP command because some services cannot be stopped.

Use the NET command with the **use** subcommand to connect to a network *share*. A network share is a resource, such as a file folder or printer, that is available to you over the network. For instance, to connect to a shared folder named DATA on the computer named Wickenburg, enter **net use \\Wickenburg\data**. Use this command if you have determined that you can ping another computer but are not able to access a shared folder on that computer.

on the **job**

At the command line, you can enter net /? **to view information about the NET command. However, this version is really a condensed version of** net help **and gives you less information. So, remember** net /? **for the exam, but use** net help **on the job.**

FIGURE 16-8

Viewing the
subcommands
for the NET
command

FIGURE 16-8

Viewing the
subcommands
for the NET
command

```
Command Prompt
C:\Users\Jane>net help
The syntax of this command is:

NET HELP
command
      -or-
NET command /HELP

   Commands available are:

   NET ACCOUNTS            NET HELPMSG            NET STATISTICS
   NET COMPUTER            NET LOCALGROUP         NET STOP
   NET CONFIG             NET PAUSE              NET TIME
   NET CONTINUE           NET PRINT              NET USE
   NET FILE               NET SESSION            NET USER
   NET GROUP              NET SHARE              NET VIEW
   NET HELP               NET START

   NET HELP NAMES explains different types of names in NET HELP syntax lines.
   NET HELP SERVICES lists some of the services you can start.
   NET HELP SYNTAX explains how to read NET HELP syntax lines.
   NET HELP command | MORE displays Help one screen at a time.

C:\Users\Jane>
```

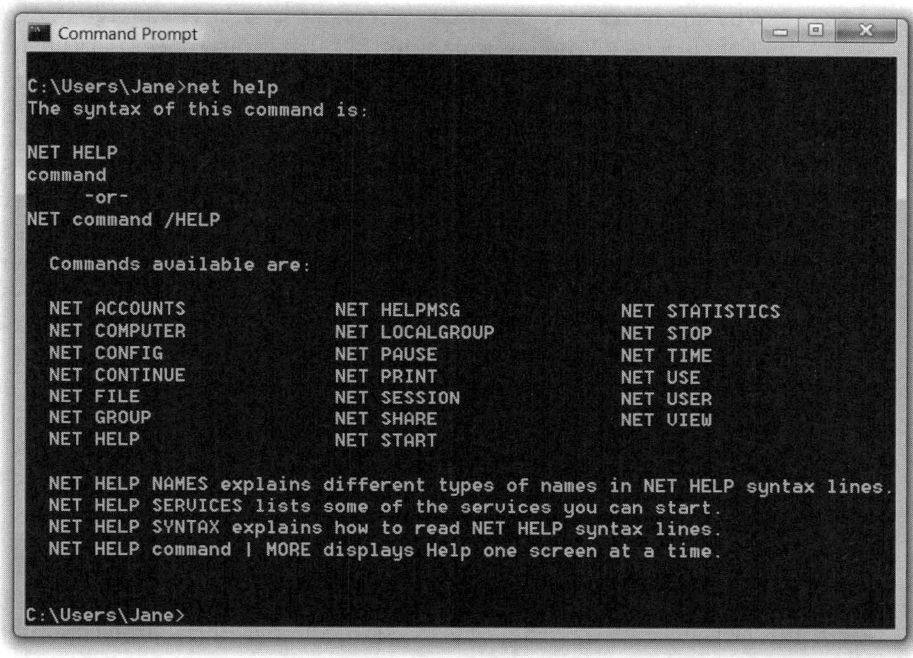

Resolving Insufficient Bandwidth

Chapter 13 described *bandwidth* as the amount of data that can travel over a network at a given time. That is deceptively simple when what is important is the user's perception of network slowness. Therefore, when a user perceives a network to be slow, increasing the bandwidth will improve its speed. The more data you can send at once, the faster data will move from beginning to end, and the faster the network will run overall. There are two ways to increase bandwidth. One is the low-cost method of reducing the broadcast sources, and the second, more costly, method is a hardware upgrade. Remember that wireless networks are shared bandwidth; 150 Mbps for an 802.11n wireless network feels fast for a single user but feels slower for 100 simultaneous network users.

Reducing Sources of Network Broadcasts

Most protocol suites have at least a few subprotocols that rely on network broadcasts. A *broadcast* is a transmission of packets addressed to all nodes on a network.

Broadcast traffic is, to some extent, unavoidable within a network segment, but too much of it takes up bandwidth needed for other traffic. Although broadcasts do not cross routers, they still persist within the network segments between routers, thus taking up valuable bandwidth. Reduce these sources by searching for the unnecessary protocol suites, and then look within the suites that are necessary and reduce the amount of broadcasting within them.

Why do unnecessary protocols exist on a network? First, more than one protocol suite can be active on a Windows computer, but that is rarely necessary anymore. If you have a TCP/IP network, and you find another protocol suite on a computer and there is no good reason to have it, remove it. Likely unnecessary (and outdated) protocol suites are Microsoft's NetBEUI, Novell's IPX/SPX, or Microsoft's NWLink (a version of IPX/SPX).

Of course, as you learned in Chapter 14, you can turn off the Service Set Identifier (SSID) broadcast from a WAP. This is not only more secure, but it reduces broadcasts. However, when it comes to the use of excess protocol suites, the most common offenders are not usually computers, but old print servers, which may have come with several protocol suites enabled. Whether a print server is a separate box or integrated into a network printer, find out how to access the print server configuration. In the case of a separate print server box, you will normally enter the print server's IP address into a web browser's address box and access it remotely. You will need the administrative user name and password to access it. For a print server integrated into a printer, it all depends on its design. The documentation for the printer will give instructions on how to access its configuration—usually through a web browser or through a control panel on the printer. In both instances, look for protocols and remove protocol suites that are not required on your network.

Unnecessary broadcasting can also hamper performance. Today's Internet users enjoy streaming audio and video, which means that users listening to Internet radio or Internet TV can have a negative impact on network throughput for others. This is a serious problem in a working environment because, aside from the ethical problem of spending work time for personal activities, using shared network bandwidth for downloading and uploading questionable content such as movies and music using a BitTorrent client can also seriously degrade network performance.

Upgrading Network Hardware

Once you have eliminated unnecessary protocol suites and unnecessary broadcasting, if there is still a bandwidth problem, increase the bandwidth by upgrading the network's components. If the network has any Ethernet hubs, replace them with switches. Recall that a hub takes a signal received on one port and repeats it on all other ports. This consumes bandwidth. A switch, on the other hand, is a more intelligent device, which takes an incoming signal and only sends it to the destination port. This saves bandwidth.

If the network already has switches, then consider upgrading to faster equipment. For example, a LAN with Ethernet (10 Mbps) or Fast Ethernet (100 Mbps) equipment can be upgraded to Gigabit Ethernet (1 to 10 Gbps).

Be sure that when you upgrade to increase bandwidth, the upgrade is thorough. That is, *all* the NICs, switches, and routers must support the new, higher speed. Although the faster equipment is downward compatible with the slower equipment, the network will only be as fast as its slowest hardware component. Also, on an Ethernet network, do not forget to upgrade the cabling to the grade required for the network speed you want to achieve. So, if you want to achieve Gigabit Ethernet speeds, you need a Gigabit Ethernet NIC, cable, and switch.

Similarly, to upgrade a wireless network, replace slower equipment with newer, faster equipment. Increase signal strength with proper placement of the wireless antenna, and install signal boosters, if necessary. Newer wireless equipment will also have better security.

Troubleshooting DNS Problems

DNS problems show themselves as messages such as "Server not found." These messages can appear in your web browser, your e-mail client, or any software that attempts to connect to a server. How do you know it is a DNS problem? You do not know this until you eliminate other problems, such as a failed NIC, a broken connection, a typo, or an incorrect IP configuration. But once you have eliminated these problems, use the following tests to troubleshoot DNS problems.

e x a m

ⓦ a t c h The CompTIA A+ 220-901 and 220-902 exams no longer cover Windows Internet Name Service (WINS), but it still persists in the A+ Acronyms list.

Using PING to Troubleshoot DNS Problems

Notice that in the steps provided for using both the PING and TRACERT commands in the previous sections, you can use either the IP address or the DNS name. When you use the DNS name with either of these commands, you are also testing DNS. For instance, if you open a Command Prompt window and enter the command ping www.mcgraw-hill.com, before the PING command can send packets to the target, www.mcgraw-hill.com, the DNS client must resolve the DNS name to an IP address. This is exactly what happens when you enter a Uniform Resource Locator (URL) in the address box of a web browser. The DNS client resolves the name to an IP address before the browser can send a request to view the page.

When pinging a DNS name is successful, you know several things: your DNS client is working, your DNS server is responding and working, and the target DNS name has been found on the Internet. Now, notice that the name we used (www.mcgraw-hill.com) has three parts to it. Reading from right to left, "com" is the *top-level domain (TLD)* name, and mcgraw-hill is the *second-level domain (SLD)* name within the com TLD. Both of these together are usually referred to as a domain name. So what is "www"? The owner of the second-level domain name defines everything else you see in the URL.

For instance, www.mcgraw-hill.com is listed in DNS servers that are probably under the control of McGraw-Hill or its ISP. The entry points to a server, named "www," are where web pages can be found. So, to the left of the second-level domain name are the names of servers or child domains of mcgraw-hill.com. This allows McGraw-Hill to organize their portion of the DNS name space and help client computers locate resources on these servers. Another example is support.microsoft.com that points to the Microsoft Support website.

And what about all those letters, numbers, slashes, and other characters to the right of the TLD? They point to specific documents on the servers. Simple? To the casual observer, yes, because DNS hides the complexity of the organization and the locations of servers and documents. Understanding this much will help you to work with DNS and perform basic troubleshooting.

So, the next time you cannot connect to a website from your browser, first double-check your spelling. If you entered the URL correctly, then open up a Command Prompt window and ping the portion of the URL that contains the TLD and SLD. In our first example, you would open a Command Prompt window and type **ping mcgraw-hill.com**. If the ping is not successful, you should immediately ping another domain name and/or try connecting to another URL through your browser. If you are successful pinging another location, then the problem may be with a router in the path to the first location. Use TRACERT, described earlier, to pinpoint the problem router.

Using IPCONFIG to Flush the DNS Cache

Before a DNS client queries a DNS server for a specific name, it checks a little chunk of memory, the *DNS cache*, where it retains a list of previously resolved DNS names and IP addresses. If the DNS client finds the name in the cache, it does not query the DNS server. However, if the server address has changed since it was recorded in the DNS cache, the DNS client will return an error and you will not be able to connect to the server. So, if you recently were able to connect to a server through your browser, but have a "server not found" error, an easy solution to try is to flush the DNS cache so that the client will query the DNS server rather than use the address in the cache. To do this, open a Command Prompt window and enter this command: **ipconfig /flushdns**. Then open your browser and attempt to connect to the server again.

ⓦatch **There isn't a direct equivalent in ifconfig to flush the DNS cache. Instead, you would restart the nscd daemon to flush the cache. In the Linux Terminal window, type** /etc/rc.d/init.d/nscd restart. **In macOS, type** dscacheutil –flushcache **in a Terminal window.**

Using NSLOOKUP to Troubleshoot DNS Problems

To further troubleshoot DNS problems, use the *NSLOOKUP* command, which lets you troubleshoot DNS problems by allowing you to query DNS name servers and see the result of the queries. In using NSLOOKUP, you are looking for problems such as a DNS server not responding to clients, DNS servers not resolving names correctly, or other general name resolution problems. NSLOOKUP bypasses the client DNS cache and talks directly to the DNS server and is thus more reliable than PING for DNS troubleshooting. NSLOOKUP has two modes:

- **Interactive mode**   In interactive mode, NSLOOKUP has its own command prompt, a greater than sign (>) within the system Command Prompt. You enter this mode by typing **nslookup** without any parameters, or **nslookup** followed by a space, a hyphen, and the name of a name server. In the first instance, it will use your default name server, as shown here, and in the second instance, it will use the name server you specify. While in interactive mode, enter commands at the NSLOOKUP prompt, and type **exit** to end interactive mode and return to the system Command Prompt.

■ **Noninteractive mode**   In noninteractive mode, you enter the NSLOOKUP command plus a command parameter for using one or more NSLOOKUP subcommands. The response is sent to the screen, and you are returned to the Command Prompt. Exercise 16-2 uses noninteractive mode.

EXERCISE 16-2

Using NSLOOKUP to Troubleshoot DNS

Use NSLOOKUP to resolve any Internet domain name to an IP address.

1. Open a Command Prompt window, and enter the following command: **nslookup mcgraw-hill.com**. If the name server is working, the result will resemble Figure 16-9.

   ■ The server and address in the first and second lines of the output are the name and IP address of the DNS server that responded to your request. This will be the name server used by your ISP or your company.

   ■ The second group of lines shows the result of the query. It is called a nonauthoritative answer because the name server queried had to query other name servers to find the name.

2. The results in Figure 16-9 show that DNS name resolution is working. Therefore, if you are unable to connect to a server in this domain, the server may be offline, or a critical link or router between it and the Internet has failed. If you were troubleshooting a connection problem to this domain, you would pass this information on to a network administrator or ISP.

FIGURE 16-9

The NSLOOKUP command queries the default name server.

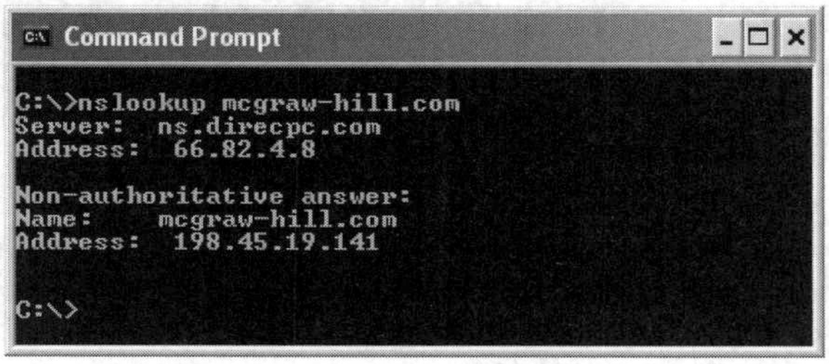

```
C:\>nslookup mcgraw-hill.com
Server:  ns.direcpc.com
Address:  66.82.4.8

Non-authoritative answer:
Name:    mcgraw-hill.com
Address:  198.45.19.141

C:\>
```

Troubleshooting with Terminal Software

Telnet is character-based terminal software that has a server component that allows a Telnet client to connect. The connected client works in a character-mode environment and can enter commands. (Windows Vista and newer versions don't include a Telnet client, but you can download one.)

Historically, network devices like routers contained a Telnet server service to which router administrators connected and used cryptic commands to configure the router. In today's SOHO network equipment, the Telnet server has been replaced by a web server, and a technician connects to the device by entering the IP address of the device in a browser.

However, Telnet still has its uses as an advanced troubleshooting tool. In Chapter 13 you learned about ports and how a port identifies the exact service targeted at a certain IP address. When you use Telnet, it uses TCP port 23, but you can direct it to use a different port number—say, TCP port 25—which is normally used by Simple Mail Transport Protocol (SMTP). Here is the scenario: Your e-mail client is unable to send messages. You have used the PING command to ping the mail server successfully. Therefore, it is possible that the physical server is up and running on the network but the SMTP service is not working. If you direct Telnet to connect to the IP address/port for the SMTP server and are unable to connect, then notify the mail server administrator because this can indicate the SMTP service is down.

Rather than use the cryptic character-based Telnet client, which has the added disadvantage of not being secure, consider downloading a GUI-based terminal client with security features. Secure Shell (SSH), described in Chapter 14, has replaced Telnet as a terminal client. It can be used to connect to terminal servers that require sophisticated security protocols. Many free terminal clients are available—many with "Telnet" in their name—but most of them are some form of SSH. One free terminal client is PuTTY, which is described on the website (www.chiark.greenend.org.uk/~sgtatham/putty/) as "a free Telnet/SSH client."

SCENARIO & SOLUTION

My network has a DHCP server. I need to see if the NIC was assigned an IP address, but when I look at the properties of the Local Area Connection, the IP address is empty. What can I do?	Open a Command Prompt window and enter the following command: **ipconfig /all**. This will display the IP configuration.
I have connected to a certain website many times, but today the connection to this one website is very slow. I would like to talk to my ISP about this, but I need more information. How can I tell where the problem is?	Because other websites do not seem as slow, use the TRACERT command to trace the route to the website and determine where the bottleneck may be.

Preventive Maintenance for Networks

It is always better to prevent problems than to spend your time solving them. In this section, you will learn the basic maintenance tasks specific to networks, which include maintaining all the equipment directly attached to the network and the media over which the signals travel. However, the value and usability of a network also depend on proper functioning of the attached computers (clients and servers), as well as other shared devices, such as printers. In Chapter 11, you learned preventive maintenance for computers. Preventive maintenance for network devices, such as NICs, hubs, switches, WAPs, and routers, is identical to that for computers.

A network also depends on the maintenance of an appropriate and secure environment for both the equipment and data. Chapters 17 and 18 explore security issues for computers and networks, and Chapter 1 presented safety and environmental issues.

Therefore, although this chapter presents some network-specific maintenance tasks, keep in mind that a computer professional must look beyond the components and software that are specific to a network and approach network maintenance holistically.

Maintaining Equipment

Network equipment, from the NICs in the computers to the bridging and routing devices that connect networks together, all have similar requirements. For instance, they all require sufficient ventilation and cooling systems to maintain the appropriate operating environment.

Reliable Power

All computer and network components must have electrical power. Providing reliable power begins with the power company supplying the power, but your responsibility begins at the meter. Do not assume that the power will always be reliable. Most of us have experienced power outages and can understand how disrupting they are. However, bad power, in the form of surges, spikes, and voltage sags, can do a great deal of damage. Prevent damage and disruption from these events by using uninterruptible power supply (UPS) devices or other protective devices discussed in Chapter 1. Versions of these power protection devices come in a form factor for mounting in equipment racks. Equipment racks are discussed in the following section.

Be aware of the number and location of circuits in the building, and the total power requirements of the equipment you have on each circuit. If you have network equipment unprotected by a UPS, be sure this equipment is not sharing a circuit with a device that has high demands, such as a laser printer or photocopier.

Consider using a dedicated circuit for the most critical equipment. A dedicated circuit has only one, or very few, outlets.

Housing Servers and Network Devices

Servers and network devices such as switches and routers should be in a physically secure room or closet with proper climate controls. The humidity should be at or near 40 percent, and the temperature should be no higher than 70 degrees. Provide adequate spacing around the equipment for proper ventilation. When dealing with more than a few servers plus network equipment, use rack-mounted servers that fit into the specially designed equipment racks for holding servers and other devices, such as UPSs, routers, and switches. These take up less space and, unlike tables and desks, allow more air to flow around the equipment.

Dedicate the room or closet to the equipment. Do not make this a multipurpose room for storage or office space, because that is inviting disaster, especially if the space is readily accessible by people who have no professional reason to be in contact with the servers or network equipment. The unintended consequences of such an arrangement can damage the equipment.

As a new technician, you may find yourself in a new and growing company. Take a professional approach to organizing and protecting the networking equipment from the beginning. This will make the changes required to accommodate a larger network easier.

Securing and Protecting Network Cabling

Regardless of the size of the network, keep network cabling neat and labeled. In the equipment room or closet, use patch panels. A patch panel is a rack-mounted panel containing multiple network ports. Cables running from various locations in the building connect to ports on the back of the patch panel. Then shorter cables, called patch cables, connect each port to switches and routers in the closet or equipment room. This keeps cables organized and even allows for labeling the ports. This will help prevent damaged cables and confusion when troubleshooting a cable run.

Secure and protect network cabling to avoid damage from mishandling or mischief and to ensure that it is well labeled so that it is easier to add new equipment and to troubleshoot.

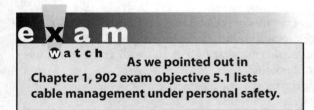

As we pointed out in Chapter 1, 902 exam objective 5.1 lists cable management under personal safety.

Horizontal runs of cabling often must run through suspended ceilings. Resist the urge to simply lay the cabling on the top of the ceiling tiles. This arrangement may be okay for a very small number of cables, but it only takes a few cables to make a tangle. Further, running additional cables into this space can be very difficult. Therefore, bundle cables together and run them through channels where possible. If the budget allows, specialized cable management systems are worth the investment. Use cable trays for running cables in the ceiling. A cable tray is a lightweight, bridge-like structure for containing the cables in a building.

CERTIFICATION SUMMARY

This chapter explored the tools and techniques for troubleshooting networks and preventive maintenance for networks. The tools discussed included physical and software status indicators, command-line utilities, toner probe, loopback plugs, punch down tools, crimpers, and cable testers. In this chapter, you learned strategies for using commands to analyze network problems.

A problem that may appear to be caused by insufficient bandwidth may actually be caused by inefficient use of bandwidth, and you solve this by removing unnecessary protocol suites from computers and network devices, such as print servers.

Analyze network connectivity problems based on error messages or other symptoms. If you see no obvious source for the problem, check the hardware, beginning with the NIC, cables, hubs, switches, WAPs, and routers. Check for any source of EMI. If you detect no physical source of a problem, check the IP configuration of the NIC and correct any errors you find.

Use command-prompt utilities to reveal the IP configuration, test connectivity, locate a bottleneck on the Internet, reveal statistics about the TCP/IP protocols and network connections involving the local computer, and detect DNS problems.

Most preventive maintenance for network devices is identical to that for computers. There are some special considerations for the servers, network devices, and the cabling, for which preventive maintenance begins with providing a proper and secure environment and carefully organizing the cabling and the cable runs through ceilings and walls. Restrict access to network-specific devices to protect them from people with no professional reason to be in contact with the servers or network equipment.

 ## TWO-MINUTE DRILL

Here are some of the key points covered in Chapter 16.

Troubleshooting Common Network Problems

- ❑ A group of command-prompt utilities installs with the TCP/IP protocol suite. Among them are IPCONFIG, PING, TRACERT, NETSTAT, NBTSTAT, and NSLOOKUP.
- ❑ Use the /? switch with any command-prompt utility to learn about the variety of subcommands and parameters that alter the behavior of the utility.

❏ Status indicators for network hardware include LED lights on physical devices and/ or status information from software installed along with the driver.

❏ A quick glance at indicator lights on a device or icons and messages on the computer screen reveals valuable information.

❏ The typical NIC installs with a configuration utility that you can open from an icon in the notification area of the taskbar. A change in status or hovering your mouse over this icon will cause a message to appear over the notification area.

❏ A cable tester connects to the ends of a cable and sends a signal down the cable in order to detect breaks in it.

❏ You can use a wireless locator to identify the source of wireless interference and to optimize WAP configuration.

❏ Sometimes simply restarting the WAP/broadband router solves connectivity issues.

❏ Media Access Control (MAC) address filtering might be preventing WLAN connections.

❏ Wireless encryption settings and passphrases must match on both the WAP and the wireless client.

❏ Make sure you are using the correct updated wireless NIC driver.

❏ A degraded wireless signal could be due to interference in the same frequency range, atmospheric conditions, or physical obstructions.

❏ Some antimalware and firewall programs can cause problems with wireless connections—check their configuration.

❏ Use the IPCONFIG command to check the IP configuration.

❏ Use the PING command to test for connectivity to another host.

❏ Find a network bottleneck on a routed network (like the Internet) using the TRACERT command.

❏ Use the NETSTAT command to view statistics about connections to the local computer.

❏ The NET command performs a variety of tasks, such as starting and stopping services.

❏ Troubleshoot DNS problems with PING and NSLOOKUP, as well as IPCONFIG.

❏ One way to increase network bandwidth is to remove unnecessary protocol suites from the network. Check computers for unneeded protocol suites and other network devices, such as print servers, which may come with several protocols enabled.

❏ A more costly method of increasing network bandwidth is to upgrade hardware. Consider changing all the network hardware (NICs, switches, cabling, etc.) to hardware capable of higher speeds than the existing equipment.

❏ When troubleshooting network connectivity problems, physically check the local network hardware. Next, check the status of the NIC driver in the Properties dialog box for the NIC.

Preventive Maintenance for Networks

❑ Preventive maintenance for network devices, such as NICs, hubs, switches, WAPs, and routers, is identical to what we described in Chapter 11 for computers.

❑ Do not overload circuits, and provide reliable power using power protection devices, as described in Chapter 1. Consider using a dedicated circuit for the most critical equipment.

❑ Locate servers and network devices in a dedicated space, such as a room or closet. Make sure the environment in this space is appropriate, and restrict access to the equipment.

❑ Secure, protect, and organize network cabling by using patch panels in the closet or room housing the network devices and by using cable management systems, such as cable trays for horizontal runs through ceilings.

SELF TEST

The following questions will help you measure your understanding of the material presented in this chapter. Read all of the choices carefully because there might be more than one correct answer. Choose all correct answers for each question.

Troubleshooting Common Network Problems

1. You suspect a network port on a switch is not functioning correctly. The indicator lights for the switch port look correct. How can you determine whether or not the switch port is working?
   A. Test with a loopback plug.
   B. Use a toner probe.
   C. Reboot the switch.
   D. Use a wireless locator.

2. What category of tool is the handiest and least expensive for troubleshooting problems with a variety of causes from those local to the computer to sources on the Internet?
   A. Status indicators
   B. Command-line utilities
   C. Ethernet NICs
   D. Cable testers

3. Which of the following is a command-line utility you would use to release a DHCP-allocated IP address from a local NIC?
   A. NBTSTAT
   B. PING

    C.   IPCONFIG

    D.   NSLOOKUP

4. What tool would you use if you suspected that a cable contained broken wires?

    A.   Cable ping

    B.   Cable tester

    C.   Status indicator

    D.   LED

5. When you see a blinking green LED (labeled "Link"), what does it usually mean?

    A.   1000 Mbps connection

    B.   100 Mbps connection

    C.   Network activity

    D.   Broken cable

6. What should you look for first on a network that seems to have a bandwidth problem?

    A.   Unnecessary protocol suites

    B.   Unnecessary servers

    C.   Unnecessary network printers

    D.   Unnecessary print servers

7. How can you quickly view the IP configuration information for all the network adapters in your computer?

    A.   Open the Network Connection Details dialog box.

    B.   Run **netstat**.

    C.   Run **ipconfig /renew**.

    D.   Run **ipconfig /all**.

8. Which of the following devices reduces network traffic within an Ethernet LAN?

    A.   Hub

    B.   Switch

    C.   Router

    D.   NIC

9. How would you check the signal strength received by a wireless NIC? Select all that apply.

    A.   Check indicator lights on the wireless NIC.

    B.   Check indicator lights on the WAP.

    C.   Open the NIC's program from the notification area.

    D.   Run **ipconfig**.

10. Which tool will show you the status of nearby Wi-Fi networks?

    A.   Punch down tool

    B.   NETSTAT

    C.   Toner probe

    D.   Wireless locator

11. What is the result of mixing Ethernet and Fast Ethernet hardware?
    A. Transmissions at 100 Mbps
    B. Transmissions at 10 Mbps
    C. Transmissions at 1 Gbps
    D. Transmissions at 10 Gbps

12. The distance between a WAP and one group of wireless hosts causes the signal to degrade so badly that the transmissions are too slow and users are complaining. What can you do?
    A. Install a signal booster.
    B. Upgrade all the wireless devices to a faster speed.
    C. Install an Ethernet network.
    D. Install a router.

13. Which type of server automatically assigns IP addresses to hosts?
    A. DHCP
    B. WINS
    C. DNS
    D. APIPA

14. What command can you use to force a DHCP client to request an IP address assignment?
    A. **ping localhost**
    B. **ipconfig /renew**
    C. **ipconfig /all**
    D. **tracert**

15. A user complains that an Internet connection to a website she needs to access for her work is extremely slow. Which of the following commands will you use first to analyze the problem?
    A. NETSTAT
    B. IPCONFIG
    C. TRACERT
    D. NSLOOKUP

16. Which of the following command-line utilities would *not* help when troubleshooting a possible DNS problem?
    A. NBTSTAT
    B. PING
    C. IPCONFIG
    D. NSLOOKUP

17. How do you stop the output from a PING command in which you used the -t switch?
    A. Type **exit**.
    B. Press the CTRL-C key combination.
    C. Type **pause**.
    D. Press the CTRL-BREAK key combination.

18. When you ping this name, you are pinging the loopback network interface as a test of the local NIC to see if it is functioning.
- A. server
- B. echo
- C. localhost
- D. gateway

Preventive Maintenance for Networks

19. Which of the following is the preferred environment for network equipment and servers in a law office?
- A. A broom closet
- B. A reception desk
- C. A dedicated, climate-controlled room
- D. A conference room

20. You need to run a group of wires through a suspended ceiling. What should you use to keep the wires organized within the ceiling area?
- A. An equipment rack
- B. A UPS
- C. Cable wraps
- D. Cable trays

SELF TEST ANSWERS

Troubleshooting Common Network Problems

1. ☑ **A.** You should use a loopback plug to test a questionable switch port. It will need an RJ-45 connector.

☒ **B** is incorrect because a toner probe is used to identify unlabeled cables. **C** is incorrect because rebooting will not identify a faulty switch port. **D** is incorrect because a wireless locator can only identify wireless networks.

2. ☑ **B.** Command-line utilities are the handiest and least expensive network troubleshooting tools for a wide range of problems.

☒ **A** is incorrect because although status indicators are handy for detecting problems local to the computer (NIC) or its local connection, they are not useful for problems far removed from the computer. **C** is incorrect because Ethernet NICs are network devices, not troubleshooting tools. **D** is incorrect because although cable testers are good troubleshooting tools for local problems, they are not the handiest or least expensive compared to the command-line utilities.

3. ☑ **C.** Use IPCONFIG to release a DHCP-allocated IP address from a NIC (**ipconfig /release**, which you would normally follow with **ipconfig /renew** to renew the address).

☒ **A** is incorrect because NBTSTAT lets you work with the NetBIOS name lists and caches, but does not release an IP address. **B** is incorrect because PING tests a connection between two hosts. **D** is incorrect because NSLOOKUP tests for DNS problems.

4. ☑ **B.** You would use a cable tester if you suspected that a cable had broken wires.

☒ **A** is incorrect because such a tool was not even mentioned and may not exist. **C** and **D** are both incorrect because neither is a tool you would use if you suspected that a cable was bad, although they would supply the clue that such a problem exists.

5. ☑ **C.** Network activity is usually indicated by a blinking green LED.

☒ **A** and **B** are both incorrect, although a multispeed NIC may have a separate Link light for each speed. **D** is incorrect because a cable break would probably result in the Link light being off.

6. ☑ **A.** Unnecessary protocol suites are what you should look for first in a network that seems to have a bandwidth problem.

☒ **B, C,** and **D** are all incorrect because none of these contribute to bandwidth as much as unnecessary protocol suites.

7. ☑ **D.** Run **ipconfig /all** to quickly see the IP configuration information for all the network adapters in a computer.

☒ **A** is incorrect because this Windows Vista and 7 GUI only shows a single network connection at a time. **B** is incorrect because running **netstat** displays information on the open connections by protocol and port number. **C** is incorrect because running **ipconfig /renew** forces a DHCP client to send an IP address renewal request to a DHCP server.

8. ☑ **B.** A switch is the device that reduces network broadcasts in an Ethernet network.

☒ **A** is incorrect because a hub sends a packet to every port, which increases traffic, whereas a switch only sends packets to the destination port. **C** is incorrect because a router connects LANs, whereas a switch is within a LAN. It is true that a router will keep broadcast traffic from traveling between LANs. **D** is incorrect because a NIC is a network adapter, which is not a device that reduces network traffic.

9. ☑ **A and C.** The indicator lights on the wireless NIC and the NIC's program, available from the notification area, are both places where you could look for the signal strength received by a wireless NIC.

☒ **B** is incorrect because since the WAP is the source of the signals, indicator lights on the WAP do not indicate the strength of the signal received by a wireless NIC. **D** is incorrect because running **ipconfig** is not how you check the signal strength received by a wireless NIC.

10. ☑ **D.** A wireless locator will show you the status of nearby Wi-Fi networks.
    ☒ **A** is incorrect because a punch down tool is used to connect cabling to a punch down block. **B** is incorrect because NETSTAT is a command-line utility that provides statistical information about the TCP/IP protocols and network connections. **C** is incorrect because a toner probe is a hardware tool for locating both ends of a cable.

11. ☑ **B.** The result of mixing Ethernet (10 Mbps) and Fast Ethernet (100 Mbps) is transmissions at 10 Mbps.
    ☒ **A** is incorrect because the presence of the slower Ethernet devices will cause communications between the slower and faster devices to run at the slower rate. **C** and **D** are both incorrect because neither Ethernet nor Fast Ethernet runs at these speeds.

12. ☑ **A.** The solution to the degraded signal due to distance is to install a signal booster.
    ☒ **B** is incorrect because the question does not mention the standard of the device in use, and it may be at the highest level available. **C** is incorrect because a wireless network is often installed where it is not possible or practical to install a wired network. **D** is incorrect because installing a router would not solve the problem of the weak signal within the wireless LAN.

13. ☑ **A.** DHCP is the type of server that automatically assigns IP addresses to hosts.
    ☒ **B** is incorrect because a WINS server resolves NetBIOS names to IP addresses. **C** is incorrect because the DNS server resolves Internet domain names to IP addresses. **D** is incorrect because APIPA does not describe a server, but an IP address (beginning with 169.254) that a DHCP client can assign to itself if it does not get a response from a DHCP server.

14. ☑ **B.** You use the **ipconfig /renew** command to force a DHCP client to request an IP address assignment.
    ☒ **A** is incorrect because **ping localhost** is used to ping the local NIC. **C** is incorrect because **ipconfig /all** is used to look at the TCP/IP configuration. **D** is incorrect because **tracert** displays a trace of the route taken by packets to the destination.

15. ☑ **C.** TRACERT is the command to use to analyze the problem of a slow connection to a website.
    ☒ **A, B,** and **D** are all incorrect because none of these is the correct command to analyze the problem described.

16. ☑ **A.** NBTSTAT would not help when troubleshooting a possible DNS problem, because NBTSTAT is for working with the NetBIOS naming system.
    ☒ **B, C,** and **D** are all useful when troubleshooting a possible DNS problem.

17. ☑ **B.** Pressing CTRL-C will stop the command and return you to the prompt.
    ☒ **A, C,** and **D** are all incorrect because none of these will stop the command output.

18. ☑ **C.** localhost is the name of the loopback network interface, and pinging it tests the NIC.
    ☒ **A, B,** and **D** are all incorrect because none of them is the name of the loopback network interface.

Preventive Maintenance for Networks

19. ☑   **C.** A dedicated, climate-controlled room is the preferred environment for network equipment and servers in any organization.
☒   **A, B,** and **D** are all incorrect; they are unsuitable locations because they do not restrict access to the equipment and do not provide the correct climate-controlled environment.

20. ☑   **D.** You should use cable trays to keep the wires organized within the ceiling area.
☒   **A** is incorrect because an equipment rack is not used within ceiling areas. **B** is incorrect because a UPS is a power protection device, not something for organizing cables. **C** is incorrect because although you could use cable wraps to organize cables, they are not the best solution for organizing cables within the ceiling (nor mentioned in the chapter).

Chapter 17

Computer Security Fundamentals

Windows and other modern operating systems have a long list of security features, as well as other features we add to our operating systems. That's good, because it's a dangerous world out there. Malware, worms, exploits, shoulder surfing, phishing, social engineering…it seems like there is a criminal lurking around every corner, just waiting to sabotage your computer or steal your private information. It's not paranoia if everyone really *is* out to get you.

This is the first of two chapters on security. This chapter surveys the overall threat landscape and provides some guidance in preventing threats to physical security. Chapter 18 looks at methods of safeguarding data security.

CERTIFICATION OBJECTIVE

■ **902: 3.1** *Identify common security threats and vulnerabilities*

CompTIA A+ 902 exam objective 3.1 requires that you compare and contrast common security threats, including social engineering, many types of viruses and malware, rootkits, phishing, shoulder surfing, spyware, and password-guessing attacks. Learn about these threats in this section. This section also provides a bit of info about the symptoms of browser and e-mail hijacking mentioned in A+ 902 exam objective 4.2. (Solutions to those and other problems are covered in Chapter 18.)

Security Threats

We need to understand security threats in order to put security concepts, technologies, and features into context and then to implement strategies for protecting against those threats. What are the threats? In this section, we list and describe some that affect individuals and entire organizations, beginning with hardware theft and disaster threats. Then we look at threats to individuals in the form of inappropriate content and invasion of privacy that can also include identity theft. You'll learn about malicious software attacks and the long list of vectors (methods) they use to infect our computers, and then consider a list of threats that may or may not do damage (grayware). Finally, we'll consider the various methods used to gain access or gather information.

Computer Hardware Theft

People steal an astounding number of computers, especially laptops, tablets, and other mobile devices, each year from businesses, homes, and automobiles. The result is loss of important tools and valuable data files—and perhaps even a loss of identity, not to mention the downtime until equipment is replaced and programs and data are restored. At one time, most computer equipment thieves simply wanted to sell the hardware quickly for cash—at a fraction of the value of your computer and data to you or your business. Today, thieves realize the value of the data itself, so the data may be their main objective in stealing hardware; they will go through your hard drive looking for bank account, credit card, and other financial data so they can steal your identity.

Disasters, Big and Small

Accidents and mistakes happen. It seems as if everyone has at one time or another accidentally erased an important file, pressed the wrong button at the wrong instant, or created a file and thereafter forgotten its name and location. To the person who made the error, this is a disaster.

Disasters happen in many forms. Just to name a few, there are fires, earthquakes, and weather-induced disasters resulting from tornados, lightning strikes, and floods. There is, of course, the possibility of a disaster of an even greater magnitude, such as a nuclear explosion, with the obvious consequences of a bomb, but also with the resulting electromagnetic pulse (EMP). This huge burst of electromagnetic energy has the potential to damage communications and power lines over a large geographic area, depending on the size of the pulse and the proximity to electrical lines and equipment. Predicting such events is imperfect at best. The principal protection against accidents, mistakes, and disasters is to make frequent, comprehensive backups.

Threats to Individuals

All the threats described in this chapter affect individuals, but certain threats specifically target them. These threats include exposure to inappropriate content and invasion of privacy, which includes the worst threat: identity theft.

Exposure to Inappropriate Content

The Internet, and especially the World Wide Web, is a treasure trove of information. It is hard to imagine a subject that cannot be found somewhere on the Internet. However, some of this content is inappropriate or distasteful. What is inappropriate or distasteful content? To some extent, only an individual can judge, but there are many circumstances in which an individual or groups should be shielded from certain content.

Invasion of Privacy and Identity Theft

Many of the threats are also clearly invasions of privacy. Protecting against privacy invasion includes protecting your personal information at your bank, credit union, retail stores, websites, health clinics, and any organization where you are a customer, member, patient, or employee. Every step you take to make your computer more secure contributes to the protection of your privacy.

Perhaps the worst form of invasion of privacy is *identity theft*, which occurs when someone collects personal information belonging to another person and uses that information to fraudulently make purchases, open new credit accounts, and even obtain new driver's licenses and other forms of identification in the victim's name. All the thieves need is your Social Security number and other key personal information to steal your identity. They can do this by physically accessing your computer, by accessing it via the Internet, or by many other low-tech means. Several websites maintained by the U.S. government offer valuable information for consumers who wish to protect themselves from identify theft.

Malicious Software Attacks

Malicious software, or *malware*, attacks are, sadly, now common on both private and public networks. Someone who initiates these malicious attacks is commonly called a *hacker* or *cracker*. They make an avocation or vocation out of creating ways to invade computers and networks. At one time, this term "hacker" described a clever programmer, or anyone who enjoyed exploring the software innards of computers.

You probably have heard of many types of software threats against computers, such as viruses, worms, Trojan horses, or spam. But have you ever heard of pop-up downloads, drive-by downloads, war driving, Bluesnarfing, adware, spyware, rootkits, backdoors, spim, phishing, or hoaxes? Do you know the difference between a vector and malware? Read on to learn about the many vectors and the various forms of deliberate attacks.

Viruses

A *virus* is a program installed and activated on a computer without the knowledge or permission of the user. At the least, the intent is mischief, but most often, the intent is malicious. Like a living virus that infects humans, a computer virus can result in a wide range of symptoms and outcomes. Loss of data, damage to or complete failure of an operating system, and theft of personal and financial information are just a few of the results of viruses infecting an individual computer. If you extend the range of a virus to a corporate or government network or portions of the Internet, the results can be devastating and costly in lost productivity, lost data, lost revenues, and more.

Denial-of-Service Attacks

Hackers and others with malicious intent have many methods for attacking network servers, and most of these techniques are beyond the scope of the CompTIA A+ 220-901 and 220-902 exams. However, two types of threats to servers are in the CompTIA A+ Acronyms list at the end of both the CompTIA A+ 220-901 and 220-902 Exam Objectives. They are DoS and DDoS. A *denial-of-service (DoS) attack* occurs when someone sends a large number of requests to a server, overwhelming it so it stops functioning on the network and therefore denying service to all other traffic. A *distributed denial-of-service (DDoS) attack* occurs when a massive number (as many as hundreds of thousands) of computers send DoS attacks to a server, making it unavailable to legitimate users.

Rootkits

A *rootkit* is malware that hides itself from detection by antimalware programs by concealing itself within the operating system (OS) code or any other program running on the computer. Someone with administrator (root) access to the computer first installs a rootkit; then the rootkit is used as a vector to install any type of malware to quietly carry out its mission.

watch For CompTIA A+ 902 exam objective 2.2, be sure you know that a rootkit hides within the OS code.

Malware Vectors

A *vector* is any method by which malware gains access to a computer or network. While some malware may use just a single vector, multivector malware uses an array of methods to infect computers and networks. Sometimes it is difficult to separate the vector from the malware, but we'll try. Let's look at a few well-known vectors. The first two, Trojan horses and worms, are each both a vector and virus.

on the job "Vector" is not a term you will see in the objectives for the CompTIA A+ 220-901 and 220-902 exams, but it is part of what you need to understand about how computers become infected so that you can work to educate yourself and others.

Trojan Horse A *Trojan horse*, often simply called a Trojan, is both a type of malware and a vector. The modern-day Trojan horse program gains access to computers much like the ancient Greek warriors who, in Homer's famous tale *The Iliad*, gained access to the city of Troy by hiding in a large wooden horse, presented as a gift to the city (a Trojan horse). A Trojan horse program installs and activates on a computer by appearing to be a harmless program that the user innocently installs. It may appear as just a useful free program that a user downloads and installs, but it is a common way for malware to infect your system. One common example is a pop-up window that looks very official, like it is part of your OS, especially since it is titled Windows Advanced Security Center. This is an example of a *rogue antivirus*. It pretends to be an antivirus, but is actually a Trojan horse hiding malware. It states that it is scanning your computer and has already found threats. Then you may see a message box with a button labeled "Prevent Attack" or a message that you are using a trial version and must purchase the full version to ensure protection. Click Activate Ultimate Protection, and you'll go to a website where you actually pay to install a Trojan on your computer. Some sources say this Trojan will steal your personal financial information. It also may install a proxy server to prevent access to the Internet.

Worm   A *worm* is a self-replicating virus. Worms travel between machines in many different ways. In recent years, several worms have moved from one computer to another as compressed (zipped) attachments to e-mail, but they can also be executable files. The file might have an innocent-sounding or enticing name to tempt the user to open and execute the program. Some of these worms, upon execution, scan the local address book and replicate themselves to the addresses. Variants of such worms as Netsky and MyDoom slowed down entire networks just through the amount of network traffic they generated.

CompTIA A+ 902 exam objective 3.1 lists just two types of viruses: worms and Trojans. Be sure you can distinguish between how each infects, even if the exam does not use the term "vector."

Zombie (Botnet)   A *zombie* is a computer that has been compromised by a virus or Trojan horse such that it becomes complicit in spreading problems throughout the network (or the Internet). For example, the malware with which it is infected might cause the computer to spread e-mail spam or launch denial-of-service attacks. A *botnet* is an army of zombies that collectively work to attack a system.

Ransomware   Some malware makes money for its owner by locking down an infected system and demanding that a ransom be paid to unlock it. This is known as *ransomware*. It might include dire warnings about having a certain limited amount of time to comply before the computer's contents will be deleted. Some ransomware purports to be from an official government agency, and accuses the computer user of having illegal content on their computer, such as child pornography.

Man-in-the-Middle   With this kind of attack, the attacking software (or person) secretly inserts itself between two parties in a secure conversation, gathering data from each. For example, one party might send an authentication code, and the other party might respond with the correct code to indicate its identity. If someone is spying on that conversation, he or she now knows both codes, and can thwart their mutual authentication, or can allow the authentication to take place and continue to spy on the conversation to collect additional sensitive data.

E-mail   Some malware infects computers via e-mail—mainly when the recipient opens an attachment or clicks a link. You may have believed it was always safe to open e-mail as long as you didn't open attachments, but the simple act of opening an e-mail containing the Nimda virus can infect a computer, depending on the software you are using to read the message. While most recent e-mail programs have protections against that particular virus and other known viruses, e-mail is still a potential vector, as long as people open attachments and click links.

The e-mail vector often depends on convincing you that it is in your interest to click a link, perhaps by stating that Microsoft or another software publisher is sending you an update. Don't fall for this; Microsoft never sends out updates through e-mail!

on the job   **Remember that Microsoft never sends out updates through e-mail!**

Malware Installation Code on Websites   Some malware infects computers by lurking in hidden code on websites. When an unsuspecting user browses to that site and clicks a link, it launches and installs malware on her computer without her knowledge. Clicking the link gives the program permission to run.

Searching for Unprotected Computers   An unprotected computer becomes a vector when discovered by malware that searches for computers with security flaws. The malware takes advantage of the flaws to install itself on the computer, and then uses that computer to gain access throughout a private network.

Backdoor   In computing, a *backdoor* bypasses authentication security so someone can gain access to a computer. Sometimes a program's author installs a backdoor into a single program so she can easily access it later for administering and/or troubleshooting the program code. Or an attacker may create a backdoor by taking advantage of a discovered weakness in a program. Then any program using the backdoor can run in the security context of the invaded program and infect a computer with malware. In one well-known situation, the Code Red worm took advantage of a specific vulnerability in Microsoft's Internet Information Services (IIS) to install a backdoor. The result was that the worm displayed a message on every web page on the IIS server. The message included the phrase, "Hacked by Chinese." Then, the Nimda worm took advantage of the backdoor left by the Code Red worm to infect computers.

Pop-up Download   A *pop-up* is a separate window that displays (pops up) uninvited from a web page. The purpose of a pop-up may be as simple as an advertisement, but some pop-ups can be vectors for malware. A *pop-up download* is a program downloaded to a user's computer through a pop-up page. It requires an action on the part of a user, such as clicking a button that implies acceptance of something such as free information, although what that something may actually be is not usually clear. The program that downloads may be a virus or a worm.

Drive-by Download   A *drive-by download* is a program downloaded to a computer without consent. Often the simple act of browsing to a website, or opening a Hypertext Markup Language (HTML) e-mail message, may result in such a surreptitious download.

A drive-by download may also occur when installing another application. This is particularly true of certain file-sharing programs that users install to share music, data, or photo files over the Internet. Some drive-by downloads may alter your web browser home page and/or redirect all your browser searches to one site. A drive-by download may also install a virus, a worm, or even more likely, adware or spyware (described later in this chapter).

Browser Hijacking   We received a call the other day from Dave, a finance officer at a large farm-implement company. Every time he opened Internet Explorer, the home page pointed to a site advertising adware removal software. This is an example of *browser hijacking* (which A+ 902 exam objective 4.2 calls *browser redirection*), a practice that has been growing. Browser hijacker malware infected his Internet browser, changing or redirecting the home page. It is not always about selling you adware removal software; there can be many reasons for browser hijacking. Sometimes the hijackers do it so that a website will register more visitors and the owners of the site can raise their rates to advertisers.

Dave was able to reverse this by changing the default page in Internet Options, but it was very annoying. He was lucky; sometimes hijackers make it very difficult to defeat the hijack by modifying the registry so that every time you restart Windows or Internet Explorer, the hijack reinstates. Or you may even find that a registry change makes Internet Options unavailable. Chapter 18 provides some suggestions for recovering from this.

E-mail Hijacking   Every week it seems like another friend or two has their e-mail account hijacked, and these accounts are most often with one of the main Internet-based e-mail providers, such as Yahoo! or Gmail. E-mail hijacking occurs when someone gains access to your e-mail account by using some method to obtain the password, and then uses the account to send messages out to your entire contact list. This may be a one-time occurrence, or it may happen over and over again.

What are the symptoms? To the recipients of the e-mail, the symptoms are most often a message with no subject line and the only content is a link. This is the most primitive use, but it can be effective, since if the hijacker does this on hundreds or thousands of accounts (they seem to have automated systems), sending messages out to all the contacts, the odds are many recipients will click the link. This could result in installing malware, or it may simply be that the hijacker is being paid for the number of clicks on a page.

Other e-mail hijackers are more sophisticated and send out messages with compelling subject lines, posing as your friends and claiming that they are stranded in a foreign country and need money wired to them immediately.

The way most people find out their e-mail has been hacked is by receiving concerned and puzzled replies from friends regarding suspicious e-mail they received from the compromised account. A person whose e-mail has been hacked may also receive automated replies from unknown recipients who have an auto-reply set up because they are out of the office or their e-mail account is temporarily out of service.

See Chapter 18 for some possible solutions, the most important of which is to change your e-mail password.

Vulnerabilities and Exploits

When an application or operating system has a security flaw that exposes it to potential compromise by malware, that's called a *vulnerability*. When such an attack actually occurs, it's called an *exploit*.

Computer criminals are constantly on the lookout for holes in OS and application software that can be exploited, and of course the makers of those software products are constantly looking too, so they can issue fixes before some malicious person finds the vulnerability. When the hacker discovers and exploits a vulnerability before the software vendor is aware that the vulnerability exists, it's called a *zero-day attack* because the vendor has zero days to patch the vulnerability before the attack.

In most large networks, there are policies for keeping computers up to date and keeping security settings consistent across all PCs and departments. For example, an IT department might require all PCs on the network to run a certain kind of antivirus software, or to disable automatic updating of the OS in favor of updates implemented on a precise schedule. When a PC on the network has changed settings that do not comply with the corporate policies, it is known as a *non-compliant system*.

CompTIA A+ 902 exam objective 3.1 includes the terms "non-compliant systems" and "violations of security best practices." You should be able to explain why non-compliant systems pose a security risk to a network.

When a new computer joins the network, such as a laptop someone has brought from home, it doesn't usually have the security policies and settings specified by the IT department, and is known as a *rogue system*. Both non-compliant and rogue systems pose a security risk, not only because they can bring malware into the network, but also because they may violate security best practices that the IT professionals have worked hard to implement and standardize.

Grayware

The term *grayware* describes threats that are not truly malicious code but still have indirect negative effects, such as decreasing performance or using up bandwidth. Grayware is undesirable, and computers should have protection against grayware, which includes spyware, adware, spam, and spim.

Spyware

Spyware is a category of software that runs surreptitiously on a user's computer in order to gather information without his or her permission and then sends that information to the people who requested it. Internet-based spyware, sometimes called "tracking software" or "spybots," may be installed on a computer by one of many means of secretly installing software. A company may use spyware to trace users' surfing patterns in order to improve its marketing efforts. Some individuals use it for industrial espionage. With appropriate legal permissions, law enforcement officers use it to find sexual predators and other criminals. Governments use forms of spyware to investigate terrorism.

Adware

Adware, which also installs on a computer without permission, collects information about a user in order to display targeted advertisements, either in the form of inline banners or pop-ups. Inline banners are advertisements that run within the context of the current page, just taking up screen real estate. Pop-ups are a greater annoyance, because each ad runs in a separate browser window that you must close before you can continue with your task. Clicking an offer presented on an inline banner or pop-up may trigger a pop-up download that can install a virus or worm.

Spam and Spim

Spam is unsolicited e-mail. This includes e-mail from a legitimate source selling a real service or product, but if you did not give the source permission to send such information to you, it is spam. Too often spam involves some form of scam—a bogus offer to sell a service or product that does not exist or that tries to include you in a complicated moneymaking deal. If it sounds too good to be true, it is! We call spam perpetrators *spammers*, and spam is illegal in many places. Some corporate network administrators report that as much as 60 percent of the incoming e-mail traffic is spam. Most often, spam is a vector for social engineering, but it can also be used to deliver malware to your computer. Spam accounts for a huge amount of traffic on the Internet and private networks, and a great loss in productivity as administrators work to protect their users from spam and individuals sort through and eliminate spam. Use the steps in Exercise 17-1 to research spam statistics.

EXERCISE 17-1

Research Spam Statistics

Find out the latest bad news on the amount of Internet e-mail identified as spam. Try this:

1. Open your browser and connect to your favorite search engine, such as Google, Bing, or Chrome.
2. Search on the words "spam statistics." For a more targeted search, include the current year in your search string.
3. In the results list, many of the links will be for antispam programs that provide individual statistics. Review the results and select a link that appears to give actual statistics on spam occurrences for Internet e-mail users. Discuss the results with your classmates.

Spim is an acronym for *sp*am over *i*nstant *m*essaging, and the perpetrators are spimmers. Small programs, called *bots* (short for robot, a program that runs automatically) and sent out over the Internet to collect information, often collect instant messaging screen names. The spimbot then sends unsolicited instant messages to the screen names. A typical spim message may contain a link to a website, where, like spam, the recipient will find products or services for sale, legitimate or otherwise.

Methods for Gaining Access and Obtaining Information

People can gain access to computers and networks through a variety of techniques that include both physical access and malicious software and grayware. Here are just a few methods.

Piggybacking and Tailgating

Physical security can include restricting access to any area by having doors guarded, requiring security badges, and using a passkey of some sort to access the area. *Piggybacking* is when someone follows an authorized person into a secure area with their consent. When someone does the same thing without the authorized person's consent, perhaps slipping into a door behind the authorized person, it is *tailgating*.

Shoulder Surfing

One method people use to gain access to your bank account, computer and corporate network, and secure physical areas is by *shoulder surfing* to steal your security code, passcode, or other security credentials as you enter them, or even as you write them on a form. The most primitive example is someone peering over your shoulder to see the keystrokes you enter at the checkout counter, ATM cash machine, or the entrance to a secure building. The thief may literally be standing at your shoulder, or may be at a distance using binoculars. More sophisticated implementations include using cameras or devices attached to the security keypad itself to log the keystrokes and either save the information for later retrieval or transmit it wirelessly to the thief.

CompTIA A+ 902 exam objective 3.1 specifically lists the term "shoulder surfing." Be sure you understand how thieves use this to steal security credentials.

When sitting at your desk, your computer screen may also be a target of shoulder surfing, and the methods are the same as those used on ATM terminals.

Cookies: The Good and the Bad

Cookies are good—mostly. Under some circumstances people can use them for the wrong purposes, but for the most part, their benefits far outweigh the negatives. There is a great deal of misinformation about cookies, the small files a web browser saves on the local hard drive at the request of a website. The next time you connect to that same site, it will request the cookie saved on a previous visit. Cookies are text files, so they cannot contain viruses, which are executable code, but they may contain the following information:

- User preferences when visiting a specific site
- Information a user entered into a form at the website, including personal information
- Browsing activity
- Shopping selections on a website

The use of cookies is a convenience to users. Thanks to cookies, you do not have to reenter preferences and pertinent information on every visit to a favorite website. The cookies act as electronic notes about your preferences and activities within a website remembering selections you have made on each page so when you return to the page you do not have to reselect them. Just one example of this is when you are at a retail site and make selections that you add to your "shopping cart." In all likelihood, cookies save these selections, and when you decide to check out, the checkout page reads the cookie files to calculate your order.

Although users are not overtly aware when the website saves or retrieves cookies on the local hard disk, most good websites clearly detail whether they use cookies and what they use them for. Look for this information in the site's privacy policy statement.

Normally, only the website that created the cookies can access them; these are called *first-party cookies*. However, some advertisers on websites have the browser create cookies, and then other sites that include this advertiser can use them. These are *third-party cookies*.

If you dig around in your browser's settings, you will find not only the settings for controlling cookies, but a list of the cookies themselves. In Chapter 15 in the section "Controlling Cookies," you learned how to configure cookie settings in your browser. Figure 17-1 shows a list of websites with cookies saved by the Chrome browser. To find this list in Chrome, do the following:

1. Click the Customize and Control Google Chrome icon (the three dots) on the right of the navigation bar to open a menu.
2. Select Settings, which opens a Settings page within the browser window.
3. Scroll to the bottom and click Show Advanced Settings.
4. Scroll down to Privacy and click the Content Settings button.
5. On the Content Setting page, click All Cookies and Site Data.

Password Theft

People use a huge number of programs and techniques to steal passwords, and once they have one password, they have access to at least one source of information or money, and maybe more. We will explain a few of those techniques.

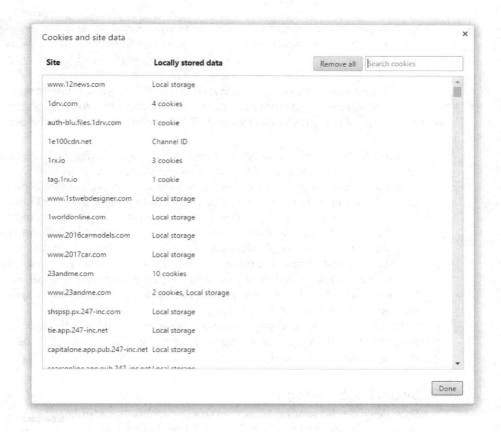

FIGURE 17-1

A list of saved cookies by site, with one site expanded

Unsecured Websites   One commonly used technique is to invade an unsecured website to access information unwitting users provide to the site, such as user names and passwords, and such personal information as account numbers, Social Security number, date and place of birth, and much more.

Password Crackers   A huge number of programs and techniques are available to people who want to discover passwords. In addition to invading an unsecured website, another technique is to use a *password cracker*, a program used to discover a password. Some password crackers fall into the *brute-force* category, which simply means the program tries a huge number of permutations of possible passwords. Because most people tend to use simple passwords such as their initials, birthdates, addresses, pets' names, and so on, the brute-force method often works. Other password crackers use more sophisticated statistical or mathematical methods to discover passwords. A *dictionary attack* is a password cracking attempt that systematically tries every word in a dictionary as the password. (It is surprising and disappointing how often this works, as many people don't use strong passwords.)

If you enter the words "password cracker" into your favorite search engine, you will discover that there are password crackers for every operating system, every type of computing device, and all the social networking services in use today.

Keystroke Loggers   A *keystroke logger* (also called a *keylogger*) is either a hardware device or a program that monitors and records a user's every keystroke, usually without their knowledge. In the case of a hardware logger, the person desiring the keystroke log must physically install it on the computer before recording keystrokes, and must then remove it afterward in order to collect the stored log of keystrokes. Some keyloggers transmit pressed keystroke data in real time wirelessly to a receiver unit. A software keystroke logger program may not require physical access to the target computer, but simply a method for downloading and installing it on the computer. Any one of several methods—for instance, a pop-up downloader or drive-by downloader (see the preceding sections)—can be used to install a keystroke logger. A keystroke logger can send the collected information over a network to the person desiring the log.

Some parents install keystroke loggers to monitor children's Internet activity, but such programs have the potential for abuse by people with less benign motives, including stalking, identity theft, and more.

Social Engineering

Social engineering encompasses a variety of persuasion techniques used for many purposes—both good and bad. People with malicious intent use social engineering to persuade someone to reveal confidential information or give something else of value to the perpetrator. The information sought may be confidential corporate data, personal identifying or financial information, user names and passwords, or anything you can imagine that could be of value to another person.

Social engineering is as old as *Homo sapiens*, and there are countless techniques employed; everyone should learn to recognize these techniques, all of which depend on the natural trusting behavior of the targeted people. Once you understand the forms of social engineering threats, you are less likely to become a victim. We will now explore social engineering threats and appropriate responses. On the Internet, the most common vehicle for social engineering communications is e-mail.

The best response to any form of social engineering is to not respond and/or not reveal any information. And you should never send money in response to a communication from a stranger, no matter how enticing the offer may be.

Fraud   *Fraud* is the use of deceit and trickery to persuade someone to hand over money or valuables. Fraud is often associated with identity theft, because the perpetrator will falsely pose as the owner of the victim's credit cards and other personal and financial information.

Phishing   *Phishing* is a fraudulent method of obtaining personal and financial information through pop-ups, e-mail, and even letters mailed via the Postal Service that purport to be from a legitimate organization, such as a bank, credit card company, retailer, and so on. They often (falsely) appear to be from well-known organizations and websites, such as various banks, eBay, PayPal, MSN, Yahoo!, Best Buy, or America Online. As such, the typical phishing attack relies on a *hoax*, meaning that it uses deception and lies to gain your confidence.

In a typical phishing scenario, the message will contain authentic-looking logos, and an e-mail may even link to the actual site, but the link specified for supplying personal financial information will take recipients to a "spoofed" web page that asks them to enter their personal data. The web page may look exactly like the company's real web page, but it's not the legitimate site. A common practice is for a phisher to use the credit card information to make purchases over the Internet, choosing items that are easy to resell, and having them delivered to an address unconnected to the phisher, such as a vacant house to which he has access.

Phishing schemes can be very clever, and can involve the forgery of an e-mail header so that the message appears to have originated from a legitimate source. This forgery is called *spoofing*.

Spear phishing is phishing that targets a specific organization, seeking access to confidential data. Unlike a regular phishing attempt, which is usually random and sent to millions of e-mail addresses, spear phishing attacks are targeted to gain access to a certain system for the purpose of gaining specific information.

Be very suspicious of e-mails requesting personal financial information, such as access codes, Social Security numbers, or passwords. Legitimate businesses will never ask you for personal financial information in an e-mail.

To learn more about phishing, and to see the latest examples, point your web browser to www.antiphishing.org, the website of the Anti-Phishing Working Group (APWG), which reports that every possible measurement of phishing activity shows huge increases. For instance, the number of unique phishing websites detected in March 2016 was 123,555. You can report phishing attacks at this site.

Would you recognize a phishing e-mail? There are websites that work to educate people to recognize a phishing scam when they receive it in e-mail or other communications. Exercise 17-2 describes how to use just one of these sites.

EXERCISE 17-2

What Is Your Phishing IQ?

You can test your Phishing IQ and learn to identify phishing scams.

1. Use your web browser to connect to the Phishing IQ test at www.sonicwall.com/ phishing.
2. You will see ten e-mails, one at a time. You must decide whether each is legitimate or phish.
3. When you finish, you can review the correct answers, along with a detailed explanation as to why each is either legitimate or phish.

If you completed Exercise 17-2, you will have noticed that phishing e-mails look very official, but in some cases, careful scrutiny reveals problems. Although the signs identified in these messages are not the full extent of the problems you can find in a phishing e-mail, this type of test helps to educate people so they do not become victims of phishing.

Although not all phishing e-mails have the same characteristics, the following lists just a few problems detected in phishing e-mails:

- The "To:" field is not your address, even though it appeared in your inbox.
- There is no greeting, or the greeting omits your name.
- The message text shows bad grammar or punctuation.
- When you click a link, the Uniform Resource Locator (URL) you are directed to does not match what appears in the e-mail.
- A link does not use Hypertext Transfer Protocol Secure (HTTPS).
- The title bar reveals that a foreign character set (e.g., Cyrillic) is used.
- What appears to be a protected account number (revealing only the last four digits) is not your number at all.
- What appears to be an account expiration date is not the correct expiration date for your account.
- A URL has a slightly misspelled domain name that resembles the legitimate domain name.
- There is no additional contact information, such as a toll-free phone number and a name and title of a contact person.

Now, to make things more confusing, some legitimate e-mails may show some of these problems or practices, and not all phishing e-mails have all of these negative characteristics.

A safer way to include a URL in a legitimate e-mail is not to make it a link, but to include it in the e-mail as unformatted text, with instructions to cut and paste it into a web browser. This way, malware cannot redirect you to a bogus website, but you must still be diligent and examine the URL before using it.

Phone Phishing   Phone phishing is another form of phishing. In order to gain the intended victim's confidence, a phishing e-mail will urge the reader to call a phone number to verify information, at which point the person on the phone will ask the victim to reveal the valuable information.

What makes this so compelling to the user is that phone phishing often involves a very authentic-sounding professional Interactive Voice Response (IVR) menu system, just like a legitimate financial institute would have. It may ask the user to enter his password or personal identifying number (PIN). To ensure that the system captures the correct password or PIN, the system may even ask the victim to repeat it. Some systems then have the victim talk to a "representative" who gathers more information.

Keep yourself up to date on the latest threats. Microsoft, Symantec, Trend Micro, and other software vendors, particularly those who specialize in security products, offer a wealth of information on their websites. You can also subscribe to newsletters from these same organizations.

Enticements to Open Attachments   Social engineering is also involved in the enticements—called "gimmes" in e-mails, either in the subject line or the body of the e-mail—to open the attachments. Opening the attachment then executes and infects the local computer with some form of malware. There are a huge number of methods used. Sadly, enticements often appeal to basic characteristics in people, such as greed (an offer too good to be true), vanity (physical enhancements), or simple curiosity. Some bogus enticements appeal to people's sympathy and compassion by way of a nonexistent charity. Or the author of the e-mail will pose as a legitimate charity—anything to get you to open the attachment.

War Driving

War driving is the name given to the act of driving or walking through a neighborhood in a vehicle or on foot, using either a laptop equipped with Wi-Fi wireless network capability or a simple Wi-Fi sensor available for a few dollars from many sources. War drivers are searching for open hotspots, areas where a Wi-Fi network connects to the Internet without using security to keep out intruders. Using a practice called *war chalking*, a war driver may make a mark on a building where a hotspot exists. People "in the know" look for these marks to identify hotspots for their use.

People who use these hotspots without permission are trespassing, and, in addition to gaining Internet access, they can prey on unprotected computers on the wireless network. With this access to the network, the intruder can capture keystrokes, passwords, and user names. Further, if the wireless network connects to an organization's internal wired network, the intruder may gain access to the resources on that network.

Intentionally created hotspots are increasing in number as more and more are made available for free or for a small charge by various businesses, such as coffee shops, bookstores, restaurants, hotels, and even campgrounds and truck stops. In fact, city-size areas are now hotspots made with overlapping Wi-Fi signals.

Bluesnarfing

Similar to war driving, *Bluesnarfing* is the act of covertly obtaining information broadcast from wireless devices using the Bluetooth standard. Using a cell phone with Bluetooth enabled, a Bluesnarfer can eavesdrop to acquire information, or even use the synchronizing feature of the device to pick up the user's information without being detected by the victim. To minimize this risk, turn off Bluetooth on mobile devices whenever it is not in use.

SCENARIO & SOLUTION

Why is it important not to use a word from a dictionary as a password?	Password cracking programs use dictionary lists to guess passwords; if your password is in the dictionary, it'll be quickly guessed by such a program.
How can you tell if an e-mail message you get from your bank is a phishing message?	Banks do not send out requests for information via e-mail. Any such request you receive is phishing.
Why is it important to install OS updates?	OSs can contain security vulnerabilities, and if a hacker finds them before the vendor does, the hacker can develop exploits and launch a zero-day attack. Installing OS updates ensures that all available security patches are applied, minimizing the risk of attack from exploits.

CERTIFICATION OBJECTIVES

- **902: 3.2** *Compare and contrast common prevention methods*
- **902: 3.6** *Given a scenario, use appropriate data destruction and disposal methods*

CompTIA A+ 902 exam objective 3.2 has four topic areas. We will detail physical security in this section and describe digital security, user education/acceptable use policy, and the principle of least privilege, the other three topics in that objective, in Chapter 18.

CompTIA A+ 902 exam objective 3.6 includes tasks required to destroy the data on a computer when you no longer need that computer. Whether you are giving it away to be used again, moving it to another user's desk in your organization, or disposing of the equipment, you need to ensure that you are not giving away personal or organizational data. A portion of this objective is the physical destruction of the storage device, and we describe those tasks in this section. This objective also includes the use of software in the form of formatting, overwriting, and drive wiping, which we will cover in Chapter 18.

Defense Against Threats: Physical Security

Physical security begins when an individual approaches the entrance to a building or campus. The level of security and the lengths to which an organization will go to secure an area depend on what they are protecting. Many organizations do not require any type of authentication until an employee is logging on to their computer—which is digital security. Others secure only small areas of their buildings, while some require authentication before you can access a campus or larger geographic area. Think of a government installation, manufacturing facility, or research institute. In this section we will look at some methods used to prevent unauthorized physical access to areas ranging in size from a computer closet to an army base.

If an unauthorized person manages to gain access to one of these areas—how do they secure the documents? We will discuss the methods for securing digitally stored documents in Chapter 18, but what about the data visible on screens and on paper documents? That is another facet of physical security, and we will address that in this section as we examine methods to secure access to paper documents and on-screen data.

Lock Doors and Enforce Policies

Locked doors and physically secured computers are the best protection from computer hardware theft. You can achieve locked doors against unauthorized access with low-tech methods ranging from limiting distribution of keys to the physical locks to other methods as low tech as human guards at entrances examining conventional badges as people enter and leave, to high-tech solutions for authentication at entrances using smart cards, radio frequency identification (RFID) badges, key fobs, RSA tokens, or biometric authentication.

You can secure special equipment such as switches, routers, and servers inside locked areas, but the typical desktop computer or laptop cannot always be physically secured. There are devices for physically securing computers, such as kiosk enclosures, but you rarely see them in use except in high-risk environments, such as schools and public buildings.

For ultra high-security areas, a *mantrap* system of security doors may be implemented. A mantrap is a set of two locked doors where the first door must close before the second door can be opened. In an automatic mantrap, there may be ID required to open each door, or possibly two different kinds of ID, like a proximity smartcard and a PIN typed on a keypad.

A secured space can also be protected with an *entry control roster*. It can be as simple as a paper roster with a guard that ensures that every person entering the area sign in, or it can be an electronic record that documents the badge number or credentials of each person who uses an electronic system of authentication.

Cable Locks

You can secure both desktops and laptops to a hard point such as a bolted-down desk or an eyebolt in a wall using a locking cable. While a determined thief can get around this, given time and privacy, use of a locking cable dramatically cuts down on hardware "walking away." When locking down a desktop PC, make sure the cable passes through the metal frame of the case, and is not simply bolted to the outside of the case. Otherwise a thief could remove the case cover and take the PC chassis.

Many laptops have a special hole or socket in the side of the case designed to work with a cable lock. Kensington makes one very popular kind of lock, and the corresponding hole in many laptops is called a k-slot.

Preventing Piggybacking and Tailgating

Campuses and buildings with restricted areas need to guard against piggybacking and tailgating practices, mentioned earlier in the description of threats. If using guards, an organization must train them to not allow this. Authorized employees must agree not to participate in piggybacking (bringing in unauthorized people) and to watch out for people following them closely in the hopes of tailgating. Using surveillance video may be necessary, along with having personnel monitor the video and taking action, watching both who comes in and who leaves.

Badges

A simple paper or plastic ID badge, with photo, is a traditional method for gaining access to areas with security guards at entrances. But unless the badge also contains one of the other technologies discussed here, such as a smart card, or RFID, it is not very good security, especially in a large facility where the guards may not recognize individuals well enough to challenge badge holders.

Smart Card Authentication

A *smart card* is a plastic card, often the size of a credit card, that contains a microchip. The microchip can store information and perform functions, depending on the type of smart card. Some smart cards only store data, whereas others may have a variety of functions, including security cards for gaining physical access to facilities or logging on to computers and networks. If configuration of the Windows domain and local Windows computers allows acceptance of smart card logons, users may use this method of presenting credentials and logging on. The domain controllers require certain software security components, and the local computer must have a special piece of hardware called a *smart card reader* or card terminal. When the user inserts the card into the reader, the reader sends commands to the card in order to complete the authentication process. As is true of a bank cash card, the user may also need to enter a PIN into the keyboard in conjunction with the smart card. The two together comprise two-factor authentication.

 on the job   **Smart cards are supported in Windows Vista and newer.**

Setup will require the device itself and the drivers and other software for the device. Further, you must install a special service called *Certificate Services* on the domain controllers for the Windows domain. Once you have installed the reader and configured the domain controllers to support Certificate Services, users can log on to the computer. Inserting the card into the reader has the same effect as pressing the CTRL-ALT-DELETE key combination, which is normally required on a Windows computer logging on to a domain. Either action constitutes a *secure attention sequence (SAS)* that clears memory of certain types of viruses that may be lurking and waiting to capture a user name and password. Smart cards are a very secure and tamper-resistant method of authentication.

on the job   **Modern debit and credit chip cards are smart cards. While American banks have been slow to move away from the old magnetic-strip technology for credit and debit cards until recently, Europe moved to smart cards for debit and credit several years ago. These are considered safer than the magnetic-strip cards, which only require a signature.**

RFID Badges

Another variation of smart card authentication includes *radio frequency identification (RFID) badges*. These cards contain an RFID chip (also called an RFID tag) with a radio antenna that can be carried by employees to allow access to secured facilities or computer systems, and which can also be used to track user activity and location. These badges work wirelessly within a few meters and do not depend on line-of-sight communication—this tends to be more convenient than swipe cards. More important, no physical contact with the authenticating device is required, as long as the RFID badge is within range of the device. You can also tie RFID badge authentication to the user network account to simplify administration.

Key Fobs

Much like a smart card, a *key fob* is a small device containing a microchip, and you can use it for gaining access to a secure facility or for logging on to a computer or a network. Also called a *security token*, it has a form factor that suggests something you might attach to a key chain, as its name implies. A common procedure for using a key fob is to enter the PIN, which identifies the user as the owner of the key fob. Then, the key fob displays a string of characters, and the user enters the string into a keypad terminal or computer to gain access. This string is a *one-time password (OTP)*. The key fob generates a different password at a prespecified interval, and this guarantees that the user has a unique, strong password protected from the vulnerabilities of ordinary user-generated passwords, which may be too easy to guess, or which the user may write down somewhere to avoid having to memorize.

Examples of key fobs are the RSA SecurID hardware security tokens from RSA Security, referred to in CompTIA A+ 902 exam objective 3.2 as *tokens*. These are very popular for authenticating to virtual private networks (VPNs), although you can also use them to authenticate to e-mail, your Windows desktop, and so on. To authenticate to a server, the user enters their PIN, and the device generates a numeric value every 60 seconds that corresponds to a server-side numeric value. RSA Security owns the *Rivest–Shamir–Adleman (RSA)* encryption and authentication system, named for the creators Ron Rivest, Adi Shamir, and Leonard Adleman. It is used in the company's key fobs and in many apps, such as web browsers and accounting systems.

Installing support for a key fob involves installing an agent that runs on the local computer and a service on the domain controller, such as Active Directory. The agent acts as a front end to the authentication process, passing encrypted authentication information to the domain controller that responded to the authentication request. On the domain controller, the service decrypts the password and provides the password and the user name to the security components for authentication. If the password and user name match a domain user account, the user is allowed access to the resources that she has been granted permissions and rights to.

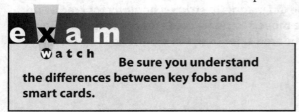

Be sure you understand the differences between key fobs and smart cards.

Biometric Authentication

Users can easily forget passwords or PINs and lose smart cards. But each person can be uniquely identified by measurements of a physical or behavioral characteristic—a *biometric*.

Biometrics are used both for physical access to buildings or areas and for logging on to computer networks. A logon based on one of these measurements is a *biometric logon*. Commonly used biometrics include fingerprints, handprints, and *retinal scans* (a scan of the retina in a person's eye). A hardware device, such as a *retina scanner* or *fingerprint scanner* (also called a *fingertip scanner*), performs that scan. A fingerprint scanner is the least expensive of the biometric devices. The built-in fingerprint scanners are the size of a Universal Serial Bus (USB) port, with a slender scanning slot. External USB fingerprint scanners are available from several vendors.

Biometric scanners require both drivers and software to integrate with the computer's or network's security system to send the scanned information to the security components for processing. If the computer is a member of a domain, you must install special software on the domain controller servers. The software will update the domain accounts database with the biometric information for each user account for which this type of logon is enabled.

Anyone traveling with a laptop with sensitive data should look into purchasing a laptop with a built-in fingerprint scanner. Follow the manufacturer's instructions for installing the software and hardware. After installing the software, configure it to recognize your fingerprint and associate it with your user account. To do this, you will need to provide a user name and password. If your computer is a member of a workgroup, you will need to provide either the computer name or the workgroup name. If your computer is a member of a domain, you must provide the domain name and your user name and password in the domain. When the configuration utility is ready to scan your fingertip and associate it with your user account, it will prompt you. To do this, swipe your finger across the scanner's sensor. You can scan one or more fingers and use any one of them for login. In most cases, the scanner's associated software will also save passwords for applications and websites and associate them with your profile.

Securing Physical Access to Documents

Securing physical access to documents can begin with the access to a building or area, described earlier, requiring some form of authentication with a password or one of the authentication devices. In addition, there are methods for guarding against shoulder surfing, securing documents in locked storage, shredding documents, and disposing of used equipment after removing all data and then following environmentally safe disposal methods.

Guarding Against Shoulder Surfing

The low-tech way to guard against shoulder surfing is to attach a *privacy filter* to any screen that may be targeted, including ATMs, desktop PCs, and laptops. Privacy filters narrow the screen's viewing angle, which ensures that only the person sitting directly in front of the system can view the screen contents.

Locked Storage for Documents

Confidential documents should be in a secure area or in locked containers. You should also control access to these areas with the methods discussed earlier.

Shredding Paper Documents

Private individuals and organizations combined generate many tons of waste paper each year. Much of that is in the form of documents holding confidential information of some sort, from credit card information on receipts to individual health status information to corporate secrets. The key to protecting that confidential information is to be diligent about shredding these paper documents and properly disposing of them. Individuals and small companies can purchase and use inexpensive cross-shredding devices that render the documents nearly impossible to reassemble, whereupon they can feel safe disposing of this shredded paper with the rest of their trash, as long as they comply with any recycling ordinances or regulations. It is, after all, a great deal of paper waste. Government agencies must use more sophisticated shredding devices and then usually dispose of the shredded documents by having them burned.

Equipment Disposal and Removal of Data

How does your organization dispose of old computer equipment? This is a topic described in Chapter 1 in regard to keeping discarded computer equipment out of the waste stream, recycling components, and disposing of hazardous waste contained in computers and related equipment. Whatever the policy on equipment disposal, it should include thorough removal of all data from hard drives and destruction of optical media containing data. The best practice is to destroy all the data on the hard drives before sending them to a recycler. Ordinary deletion of the files in Windows will not permanently delete these files, even if you reformat the hard drives. Therefore, use a program that will truly erase all the data from the hard drives so it is not recoverable, even with very sophisticated tools. We call this process *drive sanitation*, and we will describe tools you can use for this in Chapter 18 as part of digital security.

If you do not have the option of using a software tool to destroy data on old equipment, then you have other options for physically destroying the data, depending on your budget. A hand power drill is something everyone can buy from a hardware store, and unless your drives contain government secrets or data that is worth millions (or at least hundreds of thousands) of dollars, aggressively attacking a hard drive (or SSD storage) with a power drill will render the data irretrievable. Of course, the power drill method will cause metal bits and pieces to fly out of the target, so it does pose some risks to the individual doing it. Wear safety glasses, gloves, and protective clothing.

Yet another tactic is to use an electromagnetic device such as a *degaussing tool* to remove storage from hard drive platters. These devices are costly, running from several hundred for a simple handheld wand to several thousand dollars for a powerful device into which you insert a hard drive or tape drive; it first erases the data through degaussing and then physically crushes the storage device.

Incineration (burning) is also a destruction option. There are security management companies that specialize in the thorough destruction by fire of sensitive data documents and hardware, and a company can also operate its own incinerator for documents and magnetic media (like tape and disks).

In some high-security situations, you might need to have documentation that sensitive records or equipment has been destroyed: a *certificate of destruction*. The destruction management company you work with can provide this, or if you are doing your own destruction, you can document it by maintaining careful records and taking photos of destroyed equipment.

CERTIFICATION SUMMARY

A computer professional must understand the threats to people, computers, and networks. These include malicious software, social engineering tactics, and many others. To that end, this chapter began with an overview of the various threats.

Also, old hardware should be disposed of in a way that is environmentally sound (described in Chapter 1), but before disposing of old hardware, remove sensitive data previously stored on hard drives and other storage devices.

 TWO-MINUTE DRILL

Here are some of the key points covered in Chapter 17.

Security Threats

❑ Hardware theft results in the loss of important tools and valuable data files—and perhaps even a loss of identity, not to mention the downtime until equipment is replaced and programs and data are restored.

❑ Disasters that affect computers, networks, and data come in many forms, including accidents, mistakes, and natural and unnatural disasters.

❑ Identity theft occurs when someone collects personal information belonging to another person and uses that information to fraudulently make purchases, open new credit accounts, and even obtain new driver's licenses and other forms of identification in the victim's name.

❑ The wealth of information on the Internet also includes information that is generally distasteful or inappropriate for some individuals, such as children.

❑ Malicious software attacks are common on both private and public networks. Some forms include viruses, DoS and DDoS attacks, and rootkit. Many malware vectors exist, including Trojan horses, worms, zombies, ransomware, man-in-the-middle, e-mail, hidden malware installation code on websites, backdoors, pop-up downloads, drive-by downloads, browser hijacking, and e-mail hijacking.

❑ An un-updated system is at risk for exploits that target vulnerabilities in the OS. On a business network, a non-compliant system that is not fully updated and protected, such as a machine an employee brings from home, may represent a violation of the company's security best practices.

❑ Grayware is a term for threats that are not true malicious code but can have indirect negative effects, such as decreasing performance or using up bandwidth. Grayware includes spyware, adware, spam, and spim.

❑ Perpetrators use a variety of methods for gaining access and obtaining information. Some common methods include piggybacking and tailgating, shoulder surfing, cookies, password theft, social engineering, war driving, and Bluesnarfing.

❑ Cookies are small files a web browser saves on the local hard drive at the request of a website. Most cookies are harmless first-party cookies that are not program code but small text files, and they can normally only be read by the website that created them.

❑ Some advertisers on websites create cookies that the program code from the same advertiser can read from other websites. These are third-party cookies, and you can configure a web browser to disable third-party cookie reading.

❑ Password theft occurs via unsecured websites, password crackers, and keystroke loggers.

❑ Social engineering involves a variety of techniques used to persuade someone to reveal confidential information or give something else of value to the perpetrator. Phishing, phone phishing, hoaxes, and enticements to open attachments all employ persuasive social engineering tactics.

❑ Fraud is the use of deceit and trickery to persuade someone to hand over money or valuables.

Defense Against Threats: Physical Security

❑ A variety of authentication technologies is available. Just a few include ordinary logons using the standard keyboard, smart-card logons, key-fob logons, and biometric logons. RFID badges wirelessly authenticate the carrying user to secured resources such as floors within a building or locked doors.

❑ Campuses and buildings with restricted areas need to guard against piggybacking and tailgating practices.

❑ A cable lock is a cable that attaches to a portable device such as a laptop or desktop PC case to prevent it being removed from its location.

❑ A smart card is a plastic card, often the size of a credit card, that contains a microchip. The microchip can store information and perform functions, depending on the type of smart card.

❑ Another variation of smart card authentication includes radio frequency identification (RFID) badges. These cards contain an RFID chip (also called an RFID tag) with a radio antenna that can be carried by employees to allow access to secured facilities or computer systems, and which can also be used to track user activity and location.

❑ A key fob is a small device containing a microchip that you can use for gaining access to a secure facility or for logging on to a computer or a network. Examples of key fobs are the RSA SecurID hardware security tokens from RSA Security that are very popular for authenticating to VPNs.

❑ A smart card reader requires software and drivers on the local computer and Certificate Services installed on the domain controllers for the Windows domain.

❑ Commonly used biometrics include fingerprints, handprints, and retinal scans.

❑ Both the built-in and external biometric devices require drivers and software to integrate with the computer's security system.

❑ Control access to restricted spaces, equipment, files, folders, and other resources of the organization.

❑ Privacy filters narrow the screen-viewing angle, which ensures that only the computer user can view the screen contents.

❑ Government agencies must use more sophisticated shredding devices and then usually dispose of the shredded documents by having them burned.

❑ When disposing of old computer equipment, be sure to remove all data from hard drives using an acceptable disk-wiping program and destroy optical media containing confidential data. Recovery from an attack depends on how well you prepared by making good backups and protecting against the threats outlined in this chapter.

SELF TEST

The following questions will help you measure your understanding of the material presented in this chapter. Read all of the choices carefully, because there might be more than one correct answer. Choose all correct answers for each question.

Security Threats

1. What is the term for the activity that results in someone using your personal information to obtain new credit or credentials?
   A. Virus
   B. Identity theft
   C. Trojan horse
   D. Social engineering

2. Netsky and MyDoom were this type of virus, which replicates itself, moving from computer to computer.
   A. Trojan horse
   B. Password cracker
   C. Worm
   D. Keystroke logger

3. What is the term used to describe the delivery of malicious code to a user's computer through a pop-up window in a web browser?
   A. Worm
   B. Grayware
   C. Trojan horse
   D. Pop-up download

4. Which of the following is a category of software that runs surreptitiously on a user's computer to gather personal and financial information without the user's permission, and then sends that information to the people who requested it?
   A. Spam
   B. Spyware
   C. Adware
   D. Spim

5. Which of the following is a term for unsolicited e-mail?
   A. Spyware
   B. Spam
   C. Backdoor
   D. Worm

6. What type of program attempts to guess passwords on a computer?
   A. Keystroke logger
   B. Password cracker
   C. Virus
   D. Fraud

7. What type of malware is installed by an administrator and hides from detection by antimalware programs by concealing itself within the OS code or other program code?
   A. Rootkit
   B. Bluesnarfing
   C. Cookies
   D. Phishing

8. Web browsers save these small text files on the local computer at the direction of programs on a website.
   A. Backdoor
   B. Spam
   C. Cookies
   D. Trojans

9. Someone using this method may steal your password or key code as you enter it at the ATM, grocery store checkout, or security door.
   A. Trojan horse
   B. Bluesnarfing
   C. Tailgating
   D. Shoulder surfing

10. This threat installs on a computer without permission and collects information about a user in order to display targeted advertisements.
    A. Spam
    B. Spyware
    C. Adware
    D. Spim

11. The symptom of this threat is that your web browser home page changed from the one you selected, pointing to a site advertising some product.
    A. Rootkit
    B. Virus
    C. Spam
    D. Browser hijack

12. This term describes the practice of closely following someone into a restricted area without the authorized person's permission.
    A. Piggybacking
    B. Phishing
    C. Tailgating
    D. Trojan horse

13. This is the general term for any method malware uses to gain access to a computer or network.
    A. Vector
    B. Trojan horse
    C. Worm
    D. Phishing

14. You may install this type of malware because it appears to be a harmless program.
    A. Spam
    B. Worm
    C. Trojan horse
    D. Rootkit

15. This type of attack overwhelms a server with so much traffic that it stops functioning.
    A. DoS
    B. Worm
    C. Backdoor
    D. Pop-up download

16. This term describes the questionable practice of an authorized person bringing an unauthorized person into a restricted area.
    A. Piggybacking
    B. Phishing
    C. Tailgating
    D. Trojan horse

Defense Against Threats: Physical Security

17. In its most common use, this device uses a PIN and generates a new password every time a PIN is entered.
    A. Smart card
    B. Key fob
    C. Biometric logon
    D. Keyboard

18. What type of device will allow people access to secured facilities or computer systems as long as the device is within several feet of the authenticating device?
    A. Key fob
    B. RFID badge
    C. Badge
    D. Fingerprint scanner

19. Which of the following is a simple physical-security device for protecting on-screen data from prying eyes?
    A. Privacy filter
    B. Shredding
    C. Key fob
    D. Degaussing

20. Which of the following is a popular encryption and authentication system used in key fobs as well as many apps, such as web browsers and accounting systems?

   A. RSA
   B. Spim
   C. DoS
   D. Degaussing

A SELF TEST ANSWERS

Security Threats

1. ☑ **B.** Identity theft is the term for the activity that results in someone using your personal information to obtain new credit or credentials.

☒ **A** and **C** are incorrect because they are both malicious code, not an activity. **D** is incorrect because social engineering is the use of persuasion techniques for many purposes. Social engineering may be involved with identity theft, but the two terms do not identify the exact same behavior.

2. ☑ **C.** A worm (Netsky and MyDoom were worms) is a type of virus that replicates itself, moving from computer to computer.

☒ **A** is incorrect because a Trojan horse is a type of virus that hides within an apparently harmless program. A worm, like any other virus, can transfer to a computer as a Trojan horse. **B** is incorrect because a password cracker is a program that attempts to discover passwords. **D** is incorrect because a keystroke logger is a program that logs the user's keystrokes.

3. ☑ **D.** Pop-up download describes the delivery of malicious code to a user's computer through a pop-up window in a web browser.

☒ **A** and **C** are both incorrect because they are types of viruses, not the method for delivering a virus. **B** is incorrect because grayware describes threats that are not truly malicious code but that still have indirect negative effects.

4. ☑ **B.** Spyware is a category of software that runs surreptitiously on a user's computer to gather personal and financial information without the user's permission.

☒ **A** and **D** are both incorrect because they represent unwanted messages—spam being unwanted e-mail and spim being unwanted instant messaging messages. **C** is incorrect because, although adware also installs on a computer without permission and collects information, it collects information in order to display targeted advertisements.

5. ☑ **B.** Spam is a term for unsolicited e-mail.
    ☒ **A, C,** and **D** are all incorrect because they are examples of malicious program code and grayware, not e-mail. The e-mail could contain malicious code, but that is not part of the definition.

6. ☑ **B.** Password crackers attempt to guess passwords on a computer.
    ☒ **A** is incorrect because a keystroke logger does not try to "guess" passwords—it tries to *steal* passwords by capturing keystrokes. **C** is incorrect because a virus is a very general term for malicious code. **D** is incorrect because fraud is the use of deceit and trickery to persuade someone to hand over money or valuables. It does not match the narrow definition of guessing passwords.

7. ☑ **A.** A rootkit is malware that hides from detection by antimalware programs by concealing itself within the OS code or other program code.
    ☒ **B** is incorrect because Bluesnarfing is the act of covertly obtaining information broadcast from wireless devices using the Bluetooth standard. **C** is incorrect because cookies are not program code, and they do not allow access to an operating system. **D** is incorrect because phishing is a fraudulent method of obtaining personal and financial information through pop-ups or e-mail messages that purport to be from a legitimate organization.

8. ☑ **C.** Cookies are small text files saved by a web browser on the local computer at the direction of programs on a website.
    ☒ **A** is incorrect because a backdoor is program code that is used for an entirely different purpose. **B** is incorrect because spam is unsolicited e-mail. **D** is incorrect because Trojans are programs, not small text files.

9. ☑ **D.** Shoulder surfing is the method of watching over your shoulder (from nearby or long range with binoculars) while you enter a password or key code.
    ☒ **A** is incorrect because a Trojan horse is a program that appears to be a harmless and desirable program that you install, but malware is installed with it. **B** is incorrect because Bluesnarfing is the act of covertly obtaining information broadcast from wireless devices using the Bluetooth standard. **C** is incorrect because tailgating is the practice of following an authorized person into a secure area without permission.

10. ☑ **C.** Adware is a threat that installs on a computer without permission and collects information about a user in order to display targeted advertisements.
    ☒ **A** and **D** are both incorrect because they represent unwanted messages—spam being unwanted e-mail and spim being unwanted instant messaging messages. **B** is incorrect because spyware is software that runs surreptitiously on a user's computer and gathers personal and financial information without permission.

11. ☑ **D.** Browser hijack is a change in your web browser home page.
    ☒ **A** is incorrect because an administrator installs rootkit malware. **B** is incorrect because a virus relies on stealth to spread itself and would not announce its presence by changing your home page. **C** is incorrect because spam is unwanted e-mail.

12. ☑ **C.** Tailgating is the practice of closely following someone into a restricted area without the authorized person's permission.

 ☒ **A** is incorrect because piggybacking describes the practice of an authorized person bringing an unauthorized person into a restricted area. **B** and **D** are both incorrect because they describe malware vectors.

13. ☑ **A.** Vector is the general term for how malware gains access to a computer or network.

 ☒ **B,** and **C** are incorrect because Trojan horse and worm are individual examples of vectors. **D** is incorrect because phishing is an attempt to fool a user into entering private information at a fraudulent website.

14. ☑ **C.** Trojan horse is correct because it appears to be a harmless program.

 ☒ **A** is incorrect because spam is unwanted e-mail. **B** is incorrect because a worm is malware that self-replicates over a network. **D** is incorrect because an administrator installs a rootkit, which often resides in the OS code, giving access to malware.

15. ☑ **A.** A denial-of-service (DoS) attack sends so much traffic to a server that it stops functioning.

 ☒ **B, C,** and **D** are all incorrect because worm, backdoor, and pop-up download are examples of vectors.

16. ☑ **A.** Piggybacking is the practice of an authorized person bringing an unauthorized person into a restricted area.

 ☒ **B** is incorrect because phishing is an attempt to fool a user into entering private information at a fraudulent website.. **C** is incorrect because tailgating is the practice of closely following someone into a restricted area without the authorized person's permission. **D** is incorrect because Trojan horse is a vector for infecting computers.

Defense Against Threats: Physical Security

17. ☑ **B.** A key fob is a device that uses a PIN and generates a new password every time a PIN is entered.

 ☒ **A** is incorrect because, although a smart card may be similar to a key fob, people don't generally use it in the manner described in the question. **C** is incorrect because biometric logon uses a body measurement for authentication. **D** is incorrect because you cannot use a keyboard in the manner described in the question.

18. ☑ **B.** RFID badges authenticate users to secured resources wirelessly as long as the RFID badge is within range of the authentication device.

 ☒ **A** is incorrect because a key fob commonly requires that the person carrying it enter a PIN, and then it displays a one-time password (OTP) to enter for access. **C** is incorrect because a traditional badge would require that a guard inspect it before allowing someone access. **D** is incorrect because a fingerprint scanner is a hardware device, interfaced with a computer, which scans a fingerprint and transmits the scan for authentication.

19. ☑ **A.** A privacy filter is a simple device that fits over a screen and prevents unauthorized screen viewing.

    ☒ **B** is incorrect because shredding is the destruction of paper documents. **C** is incorrect because a key fob is a device for gaining physical access to a building or logging onto a computer. **D** is incorrect because degaussing is the electromagnetic erasure of magnetically stored data.

20. ☑ **A.** Key fobs and many apps use the RSA (Rivest–Shamir–Adleman) encryption and authentication system.

    ☒ **B** is incorrect because spim is unwanted e-mail over instant messaging. **C** is incorrect because denial-of-service (DoS) is an attack that sends so much traffic to a server that it stops functioning. **D** is incorrect because degaussing is the electromagnetic erasure of magnetically stored data.

Chapter 18

Implementing Digital Security

Thesecurity story is complex, which is why we spread it out over several chapters. In Chapter 14, you learned how to implement security on a wireless router. Chapter 17 looked at a variety of threats from malware, social engineering, and physical security viewpoints. In this chapter we continue our review of security features by explaining how Windows OS tools and features help make a workstation secure and private.

CERTIFICATION OBJECTIVES

- **902: 1.5** *Given a scenario, use Windows Control Panel utilities*
- **902: 3.3** *Compare and contrast differences of basic Windows OS security settings*
- **902: 3.2** *Compare and contrast common prevention methods*
- **902: 3.4** *Given a scenario, deploy and enforce security best practices to secure a workstation*

Chapter 17 described a long list of security threats. Then it detailed options for physical security and how to implement them, a topic of CompTIA A+ 902 exam objective 3.2. In this section, we will look at many of the remaining topics in that objective, including user education, user authentication, strong passwords, and the principle of least privilege. CompTIA A+ 902 exam objective 3.4 lists best practices to create a password and secure a workstation, and we describe them in this section. In this section, we will also address one topic in CompTIA A+ 902 exam objective 1.5 when we describe the User Accounts Control Panel applet, common to all versions of Windows that are included in the CompTIA A+ 220-901 and 220-902 exams. Then, we cover the Users and Groups topics from CompTIA A+ 902 exam objective 3.3.

Implementing Authentication for Digital Security

In Chapter 17, you learned the options for implementing physical security. In this section, learn how to implement the various methods of digital security, authentication, and data security.

Security Policies and User Education

In Chapter 1, you learned about *acceptable-use policy (AUP)*, also called a *security policy*, which defines what is acceptable use of all resources of the organization, of which computer equipment and data are important parts. It includes both physical and digital security, whether employees are on the organization's property or not. Therefore, a small part of this policy will be a remote access policy for how you access the network when out of the office. If you have not been informed about an acceptable-use or security policy at your organization, inquire about it because all organizations should have this spelled out and should educate all employees on the exact policies. In the United States, the *Health Insurance Portability and Accountability Act (HIPAA)* and other government regulations have made security policies mandatory for many organizations in the healthcare and finance industries. For instance, HIPAA includes the HIPPA Privacy Rule, which defines what medical information is protected and how and when it can be used and disclosed. There are significant civil and criminal consequences to organizations and individuals who fail to comply.

Personally identifiable information (PII) is data that can be used to uniquely identify an individual. PII includes many pieces of information ranging from the obvious, such as name, birth date, and Social Security number, to a person's e-mail address, home address, telephone number, schools attended, family pets, and much more. This information is scattered all over the Internet on social networking sites, as well as in what should be private databases, such as those maintained by healthcare providers, schools, and businesses. People use various means to gather this information and then use it for their own gain. This is yet another reason for a security policy that protects this information—whether it is your own information or that of clients, customers, and patients.

A security policy is not effective if no one is informed about the policy and the consequences of not complying. As an IT professional, whenever you interact with client users you have an opportunity to educate them about threats, symptoms, protections, and recovery. An educated user actively participates in the security policy and is aware of how to behave to avoid certain threats and how to notice symptoms and take action to recover on their own. This means better security and privacy for the client and fewer calls for help.

On a computer or network, the security policy that controls what happens at the individual machine level is called the *local security policy*. On a Windows client PC, you can run the Local Security Policy application to examine the settings. On a domain server you can implement local security policies that affect all the machines in the domain. Chapter 19 covers Local Security Policy in more detail.

Implementing Authentication Security

Windows requires authentication for access to a PC, and that is usually accomplished by authenticating using a local account or a domain account. A *local account* is a security account in the local accounts database, while a *domain account* resides in a database on a Windows domain controller server. You can also set a password that must be entered before a PC launches an operating system—a firmware password. In this section, you will look at how these are set. We also describe how to use the Lock Computer option in Windows to protect your computer.

Authentication and Authorization

Access control to resources on a local computer or over a network involves *authentication* (verifying a user's identity) and *authorization* (determining the level of access an authenticated user has to a resource). One of the first defenses against security threats is authentication and authorization by security systems built into the operating systems on your local computer and network servers. Windows desktop operating systems (OSs) support authenticating with a local account on a Windows computer that is a member of a workgroup. Recall from Chapter 13 that *workgroup* is a term used by Microsoft for a peer-to-peer network in which each computer can be a file-and-printer sharing client, a server, or both. There is no central authentication with a workgroup. To have central authentication, a Windows computer, must be a member of a Microsoft domain, which we will describe in Chapter 19.

Passwords   We have used the term password many times in the previous chapters of this book, but until now, we have not stopped to define it. A *password* is a string of characters that a user enters, along with an identifier, such as a user name, in order for authentication to take place. This security tool is an important one for anyone who uses a computer, especially one connected to any network, including the Internet. Do not take your passwords for granted! You may have habits or practices that make you vulnerable to identity theft and other threats. Consider the following questions:

- Do you have too many passwords to remember?
- When you have an opportunity to create a new password, do you use your favorite password?
- Do you have your password written on sticky notes or your desk calendar at school or work?
- Have you used the same password for more than a few months?

If you answered "yes" to any of these questions, you are at risk, and you need to change your behavior.

exam

ⓦatch   **Be sure you remember that passwords are case sensitive, but user names are not.**

The Windows authentication system does not require case sensitivity for user names, but it does for passwords. So, as long as you enter the correct characters for your user name, case does not matter. Case is very important for passwords, which is why Windows login will warn you when the CAPS LOCK key is turned on.

Authentication Technologies and Factors   In the vast majority of cases, especially in a small office/home office (SOHO) environment, people are authenticated to computers and networks with a user name and password. This does not require any special hardware, as the user name and password can be entered using the keyboard.

Organizations requiring more stringent authentication practices for protecting digital access will use specialized technologies, such as smart cards, radio frequency identification (RFID) badges, key fobs, and biometric scanners. All of these technologies, discussed in Chapter 17 as methods to use for physical security, also apply to digital security and provide more secure authentication at an additional cost, but the costs are decreasing, and the technologies are becoming more widespread.

The actual information or device used for authentication verification is an *authentication factor*. There are three categories of authentication factors: something you know, something you have, and something you are. An example of something you *know* is a user name and password or a personal identification number (PIN). Something you *have* may be a smart card, and something you *are* may be a measurement of a physical or behavioral characteristic (a biometric), such as a fingerprint or retina scan. Authentication involves one or more of these factors, so you can have one-factor, two-factor, or three-factor authentication. When two or more factors are used, it is called *multifactor authentication*.

w a t c h   **You should be able to identify and explain the three categories of authentication factors in multifactor authentication: something you know, something you have, and something you are.**

Local User and Group Accounts

Windows requires authentication and authorization and, therefore, requires that each user have an account. In a Windows network, the account can be a local account or a centralized domain account. Of course, whenever possible, use centralized accounts so each user only needs to sign in to the centralized database for authentication, after which, as he or she attempts to access resources on other computers in the domain, the system performs authorization to verify the user's level of access to the resource.

Each installation of Windows for desktop PCs, laptops, and tablets maintains a local accounts database containing *local user accounts* and *local group accounts*. A user account represents a single person, whereas a local group account can contain multiple users and other groups. When the computer is a member of a Windows domain, a local group may contain domain users or domain group accounts to give domain users and groups access to resources on the local computer. Logging on with a local account only gives you access to the resources on that computer, although you may have access to other resources on your network through relationships we will describe in Chapter 19.

Windows 8 and newer enable you to sign in with a *Microsoft account*, which is an e-mail address and password combination that serves as your credentials to an account with one of Microsoft's online services, such as Xbox Live or OneDrive. You are still signing on with a local account because the Microsoft account is associated with the local account. The benefit is that you have access to local resources as well as all online resources granted to the Microsoft account.

FIGURE 18-1

Windows 7 User
Accounts

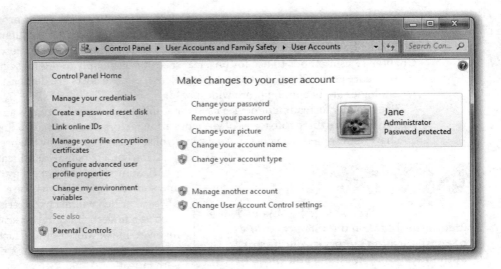

When any user logs on to a Windows computer for the first time, a local user profile is created for that user as well as a set of personal folders for that user's data. A *user profile* includes registry settings for all personal settings for that user.

Each version of Windows surveyed in this book, from Windows Vista through Windows 8.1, has two graphical user interface (GUI) tools for administering local accounts—one that is very simplified and hides many accounts and the complexity from you, and another that lets you see all local user and group accounts. As you read this section, you may want to open one or both of these tools. In Windows Vista and Window 7, the simple tool is User Accounts. The Windows 7 version is shown in Figure 18-1. The contents pane on the right contains links to allow you to make changes to your account. Because the logged-on user is an administrator, the contents pane also includes two links that only an administrator can use: Manage Another Account and Change User Account Control Settings. (You'll learn about User Account Control Settings later in this chapter.) The task pane on the left contains links to more tasks.

The simpler tool in Windows 8 and newer is the Other Accounts page of the PC Settings app. As you can see in Figure 18-2, you can select an account to manage from among the local accounts on this PC. In Windows 10 it's still in the Settings app, under Accounts, but the list of other accounts is under Family & Other People.

In all Windows versions, the more complex tool has remained much the same, and it is the Local Users and Groups node of the Computer Management console, shown in Figure 18-3. To open this in Windows Vista or Windows 7, click Start, right-click Computer, and select Manage. To open it in Windows 8.1, right-click the Start button and choose Computer Management.

FIGURE 18-2

Windows 8.1
Other Accounts

FIGURE 18-3

The Windows 8.1
Computer
Management
console showing
the Local Users
and Groups node

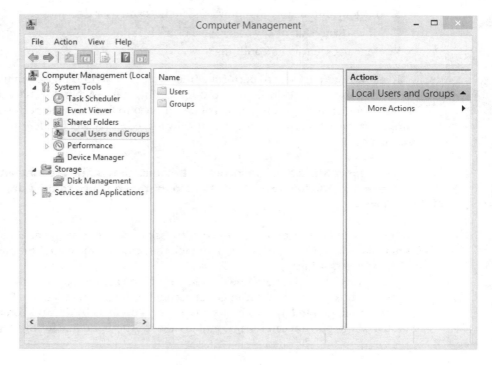

Built-in Accounts Windows also has several built-in user and group accounts, plus the installation of certain services and applications automatically creates some users and groups needed for the service or program, but not necessarily directly used by a human user. While there are several built-in groups, the important group accounts to understand are Administrators, Users, Guests, and Power Users.

The *Administrators* group has full control over the entire system and can perform all tasks on a computer, from installing a device driver to creating other security accounts. Any account added to this group gains those permissions. *Administrator* is a built-in account that is a member of the Administrators group. It cannot be renamed, disabled, or deleted. Administrators can do the following:

- Create any type of local user account
- Change permissions for any local user account
- Modify any local user account
- Install new hardware and software
- Run any program
- Modify all system settings
- Upgrade and repair Windows
- Back up and restore Windows system files and user data files
- Take ownership of any other local user's files
- Manage security and auditing logs

To allow multiple users to perform administrative functions on a computer (or network), rather than use the built-in Administrator account, make each individual account a member of the Administrators group. Then, if you ever need to find out who performed a certain administrative action (most are automatically logged), they will be identified in the logs by user name.

on the **job**

Do not confuse the Administrator account (that is, the account with the user name of Administrator) with an account that belongs to the Administrators group.

The built-in *Users* group has limited permissions, preventing members of this group from making system-wide changes, although they can run most applications that do not change system settings.

The *Guests* group has the same limited permissions of the Users group, but the default member of this group, the built-in *Guest* account, is further restricted to have fewer privileges than granted by the Guests group and is disabled by default. You cannot delete the Guest account, but you can rename and disable it. Another name for this type of account is *anonymous*, as used with older File Transfer Protocol (FTP) sites that did not require a user to sign in to upload and download files. When a member of the Guests group signs in, a user profile and personal folders are created for that user, but are immediately deleted when the user signs out.

Do you wonder why there is a Guest account? The notion of a Guest account began many years ago as a way to give individuals access without having them enter a user name or password and with very limited privileges. Use of the Guest account is discouraged, since, for audit logging purposes, it is difficult to determine who performed which action.

The *Power Users* group was created before Windows had the protection of User Account Control (UAC), and it therefore was useful in Windows 2000, Windows XP, and Windows Server 2003. Since Windows Vista and the introduction of UAC, this group is included only for backward compatibility. The Power Users group has more permissions than the Users group but fewer than the Administrators group, and has no default members. A member of Power Users can do the following:

- Create local users and groups
- Modify local user and group accounts created by that power user
- Remove users from the Power Users, Users, and Guests groups
- Install most applications
- Create, manage, and delete local printers
- Create and delete file shares

Account Types   Choosing an account type helps simplify account creation when you use the User Accounts utility on Windows Vista or Windows 7. A *Standard user account* is appropriate for an "ordinary" user without Administrator status. This account is a member of the local Users group. A user signed in with a Standard account can change her password and other personal settings, but cannot change computer settings, install or remove software and hardware, or perform other system-wide tasks. In contrast, a user signed out with an account that is an *Administrator account* type, called a Computer Administrator in Windows Vista and Windows 7, can perform system-wide tasks.

When you create a new account in Windows 8/8.1 using the PC Settings app, the account is automatically a Standard one. However, after creation you can edit the account to change it to Administrator, as shown in Figure 18-4.

Change a user's account type from Standard to Administrator if needed.

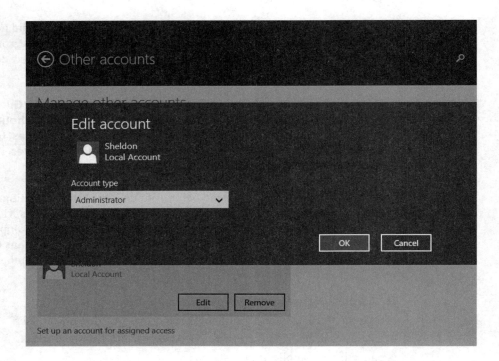

Your User Account Microsoft has long recommended not using the Administrator account as a day-to-day account. This is because prior to Windows Vista, if you signed in with an account belonging to the Administrators group (the Administrator account or other account), a program could install without your knowledge and run with full administrative rights to your computer. That is how a lot of malware infected Windows. As previously mentioned, beginning in Windows Vista, Microsoft added User Account Control, a feature that alerts the user—even an administrator—when a program attempts to install or make other unauthorized changes to Windows. Later in this chapter, you will learn more about UAC, including how it works and how to configure it.

Because UAC guards against the old threat, Windows Vista and newer versions keep the Administrator account hidden in User Accounts, but create another account during installation that is a member of the Administrators group and is seen in User Accounts. This is the account for which you provide a user name and password as you install Windows.

Windows automates the process of creating a user account at the end of setup, or in the case of preinstalled Windows, it prompts you to provide a user name and password the first time you start up your new computer. This account is a member of the Administrators group.

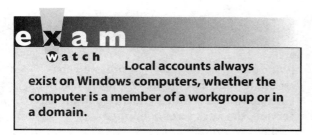

Local accounts always exist on Windows computers, whether the computer is a member of a workgroup or in a domain.

Special Groups *Special groups* are groups created by the Windows security system, and no user can create or modify these groups The membership of a special group is predefined, and the group is available to you only when you assign permissions or rights. A few important special groups are *Creator Owner* (membership consists of the user who created a file or folder), *System* (the operating system), and the *Everyone* group, which includes all users on a network, even those who have not been authenticated.

Windows Sign-in

The versions of Windows included on the CompTIA A+ 220-901 and 220-902 exams always require a sign-in, meaning you must provide a user name and password that are verified against a security database, either local or on a server on the network. Even your home computer that perhaps boots up right to the Windows desktop without asking for a user name or password is actually performing a sign-in.

If your computer is not a member of a Windows domain, but rather a member of a workgroup, and you are only signing in to the local computer, then it is possible to configure it to start up right to the desktop without a password prompt or account selection. This scenario occurs when there is only one user account on a computer and it does not have a password assigned to it—a very unsecure situation, but typical for a home computer—and the Guest account is disabled. The system simply supplies the user name and blank password to the Windows security system during sign-in.

The next step up, security-wise, is the Welcome screen, which appears in Windows Vista and Windows 7 on computers that are not on a Windows domain. The Welcome screen shows the names of all the local user accounts (except Administrator and Guest) and only requires that you select the user name and enter the password. In Windows 8/8.1 and Windows 10, when you start up the PC a Lock screen appears, with a graphic and the current date and time. Press any key to move past that, to the Welcome screen. Then click the icon for the desired user account and type the password. If you don't sign in within a short time (a minute or so), the Lock screen reappears.

The last sign-in method is the Security dialog box. If a computer is a member of a domain, it uses the Security dialog box by default, and another level of security requires the user to press the CTRL-ALT-DELETE key combination before this dialog box will appear. To sign in, you enter your user name, password, and (when appropriate) domain name into this dialog box.

In CompTIA A+ 902 exam objective 3.4, the "Timeout/screen lock" topic refers to Windows' ability to revert to the Lock screen if you don't sign in quickly after pressing a key to clear the Lock screen (Windows 8/8.1 or newer) or pressing CTRL-ALT-DELETE (if on a domain). When you use the Lock Computer feature, described in the next section, the Lock screen reappears.

Figure 18-5 shows the sign-in screen for Windows 7 in which the user, Administrator, is signing in to the domain Lachance.local. Do not be confused by the use of "local" in the domain name. For a domain that is restricted to a private network, an organization may use an invalid top-level domain name (TLD) that Internet DNS servers will not allow, such as "local," in place of a valid TLD (such as .com, .biz, and so on) to distinguish and separate the private network from the publicly accessible network. The public network can use a domain name that is identical to the internal domain, with the exception of the TLD name, which must be a valid top-level domain name.

FIGURE 18-5

The Windows 7 sign-in screen showing the user Administrator signing in to the domain Lachance.local

Lock Computer

Use the Lock Computer option to secure your desktop quickly, while leaving all your programs and files open. It is very simple to do. Before leaving your computer unattended, simply press WINDOWS KEY-L. This will lock the computer; the desktop will disappear, replaced by a screen with a message that the computer is locked. Figure 18-6 shows the Windows 8.1 lock screen. The word "Locked" appears below the user name and above the password box. When you return to your desk, simply enter your password and your desktop appears. Use this when you must leave your desk for a little while, like when you go to lunch. Do not use this when you leave for the day, unless that is required by your employer's security policy.

BIOS Passwords/DriveLock/TPM

As described in Chapter 3, you can set one or more passwords in the system BIOS or UEFI setup program. For example, BIOS may have three types of passwords: one type restricts access to the computer itself, another type restricts access to the BIOS setup, and a third, less common type, restricts access to hard drives, a feature called "DriveLock" on HP computers. As a further enhancement, an embedded Trusted Platform Module (TPM) chip restricts access to hard drives, providing more advanced security.

FIGURE 18-6

This computer is locked until someone enters the correct password.

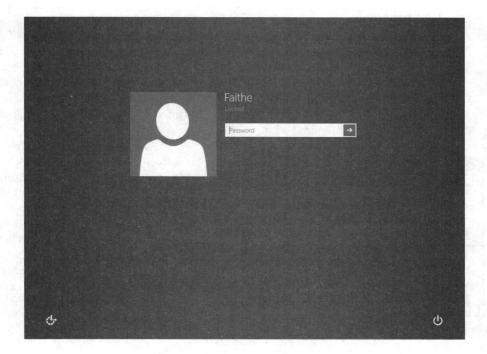

BIOS/UEFI Passwords for Setup and Startup   Recall from Chapter 3 that many BIOSs and UEFIs (let's call them *firmware* here generically, for simplicity) allow you to set a password that must be given before anyone can change firmware settings, and many allow you to set a separate password required to start up the computer. The first is reasonable if a computer is in an environment where people may tend to tamper with the firmware settings. An example would be in a student lab. The second is a bit extreme unless security requirements dictate this.

To set a firmware password for setup or startup, check the manual for the motherboard, and then go into the firmware setup program and navigate to the correct setting; it may simply be called "Set Password." Selecting this option will open a password dialog box, in which you enter the new password. On another screen, you configure the password requirement for setup and/or startup.

DriveLock   Some manufacturers provide a firmware feature (HP calls theirs DriveLock) that allows you to set a password that you must provide at startup. This password is stored on the hard drive, which means that even if you move the drive to another computer, it will be inaccessible. With some implementations, if you use the same password for firmware startup and DriveLock, you will only need to enter the password once to complete the startup; otherwise, you will need to enter two passwords.

TPM   A more sophisticated method is to store the cryptographic keys for encrypting and decrypting disk volumes in an embedded Trusted Platform Module (TPM) chip as described in Chapter 3. With TPM enabled, the user might optionally have to enter a PIN at bootup. If the PIN is correct, TPM decrypts the disk volume and allows the bootup to continue. If the drive is removed from the computer and installed into another computer, it will not be accessible unless the encryption data was transferred from the original TPM chip to the new TPM-enabled computer. TPM can also verify that the hardware boot sequence has not been tampered with.

The Windows BitLocker Drive Encryption feature (available in Windows Vista and Windows 7 Enterprise and Ultimate editions and Windows 8/8.1/10 Pro) works with TPM to secure drive contents, although this is just an option, and you can choose to use a password or smart card for unlocking the drive. The Windows BitLocker To Go feature that encrypts flash drives does not use TPM, but lets you configure it to use either a password or smart card to store the password.

When you install the Ultimate or Enterprise versions of Windows Vista or Windows 7 or

Windows 8/8.1/10 Pro on a computer with a TPM 1.2 chip on the motherboard, Windows Setup will automatically enable BitLocker and install the BitLocker applet in Control Panel.

Windows Credential Manager

Windows allows you to store credentials to automatically sign in to servers, websites, and certain applications. These are stored in local folders, called *vaults*. The user of these locally stored credentials provides a *single sign-on (SSO)*, meaning that a user only need provide credentials (usually user name and password) once and have access to multiple resources. In Windows 7 and newer, a *Credential Manager* applet in the Control Panel enables you to directly manage your credentials. Figure 18-7 shows the Windows 7 Credential Manager. We expanded one of the credentials—for connecting to a computer named W8-64-LAPTOP in a HomeGroup—so that you can see the links to edit or remove these credentials. The Edit option allows you to change the user name and password. In Chapter 19, you will learn how to create and connect to a HomeGroup.

FIGURE 18-7

Credential Manager in Windows 7

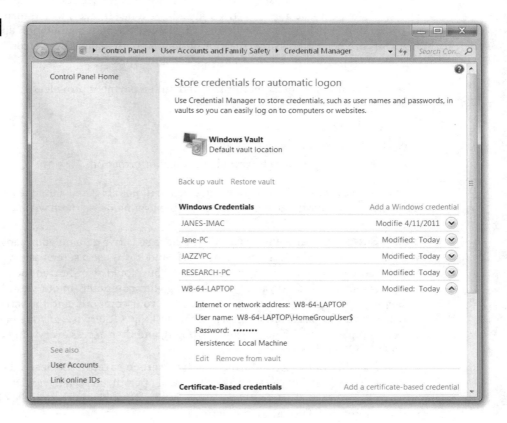

Best Practices to Secure a Workstation

This section covers all the best practices listed under 902 exam objective 3.4, except the previously covered topics BIOS/UEFI passwords, timeout/screen lock, and data encryption, and except for patch/update management, covered later in this chapter.

Require and Set Strong Passwords   Require and use passwords wherever possible. A *strong password* is one that meets certain criteria that make it difficult to crack. Passwords that do not meet these criteria are weak and ineffective and provide negligible security.

The criteria for a strong password have changed over time, as people with malicious intent (hackers) create more and more techniques and tools for discovering passwords. One definition of a strong password is one that contains at least eight characters; includes a combination of letters, numbers, and other symbols (such as _, -, $, and so on); and is easy for you to remember but difficult for others to guess.

For instance, some people take a song title or part of the lyrics from a favorite song, remove the spaces, and substitute numbers for some of the letters. For instance, the lyrics "Dance while the music goes on" (from the ABBA song "Dance") would turn into the password "dan2ewh1lethemu3i2g0es0n." The longer the better, and if nonalphanumeric characters are permitted, throw in a few of them, too, to make it even stronger.

Use strong passwords for the following account types:

- Banks, investments, credit cards, and online payment providers
- E-mail
- Work-related
- Online auction sites and retailers
- Sites where you have to provide personal information

Every account should have a unique user name (if possible) and a unique password (always). Many websites require your e-mail address as the user name, so these will not be unique.

Enable Screen Saver Password   If you have sensitive data on your computer, or available to your user account over a network, and if you use a screen saver, be sure to require that you must sign in again to resume. You should also shorten the wait period if you are using your screen saver rather than locking your computer (in our view, Lock Computer is a better practice). Then if you walk away from your computer and the screen saver turns on, it will require a password to return to the desktop. Otherwise, anyone passing by your desk can simply touch the mouse and keyboard, and then access everything on your local computer and network that you can access.

To enable this, open Control Panel and type **screen saver** in the Search box. In the results list, select Change Screen Saver. This will open the Screen Saver Settings dialog box shown in Figure 18-8. Click to place a check in the check box in the middle of the dialog box labeled On Resume, Display Logon Screen.

FIGURE 18-8

Enable On
Resume, Display
Logon Screen

on the
Job

Remember that Lock Computer is a better practice than enabling the password for the screen saver, even though "screensaver required password" is listed as a best practice in CompTIA A+ 902 exam objective 3.4.

Restrict User Permissions Use of the HomeGroups method in Windows 7 and newer for sharing files in a SOHO network gives those who have access to your computer complete control over the folders or printers to which they are granted access. However, there are other methods you will learn about in which you may apply permissions in such a way that someone has less than full control to a file, folder, or printer, giving each person or group just the level of permission they need to accomplish their work without giving them too much. This is the *principle of least privilege*. Learn more about the different methods for sharing resources over a network and about applying levels of permissions in Chapter 19.

Change Default User Names You learned in Chapter 14 that when configuring a wireless access point (WAP) or broadband router, you should change the default administrator user name and password. These devices usually come with an administrator user name of Admin, and changing it and the password makes access to that device more secure because someone would need to guess the user name as well as the password. Unfortunately, you cannot do this on the many websites that require that you use your

This Guest account is disabled.

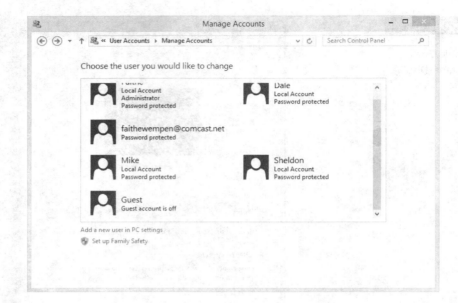

e-mail address as a user name, but you do have this option on devices such as those mentioned, and you should always change such default user names.

Disable Guest Account   By default, Windows disables the local Guest account. However, it doesn't hurt to know how to disable it in case you discover it enabled on a computer. In the Control Panel, open User Accounts and select Manage Another Account. The Manage Accounts page will, at a minimum, show the account created when installing Windows and the Guest account. The Guest account may either be on (enabled) or off (disabled); in Figure 18-9 it is disabled. If you discover that the Guest account is turned on, double-click it and select Turn Off.

Set Password Expiration   An old password is less secure than a newly set one, because nobody will have had time to snoop or guess it. For this reason, you may want to set user account passwords to expire after a certain amount of time. For example, some organizations set an expiration of six months to one year. This type of group policy is typically set at the domain level, rather than for individual workstations.

Sign-in Time Restriction   Another way to make a PC or network more secure is to limit the dates and times of sign-ins. For example, if the company is closed on Sundays, you could set a group policy to prevent Standard users from signing in on Sundays. This kind of restriction is controlled via the Local Security Policy editor or Group Policy Editor; Chapter 19 covers these utilities.

Be cautious when setting a sign-in time restriction, because there's always going to be that exceptional user who needs in the system when nobody else is there, and if he can't get in, you're going to get an irate phone call over the weekend.

Failed Attempts Lockout To prevent hackers from repeatedly trying to guess the password on an account, you can implement a failed attempts lockout policy using the Local Security Policy editor or Group Policy editor. You can set an account to be locked after a certain number of failed guesses, either permanently (until an administrator resets it) or for a certain number of minutes.

Disable Autorun/AutoPlay The *AutoPlay* feature (called *Autorun* in some earlier Windows versions) enables Windows to automatically find and run the content on removable media when it connects to a computer. The AutoPlay applet in Control Panel displays a long list of media and content types, and you can choose exactly how each is treated when it is placed in your computers. Beware, however, that AutoPlay can make you vulnerable to malware infections, because removable media is a vector for malware. The safest thing to do is to disable AutoPlay, and simply choose the action you want each time you place removable media in your computer. Figure 18-10 shows the Windows 8.1 AutoPlay Control Panel applet; clear the Use AutoPlay for All Media and Devices check box to disable the feature.

FIGURE 18-10

To turn off AutoPlay, clear the check box labeled Use AutoPlay for All Media and Devices.

AutoPlay
← → ↑ ▦ << Hardware and Sound › AutoPlay ∨ ⟳ Search Control Panel
Choose what happens when you insert each type of media or device
☑ Use AutoPlay for all media and devices
Removable drives
🖴 Removable drive — Choose a default
☐ Choose what to do with each type of media
🖼 Pictures — Choose a default
🎞 Videos — Choose a default
🎵 Music — Choose a default
🗂 Mixed content — Choose a default
Camera storage
📷 Memory card — Choose a default
Save   Cancel

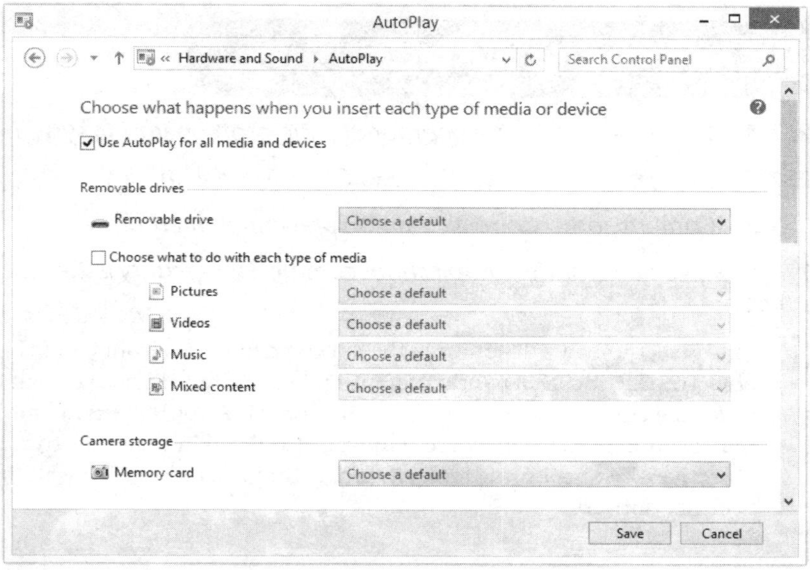

SCENARIO & SOLUTION

I am preparing a new computer for a computer lab. How can I configure the computer so students will not be able to access the system setup and change the BIOS settings, making the computer unusable?	Check out the manufacturer's documentation on the computer's system settings and look for the password settings. Set the password to the BIOS Settings menu only. Do not set the password on system startup unless the security policy for the computer lab requires this.
We are getting ready to order ten laptops for traveling auditors who will have sensitive data on the hard drives. We are looking for a secure authentication method beyond a simple user name and password for basic interactive sign-in to a Windows domain. What do you recommend?	Since you are in the process of purchasing the laptops, check out biometric devices, such as fingerprint scanners. These are more secure than the basic interactive sign-in and work with a Windows domain.
Our employees' computers are in a public area where customers and others can easily wander in and out. Employees must frequently leave their computers unattended during the workday for brief periods. How can they keep their desktops secure without shutting down their applications and Windows?	We suggest you show the employees how to use the Windows Lock Computer option (WINDOWS KEY-L).

CERTIFICATION OBJECTIVES

■ *902: 1.4*   *Given a scenario, use appropriate Microsoft operating system features and tools*

■ *902: 1.5*   *Given a scenario, use Windows Control Panel utilities*

■ *902: 3.2*   *Compare and contrast common prevention methods*

■ *902: 4.2*   *Given a scenario, troubleshoot common PC security issues with appropriate tools and best practices*

In this section we will continue the coverage of topics from CompTIA A+ 902 exam objective 3.2, including antivirus/antimalware, firewalls, and e-mail filtering. We also cover the common symptoms listed in CompTIA A+ 902 exam objective 4.2 as well as the best practices for malware removal, also listed in that objective. From the 902 exam objectives 1.4 and 1.5, we look at a single topic: Windows Firewall (including its Advanced Security option).

Implementing a Defense Against Malware

There are many small building blocks to an effective defense against malicious software. It begins with educating yourself about threats and defenses and setting up a foundation of secure authentication and data protection techniques, and continues with placing a firewall and related technologies at the junction between a private network and the Internet. Then, each computer in the private network must use a group of technologies, such as software firewalls and programs that detect and remove all types of malware, to protect it from attacks.

Self-Education

Research malware types, symptoms, and solutions to keep yourself informed. Check out the many *virus encyclopedias* on the Internet sponsored by many different organizations, including security software manufacturers such as Trend Micro, Kaspersky, and Symantec. Despite the use of the word "virus," these lists contain all types of known threats and are always up to date. Threat Encyclopedia is the title of the list maintained by Trend Micro, a security software manufacturer. Also look for antivirus support forums, which include information about threats other than viruses.

Such resources categorize the malware by type and describe symptoms and solutions. The website www.av-comparatives.org contains lists of antivirus support forums and virus encyclopedias. The U.S. government maintains excellent general information on all types of threats to computers at the United States Computer Emergency Readiness Team (US-CERT) website at www.us-cert.gov/ncas/tips/.

Network Access Control

A significant percentage of workers access their employer's network from outside—often over the Internet. Similarly, many organizations have temporary contractors working for them. Allowing access from outside the private network can expose an organization to all types of threats, and an organization with very high security needs may implement some form of *network access control (NAC)*. NAC is a group of practices for securing a private network from outside access by restricting the resources available, beginning with a specialized server called a *network access server (NAS)*. Connection to a NAS is often via a secure virtual private network (VPN), and the NAS performs authentication and authorization services. Several vendors offer NAC solutions, including both hardware and software, which include several security functions. At minimum, a NAC solution includes firewall, antivirus, antispyware, authentication, and authorization functions.

FIGURE 18-11

The UAC consent
prompt

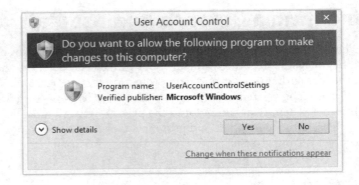

User Account Control

Malware often runs in the background without user consent, making system changes
and installing itself. To prevent this, Microsoft added User Account Control (UAC) in
Windows Vista, and improved it in Windows 7 and newer. UAC can prompt the user when
this happens to prevent malicious code from running unknown in the background. With
UAC enabled, you can expect two scenarios. In the first, a user logged on with a name and
password that is a member of the Administrators group only has the privileges of a Standard
account (member of the Users group), until the user (or a malicious program) attempts to do
something that requires higher privileges. At that point, UAC makes itself known, graying
out (dimming) the desktop, and displaying the *consent prompt* (see Figure 18-11), with a
message concerning the action. Click Continue or Yes (depending on the message) to allow
the action. You can choose to cancel the action by clicking No. If you click Yes, the task runs
with your administrative privileges, and you return to working with standard privileges in
other programs.

 UAC does not negate the need for antivirus and antispyware tools.

In the second scenario, a user logs on with the privileges of a Standard user and attempts
to do something that requires administrative privileges. In this case, UAC displays the
credentials prompt (see Figure 18-12) requiring the user name and password of an account
with administrative privileges. If you provide these, the program or task will run with
these elevated privileges, but you will return to the Standard user privileges for all other
activities. In either case, if you do not respond in a short period of time, UAC will time out,
cancel the operation, and return control of the desktop to you. By default, UAC is turned
on, although Microsoft made changes to Windows 7 and newer that reduce the number of
prompts you will see because they changed the number of Windows programs that require
approval to run.

FIGURE 18-12

The credentials prompt

Even with UAC turned off, you will not be allowed to perform all tasks and will see a message such as "The requested operation requires elevation" when you attempt to perform certain functions. In Windows Vista, you can turn UAC on or off through the User Accounts Control Panel applet. In Windows 7 and newer, modify User Account Control settings in the Action Center in the Control Panel. To modify the UAC settings, click the Change User Account Control Settings hyperlink, which opens a dialog box with a slider that lets you select a range of four settings, from Never Notify (effectively turns off UAC) to Always Notify. See Figure 18-13. The wording of the settings varies somewhat between Windows versions. Select each setting, read its description, and choose the one that's most appropriate for your needs. We recommend you stick with one of the top two settings.

on the **job**

If you choose a setting where the desktop is dimmed when a UAC dialog box appears, you can't do anything else until you respond to the UAC prompt.

System Protection

As you learned in Chapter 12, System Protection is the feature we most often call System Restore, although it also includes Shadow Copy. From the System applet of the Control Panel, select System Protection from the task list, which opens the System Properties dialog box to the System Protection tab. From this tab, you can start System Restore and undo recent system changes. You can also configure System Restore settings and create a new restore point.

FIGURE 18-13

Adjust the UAC
setting if needed.

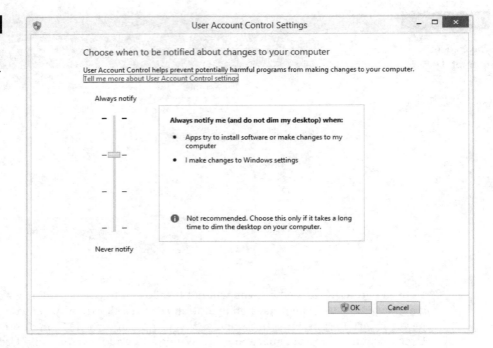

Software Firewalls

In Chapter 14, you learned that a firewall is a hardware device or software that uses several technologies to prevent unwanted traffic from entering a network. If your computer is behind a well-configured hardware firewall, it will be protected against attacks coming from outside the private network. However, many attacks come from within a private network. Therefore, whether your computer is behind an expensive well-managed hardware firewall or an inexpensive SOHO broadband router, you still need to install and configure a software firewall on every Windows computer. The best strategy is to start with the most restrictive settings and then make exceptions to allow the required traffic to pass through the firewall. Since one of the main jobs of a firewall is to maintain port security, exceptions are in the form of port numbers and can even include specific IP addresses or domain names associated with port numbers.

Windows Firewall

Windows Firewall is included in Windows Vista and newer versions. Windows Firewall is on by default, and you can open the Windows Firewall dialog box through its Control Panel applet.

FIGURE 18-14

Windows Firewall
in Windows 8.1

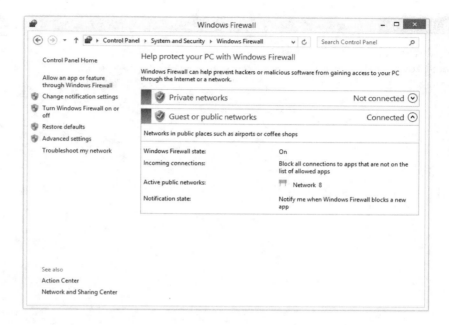

Figure 18-14 shows the Windows Firewall page in Windows 8.1. It contains simple status information and has links if you need to make any changes to the firewall. Clicking the link labeled Allow an App or Feature Through Windows Firewall will open a new page, shown in Figure 18-15. Then click the Change Settings button at the top of the page. You will need to do this to allow traffic for certain apps or services in.

on the

job

If a certain application that uses the Internet seems to be working okay but isn't connecting to its online resources, suspect a firewall issue. Make sure that the application is allowed through the firewall in the list shown in Figure 18-15.

Exercise 18-1 will help you learn more about Windows Firewall. You must be signed in with an account that has administrative privileges to work with Windows Firewall (and to complete this exercise). If you installed a third-party firewall, you should turn off Windows Firewall, because multiple firewalls on the same computer do not cooperate. Therefore, when you do Exercise 18-1, if you find that Windows Firewall is turned off, do not turn it on unless you are sure that no other firewall is installed. The exercise is for Windows 7, but the steps are very similar in Windows Vista and Windows 8.1 and newer.

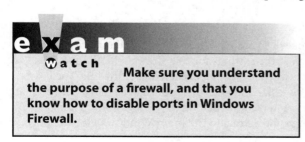

ex**a**m
watc**h**   **Make sure you understand the purpose of a firewall, and that you know how to disable ports in Windows Firewall.**

FIGURE 18-15

Windows Firewall
Allowed Apps
page

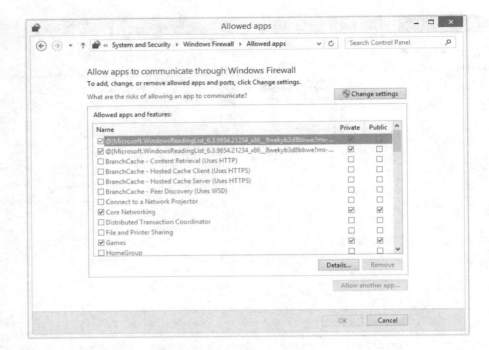

EXERCISE 18-1

Configuring Windows Firewall

In this exercise, you may encounter UAC prompts. If you are logged on with an Administrator account, simply choose to continue. If you are logged on with a Standard account, you will need to enter credentials to continue, in which case, you should obtain these credentials before you begin. Use Windows 7 or newer for this exercise.

1. Open the Control Panel and type **fire** in the Control Panel Search box. Select Windows Firewall from the results.

2. If the Windows Firewall is on, proceed to Step 3. If it is not on, find out why. If you have another firewall, you can look at the settings for that firewall. If Windows Firewall is turned off but no other firewall is enabled, then locate the link Turn Windows Firewall On or Off in the task pane and turn it on. There may be more than one location showing, so be sure you have it turned on for all locations. Then click the OK button to accept the change and return to the main Windows Firewall page.

3. On the main Windows Firewall page, select Allow an App or Feature Through Windows Firewall (a task item on the left) to open the Allowed Apps page, shown earlier in Figure 18-15.

4. In Windows 7 and earlier, the wording is a little different; it uses "Program" instead of "App" in the hyperlink wording and the page name.

5. Click the Change Settings button to enable editing. If a UAC prompt appears, respond to it.

   Here's where things are a little different between Windows versions; you don't have to click Change Settings to complete Step 5 in Windows 7, but you do in Windows 8 and newer. (However, in all Windows versions, you need to have done it to complete Step 6, so just go ahead and do it now.)

6. Select or deselect programs to allow through the firewall, and look at details that describe the program and the protocols it uses.

7. If you need to add another program/app, click Allow Another App, and then follow the prompts. We do not recommend adding a program unless you are confident that this exception is required and will not cause harm. If you need to remove an app from the list, use the Remove button.

8. When you have finished with the Allowed Apps (or Allowed Programs) page, if you have made changes, click OK. If you have not made any changes, or wish to discard your changes, click Cancel. This will bring you back to the main Windows Firewall page; close this page.

e x a m

w a t c h   So far, you have been using simple tools for working with Windows Firewall, and these will work for you most of the time. For a look at a more advanced tool, click Advanced Settings. This will open a Microsoft Management Console titled Windows Firewall With Advanced Security.

Third-Party Software Firewalls

There are many inexpensive third-party software firewalls—some commercial and some free. Examples of personal firewalls are ZoneAlarm and ZoneAlarm Pro by Check Point and Norton Security by Symantec. Each of these is available as a separate product or as part of a security software bundle. ZoneAlarm is a free program with fewer features than ZoneAlarm Pro.

Antivirus and Antimalware Software

An antivirus program can examine the contents of a disk and random access memory (RAM), looking for hidden viruses and files that may act as hosts for virus code. Effective antivirus products not only detect viruses in incoming files before they can infect your system, but also remove existing viruses and help you recover data that has been lost because of a virus. An antimalware program is similar, but provides a broader base of coverage, looking not only for viruses but for other kinds of malware too, including spyware and adware.

To keep an antivirus program up to date, always enable the update option you will find in all popular antivirus programs. Configure it to connect automatically to the manufacturer's website, check for updates, and install them. An antivirus program will update at least two components: the antivirus engine (the main program) and a set of patterns of recognized viruses, usually contained in files called definition files. Manufacturers of antivirus software commonly charge an annual fee for updates to the antivirus engine and to the definitions. Common commercial antivirus manufacturers with both home and business solutions include Symantec, Trend Micro, McAfee, and Kaspersky. There are excellent free services for home users. Even the commercial vendors who do not offer a completely free product often allow you to try their product for a period, usually 30 days.

As you learned in Chapter 17, spyware and adware are types of programs that install on your computer and perform functions on behalf of others. The intent of spyware can be very malicious, including identity theft, whereas the intent of adware is generally less malicious, even if the people responsible for the adware hope to profit by advertising their products.

How spyware and adware get installed on your computer is yet another issue. Users have a hard time believing that their actions invite in malicious programs, but that is how it happens. Perhaps you installed a wonderful free program. You may be very happy with the program itself, but you may have also installed spyware, adware, or worse along with the program.

The most insidious method used to install spyware and adware on your computer comes in the form of a pop-up window resembling a Windows alert. These bogus messages may warn you that spyware was installed on your computer and you must take some action, such as clicking OK in the pop-up window. By clicking OK, you supposedly start downloading software from Microsoft or another credible source to install on your computer to rid you of the threat. In reality, it is only a disguised method for installing spyware or adware.

Do not fall for these tricks. Fighting these threats begins with being very careful about how you respond to messages in pop-up windows and what you install on your computer while browsing the Web. If you are unsure of a message, do not click any buttons or links within the window, but close your browser. Be aware that you can infect your computer by simply viewing a website, without clicking anything.

Many free and commercial programs are available that effectively block various forms of spyware and adware, especially pop-ups. These are the easiest to block, and the most annoying because a pop-up advertisement appears in its own window and must be closed or moved before you can see the content you were seeking. Such a blocking program is a *pop-up blocker*. Configure a pop-up blocker so it will block pop-ups quietly. You can also opt to configure it to make a sound and/or display a message, allowing you to decide whether to block each pop-up.

Several years ago Microsoft offered *Windows Defender* antispyware as a free download, and they later came out with *Microsoft Security Essentials (MSE)* (antivirus and more), also offered free. Then they combined the features of both into Microsoft Security Essentials, and it is available to Windows Vista and Windows 7 at www.microsoft.com/en-us/download/details.aspx?id=5201. You cannot install Microsoft Security Essentials on a PC running Windows 8 or newer, but you don't need to, because Microsoft rolled all of its features into Windows Defender as of Windows 8.

Identifying Trusted Software Resources

One way that malware can enter a computer is through an untrusted download. If you are in charge of a group of individual users, who knows what trouble they may get into online, going to shady websites over their lunch breaks? It's important to set acceptable use policies (AUPs) about software sources that restrict users from downloading files except from trusted sources.

Which sites can be trusted? It depends on how draconian your company wants to be. The stricter the policy, the more you will impede users from doing what they perhaps legitimately need to do, but the fewer malware infections you will have to deal with. In general, we would trust sites such as the official websites for well-known hardware and software (like https://support.microsoft.com) and government sites (with domain names that end in .gov).

Implementing Security Suites

Today's security software is very different from a decade ago because today's threats are more diverse than a decade ago. Therefore, you are not as likely to install a simple antivirus program, but rather an entire security suite, so we'll talk in terms of a multifunction security suite. Symantec, Trend Micro, and many other software manufacturers offer such suites, which normally offer a full range of security products, including antivirus, antispyware, phishing filters, and even firewalls. Installing a security suite will normally disable any Windows components that provide equivalent functionality; for example, a suite that includes antimalware will disable Windows Defender, and a suite that includes a firewall will disable Windows Firewall. That's good, because running two utilities that duplicate each other's functionality can cause problems.

Part of the installation of a security suite is a thorough scan of your computer, including memory contents and all portions of all storage devices, examining all types of files, and the parts of the disk where viruses can hide, such as the boot sector or boot block. Also, as part of the installation, you can choose to turn on automatic scans (the normal default) and the frequency of those scans. Even when you configure automatic scans, you can choose to initiate a scan when you detect possible malware symptoms. In this case, boot the computer to Safe Mode, as described in Chapter 12, and run a complete antivirus scan, then follow the instructions described in the upcoming section "Removing Malware."

Microsoft Baseline Security Analyzer (MBSA) is a free Windows security auditing tool. You can analyze a single computer, analyze computers in Active Directory, or specify an IP address range to scan. You can also configure credentials to use for the scanning of remote computers. MBSA checks for security updates and the lack of valid security configurations.

You do not always have obvious symptoms of malware infections, because some malware is not detectable under normal computer operation. These infections are often, but not always, ones that occurred before a system was adequately protected. They can also occur if you have not kept up to date with updates—both to the operating system and to the security programs. If you suspect that a computer is infected, but a normal scan from within Windows does not detect malware, then you should try a special technique for detecting and removing malware. For such a scenario, the top security programs have a special Safe Mode Scan that runs in Windows Safe Mode. To do this, restart Windows in Safe Mode, and then locate the security program and have it run a full scan. If it detects malware, have it quarantine or remove it, and then restart the computer and see if the symptoms have gone away.

Although the top security programs claim to protect against all types of malware, including boot sector viruses, these are rather difficult viruses to detect and remove once they have infected a computer. Therefore, security software will, by default, scan all removable media upon insertion, not allowing access to it or programs to run from it until the scan is complete. Never disable this option.

If you suspect a boot sector virus, use the System Recovery Options menu described in Chapter 12.

Removing Malware

When malware is detected, you must remediate the infected systems, removing the malware and repairing any damage it may have done. Following is a seven-step best practices procedure for malware removal, as listed in CompTIA A+ 902 exam objective 4.2.

Identify Malware Symptoms

Malware symptoms range from no symptoms to overt, but not too obvious, symptoms, such as sudden slowness, unusual cursor movements, and unusual network activity (indicated by status lights or messages) when you are not actively accessing the network. Following is a list of other symptoms that can be associated with a malware infection or other threat. In some cases, it is a true symptom of a security problem or actual malware infection. Other symptoms can have other causes that you will need to eliminate before taking direct action against malware.

Security Alerts   Windows Action Center will display security alerts when Windows detects a security problem. Some common problems this tool detects include no antivirus or spyware protection detected or a disabled Windows Firewall. Respond to the message, for instance, by installing antivirus and antispyware software. In the case of a no-firewall message, open Windows Action Center and enable Windows Firewall, or, if you have another firewall installed, select the option that informs Windows of this.

Slow Performance   Slow performance can have several causes, depending on what there is about the computer that is actually slow. Chapter 11 described this symptom and solutions related to hard drives; Chapter 12 described slow system performance and some solutions. Chapter 16 described slow network transfer speeds and some solutions. After eliminating other causes for slow performance, follow the instructions under the sections "Quarantine Infected System," "Disable System Restore and Create a Restore Point," and "Remediate Infected Systems," later in this chapter.

Internet Connectivity Issues   Internet connectivity issues are more likely to be from the causes described in Chapter 14 than from a malware infection. Troubleshoot using the methods described in that chapter, and if you cannot find the cause and solution, boot the computer to Safe Mode, described in Chapter 12, and run a complete antivirus scan.

PC Locks Up   This term can cover several symptoms, but is usually associated with a screen that looks normal, but the system does not respond to any input from keyboard or mouse. First, restart the computer using the power button, and then see if it will start normally. If Windows does not start normally, then follow the instructions in Chapter 12. If Windows starts up normally, immediately run a complete scan with your security software. If it detects no malware, then try to duplicate the problem and see which software or device may have been associated with the lock-up. Once you isolate it to a single program or device, remove the program or device and device driver, restart your computer, and see if the system remains stable. You may need to contact the software publisher or hardware manufacturer for a solution.

Application Crashes   Applications that used to run fine may start crashing frequently as a result of malware infection. If an application is not running right, try uninstalling and reinstalling it. If it still doesn't run right, malware may be the underlying cause.

Browser Pop-Ups and Redirection   A sudden increase in the number of browser pop-up windows can indicate that adware may be present. Another symptom is a home page that redirects to a page you did not choose, especially if the page comes back after you reset it to your own favorite.

Windows Update Fails   Update failures can be a sign of a malware infection because they often disable Windows Updates so that your computer will not become more secure through security updates. When an update failure occurs, read the message, and research the cause. It may have been a network connection problem, or an incompatibility issue. If it is not clearly a network connection problem, use the error message to do an Internet search for a solution. Look at solutions from both the Microsoft site and other technical sites that you trust.

Rogue Antivirus   In Chapter 17, we described one example of a rogue antivirus when we discussed Trojan horses. A rogue antivirus is a Trojan horse masquerading as an antivirus program. Education and prevention are the best defenses, because rogue antiviruses look like the real thing, and we know several people who installed the malware. Again, the best solution is to boot the computer to Safe Mode, described in Chapter 12, and run a complete antivirus scan.

Renamed System Files   Renamed system files are less of a threat, because malware can simply infect the system files themselves. Both renaming the system files and directly infecting system files are less likely with many of the protections built into Windows. You can solve this by booting the computer to Safe Mode, described in Chapter 12, and running a complete antivirus scan. If removal of the virus leaves your system unbootable, then run the System Recovery Options from a Windows installation disc.

Files Disappearing   Disappearing files is a malware symptom, but before you assume malware has caused it, look at how it was discovered and what you or the client was doing at the time the files disappeared. Sometimes, we just forget where we stored files. However, it never hurts to run a security scan, even from Safe Mode. If you discover malware, remove it and restore your files from the latest backup.

File Permission Changes   File permission changes are also not as likely to happen in the newer versions of Windows as in Windows XP because of User Account Control. If you notice that permissions have changed, change them back (if your permissions allow), then boot the computer to Safe Mode, described in Chapter 12, and run a complete antivirus scan.

Access Denied   If access is denied to a resource a user previously was able to access, troubleshoot it as a file permission change, described earlier.

Spam   If you experience a sudden increase in the amount of spam you receive, your e-mail address may have been sold to a spamming company. Other than changing to a different e-mail address, there is not much you can do about that. Once it's in the system, it's forever exposed.

Although you can't reduce the amount of spam that gets sent your way, there are a number of ways to reduce the amount of it that actually reaches your inbox. You can turn on *e-mail filtering* at the ISP level (and in fact many ISPs have that enabled automatically). You can also enable e-mail filtering in your e-mail application, and you can install additional third-party spam filtering programs.

on the job

We use a free program called SpamBayes, which "learns" your preferences for spam filtering over time and gets better and better at it.

Hijacked E-mail   If your friends and family start receiving odd messages from your account that you didn't send, your e-mail may have been hijacked. Another symptom is automated replies from servers saying that a message could not be delivered—a message that you don't recall sending.

In the event of a hijacked e-mail, described in Chapter 17, you should do three things: immediately change your password, change your security question and answer, and verify that you are the owner of your alternate e-mail address (most e-mail accounts ask you to provide an alternate e-mail address). Hopefully the people you e-mail know that you're not stranded in Ireland and need money to get home, or whatever message the hijacker sent out from your account. You should probably send everyone an e-mail telling them what happened, reminding them not to click anything and to delete anything strange coming from your address.

Sometimes the hijacker changes your password and locks you out. In that case, contact the e-mail provider for help in resolving the problem.

Invalid Security Certificate   If you see an invalid certificate error when browsing the Web, it doesn't mean you have been infected with anything—yet. It just means that the certificate that this supposedly secure website is offering up was not issued by a trusted authority. If you see this kind of warning, click the Back button; do not proceed to that site. If you absolutely must proceed, do so in a high-security browsing mode such as InPrivate browsing in IE.

Quarantine Infected System

When you suspect a computer of infection with malware, remove it from the network in order to quarantine it and keep other computers from being infected. In addition, your security program may quarantine the malware file or it may remove it entirely. It all depends on the security software configuration. A quarantined file is disabled, but not removed from the computer. Some security software talks about the malware being in a "vault," which is the same as quarantining. Since security software can make mistakes and identify critical and uninfected files as malware, consider configuring your security program to quarantine detected malware so that you have the opportunity to review the file and decide what action to take.

Disable System Restore and Create a Restore Point

Because System Restore keeps snapshots of your computer configuration and system files, the malware can be included in those files, and your computer would be reinfected when you restored from a restore point. Therefore, after you have removed malware, disable System Restore and create a new restore point.

Remediate Infected Systems

Next, remove the infection. To do this you will probably need to boot into Safe Mode (or Safe Mode with Networking). Then use a real-time scanner such as Malwarebytes if your regular antivirus program isn't working, to find and fix the problem. If it's a really problematic infection, you might even need to boot into the Windows Preinstallation Environment and do a repair (see Chapter 12). Boot back into Windows normally and run your antivirus software scan again to confirm the infection is gone.

Schedule Scans and Run Updates

To cut down on the chance of the infection reoccurring, make sure your antivirus application is up to date. Download any available updates. Then make sure it is set for real-time scanning, and also to do a full system scan at certain intervals.

Enable System Restore and Create a Restore Point

When the system is back in order and your antivirus program is updated and working, re-enable System Restore, and create a new restore point representing the new, clean system state.

Educate the End User

Finally, if you know how the system got infected, use that information to educate yourself and everyone else who uses the PC so it won't happen again. For example, did you click a download link on a shady-looking website? Did you open an e-mail attachment from an unknown sender? Trace back to the origin of the infection and learn from it.

SCENARIO & SOLUTION

I support computers in a large organization that uses Cisco routers and firewalls at all connections to the Internet. Why should we use personal firewalls on all our Windows computers?	A properly configured hardware firewall will protect against invasions to the network, but it will not protect each computer from invasion from within the private network.
Now that I have a phishing filter enabled in Windows, do I need to be on the watch for phishing?	Yes, you still must watch for phishing attempts. Educate yourself on the techniques phishers use to obtain your personal financial information.

Preventive Maintenance for Security

As all steps you take to implement security are preventive steps, we do not need to add a long description of preventive security maintenance. There are, however, certain tasks that we should add to those described so far in this chapter that fall under preventive maintenance, beginning with backing up data, keeping up to date on service packs and patches, training users, and recognizing social engineering.

Understanding Data Loss Prevention (DLP)

Data loss prevention (DLP) is a strategy (and a type of software used for implementing it) for preventing users from sending sensitive information outside the company network. DLP systems attempt to stem two kinds of problems: data leak and data loss. A *data leak* occurs when data is made available to someone who shouldn't have it. *Data loss* occurs when the original copy of the data is no longer available.

DLP in a general sense is a broad-spectrum plan implemented as a whole in an organization, using tools such as backups, antivirus, firewalls, e-mail monitoring, and database monitoring. In addition, DLP software implements advanced measures such as learning and reasoning algorithms that look for abnormal access to data and unusual user and network activities. In other words, Big Brother is watching!

Implementing Data Backup Procedures

An important part of data security is a backup policy that includes frequent backups of data to removable media. Storage of the media should also be part of the policy. Although backup media should be handy for quick restores, a full backup set should also be stored offsite in case something occurs to the building in which the computer is housed, as well as to the computer. For offsite storage, consider encrypting the backup media. The frequency of the backups, and of the full backup that is stored offsite, depends on the needs of the organization. It is not possible to overemphasize how important it is to back up data. We discussed backup in Chapter 10. We will talk about who has the permission to back up here.

Users can back up files they created on their local NTFS volume, including the personal folders in their own User folder. Users can restore files and folders to which they have the Write permission on an NTFS volume. Members of the local Administrators and Backup Operators groups have the right to back up and restore all files. Individual users in these groups can back up and restore files that they do not normally have permissions to access. This ability does not give them any other access to these files and folders. If someone is only doing the backup function for a computer that contains other users' data, and that person does not need to do other administrative tasks, make them a member of the Backup Operators group rather than the Administrators group. This is an example of applying the principle of least privilege.

Installing Service Packs and Patches

Although this point was made previously in this book, it is important to the security of your computer and your confidential data that you keep your computer updated with the latest service packs and patches. If you have Internet access, turn on Automatic Updates in Windows. In addition, any security software you install will normally have an automatic update feature. Be sure to turn this on.

e x a m
ⓦatch

Although every security measure you take is preventive against threats, the CompTIA A+ 220-902 exam objectives stress the importance of keeping your operating system and security software up to date with service packs and patches, and the importance of user training. User training should include the use of the malware prevention technologies on users' systems and awareness of the social engineering situations they may encounter.

Training Users

Knowledge of the danger of threats and ways to prevent malicious software from invading computers is important to both the computer professional and to each PC user. Do your part to keep yourself current on security technologies. Depending on your role in an organization, take all opportunities to educate users. Make them aware of the company's security policy and the role they need to play in preventing attacks.

Recognizing Social Engineering

In Chapter 17, you learned about social engineering and ways to recognize social engineering when you encounter it in e-mails and other messages. Do your part to inform other users about social engineering by sharing what you have learned and by directing them to look at a site that educates people about these threats. We gave an example in Exercise 17-2.

■ *902: 3.6*   *Given a scenario, use appropriate data destruction and disposal methods*

In this final, short section of the chapter, we cover the "Recycling or repurposing best practices" portion of CompTIA A+ 902 exam objective 3.6. The physical destruction of hardware was covered in Chapter 17.

Securely Recycling or Repurposing Storage

When storage devices are no longer needed, you might choose to recycle them, repurpose them, or donate them to charity, but before you can do any of that, you need to make sure that the data on them cannot be read. Otherwise you are creating a security risk for your company (or for your own personal privacy, if it's your own drive.)

The level of data destruction to employ depends on how sensitive the data is—that is, how bad would it be if someone were able to read it? This can range from mildly bad (like someone could read a bunch of boring internal memos) to really bad (like someone could see customer mailing addresses) to unbelievably bad (like your customers' credit card data is sold to a criminal syndicate).

Here are some of the ways you can destroy data that you won't want others to access, listed from least to most effective:

- **Deleting files** This is the quickest and least-secure method of clearing a disk. Just select the files in File Explorer and press DELETE and then empty the Recycle Bin.
- **Reformatting** You can use the Format utility in the OS to perform a format. This erases the master file table (or file allocation table). The data is still on the disk but there is no easy way of retrieving it. Someone would have to use a special disk repair utility, or investigate the drive sector by sector, to piece it together. 902 exam objective 3.6 calls this a *standard format.*
- **Repartitioning** You can use a utility like Disk Management in Windows or GParted for Linux to delete the existing partitions on the drive, create a new partition, and format it. Deleting and re-creating the partitions adds an additional degree of difficulty for the person trying to restore data.
- **Low-level formatting (disk wiping)** What people call "low-level formatting" in the context of security is not really low-level formatting (at least not in the sense that it's done at the factory), but rather high-level formatting plus zero-filling all sectors

of the hard drive. 902 exam objective 3.6 calls this *drive wipe.* You can do this with a third-party drive utility, or in Linux you can do it from a command prompt with the dd command, like this:

```
dd if=/dev/zero of=/dev/<target device>
```

There are different security standards for different levels of disk wiping. For example, the U.S. Military standard (DoD 5220.22-M) overwrites the entire hard drive six times, through a series of wiping passes, so if you need to wipe to a certain standard, make sure the wiping software you are using conforms to the needed standard.

CERTIFICATION SUMMARY

There are no easy answers or quick fixes when it comes to computer security. Security threats go beyond simple computer invasions to inflict damage to threats against your very identity. Therefore, computer security must be multifaceted to protect computers, data, and users.

On a Windows computer, this multifaceted approach begins with implementing authentication and creating accounts using your understanding of local users and groups and how group membership gives a user his or her level of access. In Chapter 19, we will look at how you modify this level of access to files, folders, and printers. This multifaceted approach also includes implementing best practices to secure a workstation.

Be aware of the built-in security features in Windows and how to configure them, including but not limited to User Account Control, antivirus and antimalware software, phishing filters, antispyware, anti-adware, and pop-blockers. Configure firewalls on your network as well as on individual computers using Windows Firewall or another personal firewall.

TWO-MINUTE DRILL

Here are some of the key points covered in Chapter 18.

Implementing Authentication for Digital Security

❑ Each organization must have a security policy/AUP, sometimes dictated by government regulations, to protect equipment, people, and data. Among the many types of data that must be protected is personally identifiable information (PII) that uniquely identifies an individual.

❏ Access control to resources on a computer or network begins with authentication (verifying a user's identity) and authorization (determining the level of access an authenticated user has to a resource).

❏ Use the Local User and Group Accounts section of Computer Management to manage built-in accounts, change account types, enable and disable the Guest account, and create special groups.

❏ Windows Sign-in is different depending on whether you are part of an Active Directory domain or not. On a standalone or workgroup PC, you can click icons for the local user accounts. On an Active Directory system you type the user name and password, for greater security.

❏ When a user needs to walk away from a PC for short periods, the Lock Computer option will hide the desktop until the user returns and enters his or her account password.

❏ Two types of BIOS/UEFI passwords can be set—one that must be entered at startup before an operating system is loaded, and another that is required for access to the firmware system settings (also known as CMOS settings).

❏ Windows Credential Manager can store user names, passwords, and certificates in the Windows Vault to automate logging on to various network services.

Implementing a Defense Against Malware

❏ Here are some of the ways to secure a workstation: require and set strong passwords, enable a screen saver password, restrict user permissions, change default user names, disable the Guest account, set password expiration, set sign-in time restriction, set a failed attempts lockout, and disable Autorun/AutoPlay.

❏ User Account Control prevents malware from modifying your computer by prompting for your consent; this behavior can be configured in Windows 7 and newer. With Windows Vista, UAC is either on or off.

❏ A properly configured hardware firewall will protect a network from certain types of invasions from the Internet or other untrusted networks, but personal firewalls on each computer will protect from attacks that originate on the private network.

❏ Windows Firewall is enabled by default, but if you install a third-party firewall, Windows Firewall will be turned off.

❏ Antivirus/antimalware programs examine the contents of a disk and RAM, looking for hidden viruses and files that may act as hosts for virus code and malware.

❏ Always enable the update option in an antivirus program and configure it to automatically connect to the manufacturer's website, check for updates, and install them. These updates will include changes to both the antivirus engine and definition files.

❏ Encourage users to acquire applications only from trusted sources, such as the official store app for the operating system.

❏ To remove malware, (1) identify malware symptoms, (2) quarantine infected systems, (3) disable System Restore and create a restore point (4) remediate infected systems, (5) schedule scans and run updates, (6) enable System Restore and create a restore point, and (7) educate end users.

❏ Symptoms of malware include security alerts, slow performance, crashes, pop-ups, missing files, and hijacked e-mail.

❏ To prevent security problems in the future, use data loss prevention software, implement data backup procedures, install service packs and patches, and train users, including how to recognize social engineering schemes.

Securely Recycling or Repurposing Storage

❏ Erase data on a disk before recycling, repurposing, or donating it.

❏ Deleting the files and reformatting is not very secure, but better than nothing. Repartitioning requires somewhat better security, but for the best security, use a disk wiping utility that does multiple passes to wipe to the standard required for the industry.

SELF TEST

The following questions will help you measure your understanding of the material presented in this chapter. Read all of the choices carefully because there might be more than one correct answer. Choose all correct answers for each question.

Implementing Authentication for Digital Security

1. Microsoft recommends that you use a(n) _____ user account for everyday use, to minimize the risk of malware modifications to system files.
   A. Standard
   B. Administrator
   C. Guest
   D. Normal

2. When you use a smart card with a PIN, this is an example of which of the following?
   A. RFID
   B. One-factor authentication
   C. TPM
   D. Multifactor authentication

3. Which of the following is a best practice to apply to passwords?
   A. Short passwords
   B. Memorable passwords
   C. Strong passwords
   D. Blank passwords

4. This feature is quite handy, but you should disable it because it potentially could allow malware on removable media to infect your computer.
   A. Creator Owner
   B. DriveLock
   C. Screen saver
   D. AutoPlay

5. What should you set to prevent someone from changing the boot order on a PC?
   A. Guest password
   B. Screen saver password
   C. Windows Sign-in password
   D. Firmware settings password

6. This local built-in Windows account, disabled by default, is restricted in what it can do if enabled.
   A. Administrator
   B. Guest
   C. Anonymous
   D. Power User

7. This feature, introduced in Windows Vista, protects against programs running in the background, changing settings, and installing malware when a logged-on user is a member of the Administrators group.
   A. DriveLock
   B. TPM
   C. UAC
   D. Autorun

8. What Windows utility stores and manages local passwords?
   A. TPM
   B. Credential Manager
   C. BitLocker
   D. DriveLock

9. Before walking away from your computer, press WINDOWS KEY-L to enable this security feature.
   A. DriveLock
   B. Lock Computer
   C. Screen Saver
   D. TPM

10. How can you prevent hackers from trying repeatedly to guess a password?
    A. Disable Guest account
    B. Password expiration
    C. Disable AutoPlay
    D. Failed attempts lockout

11. Which of these passwords is the strongest?
    A. 1234567890
    B. Exce!!3nc3
    C. Doggedly
    D. ab34ef

12. Jason needs correct permission to back up and restore a computer containing confidential data saved by other users into their own Documents folders on an NTFS volume. Assuming he does not need to perform other administrative tasks, select the group you would put him into so that he can do these tasks. Apply the principle of least privilege.
    A. Administrators
    B. Backup Operators
    C. Guests
    D. Users

Implementing a Defense Against Malware

13. What hardware device or software program prevents unwanted traffic from entering a network?
    A. Proxy server
    B. Firewall
    C. Router
    D. Switch

14. What two antivirus components are frequently updated?
    A. Spyware and rootkits
    B. Engine and definitions
    C. Engine and spam filter
    D. Definition files and phishing filter

15. When a Standard user tries to make a system change, what feature prompts for an Administrator account's password?
    A. TPM
    B. Spam filter
    C. UAC
    D. Antivirus

16. What utility that comes with Windows 8.1 can you use to scan for and remove malware?
    A. UAC
    B. Windows Defender
    C. Pop-up blocker
    D. Windows Firewall

17. What security software examines the contents of a disk and RAM, looking for hidden viruses and files that may act as hosts for virus code?
    A. Phishing filter
    B. Antivirus
    C. Personal firewall
    D. Pop-up blocker

18. What should you do before attempting to remove malware?
    A. Sign in as a Standard user.
    B. Disable System Restore.
    C. Enable System Restore.
    D. Educate end users.

19. Your IT security office is concerned that network computers do not have the latest security updates installed. Which tool can determine this?
    A. Security Center
    B. Local security policy
    C. UAC
    D. MBSA

Securely Recycling or Repurposing Storage

20. Which is the most secure way of deleting data from a hard disk before recycling it?
    A. Repartitioning
    B. Disk wiping
    C. Deleting files
    D. Reformatting

SELF TEST ANSWERS

Implementing Authentication for Digital Security

1. ☑ **A.** Standard user accounts are suitable for everyday use because they cannot modify system settings.
    ☒ **B** is incorrect because Administrator is a type of account that has full permission to modify system settings, and so is dangerous to use on a daily basis. **C** is incorrect because Guest is a type of account that is so limited that it is not suitable for daily use. **D** is incorrect because Normal is not one of the account types.

2. ☑ **D.** Multifactor authentication. In this case, you are using something you have (the smart card) and something you know (the PIN).
    ☒ **A** is incorrect because radio frequency ID does not require entering a PIN, or even touching a computer or keypad. **B** is incorrect because it depends on only one factor, which could be a password. **C** is incorrect because TPM (Trusted Platform Module) is a chip that can be used to store passwords or keys.

3. ☑ **C.** Strong passwords are a best practice for passwords. This means a password should be both long and complex, with numbers, letters, and symbols.
    ☒ **A, B,** and **D** are all incorrect because none of them is a best practice, and you could call blank passwords a worst practice.

4. ☑ **D.** AutoPlay (or Autorun in older versions) enables Windows to automatically find and run the content on removable media when it is connects to a computer. Removable media is a potential vector for malware.
    ☒ **A** is incorrect because Creator Owner is a special Windows group. **B** is incorrect because DriveLock is a drive protection feature on some computers. **C** is incorrect because a screen saver is simply a picture or animation that displays on your screen after a period of inactivity.

5. ☑ **D.** A firmware settings password will prevent someone from changing boot order, which is a firmware setting.
    ☒ **A** is incorrect because the Guest account has no password. **B** is incorrect because the screen saver password is the same as the user's regular password for signing in to Windows; it does not protect firmware settings. **C** is incorrect because, like the screen saver password, the Windows Sign-in password also does not protect firmware settings.

6. ☑ **B.** The Guest account is built in, disabled by default, and restricted in what it can do.
   ☒ **A** is incorrect because the Administrator account is not disabled and is not restricted. **C** is incorrect because Anonymous is not a Windows account. **D** is incorrect because there is no built-in Power User account, although there is a built-in Power Users group.

7. ☑ **C.** UAC (User Account Control) prevents programs from running in the background, changing settings, and installing malware when a logged-on user is a member of the Administrators group.
   ☒ **A** is incorrect because DriveLock just allows you to set a password that you must provide at startup. **B** is incorrect because TPM (Trusted Platform Module) is a chip that can store passwords or keys. **D** is incorrect because the Autorun feature (AutoPlay in newer versions) enables Windows to automatically find and run the content on removable media when it connects to a computer.

8. ☑ **B.** Credential Manager stores and manages local passwords.
   ☒ **A** is incorrect because TPM stands for Trusted Platform Module, and is the technology for encrypting volumes using BitLocker. **C** is incorrect because BitLocker is a whole-disk encryption utility. **D** is incorrect because DriveLock is a feature on some computers that locks access to hard drives.

9. ☑ **B.** Lock Computer is enabled when you press WINDOWS KEY-L, requiring authentication before anyone can access your computer.
   ☒ **A** is incorrect because DriveLock is a feature on some computers that locks access to hard drives. **C** is incorrect because WINDOWS KEY-L does not enable the screen saver. **D** is incorrect because TPM (Trusted Platform Module) is a chip that can store passwords or keys for accessing a computer's hard drive.

10. ☑ **D.** Failed attempts lockout prevents password guessing by locking out sign-in after a certain number of failures.
    ☒ **A** is incorrect because disabling the Guest account will not prevent hacking. **B** is incorrect because password expiration will make passwords change frequently but will not prevent repeated attempts. **C** is incorrect because AutoPlay has no effect on password security.

11. ☑ **B.** Exce!!3nc3 is a strong password because it uses uppercase and lowercase letters, numbers, and symbols and is more than eight characters.
    ☒ **A** is incorrect; it is not strong, because it is only numbers and they are in an expected sequence. **C** is incorrect; it is not strong, because it contains no numbers or symbols and it is in the dictionary. **D** is incorrect; it is not strong, because it is too short and does not contain any capital letters or symbols.

12. ☑ **B.** The Backup Operators group gives the person the right to back up and restore files to which he would not normally have access, but does not give him permissions to access and open these files.
    ☒ **A** is incorrect because although a member of the Administrators group could do the tasks, the question assumes that the person does not need to do administrative tasks. **C** is incorrect because users in the Guests group cannot perform these tasks. **D** is incorrect because a member of the Users group can only back up their own files.

Implementing a Defense Against Malware

13. ☑ **B.** A firewall is the hardware device or software program that prevents unwanted traffic from entering a network.
   ☒ **A** is incorrect because although a proxy server is one of the technologies used by a firewall, it does not fully describe a firewall. **C** is incorrect because a router is a separate device (or software), although it may use one or more of the technologies associated with a firewall. **D** is incorrect because this device or software does not prevent unwanted traffic from entering a network. A switch is a cable-connecting device used within a network.

14. ☑ **B.** The engine and definitions are the two frequently updated antivirus components.
   ☒ **A** is incorrect because spyware and rootkits are two kinds of threats, not two components of antivirus programs. **C** is incorrect because although the antivirus engine is one of the updated components, the spam filter is not part of antivirus software, even though it may be bundled with antivirus software in a security package. **D** is incorrect because although definition file is part of the correct answer, phishing filter is not part of an antivirus program, but a web browser add-on or feature.

15. ☑ **C.** UAC, or User Access Control, prompts for credentials when a Standard user tries to make a system change.
   ☒ **A** is incorrect because TPM (Trust Platform Module) manages disk encryption. **B** is incorrect because a spam filter does not look for social engineering traits but for spam in your e-mail. **D** is incorrect because antivirus software does not look for social engineering traits, but for viruses.

16. ☑ **B.** Windows Defender removes viruses and other malware in Windows 8.1.
   ☒ **A** is incorrect because User Account Control (UAC) prompts for permission when system changes are being made. **C** is incorrect because a pop-up blocker prevents browser pop-ups. **D** is incorrect because Windows Firewall prevents intrusions on ports, but does not remove viruses or malware.

17. ☑ **B.** Antivirus is security software that examines the contents of a disk and RAM, looking for hidden viruses and files that may act as hosts for virus code.
   ☒ **A** is incorrect because a phishing filter works within a browser and scans websites for certain social engineering traits. **C** is incorrect because a personal firewall blocks certain types of incoming messages based on information in the packet header, but does not look at the contents to determine if it is virus code. **D** is incorrect because a pop-up blocker only works within a browser to prevent unwanted browser windows from opening.

18. ☑ **B.** Before removing malware, disable System Restore so the virus does not come back via that feature.
   ☒ **A** is incorrect because a Standard user lacks permission to make system changes. **C** is incorrect because System Restore should be disabled, not enabled. **D** is incorrect because educating end users is the last step in the malware removal process, and should not occur before attempting to remove the malware.

19. ☑ **D.** The Microsoft Baseline Security Analyzer (MBSA) can scan one or more computers for update compliance.

    ☒ **A** is incorrect because Security Center in Windows Vista (Action Center in Windows 7) allows configuration of components such as the Windows Firewall and automatic updates. **B** is incorrect because local security policy is used to configure security settings on a single computer. **C** is incorrect because User Account Control (UAC) prevents programs from running without your consent.

Securely Recycling or Repurposing Storage

20. ☑ **B.** Disk wiping is the most secure of the listed methods.

    ☒ **A** is incorrect because repartitioning is more secure than C or D but not the most secure. **C** is incorrect because deleting files is the least secure. **D** is incorrect because reformatting is the second-least secure.

Chapter 19

Configuring Windows Clients

A t work, at school, and at home, computer users depend on client software components to accomplish work—whether they are doing research over the Internet, playing an Internet game, using e-mail, or transferring files from a server to the desktop computer. Making files and devices available to network users has led to the need for securing those resources, possibly the most important set of tasks on a network. Implementing security in this environment involves many different tasks, such as implementing authentication and data security, taking all necessary steps to prevent the invasion of malicious software, and discovering if malicious software is already on a system.

This chapter continues the discussion of authentication begun in Chapter 17 where we described methods for authenticating access to buildings and campuses, and carried on in Chapter 18 where we discussed Windows OS tools and features that help secure individual workstations. Here we look at authentication of digital access to computers and networks. We begin with configuring Windows clients for file and printer sharing; then we look at how to apply permissions on NTFS volumes for both local and network users, and how to apply share permissions, which combine with NTFS permissions for network users. You will also learn about file and folder encryption on NTFS volumes versus BitLocker drive encryption.

CERTIFICATION OBJECTIVES

- **901: 4.4** *Given a scenario, troubleshoot wired and wireless networks with appropriate tools*
- **902: 1.3** *Given a scenario, apply appropriate Microsoft command-line tools*
- **902: 1.5** *Given a scenario, use Windows Control Panel utilities*
- **902: 1.6** *Given a scenario, install and configure Windows networking on a client/desktop*

In this section you'll learn how to configure Windows clients for file and printer sharing, using the three methods listed in CompTIA A+ 902 exam objective 1.6: HomeGroup, workgroup, and domain (Microsoft Active Directory domain). You will learn how to configure a client for each type and how the methods differ. This section also hits two topics from A+ 902 exam objective 1.5: HomeGroup and Network and Sharing Center, and briefly explains the NETDOM utility listed in A+ 901 exam objective 4.4 and the GPUPDATE and GPRESULT utilities from A+ 902 exam objective 1.3.

Configuring Windows Clients for File and Printer Sharing

In this section we will examine three methods for sharing files and printers from a Windows client computer. Two methods are ideal for a home or small office network that does not require a great deal of security. They are HomeGroups and workgroups. The third method is for the Windows client to join a Windows domain, which is a common method used in medium- to large-size organizations and small organizations with a greater need for security and a need for better services in-house, such as using Microsoft's e-mail server—Exchange Server—for employees' e-mail accounts.

HomeGroups

The *HomeGroup* feature is an easy-to-configure form of Microsoft's peer-to-peer file and print sharing, with only a single password protecting the HomeGroup shares on all Windows computers that join a HomeGroup. With HomeGroup enabled, you can choose to share local printers and selected Windows library folders (Documents, Music, Pictures, and/or Videos.)

 You can configure a Windows 7 or newer computer running any edition as a client to join a HomeGroup, but only certain Windows 7 editions can create and host a HomeGroup: Windows 7 Home Premium, Professional, Ultimate, and Enterprise editions. All versions of Windows 8 and newer can create and host HomeGroups.

After you create a HomeGroup on one computer, you only have to enter the password once on each client computer in the HomeGroup when the client joins the HomeGroup. Microsoft created HomeGroup to make it simple for people on a very small network to share their data with one another. It is ideal for a family or small business.

In this section, we will first describe Windows network locations, something that is important to understand in order to participate in a peer-to-peer network. Then we will summarize the rules for HomeGroups and detail how to create, configure, leave, or join a HomeGroup. Finally, we will look at the notion of libraries, and public libraries in particular, because these are the folders through which you share files and folders in a HomeGroup.

Microsoft documentation, and even the graphical user interface (GUI) tools, capitalizes the term HomeGroup inconsistently. We have decided to go with HomeGroup, and have tried to be consistent in its use.

Windows Network Locations

It is important to understand Microsoft's notion of a network location, which you need to select when you first connect to a network, because Windows will configure appropriate firewall and security settings based on the network location. This setting has an impact on your ability to use the file and printer sharing methods we discuss in this chapter. The choices in Windows 7 are Home Network (as shown in Figure 19-1), Work Network, or Public Network. In Windows 8 and newer, Private Network replaces Home Network but the settings are otherwise the same. When you connect to a network, Windows prompts you to choose the location. (You'll see how to change the network location in Exercise 19-1.)

FIGURE 19-1　　ShortMoose is a Home network.

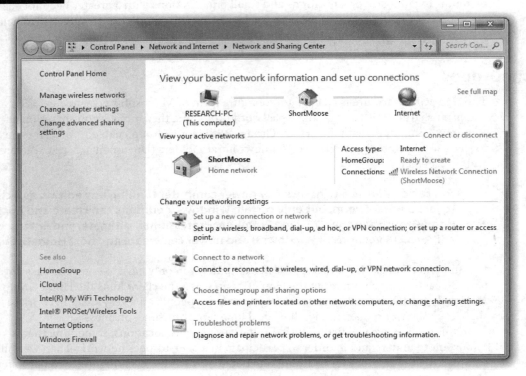

Home/Private Network　　Choose Home Network or Private Network as your location when you trust all the computers on your network, as you would at home. When you choose this, the *Network Discovery* feature is turned on, your computer will be visible to other users on the network, and you will see other computers on the network.

To manually turn Network Discovery on or off, open Network and Sharing Center and select Change Advanced Sharing Settings. Expand the current network profile if needed. Then click Turn On Network Discovery or Turn Off Network Discovery.

Work Network　　The Work Network location is your choice if you are connecting to a small network at work. Network Discovery is turned on for this setting also. While you cannot create or join a HomeGroup when in a Work network, you can participate in a workgroup, Microsoft's older and more generic form of peer-to-peer networking.

Public Network   The Public Network location is the right choice for untrusted locations, such as public waiting rooms and coffee shops. It is also the preferred choice if you are using a mobile broadband connection or if your computer connects directly to the Internet without going through a router. You will not be visible to other computers on the network because Network Discovery is automatically turned off for this location and the HomeGroup feature is disabled while on a public network. This is also the safest choice if you do not want to share your local files or printers with others on your network.

watch   Be sure you understand that Windows will configure Windows Firewall settings based on the network location and that the Public Network setting is the safest.

Network Discovery is turned on for Home and Work networks, and turned off for Public networks. HomeGroup is turned off for all except Home/Private Network.

Domain   Domain is not a network location you can select, but instead is automatically configured when your computer is joined to a Windows domain at your workplace or school. You cannot change this network location as long as your computer is part of the domain.

Creating and Configuring a HomeGroup

As discussed earlier, a HomeGroup requires the Home Network location. It also requires that IPv6 be enabled, even on a network that also supports IPv4. That is just part of the picture. Here are rules and guidelines for HomeGroups:

- HomeGroups are supported only in Windows 7 and newer.
- A computer can belong to only one HomeGroup at a time, and there can only be one HomeGroup on a local area network (LAN) or wireless local area network (WLAN).
- Computers that are part of a Windows Active Directory domain cannot create a HomeGroup but can join one.
- Your computer's network location, selected in Network and Sharing Center, must be Home Network.
- HomeGroup requires that IPv6 be enabled on the local computer. This is turned on by default in Windows 7 and newer, but if it is disabled, HomeGroup will not work.

■ All firewalls between HomeGroup computers must support IPv6 and allow file and printer sharing. Windows Firewall supports both.

■ Routers that forward IPv6 and multicast traffic allow HomeGroups to exist beyond a LAN.

■ A HomeGroup lets you share local printers and Public folders within your Windows Libraries.

Before creating a HomeGroup, check that IPv6 is enabled and that your computer is on a Home/Private network type. To check that IPv6 is enabled, open Network and Sharing Center, and in the task list on the left, select Change Adapter Settings. This opens the Network Connections page. In many cases, there will be just one connection, but you may have two or more. For instance, a laptop with both an Ethernet network interface card (NIC) and a Wi-Fi NIC will show both connections. The choice is simple if, for instance, the Ethernet NIC network connection is unplugged and you are connected to a Wi-Fi network. Double-click the network connection you will use for the HomeGroup, and this will open the Status box for that connection. Click the Properties button, and on the Networking page of the Properties dialog box, ensure that a check is in the box for Internet Protocol Version 6 (TCP/IPv6). Now you are ready to create and configure a HomeGroup. Exercise 19-1 will walk you through the steps.

EXERCISE 19-1

Creating a HomeGroup

Practice creating and configuring a HomeGroup.

1. From the Start menu/Start screen type **home** and select HomeGroup from the results list.

   Important: If you're working in Windows 8/8.1, one of the options in the search results will be HomeGroup Settings. Do not click that one, or any of the options with the Settings (cog) graphic next to it, because then you'll end up in the Settings app, and these steps won't work for you. Choose the result that just says HomeGroup to start from the Control Panel.

2. If your computer is not on a Private/Home network, switch to a Private/Home network.

   To switch between Public and Private network types in Windows 8/8.1, choose the Settings charm and click Change PC Settings. Click Network, and then click the network to change. Change the Find Devices and Content slider's setting to switch between Public and Private. (This works only if you're signed in with Administrator privileges.)

Select the resources you want to share with others on your HomeGroup.

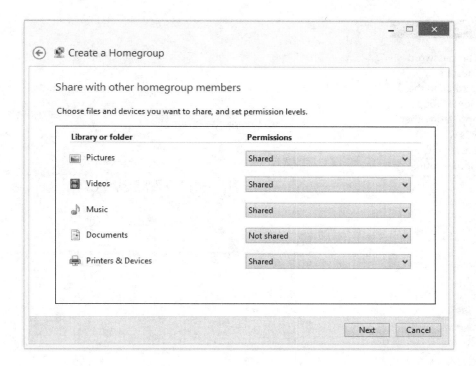

In Windows 7, from the Network and Sharing Center, click the current network type (such as Home Network) and then select a new type from the dialog box that appears.

3. Next to HomeGroup, click the Ready to Create hyperlink. Then click the Create a HomeGroup button.

4. If you're running Windows 8/8.1 or newer, click Next. (This step isn't needed in Windows 7.)

5. In the Windows 8/8.1 version, a list of libraries/folders appears. For each one, open the drop-down list and click Shared or Not Shared. See Figure 19-2. In the Windows 7 version, you have check boxes instead; click to place a check by the items you wish to share. Notice that one of the choices is Printers; use this to enable printer sharing. Then click Next.

6. Windows will generate a password for your HomeGroup, shown in Figure 19-3. Write it down or use the link to print the password and instructions. You will need to enter the password on the other computers on your network as you join them to the HomeGroup.

This password must be entered in the HomeGroup applet on other PCs when they join the HomeGroup.

7. After writing down or printing out the password, click the Finish button. Note that if you lose the password, you can open HomeGroup and view it again.

Joining or Leaving a HomeGroup

Go to another Windows computer on your network, and open the Network and Sharing Center. Next to HomeGroup, click the Available to Join hyperlink. Click Join Now, and then follow the prompts.

You cannot create a new HomeGroup when another computer on the LAN is running that is a part of an existing HomeGroup. Turn off all other computers on the network if you are having trouble creating a new HomeGroup; this should prevent your computer from seeing the existing HomeGroup, so it will allow you to create a new one.

Populating Your Public Libraries

Now that you've joined a HomeGroup, anytime you wish to share files and folders, simply place them in the Public libraries. A *library* is a virtual storage location that can display content from multiple locations. It looks like a folder that contains other folders and files, but only contains pointers to them. A single library can point to various locations on local storage or network storage, making it appear as if content from many different locations is in the same location. Libraries make it easier for you to browse and organize related information or types of files. Libraries also make it easier to back up related files because you can simply point to one library and back up files from all locations.

Figure 19-4 shows the Libraries folder with four libraries: Documents, Music, Pictures, and Videos. Each library has a Public folder in addition to the base folder for that library. (Notice in the navigation pane that the Pictures library contains two folders: Pictures and

FIGURE 19-4

Each library contains a private folder and a Public folder and any others added by the user.

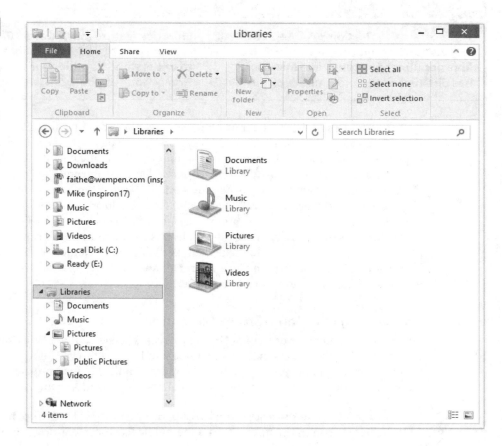

Public Pictures.) Each of these points to a different location. Users can add more locations to the libraries, and they will appear as folders under the library folders. In Windows 8.1 and newer, corresponding folders from OneDrive also appear in the libraries.

In Windows 8.1 and newer, Libraries does not appear by default in the navigation pane in File Explorer. To enable it, right-click an empty area of the navigation pane and click Show Libraries.

Anyone using a computer in the HomeGroup has full control in the Public library folders that you share. As such, they can copy, edit, delete, and move within those folders. Put anything you wish to share under those conditions into the Public folders.

e x a m
watch

The CompTIA A+ 220-901 and 220-902 exams do not explicitly list libraries under any topic, and Microsoft has diminished the prominence of the

Libraries feature in Windows 10. However, it is important to understand libraries in order to understand how file sharing works in a HomeGroup and to work with HomeGroups.

To add folders or files to a library, copy or move them directly into one of the library folders, or add a folder to a library as a location—then you do not need to move or copy the files and folders. Consider the Documents library. By default, it includes two locations, Documents (C:\Users*user_name*\Documents) and Public Documents (C:\Users\Public\Documents). In Windows 8.1 and newer it may also contain Documents (C:\Users*user_name*\OneDrive\Documents). The first location is not shared through HomeGroups, but the second location is, as long as you enabled HomeGroup sharing for Documents in the HomeGroup applet. In this case, simply copy or move folders and files into the second location to make them available to the HomeGroup. If you group a library folder by Folder Path in File Explorer (View | Group | Folder Path), you can see each folder's path, as shown in Figure 19-5.

Connecting to a HomeGroup Computer

Once you are a member of a HomeGroup, you can use File Explorer/Windows Explorer to browse to other computers in the HomeGroup and connect to the folders that were selected to share. The computer you are using will not show in the HomeGroup, just the other members. To do so, click the HomeGroup icon in the navigation pane.

You can browse the entire workgroup, not just the HomeGroup, by clicking the Network icon in the navigation pane of File Explorer/Windows Explorer.

FIGURE 19-5   Group files in a library by Folder Path to see them by location.

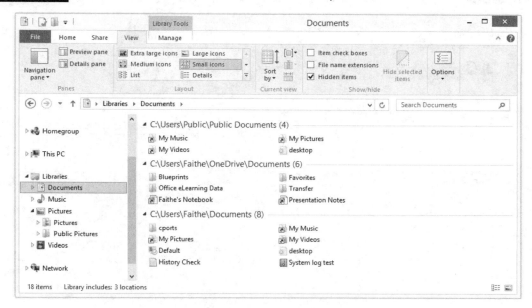

Workgroups

A *workgroup* is a uniquely named collection of networked computers participating in file and print sharing, but with no central administration. Small groups of computers band together, creating a peer-to-peer network, to share resources without relying on a server. The simple peer-to-peer network you learned how to create in Chapter 14 with a SOHO router is a workgroup.

Being part of a workgroup or HomeGroup is not an either-or proposition. All computers that are connected to a common LAN and have the same workgroup name set are automatically in a workgroup together; that doesn't go away if you create or join a HomeGroup. The computers with which your computer is a HomeGroup have a special sharing relationship with your computer, but your computer can also share with other computers outside of that HomeGroup as well.

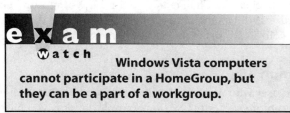

Windows Vista computers cannot participate in a HomeGroup, but they can be a part of a workgroup.

FIGURE 19-6 View and change the workgroup name.

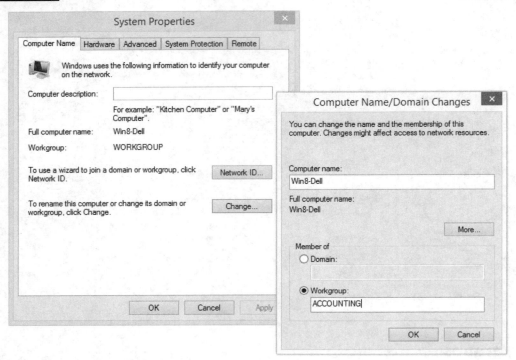

Creating and Joining a Workgroup

If your computer is not a member of a domain, it is automatically a member of a workgroup called WORKGROUP. You can join a different workgroup (or create one) by changing the workgroup name in Windows.

To change a workgroup name, open Control Panel. In the Search box type **computer name**. In the results list select Rename This Computer to open the System Properties dialog box. On the Computer Name tab, click the Change button. In the Workgroup field of the dialog box that opens (see Figure 19-6), change the workgroup name and then click OK. Follow the prompts to restart your PC to make the name change take effect.

Workgroup Administration

In a workgroup situation, each user who wants to access a remote computer's shared assets must have an account on that remote computer. So, for example, let's say you have two computers in your home, and one of those computers has three user accounts on it, one for each of your kids: Abby, Billy, and Charlie. In order for each kid's account to be able to access your PC's shared resources over the LAN, you will need to create accounts for each of the kids on your computer.

If the user name and password credentials for the account you create for each of those remote users on your PC are identical to the user names and passwords they use on their own local PC, they will not be prompted for credentials when they connect to your shared resources. If they aren't identical, they'll be prompted every time.

If you want all LAN users to be able to access certain shared content and you don't want to set up accounts for them on your PC, there's a workaround. Open Network and Sharing Center, and choose Change Advanced Sharing Settings. Expand the All Networks section, turn on Public Folder Sharing, and turn off Password Protected Sharing. Be aware, though, that if you turn off Password Protected Sharing, anyone who has access to your LAN will be able to use your shared resources. Unless your LAN is very tightly locked down, that could be a serious privacy threat.

Active Directory Domains

A Microsoft *Active Directory (AD) domain* is a collection of workstations and servers under single administrative control. The security accounts database is much more sophisticated than that on local Windows computers and resides on at least one special Windows Server computer called a domain controller. The security accounts database, or directory, is replicated across all domain controllers in the domain, allowing for more efficient access to the domain controllers from many locations. A medium-size organization might consist of a single AD domain, whereas a large multinational firm might consist of many AD domains.

When a computer joins a domain, a computer account is created for that computer and the computer itself signs in to the domain when it starts up. (This is transparent to the computer user, and is separate from a user sign-in on a local PC.) Joining a computer to a domain requires local administrative rights, and when prompted for AD domain credentials, any valid AD user account may be specified; every AD user can join up to ten computers to the domain by default. Home editions of Windows Vista and 7 cannot join a domain, nor can the regular (non-Pro and non-Enterprise) versions of Windows 8.1 or 10.

Joining a computer to a domain provides the following benefits:

- You can log on to the computer using any valid user account that exists in Active Directory or any local account.

- You will not be asked to authenticate again to resources to which you have permissions in the domain.

- The domain administrator can create centralized *Group Policy settings* for both your domain user account and your local computer that apply every time you log on (in the case of user settings) and every time the computer logs on (in the case of computer settings).

- The AD Domain Admins group is automatically added to the local computer Administrators group. This means members of Domain Admins have full control over every computer joined to the domain.

Users of nondomain-joined computers can still access network resources in an AD environment as long as they have valid AD credentials. The AD credentials of mobile laptop users will be cached locally (no expiration) so that these users can use the same credentials to authenticate to the laptop whether they are connected to the network or not. When signing in to a domain-joined computer, you can specify either a local user name and password or an AD user name and password. Remember that only passwords are case sensitive.

Domain-joined computers have the ability to share folders and printers in the same way that workgroup computers do. The only difference shows up when selecting the users and groups to which you are granting share permissions; you can select local users and groups, or you can select users and groups that exist in the AD domain.

NETDOM

New to the CompTIA A+ 220-901 and 220-902 exam objectives this time around are some command-line utilities for managing Active Directory domains. You don't need to know any syntax for these commands for the A+ exams, but you should be able to explain their purposes and uses. They are somewhat out of place on the A+ exams, in our opinion, but you should familiarize yourself with them anyway.

The first of these is the NETDOM command, which is a Windows command-line utility for managing Active Directory domains from a command prompt. On a regular Windows client PC, you might not have this tool available. Further, it must be run from an elevated command prompt.

The syntax to join a computer to a domain is as follows:

```
netdom.exe join %computername% /domain:DomainName /UserD:Domain\
UserName /PasswordD:Password
```

In this example, replace *%computername%* with the computer name, *DomainName* with the domain name, and *UserName* and *Password* with the actual user names and passwords.

For a complete look at this command and its syntax, see http://tinyurl.com/jpx6cgt.

GPUPDATE and GPRESULT

Two other domain-related commands covered are GPUPDATE and GPRESULT. The GPUPDATE command refreshes local and Active Directory–based group policy settings, including security settings. This can be helpful after making a Group Policy change.

The Group Policy Editor (gpedit.msc) is the tool used on Windows servers for managing group policies on a domain. It is not covered on the A+ 220-901 and 220-902 exams. The local equivalent of it for individual workstations is Local Security Policy (secpol.msc), covered later in this chapter.

The GPRESULT command lists the settings contained in a Resultant Set of Policy (RSOP) for a particular user or computer. The RSOP summarizes the Group Policy settings in effect. Because different group policies may apply in unexpected ways based on group memberships, viewing the RSOP can be helpful in figuring out what effective permissions are in place.

- **902: 1.5**   *Given a scenario, use Windows Control Panel utilities*
- **902: 3.2**   *Compare and contrast common prevention methods*
- **902: 3.3**   *Compare and contrast differences of basic Windows OS security settings*

This section's main focus is CompTIA A+ 902 exam objective 3.3. We describe how to create network shares and map network drives, how NTFS and share permissions interact, and how permission propagation and inheritance works.

In addition, this section picks up a few specific topics from two other objectives. The piece of A+ 902 exam objective 3.2 covered in this section concerns directory (folder) permissions and how they affect the contents of directories (folders). A+ 902 exam objective 1.5 mentions the Control Panel Folder Options applet, which we described in Chapter 10, but here we look at the Sharing option in Folder Options, not previously described.

Implementing Data Security

Now that you have learned about the ways you can configure your Windows computer for file and printer sharing, we will move on to ways in which you then protect data—shared or otherwise. In this section we will look at the file- and folder-level permissions you can set on an NTFS volume and how they apply to both local users and users connecting over a network. We will detail how to share and map resources, and then how to apply NTFS file and folder encryption as compared to BitLocker drive encryption. We will also look at Local Security Policy and how it affects user permissions. Finally, when taking a storage device out of service, learn how to remove all data before reusing or recycling it. Learn about all these data protection functions in the following sections.

NTFS Permissions

NTFS permissions apply not only to the local user sitting at the computer, but also to someone accessing a file or folder over a network. It is not necessary to understand permissions if you are sharing files only through a HomeGroup, but if you use a workgroup or AD domain, you need to understand permissions and how to apply them. Set NTFS permissions at the most restrictive level that will allow users to accomplish their work. This is an application of the principle of least privilege described in Chapter 18.

The NTFS file system in Windows supports file and folder permissions through *discretionary access control (DAC)*, in which the creator of each file or folder is the owner and can control access. Additionally, NTFS permissions are also controlled by any account that is a member of the Administrators group. NTFS permissions should be assigned based on the principle of least privilege, using an *access control list (ACL)* on each file and folder. This list is a table containing at least one *access control entry (ACE)*, which in turn is a record containing just one user or group account name and the permissions assigned to that account. Administrators, the owner, or anyone with permission to create ACEs for the file or folder, can create ACEs. You manage permissions using the Security page in the Properties dialog box of a file or folder (right-click the file or folder, choose Properties, and click the Security tab). The permissions to a file are slightly different from those applied to a folder. The standard folder permissions are:

- Full Control
- Modify
- Read and Execute
- List Folder Contents
- Read
- Write

The standard file permissions are:

- Full Control
- Modify
- Read and Execute
- Read
- Write

Allow and Deny

Each NTFS permission can be allowed or denied. Permissions explicitly denied always override allowed permissions. For example, if the Sales group is given the List Folder Contents NTFS permission to D:\Reports, and Bob is a member of Sales, Bob can list the contents of D:\Reports. If we deny Bob (or any group of which he is a member) the List Folder Contents permission for D:\Reports, Bob cannot list the contents of D:\Reports even though he is a member of a group that can.

on the **Job**

Use Deny very sparingly, as it can create some difficult-to-troubleshoot permission difficulties when someone belongs to multiple groups that have different permissions assigned. To deny permission, it's better to just clear the Allow check box.

Permission Propagation and Inheritance

When folder permissions and the permissions on the files within the folder are combined, the least restrictive permissions apply. But we also need to address the issue of *permission propagation* throughout the folder hierarchy, also called *inheritance.* When you create a new folder or file, it inherits the permissions of the parent folder, unless you choose to block propagation of permissions to child objects.

When you view permissions on a file or folder, the permissions inherited from the parent will be grayed out, and you will not be able to modify those permissions at the child (inherited) level. You can assign new permissions, but you cannot alter inherited permissions unless you modify them in the folder in which they originated. You can block inheritance on a folder or file to which you wish to assign different (usually more restrictive) permissions.

Further, you can bypass inheritance with Allow and Deny settings for a file or folder. For instance, if you explicitly allow one of the standard permissions, such as Full Control, the user will have full control over the file or folder, even if inheritance would have given the user a lesser permission. If you explicitly deny a permission, the user will be denied that permission even if it was granted to the user at a higher level in the folder hierarchy or through membership in a group. When a conflict occurs, Deny overrides Allow, and Deny creates the one exception to the rule that when NTFS folder and file permissions, including all inherited permissions, are combined, the least restrictive permission applies.

Permissions and Moving and Copying

When a file or folder is created on an NTFS volume, it inherits permissions from its parent folder; this is also true when a file or folder is copied or moved to a folder on an NTFS volume. There is one important exception to this rule that occurs when you move a file or folder to a different folder on the same NTFS volume: in this case, the file or folder takes its permissions with it.

Permissions on System Files and Personal Folders

Windows assigns permissions automatically to certain files and folders. They include system files and each user's personal folders.

System Files and Folders   Windows assigns restrictive permission on the folders in which the system files and other critical files are stored. In addition, the default setting in File Explorer/Windows Explorer is to hide these files and folders.

In Windows 7, the only way to toggle the display of hidden files and folders is through the Folder Options dialog box. (That method remains an option in Windows 8 and newer but there's an easier way, as we'll explain momentarily.) To open the Folder Options dialog box in Windows 7, in Windows Explorer, click Organize and click Folder and Search Options. To open it in Windows 8 and newer, from File Explorer, click the View tab and click Options.

Choose whether to display hidden files, folders, and drives, and also whether to hide protected operating system files.

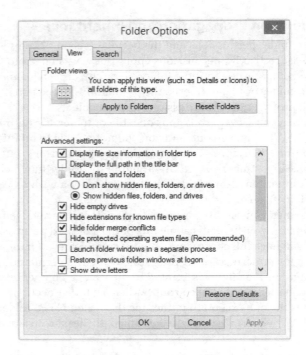

In the Folder Options dialog box (regardless of Windows version), on the View tab, expand the Hidden Files and Folders node and click the radio button next to Show Hidden Files, Folders, and Drives. See Figure 19-7.

In addition, to view system files, go down just a few items in that same list and click to clear the check box by Hide Protected Operating System Files. This is fine for learning about the hidden and system files, but for normal everyday use, we strongly recommend that you set these to the default to hide hidden files and folders and hide protected operating system files.

Personal Folders   When a user signs in to a computer for the first time, Windows creates personal folders on the local hard drive for that user. If that local drive is an NTFS partition (the default file system), Windows will assign a default set of permissions to those folders designed to keep other users out. The user has full control over his personal folders, as does the Administrators group and SYSTEM (the Windows operating system). No other user has permissions to these folders, nor can they view their contents. The default location for personal folders is in the C:\Users folder, in a subfolder for the user name.

Use Exercise 19-2 to view permissions on your personal folders on a Windows PC.

EXERCISE 19-2

Viewing Folder Permissions in Windows

In this exercise, you will view the permissions on your personal folders. Use any version of Windows for this exercise (Vista or newer). The hard disk must use the NTFS file system.

1. Open File Explorer/Windows Explorer and browse to C:\Users. Notice the folders. There should be one for each user who has signed in, plus one titled "Public." There might also be a Default.migrated folder.

2. Open the folder with the user name that you used when you signed in. View the contents of this folder. These folders make up the user profile for your user account on this computer. Close the folder.

3. Right-click the folder with the user name that you used to sign in. Select Properties, and then select the Security tab. Examine the list of users and groups that have permissions to the folder.

4. Figure 19-8 shows this dialog box with the user Faithe Wempen highlighted in the list of user names and the permissions for that user listed below. These permissions amount to full control, which is also true for the Administrators group and SYSTEM. No other user or group has full control permissions to access these folders. Close the window when you are finished.

FIGURE 19-8

The default permissions on personal folders

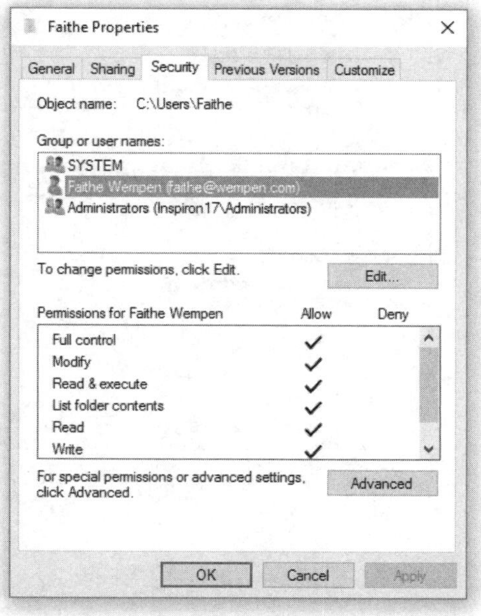

Applying Share Permissions

While we use the term "file sharing," sharing is actually done at the folder level. A share is a folder or printer that is available to network users. *Share permissions* are permissions set on a share, and they only apply to network users. If a shared folder is on an NTFS volume, a network user is affected by both share and NTFS permissions, but local users are only affected by NTFS permissions. When preparing to share a folder with network users, the recommended order is as follows:

1. Create the folder.
2. Set the appropriate NTFS permissions on the folder and individual files (if needed).
3. Create the share.
4. Set the share permissions.

To create a file share on your PC, browse to a folder you wish to share, right-click that folder, and select Properties. Click the Sharing tab in the folder's Properties dialog box. From the Sharing tab, click the Advanced Sharing button, and then mark the Share This Folder check box, as shown in Figure 19-9 in which we share the Blueprints folder.

A share has three permissions—Full Control, Change, and Read—and each permission has an explicit Allow or Deny permission level. The default permissions on a share give the Read permissions to the Everyone group. If you wish to change the default permission,

FIGURE 19-9

In the Advanced Sharing dialog, click to place a check by Share This Folder.

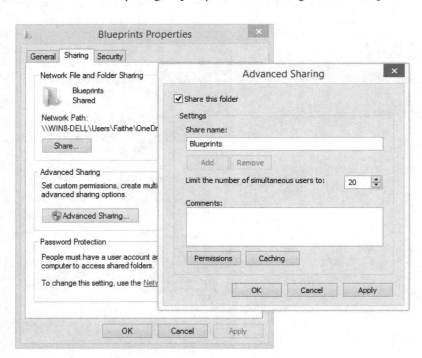

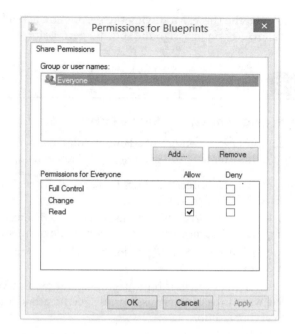

FIGURE 19-10

The default permission on a shared folder gives the Everyone group only the Read permission.

click the Permissions button to access the Permissions dialog box for the share, as shown in Figure 19-10.

Advanced sharing is simply a term for managing shares the old-fashioned way—one share at a time—turning on sharing for a folder or printer and giving users access to that share.

on the

The dialog boxes shown in this section are from Windows 8.1. The ones you see may be different depending on the Windows version and edition. For example, Windows 7 Home Premium has simpler dialog boxes for file sharing.

Now, consider what happens when a user connects to files through a share. First, the NTFS file and folder permissions (inherited and otherwise) are combined with the resulting least-restrictive permission applying at the NTFS level, and then the resulting effective NTFS permission is combined with the share-level permission, and the most restrictive permission is applied.

Because you are depending on the NTFS permissions to provide file security to a shared folder, and you know that when NTFS and share permissions are combined, the most restrictive permission applies, it follows that the default Everyone Read Only permissions on a share will be both too permissive ("everyone" can read the contents) and yet too restrictive if you wish to allow network users to modify files in the shared folder. Exercise 19-3 walks through the steps to modify the share permissions so only the users or groups you wish to give access to have the Full Control permission, and the Everyone group is completely removed from the share. Modifying the permission actually simplifies your administrative tasks by allowing you to assign the specific permission at the NTFS level.

EXERCISE 19-3

Creating a Share and Modifying Share Permissions

If your computer is a member of a HomeGroup, you will need to leave the HomeGroup in order to do this exercise. You can rejoin the HomeGroup when you are finished.

1. From File Explorer/Windows Explorer, right-click a folder you wish to share and select Properties.
2. Select the Sharing tab, and then click the Advanced Sharing button. This step is important because you wish to modify the permissions on the share you will create.
3. In the Advanced Sharing dialog box, click to mark the Share This Folder check box if it is not already marked.
4. Click the Permissions button. Notice that the Everyone group has Read permissions. We want to assign permissions to specific users or groups rather than to the Everyone group.
5. Click the Add button. Then click the Advanced button.
6. In the Select Users or Groups dialog box, click Find Now and the local accounts will appear in the Search Results box at the bottom.
7. Select the user or group you wish to give permissions to the share. Click OK twice to return to the Permissions dialog box for the selected folder. The name or group should now be included.
8. In the Group or User Names box at the top of the Permissions dialog box, select the added user or group, and then click the Allow check box for Full Control.
9. Once you have assigned the desired permission, select the Everyone group and click the Remove button.
10. Click OK twice and then click Close to close the Properties dialog box.

exam

⚙ watch   CompTIA A+ 902 exam objective 1.5 includes the topic Sharing under the Control Panel applet Folder Options. On the View tab in Folder Options, there is an option titled Use Sharing Wizard (Recommended). If you turn this on, it enables a wizard that you can use to create shares and assign permissions.

Administrative Shares

Windows has special hidden administrative shares that it creates automatically and uses when administrators, programs, and services connect to a computer over a network to perform special tasks that are mainly for use in a Microsoft domain network. Before Windows Vista, you could connect to an administrative share using a valid local account, but that feature is disabled beginning in Windows Vista, only allowing access to users with domain accounts. You cannot modify the permissions on an administrative share.

An administrative share has a special name that ends in the $ character, which marks the share as being hidden as well as being administrative. You can create a hidden share by appending the dollar sign to its name, but only the operating system can create administrative shares. These are the administrative shares:

- **Root partitions or volumes**   Only internal storage is shared, no removable drives (optical, USB flash drives, etc.). The administrative share for drive C: is C$. The complete network path to this share is \\*computername*\C$, which is a Universal Naming Convention (UNC) path, described later in the section titled "Connecting with a UNC Path."
- **System root folder**   This share points to the folder in which Windows was installed, which usually is C:\Windows. The UNC path to this share is \\computername\admin$.
- **FAX$ share**   This share points to a shared fax server.
- **IPC$ share**   This share is used for temporary connections for remotely administering a computer.
- **PRINT$ share**   This share is used for remote administration of shared printers.

Connecting to a Shared Folder

There are three ways to connect to a shared folder: browse to it for one-time use, map a drive letter to it, or connect using the UNC path.

Browsing for One-Time Use

Browsing to a share is simple—you open Windows Explorer/File Explorer and first navigate to the computer and then to the share, open it, and access files.

FIGURE 19-11

Mapping a drive
letter to a shared
folder in the GUI

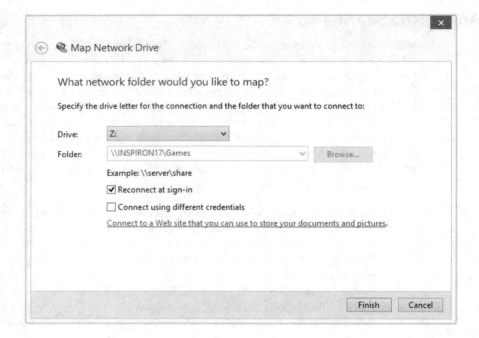

Mapping a Drive Letter

Mapping a drive letter requires that you associate a local, unused drive letter with the share on another computer. This can be automated in a logon script or through settings in Group Policy, or it can be done manually. In the latter case, you can do it in the GUI or from the command line. Figure 19-11 shows the result of browsing the network for a shared folder called Games on a computer named INSPIRON17 in the GUI and then right-clicking that folder and choosing Map Network Drive.

Mapping a drive from the command line is done using NET USE—for example, **net use z: \\192.168.1.102\games /persistent:yes** (see Figure 19-12). The Internet Protocol (IP) address or the host name can be used. The **/persistent:yes** parameter ensures that drive S: is mapped each time the user logs on. Take note that **net use * \\192.168.1.102\Shared_ Files** would consume the next available drive letter.

Connecting with a UNC Path

You can also map to a network share using a UNC path. *Universal Naming Convention (UNC)* is a method for pointing to shares on a network that begins with two backslashes (\\) followed by the name or IP address of the server, followed by a single backslash and the name of the share on the server. Do this in the Windows GUI by opening Windows Explorer/File Explorer, clicking in the address/navigation bar, and entering the UNC path. For instance, you would enter **\\INSPIRON17\research** to create a mapping to the research folder on the

FIGURE 19-12

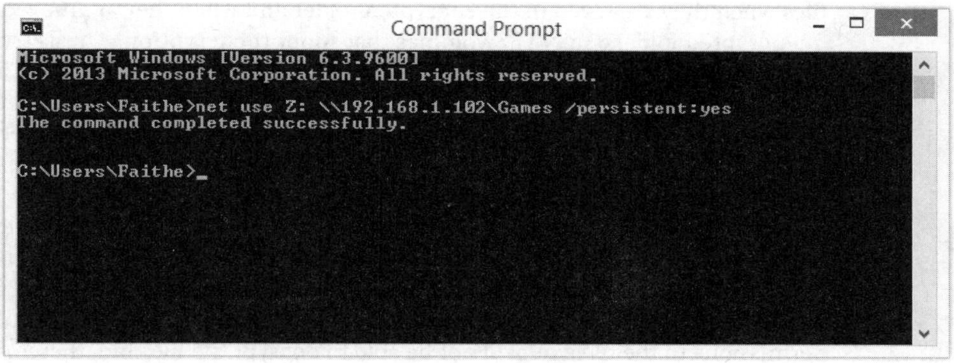

Mapping a drive letter to a shared folder from the command line

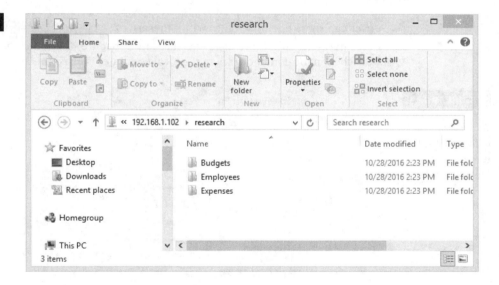

FIGURE 19-13

Connecting to a shared folder using the UNC path

computer named INSPIRON17. Figure 19-13 shows an example in which the IP address of the server is used in place of the name and the share name is research. This method does not consume a local drive letter. In a workgroup, you will be prompted for credentials unless the target computer has the same user name and password you are currently using.

Applying NTFS File and Folder Encryption

Encrypting a folder using the Encrypting File System (EFS) on a Windows NTFS volume does not actually encrypt the folder itself, but all files in the folder are encrypted, and any new files saved in the folder are automatically encrypted. NTFS encryption only applies to files when they are saved in the encrypted folder and when they are moved or copied into unencrypted folders on NTFS volumes that support encryption. This is true even if the folder to which the files are moved does not have encryption turned on. The files are not encrypted if they are copied to non-NTFS volumes or if they are e-mailed to someone.

It is simple to encrypt a folder. Simply open the Properties dialog box of the folder and click Advanced on the General tab. In the Advanced Attributes dialog box, click Encrypt Contents to Secure Data (see Figure 19-14), and then click OK.

You can only decrypt a file when logged on with the account used to encrypt it. Knowing this is important. Then decryption is transparent; simply open the file using the usual application for that file type. Both normal permissions and a special authorization to decrypt are applied. Even when logged on with another account with Full Control permissions to the file, you will not be able to decrypt the file, and, therefore, you will not be able to use it in any way.

EFS in Windows has the following features:

- A user can share encrypted files with other users.

- A user may encrypt offline files, which are files that are stored on a network server but cached in local memory when the local computer is disconnected from the server.

FIGURE 19-14

To encrypt files within a folder, turn on the Encrypt attribute.

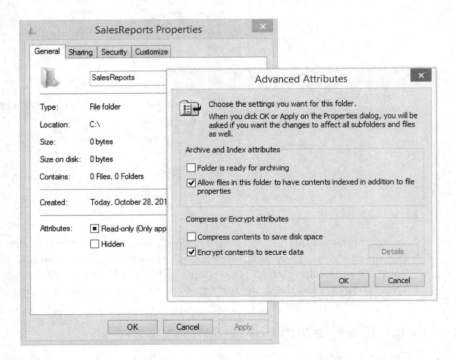

The only person who can decrypt a file or folder is the person who encrypted it, or an EFS Recovery Agent. By default, only the local or Active Directory Administrator account is an EFS Recovery Agent.

Local Security Policy

The Local Security Policy utility enables you to fine-tune the policies and permissions for the local workstation. It enables you to configure local policies that make the computer safer by enforcing policies and/or prohibiting certain activities. Local Security Policy settings apply only to the individual workstation or user. On an Active Directory domain, system administrators use the Group Policy Editor (gpedit.msc) instead to manage permissions for many clients at once.

To run Local Security Policy, click Start, type **secpol.msc,** and click secpol in search results. In the Local Security Policy window, click to expand the settings in the navigation pane at the left, and then double-click a setting on the right to change the setting in a dialog box.

For example, suppose you wanted to enforce more stringent password requirements, such as complexity level, length, and age. You could choose Account Policies | Password Policy in the Local Security Policy editor. Then you could double-click Minimum Password Length and set a minimum length in the dialog box that appears. See Figure 19-15. You could set a lockout policy for incorrect password guesses in the Account Lockout Policy section. To get a sense of what Local Security Policy can do, browse through the available settings, especially the ones under Local Policies | Security Options.

e x a m

ⓦ a t c h   There aren't any specific local policies you need to know for the 220-902 exam, but you should be able to identify Local Security Policy as the go-to place for making local security tweaks.

BitLocker

BitLocker, briefly described in Chapter 2 and Chapter 18, will encrypt your entire boot volume. It requires that the boot volume be separate from the system volume, and when you install Windows Vista or newer on a blank hard disk, Windows Setup will create two volumes in case you later decide to enable BitLocker. BitLocker is supported in the Ultimate and Enterprise editions of Windows Vista and Windows 7, and in Windows 8/8.1 Pro and Windows 10 Pro. The system volume is the active primary partition containing the boot loader accessed by the system firmware during startup. Traditionally, the system and boot volumes are one and the same, but they must be separate because BitLocker cannot encrypt the system volume. The BIOS/UEFI must be able to access the system volume at startup, and it cannot access an encrypted drive. On Windows Vista computers previous to

Use Local Security Policy to fine-tune security settings on the local PC.

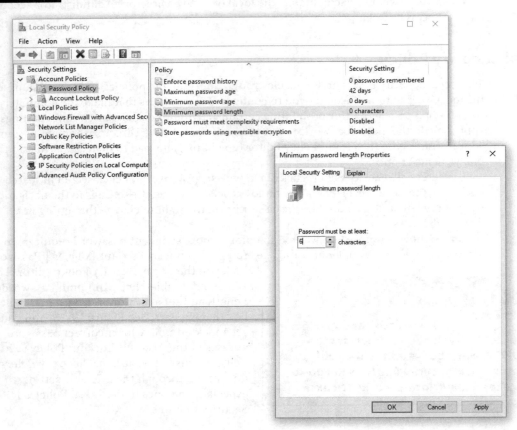

Service Pack 1 this was a problem, because when Windows Vista installed, the system and boot volumes were together. Figure 19-16 shows Disk Management on a Vista computer on which the system and boot volumes (seen on Disk 0) are one and the same: Volume C:. Realizing that two volumes on the same physical disk are required, not two physical disks, is important. Further, beginning with Windows Vista Service Pack 1, and, of course, in Windows 7 and newer, drives other than the boot volume can be encrypted with BitLocker.

Beginning in Windows 7, Microsoft changed how Windows partitions a drive during installation. If you install Windows 7 or newer on an unpartitioned hard drive, it will

FIGURE 19-16 The system and boot partitions are combined on Drive 0.

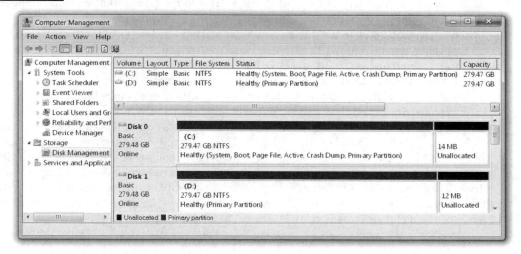

create a small (approximately 100 MB) system partition and a second partition containing the balance of the drive space as the boot partition, as shown in Figure 19-17, in which Disk 0 contains a 100 MB NTFS volume identified as System, Active, and Primary. The boot volume is drive C:. This configuration will allow BitLocker to store the encryption key on the hard drive.

FIGURE 19-17 The system volume and boot volume are separate on Disk 0.

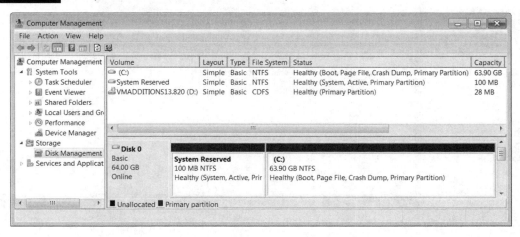

You can configure BitLocker to install the encryption key in one of several locations, including a Universal Serial Bus (USB) drive, a Trusted Platform Module (TPM) chip, or on the system volume (Windows 7 and newer). If storing encryption keys on a USB drive, this USB drive must be plugged in during computer startup for decryption to succeed. To turn on BitLocker, open Windows Explorer or File Explorer and right-click the drive. Then select BitLocker, which opens the BitLocker Drive Encryption Wizard. Select how you want to unlock the drive, and then click Next and follow the instructions.

Windows 7 and newer also have a feature called BitLocker to Go, which encrypts external hard drives and flash drives. While older versions of Windows cannot create a BitLocker to Go volume, Windows XP and Windows Vista computers can read BitLocker to Go–encrypted removable drives using the BitLocker to Go Reader, a program named BITLOCKERTOGO.EXE that is added to a drive that is encrypted with BitLocker to Go. To encrypt a removable drive, locate it in Windows Explorer or File Explorer and right-click the drive. Then select Turn On BitLocker, and after it encrypts the drive, choose how you want to unlock the drive. This page is different from that shown in Figure 19-18 in that it does not have the third choice, Automatically Unlock This Drive on This Computer.

FIGURE 19-18

BitLocker to Go
Drive Encryption
settings page

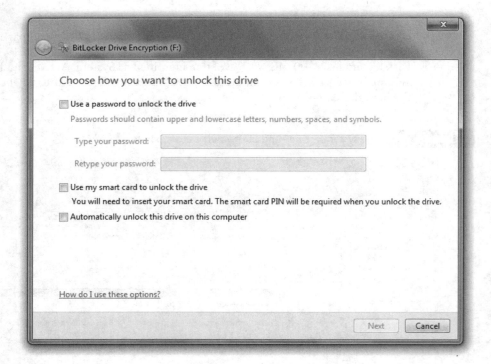

FIGURE 19-19

Setting both the hidden and read-only attributes on the file BUDGET-2013 .XLS

File Attributes

While not strictly part of security, file attributes, as you learned in Chapter 10, can affect your access to files on both File Allocation Table (FAT) and NTFS volumes. The use of hidden and system attributes is the closest thing you have to file security on a FAT volume. Attributes can be viewed, and in some cases set, by right-clicking a file or folder and choosing Properties (for advanced attributes, click the Advanced button). The ATTRIB.EXE command is the command-line equivalent. Figure 19-19 depicts applying the hidden and read-only attributes to a file from the command line using the ATTRIB command.

CERTIFICATION SUMMARY

An IT tech must know the differences between HomeGroups, workgroups, and Microsoft AD domains and how to configure Windows clients in each of these resource-sharing models. A closely related topic is the differences and features of NTFS permissions, including how NTFS permissions apply to resources for the local user as well as network users. Another important topic is NTFS permission propagation and inheritance. Compare NTFS versus share permissions, and be sure you understand how both share permissions and NTFS permissions are combined to apply to network users.

An A+ candidate should also practice and understand methods for creating shares on the server side and for mapping shares from the client side. Windows creates special hidden shares, called administrative shares, mainly for use in an AD domain.

Understand the differences between NTFS Encrypted File System (EFS) as a file encryption tool and BitLocker and BitLocker to Go as disk encryption tools.

✔ TWO-MINUTE DRILL

Here are some of the key points covered in Chapter 19.

Configuring Windows Clients for File and Printer Sharing

❑ HomeGroups facilitate sharing documents and printers on a small network.

❑ There can be only a single HomeGroup per LAN, the network location must be set to Home, and IPv6 is required.

❑ Libraries organize folders from different locations under a single entity and HomeGroup users can connect to Public libraries on HomeGroup computers where users have allowed this sharing.

❑ Workgroups are a peer-to-peer file and print sharing option, with decentralized administration, requiring creating both shares and user accounts on each computer in the workgroup that will share resources.

❑ A Microsoft Active Directory (AD) domain is a collection of workstations and servers under single administrative control, meaning that access to all computers and other resources in the domain is centrally managed.

❑ Windows Vista Business, Ultimate, and Enterprise editions can join a domain, as can Windows 7 Professional, Enterprise, and Ultimate editions. Windows 8 and 10 Pro and Enterprise editions can also join a domain.

❑ The GPUPDATE command refreshes local and Active Directory–based group policy settings, including security settings. The GPRESULT command lists the settings contained in a RSOP for a particular user or computer.

Implementing Data Security

❑ NTFS permissions apply not only to local users but also to those accessing resources over a network. Share permissions apply only to network users.

❑ Permissions that are explicitly denied always take precedence over any allowed permissions.

❑ To connect to a shared folder, browse the Network in Windows Explorer/File Explorer. UNC paths and drive letter mappings can be used to access shared folders.

❑ Use EFS encryption on the most sensitive data files. BitLocker encrypts entire volumes and is supported in the Ultimate and Enterprise editions of Windows Vista and Windows 7, and in Windows 8/8.1 Pro.

❑ Local Security Policy enables you to fine-tune the policies and permissions for the local workstation. Access it via secpol.msc.

❑ Windows 7 and newer includes BitLocker to Go for encrypting removable hard disks or flash drives.File attributes, described in Chapter 10, are not strictly part of security, but the use of hidden and system attributes is the closest thing you have to file security on a FAT volume.

SELF TEST

The following questions will help you measure your understanding of the material presented in this chapter. Read all of the choices carefully because there might be more than one correct answer. Choose all correct answers for each question.

Configuring Windows Clients for File and Printer Sharing

1. Francesca wants to set up a HomeGroup, but it appears that there is already a HomeGroup on her network, and she doesn't know its password. What can she do?
   A. Reboot her PC.
   B. Disable IPv6.
   C. Create a new HomeGroup.
   D. Ask one of the other users for the HomeGroup password.

2. Which network location, when selected in Windows 7, will cause Windows to disable both Network Discovery and HomeGroup?
   A. Home
   B. Work
   C. Public
   D. Workgroup

3. Windows 8 and newer have a network location called Private. Which location type from earlier Windows versions is it the equivalent of?
   A. Home
   B. Work
   C. Public
   D. Workgroup

4. Which editions of Windows 7 can join a HomeGroup? Select all that apply.
   A. Ultimate
   B. Home Premium
   C. Professional
   D. Enterprise

5. When someone enables sharing of documents in a HomeGroup, what is actually shared from that person's computer?
   A. Public Documents
   B. C:\Users\Public
   C. *computername*\C$
   D. Personal folders

6. What should you disable if you want people who don't have an account on your local PC to be able to access your shared folders?
   A. NTFS sharing
   B. Password protected sharing
   C. Workgroup sharing
   D. Active Directory

7. Your home network consists of a Windows Vista Business computer and two Windows 7 Home Premium computers. You would like to share music and video files among all computers. What should you configure?
   A. HomeGroup
   B. Active Directory domain
   C. Streaming server
   D. Workgroup

8. A tax auditor is at your office for the next three days. She requires access to resources stored on servers in your AD domain. What should you do to grant her access to those resources she needs?
   A. Join her computer to the domain.
   B. Provide domain administrative credentials to her.
   C. Enable the AD guest account.
   D. Create an AD account for her, grant permissions, and set the account expiration date to four days in the future.

9. Which of these Windows versions cannot join an AD domain?
   A. Windows 8.1 (non-Pro)
   B. Windows 8 Pro
   C. Windows 7 Enterprise
   D. Windows Vista Business

Implementing Data Security

10. What strategy should you use when setting NTFS permissions?
    A. Set the least restrictive level for all users.
    B. Set the most restrictive level that still allows users to accomplish their work.
    C. Give the Everyone group Read permissions.
    D. Use Allow or Deny on every permission.

11. What setting, applied directly to a file, defeats permission inheritance?
    A. Deny
    B. Allow
    C. Full Control
    D. Modify

12. What rule does Windows apply to inherited NTFS permissions to determine effective permissions?
    A. Most restrictive applies.
    B. Least restrictive applies.
    C. Full Control is calculated first.
    D. Read is calculated first.

13. What is the recommended order of tasks for creating shares and applying permissions?
    A. Create the share, apply NTFS permissions, and apply share-level permissions.
    B. Give Everyone Read access, apply NTFS permissions, apply share-level permissions, and create the share.
    C. Apply NTFS permissions, create the share, and apply share-level permissions.
    D. Apply NTFS permissions, apply share-level permissions, and create the share.

14. When a user connects over a network to a file share, how are the effective NTFS permissions and the share permissions combined for that user?
    A. Most restrictive applies.
    B. Least restrictive applies.
    C. Full Control is calculated first.
    D. Read is calculated first.

15. If an encrypted file is moved or copied into an unencrypted folder on an NTFS volume, which of the following will occur?
    A. It will be decrypted.
    B. It will remain encrypted.
    C. It will be read-only.
    D. Encrypted files cannot be moved or copied.

16. Which encryption feature comes with the Ultimate and Enterprise editions of Windows Vista and Windows 7, as well as Windows 8/8.1 and 10 Pro, and encrypts an entire volume?
    A. NTFS encryption
    B. WPA2
    C. DriveLock
    D. BitLocker

17. Where are personal folders stored in Windows Vista and newer?
    A. C:\Windows
    B. C:\Program Files
    C. C:\Personal Folders
    D. C:\Users

18. Which of the following identifies the administrative share that points to the system root folder?
    A. C$
    B. IPC$
    C. \\computername\admin$
    D. PRINT$

19. Which of the following commands will map G: to the root of drive C: on a laptop called PC424?
    A. NET USE C: \\G:\PC424
    B. NET USE G: \\PC424\C$
    C. NET USE G: \\PC424\C:
    D. NET USE G: \\PC424\C:$

20. What utility enables you to manage local security policies?
    A. gpedit.msc
    B. secpol.msc
    C. Disk Management
    D. Device Manager

SELF TEST ANSWERS

Configuring Windows Clients for File and Printer Sharing

1. ☑ **D.** Any user in a HomeGroup can view the HomeGroup password.
   ☒ **A** is incorrect because rebooting will solve nothing. **B** is incorrect because HomeGroups require IPv6. **C** is incorrect because there can be only one HomeGroup.

2. ☑ **C.** Public, when selected as a network location in Windows 7, causes Windows to disable both Network Discovery and HomeGroup support.
   ☒ **A** and **B** are both incorrect because choosing Home or Work will turn on Network Discovery and allow you to enable HomeGroup (as long as other requirements are met). **D** is incorrect because Workgroup is not a network location.

3. ☑ **A.** Private in Windows 8 and newer is the equivalent of Home in earlier versions.
    ☒ **B** and **C** are both incorrect because Work and Public have different settings than Private.
    D is incorrect because Workgroup is not a network location.

4. ☑ **A, B, C,** and **D.** All the listed Windows 7 editions can join a HomeGroup.

5. ☑ **A.** Public Documents, a folder in the Documents library, is shared.
    ☒ **B** is incorrect because C:\Users\Public is not the folder that is shared; it is the C:\Users\
    Public\Public Documents folder. **C** is incorrect because *computername*\C$ is the UNC path
    to the root directory of the C drive on the system referenced in *computername.* **D** is incorrect
    because personal folders refers to all the data folders under a particular user's folder, such as all
    the folders contained in C:\Users*username.*

6. ☑ **B.** Disabling password protected sharing enables remote users who do not have a username
    and password to connect and access your shared folders.
    ☒ **A** is incorrect because NTFS sharing is local sharing. **C** is incorrect because if workgroup
    sharing is disabled, remote users on your LAN cannot connect at all. **D** is incorrect because
    disabling Active Directory would not enable other users to connect.

7. ☑ **D.** Workgroups allow you to share folders and printers to computers running any version
    of Windows.
    ☒ **A** is incorrect because HomeGroups only apply to Windows 7 and newer. **B** is incorrect
    because Active Directory is not required on this small home network. **C** is incorrect because it is
    a generic answer, and the question does not ask about streaming; it asks about sharing files.

8. ☑ **D.** When accessing domain resources, the tax auditor will be prompted for domain
    credentials, which she will supply to get access to network resources.
    ☒ **A** is incorrect because her computer does not have to be in the domain. **B** is incorrect
    because you should never give somebody more access than they require to perform a task.
    C is incorrect because enabling the AD guest account makes audit tracking difficult and thus is
    not recommended.

9. ☑ **A.** The non-Pro versions of Windows 8/8.1 and 10 cannot join a domain.
    ☒ **B, C,** and **D** are all incorrect because all these versions can join a domain.

Implementing Data Security

10. ☑ **B.** When setting NTFS permissions, set the most restrictive level that still allows users to
    accomplish their work.
    ☒ **A** is incorrect because setting the least restrictive level for all users would expose data to
    unauthorized users. **C** is incorrect because giving the Everyone group Read permissions would
    often be too permissive. **D** is incorrect because using Allow or Deny on every permission defeats
    inheritance, which is not a good strategy.

11. ☑ **A.** Deny explicitly defeats an inherited permission when applied directly to a file.
    ☒ **B** is incorrect because Allow defeats all inherited permissions except Deny. **C** and **D** are both
    incorrect because Full Control and Modify are defeated if they are explicitly set to Deny.

12.   ☑   **B.** Least restrictive applies is the rule Windows uses for determining effective permissions on a file or folder on NTFS.
   ☒   **A** is incorrect because this is not the rule used. **C** and **D** are both incorrect because permissions are not based on which is calculated first.

13.   ☑   **C.** Apply NTFS permissions, create the share, and apply share-level permissions is the recommended order of tasks for creating shares and applying permissions.
   ☒   **A** is incorrect because if you create the share before applying NTFS permissions, the share-level default permissions will leave the shared files and folders too vulnerable. **B** is incorrect for two reasons: Everyone Read is too open for most situations, and you cannot apply share-level permissions before you create a share. **D** is also incorrect because you cannot apply share-level permissions before you create the share.

14.   ☑   **A.** Most restrictive is how effective NTFS permissions and share permissions combine for a user.
   ☒   **B** is incorrect, although this is how the effective NTFS permissions are applied. **C** and **D** are both incorrect because permissions are not based on which is calculated first.

15.   ☑   **B.** The file will remain encrypted if moved or copied into an unencrypted folder on an NTFS volume.
   ☒   **A** is incorrect because as long as the move or copy is not performed as a drag-and-drop operation, an encrypted file will remain encrypted. **C** is incorrect because this is not the result of moving or copying an encrypted file into an unencrypted folder on an NTFS volume. **D** is incorrect because encrypted files can be moved or copied.

16.   ☑   **D.** BitLocker is the encryption that comes with the OS and protects an entire volume on a computer running the Ultimate and Enterprise versions of Windows Vista and Windows 7, or Windows 8/8.1 and 10 Pro.
   ☒   **A** is incorrect because NTFS encryption only encrypts at the folder level on an NTFS volume. **B** is incorrect because WPA2 is a Wi-Fi encryption standard. **C** is incorrect because DriveLock is not an encryption technology, but a system for controlling access to an entire hard drive without data encryption.

17.   ☑   **D.** Personal files are stored in C:\Users in subfolders for each user.
   ☒   **A** is incorrect because C:\Windows is used for storing Windows files. **B** is incorrect because C:\Program Files is used for storing programs. **C** is not a system-created location.

18.   ☑   **C.** *computername**admin$* identifies the system root folder administrative share.
   ☒   **A, B,** and **D** are all incorrect because although all are administrative shares, they do not point to the system root folder.

19.   ☑   **B.** Drive C: is a hidden share (suffixed with a $). The correct syntax is the drive letter to assign, two slashes, the computer name, a slash, the letter of the drive to be mapped, and a dollar sign.
   ☒   **A, C,** and **D** are all incorrect because they do not follow this pattern.

20.   ☑   **B.** Local Security Policy has an executable filename of secpol.msc.
   ☒   **A** is incorrect because gpedit.msc is the Group Policy Editor for AD domains. **C** is incorrect because Disk Management is the utility for managing local disks. **D** is incorrect because Device Manager is the utility for managing local hardware.

Chapter 20

Supporting Mobile Devices

■ **902: 4.4** Given a scenario, troubleshoot common mobile OS and application security issues with appropriate tools

✓ Two-Minute Drill

Q&A Self Test

Mobile computing was once solely the territory of the business traveler with laptop in tow, resting what was sometimes a hefty computer on knees in waiting rooms and on trays on airliners. Today that model of mobile computing seems rather quaint as more and more ordinary people are doing mobile computing with smaller, faster devices in more places—many of them not far from home. Tablets are issued to schoolchildren of all ages for delivering courseware content. And let's not even begin to talk about the use of smartphones among even the youngest of children. In this chapter we will explore mobile devices from the CompTIA A+ technician's perspective, focusing on smartphones and tablets, and making comparisons between these devices and laptops, which were previously covered in Chapters 7 and 12. We also look at troubleshooting mobile devices in this chapter, helping you understand what can go wrong with these devices and how you can narrow down and solve the problems.

CERTIFICATION OBJECTIVES

■ **901: 3.4** *Explain the characteristics of various types of other mobile devices*
■ **901: 3.5** *Compare and contrast accessories and ports of other mobile devices*
■ **902: 2.5** *Identify basic features of mobile operating systems*
■ **902: 2.6** *Install and configure basic mobile device network connectivity and e-mail*

In this section, we review several types of mobile computing devices, including tablets, smartphones, wearable devices, e-readers, and so on, as enumerated in CompTIA A+ 901 exam objective 3.4. We also cover the connection types and accessories from 901 exam objective 3.5 (except hotspot/tethering, which is covered later in the chapter). We also explain how smartphones are identified by a variety of ID numbers such as IMEI and IMSI, as outlined in 902 exam objective 2.6. Finally, we look at some basic features of Android, iOS and Windows Phone devices, as listed in 902 exam objective 2.5.

Overview of Mobile Devices

The most popular mobile devices today are smartphones and tablets—both of which can perform a huge number of computer functions, depending on the apps you install. A *smartphone* fits in the palm of your hand and functions as a cell phone handset, as well as your personal Jack-of-all gadgets. When you select a smartphone, you are also selecting a certain operating system (OS), such as Android or iOS.

A *tablet* is a portable computer without an integrated keyboard. A tablet is smaller than most laptops, larger than a cell phone, and has a touch screen display. Most tablets do not function as cell phones, because they are simply too big and heavy to use as a handset, although one may have an optional connection (with service fee) to a cellular data network for Internet connectivity. Some small tablets do also have phone capabilities, and such devices are called *phablets*, which is a blending of the words *phone* and *tablet*.

Some mobile devices are wearable. For example, *smart watches* like the Apple Watch not only tell time, but also connect wirelessly to a smartphone or tablet. They run simple applications, provide calendar and schedule reminders, and accept voice commands for activities like sending text messages. *Fitness monitors* like the Fitbit track your movements and activity levels and report those back to a monitoring application. Glasses and headsets are also available that include computer components. Google Glass, which consists of a small computer built into an eyeglass frame, has been taken off the market for retooling, but is expected to be re-released soon.

E-readers like the Kindle store and display books. A *global positioning system (GPS)* receives data broadcast from orbiting satellites to determine and report the user's current location. A *smart camera* not only takes digital photos, but also has applications built in that can edit photos and transfer them to storage devices.

Many of these special-purpose mobile devices were wildly popular when first introduced but have fallen out of favor as their features have been incorporated into general-purpose mobile devices like smartphones and tablets. For example, the average smartphone today includes a GPS and a smart camera, and e-reader software is available for most tablets.

In this section we will give a user's perspective on smartphones and tablets, and then look at the hardware and software features that set each type of mobile device apart from the others.

Hardware Features

While there are exceptions, the user should not open up smartphones, tablets, or other mobile devices. They are not designed to be user-serviced, and they rarely allow for hardware upgrades. Therefore, this section focuses on understanding the existing hardware in mobile devices, rather than adding or upgrading hardware components.

Nothing is impossible, and if you search YouTube, you will find videos of people dismantling a variety of tablets, including Apple's latest iPad (on the first day it was available). Although possible, there is risk in dismantling a $600 tablet. You can easily render it useless, and even opening one up voids the warranty!

Screens

All popular smartphones and tablets now have touch interfaces in the form of touch screens that accept and interpret multiple touch gestures at a time—something called *multi-touch*. The touch screen is the main input device on a smartphone or tablet, and also the main output device.

Most smartphones and tablets use some form of liquid crystal display (LCD) screen with a touch-sensitive overlay, although some smartphones use some form of organic light-emitting diode (OLED) technology described in Chapter 5. The benefit of OLED over LCD technology is that OLED is lighter and uses less power because it does not use backlighting. The present technology for OLED is too expensive to economically produce screens larger than the size of a smartphone, however.

The touch screens in current smartphones and tablets are *capacitive screens* that sense capacitance (the electrical charge) from your body when you touch the screen. Capacitive touch screens really work best when you use your finger. However, several manufacturers make a pen-shaped device called a *stylus* just for these screens. This stylus is very different from the stylus you may use with an input device like a Wacom tablet, because they work passively, using a special material, such as rubber that mimics a finger. We have tried them with our smartphones and tablets, and find they work okay on a tablet, and are a bit more helpful on the smaller screen of a smartphone. A stylus keeps the screen cleaner, but it is one more thing to keep track of and easy to misplace!

Older smartphone touch screens used a different, noncapacitive technology that responded better to a stylus than to a finger.

Calibration   Older screen technology required screen *calibration* to align touch actions, and you may encounter some smartphones that still require this. The calibration utility prompts you to touch a symbol that appears sequentially in each corner of the screen and then one in the screen's center. The software then adjusts the touch calibration to match. If your mobile device has no calibration utility in its Settings, it does not need to be calibrated.

Screen Orientation   All modern mobile devices support *screen orientation*, also called *screen rotation*, that keeps the image on the screen upright no matter how the device rotation changes. This is based on the angle at which you hold the device, and it is made possible by an *accelerometer*, a built-in component that measures acceleration of the

FIGURE 20-1

The iPad home page in "landscape" and "portrait" orientations

smartphone or tablet, and a *gyroscope*, which measures the tilt and direction. These two features, along with a built-in compass, help the device determine which side of the screen is "up" at any given moment. Figure 20-1 shows the screen of an iPad when held in "landscape" orientation and in "portrait" orientation.

If you perceive that a smartphone or tablet is not responding correctly to change in orientation, consult the manufacturer because the device may be defective or may need to be calibrated to respond to rotation.

Some Android devices have a program to calibrate for screen orientation. For instance, on a Galaxy Tab, you place it on a level surface with the screen up and start the screen orientation calibration program from Settings. Then you tap Calibrate and an image of a ball moves to the center of the screen. Supposedly that solves the problem.

Gestures There are a variety of touch gestures, and we will look at the most common. A *tap* gesture is a firm, but brief, touch to the screen. This will open the tapped app or other object. When you want to move the contents of the screen to see what is outside the viewing area, touch the screen and flick your finger right, left, up, or down. This gesture is called a *swipe* or a *flick*. There are several multi-touch gestures that use two or more fingers. If you place two fingers on the screen at a small distance from each other and draw them together, this is a *pinch*. Reverse that gesture, and it is still called a pinch. *Press and hold* is a touch without releasing. On some mobile devices, this will open a context menu; on others it allows you to move the icon you pressed—or some other action. Where you touch the screen is also significant.

FIGURE 20-2 A virtual keyboard opens on the screen when you need it.

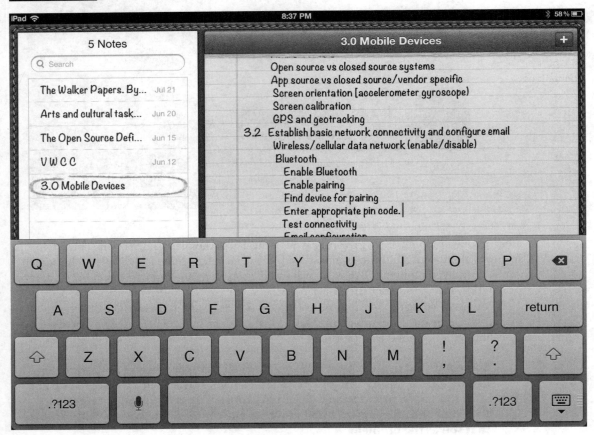

FIGURE 20-2 A virtual keyboard opens on the screen when you need it.

Our last word on screens is about keyboards. The operating system on a smartphone or tablet provides you with a *virtual keyboard*, an on-screen keyboard that appears when you tap inside a box requiring text or number entry, as shown in Figure 20-2.

Storage

Smartphones and tablets exclusively use solid-state drives (SSDs) for installed programs and for storing your data. They do not use magnetic hard drives due to the bulk, weight, slower speed, and sensitivity to vibration. Most SSDs in mobile devices are permanently built-in and cannot be replaced or upgraded.

Multimedia Support

While individual device models vary, multimedia support in smartphones and tablets includes built-in speakers and connectors for headsets, microphones, and speakers. The number and location of the speakers varies depending on the model. Some smartphones have a single speaker that serves both for voice calls and general-purpose audio (such as music playback), changing its volume according to the use. Others have two speakers, for better quality sound.

Mobile devices that include Bluetooth can also support a variety of external multimedia device connections, such as *headsets* (useful for hands-free phone calls), external speakers, and transceivers that connect a tablet or smartphone to a car stereo or other external input or output sources.

Smartphones and tablets also have feature-rich digital cameras for photos and videos, including optical zoom and flash. In fact, many have two cameras: one on the back of the device to be aimed away from the user, and one aimed at the user, handy for taking self-portraits and for participating in video conferencing.

Ports and Connectors

Smartphones and tablets need a way of transferring data to and from the device, and also of supplying it with AC power to charge the battery. Wireless communication is fine for some data transfer (see the next section), but it can't fulfill all the needed functions. Therefore, at least one port is required on a device.

On many devices, a single connector transfers both data and power. Apple devices use a connector called Lightning, shown in Figure 20-3. Other brands of smartphones and tablets may use mini USB or micro USB connectors, or a proprietary connector.

FIGURE 20-3

A Lightning connector serves for both data and power transfer on Apple devices. (Photo: https://commons.wikimedia.org/wiki/File:Lightning_connector.jpg [Creative Commons license])

At the other end of the cable is either a standard USB connector or a power plug (either for an AC wall outlet or a car connection). A USB connector can attach the device to a computer to transfer data. Devices are plug and play, so most computer operating systems immediately recognize and connect to the tablet or smartphone and treat it like an external drive.

Some devices also have a 3.5-mm headphone jack, for connecting wired headphones. The iPhone 7 does not have a headphone jack, however; as phones become slimmer, the trend is moving away from external ports.

Wireless Communication

Smartphones and tablets today offer several wireless connection options. To begin with, a smartphone, by definition, connects to a cellular network as a phone, but also, as an option, will connect to the cellular data network. This depends mainly on what level of service you subscribe to from a cellular provider.

exam

watch CompTIA A+ 902 exam objective 2.5 mentions "WiFi calling." This refers to a smartphone's ability to place a phone call using Wi-Fi rather than the cellular network. This is useful when no cellular network is available, or when using a cellular network would cost extra but there is a free Wi-Fi connection, such as when visiting another country.

A tablet would make a rather awkward cell phone, but a tablet may come with a cellular modem so that it can connect to a cellular data network. You pay extra for this option—both for a cellular modem and for the cellular data service.

Today both types of devices normally come with two other wireless network options: Bluetooth and Wi-Fi. You learned about both of these in Chapter 7 in the context of laptops, and they work similarly on smartphones and tablets. You enable and configure them in the Settings app in the mobile OS.

Some smartphones also support another wireless standard called near field communication (NFC). As explained in Chapter 14, NFC is a specialized, low-power, short-range radio frequency (RF) wireless method. You may have encountered NFC at a cash register at your local superstore, where you had the option to tap your credit card on the reader instead of swiping it. Bringing your card near the reader (within a few inches) reads it. NFC is found more often on smartphones than on PCs. If a smartphone has NFC, it can share certain kinds of files with other nearby phones. It works great with photos, but it doesn't share most other types of files.

Infrared (IR) is a line-of-sight wireless technology that was popular before Bluetooth for connecting wireless peripherals and quick device-to-device transfers. It's not popular anymore because the line-of-sight requirement limits its flexibility. You may find an IR port on a very old laptop or handheld device.

Mobile Device Accessories

In addition to the standard equipment that comes built into a mobile device, you may be able to add extra peripherals or equipment that can enhance your experience as a user. These include the following:

- **Game pad**   Similar to a game controller on an Xbox or other console system, enables you to have more control when playing games on a smartphone or tablet.
- **Docking station**   Enables the device to connect with a variety of extra peripherals with a single connection, including more ports, external keyboards, external pointing devices, and external monitors.
- **Extra battery**   On devices with removable batteries, enables you to swap out your spent battery for a fresh one to continue working.
- **Battery charger**   Functions in the same way that an AC outlet would, recharging the battery when away from AC power.
- **Protective cover**   Protects the device from damage, such as from short-circuiting from water or cracking the screen or the plastic housing when dropped. Some covers, such as on tablets, can also put the device into and out of sleep mode when they are closed or opened.
- **Credit card reader**   Attaches to a port on the device and allows credit cards to be swiped or scanned. Some models include a chip reader, for greater security. Devices have traditionally used the headphone jack for this connection, but with newer models coming without headphone jacks, this will be changing.
- **Memory card**   Usually some form of Secure Digital (SD) card, such as MicroSD, adds more storage space to devices that have a card slot.

on the Job   **Don't confuse a memory card with a SIM (subscriber identity module) card, which is a very small electronic chip installed in a smartphone that connects it with the phone service provider and also provides space for personal data to be stored.**

How Smartphones Are Identified

Hidden inside your smartphone are some important identification numbers. You don't need them for everyday use, but you might occasionally need to know them when troubleshooting.

Each smartphone contains a SIM card, which associates it with a particular cell service provider. The *Integrated Circuit Card ID (ICCID)* is the unique identifier for the SIM card.

The *International Mobile Subscriber Identity (IMSI)* is your unique ID as a subscriber to cellular service. It is stored on the phone's SIM card. Your phone company uses this code to identify you. This ID number is different from your *Mobile Station ISDN Number (MSISDN)*, which is your phone's telephone number. A single subscriber (that is, a single IMSI) might be associated with multiple MSISDNs, such as when someone has a single phone that takes calls from both their business and personal phone numbers.

Another identifier is the *International Mobile Equipment Identity (IMEI)*, which is the unique number assigned to your mobile phone. On a phone with a removable battery, you might find the number behind the battery. This serves as a tracking number for the device. Cell providers maintain an Equipment Identity Register (EIR) that contains all valid mobile phone codes. If you report a phone stolen, the IMEI for that phone is marked invalid. On some phones it is called the *MEID (Mobile Equipment ID)*.

You can find out your phone's ID numbers by looking in the Settings app. On an iPhone, for example, they're under Settings | General | About.

Mobile Operating Systems

While there are several mobile operating systems, we will concentrate on the most popular ones. The three mentioned for smartphones in the A+ objectives are Apple iOS, Google Android, and Microsoft Windows Phone.

On tablets, it is almost the same lineup, except for Windows Phone. Microsoft Windows RT is on some tablets (a mobile-optimized version of Windows 8), and others have a full desktop version of Windows on them, such as the Surface Pro, Microsoft's hybrid laptop/tablet with a detachable keyboard.

Each mobile operating system has an easy-to-use graphical user interface (GUI) optimized for touch screens, and each has a home page (expandable to multiple pages) where icons for settings, utilities, and apps reside. We will talk about some differences among these OSs.

The operating system on Apple's iPhone and iPad is *iOS*, Apple's operating system for Apple mobile devices. You will only find iOS on devices manufactured by Apple, making it a vendor-specific, *closed source* operating system. It is vendor specific because it is only offered on Apple hardware. It is closed source because Apple does not publish iOS source code and does not allow others to modify it in any way. There are closed source applications as well as operating systems.

The *Android* mobile OS runs on devices from many manufacturers worldwide. This is *open source* software, meaning that the source code is available to anyone to use or modify, and the software is not controlled by a single entity. As a result, different devices that run Android may have differently configured user interfaces and options. Android is a very popular OS for non-Apple mobile devices. Manufacturers do make some vendor-specific changes to the OS, and some even change the GUI.

While standard Microsoft Windows runs on some tablets, Microsoft has a long history of mobile versions, going back to the 1990s. Concurrent with Windows 8, they released a line of tablets with a mobile-specific version called Windows RT. It is similar to the Start screen interface from Windows 8/8.1; it lacks a desktop environment and can't run standard desktop applications. Current Windows tablets are convertible to laptops and run the full version of Windows 10.

Mobile Apps

All mobile devices come with some built-in apps, and you can customize your device by choosing from the huge number of available apps—some free and many for sale. There are literally hundreds of thousands of mobile apps. Apps are OS specific, so you must find apps that work with your OS and device.

App Stores

The home screens on mobile devices normally have an icon for connecting to an online retail site for buying apps. The differences in your choices for sources depend on the operating system.

As you browse through apps for any mobile device, you will find that many of them have requirements to install—mainly that certain services are turned on—so read through the description of each app and pay attention to the requirements. You may need to give the app full control of your device or turn on the locator service and/or GPS service.

Some apps are free; others cost a small amount (usually under $10). If you choose an app that isn't free, you'll be prompted for a payment method unless you already have a credit card set up in the app store. (You might have been prompted for a payment method when you created your account initially.)

Apps for Apple iOS

For Apple iPhones and iPads, the only source of apps is Apple via the online App Store or the brick-and-mortar Apple Stores, selling only Apple-sanctioned software from many

FIGURE 20-4   The Apple online App Store

publishers. Apps written for iOS run on both types of Apple devices, but apps display best on the device for which they were written because of the screen size differences. There is no other Apple-sanctioned source of apps for iOS systems. Tap the App Store icon on the home page of an iPhone or iPad to connect to the App Store; the first time you connect you will need to provide your Apple ID and password. Figure 20-4 shows the App Store. Your apps are updated through the App Store, and when one or more updates are ready, the number of updates will appear on the App Store icon. When you open the App Store, the updates will display, and if you decide to update, you will need to enter your Apple ID and password before it will download and update.

Apps for Android

Play is an Android app that connects you to the Google Play online app store. Google Play is Google's official source for Android apps, but since this is an open OS, there are

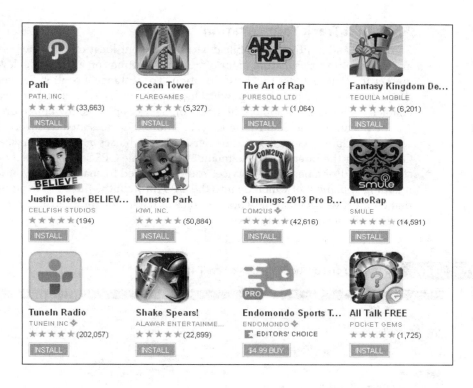

FIGURE 20-5

A small sampling of apps at the Google Play online app store

other sources in the open source market, such as GetJar at www.getjar.com. Pay very close attention to the specs for an app, as there are many versions of Android, with features that are only supported on some devices. Figure 20-5 shows a small sampling of the Android apps at the Play Store.

Apps for Microsoft Windows

The Microsoft Store has apps from many publishers for all their Windows OSs on all devices, including those for devices running Windows 8 and newer and smartphones running Windows Phone. Some are free, but there is a charge for many of them. The Microsoft model is, in part, like the Apple model. Apps written for the new Windows Modern/Metro GUI (regardless of the device it is intended for) must be purchased exclusively through the Microsoft Store; apps written for traditional Windows or the Windows Desktop GUI are available at the Microsoft Store and through other sources that sell software.

Apps that Track Your Location

Some apps and utilities for mobile devices track your location with the help of the Internet, and you can turn this feature on or off. Go into Settings on any mobile device and look for any setting that includes the word "location." For instance, Location Services on the Apple iPad will determine the iPad's physical location by using Wi-Fi hotspot locations. This is enabled in the Settings app on the Location Services page, shown in Figure 20-6.

The Locations and Security settings in Android devices include several location-specific settings, including Google Location Services, which uses a location service supplied by Google over the Internet. It also includes standalone GPS services based on third-party software and/or a peripheral device. You would need to enable this if you wanted to use a mapping app, most of which tie into the GPS through the Internet. In addition, in all devices that connect to a cellular network for voice or data, look for a setting to enable or disable location services over that network.

FIGURE 20-6   Turning on Location Services on an iPad

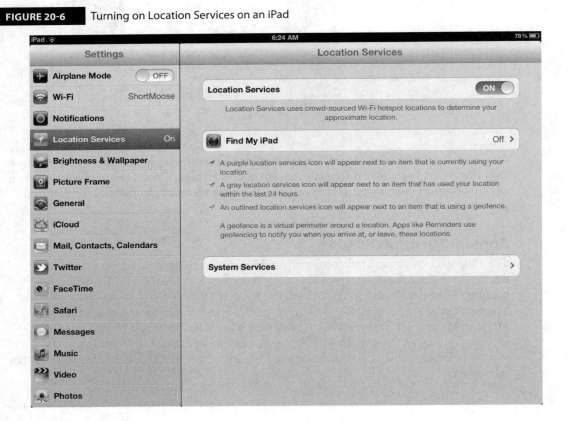

on the Job **Enabling Location Services in iOS and Google Location Services or GPS Services also means that technically you can be tracked through your device, a practice called** *geotracking*. **To do it legally would require government action and, in some cases, the cooperation of the phone company.**

Virtual Assistants

Each of the "big three" mobile operating systems include a virtual assistant utility, which enables you to ask questions and issue commands by speaking and receive a spoken answer. Windows has Cortana, Apple has Siri, and Android has Google Now. Each of them works basically the same way. You activate the assistant to get its attention, ask a question, and get an answer. You can enable or disable the virtual assistant in the Settings app.

SDK and APK

CompTIA A+ 902 exam objective 2.5 lists two mysterious acronyms: SDK and APK. Furthermore, it lumps them together on a single line, when in fact they are very different.

SDK stands for *software development kit*, which is a set of software tools for developing apps on a specific platform. Different SDKs are available for creating apps for each platform. For example, Android apps require an SDK with Java. For iOS apps, you need an SDK with Swift. For Windows Phone apps, you need the .NET Framework SDK with .NET.

APK, *Android application package*, is the package file format for Android apps. A package enables the executable file and all its support files to be distributed in a single archive file that can be easily downloaded to the device. The device's OS then invisibly unpacks the needed files and installs the program without any user intervention. Application packages are available for iOS and Windows Phone platforms as well, although the A+ exam objectives only mention the Android type.

Emergency Notifications

All of the major mobile app OSs include an emergency notification system that shows a warning message on the screen and makes some loud noises whenever the national Emergency Alert System (in the United States) is activated. That means you may get warnings for weather-related issues like tornadoes and flooding, even if the phone's sound is muted.

Mobile Payment Services

Each phone platform also has some sort of mobile payment system. You enter your credit card number(s) or other payment method, and then at some retail outlets, you can easily pay with your phone, using NFC to communicate with the payment processing terminal at the register. Apple Pay is the service for iOS, and Google Pay is the service for Android. For Windows Phone, it is Microsoft Wallet. You can set it up via the Settings app.

CERTIFICATION OBJECTIVES

- ■ *901: 2.7* *Compare and contrast Internet connection types, network types, and their features*
- ■ *901: 3.5* *Compare and contrast accessories and ports of other mobile devices*
- ■ *902: 2.6* *Install and configure basic mobile device network connectivity and e-mail*
- ■ *902: 2.7* *Summarize methods and data related to mobile device synchronization*
- ■ *902: 3.5* *Compare and contrast various methods for securing mobile devices*

To prepare for CompTIA A+ 902 exam objective 2.6, this section details how to enable or disable Wi-Fi or cellular connections and how to configure them. It also describes how to enable Bluetooth for pairing with another device or computer, including the use of a PIN code for some devices and how to test the connectivity. For 902 exam objective 2.7, you need to know the options for mobile device synchronization, including the software requirements to install synchronization apps on a PC, the connection types for synchronization, and the types of data to synchronize. Creating a mobile hotspot (tethering), also covered in this section, is listed under three different exam objectives: 901: 2.7, 901: 3.5, and 902: 2.6. This section covers two topics from 902 exam objective 3.5—patching/OS updates and remote backup applications.

Configuring and Using Mobile Device Connections

In this section we will describe how to connect your mobile device to three types of wireless networks: cellular, Wi-Fi, and Bluetooth. We also examine some useful tasks that rely on connectivity, including configuring e-mail, tethering, and data synchronization.

Connecting to Wireless Networks

As described earlier, smartphones and tablets come with network adapters for cellular data networks, Wi-Fi networks, or both. They also have Bluetooth connections for connecting to nearby devices. Now learn how to connect to these wireless networks.

Connecting to Cellular Networks

When you buy a smartphone or a tablet with cellular data capability, you make the choice at the point of sale concerning the cellular network to which you will subscribe, and you normally sign a contract for a certain level of service before you gain possession of the device (whether in person or over the Internet). Therefore, the actual configuration is done in the store; or in the case of a purchase over the Internet, all you need to do is enter credentials received from the cellular provider on the first use.

Connecting to Wi-Fi Networks

To connect to a Wi-Fi network for the first time, open the Settings app on your device. Then select the option for Wireless (or Wi-Fi) and turn on Wi-Fi, if necessary. In the list of available cellular networks, displayed by SSID, select one and enter the required password. Windows will remember this network, maintaining a list of Wi-Fi networks it has successfully connected to, as shown in Figure 20-7, and providing the password whenever it detects a network. If you travel, you will need to do this for each new Wi-Fi network you connect to.

exam
watch
      All radio frequency (RF) signals coming from mobile devices must be turned off when you fly on a commercial airliner. Therefore, smartphones and tablets have a mode called *airplane mode* that does **just that, allowing you to continue using your device for access to locally stored data, while complying with the regulations. Look for it in the Settings app.**

FIGURE 20-7   Turn on Wi-Fi and then connect to a detected network.

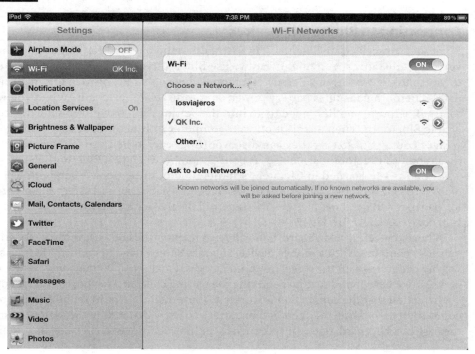

Creating a Mobile Hotspot (Tethering)

You can use a smartphone's cellular network connection to access the Internet when no Wi-Fi is available. Furthermore, you can share that cellular connection to the Internet with other nearby devices. For example, you can share your phone's Internet connection with your laptop when you are somewhere that cell service is available but Wi-Fi is not. The phone becomes a *mobile hotspot*. This is also known as *tethering*. (Some people use the term *tethering* only when referring to a situation where you physically connect a smartphone to a computer via cable, but Android's OS settings use the term for a Wi-Fi hotspot too, and so do we.) You assign a PIN or password to the connection so that only authorized devices may access the connection.

In iOS, from the Home screen, tap Settings | Personal Hotspot and drag the slider to On. In Android, tap Settings, and in the Wireless Network section, tap More | Tethering & Portable Hotspot. In Windows Phone, tap Settings and then scroll down and tap Internet Sharing. Drag the slider to On.

on the job

Remember that creating a mobile hotspot means that other devices are going to be using up your cell plan's data allotment. Make sure you are aware of any potential overage charges you may incur. Even if you have unlimited data, you might still want to monitor and restrict usage because after a certain amount of data is used, some carriers reduce your data speed (known as *throttling*).

Connecting to Bluetooth Devices

Bluetooth, described in Chapter 7, is a wireless standard used for communicating over very short distances. You might want to use Bluetooth to connect a Bluetooth keyboard to your mobile device, or to connect a mobile device to a PC or Mac to synchronize data. Bluetooth consumes battery power, so it is disabled by default. When you want to use Bluetooth, you first need to go into the Settings app on your mobile device and enable Bluetooth. Then enable it on your computer or Bluetooth device with which you wish to connect to so that they can discover (find) each other, which they will attempt to do as soon as Bluetooth is enabled. A connection between two Bluetooth devices is called a *pairing*, as you learned in Chapter 14 in the Bluetooth section. When both devices have discovered each other, go to the Settings screen on each one and select the other device for pairing. After a short pause, a message will display with a pairing code (also called a PIN code), as shown in Figure 20-8.

When connecting a keyboard, you will need to enter the code using the keyboard. When pairing a computer with a mobile device, you may simply need to confirm that the same pairing code shows on the screen for both devices. Finally, test connectivity between the devices. We have found that just entering the pairing code on a keyboard is not enough confirmation that the connection is working. You wouldn't want to set up a Bluetooth connection for a client and then find out after you leave that it didn't work for them. So in the case of a keyboard, open an app, such as an Internet browser, click in a box requiring

FIGURE 20-8   Pairing a Bluetooth keyboard with an iPad

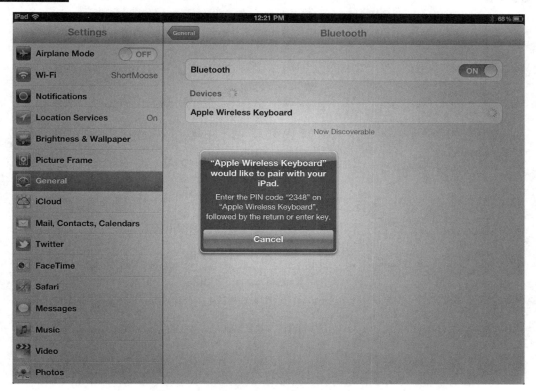

CompTIA A+ 902 exam objective 2.6 lists steps in this order for setting up Bluetooth: enable Bluetooth, enable pairing, find device for pairing, enter PIN code, and test connectivity.

text (such as an address box), and then start typing on the keyboard. If it does not work, you may not have confirmed the pairing on both sides (not always necessary). Although we have found that a failure to connect is often a case of impatience, if you have a problem with the pairing, disable Bluetooth on both devices and start over again.

E-mail Configuration

If you would like to use your mobile device to access your e-mail, you begin by adding the account, which requires first that you select the type of account. Mobile devices support several types of accounts for e-mail, social networking, data backup, and more—for which

FIGURE 20-9   A list of supported account types on an iPad

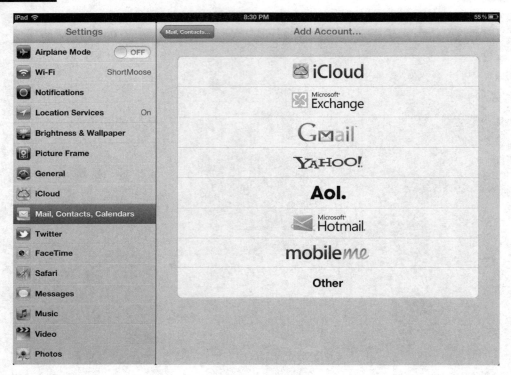

they know the basic connection information. Therefore, for these accounts, you only need to provide your personal login, which is usually an e-mail address and password to the account. Figure 20-9 shows a list of account types supported on an iPad. For all account types, you need your e-mail address and a password for your account that allows your device to send and receive e-mail using that account.

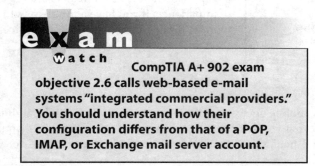

Web-Based E-mail Accounts

For recognized web-based e-mail accounts, such as Outlook.com, Gmail, iCloud, or Yahoo mail, you do not have to specify a sending and receiving server. All you need to enter is your user name and password. That's because your mobile OS already knows the incoming and outgoing mail server addresses and ports for these commonly used systems.

POP3 and IMAP Accounts

If you want to use an account type other than a web-based e-mail service, you will need server addresses obtained from your e-mail server administrator. To receive mail, you will need an address for either a Post Office Protocol 3 (POP3) server or Internet Message Access Protocol (IMAP) server that receives your incoming mail and forwards it to you. An e-mail client uses one or the other of these. To send mail, you usually need the address of your Simple Mail Transfer Protocol (SMTP) server that accepts your outgoing mail and forwards it to an e-mail server.

The addresses for these servers are not numerical. A POP3 address will simply be the name of a mail server in an Internet domain, and may resemble this: pop.domainname.com. The address for an IMAP server might look something like this: imap.domainname.com. The SMTP address might look like this: smtp.domainname.com. These are just examples, so you need to get the actual addresses for these servers from your e-mail administrator. Some ISPs use mail server names that don't have anything to do with the actual domain name; for example, one of our ISPs uses pop.secureserver.net, imap.secureserver.net, and smtp-out.secureserver.net for all of the hundreds of domain names that it hosts.

Armed with the needed information, locate the e-mail settings on your mobile device and carefully enter the information. On an iPad open the Settings app and tap Mail | Contacts | Calendars. Then, in the right pane, tap Add Account. Is the type of e-mail account you need to use listed? If it is, tap it and continue. If not, tap Other at the bottom of the list and then tap Add Mail Account. The New Account dialog box will display, along with the virtual keyboard (unless you have an external keyboard connected). Enter your name (not a user account name), e-mail address, password for that e-mail account, and a description for the e-mail account that will identify it for you in the list of accounts. Tap Next and follow the instructions, using the addresses you obtained from your e-mail server administrator. Figure 20-10 shows the configuration for a POP account being verified for the first time (notice the word "Verifying" at the top of the box).

The "Corporate and ISP email configuration" topic in CompTIA A+ 902 exam objective 2.6 only lists POP3, IMAP, and port and Secure Sockets Layer (SSL) settings. It does not include SMTP.

On an Android device, you will have a Google account for accessing Google services, as well as a required Gmail account. In fact, the Email icon opens to Gmail. To configure another type of account in Android, open Settings, select Accounts, and then select Add Account. This opens the Setup Accounts screen that lists a variety of account types, not just e-mail accounts but social networking sites, photo sharing sites, data backup sites, and other accounts added as you install certain apps.

Tap Email and enter the account information described earlier. If your administrator indicates that your account requires a different port setting or needs a special SSL setting, tap Advanced Settings at the bottom of the Outgoing Server page. This will bring up a page for the port settings, as well as the security settings. The default port is 25 for outgoing

FIGURE 20-10 Configuring a POP e-mail account

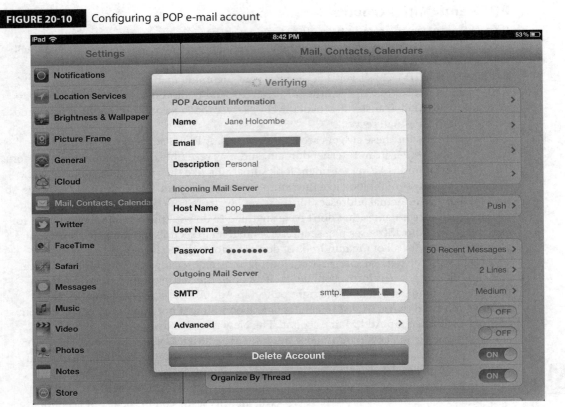

e-mail. This page shows settings for Transport Layer Security (TLS), which is a protocol based on SSL. Do not change these settings, unless your administrator requires it.

Configuring an Exchange Client

Many organizations use internally maintained Microsoft Exchange e-mail servers for employee e-mail accounts and for sending e-mail within the organization as well as over the Internet. Also, many hosting services for Internet domain names offer Exchange e-mail services to their clients. Exchange gives the organization full administrative control, while providing users with a central location for their e-mail history, contacts, tasks, and many collaborative tools. If you need to connect your device to an Exchange server, first open Accounts from Settings and see if your device lists Microsoft Exchange as an account type.

If it does, select it and enter the e-mail address, user name, password, and a description for the list of accounts. If Microsoft Exchange is not listed as a supported account type, you will need to manually configure it, as previously described under "POP3 and IMAP Accounts."

Updating a Smartphone

Your smartphone will periodically receive updates from your cellular provider. The most common of these is an OS update; these updates are pushed out fairly regularly. There are also some other, less-common ways to update a smartphone too, such as updating the baseband/radio firmware and the preferred roaming list (PRL).

OS Updates

Installing OS updates can correct system problems, add more features, and in some cases even change the user interface. The process of updating the OS is somewhat like that of updating the BIOS/UEFI on a PC motherboard, in that it is stored in read-only memory and updates are "flashed" to it.

When an update is available for a smartphone, you might see an onscreen message alerting you, and inviting you to tap a button to allow the update to proceed. On the other hand, you might have to go looking for an update in the Settings app to see whether one is available. In iOS, choose Settings | General | Software Update, for example. Just follow the prompts to install the update, after making sure that the device has sufficient battery charge left (at least 50 percent) or is plugged into AC power. An OS update may take a half-hour or more, so be prepared to be without the use of your phone for that time.

Baseband/Radio Firmware

The *modem* in the phone is the part of the device that modulates and demodulates—that is, converts between analog and digital, and sends and receives data. This is sometimes called the device's *baseband* or *radio*. This modem/radio has *firmware*, like a motherboard has firmware.

In most cases, your cellular provider will partner with your phone's hardware manufacturer to push out updates to the firmware whenever they become available. This is true for Apple and Windows Phone products, and for Android phones that use the default user interface. However, if you are a power user who uses a custom OS version on an Android device, like Paranoid Android, Android Open Kang Project (AOKP), or CyanogenMod (CM), you might want to look into updating the firmware, because it might not get updated automatically with new OS versions.

The process of updating the modem firmware is somewhat complex, and involves finding out the OS version and the phone's firmware version and reconciling them if needed. You can find online articles about doing this.

To find out your Android phone's radio firmware version, choose Settings | About Phone | Baseband Version.

Updating the Preferred Roaming List (PRL)

The PRL is a database stored in your smartphone that contains information used for connecting to cellular service towers. It is necessary for the device to be able to *roam*, which means to get service when outside of the cellular network area of your provider. The PRL is installed at the factory for the phone, and is not normally updated during the life of the phone. However, updating it may make the phone slightly better able to connect to the best roaming carriers. If you travel a lot outside your network, this might be appealing.

Some cell service providers allow the user to download the latest PRL to their phone by dialing a certain feature code. For example, in the United States, for Sprint it is ##873283#, and for Verizon, MetroPCS, and US Cellular it is *228. Check with your provider to find out if a code is available for your phone to perform this update.

e x a m
w a t c h   PRL updates and baseband   nor are they recommended by most phone
updates are specified in CompTIA A+ 902   manufacturers for most users. Know about
exam objective 2.6. We're not sure why, as   them, but don't rush to try them.
they're not common activities to perform,

Connecting to a VPN

As you know from Chapter 14, a virtual private network (VPN) is a secure network tunnel created on an unsecured network (the Internet). Smartphones can connect to VPNs.

To create a VPN connection, use the VPN configuration utility in the Settings app in the mobile OS. For example, on an iPhone, choose Settings | General | VPN, and tap Add VPN

Configuration. Then work through the steps that appear to set up the connection. On an Android phone, in the Settings app, in the Wireless & Networks section, tap More and look for VPN. You can also use a third-party VPN connection app, such as one provided by your employer. Refer to the section "Virtual Private Networking," in Chapter 14, for more details about VPN.

Synchronization

When you have multiple computing devices, who knows which device you might be using at any given moment? Desktop...tablet...cell phone...they're all in constant rotation. You might send an e-mail or create a document on any one of them, and then want to refer to it later on another. To make that possible, you need to *synchronize*, or *sync*, certain data. When data is synchronized between two devices or locations, the files are examined and newer files replace the older files—sometimes, but not always, in both directions. Synching data can also be a backup, an insurance policy against losing your data if a mobile device is lost or stolen.

What kind of data can/should you sync? CompTIA A+ 902 exam objective 2.7 recommends this list:

- Contacts
- Programs
- E-mail
- Pictures
- Music
- Videos

- Calendar
- Bookmarks
- Documents
- Location data
- Social media data
- eBooks

You can synchronize either to another device, such as a desktop PC, or to a cloud service, such as iCloud. Many synchronization programs offer you the opportunity to choose between those two options, and to specify an exact location in each one.

If you synchronize with a computer, you can do it either with a cable (usually USB) or in some cases wirelessly, via a Wi-Fi connection. Syncing to a cloud-based service occurs through an Internet connection—whether it is via a Wi-Fi connection or through a cellular connection.

ⓦatch **Another name for a cloud synchronization app is *remote backup application*; that's how it's listed in CompTIA A+ 902 exam objective 3.5.**

Depending on the device and OS, a specific cloud service may be the recommended default. For example, for Apple devices, iCloud is the default service. Synchronizing with iCloud has many advantages, such as being able to restore your data and personal information easily if your device locks up and has to be reset to factory settings.

You don't necessarily have to choose between local and cloud synchronization. You can do both. Alternatively, you can set up both devices to synchronize to the same account on the same cloud service, so they keep each other synchronized that way.

Connecting Mobile Devices for Syncing

You can sync your smartphone or tablet with your computer, either locally with a USB cable or over the Internet using a cloud-based service. For the local option, use the USB cable that came with the smartphone, usually attached to an alternating current (AC) adapter for charging. Disconnect it from the AC adapter. Connect the end previously connected to the power supply (usually a standard USB connector) to the computer and connect the other end to the device. On smartphones, this will usually be a micro USB connector; on an iPad and some other tablets, it is a Lightning connector. On some devices, this connection will cause two programs to run on the computer—one from your cell provider (if the device has cellular service) for configuring your online account (if you already have one, you simply log in), and a second one that is device-specific and aids in transferring files.

Syncing iPhones and iPads

You can use Apple iTunes for syncing an iPhone and iPad with a Mac or PC. iTunes comes with all Apple computers, and is a free download for Windows PCs. Although it is best known as a music player, it also has the side use of being a synchronization utility for Apple devices.

You may also want to explore the iCloud desktop app for Windows or Mac. This app enables you to configure your cloud-based storage. You can specify what kinds of data should be synched in the cloud (Photos, Contacts, Bookmarks), and how it is stored. See Figure 20-11.

CompTIA A+ 902 exam objective 2.7 includes "Software requirements to install the application on the PC." The system requirements for installing synchronization software are usually very modest, but make sure you check them before you purchase a synchronization application (assuming you don't like any of the free ones available).

Another option that is more of a backup than a syncing option is iCloud. This data is available to all devices from any location with Internet access.

FIGURE 20-11   Use the iCloud desktop app to configure cloud-based storage.

Syncing Android Devices

When you connect an Android device to your computer, it is treated like an external drive, and you can copy files back and forth. Strictly speaking, this isn't syncing. There are individual solutions for various types of data. For instance, when you create a contact in Android, it asks you to pick an account to store (or back up) the contact information. The choices are Google or one provided by your cellular carrier. Select Google and your contacts will be automatically backed up and synced to Google over the Internet, either through a cell connection or via Wi-Fi. After all, who do you expect to have the longest relationship with, Google or your cell provider? We use Google to back up our contacts because it will be available to use if we cancel the contract with the cell provider.

Using a Different Cloud Sync/Backup Service

Phone OSs make it painless and easy to back up using their preferred provider, but you can also use other cloud backup providers, regardless of your phone model.

For example, Google Sync works with Windows Phone and iOS devices to synchronize them with a Google account. This can be useful if your phone is Apple or Windows but you prefer Google's cloud as your backup location. Android devices don't require Google Sync. Similarly, there are OneDrive synchronization apps for Android and iOS. OneDrive is Microsoft's cloud storage system; it's used by default for backing up Windows Phones. iCloud is available on Android and Windows phones via a synchronization app as well.

CERTIFICATION OBJECTIVES

- **902: 3.5**   *Compare and contrast various methods for securing mobile devices*
- **902: 4.4**   *Given a scenario, troubleshoot common mobile OS and application security issues with appropriate tools*

This section covers the many methods of hardware- and software-based security and user authentication available on mobile devices, including a long list of topics from CompTIA A+ 902 exam objective 3.5 such as OS updates, antimalware software, screen locking, authentication, and corporate policies and procedures that promote good security. It also looks at OS and application security issues and security software tools covered in A+ 902 exam objective 4.4.

Securing Mobile Devices

Mobile devices have become a security issue in many organizations for the very reason mobile devices are part of the CompTIA A+ 220-901 and 220-902 exams: they have become ubiquitous and have come into the workplace, both by invitation when required for work and as party crashers when users bring their favorite mobile devices to work, even connecting them to the corporate intranet. The act of bringing your own device from home to a workplace or organization is known as *Bring Your Own Device (BYOD)*. System administrators have much less control over BYOD devices than they do corporate-owned devices.

One way that businesses combat the potential security problems from BYOD is with firm *policies and procedures* that dictate how personal devices should be configured and should connect to the company network. This policy is often called an *acceptable-use policy (AUP)*, and employees may have to sign it as a condition of employment. For example, an AUP might specify that employees cannot use mobile devices that have been "cracked," meaning the devices have been modified to allow them to run untrusted applications from nonstandard app stores. Such applications can make the device (and the network) more vulnerable to malware. An AUP might also have profile security requirements, such as requiring a complex password (rather than a simple four-digit passcode).

To meet the challenges of supporting mobile devices in the workplace, you need to know about the hardware and software tools and features available for making mobile devices more secure, thereby protecting not only the devices but the valuable (and perhaps confidential) data that they can access.

Mobile Security Risks

There are several risks in using a mobile device, including unauthorized device access, spying, unauthorized use of the cellular data plan to access the Internet (on smartphones and tablets with cellular service), and malware. Let's look at each of those risks in more detail.

Unauthorized Device Access

Unauthorized device access occurs when someone other than the owner is able to physically gain access to the device without permission. This can happen if there is no lock password on the device, or if the person is able to circumvent or guess the password. *Unauthorized account access* occurs when the intruder is able to gain access to the owner's personal accounts or data as a result of gaining physical access to the device. The intruder is then able to snoop personal documents and notes and even sign into online services where data is stored.

On an Android device, it is also possible for an intruder to gain root access, which allows the user to access the Android operating system itself, to make changes to system files. This can result in malware being installed or the OS not working properly. This is called *rooting*, and it usually requires specialized rooting software.

By default, Android devices don't allow root access. However, some users choose to "root their phones" to install unauthorized applications or to remove preinstalled applications put there by the wireless carrier.

Someone gaining unauthorized access to a device may also surreptitiously enable location-tracking software that can send data back to the hacker remotely to track the location of the device owner without his or her knowledge.

The best way to prevent unauthorized device access is with a strong screen sign-in authentication. See "Sign-in Authentication," later in this chapter, to learn about the available options.

Spying

Spying can take many forms. The simplest kind is ordinary shoulder surfing, where someone watches you as you use your device. It's harder to spy on a smartphone or tablet screen from a distance because it's smaller than a desktop or laptop screen, but it still happens.

Spying can also include unauthorized location tracking, as we mentioned in the previous section. Someone who has had physical access to your device can install a tracking device or tracking software on it. With certain spyware installed on your device without your knowledge, the hacker can also access your microphone and camera, to spy on you visually or aurally.

Unauthorized Use of Your Internet Access

If your smartphone includes a tethering/mobile hotspot feature, you can share your Internet connection with others. The downside of that is that someone could guess or hack the password for that connection and use your phone as a hotspot without your permission. This might result in data overages for you, as well as slow application performance as your phone's processor handles the increased processing load.

Malware Infection and Exploits

Malware creators historically haven't paid much attention to mobile OSs, and in fact Apple doesn't even recommend antivirus software for its operating systems. However, malware is still a threat, especially on Android devices, and can result in the same kinds of problems as on a desktop computer.

OS exploits are also a potential threat, at least theoretically. Recall from Chapter 17 that an exploit is a security flaw in the OS code that a malware writer finds before the OS manufacturer can find it and fix it.

Mobile Security Tools

Now that you're aware of the security risks, let's look at how those risks can be mitigated.

Sign-in Authentication

Mobile devices usually have a setting for a passcode lock. A *passcode lock* restricts access to a device by requiring a login to the device using a pattern (screen gestures you choose), a PIN, or password. On Android devices look for Set Up Screen Lock Settings under Location and Security Settings.

You should require a login for access to your mobile device. On an iOS device, you can make your login more secure by using a complex password, rather than the standard simple passcode. Note that the Auto-Lock option only sets the amount of time of inactivity before a device locks, but this does not, on its own, require a passcode. If you don't require a passcode, you simply use a swipe to close the lock screen and access the device.

Some devices also employ *biometric authentication* as an option. Biometric authentication verifies the user's identity by examining some part of their body. For example, newer iPhones include a fingerprint scanner on the Home button, and some other devices use the built-in camera to do facial recognition for authentication, also called a *face lock*.

When a device requires more than one authentication method, it's known as *multifactor authentication*. For example, a device might ask for both a passcode and a fingerprint, for extra security. Most devices don't offer multifactor authentication in the OS, but you can install *authenticator applications* that enable that option.

Restrictions for Failed Login Attempts

Some devices put restrictions (or consequences) on multiple consecutive failed password attempts. For example, you can set up a smartphone so that there is a lockout period of several minutes after a certain number of failed password attempts. This prevents someone from repeatedly guessing the password quickly. Eventual guessing it is still possible, but it will take the hacker much longer. Some devices also enable you to turn on a feature that will erase the data on the device after a certain number of failed login attempts.

Security Software

Many security programs are available for Android systems with such features as antivirus, antispam, browsing protection, and privacy features that will alert you if an app attempts to access your private information (e.g., location, contacts, and messages). These inexpensive security suites also include backup features and missing device features. If a device is missing, you can use this software to locate it (if location services is enabled), initiate a loud alarm on the device, and/or do a *remote wipe* (deleting all contents) of your device, making it effectively unusable by anyone who steals or finds it.

Apple iOS devices do not come with antivirus software, and the Apple Store at this time does not have antivirus software. Apple claims that their products do not get viruses because of the closed nature of the system (only Apple hardware and only Apple-tested software).

Application Security

On Android devices, you can choose to acquire applications from unofficial sources, in addition to getting them from the Play Store. CompTIA A+ 902 exam objective 3.5 calls these *untrusted sources*. (In contrast, officially sanctioned stores are *trusted sources*.) When you use an untrusted source, you run the risk of introducing malware into your system, or installing poorly written apps that crash.

This same exam objective also mentions uninstalling and reinstalling applications, as well as force stopping applications. These topics are covered later in this chapter.

Full Device Encryption

Full device encryption encrypts all the data on the phone that so it cannot be booted except by someone with the PIN code or password. On some devices, encryption is synonymous with the lock screen passcode that you learned about earlier in this chapter. On other devices, notably some Android devices, you can choose to encrypt your data separately from setting a passcode. You still use the same passcode to gain entry, but if you don't know the passcode, it's harder to hack into the device to get at the data than if encryption is not enabled. Some versions of Android also let you set a separate encryption password.

Why would you set a separate encryption password from the lock screen password? It's primarily to balance security with convenience. The encryption password is required only when rebooting, so you can use a stronger, more complex password for it. You can leave the lock screen passcode as a simple number, for quick availability.

Protecting Data

Just like on a desktop or laptop PC, it is important to back up your mobile device data frequently. Synching your data with a local PC or a cloud storage system, as you learned earlier in the chapter, is the most effective way of protecting your device's data.

Network Security

Be aware when you are using your mobile device on a Wi-Fi network, especially when using a public access point that is not password protected. All the devices connected to the same router are effectively on a LAN together. Do not send and receive sensitive information on an unsecure network, no matter what kind of device you are using.

CompTIA A+ 902 exam objective 4.4 lists these two tools to be aware of:

- **Wi-Fi analyzer**   This software for a smartphone or a tablet (or separate handheld device) provides information about nearby Wi-Fi networks, including the SSID, the channel, and the security type.
- **Cell tower analyzer**   This device (or software) provides information about the cell phone towers within range. Most of this information will not be meaningful to anyone except a cellular service technician.

Recovering After a Device Is Lost or Stolen

All the major mobile device OSs include features that help you when your device is lost or stolen, so don't panic. These are the major tools in the arsenal:

- Locators, which can use Internet and cell tower usage to determine your device's location
- Remote wipe features, which can erase all the data on the device remotely the next time it connects to the Internet
- Information utilities that enable you to send a message to your lost device so that whoever has it will see it and be able to contact you (if it was lost, rather than stolen)

If it's an Android device and is signed into a Google Account, you can use the Android Device Manager (on any device with a web browser) to show your device's location. For this to work, the device has to have a Wi-Fi connection or mobile data connection and an active SIM card. In other words, it doesn't work for devices where the finder doesn't want it to be located. The Android Device Manager also allows you to remotely contact, lock, or erase the device.

On an iOS device, sign into iCloud using a web browser and select Find iPhone. Then click All Devices and select the desired device. The next step depends on whether you think you lost the iOS device or it was stolen. If you think you lost it and that someone has found it, and the person who has it might want to return it to you, click Lost Mode. Lost Mode locks the device with a passcode (if you didn't already have one set) so that others can't access your personal information. It also displays a custom message on the screen, such as how to contact you. If you think your device was stolen, and you want to delete all the data on it, click Erase iPhone.

CERTIFICATION OBJECTIVES

- ***901: 4.5***   *Given a scenario, troubleshoot and repair common mobile device issues while adhering to the appropriate procedures*
- ***902: 4.3***   *Given a scenario, troubleshoot common mobile OS and application issues with appropriate tools*
- ***902: 4.4***   *Given a scenario, troubleshoot common mobile OS and application security issues with appropriate tools*

This section covers parts of three major objectives, all having to do with mobile troubleshooting. CompTIA A+ 901 exam objective 4.5 looks at hardware issues with mobile devices, such as overheating, short battery life, and display problems, and the procedures used to remediate those issues. A+ 902 exam objective 4.3 contains software troubleshooting topics like applications running slowly and lack of wireless connectivity. These objectives actually have a lot of topics in common, so you'll see quite a bit of overlap. Also covered are a few items that are listed under 902 exam objective 4.4, such as reasons for signal drop, power drain, low data speeds, and unintended wireless connectivity.

Mobile Device Troubleshooting

To round out this chapter, we will next take a look at some of the many things that can go wrong with mobile devices and how to fix them.

Hardware Issues

Hardware issues include problems with the hardware components on the device, such as the display, the touch screen, and the battery. Be aware, however, that sometimes software issues will manifest themselves as problems with hardware. For example, background-running applications might be the underlying cause of short battery life.

Dim Display

A dim display could be the result of defective hardware, but it is more likely caused by a setting that is telling the device to conserve battery power by placing the display in a low-power-consumption mode. Check the device's power management settings, and do a soft reset (explained later in this chapter), before you assume that your device is defective. When a battery gets below a certain charge level, the OS may dim the display automatically.

On an iOS device, choose Settings | Display and Brightness and turn Auto-Brightness off. Then restart the device by powering it off and back on again. Then go to Settings | General | Accessibility | Increase Contrast. While you're there, turn on Reduce Transparency and turn on Reduce White Point.

On Android devices, choose Settings | Display | Brightness and clear the Automatic Brightness check box. Then drag the slider to manually adjust brightness. You can also download an app that will enable you to control brightness and contrast settings.

A dim display can also be the result of a malfunctioning ambient light sensor. This sensor allows your device to change the brightness of the screen depending on the lighting conditions in the room.

On iOS devices, occasionally the Zoom setting may cause dimness problems, although it's not an obvious connection. Choose Settings | General | Accessibility and make sure Zoom is turned off.

One more thing to try is to reset all settings. This has some of the same effects as a hard reset but it doesn't delete your data or media. On an iPhone, choose Settings | General | Reset | Reset All Settings | Confirm. (This option isn't available for Android.)

Out of options and still having the problem? Sync your device to a backup source to save everything, and then do a hard reset, as described later in this chapter.

Cannot Broadcast to External Monitor

To use an external monitor such as a TV with your Android mobile device, you can connect them with a cable (such as micro USB or Micro-HDMI), or you can wirelessly cast your screen using an app. HDMI is the best option, if available. The TV will simply mirror the mobile device's screen.

When mirroring a mobile screen to a TV, keep in mind that the mobile device must remain powered on the whole time. If it goes to sleep after 5 minutes, so will the TV display. Adjust settings as needed, and plug the device into an AC charger to prevent battery drain.

If you're going wireless, use an app and adapter such as Chromecast. Chromecast provides an inexpensive HDMI dongle that plugs into your TV and talks to your Android phone or other mobile devices wirelessly.

Apple devices don't support streaming to an external monitor except with Apple TV. It supports AirPlay mirroring of the screen from iOS devices, and is similar to Chromecast.

If you are watching copyright-protected content, it might not stream to a TV or other external monitor unless you sign up for a subscription and pay a fee. You'll be prompted if that's the case.

Touch Screen Nonresponsive

As mentioned earlier, most touch screens are *capacitive*, which means they respond to the electrical charge in a person's finger. They don't respond very well to gloved fingers or styluses not specifically designed for touch screen use. So first of all, make sure you are using a clean, dry finger on the screen.

Next, make sure the screen is clean and accessible. Wipe it with a soft, slightly damp, lint-free cloth. If you are using a screen protector on the device, remove it.

Restart the device. If it won't restart normally, force stop it and restart it, as explained later in this chapter. After you restart the device, if the touch screen fails its startup diagnostic, you likely have a hardware problem. You can attempt to replace the touch screen yourself, but if you're not familiar with disassembly and assembly of mobile devices, you could easily break something; it's better to enlist the help of someone who repairs mobile devices for a living.

You can also employ diagnostics tools to check the screen. On an Android phone, you can use the Device Diagnostics Tool, for example. For more information about this tool, check out online resources.

No Display

If the device appears completely lifeless, its battery is probably drained. If charging the battery does not solve the problem, the display hardware may have failed, or the device may need a soft or hard reset. See "Resetting a Mobile Device" later in this chapter.

Inaccurate Touch Screen Response

If you touch one spot and your touch registers in another spot, that's a screen calibration issue, which is a disparity of positions between the display part of the screen and the touch-sensitive input part of the screen. Lack of calibration should not be a problem on capacitive screens because of their technology, so this is not an issue on devices that have capacitive screens (like most modern iPhones, for example). Check in the Settings app for a calibration utility. If there isn't one, your screen is probably capacitive.

It's easy to say that calibration shouldn't be an issue, of course, but what if it is anyway? If you experience calibration problems and you don't have access to a calibration utility, try doing a hard reset on the device, or take it to a repair shop to have them replace the digitizer.

Overheating

Does your mobile device get hot? This used to be a bigger problem than it is today, back when phone batteries were bigger and bulkier. On some models overheating may still occur today, however, especially on devices with removable batteries. In 2016, the Samsung Galaxy Note 7 had an issue with overheating and catching fire, for example, and a massive recall was issued.

First of all, where is your device getting hot? If it's on the back, it might be a problem with the battery. Try a different battery.

If it gets hot on the bottom, and only when plugged into AC power, there may be an issue with the charger. Try a different charger if possible.

If it gets hot above the battery compartment (if there is one), it's probably the device itself that is overheating. This is also true if the device heats up near the speaker (where you put your ear when talking if it's a phone), or if the heat seems to be coming from the screen.

Overheating can occur when you have many applications open simultaneously because this puts a strain on the CPU to run continuously (generating heat). Watching downloaded movies or streaming video on a device can also cause it to overheat because of the constant activity of the screen, memory, and CPU. Give your device time to rest and cool off.

Carrying your phone in a pocket or other enclosed area can also contribute to overheating, as can using a tight case that doesn't allow for any ventilation.

Disabling unneeded background applications and features can also help keep the device cool. For example, if you aren't using Bluetooth or Wi-Fi, turn them off in the Settings app.

Do not put a mobile device into a refrigerator or freezer to cool it off. Moisture can condense on the circuitry, causing a short-circuit.

Frozen System

If your phone suddenly seizes up when you are using it, there could be a number of different root causes. If the screen goes dark, you have probably run out of battery. Try connecting it to AC power.

If power wasn't the issue, try a soft reset. If that doesn't work, try a hard reset. See "Resetting a Mobile Device," later in this chapter.

No Sound from Speakers

If you aren't hearing any sound, the sound is probably muted. Check the volume level by pressing the Volume Up button on the device. Some devices also have a Mute switch or button that kills the sound instantly regardless of the volume level setting. (An iPhone has this on the upper-left corner, for example.) Make sure the Mute switch hasn't been flipped.

System Lockout

A system lockout occurs when you forget the device's passcode. The only way to get around a system lockout is to do a hard reset. (We hope you backed up/synched your data.)

Power Drain/Short Battery Life

Devices are designed to put themselves into a low-power mode after a few minutes of inactivity. If they're on constantly, the battery gets drained fairly quickly. Make sure that the device's Lock Timeout setting is set as low as you can tolerate without finding it annoying, for maximum battery life.

A battery that just plain drains quickly may be in need of replacement. On a device with a replaceable battery, just buy the kind you need and swap them out. On a device with a built-in battery, battery replacement can be complicated and can void the warranty, so consider using an authorized repair shop or an Apple Store. Before you replace the battery, though, try restarting the device; occasionally a device will get an application that is "stuck" running, and that application's activity will cause the battery to drain quickly. Restarting can shake that off.

Data Transmission Issues

In this section we look at problems involving data and connectivity, including cell service, Bluetooth, and Wi-Fi.

Weak Cell Signal and Dropped Calls

A weak cell signal can occur when not close enough to a cell tower, of course, but there are also other reasons you might have a weak signal, including these:

- Being inside a building with walls that don't allow a cell signal to penetrate easily. For example, sometimes you might lose signal in an elevator or a basement.

- Being on or near water can degrade cell service, such as being in a boat or near a decorative waterfall or fountain.

- Many different cell signals bouncing around in a small area (like in a large city) can create *destructive interference*, resulting in poor service. Using a cellular repeater device may help in this situation.

- Your grip on your phone can actually interfere with its signal, if it's iffy to begin with. Use a hands-free headset and your reception may improve a bit.

The main cure for weak signal strength is to simply move to a different location, move away from the obstacle, or open a window. However, resetting the phone (soft reset) or turning on airplane mode and then turning it off again may increase signal strength. This is because a phone doesn't always connect to the closest tower; it might connect to a more distant one if it thinks you are moving in that direction. Resetting the phone reconnects with the closest tower.

Another option in an area of bad cell service is to use *Wi-Fi calling*. Most smartphones enable you to make calls over Wi-Fi. Check the Settings app.

No Wireless Connectivity

Using cellular data to surf the Internet on a wireless device can eat up your data plan allotment quickly, so you will want to connect to a Wi-Fi network whenever it is available. When a wireless network is in range that you have already connected to, it may reconnect automatically. If you aren't getting a wireless connection, however, check these things:

- Make sure there is a WAP or router nearby that is offering Wi-Fi service. If you have another Wi-Fi-enabled device, connect to that access point with it if you can.

- Make sure Wi-Fi is enabled on your device. Sometimes you might turn it off to save battery life when you don't need it, and then forget you have done so.

- Verify that you have the right password for the router or WAP.

Intermittent or Slow Wi-Fi

Intermittent Wi-Fi access can be the result of the same sort of problems that you might face on a desktop or laptop computer that has Wi-Fi. Check the following:

- Check the distance from the WAP or router. Get closer to it if possible.
- Make sure there are no 802.11b devices connecting to the router or WAP, as that can slow down everyone else's access on the same LAN.
- Do a soft reset of the device.
- Reset the router or WAP if you are able to access it.
- Look for interference from cordless landline phones in the vicinity. Some of them operate on the 2.4 GHz band, which is also where 802.11b, g, and n devices operate.

No Bluetooth Connectivity

Bluetooth can be turned on/off in the device's Settings app; don't forget to check that setting if Bluetooth isn't working.

If your Bluetooth adapter is working but you can't pair with devices, here are some tips:

- Determine what pairing process the device uses. The process can vary. Sometimes you can enter a code; other times you just touch the device to the accessory you want to pair it with, or hold down a button.
- Move away from nearby Wi-Fi routers and USB 3.0 ports, both of which may generate interference.
- Make sure the devices you are trying to pair are able to connect with each other.
- Make sure your device's Bluetooth is set to be Discoverable.
- Make sure the two devices are close enough to one another.
- Power cycle each device.
- Power down any devices that may be interfering with the pairing, such as other Bluetooth devices in the area.
- If the device has been paired in the past but won't pair now, delete its information from your device and rediscover it.
- Investigate whether you need to install a driver for the accessory.
- Investigate whether a firmware update is available for either device.

Data Transmission Overlimit

Many mobile devices have warnings you can set to alert you when you are nearing your data allotment limit for the billing period. Check in the Settings app or in the proprietary software installed on your device by your cell provider.

Unintended Wi-Fi Connection or Bluetooth Pairing

If you have established a Wi-Fi connection with a WAP or router in the past, it may connect automatically when the device is within range, even if you don't intend it to. To prevent this, go into Settings and disconnect manually from the access point. To be extra sure it won't happen again, turn off Wi-Fi.

The same goes for Bluetooth. A previous pairing may repeat itself automatically. Disconnect it manually in Settings. Turn off Bluetooth for extra assurance that it won't connect.

Application Issues

Issues with individual apps may manifest as applications not loading at all, performing poorly, locking up, or using more system resources than they should.

When an application is using more resources (such as too much memory), other applications running concurrently may suffer in performance. This problem is usually caused by an error in the application. If it's an error in the copy of the application on your device, you might be able to fix it by uninstalling and reinstalling the application. If it's a bug in the application itself, there's not much you can do, other than search for a newer version of it. The same goes for an application that runs poorly (slowly in general, or starting and stopping).

If an application won't run at all, resetting the device is likely to help. If not, try reinstalling the application, or perhaps just giving up on it and trying a different application.

E-mail Encryption Issues

CompTIA A+ 902 exam objective 4.3 refers to these issues as "Unable to decrypt email." E-mail encryption issues are not common on mobile devices, but occasionally you may have an issue. Here are some of the possibilities to investigate when you get an e-mail message that you can't decrypt:

- Make sure Secure/Multipurpose Internet Mail Extensions (S/MIME) are enabled in the OS.

- If you are receiving an encrypted e-mail in your Exchange account from someone on a different Exchange server, you might need to install their certificate on your device in order to read it.

- If the sender is using an old version of Microsoft Outlook 2010, they may need to install Office 2010 Service Pack 1.

Troubleshooting with Safe Mode

Android phones have a Safe Mode, similar to the Safe Mode on a Windows PC. It boots into the OS without any third-party applications. If you have a problem, and the problem goes away when you boot into Safe Mode, you know that the problem is due to a third-party application. There is usually a key combination you can press that will enter Safe Mode. For example, with the device turned off, you might press the power button and hold it until you see a logo, and then release the power button and immediately press and hold a different key, such as Volume Down. (That's the procedure for a Samsung Galaxy S5.)

Closing, Uninstalling, and Reinstalling Mobile Applications

If you suspect a problem with an application, uninstall it. The process for doing so depends on the OS. You can then reinstall a clean copy of it from a trusted source.

If an application is running, you might not be able to remove it until you shut it down completely. One way is to reboot the device. Another way is simply to close the application.

Quitting an app on iOS is easy. Double-press the Home button, swipe to the app you want to force quit, and then swipe it up to close it.

On Android devices there is an option called *Force Stop* that enables you to shut down an application completely so it can be removed. If you attempt to remove an application but its Uninstall or Remove button is unavailable, use the Force Stop button to shut it down, and then remove it. If both the Uninstall and Force Stop buttons are unavailable, it's a system app and you cannot uninstall it.

Resetting a Mobile Device

There are two kinds of resets. A *soft reset* is basically just a reboot. Sometimes when a device locks up or starts acting squirrelly, a soft reset will do the trick. A *hard reset* (also called a *factory reset* or *clean install*) wipes out everything on the device and takes it back to its original factory settings. (You want to avoid doing that if possible because you lose everything you've stored.)

Sometimes a hard reset is the fastest and easiest way to ensure that your device doesn't have any virus or other security-compromising malware on it. Some may say a hard reset is overkill, but if your device is experiencing puzzling symptoms, a hard reset beats spending weeks of trying various fixes and hoping for the best.

Resetting a Device

To reset an Android device, you will want to access the Factory Data Reset screen. The tricky part is that different phone brands and models access this screen differently. Look up the exact steps for your model online. On one of our phones, for example, with it powered off, you can hold down Volume Down and Power together. When you see the brand logo, you release the Power button only, and then immediately press it again, and then you release both buttons when the Factory Reset Data screen appears. If that sounds as awkward as a game of Twister…it is. It's difficult on purpose, so you don't do it accidentally.

To reset an iOS device, you need a computer with iTunes installed. Connect the device to the computer and open iTunes. Then press and hold Sleep/Wake and Home at the same time, but *don't* release the buttons when you see the Apple logo. Keep holding them until you see the Recovery Mode screen. A message appears in iTunes that there's a problem with the device that requires it to be updated or restored. Click Update and wait for iTunes to fix the device.

Getting Your Data Back After a Hard Reset

If you're lucky enough to have backed up or synched the device's settings before the disaster occurred, you can restore them as follows.

On an Android device, after a hard reset, you are prompted to walk through a setup process. As part of it, you're prompted to sign in to Google. When you do so with the same Gmail account you used for synching, your data is automatically restored to the device.

On an iOS device, when the device comes back up after a hard reset, the Setup Assistant runs. Go to Set Up Your Device, tap Restore from a Backup, and sign in to iCloud. Tap Choose Backup, and then select the backup you want to use and follow the prompts.

CERTIFICATION SUMMARY

Because mobile devices have come into all areas of our daily life and are used more and more at work (officially and unofficially), a CompTIA A+ certification candidate needs to be prepared to support users of these small but useful devices. Understand their hardware features and the sources of apps for the most popular devices, which run the Apple iOS or Android OS. Mobile devices have locator and GPS services that you can enable for pinpointing the location of the device. This is handy for using mapping programs, but is also useful for finding your device, should it be lost or stolen. It also means that you could be tracked through your device, if necessary.

A smartphone, because it is first of all a cell phone, comes configured with a connection to a cellular network, including both voice and data services. Tablets do not function as phones, so a connection to a cellular network for data access is optional. Beyond that, both smartphones and tablets come with Wi-Fi and Bluetooth options. Know how to configure a device to receive and send e-mail through e-mail accounts, and synchronize devices with computers or cloud-based services.

There are many options for securing mobile devices, from security apps for Android devices to a variety of security settings on both Android and iOS devices.

Mobile devices, because of their on-chip OS, don't get easily corrupted, and aren't particularly vulnerable to malware. However, they do get confused sometimes and need to be reset, either with a soft or hard reset. Settings can also be misadjusted, resulting in certain components not appearing to work. Know where the basic settings are located for various types of mobile devices, and how to reset them.

TWO-MINUTE DRILL

Here are some of the key points covered in Chapter 20.

Overview of Mobile Devices

❑ Mobile devices include smartphones, tablets, phablets, smart watches, fitness monitors, e-readers, GPS devices, and smart cameras.

❑ Modern touch screens are capacitive screens and do not need calibration, although that was required in many older devices.

❑ Screen rotation (also called screen orientation) is a feature that changes the screen orientation based on the angle at which you hold the device. This is accomplished with an on-board accelerometer in most devices, but some devices aimed at gamers use a gyroscope.

❑ Mobile devices use SSDs for storage. Most include a microphone and speaker and one or more ports, such as a Lightning port on Apple devices. Most include multiple wireless connection capabilities, including Wi-Fi, Bluetooth, and NFC.

❑ Mobile device accessories include game pad, docking station, battery charger, protective cover, credit card reader, and memory card.

❑ Android is an open source operating system for mobile devices, while Apple iOS is closed source and vendor specific.

❑ Mobile devices have location services that use Internet-based tracking services and/or GPS, allowing for use of mapping programs and also allowing geotracking of the device.

❑ Apps for Apple iOS are only available from the Apple Store. The Google Play online app store is Google's official source for Android apps, but since this is an open OS, there are other sources in the open source market.

❑ Most mobile apps have virtual assistant applications that accept voice commands.

Configuring and Using Mobile Device Connections

❑ When you purchase a smartphone, it has a configured cell connection, but you need to configure Wi-Fi and Bluetooth separately.

❑ When traveling by commercial airliner, use airplane mode to turn off all RF broadcasts.

❑ Tethering, or creating a mobile hotspot, enables a smartphone to serve as a wireless access point for other devices.

❑ To set up a Bluetooth pairing, first you enable Bluetooth, have the devices discover each other, then enable pairing, then either enter a PIN code on one side or confirm that the same code displays on both devices, and finally test connectivity.

❑ To configure e-mail on a mobile device, you need certain information that you may need to obtain from an e-mail administrator if you do not already have it. For connection to popular web-based e-mail systems like Gmail, you only need the e-mail address and password. For other e-mail connections, you may also need server addresses for POP3 or IMAP4 and SMTP, and port and SSL settings.

❑ Install OS updates to make sure a mobile device has all the latest patches and security features. Use the Settings app. You might be able to update the baseband/radio firmware and/or the preferred roaming list on some Android devices.

❑ You can synchronize devices by connecting the device to a computer or over an Internet connection to a cloud-based service. Data you can sync includes contacts, programs, e-mail, pictures, music, and videos.

Securing Mobile Devices

❑ Securing mobile devices is a challenging, but necessary, task for a support person, especially since so many people use their personal mobile devices at work, a practice (sanctioned or not) called bring your own device (BYOD).

❑ Mobile security risks include unauthorized device access, unauthorized account access, malware, spying, and unauthorized use of Internet access.

❑ Mobile security begins with sign-on authentication, such as a passcode lock, biometric authentication, multifactor authentication, and restrictions for failed login attempts.

❑ To avoid malware and crashing applications, acquire applications only from trusted sources.

❑ To protect data stored on a device, consider full device encryption, strong authentication, and frequent data backup via synchronization.

❑ Before a device is lost or stolen, enable remote backups and be prepared to do a remote wipe. For iOS devices, keep data synced to iCloud, and use its remote-wipe feature on the lost or stolen device. On an Android device, install a security suite that includes remote wipe. You can also use Android Device Manager to remotely erase the device.

❑ If you enable locator features, you can use a locator app to find your lost or stolen mobile device using a map on another device or computer.

❑ If the device is stolen, use a remote wipe to prevent the thief from having access to your data.

Mobile Device Troubleshooting

- ❏ A dim display may be caused by defective hardware, power management settings, or a low battery. First try adjusting the device's power management settings.
- ❏ A nonresponsive touch screen can sometimes be corrected with a reboot. Also make sure the screen is clean and dry. Some types of screens may need calibration.
- ❏ Overheating can occur from a defective battery, charger, or motherboard. Let the device breathe; don't store it in a pocket or an unventilated case.
- ❏ Try a soft reset in the event of a frozen system; then try a hard reset if that doesn't work.
- ❏ If there is no sound, sound is probably muted. Check the volume level and the Mute switch (if there is one).
- ❏ A weak signal or dropped calls may be related to location or interference.
- ❏ For lack of wireless connectivity, make sure the interface is enabled in Settings. For intermittent or slow wireless, check location and interference.
- ❏ For application issues, uninstall and reinstall.
- ❏ A soft reset keeps all data and settings. A hard reset should be used only if all else fails; it wipes all data and settings.
- ❏ To get your data back after a hard reset, use your backup created with synchronization.

SELF TEST

The following questions will help you measure your understanding of the material presented in this chapter. Read all of the choices carefully because there might be more than one correct answer. Choose all correct answers for each question.

Overview of Mobile Devices

1. Which of these is not a mobile computing device?
   A. Phablet
   B. Tablet
   C. Smartphone
   D. Router

2. What component enables automatic screen rotation on a device?
   A. Gyroscope
   B. Portrait
   C. Landscape
   D. SSD

3. A typical mobile device uses this component for local storage.
   A. Virtual disk
   B. Tethering
   C. Hard drive
   D. SSD

4. What kind of connector is used to charge an iPad?
   A. Micro USB
   B. Mini USB
   C. Lightning
   D. Thunderbolt

5. Which of these is the unique ID assigned to a mobile phone?
   A. ICCID
   B. IMSI
   C. IMEI
   D. WAP

6. Where can you find apps for an iOS device?
   A. Amazon
   B. Play Store
   C. Software retailer
   D. Apple Store

7. Which of these is the package file format for Android applications?
   A. SDK
   B. APK
   C. .NET Framework
   D. Swift

Configuring and Using Mobile Device Connections

8. When you purchase a smartphone, it has this type of connection configured for you.
   A. Wi-Fi
   B. Cell
   C. Bluetooth
   D. Tethered

9. _____ means sharing your phone's Internet connection with another Wi-Fi-enabled device.
    A. Airplane mode
    B. Pairing
    C. Near field communication
    D. Tethering

10. _____ means connecting a Bluetooth-enabled accessory to a smartphone, tablet, or other mobile device.
    A. Airplane mode
    B. Pairing
    C. Near field communication
    D. Tethering

11. What mode on mobile devices turns off all RF broadcasts?
    A. Pairing
    B. Airplane
    C. Tethering
    D. Wi-Fi

12. What information do you need to configure your mobile device to connect to a Gmail account?
    A. Server addresses for IMAP and POP3
    B. URL of the web-based e-mail interface
    C. E-mail address and password
    D. Port numbers

13. The _____ is a database stored in your smartphone that contains information used for connecting to cellular towers.
    A. Baseband
    B. NFC
    C. SSL
    D. PRL

14. What type of e-mail service is internally maintained for an organization's employees, with all accounts centrally administered by the organization's e-mail administrator?
    A. Gmail
    B. Hotmail
    C. Microsoft Exchange
    D. Work

Securing Mobile Devices

15. What security feature requires you to enter a PIN for access to a device?
A. Remote wipe
B. Failed login attempts restrictions
C. Multi-touch
D. Passcode lock

16. Which of these would you *not* use after your mobile device is lost?
A. Locator
B. Remote wipe
C. Disable Wi-Fi and Bluetooth remotely
D. Configure a passcode lock remotely

Mobile Device Troubleshooting

17. Which problem would a soft reset *not* fix?
A. Touch screen not responding
B. Dim screen
C. Frozen system
D. System lockout due to forgotten passcode

18. When you are outdoors in a rural area and have a weak cell signal, what is likely the problem?
A. Destructive interference
B. Distance from a cell tower
C. No nearby WAP
D. Constructive interference

19. Which of these would *not* help a problem with slow or intermittent Wi-Fi?
A. Soft reset of the mobile device
B. Reset the router
C. Reduce 2.4 GHz band interference
D. Calibrate screen

20. When two nearby Bluetooth-enabled devices don't recognize each other, what is likely the problem?
A. The devices need to be touching.
B. One of the devices isn't set to be discoverable.
C. Wi-Fi is not enabled.
D. Interference exists from a nearby cordless landline phone.

A SELF TEST ANSWERS

Overview of Mobile Devices

1. ☑   **D.** A router is not a mobile device.
    ☒   **A, B,** and **C** are all incorrect because they are all mobile devices.

2. ☑   **A.** A gyroscope, along with an accelerometer, enables automatic screen rotation.
    ☒   **B** and **C** are both incorrect because portrait and landscape are screen orientations. **D** is incorrect because SSD stands for solid-state drive, a type of storage in a mobile device.

3. ☑   **D.** A solid-state drive (SSD) is used in a mobile device for local storage.
    ☒   **A** is incorrect because a virtual disk is not a component of mobile devices. **B** is incorrect because tethering describes a cable connection between a mobile device and a PC. **C** is incorrect because a hard drive is too bulky, heavy, slow, and vulnerable to head crashes for use in a mobile device.

4. ☑   **C.** A Lightning connector is used to charge Apple iOS devices.
    ☒   **B** and **C** are both incorrect because they are types of USB connectors used on some non-Apple mobile devices. **D** is incorrect because Thunderbolt is the type of connector used on a desktop Mac to attach monitors and some other devices.

5. ☑   **C.** The International Mobile Equipment Identity (IMEI) is the unique identifier assigned to a mobile phone.
    ☒   **A** is incorrect because the Integrated Circuit Card ID (ICCID) is the unique identifier for the SIM card. **B** is incorrect because the International Mobile Subscriber Identity (IMSI) is the unique identifier for the subscriber account for cellular service. **D** is incorrect because a WAP is a wireless access point.

6. ☑   **D.** The Apple Store is the only source for apps for iOS.
    ☒   **A, B,** and **C** are all incorrect because the Apple Store is the only source for iOS apps.

7. ☑   **B.** APK is the Android application package format.
    ☒   **A** is incorrect because SDK stands for software development kit. **C** is incorrect because .NET Framework is a type of SDK used for Windows Phone applications. **D** is incorrect because Swift is a type of SDK used for iOS applications.

Configuring and Using Mobile Device Connections

8. ☑   **B.** When you purchase a smartphone, it has a configured cell connection.
    ☒   **A, C,** and **D** are all incorrect because you need to configure Wi-Fi, Bluetooth, and a tethered connection separately.

9. ☑   **D.** Tethering means sharing your phone's cellular Internet connection via Wi-Fi.
    ☒   **A** is incorrect because airplane mode turns off all wireless services on the device. **B** is incorrect because pairing means to connect two devices via Bluetooth. **C** is incorrect because near field communication (NFC) is a very short-range kind of wireless connectivity used for credit card terminals and payment systems.

10. ☑   **B.** Pairing means to connect two devices via Bluetooth.
    ☒   **A** is incorrect because airplane mode turns off all wireless services on the device. **C** is incorrect because near field communication (NFC) is a very short-range kind of wireless connectivity used for credit card terminals and payment systems. **D** is incorrect because tethering means to share your phone's cellular Internet connection via Wi-Fi.

11. ☑   **B.** Airplane mode turns off all RF broadcasts.
    ☒   **A** is incorrect because pairing is done between two Bluetooth devices. **C** is incorrect because tethering describes a cable connection between a mobile device and a computer. **D** is incorrect because Wi-Fi describes a wireless network using one of the 802.11 standards.

12. ☑   **C.** The e-mail address and password are all you need to configure your mobile device to connect to a Gmail account.
    ☒   **A** is incorrect because that address information is needed only for IMAP or POP accounts. **B** is incorrect because you connect to web-based e-mail accounts via your mail app on a mobile device. **D** is incorrect because port numbers are not required when configuring a Gmail account.

13. ☑   **D.** The preferred roaming list (PRL) is the database that contains cell tower information; your phone uses it to choose the best tower to connect to wherever you are.
    ☒   **A** is incorrect because baseband refers to the cellular radio in the phone. **B** is incorrect because NFC refers to near field communication, a type of wireless connection. **C** is incorrect because SSL stands for Secure Sockets Layer, a type of web security.

14. ☑   **C.** Microsoft Exchange is a type of e-mail service that is internally maintained for an organization's employees, and all accounts are centrally administered by the organization's e-mail administrator.
    ☒   **A** is incorrect because Gmail is not maintained internally, nor is it centrally administered by anyone other than Google. **B** is incorrect because, like Gmail, Hotmail is not internally maintained within an organization for their employees; it is administered by Microsoft. **D** is incorrect because "Work" is not a type of e-mail service.

Securing Mobile Devices

15. ☑ **D.** Passcode lock is a security feature that requires you to enter a PIN for access.
☒ **A** is incorrect because remote wipe does not restrict access by requiring a login. **B** is incorrect because this is simply a setting for consequences of entering the wrong password too many times. **C** is incorrect because multi-touch just describes a feature of a touch screen.

16. ☑ **C.** You would not disable Wi-Fi and Bluetooth remotely after a device has been lost.
☒ **A** is incorrect because a locator service might be used to locate the lost device. **B** is incorrect because remote wipe might be used to prevent a privacy breach. **D** is incorrect because configuring a passcode lock remotely can be done on some mobile OSs, such as in Lost Mode for iOS.

Mobile Device Troubleshooting

17. ☑ **D.** Only a hard reset can fix system lockout.
☒ **A, B,** and **C** are all incorrect because they can all likely be fixed by a soft reset.

18. ☑ **B.** Distance from a cell tower is the most likely cause of a weak cell signal.
☒ **A** is incorrect because destructive interference is likely to occur in crowded urban areas with many cell towers. **C** is incorrect because cell service doesn't come from a WAP. **D** is incorrect because there is no such thing as constructive interference.

19. ☑ **D.** Calibrating the screen would have no effect on Wi-Fi.
☒ **A, B,** and **C** are all incorrect because they could all potentially help with slow or intermittent Wi-Fi.

20. ☑ **B.** Both devices must be discoverable in order for a pairing to work.
☒ **A** is incorrect because Bluetooth devices do not need to touch; this would apply more to near field communication (NFC). **C** is incorrect because Bluetooth is not dependent on Wi-Fi. **D** is incorrect because interference from a cordless landline phone is an issue with some Wi-Fi, not with Bluetooth.

Chapter 21

Using and Supporting Printers

CERTIFICATION OBJECTIVES

- **901: 1.13** Install SOHO multifunction device/printers and configure appropriate settings

- **901: 1.14** Compare and contrast differences between the various print technologies and the associated imaging process

- **901: 1.15** Given a scenario, perform appropriate printer maintenance

- **901: 4.6** Given a scenario, troubleshoot printers with appropriate tools

- **902: 1.4** Given a scenario, use appropriate Microsoft operating system features and tools

- **902: 1.5** Given a scenario, use Windows Control Panel utilities

✓ Two-Minute Drill

Q&A Self Test

I n this chapter, you will examine printers to understand the types in use and the technologies, components, and consumables involved. You will learn about the typical issues involved with installing and configuring printers, the typical upgrading options, and preventive maintenance and troubleshooting.

CERTIFICATION OBJECTIVE

- **901: 1.14** *Compare and contrast the differences between the various print technologies and the associated imaging process*

CompTIA requires that A+ certification candidates recognize the various types of printers available for use with PCs, and understand the differences among these device types so you can make purchasing decisions and determine the consumables required for each.

Printer Basics

Printers are among the most common peripherals used with PCs. Understanding such printer basics as printer types and their related technologies, paper-feeding technologies, printer components, and printer interfaces is important to your success on the exams and on the job.

Printer Types and Technologies

There are several types of printers in use, including impact, laser, inkjet, and thermal printers. Laser and inkjet printers may be the most commonly used by the average home or business user, but the other types have their place in the world, and we will describe the characteristics of all types. Each has its own set of steps for taking output from your computer (or a scanned image) and printing it for you, called an *imaging process*.

Be sure you can distinguish among the four types of printers listed in CompTIA A+ 901 exam objective 4.1: laser, inkjet, thermal, and impact.

Impact

Impact printers were the original computer printers, decades ago. An *impact printer* has a roller or platen the paper presses against and a *print head* that strikes an inked ribbon in front of the paper, thus transferring ink to the paper, like on a typewriter. The only kind of impact printer still in use today is a dot matrix printer. The print head in a *dot matrix printer* uses a matrix of pins to create dots on the paper, thus forming alphanumeric characters and graphic images. Each pin is attached to an actuator, which, when activated, rapidly pushes the pin toward the paper. As the print head (containing the pins) moves across the page, different pins move forward to strike a printer ribbon against the paper, causing ink on the ribbon to adhere to the paper. Because they create printouts one character at a time, we call dot matrix printers *character printers*. The most common use for dot matrix impact printers today is for printing multiple-page receipts or forms that require an impact to make an impression on the second and third sheet of paper.

Impact printers have many disadvantages. The impact of the print head is often very loud, and the wear and tear of the repeated hammering makes these printers prone to mechanical failures. Impact printers do not provide very good resolution. Text and images appear grainy, and you can usually see each individual printed dot. Furthermore, impact printers are limited in their ability to use color, and they usually can only use one printer ribbon color (typically black, although you can substitute another color available for that printer, if available). Even if you manage to find am impact printer that can use ribbons with up to four colors and/or up to four printer ribbons, it will not have as many color combinations as other printer types.

Laser

Most *laser printers* use a concentrated light beam (called a *laser beam* because a laser generates it) in the imaging process. Some less expensive ones use light-emitting diodes (LEDs) for this purpose. Laser printers are generally faster than other types of printers, provide the best quality output, and have the most complex structure and process. Laser printers use very small particles of toner, so they are able to provide excellent resolution, and because of this and their speed, these are perhaps the most commonly used printers in business environments, especially for shared network printers. Figure 21-1 shows a typical laser printer for a home or small office.

A laser printer is a nonimpact printer, because it does not require any form of physical impact to transfer an image to a printout. Because it creates printouts one page at a time (rather than one character or line at a time), a laser printer is called a *page printer*.

Laser Printer Imaging Process   Although some laser printers use a slightly different imaging process, we'll describe a typical order of events that occurs in the laser imaging process. Note that these events occur in repeating cycles, so it is not as important to know

A desktop laser printer with the manual tray open. The toner cartridge is hidden behind the panel above the paper feeder.

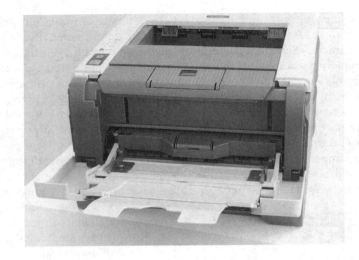

which step is first or last, as it is the sequence of events. For example, some sources list charging as the first step, whereas others list cleaning as the first step.

In a laser printer, the *imaging drum* (the technical term is *electro-photosensitive drum*) is made of metal with an electro-photosensitive coating. The drum is actually more like a slender tube, with a typical circumference of less than an inch, so the imaging process must repeat several times per printout page. Both the drum and the primary corona wire are often contained within the toner cartridge. When printing a page, the feed mechanism moves the paper into the printer and the drum rotates. The steps that follow occur repeatedly while the paper is moving and the drum is turning, although even the processing step will need to repeat for large, multipage documents.

■ **Processing** During the *processing* stage, the printer takes the file sent from a computer (or a scanned image) and creates a bit-mapped image (consisting of dots), called a *raster image*. Then it breaks this image up into its individual horizontal lines of dots, called *raster lines*, and the imaging process prints each raster line in turn until completing the page, processing each page in the document in turn.

■ **Charging** In the *charging* step, the printer's high-voltage power supply (HVPS) conducts electricity to a *primary corona wire* that stretches across the printer's photosensitive drum, not touching it, but very close to the drum's surface. The charge exists on the wire and in a corona (electrical field) around the length of the wire. The high voltage passes a strong negative charge to the drum. In more recent printers, a primary charge roller is used for this purpose.

■ **Exposing** The surface of the electro-photosensitive drum now has a very high negative charge. In the *exposing* (also called *writing*) stage, the printer's laser beam moves along the drum, creating a negative of the image that will eventually appear on the printout. Because the drum is photosensitive, each place that the laser beam touches loses most of its charge. By the end of the writing step, the image exists at a low voltage while the rest of the drum remains highly charged. The laser that generates this laser beam is normally located within the printer body itself, rather than in the toner cartridge.

■ **Developing** In the *developing* stage, the "discharged" areas on the drum attract microscopic toner particles through the open cover on the printer's toner cartridge. By the end of this stage, the drum contains a toner-covered image in the shape of the final printout.

■ **Transferring** During the *transferring* step, *pickup rollers* extract a single page of paper, and the paper moves through the printer close to the drum. The *transfer corona wire*, located within the body of the printer and very close to the paper, applies a small positive charge to the paper as it passes through on the *transfer roller*. This positive charge "pulls" the negatively charged toner from the drum onto the paper. At this point the only thing holding the toner to the paper is an electrical charge and gravity.

■ **Fusing** As the paper leaves the printer it enters the *fusing* stage, passing through a set of *fusing rollers* that presses the toner onto the paper. These rollers are heated by a *fusing lamp*. The hot rollers cause the resin in the toner to melt, or fuse, to the paper, creating a permanent nonsmearing image. These components, collectively called the *fuser assembly*, are normally located within the body of the printer rather than in the toner cartridge.

■ **Cleaning** There are two parts to the *cleaning* stage. First, when the image on the drum transfers to the paper, a *cleaning blade* (normally located within the toner cartridge) removes residual toner, which drops into a small reservoir or returns to the toner cartridge. Next, one or more high-intensity *erasure lamps* (located within the body of the printer) shine on the photosensitive drum, removing any remaining charge on that portion of the drum. The drum continues to rotate, and the process continues.

Imaging Process Variations in Color Laser Printers Color laser printers are able to blend colors into practically any shade, typically using four toner cartridges. Therefore, the writing and developing stages take place four times (once for each color: black, cyan, magenta, and yellow) before the image transfers to the paper. Some color laser printers use a *transfer belt* to transfer colors from each cartridge to the final printed page.

Ozone and Laser Printers   The side effect of a laser printer's use of coronas in the imaging process is the creation of ozone (O_3), which can harm other printer parts, and if at sufficient levels in a closed area has the potential to be harmful to humans. Therefore, laser printers that produce ozone above certain levels have an *ozone filter* to remediate this, but others do not. If a printer has an ozone filter, your printer documentation will identify it. Ozone is only created when a printer is printing, and only some laser printers produce an amount of ozone requiring an ozone filter.

Inkjet

The printers categorized as *inkjet* printers use several technologies to apply wet ink to paper to create text or graphic printouts. Inkjets use replaceable *ink cartridges*—one for each color. Some combine multiple ink reservoirs into a single cartridge, and other inkjet printers have a separate cartridge for each ink reservoir. An inkjet cartridge will only fit certain printer models. These printers provide much better resolution than impact printers, and many of them create wonderful color output because, unlike impact printers, inkjets can combine basic colors to produce a wide range of colors. Inkjet printers are very quiet, compared to impact printers and even laser printers.

The *print head* in an inkjet ink cartridge is an assembly of components, including a tiny pump that forces ink out of the reservoir, through nozzles, and onto the page. There are many kinds of nozzles that make microscopic droplets measured in picoliters (one-millionth of a millionth of a liter); a typical droplet measures 1.5 picoliters. Ink cartridges move back and forth across the page. They sit in a cartridge *carriage* mechanism driven by a *carriage belt* that allows the print heads to move over the paper. As in a laser printer, a feeder assembly feeds paper into the printer and a series of rollers moves the paper through.

When printing text, inkjet printers print a character at a time, so they are *character printers*, and their print mechanisms do not contact the page, making them nonimpact printers as well. The printers themselves are usually inexpensive, but the significant operating costs of these printers are the ink cartridges, which can cost between 10 and 25 cents per printed color page. Black and white pages are less expensive. So, although these printers are inexpensive to buy, the cost of the consumables (ink) can be high.

Thermal

A *thermal printer* uses heat in the image transfer process. Thermal printers for PCs fall into two categories: direct thermal printers and thermal wax transfer printers.

In a *direct thermal printer*, a *heating element* heats a print head that burns dots into the surface of *thermochromic paper*, commonly called *thermal paper*. Early fax machines used this technology for printing, and direct thermal printers are commonly used as receipt printers in retail businesses. Thermal paper has a coating consisting of a dye and an acid in a suitable stable matrix. When the matrix heats above its melting point, the dye reacts with the acid and shifts to its colored form in the areas where it is heated, producing an image. Thermal printers are actually dot matrix printers, although no one calls them that. Thermal printers are roll fed with a *feed assembly* that moves the paper appropriately past the print head.

Thermal wax transfer printers use a film coated with colored wax that melts onto paper. These printers are similar to dye-sublimation printers but differ in two major ways: the film contains wax rather than dye, and these printers do not require special paper. Thermal wax transfer printers are, therefore, less expensive than most dye-sublimation printers, but the dye-sublimation printers create higher-quality output.

All-in-One Printers

Not many years ago, printers, scanners, copiers, and fax machines were each separate devices. Today, combination devices abound. These types of devices, often categorized as a *multifunction device (MFD)* or an *all-in-one printer*, combine the scanner, printer, and copier in one box, often with a built-in fax as well. Although an MFD can function like a copier or a fax machine (when you place an image to copy on the platen and the copied image comes out or a fax is sent over a phone line), there are significant differences between the old and the new. An MFD shines as a PC-connected device that provides all the functionality of a printer as well as a copier and scanner while using up the desk space of just one of these devices. The printing component of an all-in-one printer is usually either a laser printer or an inkjet printer. Figure 21-2 shows an MFD combining an inkjet printer, scanner, copier, and fax in one machine.

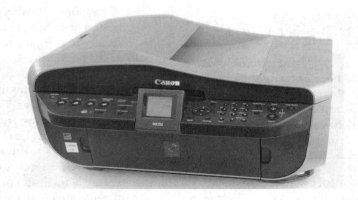

An all-in-one
inkjet printer
that combines
scanner, printer,
fax, and copier in
one machine

Paper-Feeding Technologies

While each type of printer has unique qualities, each one has a set of components called the feed assembly that moves paper through the printer so that the image can be placed on it.

The two most common paper-feeding technologies are friction feed and tractor feed. A printer using *friction feed* prints on individual pieces of paper, moving the paper by grasping each piece of paper with rollers. *Tractor feed* requires *continuous form paper*, sheets of paper attached to each other at perforated joints, with perforations on the sides that fit over sprockets that turn, pulling the paper through the printer. Further, continuous-form paper has about a half-inch-wide border at each side that contains holes that accommodate the sprockets on the tractor feed mechanism, thus pulling the paper through the printer. These borders are removable. When using continuous form feed, you must disable the friction feed. Checks, receipts, and other forms, including multiple-part forms, use continuous form feed paper. Because these forms often have specific areas in which the information must print, a necessary step when inserting this paper into the printer is to register or align the perforation accurately between each form with a guide on the printer.

All the printer types discussed here can and usually do use friction feed to move paper through the printer. Some, especially laser printers, use more than one set of rollers to keep the page moving smoothly until ejecting it. Many laser printers use a *separation pad* to get proper feeding of a single sheet of paper. The pickup rollers press down on the paper to move it through the printer, while the separation pad keeps the next sheet from advancing. The separation pad is a replaceable item when paper stops feeding properly. Friction-fed printers usually have more than one paper source available: one tray that can hold a lot of paper, and another that holds a smaller amount of paper. These trays can hold from a few pages up to several reams in the large paper feeders of high-end network printers.

Once in the printer, the path the paper takes during friction feed varies from printer model to printer model. Normally, *rollers* pick paper from the feed stack one sheet at a time and move it to the *feeder* mechanism that controls movement of the paper through the printer.

The feeder moves the paper one line at a time either past a fixed point for printing or, in some printers, past a print head that moves back and forth printing each line.

Some friction feed assemblies are designed to allow selection of single-sided or double-sided printing. Some printers contain a *duplexing assembly* to print on both sides of the page, but many will require you to feed pages already printed back into the printer again to print on the other side of the page.

All printers eventually deposit the printed page in a tray where the user can retrieve it, and some support the *collating* of documents, placing them in page order—sometimes even for multiple copies.

on the
on the
Job

Prevent paper jams and component wear and tear by using the proper paper for your printer. Read the documentation for the printer to determine the best paper for the results you desire.

Printer Components

The actual printer components vary, depending on the printing and paper-feed technology of the printer. However, regardless of the printing technology used, all printers have a certain set of components in common, which includes the system board, memory, driver and related software, firmware, and consumables.

System Board   Each printer contains a system board that serves the same purpose as a PC's motherboard. Often referred to simply as a printer board, this circuit board contains a processor, read-only memory (ROM), and random access memory (RAM). The processor runs the code contained in the ROM, using the RAM memory as workspace for composing the incoming print jobs (in most printers) and storing them while waiting to print them.

Firmware   A printer, like a computer and most devices, has its own firmware code, including basic firmware that contains the low-level instructions for controlling it. Printer firmware is accessed by the driver, which is installed into the operating system. Another type of firmware code in printers is an interpreter for at least one printer language.

Driver   A new printer comes packaged with a disc containing drivers, usually for several operating systems. Like drivers for other devices, a print driver allows you to control a printer through the operating system.

Printer Language   Beyond a driver that physically controls the action of a printer, the computer must also have special software printer language that translates the characters and graphics of your computer-generated document into a form that the printer can compose and print out. Common printer languages include PostScript, Hewlett-Packard Printer Control Language (PCL), Windows GDI, and other vendor-specific printer languages.

CERTIFICATION OBJECTIVES

- ■ *901: 1.13* *Install SOHO multifunction device/printers and configure appropriate settings*
- ■ *901: 1.14* *Compare and contrast differences between the various print technologies and the associated imaging process*
- ■ *902: 1.4* *Given a scenario, use appropriate Microsoft operating system features and tools*
- ■ *902: 1.5* *Given a scenario, use Windows Control Panel utilities*

In this section we tie up more loose ends by including one item in CompTIA A+ 902 exam objective 1.4, print management. We also describe the use of the Windows Control Panel's Devices and Printers applet, listed in 902 exam objective 1.5. We thoroughly cover 901 exam objective 1.13, which requires that you understand printer drivers, print interfaces, and printer device sharing options, and how to install a local printer versus a network printer. We also pick up the topics of calibration and virtual printer drivers from 901 exam objective 1.14.

Installing and Configuring Printers

The plug and play nature of Windows, as well as of printers and scanners, makes installing and configuring these devices quite easy, even for the ordinary PC user. Before you install a printer, make sure that you have a print driver for that printer that will run in the version of Windows running on the computer. Not only must the version level be correct, but you must also match 32-bit Windows with 32-bit drivers and 64-bit Windows with 64-bit drivers. In this section, we will begin with an overview of printer interfaces, and then explore the issues related to installing and configuring printers.

Printer Interfaces

There are a number of interfaces for connecting a printer to a computer. For example, you can configure a printer so it attaches directly to a computer or indirectly through a network. You can also configure a printer so it is accessible to only one person or to an entire network of people. Printers use the common interfaces described in Chapter 4, and the following text describes usage of each of these interfaces with printers and scanners.

e x a m
w a t c h
The legacy parallel (LPT) port used to be the main interface for printers, but it is not even mentioned anymore in the CompTIA A+ 220-901 and 220-902 exam objectives dealing with printers. We include it here for historical purposes, and because the serial interface inexplicably remains in 901 exam objective 1.13. Legacy serial printing predates parallel printing and has been obsolete for more than 20 years.

A legacy parallel port on an old computer (Photo: https:// commons. wikimedia.org/ wiki/File:Parallel_ computer_ printer_port .jpg [Creative Commons license])

Parallel

The parallel interface is seldom found on a modern computer, but you can recognize it as a 25-pin female D-Sub connector built into the PC, as shown in Figure 21-3. A parallel printer cable has a 36-pin Centronics connector on the printer end, connecting to a corresponding Centronics port on the printer (see Figure 21-4).

A Centronics connector on an old printer (Photo: https://commons.wikimedia.org/wiki/ File:InputOutput_Port.png [Creative Commons license])

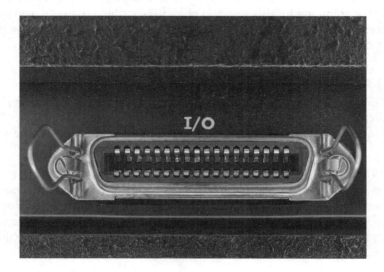

The parallel interface dominated for a long time and was the hands-down favorite over another common, but slower, interface, serial, that shared its long history. The parallel printer standards are documented in IEEE 1284. (Recall from earlier chapters that IEEE is a standards organization that dictates the operating specifications for various types of computing ports and devices.)

Serial

The serial interface was also once a common printer interface, back in the days when printing was a painfully slow process. Serial printing is obsolete, but it used a type of port known as RS-232 (now called legacy serial). An RS-232 port could be either 9-pin or 25-pin. The 25-pin version looked just like a legacy parallel port (see Figure 21-3) except it was male, rather than female, on the computer. The 9-pin version was a D-sub connector with pins arranged in two rows (5 and 4). If you ever do see a serial printer interface in the field, it will probably be on an old dot matrix printer or point-of-sale terminal on a cash register.

USB

Universal Serial Bus (USB) is the current dominant printer interface. As its name implies, data travels one bit at a time over the USB interface. However, as described in Chapter 4, USB is fast and requires only a very small connector on each end. The PC end uses a USB type-A connector, and the device end of the cable is usually a type-B connector. Printers do not always come with a USB cable, and you may need to supply your own.

Because printers normally require more power than the small amount of electrical power a USB interface can provide from the PC, printers use an external power supply. To attach a USB device, simply plug it into a USB external socket or root hub. There is no need to even turn off the computer for this plug and play interface, but be sure to read the instructions first, because for some USB printers, you must install the device driver before plugging in the device.

IEEE 1394/FireWire

The IEEE 1394 interface, also known as FireWire, was popular for a while, but few manufacturers include it on new printers, and even Apple, who originated this standard, no longer includes FireWire on their devices. Virtually all new printers come with USB.

Network Printing (Ethernet or Wi-Fi)

A printer connected to your PC for your own use is a *local printer*. A printer connected directly to the network is a *network printer*. However, this line blurs because it has long been common to share locally connected printers over a network or to connect one or more printers to a network-connected hardware print server. We will examine these three ways to connect a printer to a network.

■ Use a *hardware print server*, a device connected to a network that controls the printing jobs to one or more printers, which are usually connected directly to the print server. Using the manufacturer's instructions, you configure this type of print server much as you do a wireless access point (WAP), by connecting your computer and the print servers with an Ethernet cable and entering its Internet Protocol (IP) address into a browser and configuring the device. As with a WAP or router, be sure to change the password.

■ Use a true network printer that contains a network interface card (NIC) and that you configure in the same manner as any computer on the network. The printer acts as a print server, accepting print jobs over the network. If the printer is powered on and online, it is available to network users. The NIC may be an Ethernet NIC or a wireless NIC, or the printer may contain both types. Although this is not a hard-and-fast rule, high-end network printers most often have Ethernet NICs for use in businesses and large installations.

The most common wireless printers use one of the 802.11*x* standards for Wi-Fi technology, although some may use infrared (IR) or Bluetooth. We described Wi-Fi and Bluetooth in Chapter 7, and infrared in Chapter 14.

■ A computer with a network connection can share a local printer attached to that computer's local interface (USB or other). This computer becomes the print server. In this case, you can only access the printer from the network if the computer attached to it is on and has network access.

e x a m
ⓦatch   In each method of sharing printers over a network, there is a print server. However, CompTIA A+ 901 exam objective 1.13 only lists a hardware print server.

Wireless Printer Interfaces

Modern printers may have a variety of wireless interfaces. Some of these may be network-related, like Wi-Fi. Depending on the printer's age, it might support 802.11a, b, g, n, and/or ac. Other interfaces may be personal one-to-one connections, like Bluetooth. Consult the manual that comes with the printer to learn the details of configuring the wireless interfaces. A Bluetooth printer interface requires pairing, which you learned about in Chapter 20.

e x a m
ⓦatch   CompTIA A+ 901 exam objective 1.13 mentions "infrastructure vs. ad hoc" with regard to wireless device sharing. Because recent versions of Windows have removed the ability to create ad hoc Wi-Fi networks, a Wi-Fi network interface can be assumed to be in infrastructure mode (that is, going through a WAP or router). A Bluetooth connection, on the other hand, is by definition ad hoc.

Cloud/Remote Printing

It is also possible to connect to a printer via the Internet, for cloud/remote printing. This is similar to network printing except the printer isn't on your local LAN, but somewhere on the larger network—the Internet itself. See the section "Installing the Internet Printing Client," later in the chapter.

Virtual Printers

A virtual printer is a printer driver installed in the OS that doesn't actually print to a physical printer. Instead it prints to an application that converts the data into some type of file. When you print to one of these drivers, you are prompted for a filename and location, and you might also be prompted for additional settings.

The following are most common types (and the ones mentioned in CompTIA A+ 901 exam objective 1.14):

- **Print to PDF**   This driver creates an Adobe PDF file, which is a platform-independent page description. The resulting file can be distributed easily via e-mail to any platform that has a PDF reader application available for it, and it will look exactly the same there as it did originally. Many different applications install their own PDF driver, so you may end up with several PDF virtual printers, each one usable in only certain applications. For example, Quicken installs the Quicken PDF Printer, and it works only when printing from within Quicken.

- **Print to XPS**   This driver creates a Microsoft XPS document, which is a page description layout like PDF but Microsoft-branded. The driver may be called Microsoft XPS Document Writer.

- **Print to image**   A driver that prints to an image creates a bitmap image file out of the page to be printed. This is no longer common now that PDF has become such a popular format for printing to file, because PDF files look good on any platform and don't distort when resized.

- **Print to file**   Printing to a file can have several different meanings. In a generic sense, all the virtual printers print to a file of some sort. Some virtual printer drivers print to a specific type of file for the application they are associated with. It is also possible to print to a file that contains the raw data to send to a printer that is not currently available; the file created contains the actual stream of data that would be sent to the printer. That file can later be copied to the real printer when it becomes available. This is not common.

Installing a Printer

Before installing any printer, you need to unpack it (if new) and test it. The actual steps you take to install it will depend on the individual printer and whether it is plug and play or non–plug and play. Any new printer today is plug and play, but on the job, you may run into some old printers that are not plug and play and be asked to install them on new computers.

Some Windows terminology is helpful at this point. To Windows, the *printer* is the software installed in Windows that controls a physical printer (or more, if other similar printers are available). To Windows, a physical printer is a *print device*. So, when you install a printer into Windows, you are installing a software printer as well as the print driver. The printer uses the driver and spooler (queueing software) to process and send your print jobs to the print device. This explains why you can install multiple "printers" in Windows that all refer to the same physical device, and configure different settings for each copy.

Unpacking and Testing a Printer

Follow the manufacturer's instructions to unpack a new printer, removing all the shipping material. Normally packed with the printer is an optical disc containing the printer driver (usually several for different operating systems) and additional software for working with the printer's features. Immediately check that you have a correct print driver for the operating system on the computer it will be connected to, or computers if it will be shared.

Next, plug in the power cable, but do not connect the printer to the computer, and follow the instructions to install toner or ink cartridges and to load paper. You must power up some printers before you can install the cartridges. Follow the manufacturer's instructions for printing a test page directly from the printer. Then move on to installing the printer in Windows.

Installing a Local Printer

You might not have to install a local printer; if it's connected via USB port, Windows should find the printer immediately after you connect it, and offer to install it automatically. If that fails for some reason, your next recourse is to run the setup utility on the disc that came with the printer (or a downloaded equivalent of that). If that still doesn't work, the next thing to try is the Add Printer Wizard.

To use the Add Printer Wizard, open the Control Panel and navigate to Hardware and Sound | Devices and Printers. Then click Add a Printer and follow the prompts to discover and install the printer (see Figure 21-5). The steps are somewhat different depending on the Windows version; it's the same basic process, but the steps may be in a different order, and more or fewer prompts may appear. For example, in Windows 7 the wizard asks whether you want to add a local or network printer, whereas Windows 8/8.1 looks for both types automatically.

Sharp-eyed readers may notice that the printer found in Figure 21-5 is actually a network printer, because it is found by its IP address. The Add Printer Wizard works the same for network-enabled printers on the same workgroup (LAN) as the computer setting it up, as you will see in the next section.

Adding a printer using the Add Printer Wizard in Windows 8.1

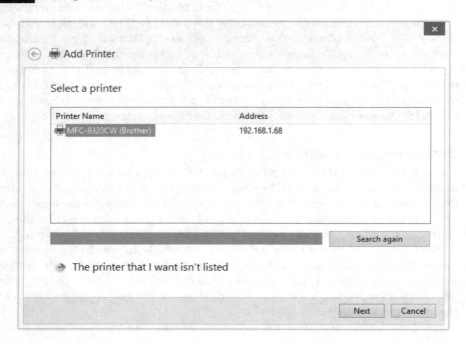

As you set up a local printer, you might be asked whether you want to share it with others on your LAN. On a Windows system, this sharing will occur via the workgroup, using TCP/IP. On a Mac, the sharing may occur via Bonjour or AirPrint.

CompTIA A+ 901 exam objective 1.13 mentions both Bonjour and AirPrint. You don't need to know how to configure them, but you should understand that they are Mac technologies that can help with printer sharing. AirPrint is a protocol supported in both macOS and iOS for sharing printers via Wi-Fi. It requires a WAP. Bonjour is Apple's version of plug and play, discovering services and assigning technologies to them automatically.

Installing a Network Printer

When preparing to connect a printer directly to a network via the printer's built-in NIC, first unpack the printer, install ink or toner cartridges, load the paper, connect to a power source, and then connect the appropriate cable to a switch. If the printer has a Wi-Fi NIC, ensure that an appropriate wireless router is configured and within signal range of the printer. Then power up the printer and follow these general steps:

1. *Configure the IP address for the printer's network adapter.* Networks come with network protocols built in, including Transmission Control Protocol/Internet Protocol (TCP/IP). On a SOHO LAN, if your router assigns IP addresses via Dynamic Host Configuration Protocol (DHCP), it may assign one to the printer automatically. On a corporate network, you will likely need to configure an IP address for the printer's NIC. You usually do this through a menu on the printer's control panel, or via special software on a PC directly connected to one of the printer's ports, such as a USB port. The manufacturer's instructions will give you the details on the method, but you may want to talk to a network administrator to discover the correct IP address to assign to the printer's network adapter.

2. *Test the IP address.* Once you have assigned the IP address, test that you can reach the printer over the network. Testing will require going to a computer proven to be connected to the network and running the following command from a command line: **ping <*ip_address*>**, where <*ip_address*> is the IP address assigned to the printer. IP addresses were described in Chapters 13 and 14. You might also be able to access the printer's configuration page via a web browser using its IP address, the way you did a SOHO router in Chapter 14.

3. *Prepare each network computer.* Install the printer driver and other utilities on each computer that will print to the printer. If the printer connected successfully to the LAN, the printer should be automatically detected when you run the Add Printer Wizard from Devices and Printers in the Control Panel.

4. *Adjust any data privacy and security settings.* You may be able to set up user authentication on the printer, for example, so that only certain users can print to it. You might also be able to control caching of print jobs, for greater security.

Installing the Internet Printing Client

The Internet Printing Client is installed and enabled by default along with TCP/IP protocols and services in Windows Vista and newer. If it's not enabled, open the Programs applet in Control Panel, then choose Programs and Features and select the Turn Windows Features On or Off. Then open the Print Services node (Print and Document Services in Windows 8), and select the check box for Internet Printing Client.

Installing an All-in-One Printer

When installing an all-in-one printer containing a scanner, copier, and fax, you will have a few additional tasks. When unpacking a new device, pay extra attention to the setup instructions because the scanner in the all-in-one may have a lock to secure the fragile internal components from damage during shipping. Release this lock once you have the device positioned properly on a clean surface. The setup program on the disc that comes with the device will have all the software for the various types of devices. You might already have software that will run some of the components. For example, Windows Fax and Scan will work with most multifunction devices to send and receive faxes and scan images.

If the all-in-one includes a fax, and if you plan to use that feature, then you will need to connect a phone cable to the device's RJ-11 (landline phone) connector and connect this to a phone wall jack. Then follow the manufacturer's instructions for configuring the fax to send and receive fax messages.

Configuring a Printer

After a printer is installed, it appears on the list of printers in the Control Panel (Hardware and Sound | Devices and Printers). If you right-click the printer's icon, a context menu appears, as shown in Figure 21-6. There are three very similar commands to note on this menu: Properties, Printer Properties, and Printing Preferences.

FIGURE 21-6   Right-clicking a printer's icon produces a menu with several similar-sounding commands on it.

A few settings overlap between the dialog boxes that open when you select these commands, but generally the settings for each are very different. We'll look at those differences in the following sections. Your printer driver might not have exactly the same dialog box features and tabs as the ones shown, as printer manufacturers tend to tweak the available settings based on the printer's features.

Properties

The dialog box that opens when you choose Properties from the context menu is read-only; there are no settings you can change here. It focuses on the printer hardware, as shown in Figure 21-7. Notice that the files installed for this printer include a hardware driver and some helper files, including one for the device's print queue.

On the Hardware tab there is a Properties button; if you click that, the Properties dialog box that opens is the same as the one that opens when you right-click the printer's icon in Device Manager and choose Properties.

This dialog box appears when you choose Properties; it contains hardware and driver information for the printer.

Printer Properties

The dialog box that opens when you choose Printer Properties from the context menu shown in Figure 21-6 gives you access to a variety of customizable settings for the printer, including sharing, ports, duplexing, and security. On the General tab (shown in Figure 21-8) you can change the printer's name and add a location and comment for it. This information may be useful if you share it with others on your LAN.

on the job **The actual tabs in the Printer Properties dialog box vary by printer, and depend on the device driver, the Windows version, and in some cases certain Windows settings.**

Some of the settings you may be able to adjust in this dialog box include the following, listed by tab:

■ **Sharing** On this tab you can share the printer with other computers on your LAN. This option is available even if you access the printer via the LAN yourself, although it would be better for each of the clients to connect to the printer independently rather than go through your share.

FIGURE 21-8

This dialog box appears when you choose Printer Properties; you can adjust many printer settings here.

■ **Ports** On this tab you can specify which port the computer uses to connect to the printer. Various parallel (LPT) and serial (COM) ports are listed, but you can ignore those; they're for backward compatibility with very old printers. As long as the printer is working correctly, you should not have to change this setting.

■ **Advanced** The Advanced tab, if present, may contain settings such as when to make a shared printer available on the network (a time range), whether to use the Windows print spooler (hint: use it), and whether to eject a blank separator page between each print job (wasteful, but useful in some situations).

■ **Color Management** On a color printer, this tab may provide options for calibrating the colors or installing color profile files that help match up colors with a professional printing service.

■ **Security** If present, this tab enables you to assign permissions to other accounts to use the printer.

■ **Device Settings** If present, this tab may contain a list of automatically adjusted settings and their current values, such as whether or not a duplexing unit or photo tray is installed or what size paper is in a particular paper tray.

**o n   t h e
⓿ o b**

Duplexing **is the ability to print on both sides of the paper without the user manually flipping over the paper and reinserting it into the printer. If your printer has this feature, it may have a special hardware component that stores and flips pages.**

Printing Preferences

If you select Printing Preferences from the printer icon's right-click context menu (see Figure 21-6), you get a dialog box containing settings that pertain to the individual print jobs (see Figure 21-9). This dialog box varies greatly depending on the printer; some printers have many more settings here than others.

Somewhere among these settings you will find an Orientation command that lets you choose between Portrait and Landscape orientation. It's better not to change to Landscape orientation here, because Landscape then becomes the default for all documents printed from all applications, and that's probably not what you want. Make orientation changes from within the individual applications that you print from.

There should also be settings that allow you to change the paper source (for example, choose between paper trays) and specify the type of paper you are using. This is significant on some photo-quality inkjet printers because if special photo paper is used, it can print at a higher resolution. There may also be a separate Quality setting where you can manually adjust the print resolution (such as Best, Better, or Draft). A lower-quality print mode might print more quickly or use less ink/toner.

In addition, there is probably going to be a Color setting where you can toggle between Black and White and Color (again, for *all* print jobs). We have used this setting to temporarily switch to black-and-white printing when the printer was out of colored ink or toner, for example.

FIGURE 21-9

The available printing preferences will vary depending on the printer model.

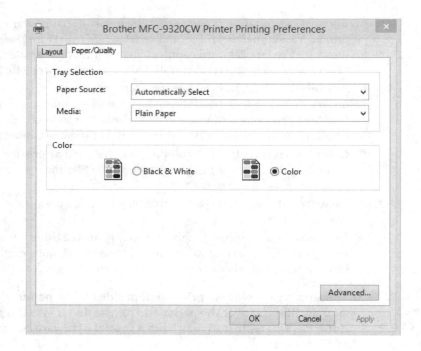

A Collation option may be available for some printers. *Collation* refers to the order in which pages print when you print multiple copies of a multipage document. A collated document prints entire copies together, like pages 1, 2, 3, 1, 2, 3. An uncollated document prints all of one page, then all of the next page, like this: 1, 1, 2, 2, 3, 3.

There might also be an Advanced button that opens an Advanced Options dialog box. From it you might be able to turn on special modes for the printer, like a toner-saving mode, or specify a watermark that appears on each page.

Windows Print Processing

You've just created a report in Word and click Print. Normally you see your printer spring to life and you hear the hum of a busy printer. Then, you reach over and snatch the paper as it leaves the printer. However, there's more to the print story than a mouse click and an instant printout. Windows plays a big part in this frequent and ordinary transaction, doing some processing to prepare the job for the printer via the printer driver that controls how the document is prepared for the capabilities of the printer. Once Windows has the print job ready to send, it doesn't leave the computer right away, but is sent to the *print spooler*, a Windows component that uses memory or disk to store print jobs in a queue, sending each one to the printer as it is ready to print. This feature is on by default, and is especially important when sending several jobs to a printer at once, whether to a local printer or to a network printer. Once a job is sent to the printer, additional processing is done by the printer before the document is printed. The extent of that processing depends on the printer, so we will look at printer types and technologies next.

Devices and Printers

The main Windows location for managing the installed printers is called Devices and Printers. You saw the Windows 8.1 version in Figure 21-6, where we were checking out a printer's context menu commands. To get to it, open the Control Panel, click Hardware and Sound, and click Devices and Printers.

The Devices and Printers window might have several sections, but the one we're interested in right now is Printers. Icons for each printer appear in this section. (Remember, from Windows' perspective, a printer is a driver, not the physical device.)

Here's a key to what you see there:

- The default printer has a green check mark on its icon. You can change the default printer by right-clicking the desired printer and choosing Set As Default Printer. (You can't see the check mark in Figure 21-6 because the context menu is in the way.)

- A printer with a dimmed icon, or one with a black clock face on it, is not currently available, or offline. In Figure 21-6, for example, the ABS PDF Driver v400 (redirected 2) printer has a clock face on its icon.

- When you select a printer, the status bar in the Devices and Printers window shows information about that printer. In Figure 21-6, you see that the selected printer is network connected, and that it's a multifunction device with 0 documents in queue.

Print Management

Print Management is a utility in some Windows versions that gives you a central location for administering all printers—both local and network. It is listed in Administrative Tools in both Windows 7 and Windows 8, and you can also open it in Windows 7 by searching for **print management** from the Start menu's Search box. It is also available as a snap-in for Microsoft Management Console (MMC), as described in Chapter 12 (enter **mmc.exe** in the Run dialog box and choose File | Add/Remove Snap-ins | Print Management).

CompTIA A+ 902 exam objective 1.4 includes Print Management among the OS features and tools you should know about. Some exam prep guides interpret this to mean managing print jobs in a generic sense, but it actually refers to the Print Management utility. Make sure you know about both Print Management and Devices and Printers, two different ways to work with printers.

FIGURE 21-10   The Print Management utility in Windows 8.1

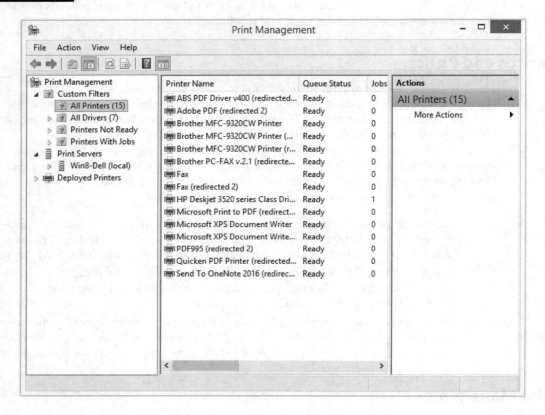

Figure 21-10 shows the Print Management console showing one of the filtered views, All Printers. You can also view all print drivers, printers that are not ready, and printers with jobs. Notice that the local computer, because it is sharing printers, is listed as a print server.

Sharing a Printer

If you are sharing a local printer, how you enable printer sharing depends on how you configured your client for file and printer sharing in a HomeGroup, a workgroup, or a Microsoft Active Directory domain. These methods were described in Chapter 19.

Sharing a Printer in a HomeGroup

If your computer is part of a HomeGroup and you wish to share a local printer, open the HomeGroup app in Control Panel and choose to share printers. (In Windows 7 you mark a check box and in Windows 8/8.1 and newer you choose Shared from a drop-down list.)

Sharing a Printer in a Workgroup or a Microsoft Active Directory Domain

If your computer is part of a workgroup or Microsoft Active Directory domain, you can share printers through the Sharing tab on the printer's Properties dialog box, shown in Figure 21-11. Click to place a check mark in the box labeled Share This Printer. If you have administrative rights and your computer is a member of a domain, there will be another check box labeled List In the Directory. Checking this will publish the printer in Active Directory, making it available to others in the domain to search Active Directory for your shared printer.

FIGURE 21-11   The Sharing tab in a printer's Properties dialog box

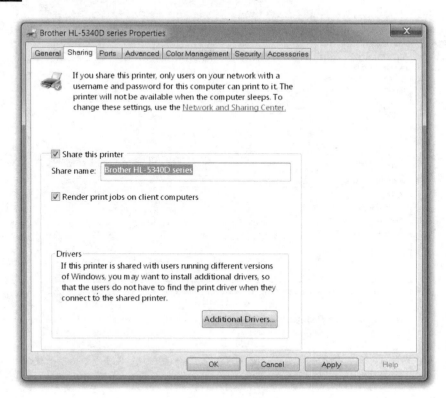

The Render Print Jobs on Client Computers option should be selected by default. If not, select it, because it moves the task of preparing a document for the printer to the client computer, saving your computer's processing power. Also, click Additional Drivers if computers that will be connecting to access the printer are running versions of Windows other than the one on this computer. Then select drivers for those printers, and when they connect, the correct driver will automatically be sent to their computer and installed.

As with file sharing, when you share a printer in a workgroup or domain, you must assign permissions manually to the users connecting over the network, unless you leave the default permissions. In the case of a printer, the default permission gives the Everyone group Print permission, as shown on the Security tab in Figure 21-12. Creator Owner has Manage Documents permission, and the user Yoda is a member of the Administrators group and therefore has Print, Manage This Printer, and Manage Documents permissions.

FIGURE 21-12   The Security tab in a printer's Properties dialog box

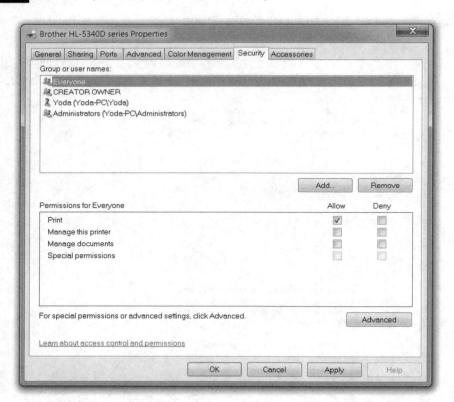

The four printer permissions are as follows:

- **Print**   Allows a user to print, cancel, pause, and restart only the documents that they send to the printer.
- **Manage This Printer**   Allows a user to rename, delete, share, and choose printer preferences. Also permits a user to assign printer permissions to other users and manage all print jobs on that printer.
- **Manage Documents**   Permission to manage all jobs (for all users) in the printer's print queue.
- **Special Permissions**   Primary use of specials printers is by an administrator in order to change the printer owner. The person who installs a printer is the Creator Owner, who is automatically assigned the Manage Documents permission.

Upgrades

Printers are somewhat limited in how you can upgrade them, unlike computers, which you can upgrade in many ways, such as by adding memory, installing a large selection of new peripherals, upgrading the ROM BIOS, and upgrading the software. We will describe some possible software and hardware upgrades for printers.

Device Driver and Software Upgrades   Like other software, software associated with printers and scanners calls for occasional upgrades, with drivers being the most frequently upgraded. When an updated driver is available for your printer, follow the manufacturer's instructions to install it. If it comes with its own installation program, run it. Alternatively, the instructions may tell you to use the Update Drivers option. To update a printer driver in this fashion, open the printer's Properties dialog box, select the Advanced tab, click New Driver, and follow the instructions in the Add Printer Driver Wizard.

Hardware Upgrades   Popular hardware upgrades for printers and scanners are automated document feeders for scanners and larger-capacity paper trays for laser printers. Higher-end devices in both categories are most likely to have upgrade options, usually offered by the manufacturer.

Another popular hardware upgrade is memory, particularly for laser printers. Adding memory can increase the speed when printing complex documents or graphics. A search of the Internet will turn up many manufacturers of memory upgrades for laser printers.

Firmware Upgrades   Some printers—in particular, laser printers—support firmware upgrades. This, of course, depends on the manufacturer releasing firmware upgrades.

First, determine the firmware version currently in your printer, and then check on the manufacturer's website for notices of upgrades. Instructions from the manufacturer will guide you through upgrading the firmware, which you do from your computer.

SCENARIO & SOLUTION

We need a printer that will print an image to multipart forms for retail receipts. What should we buy?	Buy an impact printer, which will be able to print to carbon-copy forms.
In a laser printer, how does the image get from the drum to the paper?	The transfer corona wire applies a positive charge to the paper. As the paper passes the drum, the negatively charged toner is attracted to the page.
What cleans the photosensitive drum in a laser printer?	A cleaning blade removes residual toner from the drum, and an erasure lamp removes any remaining charge from the drum.

Deleting a Printer

When you no longer use a printer, delete it from Windows by opening the Devices and Printers applet in the Control Panel, right-clicking the printer, and selecting Delete or Remove Device. Respond to the confirmation dialog box ("Are you sure...?"), and the printer will be deleted.

CERTIFICATION OBJECTIVES

■ **901: 1.14** *Compare and contrast differences between the various print technologies and the associated imaging process*

■ **901: 1.15** *Given a scenario, perform appropriate printer maintenance*

This section covers printer maintenance tasks for the four major types of printers covered on the CompTIA A+ 220-901 exam: laser, thermal, impact, and inkjet. It also covers calibration, a topic from 901 exam objective 1.14.

Printer Maintenance

Because of the frequency with which printers are used, they require almost constant maintenance. Fortunately, the maintenance procedures are usually easy—the most frequent tasks involve consumables. Consider scheduling regular maintenance, such as cleaning, based on the amount of usage for each printer and scanner. Manufacturers may provide a list of other maintenance tasks, such as vacuuming or replacing the ozone filter in laser printers, which should occur along with a regular cleaning, but not at the same frequency.

Check with the manufacturer for recommendations for how to maintain the ozone filter. Some can be vacuumed, while others must be replaced at a specified interval.

Maintenance Tools

The basic tool set that you use for maintaining a computer is appropriate for printers too. It includes using compressed air from pressurized cans for blowing out the paper dust and debris inside a printer and a small vacuum cleaner. Because the particles of toner in a laser printer are so microscopic, it isn't a good idea to use a conventional vacuum because the toner can clog it up, and because the filters may not be as fine on a regular vacuum, so toner particles might become airborne. Manufacturers do make special vacuums for laser printers, but they tend to be expensive. Laser printer manufacturers also make maintenance kits for replacing aging parts at predetermined intervals.

Replacing Consumables

The most common maintenance tasks involve replacing consumables. Printer consumables include the printer medium, some components, and paper. The printer medium is a consumable that contains the pigment for the image that a printer creates. The medium comes in a special form for the technology and is specific to the model of printer. The most common forms are ink ribbons, ink cartridges, and laser printer toner cartridges. A printer cannot work without consumables, such as paper and ink or toner cartridges. If you are the one responsible for purchasing and storing these products, letting these supplies run out is bad for your career!

For the best results, use the manufacturer's recommended consumables. This includes ink and toner cartridges as well as paper for printers. In the case of the major printer manufacturers, their branded ink and toner products may only be available at premium prices. To save money, consider third-party sources, but be prepared to buy and test one set of cartridges before ordering quantities.

Shelf Life

The shelf life of both laser printer toner cartridges and inkjet cartridges is similar, and is usually two years from production date or six months from when you first open the package or first put it into use. Even printer paper has a shelf life because paper for friction-feed printers must contain a certain range of moisture content in order to feed properly without causing jams. Old paper also may discolor unless it is of very high quality. Used printer consumables can negatively affect the environment and should be disposed of in a manner that is both legal and respectful of the environment, as described in Chapter 1.

Paper

All printers have the dreaded "paper out" light and Windows desktop error message (if connected to a computer). A printer in a cash register, a point-of-sale (PoS) printer, typically has an alarm. Replacing paper is the most frequent maintenance task. So, be prepared for this, and aid any user who does not know how to do this, because support techs simply can't be available at every printer.

With the exception of thermal printers and some impact printers that require tractor-feed paper, most printers, including laser and inkjet, can use standard-sized sheets of ordinary copier paper for drafts and everyday casual printing. For the best results, however, consult the printer documentation for the type and quality of paper to use. Paper should be stored in its packaging and in a cool, dry place. For instance, copier paper often comes in paper-wrapped one-ream (500-page) packages, but is also available in bulk boxes, in which the paper is not wrapped. Do not unwrap or remove paper from its container until ready to install in a printer. If you are using a tray to feed a friction-feed printer, simply pull out the appropriate paper tray. Gently ripple a stack of fresh paper and then insert it into the tray. If there is a lid for the tray, replace that before inserting the tray into the printer.

Tractor-feed impact printers printing multiple copies use either carbon paper or *impact paper* that contains encapsulated ink or dye on the back of each sheet except the last one so that the impact of the print head on the first sheet breaks the encapsulation on all sheets and causes a character image to appear on the subsequent sheets.

To replace paper in a tractor-feed printer, you will need to lift the printer lid, feed the first sheet of the new stack through the paper path, and line up the holes with the sprockets on the feed wheels. As this procedure varies from model to model, consult the manufacturer's documentation. Finally, stack the continuous form paper in a bin or next to the printer neatly so that it can easily feed into the printer.

When feeding card stock or sheets of labels through a printer, be sure to use the straightest paper path to avoid jams. And never feed a sheet of labels through a laser printer if one or more labels have been removed, because the "Teflon-like" material on the paper carrier will melt on the fusing roller and ruin it. A fusing roller is an expensive component to replace because you normally must replace the entire fusing assembly.

Adding paper to any printer should only take a few seconds because it does not involve turning off the printer's power. The error message should go away on its own. If you do not close or insert the tray properly, a Tray Open or Close Tray message may appear. If the printer uses an upright friction feed, follow the steps in Exercise 21-1 to add more paper.

EXERCISE 21-1

Adding Paper to an Upright Friction-Feed Tray

If you have access to a printer with an upright friction-feed tray, you can follow these instructions.

1. Release the tray lever at the back of the printer (if so equipped). This will cause the paper tray to drop away slightly from the friction rollers.
2. Place a small stack of paper in the tray, using the paper guides.
3. Engage the tray lever to bring the paper closer to the feed rollers.
4. The printer might automatically detect the paper and continue the print job. If not, look for and press the Paper Advance button on the printer. This instructs the printer to detect and try to feed the paper.

Multipart forms are not always available as continuous-feed paper, in which case, you need an impact printer capable of friction feed. Usually, this only requires removing the tractor feed assembly and making sure that the friction-feed mechanism is engaged (it is disengaged while tractor feed is in use).

Paper for a thermal printer comes in rolls. Perhaps the most common thermal printers are in cash registers; you have probably witnessed a cashier changing thermal paper while you waited in line with a shopping basket full of frozen food. To change the thermal paper roll, you first open the feed assembly compartment and remove the plastic or cardboard roll from the spent roll and remove any torn paper or debris in the compartment. Then place the new roll on the spindle, taking care to have the paper feed in the correct direction from the roll, and thread it through the assembly (look for directions mounted in the compartment or arrows on the components), making sure to thread the end of the roll outside. Close the door, give a gentle tug to the paper, and tear off the leading edge. Most thermal printers have a paper cutter where the paper exits.

Ink

The most common forms of ink for printers are ink ribbons for impact printers and ink cartridges for inkjet printers.

An impact printer uses a fabric ribbon embedded with ink. The ribbon is usually a closed loop on two spools (for unused and used ribbon) enclosed within a cartridge. This cartridge is either a movable cartridge mounted on the print head assembly, or a stationary cartridge that stretches the ribbon the width of the paper, allowing the moving print head assembly to move back and forth. The used portion of the ribbon simply spools back into the ribbon cartridge. To install, follow the manufacturer's instructions, which will include carefully bringing the ribbon over the print head.

FIGURE 21-13

An open inkjet printer with the ink cartridges exposed

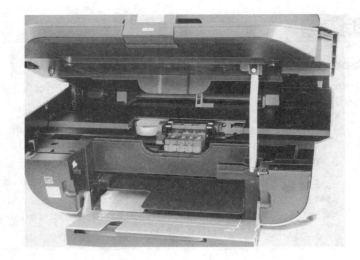

The medium for inkjet printers is ink contained in reservoirs. In the case of inkjet printers, this reservoir is part of a small cartridge that also may contain the print head that sprays the ink on the paper. Figure 21-13 shows an open inkjet printer with the cartridges exposed. You must turn this model on when you change the cartridges because when it is turned off, the cartridges are "parked" out of sight. Lights on each cartridge give the status of the cartridge: steady when there is adequate ink, blinking when ink is low.

If you search the documentation or the manufacturer's website, you can discover the expected yield of a cartridge. The yield of a typical inkjet cartridge is in the hundreds of pages. One printer shows a black ink cartridge yield of 630 pages of text and 450 pages for graphic printouts that have 5 percent coverage. The same printer shows a color ink yield of 430 pages with 5 percent coverage per color. If your printouts use more ink per page, then the yield will be smaller.

Toner

Toner cartridges for a typical desktop laser printer run around $50 and up, and if you've got a color laser printer, you'll need four cartridges (cyan, magenta, yellow, and black). However, they last for several thousand pages, making these printers relatively inexpensive per page to use.

Several companies take used printer cartridges, recondition the drum and other components, refill the toner reservoir with fresh toner, and offer them at significantly lower cost than the manufacturer's fresh cartridges. We have had mixed experiences with these "refilled" cartridges. Some refilled/reconditioned cartridges have performed as well as the best brand-name new toner cartridges, whereas others have been very poor. Caveat emptor!

The brand-name cartridges from your printer's manufacturer will normally produce the highest quality and demand the highest price. We often buy new cartridges from a company that sells both new and reconditioned cartridges. No matter what vendor we use for our toner cartridges, we always buy from one that takes our old toner cartridges for recycling at no cost to us.

The yield of a laser cartridge for a typical desktop monochrome black laser printer is several thousand pages. The actual number of pages depends on the coverage level—that is, the amount of each color used on each page. A page with a full-page, full-color graphic will use up a lot more toner than a business letter with a tiny full-color logo in the corner. Numbers such as 3000 to 8000 pages are common. The yield for a color laser printer generally runs over 1000 pages per cartridge. For instance, the documentation for one printer estimates the yield for a standard-capacity black toner cartridge at 4000 pages, whereas the estimate for each of the standard cyan, magenta, yellow, and black (CMYK) cartridges is 1500 pages. The high-capacity color toner cartridges show an expected yield of 4000 pages.

To replace a toner cartridge, turn off the printer and gently remove the old cartridge. Turning off the printer is not required for replacing the cartridge, but we recommend doing it because this is a good time to give the printer a quick cleaning, removing paper and toner debris, as described later in this chapter. After cleaning the printer, remove the new cartridge from its packaging and set it aside while you insert the old cartridge into the packaging for disposal. Then remove any tape or plastic components labeled to be removed before installing. Gently rock the cartridge from side to side, and then insert into the printer, per the manufacturer's instructions.

Cleaning a Printer

The best thing you can do to prolong the life of a printer and prevent problems from occurring is to clean it regularly. In all printers, whether laser, thermal, or impact, small particles of paper and other debris can be left behind and cause a potentially harmful build-up. This build-up can hold a static charge, which can, in turn, damage components through electrostatic discharge (ESD) or cause pages to stick together.

We do not recommend using any solvents to clean a printer, and you should never spray a liquid on or into a printer for any reason. Use a very dilute mixture of water and white vinegar to dampen a cloth, and thoroughly wring it out before wiping off the exterior of the printer. Do not use liquids inside the printer unless following the advice of the manufacturer.

Before opening up a printer for cleaning, power it down and unplug it. Do not touch the printer's power supply, and allow the fusing roller in a laser printer to cool down before you clean inside.

Removing the build-up will also keep the paper path clear, thus reducing paper jams and ensuring there is no inhibition of moving parts. You can remove dust and particle build-up using compressed air or a vacuum. As you clean the printer, be on the lookout for small paper corners left behind during the print process or after you cleared a paper jam.

In an inkjet printer, you should look for and remove ink from the inside of the printer. Ink can leak and cause smudges on the paper. As the ink dries, it can cause moving components or paper to stick.

Laser printers can accumulate toner. Remove excess toner using a paper towel or cotton swab, but beyond that, only clean laser printer internal components using the manufacturer's instructions, which may include using a *toner vacuum*, a vacuum with filters to protect you from inhaling the super-fine toner particles. This is essential if you support many laser printers.

You may have to replace the ribbon and the print head in an impact printer, and in a thermal printer you should clean the heating element. Figure 21-14 shows the interior of a laser printer.

e x a m
ⓦatch **The maintenance tasks listed for a thermal printer in CompTIA A+ 901 exam objective 1.15 are replace paper, clean heating element, and remove debris.**

Some manufacturers add a Maintenance tab to the Printer Properties dialog box for tasks such as those shown in Figure 21-15 for an inkjet printer. Notice the four buttons for cleaning various components, plus the buttons for Print Head Alignment and Nozzle Check.

FIGURE 21-14

A desktop laser printer opened and ready for cleaning

FIGURE 21-15   A Printer Properties dialog box showing maintenance options

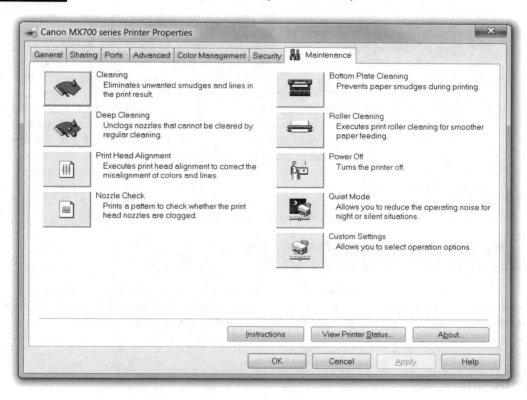

Replacing Print Heads

The print head is the hardest-working component in an impact printer, so be prepared to replace one if necessary. We will describe symptoms of problems with print heads later in "Troubleshooting Printers." If the solutions provided there do not eliminate the symptoms, then replace the print head. Contact the manufacturer for a replacement, and follow the instructions for removing the old print head and installing the new one.

exam

ⓦatch   **The maintenance tasks for an impact printer listed in CompTIA A+ 901 exam objective 1.15 are replace ribbon, replace print head, and replace paper.**

Maintenance Kits and Page Counts

Some printers, mainly professional-quality and high-production laser printers, have "maintenance counts." The printer counts the number of pages printed over the lifetime of the printer, and when this page count reaches a certain number, called the maintenance count, a service message will appear on the printer's display. This message indicates that the printer has reached the end of the expected service life for some of its internal components, such as the various types of rollers, pads, and entire assemblies. When this occurs, you must install the manufacturer's maintenance kit of replacement parts, after which you must reset the page count so it can track the expected life of the parts in the new maintenance kit.

If you do not reset the page count, the printer will continue to issue the maintenance warning. Use the manufacturer's instructions for resetting the page count. In the rare instance when you must install a new maintenance kit before the page count reaches the maintenance count, on some models you must reset the maintenance count to match the page count. Then, when the next page is printed, you will receive the maintenance message and can proceed with the maintenance and reset the page count.

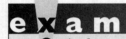

Be sure you are clear on the difference between page count and maintenance count. "Page count" is the count you will reset whenever you install a new maintenance kit. You rarely, if ever, will need to reset the "maintenance count."

Calibration

Calibration is a process that matches colors seen on the screen to colors printed on paper. To get the best quality out of a color printer, look for a calibration tool in the Color Management tab of the printer's Properties dialog box. We opened the Color Management dialog box shown in Figure 21-16 by selecting the Color Management tab, and then clicking the Color Management button. Notice the list (two items) in the box under ICC Profiles. These are sets of specifications used by your printer to print color, per *International Color Consortium (ICC)* standards. ICC is a standards organization for color management systems. Find additional profiles on the All Profiles tab, which in this case contains *Windows Color System (WCS)* profiles. WCS is a color management system that Microsoft is promoting as a standard. You can select profiles from this list and add them to the printers list on the Devices page. Then print out samples and compare the screen image of each sample with the printed image. Using a utility like this, you are depending on your eyes to judge the correct settings. Of course, none of these profiles will work if your display's color is not right. So, click the Advanced tab and click Calibrate Display. Follow the instructions for calibrating the display.

FIGURE 21-16 The Color Management dialog box

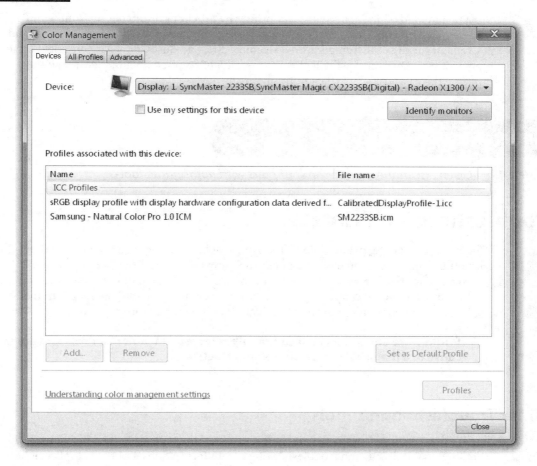

 **The maintenance tasks for a laser jet printer listed in CompTIA A+ 901 exam objective 1.15 are replacing toner (cartridge), applying maintenance kit,** **calibration, and cleaning. Note that for laser printers, calibration only applies to color laser printers.**

Ensuring a Suitable Environment

Prevent a myriad of problems with your printer by providing a suitable environment. Be sure the printer is on a level surface, close to the computer to which it is connected, and convenient for the user. Temperature extremes, dirt, and dust will negatively affect either type of device. Dirt and dust will affect the quality of scanned documents, and, if they infiltrate the case, can cause heat build-up in any device.

CERTIFICATION OBJECTIVE

■ *901: 4.6   Given a scenario, troubleshoot printers with appropriate tools*

Troubleshooting Printers

When troubleshooting printers, apply the same troubleshooting theory and procedures used with other computer components and use the same toolkit, as described in Chapter 3. When a printer needs a major repair, first evaluate the cost/benefit of the repair by finding out how much it would cost to replace the printer versus the cost of the repair. In this section, learn about common printer problems and their solutions.

Printers are one of the most commonly accessed network resources and are the cause of a majority of network-related trouble calls.

Printer Troubleshooting Tools

Troubleshooting tools for printers include a subset of the tools described in Chapter 3 for installing, maintaining, and troubleshooting computers. A subset of those tools will be your most useful tools, including an assortment of screwdrivers, a selection of printer-specific field replaceable units (FRUs), multimeter (for testing wall outlets), and printer-specific tools, such as those listed in CompTIA A+ 901 exam objective 4.6, which include a maintenance kit, toner vacuum, compressed air, and printer spooler. We'll discuss each of these last four in context with specific printer problems.

Enabling or Disabling Print Spooling

As introduced earlier in the chapter, a print spooler is a utility that manages the jobs that are waiting to be printed. By default the print spooler is on. That means that when an application sends a print job to the printer, Windows manages that job until it is fully fed to the printer. If the printer isn't ready for it, Windows holds the job as long as needed. Having Windows take care of this function means that the application itself doesn't have to, so the application returns back to normal operation immediately. If you turn off the print spooler, the application may be unusable until the job finishes being sent to the printer.

To access print spooler settings, from the Devices and Printers window, right-click the printer and choose Printer Properties, and then click the Advanced tab. The wording of the spooling options varies slightly depending on the Windows version.

- **Spool Print Documents So Program Finishes Printing Faster**   Enables the spooler. In Windows Vista and Windows 7, the word *documents* is replaced by *jobs*. If you enable spooling you can choose whether to start printing after the last page is spooled or start printing immediately.
- **Print Directly to the Printer**   Disables the spooler.

Unable to Install a Printer

With plug and play and Windows' ability to discover network printers, you will have fewer instances in which a printer will not install. In all cases of printer installation problems, check that you are using the correct driver version for your version of Windows, including 32-bit versus 64-bit. Then concentrate on the type of connection. If you are unable to install a local printer with a USB connection, be sure that the print device is not connected to the computer until after you install the printer driver. Then connect the printer and turn it on.

If the problem is with a print device connected via parallel printer, ensure that the port is configured correctly in Windows and BIOS settings.

For a network printer, go to the print device itself and make sure it is turned on and connected. Check connections to it from other computers. If you receive an access denied message when trying to install a printer, you will need to have the administrator of the printer share give you administrative access to the printer. After doing this, repeat the steps for installing the printer.

Access Denied to an Installed Printer

If a user attempts to print to a local or network printer and sees an access denied message, the printer administrator will need to change the permissions on the printer or printer share for your account or group so that the user can print. Recall that to print requires the Print permission. A user who has the responsibility of managing all jobs on a printer needs Manage Documents permission, and someone who does all printer management tasks must have the Manage This Printer permission.

Non-Windows Clients Cannot Connect to a Shared Printer

If you need to share a printer connected to a Windows computer with computers on your network running other operating systems, such as macOS, you may need to enable the line printer daemon (LPD) service on the Windows computer. On a Windows 7 computer, open Control Panel, select Programs and Features (in icons view), and then select Turn Windows Features On or Off. In the Windows Features dialog box, browse to the Print and Document Service node and expand it. Then enable the LPD Print Service.

On an Apple computer running macOS, open an app that you would normally print from and then open the Print menu (File | Print in Microsoft Word for Mac). From the Print dialog box, open the Printer pop-up menu and select Add Printer. In the Add Printer dialog box, click the IP button. In the Protocol box, select Line Printer Daemon. In the Address box, enter the IP address of the Windows computer to which the printer is connected. It will then attempt to detect the printer and the Print Using box will suggest a printer (a driver). For our laser printer, it will select a Generic PostScript Printer. Click Add. On the Installable Options page, select the options you wish to use, such as duplex printing, and click Continue. Then send a print job to the printer as a test.

<table>
<tr><td>

e x a m

ⓦ a t c h   **The CompTIA A+ Acronyms list includes** line printer daemon/line printer remote (LPD/LPR) **and** Internet Printing Protocol (IPP). **Both are protocols for printing to a networked printer over TCP/IP networks,**

</td><td>

using the IP address of the printer. LPD/LPR itself is also sometimes broken down into the two named protocols. IPP is a newer, more secure protocol that supports authentication and encryption.

</td></tr>
</table>

Paper Feed Problems

Common to all printers, paper feed problems have a variety of causes, and the symptoms are not just paper jamming and stopping the printing. Paper feed problems result in creased paper and paper simply not feeding at all because it never leaves the paper tray. Here are just a few possible causes and solutions:

- **Too much paper in a paper tray** Too much paper can cause more than one page to feed through the printer at a time. The extra page can cause problems with the print process itself and jam within the printer. To avoid this, reduce the amount of paper you place in the tray.
- **Static electricity** If static builds up within the pages, it can cause the pages to stick together. Use your thumb to "riffle," or quickly separate, the pages before you load them into the paper tray. Riffling allows air between the pages and can reduce "static cling." Remove dust from the printer, as this can also cause static build-up.

■ **Moisture in the paper**   Moisture can cause pages to stick together or not feed properly. To protect paper from moisture changes, keep it in its packaging until needed. Store paper in a cool, dry place.

■ **Worn out friction-feed parts**   Worn parts will fail to move the paper smoothly. Check feed rollers for wear. Feed rollers are often rubber or plastic, and you should replace them (depending on the cost of replacing parts versus replacing the printer). You may also need to replace the separation pad.

■ **The wrong paper**   Use paper that is not too thin, not too thick, and that has a certain range of moisture content to avoid static build-up. Try using a different weight paper. Try feeding from an alternative (straight-through) paper path. Most printers have the option of a more direct paper path that can handle heavier-weight paper than the standard path.

■ **Too few sheets in an upright paper tray**   If the stack of paper in an upright paper tray is too small, the friction rollers might not be able to make good contact with the top page. Try putting a larger stack of paper in (without making it too large).

■ **Broken parts in the paper path**   Inspect for any broken parts in the paper path. If you find any, you will have to investigate repairing or replacing the printer. If necessary, clean the printer, and once you have finished clearing the jam, either resume the print job or send another print job. Most printers will not resume operation until you have completely cleared the jam. Many printers also require you to press the reset or clear button to restart the printer.

■ **Misalignment of paper in tractor feed**   Tractor feed has its own problems. These feed mechanisms are notorious for feeding paper incorrectly through the printer. Misalignment of the paper in the printer usually causes the problem. Tractor feeds require special continuous-form paper, in which each page of paper attaches to the one before it, much like a roll of paper towels. If the perforations between pages do not line up properly, the text for one page will print across two pages. When this happens, look for a Paper Advance button on the printer that will incrementally advance the paper until it is properly aligned. If you do not have the documentation for the printer, this task may take trial and error.

■ **Friction feed not disabled for tractor feed**   Another problem with tractor feeds occurs when the friction-feed mechanism is not disabled. The most obvious symptom of this problem will be torn paper if the tractor pulls faster than the friction feed moves, or bunched paper if the opposite condition exists.

Clearing a Paper Jam

Most paper jams will stop the current print job. If you suspect a paper jam, consult your printer documentation. In general, turn off and open the printer, and carefully remove any paper jammed in the paper path, following the manufacturer's instructions. Some printers

include levers that you can release to more easily remove jammed paper. Normally, you will need to gently pull the paper in the direction the paper normally moves through the printer. Pulling in the opposite direction could damage internal components, such as rollers. This is especially true of the fusion roller in a laser printer. Avoid tearing the paper. If it tears, be sure you locate and remove all pieces from the printer.

No Connectivity to Printer

A problem with printer connectivity begs the question, "Was it ever connected?" If this is the first time you are attempting to connect the printer, then troubleshoot based on the connection method you are attempting. This is rarely a problem with USB, unless the connector is not properly connected. USB is the least troublesome of your connection options. If this is a parallel printer connection (we'll try not to ask, "Why are you still using parallel?"), check the cable connection, and verify that the cable is an IEEE 1284–compliant cable. Then check the computer's parallel port settings in BIOS settings to ensure that the port is enabled, and that it is using the correct mode, which is ECP mode if you have an IEEE 1284–compliant cable and printer. See Chapter 4 to review how to enter BIOS settings. If connecting via Ethernet, Wi-Fi, or Bluetooth, troubleshoot the network connection.

Unable to Install Printer

If you attempt to install a printer and are unable to do so, there are several possible causes and solutions, depending on the printer model and the version of Windows. Note any error messages, and if you cannot interpret them or do not understand what action you should take, contact the manufacturer, or check out the support page on their website for a solution. If you are using the driver disc that came with the printer, the problem may be with the installation program itself rather than the printer driver, and the manufacturer's support personnel may give you instructions on how to install the driver manually, bypassing the installation program. Another possible cause is that the printer did not come with a driver for the version of Windows you are using, and you will need to request an appropriate driver from the manufacturer. If they do not have an exact match, they may be able to recommend a similar driver from one of their models that will allow you to use most of the printer's capabilities.

Printer Will Not Print

If you send a print job to a printer and nothing happens, check the connection first (local connection or network connection), and check to see that the printer is powered on.

Check the printer status lights or display, if it has one, to see if there are any printer errors or if it is perhaps out of paper, ink, or toner. If you see errors, troubleshoot the errors.

If everything about the printer seems normal except for it failing to print (or stopping in the midst of a print job), then treat it like a print spooler problem. Print spooler problems can cause a print job to not arrive at a printer or a job in progress to inexplicably stop. The print queue may be backed up because it is overwhelmed, or the print spooler service may have stopped. When this service stops, nothing prints until it is restarted. This is referred to as a "stalled print spooler."

You need to determine if the spooler is stalled. For this, you must have the Manage Documents permission to the printer. Assuming you logged on as a member of the Administrators group, which is automatically assigned this permission, open the Printers folder and double-click the printer. Doing this opens the user interface for the print queue from which you can manage the print jobs the print spooler is holding. Check the status of the print job. If the print job status is Paused, right-click it and select Restart. If this fails, attempt to cancel the print job. Sometimes canceling the first job in the queue will allow the other jobs to print.

If this does not help, then cancel each job in the queue. If you are not able to restart or cancel jobs in the queue, you will need to restart the Print Spooler service. Follow the steps in Exercise 21-2 to restart this service.

EXERCISE 21-2

Restarting the Print Spooler Service

Use the Services node in Computer Management to restart a stalled print spooler.

1. In File Explorer/Windows Explorer, right-click This PC or Computer, and select Manage from the context menu.
2. In the Computer Management Console, select Services and Applications, and then double-click Services.
3. In the contents pane, scroll down to Print Spooler.
4. Right-click Print Spooler and select Restart (see Figure 21-17).
5. If restarting the service fails, then close all open windows and restart the computer. When Windows restarts, the Print Spooler service will restart.
6. Restart the printer.
7. Resend the print jobs to the printer.

FIGURE 21-17

Right-click the
Print Spooler
service and select
Restart.

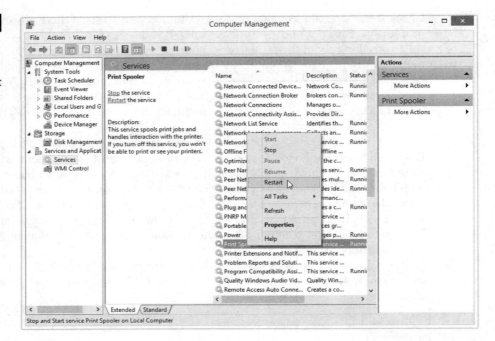

Blank Pages

If a printer produces blank pages, troubleshoot the possible cause based on the type of
printer, as described next.

Blank Pages from an Impact Printer   If an impact printer produces blank pages, pay
attention to the sound coming from the printer. If the pins are striking the page but not printing,
you have a ribbon problem. Make sure the ribbon lines up with the print head; if it does not,
move it into position. You may have to find a way to remove slack from the ribbon, which you
can do by removing the ribbon cartridge and manually rewinding the ribbon before reinserting
it into the printer. If the ribbon does line up properly but there is no print or just very faint print,
the ribbon has probably worn out, and replacing the ribbon will resolve the problem.

If carbon copies printed on an impact printer are blank or dim, consult the documentation
to adjust the distance between the print head and the paper. If you cannot hear the pins
striking the page, try replacing the print head.

Blank Pages from an Inkjet   If an inkjet printer produces blank pages, the likely cause is
an empty ink cartridge. Use the printer software to determine the amount of ink left in an ink
cartridge. The printer software may be a separate program that you will start from an icon
in the Windows GUI, or it may be integrated into the Windows Printer Properties dialog box.
If the printer software is integrated into the Printer Properties dialog box, it may be in the form
of a custom tab or a special button.

FIGURE 21-18

A printer status message generated by the printer's management software

A warning that the printer is running low on ink, as shown in Figure 21-18, does not necessarily mean that you should immediately replace the cartridge. We go for weeks with this status showing and warnings popping up when we print. We simply tell it to continue. We normally only replace a cartridge if the quality of the printout is not adequate for our purposes, or if the print job will not continue without changing it.

If there is ink, the problem could be clogged nozzles. Follow the printer manufacturer's instructions for cleaning the nozzles in the print head. Software installed with the printer driver usually does this and should be available on the Maintenance tab of the printer's Properties dialog box (such as the Deep Cleaning option shown earlier in Figure 21-15). If it isn't, check the documentation for a way to initiate this from the printer's controls. In the extreme, follow the manufacturer's instructions for manually cleaning the print head, perhaps with a lint-free cloth slightly dampened with distilled water.

Blank Pages from a Laser Printer   If a laser printer is producing blank pages, suspect some component of the printing process. For instance, a blank page can result if the image fails to transfer to the paper, which could be a problem with the transfer corona wire. Shut down the printer, disconnect the power cable, open the printer, and inspect the corona wire (consult your manual for its location). You may find dirt or debris (like a staple) shorting out the wire. You may discover that the wire itself is broken, although it would take rough treatment indeed to do this. If the wire is intact but has debris on it, it could be shorting out. Clean the printer, and then try to print again.

It is rare for a laser cartridge to be the cause of a completely blank page, unless it contains a drum and the drum has failed. If it has, you must replace it. If the drum is part of the cartridge, replace the cartridge. You are more likely to see some of the other problems described next when the cartridge has a problem.

Print Quality

Print quality problems are very common with all types of printers. In laser printers, print quality problems are most often (but not always) associated with a component in the toner cartridge. When troubleshooting a print quality problem on a laser printer, swapping the toner cartridge often solves many of the problems listed here. Following are several common print quality problems and their suggested solutions.

Faded Prints

Several things can cause faded prints from a laser printer. The toner in the cartridge could be low, the corona wire could be dirty and not passing the correct charge to the paper, or the drum could be dirty or defective. If the drum is part of the toner cartridge, replacing the cartridge could solve the problem. If the drum is separate from the toner cartridge, try replacing it. Most laser printers include a way to clean the corona wires. You must first power off the printer and disconnect the power cable. Then, using either a special felt-lined tool or a built-in slider, gently move the tool along the wire.

Faded prints on an impact printer are almost always due to ribbon problems. Replace the ribbon cartridge.

Printouts from thermal printers have a unique problem, especially since thermal printers are frequently used to print receipts. The paper darkens over time, and the image fades and becomes unreadable. There are several solutions to this, but thermal paper quality varies, so you may completely lose the image when you try some of these techniques. The best action to take is to immediately scan or copy all receipts before they fade. Then you either have a paper copy or an image of the receipt stored in your computer. Even this proactive technique has its risks, since the light from the copier can darken the thermal printout.

Another technique used after an image has faded is to copy or scan it after adjusting the contrast settings to try and recover the image. And yet another technique uses a laminating machine with the hope that the heat from the laminator will restore the image. None of these techniques is guaranteed to work.

Ghost Image from the Previous Page

A ghost image occurs when a usually very faint image from a previous page appears on subsequent pages. This problem occurs only in laser printers and indicates a cleaning stage failure. The drum might have lost the ability to drop its charge in the presence of light. Replace the drum to resolve the problem. If the drum is not the cause, it could be either the cleaning blade or the erasure lamps. Because both the cleaning blade and drum are inside the toner cartridge in many laser printers, you can resolve this problem by replacing the toner cartridge. The erasure lamps are always (to our knowledge) in the printer itself, and they are not easy to replace. You will probably have to send the printer back to the manufacturer or to a specialized printer repair shop.

Toner Not Fused to the Paper

If the toner is not sticking to the paper, the fusing roller is defective or the fusing lamp (inside the roller) is burned out and not heating the roller enough to melt the toner to the paper. Similarly, a scratched nonstick coating on the fusing roller, or baked-on debris on it, can cause smeared toner on the printout. Either way, replace the fusing lamp and/or the fusing roller to fix the problem.

Random Speckles, Smudging, Smearing, and Streaking

Ribbon ink, cartridge ink, and toner residue can be within the printer itself and transfer onto the paper. If any type of printer produces a page with speckles, smudging, smearing, or streaking of the ink or toner, try cleaning the printer. This includes manually cleaning it and/or using the printer software to instruct the printer to perform cleaning and other maintenance tasks. We described printer cleaning in this chapter in "Printer Maintenance."

If an impact printer produces a smudged, smeared, or streaked printout, check the pins on the print head. Stuck pins can cause printouts to have a smudged appearance as they continue to transfer ink to the page, even when they do not create a character or image. If this is the case, notify the manufacturer, and replace the print head or the entire printer.

If the output from an inkjet printer appears smudged or smeared, the most likely cause is someone touching the printed page before the ink dries. The ink used in an inkjet printer must totally dry before it is touched, or it will smear. Most inkjet printers do not use permanent ink, and even after it has dried, these inks may smear if they become wet.

The heat and pressure of the fusion stage in a laser printer creates a smudge-proof permanent printout. Smudged or streaked laser printouts could be caused by a dirty corona wire, but are usually the result of a failed fusing stage. Depending on the exact source of the problem, you may need to replace the fusing rollers, the halogen lamp, or the entire fuser assembly.

Repeated Pattern of Speckles or Blotches

A repeated but unintended pattern on a printout is another indication of ink or toner residue in the printer. Clean the printer, paying attention to the feed rollers in an inkjet and the transfer corona wire in a laser printer. If a repeated pattern is on the printout of a laser printer, suspect the drum. A small nick or flaw in the drum will cause toner to collect there, and it will transfer onto each page in a repetitive pattern. In addition, some drums lose their ability to drop their charge during the cleaning step. The drum has a very small diameter, so this same pattern will repeat several times down the length of the page. In either case, replacing the drum should solve the problem.

Wrong Colors

Wrong colors may be a problem with the ink or toner cartridges, or it may be a software problem of some sort. Modern color printers don't allow you to print if a cartridge is out of ink or toner, so we can usually rule out an empty color cartridge. However, open up the printer and take a look at the cartridges. Things have improved in this area, but if a color cartridge is low, some printers cannot produce the correct shades. To get the desired results in a printout, you may simply need to replace the cartridges.

Also, if the nozzles on an inkjet clog, the colors may come out "dirty" or might not appear at all. Follow the manufacturer's instructions for cleaning the nozzles.

Wrong colors can be an application-related issue, and you should test a document using similar colors from another application. If the colors print out correctly from another app, there may be a problem with a setting in the first app.

Lines

If lines appear in a printout from an impact printer, the print head may have a malfunctioning pin, in which case, replace the print head. In any printer, parallel lines of print can indicate an incompatible driver, a problem you may solve by updating or replacing the driver. This symptom can also be a sign of a malfunction in the printer's electronics, so you need to repair or replace the printer, depending on its value and the cost of repair.

In a laser printer, a leaking toner cartridge or a dirty printer that has toner where the paper can pick it up as it passes through can cause vertical lines. Remove the toner cartridge, set it on a paper towel to see if it's leaking, clean it with a small vacuum cleaner, and then clean the interior of the printer until all the toner and paper dust are removed.

Garbled Output

Garbled output—often called "garbage"—usually indicates a communications problem between the computer and printer. The most common cause of this is an incorrect or corrupted print driver, but first check that the data cable is firmly and properly attached, and then try doing a power cycle (turning the printer off and then back on) because it may have simply experienced a temporary problem. Restarting the computer may also solve the problem.

If there are no connection problems and a power cycle of the printer and computer does not improve the printing, then check that the computer is using the correct printer driver. Look at the printer settings by opening the Devices and Printers folder and display the printer's Properties dialog box, as in Figure 21-7. Ensure that the physical printer matches the printer model shown in this dialog box. If the driver is not correct, uninstall it and reinstall the correct driver. If the driver appears to be correct, look at the manufacturer's site for an update and install the update. If the version of the driver is the most current, try reinstalling the driver.

Finally, this problem could be the result of insufficient printer memory. You can test this by trying to print a very small document. If it works, there is a chance that the original document was too large for the printer's memory. You can add more RAM. Check the documentation to find out how to check on the amount of memory, what type of memory to install, and how to install the memory.

Printer Error Messages

Printers generate a variety of error messages. They often come with their own configuration and monitoring utility installed on your computer when you install the printer driver. We'll describe some of the more common error messages that could appear on the computer screen or the printer's console, or both. The OS generates some of these messages. Any time you get a printer error message that you do not understand, check the message or error code number in the manufacturer's documentation. You may need to do a search on the manufacturer's website, where a more complete list is often available.

Paper Out   A paper out message normally indicates that there is no paper in the printer, and the solution is simple: add paper. However, it can also appear on an older printer when there is paper in the tray. Over time, the surface of the rollers used to feed the paper may lose their ability to grip and move the paper. This issue occurs especially as the paper becomes low in the tray and the rollers cannot benefit from the pressure of a full stack of paper to grip and feed the paper. Locate the rollers and clean them, first wiping the dust and grime off, and then using isopropyl alcohol to clean any residue that may make the rollers slippery.

Out of Memory/Lost Memory Errors   A laser printer composes each page of a print job, using its own memory as it creates the raster image. This can require a great deal of memory, depending on the complexity and resolution of the page. Therefore, if an out of memory, lost memory, or memory overflow error appears on a printer's display, the printer does not have enough memory for the print job. For the short term, reduce the resolution of the image or reduce the dimensions of graphics on a page and try again. In most cases, the more permanent solution is to add more RAM to the printer, as described previously when we discussed the symptom of garbage or "garbled" printing.

Processing Error   If a printer has a processing error, such as the error 21 displayed on an HP laser printer, the cause is a document that is too complex for the printer's print processor. Adding memory will not help this problem. If the printer cannot print it as is, simplify the document by minimizing the number of fonts, reducing the resolution, and making graphics images smaller. Since you still want the best quality document possible, experiment by making one change that affects your document the least and testing to see if it will print out. Go with the fewest changes that result in a successful printout.

I/O Error or Connectivity Problem   An I/O error message can take many forms, including "Cannot communicate with printer" or "There was an error writing to LPT# or USB#." Windows typically reports this message, and it indicates that the computer cannot properly communicate with the printer, clearly identifying it as a connectivity problem. Or is it? Start by ensuring that the printer is on. If it is not, turn it on, and then try to print.

Next, make sure the printer data cable firmly and properly attaches to both the printer and the computer and that a proper driver is loaded. If you suspect the driver is corrupt, remove it, and then reload it. Ensure that the driver uses the correct port by checking the Ports tab in the Printer Properties dialog box for the printer (right-click the printer's icon in Devices and Printers and choose Printer Properties).

Low Toner or Ink The low toner (or similar) message applies to laser printers, and it appears well before the toner is completely gone as an early warning. The printer should continue to print normally. You can often make the error message go away by removing the toner cartridge and gently rocking the cartridge back and forth. This will resettle and redistribute the toner within the cartridge. Note, however, that this is not a solution to the problem. The reason for the error is to warn you to replace the toner cartridge soon. Most laser printers will not work at all if the toner cartridge is empty.

When you are using an inkjet, the ink low (or similar) message will appear on your computer screen or an ink level bar will be displayed. Replace the cartridge.

When an ink cartridge gets low, you should replace rather than refill it. By refilling an old cartridge, you are reusing old, possibly worn-out components.

Blank Printer Display Screen If the LCD screen on the printer is completely blank, the most likely cause is that the printer isn't getting power. If other lights on the printer are illuminated, the LCD screen is probably malfunctioning.

SCENARIO & SOLUTION

The output from my laser printer is smeared. What should I do?	Clean the printer, especially the fusing roller. If this doesn't work, replace the drum. If the drum is in the toner cartridge, replace the toner cartridge. If none of this works, the problem may be with the fuser assembly, which will need replacing.
I am careful not to handle the printouts from my inkjet printer, but they are coming out with smudges. What can I do?	Check the paper path. Something may be contacting the page before the ink has had a chance to dry, or people may be handling the printout before it is dry.
Why do printouts from my color inkjet printer have the wrong colors?	The printer is probably low in one or more colors or has a clogged nozzle.

CERTIFICATION SUMMARY

This chapter explored printer issues for IT professionals. The focus of this chapter was the components, procedures, troubleshooting, and maintenance procedures for common printer types. Impact printers provide the lowest quality, and today they mainly print multiple-part forms. Laser printers, the most expensive, can provide excellent printouts and are the most common type used in offices. For this reason, you are likely to deal with laser printers in businesses more frequently than with other printer types. Inkjet printers are extremely popular as inexpensive desktop color printers.

Before installing a printer, carefully read the manufacturer's instructions. When working with printer problems, apply the troubleshooting procedures learned in Chapter 11, and become familiar with the symptoms and problems common to the printer or scanner. Printers require maintenance to replenish paper and, less frequently, ink or toner. Clean printers regularly to ensure high-quality results, and to avoid many problems that dirt, dust, and grime can create.

TWO-MINUTE DRILL

Here are some of the key points covered in Chapter 21.

Printer Basics

- ❑ Printers are the most common peripheral used with PCs.
- ❑ Impact printers are usually of low quality, use a ribbon, move paper with friction feed or tractor feed, and their most common use is for printing multiple-part forms, such as retail receipts.
- ❑ Laser printers use laser light technology in the printing process. The stages of the laser printing imaging process are charging, exposing, developing, transferring, fusing, and cleaning.
- ❑ The term "inkjet" refers to printers that use one of several technologies to apply wet ink to paper to create text or graphic printouts.
- ❑ Thermal printers use heat in the image transfer process.
- ❑ The two most common paper-feed technologies are friction feed and continuous form feed.
- ❑ The typical printer has a system board, ROM (containing firmware), and RAM memory, as well as various components related to the specific printing technology and paper-feed mechanism. Additional components include the device driver and related software, and consumables in the form of paper, ink ribbons, ink cartridges, or toner cartridges.

❑ Manufacturers offer all-in-one printers, multifunction products that include a scanner, printer, copier, and fax integrated within the same case.

❑ Printer interfaces include parallel, serial, USB, IEEE 1394/FireWire, Ethernet, and wireless.

Installing and Configuring Printers

❑ Before installing a printer, be sure to read the manufacturer's instructions.

❑ Installing a printer in Windows is a simple job, especially for plug and play printers. Even non–plug and play printers are easy to install using the Add Printer Wizard.

❑ After installing a printer, perform a test print.

❑ Configure a printer through the printer's Properties dialog box, the Printer Properties dialog box, and the Printing Preferences dialog box.

❑ There are a few common upgrades to printers, including device drivers and other software, document feeders, memory, and firmware.

Printer Maintenance

❑ Some laser printers track the number of pages printed in a page count and require that critical components be replaced using a maintenance kit. After installing the maintenance kit, you must reset the page count.

❑ Clean each printer according to the manufacturer's recommendations to avoid poor output and other problems.

❑ Provide a suitable environment for each printer to avoid problems that dirt and temperature extremes can cause in these devices.

❑ For the best results, use the recommended consumables in printers. This may require using the media and paper provided by the manufacturer or less expensive substitutes of equal quality from other sources.

Troubleshooting Printers

❑ The troubleshooting process for printers is identical to that used for computers.

❑ Common printer problems include those involving paper feed and print quality. Printer error messages on your computer screen or the printer display panel will alert you to common problems, such as paper out, I/O errors, and print spooler problems.

SELF TEST

The following questions will help you measure your understanding of the material presented in this chapter. Read all of the choices carefully, because there might be more than one correct answer. Choose all correct answers for each question.

Printer Basics

1. What is a common use for impact printers?
   A. High-quality color images
   B. High-speed network printers
   C. Multipart forms
   D. UPC code scanning

2. What type of printer is the most often-used shared network printer in businesses?
   A. Laser
   B. Impact
   C. Thermal
   D. Inkjet

3. In what stage of the laser printing process does a laser beam place an image on the photosensitive drum?
   A. Cleaning
   B. Developing
   C. Charging
   D. Exposing

4. Which stage in the laser printing process is responsible for creating a permanent nonsmearing image?
   A. Cleaning
   B. Fusing
   C. Transferring
   D. Exposing

5. What type of printer applies wet ink to paper?
   A. Laser
   B. Impact
   C. Thermal
   D. Inkjet

6. What is the unit of measure used to describe the size of droplets created by the nozzles in an inkjet printer?
   A. Millimeter
   B. Meter
   C. Picoliter
   D. Liter

Installing and Configuring Printers

7. What Windows GUI tool can you use to install a non–plug and play printer?
   A. Add Printer Wizard
   B. Device Manager
   C. This PC/Computer
   D. Add or Remove Programs

8. What important configuration task must you perform on a network printer before it will be recognized on the network?
   A. Install TCP/IP.
   B. Assign an IP address.
   C. Give it the address of each client.
   D. It must be detected by the clients.

9. Which of the following would you use to turn on sharing local printers in a HomeGroup?
   A. Devices and Printers
   B. Printer Properties
   C. Printing Preferences
   D. HomeGroup applet

10. Which of the following is a Windows 7 and Windows 8 tool for viewing and centrally administering all local and network printers?
    A. Devices and Printers
    B. HomeGroup applet
    C. Printer Properties
    D. Print Management

Printer Maintenance

11. What should you do after installing a maintenance kit in a laser printer?
    A. Reset the maintenance count.
    B. Reset the page count.

C.   Reset the printer.

D.   Call the manufacturer.

12.   What simple maintenance task for printers helps maintain high-quality results?

A.   Performing a memory upgrade

B.   Installing a maintenance kit

C.   Replacing the fuser

D.   Cleaning

Troubleshooting Printers

13.   When a print job will not print, check to see if this Windows service is still holding it in its queue.

A.   Printer

B.   Spooler

C.   Print driver

D.   Print device

14.   What can contribute to static build-up in a printer?

A.   Dust

B.   Ink

C.   Overloaded paper tray

D.   Paper jams

15.   You have shared a printer on your Windows 7 computer, and the Windows clients on your network can connect and print, but your Apple computer running macOS cannot. What service should you enable on your Windows 7 computer?

A.   IPP

B.   Network Discovery

C.   LPD

D.   Printer

16.   What component on an inkjet printer may clog with ink?

A.   Nozzles

B.   Hammers

C.   Friction-feed rollers

D.   Tractor feeder

17.   What is a possible source of a problem causing blank pages to print out on a laser printer?

A.   Paper path

B.   Transfer corona wire

C.   Power supply

D.   Paper tray

18. What component in a laser printer could be the source of a repeated pattern of speckles?
    A. Fusion roller
    B. Drum
    C. Toner
    D. Primary corona wire

19. When a ghost image from a previous page occurs on subsequent pages printed on a laser printer, what component is a probable source of the problem?
    A. Fusion roller
    B. Drum
    C. Toner
    D. Primary corona wire

20. Of all the possible solutions for "garbage" printing, which two are the first ones you should try?
    A. Check for loose data cable.
    B. Upgrade driver.
    C. Power-cycle the printer and computer.
    D. Uninstall and reinstall driver.

SELF TEST ANSWERS

Printer Basics

1. ☑ **C.** Multipart form printing is a common use for impact printers.
   ☒ **A** is incorrect because impact printers do not create high-quality color images. **B** is incorrect because impact printers are not high-speed printers. **D** is incorrect because no standalone printer can scan.

2. ☑ **A.** The laser printer is the most often-used shared network printer in businesses.
   ☒ **B, C,** and **D** are all incorrect because these types of printers seldom are shared network printers in businesses.

3. ☑ **D.** Exposing is the laser printing stage in which the laser beam places an image on the photosensitive drum.

☒ **A** is incorrect because cleaning is the stage in which the drum is cleaned. **B** is incorrect because developing is the stage in which toner is attracted to the image on the drum. **C** is incorrect because charging is the stage in which a charge is applied to the drum.

4. ☑ **B.** Fusing is the stage in the laser printing process in which the image permanently fuses to the paper.

☒ **A, C,** and **D** are all incorrect because none of these is the stage that creates a permanent nonsmearing image.

5. ☑ **D.** Inkjet is the type of printer that applies wet ink to paper.

☒ **A** is incorrect because in a laser printer dry toner is fused to the paper. **B** is incorrect because an impact printer uses an ink ribbon. **C** is incorrect because a thermal printer uses heat to print an image.

6. ☑ **C.** Picoliter is the unit of measure used to describe the size of droplets created by the nozzles in an inkjet printer.

☒ **A** and **B** are both incorrect because neither one is the unit of measure used for the size of droplets from the nozzles in an inkjet printer, which is a measurement of liquid volume. Both millimeter and meter are units of distance measure. **D** is incorrect because although liter is a measure of liquid volume, it is far too large a volume for such small drops.

Installing and Configuring Printers

7. ☑ **A.** The Add Printer Wizard is the Windows GUI tool for installing a non–plug and play printer.

☒ **B, C,** and **D** are all incorrect because none of these is the GUI tool for installing a non–plug and play printer.

8. ☑ **B.** Assign an IP address is the important configuration task you must do on a network printer before it will be recognized on the network.

☒ **A** is incorrect because a network printer comes with TCP/IP installed. **C** is incorrect because the network printer does not need the address of each client; each client needs the address of the network printer. **D** is incorrect because the network printer must have an IP address before it can be recognized on the network.

9. ☑ **D.** The HomeGroup applet is where you turn on sharing of local printers.

☒ **A** and **B** are both incorrect because once your computer is joined to a HomeGroup, you cannot turn on sharing by going into Devices and Printers, selecting your printer, and opening the Printer Properties, as you would if the printer belonged to a workgroup or domain. **C** is incorrect because the Printing Preferences dialog box only controls how documents are printed and has nothing to do with sharing.

10. ☑ **D.** Print Management is a Windows 7 and Windows 8 MMC snap-in for viewing and centrally administering all local and network printers.
    ☒ **A** is incorrect because Devices and Printers does not give you access to centrally administer all local and network printers. **B** is incorrect because the HomeGroup applet hides file and print sharing administrative tasks. **C** is incorrect because Printer Properties only gives access to the properties on a single printer.

Printer Maintenance

11. ☑ **B.** Reset the page count of a laser printer after installing a maintenance kit.
    ☒ **A** is incorrect because resetting the maintenance count will set to zero pages the number at which the printer should receive maintenance. **C** is incorrect because resetting the printer will not turn the page count to zero, and the printer will display a maintenance warning. **D** is incorrect because calling the manufacturer is unnecessary when all you need to do is reset the page count.

12. ☑ **D.** Cleaning is the simple maintenance task for printers that helps maintain high-quality results.
    ☒ **A** is incorrect because upgrading memory is not a simple maintenance task, and it will not help maintain high-quality results. **B** is incorrect because installing a maintenance kit is not a simple maintenance task. **C** is incorrect because replacing the fuser is not a simple maintenance task but a complex repair task.

Troubleshooting Printers

13. ☑ **B.** Spooler is the Windows component that holds print jobs in its queue before sending them to the printer. The spooler can be stalled, preventing a job from printing.
    ☒ **A** is incorrect, although printer is the term for software in Windows that manages print jobs and sends them to print devices via the spooler. **C** is incorrect because this is a device driver for the printer. **D** is incorrect because the print device is the physical printer.

14. ☑ **A.** Dust can contribute to static build-up in a printer.
    ☒ **B** is incorrect because, although ink residue may build up in a printer, it does not appreciably contribute to static buildup. **C** is incorrect because an overloaded paper tray is not a cause of static build-up in a printer. **D** is incorrect because, although static build-up in a printer may occasionally cause a paper jam, it is not a primary cause.

15. ☑ **C.** You must enable the line printer daemon (LPD) service on the Windows computer for the Apple computer running macOS.
    ☒ **A** is incorrect because although Internet Printing Protocol (IPP) is also a service for printing over a TCP/IP network, it is not the one that will correct the problem described. **B** is incorrect because Network Discovery is also not the service that will correct the problem described. **D** is incorrect because "Printer" is not a service.

16. ☑ **A.** Nozzles in an inkjet printer can become clogged with ink.

☒ **B, C,** and **D** are all incorrect because these components do not become clogged with ink.

17. ☑ **B.** The transfer corona wire is a possible source of a problem causing blank pages to print on a laser printer.

☒ **A, C,** and **D** are all incorrect because they are not considered possible sources for blank pages printing out on a laser printer.

18. ☑ **B.** The drum could be the source of a repeated pattern of speckles on printouts from a laser printer.

☒ **A, C,** and **D** are all incorrect because none of these is a probable source of a repeated pattern of speckles on printouts from a laser printer.

19. ☑ **B.** The drum is the probable source of a ghost image printing on subsequent pages from a laser printer.

☒ **A, C,** and **D** are all incorrect because none of these is a probable source of a ghost image.

20. ☑ **A** and **C.** These are the first two solutions you should try for "garbage" printing because they are simple and easy to try.

☒ **B** and **D** are incorrect because they are not as simple and fast to try as the first two.

Appendix

About the CD-ROM

The CD-ROM included with this book comes complete with Total Tester customizable practice exam software, 400 practice exam questions, video training from the authors, a comprehensive glossary, and a secured PDF copy of the book.

System Requirements

The software requires Windows Vista or higher and 30 MB of hard disk space for full installation, in addition to a current or prior major release of Chrome, Firefox, Internet Explorer, or Safari. To run, the screen resolution must be set to 1024 × 768 or higher. The secured book PDF requires Adobe Acrobat, Adobe Reader, or Adobe Digital Editions to view.

Installing and Running Total Tester Premium Practice Exam Software

From the main screen you may install the Total Tester by clicking the Total Tester Practice Exams button. This will begin the installation process and place an icon on your desktop and in your Start menu. To run Total Tester, navigate to Start | (All) Programs | Total Seminars, or double-click the icon on your desktop.

To uninstall the Total Tester software, go to Start | Control Panel | Programs And Features, and then select the Total Tester program. Select Remove, and Windows will completely uninstall the software.

Total Tester Premium Practice Exam Software

Total Tester provides you with a simulation of the CompTIA A+ 220-901 and 220-902 exams. Exams can be taken in Practice Mode, Exam Mode, or Custom Mode. Practice Mode provides an assistance window with hints, references to the book, explanations of the correct and incorrect answers, and the option to check your answer as you take the test. Exam Mode provides a simulation of the actual exam. The number of questions, the types of questions, and the time allowed are intended to be an accurate representation of the exam environment. Custom Mode allows you to create custom exams from selected domains or chapters, and you can further customize the number of questions and time allowed.

To take a test, launch the program and select the CompTIA A+ pack from the Installed Question Packs list. You can then select Practice Mode, Exam Mode, or Custom Mode. All exams provide an overall grade and a grade broken down by domain.

Video Training from the Authors

Video MP4 clips provide detailed examples of key certification objectives in audio/video format from the authors of the book. You can access the videos directly from the Video table of contents by clicking the Video link on the main page.

Glossary

In addition to providing access to the testing and training materials, the CD-ROM also includes a bonus glossary of key terms from the book. The glossary is in PDF format and more information on viewing the file is in the following section.

Secured Book PDF

The entire contents of the book are provided in secured PDF format on the CD-ROM. This file is viewable on your computer and many portable devices.

- **To view the PDF on a computer**, Adobe Acrobat, Adobe Reader, or Adobe Digital Editions is required. A link to Adobe's website, where you can download and install Adobe Reader, has been included on the CD-ROM.

  Note: For more information on Adobe Reader and to check for the most recent version of the software, visit Adobe's website at www.adobe.com and search for the free Adobe Reader or look for Adobe Reader on the product page. Adobe Digital Editions can also be downloaded from the Adobe website.

- **To view the book PDF on a portable device**, copy the PDF file to your computer from the CD-ROM and then copy the file to your portable device using a USB or other connection. Adobe offers a mobile version of Adobe Reader, the Adobe Reader mobile app, which currently supports iOS and Android. For customers using Adobe Digital Editions and an iPad, you may have to download and install a separate reader program on your device. The Adobe website has a list of recommended applications, and McGraw-Hill Education recommends the Bluefire Reader.

Technical Support

For questions regarding the Total Tester software or operation of the CD-ROM, visit **www.totalsem.com** or e-mail **support@totalsem.com**.

For questions regarding the secured book PDF, visit **http://mhp.softwareassist.com** or e-mail **techsolutions@mhedu.com**.

For questions regarding book content, e-mail **hep_customer-service@mheducation.com**. For customers outside the United States, e-mail **international_cs@mheducation.com**.

INDEX

G

H